JEWISH LAW | HISTORY, SOURCES, PRINCIPLES | *Ha-Mishpat Ha-Ivri*

VOLUME I

PART ONE

The History and Elements of Jewish Law

and

PART TWO

The Legal Sources of Jewish Law

SECTION 1

Exegesis and Interpretation

VOLUME II

PART TWO (*continued*)

The Legal Sources of Jewish Law

SECTION 2

Legislation, Custom, Precedent, and Legal Reasoning

VOLUME III

PART THREE

The Literary Sources of Jewish Law

VOLUME IV

PART FOUR

Jewish Law in the State of Israel

and

Appendixes, Glossary, Bibliography, Indexes

A PHILIP AND MURIEL BERMAN EDITION

M E N A C H E M   E L O N

D E P U T Y   P R E S I D E N T,   S U P R E M E   C O U R T   O F   I S R A E L

JEWISH LAW

HISTORY, SOURCES, PRINCIPLES

Ha-Mishpat Ha-Ivri **VOLUME IV**

Translated from the Hebrew
by Bernard Auerbach
and Melvin J. Sykes

THE JEWISH PUBLICATION SOCIETY Philadelphia Jerusalem 5754 / 1994

Originally published in Hebrew under the title
Ha-Mishpat Ha-Ivri
by the Magnes Press, The Hebrew University, Jerusalem

First English edition

Manufactured in the United States of America

The author and publisher gratefully acknowledge the support of the Philip and Muriel Berman Book Fund of The Jewish Publication Society, sponsored by Mr. and Mrs. Philip I. Berman, Allentown, Pennsylvania, in the publication of this book.

Library of Congress Cataloging-in-Publication Data

Elon, Menachem.
[Mishpaṭ ha-ʻIvri. English]
Jewish law : history, sources, principles / Menachem Elon ; translated from the Hebrew by Bernard Auerbach and Melvin J. Sykes.
p. cm.
Includes bibliographical references and index.
Volume I, ISBN 0–8276–0385-1
Volume II, ISBN 0-8276-0386-X
Volume III, ISBN 0-8276-0387-8
Volume IV, ISBN 0-8276-0388-6
Four-volume set, ISBN 0-8276-0389–4
1. Jewish law—History. 2. Rabbinical literature—History and criticism. 3. Law—Israel—Jewish influences. I. Title.
BM520.5.E4313 1993
296.1′8′09—dc20 93–9278
CIP

Designed by Arlene Putterman

Typeset in Meridien and Perpetua by Graphic Composition, Inc.
Printed by Hamilton Printing Company

PHILIP AND MURIEL BERMAN EDITION

The Author

JUSTICE MENACHEM ELON was first appointed to the Supreme Court of Israel in 1977 and was named Deputy President of the Court in 1988. A legal scholar and teacher, he was awarded the Israel Prize in 1979 for *Ha-Mishpat Ha-Ivri.*

Justice Elon has published many works on the history and nature of Jewish law and the relation between it and the modern State of Israel, including *The Freedom of the Person of the Debtor in Jewish Law* (1964) and *Religious Legislation in the Laws of the State of Israel and Within the Jurisdiction of the Civil and Rabbinical Courts* (1968). From 1968 to 1971 he was editor of the Jewish Law section of the *Encyclopaedia Judaica,* which was subsequently collected in his *Principles of Jewish Law* (1975). By 1984 he had edited 10 volumes of *The Annual of the Institute for Research in Jewish Law of The Hebrew University of Jerusalem* and was also editing a digest of the responsa of the medieval authorities. He has been a member of government committees for the preparation of various bills of the Israeli Civil Law Coordination.

An ordained rabbi, Justice Elon earned his diploma from the Tel Aviv School of Law and Economics in 1948, received a master's degree in humanities, and was awarded a doctor of laws degree *cum laude* from The Hebrew University of Jerusalem. He began his affiliation with The Hebrew University in 1954 as an instructor of law and was subsequently appointed teaching associate, senior lecturer, associate professor, and, in 1972, Professor of Jewish Law.

Translators

BERNARD AUERBACH, Professor of Law, University of Maryland School of Law (retired, 1992). B.A. (Yeshiva University), J.D. (New York University), LL.M. (Yale University), Rabbinic Ordination (Rabbi Isaac Elchanan Theological Seminary, Yeshiva University), Sterling Fellow, (Yale University). *Consultant:* Court of Appeals of Maryland Standing Committee on Rules of Practice and Procedure (1965–1980). *Reporter:* Maryland Judicial Conference (1967–1970). *Recipient:* Bernard Revel Memorial Award for Arts and Sciences, Yeshiva College Alumni Association. *Member:* Jewish Law Association; American Bar Association.

MELVIN J. SYKES, A.B. (Johns Hopkins University), LL.B. (Harvard University), Diplomate, Baltimore Hebrew College. *Fellow:* American College of Trial Lawyers, American College of Trust and Estate Counsel, American Bar Foundation, Maryland Bar Foundation (former president). *Member:* American Law Institute, Court of Appeals of Maryland Standing Committee on Rules of Practice and Procedure; American and Maryland State Bar Associations, Bar Association of Baltimore City. *Sole Practitioner, Baltimore, Maryland:* General practice, trial and appellate litigation, probate and trusts. *Adjunct Faculty Member:* University of Maryland School of Law.

Editorial Consultant

DANIEL D. CHAZIN, *Member:* New Jersey and New York Bars. B.A. (Yeshiva University), J.D. (New York University). *Member:* American Bar Association, New Jersey and New York State Bar Associations. Gruss Fellow, 1989–90, New York University School of Law.

Assistant Editorial Consultant

NORMAN MENACHEM FEDER, A.B., M.A. (Columbia University), J.D. (New York University). Editor-in-Chief, N.Y.U. Journal of International Law & Politics (1986–1987). Luce Scholar (1987–1988). Law Clerk to Judge Roger J. Miner, United States Court of Appeals for the Second Circuit (1988–1989). Law Clerk to Deputy President Menachem Elon, Supreme Court of Israel (1989–1990). Associate, Cleary, Gottlieb, Steen & Hamilton, New York.

SUMMARY OF CONTENTS

BIBLIOGRAPHICAL ABBREVIATIONS OF BOOKS AND ARTICLES FREQUENTLY CITED xix

ABBREVIATIONS USED IN CITING RABBINIC WORKS AND SCHOLARLY LITERATURE xxiii

ABBREVIATIONS USED IN CITING MODERN LEGAL MATERIALS xxv

ACRONYMS AND APPELLATIONS OF HALAKHIC AUTHORITIES xxvii

TRANSLITERATION GUIDE xxxi

VOLUME I

PART ONE
The History and Elements of Jewish Law

Chapter 1	THE HISTORY OF JEWISH LAW	1
Chapter 2	THE DEVELOPMENT OF JEWISH LAW: SOME IMPORTANT FACTORS	46
Chapter 3	THE SCIENTIFIC STUDY OF JEWISH LAW	75
Chapter 4	*MISHPAT IVRI:* DEFINITION AND NATURE	92
Chapter 5	THE ORAL LAW: DEFINITION AND GENERAL PRINCIPLES	190
Chapter 6	THE BASIC NORM AND THE SOURCES OF JEWISH LAW	228
Chapter 7	THE PREROGATIVES OF THE HALAKHIC AUTHORITIES	240

PART TWO
The Legal Sources of Jewish Law
SECTION 1 *Exegesis and Interpretation*

Chapter 8	EXEGESIS AND INTERPRETATION (MIDRASH AND *PARSHANUT*): INTRODUCTION	275
Chapter 9	EXEGETICAL INTERPRETATION OF THE TORAH	281
Chapter 10	INTERPRETATION OF THE *HALAKHAH*	400
Chapter 11	INTERPRETATION OF DOCUMENTS	422
Chapter 12	INTERPRETATION OF COMMUNAL ENACTMENTS	444

GLOSSARY G•1

VOLUME II

PART TWO *(continued)*
The Legal Sources of Jewish Law
SECTION 2 *Legislation, Custom, Precedent, and Legal Reasoning*

Chapter 13	LEGISLATION: INTRODUCTION	477
Chapter 14	LEGISLATION: NATURE, OBJECTIVES, AND PRINCIPLES OF LEGISLATION BY THE HALAKHIC AUTHORITIES	494
Chapter 15	LEGISLATION: ENACTMENTS THROUGH THE END OF THE TANNAITIC PERIOD	545
Chapter 16	LEGISLATION IN THE AMORAIC PERIOD	622
Chapter 17	LEGISLATION IN THE GEONIC PERIOD	643
Chapter 18	POST-GEONIC LEGISLATION: INTRODUCTION	666
Chapter 19	COMMUNAL ENACTMENTS	678
Chapter 20	SURVEY OF LEGISLATION FROM THE TENTH CENTURY C.E. TO THE PRESENT	780
Chapter 21	CUSTOM *(MINHAG)*: ITS NATURE AND THE SOURCE OF ITS BINDING FORCE	880
Chapter 22	CUSTOM: OPERATION AND CATEGORIES	895
Chapter 23	*MA'ASEH* AND PRECEDENT	945
Chapter 24	LEGAL REASONING *(SEVARAH)*	987
	GLOSSARY	G•1

VOLUME III

PART THREE
The Literary Sources of Jewish Law

Chapter 25	THE LITERARY SOURCES OF JEWISH LAW: NATURE AND DEFINITION	1017
Chapter 26	THE LITERARY SOURCES FROM THE SINAITIC REVELATION UNTIL THE *TANNAIM*	1020
Chapter 27	THE LITERARY SOURCES FROM THE TANNAITIC PERIOD UNTIL THE REDACTION OF THE TALMUD: INTRODUCTION	1038
Chapter 28	THE LITERARY SOURCES IN THE TANNAITIC PERIOD	1041
Chapter 29	THE LITERARY SOURCES IN THE AMORAIC PERIOD	1083
Chapter 30	THE LITERARY SOURCES AND OTHER HALAKHIC	

LITERATURE IN THE POST-TALMUDIC PERIOD: INTRODUCTION 1101
Chapter 31 COMMENTARIES AND NOVELLAE 1104
Chapter 32 THE CODIFICATORY LITERATURE: NATURE AND STRUCTURE; THE PROBLEM OF CODIFICATION 1138
Chapter 33 THE CODIFICATORY LITERATURE: FROM THE GEONIC PERIOD UNTIL MAIMONIDES' *MISHNEH TORAH* 1149
Chapter 34 THE CODIFICATORY LITERATURE: MAIMONIDES' *MISHNEH TORAH* 1180
Chapter 35 THE CODIFICATORY LITERATURE: FROM MAIMONIDES UNTIL THE *SHULḤAN ARUKH;* THE *SEFER HA-TURIM* 1236
Chapter 36 THE CODIFICATORY LITERATURE: THE WORKS OF JOSEPH CARO AND MOSES ISSERLES 1309
Chapter 37 THE CODIFICATORY LITERATURE: REACTIONS TO THE *SHULḤAN ARUKH,* AND ITS FINAL ACCEPTANCE 1367
Chapter 38 THE CODIFICATORY LITERATURE: COMMENTARIES ON AND CODIFICATION AFTER THE *SHULḤAN ARUKH* 1423
Chapter 39 THE RESPONSA LITERATURE 1453
Chapter 40 LITERATURE FACILITATING RESEARCH IN JEWISH LAW: COMPILATIONS OF LEGAL DOCUMENTS, REFERENCE WORKS 1529

GLOSSARY G•1

VOLUME IV

PART FOUR
Jewish Law in the State of Israel

Chapter 41 INTRODUCTION: JEWISH LAW FROM THE ABROGATION OF JEWISH JURIDICAL AUTONOMY TO THE ESTABLISHMENT OF THE STATE OF ISRAEL 1575
Chapter 42 JEWISH LAW IN THE GENERAL LEGAL SYSTEM OF THE STATE OF ISRAEL 1619
Chapter 43 THE LAW OF PERSONAL STATUS IN THE RABBINICAL AND GENERAL COURTS: ADDITIONAL ASPECTS OF THE PROBLEM OF THE STATUS OF JEWISH LAW IN THE LAW OF THE STATE OF ISRAEL 1752
Chapter 44 THE FOUNDATIONS OF LAW ACT, 1980 1827
Chapter 45 THE RELIGIOUS AND CULTURAL ASPECTS OF THE QUESTION OF THE STATUS OF JEWISH LAW IN THE JEWISH STATE 1898

Appendixes, Glossary, Bibliography, Indexes

Appendix A CROSS-REFERENCE TABLE—THE *MISHNEH TORAH* AND THE *SHULḤAN ARUKH* 1949

CONTENTS

BIBLIOGRAPHICAL ABBREVIATIONS OF BOOKS AND ARTICLES FREQUENTLY CITED xix

ABBREVIATIONS USED IN CITING RABBINIC WORKS AND SCHOLARLY LITERATURE xxiii

ABBREVIATIONS USED IN CITING MODERN LEGAL MATERIALS xxv

ACRONYMS AND APPELLATIONS OF HALAKHIC AUTHORITIES xxvii

TRANSLITERATION GUIDE xxxi

VOLUME IV

PART FOUR
Jewish Law in the State of Israel

Chapter 41 INTRODUCTION: JEWISH LAW FROM THE ABROGATION OF JEWISH JURIDICAL AUTONOMY TO THE ESTABLISHMENT OF THE STATE OF ISRAEL 1575

I. The Period of the Emancipation, 1576
A. Internal-Spiritual and External-Political Changes, 1576
B. The Change with Regard to the Hebrew Language, 1577
C. The Change in Attitude to Jewish Law, 1578
D. Warnings by the Halakhic Authorities at the Onset of the Change in Attitude to Jewish Law, 1579
E. The Abrogation of Juridical Autonomy and the Reconciliation of the Halakhic Authorities to the New Situation, 1582
F. The Continuation of Juridical Autonomy among the Jews of the Eastern Countries, 1584
G. Consequences of the Abrogation of Jewish Juridical Autonomy, 1586
II. The Era of National Awakening, 1588
A. Ha-Mishpat Ha-Ivri (Jewish Law) Society, 1588

B. Mishpat Ha-Shalom Ha-Ivri (The Jewish Court of Arbitration), 1592
C. Jewish Law in the Rabbinical Courts in the Land of Israel, 1596
1. Establishment of the Chief Rabbinate and Setting the Course of Its Activity in the Area of Jewish Law, 1596
2. Judicial Procedure and the Law of Personal Status, 1598
3. Civil Law, 1600
D. The Religious Leadership and Jewish Law, 1605
E. Jewish Law and the Hebrew Language, 1607
1. The Restoration of the Hebrew Language as the Language of Daily Life, 1607
2. The Position of Jewish Law, 1608
III. On the Eve of the Establishment of the State of Israel, 1611
A. The Legal System under the British Palestine Mandate Immediately before the Establishment of the State of Israel, 1611
B. The Deliberations Regarding the Place of Jewish Law in the Legal System of the State of Israel, 1612
C. Proposals to Require Recourse to Jewish Law, 1617

Chapter 42 **JEWISH LAW IN THE GENERAL LEGAL SYSTEM OF THE STATE OF ISRAEL** **1619**
I. The Official Position of Jewish Law and the Hebrew Language in the State of Israel, 1620
A. Section 11 of the Law and Administration Ordinance, 1948, 1620
B. The Hebrew Language, 1621
C. Dependence on English Law and Non-Recourse to Jewish Law, 1621
II. The Actual Position of Jewish Law in the State's Legal System, 1623
III. Jewish Law in Legislation, 1624
A. The Two Legislative Periods, 1624
B. Legislative Policy, 1625
C. Legislation Based on Principles of Jewish Law, 1627
1. The First Legislative Period, 1627
a. Civil Law, 1627
(1) The Cooperative Houses Law, 1627
(2) Labor Law, 1629
(3) Imprisonment for Debt, 1635
b. Criminal and Public Law, 1639
(1) The Penal Law Revision (Bribery) Law, 1640
(2) The Defamation Law, 1642
(3) Immunity of Judges, 1645
(4) Laws Incorporating Basic Tenets of the Jewish Tradition, 1646
(5) The Law of Return, 1647
(6) The Basic Law: Israel Lands, 1651
c. Personal Status, Family, and Succession Law, 1652
(1) The Marriage Age Law, 1654

(2) The Woman's Equal Rights Law, 1656
(3) The Family Law Amendment (Maintenance) Law, 1660
(4) The Capacity and Guardianship Law, 1663
(5) The Succession Law, 1671
(a) Provisions Generally Incorporating Jewish Law, 1671
(b) Provisions Not in Accord with Jewish Law, 1683
(6) Who Is a Jew?, 1688
2. The Second Legislative Period, 1690
a. The Bailees Law, 1692
b. The Unjust Enrichment Law, 1696
c. Admonition of Witnesses and Abrogation of the Witness Oath, 1697
d. The Crime Register and Rehabilitation of Offenders Law, 1707
e. Self-Help—The Land Law, 1709
f. Illegal Contracts, 1716
D. Legislation Contrary to Jewish Law, 1721
1. Suretyship—The Guarantee Law, 1721
2. The Gift Law, 1724
3. Limitation of Actions, 1724
E. Self-Sufficiency of the Law of the State of Israel, 1728
IV. Jewish Law in Israeli Judicial Decisions, 1729
V. Jewish Law in the Interpretation of Israeli Legislation, 1731
A. Problems of Statutory Interpretation and Interpretive Approaches to Israeli Legislation, 1732
B. The Proper Method of Interpreting Israeli Legislation, 1735
1. Value-Laden Legal Terms, 1738
2. Other Problems of Statutory Construction, 1737
3. *Bank Kupat Am v. Hendeles*—The First Hearing, 1739

Chapter 43 **THE LAW OF PERSONAL STATUS IN THE RABBINICAL AND GENERAL COURTS: ADDITIONAL ASPECTS OF THE PROBLEM OF THE STATUS OF JEWISH LAW IN THE LAW OF THE STATE OF ISRAEL** **1752**

I. Adjudication in Matters of Personal Status, 1753
A. Continuation of the Basic Allocation of Jurisdiction, 1753
B. The Nature of the Problems Discussed in This Chapter, 1756
II. The Law Applied by the Rabbinical Courts in Matters of Personal Status, 1758
A. Jewish Law, 1758
B. Statutes Mandating Their Application by the Rabbinical Courts, 1760
III. Application of the Jewish Law of Personal Status by the General Courts, 1765
A. Conflict of Laws, 1766
B. Evidence and Procedure, 1767
C. Privately Performed Marriages, 1770

1. Marriage Between a *Kohen* and a Divorcée, 1771
2. Marriages Permitted under the *Halakhah*, 1782

IV. The Weight Given by the General Courts to the Decisions of the Rabbinical Courts Interpreting Jewish Law, 1784
A. The Earnings of a Wife from Her Employment, 1785
B. The Rights and Obligations of Parents in the Education of Their Children, 1794

V. Legislation Contrary to Jewish Law—A Case Study of the Solution to a Problem, 1802
A. The Obligation of a Husband to Support His Wife as Affected by Her Income from Employment and from Her Property, 1802
B. Amendment of the Woman's Equal Rights Law, 1805

VI. Differing Trends in Regard to the Employment of Legislation in the Rabbinical System, 1807
A. Decline in Legislation as an Instrument of Halakhic Creativity, 1807
B. The Rabbinical Court of Appeals—Accomplishments and Limitations, 1809

VII. Civil Law in the Rabbinical Courts, 1818

VIII. The Rabbinical Courts and the General Legal System of the State, 1819
A. The *Wiloszni* Case, 1820
B. The *Nagar* Case, 1824

Chapter 44 **THE FOUNDATIONS OF LAW ACT, 1980** **1827**

I. The Purpose and Meaning of the Foundations of Law Act, 1827
A. Repeal of Article 46 of the Palestine Order in Council, 1828
B. The Principles of the Jewish Heritage as a Part of the Positive Law of the Israeli Legal System, 1831
C. According Full Operative Force to the Fundamental Principles of the Israeli Declaration of Independence, 1832
D. Legislation, Judicial Precedent, Analogy, 1834
E. "A Legal Issue Requiring Decision"; Lacuna, 1835
F. The Principles of Freedom, Justice, Equity, and Peace of the Jewish Heritage, 1839
G. The Principles of the Jewish Heritage in the Decisions of the Courts, 1841
1. The Fundamental Rights of Detainees and Prisoners, 1841
2. Freedom from Detention, 1842
3. Freedom of Thought and Speech, 1846
4. Human Dignity and Equality, 1850
5. Attitude toward National and Religious Minorities, 1854
6. The Right of Privacy, 1856
7. Other Court Decisions Discussing the Principles of the Jewish Heritage, 1860

8. How the Sources of the Jewish Heritage Are to Be Used, 1861
II. The Interpretive Function of Jewish Law in the Israeli Legal System in Light of the Foundations of Law Act, 1863
A. Uncertainty as to the Meaning of a Statute—The *Hendeles* Case, Additional Hearing, 1863
B. The Interpretation of Value-Laden Legal Terms, 1871
C. Terms and Expressions Unique to Jewish Law, 1874
D. An Institution of Jewish Law Incorporated Into Israeli Law—The *Koenig* Case, Additional Hearing, 1875
III. The Foundations of Law Act, 1980, and the Incorporation of the English Statute of Elizabeth, 1571, 1885
IV. Conclusion, 1894

Chapter 45 **THE RELIGIOUS AND CULTURAL ASPECTS OF THE QUESTION OF THE STATUS OF JEWISH LAW IN THE JEWISH STATE** **1898**
I. In General, 1898
II. Jewish Law in the Independent Israeli Legal System from the Perspective of the Traditional Jewish Legal System, 1906
A. The Nature of the State's Incorporation of Jewish Law, 1906
B. The Prohibition Against Litigating in Non-Jewish Courts, 1914
C. The Problems When Jewish Legislation and Adjudication Are Not Based on Jewish Law, 1917
III. Jewish Law in the Independent Israeli Legal System from the Perspective of the Law of the State, 1918
A. The Legislature, 1918
B. The Courts, 1920
IV. Subjective and Objective Factors Affecting Recourse to Jewish Law, 1923
A. Subjective Factors, 1924
B. Objective Factors, 1931
C. Observations Concerning Fears and the Fearful, 1938
V. Concluding Reflections, 1940

Appendixes, Glossary, Bibliography, Indexes

Appendix A **CROSS REFERENCE TABLE—THE *MISHNEH TORAH* AND THE *SHULḤAN ARUKH*** **1949**

Appendix B **ADDITIONAL COMPARISONS OF THE LANGUAGE AND STYLE OF THE *MISHNEH TORAH*, THE *TURIM*, AND THE *SHULḤAN ARUKH*** **1979**

Appendix C **A LISTING OF THE MOST WIDELY KNOWN COMPILATIONS OF RESPONSA** **1989**

BIBLIOGRAPHICAL ABBREVIATIONS OF BOOKS AND ARTICLES FREQUENTLY CITED

H. Albeck, *Mavo la-Mishnah* [Introduction to the Mishnah], Jerusalem, 1959 = Albeck, *Mavo.*

G. Alon (or Allon), *Meḥkarim be-Toledot Yisra'el bi-Mei Bayit Sheni u-vi-Tekufat ha-Mishnah ve-ha-Talmud* [Studies in Jewish History in the Days of the Second Temple and in the Mishnaic and Talmudic Period], 2 vols., Tel-Aviv, 1957–1958 = Alon, *Meḥkarim.* (For an English version, *see Jews, Judaism and the Classical World: Studies in Jewish History in the Times of the Second Temple and Talmud,* I. Abrahams and A. Oshery trans., Jerusalem, 1977.)

——— *Toledot ha-Yehudim be-Ereẓ Yisra'el bi-Tekufat ha-Mishnah ve-ha-Talmud* [History of the Jews in the Land of Israel in the Mishnaic and Talmudic Period], 3rd ed., Tel-Aviv, 1959 = Alon, *Toledot.* (For an English version, *see The Jews in Their Land in the Talmudic Age,* G. Levi trans. and ed., Jerusalem, 1 vol., Magnes Press, 1980–1984; reprinted, Harvard University Press, 1989.)

S. Assaf, *Battei ha-Din ve-Sidreihem Aḥarei Ḥatimat ha-Talmud* [Jewish Courts and Their Procedures after the Completion of the Talmud], Jerusalem, 1924 = Assaf, *Battei Din.*

——— *Ha-Onshin Aḥarei Ḥatimat ha-Talmud* [Penal Law After the Completion of the Talmud], Jerusalem, 1922 = Assaf, *Onshin.*

——— *Tekufat ha-Geonim ve-Sifrutah* [The Geonic Period and Its Literature], Jerusalem, 1956 = Assaf, *Geonim.*

Y. Baer, *Toledot Ha-Yehudim bi-Sefarad ha-Noẓrit* [A History of the Jews of Christian Spain], 2nd ed., Tel Aviv, 1965. An English translation, *A History of the Jews in Christian Spain,* JPS, 2 vols., 1961–1966 = Baer, *Spain.*

S.W. Baron, *A Social and Religious History of the Jews,* JPS-Columbia, 18 vols. 1952–1983 = Baron, *History.*

M.A. Bloch, *Sha'arei Torat ha-Takkanot* [On Legislative Enactments], Vienna *et al.*, 7 vols., 1879–1906 = Bloch, *Sha'arei.*

P. Dykan (Dikstein), *Toledot Mishpat ha-Shalom ha-Ivri* [History of the Jewish Court of Arbitration], Tel Aviv, 1964 = Dykan, *Toledot.*

M. Elon, *Ḥakikah Datit be-Ḥukkei Medinat Yisra'el u-va-Shefitah Shel Battei ha-Mishpat u-Vattei ha-Din ha-Rabbaniyyim* [Religious Legislation in the Statutes of the State of Israel and in the Decisions of the General and Rabbinical Courts], Tel Aviv, 1968 = Elon, *Ḥakikah.*

——— "Ha-Ma'asar ba-Mishpat ha-Ivri" [Imprisonment in Jewish Law], *Jubilee Volume for Pinḥas Rosen,* Jerusalem, 1962, pp. 171–201 = Elon, *Ma'asar.*

——— *Ḥerut ha-Perat be-Darkhei Geviyyat Ḥov ba-Mishpat ha-Ivri* [Individual Freedom and the Methods of Enforcing Payment of Debts in Jewish Law], Jerusalem, 1964 = Elon, *Ḥerut.*

——— (ed.) *Principles of Jewish Law,* Jerusalem, 1975 = *Principles.*

——— "Samkhut ve-Oẓmah ba-Kehillah ha-Yehudit, Perek be-Mishpat ha-Ẓibbur ha-Ivri" [Authority and Power in the Jewish Community, A Chapter in Jewish Public Law], in *Shenaton ha-Mishpat ha-Ivri* [Annual of the Institute for Research in Jewish Law], Hebrew University of Jerusalem, III–IV (1976–1977), pp. 7ff. = Elon, *Samkhut ve-Oẓmah.* (For an English translation, *see* "Power and Authority—Halachic Stance of the Traditional Community and Its Contemporary Implications," in *Kinship and Consent, The Jewish Political Tradition and Its Contemporary Uses,* D. Elazar ed., Turtledove Publishing, 1981, pp. 183–213).

——— "Yiḥudah Shel Halakhah ve-Ḥevrah be-Yahadut Ẓefon Afrikah mi-le-aḥar Gerush Sefarad ve-ad Yameinu" [The Exceptional Character of *Halakhah* and Society in North African Jewry from the Spanish Expulsion to the Present], in *Halakhah u-Fetiḥut, Ḥakhmei Morokko ke-Fosekim le-Doreinu* [Halakhah and Open-Mindedness: The Halakhic Authorities of Morocco as Authorities for Our Own Time], 1945, pp. 15ff. = Elon, *Yiḥudah Shel Halakhah.*

J.N. Epstein, *Mavo le-Nusaḥ ha-Mishnah* [Introduction to the Text of the Mishnah], 2nd ed., Jerusalem, 1964 = Epstein, *Mavo.*

——— *Mevo'ot le-Sifrut ha-Tannaim,* [Introduction to Tannaitic Literature], Jerusalem, 1957 = Epstein, *Tannaim.*

——— *Mevo'ot le-Sifrut ha-Amoraim,* [Introduction to Amoraic Literature], Jerusalem, 1963 = Epstein, *Amoraim.*

L. Finkelstein, *Jewish Self-Government in the Middle Ages,* New York 1924 (second printing, New York, 1964) = Finkelstein, *Self-Government.*

Z. Frankel, *Darkhei ha-Mishnah* [The Methodology of the Mishnah], Leipzig, 1859 (facsimile ed., Tel Aviv, 1969) = Frankel, *Mishnah.*

——— *Mevo ha-Yerushalmi* [Introduction to the Jerusalem Talmud], Breslau, 1870 (facsimile ed., Jerusalem, 1967) = Frankel, *Mevo.*

A.H. Freimann, *Seder Kiddushin ve-Nissu'in Aḥarei Ḥatimat ha-Talmud, Meḥkar Histori-Dogmati be-Dinei Yisra'el* [Law of Betrothal and Marriage after the Completion of the Talmud: A Historical-Dogmatic Study in Jewish Law], Mosad ha-Rav Kook, Jerusalem, 1945 = Freimann, *Kiddushin ve-Nissu'in.*

L. Ginzberg, *Perushim ve-Ḥiddushim ba-Yerushalmi* [A Commentary on the Palestine Talmud] (English title by Prof. Ginzberg), New York, 1941 (facsimile ed., New York, 1971) = Ginzberg, *Perushim.*

A. Gulak, *Yesodei ha-Mishpat ha-Ivri* [The Foundations of Jewish Law], Jerusalem, 1923 (facsimile ed., Tel Aviv, 1967) = Gulak, *Yesodei.*

I. Halevy, *Dorot ha-Rishonim* [The Early Generations—A History of the Oral Law to the *Geonim*], Frankfort, 1897–1906 (facsimile ed., Jerusalem, 1957) = Halevy, *Dorot.*

I. Herzog, *The Main Institutions of Jewish Law,* 2nd ed., London, 2 vols., 1965–1967 = Herzog, *Institutions.*

D.Z. Hoffmann, *Das Buch Deuteronomium Übersetzt und Erklärt* [The Book of Deuteronomy: Translation and Commentary] = Hoffmann, *Commentary on Deuteronomy.*

Kovez̤ Teshuvot ha-Rambam ve-Iggerotav [Compilation of Responsa and Epistles of Maimonides], Leipzig, 1859 = *Kovez̤ ha-Rambam.*

J. Levy, *Wörterbuch über die Talmudim und Midraschim* [Talmudic and Midrashic Dictionary], 2nd ed., Berlin, 1924 = Levy, *Wörterbuch.*

S. Lieberman, *Greek in Jewish Palestine* = Lieberman, *Greek.*

——— *Hellenism in Jewish Palestine* = Lieberman, *Hellenism.*

A. Neubauer, *Seder ha-Ḥakhamim ve-Korot ha-Yamim* [Medieval Jewish Chronicles], Oxford, 1895 (facsimile ed., Jerusalem, 1967) = Neubauer, *Seder ha-Ḥakhamim.*

J.W. Salmond, *On Jurisprudence,* 12th ed., London, 1966 = Salmond.

Shenaton ha-Mishpat ha-Ivri [Annual of the Institute for Research in Jewish Law, Hebrew University of Jerusalem] = *Shenaton.*

M. Silberg, *Ha-Ma'amad ha-Ishi be-Yisra'el* [Personal Status in Israel], 4th ed., Jerusalem, 1965 = Silberg, *Ha-Ma'amad.*

H. Tykocinski, *Takkanot ha-Geonim* [Geonic Enactments], Jerusalem, 1960 = Tykocinski, *Takkanot.*

E.E. Urbach, *Ḥazal, Pirkei Emunot ve-De'ot* [The Sages: Doctrines and Beliefs], rev. ed., Jerusalem, 1971 = Urbach, *The Sages.* (For an English version *see The Sages, Their Concepts and Beliefs,* I. Abrahams trans., Magnes Press, 2 vols., Jerusalem, 1975.)

——— *Ba'alei ha-Tosafot, Toledoteihem, Ḥibbureihem ve-Shittatam* [The Tosafists, Their History, Writings and Methodology], 2nd ed, Jerusalem, 1968 = Urbach, *Tosafot.*

Z. Warhaftig, (ed.); *Osef Piskei ha-Din Shel ha-Rabbanut ha-Rashit le-Erez̤ Yis-*

ra'el [A Compilation of the Rulings of the Chief Rabbinate of the Land of Israel], 1950, = *Osef Piskei ha-Din.*

I.H. Weiss, *Dor Dor ve-Doreshav* [The Generations and Their Interpreters—A History of the Oral Law], 6th ed., Vilna, 1915 = Weiss, *Dor Dor ve-Doreshav.*

ABBREVIATIONS USED IN CITING RABBINIC WORKS AND SCHOLARLY LITERATURE

ad loc.	*ad locum*, "at the place," used after a citation to designate commentary on the passage cited
A.M.	*anno mundi*, "in the year [from the creation] of the world"
b.	ben, bar, "son of"—as in Simeon b. Gamaliel
Baḥ	*Bayit Ḥadash*, a commentary on *Tur* by Joel Sirkes.
B.C.E.	before the common era, equivalent of B.C.
ca.	*circa*, "approximately"
C.E.	common era, equivalent of A.D.
cf.	*confer*, "compare"
EH	*Even ha-Ezer*, part of the *Shulḥan Arukh*
EJ	Encyclopaedia Judaica
ET	*Enẓiklopedyah Talmudit* [Talmudic Encyclopedia]
ḤM	*Ḥoshen Mishpat*, part of the *Shulḥan Arukh*
HUCA	*Hebrew Union College Annual*
ibn	"son of," equivalent of "b." (which *see*)
id.	*idem*, "the same," used instead of repeating the immediately preceding citation
JJGL	*Jahrbuch für jüdische Geschichte und Literatur* [Jewish History and Literature Annual]
JJLG	*Jahrbuch der jüdisch-literarischen* Gesellschaft [Jewish Literary Society Annual]
JPS	The Jewish Publication Society
JQR	*Jewish Quarterly Review*
lit.	literally
loc. cit.	*loco citato*, "in the place [previously] cited"
M	Mishnah, used to designate a Mishnaic tractate
MGWJ	*Monatsschrift für Geschichte und Wissenschaft des Judenthums* [Monthly for the History and Science of Judaism]
ms., mss.	manuscript(s)
MT	*Mishneh Torah* (Maimonides' code)

n.	note
nn.	notes
OḤ	*Oraḥ Ḥayyim,* part of the *Shulḥan Arukh*
op. cit.	*opere citato,* "in the work [previously] cited"
R.	Rabbi, Rav, or Rabban, used in the present work for the Talmudic Sages
Resp.	Responsa
Sema	*Sefer Me'irat Einayim* by Joshua Falk
Semag	*Sefer Miẓvot Gadol* by Moses of Coucy
Semak	*Sefer Miẓvot Katan* by Isaac of Corbeil
Shakh	*Siftei Kohen* by Shabbetai b. Meir ha-Kohen
Sh. Ar.	*Shulḥan Arukh*
"Shum"	Hebrew acrostic for the communities of Speyer, Worms, and Mainz
s.v.	*sub verbo, sub voce,* "under the word," designating the word or expression to which commentary is appended. Equivalent of Hebrew "d.h." (*dibbur ha-matḥil*)
Taz	*Turei Zahav* by David b. Samuel ha-Levi
TB	Talmud Bavli [Babylonian Talmud]
TJ	Talmud Yerushalmi [Jerusalem Talmud, sometimes called Palestine Talmud]
Tur	*Sefer ha-Turim* by Jacob b. Asher
v.l.	*varia lectio,* pl. *variae lectiones,* "variant reading(s)"
YD	*Yoreh De'ah,* part of the *Shulḥan Arukh*

ABBREVIATIONS USED IN CITING MODERN LEGAL MATERIALS

A.2d	Atlantic Reports, Second Series (U.S.)
A.B.A.J.	*American Bar Association Journal*
A.C.	Law Reports Appeal Cases (Eng.)
All E.R.	All England Law Reports, formerly All England Law Reports Annotated
Atk.	Atkyns English Chancery Reports (1736–1755)
Ch.	Chancery (Eng.)
C.L.R.	Current Law Reports (cases decided during the British Mandate)
Colum. L. Rev.	*Columbia Law Review*
D.C. App.	District of Columbia Court of Appeals
DK	*Divrei ha-Keneset* [The Knesset Record]
E.R., Eng. Rep.	English Reports, Full Reprint (1220–1865)
Ex.	Court of Exchequer (Eng.)
Harv. L. Rev.	*Harvard Law Review*
H.L.C.	Clark's House of Lords Cases (Eng.)
I.C.L.Q.	*International and Comparative Law Quarterly*
I.S.C.J.	Israel Supreme Court Judgments
Jur.	Jurist Reports (Eng., 18 vols.)
K.B.	King's Bench (Eng.)
L.J.	Law Journal
L.J.Q.B.	Law Journal Reports, New Series, Queen's Bench (Eng.)
L.Q.	Law Quarterly
L. Rev.	Law Review
Md. L. Rev.	*Maryland Law Review*
Minn. L. Rev.	*Minnesota Law Review*
Mod.	Modern Reports, 1669–1732 (Eng.)
N.E.2d	Northeastern Reporter, Second Series (U.S.)
Ohio App.	Ohio (Intermediate) Appellate Court reports

Osef Piskei ha-Din	a collection of rabbinical court decisions compiled by Zeraḥ Warhaftig
P.D.	*Piskei Din,* Israel Supreme Court Reports
P.D.R.	*Piskei Din Rabbaniyyim,* Israel Rabbinical Court Reports
P.L.R.	Palestine Law Reports (Court Decisions during the British Mandate)
P.M.	*Pesakim Meḥoziyyim,* Israel District Court Reports
Q.B.	Queen's Bench (Eng.)
SCJ	Supreme Court Judgments Annotated (Reports of cases in the Supreme Court of the Land of Israel during the British Mandate)
Vand. L. Rev.	*Vanderbilt Law Review*
Wis. L. Rev.	*Wisconsin Law Review*
W.L.R.	Weekly Law Reports (Eng.)

ACRONYMS AND APPELLATIONS OF HALAKHIC AUTHORITIES

Alfasi	Isaac b. Jacob ha-Kohen of Fez, Rif
Asheri	Asher b. Jehiel, Rosh
Ba'al ha-Roke'aḥ	Eliezer b. Judah
Ba'al ha-Turim	Jacob b. Asher
Baḥ	Joel Sirkes
Ḥafeẓ Ḥayyim	Israel Meir ha-Kohen
Ha-Gra	Elijah b. Solomon Zalman (Gaon of Vilna)
Ha-Kala'i	Alfasi
Ḥakham Zevi	Zevi Hirsch b. Jacob Ashkenazi
Ḥatam Sofer	Moses Sofer
Ḥayyim Or Zaru'a	Hayyim b. Isaac
Ḥazon Ish	Abraham Isaiah Karelitz
Ḥida	Ḥayyim Joseph David Azulai
Mabit	Moses b. Joseph Trani
Maharaḥ	Ḥayyim b. Isaac, also known as Ḥayyim Or Zaru'a
Maharai	Israel Isserlein
Maharal of Prague	Judah Loew b. Beẓalel
Maharalbaḥ	Levi b. Ḥabib
Maharam Alashkar	Moses b. Isaac Alashkar
Maharam Alshekh	Moses b. Ḥayyim Alshekh
Maharam of Lublin	Meir b. Gedaliah of Lublin
Maharam Mintz	Moses b. Isaac Mintz
Maharam of Padua	Meir Katzenellenbogen
Maharam of Rothenburg	Meir b. Baruch of Rothenburg
Maharash Kastilaẓ	Simeon Kastilaẓ
Maharashdam	Samuel b. Moses Medina
Maharaẓ Chajes	Ẓevi Hirsch Chajes
Mahardakh	David ha-Kohen of Corfu

Maharḥash	Ḥayyim Shabbetai of Salonika
Mahari Bruna	Israel b. Ḥayyim Bruna
Mahari Caro	Joseph Caro, also known as Maran
Mahari Minẓ	Judah Minẓ
Mahari Weil	Jacob b. Judah Weil, also known as Maharyu
Maharibal	Joseph ibn Lev
Maharif	Jacob Faraji
Maharik	Joseph b. Solomon Colon
Maharikash	Jacob b. Abraham Castro
Maharil	Jacob b. Moses Moellin
Maharit	Joseph b. Moses Trani
Maharit Algazi	Yom Tov b. Israel Jacob Algazi
Maharitaẓ	Yom Tov b. Akiva Ẓahalon
Mahariẓ	Yeḥaiah (Yaḥya, Yiḥye) b. Joseph Ẓalaḥ (Saliḥ)
Maharsha	Samuel Eliezer b. Judah ha-Levi Edels
Maharshak	Samson b. Isaac of Chinon
Maharshakh	Solomon b. Abraham
Maharshal	Solomon b. Jehiel Luria
Maharsham	Shalom Mordecai b. Moses Schwadron
Maharyu	Jacob b. Judah Weil, also known as Mahari Weil
Malbim	Meir Leib b. Jehiel Michael
Maran	Joseph Caro, also known as Mahari Caro
Neẓiv (Naẓiv)	Naphtali Ẓevi Judah Berlin
Noda bi-Yehudah	Ezekiel b. Judah ha-Levi Landau
Rabad (Rabad I)	Abraham b. David (ibn Daud) of Posquières
Rabad (Rabad II)	Abraham b. David (ibn Daud) ha-Levi
Raban	Eliezer b. Nathan of Mainz
Rabi	Abraham b. Isaac of Narbonne
Radbaz	David ibn Zimra
Ralbag	Levi b. Gershom, Gersonides
Ralbaḥ	Levi ibn Ḥabib
Ramah	Meir Abulafia
Rambam	Moses b. Maimon, Maimonides
Ramban	Moses b. Naḥman, Naḥmanides
Ran	Nissim of Gerona (Gerondi)
Ranaḥ	Elijah b. Ḥayyim

Rash	Samson b. Abraham of Sens
Rashba	Solomon b. Abraham Adret
Rashbam	Samuel b. Meir
Rashbash	Solomon b. Simeon Duran
Rashbeẓ (Rashbaẓ)	Simeon b. Ẓemaḥ Duran
Rashi	Solomon b. Isaac of Troyes
Rav Za'ir	Chaim Tchernowitz
Raviah	Eliezer b. Joel ha-Levi
Redak (Radak)	David Kimḥi
Re'em	Elijah b. Abraham Mizraḥi; Eliezer b. Samuel of Metz
Re'iyah	Abraham Isaac ha-Kohen Kook
Rema	Moses Isserles
Remakh	Moses ha-Kohen of Lunel
Reshakh	Solomon b. Abraham, Maharshakh
Rezah	Zeraḥia ha-Levi Gerondi
Ri	Isaac b. Samuel, also known as Isaac the Elder
Ri Migash	Joseph ibn Migash
Riaz	Isaac b. Moses of Vienna; Isaiah b. Elijah of Trani
Ribash	Isaac b. Sheshet Perfet
Rid	Isaiah b. Mali di Trani the Elder
Rif	Isaac b. Jacob ha-Kohen, Alfasi
Ritba	Yom Tov b. Abraham Ishbili
Riẓag	Isaac ibn Ghayyat
Rogachover	Joseph Rozin (Rosen)
Rosh	Asher b. Jehiel, Asheri
Shadal (Shedal)	Samuel David Luzzatto
Tashbaẓ (Tashbeẓ)	Samson b. Ẓadok
Tukh	Eliezer of Touques
Yaveẓ	Jacob Emden
Yaveẓ of North Africa	Jacob ibn Ẓur of Morocco

TRANSLITERATION GUIDE

LETTERS

NAME OF LETTER	SYMBOL	TRANSLITERATION	SOUND	REMARKS
aleph	א	not transliterated		
bet	בּ	b	as in *b*oy	
vet	ב	v	as in *v*alue	
gimmel	גּ, ג	g	as in *g*ate	no distinction between gimmel with *dagesh lene* and *gimmel* without *dagesh*
dalet	דּ, ד	d	as in *d*ance	no distinction between *dalet* with *dagesh lene* and *dalet* without a *dagesh*
he	ה	h	as in *h*ome	
vav	ו	v	as in *v*alve	when used as a vowel, transliterated as "o" or "u"
zayin	ז	z	as in Zion	
ḥet	ח	ḥ	ch as in German *Achtung*	no English equivalent
tet	ט	t	t as in *t*ag	
yod	י	y or i	y as in *y*es or when i, like ee in sh*ee*n	y except when vowel, and then "i"
kaf	כּ	k	k as in *k*ing or c as in *c*ome	English has no equivalent for the difference between *ḥet* and *khaf* in Hebrew
khaf	כ,ך	kh	like ch as in *Achtung*	

LETTERS (*continued*)

NAME OF LETTER	SYMBOL	TRANSLITERATION	SOUND	REMARKS
lamed	ל	l	l as in *l*ean	
mem	מ,ם	m	m as in *m*other	
nun	נ,ן	n	n as in *n*o	
samekh	ס	s	s as in *s*ing	
ayin	ע	not transliterated		indicated by apostrophe
pe	פּ	p	p as in *p*ost	
fe	פ,ף	f	f as in *f*ine	
ẓade / sade / tsade	צ,ץ	ẓ	like ts in fi*ts*	
kof	ק	k	like ck as in lo*ck*	
resh	ר	r	r as in *r*ain	may be rolled
shin	שׁ	sh	sh as in *sh*ine	
sin	שׂ	s	s as in *s*ong	
tav / taw	תּ / ת	t	t as in *t*ame	no distinction between *tav* with *dagesh lene* and *tav* without a *dagesh*

VOWELS

NAME OF VOWEL	SYMBOL (PLACED BELOW LETTER)	TRANSLITERATION	SOUND	REMARKS
kamatz / kameẓ / kamaẓ	ָ	a	like a in f*a*ther	if "long" kamaẓ
		o	like aw in l*aw*	if "short" kamaẓ
pataḥ	ַ	a	like a in f*a*ther	
ḥataf-pataḥ	ֲ	a	like a in *a*lignment	but no precise English equivalent

VOWELS (*continued*)

NAME OF VOWEL	SYMBOL (PLACED BELOW LETTER)	TRANSLITERATION	SOUND	REMARKS
ẓere / tsere	ֵ	e or ei	like *ai* as in pl*ai*n, ei as in "v*ei*n"	except *bet* not *beit*
segol	ֶ	e	like e in l*e*d	
ḥataf-segol	ֱ	e	like second e in heg*e*mony	
sheva	ְ	e	like e in sh*e*nanigan	*sheva na* is transliterated, *sheva naḥ* is not
ḥirek / ḥireq	ִ	i	between ee in sh*ee*n and i in p*i*n	
holam	וֹ, ֹ	o	o as in h*o*me	dot placed above letter
kubbuẓ / kibbuẓ	וּ, ֻ	u	u as in bl*ue*	

Notes

1. *Dagesh forte* is represented by doubling the letter, except that the letter *shin* is not doubled.

2. The definite article "ha" is followed by a hyphen, but although the following letter always has a *dagesh forte* in the Hebrew, it is not doubled in the transliteration. The transliteration of the definite article starts with a small "h" except in the name of Rabbi Judah Ha-Nasi, Rosh Ha-Shanah (the holiday) and the beginning of a sentence or title.

3. An apostrophe between vowels indicates that the vowels do not constitute a diphthong, but each is to have its separate pronunciation.

PART FOUR

Jewish Law in the State of Israel

Chapter 41

INTRODUCTION: JEWISH LAW FROM THE ABROGATION OF JEWISH JURIDICAL AUTONOMY TO THE ESTABLISHMENT OF THE STATE OF ISRAEL

I. The Period of the Emancipation
- A. Internal-Spiritual and External-Political Changes
- B. The Change with Regard to the Hebrew Language
- C. The Change in Attitude to Jewish Law
- D. Warnings by the Halakhic Authorities at the Onset of the Change in Attitude to Jewish Law
- E. The Abrogation of Juridical Autonomy and the Reconciliation of the Halakhic Authorities to the New Situation
- F. The Continuation of Juridical Autonomy among the Jews of the Eastern Countries
- G. Consequences of the Abrogation of Jewish Juridical Autonomy

II. The Era of National Awakening
- A. Ha-Mishpat Ha-Ivri (Jewish Law) Society
- B. Mishpat Ha-Shalom Ha-Ivri (The Jewish Court of Arbitration)
- C. Jewish Law in the Rabbinical Courts in the Land of Israel
  1. Establishment of the Chief Rabbinate and Setting the Course of Its Activity in the Area of Jewish Law
  2. Judicial Procedure and the Law of Personal Status
  3. Civil Law
- D. The Religious Leadership and Jewish Law
- E. Jewish Law and the Hebrew Language
  1. The Restoration of the Hebrew Language as the Language of Daily Life
  2. The Position of Jewish Law

III. On the Eve of the Establishment of the State of Israel
- A. The Legal System under the British Palestine Mandate Immediately before the Establishment of the State of Israel
- B. The Deliberations Regarding the Place of Jewish Law in the Legal System of the State of Israel
- C. Proposals to Require Recourse to Jewish Law

I. THE PERIOD OF THE EMANCIPATION

A. Internal-Spiritual and External-Political Changes

A fundamental change in the historic course of Jewish law took place in the eighteenth century with the advent of the Emancipation and the abrogation of Jewish autonomy. The story of the termination of Jewish autonomy in general, and of Jewish juridical autonomy in particular, has been widely documented in recent historical studies and need not be repeated here.[1] As already noted,[2] two factors supported and explain the persistence of a living and functioning Jewish legal system notwithstanding the lack of political sovereignty and of a territorial center. The first factor was the internal discipline of traditional Jewish society, which, rooted in religious and national imperatives, felt bound to govern its everyday life by Jewish law. The second factor was the existence of the corporative state; by virtue of its political structure, the state allowed autonomous bodies possessed of juridical authority to exist within its boundaries and, indeed, for various reasons already discussed, even had a positive interest in promoting the existence of such autonomy.

In the eighteenth century, however, both these factors underwent a radical change. From the political perspective, as a result of the movement toward equality before the law for all citizens, including Jews, the European countries, in quick succession, withdrew from their Jewish communities the power, even in civil litigation, to compel Jews to submit to adjudication before Jewish courts. The use of the ban, as well as other methods of enforcing the judgments of Jewish courts, was also prohibited. Important as the political factor was, however, the primary cause of the progressive disuse of Jewish law in practical life was the change wrought by the Emancipation in the social and spiritual life of the Jewish people, and the consequent erosion of the internal discipline that had been largely responsible for the vitality of Jewish law in the everyday life of the community. Up to

1. *See* S.W. Baron, *The Jewish Community,* II, pp. 351ff.; Y. Kaufmann, *Golah ve-Nekhar* [Exile and Estrangement], II, 1930; J. Katz, *Tradition and Crisis,* ch. XX, pp. 213ff.; Assaf, *Battei ha-Din,* pp. 5–6; A.H. Freimann, "Dinei Yisra'el be-Ereẓ Yisra'el" [Jewish Law in the Land of Israel], *Luaḥ ha-Areẓ,* 1946, pp. 110ff.; S. Ettinger, "Toledot Yisra'el ba-Et ha-Ḥadashah" [History of the Jews in the Modern Period], in H.H. Ben-Sasson, *Toledot Am Yisra'el* [History of the Jewish People], vol. 3, 1970, pp. 17–137.

2. *Supra* pp. 3–39.

that time, the Jewish community had regarded Jewish law as the supreme value by which all activities were to be measured; but the Emancipation split the community—some still followed the tradition, but others felt no obligation to do so.

B. The Change with Regard to the Hebrew Language

This radical change in spiritual outlook cut far more deeply than the matter of the observance of religious precepts. Among other results, it produced a change in attitude to the Hebrew language. As Yeḥezkel Kaufmann has written:[3]

> Previously, Jewry was able to preserve the Hebrew language as a cultural medium. The source of its vitality was its religious sanctity. As long as the culture was religious, the people strove to maintain the "holy tongue" as part of it. In the mundane world of everyday life, such as the marketplace, Jews used the vernacular, either unchanged or in some modified form. However, the other languages used by the Jews could not dislodge Hebrew as the medium of religious-cultural creativity. Hebrew (sometimes together with its sister language, Aramaic) was the language of the literature of "Torah," of *Halakhah,* of *Aggadah,* and of sacred poetry. The power it derived as a result of this basic role sometimes enabled it to serve as a medium of creative secular expression as well.
>
> It is true that in spite of its special cultural value in pre-modern Jewish life, Hebrew was not always able to maintain itself against its foreign rivals during that period, even in the cultural sphere. In various periods, the Jews produced complete literatures in the vernacular (including works of religious Jewish content), such as the Hellenistic and Judeo-Arabic literatures. Nevertheless, so long as religion was the focus of intellectual life and the Torah remained the supreme cultural ideal, the position of Hebrew, the language of the Torah, remained strong.
>
> However, when the old cultural pattern began to be undermined, the Hebrew language could no longer maintain its position. From the time that the new secular culture began to prevail over traditional Judaism, the language of the new culture also began to make inroads against the position of Hebrew. In the sphere of secular culture, Hebrew could not compete against living foreign languages rooted in practical life. As the secular culture replaced the Torah culture, so the secular language supplanted the Torah language. Given that Judah Halevi wrote his religious-national work, the *Kuzari,* in Arabic, what could Hebrew now hope for in the face of the waning power of the traditional cultural ideal? The languages of the gentiles began to prevail among Jews, not only as languages of the marketplace but even as vehicles

3. Kaufmann, *supra* n. 1 at 38–39.

of cultural expression. The Hebrew language was forced to make its stand within the narrow confines of religion.

C. The Change in Attitude to Jewish Law

The change in the attitude of the Jewish community toward Jewish law was even more drastic. Here again Kaufmann has put it well:[4]

> Together with the loss of place suffered by the [Hebrew] language, another fundamental institution of the pre-modern Jewish community, which performed a function of incomparable significance, also began to crumble. Jewish law began to lose its force as an active social institution. This was, perhaps, the most profound change in Jewish life that occurred at that time.

This was a development which, as Kaufmann proceeded to point out, was rooted in the general trend of the time:

> [This trend was the] overall change that took place in European culture—the end of the old religious-cultural worldview. . . . The more the desire to free life from the control of religion spread its roots in the Jewish community, the greater was the tendency to consign the old religious law to the archives. The modern state withdrew only the governmental sanction this law previously enjoyed, but did not prohibit its use or prevent the Jews from being judged according to their own laws. Nevertheless, the importance of the Jewish court in matters not strictly religious continued to decline over the course of time. Jewish law was part of the old religious worldview that established religion as the arbiter of all of life. When this worldview lost its hold, Jewish law lost its power.

As already pointed out, the drastic spiritual change in religious outlook during the era of the Emancipation also engendered a blindness to the distinct national element of Jewish law:

> From the fate of Jewish law, one can clearly discern the nature of the factors that operated to bring about assimilation in modern times. It was Jewish law that was the basis for a clearly distinctive national life and truly fashioned the pre-modern Jewish community into a "nation within a nation." But this law was also the foundation for a unique religious culture. . . . The secular outlook on life and culture in this period destroyed this strong pillar of pre-modern Jewish life. . . . The natural heir of Jewish religious law was the law of the non-Jewish secular state. Other cultural areas followed the same pattern. Each area that became disengaged from religion was vanquished (or would in the future be vanquished) by non-Jewish culture.[5]

4. *Id.* at 40.
5. *Id.* at 40–41.

The consequence of this drastic change in attitude toward the significance and function of Jewish law in the life of the Jewish people was that not only did Jewish communal leaders offer no resistance to the termination of Jewish juridical autonomy, but a substantial number even welcomed the end of this segregation of the Jewish community from the general society. They viewed this development as helping to achieve the freedom and equality long hoped for and promised, and as an opportunity to become an organic part of the emancipated European society.

D. Warnings by the Halakhic Authorities at the Onset of the Change in Attitude to Jewish Law

At the beginning of this critical change, many leading halakhic authorities voiced stern and severe warnings of the religious and national peril lurking in the abrogation of Jewish juridical autonomy. In the second half of the eighteenth century, Ezekiel Landau, the Rabbi of Prague, admonished those

> who go to non-Jewish courts and thereby undermine divine justice.[6]
>
> Many breaches have occurred in our generation; and the three pillars on which the entire world rests—justice, truth, and peace—have been shaken. We witness in our own land [Bohemia] the weakening of [our] law; and it is only by chance that parties sometimes agree to submit their case to adjudication by arbitrators chosen according to the law of the Torah. It never occurs to anyone to subject himself to the law of the Torah on account of the respect due to it and on account of the fear of God, the Judge of all the world, Who has commanded us to judge according to the law of the Torah. The laws of the Torah are thus treated with scorn.[7]

A strong and particularized admonition was delivered by Raphael ha-Kohen, who, during his lifetime (1723–1804), was the spiritual leader of various Jewish communities in Poland, Lithuania, and Germany.[8] Raphael ha-Kohen considered one of his major tasks to be the strengthening and sustaining of an autonomous Jewish legal system, and he devoted great effort to this end.[9] A major part of his last two sermons to the community of Altona in 1799 consisted of a description of the gradual erosion of Jewish

6. *Derushei ha-Ẓelaḥ*, Homily #8, end of par. 14, p. 16b.

7. *Id.*, Homily #22, par. 24, p. 33d.

8. Among these communities were Minsk, Wilkomir, Pinsk, Posen, and the three associated communities of Altona, Hamburg, and Wandsbeck. *See* Eliezer (Lazarus) Katzenellenbogen, *Zekher Ẓaddik* [Remembrance of a Righteous Man], 1805, section "Ma'alelei Ish" [The Great Deeds of a Man], pp. 4ff. (hereinafter, *Zekher Ẓaddik*); J.A. Kamelhar, *Dor De'ah* [An Enlightened Generation], 1953, pp. 81–86.

9. *See Zekher Ẓaddik*, pp. 7–8, 17 *et al.*

juridical autonomy in Europe, an analysis of the causes of this development, and words of admonition and reproof:[10]

> If we pay attention, we will see . . . that most of the reproofs of the earlier and later prophets concerned matters of justice . . . and that instead of carrying out our obligation of doing justice, by the merit of which God would rescue us from our captivity, we have sinned even more than our fathers. . . .
>
> Consider, and look about you to all the lands where the Jewish people are scattered. In former times, they had law and justice, a rod and a lash with which to rescue the oppressed from the oppressor and to break the teeth of iniquity in all the lands of their habitation. Even in those days of darkness and eclipse, times of ever-imminent danger, expulsions, calamities, and afflictions which we underwent everywhere—in spite of all, the "scepter did not depart from Judah" nor the "ruler's staff" from between our feet [*cf.* Genesis 49:10]. From it, our justice became manifest according to the customs and laws which were our heritage.
>
> But now (woe to a generation in whose days this happens!) there remains no remembrance or trace of God's just laws; "Our enemies are now our judges" [*cf.* Deuteronomy 32:31]. The honor of Jacob has dimmed among the nations, and his laws are no longer remembered. . . . These are no trivial things that we have experienced—the tribulations that we see in all the lands and places of our habitation in Europe. The very source of our life is dishonored; law and justice have departed, and the law of Israel is no longer remembered in our land. How shall we earn deliverance from our exile? By what means shall we obtain the favor of our God?[11]

Raphael ha-Kohen acknowledged the religious and social significance of the fact that observance of the commandments and obedience to the Torah had declined among part of the Jewish population of his time. It was, however, the cavalier attitude toward the requirement that disputes among

10. He delivered this sermon, entitled *Ẓiyyon be-Mishpat* [Zion with Justice; *cf.* Isaiah 1:27—"Zion shall be redeemed with justice"], on the eve of Rosh Ḥodesh Adar II, 1799. *See Zekher Ẓaddik,* pp. 18a/b. The description of his speech by a member of the audience who recorded what he said is fascinating: "It was amazing to see a man nearly in his eighties speak with such fire. . . . On that day, he renewed his strength, restored his vigor, and stood before us like a man who had become a youth once again; the fire of God burned in his words; the flames emitted from his mouth entered the hearts of the listeners—the flames of the Lord! The entire audience responded as one, saying: 'We have never heard a voice like this, speaking from the midst of the fire, as we have heard today' [*cf.* Deuteronomy 4:33]." *Id.* at 8b.

11. *Id.* at 7b–8a. This should not be understood to mean that juridical autonomy was completely abrogated during the life of Raphael ha-Kohen. He himself (as explained further on, *id.*) stated that such autonomy existed in Altona during his lifetime. He was forcefully pointing out the critical and fundamental turn of events taking place in his time, which he foresaw would result in the complete abrogation of juridical autonomy.

Jews be adjudicated according to Jewish law that he viewed as the most severe consequence of the abandonment of the law of the Torah:

> Even with all the sinful deeds . . . if only they would hold fast to the law and not turn their backs on it, they would retain the power of survival, because God would be gracious to them. . . . For if there is no law, there will be no graciousness. Of all the evil deeds they have done, the most sinful toward Him has been the abandonment of the law; this alone is the cause of His failure to show favor toward them.[12]

Raphael ha-Kohen repeatedly emphasized that the most distressing aspect of the abrogation of Jewish juridical autonomy was the support and encouragement of this development by part of the Jewish community, which viewed it as a step toward equality of rights and obligations with the rest of the general population. Those [he stated]

> who neither rested nor paused . . . [in their efforts] to take away the "ruler's staff" from the judges of Israel—how can they not be abashed and ashamed? . . . They have left neither root nor branch of the laws of God and Israel. Let them be ashamed and mortified, these partners of the destroyer! . . . They were at the forefront of this heinous removal of all trace of even the slightest authority from Israel.[13]

Accordingly, Raphael ha-Kohen's last request to the community of Altona was the following:

> One thing more do I ask of the house of Israel. Awake! I entreat you to serve God valiantly. Strengthen the pillar of the law, this remaining precious asset, which God's grace has inclined the heart of our master, the gracious king (may his glory increase), to bestow on us in his land—the privilege of adjudicating our disputes according to the Torah, the laws, and the ordinances which God has commanded us. Hold dear this remaining privilege we have in this land, for which your ancestors have ever sacrificed their lives and possessions. Let them always be remembered for their courageous efforts for our people to establish and protect God's throne.
>
> You who have taken the place of your fathers—follow their good deeds and strengthen the hands of the judges in your towns by giving them the capacity and the power to break the teeth of iniquity and to render judgments of truth and peace in your gates. Who knows but that it is because of the rule of law and justice that God has given you all these good things which you have seen?

12. *Id.* at 8b.
13. *Id.* at 8a, 9a/b.

> For while all the other lands reverberate with the clamor of war, you live here in peace and tranquillity and there is no one of whom you need be afraid. May the blessings of God be upon you and may God increase them a thousandfold. May the pillar of the law, upon which the world rests, support and protect you.[14]

E. The Abrogation of Juridical Autonomy and the Reconciliation of the Halakhic Authorities to the New Situation

The entreaties of Raphael ha-Kohen to the communal leaders were unsuccessful. Indeed, the situation worsened. The external-political and internal-spiritual changes that progressively developed during the nineteenth century affected even that part of the Jewish people that continued to observe the religious tradition. Among the Jews of Western and Central Europe, it soon became the widespread and accepted practice among all elements of the Jewish community to litigate in the courts of the state.[15] The traditional Jewish population of Eastern Europe continued for a considerable time to maintain its adherence to Jewish law, and the Jews there still turned to the rabbis and their courts to adjudicate legal disputes according to the Torah.

14. Sermon entitled *Torat Ḥesed* [Torah of Lovingkindness], *Zekher Ẓaddik,* p. 20a/b. Raphael ha-Kohen resigned his position in the communities of Altona, Hamburg, and Wandsbeck for two reasons: (a) he believed that because of his advanced age (79) he was unable adequately to safeguard the strength and effectiveness of the Jewish court system and (b) he wanted to settle in the Land of Israel (*Zekher Ẓaddik,* p. 17a/b). The Napoleonic Wars, adverted to in the passage quoted in the text, prevented his trip; and he moved to Hamburg, where he died. During those wars, many hoped that the redemption of the Jewish people and the rebuilding of the Temple in Jerusalem were at hand. It is told of Raphael ha-Kohen that he began to study the laws relating to sacrificial offerings (the Order of *Kodashim*) so that he would be able to fulfill his priestly function in the Temple service. *See Zekher Ẓaddik* and *Dor De'ah, supra* n. 8; A. Marcus, *Ha-Ḥasidut* [Hasidism], 1954, pp. 94–95.

15. The traveler Jacob Sapir's description of the fate of Jewish juridical autonomy as a result of the institution of the Napoleonic Code in 1803 is revealing:

> In his [Napoleon's] days, the Jewish people, while delighted with their new physical freedom, were stunned by their new spiritual slavery. The Torah was draped in sackcloth; for all its glory, majestic beauty, and splendor had been taken away. Napoleon was the first to give the Jews freedom, including freedom of religion, together with equal rights with all citizens of the land without regard to nationality; but, at the same time, he took from them their rootedness in their religion by persuading them to acquiesce in the removal of [their jurisdiction over] civil and domestic relations cases. He impaired their most precious possession by tampering with their holy marriage laws and other basic tenets of the Torah, leaving for the Jewish religion only matters relating to each individual's worship of God. . . . The glory of the Torah and of the religion has fallen low to the very ground. There is no longer a Jewish court that can judge God's people in civil matters according to the holy Torah.

Edut bi-Yehosef, Mayence, 1875, pp. 36–37, quoted in Freimann, *Kiddushin ve-Nissu'in,* p. 327.

However, this dispute resolution by the rabbinical courts took on more and more the character of arbitration and compromise, lacking the qualities of adjudication within the framework of an organic and living legal system; and even among that population, in the course of time, resort to the courts of the state continued to increase.[16]

Halakhic authorities also reconciled themselves to the new circumstance of the loss of Jewish juridical autonomy and in fact justified it under the doctrine of *dina de-malkhuta dina* ("the law of the land is law")—a position directly contrary to that held by earlier authorities.[17] The largest and most significant areas of *mishpat ivri*—civil, criminal, administrative, and public law—were no longer applied in practice "at this time" and became relegated to the same category as the laws in the Talmudic Orders of *Kodashim* [Consecrated Things] and *Tohorot* [Ritual Purity]; their study became a matter of "study and receive a reward"—for theoretical contemplation but not practical application.[18] The only branch of *mishpat ivri* that was

16. In a parallel development, the vernacular also took the place of Hebrew in Jewish creative efforts in literature and research, and occasionally even in purely halakhic writings.

17. *See supra* p. 15 and nn. 41–42, and pp. 64–74; *Resp. Tashbeẓ,* I, #158, quoted *supra* pp. 133–135; *see also infra* pp. 1916–1917. In every previous period, resort to non-Jewish courts was strictly forbidden: the entire discussion among halakhic authorities regarding the doctrine of *dina de-malkhuta dina* revolved around whether this doctrine justified Jewish courts in recognizing or giving effect to the law of a foreign system, but litigating before non-Jewish courts was unanimously forbidden. Prior to the Emancipation, this prohibition could be complied with, since the general government had then accorded the Jewish community juridical autonomy, which the Emancipation withdrew. The development of the *Halakhah* relating to litigation in non-Jewish courts is an example of the reciprocal relationship between historical reality and halakhic decision making. *See also infra* nn. 18 and 23.

18. *See,* for example, the remarks of Meir Dan Plotzki, head of the Rabbinical Court of Ostrava, Poland, at the end of the nineteenth and the beginning of the twentieth centuries, in *Keli Ḥemdah,* Mishpatim, #1. After dealing at length with the prohibition against litigating in non-Jewish courts, and expressing his astonishment at the permission granted as early as the geonic period to resort to such a court when the defendant is a violent person who refuses to appear before a Jewish court (*see supra* pp. 15–16 and nn. 43 and 45), he concluded:

> It is, of course, true that this law [forbidding litigation before non-Jewish courts] has no practical relevance, because it does not apply to [non-Jewish] judges in our time, who are not, God forbid, "idol worshippers," and are not included in the prohibition; clearly one may litigate before them on a basis like that of *dina de-malkhuta.* What I have written [on this subject] is for the benefit of [those who reside in] distant countries such as China and Japan, where there are idol worshippers and the prohibition against resort to non-Jewish courts applies.

See also the declaration by Isaac Elhanan Spektor, the Rabbi of Kovno and the outstanding author of responsa of his time (1817–1896), in *Resp. Ein Yiẓḥak,* II:

> If in various places [in this book] the legal aspects of civil and monetary matters are discussed, the discussions relate only to past eras. Today, such matters are to be resolved only according to the laws of the land, and we must not, Heaven forbid, question their objective or the basis of their authority. Nevertheless, the sources [of the Torah laws] still retain their validity and importance from the standpoint of "study

still actually applied was a portion of family law—marriage and divorce according to "the law of Moses and Israel." In this area of the law, which has a distinct religious component, the traditional segment of the Jewish people continued to maintain strong internal discipline; and, to a certain extent, even Jews who did not ordinarily carry out religious precepts submitted to such discipline in these matters. However, the extent to which governments recognized these marriages varied from country to country throughout the Jewish diaspora.[19]

F. The Continuation of Juridical Autonomy among the Jews of the Eastern Countries

Interestingly, among the Jews of the Eastern countries, such as Turkey and North Africa, Jewish law still continued to a certain extent to develop creatively as a living law with practical relevance.

We have elsewhere described the reasons for this phenomenon:[20]

> The Jewish centers in Morocco and elsewhere in North Africa, as well as in all the Eastern countries, were able to continue the creative activity incident to juridical autonomy long after the Jewish centers of Europe ceased to do so. The differences in the general historical and political situation at the end

---

> and receive a reward," which is true of many other laws that are not applicable today, as many great scholars have written in their books, and as is well known to the initiate. This [study of these Jewish civil laws] is also of great help in understanding numerous religious laws which always have practical relevance.

Of course, the chilling effect of the censor is reflected in the statements of these two halakhic authorities, but that fact itself demonstrates the lack of Jewish juridical autonomy and the absence of Jewish adjudication in everyday life.

Solomon Kluger (1785–1869) described the situation at that time as follows (*Resp. Ha-Elef Lekha Shelomo,* ḤM #2): "Especially in our time, the custom has spread of taking cases to the non-Jewish courts without first obtaining the permission of a Jewish court."

On the other hand, some halakhic authorities continued to protest against this "spreading custom." *See, e.g., Resp. Ḥatam Sofer,* ḤM #22, p. 14b, where Moses Sofer wrote to Wolf Treves, who filed a claim in a non-Jewish court, that the result of Treves's action would be that when members of his community "will bring their claims before non-Jewish judges and abandon the laws of Israel, then even if he [Treves] vehemently protests, they will not listen, for they will say: 'You see the mote in another's eye but not the beam in your own'" (*see* TB Arakhin 16b).

19. *See* Freimann, *Kiddushin ve-Nissu'in,* pp. 300ff.; J. Katz, *Exclusiveness and Tolerance,* pp. 191–193.

20. Elon, *Yiḥudah Shel Halakhah,* pp. 25–27; *id., Ḥerut,* pp. 225ff. *See also* Freimann, *Kiddushin ve-Nissu'in,* pp. 327ff.; *id.,* "Dinei Yisra'el be-Ereẓ Yisra'el," *supra* n. 1 at 113–114; Ben-Zion Gat, *Ha-Yishuv ha-Yehudi be-Erez Yisra'el bi-Shenot 5600–5641* [The Jewish Community in the Land of Israel, 1840–1881], Jerusalem, 1963, pp. 76–80.

of the eighteenth century between Europe, on the one hand, and the Eastern countries on the other, resulted in a difference in halakhic development: while in North Africa and the other Eastern countries there was continued rich and impressive development in all fields of the *Halakhah,* including civil law, the European Jewish centers experienced the decline—indeed the complete cessation—of the creativity of Jewish civil law as applied to practical life. These differences in regard to legal creativity are directly related to the rise of the Emancipation in Europe, which led to the abrogation of Jewish autonomy in general, and Jewish juridical autonomy in particular. . . .

The situation was different in the Jewish centers of North Africa and the Eastern countries. Jewish juridical autonomy continued to exist in most of the North African countries for a long time [after the Emancipation in Europe]. Even in Algeria, which was the first of the North African countries to come under French rule, Jewish juridical autonomy existed until close to the middle of the nineteenth century. Jurisdiction over all legal matters except family law was withdrawn in 1834, and this last vestige was taken away in 1842. However, the Jews of Algeria for a long time thereafter devotedly and unyieldingly stood fast to protect Jewish juridical independence, as witness the following description by Jacob Sapir, a Jerusalemite who visited North Africa in the 1860s:

> The Jews of Algeria, although under the rule of the French government, . . . have not been accorded equality of rights with all other French citizens because they have not accepted the French Code, which would involve abandoning the fundamentals of our holy Torah. The devout among them say, "[We wish] neither your sting nor your honey. We have no share in Napoleon nor any portion in his Code. Return to your God, O Israel."

This resolute and vigorous stand by the Jews of Algeria resulted in continued creativity and development there in all areas of Jewish law for a considerable time after Jewish juridical autonomy ended. This creativity persisted even later among the Jews of Morocco, where juridical autonomy continued considerably longer than in Algeria. Jurisdiction by Jewish courts over matters of family law among Jews—marriage, divorce, family status, adoption, wills, inheritance, and endowments—existed in Morocco until its independence in 1956, and Moroccan Jewry continued its creative application of Jewish law to practical life until close to our own time.[21]

A clear manifestation of the continued existence of this juridical autonomy is the far-ranging responsa literature produced by Eastern Jewry as late as the nineteenth century—a literature containing extensive discussion

21. *See* Shuraki, *Korot ha-Yehudim bi-Ẓefon Afrikah* [History of the Jews of North Africa], Tel Aviv, 1975, pp. 109–110, 158. For the source of the quotation from Sapir, *see supra* n. 15.

of issues that arose in actual cases in various fields of law and were brought to the rabbinical courts for adjudication.[22] Even a superficial comparison of the responsa literature of the Eastern countries in the nineteenth century with that produced in Europe clearly indicates the vast difference between these two diasporas in regard to juridical autonomy.

The responsa literature in the Eastern countries continued, to a substantial and significant extent, to deal with the subjects of *Ḥoshen Mishpat*, *i.e.*, civil-law questions that arise out of concrete situations in practical life. By contrast, in the European countries in this period, questions on the subjects of *Ḥoshen Mishpat* were scant, and were dealt with in the responsa more as theoretical questions than as practical problems such as would arise in an autonomous legal system. It is true that in the eastern part of Europe the leading halakhic authorities and the students of the large and renowned *yeshivot* (academies) still continued during the nineteenth century to study in depth the civil-law portions of the halakhic system; tractates such as *Bava-Kamma, Bava Meẓi'a,* and *Bava Batra,* all of which deal with civil law, constituted a venerable and important segment of the program of study of these *yeshivot.* However, their study was merely theoretical—to "learn Torah for its own sake"—and did not even purport to address the solution of the novel practical problems constantly posed by ever-changing circumstances.

G. Consequences of the Abrogation of Jewish Juridical Autonomy

The abrogation of Jewish juridical autonomy brought on by the Emancipation had two serious consequences for Jewish law. First, since Jewish law no longer operated within a functional legal system, its organic development was severely stunted. The harm was compounded by the fact that this historically crucial development in the evolution of Jewish law occurred at the dawn of the nineteenth century, when social, economic, and industrial revolutions were profoundly affecting the law in many fields, especially commercial and public law.

Secondly, the deep-seated and until then unchallenged axiom that Jewish life could not be lived apart from Jewish law faded from Jewish national and religious consciousness in the nineteenth century in most of

22. *See, e.g.,* the responsum of Ḥayyim Palache, Rabbi of Izmir in the mid-nineteenth century, *Resp. Ḥikekei Lev,* II, ḤM #5, which deals comprehensively and at length with the real-life question of the terms and conditions under which debtors may be imprisoned for failure to pay their debts. *See* Elon, *Ḥerut,* pp. 228ff. For additional examples, *see* Elon, *Yiḥudah Shel Halakhah,* pp. 22ff., 28ff.

the diaspora; and with the passage of time it has become clear that this second consequence was even more serious than the first.[23]

The new political and social situation, as it became more firmly established, left not even the slightest hope that Jewish juridical autonomy in the diaspora would ever be restored. Even were a national minority to dedicate all its energies to an attempt to establish an autonomous juridical system of its own, no modern state would permit such autonomy or recognize its authority. The only possibility for the renewal of a fully functional Jewish legal system was to incorporate Jewish law into the legal system of a sovereign state which would have both juridical and political autonomy. Thus, the future destiny of Jewish law as a living and functional system became entwined with the destiny of the Jewish national aspiration for the reestab-

23. *See infra* pp. 1605–1606, 1610–1618. Another consequence of the abrogation of juridical autonomy relates to the approach to decision making by the halakhic authorities. Halakhic creativity and development have always been influenced by changes in social or historical conditions. The influence has not been merely the indirect influence of mood and outlook, which are solely matters of conjecture, but direct influence perceived and explicitly acknowledged by the halakhic authorities themselves when they enact legislation or decide legal issues.

A number of examples have been previously discussed. Thus, when, beginning with the tenth century, there was no longer a single center exercising spiritual hegemony over the entire Jewish people, such as the Land of Israel and, later, Babylonia during most of the geonic period, each Jewish center began to exercise its own spiritual autonomy. This historical transformation influenced the methods of legal decision making and also affected the scope of legislation: legislation binding on the entire Jewish people ceased to be enacted, and the legislation thereafter adopted was applicable only in particular localities. (For detailed discussion, *see supra* pp. 666–677.)

Again, on account of the same historical transformation, the halakhic authorities refrained from legislative enactments to annul marriages; because of the local nature of legislation, they were fearful of serious difficulties were a marriage to be valid in one place and invalid in another. (For detailed discussion, *see supra* pp. 846–879. *See also* Elon, *Mi-Ba'ayot ha-Halakhah ve-ha-Mishpat bi-Medinat Yisra'el* [On the Problems of *Halakhah* and Law in the State of Israel], Reports of the Society for the Study of the Jewish People in the Diaspora, The President's House, Institute for Contemporary Judaism, 1973, Sixth Series, Seventh Booklet, pp. 12–13, 30–33.) For another interesting example of the effect of historical changes on Jewish law, *see supra* n. 17.

Still another consequence of the abrogation of Jewish juridical autonomy at the end of the eighteenth century was that the halakhic authorities were no longer called upon to adopt enactments or make legal rulings for the community as an entity, but only for particular groups of individuals; consequently, even had there been no split between religious and secular Jews, halakhic decisions would have lost much of their community-wide significance. The legal rulings of an organized autonomous juridical authority on matters such as communal administration, taxes, public order, etc. necessarily reflect the exercise of responsibility for the continued well-being of the entire community, as an entity, for which the authority acts. On the other hand, without such autonomy, no matter how many individuals accept the decision as binding, the decision is addressed to them as a group of individuals and not as a total Jewish community. Certainly, when the decisionmaker is aware that his ruling is directed to only part of the community, broader considerations of the interests of the total community play less of a part in his decisions.

lishment of political independence. Indeed, as will be seen, the call for the renewal of Jewish law was an integral part of the rise of the Zionist movement. The response that the call evoked and the problems to which it gave rise are the subjects of the remainder of this work.

II. THE ERA OF NATIONAL AWAKENING

The National Awakening and the Zionist movement, which proclaimed the need for return to the Jewish homeland and independent national life there for the Jewish people, were naturally accompanied by a radical change in the attitude of the Jewish people toward Jewish law. It was recognized that Jewish law embodied not only religious but also essential national values. Consequently, a movement arose among Jewish jurists and intellectuals, together with others from all segments of the Jewish people, that viewed the restoration of Jewish law in Jewish society as having national significance paralleling that of the return to the Jewish homeland and the rebirth of the Hebrew language.

A. Ha-Mishpat Ha-Ivri (Jewish Law) Society

Soon after the Balfour Declaration, the Ha-Mishpat Ha-Ivri (Jewish Law) Society was founded in the Central Synagogue in Moscow on December 17, 1918.[24] Its purpose was to create in Jerusalem, the "center of our national life," an institute for research into and renewal of Jewish law. The institute was to be the first stage of a "Faculty of Law of the Jerusalem University." It would engage jurists whose expertise included Jewish law to do research in Jewish law and to prepare that law to become an active force in Jewish life; and it would establish a library for general and Jewish law, and publish in Hebrew a scholarly legal journal, as well as books on law, and Hebrew translations of basic legal treatises.[25] Among the objectives of the society was the preparation of a comprehensive work, *Sha'arei ha-Mishpat ha-Ivri* [The Gates of Jewish Law], which was to "compile all of the sources contained in the Jewish legal literature of all periods . . . in a clear

24. *See* the interesting minutes of the founding session of this group included in the article "Le-Toledot Ḥevrat ha-Mishpat ha-Ivri" [History of the Ha-Mishpat Ha-Ivri Society], *Ha-Mishpat,* II (1927), pp. 220–222. The founders were S. Eisenstadt, Y. Yunovitz, A. Gulak, and Y. Persitz. As to the activity prior to the founding of this society, *see* Eisenstadt, *Ẓiyyon be-Mishpat* [Zion with Justice], pp. 31–34, 167–168.

25. *Ha-Mishpat, supra* n. 24 at 221.

and systematic order to facilitate research and study, such that anyone may easily find in it whatever he seeks."[26]

Some of the statements in the Introduction to the first issue of the periodical *Ha-Mishpat ha-Ivri,* written in Moscow in 1918, are noteworthy. After first explaining the importance of scientific research into Jewish law, the Introduction stated:

> Research into Jewish law throughout the ages, and revitalization of authentic Jewish legal thought—the two objectives before us in our work—may have at this time not only scientific and theoretical significance but also practical political importance. In recent times, our people have been gradually gaining political freedom and achieving the right of national self-determination in many aspects of communal life in various countries of the diaspora. Simultaneously, it is building a national center in our land which, in the future, will be independent; and its life will be free, and consonant with the needs, characteristics, and temperament of its people. Both the diaspora and the

26. *See Ha-Mishpat ha-Ivri,* I (a scientific quarterly, Moscow, 1918), p. 122. It should be noted that not all those who participated in founding the Ha-Mishpat Ha-Ivri Society were in agreement as to the place of Jewish law in the Jewish national movement. The minutes (*Ha-Mishpat,* II, pp. 221–222) indicate that the majority held that the goal was

> historical and dogmatic [*i.e.,* analytical] research of ancient [Jewish] law, in order to reveal its distinctive approach and character. . . . Despite the similarities in life-styles and cultures of various nations, and despite [the contacts in] international trade and commerce, there is no branch of the law upon which any nation fails to impress its own distinctive seal. . . . Since our national revival includes a return to our original creativity, we cannot restore that creativity as a community without studying the essential character of our own law; such study is a prerequisite for Jewish legal reform and renaissance.

Those professing "the new orientation" differed:

> We are living in an era in which all law is becoming universal. Consequently, Jewish law in the future cannot regain the centrality in our national existence that it had in the past. National boundaries are currently of less and less significance in the civil law. . . . The study of ancient Jewish law has only cultural and historical, but not practical value. To actually create a legal structure, we need to study general law, which continues to develop in modern times, while analyzing the methods of Jewish legal creativity in those fields in which it has continued to develop down to our day.

Id. at 222. According to this latter view, the important function of the Ha-Mishpat Ha-Ivri Society was scientific research, but this research was not likely to yield any significant practical results. As will be seen, the former opinion prevailed; but even in later periods, a minority refused to acknowledge that the regeneration of Jewish law was indispensable to the national renaissance. *See, e.g.,* the discussion by P. Dykan (Dikstein), *Mishpat ha-Shalom ha-Ivri, She'elotav le-Halakhah u-le-Ma'aseh* [The Jewish Court of Arbitration—Its Theoretical and Practical Problems] (hereinafter, pamphlet, *Mishpat ha-Shalom ha-Ivri*), 1925, pp. 9–13, and other essays in Dykan's book *Toledot Mishpat ha-Shalom ha-Ivri* [History of the Jewish Court of Arbitration], Tel Aviv, 1964 (hereinafter, *Toledot*). A similar debate, although with somewhat different arguments, arose years later with regard to the question of the incorporation of Jewish law into the law of the Jewish state. *See infra* pp. 1612–1618, 1918–1920.

> Land of Israel will thus require a legal code to govern the conduct of the people.
>
> It is self-evident that this law simply cannot be adopted *in toto* from others. Surely, it must be "native born" and not a foreign growth. Even those foreign legal principles that merit being treated as models or incorporated into Jewish law must first be adapted to fit our own historical legal characteristics and must pass through the channels of our nation's creative processes to take on a national form consistent with the needs and temperament of the people. Our new national life, daily enriched by new political and communal ideas and activities, makes it necessary to grapple with political and civil problems of a legal nature. Thus, it is the obligation of the scholarly literature in the field of Jewish law to establish the necessary foundation and prepare the soil for authentically Jewish legal creativity. . . .
>
> We therefore will particularly examine the law in its Jewish national forms, as it has developed during the thousands of years of our people's existence in its own land and in the diaspora, and we will collect the materials essential for its continued development and for new creativity in our land, the land of our past and our future, in accordance with our historical foundations and accepted scientific method.

These comments reflect an important change in the attitude of many leaders of the Jewish community—even the secularists—toward the place of Jewish law in the life of the Jewish people. Although this approach had significant potential for restoring Jewish law to practical life, it also involved from the very beginning a basic problem inherent in the attempt to put Jewish law into practice in the new intellectual climate of Jewish society. The Introduction continued:

> Of course, during the thousands of years of our history, our entire culture bore a religious stamp, and our legal system was closely tied to religious law, to the extent that even today it is difficult in many subject areas to discern the boundary between law and religion. In the literature of the last few decades, there has begun a process of separating law from ethics and religion. We propose to continue this process and prepare Jewish law to exist as a secular legal system.

These words, read today, tend to arouse at least a little twinge of envy at the tranquillity of spirit that permeates them. Today, we are aware of the magnitude of the difficulties involved in this "process"—especially after the establishment of the State of Israel and the emergence of the problem of choosing the basic norm for its legal system. For example, can the creative development of Jewish law continue if its national and religious aspects are uncoupled? Does this new direction for the future evolution of Jewish law bode well for Jewish law itself? And if this "process" is desirable, how will it be accomplished, since it is so different from what had previously occurred throughout the course of the long history of the growth and development of Jewish law, during which the two primary bases of that law—the religious and the national—were inextricably intertwined? The full range of these problems is discussed later;[27] but at this point, it is interesting and indeed important to note that the basic problem, which often now arises in connection with the issue of the incorporation of Jewish law as part of the law of the State of Israel, was clearly and explicitly raised at the very beginning of the movement to apply Jewish law to the practical problems of daily life.[28]

27. *See* (in addition to the discussion *supra* pp. 38–39) *infra* pp. 1592 n. 31, 1655–1660, 1668–1671, 1758–1759, 1906–1914, 1923–1931, 1942–1946.

28. In that same year (1918), a project to prepare Jewish law to become the basis of a living national law was also planned in Jerusalem. Among the project's initiators was Gad Frumkin, who served afterward as the only Jewish judge of the Supreme Court of Palestine during the period of the British Mandate. Later, when some of the founders of the Ha-Mishpat Ha-Ivri Society moved from Moscow to the Land of Israel, this society was also organized in Jerusalem, with Frumkin as its head. The program of the society in Jerusalem was similar in its general outline to that of the society in Moscow. Frumkin, *Derekh Shofet bi-Yerushalayim* [The Way of a Judge in Jerusalem], Tel Aviv, 1955, pp. 231–232, relates:

> At that time, we began to consider the task of preparing legislation for "the future governance of the Land of Israel. This legislation will be based on ancient Jewish law, but will also include all the improvements found in the laws of other nations, and will be consonant with present-day conditions." I will quote here a complete text of my own handwritten draft, dated 1918. I do not remember who my colleagues and associates were when this idea was first suggested. After some time, when M. Eliash, Dr. Paltiel Dikstein, Dr. S. Eisenstadt, Kalman Friedenburg, and others came to the Land of Israel, we heard that a similar idea had also occurred to Jewish jurists in Moscow; and together we established here the Ha-Mishpat Ha-Ivri Society which I had the honor to head for as long as it existed. The draft reads as follows:

A society of Jewish jurists residing in Jerusalem has been established with the purpose of uniting with jurists throughout the Land of Israel and, subsequently, making contact with individuals or groups of Jewish jurists abroad, in order to achieve the following goal:

To conduct research into Jewish law and its development from its beginnings to the present time, to make it compatible with the legal systems of the West and the East, and to formulate proposals for legislation prescribing the future governance of the Land of Israel. This legislation will be based on ancient Jewish law, but will also include all the improvements found in the laws of other nations, and will be consonant with present-day conditions. In order to achieve this goal, the society will proceed as follows:

A. Preparation

1. Organize all the jurists in the country—those who completed their [legal] training in universities, together with Talmudists who are expert in Jewish law.

2. Cooperate with similar societies abroad and with individuals who are involved in such activity or whose participation in the work would be beneficial.

3. Lay the foundations for a large legal library which will contain everything that has been published in the field of Jewish law from the Torah of Moses to the present.

B. Research

Assign to the members of the society here and abroad, according to their fields of expertise, research on individual points of Jewish law, with a view to ultimately gathering the entire *corpus juris* of Jewish law into a single compendium.

B. Mishpat Ha-Shalom Ha-Ivri (The Jewish Court of Arbitration)

A significant practical expression of the new movement at the beginning of the twentieth century to apply Jewish law to practical life[29] was the organization of Mishpat Ha-Shalom Ha-Ivri (the Jewish Court of Arbitration) in 1909–1910 in Jaffa, at the instance of the heads of the Israel office of the Zionist Organization.[30] Mishpat Ha-Shalom Ha-Ivri was intended to be

> a stage in the achievement of a full national renaissance. Our law is one of the most valuable assets of our national culture, and a unifying force [among Jews] throughout the world. The Jewish people have developed and maintained a remarkable system of law, whose foundations were laid at the dawn of our national existence; hundreds of generations have toiled over it, perfected it, and adorned it, and even today it retains the power to renew its youth and to develop in a manner appropriate to the outlook of our generation and the needs of our time. During the thousands of years of the existence of the nation, this law was influenced by many material and spiritual factors. It absorbed religious and ethical concepts; it reflected cultural, economic, and social values; and it can still faithfully reflect the life of the people throughout the future.[31]

C. Action

After completing the preparation and research, appoint special committees to draft laws on subjects relevant to practical affairs.

See Frumkin, *supra* at 231, regarding the request of the Zionist Executive in London "to prepare a detailed program and budget for a school of law at the Hebrew University in Jerusalem, the cornerstone of which had then been laid," and *id.* at 406. *See also* A. Gulak, "Le-Siddur Ḥayyeinu ha-Mishpatiyyim ba-Areẓ" [On the Organization of Our Legal System in the Land of Israel], *Ha-Toren,* New York, 1921, reprinted in *Ha-Mishpat ha-Ivri u-Medinat Yisra'el* [Jewish Law and the State of Israel], ed. J. Bazak, pp. 28–35, where Gulak identified additional founders of the Ha-Mishpat Ha-Ivri Society. As to the reason why the society ceased to be active, he wrote: "The Bolshevistic turmoil which engulfed Russia scattered the members of this society and put an end to its fruitful work" (*id.* at 33–34).

29. The movement for the return to Jewish law also led some scholars to direct their attention to researching and remolding Jewish law so as to make it ready for reception into the functioning legal system of the future Jewish state. *See supra* pp. 86–87.

30. *See* Mordecai b. Hillel ha-Kohen, "Le-Toledot Mishpat ha-Shalom ha-Ivri be-Ereẓ Yisra'el" [On the History of the Jewish Court of Arbitration in the Land of Israel], pamphlet, *Mishpat ha-Shalom ha-Ivri,* pp. 3–4.

31. Dykan, *Toledot,* p. 68. This approach to Jewish law was given further emphasis with the founding of the Jewish Court of Arbitration:

> The Jewish Court of Arbitration (Mishpat Ha-Shalom Ha-Ivri) committed itself to the mission of renewing the fundamentals of Jewish law without any admixture of religion . . . , *i.e.,* to the goal of renewing that traditional Jewish law which strives to govern the relation of man and his fellow with justice, equity, lovingkindness, and truth. . . . Mishpat Ha-Shalom Ha-Ivri respected the [Jewish] religion and faith, but it viewed Jewish law as something apart—something of value to everyone, religious or not (*id.* at 14–15).

In the course of time, branches of Mishpat Ha-Shalom Ha-Ivri were founded in various places in the Land of Israel; and at the end of World War I, at the organizational conference in 1918 of the institutions of the *yishuv* (the pre-State Jewish community in the Land of Israel), a resolution was adopted "charging all of the Jewish inhabitants of the Land of Israel to submit their disputes for adjudication exclusively to Mishpat Ha-Shalom Ha-Ivri."[32] At various locations in the country, district courts were established, and above them a Supreme Court.[33] Various regulations and procedural rules were adopted and published, with periodic supplementation in 1918, 1922, 1928, and 1936, covering such matters as judicial administration and rules of procedure and evidence.[34]

Mishpat Ha-Shalom Ha-Ivri coexisted with other judicial institutions. On the one hand, there were the courts of the Ottoman Empire[35] and, later, those of the British Mandatory Power. So far as these governments were concerned, Mishpat Ha-Shalom Ha-Ivri operated as an arbitration tribunal, and its work was facilitated by the promulgation of the Arbitration Ordinance, 1926, which authorized submission of disputes not only to a single arbitrator or an *ad hoc* tribunal but also to a permanent court of arbitration with a regular roster of panel members, such as Mishpat Ha-Shalom Ha-Ivri.[36]

On the other hand, there were the rabbinical courts. Prior to the establishment of the Chief Rabbinate of the Land of Israel in 1921, these courts were not organized into a coherent system; each rabbinical court served its own particular community of adherents. Starting in 1921, most of these courts became part of the judicial system under the aegis of the Chief Rabbinate. Except, perhaps, at the beginning, the rabbinical courts distanced themselves from Mishpat Ha-Shalom Ha-Ivri. (Their relationship is more fully discussed later.) In any case, the leaders of Mishpat Ha-Shalom Ha-Ivri viewed the rabbinical courts and Mishpat Ha-Shalom Ha-Ivri as two

32. *Id.* at 28. *See also* the resolutions of the First Conference of the Representatives of the Mishpat Ha-Shalom Ha-Ivri Courts in the Land of Israel, 1922, par. 4, quoted in pamphlet, *Mishpat ha-Shalom ha-Ivri,* p. 35.

33. Dykan, *Toledot,* pp. 39ff.; *see also id.* at 43–50 for a full list of the judges, among whom were some of the most highly respected leaders of the *yishuv.* The first head of Mishpat Ha-Shalom Ha-Ivri was Dr. Arthur Ruppin, and the first secretary was S.Y. Agnon. *See* Mordecai b. Hillel ha-Kohen, *supra* n. 30 at 4. For an interesting and instructive description of Mishpat Ha-Shalom Ha-Ivri, the reasons for its creation, and the names of its members and judges, *see* S.Y. Agnon, *Me-Aẓmi el Aẓmi* [From Myself to Myself], Tel Aviv, 1976, pp. 187–189.

34. Dykan, *Toledot,* pp. 57ff.

35. The corruption prevalent in the Ottoman legal system was one of the factors that encouraged the fledgling Jewish community to turn to Mishpat Ha-Shalom Ha-Ivri. *See* Mordecai b. Hillel ha-Kohen, *supra* n. 30 at 3–4; Agnon, *supra* n. 33 at 187.

36. Arbitration Ordinance, 1926, sec. 2.

parallel national institutions engaged in adjudicating civil disputes involving monetary claims.[37]

The effort of Mishpat Ha-Shalom Ha-Ivri to apply Jewish law to practical life was no doubt laudable, but it did not succeed in accomplishing its goal. Although during the decade 1920–1930 a considerable number of disputes were submitted to Mishpat Ha-Shalom Ha-Ivri, the caseload steadily diminished thereafter,[38] and no real contribution to Jewish law appears to have resulted from its deliberations or judgments.[39] To be sure, one reason for the failure of Mishpat Ha-Shalom Ha-Ivri was the hard fact that it had no power to enforce its judgments.[40] Another reason was the strong opposition of the rabbinical courts,[41] of the leaders of the national-religious (religious Zionist) sector of the Jewish community,[42] and of prominent scholars such as S. Assaf[43] to the existence of any permanent judicial structure outside of and in opposition to the framework of the rabbinical courts. But the main reason for the failure of Mishpat Ha-Shalom Ha-Ivri was twofold: (1) Mishpat Ha-Shalom Ha-Ivri did not undertake to apply the existing Jewish law as contained in the *Shulḥan Arukh Ḥoshen Mishpat* and the subsequent halakhic literature, and (2) it had no normative system of Jewish or, for that matter, any other law, to govern its adjudication. It was a lay court which applied general principles of equity, justice, morality, and social welfare; and the overwhelming majority of its judges, although generally intelligent, not only were ignorant of Jewish law but often had no legal training at all.[44]

Both the supporters and the opponents of Mishpat Ha-Shalom Ha-Ivri

37. *See* par. 2 of the resolutions of the First Conference of 1922, cited *supra* n. 32; Mordecai b. Hillel ha-Kohen, *supra* n. 30 at 6–7; Dykan, *Toledot,* pp. 29–30, 51–52.

38. Dykan, *Toledot,* pp. 31–38. Mishpat Ha-Shalom Ha-Ivri "officially" came to its end in June of 1949, after the establishment of the State (*see id.* at 13, 37), but for practical purposes it had ceased to function about 1930.

39. As to the nature of the cases decided by Mishpat Ha-Shalom Ha-Ivri, *see* Dykan, *Toledot,* pp. 70ff., and the various source references there cited.

40. *See supra* n. 36. There were those who objected to the very establishment of Mishpat Ha-Shalom Ha-Ivri and preferred to litigate before the governmental courts. *See* pamphlet, *Mishpat ha-Shalom ha-Ivri,* pp. 9–13; Dykan, *Toledot,* pp. 35–38.

41. *See* the sources cited *supra* n. 37.

42. *See Ha-Tor,* XX (1921), articles by M. Berlin and M. Ostrowsky, two religious Zionist leaders.

43. *See* Assaf, *Battei ha-Din,* pp. 6–9, discussing the basic difference between the courts of the Mishpat Ha-Shalom Ha-Ivri and the lay courts of the various periods of Jewish law—namely, that although the decisions of the earlier lay courts also did not always strictly conform to the halakhic rules, their nonconformance, unlike that of Mishpat Ha-Shalom Ha-Ivri, was not programmatic or based upon principled opposition to the longstanding legal tradition. As to the Jewish lay courts, *see supra* pp. 20–33.

44. For a list of the judges, *see* Dykan, *Toledot,* pp. 43–50. The same criticism may be found in Agnon, *supra* n. 33 at 189.

noted this weakness. Prof. P. Dykan (Dikstein), after discussing the lack of a code and of judges familiar with either general or Jewish law, commented:

> As a result of all of these objective factors, some of which cannot be changed in the near future, Mishpat Ha-Shalom Ha-Ivri has become a court that reflects the personal conscience and the wide discretion of the judges, who have been chosen by the community and who know the practices, outlook, and opinions of the people. Some of those involved with this institution proclaim this to be a great virtue. They find particular value in an independent court, freed from the shackles of rigid law, that dispenses justice and equity on the basis of the individual conscience and the personal responsibility of the judge.[45]

Dykan, however, pointed out that part of the community, and some of the judges, disapproved of this absolute freedom. As a result, in matters involving promissory notes, general law was followed; formalities of written contracts and other documents were increasingly emphasized; and, "most important, the traditionally accepted Jewish law was declared to be the principal source of guidance for the judicial process, and sometimes even the provisions of *Ḥoshen Mishpat* were recognized as obligatory to the extent that they could be adapted to the needs of the time and the outlook of our generation."[46]

However, these steps did not go far enough. For the most part, decisions continued to be based largely on sentiment and good will. Looking to Jewish law as a source of "guidance" may be useful to the legislator[47] but cannot be of practical benefit in the arbitral process. Adjudication cannot function on a proper basis when it looks to law merely as a guide,[48] especially when the judges are not sufficiently knowledgeable to be able to make use of such "guidance."[49]

It was one of the founders of the Ha-Mishpat Ha-Ivri Society, a prominent activist in the campaign to prepare Jewish law for the restoration of Jewish sovereignty, who most perceptively pointed out this weakness in Mishpat Ha-Shalom Ha-Ivri. Y. Yunovitz, after criticizing the weakness of

45. Pamphlet, *Mishpat ha-Shalom ha-Ivri,* pp. 17–18.

46. *Id.* at 18–19.

47. *See infra* p. 1626, regarding guidelines for the Legislature of the State of Israel.

48. At the Second National Conference in 1927, the expression "principal source of guidance" was changed to "basis," on the understanding, as Dykan stated, "that a 'basis' is much more than a source of guidance, but is still a sufficiently flexible concept" (Dykan, *Toledot,* p. 72). Obviously, this change was not sufficient to achieve all the improvement that was required.

49. *See also* Dykan, pamphlet, *Mishpat ha-Shalom ha-Ivri,* pp. 17–18, and *Toledot,* pp. 70–74; Eisenstadt, *supra* n. 24 at 64–68.

the rabbinical courts and their failure to understand how to develop and properly prepare Jewish law to meet the new circumstances, continued:[50]

> On the other side, corresponding to them [the rabbinical courts], are the advocates of the "secular" law, with their "Mishpat Ha-Shalom," which does not purport to be *ad hoc* arbitration, but a permanent national institution, as it were, deserving the respect and obedience of everyone, to the point that anyone who falls short in these duties is accused of being unfaithful to Jewish law. This new creation, which completely wraps itself in the cloak of the national spirit even though it has no root in our past, appears to us as a new "Ugandism" [an abortive proposal, early in the history of Zionism, to establish a Jewish state in Uganda] on the holy soil—a legal "Ugandism," with judges from the marketplace, almost none of whom is worthy of the title "master" or "scholar." With only a few exceptions, not only are they totally ignorant of the Talmud and of the recognized arbiters of halakhic questions, but they do not even have a secular professional education. They are without knowledge or learning. They have no practical training in Jewish law; or, at the very least, their training is inadequate. Yet they consider themselves judges over Israel and render judgments in all kinds of cases, not on the basis of principles or defined legal concepts or the rule of law or legal analysis, but solely according to their personal whims or untutored lay opinions.

This method of operation, in spite of the good intentions of those who fostered it because of the national character of its background and objectives, could not adequately take the place of a regular judicial system. Mishpat Ha-Shalom Ha-Ivri may well be of some interest for the light it sheds on the renewal of Jewish national creativity during the existence of this tribunal, but it cannot be considered in any respect a continuation of the authentic Jewish legal tradition.[51]

C. Jewish Law in the Rabbinical Courts in the Land of Israel

1. ESTABLISHMENT OF THE CHIEF RABBINATE AND SETTING THE COURSE OF ITS ACTIVITY IN THE AREA OF JEWISH LAW

As stated, the rabbinical courts in the Land of Israel opposed the program of Mishpat Ha-Shalom Ha-Ivri. Logic and good sense would therefore

50. Y. Yunovitz, Introduction to Assaf, *Onshin,* pp. 5–6.

51. In addition to the Mishpat Ha-Shalom Ha-Ivri courts, mention should be made of the "Court of Comrades," established by the labor community. All members of that community were required to submit their disputes to this tribunal and to obey its rulings. Judges of this court were appointed from among the workers. Their decisions were not based on any system of laws, but on notions of justice and equity according to the circumstances of each case. *See* Dykan, *Toledot,* pp. 53–54; Freimann, "Dinei Yisra'el be-Ereẓ Yisra'el," *supra* n. 1 at 114–118.

appear to have dictated that the rabbinical courts would themselves undertake the historic task of continuing to nurture and develop Jewish law so as to make it responsive to the needs of the times. The organizational structure and the internal conditions of the rabbinical courts in the Land of Israel at the beginning of the twentieth century did not afford very much hope that these courts would be equal to the task. However, with the establishment of the Chief Rabbinate of the Land of Israel in 1921, there were promising indications that the halakhic authorities were aware of how crucial that juncture was in the history of Jewish law.

In the early days of the British Mandate, when the institutional framework of the Jewish community was in the first stages of organization, the halakhic leaders and the representatives of the public met to consider action to establish the Chief Rabbinate and confer jurisdiction over matters of personal status on the rabbinical courts.[52] At the same time, a special commission was formed to make the necessary preparations and select the members and officers of the Council of the Chief Rabbinate. The chairman of the commission was Norman Bentwich, the Attorney General of the British Mandatory Government. At these conference sessions, Bentwich spoke at length about the historical significance of the establishment of the Chief Rabbinate of the Land of Israel. He compared this event to the establishment of the Great Assembly in the days of Ezra and Nehemiah, when the exiles returned to the Land of Israel from Babylonia in the fifth century B.C.E. He expressed the wish that the rabbinical court system would perform its historic task in the new national renaissance—to solve the legal problems facing it in the new era, and become recognized by Jews throughout the world as the ultimate institutional authority for resolving issues of Jewish law.[53]

This was certainly Bentwich's wish not only as a representative of the British Mandatory Government, but also as a Jew who expressed the views and hopes of the entire community in the Land of Israel, which was then in the midst of organizing its national institutions. Indeed, the Chief Rabbi, Abraham Isaac Kook, fully endorsed the goal expressed by Bentwich:

> It is well known that there are two major sources of the *corpus juris* of Jewish law: received laws (*dinim*) and legislative enactments (*takkanot*). It is not possible for us to make any changes within the category of received laws that are firmly established. However, we are free, by using the method of *takkanot,* to

52. *I.e.,* exclusive jurisdiction in matters of marriage, divorce, and probate; concurrent jurisdiction in matters involving support, intestate succession, and several other areas. All other legal matters remained under the jurisdiction of the courts of the Mandatory Government.

53. *See Ha-Tor,* XVIII (1921) (12 Shevat) and XXI–XXII (1921) (24 Adar I).

> make new law and to institute those improvements which the court, acting "for the sake of Heaven," and with public approval, will find necessary for the general welfare. The halakhic authorities throughout the generations have enacted many important *takkanot;* not only the *tannaim* and *amoraim* in earlier times, but also the courts of the *geonim* and later authorities exercised this power.
>
> In our new national life in the Land of Israel, there will sometimes surely be a great need to enact important *takkanot,* which, as long as they are approved by the majority of the generally recognized halakhic authorities of Israel and then accepted by the community, will have the same force as a law of the Torah.[54]

Thus, Rabbi Kook desired to see the continued creativity of Jewish law in the rabbinical courts by means of the same two major legal sources that have contributed to the development of the *Halakhah* in every age: (1) midrash, *i.e.,* interpretation and application of the law to actual cases so that the law continues to develop, as Rabbi Kook expressed it, "within the category of received laws," through finding new legal solutions by interpreting existing law,[55] and (2) *takkanah, i.e.,* legislation, by which Jewish law meets the needs of new legal and social situations through the enactment of new laws that are added to existing law.[56]

To what extent were these great hopes realized? A study of the methods and accomplishments of the Council of the Chief Rabbinate and the rabbinical courts up to the establishment of the State of Israel reveals that in the areas of judicial procedure and personal status (over which the government, by law, granted jurisdiction and enforcement powers to these courts), the methods above described did engender some creativity. However, even in these branches of the law, creative development was sporadic, fragmentary, and overly cautious, and did not achieve the progress that might have been possible if the halakhic leaders had fully exercised their authority and power to meet the needs of the time. As for all the other areas of Jewish law, particularly the various branches of civil law, almost nothing was accomplished.

2. JUDICIAL PROCEDURE AND THE LAW OF PERSONAL STATUS

An important and fundamental procedural enactment, adopted in 1921 as one of the first acts of the Chief Rabbinate, established the Rabbinical Court of Appeals—an institution that did not exist in Talmudic law, although a somewhat similar institution had existed in the rabbinic period.

54. *Id.*
55. *See supra* pp. 275ff.
56. *See supra* pp. 477ff.

However, for more than twenty years thereafter, the rabbinical courts, whose continuity had been broken during a long period in the diaspora, were unable to organize themselves into a well-ordered court system run according to clearly established rules.

A change for the better occurred in 1943, when the Council of the Chief Rabbinate adopted procedural enactments for the rabbinical courts. These enactments contained detailed regulations on the manner of initiating claims, trial procedure, evidence, and appeals and appellate practice. An appendix of forms included forms for complaint, summons, subpoena, and initiation of appeals. Some of the enactments were based on Jewish law, while others were influenced by the practice in the general court system. The enactments also included detailed provisions for the payment of court costs in connection with various types of actions, as well as provisions relating to the adoption of children—both of which were innovations in Jewish law. The greatest change introduced by these enactments was the undertaking by the rabbinical courts to distribute a decedent's estate according to the Succession Ordinance enacted by the Mandatory Government in 1923, under which daughters had equal rights with sons, and wives with husbands.[57]

This type of beneficial legislation continued during the following year with enactments that increased the minimum amount of the *ketubbah* (providing financial benefits to a wife in case of divorce or the husband's death), required a *levir* to support his deceased brother's widow so long as he refuses to perform *ḥaliẓah* and thus free her for remarriage, and, very importantly, made fathers legally liable to support their children until the age of fifteen.[58]

From this time on, *i.e.*, after 1944, the legislative activity of the halakhic institutions in the Land of Israel virtually ceased. Only three additional *takkanot* were enacted, all in 1950. The most important of these prohibited the marriage of females under the age of sixteen.[59] This lapse of legislative activity is cause for keen disappointment, inasmuch as many pressing problems in the law of personal status await legislative solution.[60]

By contrast, progress since 1950 has occurred in the development of the Jewish law of personal status by means of judicial interpretation. For

57. For full details of these enactments and the changes they introduced into Jewish law, *see supra* pp. 824–835. Later, when legislative activity ceased, various halakhic authorities had second thoughts and narrowed the scope even of the enactments that had previously been adopted. For detailed discussion of this development, *see infra* pp. 1807–1809.

58. For further details, *see supra* pp. 829–833. As to the enactment concerning child support, *see also supra* pp. 116–117 and *infra* pp. 1660–1663.

59. *See supra* p. 834. As to the age of marriage, *see also infra* pp. 1654–1656.

60. For detailed discussion, *see supra* pp. 846–879 concerning legislation on annulment of marriage.

example, the rabbinical courts created an important legal right in connection with divorce, namely, the right of a wife during divorce proceedings to obtain not only the amount provided in her *ketubbah,* but also a specified additional sum as "compensation." The amount depends on the circumstances of each case; and an important consideration is that the wife should share with her husband in the property that was accumulated during the marriage through their joint efforts.[61]

3. CIVIL LAW

While the rabbinical courts displayed significant creativity in the law of personal status, the same cannot be said with regard to the other areas of Jewish law. It is, of course, true that the rabbinical courts had no judicial jurisdiction in other areas of the law, in which they could act only as arbitration tribunals when the parties so agreed. Nevertheless, the great excitement that then seized the Jewish community in the Land of Israel at the prospect of the renewal of Jewish law should have caused the halakhic leaders to take the necessary steps to prepare Jewish law for adaptation to the economic and social needs of the Jewish community of that time. It is disheartening that the halakhic leaders confined themselves to resisting Mishpat Ha-Shalom Ha-Ivri, and had no positive program for preparing a suitable code of Jewish civil law that would motivate the submission of civil disputes to the rabbinical courts.

It is true that their intentions were laudable:

> In 1919, . . . the rabbis of the Land of Israel, assembled in their first conference, strongly demanded that the law of the land be the law of our Torah and that the judges be those designated according to the Torah; and at the same time, they pledged to institute improved rules of procedure for the convenience of the public and to draft and publish legal forms for general use, including commercial instruments and other contracts conforming to the law of the Torah. The rabbis also declared that their courts would recognize as legally binding [to the same extent as if the transaction had been effected by

61. For detailed discussion, *see* Elon, *Ḥakikah,* pp. 165–167; *id.,* "The Sources and Nature of Jewish Law and Its Application in the State of Israel," Part III, 3 *Israel L. Rev.* 416, 432–433 (1968); Lieberman v. Lieberman, 35(iv) *P.D.* 359, 372–373 (1981). *Cf.,* in other legal systems, the wife's right, generally created by statute, to a monetary award based on her contribution to the accumulation of "marital property." Another interesting example is the alimony *pendente lite* awarded by the rabbinical courts; *see* M. Corinaldi, "Sa'ad ha-Hafradah ha-Zemanit Bein ha-Ba'al ve-ha-Ishah ve-Hitpatḥuto bi-Fesikat Battei ha-Din ha-Rabaniyyim be-Yisra'el" [Alimony *Pendente Lite* between Husband and Wife and Its Development in the Decisions of the Rabbinical Courts in Israel], *Shenaton,* I (1974), pp. 184–218. *See also infra* pp. 1785–1787. for additional examples of creative interpretation by the rabbinical courts.

> one of the traditional modes of acquisition] all methods of transfer of title currently in use among merchants.[62]

However, these intentions were never translated into action,[63] and the vast majority of the community did not submit their civil disputes to the rabbinical courts for decision.

When the procedural enactments for the rabbinical courts were adopted in 1943, the call was again heard to make Jewish law applicable in every legal field. In their Introduction to these enactments, Chief Rabbis Isaac Herzog and Ben-Zion Uziel, commenting on the limitation of the jurisdiction of the rabbinical courts to matters of personal status, stated:[64]

> This limited scope was broadened by the law passed by the legislative authorities of the Jewish community in . . . 1928, which conferred upon every rabbinical court the authority to act as a permanent court of arbitration as well. The way has been opened by which all kinds of controversies and disputes between individuals, between individuals and public bodies, and between one public body and another, can be submitted to the rabbinical courts for adjudication, including even those cases that, because of their subject matter, are beyond the jurisdiction of those courts under the general law. This provides a magnificent opportunity to advance toward the great and holy objective of restoring Jewish law, administered by its own judges, as the vital governing law of our communities.

However, this "opening of the way," which could have been a strong impetus to the development of Jewish law so as to enable it—even at that late date—to be applied in daily life, produced meager results, and those only in judicial decisions. This is apparent from the published opinions of the Rabbinical Court of Appeals:[65] of the approximately fifty such decisions during 1943–1948, only ten deal with matters other than personal status. These ten decisions involve contracts, labor relations, partnership, fair and unfair competition, procedure, evidence, and enforcement of judgments. A few of these cases evince a grappling with the changing general and social conditions of contemporary life. Two cases are illustrative.

62. Freimann, *supra* n. 1 at 114–115.

63. After a time, the rabbinical courts, using custom (*minhag*) as a legal source, began to give effect to the modes of acquisition in use under the general law and to recognize other legal institutions as well on the same basis. *See supra* pp. 924–926. Over the course of time, other laws of the general legal system were given effect on various bases. *See* the extensive discussion in Wiloszni v. Rabbinical Court of Appeals, 36(ii) *P.D.* 733, 741ff. (1982); *infra* pp. 1820–1824.

64. Introduction to the Procedural Enactments of the Rabbinical Courts in the Land of Israel, 1943, p. 6.

65. *See* Warhaftig, *Osef Piskei ha-Din.*

In one case,[66] which involved a dispute over a decedent's estate, an important question in the Jewish law of evidence arose out of the contemporary socio-religious situation. A woman produced witnesses who were present when she went through a marriage ceremony with the decedent. On the strength of the testimony of these witnesses, the woman claimed to be the decedent's widow. Significantly, these witnesses were the only witnesses to the marriage ceremony, which was not conducted by a rabbi because the decedent was a *kohen* (priest) and the woman a divorcee. (Marriage between a *kohen* and a divorcee is forbidden by Jewish law, but is valid once performed.) According to Jewish law, the testimony of witnesses to a marriage is "constitutive" or substantive (*i.e.*, essential to a valid ceremony) and not merely "probative" or procedural in nature (*i.e.*, merely one method of proof of an otherwise valid ceremony).[67] The husband's heirs, who opposed the wife's claim, argued that she was not the deceased's widow, because the ceremony was legally ineffective. One of their arguments for invalidity of the marriage was that the witnesses had been proved to be habitual violators of the sabbath and therefore, according to Jewish law, they could not be competent witnesses.[68]

The court rejected the arguments of the decedent's heirs and affirmed the validity of the marriage.[69] As to the incompetency of the witnesses, the court made the following instructive observations:

> With regard to the question of whether the witnesses are not competent to testify because of their violations of the law as between man and God, one must take into consideration that under present circumstances—in which, due to our own sins, and to factors which are worldwide, disregard of the obligations of religion has increased and become widespread—these types of transgressions do not impair the credibility of the witnesses. During the present condition of such profound withdrawal of God's presence from the world, they are virtually in the category of unintentional transgressors. The disqualification of transgressors to be witnesses rests on the suspicion of perjury, and is based on reason, not simply on a Scriptural fiat [lit. "a decree of the King without a rationale"]. . . . Indeed, the rule that religious transgressors are incompetent to testify is not based on Biblical law.[70] Therefore, in such matters,

66. B. v. A. (1946), Warhaftig, *Osef Piskei ha-Din,* p. 132.

67. "If one marries a woman without the presence of witnesses . . . his marriage is not valid, even if both acknowledge that it took place." Sh. Ar. EH 42:2.

68. Sh. Ar. ḤM 34:2; *see also* 34:24.

69. The marriage was effective even though it took place without a *ḥuppah* (marriage canopy), benedictions, or a rabbi, since, *ex post,* the absence of any of these does not invalidate a marriage. Even the additional problem that the parties were a *kohen* (priest) and a divorcee does not invalidate the marriage, since such a marriage, although forbidden *ex ante,* is nevertheless valid once performed. *See* Sh. Ar. EH 18:1.

70. This additional argument is surprising in view of the fact that the disqualification of a transgressor to be a witness is Biblical in origin; *see* Sh. Ar. ḤM 34:2–3. It seems likely

> assessment of the credibility of witnesses depends in large measure upon the conditions of the time and place. If the court is convinced that a particular person is not likely to commit perjury for gain, he should be accepted as a competent witness.[71]

This significant ruling was necessary to proper judicial administration in view of the social situation of our time, when a substantial part of the community is not religiously observant; and the rabbinical courts have subsequently applied this ruling without being troubled by any misgivings.[72]

The second case involved an illegal contract. The general principle applicable to such a contract in Jewish law is that the court will not entertain an action on the contract if the relief sought is the specific performance of the illegal act; but the contract itself is not invalid, and damages may be recovered for breach of the contractual obligations undertaken by the parties.[73] In this case, A sued B for a sum of money, alleging that A was entitled to the money as a result of the purchase of foreign currency which B bought on A's behalf at a time when trading in foreign currency was illegal. On appeal from the judgment of the local rabbinical court, the Rabbinical Court of Appeals decided that since the claim was based on a transaction that

---

that Rabbi Uziel's original opinion was incorrectly copied. (The collection includes a summary, not the full original opinion.) The original does not state that transgressors are disqualified as witnesses only according to rabbinic law, but rather that the reason why they are incompetent is that they are suspected of testifying falsely; and it is not a "decree of the King," *i.e.*, a Scriptural fiat. The sources cited in that opinion also indicate that the intent was to the effect here set out. *See, e.g., Urim ve-Thummim,* Sh. Ar. ḤM 28, Urim, subpar. 3: "The reason a transgressor is incompetent to testify is that it is suspected that he will testify falsely; it is not merely fiat—a 'decree of the King without a rationale.'" As to disqualification of a witness for committing a transgression involving financial greed, *see Sema* to Sh. Ar. ḤM 34, subpar. 5, concerning a violator of a rabbinic law.

71. Warhaftig, *Osef Piskei ha-Din,* pp. 137–138. The decision continues: "Indeed, this matter needs further clarification and refinement, but that is not necessary here, in view of the other grounds mentioned above." (The court relied on another ground for holding the witnesses to be competent: The testimony that they were seen smoking on the sabbath referred to a time subsequent to the marriage ceremony, and until then they are entitled to the presumption that they are competent to testify. In addition, their confession that they do not observe the sabbath is inadmissible, since "one cannot incriminate oneself." *See id.* at 137.) These comments were apparently written in order to soften the impact of the court's innovative approach. In actuality, it is a widespread and accepted practice in the rabbinical courts to accept the testimony of all witnesses, even though many do not fulfill the religious commandments and therefore, according to the law in the *Shulḥan Arukh,* their testimony should not be accepted. *See also supra* n. 70.

72. However, in one instance the Rabbinical Court of Appeals later rendered a decision contrary to this case. *See infra* p. 1754 n. 8.

73. *See, e.g.,* Maimonides, *MT,* Mekhirah 30:7, Malveh ve-Loveh 4:6, 6:5; Sh. Ar. YD 161:1–11.

violated the law of the State, the lower court should not have entertained the action. The opinion stated:[74]

> Since the subject of the arbitration is a monetary claim in connection with the purchase and sale of foreign currency, which has been made illegal by the law of the State on grounds of public policy, and the parties were not only obligated to be aware of the prohibition, but in fact they had full knowledge of it, as appears from the proceedings in the lower court, we are not permitted to entertain the matter and, under the law of the State, the court below was similarly not permitted to do so. The decision below is therefore vacated.

Although it is possible to find some support for this decision in relatively recent sources of Jewish law[75] it was, in essence, a fundamentally new approach to the important subject of illegal contracts under Jewish law—an approach guided, first and foremost, by the desire to help achieve the objective of a law enacted by the State to promote the public welfare.[76]

Two procedural decisions are interesting examples of the care taken in regard to the incorporation of principles generally applicable in other legal systems. One case followed the rule—accepted in most legal systems—that findings of fact by the trial court will be accorded deference on appeal, and only conclusions of law are reviewable *de novo*.[77] The second case rejected a rule generally accepted in other systems and held instead that courts must entertain claims that are closely related to the claims of the complaint, notwithstanding that the related claims are not specifically mentioned in the complaint.[78] The court said:

74. A. v. B. (1945), Warhaftig, *Osef Piskei ha-Din*, p. 63.

75. Unfortunately, no authority is cited in the decision. *Pitḥei Teshuvah*, Sh. Ar. ḤM ch. 34, subpar. 1, offers some support for the conclusion reached.

76. As to illegal contracts, *see also supra* pp. 128–130; *infra* pp. 1716–1720. An additional interesting example can be found in A. v. B. (1945), Warhaftig, *Osef Piskei ha-Din*, p. 86, which raised the question of the validity of a contractual provision for liquidated damages in case of breach. According to Jewish law, such a clause is invalid because, as a general rule, it has the defect of *asmakhta* (*i.e.*, lack of full intent by the obligor to be bound) unless the obligation was undertaken before a "distinguished court" (*bet din ḥashuv*) or it was stated to be *she-lo ke-asmakhta* (not in the manner of *asmakhta*), thus demonstrating the seriousness of the commitment. *See* Gulak, *Yesodei*, I, pp. 67–75; ET, II, pp. 108–115, s.v. Asmakhta (2). These precautionary provisions were not contained in the contract involved in the case before the rabbinical court, but the court nevertheless gave full effect to the liquidated damage clause on the ground that "otherwise, most business transactions and contractual agreements would have to be voided. A provision like this one should be deemed to have included '*she-lo ke-asmakhta*' and regarded as if it had been agreed upon before a distinguished court, and there is stronger justification [for enforcing a liquidated damage provision] than [for according effectiveness to] a *sitomta*" (Warhaftig, *supra* at 89). As to *sitomta*, *see supra* pp. 914–915.

77. B. v. A. (1944), Warhaftig, *Osef Piskei ha-Din*, p. 41.

78. Administration of Yeshivah B. v. Trustees of Endowment A. (1944), Warhaftig, *Osef Piskei ha-Din*, p. 33.

> The lower court decided correctly . . . and did not yield to an excessively formalistic technicality. . . . In the case at bar, the members of the synagogue demanded that the room be vacated; and after the court rejected this demand, the question of the amount of the rent inevitably arose as part of the dispute and required an appropriate disposition. In this situation, it was the court's prerogative, and even its duty, to decide this dispute as well, and not to be confined by the formal limitations of the complaint. It is the duty of every Jewish court to try to achieve a final resolution that sets at rest all controversy, to make peace between the parties, and not leave undecided any points that might be sources of future contention. The court below was therefore correct in considering and deciding all issues involved in this matter and in no wise exceeded its authority.[79]

These examples illustrate the vitality of Jewish law in solving new problems posed by contemporary social and economic conditions. What is so disheartening is that they remain isolated examples. The rabbinic institutions failed to replicate them and did not meet the basic challenge—to prepare Jewish law to enable it to govern the practical life of the Jewish community, which was then on the road to national independence.

D. The Religious Leadership and Jewish Law

The national-religious (religious Zionist) leaders of the *yishuv* (the pre-State Jewish community in the Land of Israel) who should, in the nature of things, have been particularly interested in preparing Jewish law, as both a religious and national treasure, for practical application in daily life,[80] were not alert to the need to take action to achieve this goal. Probably one of the main reasons for this failure is the historical circumstance that, after the Emancipation, Jewish civil and criminal law were no longer applied in practice.[81] From the beginning of the nineteenth century, religious Jews in the diaspora limited their efforts to education, and the observance of religious law in such matters as the sabbath, *kashrut,* marriage, and divorce. The application of Jewish law to the practical affairs of everyday life ceased to be in the forefront of their consciousness. Similarly, in the *yishuv,* the national-religious movement limited its attention to the same areas, and paid its respects to Jewish civil law with a few articles and proclamations that had no practical use or effect.

This failure has proved to have been one of the gravest errors in the history of the national-religious movement. The movement is entitled to

79. *Id.* at 36–37.

80. It was because of their particular interest in this regard that the national-religious leadership sharply rejected Mishpat Ha-Shalom Ha-Ivri; *see supra* p. 1594.

81. *See supra* pp. 1576–1588.

great credit for its many accomplishments in connection with the building of the *yishuv* and of the Jewish state and for its concern that the spiritual and social character of the *yishuv* and of the Jewish state be organically linked with the national-religious past of the Jewish people. Its leaders, however, failed to realize, at the time when the *yishuv* was beginning to establish itself as an autonomous community, that one of the most important and effective means of connecting the nascent Jewish state with the great spiritual past of the Jewish people would be to restore Jewish law as a fully operational legal system.[82] Moreover, it is precisely in all the branches of Jewish law other than marriage and divorce that it is possible by means of appropriate and thorough preparatory work to arrive at a common language and understanding among the various elements of the people who differ in their religious and social outlook. This is so because matters of marriage and divorce are much more closely entwined with ideology and views of morality and religion than are questions of partnership, agency, suretyship, mortgages, pledges, and all the other branches of civil law; yet these latter areas of Jewish law have no less potential than the law of personal status for contributing to the preservation of Jewish historical continuity.[83]

It was not until immediately before the establishment of the State that religious Jewry first dealt seriously with the question of the place of Jewish law in the legal system of the Jewish state, but at that point there was insufficient time to prepare Jewish law for its natural role in that legal system.[84]

82. *See* the comments of Rabbi Meir Bar-Ilan (Berlin), the religious Zionist leader, written immediately after the founding of the State:

> Had we been more fortunate, the leaders, rabbis, and scholars of observant Jewry would many years ago have prepared a code of law for the State of Israel for the time when we would be privileged to see it established. But because we lacked faith, the State of Israel caught us suddenly unaware, without our having adequately prepared a civil and criminal legal system for it. We cannot, therefore, criticize those legislators for using Mandatory law as their guideline and setting up courts accordingly. What they can be criticized for, however, is that they did not declare that that system was only a temporary expedient for an emergency situation.

Yavneh, Koveẓ Akadema'i Dati, 1949 (hereinafter, *Yavneh*), p. 29. Surprisingly, in Rabbi Bar-Ilan's collected writings (*Kitvei Rabbi Meir Berlin,* I, 1950, pp. 274–279), this article is reproduced, but the portion that includes this quotation is omitted. As to the failure of the national-religious leaders to take action to prepare Jewish law for use as the legal system of the State, *see* M. Unna, *Bi-Derakhim Nifradot—Ha-Miflagot ha-Datiyyot be-Yisra'el* [With Diverse Approaches—The Religious Parties in Israel], 1984, pp. 83ff.

83. *See* Elon, *Mi-Ba'ayot ha-Halakhah ve-ha-Mishpat bi-Medinat Yisra'el, supra* n. 23 at 9ff.

84. *See infra* pp. 1612–1618.

E. Jewish Law and the Hebrew Language

1. THE RESTORATION OF THE HEBREW LANGUAGE AS THE LANGUAGE OF DAILY LIFE

The Hebrew language had a happier fate than Jewish law, even though, in one respect, it was more difficult to restore the Hebrew language as a spoken language than to renew Jewish law as living law. Not only had the use of Hebrew gradually declined in Jewish spiritual and cultural life as a consequence of the Emancipation,[85] but even from the beginning of the long exile of the Jews from their land, Hebrew served only as a medium for intellectual and literary expression and was not spoken in daily social and economic life. Any mundane use of Hebrew during that long period was due, paradoxically, to the holiness of the language (there were Jews who refrained from speaking in any "secular" language on the sabbath), or to its usefulness as a means of written communication, or to other similar factors. Moreover, many of the leaders of the nascent Zionist movement were skeptical about whether Hebrew had the capacity to be a vehicle for communication and creativity in the modern environment; Theodor Herzl, the leader of the Zionist movement, himself thought it quite conceivable that a Jewish state could exist without Hebrew as its language.[86]

What brought about the use of Hebrew in the *yishuv*—not only as a holy tongue but as the national language, spoken as well as written, of the Jewish people returning to its land—was the innate realization that with-

85. *See supra* pp. 1577–1578.

86. Herzl (*The Jewish State,* translated from the German in L. Lewisohn, *Theodore Herzl, A Portrait for This Age,* World Publishing Co., 1955, pp. 294–295) wrote:

> It might be suggested that our lack of a common current language would present difficulties, for we cannot converse with one another in Hebrew. Who among us knows enough Hebrew to ask for a railway ticket in that language? We have no such people. But it is really a very simple matter. Every man retains his own language, the cherished homeland of his thoughts. Switzerland offers conclusive proof of the possibility of linguistic federalism. . . .
>
> The language which proves itself to be of greatest utility for general intercourse will without compulsion establish itself as the national tongue. Our community of race is peculiar and unique. We know ourselves as bound together only by the light of our ancestral faith.

In the Hebrew edition of Herzl's collected writings published by Ha-Sifriyyah Ha-Ẓiyyonit (The Zionist Library), 1960, vol. I, p. 84, A. Bein reports that M. Berkowitz, the translator of the first Hebrew edition, said that when Herzl saw that his book was being read in Hebrew and that journals were regularly being published in Hebrew, "he changed his opinion and became convinced that the Hebrew language could be revived and that it had the exclusive claim to become the language of the Jewish state in the near future," and he requested Berkowitz to publicize this change of mind.

out the use of the Hebrew language in the everyday social, economic, and spiritual life of the people, the national renaissance could never be complete.

In 1913, at the time of the "language war" in the Land of Israel, the bold step was taken to make Hebrew the language of instruction in the schools of the *yishuv;* and in 1919, Herbert Samuel, the British High Commissioner, proclaimed Hebrew as one of the three official languages of Palestine. From that time, Hebrew has been a living language. The untiring efforts of public bodies and intensely dedicated individuals (led by Eliezer Ben Yehudah, whose forty-year struggle until his death in 1922 succeeded in reviving Hebrew as a spoken language) led to the creation of a new style and new terms, expressions, and forms of speech, all to a large extent drawn from the age-old resources of the language. Thus, Hebrew was able to satisfy the constantly changing demands made on a contemporary language, yet at the same time maintain the continuity and the essential identity between the contemporary national language and the holy tongue thousands of years old.

When compared with similar attempts by other peoples to revive their national language, the success of Hebrew is truly "an event that has no precedent in human history."[87] Even before the establishment of the State of Israel, the use of Hebrew was of prime importance as a manifestation of the Jewish national spirit. Today, it is simply impossible to conceive of social and cultural life in the State of Israel without Hebrew; all the debates and concerns about whether Hebrew could be revived as a language of daily life are now merely matters of historical and philological interest. All segments of the Jewish population of Israel—the secularists, who view the Hebrew language solely as a national asset, and the religious, who consider Hebrew a holy tongue as well—have had a part in this great and remarkable achievement. There is no Jew in our day who would reverse the revival of the Hebrew language; indeed, Hebrew as an everyday language has become one of the most important spiritual and practical assets shared by all segments of the people; it is a force for unifying the entire people into a single and harmonious entity.

2. THE POSITION OF JEWISH LAW

What was accomplished for the Hebrew language during the era of Jewish national reawakening was not accomplished for Jewish law. There are, of course, real differences between the feasibility of restoring Jewish law as a living legal system and the feasibility of reviving Hebrew as a living language. First, the revival of Hebrew depended mainly on independent

87. *See* J. Klausner, *Enẓiklopedyah ha-Ivrit* [Hebrew Encyclopedia], IX, p. 131, s.v. Ben Yehudah, Eliezer.

decisions by individuals and public institutions, whereas the renewal of Jewish law as a living legal system is heavily dependent on the existence of Jewish political sovereignty, or, at the least, the cooperation of the non-Jewish government. Secondly, legal norms have greater impact on ideas and perceptions of morals and justice than do modes of linguistic expression; and the restoration of Jewish law to practical life, even after only a relatively brief period of desuetude, also requires wider and deeper preparatory work.

All these considerations were obstacles, but they did not render the renewal of Jewish law impossible; and they certainly cannot justify the failure to accomplish that renewal, particularly in view of the fact that the situation of the Jewish community in the Land of Israel prior to the establishment of the State was quite favorable for serious effort toward this end.

Many factors made this time of preparation for full Jewish national sovereignty appropriate for the renewal of Jewish law. The situation of the *yishuv* in regard to political autonomy was similar, in many respects, to the situation enjoyed by the western Jewish diaspora centers before the Emancipation. A large Jewish community imbued by a strong and developing national consciousness had once again achieved internal autonomy, with institutions governed by elected officials and full juridical autonomy as to matters of personal status.

As noted, this autonomy produced the beginnings of a new creativity in the law of personal status, which, though not fully meeting all the needs of a modern Jewish society, made substantial progress in that direction. Moreover, although the Jewish community was not granted juridical autonomy in civil-law matters, there was initially strong enthusiasm for the restoration of Jewish civil law as a living legal system, and methods for translating that enthusiasm into action were available.

However, actual results along these lines swiftly proved disappointing. Mishpat Ha-Shalom Ha-Ivri attempted to revive lay courts like those in the diaspora during the period of Jewish internal autonomy prior to the end of the eighteenth century;[88] however, this institution, whose judges did not use the settled and explicit norms of Jewish law but instead ruled according to personal and subjective notions of ethics and justice, could not carry forward the Jewish legal tradition. The rabbinical courts, for their part, did almost nothing to grapple with new conditions in the broad field of civil law, and consequently the people—even those who as a matter of religion accepted rabbinical authority—did not submit their disputes to these courts.

The rabbinical institutions did try for a short time to revive the pow-

88. *See supra* pp. 20–29.

erful instrument of *takkanot ha-kahal* (communal legislation),[89] as appears from the enactments promulgated in 1944 "by the Chief Rabbinate of the Land of Israel . . . with the approval of the communities through their councils and committees."[90] This action could have provided an important precedent for the enactment of *takkanot* in all the various areas of law in the future Jewish state. Nevertheless, this approach also was abandoned soon after it began to be used;[91] and there was virtually no further halakhic legislative activity by either the Chief Rabbinate or the representative institutions of the *yishuv*—the modern forms of the two historic legislative agencies of the Jewish legal system, namely, the halakhic authorities and the lay communities.

This period, although in general one of the most dynamic and creative in Jewish history, was for Jewish law a period of eclipse and stagnation. The segment of the Jewish community that esteemed Jewish law solely for its national value and attempted to revive Jewish law through Mishpat Ha-Shalom Ha-Ivri failed to take even the first steps necessary to achieve this objective; Mishpat Ha-Shalom Ha-Ivri failed to realize that the revival of Jewish law (which was the goal of the Ha-Mishpat Ha-Ivri Society), like the strikingly successful revival of the Hebrew language, requires that development and renewal be rooted in the past while being fashioned to meet contemporary needs.

On the other hand, the spiritual leaders of those in the Jewish community who viewed Jewish law as having not only national but also religious significance lacked the vision to remold the Jewish legal system to enable it to respond to the demands of contemporary social and economic life. Indeed, the religious population as a whole lacked the internal discipline that would motivate them to submit their legal disputes to the rabbinical courts and thus provide an opportunity to develop a corpus of case law consonant with traditional Jewish law and yet appropriate to contemporary conditions. Even if only the religious population of the *yishuv* had taken this course, so that, instead of the ten opinions in civil-law cases noted above, there had been a thousand in that period of almost thirty years, this would have added many scores of seminal decisions on various modern problems of civil law, which could have provided a solid foundation for the preparation of a modern code of Jewish law. As it turned out, the depressing result was that Jewish law failed to achieve the success achieved by the Hebrew language at that time: to become—at least in the area of civil and administrative law—a spiritual and cultural resource shared by all segments

89. *See supra* pp. 678ff.

90. *See* Elon, *Ḥakikah,* p. 163; *supra* p. 832.

91. The only exceptions were a few *takkanot* enacted in 1950, which are of no special significance. *See supra* pp. 833–834.

of the Jewish population and linking the contemporary renaissance with the great traditions of the past.

This failure on the part of all elements of the Jewish population dulled the *yishuv*'s awareness of the value of Jewish law to the national renaissance in the pre-State period and was responsible for the failure to take the steps necessary to prepare the Jewish legal system to become a significant and powerful cultural and national force in the life of the nascent Jewish state.

The plight of Jewish law in this period was more serious than in the preceding post-Emancipation period in the nineteenth century when there was no juridical autonomy. Immediately following the Emancipation, the Jewish community, as a result of factors both internal and external to it, was compelled to forgo the use of autonomous Jewish tribunals. This was not the case, however, from the time the Jewish people began to return in large numbers to their ancestral homeland; if they had truly wished to make the necessary preparations for a legal order based on Jewish law, they could have done so. They had a historic opportunity, rare even in the extraordinarily long history of Jewish law, to lay the foundations for such a legal order; but that opportunity was tragically missed. This failure had crucial consequences in the following period that witnessed the full restoration of Jewish sovereignty—an integral part of which, in the normal course of events, should have naturally been a legal order based on the restoration of Jewish law. Hebrew was ready to become the prevailing language in the future Jewish state. Jewish law, however, was not ready to become the governing legal system. Not only was Jewish law completely unprepared to assume this status, but independent Jewish statehood in the mid-twentieth century confronted Jewish law with yet new problems.

III. ON THE EVE OF THE ESTABLISHMENT OF THE STATE OF ISRAEL

A. The Legal System under the British Palestine Mandate Immediately before the Establishment of the State of Israel

An important factor that could have served to advance the incorporation of Jewish law into the legal system of the nascent Jewish state was the unique structure of the legal system under the British Palestine Mandate just before the State of Israel was established. The principles governing the legal system during the British Mandate were set forth in Article 46 of the Palestine Order in Council of 1922. This article provided that the Ottoman law in force in the country on November 1, 1914, was to be recognized as binding, subject to the ordinances and regulations thereafter promulgated by the Mandatory Government. All problems for which the existing legal system provided no solution were to be resolved by the courts on the basis of the principles of English common law and equity, "so far only as the circumstances of Palestine and its inhabitants and the limits of His Majesty's jurisdiction permit, and subject to such qualification as local circumstances render necessary."

In accordance with these principles, a number of legal systems provided the sources for the system that crystallized in the Land of Israel prior to the establishment of the State of Israel. Thus, the law of sales, suretyship, and pledges derived from the *Mejelle,* which was based on Moslem religious law. The law of damages for breach of contract was partly based on paragraphs 106 to 111 of the Ottoman Code of Civil Procedure of June 21, 1879, which in turn was based on French law. Tort law was based on a Mandatory ordinance of 1944–1947 which was derived from English law. The law of specific performance and equitable title was based on the doctrines of English equity. A considerable part of the law of personal status was governed by the religious law of each religious community, which the Mandatory government recognized as binding on members of the respective communities.[92]

The existence of these different sources made it necessary to turn to the different languages in which the sources were written, such as Turkish (the language of the *Mejelle*), English (for English law), and Hebrew (for the substantive law of personal status of Jews). Such a legal structure could hardly inspire enthusiasm; in the words of the late Justice Silberg, it is not a legal system but "a mosaic, destined perhaps to excite the eye of an archeologist, but not able to serve as a firm basis for healthy and normal legal relations."[93]

B. The Deliberations Regarding the Place of Jewish Law in the Legal System of the State of Israel

The eve of the establishment of the State of Israel once again presented an opportunity to deal with the question of the place of Jewish law in the future sovereign state. As previously noted, the question was discussed by the scholars and advocates of Jewish law at the beginning of the national renaissance; and various opinions were expressed at that time concerning the preparation of Jewish law for incorporation into the legal system of the new Jewish state and concerning the necessity and extent of such incor-

92. *See* Articles 47, 51–57, 64–65 of the Palestine Order in Council, 1922.

93. M. Silberg, *Talmudic Law and the Modern State,* New York, 1973, p. 148; *id.*, "Li-She'elat Arikhat Kodex Ivri" [On the Question of Preparing a Jewish Legal Code], *Ha-Praklit,* IV (1948), p. 262.

poration.[94] These various approaches were once again a focus of attention on the eve of statehood, when the existing legal system was such a patchwork of disparate and mutually inconsistent elements as to invite the reception of Jewish law if only in order to achieve a coherent and homogeneous system. The debate was opened by A.H. Freimann in his programmatic essay "Dinei Yisra'el be-Ereẓ Yisra'el" [Jewish Law in the Land of Israel],[95] and many other scholars of Jewish law participated.[96] The discussion centered on how to prepare Jewish law for modern conditions and how to solve contemporary legal problems.

The first thorough discussion by the religious Jewish community of the place of Jewish law in a future Jewish state also took place during this period. Two documents were written by leaders of the Agudat Israel organization in 1938, following the hearings of the Peel Commission on the establishment of a Jewish state in part of the Land of Israel.[97] The first, entitled "Tokhnit la-Ḥukkah ba-Medinah ha-Yehudit" [A Constitutional Program for the Jewish State], was written by Dr. Isaac Breuer, a lawyer and ideologue of Agudat Israel. The first chapter sets forth the basic constitutional principles: the Torah is the law of the Jewish people; its binding force is independent of acceptance or non-acceptance by the people; and it must govern all aspects of life, including the form of government and the judicial system. To this end, detailed provisions in accordance with the law of the Torah should be worked out for constitutional, public, and private law. Breuer essentially rejected the principle that religion and state should be kept separate. He recognized only one exception: "where circumstances make it clear that without the separation of religion from the state the strictly religious element will not have the freedom to develop an internal

94. *See supra* pp. 1588–1591.

95. *Lu'aḥ ha-Areẓ,* 1946, pp. 110, 119ff. *See also* Freimann's proposals as head of the Jewish Law Section of the International Congress of Jewish Studies at Mt. Scopus, Jerusalem, in 1947, as quoted in J.P.D., "Le-Darkhei ha-Ḥakikah bi-Medinateinu" [On Approaches to Legislation in Our State], *Ha-Praklit,* X (1949), pp. 144, 146.

At that time, Freimann, in his article in *Luaḥ ha-Areẓ,* had already mentioned the possibility of recognizing the halakhic validity of legislation adopted by the legislative body of the Jewish state, on the basis of the principle of the validity of communal legislation. This issue was later dealt with in the decisions of the Supreme Court of Israel and in the rabbinical courts. *See infra* pp. 1820–1826, 1944–1945. As to these discussions, *see also* M. Elon, "The Sources and Nature of Jewish Law and Its Application in the State of Israel," *supra* n. 61 at 443–445.

96. *See, e.g.,* Silberg, "Li-She'elat Arikhat Kodex Ivri," *supra* n. 93; H. Cohn, "De'agah le-Yom Maḥar" [Concern for the Future], *Ha-Praklit,* II (1946), p. 38; *id.,* "De'agah Shel Yom Etmol" [Concern for the Past], *Sura,* 1957–1958, p. 745; A.L. Globus, "Al Bet Din Ivri" [Concerning the Jewish Court], *Ha-Praklit,* IV (1948), p. 111; S. Eisenstadt, "Medinah u-Mishpat" [State and Law], *Ha-Praklit,* V (1946), p. 113.

97. Both documents are printed in *Yavneh,* pp. 33–40.

religious communal life." The subsequent chapters deal with the minimum standards that Breuer felt should exist in the Jewish state during the time that the law of the Torah is accepted by less than the entire Jewish community, namely, that matters of personal status should be governed by the law of the Torah and that jurisdiction over all other civil-law matters should be exercised by a "Torah *bet din* . . . unless the parties agree otherwise."

The second plan, devised by Moshe Blau, a leader of Agudat Israel in Jerusalem, entitled "Yesodot ha-Ḥukkaḥ ba-Medinah ha-Yehudit" [The Constitutional Foundations of the Jewish State], was more modest with regard to the application of Jewish law. This document, too, stated as the basic constitutional principle that the authority of the Torah over public life was "immutable." It proposed that the constitution of the State provide that the rabbinical courts have exclusive jurisdiction over matters of personal status; the general courts would have jurisdiction over all other civil-law matters, but would be obligated to conform to "the basic rules of Torah law . . . such as the rules governing the competence of witnesses." The rabbinical courts would also have jurisdiction over all other civil-law matters as arbitration tribunals if the parties agree; and the arbitration awards would be directly enforced by an agency established for this purpose without the need to apply to the general courts for enforcement.

Immediately prior to the establishment of the State, the leaders of Agudat Israel returned to the problem of the relationship between religion and state. In a June 1947 letter from the Jewish Agency to the World Union of Agudat Israel[98] summarizing the discussions between the two bodies concerning the religious guarantees in the future state, the Jewish Agency Executive obligated itself to do all in its power to ensure that the State would be responsible to guarantee: (1) the sabbath as the official day of rest; (2) kosher food in all state facilities used by Jews; (3) all necessary action to ensure that matters of personal status are governed by religious law in order "to prevent the Jewish people from being split (God forbid!) in two"; and (4) religious education for all those desiring it. Interestingly, this "constitutional" letter says nothing at all about the place of any aspect of Jewish civil law in the new state.

A different note was sounded by Chief Rabbi Herzog in an article written just prior to the establishment of the State, entitled "Ha-Teḥikkah veha-Mishpat ba-Medinah ha-Yehudit" [Legislation and Law in the Jewish State].[99] The article begins:

98. The letter is printed in *Yavneh,* pp. 40–41, and is dated June 19, 1947. It is signed by David Ben-Gurion, J.L. Fishman, and I. Greenbaum.

99. *Yavneh,* pp. 9–13.

> The aspiration of religious Jewry in this country and in the diaspora must be that the constitution include a basic provision that the legal system of the Land of Israel is based on the fundamental principles of the Torah. However, in order that such a provision be acceptable to a large part of the population of the Land of Israel (who are far from knowledgeable about the Torah and, to our sorrow, so remote from our sacred tradition, that they believe that the Torah and democracy are inconsistent), it is essential at this time to work out a proposal for a legal system that will take into account the democratic nature of the state. This is also essential because the State will be established under a resolution of the United Nations, which calls for a state founded on democratic principles, and because a considerable and important minority of the citizens of the State will be non-Jews, so that although the State will be a Jewish state it will include, in no small measure, non-Jews as well as Jews.[100]

Rabbi Herzog went on to discuss the difficulties in fulfilling the requirement that the legal system be based on the principles of Jewish law, and the manner in which these difficulties could be overcome. Thus, he pointed out the necessity of finding a way, consistent with Jewish law, to enable those who are not religiously observant to be appointed as judges or to act as witnesses, although the strict *Halakhah* disqualifies them. He also stressed the need for the proper preparation and the adoption of *takkanot*[101] in both civil and criminal law[102] to meet the needs of the new social and economic environment.

Rabbi Herzog proposed that the rabbinical courts be given exclusive jurisdiction over matters of personal status as well as concurrent jurisdiction over cases involving the other areas of civil law, since "even on the assumption that the government will agree to enact legislation that the legal system shall be based on Jewish law, it is inconceivable that the traditional Jewish courts should not have power to deal with the entire range of civil law."[103] Rabbi Herzog considered the problems posed by two separate and parallel court systems, and suggested the possibility of resolving the problems by

100. *Id.* at 9–10.

101. In order to solve the many immediate problems regarding religion and the state in the contemporary setting, Chief Rabbi Uziel proposed (*Yavneh*, pp. 14ff.) reconvening the Great Assembly (*Keneset ha-Gedolah*) and reestablishing the Sanhedrin, following the model of what had been done in similar circumstances in the time of Ezra and Nehemiah.

102. Rabbi Herzog strongly maintained that the Jewish state should ban capital punishment and replace it with the penalty of imprisonment. *See Yavneh*, p. 10. The death penalty for murder was indeed abrogated in the Penal Law Revision (Abolition of the Death Penalty for Murder) Law, 1954.

103. *Yavneh*, p. 11.

giving the defendant the option to choose which court should try the case.[104]

Still another approach was taken by Rabbi Meir Bar-Ilan (Berlin), a leader of the religious Zionist movement.[105] He expressed his regret for the grossly negligent failure of the rabbis and religious leaders to prepare Jewish law for incorporation into the legal system of the Jewish state[106] and stressed the need to begin without delay the task of making the entire corpus of Jewish law a suitable foundation for the legal system of the State of Israel by enacting appropriate *takkanot* and formulating the law in a manner consonant with contemporary legal conditions. In his view, there was no choice but to base the legal system on Jewish law; and he strongly opposed the idea of two parallel court systems having concurrent jurisdiction—one system for the religious and the other for the secular:[107]

> There is great danger in a sort of tacit agreement that appears to exist in our religious circles to the effect that if the State of Israel will have a dual system of both religious "rabbinical" courts and secular courts, with the parties having the option to choose which court will try their cases, and if they [the religious courts] will be accorded official recognition, this will be all that is required and nothing more will be sought. This policy, which is based on purely parochial concern for being able to remain separate and apart and is content to "relegate the Torah to a corner," was our bane over the last two generations and could have calamitous consequences for the Jewish state for generations to come.
>
> The only course open to every true Jew is to exert every effort to see to it that there is but one law throughout our country, not only for ourselves but for all the people, including non-Jews. As in all other countries, the law should be based on territorial authority and not personal affiliation, except, of course, as to cases involving matters of religion. And this one law must be based on the Torah of Israel in all its ramifications, and not on some other law.

Convinced of the validity of this basic juridical approach, Rabbi Bar-Ilan pressed for an urgent search for the solution (including the adoption of necessary *takkanot*) to all the problems impeding the acceptance of Jewish law as the law of the State, such as, for example, the problems relating

104. A similar provision, giving the option to the plaintiff, is contained in the Rabbinical Courts Jurisdiction (Marriage and Divorce) Law, 1953, sec. 4, pursuant to which an action for support not incident to a divorce proceeding may be brought by the wife either in a rabbinical court or in a general court.

105. "Ḥok u-Mishpat bi-Medinateinu" [Statute and Law in Our State], *Yavneh,* p. 29.

106. *Id.*

107. *Id.* at 31.

to the disqualification of witnesses and judges, and the law of inheritance. He continued:

> If we are not flexible enough to find a practicable and acceptable solution, our rigidity will lead to ultimate disrespect [for Jewish law]. In that event, the governing law will certainly not be our own, and societal life in our state will not reflect our spirit or outlook. The pattern that emerges will reflect and influence all of life—all our public and private actions, even those pertaining to religious matters—for when one foundation stone is removed, the whole superstructure crumbles.[108]

C. Proposals to Require Recourse to Jewish Law

None of the foregoing views as to the necessity and method of preparing Jewish law for incorporation into the legal system of the State could be implemented before the State was established, if only because of the short time before Jewish statehood would become a fact. Consequently, an original proposal ardently espoused by P. Dykan (Dikstein), a veteran in the campaign for restoring Jewish law to daily life, took on particular significance. In a series of articles,[109] Dykan proposed that, in addition to taking urgent steps to prepare Jewish law for its restored role and in addition to teaching Jewish law to the legal community, an appropriate declaration concerning Jewish law should be included in the very first document proclaiming the restoration of Jewish sovereignty. This declaration would be implemented by repeal of the provision of Article 46 of the Palestine Order in Council that designated English common law and equity to fill lacunae in the law and would designate Jewish law instead. At the same time, Dykan proposed to retain a different provision of Article 46 that would make the application of Jewish law subject to modification (as the application of English law had been) as required by contemporary conditions. Dykan proposed the following as a substitute for Article 46 of the Order in Council:

> Wherever the existing law does not deal with any particular issue or is ambiguous or inconsistent, the courts and other governmental agencies shall be governed by the rules of Jewish law, in accordance with the needs of the time.[110]

108. *Id.* at 32; *see also* Unna, *supra* n. 82 at 83ff.

109. P. Dikstein (Dykan), "Lo Titakhein Medinah Ivrit le-Lo Mishpat Ivri" [A Jewish State Is Inconceivable without Jewish Law], *Ha-Praklit,* IV (1948), p. 328; *id.* "Hakhrazah al ha-Mishpat ha-Ivri" [A Declaration Regarding Jewish Law], *Ha-Praklit,* V (1948), p. 3; *id.*, "Aẓma'ut Medinit ve-Aẓma'ut Mishpatit" [Political Independence and Juridical Independence], *Ha-Praklit,* V (1948), p. 107.

110. A number of additions to this formulation were proposed, including abrogation of the binding authority of English decisions, and repeal of the provisions in various statutes (such as Section 4 of the Criminal Law Ordinance, 1936, and Section 2(a) of the Civil Torts

This proposal would have achieved three important objectives: (1) it would have eliminated the dependence by a sovereign Jewish state on a foreign (namely, the English) legal system; (2) it would have linked, however tenuously and modestly, the law of the sovereign Jewish state with the entire system of Jewish law; and (3) it would have stimulated all interested parties to take the necessary action to prepare Jewish law to become suitable for use whenever recourse to Jewish law is required by the law of the State. It was believed at that point that, over the course of time, this most important stimulus, backed by official governmental authority, would lead to a central role for Jewish law in the legal system of the State.

What was the outcome of all these deliberations and proposals with regard to the revival of Jewish law as part of the legal system of the State? At the end of 1947, immediately after the United Nations' resolution on the establishment of a Jewish state, the Supreme National Institutions of the *yishuv* set up a council charged with taking all steps necessary to prepare the legal system of the state then about to be established. This council appointed a committee to deal with the religious courts, the law of personal status, and all questions pertaining to Jewish law. A.H. Freimann, who was eminently suited for such an important office, was appointed chairman. However, the hour was very late. There were only a few months remaining before the establishment of the State, and the *yishuv* faced urgent political problems, chief among which were the formidable problems of national security. In this brief interval before the establishment of the State, Freimann met his death in a convoy massacred while on its way to Mount Scopus, and this undoubtedly was a factor in the failure of his committee to achieve any practical result.[111]

The Declaration of Independence of the Jewish state was imminent. However, the Jewish legal system had not been adequately prepared for this historic event; not even the outlines of a policy had been adopted for the incorporation of the historic legal system of the Jewish people into the legal system of the nascent state. Time would tell how critical this situation was for one of the most fundamental legal-cultural issues facing the Jewish state.

Ordinance, 1944–1947) which required that the statutes be construed in accordance with English law. However, inasmuch as the ordinances had their source in the laws of Britain, Dikstein did not propose that these ordinances be construed in accordance with Jewish rather than English law. The purpose of his proposal to repeal the requirement to refer to English law was essentially to declare officially the end of subservience to other legal systems. It was assumed that the judges, as a matter of course, would generally continue to interpret these ordinances in accordance with English law, since the ordinances originated in that system.

111. *See* P. Dikstein, "Le-Zekher Dr. Avraham Ḥayyim Freimann z"l" [Dr. A.H. Freimann: In Memoriam], *Ha-Praklit,* V (1948), pp. 67, 69–70.

Chapter 42

JEWISH LAW IN THE GENERAL LEGAL SYSTEM OF THE STATE OF ISRAEL

I. The Official Position of Jewish Law and the Hebrew Language in the State of Israel
    A. Section 11 of the Law and Administration Ordinance, 1948
    B. The Hebrew Language
    C. Dependence on English Law and Non-Recourse to Jewish Law
II. The Actual Position of Jewish Law in the State's Legal System
III. Jewish Law in Legislation
    A. The Two Legislative Periods
    B. Legislative Policy
    C. Legislation Based on Principles of Jewish Law
        1. The First Legislative Period
            a. Civil Law
                (1) The Cooperative Houses Law
                (2) Labor Law
                (3) Imprisonment for Debt
            b. Criminal and Public Law
                (1) The Penal Law Revision (Bribery) Law
                (2) The Defamation Law
                (3) Immunity of Judges
                (4) Laws Incorporating Basic Tenets of the Jewish Tradition
                (5) The Law of Return
                (6) The Basic Law: Israel Lands
            c. Personal Status, Family, and Succession Law
                (1) The Marriage Age Law
                (2) The Woman's Equal Rights Law
                (3) The Family Law Amendment (Maintenance) Law
                (4) The Capacity and Guardianship Law
                (5) The Succession Law
                    (a) Provisions Generally Incorporating Jewish Law
                    (b) Provisions Not in Accord with Jewish Law
                (6) Who Is a Jew?
        2. The Second Legislative Period
            a. The Bailees Law
            b. The Unjust Enrichment Law
            c. Admonition of Witnesses and Abrogation of the Witness Oath
            d. The Crime Register and Rehabilitation of Offenders Law
            e. Self-Help—The Land Law
            f. Illegal Contracts
    D. Legislation Contrary to Jewish Law
        1. Suretyship—The Guarantee Law
        2. The Gift Law
        3. Limitation of Actions
    E. Self-Sufficiency of the Law of the State of Israel

IV. Jewish Law in Israeli Judicial Decisions
V. Jewish Law in the Interpretation of Israeli Legislation
  A. Problems of Statutory Interpretation and Interpretive Approaches to Israeli Legislation
  B. The Proper Method of Interpreting Israeli Legislation
    1. Value-Laden Legal Terms
    2. Other Problems of Statutory Construction
    3. *Bank Kupat Am v. Hendeles*—First Hearing

I. THE OFFICIAL POSITION OF JEWISH LAW AND THE HEBREW LANGUAGE IN THE STATE OF ISRAEL

A. Section 11 of the Law and Administration Ordinance, 1948

In order that the young State of Israel not find itself in a legal vacuum, it was necessary, as soon as the State was established, to adopt the now familiar Section 11 of the Law and Administration Ordinance of 1948, which provides:

> The law in effect on the 5th day of Iyyar, 5708 (May 14, 1948) shall remain in force insofar as not inconsistent with this ordinance or with the other laws that may be enacted by or under the authority of the Provisional Council of State, and subject to such modifications as may result from the establishment of the State and its agencies.

Thus, the State of Israel continued in effect the entire legal system, with all its diverse sources and tendencies, that existed just prior to the State's establishment. With the sole exception of the law of personal status, Jewish law was not officially incorporated into the State's legal system. Some questions of the personal status of Jews, particularly marriage and divorce, were within the exclusive jurisdiction of the rabbinical courts. Others were within the concurrent jurisdiction of the rabbinical courts and the general courts, but Jewish law applied to such issues even in the general courts. Thus, statehood left the operation of the legal system of the country essentially unchanged.[1]

1. For detailed discussion, *see supra* pp. 1596–1600; *infra* pp. 1652, 1752ff.

B. The Hebrew Language

At the very same time, the Hebrew language celebrated its ultimate victory, which the State formally acknowledged. The Declaration of Independence, in reciting the chain of events marking the national reawakening and the return to the land, refers to "the revival of the Hebrew language"; and the same statute that enacted Section 11, quoted above, stated in Section 15(b): "Every provision of law requiring the use of the English language is hereby repealed." Thus, Hebrew became the language of the State, the law, and all areas of life.

C. Dependence on English Law and Non-Recourse to Jewish Law

The failure to prepare Jewish law for reception by the State left no alternative but to continue the entire existing legal system in effect. However, it would still have been possible, if Dykan's proposal had been accepted, to proclaim the independence of the new state's legal system by abrogating Article 46 of the Palestine Order in Council, which required the courts to resort to English common law and equity when faced with a lacuna, and by abrogating the binding force of English precedents. It would also have been possible, if Dykan's proposal had been adopted, to link the legal system of the Jewish state with Jewish law, even if only to a very modest extent, through a declaration of principle that the State's future legislation should be based on the fundamentals of Jewish law, and that resort to Jewish law would thenceforth be obligatory when the existing law did not provide a solution. Indeed, such a proposal was formally considered by the Constitution Committee of the Provisional Council of State very soon after the State was established. The basis for the committee's discussion was a draft constitution prepared by Leo Kohn, who had been Secretary of the Political Department of the Jewish Agency Executive and became the Political Adviser to the Foreign Ministry after the establishment of the State.[2] Section 77 of this draft constitution stated:

> The law existing in Israel on the day this Constitution takes effect shall remain in force insofar as consistent with the provisions of the Constitution and so long as it has not been repealed or amended by the elected legislative body.

2. The draft was entitled *Ḥukkah le-Yisra'el* [A Constitution for Israel], and was published in Tel Aviv in 1949. It was prepared at the request of the Jewish Agency Executive. The Constitution Committee of the Provisional Council of State, during its consideration of the draft, stressed that the draft had no official status and the author alone bore responsibility for it. *See* the remarks of Dr. Zeraḥ Warhaftig, Chairman of the Committee, in the Introduction to the draft.

> The legislation of the State shall be based on the fundamental principles of Jewish law, which shall guide the courts in filling gaps in existing laws.[3]

The Knesset did not adopt a constitution as a part of the State's legal system; and, although the proposed Section 77 itself could have been enacted as a statute, not even that much was accomplished. The proposal's opponents successfully argued: (1) there is no assurance that Jewish law provides a ready solution for the problems for which Israeli law affords no clear answer, and (2) the vast majority of lawyers and judges are not sufficiently knowledgeable and proficient to be able to research the sources of Jewish law for answers to problems that might arise. The outcome was that not only was no link forged between Jewish law and the legal system of the State, but the legal system of the State continued to be linked officially to English law.[4]

The validity of the arguments raised to prevent the acceptance of this seminal proposal is open to question. The proposal speaks of recourse to Jewish law when there is a gap in the existing law, *i.e.*, a lacuna,[5] which,

3. The first part of the section essentially restates the content of Section 11 of the Law and Administration Ordinance, 1948, quoted above. The Explanatory Notes (pp. 38–39) comment as follows on the significance of the second part of the section:

> It is proposed here that, when new laws are prepared, the fundamentals of Jewish law should be used as guiding principles, and that until new laws are enacted, judges will be required to draw on that [*i.e.*, Jewish] law when they fill gaps in the existing law. The underlying theory is that, although it is impossible to substitute another legal system for the Mandatory system overnight, new legislation in Israel should be based on the fundamentals of Jewish law. This law is one of the most fascinating manifestations of the Jewish spirit. Being firmly rooted in the Bible and in the Oral Law, it has been developed through a rich literature of responsa which has adapted it to the changing conditions of the life of the Jewish people. . . . Jewish law never stagnated. Theoretical study and practical application provided constant fine-tuning. This law is an integral part of our national Jewish heritage. It must be adapted to our present conditions and become the foundation of the new legal system of the State of Israel.

4. As to the proposal of P. Dykan, *see supra* pp. 1617–1618. Later, similar proposals were made from time to time in the Knesset, but with no greater success. Proposals for recourse to Jewish law were sometimes made in connection with the legal system as a whole, and sometimes in connection with specific statutes. For a proposal of the first kind, *see, e.g.*, the private member's bill introduced by MK Warhaftig entitled "A Bill for the Application of the Principles of Jewish Law, 1958," 25 *Divrei ha-Keneset* [The Knesset Record] (hereinafter, *DK*) 231 (1958), and the response of the Minister of Justice, P. Rosen, *id.* at 232. For proposals of the second kind, *see, e.g.*, with regard to the Cooperative Houses Law, 1953, 8 *DK* 765, 775 (1951); 12 *DK* 2786 (1952); 13 *DK* 266–267 (proposal of MK Warhaftig and response of Minister of Justice H. Cohn); the Key-Money Law, 1958 (a rent control act), 24 *DK* 2478, 2513–2514 (1958); and the Capacity and Guardianship Law, 1962, 32 *DK* 56–57 (1962). *See also* the comments of Minister of Justice I.S. Shapiro, 46 *DK* 1707 (1966).

5. For a discussion of lacunae, *see* G. Tedeschi, "Ba'ayat ha-Likkuyim be-Ḥok ve-Siman 46 li-Devar ha-Melekh be-Mo'aẓato" [The Problem of Lacunae in the Law, and Article 46 of the Palestine Order in Council], in *Meḥkarim be-Mishpat Arẓeinu* [Studies in the Law of Our Land], 2nd ed., 1959, pp. 132ff.

in the nature of things, will probably occur in very few cases,[6] since the vast majority of legal questions are answered by the State's current law. Nor should it be overlooked that recourse to English law is not to a clear and explicit code, but to English case law, which is voluminous, obscure, and scattered throughout different legal sources. Moreover, access to these English-language sources is far from convenient for the overwhelming majority of Israeli citizens, who have a right to know what the law of the State provides. Even Israeli lawyers, in increasingly large numbers, experience the same difficulties with English precedents.

Consequently, was it not desirable that the State take the minimal "risk" in having its legal system, in case of a lacuna, look to the principles of Jewish law? Balanced against the "risk" involved, was there not a great advantage in creating a formal, even if slight, link between the law of the Jewish state and the historic national law of the Jewish people? Creating such a link would have forced the appropriate agencies to define the attitude of Jewish law toward those legal problems that Article 46 would otherwise require to be decided according to English law. This material on Jewish law, when properly prepared, would then have been available to the legal community, as well as to the educated laity, for practical use as well as for study and critical analysis. Once a start was made with regard to these particular legal problems, the same kind of work could have been done in other areas of Jewish law to enable them to be incorporated into the law of the State. In the final analysis, the period of Jewish national awakening produced more than a few significant achievements by taking even greater and more serious chances. Jewish law, too, was certainly worth some risk.

II. THE ACTUAL POSITION OF JEWISH LAW IN THE STATE'S LEGAL SYSTEM

As stated, apart from matters of personal status, Jewish law was not officially incorporated into any area of the new state's legal system. The legal principles of the State were not grounded on the principles of Jewish law, nor was there any type of link between the two systems that required recourse to Jewish law in order to fill lacunae in the existing law or for any similar purpose. The resulting situation in regard to Jewish law was much different than it was before the establishment of the State. In the pre-State period, Jewish law laid claim to the right to replace the existing non-Jewish legal system when the State would be established; and if Jewish law had

6. For examples of incorporation of English law by way of Article 46, *see* Tedeschi, *supra* n. 5 at 165–167.

been properly prepared, this substitution could have been accomplished at once, or at least a general proclamation of this goal could have been adopted or specific Jewish legal principles enacted. However, once statehood had been achieved, the legal system with which Jewish law had to contend was that of the Jewish state, and the reception of Jewish law could only be piecemeal, one step at a time, as changes were made in the State's legal system either by the Knesset or by the courts.

As will be seen, a fundamental change did occur in the official status of Jewish law in the Jewish state when the Knesset enacted the Foundations of Law Act, 1980. However, before the change and its consequences for the State's legal system are discussed, it is important to examine the actual position of Jewish law in the legal system of the State before the Foundations of Law Act was adopted. This examination is essential not only because of the intrinsic historical interest of the inquiry, but also because of the light it sheds on the various approaches that have been taken with regard to the position of Jewish law in the legal system of the State after the adoption of that Act.

An understanding of the actual relationship between Jewish law and the law of the State of Israel requires an examination of the two major processes that shape and develop the legal system of the State, namely, legislation by the Knesset and adjudication by the courts.

III. JEWISH LAW IN LEGISLATION

A. The Two Legislative Periods

Legislative activity with regard to the State's legal system can be divided into two major periods: first, from the establishment of the State until the middle of the 1960s, and second, from the middle of the 1960s, when the major work on codification of the civil law was begun, until the culmination of that effort in the enactment of the Foundations of Law Act, 1980. That statute repealed Article 46 of the Palestine Order in Council, which required recourse to English equity and common law to fill lacunae, and instead requires the Israeli courts in such a situation to reach a decision "in the light of the principles of freedom, justice, equity, and peace of the Jewish heritage."

This division, like all designations of historical periods, is not precise and inflexible. In the early 1950s, the Ministry of Justice undertook the codification of Israeli law and published three comprehensive draft proposals for legislation on succession (inheritance), evidence, and family law. These drafts, prior to their acceptance by the Government, were published by the Legislative Drafting Department of the Ministry of Justice to elicit comments and suggestions from jurists and the general public.[7] The Succession Law was not adopted until 1965; however, based upon the Draft Individual and the Family Bill, the Knesset adopted the Family Law Amendment (Maintenance) Law, 1959, the Adoption of Children Law, 1960, and the Capacity and Guardianship Law, 1962. In addition, various parts of the Draft Evidence Bill were adopted during the 1950s.[8] However, the greater part of the codification of civil law began in the middle of the 1960s with the adoption of the Agency Law, 1965, and continued with the codification of all aspects of the law relating to obligations and acquisitions. This was the beginning of the most important period of the codification and systematization of the bulk of the Israeli civil law.

This division into the two legislative periods outlined above also conveniently fits the subject matter of the discussion that follows. Beginning with the early 1950s, the discussions in the Knesset on the various proposals were concerned not only with the substance of the laws, but also, to a considerable extent, with two other principal problems: (1) what the policy of a Jewish legislature should be with regard to the sources for its legislation, and (2) what the legislature's expectations are as to how statutory interpretation by the courts will be affected by the source of the provision being construed. These problems were discussed by the Knesset over a lengthy period during the codification of the civil law, especially during the enactment of the Family Law Amendment (Maintenance) Law, 1959, the Capacity and Guardianship Law, 1962, and the Succession Law, 1965; but these discussions then gradually subsided. Our treatment of the legislation enacted during the first period will largely focus on the nature and implications of these more general discussions. That frame of reference reinforces the appropriateness of drawing the line between the two legislative periods at the middle of the 1960s.

B. Legislative Policy

Soon after the State was established, the first Minister of Justice, Pinḥas Rosen, discussing the functions of the Ministry of Justice under the provisional government, described, in general terms, the legislative policy of his ministry:[9]

7. *See* Introductions and Prefaces to the Draft Succession Bill, 1952, the Draft Evidence Bill, 1952, and the Draft Individual and the Family Bill, 1955, respectively—all published by the Ministry of Justice.

8. *See infra* pp. 1640–1690 for discussion of these statutes; as to the Draft Evidence Bill, *see infra* pp. 1702–1703.

9. *Ha-Praklit,* V (1948), p. 101.

> Law and governmental administration will for the time being remain as they were when the Mandate came to an end. We have adopted this course reluctantly. It is not our intention to continue to maintain the old Ottoman laws and all the legislation of the Mandatory government. It is our hope that we shall soon be able to undertake to replace them with new laws that will be more progressive and will also be drawn from the sources of our own national law.

These general remarks provide little detail as to the specifics of legislative policy. Four years later, in 1952, a clearer and more specific statement was contained in the Ministry of Justice's Draft Succession Bill, which was the first of a series of draft proposals for legislation covering an entire area of civil law. In their Introduction, the draftsmen stressed that although the proposal was only "part of a wider legislative program, we regard this bill as a model for the laws which will follow it. The basic guidelines pursuant to which this bill was drafted will also apply to other civil legislation."[10]

What were those basic guidelines? The goal was to achieve legal self-sufficiency and to end dependence on any foreign legal system. In formulating its specific provisions, the draft bill relied on the following:

> (1) The legal and factual situation presently existing in the Land [of Israel]; (2) Jewish law, which is one of our national cultural treasures that we must renew and carry forward; and (3) the laws of other countries, western and eastern, from which our people have been gathered to become fused into one community.

That the law must, first and foremost, fit the factual situation in the country where it applies, cannot be disputed; this is also a basic requirement of Jewish law. However, what should be the law when there are conflicts between the viewpoints and approaches of Jewish law and the laws of other countries? Which has priority? The Introduction to the draft bill gave this response:

> We have regarded Jewish law as the primary but not the sole or binding source. . . . As for the laws of other nations, we think that the practical experience they represent as well as their underlying jurisprudential basis should serve as an ancillary source of enlightenment and guidance.[11]

Thus, in the guidelines laid down as the basis for legislation by the Knesset, the primary source is Jewish law; foreign law is a secondary source for

10. Draft Succession Bill, 1952, p. 5.

11. *Id.* at 6–7. This statement was repeated in the Explanatory Notes to the Succession Bill, 1958 (Bill No. 344). For further discussion of the legislative objective, *see* M. Elon, "The Sources and Nature of Jewish Law and Its Application in the State of Israel," Part IV, 4 *Israel L. Rev.* 80 (1969).

enlightenment and guidance. However, an examination of the legislation by the Knesset during more than thirty years of the State's existence prior to the enactment of the Foundations of Law Act, 1980, reveals that those involved in the legislative process were not always clear as to the extent to which priority should be accorded to the principles of Jewish law. Consequently, although a considerable number of Israeli statutes are based on principles of Jewish law, that number, relatively speaking, is meager and much smaller than it need have been; and, in fact, various laws are in conflict with Jewish law for no good reason.[12]

C. Legislation Based on Principles of Jewish Law

1. THE FIRST LEGISLATIVE PERIOD[13]

a. CIVIL LAW

(1) The Cooperative Houses Law. In 1952, the Knesset passed the Cooperative Houses Law, which, contrary to the then existing law, provided for separate ownership of cooperative apartments. When the Minister of Justice introduced the bill in the Knesset, he explicitly relied on Jewish law, which recognizes separate ownership in buildings and parts of buildings,[14] as opposed to Roman law—and most Continental law, which follows Roman law in this respect—pursuant to which there can only be a single and undivided ownership of land and all improvements built upon it.[15] In the

12. As to the extent that legislation of the Knesset has drawn upon Jewish law since the adoption of the Foundations of Law Act, 1980, *see* the remarks of Minister of Justice Moshe Nissim, in his report to the Tenth Knesset, June 6, 1982, on the activities of the Ministry of Justice, *DK*, 10th Sess., 99th meeting, p. 2775 (1982), quoted *infra* p. 1895 n. 260.

13. The discussion in the present work of the legislation adopted in this period and in the first part of the second legislative period is largely based on Part IV of the article cited *supra* n. 11 and on Part III of that article, 3 *Israel L. Rev.* 416 (1968), which clarify the nature and the extent of the incorporation of Jewish law in Knesset legislation and the problems attendant upon that incorporation; the only changes or additions are those necessitated by events subsequent to the appearance of that article.

14. *See* TB Bava Meẓi'a 116b *et seq.*: "A house and an upper story which belong to two owners . . . ," and other sources. The common law is similar to Jewish law on this point. *See infra* n. 15.

15. *See* 8 *DK* 761 (1951), statement of P. Rosen:

> It may be noted that the difficulties I have mentioned arise not only in our country, but also in other countries which, following Roman law, do not recognize the ownership of a building or part of a building separate from ownership of the land. Such difficulties do not exist in common-law countries. In England, there can be separate ownership of buildings, apartments, and even parts of apartments. Similarly, American common law follows English law on this point and allows for the separate ownership of apartments. It should be noted that, contrary to Roman law, under which there can only be a single and undivided ownership of land and all improvements

ensuing Knesset debate, it was emphasized that the bill embodied principles of Jewish law.[16]

It is interesting to note the differences in conceptual approach expressed regarding this statute. Some pointed out that in view of the "historic" difference between Roman law and Jewish law as to the possibility of separate ownership of parts of buildings, land, trees, and the like, the enactment of the Cooperative Houses Law should be considered "a victory for the view of Jewish law . . . and a beginning of the incorporation of Jewish legal principles into our legislation."[17] Others pointed out that "it can be seen that the proposed legislation has been conceived and nurtured by Jewish law. I would not go too far. . . . It is an original proposal, yet it is Jewish legislation and not just a patching up of existing laws."[18] The statement of the Minister of Justice is of particular interest:[19]

> I wish to conclude with a basic observation in connection with Jewish and Roman law. I do not wish to delve deep into a subject which is not in my field, but I share the satisfaction of the members of the Knesset . . . that this legislation embodies the principles of Jewish law.
>
> Nevertheless, I doubt whether, as a general rule, in all aspects of land law, the position of Jewish law should be preferred over Roman law; and I would not be so willing to recommend abandonment of the Roman law principle that rejects the separate ownership of the land and of the dwelling . . . if not for the fact that the economic situation requires this course in the case of cooperative housing. The economic situation is that people invest their funds in apartments; financially, they are owners. It is therefore necessary to

---

built upon it, the concept of separate ownership of buildings and parts of buildings is known to Jewish law. Jewish law encounters no difficulties at all with the possibility of co-ownership of a cooperative dwelling by its members [lit. partners]. On the contrary, the rule is that each co-owner has an enforceable right to partition of the property—both the land and the building.

The question that has occupied the students of Jewish law in connection with the partition of property is: What are the reciprocal rights and obligations of the owners after the partition, in the absence of an explicit agreement at the time of the partition? For example, what is the law as to the roof, walls, ceilings, foundations, corridors, stairways, and other common areas and instrumentalities, and as to extending an individual apartment, building an additional story, rights of first refusal and, in later times, the law relating to insurance? There are differences of opinion on all these matters among the halakhic authorities, but these differences concern the relations among neighbors. As to the recognition of separate ownership itself, there was no doubt.

16. *See* 8 *DK* 765–766, 771–775 (1951). The Cooperative Houses Law is now Sections 52–77 of the Land Law, 1969.

17. Remarks of MK Warhaftig, 8 *DK* 765–766 (1951).

18. Remarks of MK Shag, *id.* at 771.

19. *Id.* at 775.

> bring the law into harmony with the economic reality. The fact that we thus tread the path of Jewish law gives us all great satisfaction; but the starting point is—at least for me, as I must admit—the economic situation that compels us to adopt this course.

(2) Labor Law. Instructive examples of legislation drawing upon the sources of Jewish law appear throughout the broad field of labor law. There have been major changes in this field throughout the world since the Great Depression of the 1930s, and labor law has been regarded as a particularly significant field in the Land of Israel both before and after the establishment of the Jewish state. The Knesset has enacted an extensive array of labor legislation, and it is instructive how these modern statutes have been rooted in the principles of Jewish law first laid down in the Torah and then developed up to the present time. Two pivotal labor law statutes enacted in this period are illustrative.

The first statute is the Wage Protection Law, 1958, which protects against delay in the payment of wages. In 1955, a private member's bill entitled "Wage Delay Prohibition Law, 1955," was introduced but failed to pass. As its Hebrew title (*Ḥok Issur Halanat Sakhar*) indicates, the bill was based on Leviticus 19:13, "The wages of a laborer shall not remain with you until morning," and on Deuteronomy 24:15, "You must pay him his wages on the same day." Indeed, the bill was supported by specific reference to those verses and to other Jewish legal sources which consider the failure to pay wages promptly to be a serious transgression.[20] Two years later, the Government introduced its own detailed bill,[21] which was enacted in 1958.

When introducing the Government's bill, the Minister of Labor related it to the Wage Protection Convention adopted in 1949 by the International Labor Organization.[22] However, he went on to say:

> This bill . . . is intended to regulate one of the very distressing chapters in the history of labor relations . . . to prevent a troublesome situation which the moral, social, and legal conscience of our people has condemned since ancient times, as stated in Leviticus: "The wages of a laborer shall not remain with you . . . ," and also in Proverbs:[23] "Do not say to your fellow: 'Come back again; I'll give it to you tomorrow.'"[24]

20. Remarks of MK Unna, 18 *DK* 1659–1660, 1672 (1955); 19 *DK* 886–889 (1956).
21. Wage Protection Bill, 1957 (Bill No. 280).
22. 21 *DK* 373 (1957); *see also* the explanatory comments to the bill by MK Namir.
23. Proverbs 3:28.
24. 21 *DK* 376 (1957).

Knesset members from all parties also saw in the bill "a faithful expression of the ancient Jewish tradition"[25] resting on innumerable Biblical, Talmudic, and post-Talmudic sources,[26] including an observation of one of the outstanding halakhic authorities of the last generation, Israel Meir ha-Kohen (the Ḥafeẓ Ḥayyim), who deplored that

> there are people who treat the prohibition against delay in the payment of wages lightly, and are quick to delay payment on even the slightest excuse. . . . They readily reduce the laborer's wages without realizing that they are imperiling their souls by transgressing Biblical prohibitions. . . . Have you seen a Jew who delays making the benediction over the *shofar* or *lulav* until nightfall? On the contrary! Every Jew hastens to perform the commandment as early as possible and is happy to do God's will as prescribed by the law. But as to this commandment [against delay in the payment of wages], which is also an affirmative Biblical commandment that the Torah has hedged about with several prohibitions, how the Evil Inclination prevails![27]

One Knesset member in particular expressed incisively the profound relationship between the bill's provisions and the principles of justice and morality reflected in Jewish law:

> It is no accident that the entire bill has everyone's blessings. There is no difference between us, be we religious or free-thinking, progressive or conservative. Deep down in our hearts is rooted the age-old feeling of concern for social justice for the weak and [therefore] for the worker and his wages. It is not by chance that divine law enjoins us on this matter and that the blood of so many of our brethren has greased the wheels of all the revolutions to assure this right.[28]

25. Remarks of MK Almogi, 23 *DK* 1234 (1958).

26. *See* the remarks of MKs Shustock, 21 *DK* 376 (1957); Kelmer, *id.* at 380; Raphael, *id.* at 404; Katz, *id.* at 385; Kargman, *id.* at 390; Yeshayahu, *id.* at 398; Lorenz, *id.* at 400. *See also* Y. Gross, "Haganat Sekhar Ha-Oved" [Wage Protection for the Laborer], *Ha-Praklit,* XVI (1960), pp. 72–86, 153–178; S. Warhaftig, *Dinei Avodah ba-Mishpat ha-Ivri* [Labor Law in Jewish Law], Tel Aviv, 1969, pp. 345–369.

27. *Ahavat Ḥesed,* beginning of ch. 9. It should be pointed out that Jewish law imposes on the laborer the reciprocal obligation to perform his work faithfully. *See* Maimonides, *MT,* Sekhirut 13:7: "Just as the employer is admonished not to steal or hold back the wages of the poor [laborer], so is the poor [laborer] admonished not to rob the employer of the work due him, by malingering a little here and a little there so that the whole day is spent deceitfully, but he must be scrupulously accountable for the time [agreed upon] and must . . . work to the best of his ability."

28. 21 *DK* 406 (1957). For further sources, *see* the detailed studies of Gross and Warhaftig, *supra* n. 26. *See also* the remarks of the Minister of Labor, Y. Allon, 37 *DK* 2462 (1962). It is surprising that the statute was not entitled "Wage Delay Prohibition Law" (*Ḥok Issur Halanat Sakhar*), as had been previously proposed in the private member's bill introduced by MK Unna, in order to indicate by its name its source in Jewish law. *Cf.* the title of the Prohibition of Defamation Law (*Ḥok Issur Leshon ha-Ra*), which does so indicate; *see infra* pp. 1642–1644.

The second labor-law statute rooted in principles of Jewish law is the statute governing severance pay for dismissed employees. Jewish law on this subject has undergone an interesting development. While the Torah itself expressly provides for the prompt payment of wages, the right to compensation on dismissal is not mentioned explicitly either in the Torah or in the Talmud. Halakhic authorities, however, derived such a right by analogy from a similar Biblical legal institution—the gratuity that a master must pay a slave upon the slave's release after six years of service:

> If a fellow Hebrew, man or woman, is sold to you, he shall serve you six years, and in the seventh year you shall set him free. When you set him free, do not let him go empty-handed: Furnish him out of the flock, threshing floor, and vat, with which the Lord your God has blessed you.[29]

This obligation to give a gratuity is unique to Jewish law among the ancient legal systems; its source lies in the special position the Hebrew slave had in Jewish law, which gave him the same status as a worker indentured for a fixed term.[30] The Talmud established that the slave was entitled to a gratuity even if his work was terminated before the end of his term of service, so long as he was not the cause of the termination.[31] A number of fundamental issues in regard to the gratuity underwent several stages of development. Thus, for example, in the tannaitic period, the gratuity was regarded as a personal right of the slave, which did not pass to his heirs at his death ("'Furnish him'—but not his heirs");[32] but in the amoraic period, it was held to be part of the compensation for his work and therefore part of his estate.[33]

In the post-Talmudic period, there were two conflicting views as to the nature of the gratuity: (1) that it was not compensation for work done, but was given "out of charity"[34] or was in the nature of "contribution and gift";[35] (2) that, in accordance with the rule from the amoraic period pursuant to which the gratuity may be inherited, the gratuity was essentially compensation for work beyond that performed as consideration for the stipulated wage[36] and was therefore to be treated as additional wages. Another rule laid down in the Talmudic period was that the gratuity was not subject to attachment by the slave's creditors ("'Furnish him'—but not his

29. Deuteronomy 15:12–14.

30. "For in six years he has given you double the service of a hired man." Deuteronomy 15:18. *See also* Elon, *Ḥerut,* p. 2.

31. *Sifrei,* Deuteronomy, Re'eh, sec. 119 (p. 178); TB Kiddushin 16b.

32. *Sifrei,* Deuteronomy, Re'eh, sec. 119 (p. 178).

33. TB Kiddushin 15a.

34. *Shakh* to Sh. Ar. ḤM ch. 86, subpar. 3.

35. *Sema* to Sh. Ar. ḤM ch. 86, subpar. 2.

36. Meiri, *Bet ha-Beḥirah,* Kiddushin 15a.

creditor").[37] Most halakhic authorities also held that the obligation to pay the gratuity bore no relationship to the amount of profit derived by the master from the slave's labors. All agreed that there was a minimum payable, but opinion was divided as to the amount of this minimum. Beyond this minimum, it was generally agreed that the master should add "generously" according to his resources.[38]

After slavery disappeared from Jewish law, and legal discussion of the gratuity became purely theoretical, the halakhic authorities applied the principle underlying the slave's gratuity to ordinary employees. The first record of this adaptation dates from the end of the thirteenth century. According to *Sefer ha-Ḥinnukh,* "the purpose of this commandment is to instill in people's minds the worthy, admirable, and desirable qualities . . . of dealing mercifully with those who work for us and generously giving them of our possessions beyond what we have agreed to give them as their wages."[39] *Sefer ha-Ḥinnukh* then points out that although, since the destruction of the Temple, the law of the slave's gratuity is not applicable,[40] it is still not without practical significance:

> In any case, even at the present time, the wise man should consider the implication: Whoever hires an individual who works for him for a long or even a short time should pay him [the employee] a gratuity out of that with which God has blessed him [the employer] when the employee departs from his work.

These observations mark the beginning of the development in Jewish law of the institution of employees' severance pay. Because the source of severance pay was the slave's gratuity, the specific rules that governed the gratuity—such as its being in the nature of wages, its not being subject to attachment by creditors, the minimum payment required, etc.—were applied to severance pay. Mishpat Ha-Shalom Ha-Ivri[41] succeeded in devel-

37. TB Kiddushin 15a, 16b.

38. *Sifrei,* Deuteronomy, Re'eh, sec. 120 (p. 179); TB Kiddushin 17a/b. For further rules concerning the gratuity, *see* ET, IX, p. 679, s.v. Ha'anakah; M. Elon, *Ha-Enẓiklopedyah ha-Ivrit* [Encylopaedia Hebraica], XV, pp. 69–70, s.v. Ha'anakah ba-mishpat ha-ivri; *id.*, EJ, VII, pp. 1003–1007, s.v. Ha'anakah (reprinted in *Principles,* pp. 315–319); Warhaftig, *supra* n. 26 at 643–653.

39. *Sefer ha-Ḥinnukh,* ed. Chavel, Commandment #450.

40. The law of the Hebrew slave is applicable in practice only when the jubilee year is observed; and the observance of the jubilee year ceased when the tribes of Reuben, Gad, and the half-tribe of Manasseh went into exile; TB Arakhin 32b. *See also* E.E. Urbach, "Hilkhot Avadim ki-Mekor la-Historyah ha-Ḥevratit bi-Mei ha-Bayit ha-Sheni u-vi-Tekufat ha-Mishnah ve-ha-Talmud" [The Laws of Slavery as a Source for the Social History of the Second Temple, Mishnaic, and Talmudic Periods], *Zion,* XXV (1960), pp. 141–189.

41. For discussion of Mishpat Ha-Shalom Ha-Ivri, *see supra* pp. 1592–1596.

oping the law of severance pay to a considerable extent on the basis of the principles relating to the gratuity,[42] and the decisions of Mishpat Ha-Shalom Ha-Ivri on this subject have been cited by the Israeli courts.[43] As the Israeli Supreme Court has pointed out:[44]

> It is well known that the source of the idea of this form of compensation lies in the Biblical obligation to give a gratuity: "Furnish him out of the flock, threshing floor, and vat" (Deuteronomy 15:14, and *see also* TB Kiddushin 17a/b).

The rabbinical courts also developed the institution of severance pay in an instructive manner, the guiding principles being that "the source for severance pay is the gratuity that was required to be paid to the Hebrew slave" and that "this claim is not merely one of grace but is based on law."[45]

As indicated, the law relating to severance pay developed in the Jewish community in the Land of Israel as early as the 1920s, and a judgment of the Mandatory High Court in 1940[46] recognized the admissibility of proof of the custom to give severance pay. However, the lack of a clear and detailed statute created many difficulties in making severance pay an effective legal obligation, in proving the existence of such a custom in all occupations, and in other important respects. During the 1950s, Knesset members representing various parties introduced private bills on the subject; and, in 1962, the Government introduced its own bill,[47] which was adopted as the Severance Pay Law, 1963. Explaining this bill on first reading, the Minister of Labor pointed out:[48]

> Knesset members will certainly associate the bill with the age-old tradition which is the pride of the Jewish people. . . . Compensation to the dismissed employee is perhaps the first social right that employees in this country achieved, even before they came to be organized in a strong general union. It represents a continuation of the ancient Jewish tradition rooted in the concept of the Biblical gratuity.

42. *See* M. Vager and P. Dykan (Dikstein), *Pizzuyei Pitturin, Perek be-Hitpathut Dinei Avodah ba-Yishuv ha-Ivri bi-Zemaneinu* [Severance Pay: A Chapter in the Development of Labor Law in the Contemporary Jewish *Yishuv*], Jerusalem, 1940; P. Dykan, *Toledot*, p. 90.

43. *See* Wolfsohn v. Spinneys Co., Ltd., 5 *P.D.* 265, 275 (1951); Goldstein v. Neuman, 5 *P.M.* 329 (1950).

44. Wolfsohn v. Spinneys Co., Ltd., *supra* n. 43.

45. Kaiserman v. Direnfeld, 3 *P.D.R.* 272, 286–287 (1959). *See also supra* pp. 924–926.

46. S. Cohen and Company v. Capun, 7 *P.L.R.* 80, 1 *I.S.C.J.* 63, 7 *C.L.R.* 61 (1940).

47. Severance Pay Bill, 1962 (Bill No. 493).

48. Remarks of MK Allon, 33 *DK* 1050 (1962).

The overwhelming majority of Knesset members of all parties who participated in the debate referred to many sources for the bill in the Bible and in Talmudic and post-Talmudic literature.[49] One member even suggested that "we would save a great deal of time if, instead of enacting this bill as it stands, we simply provided that Jewish law governs severance pay . . . and that the rabbinical courts shall decide all questions which may arise concerning severance pay. If we did so, all problems would be solved, for all the good things we are seeking [to accomplish] by this bill are already contained in Jewish law."[50] The Minister of Labor, however, did not agree with this "interesting" suggestion, preferring rather that the Knesset itself adopt "the positive values that form an inseparable part of the magnificent Jewish tradition."[51]

49. *See* the remarks of MKs Tayer, *id.* at 1070; Sanhedrai, *id.* at 1081–1082; Gross, *id.* at 1160; Katz, *id.* at 1161–1163; and Kargman, 22 *DK* 1623 (1957).

50. 33 *DK* 1300 (1962). MK Ben-Meir pointed to a rabbinical court decision, Nast v. Management Committee of Bet ha-Midrash ha-Merkazi, Haifa, 1 *P.D.R.* 330 (1955), which was more liberal than the decisions of the general courts in regard to severance pay. It should be noted that the rabbinical courts have also developed this area of law on the basis of custom; *see supra* p. 926.

51. 33 *DK* 1303 (1962). On the Jewish sources of labor legislation, *see also* 7 *DK* 354, 361 (1951); 8 *DK* 1201 (1951); 20 *DK* 1079 (1956); 21 *DK* 1082 (1957). Here, too, it would have been appropriate to use traditional Jewish legal terminology for the gratuity (*ha'anakah*) in naming the law, so as to link it to its original source.

In 1985, a bill on labor contracts (Bill No. 1718) was published. The Introduction to the bill states that "the earliest sources of Jewish law contain provisions protecting the rights of the worker. Basic rights of the worker as against his employer were defined and established in the Bible and in the Mishnaic and Talmudic periods. The bill adopts the approach of Jewish law." The intention to adopt the approach of Jewish law was also explicitly expressed in the Explanatory Notes and reflected in the provisions of the bill. Two instances are noteworthy.

Section 10 of the bill contains an innovative provision that even when the court concludes that the worker has caused damage to the employer, the court may relieve the worker from liability if it finds that the worker acted in good faith for the purpose of carrying out his assigned task. The Explanatory Note to this section states: "It should be noted that Jewish law recognized that, in certain circumstances, the rights of the worker should be determined according to the principle of *lifnim mi-shurat ha-din* (acting more generously than the law requires) on the basis of the verse in Proverbs 2:20, 'So follow the way of the good, and keep to the paths of the just.' It was on the basis of this principle that the *amora* Rav excused certain laborers from paying for damage caused by them and even ordered the payment of their wages, as is recorded in TB Bava Meẓi'a 83b [83a]."

Section 11 of the bill also adopts the approach of Jewish law. That section distinguishes between the employer and the worker in the following manner: While the employer may terminate an employment agreement entered into for an indeterminate period only "for good cause," the worker may terminate it "for any reason." The Explanatory Note gives the following reason for this distinction: "We should note here the words of the *amora* Rav (of the first generation of *amoraim,* the first part of the third century) that 'a laborer may leave his work even in the middle of the day.' The basis for this rule is the verse (Leviticus 25:55), 'For it is to Me that the Israelites are servants,' which was interpreted by the Sages

(3) Imprisonment for Debt. Another interesting instance in which the Knesset adopted the position of Jewish law (this time contrary to the original proposal of the Government) concerns imprisonment for debt.[52]

In 1957, the Government introduced a bill on the execution of judgments that was intended to replace the existing Ottoman law and "to render procedures for enforcement of judgments more speedy and efficient and less expensive, and to confine them, in accordance with Jewish legal tradition, to proceedings against the assets of the debtor as distinct from execution against the debtor's person, such as by imprisonment."[53] Indeed, a number of the provisions of the bill did accord with Jewish law.[54] The discussion here, however, will focus primarily on the subject of imprisonment for debt.

The bill would have totally abolished imprisonment for debt,[55] on the theory that the proposed statute provided other sufficient means for speedy and efficient enforcement of judgments, and that "imprisonment for nonpayment of a debt is not consonant with Jewish tradition or the laws of the Torah."[56] In support of this statement as to Jewish law, a ruling of Maimonides was cited that completely rejects the legality of such imprisonment.[57] Actually, however, Maimonides' ruling on this question does not fully express the position of Jewish law as it developed and crystallized over the course of time. The ruling stated the law applicable in Maimonides' own time. However, beginning in the fourteenth century, the Jewish law on this subject changed in response to changes in social and economic conditions, and imprisonment for debt became available when the debtor was known to have means but refused to pay.[58] The discussion in the Knesset focused on this issue, and many members argued that modern conditions require that imprisonment be an available sanction to assure payment of debts.

---

to mean 'They are servants of Mine and not servants of [My] servants' (TB Bava Meẓi'a 10a)."

52. For a detailed study of this subject, also discussing how Jewish law develops and is researched, *see* Elon, *Ḥerut,* pp. 111–237. This study served as the basis for the discussion in the Knesset and the final text of the law.

53. Bill No. 321, Introduction.

54. *See* the opening statement of Minister of Justice P. Rosen at the first reading of the bill, 23 *DK* 93, 257 (1958); and the remarks of MK Warhaftig, *id.* at 100, and MK Lorenz, *id.* at 130. *See also* the Explanatory Notes to the respective sections of the bill.

55. *See* sec. 82(3) of the bill.

56. Explanatory Notes, p. 35.

57. Maimonides, *MT,* Malveh ve-Loveh 2:1. *See* P. Rosen's remarks, 23 *DK* 259 (1958).

58. *See* Elon, *Ḥerut,* pp. 133ff. MK Warhaftig, 23 *DK* 100–101 (1958), was of the opinion that Jewish law does not permit imprisonment for debt, except where the obligation is for spousal support. This distinction between ordinary debts and obligations for support of a wife is erroneous; *see* Elon, *Ḥerut,* p. 267 n. 46. MK Lorenz correctly pointed out (23 *DK* 131) that Jewish law does permit the imprisonment of a debtor who has the means to pay but refuses to do so.

The 1957 bill did not pass. It was reintroduced in July 1960; and, although it still proposed to abolish imprisonment for debt, the Minister of Justice, in presenting the bill for its first reading,[59] drew the Knesset's attention to the correct position of Jewish law, as described above. He said:

> While it is true that in Maimonides' time Jewish law completely rejected imprisonment for all debts—whether an ordinary debt or a debt arising out of non-payment of support—nevertheless, in later periods of its development, Jewish law did permit such imprisonment under certain circumstances. Just as in any other legal system, a particular position taken, for example, in the twelfth century cannot be put forth as the current position of that system, so too one may not point to a specific rule in a specific period of Jewish law as reflecting the position of Jewish law today without examining the stages of development of that rule in subsequent periods.

To support this view, the Minister relied on the research that had been done on the subject, and observed that "the conclusion to be drawn . . . is that if you decide to follow Jewish law, there is no need to repeal the substance of this Ordinance [*i.e.*, the British Mandatory law, which provided for imprisonment for debt] but only to make some changes in its language."[60] Most of the Knesset members who participated in the debate on the first reading accepted the position of Jewish law; the majority explicitly,[61] and the others implicitly.[62]

Incidentally, the debate was the occasion for an enlightening discussion on the process of development of Jewish law. The Minister's description of the stages of development of the Jewish law of imprisonment for debt led one Knesset member to protest:[63]

> The Minister of Justice has informed us that this part of his presentation was formulated with the agreement of the Adviser on Jewish Law. Whether it is his own view or that of his adviser, I am amazed at the approach and at the manner in which the development of the *Halakhah* has been described, as well as at his statement concerning "its [Jewish law's] ability and readiness to respond to social and economic needs as they changed from period to period until the time of the *Shulḥan Arukh,* when the law was established as it is today." Distinguished members of the Knesset! I hereby unequivocally state that all who speak that way of the development of the *Halakhah* based

59. This was before the Continuity of Debate Law, 1964; because the Third Knesset had dissolved before the second and third readings had been completed, the bill had to be reintroduced for a first reading.

60. 29 *DK* 1781, 1783 (1960). *See also* Elon, *supra* n. 52.

61. MKs Meridor, 29 *DK* 1784 (1960); Azanyah, *id.* at 1786; Nistam, *id.* at 1789; Ẓadok, *id.* at 1827; Porush, *id.* at 1833; Ben-Yisrael, *id.* at 1862.

62. MKs Bar Rav Hai, *id.* at 1836; Zimmerman, *id.* at 1863.

63. Remarks of MK Porush, *id.* at 1833.

> on the laws of the Torah demonstrate that their understanding of the Torah and its rules is merely superficial; for the entire Holy Torah, both Written and Oral, was spoken by God and revealed to Moses at Sinai, and is everlasting and immutable. The rules and *takkanot* laid down by halakhic authorities . . . are of abiding validity, and it is our duty to observe them. . . . Now, regarding imprisonment for debt, no "development" whatsoever has occurred.

The Minister of Justice responded:

> This time, Jewish law has taken an honorable place in this "opulent symphony." After having spoken at length on this subject in my introductory remarks, on the basis of research which I presented to the Knesset, the research of the Adviser on Jewish Law,[64] I must now, in my reply—and I do so willingly—turn to the subject once more.
>
> The member of the Knesset . . . attempted to convince us that the rule that a debtor who has assets but refuses to pay may be imprisoned has always been the rule of Jewish law, and he was extremely upset that in the survey by the Adviser on Jewish Law, which I presented to you, this position was described as a development in Jewish law which changed the preexisting rule that had completely rejected imprisonment for debt.
>
> The member of the Knesset . . . contended that whoever speaks in this way about the development of the *Halakhah* based on the laws of the Torah demonstrates that his understanding of the Torah and its rules is merely superficial. Apparently, he thought that my remarks were the fruits of my own investigation and research; otherwise, he undoubtedly would have been more careful about his choice of words. In any case, I have inquired into the subject and I suspect, with all due respect, that the Knesset member overlooked . . . a number of *halakhot* which clearly indicate that, until the fourteenth century, Jewish law completely rejected imprisonment for nonpayment of debt, with one exception that had already existed before that time, as I pointed out in my introductory statement.[65]

The Minister of Justice then went on to cite additional sources to prove the correctness of his description of the development of Jewish law of imprisonment for debt.

It is difficult to argue with the dogmatic approach that denies the existence of any development in Jewish law, but what can be said is that not only is such development obvious to the modern scholar who studies in historical perspective the institutions of Jewish law, but the halakhic authorities themselves also fully understood and explicitly stressed its occurrence.[66]

64. *See* Elon, *supra* n. 52
65. 29 *DK* 2111 (1960).
66. *See* Elon, *Ḥerut,* particularly pp. 254–255; *see also supra* pp. 46–50.

This extremely interesting debate in the legislature of the Jewish state, with significant implications in regard both to the grounding of the statute on imprisonment for debt in Jewish law, and to the way in which Jewish law develops, soon had its practical repercussions. The 1960 bill likewise did not obtain final Knesset approval; and, in 1965, the Government introduced a third bill on the execution of judgments.[67] This time a fundamental change was made in the Government's proposal. The Explanatory Notes state that "many—jurists and judges alike—have objected [to the previous bills] because they believe that in the present circumstances imprisonment for debt should not be totally abolished."[68] Therefore, it was explained, the new bill does not bar such imprisonment if the Chief Execution Officer is convinced that the debtor has the means to pay. The maximum period of imprisonment was set at twenty-one days.[69] Because the introduction of this bill,[70] and the opening presentation of the Minister of Justice on its first reading,[71] came just before the dissolution of the Fifth Knesset, only one member spoke on the bill, and then only to state that such a comprehensive bill should not be introduced at such an inopportune moment when there was no time to give it proper consideration.[72]

In the Sixth Knesset, the Legislative Committee dealt at length with the question of imprisonment for debt in the course of its consideration of the proposed Execution Law. The committee considered the position of Jewish law with regard to imprisonment for debt, and a majority of the committee agreed to accept this position. The Execution Law, 1967, as adopted by the Knesset, provides that if a debt, or any installment thereof, has not been paid within the time prescribed by the Chief Execution Officer after he has ascertained the debtor's ability to pay, and if no other means exist to compel compliance with the judgment, the Chief Execution Officer may order the imprisonment of the debtor for a period not to exceed twenty-one days. The statute also provides that the debtor may not be imprisoned twice for the same debt or installment.[73] These provisions repre-

67. Bill No. 659.

68. *Id.* at 272.

69. Secs. 80–83. Sec. 84 provided that imprisonment may be ordered for failure to comply with an order to support one's wife, children, or parents, even without an investigation of ability to pay, since ability to pay would already have been taken into account during the proceedings adjudicating the liability for support.

70. *See supra* text accompanying n. 67.

71. *See* the remarks of Dr. Joseph, 43 *DK* 2528 (1965).

72. MK Kelmer, *id.* at 2567. For the same reason, MK Meridor proposed that the bill be returned to the Government (*id.* at 2568). By a vote of 7–5, the bill was referred to the Legislative Committee.

73. Execution Law, 1967, secs. 70–74. These sections also contain additional provisions designed to make clear that such imprisonment is not punitive, and that its sole purpose is to compel payment of a debt by one who has the means to pay.

sent a complete adoption of the approach of Jewish law as it crystallized after a long history. As the chairman of the committee eloquently stated in his reply to those members who sought to delete that part of the bill providing for imprisonment for debt:

> I believe that it would be wrong to view this legislation as reflecting the draconian approach of Roman law. A closer look at Jewish law would demonstrate that our [*i.e.*, Jewish] law originally was totally opposed to imprisonment for debt in any form, but that, in the course of time, circumstances arose that required the use of this sanction to ensure payment of debts, inasmuch as defaults would have serious adverse effects on the economic order.
>
> The point that imprisonment for debt subordinates personal freedom to monetary considerations does not conclude the argument. All aspects of the matter must be considered, including the extent to which economic life and relationships will be disrupted unless there are sound and efficient procedures to assure the payment of debts.
>
> The question is thus one of the climate of public opinion and of the particular circumstances and conditions in which the law is to operate. It is not sufficient to cite principles of other legal systems to demonstrate that we should reach the same result they do. We must ascertain whether, under the conditions in which we live, we can follow a particular path or should find an alternative way. That is the question before us, and not whether the path is fitting for a democratic and enlightened country or whether there are other countries that have taken that path.
>
> After many years of debate, . . . we have reached the conclusion that in our circumstances we cannot completely give up this means of enforcement. It has already been stated here that imprisonment for debt . . . is not punitive, . . . but is a method of compelling the fulfillment of the debtor's obligation to the creditor, who is often greatly in need of what the debtor does not wish to pay him. . . . I wish to reiterate strongly that specifically with regard to this issue we are following Jewish law, which fundamentally rejects imprisonment for debt but is prepared, when the public welfare and a sound social order so require, to adapt to the circumstances of time and place and to the climate of public opinion. It seems to me that this is a good example of how we can learn something from the approach of Jewish law, and how we may correctly deal with contemporary problems.[74]

b. CRIMINAL AND PUBLIC LAW

Jewish law has been the basis for legislation not only in the area of civil law. In both criminal and public law, statutes have been based, wholly or in part, on the principles of Jewish law. The following are a few examples:

74. Remarks of MK Unna, 49 *DK* 2926–2927 (1967). *See also* Elon, *Ḥerut,* pp. 265–269; State of Israel v. Tamir, 37(iii) *P.D.* 201, 207–208 (1983).

(1) The Penal Law Revision (Bribery) Law. An instance of legislation based on the principles and sources of Jewish law and covering an entire area of criminal law is a bill introduced in 1951 under the title "Penal Law Revision (Bribery and Rewards) Law." The title "Bribery and Rewards" was taken, as the Minister of Justice pointed out at the bill's first reading,[75] from the Book of Isaiah, which records the prophet's castigation of the people for having departed from the right path: "Your rulers are rogues and cronies of thieves, every one avid for bribes and greedy for rewards."[76] "Bribery" was defined in the bill as the giving of money or some other benefit in exchange for a specific act; "reward" was defined as the giving of money or some other benefit not in exchange for a specific act[77] or in connection with any particular matter, but "in order to secure the goodwill of the recipient and incline him to show favor at an opportune moment."[78] This reflects the approach taken by Jewish law, which is to treat these two offenses as equally serious,[79] as the Explanatory Notes to the bill emphasize.[80]

The bill prescribed penalties of varying degrees of severity: for a bribe taken by a judge or anyone acting in a judicial capacity, imprisonment for up to five years; for a bribe taken by any other government employee or public functionary, imprisonment for up to three years. The more severe penalty for a judge who accepts a bribe was based on Jewish law,[81] as pointed out in the Explanatory Notes.[82]

The bill provided that not only the recipient but also the giver of the bribe is criminally liable, and this too reflects Jewish law.[83] "Thus the bill renews one of the principles of Jewish law and aligns itself with the laws of the United States, the state of New York, Italy, France, England, and other

75. Remarks of P. Rosen, 8A *DK* 802 (1951).

76. Isaiah 1:23. The Hebrew for "Bribery and Rewards" is *shoḥad ve-shalmonim.* The 1985 JPS *Tanakh* translates *shoḥad* as "presents," and *shalmonim* as "gifts." However, *shalmon* connotes that something in return has been given or is expected.

77. *See* the Penal Law Revision (Bribery and Rewards) Bill, 1950, p. 62, sec. 2.

78. *See id.,* secs. 5, 6 and Explanatory Notes, p. 65.

79. *See, e.g.,* Maimonides, *MT,* Sanhedrin 23:3 with regard to "verbal" bribery, and as to a judge whose tenant farmer was in the habit of bringing him produce every week, and who therefore disqualified himself from sitting on a case in which the tenant had an interest.

80. Explanatory Notes, p. 65.

81. The classic situation of bribery dealt with in Jewish sources involves bribery of judges. *See* Deuteronomy 16:18–19, 27:25; Micah 3:11; and other Biblical sources. The same is true of Maimonides, *MT,* Sanhedrin ch. 23, and *Tur* and Sh. Ar. ḤM ch. 9.

82. Explanatory Notes, p. 63.

83. Maimonides, *MT,* Sanhedrin 23:2 states: "Just as one who accepts [a bribe] transgresses . . . , so too does the one who gives, as it is written [Leviticus 19:14]: 'You shall not place a stumbling block before the blind.'" The same rule is stated in Sh. Ar. ḤM 9:1.

jurisdictions."[84] Another provision makes clear that the crime of bribery takes place not only when the purpose of the bribe is to induce an unlawful act or to pervert justice, but also when the object is to obtain performance of a lawful act which it is the duty of the recipient to perform in any case. Some legal systems treat these two situations differently. The Explanatory Notes[85] point out that the approach of Jewish law is: "'You shall not take bribes' [Deuteronomy 16:19]—obviously, this is forbidden when the intention is to pervert justice; but even if the intention is to acquit the innocent and convict the guilty, it is still forbidden."[86]

While in most respects the bill followed Jewish law, it is interesting to examine the reasons why two provisions of the bill did not. As to the first, the Explanatory Notes state that it was not thought desirable to follow the rule of Jewish and Ottoman law that requires the return of the bribe to the briber; "the modern view rejects this."[87] The second provision, relating to the law of evidence, permitted conviction of either party to the bribe solely on the basis of the testimony of the other party; the traditional rule of Jewish law requires two witnesses.

All who spoke at the first reading of the bill pointed out that its provisions, most of which were at variance with the law then in force in the State of Israel, accorded with Jewish law; and many sources of Jewish law were cited in support of the bill.[88] Interestingly, no one challenged the rejection of the rule of Jewish law requiring the return of the bribe to the briber.[89] On the other hand, serious doubt was expressed with regard to the provision making the testimony of an accomplice legally sufficient for conviction. One of the members of the Knesset reacted to this provision as follows:

> I strongly oppose Section 7, which permits the conviction of one of the participants in the crime solely on the basis of the testimony of an accomplice.

84. Explanatory Notes, p. 64. Under British Mandatory law, giving a bribe was not a criminal offense.

85. *Id.*

86. Maimonides, *MT,* Sanhedrin 23:1, on the basis of *Sifrei,* Deuteronomy, Re'eh, sec. 144, and TB Ketubbot 105a; *see also* Sh. Ar. ḤM 9:1.

87. Explanatory Notes, pp. 65–66. For the Jewish law, *see* Maimonides and Sh. Ar., *supra* n. 86.

88. *See* the remarks of MKs Shag, 8A *DK* 803 (1951); Ben-Zvi, *id.* at 815; Genichovsky, *id.* at 815; Gil, *id.* at 817; Warhaftig, *id.* at 818.

89. *Cf.* the reaction in the Knesset to the statement in the Explanatory Notes to the Gift Law that a particular provision did not accord with Jewish law; *see infra* p. 1724. The deviation from Jewish law in regard to bribery was generally agreed upon because returning the bribe would be contrary to currently prevailing social and moral sentiments. There was no such clash between Jewish law and contemporary mores in regard to the issue of whether a gift is a strictly unilateral transaction. *See also infra* pp. 1683–1684.

> This could result in many instances of blackmail. We must search for a different method of obtaining proof. I do not agree with the opinion expressed here that we should insist on the requirement of two witnesses. As I have previously stated, in our time we must adopt the approach that cases may be decided on the basis of strong probabilities, *i.e.,* the court should be able to evaluate the evidence. However, I do not at all agree that a conviction may rest solely on the testimony of an accomplice.[90]

This issue thus involved a dispute on a substantive question that is subject to reasonable difference of opinion.

The Penal Law Revision (Bribery) Law (as the statute was finally entitled) was passed by the Knesset in 1952 after a number of minor amendments.[91] As the Explanatory Notes to the bill and the Knesset debates make clear, this statute covering an important area of criminal law was based mainly on the principles of Jewish law. The legislation is particularly significant in that it concerns criminal law—a field in which many had thought that Jewish law was unable to make any contribution to Knesset legislation.[92]

(2) The Defamation Law. The Defamation Law is another illustration of a criminal statute based in general on Jewish legal principles, with specific provisions designed to meet modern social conditions. This statute was first introduced into the Knesset in 1962,[93] and it passed through numerous stages and debates before being finally enacted. The term for "defamation" in its Hebrew title is *leshon ha-ra* (lit. "language of evil"), a term unique to Jewish law. Elaborating on this theme,[94] the Explanatory Notes stated:

90. Remarks of MK Warhaftig, 8A *DK* 819 (1951), and *see id.* for the reply of Minister of Justice P. Rosen that, notwithstanding justified misgivings, it was necessary to permit conviction on the basis of the testimony of an accomplice, because otherwise a conviction would hardly ever be possible, inasmuch as the offense, by its very nature, is committed in the strictest secrecy.

91. The term "rewards" was omitted from the title, but the offense it denotes, *i.e.,* the giving of money or some other benefit in order to secure the goodwill of the recipient unconnected with any particular matter, was retained in the statute (sec. 4(c)) as part of the general definition of the crime of bribery. MK Ami'assaf, on behalf of the Legislative Committee, explained the omission as being due to the fact that the statute as adopted prescribed the same penalty for gifts intended to secure goodwill as for bribery, whereas the bill punished bribery (in the strict technical sense) more severely. (11B *DK* 1413 (1952)). The statute as adopted also differs from the bill in that the penalty for giving a bribe is only half of the penalty for taking it (sec. 3).

92. *See also* Samuel Flato-Sharon v. State of Israel, 38(ii) *P.D.* 757 (1984) (Dov Levin, J., discussing bribery in Jewish law).

93. Defamation Bill, 1962 (Bill No. 504), p. 141.

94. In addition to its innovations, the bill's objective was to consolidate the existing statutory provisions on defamation—both civil (Civil Wrongs Ordinance, 1944, secs. 16–22) and criminal (Criminal Law Ordinance, 1936, secs. 201–203, 205–209).

> The specific rules and prohibitions with regard to *leshon ha-ra* are rooted in the ancient tradition of Jewish law. Leviticus (19:16) contains the precept "Do not go about as a talebearer among your countrymen." The authorities of Jewish law throughout its history have regarded defamation as "a great sin and a cause of the death of many Jews" (Maimonides, *MT*, De'ot 7:1).
>
> . . . Many of the principles and innovations of the bill have been extensively discussed in the wide literature of Jewish law; and, close to our own time, one of the leading halakhic authorities dealt with the law on this subject in detail in his book *Ḥafeẓ Ḥayyim* [Eager for Life], whose title comes from Psalms 34:13–14: "Who is the man who is eager for life (*ḥafeẓ ḥayyim*), who desires years of good fortune? Guard your tongue from evil, your lips from deceitful speech." A survey of these sources discloses that, as is provided in the bill, defamation includes both written and oral statements, whether concerning a single person or a group, or persons living or dead. In cases of defamation, Jewish courts, at various times and places, have imposed criminal penalties and have compelled the payment of compensation to the victim. It was also their practice to compel the wrongdoer to make a public apology.[95]

The bill as originally introduced evoked a storm of public criticism because of its limitations on freedom of the press and on public debate. As a result, the Government reintroduced, over a year later, a modified bill[96] which took into consideration most of the criticisms directed against the original bill.[97] At the first reading of the revised bill, the Minister of Justice again stressed the Jewish sources of a number of the bill's principles.[98] As to the central problem of striking the proper balance between the prohibition of defamation, on the one hand, and freedom of the press and public debate, on the other, he observed:[99]

95. Defamation Bill, *supra* n. 93 at 145, 147. The 1985 JPS *Tanakh* notes that the meaning of the Hebrew text of Leviticus 19:16 is uncertain. It gives the translation in the foregoing quotation as an alternate rendering. *Tanakh* translates the verse: "Do not deal basely with your countrymen."

96. Defamation Bill, 1963 (Bill No. 564).

97. *Id.* at 290.

98. Remarks of Dov Joseph, 37 *DK* 2401 *et seq.* (1962). *See, e.g., id.* at 2404:

Another innovation to which I attach great importance is Section 3 (Group Defamation). This is a problematic subject in many countries . . . , and if that is the case in the world at large, how much more so is it with us. For not only has the Jewish people in the diaspora been—and too often is still—the primary victim of group defamation, but Jewish lawyers and members of parliaments in the diaspora have fought for generations for just such protection as is assured by our bill. It can be said that we have created here a secular Jewish tradition, uniformly endorsed by Jewish jurists in many countries, which can serve as a guide for the State of Israel. But it is not only a secular tradition, for we read in the book *Ḥafeẓ Ḥayyim* [10:12]: "Certainly if one defames an entire city, that is clearly a criminal violation, for the prohibition against *leshon ha-ra* applies . . . even if one defames a private individual; how much more so [if one defames] an entire Jewish city!"

99. 37 *DK* 2402 (1962).

> Ancient Jewish law, too, did not tolerate defamation. In chapter 19 of Leviticus, the precept "Do not go about as a talebearer among your countrymen" (verse 16) is immediately followed by the precept "Reprove your kinsman" (verse 17). The first precept became the foundation in Jewish law for the prohibition of defamation, and the second for the freedom of public debate. There is no need in this House to belabor the fact that sharp public debate has freely taken place among Jews since the beginning of Jewish history. The prohibition of defamation has not prevented free debate, inasmuch as free debate does not necessitate freedom to defame. These principles are undisputed. Any disagreement concerns the balance to be struck between the two principles—where to set the boundary between them. In the bill, which I now have the honor to present on behalf of the Government, we have attempted to draw the correct boundary line.

In the debate on this draft as well, members of the Knesset continued to intersperse their remarks with references to the sources of Jewish law.[100] The bill was enacted as the Defamation Law (*Ḥok Leshon ha-Ra*), 1965. Certain amendments that were introduced in 1966,[101] reflecting the recommendations of a special committee appointed by the Prime Minister, were enacted in 1967. An amendment suggested by the Legislative Committee of the Knesset changed the Hebrew title of the statute to *Ḥok Issur Leshon ha-Ra* (Prohibition of Defamation Law), 1965.[102]

This statute illustrates how an important halakhic concept can influence penal legislation, not so much with regard to specific provisions as by way of general approach. In this instance, this was the proper method of drawing upon Jewish law, since the detailed provisions of the *Halakhah*, and especially the many stringencies in the halakhic rules relating to *leshon ha-ra*, are not appropriate for legislative enactment but are essentially religious proscriptions that should not be transformed into laws enforceable by the police and the Office of Execution.[103]

100. *See* the remarks of MKs Ẓadok, *id.* at 2454; Unna, *id.* at 2460; Sanhedrai, *id.* at 2572; Porush, *id.* at 2581.

101. Defamation (Amendment) Bill, 1966 (Bill No. 693).

102. *Id.*, sec. 1. *See* 48 *DK* 1730 (1967) for the explanation by MK Raphael, speaking for the Legislative Committee, of the reason for the change of title: "Henceforth, the title of the statute will be the 'Prohibition of Defamation Law' (*Ḥok Issur Leshon ha-Ra*). In the view of the Committee, the new name better expresses the content and essence of the law. . . . I personally believe that the change of name will atone for guilt, as stated in the *Zohar* (Genesis), and that with the change of name, the fortune of this law which, as is known, was born in dispute and differences of opinion, will improve."

103. *See* 46 *DK* 2451 (1966) for the remarks of Minister of Justice I.S. Shapira, responding to critics in the debate on the first reading of the Defamation (Amendment) Bill. For a discussion of the Jewish law of defamation, *see* N. Rakover, "Al Leshon ha-Ra ve-al ha-Anishah Alehah ba-Mishpat ha-Ivri" [On Defamation and Its Penalties in Jewish Law], *Sinai*, LI (1962), pp. 197–209, 326–345.

(3) Immunity of Judges. Another interesting example of a modern Israeli statute with deep roots in Jewish law concerns a judge's absolute immunity from civil or criminal liability for any act done in the course of carrying out his judicial function. Under the law of the British Mandatory government, a magistrate enjoyed a limited civil immunity, whereas the immunity of judges of higher courts was absolute. A bill to amend the Civil Wrongs Ordinance (Amendment No. 3), 1959,[104] proposed the extension of absolute immunity to magistrates. At the first reading of the bill, the Minister of Justice extensively discussed the approach of Jewish law to this question.[105]

Jewish law considers the following factors to be significant: (1) whether the *dayyan* (judge) is an expert and was duly appointed by competent authority; (2) whether the error involves clear and binding law (*ta'ut bi-devar mishnah,* lit. "a mistake in a matter set forth in the Mishnah") or the judge's reasoning; (3) whether the judge merely renders an opinion or goes on to execute the judgment.[106] If the judge is an expert and was duly appointed, he is not liable for damages resulting from an error in his decision.[107] Two reasons are given for this rule: (1) the practical reason that if judges were subject to liability, no one would agree to act as a judge, and (2) the juridical reason that the judge must, by virtue of his office, hear and decide the case, and thus any error in the outcome can be considered an act resulting from unavoidable compulsion.[108] After discussing the position of Jewish law on this issue, the Minister of Justice concluded:[109]

> Under Jewish law, a qualified person duly appointed to judicial office—at one time by the exilarch [in Babylonia] and today by the President of the State pursuant to the Judges Law, 1953—is exempt from liability for any damages caused as a result of any error in his judgment. . . . My statement up to this

---

The relationship of the Defamation Law to its sources in Jewish law was discussed by the Israeli Supreme Court in Avneri v. Shapiro, 42(iv) *P.D.* 20, 25–26 (1988). Deputy President Elon, speaking for the court, stressed that even apart from the Foundations of Law Act, 1980 (discussed in chapter 44), the legislative history of the Defamation Law demonstrates that the statute is based on Jewish law. Jewish law should therefore be the primary interpretive source for the statutory provisions, including the provisions for temporary and permanent injunctions, and English law may be looked to only for comparative purposes.

104. Bill No. 380.

105. Remarks of P. Rosen, 28 *DK* 643–644 (1960).

106. *See* TB Bekhorot 28b; Sanhedrin 5a; Maimonides, *MT,* Sanhedrin 6:1–2; Sh. Ar. ḤM ch. 25.

107. *See* Maimonides and Sh. Ar., *supra* n. 106.

108. The first reason was given by Alfasi and the second by Naḥmanides and Nissim Gerondi; *see* Alfasi's *Sefer ha-Halakhot* and the commentaries of Naḥmanides and Nissim Gerondi on TB Sanhedrin 5a. *See also* P. Rosen's remarks, *supra* n. 105.

109. 28 *DK* 644 (1960).

> point is the opinion of my Adviser on Jewish Law. I believe that the subject is of great interest—particularly the extent to which the matter is treated in Jewish law.[110]

(4) Laws Incorporating Basic Tenets of the Jewish Tradition. Various Knesset statutes in the area of public law incorporate basic tenets of the Jewish tradition (as well as other religious traditions), as in the following section of the Law and Administration Ordinance, 1948:

> The sabbath and the Jewish festivals—the two days of *Rosh Ha-Shanah,* the Day of Atonement, the first and eighth days of *Sukkot,* the first and seventh days of Passover, and the festival of *Shavu'ot*—are legal holidays in the State of Israel. Non-Jews have the right to observe their own sabbaths and holidays.

The Jewish sabbath and festivals have also been given special status in a number of other laws.

110. The extent to which Jewish law was relied upon can be seen from the Minister's subsequent remarks (p. 645) regarding the concern that, under the language of the bill, a judge could act maliciously and still enjoy the absolute immunity provided for in the bill: "And as you have certainly realized from my remarks, according to Jewish law a judge is exempt from liability only if he acted erroneously but not if he acted maliciously. But it seems to me that there need be no such concern [that a judge will act maliciously]." *See also id.* at 711 for MK Warhaftig's further remarks on the relevant Jewish law.

It should be pointed out that as a result of the influence of Jewish law an important change was made in the composition of the courts when the State of Israel was established. A fundamental principle of Jewish law is: "Judge not alone, for none may judge alone save One [*i.e.,* God]" (M Avot 4:8). In special cases, an "expert" may be the sole judge; *see* TB Sanhedrin 3a, 5a; Maimonides, *MT,* Sanhedrin 2:10–11; *Tur* and Sh. Ar. ḤM ch. 3. Another principle is that a court may not consist of an even number of judges, because if it did, there could be a tie vote and no majority decision. (M Sanhedrin 1:6: "A court may not be evenly divided.") For a variety of halakhic and historical reasons, a single judge is sometimes permitted to hear a case (*see supra*), but the general approach of Jewish law is that there must be at least three judges. Rabbinical courts still adhere to this practice.

This principle was adopted in part in the Courts Law, 1957, which departed from the prior British Mandatory law. A panel of the Supreme Court is always three (except for interlocutory orders, orders *nisi,* and the like), and the President of the Court or his permanent Deputy may direct that the panel be larger, so long as the panel does not consist of an even number of judges (Courts Law, 1957, secs. 3, 8; currently, Courts Law (Consolidated Version), 1984, secs. 26, 30). In the district court, a case is generally heard by one judge, but when that court sits as an appellate court (not in interlocutory matters) or in a case involving the death penalty or where the sentence may be more than ten years imprisonment, the court consists of three judges. *See* Courts Law, 1957, sec. 15; *see also* sec. 25 for the composition of the magistrates' court. Currently, these provisions are in the Courts Law (Consolidated Version), 1984, secs. 37, 47. At the first reading of the Courts Bill, 1955, the Minister of Justice stated that it was desirable that all courts sit in panels of at least three judges in every case, but that budgetary considerations and the lack of a sufficient number of judges necessitated the compromise set forth in the bill (*see* 17 *DK* 1712 (1955)).

Another example of a public law reflecting Jewish tradition is the Kosher Food for Soldiers Ordinance, 1949, which states: "Kosher food must be provided for every Jewish soldier in the Israel Defense Forces. The Minister of Defense and the Minister of Religions are charged with the implementation of this ordinance." Still another example is the Pig-Raising Prohibition Law, 1962, which prohibits the raising, keeping, and slaughtering of pigs in the State of Israel (except for certain regions having a Christian population). These laws are beyond the scope of our discussion here, and have been thoroughly dealt with elsewhere.[111]

(5) The Law of Return. Section 1 of the Law of Return, 1950, underscores the fundamental character and mission of the State of Israel: "Every Jew has the right *la'alot* [to immigrate, lit. "to go up"] to the Land [of Israel]." This provision not only resonates with overtones of Jewish history and Jewish national-religious philosophy, but also is closely tied to Jewish law. The idea that the Land of Israel was and will always remain the property of every single Jew, wherever he may be, as well as the property of the Jewish people as a whole, was expressed in the geonic period (Nahshon Gaon, ninth century, Babylonia) in a purely legal context. At that time, it was ruled that chattels can be acquired incidentally to the acquisition of land (*kinyan agav karka*), even if the transferor actually owns no land, on the theory that every Jew is deemed by the law to own four cubits of the Land of Israel:

> The Rabbis have affirmed that there is no Jew who does not own four cubits in the Land of Israel, for the nations who have captured and taken possession of the Land do not own it, because the rule is that land can never be effectively stolen or taken by force. The Land of Israel is thus ours forever, even though we do not exercise dominion over it.[112]

The Knesset debates on the Law of Return, the Jewish legal sources which they cited,[113] and the halakhic, historical, and jurisprudential basis of the

111. *See* Elon, *Ḥakikah*, pp. 14ff. *See also id.* for legislation regarding education, the Chief Rabbinate, etc. These statutes have been the focus of debate on the issue of "religious coercion"; *see id.* at 4–5.

112. B.M. Lewin, *Oẓar ha-Geonim*, Kiddushin, Responsa, pp. 60–63. *See also supra* pp. 649–651.

113. *See, e.g.*, the remarks of MK Warhaftig, 15 *DK* 823 (1954). *See also* the Explanatory Notes to the bill (Bill No. 48, June 27, 1950) and the Knesset debates, 6 *DK* 1207ff., 2035ff. (1950), on the Law of Return, in which the Prime Minister, David Ben-Gurion, participated. The place of this law in Jewish history has also been extensively discussed by the Supreme Court of Israel; *see, e.g.*, Rufeisen v. Minister of the Interior, 16 *P.D.* 2428 (1962); Lansky v. Minister of the Interior, 26(ii) *P.D.* 337 (1972); Clark v. Minister of the Interior, 27(iii) *P.D.* 148 (1973). As to the issue of "who is a Jew" for purposes of the Law of Return, *see infra* pp. 1688–1690.

Law of Return were extensively reviewed in the opinion of Deputy President Elon in *Ben Shalom v. Central Elections Committee.*[114] This review, to which none of the other justices took exception, noted:[115]

> It is axiomatic that in the Land of Israel "the spiritual and religious identity" of the Jewish people "was shaped" and there "it created cultural values of national and universal significance and gave to the world the eternal Book of Books. After being forcibly exiled from their land, the people kept faith with it throughout their dispersion and never ceased to pray and hope for their return to it and for the restoration in it of their political freedom."[116] This spiritual-religious link has been reflected in every aspect of the spiritual heritage of the Jewish people—the Torah and the religious precepts, the laws and practices of the people, the studies of young and old, and the earliest training of children. . . .
>
> Immigration to and settlement of the Land of Israel, and the precepts and laws directly related to the Land, have been central to the spiritual heritage of all Jews everywhere. . . .
>
> Thus, it is recorded:[117]
>
>> R. Eleazar b. Shammua and R. Johanan ha-Sandelar were traveling to Neẓivim [a Babylonian town] to learn Torah from R. Judah b. Bathyra. They reached Sidon, and thoughts of the Land of Israel came to mind. They began to weep, and they rent their garments and recited the verse "You shall occupy it and settle on it, and you shall take care to observe all the laws and rules that I have set before you this day."[118] They said, "Dwelling in the Land of Israel is equivalent to all the [other] precepts of the Torah," and they retraced their steps and returned to the Land of Israel. . . .
>
> Whenever a Jew prays anywhere in the diaspora, "he shall direct his thoughts[119] toward the Land of Israel, as is written, 'And they pray to You in the direction of their land.'"[120] All the weekday, sabbath, and festival prayers, as well as the grace after meals, are imbued with the love of the Land of Israel, the desire for the return with proud bearing from the four corners of the earth to our land, and the yearning for the ingathering of the Jewish exiles. When a Jew prays for rain, he does not do so at the time of rains in his place of

114. 43(iv) *P.D.* 221 (1989). For the convenience of the reader, the source references in the text of the opinion are cited here as footnotes. Source references in lengthy quotations from other opinions are cited in the same manner.

115. 43(iv) *P.D.* 264ff.

116. The quoted language is from the Israeli Declaration of Independence.

117. *Sifrei,* Deuteronomy, Re'eh, sec. 80 (ed. Finkelstein, p. 146).

118. Deuteronomy 11:31–32.

119. Maimonides, *MT,* Tefillah 5:3 states: "he shall face"; *see Kesef Mishneh, ad loc.*

120. TB Berakhot 30a; Maimonides, *supra* n. 119; *Tur* and Sh. Ar. OḤ 95:1.

dispersion in Germany, Poland, or Russia, but rather during the rainy season of the Valley of Jezreel; and [he prays] for the crops of the Galilee and the Negev in the Land of Israel. . . .

The Land of Israel also has special importance with regard to other principles that are significant for communal life and governance. The calculation and determination of the lunar months and the intercalation of the calendar were committed to the halakhic authorities of the Land of Israel, as is written: "For instruction (*Torah*) shall come forth from Zion, the word of the Lord from Jerusalem,"[121] and the entire nation in the diaspora acted according to their decision.[122] . . . Inhabitants of the Land of Israel occupy a preferred status with regard to certain precepts. Thus, they have priority over those living outside the Land in regard to receipt of charity. The Jews of the diaspora at all times and places have assisted and supported individuals, institutions, and settlements in the Land of Israel. This has forged a strong permanent bond between the Jews in the Land of Israel and the Jewish communities of the diaspora—a relationship much more profound than mere financial support. . . .

Our Sages have considered the Land of Israel "a gift, an inheritance, and a precious possession." . . . The *Halakhah* gave these terms practical legal meaning, *e.g.*, . . . in connection with *kinyan agav karka, i.e.*, acquisition of chattels incidental to the acquisition of land.[123] . . .

As was aptly stated by the late Deputy President Silberg of the Israeli Supreme Court:[124]

> This heritage to which virtually all of us to a greater or lesser extent are bound is one of the foundation stones of our right to possess and settle this land. We were exiled from the Land 1900 years ago, but were not absent from it for even a single day. We thought of it unceasingly, whether awake or dreaming; and it was the focus of our attention from the beginning of the year to the end. Our spiritual presence in this land was far more intensive than the physical presence of all the nations and peoples—Romans, Greeks, Crusaders, Persians, Tatars, Mamelukes, Turks, and Arabs—who ruled or inhabited it in the nineteen centuries after the destruction [of the Temple].

Even the physical presence of Jews in the Land of Israel . . . was maintained with utmost zeal and almost superhuman effort. . . .

This wondrously stirring record of immigration and return to Zion from all the lands of dispersion and throughout the generations was marked by such deep yearning of those who returned that "they would kiss the borders

121. Isaiah 2:3.

122. Maimonides, *MT,* Kiddush ha-Ḥodesh 1:8; *id., Sefer ha-Mizvot,* Affirmative Commandment #153.

123. TB Kiddushin 26a. *See also supra* pp. 650–651; *infra* pp. 1651–1652.

124. Schalit v. Minister of the Interior, 23(ii) *P.D.* 477, 498 (1970).

of the Land of Israel and its stones, and roll about on its soil. Thus, it is written, 'Your servants take delight in its stones and cherish its dust.'"[125]. . .

Scholars, researchers, and writers have described this historical phenomenon in great detail, from the first return of the Babylonian exiles following the proclamation of Cyrus—"Anyone of you of all His people, may his God be with him, and let him go up to Jerusalem that is in Judah"[126]—through the immigrations in the Second Temple period, and after the destruction of the Temple up to our own days. . . . The historian Dr. Alex Bein put it well in his discussion of the background and significance of the Israeli Declaration of Independence:[127]

> Every nation exists not only within the boundaries of a particular land, but also by virtue of a particular land. . . . However, the link between the Jewish people and its land is *sui generis,* unlike that of any other nation. . . .
>
> Other nations expelled from their lands met either of two fates: they were scattered among other peoples, assimilated with them, and lost their separate national identity, or they stayed together and conquered some other land which they turned into a new "homeland." However, the Jewish people took a road followed by no other nation, thereby disproving, as it were, an accepted principle of national history. They were scattered throughout the world, but wherever they went, they refused to forget that only the Land of Israel was their true homeland. . . .

The proposition that the State of Israel is the State of the Jewish People is also grounded in international law:

> This right was recognized in the Balfour Declaration of the 2nd November, 1917, and reaffirmed in the Mandate of the League of Nations, *which, in particular, gave international sanction to the historic connection between the Jewish people and the Land of Israel and to the right of the Jewish people to rebuild its National Home.* . . . On the 29th November, 1947, the United Nations General Assembly passed a resolution calling for the establishment of a Jewish State in the Land of Israel. . . . This recognition by the United Nations *of the right of the Jewish people to establish their state* is irrevocable.[128] . . .

In sum, the natural right of every Jew, wherever he may be, to return to his land, the Land of Israel, is founded upon the religious and national heritage of the Jewish people and its political and historical experience. This right is the basis for the establishment of the sovereign State of Israel, and was recognized in the legal system of the State as a legal-constitutional right, and an

125. Maimonides, *MT,* Melakhim 5:10 (on the basis of TB Ketubbot 112a/b), quoting Psalms 102:15.

126. Ezra 1:3; II Chronicles 36:23.

127. *Im Megillat ha-Aẓma'ut Shel Medinat Yisra'el* [On the Declaration of Independence of the State of Israel], Jerusalem, 1949, pp. 9–10.

128. Israeli Declaration of Independence (emphasis in the opinion).

axiomatic legal principle undergirding the entire legal system. Shortly after the State of Israel was established, this basic legal right was embodied in the Law of Return.

(6) The Basic Law: Israel Lands. The Basic Law: Israel Lands provides: "The ownership of Israel lands, namely, the lands of the State, the Development Authority, and the Jewish National Fund, shall not be transferred by sale or in any other manner"—with certain limited exceptions as to various types of land and particular transactions.[129] These two provisions—the general rule and the exceptions—are deeply rooted in Jewish law and reflect Jewish values, as the chairman of the Legislative Committee eloquently explained when he presented the bill for its second and third readings in the Knesset:[130]

> The law covers land, the national heritage; its purpose is to articulate a basic principle of our national life, namely, that ownership of the land cannot be transferred in perpetuity.
>
> The purposes of this bill, as I present it, are as follows: [First,] to give legal form to the essentially religious principle that "the land must not be sold beyond reclaim, for the land is Mine" (Leviticus 25:23). Whether or not this verse from Scripture is mentioned in the law, as was proposed, this law gives legal form to that principle of our Torah. . . .
>
> The second purpose is a practical one. The land was acquired and settled by the whole nation. God first promised it to our ancestors Abraham, Isaac, and Jacob. It was settled for the first time by the entire nation under Joshua, and then under King David. It was settled a second time by the exiles who returned from Babylonia, and a third time, in our generation, by all the Jews who dwell in Zion with assistance from the entire Jewish people throughout the world.
>
> The lands belonging to the Jewish National Fund were acquired with the pennies contributed by all Jews everywhere, and the lands of the Development Authority were consecrated by the blood of our young soldiers. We have no right to transform this property, acquired and conquered by the entire people, into the private property of individuals. . . .
>
> The purpose of the second section of the bill is to express a principle that we have previously accepted in several other laws. I refer to the distinc-

129. Basic Law: Israel Lands, *Laws of Israel*, 1960, No. 312, p. 56, secs. 1 and 2. As to the nature of a "Basic Law," *see* P. Elman, "The Basic Law: The Government," 4 *Israel L. Rev.* 242 (1969). The statute permits transfers of ownership of land (particularly urban land) in certain instances (sec. 2). Section 3 of the law is also of interest. It provides that the law "shall not affect acts designed solely to enable observance of the sabbatical year," *i.e.*, "sales" rendering it halakhically permissible to work the land in the sabbatical year. *See* Elon, *Ḥakikah*, p. 55.

130. Remarks of MK Warhaftig, 29 *DK* 1916–1917 (1960).

> tion between agricultural and urban land. . . . We have provided here that the prohibition of transfer in perpetuity does not apply to urban or industrial land. Such land may be transferred.
>
> In other words, we have adopted in our statutes the distinction made by our Torah, the Torah of Moses, between agricultural land and residential buildings in walled cities: "If a man sells a dwelling house in a walled city, it may be redeemed until a year has elapsed since its sale. . . . If it is not redeemed before a full year has elapsed, the house in the walled city shall pass to the purchaser beyond reclaim throughout the ages; it shall not be released in the jubilee" (Leviticus 25:29–30). This distinction . . . is clear and understandable, since the land itself is of primary importance only when it is used for agriculture. In the case of urban and industrial land, on the other hand, it is the activity on the land or what is extracted from the land that is of primary importance. The same distinction has been accepted in two other laws: the Development Authority (Transfer of Property) Law, 1950, and the State Property Law, 1951.

c. PERSONAL STATUS, FAMILY, AND SUCCESSION LAW

Jewish law has been the wellspring of a large and significant portion of Israeli legislation concerning personal status, and family and succession law. Two principal methods have been used for the incorporation of Jewish law in these areas. One is blanket incorporation by reference without setting forth in the statute the specific provisions of the law being incorporated. The classic example of this method is the law of marriage and divorce. Section 2 of the Rabbinical Courts Jurisdiction (Marriage and Divorce) Law, 1953, states: "Marriage and divorce between Jews in Israel shall be effected according to Torah law." The law does not specify the contents of Torah law nor does it prescribe specifically how marriages and divorces are to be effected. The Legislature simply adopted by reference the whole of Jewish law on that subject as the law of the State.

The second method of adopting Jewish law is for the Knesset to set forth in its statute the precise norms and provisions it intends to incorporate. In the pre-State period, the first method was generally employed in the entire area of family law, but after the establishment of the State this method was limited to the law of marriage, divorce, and spousal and child support. On other subjects in the law of personal status, the Knesset did not employ the method of blanket incorporation by reference, but enacted specific and detailed provisions based to a great extent on Jewish law.

The technique of blanket incorporation by reference employed in regard to the Jewish law of marriage, divorce, and spousal and child support has been much discussed both by scholars and commentators. Particular attention has been given to such questions as how and to what extent the general courts, as distinguished from the rabbinical courts, should apply

Jewish law when such issues come before them. Some of these questions will be discussed later.[131] At this point, however, it is appropriate to review certain provisions of Knesset legislation in other areas of family law as they relate to sources in Jewish law, and to note the problems of legislative policy encountered in the enactment of this legislation that are relevant to the general question of the relation of Knesset legislation to Jewish law.

The change from blanket incorporation to incorporation of specific provisions began modestly in 1950–1951 with the adoption of the Marriage Age Law and the Woman's Equal Rights Law, and broadened thereafter with the passage of the Family Law Amendment (Maintenance) Law, 1959, and subsequent legislation. This detailed legislation concerning family and succession law reflects a tension between two conflicting tendencies. On the one hand, the adoption of Jewish law in this area[132] is considerably more extensive and more consistent than in other legislation because, in this area, Jewish law had always governed the Jewish population of the Land of Israel, and most of the problems covered by the legislation had already been dealt with—by the general as well as by the religious courts—in accordance with that law. As a result, lawyers and judges had become familiar with the basic principles of this area of Jewish law and had learned to appreciate its approach to the solution of such important problems as support, guardianship, and particular aspects of inheritance.

On the other hand, from time to time, opposition has arisen to legislating by way of statutory incorporation of specific provisions of Jewish law in this area, particularly on the part of those who in other legal areas are strong proponents of Knesset enactment of legislation containing detailed provisions based on Jewish law. This opposition is based on two considerations: (1) changes introduced in the course of legislation are more likely to arouse religious sensitivities in matters of family law than in other legal areas; and (2) where Jewish law is incorporated by blanket reference, the interpretation of the law will be based on the sources of Jewish law, but where the Knesset formulates a law, even when the formulation adopts a rule of Jewish law, the interpretation of the Knesset's legislation by the courts of the State will not necessarily conform to the interpretation of the rule in the *Halakhah*. In addition, legislation by the Knesset in this sensitive area provokes divisive discussion of the delicate problem of the proper relation between religion and state in Knesset legislation.

131. *See infra* pp. 1752ff.; *see also* Elon, *Ḥakikah*, pp. 3–4, 31–33, 59ff.; I. Englard, "Ma'amado Shel ha-Din ha-Dati ba-Mishpat ha-Yisra'eli" [The Status of Religious Law in the Israeli Legal System], *Mishpatim*, II, pp. 294ff.; *id.*, *Religious Law in the Israel Legal System* (1975), pp. 49ff. For a listing of sources discussing issues of marriage, divorce, and spousal and child support, *see infra* p. 1753 n. 3.

132. Except for certain matters which will be discussed *infra*. *See, e.g.*, pp. 1683–1688.

Each of these two positions (which are instructive not only in themselves but also for the light they throw on the general problem of the incorporation of Jewish law in the law of the State, as well as on a whole complex of related questions) will be treated by examining some illustrative Knesset statutes.

(1) The Marriage Age Law. The Marriage Age Law raised the minimum age of marriage for women.[133] Under the British Mandate, the minimum age was generally fifteen (and in some instances even lower), and the sanction for violation of the law was relatively light—six months imprisonment. With the advent of large-scale Jewish immigration from North African and Middle-Eastern countries where child marriage was practiced, it became essential to amend the law. Because of the dangers resulting from pregnancy, and because of other difficulties associated with marriage under the age of sixteen years and one day, the Chief Rabbinate, the religious legislative body, enacted a *takkanah* in 1950 forbidding marriage to girls under that age.

In the Knesset, the Government originally proposed a minimum age of seventeen years. During the debate on the bill, it was suggested that the minimum age should be the same as in the *takkanah* of the Chief Rabbinate.[134] A later draft would have set the age of sixteen as the minimum and would have permitted marriage between sixteen and eighteen years of age only with the consent of the girl's parents or guardian.[135] Ultimately, the age of seventeen was established as the minimum for all marriages,[136] except that a district court could permit the marriage of a female under that age who had borne a child to, or was pregnant by, the man she wished to marry.[137] Ten years later, the law was amended to permit marriage of a girl who is not pregnant but has reached the age of sixteen, provided that "in the opinion of the court, special conditions exist to justify such permission."[138]

133. A private member's bill (MK Ada Maimon) was first introduced for this purpose; *see* 4 *DK* 639 (1950). The Government's bill of 1950 was published as a proposed amendment to the Criminal Code Ordinance (Bill No. 31, 1950).

134. *See* the remarks of MKs Warhaftig, 4 *DK* 655 (1950), and Shag, *id.* at 661.

135. 5 *DK* 1740 (1950).

136. *Id.* at 1705, 1726, 1832. The proposal to fix the age at seventeen was by MK Bar Rav Hai.

137. Marriage Age Law, 1950, sec. 5.

138. Marriage Age (Amendment) Law, 1960. The explanation given was that experience had shown that there was a need in some cases to permit marriage at the age of sixteen years and that the law then in force encouraged becoming pregnant so as to be able to marry. As to the relationship between the amendment to the Marriage Age Law and the *takkanah* of the Chief Rabbinate, *see* the remarks of Minister of Justice Rosen, 28 *DK* 9 (1960), and

During the debates on this law, the problem of the relation between state and religion in Knesset legislation arose in the context of the question of the sanctions to be prescribed for violation of the law. According to Jewish law, the marriage is effective if the girl is above the age of twelve years and one day, and this was also the result under the enactment of the Chief Rabbinate, notwithstanding that the marriage was in violation of the *takkanah*.[139]

The question was whether the Knesset should provide, contrary to Jewish law, that a marriage in violation of the law is void, or should provide only for penal sanctions. The policy of the Government as to the validity of marriage and divorce (which remains in force to the present) was stated by the Minister of Justice as follows:[140]

> This minimum age requirement may be enforced by invalidating marriages at an age below the minimum, or by penal sanctions, or by both these methods. Some countries approach the question as essentially one of civil law. As is known to the members of the Knesset, marriage in our country is governed by the religious law, and the validity of marriages is determined by the provisions of the religious law, whether Jewish, Christian, or Moslem. I should like to state, first, that the government, after prior debate on this question in the Legislative Committee, does not treat the question, in its bill, as a matter of civil law, which in this instance is the religious law. We do not propose that a marriage under the minimum age should be declared void. . . . We treat the question as a matter of criminal law.

This was the approach adopted in the statute passed by the Knesset. The validity of a marriage under the minimum age is to be determined by the personal law applicable to the parties; and if that law so provides, nonage may warrant a divorce before a religious court of competent jurisdiction.[141]

However, the debate on the question of the relation between religion and state as regards legislation did not end at this point. One Knesset mem-

---

MKs Warhaftig, *id.* at 10; Rubin, *id.* at 23; Sanhedrai, *id.* at 24; Katz, *id.* at 26; and Lorenz, *id.* at 29.

139. This is also the halakhic rule in regard to a large number of prohibited marriages that are nevertheless valid after the fact. The classic example is the marriage of a *kohen* (priest) and a divorcée, which is Biblically prohibited but, once performed, is valid and may be dissolved only by divorce. Only where the prohibition is stringent, as in the case of marriage between relatives of the first degree or with a woman who is already married, is the marriage itself void.

140. Remarks of P. Rosen, 4 *DK* 638 (1950).

141. Marriage Age Law, 1950, sec. 3.

ber objected to the entire consideration of the bill by the Knesset, "as it touches on family law, which is under the jurisdiction of the rabbinate. . . . The agency authorized by the bill to decide the matter has no authority under the *Halakhah,* because it is not a religious body."[142] This far-reaching argument, which has apparently not been repeated in such an extreme form, elicited the following response by the Minister of Justice, who pointed out the change effected, so far as the State is concerned, in the basic nature of a halakhic norm when that norm is embodied not only in a halakhic rule but also in a statute enacted by the State:

> With all the respect that I have for the traditional law, that law is effective in this country [only] to the extent that it is recognized and enacted as law by the State. We must all understand that the religious law on marriage is today not only religious law but also the law of the State, in accordance with what we laid down in the Law and Administration Ordinance, which provided that the law in effect on the 5th day of Iyyar, 5708 (May 4, 1948) remains in force. The conclusion is that the religious family law is the law of the State; however, it binds the State only to the extent that the State wishes to be so bound. In this instance, the Government did not wish to propose a bill that would amend currently existing family law.[143]

(2) The Woman's Equal Rights Law. The same set of problems was again discussed a year later, this time more intensively and at greater length, when the Woman's Equal Rights Law was debated. The main purpose of this statute is to establish equality of legal rights for men and women with regard to such matters as testimonial competence, acquisition of property during marriage, guardianship of children, and succession. This statute also prohibits bigamy, which had previously been permitted to Moslems, and provides criminal penalties for divorcing a wife without her consent. In the main, these provisions are in accord with Jewish law as it has evolved;[144]

142. Remarks of MK Levinstein of the Agudat Israel Party, 4 *DK* 659 (1950).

143. *Id.* at 667. During this debate, MK Prof. Dinabourg (Dinur) discussed from the halakhic perspective the authority of the Knesset to adopt enactments concerning the minimum age at which marriage could take place, as well as the registration of marriages, which are similar to the rabbinic legislation and the communal enactments (*takkanot ha-kahal*) adopted throughout the history of the Jewish law (*id.* at 665–666). MK Dinabourg made a more explicit statement of his position on this question in the debate on the Woman's Equal Rights Law; *see infra.* The merits of the issue are discussed *infra* pp. 1820–1826, 1944–1945. *See also supra* p. 1613 n. 95.

144. *See, e.g.,* remarks of MKs. Shag, 9 *DK* 2100 (1951), and Warhaftig, *id.* at 2118, 2124, 2129, regarding a woman's testimony, her competence to engage in legal transactions after marriage, and her position as a guardian. *See also infra* pp. 1664–1667, 1684, and accompanying notes. In Shakdiel v. Ministry of Religions, 42(ii) *P.D.* 221 (1988), the Supreme Court held that a woman has the right to be a member of a local religious council. The court discussed public service by women as members of administrative and governmen-

and where this is not the case, the halakhic authorities have the power to enact *takkanot* appropriate to the needs of contemporary society. The basic provisions of the statute are also in conformity with the halakhic principle that in monetary matters, individuals—and certainly the public as a whole—may agree to contract out of a Biblical norm.[145] As was rightly said in the debate in the Knesset:[146]

> All family law, insofar as it relates to monetary matters—and this is what this bill is concerned with—is a matter for legislation by way of *takkanah* and as such is subject to modification. . . . The Legislative Committee may deal with the subject on the basis of both principle and practicality, for this is an area in which the fundamentals of Jewish law should be organically integrated with the requirements of modern life. . . . The Committee should be thorough and should not avoid the difficult questions; it should examine all aspects of life with the help of the experts, including the rabbinate and others learned in Jewish law, in order to formulate legislation acceptable to the general public. It is certainly possible, under the Torah, the Talmud, and the codificatory literature, to find the means for resolving the very many demands of contemporary life in a manner that would be an exemplary model for Jews the world over.

In this instance, in contrast to the *takkanah* concerning under-age marriage, the Chief Rabbinate did not adequately respond to the situation and failed to enact detailed and comprehensive *takkanot*.[147]

The Woman's Equal Rights Law provides that it does not affect the religious law governing marriage and divorce; it thus continues the policy of the Marriage Age Law not to interfere with the rules relating to the creation and dissolution of the marital status, even if in some instances these rules may adversely affect the legal position of women. In this connection, many members of the Knesset looked to the Chief Rabbinate to exercise the

---

tal bodies, both under Israeli statute and Jewish law, and reviewed the development of the law on this issue over the course of time. *See infra* pp. 1900–1903.

145. This was also the case with the Procedural Enactments of the Chief Rabbinate of the Land of Israel, 1943, relating to equality of the sexes in regard to inheritance; *see* Elon, "The Sources and Nature of Jewish Law and Its Application in the State of Israel," Part III, 3 *Israel L. Rev.* 416, 428ff. and n. 56 (1968); *id.*, *Ḥakikah*, pp. 37–43. *See also supra* pp. 123–127, 828–829, and *infra* pp. 1761–1762, 1824–1826, as to the remarks of Rabbi Kafaḥ that the provisions of the Woman's Equal Rights Law are halakhically valid since they concern monetary matters (*mamon*), as to which the public may legislate.

146. Remarks of MK Dinabourg, 9 *DK* 2105–2106 (1951).

147. As to how the rabbinical courts have applied the Woman's Equal Rights Law, *see infra* pp. 1761–1762, 1824–1826 (statement of Rabbi Kafaḥ). As to the amendment to the Woman's Equal Rights Law in 1976, *see infra* pp. 1802–1807. *See also* Schereschewsky, *Dinei Mishpahah* [Family Law], 3rd ed., Jerusalem, 1984, pp. 279ff.

traditional halakhic legislative authority to adopt, on its own initiative, appropriate *takkanot* to resolve a number of problems connected with the *agunah*—*e.g.*, a husband's chronic mental illness or willful refusal to consent to a divorce, and some situations involving *halizah*.[148]

This statute was the first enactment of the Knesset to prescribe substantive provisions with regard to personal status (though only as to financial matters) and to require the religious courts to abide by those provisions. It was, therefore, to be expected that the problem of the relation between state and religion in Knesset legislation should again arise. Some Knesset members argued that in the area of personal status the Knesset should not enact substantive provisions that these members believed to be contrary to the *Halakhah*.[149] The main debate, however, centered on the obligation of the religious courts to apply the statutory provisions enacted by the Knesset. Under the Government's proposal, as well as the Legislative Committee's draft for the second and third readings of the bill,[150] the relevant section read as follows:

> Every general court and religious court having jurisdiction over matters of personal status shall act in accordance with this statute.

Members of the Knesset from the religious parties regarded this as interference by the State with the substance of the law applied in the religious courts, and as infringing the freedom of conscience of the judges of those courts by compelling them to act contrary to religious law. Some proposed to delete the reference in the section to the rabbinical courts.[151] The response to this position was that to the extent that the religious courts claim from the State recognition of their authority, the State on its part may determine the limits of the jurisdiction that it confers. The Prime Minister, David Ben-Gurion, made this point as follows:[152]

> A second argument has been made here. I regard it with respect, in spite of my disagreement with it. We have been asked: "Are you directing the rabbis

148. *See* the remarks of Minister of Justice Rosen, 9 *DK* 2007 (1951); and MKs Dinabourg, *id.* at 2105–2106; Persitz, *id.* at 2116–2117; and Ben-Zvi, *id.* at 2125–2126. *See also* Elon, *Ḥakikah*, pp. 182–184, and *supra* pp. 522–530, 846–879.

149. *See, e.g.*, the remarks of Minister of Social Welfare Levin, and the pertinent remarks of MKs Warhaftig and Shag, 9 *DK* 2090 (1951); and the response of MK Harari, *id.* at 2102.

150. Woman's Equal Rights Bill, 1951 (Bill No. 75), sec. 7; 9 *DK* 2193 (1951).

151. *See id.* at 2196 for MK K. Kahana's proposed amendment to the effect that the provision would not apply to "matters as to which both the religious and the general courts have concurrent jurisdiction." The reason for this formulation was that language specifically excepting matters over which the religious courts have exclusive jurisdiction, *i.e.*, marriage and divorce, was deemed unnecessary because such matters are in any case beyond the reach of the statute. *See also* Kahana's remarks, *id.* at 2187.

152. *Id.* at 2132.

> how to decide a dispute under Jewish law?" . . . This argument . . . raises a grave and serious problem. If the State cannot give directives to the rabbis, on what basis can the rabbis exercise governmental authority? All of us, all parties in Israel, have promised freedom of religion and of conscience. The State will certainly not infringe the right of any person to live according to the principles of his faith. And you may demand that the Knesset not instruct the rabbis how they are to reach their judgments, if the rabbis wish or are required to decide only in accordance with the *Shulḥan Arukh.* But the conclusion to be drawn from this argument is that rabbinic judgments should have the authority only of the *Shulḥan Arukh.* Whoever accepts such authority will accept it; whoever does not, will not. For the State has guaranteed freedom of conscience not only to the religious, but to every citizen.
>
> The authority that the rabbinate has today derives not from the *Shulḥan Arukh* but from the law of the [British] Mandate, which has been given legal validity in the State of Israel by the Provisional Council of State. . . . As long as a rabbi acts pursuant to the authority of the Knesset, the Knesset may tell him how to act. If the rabbinate and the "religious bloc" do not wish the Knesset to give the rabbis directives—and I believe they have this right—then the necessary conclusion is that the rabbis will be acting solely by virtue of the authority of the *Shulḥan Arukh,* and the Knesset will withdraw all the governmental authority given them by the State. You cannot hold the string at both ends. You must choose the path along which you wish to proceed. Either the rabbis will be independent of the law of the State and will enjoy no governmental authority but only a voluntary religious authority . . . , or in certain areas they will be vested with governmental authority, and their religious rulings will be enforced by government officials in those matters expressly provided for in the law. However, in that case, the State may tell the rabbis how to act, and determine the conditions on which their governmental authority rests, just as it does with regard to the Government, the judges, members of the Knesset, State officials, the police, the army, and all those who act on behalf of the State. There is no escape from this choice. . . . What is inconceivable is that rabbis will be given governmental authority that is in no way subject to the limitations established by the State.

Ultimately, the Knesset decided to take a middle course on this sensitive question. The following compromise was proposed by a number of members during the second and third reading of the bill:[153]

> Every general court shall act in accordance with this statute; every religious court having jurisdiction over matters of personal status shall also act in accordance with this statute, unless all the parties are eighteen years of age or over and have consented before the religious court, of their own free will, to have their case tried according to the laws of their own religious community.

153. *Id.* at 2196 (MKs Warhaftig and Klebenov).

This change in the statute, permitting the parties to agree of their own free will (hence the requirement that they be adults and that they consent in open court) to have their dispute decided according to their religious law, was supported by the following argument:

> Why should the right not be given to adults to waive a material benefit in order to maintain their faithfulness to traditional Jewish law? . . . In our view, the State may abridge freedom of conscience and religious belief only when such abridgement is essential and unavoidable.[154]

This argument prevailed and the compromise proposal was adopted.[155]

With respect to the Marriage Age Law and the Woman's Equal Rights Law, the crux of the problem was: To what extent may the Knesset intervene in the substantive religious law when, in addition to the law's religious authority, it is sought to buttress that law with the authority and the enforcement powers of the State?

After a hiatus of some years, the Knesset greatly increased the number of substantive provisions in its family-law legislation. These were, to a considerable degree, based upon the principles of Jewish law, but they also had special objectives and raised distinct problems, which were not dealt with when Jewish legal principles were adopted in other areas of the law.

(3) The Family Law Amendment (Maintenance) Law. The first of this latter type of family-law legislation is the Family Law Amendment (Maintenance) Law, 1959.[156] This statute deals with the problem of support in two principal ways. Support of one's spouse and minor children, like marriage and divorce, is governed by the personal law of the parties.[157] However, support of other members of the family—parents, spouse's par-

154. Remarks of MK Klebenov, *id.* at 2187. The debate on Section 1 of the statute is also interesting. This section provides that "any provision of law insofar as it discriminates against women as women in regard to any legal transaction or proceeding shall not be given effect." It was suggested by MKs Nir and Harari that "shall not be given effect" should be replaced by "is repealed" (*id.* at 2193), but the Knesset rejected the suggestion, since "the precepts of religious law cannot be repealed by a vote of the Knesset. . . . The concern of the Knesset is not whether a halakhic rule is to be abrogated, but whether it should be given effect in the State of Israel. . . . We do not seek to abrogate the provisions of the *Shulḥan Arukh;* that is tradition." (Remarks of MK Bar Rav Hai, speaking for the Legislative Committee, *id.* at 2168.) Subsequently, a similar debate took place in the Supreme Court, in the opinions of President Y. Olshan and Justice M. Silberg; *see* Elon, *Ḥakikah,* pp. 38–41.

155. A rabbinical court which, without the consent of the parties, disregards an applicable provision of the Woman's Equal Rights Law is subject to the supervisory jurisdiction of the High Court of Justice; *see infra* pp. 1758–1759.

156. The bill was published in 1956 (Bill No. 267); it was patterned on Sections 122–136 of the Draft Individual and the Family Bill, published in 1955 by the Ministry of Justice, in which many of the Jewish legal sources on which it is based are cited.

157. Secs. 2 and 3.

ents, adult children and their spouses, grandchildren, grandparents, and spouse's grandparents—is expressly regulated by the statute itself.

Under the statute, the duty to support other members of the family arises only when one has more than sufficient means to support himself and his spouse and minor children, and the family member to whom the duty would run is unable to be self-supporting. The extent and mode of the support required by the statute are to be determined "having regard to the circumstances . . . according to the need of the person entitled and the ability of the person liable."

These provisions accord with the attitude of Jewish law, which requires support of other family members on the basis of the principle that "charity can be compelled"[158] so long as one's resources are adequate to satisfy the needs of one's immediate family and there is someone dependent on the charity for his livelihood. Jewish law also establishes priorities as to those entitled to charity: "The poor of one's household have priority over the poor of one's town, and the poor of one's town have priority over the poor of any other town."[159] The Minister of Justice and most of those who participated in the Knesset debates on the bill emphasized that its provisions regarding the obligation to support members of the family, the extent and mode of the support,[160] and the order of priority of claims to support[161] were based on Jewish law; and they cited many Jewish legal sources, both Talmudic and post-Talmudic.[162]

This statute, based as it was largely on Jewish law, gave rise to two fundamental questions concerning the incorporation of Jewish law into Knesset legislation. The first is, What should be the method of incorpora-

158. TB Ketubbot 49b; Sh. Ar. YD ch. 251. *See also supra* pp. 116–117.

159. For further details, *see* Sh. Ar. YD chs. 247–251. *See also supra* p. 101 n. 37 and pp. 117, 831; I. Kister, "Dinei Ẓedakah ve-Shimmusham ba-Mishpat be-Yisra'el [The Laws of Charity and Their Application in Israeli Law], *Ha-Praklit,* XXIV (1968), pp. 168–177.

160. *See* the remarks of Minister of Justice P. Rosen, 20 *DK* 1974 (1956):

> The religious courts generally compel family members to support relatives—even somewhat beyond the immediate family—on the basis of the principle that charity may be compelled. . . . When we determined those who are eligible for support, we realized that we could have recourse here to Jewish legal principles, and so we did, because, generally speaking, the subject of support is well developed in Jewish law in terms of principles. . . . The fact is that this statute is based on the principles of Jewish law.

161. *See* the remarks of MK Warhaftig, 26 *DK* 1147 (1959): "We even accepted the degrees of kinship and the order of priorities in Section 4 after research into Jewish law; and, after negotiation with the Ministry of Justice, we unanimously agreed on these provisions on the basis of Jewish law."

162. *See* the remarks of MKs Rosenberg (Ben-Meir), 20 *DK* 1933–1934 (1956); Raphael, *id.* at 1942; Lorenz, *id.* at 1945; Ben-Yaakov, *id.* at 1968–1969; and MK Azanyah, on behalf of the Legislative Committee, 26 *DK* 1147 (1959). Some of these MKs felt that Jewish law could have been adopted more fully.

tion? As stated, the statute provided that support of spouses and minor children was to be governed by the personal law of the parties, but did not itself set forth the specific provisions of that law. Some members queried why, inasmuch as spousal and child support is by far the most frequent and pressing problem, the Knesset did not itself directly set forth detailed provisions concerning spousal and child support but did so in the case of other members of the family:

> Can the State of Israel not determine this by means of a statute of the Knesset? Does the fact that religious law prescribes the duty of support prevent the duty from also being prescribed by a secular body, *i.e.*, the State? . . . Parents must support their children, a husband must support his wife, and a wife must support her husband; and these take priority over grandparents, grandchildren, brothers, and sisters.[163]

These Knesset members pointed out that there was a strong desire expressed by some Knesset members that Jewish law be the basis of provisions of other bills on civil, criminal, and public law; they argued that there was no justification for a double standard (lit. "two sets of books")[164] in regard to the method of incorporating Jewish law in the Knesset's legislation.

The second question is, How should statutes incorporating the specific provisions of Jewish law on the subject involved be interpreted? As has been mentioned, Article 46 of the Palestine Order in Council required the courts to turn to English common law and equity when faced with a gap in the existing law.[165] Some Knesset members proposed to add a section to the Family Law Amendment (Maintenance) Law stating: "This law shall be construed in accordance with the principles of Jewish law."[166] They argued:

> This statute is based on the principles of Jewish law, and most of its detailed provisions are based on Jewish law. On the subject of this legislation up to recent time, English law, particularly, made no provision for support of relatives other than immediate family. Only recently has a statute known as the "Poor Relief Act" been enacted, which recognizes a claim of more distant relatives for support. The law there on this subject is much less developed than Jewish law. Why make a patchwork of Jewish and English law? Let us link this statute to Jewish law. . . . It will thus be possible to develop it more justly and more properly.[167]

163. Remarks of MK Rubin, 26 *DK* 1126–1127 (1959). MK Harari had advanced the same argument, 20 *DK* 1944 (1956). *See also* Elon, *Ḥakikah,* pp. 60ff.

164. *See* the remarks of MK Rubin, 20 *DK* 1947 (1956).

165. *See supra* pp. 1611–1612.

166. *See* the remarks of MK Warhaftig, 26 *DK* 1138 (1959).

167. *Id.* at 1147. MK Rosenberg (Ben-Meir) made the same proposal in the debate on the first reading of the bill; *see* 20 *DK* 1934 (1956).

The opponents of this proposal argued:

> There cannot be a blind reception. Whatever we receive from Jewish law into the Knesset's legislation (and this is not an insignificant quantity) we set forth specifically. But a blanket provision . . . does not make clear to us what we are accepting.[168]

The author's view regarding recourse to Jewish law has already been expressed.[169] It should be noted that the proposal for such a provision in the Family Law Amendment (Maintenance) Law involved only a limited measure of reference to Jewish law: it did not relate to the entire Israeli legal system, but rather to a particular statute which everyone agrees is based largely on Jewish law. Hence, the proposal for recourse to Jewish law was not merely to fill possible lacunae but also for the purpose of construing the statute.

The proposal was rejected. This rejection may very well have weakened the argument for including in the statute detailed provisions concerning spousal and child support rather than providing in general terms that the religious law should govern. For if a statute sets forth detailed provisions based on Jewish law but does not also require recourse to Jewish law to interpret those provisions, there is good reason to be concerned that the statute will be cut off from its sources.[170] On the other hand, where the legislature provides in general terms that Jewish law will govern a particular subject, the governing law remains linked to its sources. For this reason, apparently, a number of Knesset members felt that, under the circumstances, incorporating Jewish law in general terms was preferable to enacting specific provisions based on Jewish law; rejection of the proposal to include a provision that the statute should be construed in accordance with Jewish law meant that there was no assurance that the specific provisions of Jewish law incorporated in the statute would be interpreted in a manner consonant with their Jewish legal sources.

(4) The Capacity and Guardianship Law. A similar situation involving the same questions arose with respect to another important statute in the area of personal status, namely, the Capacity and Guardianship Law, 1962,[171] which fixed the minimum age for capacity to engage in legal trans-

168. Remarks of MK Azanyah, 26 *DK* 1147 (1959).

169. *See supra* pp. 1617–1618, 1621–1623.

170. This argument was indeed made at the additional hearing of Koenig v. Cohen, 36(iii) *P.D.* 701 (1982), concerning the construction of the will of a *shekhiv me-ra* under the Succession Law; *see infra* pp. 1878–1884.

171. The Knesset had previously enacted the Adoption of Children Law, 1960. A critical issue in connection with this statute was whether to sever all ties between the

actions, prescribed other limitations on capacity (such as in case of mental illness), and established procedures for the appointment of guardians of the person and of the property for persons wholly lacking, or possessing only limited, legal capacity. The Explanatory Notes to the bill[172] stated:

> In substance, almost all of its provisions accord with Jewish law. The only important difference . . . derives from the principle of equal status of women, in consequence of which the responsibility for the care of children is placed not on the father alone, but on the father and the mother jointly. This principle was already established in Section 3 of the Woman's Equal Rights Law, 1951, of which the second part of the instant law can be considered a continuation and development.

This statement is not completely accurate, for Jewish law, in its present state, places the responsibility for the care of children on both parents, as is more fully discussed later in this section.[173] At this point, however, our discussion will focus on the main points of this legislation. The age at which an individual achieves legal capacity in Jewish law, *i.e.*, the age of majority, is thirteen years and one day for a male, and twelve years and one day for a female. In the course of time, as a result of social and economic changes, Jewish law became quite flexible in this regard, reducing the age of majority for some purposes and increasing it for others. As early as in the Mishnah,[174] Jewish law provided that the purchase and sale of movables by "young children" is valid. Some Talmudic Sages held that "young children" for this purpose were children of age six or seven; others held that the minimum age was ten. The Talmud concluded that the minimum age depends on the intelligence of the particular child in relation to the specific transaction.[175] R. Johanan explained that the reason for according legal capacity to a child for certain sales and purchases is "to provide for his livelihood," since if the law were otherwise, no one would be willing to sell to or buy from a child, even to provide the child with food, education, or other

---

adopted child and his natural parents. On this issue, Jewish law diverges sharply from many other legal systems based on Roman law. The Adoption Law passed by the Knesset represents a compromise. For detailed discussion, *see supra* pp. 827–828 and n. 178; Elon, *Ḥakikah*, pp. 45–46.

172. Capacity and Guardianship Bill, 1961 (Bill No. 456), p. 178.

173. *See supra* pp. 1656–1657; *infra* pp. 1667, 1794–1802, pointing out that under current halakhic rulings, a father and a mother are equally entitled and obligated to support and educate their children. *See also* the statement of Chief Rabbi Uziel, quoted in Nagar v. Nagar, 38(i) *P.D.* 365, 396–397 (1981).

174. M Gittin 5:7.

175. TB Gittin 59a: "They [the Sages] do not disagree—[the age is fixed for] each one according to his intelligence."

necessities; if these types of transactions were not valid, the very survival of the child might be jeopardized.[176] On the other hand, there were times when the minimum age was fixed higher than thirteen for certain matters: *e.g.*, in some land transactions, one view was that eighteen was the minimum age, and the accepted view held that the minimum age was twenty.[177] This flexibility continued in post-Talmudic times. An enactment adopted in 1624 by the Council of the Four Lands in Poland provided that a promissory note signed by anyone under twenty-five years of age was a nullity,[178] and there is a record of an instrument executed by a father appointing a guardian for his children and designating eighteen years as the age of majority at which the guardianship would terminate.[179]

The statute as passed by the Knesset adopted the guiding principle of flexibility that characterizes Jewish law: the age of legal capacity depends on the degree of the individual's intelligence and understanding of the specific transaction, and the prevailing social conditions. The statute fixes eighteen as the age of majority for most purposes, including military service and voting, but goes on to provide that a juristic act performed by one below that age is effective if the act is commonly performed at the lesser age, unless the act causes substantial harm to the minor or his property.[180] During the various readings of the bill, the position of Jewish law as to the age of majority was discussed at length.[181] It should be noted that the law continues to prescribe different minimum ages for a number of substantive matters, such as criminal responsibility, tort liability,[182] and acts that determine or change personal status.[183]

The Capacity and Guardianship Law adopts the principle, already laid down in the Woman's Equal Rights Law, 1951, that both parents are the

176. *Id.*; Maimonides, *MT*, Mekhirah 29:1; Sh. Ar. ḤM 235:1.

177. TB Bava Batra 155a; Maimonides, *MT*, Mekhirah 29:13; Sh. Ar. ḤM 235:9.

178. I. Halpern, *Pinkas Va'ad Arba Araẓot* [The Record Book of the Council of the Four Lands], Jerusalem, 1945, p. 48, Enactment #125.

179. A Gulak, *Oẓar ha-Shetarot*, p. 145, Instrument #157; *see also id.*, *Yesodei*, I, pp. 38ff., 41; Elon, *Principles*, Index, s.v. Minor; *supra* pp. 585–587; and Index, *infra*, s.v. Minors.

180. Secs. 3, 6.

181. *See* remarks of Minister of Justice Rosen, 32 *DK* 46–47 (1962), and MK Unna, 34 *DK* 3081 (1962).

182. *See* the Capacity and Guardianship Law, sec. 13. Until the age of nine, there is no criminal responsibility; between nine and twelve, it must be shown that the child understood that what he was doing constituted a criminal offense. Above the age of twelve, the child is fully responsible for any criminal act (Penal Law, 1977, sec. 13); an amendment to the law fixed the age at thirteen, but it was later restored to twelve. For civil tort liability, the age is twelve (Civil Wrongs Ordinance (New Version), 1968, sec. 9).

183. Primarily in connection with the minimum age for marriage. For details as to the civil and criminal consequences of marriage at a lesser age than the prescribed minimum, *see* the discussion of the Marriage Age Law, 1950, *supra* pp. 1654–1656.

natural guardians of their minor children.[184] It also provides that "the guardianship of the parents includes the duty and the right to care for the needs of minors (including education, vocational and occupational training, and employment); to preserve, manage, and develop the minors' property; to have custody of the minors; to determine the minors' place of residence; and to act on the minors' behalf."[185]

In explaining "the duty and the right to care for the needs of minors," the Minister of Justice stated:[186]

> From the point of view of the law, the essence of parenthood is the obligation to care for the children. As a practical matter, the parent-child relationship essentially imposes obligations on the parents. Parental rights are rights to exercise the authority necessary to discharge their obligations.
>
> These principles have been developed by a long line of Israeli court decisions, and are based upon the principles of Jewish law.

Among the sources cited were the statements in the Talmud[187] that a father is required to have his son ritually circumcised, to redeem his first-born son, to teach his son Torah, to find him a wife, and to teach him a trade and how to swim, and the statement that "anyone who does not teach his son a trade is considered as having taught him to be a bandit," for if one has learned no honest trade from which to make a living, he will turn to robbery. The Minister of Justice also cited Samuel de Medina (sixteenth century, Salonika), who stated that wherever the halakhic rule is that the mother or father has certain rights regarding their children (such as the rule that in the event of divorce, daughters remain with the mother, and sons over the age of six with the father, unless the best interests of the children require a different arrangement),[188] the underlying policy is to benefit the children rather than promote the interests of the parent.[189] Radbaz (David ibn Zimra, sixteenth century, Egypt) succinctly summarized the principle: "It all depends on what the court thinks best for the child."[190] This is precisely the principle adopted by the Woman's Equal Rights Law, and subsequently by the Capacity and Guardianship Law.[191]

184. Sec. 14. *See supra* p. 1656.
185. Sec. 15.
186. Remarks of P. Rosen, 32 *DK* 48 (1962).
187. TB Kiddushin 29a and Rashi, *ad loc.*
188. This distinction was also adopted in the statute; *see* sec. 25. *See also* Nir v. Nir, 35(i) *P.D.* 518, 523 (1980).
189. *Resp. Maharashdam,* EH #123.
190. *Resp. Radbaz,* I, #123.
191. *See* Steiner v. Attorney General, 9 *P.D.* 241, 251 (1954). For detailed discussion, *see* Nagar v. Nagar, 38(i) *P.D.* 365, 392–395 (1981).

The Minister of Justice described the statute's adoption of the approach of Jewish law in the following terms:[192]

> We have rejected in regard to this entire subject the concept, still prevailing in the laws of many nations, that the father or the parents are entitled to exercise dominion over the person, property, and income, of the child, whether in the form of *patria potestas* or in some other manner.

As stated, the law places the duty and the privilege of educating sons and daughters alike on both the father and the mother. A district rabbinical court has ruled that only the father has the duty of educating his son and, therefore, he has the right to determine the form of education to be given. This decision was not appealed to the Rabbinical Court of Appeals, but it may be assumed that if it had been appealed, it would have been reversed. A decision of a Special Tribunal,[193] consisting of two Supreme Court justices and a *dayyan* (judge) of the Rabbinical Court of Appeals, in referring to this decision of the district rabbinical court, noted that in recent generations, in the wake of changing social and educational conditions, Jewish law has obligated both men and women to study Torah and *Halakhah,* and therefore both the father and the mother have the right and the duty to educate their children—daughters as well as sons. The provisions of the Woman's Equal Rights Law and the Capacity and Guardianship Law on this question thus accord with contemporary Jewish law.

Another legal principle, reflected in a number of provisions, confers upon the court supervisory power over all aspects of guardianship, whether natural (*i.e.,* parental) or legal (*i.e.,* established by the court for minors or others lacking full legal capacity). When required for the welfare of the child, the court may appoint a guardian other than the natural parents to take control of the child's person or property.[194] The court supervises the conduct of the guardian, resolves any disagreement on what is in the best interests of the ward, and receives accounts and reports on the state of the ward's property. The Minister of Justice stated that these provisions were based on the ancient Jewish concept that the court is "the father of orphans," which was extended in Jewish law to apply to all those incapable of looking after themselves.[195]

192. Remarks of P. Rosen, 32 *DK* 48 (1962).

193. Nagar v. Nagar, *supra* n. 191. This case is discussed *infra* pp. 1794–1802.

194. This provision is also in the Woman's Equal Rights Law, 1951, sec. 3(b).

195. TB Gittin 37a; *Resp. Radbaz,* I, #263, #360; Rema to Sh. Ar. EH 82:7 and *Pitḥei Teshuvah, ad loc.,* subpar. 7; Gulak, *Yesodei,* III, pp. 146–154; Nagar v. Nagar, *supra* n. 191 at 396.

Still another principle of Jewish law given effect in the Capacity and Guardianship Law is contained in Section 67:

> Anyone acting as a guardian shall have the obligations and responsibilities to his ward which are prescribed by this chapter even if he has not been formally appointed as such, or there was a defect in his appointment, or he has resigned or has been discharged, or his guardianship has terminated.

In explaining this section, the Minister of Justice pointed out:

> For those members of the Knesset who grew up on the Continental codes, this provision has a certain novelty. But we have found a prototype in [*Shulḥan Arukh*] *Ḥoshen Mishpat* 290:24, which states: "A householder who supports minor orphans at their request is bound to comply in all respects with the legal obligations incident to guardianship." The common law has also extensively developed this concept because its practical consequences are so important.[196]

Apart from these substantive matters, the Capacity and Guardianship Law also relied on Jewish law for the administrative agencies established to deal with guardianship. The statute established the office of Administrator General to assist the court in its supervisory function. As the Minister of Justice observed, "This is a well-known and venerable personage in Jewish law, which sentimentally refers to him as 'the father of orphans.'"[197] A *takkanah* enacted by the Council of Lithuania in 1623 provided:

> When a person dies and has not appointed guardians in his lifetime, the court . . . shall accurately inventory the estate and appoint guardians . . . who shall supervise it for the orphans, . . . and . . . [the court] shall appoint auditors to review the accounts of the guardians. Each of the three communities shall appoint three "fathers of orphans" to review annual accountings from the guardians and record in a special book of theirs the yearly accountings for each orphan.[198]

This statute also produced sharp and extensive debate concerning the method of incorporating Jewish law into Knesset legislation. The bill as

196. 32 *DK* 49 (1962).
197. *Id.*
198. S. Dubnow, *Pinkas ha-Medinah o Pinkas Va'ad ha-Kehillot ha-Rashi'ot bi-Medinat Lita* [The Record Book of the Land or the Record Book of the Council of the Principal Communities of Lithuania], Berlin, 1925, p. 9, Enactment # 37.

originally introduced contained a provision that would have deprived the religious courts of jurisdiction over all matters within the purview of the bill except those affecting the law of marriage and divorce.[199] In contrast, the Family Law Amendment (Maintenance) Law, discussed above, had preserved the preexisting jurisdiction of the religious courts.[200] The Capacity and Guardianship Law, like the earlier statute, neither requires the courts to turn to Jewish law to fill a lacuna nor cuts the link with English law established by Article 46 of the Palestine Order in Council. This raised the possibility that the Jewish legal principles relating to this significant area of the law, although incorporated in the statute, would be severed from their sources in Jewish law; and since only the general courts, to the exclusion of the rabbinical courts, would have jurisdiction over cases arising under this law, the Jewish legal sources would play no part in actual decisions concerning legal capacity and guardianship.[201]

In the course of the debate, an argument was made that seemed to imply that Jewish law, as a matter of principle, should not be incorporated into the Knesset's statutes. Section 20 of the bill provided that a minor must obey his parents in all matters within their responsibility and that the parents may take all proper steps for the minor's upbringing. Several Knesset members opposed this section on the ground that the Knesset should not pass legislation interfering with the personal relations between parents and children, and therefore the statute should not provide that children must obey their parents.[202] One member supported this position with the following more fundamental argument:[203]

> A well-known story has it that a certain community once copied the Ten Commandments into its communal register. They were asked: "Why are you copying the Ten Commandments into your register?" They answered: "The people do not obey what is written in the Torah. Maybe they will obey what is written in the communal register."
>
> Do you wish to put the Ten Commandments into the communal register? Will that assure that they will be obeyed? . . . There are things that do not require legislation. With regard to them, we have the Ten Commandments. I would understand if you proposed a sanction—for example, that a child who does not obey his parents will be imprisoned until he obeys. If you do not and cannot propose a sanction, why repeat the Ten Commandments

199. Secs. 76 and 78 of the bill.
200. Sec. 19.
201. *See* remarks of MKs Warhaftig, 32 *DK* 55, 57 (1962), and Kahane, *id.* at 407.
202. *See, e.g.*, remarks of MKs Meridor, *id.* at 51, and Nir (Rafalkes), *id.* at 54.
203. Remarks of MK Warhaftig, *id.* at 56.

> and, thereby, if you will forgive me [for saying this], reduce this eternal commandment from its lofty height to the level of a transient statute?

This argument, with its less than apt analogy, implies that it is undesirable for Knesset legislation to incorporate Jewish legal principles, because such incorporation diminishes the value of those principles by changing their *Grundnorm* from divine precept to human enactment. Others sharply disagreed with this view, because it denies all possibility of the incorporation of Jewish law into Knesset legislation. Even if a statute requires the courts to turn to Jewish law to construe the statute, this argument would still contend that the status of Jewish law is being diminished by the very fact that this requirement, from the standpoint of the legal system of the State, derives its force from the Knesset. Acceptance of this argument stands in direct contradiction to the aim of the Knesset to incorporate Jewish spiritual and legal values into its legislation.[204] Indeed, one Knesset member rejected this argument specifically on the basis of Jewish spiritual values. He defended the section requiring children to obey their parents and even advocated a direct reference to the Fifth Commandment,[205] since this would "express a link with the commandment to honor one's parents. . . . This link should be explicit in the statute to indicate the ancient and hallowed source of the provision in Jewish thought. . . . In short, we should identify the basis on which we have rested this law and its provisions."[206]

The argument over this peripheral point might have diverted attention from the main question, namely, the need to sever the link between English law and an Israeli statute based on Jewish legal principles, and to direct the courts to turn to Jewish law in case of a lacuna.[207] However, the Knesset

204. *See, e.g.*, remarks of MKs Ẓadok, *id.* at 156; Klinghoffer, *id.* at 158–159; Rosen, *id.* at 413; Korn, *id.* at 292–293.

205. The final text of the statute (sec. 16), while not referring to the commandment, echoes its language: "A minor, duly honoring his father and mother, shall obey his parents in all matters within the scope of their parental responsibilities." *See* 36 *DK* 1123–1124 (1962).

206. Remarks of MK Unna, 34 *DK* 3078, 3086 (1962). This debate is especially significant in regard to the basic question of the incorporation of Jewish law into the law of the State, as to which *see infra* pp. 1906–1917.

207. It may be assumed that the failure to sever the link with English law was the decisive factor in the far-reaching assertion of MK Warhaftig that the value of a halakhic principle is diminished when it is adopted as a legal norm by the Knesset. He generally fought for the incorporation of Jewish law into Knesset legislation, and on one occasion even relied on the duty to respect one's parents contained in the Fifth Commandment as the basis for the inclusion in legislation of a provision obligating an adopted child to support his natural parents. 26 *DK* 1123–1124 (1959). *See* 32 *DK* 160 (1962) for MK Gross's remarks interpreting in this way the statement of MK Warhaftig concerning the Capacity and Guardianship Law. Prof. Tedeschi's criticism ("Mashber ha-Mishpaḥah va-Ḥasidei ha-Masoret"

did manage to address this latter question. A number of members advocated that at least the formal link to English law should be explicitly severed.[208] As to a specific directive to the courts to construe the statute by referring to Jewish law, the Minister of Justice confined himself to expressing the hope that "the Israeli courts will surely interpret the law according to its own terms and in the light of the sources from which it was derived. We know that in all matters of personal status, the courts in fact will be governed by Jewish law."[209] However, this hope has not always been realized.[210]

The statute as finally enacted did not include a provision, advocated by most of those who participated in the debate during the first reading, that would have severed the formal link to English law. On the other hand, the provision in the bill denying jurisdiction to the religious courts was also not adopted. Instead, the law provides that it shall "neither add to nor derogate from the jurisdiction of the religious courts; where a religious court has jurisdiction, any provision of this law which refers to a court . . . shall be deemed to refer to a religious court."[211]

(5) The Succession Law. (a) *Provisions Generally Incorporating Jewish Law.* An excellent example of the incorporation of principles of Jewish law into the law of the State is one of the most comprehensive statutes ever passed by the Knesset, the Succession Law, 1965. A Draft Succession Bill was first presented by the Ministry of Justice for public consideration in

---

[The Crisis in Family Life and the Devotees of Tradition], *Studies in Memory of Avraham Rosenthal,* Jerusalem, 1964, pp. 282, 290) of "the extreme stand of the devout," on the basis of Warhaftig's statement, is exaggerated and ignores the main problems arising out of: (a) formally linking to English law a statute based essentially on Jewish law, and (b) severing the principles of Jewish law permeating the statute from the Jewish legal sources. For a detailed discussion of the Knesset debate on the matter, *see* Elon, *Ḥakikah,* pp. 62–68. As to the question of the change of the *Grundnorm* when a rule of Jewish law is adopted as a law of the Knesset, *see supra* p. 234 n. 24; *infra* pp. 1907–1908.

208. Remarks of MKs Klinghoffer, Rosen, Korn, and Bar Rav Hai, 32 *DK* 173 (1962); remarks of MK Uziel, *id.* at 190.

209. Remarks of MK Rosen, *id.* at 413.

210. *Cf.* Koenig v. Cohen, 36(iii) *P.D.* 701 (1981), for a discussion of the similar question of the incorporation into Israeli law of the form of testamentary disposition known as the will of a *shekhiv me-ra.* The *Koenig* case is discussed *infra* pp. 1875–1884.

211. Sec. 79. Minister of Justice Dov Joseph had already announced this change in his summation of the debate on the first reading of the bill; *see* 32 *DK* 552 (1962). MKs Klinghoffer and Nir proposed an amendment to the section, according to which the rabbinical courts would retain their jurisdiction over the matters covered by the statute, but would be obligated to apply the statutory provisions (34 *DK* 3140 (1962)). They argued in support of the amendment (*id.* at 3095) that it would be similar to the provisions of the Woman's Equal Rights Law and the Adoption Law that require the religious courts to apply those statutes. The Knesset rejected the amendment; *see id.* at 3096. As to the interpretation of sec. 79, *see* Omri v. Zouavi, 39(ii) *P.D.* 113 (1985).

1952, and the Succession Law Bill was introduced in the Knesset by the Government in 1958. It received a first reading in that year, but the Legislative Committee was unable to complete its deliberations before the end of the Third Knesset, and the bill was reintroduced in the Fourth Knesset in 1960. Once again, consideration of the bill was not completed during the life of the Fourth Knesset, and the bill was reintroduced in the Fifth Knesset at the end of 1961 and eventually passed its second and third readings early in 1965. During all this time, while the bill was intensely debated both in the Knesset and by the general public, one of the main points of contention involved the problem of incorporating Jewish law in the statute.

As already indicated, the Introduction to the 1952 bill set out the basic legislative guidelines for this bill and for Israeli civil legislation generally.[212] The objective of making the law independent of any foreign legal system was fully expressed in a section entitled "Self-Sufficiency of this Law," which reads: "In matters of succession, Article 46 of the Palestine Order in Council, 1922–1947, shall not apply."[213] As will be recalled, the guidelines also prescribed an eclectic approach pursuant to which the statute drew on a variety of sources—the existing legal and factual situation in Israel, Jewish law, and the laws of other countries—with Jewish law being given the status of "the primary but not the sole or binding source."

How successful was the Succession Law in achieving its objectives? Problems of inheritance occupy a prominent place in the social and economic philosophy of all legal systems and are particularly important in Jewish jurisprudence, which views the inheritance of material possessions as a reflection of the unbroken continuity of the generations that is independent of, and in fact transcends, the personal wishes of the deceased.[214]

According to Jewish law, the heirs of a decedent are: (1) his issue,[215] and if none, then (2) his father[216] and his father's issue, and if none, then

212. *See supra* pp. 1626–1627.

213. Sec. 151 of the bill; sec. 150 of the statute as enacted.

214. According to Maimonides, one is not free to bequeath one's property as one chooses. *MT,* Naḥalot 6:1; similarly Sh. Ar. ḤM 281:1. *See also supra* p. 127 n. 145.

215. According to the Torah (Numbers 27:8; *see* M Bava Batra 8:2), a daughter does not inherit when there are sons. By rabbinic legislation, a daughter is entitled to support out of the estate of her father, and if the estate is small, "the daughters receive support and the sons go begging" (M Ketubbot 4:11, 13:3). Over the course of time, various *takkanot* were enacted which gave a daughter a share in her father's estate; some post-Talmudic enactments even provided that an unmarried daughter should share in the estate equally with sons. For detailed discussion, *see supra* pp. 575–580, 655–656, 828–829, 842–846, and p. 152 n. 250 (concerning *Resp. Tashbeẓ,* III, #190); *see also* Elon, *Yiḥudah Shel Halakhah,* pp. 15, 29–31, concerning the enactments of the Moroccan halakhic authorities on the right of a daughter to inherit.

216. According to Jewish law, a mother does not inherit from her children (Maimonides, *MT,* Naḥalot 1:6; Sh. Ar. ḤM 276:4). However, as early as the thirteenth century,

(3) his grandfather and his grandfather's issue. "In this way, it [the line of succession] ascends to the most remote ancestor; there can therefore be no Jew who has no heirs."[217]

Jewish law also permits free disposition of property in a will, even if the result is that nothing remains for the heirs; but such a disposition, although testamentary in effect, is regarded by the law as in the nature of a gift *inter vivos* (a lifetime gift). Thus, an heir may not be expressly disinherited—though disinheritance may be the practical effect—and the recipient of the property is not termed an heir but a donee of the gift.[218] Still, despite the legality and efficacy of this form of testamentary disposition, the order of intestate succession as prescribed by law is the norm and is preferable: "When a person disinherits his sons and bequeaths his property to others, his act is legally effective, but the Sages are displeased with him." The sole exception, according to Rabban Simeon b. Gamaliel, is that "if the sons were not conducting themselves properly, his act is praiseworthy [lit. he should be remembered for good]."[219]

A number of legal consequences follow from this stance of Jewish law with regard to inheritance. The following discussion notes the most important ones relevant to the Succession Law as enacted by the Knesset. Upon the decedent's death, the estate devolves automatically on the heirs. Consequently, the heirs cannot disclaim their inheritance (although they, like

---

enactments were adopted in Spanish communities that gave a mother the right to inherit from her children in certain circumstances. *See supra* pp. 840–841.

217. Maimonides, *MT*, Naḥalot 1:3; Sh. Ar. ḤM 276:1.

218. Sh. Ar. ḤM 253:2, 281:1,7. This distinction is also reflected in the organization of the various rules in the codificatory literature. The order of succession in Maimonides' *Mishneh Torah* appears in *Hilkhot Naḥalot* [Laws of Inheritance]; testamentary dispositions are treated in *Hilkhot Zekhiyyah u-Mattanah* [Laws of Entitlement and Gifts], chs. 8–12. Similarly, in *Tur* and Sh. Ar. ḤM, succession is treated in chs. 276–289, testamentary disposition by a person in good health is dealt with in chs. 241–249, and the will of a *shekhiv me-ra* is discussed in chs. 250–258. *See also Resp. Asheri* 55:9 in regard to Asheri's dispute with Rabbi Israel as to whether the phrase in a *takkanah* of Toledo (Spain)—"one who takes by inheritance" (*ha-zokheh bi-yerushah*)—also includes a legatee under a will.

219. M Bava Batra 8:5. *See* Rema to Sh. Ar. ḤM 282:1: "Where a person directs by will that his property be distributed in the best possible manner, the property is to be given to his heirs, for nothing is better than this." *Cf.* the ancient "Doctrine of Worthier Title" in English property law. Pursuant to this doctrine, where the same quality and quantity of estate is devised that the devisee would have acquired by descent, the title passes by descent—"the worthier title"—and not by "purchase" (*i.e.*, the devise). *See* 2 Blackstone, *Commentaries*, 241–242. The doctrine was abolished in England in 1833 by the Statute of 3 and 4 William IV, ch. 106, sec. 3. The purpose of the English doctrine was to protect creditors, whereas the preference for intestate succession in Jewish law reflects the high value placed on family and generational continuity. *See also supra* pp. 151–154; and *see* Gulak, *Yesodei*, III, pp. 71–75, 79–81, for the essential difference between the Jewish and Roman law of succession.

any other owner of property, may abandon it).[220] Anyone who claims under a will or makes any other claim to the estate has the burden of proving his claim.[221] The heirs include those born out of wedlock and those born of a prohibited marriage (such as the marriage of a brother and sister) or an adulterous union. In the latter two instances the child is a *mamzer,* but for purposes of inheritance he is considered the child of the decedent, and has the full rights of an heir.[222] Likewise, an heir who is a "transgressor," or otherwise does not conduct himself properly, also inherits unless, as Rabban Simeon b. Gamaliel held was praiseworthy, the decedent previously bequeathed his property to someone else. This is true even of an apostate, who inherits from his Jewish relatives on the principle that "a Jew—even one who has sinned—is nevertheless still a Jew." But "if the court sees fit to deprive him of the property and penalize him by disinheriting him in order not to strengthen the hands of the wicked, it may do so. If he has children who have remained in the Jewish fold, the inheritance of their apostate father should be given to them. This is always the custom in the West."[223] Others take the view that the apostate's share is held by the court, to be given to him if he returns to Judaism.[224]

In many respects, the Succession Law gives expression to the Jewish view of the continuity of the generations; this is especially demonstrated by the evolution of the final text of the statute. Section 1 provides: "Upon death, a person's estate passes to his heirs."[225] The first clause of Section 2 as originally drafted was in conflict with Jewish law, while the second part agreed with it. The original draft of Section 2 read: "Heirs may inherit pursuant to law or under a will; to the extent that inheritance is not governed by a will, it is prescribed by law." The second clause accorded with the notion of the priority of intestate over testate succession,[226] but the first clause used the term "heir" equally for heirs who take in intestacy and

220. Geonic responsum quoted in *Bet Yosef* to *Tur* ḤM 278:1: "From the death of the decedent, all property is vested in the heir even if it is not in his possession." *Sema* to Sh. Ar., *ad loc.*, subpar. 27, states that an heir cannot disclaim his inheritance "but may only, by appropriate declaration, completely abandon it." *See also* Gulak, *Yesodei,* III, pp. 77–79.

221. Sh. Ar. ḤM 246:5, 251:2, EH 93:2.

222. Maimonides, *MT,* Naḥalot 1:7; Sh. Ar. ḤM 276:6. *See also supra* p. 827 n. 178.

223. Maimonides, *MT,* Naḥalot 6:12; Sh. Ar. ḤM 283:2.

224. Rema to Sh. Ar. ḤM 283:2.

225. This contrasts with English law, pursuant to which the estate vests in the executor or administrator, the personal representative of the decedent, until it is distributed to those entitled. *See* M. Elon, "Ha-Yesh li-Menahel ha-Izavon Kinyan Bo" [Does the Administrator Have a Property Right in the Assets of the Estate?], *Ha-Praklit,* XI (1955), pp. 205ff.

226. In this, it diverged from English and Roman law. *See* Draft Succession Bill, 1952, published by the Israeli Ministry of Justice, pp. 39–40.

legatees under a will. The Explanatory Notes to the bill explicitly pointed out that this usage is contrary to Jewish law.[227]

In the final version, after extensive debate in the Legislative Committee, the first clause was changed to accord with Jewish law. This clause now reads: "Those who inherit include the heirs, who inherit pursuant to law, and the legatees, who take under a will." The difference is not only semantic; it points up the basic distinction, maintained throughout the statute, between succession, on the one hand, and entitlement under a will, on the other.[228] Again, Section 3(c)[229] adopts the rule that "for the purpose of succession it is immaterial whether a child was born out of wedlock." The Explanatory Notes emphasize the Jewish legal sources of this principle:

> We know of no legal system that treats "legitimate" and "illegitimate" children with such complete equality as does Jewish law. All other legal systems—even the most modern and progressive in this respect, such as the Italian Law of 1962 or the Soviet Law—discriminate in regard to inheritance against children born out of wedlock. . . . Our bill here gives new life to the Jewish law.[230]

Section 50 of the bill, as originally drafted, which provided that "the testator may disinherit anyone (except the State) entitled to inherit pursuant to law," was deleted from the final version of the bill. This reflects to a certain extent the position of Jewish law, which does not permit an heir to be expressly disinherited,[231] although there is no provision in the statute directly prohibiting such disinheritance.[232]

227. *Id.* at 39.

228. *Compare, e.g.*, secs. 10, 11, and 17, which deal with intestate succession, where the inheritor is called an "heir," *with* secs. 49–52, where a legatee under a will is called "one who takes [*zokheh*, lit. "is entitled"] under a will." *Compare also* sec. 55 of the 1958 bill (which refers to one who takes under a will as an "heir") *with* its parallel, sec. 49 of the final version.

229. Succession Bill, 1958 (Bill No. 344), sec. 18.

230. Explanatory Notes to the Draft Succession Bill, 1952, pp. 42–43. *See also* 24 *DK* 2105 (1958) for the remarks of Minister of Justice P. Rosen and other MKs during the debate on the first reading of the bill.

231. M Bava Batra 8:5: "If one says . . . 'So-and-so, my son, shall not inherit with his brothers,' he has said nothing [*i.e.*, his statement is ineffective], since he has stipulated out of a law contained in the Torah. . . . If one apportions his property to his sons and gives more to one than to another . . . , if he says [it should be] 'by inheritance,' he has said nothing . . . , but if [he states that it is conveyed] 'as a gift,' his words are effective."

232. *See also* the explanation for this deletion given by the chairman of the Legislative Committee, MK Unna, when he brought the bill up for second and third readings. 42 *DK* 954 (1965).

In contrast to these provisions, there are a number of others that are not in accord with the approach of Jewish law. The order of intestate succession prescribed by the original bill was: children and their issue; parents and their issue; grandparents and their issue; the decedent's spouse;[233] and the State.[234] Terminating the line of succession at the grandparents and making the State a legal heir are contrary to Jewish law, which "ascends to the most remote ancestor; there can therefore be no Jew who has no heirs." Under Jewish law, if no heir is found, the estate passes into the control of the court until such time as it is established who is the proper heir.[235] Because such a provision may make it difficult to wind up the estate within a reasonable time, it was suggested that if no heirs can be found up to the line of the grandparents, the State should become trustee of the estate for a prescribed time, and if no other heirs are found within that time, the estate would then escheat to the State.[236] This proposal failed.

An alternative proposal would have ended the order of succession at the line of the grandparents, but instead of the State's being referred to as a "legal heir," the State would be described in the law as "taking" the estate. This proposal, too, was defeated.[237] The final text of the statute differs from the original bill only in that the State is not listed among the legal heirs at the beginning of the chapter on intestate succession, but at the end of that

233. In the statute as enacted (sec. 10), the spouse is given priority over the children. *See* MK Unna's explanation of his proposal, made at the second and third readings, to restore the previous order of priority; 42 *DK* 964 (1965). As to the position of Jewish law regarding inheritance by a spouse, *see* the discussion *infra* pp. 1678–1679.

234. Succession Bill, 1958, sec. 13.

235. *See* Gulak, *Yesodei,* III, p. 84.

236. Proposal by MK Warhaftig, 28 *DK* 466 (1960).

237. This proposal was made by MK Unna at the second and third readings. His argument, 42 *DK* 972 (1965), was as follows:

> There is here no difference in the practical outcome, but as a matter of principle I do not believe that the State should be described as an heir. The concept of "succession" has precise meaning and refers to the link between the generations. . . . Even if we include a spouse, "succession" connotes more than pecuniary relationship and a legal basis for the acquisition of property; it also connotes the personal connection between members of a family. In my opinion, it is not proper for the State to be referred to as a legal heir.

MK Azanyah, on behalf of the Legislative Committee, replied (*id.* at 974) that under MK Unna's proposal the State might not be able to obtain the property of an estate of an Israeli citizen who lived abroad in a country whose law provides that the estate passes only to a legal heir. MK Unna expressed a strong doubt that any country would refuse to transfer the estate to the State of Israel on the basis of a semantic distinction, in view of the principles of comity and reciprocity between states. Even if such a thing were to happen, "we should not yield on a matter of principle for the sake of some [practical] advantage which may never come about" (*id.* at 972).

chapter it is provided that "if there is no heir under Sections 10 through 16, the State shall inherit as a legal heir."[238]

Another section of the statute prohibits inheritance by anyone who has been convicted of intentionally causing or attempting to cause the death of the decedent or who has been convicted of concealing, destroying, or forging the last will of the decedent, or making a claim on the basis of a forged will.[239] The Explanatory Notes state that the prohibition of inheritance on the ground that the heir caused or attempted to cause the decedent's death "is based on the prophet's [Elijah's] question [to Ahab in the matter of Naboth's vineyard]: 'Would you murder and take possession too?' (I Kings 21:19). This rebuke, however, apparently did not give rise in Jewish law to a rule prohibiting a murderer from inheriting from his victim."[240] It seems that at least some halakhic authorities have regarded it appropriate to enact a *takkanah* to disinherit the murderer.[241] On the other hand, that part of the section which prohibited inheritance by those convicted of other crimes, even as grave as forging the will, is clearly inconsistent with Jewish law, which differentiates between the penalty a person is to suffer for his criminal acts and his natural right to inherit, which cannot and should not be curtailed.[242]

238. Sec. 17. The general list of heirs appears in sec. 10. Another addition in the final version is that the State must use the estate for "purposes of education, science, health, and welfare."

239. Sec. 5. In the final version of the statute, in contrast to the 1958 bill, a provision was added to the effect that if the decedent forgives an heir who has been convicted of attempting to murder him, that heir regains his right of inheritance. A similar provision was contained in the 1952 bill.

240. Draft Succession Bill, 1952, p. 44.

241. Maimonides, *MT*, Mamrim 7:14 states: "A rebellious son is like any other person executed by the court in that his property passes to his heirs. Even though it was his father's complaint that led him to be executed, he [the father] inherits all his property." Radbaz, *ad loc.*, queried whether the second sentence of Maimonides' rule is not superfluous, since the father would clearly inherit under the rule stated in the first sentence. Radbaz concluded that the second sentence was not superfluous. He reasoned that the son would not have been convicted as a rebellious son if the father had forgiven him (*id.* 7:10), and one might therefore suspect that the father made the complaint because he desired his son's property and that, in order to obviate this possibility, "the Sages should . . . enact that he does not inherit. Therefore, he [Maimonides] made clear that we do not entertain this suspicion, and the father inherits." This implies that an enactment should be adopted to the effect that if such a suspicion is in fact well grounded, the murderer shall not inherit.

242. Some members of the Knesset opposed the provision that disqualifies an heir who has committed forgery; they argued that the criminal offense should be regarded as separate and distinct from the right to inherit; *see* remarks of MKs Edelson, 28 *DK* 441 (1960) and 32 *DK* 959 (1962), and Zimmerman, 28 *DK* 478 (1960). It should be noted that the final version of the statute, in contrast to the 1958 bill, mitigated the discrepancy with Jewish law by providing (sec. 14) that the child or relative of the disqualified heir stands in

Several other important provisions of the Succession Law exemplify an interesting method of incorporating principles of Jewish law. The provisions for maintenance out of the estate, to which an entire chapter of the statute is devoted, constitute an instructive example.[243]

The law of inheritance, testate and intestate alike, is beset by a basic problem with which various legal systems have struggled: how to assure the subsistence of the decedent's family—his wife, children, and parents—who were dependent on the decedent during his lifetime and who after his death are left with insufficient support or none at all. Their legally prescribed share in the estate is not always enough for their needs; freedom of testation—which, in practical effect, also exists in Jewish law—enables the decedent to transfer his property to others and thus leave either some or all of his dependents without support.

Many solve the problem by setting up a "reserved portion," sometimes called "statutory share" or *Pflichtteil,* whereby certain portions of the estate are reserved for family dependents and are beyond the power of testamentary disposition. The source of this device, used in Continental law and other legal systems, is Roman law. However, this solution is defective in that the size of the reserved portion is fixed in advance and may not be commensurate with the actual needs of the dependent relatives. Another method of dealing with this problem, which was adopted in 1900 in Australia and subsequently in England and elsewhere, is the "family provision" allowance, whereby the court may grant to the dependents appropriate sums out of the estate in those cases where the testator has not made sufficient provision for their maintenance. Under both of these methods, the proportionate shares of the estate provided for in a will may be changed, but neither of these methods affects the shares prescribed by law for the distribution of intestate property.[244]

Jewish law solved this problem in an instructive manner, using the "family provision" approach, and the Succession Law followed Jewish law in this respect. On this point the Explanatory Notes commented:

---

the heir's place. (Such a provision was also included in the 1952 draft.) *Cf.* the rule in Jewish law, stated *supra* p. 1674, that the court may disqualify an apostate heir from inheriting, and give the inheritance to the apostate's son, the grandson of the decedent.

243. Chapter 4, secs. 56–65.

244. In 1951, in England, a special commission recommended that allowances also be given out of the part of an estate that passes by intestacy. *See* Explanatory Notes to the Draft Succession Bill, 1952, p. 100. Similarly, several legal systems have recently provided that minor children are entitled to support from the entire estate, whether passing by will or by intestacy. *See* Explanatory Notes, *id.*

> The main source of our proposal is Jewish law. As far as we know, no legal system today is comparable to Jewish law in developing and perfecting the concept that the right to receive the assets of an estate is subordinate to the needs of the decedent's dependents. We have drawn from Jewish law, more than from any other source, the elements of this chapter, which is, as it were, the "center of gravity" of the entire statute. The law as to maintenance out of the estate in special measure exemplifies the breathing of new life into Jewish law and incorporating that law into the law of the State of Israel.[245]

This is an illuminating example of the integration of a principle of Jewish law into an existing legal framework that differs from that of Jewish law. Jewish law provides for maintenance for a widow, and for a daughter when she does not inherit because there is a son. The widow is not an heir of her husband but, instead, all her needs—food, shelter, etc.—are provided for out of the estate during her widowhood;[246] and the daughter is maintained out of the estate until she attains her majority or is married.[247] This right of the widow and daughter is without limit; even where the estate has only enough assets for their maintenance, the assets must be used for that purpose until the estate is exhausted.[248] As the Mishnah graphically states: "If one dies and leaves sons and daughters, and the estate is substantial, the sons inherit and the daughters receive support. If the estate is small, the daughters receive support and the sons go begging."[249]

The Succession Law incorporates the principle of maintenance out of the estate not only for a widow but also for a widower, and not only for daughters but also for sons; maintenance is payable when any of them are in need of support and no other means of providing for them are available.[250] This is the essence of the concept of maintenance under Jewish law. Under the statute, children are entitled to maintenance up to the age of eighteen, and in special circumstances up to twenty-three years of age; invalids are entitled for the duration of their infirmity; and entitlement to maintenance was broadened to include parents for their entire lives, to the

245. Draft Succession Bill, 1952, p. 101. *See also* the 1958 Bill (No. 344), p. 235, and the Minister of Justice's opening remarks and his reply at the bill's first reading, 24 *DK* 2106, 2357 (1958), and 28 *DK* 356 (1960).

246. TB Ketubbot 52b; Sh. Ar. EH chs. 93–94.

247. TB Ketubbot 52b; Sh. Ar. EH ch. 112.

248. *See* Gulak, *Yesodei,* III, pp. 88–90.

249. M Ketubbot 13:3; Bava Batra 9:1. It is this law that provoked the reaction of the Sage Admon: "Should I lose out because I am male?" (*id.*). The law, however, did not follow his view. *See* Sh. Ar. EH 112:11 and *supra* n. 215.

250. *See* sec. 56, which defines who is in need of support, and sec. 59, which establishes the manner in which the entitlement to maintenance is adjudicated and the amount is determined.

extent that they were dependent on the decedent immediately before his death.[251] The statute voids any clause in a will that denies or limits the right to maintenance.[252] In this respect, it directly follows the rule of Jewish law: "If one says at the time of his death, 'Do not support my widow out of my assets,' his statement is disregarded. . . . 'Do not support my daughters out of my assets,' his statement is disregarded."[253]

A further example of the incorporation of Jewish law relates to the complex problem of "commorientes," or simultaneous deaths in an accident where the precise determination of the rights of the respective heirs is impossible because it is unknown who died first. The bill[254] proposed what was stated in the Explanatory Notes to be a solution based on various Continental law systems:[255] "If two or more persons die and it is not established who died first, the rights in their estates shall be determined as if each decedent was the last to die, but his estate shall not be augmented by reason of the death of any of the others." During the debate, a proposal was made to solve this problem on the basis of Jewish law, which applies two general principles: (1) where, as between two claimants to the inheritance, one is an heir irrespective of who died first (the definite heir) and the only question is the amount he takes, and the other becomes an heir only in the event of one death having occurred first (the doubtful heir), the definite heir takes all; and (2) where both claimants are doubtful heirs and one of them is a blood relative of the decedent, while the other is not but has become entitled to an inheritance through the spouse of the decedent, the blood relative has priority.[256] This solution does not purport to determine

251. Sec. 57. The reason given for including parents is: "The family structure in the country, as it is today after the Holocaust and in the period of the Ingathering of the Exiles, requires and justifies the inclusion of parents together with children and spouses." Draft Succession Bill, 1952, p. 101.

252. Sec. 65.

253. Sh. Ar. EH 93:3, 112:10. During the debate, it was argued that the Succession Law's provision for maintenance is contrary to Jewish law in that (a) it applies not only to a widow but also to a widower, (b) it applies not only to daughters but also to sons, and (c) unlike Jewish law, this provision does not end the right to support at adolescence or marriage, but rather at the age of eighteen or twenty-three. *See* remarks of MKs Ben Meir, 24 *DK* 2192 (1958); Nissim, 28 *DK* 442 (1960); Nurock, 32 *DK* 962 (1962); and Porush, 42 *DK* 1005 (1965). This argument is excessively formalistic and would negate all possibility of incorporating principles of Jewish law into Israeli law. It is submitted that the statute correctly incorporates the central concept of Jewish law concerning maintenance out of the estate for whoever is in need of it, together with the most significant provisions filling out the details. The changes that have been noted are consistent with the central concept as adapted to present-day social and economic conditions; they are not contrary to the basic position of Jewish law. *See also* Draft Succession Bill, 1952, p. 101; *infra* n. 263.

254. Succession Bill, 1958 (Bill No. 334), sec. 9.

255. Draft Succession Bill, 1952, pp. 48–49.

256. *See* Maimonides, *MT,* Naḥalot 5:5–9; *Tur* and Sh. Ar. EH 163:4–8, ḤM 280:10–12.

who died first—a determination which is impossible to make and which is the weakness in the solutions of other legal systems—but sets up an order of priorities among the claimants. The substance and even the phraseology of Jewish law on this issue was unanimously accepted by the Knesset, with only minor changes to fit into the general structure of the Succession Law.[257]

Still another example of the incorporation of Jewish law into the statute relates to the law of wills. As described above, while Jewish law regards the order of succession in intestacy as the preferred order of devolution of property on death, it nevertheless accords complete freedom of testation,

---

The Uniform Simultaneous Death Act in the United States provides that, with stated exceptions, "Where title to property or its devolution depends on priority of death and there is no sufficient evidence that the persons have died otherwise than simultaneously, the property of each person shall be disposed of as if he had survived." The exceptions relate to (1) when two or more beneficiaries are designated to take successively because of survivorship under another person's disposition of property, in which case "the property disposed of shall be divided into as many equal portions as there are successive beneficiaries, and these portions shall be distributed to those who would have taken in the event that each designated beneficiary had survived"; (2) when property is held in joint tenancy, in which case the fractional share of each tenant is distributed as if that tenant had survived; and (3) when the property involved is life insurance, in which case the proceeds of the policy are distributed as if the insured survived the beneficiary. The Uniform Act does not apply where a will, *inter vivos* trust, deed, or contract of insurance provides for distribution different than that provided by the Act.

American statutes also frequently provide that an heir or beneficiary who fails to survive the decedent for a stated number of days is considered to have predeceased the decedent; the burden of proving the survivorship for the required length of time is on those who claim through the heir or beneficiary, and in case of failure of such proof, the heir or beneficiary will be considered not to have met the survival requirement. *See, e.g.,* Uniform Probate Code, sec. 2–104.

For the position of Jewish law as well as that of other legal systems, *see* M. Silberg, *Ha-Ma'amad ha-Ishi be-Yisra'el* [Personal Status in Israel], Jerusalem, 1958, pp. 285–322; and *see id.* at 314, 321–322, as to the superiority of the solution reached under Jewish law.

257. Section 9 of the Succession Law reads as follows:

> (a) If two or more people die, and it is not known who died first, the rights in the estate of each of them shall be determined as follows:
>
> (1) If one of the claimants is a definite heir and the other is a doubtful heir, the definite heir shall have priority.
>
> (2) If both claimants are doubtful heirs, the claimant who is a spouse or blood relative of the decedent shall have priority.
>
> (3) In the absence of a will, the estate shall be divided among other claimants of equal rank according to the principles governing succession pursuant to law.
>
> (b) For purposes of this section, a "definite heir" is one who would be an heir irrespective of which decedent was the first to die; a "doubtful heir" is one who would be an heir only if [a particular] one of the decedents was the first to die.

See the comments of MK Unna during the debate on the second and third readings of the bill, 42 *DK* 953 (1965). For details of the debate in committee, *see* M. Unna, *Ha-Mishpat ha-Ivri be-Ḥakikat ha-Keneset* [Jewish Law in Knesset Legislation], Lecture delivered at Bar-Ilan University (undated), p. 13. *See also* U. Yadin, "The Law of Succession and Other Steps towards a Civil Code," *Scripta Hierosolymitana,* XVI (1966), pp. 115–116.

provided the testator does not purport to designate his legatees as "heirs" but disposes of his property by way of "gift." This conceptual framework creates difficulty, since a gift is a bilateral transaction that must be consummated during the life of the donor—something not always consistent with the testator's desires. Jewish law gradually evolved various means by which an essentially testamentary disposition could satisfy the necessary legal requirements of a gift but at the same time retain ownership (or at least possession) in the testator during his life, include after-acquired assets as part of the property passing to the designated beneficiaries at the testator's death, and otherwise partake of the nature of a will. A "will" of this kind is called *mattenat bari* (the gift of a healthy person), and one of the usual modes of acquisition (*kinyan*) is necessary to render it effective.

Jewish law also provides for another kind of will, similar in character to wills in other legal systems, which takes effect only upon death. This is the *mattenat shekhiv me-ra, i.e.,* the will of "a sick person who is totally infirm because of his sickness and who cannot walk out of his house to the market-place and is bedridden."[258] Such a will need not be in writing and "does not require any act of acquisition (*kinyan*), for the words of a *shekhiv me-ra* are as though written and delivered."[259] This also applies to the will of a "testator on the brink of death" (*meẓavveh meḥamat mitah*), *i.e.,* anyone who is in imminent danger of death, such as "one who sets out on a sea voyage, or goes with a caravan into the desert, or is condemned to death, or has a life-threatening illness."[260] If the testator completely recovers from his sickness or the danger passes, the will becomes ineffective.[261]

Among the four forms of will provided for in the Succession Law is the *mattenat shekhiv me-ra.* The statutory provision incorporates both the substance and the language of Jewish law. Section 23, which is entitled "Oral Will," reads as follows:

> (a) A person on his deathbed (*shekhiv me-ra*) or one who, under the circumstances, reasonably apprehends imminent death may make an oral will in the presence of two witnesses who understand his language.
>
> (b) The testator's declaration, with a notation of the date and the circumstances under which the will was made, shall be recorded in a memorandum which the two witnesses shall sign and file in a district court; the memorandum shall be made, signed, and filed as soon as practicable.

258. Maimonides, *MT,* Zekhiyyah u-Mattanah 8:2; Sh. Ar. ḤM 250:5.
259. Maimonides, *supra* n. 258; Sh. Ar. ḤM 250:1.
260. Maimonides, *MT,* Zekhiyyah u-Mattanah 8:24; Sh. Ar. ḤM 250:8.
261. Maimonides, *MT,* Zekhiyyah u-Mattanah 8:25–26; Sh. Ar. ḤM 250:2: "If he does not recover completely, but goes from sickness to sickness [and then dies], his gift is valid so long as he had not walked in the market place (albeit with the aid of a walking stick), even if he had been walking about in his home with a cane."

(c) An oral will becomes void one month after the circumstances that warranted its making have ceased to exist, provided the testator is still alive.[262]

These provisions constitute a full adoption of Jewish law with respect to permissible oral wills: nomenclature (*shekhiv me-ra* and *meẓavveh meḥamat mitah*), force and effect, procedures to be followed, and automatic lapse after a specified period.[263] However, subsequently, various opinions were expressed in the Supreme Court of Israel regarding the nature and the scope of the incorporation of the Jewish law on the will of a *shekhiv me-ra*. These opinions are discussed later.[264]

(b) *Provisions Not in Accord with Jewish Law.* A number of provisions of the Succession Law in addition to those already discussed did not adopt the position of Jewish law. Such divergences from Jewish law are of two types. The first type involves rules that are undoubtedly basic to Jewish succession law, such as: the right of the first-born son to a double share; the rule that where there is a son, a daughter does not inherit but is entitled to maintenance; the rule that a wife does not inherit from her husband but is entitled to maintenance; and the rule that a mother does not inherit from her sons. As indicated above, the Succession Law does not recognize any right of primogeniture, and treats equally daughters and sons, wives and husbands, and mothers and fathers. Indeed, a number of Knesset members were opposed to those sections as being contrary to Jewish law.[265] However, an honest advocate of the position that Jewish law should be incorporated in Knesset legislation to the extent that Jewish law accords with the societal circumstances and the outlook of the vast majority of the people of Israel, including most of the religious population itself, cannot argue in good faith that these rules of Jewish law should have been incorporated in the Succession Law.

262. In the 1952 draft bill and in the 1958 bill (sec. 28), the Hebrew term *shekhiv me-ra* does not appear; the bills mention only "one who apprehends imminent death."

263. Some Knesset members asserted that subsection (c) varied from Jewish law in specifying one month as the period which must elapse before the will becomes void, whereas Jewish law provides that the will becomes void when there is no longer any danger of death or when the testator has recovered. *See* the remarks of MKs Lewin, 24 *DK* 2182 (1958), and Nurock, 32 *DK* 962 (1962). However, this would seem to be another example of unjustified formalistic criticism of the method of incorporating Jewish law into Israeli legislation. The central concept of Jewish law is that when the circumstances that permit the making of an oral will are no longer operative, the will becomes void. This concept was fully adopted by the statute; the statute also prescribed an additional fixed period of one month in order to make the law more precise and certain.

264. *Infra* pp. 1875–1884.

265. *See* the remarks of MKs Lewin, 24 *DK* 2181 (1958); Nurock, 32 *DK* 962 (1962); Porush, 42 *DK* 958, 970, 997, 1005 (1965).

As has already been shown, Jewish law itself includes a long series of legislative enactments in the direction of equality of succession rights as between the sexes.[266] The Israeli rabbinical courts themselves have also followed the same path, even with regard to primogeniture, for over sixty years, since the Succession Ordinance of 1923[267] and, thereafter, under Section 4 of the Woman's Equal Rights Law, 1951.[268] Moreover, with the establishment of the State, Chief Rabbis Herzog and Uziel both made proposals for legislation within the framework of the *Halakhah* that would have granted daughters succession rights, and wives the right to inherit from their husbands; these proposals were opposed by the other members of the Council of the Chief Rabbinate and were not enacted.[269] One can only deeply regret this inaction. It cannot reasonably be argued, in contravention of the clear trend in Jewish law itself, that the Knesset should adopt provisions in the Succession Law that should and could have been rectified by means of appropriate *takkanot* within the halakhic system.[270]

The second type of divergence from Jewish law involves statutory pro-

266. *See supra* n. 215.

267. *See supra* pp. 828–829.

268. *See supra* p. 829 n. 183; pp. 1656–1657.

269. *See supra* p. 1494 n. 124.

270. MK Warhaftig referred to this attempt by the Chief Rabbis to enact *takkanot* concerning succession (*see* 28 *DK* 465 (1960)) and contended that the reasons they were not adopted were that (a) there was no prospect that the Government would accept them, and (b) historically, halakhic legislation develops when Jewish law is accepted as binding. Although the latter observation is correct, it is unsatisfactory as an explanation for the failure to enact *takkanot* in this instance. When the Chief Rabbis made their proposal, the rabbinical courts had had jurisdiction over matters of succession for over forty years, and there was no reason why the *takkanot* could not have been applicable in the rabbinical courts, which would then have adjudicated on the basis of Jewish law, and not by virtue of the obligatory provisions of Section 23 of the Succession Ordinance.

The late Chief Rabbi Herzog explained the reason for the failure to enact his proposal as being that "most of the rabbis on the Council were not inclined to adopt any enactment." *See* his remarks at the beginning of his article "Haẓa'at Takkanot bi-Yerushot" [Proposed Enactments on Inheritance], *Talpiot,* VI (1953), pp. 36–37, which are quoted in full *supra* p. 1494 n. 124.

It is of interest to note that as the debate on the Succession Law ended, no reservation was expressed by MK Warhaftig with regard to the equality of male and female rights of inheritance. As to the many *takkanot* that were enacted on the subject of succession at various times, *see supra* pp. 835–846. As to the attempt by the Chief Rabbis to enact *takkanot* on succession, *see also* Chief Rabbi Ben-Zion Uziel, "Mishpetei Yerushat ha-Bat" [The Law Relating to Inheritance by a Daughter], *Talpiot,* V (1952), pp. 451ff., VI (1953), pp. 51ff.; *id.*, "Takkanot Ḥakhamim bi-Yerushat ha-Ishah" [Legislation by the Halakhic Authorities on Inheritance by Women], *Or ha-Mizraḥ,* 1957; *id.*, "Ha-Ishah be-Naḥalat Ba'alah" [Inheritance by Women from Their Husbands], *Ha-Torah ve-ha-Medinah,* II, pp. 9ff.; Elon, *supra* n. 11 at 127, 134–135 and n. 262, 138–140. In practice, the rabbinical courts treat women equally with men in matters of succession and in regard to competence to testify. *See supra* pp. 1599–1605. *See also* p. 1494 n. 124, p 1672 n. 215.

visions entirely contrary to Jewish law. These provisions give a share of the estate, equivalent to the share of a lawful spouse, to one who was not legally married to, but cohabited with, the decedent, and was commonly reputed to be the decedent's spouse. The concept of "the commonly reputed spouse" had become part of Israeli law by virtue of some fifteen statutes enacted prior to the Succession Law. These statutes were mainly of a socio-economic character, concerning such matters as pension rights and tenant protection, except for one statute—the Names Law, 1956—that has some relationship to personal status.[271] Those statutes provide that the various social and economic benefits granted to a widow or widower should also be conferred upon the "commonly reputed wife," "the commonly reputed husband," or "the commonly reputed spouse" of the decedent.[272] As was often pointed out in the many debates in the Knesset and in the opinions of the Supreme Court,[273] these provisions were enacted because there are couples who either do not wish to enter into a religious marriage (which is the sole form of marriage in the State of Israel) or are ineligible for such a marriage on account of some halakhic impediment such as the prohibition of the marriage of a *kohen* (priest) and a divorcée, and it is necessary to protect the rights of these partners.

A decision of the Supreme Court has gone so far as to apply these laws even when the "commonly reputed wife" is legally married to another man;[274] and a majority decision of the court has held that an agreement between a couple to live together as man and wife, even if either or both are married to others, "is not in any way prohibited, immoral, or contrary to the public interest," and that the courts may not refuse to entertain actions based on such an agreement.[275] The provisions for the "commonly reputed spouse," as judicially interpreted, are contrary to the position of Jewish law, which regards the preservation of the family unit created by marriage as the fundamental objective of family law.[276]

271. For detailed discussion of these laws, *see* Elon, *Ḥakikah,* pp. 119ff. The relevant section in the Names Law provides that a child born out of wedlock takes his mother's family name "unless the mother desires him to have his father's name and the father agrees, or unless the mother has been the father's commonly reputed wife."

272. These are the terms used in the various statutes.

273. For detailed discussion, *see* Elon, *Ḥakikah,* pp. 119ff.

274. State of Israel v. Pesler, 16 *P.D.* 102 (1962); *see* Elon, *Ḥakikah,* pp. 112ff.

275. Yeager v. Palevitz, 20(iii) *P.D.* 244, 249 (1966); *see* Elon, *Ḥakikah,* pp. 131ff.

276. In the debate concerning the "commonly reputed wife," proponents of that concept often point to cases where women become *agunot* because their husbands maliciously refuse to consent to a divorce, or lack capacity to do so on account of chronic mental illness. Although such cases are few, they do urgently require solution; and solution is possible within the framework of the *Halakhah. See* Elon, *Ḥakikah,* pp. 182–184; *supra* pp. 878–879. However, the rights accorded to a "commonly reputed wife" legally married to someone else are not limited to cases where her lawful husband maliciously refuses or lacks capacity

The Draft Succession Bill first proposed in 1952 took the position that the "commonly reputed spouse" should not be accorded any right to inherit:[277]

> The preservation of the family as the basic unit of society and of the state requires that only a lawful spouse should be considered a legal heir. Those other statutes [*i.e.*, those that give the commonly reputed spouse certain economic benefits] are based on considerations that are completely irrelevant in the context of succession. Cases of extramarital unions should be dealt with by appropriate provisions in the parties' wills. This was also the view taken in England by the above-mentioned special commission which studied what benefits should be given to the "unmarried wife."

The same position was taken in the 1958 bill and was supported by two respective Ministers of Justice at the first three readings of the bill.[278] This position was also consistent with the pronouncement of the Supreme Court of Israel that the statutes conferring benefits on the commonly reputed spouse did not confer any "status" on the individual concerned similar to the status attained upon marriage;[279] a right of succession would necessarily constitute the recognition of a "status" incident to extramarital cohabitation.

Various views were expressed in the debate in the Knesset concerning the rights of one reputed spouse in the other's estate. The opposition to granting such rights cut across party lines and was based on the arguments that succession should depend on biological or family kinship,[280] that no other legal system provides for such rights, and that it is always possible to bequeath the property to the "commonly reputed spouse" by will.[281] In

---

to divorce her; a "commonly reputed wife" has all the rights incident to that status regardless of whether she is an *agunah*.

277. Draft Succession Bill, 1952, p. 63.

278. These Ministers were Pinḥas Rosen and Dov Joseph. *See* 24 *DK* 2358 (1958); 28 *DK* 569 (1960); 33 *DK* 1068 (1962).

279. State of Israel v. Pesler, *supra* n. 274 at 109–111.

280. *See, e.g.*, the remarks of MK Shofman, 24 *DK* 2141 (1958), 42 *DK* 1007–1008 (1965):

> The entire concept of intestate succession is linked to another concept, that of the family. There is no intestate succession except within the family. The family is the social unit upon which society is based. No expedient, experiment, or scheme has succeeded in changing the fact that the family is the basic unit and the very foundation of society. No one calling himself "progressive" has suggested any alternative more satisfactory, more just, or more important for society.

281. *See* the remarks of Minister of Justice Dov Joseph, 33 *DK* 1068 (1962):

> In Israel, as in all other countries, there are laws that govern marriage and divorce. These laws may indeed be criticized, but the legislation under discussion is not the place to correct them, although we are not at liberty to pretend that they do not exist.

spite of these arguments, the "commonly reputed spouse" was given recognition in two highly significant provisions of the final text of the Succession Law. One (Section 55) pertains to the right of succession and is entitled "Quasi-Will":

> Where a man and woman, though not married to each other, have lived together as a family in a common household, and one of them dies, neither being then married to another person, the deceased is deemed, subject to any contrary direction expressed or implied by will, to have bequeathed to the survivor what the survivor would have inherited as a legal heir if the parties had been married to each other.

The other (Section 57(c)) concerns maintenance from the estate:

> Where a man and woman, though not married to each other, have lived together as a family in a common household, and one of them dies, neither being then married to another person, the survivor is entitled to maintenance out of the estate as if the parties had been married to each other.

The term "commonly reputed spouse" does not appear in either of these two sections. Instead the statute refers to "a man and woman" who "have lived together as a family in a common household"—which, as pointed out in the debate, could be interpreted as including a father and daughter, or a brother and sister, sharing the same dwelling.[282] Nor does either section prescribe a minimum period for the couple to live together in order for rights in the decedent's estate to arise.[283] (It should be noted that the two sections do require, unlike the other statutes referred to above, that neither be married to another person.) These two provisions provoked sharp opposition in the Knesset[284] and among the public at large; and it was largely because these provisions are so contrary to Jewish law that the oft-made proposal in the area of family and succession law to require the courts to refer to Jewish law in the event of a lacuna was not made in this instance.[285]

> I know of no country in which the "commonly reputed spouse," in the wider sense of the term, has inheritance rights equivalent to those of a lawful spouse. . . . I agree that certain facts and circumstances must be taken into consideration, but the proper solution to the problems they raise in regard to inheritance is through a bequest in a will, which is an expedient available to everyone.

282. *See* the remarks of MK Meridor, 42 *DK* 1008 (1965).

283. *See* the remarks of MK Klinghoffer, *id.*

284. Some members abstained in the voting for the Succession Law at the second and third readings, primarily because of these sections; *see id.* at 1115. Other opponents of these sections voted against the bill.

285. *See* the remarks of MK Unna, Chairman of the Legislative Committee, when presenting the bill for its second and third readings; *id.* at 952. The Knesset members who

The Succession Law also contains a provision similar to those found in other statutes discussed above. Section 148 provides:

> This law shall not affect the financial relations between a husband and wife or the rights arising from the marital relationship; however, this law, to the exclusion of all other laws, shall govern rights of succession and rights of maintenance out of the estate.

The proposals as to the jurisdiction of the religious courts and the law they are to apply in the matters dealt with in the Succession Law passed through various stages until it was finally decided to vest jurisdiction in the general courts. However, the religious courts may, pursuant to the applicable religious law, also issue succession orders, grant probate, and determine the maintenance to be given out of an estate, provided that (1) all the interested parties (as defined by the Succession Law) consent in writing, and (2) "if one of the parties is a minor or has been declared incompetent, his rights of inheritance, whether pursuant to law or under a will, and his right to support . . . shall be no less than the rights provided under this statute."[286]

(6) Who Is a Jew? To conclude this discussion of legislation concerning personal status, note should be taken of the incorporation of a fundamental principle of Jewish law adopted in 1970 in an amendment to the Law of Return, in the wake of the Supreme Court's decision in *Shalit v. Minister of the Interior.*[287] The subject of the amendment, popularly known as "Who is a Jew?" has been widely discussed in both legal and general literature;[288] here it will suffice to quote the text of the amendment found in Section 4(b):

would ordinarily have proposed to add a provision to look to Jewish law to fill any lacuna made no such proposal in regard to the Succession Law. Such a suggestion was made by MK Korn at one of the first readings. 28 *DK* 435 (1960). However, he did not persist with it. *See* his remarks, 32 *DK* 960 (1962). He later proposed the repeal of Article 46 of the Palestine Order in Council with regard to all laws and not merely the Succession Law. This proposal was supported by MK Nir, *id.* at 966; but it was rejected by Dr. Joseph, the Minister of Justice. 33 *DK* 1066 (1962).

286. *See* secs. 151, 155. It should be noted that, under this provision, if all interested parties agree to the jurisdiction of the religious court, the court can distribute the estate pursuant to the religious law even though a woman may not inherit under that law. Under the previous statute (Succession Ordinance, 1923, sec. 21—repealed by the Succession Law, 1965), the religious courts were required to distribute an estate's *miri* property in accordance with the schedule attached to the Ordinance. *See further* the remarks of MKs Shofman, 24 *DK* 2140 (1958), and Kushnir, 42 *DK* 1031, 1116 (1965).

287. 23(ii) *P.D.* 477 (1968).

288. The following two sources discuss the subject from a legal point of view: A.H. Shaki, *Mi Hu Yehudi be-Dinei Medinat Yisra'el* [Who Is a Jew According to the Laws of the

> For the purpose of this law, "a Jew" is one who was born to a Jewish mother or who converted to Judaism, and who does not profess another religious faith.

This definition reflects the position of Jewish law in regard to establishing a Jew's personal status,[289] and the definition has great historical and concep-

---

State of Israel], Jerusalem, 1977, Part I, particularly pp. 173–198; M. Shava, "Comments on the Law of Return (Who Is a Jew)," 3 *Tel Aviv University Studies in Law* 140 (1977). *See also* Elon, *Ḥakikah,* pp. 52–53.

289. As to the principle of matrilineal descent as determining Jewishness, *see* TB Kiddushin 66b, 68b and the pertinent codificatory literature.

The meaning of the term "converted" in connection with registration as a Jew in the population registry and on one's identity card was discussed by the Supreme Court in Organization of Torah-Observant Sephardim (Shas Movement) v. Kahana, Director of Population Registry of the Ministry of the Interior, 43(ii) *P.D.* 723 (1989).

The majority view, expressed by President Shamgar, was that a certificate of conversion issued by any Jewish congregation outside the State of Israel, whether Orthodox, Conservative, or Reform, suffices to require that an applicant be registered as a Jew under the Population Registry Law, 1965. Accordingly, the Registrar may not inquire into the validity of the conversion.

Deputy President Elon, on the other hand, argued that since the Population Registry Law incorporates the definition of "Jew" contained in Section 4(b) of the Law of Return, the Registrar must satisfy himself of the validity of the applicant's conversion before registering the applicant as Jewish, if the Registrar has reasonable ground to believe that the conversion is not valid. The dissent stated:

> The term "converted to Judaism" (*nitgayyer*) was not an invention of the legislature. It is a normative legal term originating in Jewish law, and exists in no other normative system. In construing this term, the court must turn to the legal system in which it originated, *i.e.,* the *Halakhah* as expounded in the Talmud, its commentaries, and the codificatory and responsa literature (*see* TB Yevamot 46a–47b; Gerim, chs. 1–2; Maimonides, *MT,* Issurei Bi'ah chs. 13–14; *Tur* and Sh. Ar. YD chs. 268–269).
>
> [The majority decision] disregards the meaning of "conversion to Judaism" (*giyyur*) in the normative system where the term originated, and is contrary to the objective denotation of this term. For example, conversions in Reform congregations are not governed by uniform and binding rules. The process differs from congregation to congregation, and depends in each instance on the views and opinions of the person officiating. Thus, in the case before us, the court has been advised by the attorney for the appellants that their conversion did not include immersion in the ritual bath, which, of course, is a basic halakhic requirement for conversion.

The dissent contended that, construing the entire statute *in pari materia,* the fact that the statute adopts the halakhic matrilineal criterion for Jewish descent argues for the halakhic interpretation of "converted to Judaism." On a practical level, the dissent added:

> It is vitally important that the act of joining the Jewish people should be effected by a method whose validity is recognized by all segments and elements of the Jewish people. . . . Only the historical and halakhic procedures for conversion to Judaism can meet the requirement of universal recognition of their validity by the entire Jewish people. The acceptance of these procedures in no way abridges anyone's right to live his life according to his own beliefs and practices.
>
> Let us take counsel to find a way to willingly accept these requirements, as is the wish of the Knesset, and, I am certain, of the nation.

tual significance far beyond its importance from the purely legal point of view.

2. THE SECOND LEGISLATIVE PERIOD

The foregoing study of the legislative process in the Knesset during the first legislative period has disclosed various fundamental problems in connection with the incorporation of Jewish law into the legal system of the State. The discussions of these problems during the debates in the Knesset are extremely important to an understanding of the role of Jewish law in the State of Israel. These discussions were particularly extensive in the first legislative period, when the problems first arose in a practical setting. Some of the problems were resolved during the second legislative period—*e.g.*, the substitution of the "principles of freedom, justice, equity, and peace of the Jewish heritage" for English common law and equity as the source to

---

As to the part of the definition of Jew that requires that one "does not profess another religious faith," the Supreme Court, in Beresford v. Minister of the Interior, 43(iv) *P.D.* 793 (1989), held that one who was born Jewish but is a member of a congregation of Messianic Jews, or Jews for Jesus, or similar groups, is one who professes another religious faith and therefore is not eligible for the benefits of the Law of Return. (A Jew who has changed his religion may, like anyone else who seeks Israeli citizenship, apply to become a naturalized citizen of Israel pursuant to the Citizenship Law, 1952.) The decision was unanimous, although Justices Elon and Barak reached the conclusion by different routes.

Another important decision, Miller v. Minister of the Interior, 40(iv) *P.D.* 436 (1986), held that the word "converted" may not be added after the word "Jew" in the Population Registry or on one's identity card. Such an addition is prohibited both by the Population Registration Law, 1965, as explained by Court President Shamgar, and by Jewish law, as explained by Justice Elon, who said:

> When a non-Jew joins the Jewish people, he becomes a member of the Jewish people in all respects—entitled to all rights and subject to all obligations of such membership. . . .
>
> There is no other instance in the Torah comparable to its treatment of the stranger, about which the Torah admonishes again and again, a total of thirty-six times (*see* TB Bava Meẓi'a 59b; *Resp. Maimonides,* ed. Blau, #448). A stranger is not to be mistreated, whether by word, by deed, or by halakhic-legal means. Two basic factors underlie these prohibitions: (1) the historical memory of the people—"You too must befriend the stranger, for you were strangers in the land of Egypt" (Deuteronomy 10:19), and (2) the special sensitivity of a person who has left behind the social and spiritual environment in which he was born, raised, educated, and lived, and who has become part of an entirely different spiritual and social environment and taken upon himself to observe its precepts and way of life. "You shall not oppress a stranger, for you know the feelings of the stranger" (Exodus 23:9). One may not remind a convert of his status and of his prior conduct, and one may not treat him disrespectfully (*Mekhilta,* Mishpatim, sec. 18; TB Bava Meẓi'a 59b; Maimonides, *MT,* De'ot 6:4; *Sefer ha-Ḥinnukh,* Commandment #431, *et al.*). . . . It is beyond dispute that adding the word "converted" in parentheses—an addition that is not made in the case of an "ordinary" Jew—treats one as different from other members of the Jewish people. Such an addition is therefore prohibited.

be looked to when it is necessary to fill a lacuna in the law. However, a considerable number of the problems that arose in the first legislative period have remained unresolved—most importantly, the much more common and typical question of how to interpret a statute when there is no lacuna, but rather an ambiguity in a statutory provision.

Commencing in the second legislative period, the problems encountered with regard to incorporating Jewish law into the legal system of the State were dealt with mainly by jurists, commentators, and courts—particularly the Supreme Court—and to a much lesser extent by the Knesset as part of the legislative process. At the same time, in the civil legislation of the second legislative period (which in effect codified the entire civil law of Israel), and in legislation in criminal law and other legal areas, Jewish law continued to be incorporated into the Knesset's legislation to an even greater extent than before. As in the first legislative period, it was often stated either in the Explanatory Notes or in the Knesset debates on a particular statute that to a greater or lesser degree the source of the statute was Jewish law.[290] In some cases, Jewish law was the pivotal influence on the

290. *See, e.g.*, the Knesset debates on the following statutes:

Agency Law, 1965—41 *DK* 475–477 (1965) (MK Kelmer); *id.* at 477–478 (MK Gross); *id.* at 479–480 (MK Bar Rav Hai); *id.* at 664 (MK Kushnir).

Pledges Law, 1967—44 *DK* 38 (1966) (MK Gross).

Guarantee Law, 1967—41 *DK* 667–669 (1965) (MK Kelmer); *id.* at 669–670 (MK Gross).

Transfer of Obligations Law, 1969—43 *DK* 2525–2526 (1965) (Minister of Justice Dov Joseph); 45 *DK* 3831 (1969) (MK Unna).

Hire and Loan Law, 1971—59 *DK* 273–275 (1971) (MK Ben-Meir); *id.* at 280–282 (MK Porush); *id.* at 288–289 (MK Neriyah); *id.* at 528–530 (Minister of Justice Joseph).

Fiduciary Law, 1975—73 *DK* 2896 (1975) (Minister of Justice Ẓadok).

Defective Products (Liability) Law, 1980—85 *DK* 1303 (1979) (MK Sheinman).

Protection of Privacy Law, 1981—89 *DK* 3487 (1980) (Minister of Justice Tamir).

Consumer Protection Law, 1981—90 *DK* 48 (1981) (MK Gross).

Amendment of Evidence Ordinance Bill (Amendment No. 6), 1980 (Bill No. 1477)—90 *DK* 310–313 (1981) (in connection with the repeal of the requirement of full corroboration of the testimony of an accomplice in the trial of a defendant charged with a sexual offense, and the sufficiency of a lesser degree of corroboration to support a conviction), including the remarks of Minister of Justice Nissim with regard to the developments in the Jewish law of evidence in criminal cases on the basis of the doctrine that the court may impose punishments not provided for in the Torah. *See also supra* pp. 691–698; Nagar v. State of Israel, 35(i) *P.D.* 113, 163ff. (1980); and the text of the Evidence Ordinance, sec. 54a.

Amendment of Courts Law Bill (Amendment No. 13), 1980 (Bill No. 1478)—90 *DK* 319 (1981) (in connection with holding closed court sessions to prevent intimidation of witnesses), including the remarks of Minister of Justice Nissim as to the position of Jewish law that where a party is a violent person whom the witnesses fear, their testimony may be taken in his absence. *See also* the Explanatory Notes to the bill, p. 404. For the final text, *see* Courts Law (Consolidated Version), 1984, secs. 68(b)(7), 69(b).

Amendment of Copyright Ordinance Bill (Amendment No. 4), 1981 (Bill No. 1517)—91 *DK* 2153 (1981) (in connection with the protection of intellectual property), including the statute's basic concepts. In other instances, some of the specific statutory provisions were directly influenced by Jewish law. Examples of these two types of relationships are discussed in turn in the following sections.

a. THE BAILEES LAW

One of the first statutes enacted as part of the codification of Israeli civil law was the Bailees Law, 1967. The original bill was entitled the Safekeeping of Property Law, 1965,[291] and it set forth various rules governing the classification and modes of bailments, the liability of bailees, and other pertinent matters. The Explanatory Notes stated:[292]

> In regard to the liability of bailees, the bill distinguishes between various categories of bailees in a manner similar to Jewish law. Mishnah Shevu'ot 8:1 [states]: "There are four types of bailees: the unpaid bailee (*shomer ḥinam*), the borrower (*sho'el*), the paid bailee (*shomer sakhar*), and the hirer (*sokher*)."

Not only did the bill follow Jewish law with regard to the liability of bailees, but it also adopted the terminology of Jewish law for the names of the various categories of bailees.

During the Knesset debates, the Minister of Justice, in his opening statement and especially in his reply, as well as other Knesset members from various political parties, stressed that the bill was based on Jewish law, and

---

remarks of Minister of Justice Nissim on the positions taken in other legal systems and in Jewish law. *See also* the Introduction to the bill, p. 238; and Sections 3 and 3A of the Copyright Ordinance.

These debates, generally speaking, identified provisions of the statute that were based on Jewish law, although sometimes there were differences of opinion as to whether a particular provision was in fact derived from Jewish law (*see, e.g.*, the discussion with regard to the Agency Law, *supra*). However, in this legislative period, there was almost no discussion, such as there was in the first legislative period, of such questions as the nature of the incorporation of the principles of Jewish law and the resulting problem of the relation between Jewish law and the State.

Some of the Explanatory Notes to the bills and the Knesset debates with regard to various statutes have been discussed in opinions of the Supreme Court. *See, e.g.*, Muberman v. Segal, 32(iii) *P.D.* 85 (1978) (Succession Law, 1965); Zikit v. Eldit, 32(iii) *P.D.* 487 (1978) (Contract for Services Law, 1974); Feld v. State of Israel, 33(i) *P.D.* 540 (1979) (Succession Law, 1965); Roth v. Yeshufeh, 33(i) *P.D.* 617 (1979) (Contracts Law (General Part), 1973); Bank Kupat Am v. Hendeles, 34(iii) *P.D.* 57 (1980) (Restoration of Lost Property Law, 1973), *Additional Hearing*, Hendeles v. Bank Kupat Am, 35(ii) *P.D.* 785 (1981) (same); Howard v. Miarah, 35(ii) *P.D.* 505 (1980) (Contracts Law (General Part), 1973); Illit v. Eleko, 34(iv) *P.D.* 673 (1980) (same); Rosenstein v. Solomon, 38(ii) *P.D.* 113 (1984) (Land Law, 1969).

291. Bill No. 676 (1965).

292. *Id.* at 54.

much of the discussion was devoted to examining the relevant Jewish legal sources.[293]

The Bailees Law contains sixteen sections, the great majority of which are based on Jewish legal principles. An interesting question with regard to the title of the statute arose at the second and third readings of the bill. As stated, the title originally proposed was the "Safekeeping of Property Law" (*Ḥok Shemirat Nekhasim*), a term unknown to Jewish law. On the other hand, the term "bailees" (*shomerim*) is well known in Jewish law, which speaks of the four types of bailees (*arba'ah shomerim*). The proposal to call the statute the "Bailees Law" was rejected in the Legislative Committee on the ground, among others, that statutory titles generally set forth the activity or transaction and not the identity of the persons involved—*e.g.*, the "Sale Law," rather than the "Sellers Law."[294] However, when the bill was brought for its second and third readings, the title was changed to the "Bailees Law, 1967." Some of the reasons for the proposed change merit quotation:[295]

> When we began to deal in committee with this law, which in effect transforms or translates the *Mejelle* and other legal rules into an Israeli code based on Jewish law, I did not understand what was meant by "safekeeping of property" until I saw the text of the various sections. Then I realized that we were concerned with the law of bailees (*shomerim*), as I had learned at school from the Bible and the Talmud; and, understandably, that was the primary association when I went over the material. In all innocence, I then asked why the statute is not entitled the "Bailees Law" rather than the "Safekeeping of Property Law," and I was told that that indeed had been the original intention, but that the word *shomerim* [bailees, which also means "watchmen" or "guards"] evoked in many people an association with the Ha-Shomer (the "watchmen") in the Galilee, with Ha-Shomer ha-Ẓa'ir [the Young Guard—a political movement], and with other such worthy organizations.
>
> It seems to me that . . . we are dealing with Jewish legislation governing the bailment of property that is entirely structured according to the four types of bailees in Scripture, and yet this statute fails to declare its connection with those [Scriptural] rules concerning bailees. These being the facts, serious doubts arise as to whether the Knesset has acted properly up to this point—and we have very many years ahead of us—in cutting out associative words,

293. *See* remarks of Minister of Justice Joseph, and MKs Raphael, Abramov, and Hausner, 44 *DK* 215–218 (1966).

294. *See* remarks of MK Azanyah, 49 *DK* 2149 (1967), and also those of MK Aloni, quoted *infra*.

295. Remarks of MK Aloni, 49 *DK* 2148 (1967). *See also id.* for MK Azanyah's reply, admitting that the bill included many legal concepts of Jewish law but claiming that the Hebrew term *shomer* (bailee) did not sufficiently indicate the contents of the law.

symbols, concepts, and linkages which could promote attachment to our heritage, our history, and our cultural values, particularly in a field of which we are so proud. For it is our people who laid the foundation for social legislation in western thought.

I was a teacher for a number of years and I regretted that the Wage Protection Law was not called the "Wage Delay Prohibition Law," so that when teaching the Scriptural verse "The wages of a laborer shall not remain with you . . . ," a teacher could drive the point home by telling his pupils that this law of the Torah still applies today.[296] That is the significance of continuity. Thus is fashioned the associative link that is educationally so important. This is perhaps the best kind of continuity, because it unites us all without religious or national compulsion, in that this ethical and legal basis serves as a general foundation for modern legal thought, and there is no need to be embarrassed or to hide the fact that its source rests on the foundation laid down by the Jewish people when the Torah came into being.

It similarly pained me when we adopted the Severance Pay Law, the source of which is the verse "Do not let him go empty-handed: Furnish him (*ha'aneik ta'anik lo*) [out of the flock, threshing floor, and vat]," that the word *ma'anak* ("gratuity") is not a part of the title.[297] It is a pity that a school teacher cannot point out the association between that law and the Scriptural verse. Not only in grade school, but even in the university, many do not realize the connection between the two. I want my children to know when they study this subject that this is not a legally unenforceable Biblical precept; it is intimately connected with daily life in Israel.

This is not the place for a detailed review of the Bailees Law and how its provisions rest on principles of Jewish law.[298] The first two sections of the statute are sufficient to illustrate the point here sought to be made.

After first defining a "bailment" as "lawful possession not by virtue of ownership," Section 1 provides:

. . . (b) A bailee of property who derives no benefit for himself from the bailment is an unpaid bailee (*shomer ḥinam*).

(c) A bailee of property who receives payment or derives some other benefit for himself from the bailment, and is not a borrower, is a paid bailee (*shomer sakhar*).

(d) A bailee of property for the purpose of using or benefiting from it without paying consideration is a borrower (*sho'el*).

296. *See supra* pp. 1629–1630.

297. *See supra* pp. 1631–1634.

298. For such a review, *see* Gulak, *Yesodei,* pp. 65ff.; Herzog, *Institutions,* II, pp. 175–196; N. Rakover, "Mekorot ha-Mishpat ha-Ivri le-Ḥok ha-Shomerim" [The Jewish Law Sources of the Bailees Law], *Ha-Praklit,* XXIV (1968), p. 208; M. Corinaldi, "Shomer she-Masar le-Shomer ba-Mishpat ha-Ivri u-ve-Ḥok ha-Shomerim, 1967" [A Bailee Who Delegates to Another Bailee, in Jewish Law and in the Bailees Law, 1967], *Shenaton,* II (1975), p. 383.

The very names given in Hebrew to these three types of bailees,[299] as well as their definitions, are based on Jewish law;[300] anyone who has ever studied the passages on bailees in the Torah and the Talmud will immediately perceive the close connection between these definitions and those sources.

Section 2 concerns the liability of bailees. Section 2(a) provides: "An unpaid bailee is liable for loss or damage to the property, if caused by his own negligence." This follows the rule of Jewish law that "an unpaid bailee is liable only for negligence (*peshi'ah*),"[301] which is defined as "failing to guard [the property] in the manner of bailees"; but "if he guarded [the property] in the manner of bailees, he is not liable."[302] Section 2(b) provides: "A paid bailee is liable for loss or damage to the property, unless caused by unforseeable circumstances whose results he could not have prevented." This is similar to the rule of Jewish law that a paid bailee is liable except where the damage has been caused by *force majeure* (Hebrew, *ones*), *i.e.*, when he could not have prevented the damage.[303] Section 2(c) reads: "A borrower is liable for loss or damage to the property from whatever cause, but his liability shall not be greater than that of a person who holds the property unlawfully." This is also the position of Jewish law, *i.e.*, that a borrower is liable for damage even if caused by *force majeure*.[304] Most of the

299. The four types of bailees in Jewish law, so far as the applicable legal rules are concerned, actually are three; *see* Maimonides, *MT*, Sekhirut ch. 1.

300. Exodus 22:6–14; M Bava Meẓi'a 7:8; Maimonides, *MT*, Sekhirut 1:1. TB Bava Meẓi'a 43a defines a paid bailee as "one who derives a benefit" from the possession of the article; the *Minḥat Ḥinnukh* commentary (by Joseph Babad, nineteenth century, Galicia) to *Sefer ha-Ḥinnukh*, Commandment #59, comments: "It is not only when the bailor pays him a fee for being a bailee that he becomes a paid bailee; even when he does not pay him a fee for being a bailee, but the bailee derives some benefit [from the bailment], he is a paid bailee. For example, a craftsman given an object to repair or alter and paid for his work but not for being a bailee is nevertheless considered a paid bailee because of the benefit he derives from what has been entrusted to him." TB Bava Meẓi'a 94b defines a borrower as one who "receives all the benefits." *See also* Yeinot Eliaz Co. v. Eshkolot Anavim Co., 1 *P.D.R.* 178, 189 (1953). An unpaid bailee, as the term itself indicates, is one who safeguards the bailed property but derives no benefit from the bailment.

301. Sh. Ar. ḤM 291:1; *see also* Maimonides, *MT*, Sekhirut 1:2.

302. M Bava Meẓi'a 3:10.

303. Maimonides, *MT*, Sekhirut 1:2; Sh. Ar. ḤM 303:2–3. Section 2(b) goes on to limit a paid bailee's liability if "the purpose of safeguarding the property was secondary to the main purpose of his having possession." There is a difference of opinion in Jewish law as to whether a bailee who benefits from the bailment but receives no payment for safeguarding the property is liable to a lesser extent than a bailee who is paid for his services as such.

304. Maimonides, *MT*, Sekhirut 1:2; Sh. Ar. ḤM 340:1. Jewish law does not impose liability on a borrower if the borrowed article was damaged as a result of its use for the purpose for which it was borrowed, such as "if it died as a result of the work [for which it was borrowed]" (Sh. Ar., *id.*). This limitation on the borrower's liability was not included in the statute.

other provisions of the Bailees Law are similarly based on Jewish law, but these examples are sufficient to illustrate how an entire subject in the Israeli civil code rests on Jewish legal principles; and, indeed, the Supreme Court of Israel has recently looked to Jewish law for assistance in understanding the statutory distinctions between the various types of bailees.[305]

b. THE UNJUST ENRICHMENT LAW

Another instructive example of extensive incorporation of Jewish law is the Unjust Enrichment Law, 1979. The Introduction to the bill[306] quotes the expressions traditionally used by Jewish law on this subject, such as "one who appropriates his neighbor's property (*yored le-nikhsei ḥavero*)," "one who makes profit from his neighbor's cow (*oseh seḥorah be-farato shel ḥavero*)," and "the one gains without the other's losing (*zeh neheneh ve-zeh eino ḥaser*)." The Introduction also cites the relevant legal principles:

> The proposed law adopts the approach of Jewish law. . . . It grants restitution to one who improves another's property; it adopts the principle of "the one gains without the other's losing" as a rationale for exempting the recipient of such a benefit from making restitution; and, in order to encourage acts of rescue, it reimburses the loss suffered by one who rescues another's property.

The Minister of Justice, when introducing the bill in the Knesset, accurately summed up:

> The basic concept upon which this bill is founded is the principle that underlies the rules of equity in Jewish law: Do what is right and good between man and his neighbor.[307]

305. Ali v. Sasson, 36(iii) *P.D.* 281, 289ff. (1982) (A. Sheinbaum, District Judge specially assigned).

306. Unjust Enrichment Bill, 1978 (Bill No. 1353).

307. Remarks of Minister of Justice Tamir, 83 *DK* 3917 (1978). *See also* the remarks of MK Glass, Chairman of the Legislative Committee, 84 *DK* 1113 (1979): "This law is nourished most significantly from the sources of Jewish law, . . . which recognizes the rights of one who rescues or otherwise helps another. Also, as to a volunteer who pays another's debt, we have reiterated strongly the rule of Jewish law that such a person need not be reimbursed." D. Friedmann, "Yesodot be-Dinei Asiyyat Osher ve-Lo ve-Mishpat le-Or ha-Ḥakikah ha-Yisra'elit ha-Ḥadashah" [Basic Principles of the Laws of Unjust Enrichment in the Light of the New Israeli Legislation], *Iyyunei Mishpat,* VIII (1981), p. 22, discusses the influence of the Continental and common law on the Unjust Enrichment Law, but ignores the decisive influence of Jewish law. *See also id., Dinei Asiyyat Osher ve-Lo ve-Mishpat* [The Laws of Unjust Enrichment], 1982, pp. 18ff.

It is interesting to note that the modern Hebrew term for unjust enrichment, which is the Hebrew title of the statute, *Asiyyat Osher ve-Lo ve-Mishpat* (lit. "Obtaining Riches and Not by Right"), is taken from a verse in the Book of Jeremiah: "As the partridge sits on eggs and does not hatch them, so he who obtains riches and not by right shall leave them in the midst of his days, and at his end he shall be a fool" (Jeremiah 17:11). It was the Deputy President of the Supreme Court, the late Justice Cheshin, who suggested this elegant and appropriate

c. ADMONITION OF WITNESSES AND ABROGATION OF THE WITNESS OATH

Another statute adopted toward the end of the second legislative period is entirely based, not only in concept but also in detail, on the rules of Jewish law. This statute is the Rules of Evidence Amendment (Warning of Witnesses and Abolition of Oath) Law, 1980. The final form in which this statute was enacted represents the culmination of a legislative history of almost thirty years. Because of the statute's importance and its uniqueness in having totally incorporated the rules of Jewish law, it is appropriate first to examine in general outline the position of Jewish law on the subject, and then to review the various stages of the statute's legislative history.

One of the most stringent prohibitions in Jewish law is that against giving false testimony. This prohibition is one of the Ten Commandments: "You shall not bear false witness (*ed sheker*) against your neighbor."[308] Consequently, Jewish law took the position that there is neither reason nor logic in administering an oath to a witness to tell the truth, as "he has already been adjured at Mt. Sinai" not to bear false witness. According to Jewish law, a witness likely to violate the commandment "You shall not bear false witness against your neighbor" is equally likely to violate the precept "You shall not take the name of the Lord your God in vain," which is also one of the Ten Commandments.[309] Not only does swearing a witness not assure truthful testimony, it arguably violates a religious prohibition; an additional oath by a witness already adjured to tell the truth would itself be taking the name of God in vain.[310]

In order to prevent any misunderstanding, it should be pointed out that Jewish law fully recognizes the utility of an oath; however, in Jewish civil law the oath serves mainly as one of the methods by which a party proves the truth of his allegations.[311] There is also in Jewish law a "witness's oath" glossary, but this has no connection with the swearing of witnesses to assure the truth of their testimony. The "witness's oath" is taken when

---

term for unjust enrichment while still a district court judge, four months before the establishment of the State of Israel, in his opinion in Shoresh v. Ha'avarah, 3 *Ha-Mishpat* (a compilation of the Hebrew opinions of the district courts of Palestine) 71, 73, sec. 3 (1948). The term became widely used in the Israeli legal community and was then adopted as the Hebrew title of the statute.

308. Exodus 20:16. *Cf.* the text of the commandment in Deuteronomy 5:17: "You shall not bear vain witness [*ed shav*] against your neighbor."

309. *See* Exodus 20:7; Deuteronomy 5:11.

310. *See* TB Nedarim 8a for the dispute as to whether it is permitted to take an oath to observe a commandment. *See also Resp. Tashbeẓ*, III, #15 (quoted *infra* p. 1701); *Tur* and Sh. Ar. OḤ ch. 156.

311. *See supra* pp. 614–626.

one person asserts that another has information on a particular litigated matter, and demands that he come forward to testify in court as to what he knows:

> What is the witness's oath? When witnesses [may] have knowledge of a monetary matter and one of the parties demands that they give testimony, but they deny knowledge and, instead of testifying, they swear that they have no knowledge of the matter on which they have been called upon to testify—this is called the witness's oath.[312]

However, Jewish law at its origin never recognized or demanded an oath in order to assure the truth of a witness's testimony. Moreover, it has even been said:

> They are not to be believed once they have taken an oath, since Scripture states that "a case can be valid only on the testimony of two witnesses"[313]—which contemplates that witnesses are to be credited on their word alone; the evidence of witnesses who require an oath to buttress their testimony has no probative value.[314]

Jewish law does recognize that it is proper to put a witness on notice, before he testifies, that he must tell the truth; it provides that before testimony is given, "the witnesses are admonished," *i.e.*, cautioned to tell the truth and given notice of the strict prohibition against giving false testimony and of the punishment awaiting one who violates the prohibition. The admonition in a civil case is different from that in a capital case; it varies with the gravity of the matter. The Mishnah and the Talmud[315] contain a detailed discussion concerning the form of admonition. For present purposes, it is sufficient to note Maimonides' summary of the substance of the admonition:[316]

> Witnesses in a civil case are also admonished. How are they admonished? They are admonished in the presence of everyone [*i.e.*, before all those present in court at that time—the reason being to make them feel ashamed to give false testimony—Radbaz, Commentary on the *Mishneh Torah*], and they are informed of the potency of false testimony and the shame that attaches, in this world and in the next, to one who gives such testimony.

312. Maimonides, *MT*, Shevu'ot 1:12. *See also id.*, ch. 9 *et seq.*; TB Shevu'ot 30a *et seq.*

313. Deuteronomy 19:15.

314. *Tosafot* (in the name of Ri), Kiddushin 43b, s.v. Ve-hashta de-tikkun rabbanan. This is also the conclusion in *Resp. Ḥatam Sofer*, ḤM, #162. *See also id.*, Hashmatot, #207; Ben-Zion Uziel, *Resp. Mishpetei Uziel*, III, ḤM, #13.

315. TB Sanhedrin 29a, 37a.

316. Maimonides, *MT*, Edut 17:2.

In the *Shulḥan Arukh,* Joseph Caro added, "and that he is contemptible in the eyes of those who suborn him."[317]

In a capital case, where the fate of the accused depended on the witness, the admonition was as follows:[318]

> Perhaps your testimony is a matter of conjecture, or rumor, or hearsay, even from a trustworthy person. Perhaps you are not aware that we are going to subject you to a probing examination.
>
> You should know that a capital case is not like a civil case: in a civil case, a person pays and is then forgiven; in a capital case, the victim's blood and the blood of his descendants until the end of time will be on the witness, as Scripture states with regard to Cain: "Your brother's blood [the Hebrew for "blood" is in the plural] cries out to Me" [Genesis 4:10]—his blood and the blood of his descendants.
>
> The creation of humankind started with the creation of a single individual to teach that whoever removes one single soul from this world[319] is regarded as if he had caused the whole world to perish; and whoever keeps one single soul alive in this world is regarded as having preserved the whole world. All people are created in the form of Adam, the first man; and yet each person is different from every other. Therefore, everyone can say: "It is for me that the world was created."
>
> Perhaps you will say: "Why should we become involved at all and subject ourselves to such trouble?" It is written: "[If one is] able to testify as one who has either seen or learned of the matter . . ." [Leviticus 5:1. The verse concludes: "if he does not give information, . . . he is subject to punishment."] Perhaps you will say: "Why should we take upon ourselves responsibility for the blood of this man?" It is written: "When the wicked perish there are shouts of joy" [Proverbs 11:10].

To summarize: A witness about to testify does not take an oath to tell the truth, since he is already adjured to do this—"You shall not bear false witness against your neighbor." Instead of an oath, he was given a cautionary admonition, the general substance of which was to make him aware of the nature of testimony and that it must be on the personal knowledge of the witness and not hearsay, and to point out the seriousness of the prohibition against giving false testimony and the punishment awaiting one who testifies falsely.[320]

317. Sh. Ar. ḤM 28:7, following TB Sanhedrin 29a.

318. Maimonides, *MT,* Sanhedrin 12:3.

319. The current printed version of the Mishnah reads: "Whoever removes one single soul of Israel . . ." and "whoever keeps one single soul of Israel alive . . ." (M Sanhedrin 4:5). Other versions have the same as Maimonides: "one single soul from this world." *See* Albeck, *Commentary on M Sanhedrin,* Hashlamot, p. 445.

320. A review of the law relating to the witness's oath in ancient legal systems reveals that the requirement that a witness be sworn to tell the truth was accepted in those systems

Beginning in the first part of the fifteenth century in Spain and North Africa, the position of Jewish law on the subject of a witness's oath changed substantially. For the purposes of the present discussion, it will suffice to review two responsa which indicate the nature, extent, and underlying social and psychological causes of this change.

In 1405 C.E., the leaders of the Jewish community of Barshak, Algeria, turned to Isaac b. Sheshet Perfet (Ribash),[321] and asked him whether testimony may be taken "when the court desires to receive it under oath administered on a scroll of the Torah, and the witnesses absolutely refuse to be sworn, for fear of incurring the penalty attached to any swearing." The very terms of this question indicate the revolutionary change in the legal situation: the question was not, as it would have been under the original rule, whether evidence is competent notwithstanding that the witness has taken an oath, but the converse, *i.e.*, whether unsworn evidence is competent when the court requests that the witness be sworn. Ribash responded:

> The acceptance of testimony by the courts without an oath is not contrary to law; we do not find that the giving of testimony requires an oath by the witnesses to tell the truth, since they are already adjured from Mt. Sinai. . . . It is true that there are places where it is customary to swear witnesses in order to instill fear in them, but this practice is not required by law.
>
> Here we follow the practice of swearing witnesses before accepting testimony against a defendant in a criminal case, to prevent the witnesses from withholding true evidence in order to help the accused, by claiming that they did not see what they actually saw. The witnesses themselves wish to be sworn so as to be able to explain to the accused that they gave incriminating evidence against him because "the oath forced us to tell the truth."

At the very same time, Simeon b. Ẓemaḥ Duran (Rashbeẓ), a younger contemporary of Ribash, responded to the scholar Amram of Granada

---

long before the rise of Christianity. According to Lord Chief Justice Willes in Omychund v. Barker, 1 Atk. 22, 45, 26 Eng. Rep. 15, 30 (Ch. 1744), "Oaths are as old as the creation." *See also* W.M. Best, *The Principles of the Law of Evidence* (12th ed.), London, 1922, pp. 42–43. This requirement remained obligatory until recently, when affirmation was permitted in lieu of an oath. Interestingly, leaders of the Christian church based the requirement of a witness's oath on Scriptural verses, such as Numbers 30:3: "If a man makes a vow to the Lord or takes an oath imposing an obligation on himself, he shall not break his pledge; he must carry out all that has crossed his lips." (*See* the remarks of Archbishop Secker, quoted by Best, *supra* at 44–45.) That verse, however, is in no way connected, either by content or context, with the requirement that a witness take an oath to the truth of his testimony. *See also* 6 *Wigmore on Evidence* (J. Chadbourne rev. 1976), pp. 380ff.; Note, "Oaths in Judicial Proceedings and Their Effect upon the Competency of Witnesses," 51 *Amer. L. Reg.* 373, 384–389 (1903).

321. *Resp. Ribash* #170; the precise date appears at the end of the question.

(southern Spain) on the same subject.[322] Rashbeẓ provided additional important details concerning the factors that brought about the change in the law concerning the swearing of witnesses, and the extent to which this change was accepted in the Jewish judicial systems in various communities. The responsum reads:

> You wish to know my opinion as to whether the practice in Spain of swearing witnesses has any basis. You are astonished at the practice although you are aware that many important rabbis follow it. I can also confirm your own report that Rabbi Isaac b. Sheshet, of blessed memory, also followed this practice here, and I have also been told that Rabbenu Nissim[323] used to say concerning testimony given in Barcelona: "I wish an oath to be taken on this testimony."
>
> Apparently, although an oath to testify truthfully is not required, it is not a vain oath, for the law is that one may take an oath to fulfill the commandments. . . . In any case, even on this theory, witnesses are not required to take an oath; the most that we can say on this is that it is permissible and it does not involve the taking of the name of Heaven in vain.
>
> I should also say that a court may require an oath to be taken if it sees that the people are not taking seriously the prohibition against giving false testimony. [This is true] notwithstanding that one may argue that both giving false testimony and taking a false oath violate a negative commandment, and therefore if someone is suspected of giving false testimony and thus violating that commandment, how can he be believed on an oath? In other words, will this negative commandment [against taking a false oath] be more effective than the other one [against giving false testimony] . . . ?
>
> Notwithstanding all this, when we see that the present generation has become lax and takes the view that it is not forbidden to lie when giving evidence without an oath, we are compelled to conduct our judicial procedure in a manner that takes account of their views. . . .
>
> Personally, I do not swear any witnesses unless the defendant so requests and the witness remains silent, because those reared in this country [Algiers], like the local people, find it difficult to follow this practice; but in Spain, witnesses [in Jewish courts] are sworn, as is the custom of that people [the Spanish Christians]—not that one may follow their laws, but because the witnesses brought up on their practice think that it represents the law of the Torah.

This important change in the law was the result of moral, social, and psychological changes that occurred in that period. Swearing of witnesses

322. *Resp. Tashbeẓ*, III, #15; as to the questioner, *see* the beginning of #13.

323. The reference is to Nissim Gerondi (Ran), one of the leading halakhic authorities in fourteenth-century Spain. Ribash was one of his outstanding disciples and greatly praised the knowledge and ability of his teacher; *see Resp. Ribash* ##375–376.

gradually became accepted as part of the Jewish legal system to the point that Moses Isserles (Rema), in Poland in the sixteenth century, could say in his glosses to the *Shulḥan Arukh* that "if the court sees a temporary need to swear the witnesses to tell the truth, it may [require the oath]."[324]

This approach of Jewish law was adopted by the Ministry of Justice in 1952 in a draft bill on the law of evidence, published for public comment.[325] Sections 19 and 20 read:

> 19. Before giving evidence, a witness should be admonished by the court in language he understands that he must tell the whole truth, and that if he does not do so he is subject to the penalties prescribed by law. After the witness has been admonished, his testimony is regarded as testimony given under oath for the purposes of Section 117 of the Criminal Law Ordinance, 1936.
>
> 20. If the court has reason to believe that swearing a witness will assist in the disclosure of the truth, the court may administer the following oath: "I swear that my testimony in this court will be the truth, the whole truth, and nothing but the truth."

The Explanatory Notes to the draft of these sections pointed out that the oath had become a rote formula mouthed by witnesses without thought or attention, and that the draft adopted the position of Jewish law:

> It is an ancient Jewish tradition that the court admonishes the witnesses before they testify, or, in the language of the *Halakhah*, "the witnesses are admonished as to the solemnity of their undertaking and are informed of the potency of false testimony and the shame that attaches, in this world and in the next, to one who gives such testimony, and that he is contemptible in the eyes of those who suborn him" (*Shulḥan Arukh Ḥoshen Mishpat* 28:7). Such an admonition, when given by the judge in a manner and in words calculated to make the witness understand, is likely to influence the witness and to bring home to him the importance of the testimony, and this is the purpose of the law in requiring any oath.

The Explanatory Notes explained Section 20 on the basis of the rationale of Ribash and Rashbeẓ for making the oath discretionary with the court:

324. Rema to Sh. Ar. ḤM 28:2. *See also* Wigmore, *supra* n. 320 at 387: "It follows that the *form* of the administration of the oath *is immaterial,* provided that it involves, in the mind of the witness [*cf.* Rashbeẓ's remarks!], the bringing to bear of this apprehension of punishment." Wigmore concludes (*id.* at 413–414): "The true purpose of the oath is not to exclude any competent witness, but merely to add a stimulus to truthfulness wherever such a stimulus is feasible. Until the 1800s, however, this advanced notion of its purpose had not been reached." In fact, Jewish law had reached this "advanced notion" some 1800 years earlier.

325. Draft Evidence Bill, 1952, published by the Ministry of Justice.

> There are those, particularly among the judges, who say that in a land such as ours the time is not ripe for abolishing the oath. According to those who take this view, primitive people will recoil from giving a false oath but will not recoil from giving false testimony. Under this section, a court before whom such a witness appears has the authority to swear him, either before he has begun to testify or afterward. The name of God has been omitted from the form of oath in order to avoid objections based on religious scruples.[326]

Shortly thereafter, a portion of the draft was placed on the Knesset's legislative agenda. In 1955, a bill was introduced[327] which provided that a written statement, required to be given under oath or affirmation before a justice of the peace or a registrar of the district court (pursuant to the still subsisting British Mandatory law), was also competent evidence if given before a *dayyan* (judge of a rabbinical court), an attorney, or others specified in the law, and that, in lieu of the oath or affirmation, it sufficed if "the witness has been admonished that he must declare the truth and that he is subject to the penalties prescribed in the law if he fails to do so." The bill also provided that the statement was subject to the penalties of perjury. The Explanatory Notes to this bill pointed to the bill's reliance on Jewish law; and, soon afterward, the bill was enacted by the Knesset.[328]

Over a year later, there began to be circulated an internal interoffice draft of a bill which included two sections substantially similar to Sections 19 and 20 of the 1952 draft bill quoted above, with only minor stylistic changes. The proposal was not acted upon for a considerable time, and was finally adopted in a truncated and watered-down form far removed from the position of Jewish law. At first, this approach was adopted in Rule 182(a) of the Civil Procedure (Amendments) Law, 1963:

> The court shall admonish the witness before receiving his testimony that he must tell the truth and that if he does not do so, he is subject to the penalties prescribed by law. The witness shall swear to tell the truth, but upon declaring that he does so for reasons of religion or conscience, he may make a solemn affirmation in lieu of an oath, unless the court is convinced that the witness's declaration is not made in good faith.

In this manner, the statute adopted the rule of Jewish law that a witness should be admonished that he must tell the truth; but unlike Jewish law, pursuant to which the court administers an oath to witnesses only when necessary in a particular case, and not as a matter of course, Rule

326. *Id.* at 24–25.
327. Amendment of Evidence Ordinance Bill, 1955 (Bill No. 249), p. 6.
328. Amendment of Evidence Ordinance Law, 1955.

182(a) required not only the admonition but also that every witness be sworn as a matter of course in every case.

The text of amended Civil Procedure Rule 182(a) was also adopted a short while later as Section 154 of the Criminal Procedure Law, 1965. This section did not appear in the original draft of the Criminal Procedure Law but was added on the initiative of the Legislative Committee of the Knesset. The discussions that took place in the Knesset on the adoption of Section 154 on second and third reading make clear the reasons for this fragmented reception of Jewish law. Knesset members holding different points of view, each for his own reasons, proposed that in place of the words "the witness shall swear to tell the truth" the law should read: "the witness shall solemnly affirm that he will tell the truth."[329] However, a majority of the committee rejected the proposal. One explanation for the text as adopted was the following:

> All those who propose today to abrogate the oath are . . . anticipating a particular development. It is possible that, in a generation or two, the Israeli population will reach the point that it will regard the court's admonition and cautionary statement prior to the giving of testimony as a sufficient deterrent [to perjury] so that it may replace the oath.[330]

This was the legal situation until 1978, when the subject came up again before the Supreme Court sitting as the High Court of Justice in the case of *Becker v. Judge Ḥayyim Eilat.*[331] The specific question dealt with by the court concerned a witness called to testify in the magistrate's court, whom the judge asked to be sworn. The witness, who claimed to be an agnostic, refused to be sworn and requested to be permitted to make an affirmation pursuant to Section 154 of the Criminal Procedure Law. The witness stated: "I am not prepared to swear on the Bible because, for rea-

329. *See* 43 *DK* 2370 (1965), and the reasons given for the proposed change, p. 2434.

330. *Id.* at 2435 (remarks of MK Azanyah). *See also* the statement of Jonathan Eybeschütz, a leading halakhic authority in Germany in the first half of the eighteenth century: "It is a need of the time, since they have become accustomed to the procedure of the gentiles who swear witnesses to tell the truth. As a result, the great majority of the people believe that as long as they have not taken an oath, it is permitted to give false testimony. That is why the *bet din* has become accustomed to swear the witnesses"; *Urim ve-Thummim* to Sh. Ar. ḤM ch. 28, Urim, subpar. 10. The statement that "the *bet din* has become accustomed" implies that it was done generally for all witnesses; and, if so, it also implies that this procedure was followed in Eybeschütz's days, because of the common belief of "the great majority of the people." A provision similar to Rule 182(a) and Section 154 was also inserted into the Arbitration Law, 1968; *see* Section 14 of that statute and par. 11 of the schedule appended to the statute.

331. 32(iii) *P.D.* 370 (1978) (Elon, Asher, and Bekhor, JJ.). The Supreme Court, sitting as the High Court of Justice (*Bet Din Gavo'ah le-Ẓedek*), has original jurisdiction over cases challenging allegedly arbitrary or capricious governmental acts or omissions.

sons of conscience, I do not believe in God as the Bible presents Him, and I will therefore make a solemn affirmation." The judge decided that this reason did not qualify as a "reason of religion or conscience" within Section 154, which would permit an affirmation in lieu of an oath. The judge reasoned as follows:

> In this case, the witness does not associate himself with any group when he states that he believes in God but not in the way that the Bible presents Him. I do not understand this distinction, and I suspect that the witness's reasons are not given in good faith. Therefore, so long as the witness will not swear as required by law, I will not permit him to testify.

The issue was presented to the Supreme Court, sitting as the High Court of Justice. The Supreme Court, after extensively discussing the meaning of Section 154 and the Jewish legal sources on which that section was based, came to the conclusion that, in both letter and spirit, Section 154 entitled an agnostic witness to affirm rather than take an oath.

Counsel for the appellant raised this additional argument:

> The foregoing conclusion [that an agnostic should not be forced to take an oath] not only is compelled by the language of Section 154 but is also desirable policy, which counsels requiring oaths in as few instances as possible, both in order to protect freedom of religion and conscience (and this includes the right of nonbelievers to be protected against forced oaths), and because there is grave doubt whether an oath is more effective than a solemn affirmation as a means of inducing witnesses to testify truthfully.

On this point the Supreme Court stated:[332]

> We agree that this is indeed the desirable policy, and we have seen that this is the view of the Legislature . . . , which looks forward to the day when it will be possible to abolish the requirement of an oath completely. For our part, there is an additional reason why this policy is desirable. It is distressing to see the widespread disregard for oaths, and how the act of swearing, which has a profound meaning for persons of faith, has daily become trivialized, mouthed by rote, and taken lightly. Indeed, the halakhic authorities have repeatedly warned against habitual swearing even to the truth.[333] The governing rule has been succinctly stated: "One should do business with integrity, and be careful not to mention the name of Heaven in vain. . . . A person should be extremely careful with regard to oaths, for our Rabbis have expressed grave concerns about false oaths and even about swearing to the

332. *Id.* at 386.

333. *See Midrash Tanḥuma,* ed. Buber, Mattot, sec. 1; *Leviticus Rabbah* 6:3, ed. Margaliot, p. 132, and *see* additional sources listed there in n. 2; *Midrash Aseret ha-Dibberot,* ed. Jellinek, Ḥeder Rishon, p. 72; *Ḥovot ha-Levavot,* "Love of God" section, ch. 6.

> truth."[334] Every person is presumed not to bear false witness against his neighbor, and we need only remind and caution him that he has already been adjured not to violate this commandment. This is the desirable policy we should hope to achieve.

Subsequently, in 1980, a private member's bill was introduced[335] to abolish the oath and substitute an admonition to the witness that he tell the truth, and that he is subject to the penalties set forth in the law if he fails to do so. The bill also provided that if the court has grounds to believe that swearing the witness will assist in disclosure of the truth, it may require the witness to be sworn, but that if the witness declares that reasons of religion or conscience so require, he may instead affirm. The explanation accompanying the bill relied on the position of Jewish law on this subject, as discussed above, and also on the opinion of the Supreme Court in the *Becker* case above referred to, particularly the passage about abolishing the requirement of witness oaths. The Knesset passed the bill under the title "Rules of Evidence Amendment (Warning of Witnesses and Abolition of Oath) Law, 1980." It is appropriate to quote this statute in full:

1. **Abrogation of the Oath.** Notwithstanding any other provisions of law, a witness about to testify in any judicial or quasi-judicial proceeding is not required to be sworn.
2. **Admonition of Witnesses.** A witness about to testify in any judicial or quasi-judicial proceeding shall first be admonished, in language he understands, that he must tell the whole truth, and nothing but the truth, and that if he fails to do so, he is subject to the penalties prescribed by law.
3. **Admonition in Place of Oath.** Whenever a statute permits or requires an oath, an admonition in the manner prescribed in Section 2, with whatever changes are necessary under the circumstances, shall be given; whoever is authorized under the statute to administer an oath is authorized to give the admonition as above provided.
4. **Effect of Admonition.** An admonition pursuant to this statute has the same legal effect as an oath under the Penal Law, 1977.
5. **Administration of Oath by Order of Court.** If the court has reason to believe that swearing a witness will assist in disclosing the truth, the court, *sua sponte* or on request of a party, may require the witness to be sworn; but the witness, upon declaring that he does so for reasons of religion or conscience, may make a solemn affirmation in lieu of an oath, unless the court is convinced that the witness's declaration is not made in good faith. If the court decides to swear the witness, the form of the oath is as follows: "I swear by God that my testimony in this court will be the truth, the whole truth, and nothing but the truth."

334. *Tur* and Sh. Ar. OḤ ch. 156.
335. The bill was introduced by MK Gross.

This statute fully incorporates the position of Jewish law as crystallized over the course of time. The first section establishes the general principle that a witness should not be sworn; the second section requires that a witness be admonished to tell the truth and that if he fails to do so, he is subject to the penalties prescribed by law. This is the original position of Jewish law. The fifth section of the statute, which confers discretion on the court to require a witness to be sworn if the court is convinced that an oath will assist in disclosure of the truth, accords with the rulings in the responsa of Ribash and Rashbeẓ which were accepted as law by Rema, as discussed above.[336] On this subject, Jewish law was accepted in its entirety. This acceptance occurred in stages, consistent with the social-psychological conditions existing during each stage, and through cooperative interaction between the legislature and the judiciary. The factors leading to this result were similar to those which shaped the law on this subject within the halakhic system.[337]

d. THE CRIME REGISTER AND REHABILITATION OF OFFENDERS LAW

Another interesting example of a statute adopting the basic content of Jewish law, this time in the area of criminal law, is the Crime Register and Rehabilitation of Offenders Law, 1981.[338] This statute regulates the recording of convictions, sentences, and other dispositions of criminal cases, and the procedures for disclosing such information. In addition, the statute in-

336. *See also* Criminal Procedure Law (Consolidated Version), 1982, sec. 173, which replaced Criminal Procedure Law, 1965, sec. 154: "The court shall admonish the witness before taking his testimony, and Sections 4 and 5 of the Rules of Evidence Amendment (Warning of Witnesses and Abolition of Oath) Law, 1980, shall apply." The heading in the margin of Section 154 of the 1965 statute reads: "Admonition and Swearing of Witnesses," while that of Section 173 of the 1982 statute reads: "Admonition of Witnesses."

337. A little more than three years later, a number of changes were made in the law. *See* Rules of Evidence Amendment (Warning of Witnesses and Abolition of Oath) Law, 1984. At the end of Section 2 of the statute, the amendment added the following: "The witness shall respond that he has understood the admonition and that he commits himself to conform to it." This addition was intended to assure that the witness understands the import of the admonition as to the seriousness of giving false testimony. Another provision of the amendment applied Section 4 of the statute to a military court under Section 111 of the Military Justice Law, 1955. The amendment also added a new section, Section 6: "This statute is not intended to prohibit a person from giving sworn testimony or making an affidavit if he expressly agrees to do so and if such sworn testimony or affidavit is required for use in a foreign country." This amendment was required because "the absence of an oath in Israel might weaken the weight of testimony given in Israel for submission in proceedings abroad. It is therefore proposed to make it clear that the statute does not prohibit voluntary oaths for use in foreign proceedings or for other purposes abroad." *See* Explanatory Notes to the 1982 bill (Bill No. 1561), p. 62. This amendment, of course, does not limit the statute's effect on the swearing of witnesses in legal proceedings before Israeli courts.

338. This statute was enacted by the Knesset after the Foundations of Law Act, 1980, went into effect.

cludes provisions having "a social purpose of encouraging rehabilitation of penitents"[339] by making it possible to prevent the disclosure of information about prior convictions and to expunge criminal records after the expiration of certain prescribed periods. This possibility of expunction, "as if the conviction had never occurred,"[340] is based on the Jewish concept of repentance (*teshuvah*), as indicated in the Hebrew title of the statute, *Takkanat ha-Shavim,* a halakhic term connoting assistance to the criminal offender in achieving repentance and rehabilitation. On this point, the Explanatory Notes to the bill stated:[341]

> Many citizens once convicted, however long ago and for whatever crime, major or minor, can neither obtain certain permits and licenses nor return to their occupations and take part in certain work (*e.g.*, as a member of the crew of an airplane or ship) and cannot even travel to certain foreign countries. . . . The basic principle upon which this bill rests is that, with certain exceptions, one should not be stigmatized all one's life because of a transgression but should be given the opportunity to turn over a new leaf; rehabilitation and full integration into society should be encouraged.
>
> The bill adopts the approach of the *Halakhah* expressed in the Enactment for the Encouragement of Penitents (*Takkanat ha-Shavim*), first referred to in Mishnah *Gittin* 5:5, and later extended to other legislative and judicial measures to facilitate the offender's repentance and return to society. In this connection, Hai Gaon, the head of the *yeshivah* in Pumbedita approximately a thousand years ago, wrote in one of his responsa:
>
>> The law is clear that nothing can stand in the way of repentance; God forgives every penitent who He knows has regretted his ugly deeds and has resolved not to commit them again. Although human beings do not know what is hidden but only that which has been openly revealed, if a long period of time has passed and the offender has given no indication of covert or overt impropriety, and it is truly believed that he has repented, he is to be welcomed back in good standing.
>
> On the other hand—and this too is consistent with halakhic principles—the bill includes a number of limitations on the right of the offender to confidentiality of information concerning his crimes. These limitations are based on considerations such as the seriousness of the offense, whether the information is needed to assess fitness for a position whose occupant should exemplify high personal standards, and whether confidence in a person occupying a position of trust would be impaired by reason of the crime.[342]

339. Crime Register and Rehabilitation of Offenders Bill, 1981 (Bill No. 1514), p. 216.

340. Crime Register and Rehabilitation of Offenders Law, 1981, sec. 21.

341. Explanatory Notes to Bill, *supra* n. 339 at 216–217.

342. Minister of Justice Moshe Nissim, presenting the bill for its first reading in the Knesset, dwelt at length on statute's roots in the principles of Jewish law, above discussed, and added (91 *DK* 1892 (1981)):

This statute was extensively discussed by the Supreme Court in *Carmi v. State's Attorney.*[343] The opinion, for a unanimous court, made clear that Jewish law should be the major and primary source for the interpretation of this statute.

As stated, even those statutes enacted in the second legislative period that were not based on Jewish legal principles to the same extent as in the examples just discussed, contain, to a greater or lesser degree, various provisions that are based on Jewish law.[344] The following discussion reviews two instructive examples of such incorporation of Jewish legal principles into the law of the State, as reflected in the decisions of the Supreme Court.

e. SELF-HELP—THE LAND LAW

The Land Law, 1969, provides an interesting example of the incorporation of a principle of Jewish law in order to change the preexisting law. The Land Law is one of the comprehensive statutes of the Israeli civil codification. It replaces the Ottoman Land Law of 1858 and many subsequent Ottoman and Mandatory laws, and it represents a new approach in Israeli law. The Land Code Bill, published in 1964, contained a number of principles inconsistent with Jewish law that need not be discussed at length here.[345] However, in this connection, the remarks of Moshe Landau (later

---

> When ignorance of the criminal record of an individual is likely to cause serious damage, the *Halakhah* requires that past crimes be made known. *See Hafeẓ Ḥayyim* by Rabbi Israel Meir ha-Kohen of Radin, II, 9:1. The draft adopts this approach. It does not provide for the physical expunction of the record, but limits the disclosure of information the record contains. . . . I could quote many other halakhic sources . . . that exemplify the lofty ethical approach which views the [criminal as a] human being and sees the need to rehabilitate him and turn him into an upstanding member of society. In the interest of brevity, I will not quote more than I have already done. . . . The bill before you will have extremely significant consequences, and it is a guidepost for the improvement of society.
>
> At the same time, I must emphasize the difficult challenge this legislation puts before us, namely, achieving the correct balance between the requirements of the rehabilitative approach, which is based on the needs of the individual, and the protection of the public interest, which demands the setting of limits, harsh by their very nature, that to a certain extent are inconsistent with the approach which stresses the needs of the individual. The bill before you is the result of a compromise. As I said, it draws from, and follows the path of, Jewish law.

See also DK, 10th Knesset, 2d Sess., 83d meeting, p. 2319 (1982); *supra* pp. 601–602.

343. 44(i) *P.D.* 353 (1990).

344. For a detailed listing of these provisions, *see supra* p. 1691 and n. 290; *infra* n. 412.

345. *See* the critical comments of various MKs, 40 *DK* 2131, 2278, 2282, 2342 (1964). *See also* Elon, *supra* n. 11 at 90–91.

President of the Supreme Court), who headed the committee that prepared the bill, are noteworthy:[346]

> As regards Jewish rabbinical law, it must regretfully be admitted that more should perhaps have been done to incorporate this part of the Jewish national heritage into the provisions of the new Code. The failure to do so may be explained partly by the monolithic nature of rabbinical law, which makes piecemeal adoption seem a half-measure satisfactory to no one, and partly by the lack of a modern restatement of the body of that law which could serve as a sure basis for its adaptation to present-day conditions.

With all respect, this rationale is not convincing. First, although it is true that "piecemeal adoption" may become problematic if it results in a conceptual incongruence between different legal provisions, there is actually no such incongruence in the overwhelming majority of instances. An excellent example is the law of self-help, as the following discussion demonstrates. Second, the fact that the lack of a modern restatement may require greater effort to present the stance of Jewish law certainly is no justification for refusing to undertake the important and historic task of basing the legislation of the State of Israel on the Jewish legal heritage.[347]

Indeed, in the case of the Land Law, the Legislative Committee of the Knesset rejected the bill that would have continued the preexisting legal regime as to self-help, based on Ottoman law and rooted in Roman and Continental legal concepts, and instead adopted the approach of the Jewish legal system. The question of self-help (*i.e.*, taking the law into one's own hands) is a major topic in the law of real property as well as in other areas of the law.

The difference between the bill and the final text of the law was extensively discussed in *Rosenstein v. Solomon*, a relatively recent decision of the Israeli Supreme Court.[348] Section 173 of the bill provided:

> Whoever seizes land without the consent of the possessor and without a court order . . . must restore the land to the possessor, even if his right [*i.e.*, the right of the one who seized the land] to possession is superior to the right of the possessor.

This section would have carried forward in substance the provision of Section 24 of the Ottoman Land Law, which required the restoration of the *status quo ante* in all instances of self-help before permitting adjudication of

346. M. Landau, "Legislative Trends in the Land Code Bill, 1964," *Scripta Hierosolymitana*, 1966, p. 136.

347. *See also infra* pp. 1867–1868, 1927–1928, for the comments of Justice Landau in Hendeles v. Bank Kupat Am, 35(ii) *P.D.* 785, 798 (1981).

348. 38(ii) *P.D.* 113 (1984) (Elon, J.).

the rights of the parties, even if the particular circumstances justified adjudication prior to restoration of the *status quo.*[349] The Knesset rejected this proposal; the bill's inflexible approach may perhaps have appeal as an abstract legal doctrine, but it is not feasible in the real world, in which, under certain circumstances, the natural and justified desire of an owner to retake property stolen from him is entitled to be respected.

Justice Oliver Wendell Holmes has aptly expressed this point:[350]

> Those who see in the history of law the formal expression of the development of society will be apt to think that the proximate ground of law must be empirical, even when that ground is the fact that a certain ideal or theory of government is generally entertained. Law, being a practical thing, must found itself on actual forces. It is quite enough, therefore, for the law, that man, by an instinct which he shares with the domestic dog, and of which the seal gives a most striking example, will not allow himself to be dispossessed, either by force or fraud, of what he holds, without trying to get it back again. Philosophy may find a hundred reasons to justify the instinct, but it would be totally immaterial if it should condemn it and bid us surrender without a murmur. As long as the instinct remains, it will be more comfortable for the law to satisfy it in an orderly manner, than to leave people to themselves. If it should do otherwise, it would become a matter for pedagogues, wholly devoid of reality.

It was regarding such matters that the Sages said, "The Torah fathomed the character of human beings and spoke taking account of their evil inclination."[351] Furthermore, a property owner should be entitled on occasion to repossess his property by the quickest and most convenient method available.

The change made by the Legislative Committee is contained in Section 19 of the statute, regarding which the Supreme Court stated:[352]

> The final text of the last part of Section 19 of the Land Law, 1969, effected a substantial change in regard to the issue before us. Section 18 of the statute, like Section 174 of the bill, prescribed two conditions that had to be met before self-help would be justified: (1) the purpose of the self-help must be to prevent a trespass about to be committed or to eject the trespasser from property he has succeeded in taking, and (2) the self-help must be carried out

349. Sec. 174 of the bill provided for an exception to this rule only where the land was repossessed by self-help immediately or within a reasonable time after it was trespassed upon.

350. O.W. Holmes, *The Common Law,* Harvard U. Press, 1963, p. 168.

351. *See* TB Kiddushin 21b and Meiri, *Bet ha-Beḥirah, ad loc.*; Rashi on Deuteronomy 21:11.

352. Rosenstein v. Solomon, 38(ii) *P.D.* 113, 125–126 (1984).

without excessive force, "according to the circumstances of the matter, and within a reasonable time."[353]

The change came at the end of Section 19. The first part of Section 19 states: "Whoever dispossesses the possessor of land otherwise than pursuant to Section 18(b) must return the land to the possessor," *i.e.,* upon the expiration of thirty days following the wrongful taking of the land, self-help is no longer available to the lawful owner; and if he nevertheless resorts to self-help, the *status quo ante* must be restored.

Thus, the Land Law adopted generally the principle embodied in Section 24 of the Ottoman Land Law. Section 19 then goes on to include the changes made by the Legislative Committee after the bill's first reading:

> However, this provision does not detract from the authority of the court to adjudicate the rights of both parties at the same time; and the court may award possession as it deems just and under such conditions as it deems appropriate, pending the final decision on the merits.

Thus, the court, at its discretion, may adjudicate at the same time the property rights of both parties—the party who used self-help and the party against whom the self-help was directed. While the court considers the merits, it may, on terms and conditions it deems appropriate, issue an interlocutory order concerning the possession of the land pending final judgment.

This provision permitting the court to adjudicate the rights of the parties without restoring the *status quo ante* constitutes a substantial change from the preexisting law. The decision as to whether to leave undisturbed, *pendente lite,* the situation as it exists after the self-help, or whether to restore the previous situation or make any other arrangement as to the possession of the property, is to be made by the court "as it deems just and under such conditions as it deems appropriate." This is a very vague and general standard which gives the court broad discretionary power, similar to many other such general standards contained in the Land Law and in our legal system generally.

The Supreme Court's opinion went on to discuss the background of the Knesset's adoption of this change in the final text of the statute, and the source from which the Knesset drew its approach to the question of self-help:[354]

> As stated, this innovation in Section 19 was not in the original bill, but was adopted, together with many other changes, by the Legislative Committee of the Knesset. Particularly in such an instance, it is apposite to examine the explanation given by the Legislature as to why it inserted this change into the final text of the statute rather than adopt the [original text of the] bill. When

353. In the Public Lands (Removal of Squatters) Law, 1981, "within a reasonable time" was changed to a fixed period: "within thirty days after the taking."

354. Rosenstein v. Solomon, 38(ii) *P.D.* 113, 126–127 (1984).

the chairman of the Legislative Committee, MK Unna, presented the bill for its second and third readings, he said:[355]

> Section 19 establishes the general rule that whoever dispossesses a person in possession of land otherwise than pursuant to Section 18(b) must return the land to the person dispossessed. If the dispossessor is a robber [*i.e.,* has no claim of right to possession], the obligation to return the land is absolute. However, if the dispossessor is the true owner, various approaches can be taken. Under Roman law, the dispossessor must first restore the land to the person he dispossessed even if that person had stolen the land. Jewish law, on the other hand, takes the view that the land need not be returned to a robber, and that a person who dispossesses a robber is entitled to prove his own ownership and retain possession.
>
> While the Government's bill provided, in Section 173, that the land had to be restored even if the right of the dispossessor was superior to that of the person dispossessed, most members of the Legislative Committee were of the opinion—which conforms to Jewish law—that it is pointless to take the land away from its lawful owner and require him to litigate a claim . . . in order to retrieve his property. It was therefore provided that the court could decide the rights of both parties at the same time and award possession pending final judgment on the merits, as it deems just and under such conditions as it deems appropriate.

In reply to objections raised by MK Arazi, who sought to retain, essentially, the text of Section 173 of the bill, MK Unna added:

> I believe that MK Arazi was not accurate when he described the proposal of the Committee, this section of which was adopted by a majority, as offering an opportunity for taking the law into one's own hands and, as he put it, permitting "might to make right." Nothing was further from the intention of the majority of the Committee.
>
> In actuality, this is more a legal than a factual question. Once we stated at the beginning of the section, "Whoever dispossesses the possessor of land otherwise than pursuant to Section 18(b) must return the land to the possessor"—which is the text of both versions—we have stated the general rule concerning the wrongful taking of land. The question is . . . , What does this addition [proposed by MK Arazi] say? [It says] that it shall make no difference to the judge whether the one who took the land is the lawful owner or a robber. In other words, even if the lawful owner retook land or a dwelling of which someone else had forcibly dispossessed him, the lawful owner must restore it to the person known to be a robber. This was unacceptable to us.
>
> Once we had laid down the principle that it is forbidden to retake possession by force, we were faced with the question how to deal with

355. 45 *DK* 3759 (1969).

> cases such as the following: Someone breaks into a dwelling belonging to one who was on a mission abroad, and proceeds to live there. The owner returns and finds that a stranger has taken over his home. According to the original draft, he can [do nothing but] wait until the court decides his case, which could take months or even years. Our conception, however, was that this entire matter should immediately come before the court, and the court, without delay, should investigate and determine whether the true owner has irrefutable proof that the dwelling is indeed his, in which case the court would allow him to retain possession until the final judgment. If, however, his proof is not clear and convincing, the court would order the immediate return of the property. . . . The matter should be speedily resolved by the court, which must have the discretion to deal with the question of possession from the initial stage of the case until final judgment on the merits. . . . The Committee's proposal is a balanced one, since it establishes the principle that seizure by force is prohibited, but, on the other hand, it grants to the court the power to afford relief in view of the court's ability to weigh the respective contentions when they are submitted.[356]

Thus, the Land Law adopted as the general rule the provision that self-help is forbidden and that the rights of the parties will not be adjudicated until the *status quo ante* has been restored. However, if the court finds that the rights of the person who retook the property by self-help are *prima facie* superior, the court may try the case on the merits without ordering the restoration of the *status quo ante,* and may award possession *pendente lite* on such terms and conditions as it deems just.

As MK Unna pointed out, this provision of Section 19 is contrary to the position of Roman and Continental law and to Section 24 of the Ottoman Land Law (which followed the Continental law) but accords with Jewish law. The subject of self-help in Jewish law underwent a long and tor-

356. *Id.* at 3811–3812, quoted in Rosenstein v. Solomon, *supra* n. 354 at 127–128. *See also* the remarks of MK Unna, *id.,* in regard to the approach of the justices of the Supreme Court to this subject:

> MK Arazi seeks to rely on the justices of the Supreme Court. His quotations are indeed accurate. But he forgets a whole array of contrary quotations which demonstrate that the justices of the Supreme Court are divided in their views. Moreover, there is a trend in recent years, in contrast to the situation in 1949 and 1950, to follow the path taken by the Committee. Almost the only justice who has held fast to his earlier position is Justice Landau, whom MK Arazi quoted. Justice Landau prepared the bill, and it was his proposal that was submitted to the Committee. It is not correct to view the matter as if this [Justice Landau's view] is the consensus of the members of the Supreme Court. The text which the Committee has proposed is therefore a balanced one.

See also supra pp. 1709–1710, quoting the remarks of Justice Landau concerning the failure to incorporate Jewish law to a sufficient extent in the Land Law. The question of self-help was appropriately resolved by the Legislative Committee of the Knesset.

tuous development, which is discussed at length in the *Rosenstein* case.[357] In short, most halakhic authorities hold that one from whom real or personal property has been stolen may resort to self-help as long as it is clear that he is the owner and had in fact been wrongfully dispossessed; and if the owner has suffered no loss or damage, self-help may not be accomplished by force and must be done with as little injury to the wrongdoer as possible.

Jewish law does not ignore the danger posed by self-help—even with the stated reservations and qualifications—to the public peace and to law and order. The opinion in the *Rosenstein* case had the following to say on this point:[358]

> We are not unmindful that Jewish law has pursued as a basic policy the maintenance of public peace and the prevention of any form of violence, and that this policy is reflected in innumerable rules and precepts in all areas of the law.
>
> Thus, the Sages adopted numerous enactments to "promote peace and tranquillity"[359] and to "prevent strife and enmity."[360] The goal of preventing breach of the peace is of primary concern in the decision-making process of the halakhic authorities.[361] For example, in a case where a litigant is known to be violent, the rules of evidence and procedure are radically different from those normally applicable; if the violent character of a defendant intimidates the witnesses against him to the point that they are afraid to testify, then the burden of proof is placed on the defendant rather than the plaintiff.[362] Maimonides summarized the point as follows:[363]
>
>> If a party has witnesses [to support his case], he should look after the witnesses until he brings them to court. If the court knows that the defendant is a violent person and the plaintiff alleges that the witnesses are afraid of the defendant [and therefore refuse] to testify, the court may require the defendant to bring witnesses [to prove his case]. All such matters are similarly dealt with in the case of violent persons.[364]
>
> In the matter of self-help, Jewish law also set as its guiding policy the maintenance of public order and the prevention of violence. As Isaac b. Moses of

357. 38(ii) *P.D.* at 128–134. The basic Talmudic discussion is in TB Bava Kamma 27b and TJ Bava Kamma 3:1, 12a (3:1, 3c), and was extensively discussed—with varying opinions—in geonic literature (*She'iltot le-Rav Aḥa mi-Shabḥa, she'iltah* 2) and by the commentators, codifiers, and authors of responsa. *See* Rosenstein v. Solomon, *supra.*

358. 38(ii) *P.D.* at 132–133.

359. M Gittin 5:8.

360. TB Ḥagigah 22a; Ketubbot 47a, 58b; Kiddushin 63a; Bava Meẓi'a 10a, 12b; TJ Ketubbot 9:4, 52b (9:4, 33a); Maimonides, *MT,* Ishut 21:9. *See also supra* pp. 628–631.

361. *See, e.g.,* Menahem Krochmal, *Resp. Ẓemaḥ Ẓedek* #2; Maimonides, *MT,* Megillah va-Ḥanukkah 4:14.

362. TB Ketubbot 27b; Bava Meẓi'a 39b: "Thus we will judge you and all your violent companions."

363. *MT,* Edut 3:12.

364. *See also Resp. Ribash* #170.

Vienna, the author of *Or Zaru'a* (first part of the thirteenth century), pointed out, self-help is permitted only when it is clear that the person who resorts to it is in fact the owner and has been wrongfully dispossessed; the reason is that [if the law were] otherwise "everyone will say to his neighbor, 'This is mine,' . . . and no one will be left in peace."[365] Solomon Luria (Maharshal, Poland, sixteenth century) elaborated on this rationale: "Because otherwise no one will be left in peace, since everyone will seize the cloak of his fellow and say, 'It is mine,' and will prevail on his claim; thus, might will make right!"[366] When, however, the facts clearly show that property has been stolen, Jewish law recognizes the owner's right to retake his property by self-help; and in such a case, that right outweighs the concern that permitting self-help will tend to increase breaches of the peace.[367]

f. ILLEGAL CONTRACTS

An interesting example of the incorporation of a principle of Jewish law, in substance though not in full detail, appears in Sections 30 and 31 of the Contracts Law (General Part), 1973, concerning illegal contracts. The position of Jewish law on this subject, as has been pointed out earlier in this work,[368] is essentially different from that of other legal systems. Under Jewish law, an illegal contract may not be enforced where the effect would be to bring about the performance of the illegal act. Thus, an agreement to lend money at interest, which is prohibited by Jewish law, may not be enforced, because enforcement would make the court an accomplice in violating the prohibition. However, if the purpose of the agreement itself is not unlawful but the factum is tainted by violation of a religious prohibition (*e.g.*, a contract made on the sabbath), the validity of the contract is not affected by the fact that it was entered into in a manner prohibited by law, and the court will enforce it. Thus, if, in order to deceive the tax authorities, a contract for the sale of property specifies a price less than the amount actually agreed upon, the basic purpose of the contract to sell land is in no way unlawful; such a contract is binding and enforceable. Of course, the guilty parties are criminally liable for cheating the tax authorities, but they cannot be allowed to "transgress and be rewarded"; their crime cannot be permitted to be a shield against civil liabilities flowing from the contract. Consequently, each party to the transaction is entitled to enforce his con-

365. *Or Zaru'a,* Piskei Bava Kamma 3:145.

366. *Yam Shel Shelomo,* Bava Kamma, ch. 3, #5.

367. *See* the subsequent remarks in the opinion to the effect that when social and moral conditions so require, the interest in preserving the public peace is to be given priority over the right of the victim to retake his stolen property through self-help, even if as a general rule such a right is recognized. *See* Jacob Reischer, *Resp. Shevut Ya'akov,* II, ḤM #167; *infra* p. 1911 n. 38.

368. *Supra* pp. 128–130.

tractual rights, so long as performance does not itself constitute a violation of the law.[369]

Sections 30 and 31 of the Contracts Law (General Part) deal with the problem of illegal contracts differently than the common-law and the Continental legal systems; these sections, although not completely congruent with Jewish law, are based on the policy of Jewish law described above. An opinion in *Howard v. Miarah*[370] extensively discussed the question of illegal contracts:

> Sections 30 and 31 effected a substantial innovation in regard to defective contracts (which is the term used in the marginal heading to describe contracts tainted by a defect described in the section). The new approach is manifest from the result when the two sections are read together. Section 30 provides that "a contract whose execution, content, or purpose is illegal, immoral, or contrary to public policy is void." This absolute and unqualified provision, if it stood alone, could have only one meaning: a contract which suffers from a defect described in the section is absolutely null and void—as worthless as a broken shard. However, this section does not stand by itself; Section 31 stands with it *in pari materia,* and each section throws light on the other.
>
> There are two main provisions in Section 31: (a) benefits received pursuant to an illegal contract are ordinarily subject to restitution . . . except to the extent that the court determines that justice requires otherwise; and (b) if one party has performed its obligations under the contract, the court may, if it determines that justice so requires, order the other party to perform its corresponding obligations, in full or in part. Section 31 thus provides that not only may the court order restitution of what was received under the illegal contract, but it may also "revive" the void contract, and, under certain circumstances, order performance of the contractual obligations. Since it may be presumed that the Legislature is not interested in "resurrection of the dead" or *creatio ex nihilo,* it becomes perfectly clear what Section 30 means when it says that the contracts to which it refers are "void."

A comprehensive article by Professor D. Friedmann has discussed the novel features of Section 31. It states:[371]

369. In the course of time, the rule was qualified: where recognizing a contractual right will encourage illegal acts, the court will deny recognition. For example, if witnesses fail to testify after being paid to testify falsely, the court will not order restitution of the money paid. *See Resp. Shevut Ya'akov,* I, #145, and *see supra* pp. 129–130.

370. 35(ii) *P.D.* 505, 516–517 (1980) (Elon, J.).

371. D. Friedmann, "Toẓa'ot I-Ḥukkiyyut ba-Din ha-Yisra'eli le-Or Hora'ot Se'ifim 30–31 le-Ḥok ha-Ḥozim (Ḥelek Kelali)" [The Consequences of Illegality in Israeli Law in the Light of the Provisions of Sections 30–31 of the Contracts Law (General Part)], *Iyyunei Mishpat,* V (1976–1977), pp. 618–619.

> This provision is not taken from any foreign legal system. It does not follow English, German, or French law. In all those systems, the general rule, subject to certain exceptions, denies any relief when the parties are *in pari delicto*. However, Section 31 of the Contracts Law establishes as the general rule the right of restitution in case of an illegal contract, subject to exceptions depending on the court's discretion. . . . Section 31 devises an original solution, which does not rest on the sources on which Israeli legislation is generally based.

These observations by Professor Friedmann were the subject of the following comments in the *Howard* opinion:[372]

> I agree with these statements, except for the very last one. The distinguished author was not completely accurate in his generalization concerning the sources upon which Israeli legislation is generally based, or in his specific statement concerning the source and pedigree of the legislation on the subject before us. His general statement is not fully accurate because he overlooked a singularly important source on which Israeli legislation is generally based, *i.e.*, Jewish law, which—as the drafters of the civil statutes attest—the Legislature viewed as a primary source for civil legislation; other legal systems served the Legislature as "an ancillary source of enlightenment and guidance." (The reader is referred to our discussion of this matter elsewhere.)[373]
>
> This point has been repeatedly made with regard to the subject before us. The Introduction to the Contracts Bill (General Part), 1970, states that "the principles upon which the bill is based were discussed in the Public Committee after a review of various legal systems, with particular attention to the approach of Jewish law." The Introduction makes clear that this statement is particularly true in regard to the matter of illegal contracts:
>
> > Under the English rule, the court does not dirty its hands by dealing with such a contract, and prefers to let the loss resulting from nonperformance lie where it falls. This rule has caused great injustice, as shown by Justice Dr. M. Silberg's research and the discussion in *Jacobs v. Kartoz*[374] and its progeny. The bill provides that an illegal contract is void, but at the same time it lays down a number of alternative remedies that the court may employ according to the circumstances of the case: complete or partial restitution; denial of restitution; and, to the extent that one of the parties has performed, requiring full or part performance by another party.
>
> Further on, the Explanatory Notes to Sections 31 and 32 of the bill (which are almost completely identical to Sections 30 and 31 in the statute as en-

372. 35(ii) *P.D.* at 517–518.
373. Roth v. Yeshufeh, 33(i) *P.D.* 617, 632–633 (1979).
374. 9 *P.D.* 1401 (1955).

acted) state: "This broad range of possible solutions allows the court to decide each case on its own facts, and to do justice between the parties in each instance."

The *Howard* opinion goes on to describe the method of the incorporation of the Jewish law on the subject of illegal contracts:[375]

> The law of illegal contracts is an interesting example of how Israeli law can incorporate principles and policies of Jewish law without adopting in detail all the rules and legal positions of Jewish law. The position of Jewish law that an illegal contract is generally binding as a matter of civil law was not adopted; the general rule, as enacted in Section 30, is that such a contract is void. However, the Contracts Law did adopt two fundamental principles basic to the Jewish law of illegal contracts. The first acknowledges that the court is empowered to entertain a claim based on an illegal contract; the position that a claim on an illegal contract is "too tainted to touch" was completely rejected. The court is required to "dirty its hands" and adjudicate such a claim in order to do justice between the parties. It is true, of course, that in using its discretion, as stated in Section 31, the court is to take into account, among other considerations, the conduct of each of the parties and the extent of each party's role in the illegality of the contract, and the need "to educate the public to avoid tactics that every honest person must view as suspect."[376] As we have seen, this last factor was also given significant weight in the Jewish law of illegal contracts, so as to prevent undesirable conduct under certain social conditions. But these are all considerations that are relevant when a claim on an illegal contract is litigated. The court sitting in such a case no longer refuses to entertain such a claim; it accepts the responsibility of examining the contract and its terms, weighing the circumstances of the case and, most importantly, treating the parties as justice requires.
>
> The other principle with regard to illegal contracts that has been adopted by the Israeli Contracts Law is the basic objective of Jewish law that "the wrongdoer should not be rewarded"—that one who violates the law should not be enabled by the violation to avoid contractual obligations imposed by the civil law. In order to achieve this goal, the Legislature provided in Section 31 that, as a general rule, restitution should be made of moneys received; and the court was given discretionary authority to order, in particular circumstances, the performance of the obligations arising out of the contract, all in order "to decide each case on its own facts, and to do justice between the parties in each instance."[377]

375. 35(ii) *P.D.* at 519–520.
376. *See* Nili v. Shelomi, 30(ii) *P.D.* 3, 6 (1976).
377. Explanatory Notes to Contracts Bill (General Part).

These objectives of the Jewish law of illegal contracts, which were accepted in the Contracts Law, suggest the following conclusions, which are unique to Israeli contracts legislation:[378]

> We must avoid as far as possible, consistent with Sections 30 and 31, any result that would deny to the parties rights to which they are entitled under the contract they have agreed upon. This policy is realized by giving effect to two guiding principles: (1) the parties should be held to their contractual obligations to the fullest extent permitted by Section 31; and (2) the consequences of illegality pursuant to Section 30 should be limited to the fullest possible extent by making a distinction, for example, between illegality by reason of the essential nature of the transaction embodied in the contract (such as a contract for the performance of an illegal act) and illegality which is only incidental to the essence of the transaction. . . .
>
> All this leads to an additional conclusion, alluded to at the beginning of this opinion. It is true that Section 30 states that an illegal contract is void. However, the provisions of Section 31 reveal the nature and extent of this invalidity. The court has the power to order the performance of obligations contained in the contract; and, as stated above, this power is to be exercised as sympathetically and generously as possible. It follows that we have before us a contract which actually is alive and which, at the appropriate time, when the court so orders, is given effect both as a contract and—when the court exercises its authority under Section 31 and denies the right of restitution—as a conveyance of property.
>
> An illegal contract under Israeli contract law is thus not like "the dust of the earth," as worthless as a broken shard or, as my distinguished colleague put it, "completely valueless," for the court is not in the business of creating *ex nihilo* and ordering the performance of nonexistent obligations. The invalidity referred to in Section 30 thus means, as it were, that the contract . . . is dormant, and the court's decree awakens the contract from its "slumber" to make it as fully effective as the court orders. The term "void" in Section 30 thus does not mean "nonexistent," but rather "existing but not operative." Because it does have life, it may also, within the framework of the provisions of Section 31, be given effect.[379]

378. 35(ii) *P.D.* at 520–521.

379. For further discussion of the specific approach of the Contracts Law to illegal contracts, *see* Edrei v. Gedalyahu, 36(iv) *P.D.* 281, 290ff. (1982). It is there pointed out (p. 292) that the term "void" in its legal sense—in other areas of the law as well—"does not mean non-existent. Voidness as a legal rather than a natural concept is always relative and flexible. A legal norm can be completely without force in one context and yet binding in another. . . . This is true in all areas of the law." A subsequent article by Friedmann concerning illegal contracts, "Consequences of Illegality under the Israeli Contracts Law (General Part), 1973," 33 *Int. and Comp. L.Q.* 81 (1984), discusses in detail the *Howard* and *Edrei* cases and the differences of opinion in the Supreme Court as to the interpretation of Sections 30 and 31. Friedmann reiterated that "a wholly new approach has, however, been adopted with regard to the consequences of illegality" (p. 81), and pointed out that this new ap-

D. Legislation Contrary to Jewish Law

There are some rules of Jewish law whose incorporation into the law of the State cannot reasonably be expected in view of contemporary economic and social conditions. Such rules include gender-discriminatory laws applicable to various legal transactions or to inheritance. If contemporary halakhic authorities were not so diffident about exercising their decision-making authority, they could, within the halakhic system itself, adapt these rules to current needs through the traditionally accepted methods for the continued creative development of Jewish law. These methods had always been employed by halakhic authorities of previous generations and, in fact, Chief Rabbis Herzog and Uziel sought to employ them at the time the State was established, but their efforts met resistance from others.[380]

A considerable amount of Israeli legislation, however, involves failure to incorporate Jewish law due only to indifference and lack of awareness of the place of Jewish law in the spiritual life of the Jewish people. This astonishing fact is an indictment which, at least in the author's view, is extremely serious and, therefore, requires proof by a number of explicit examples.

1. SURETYSHIP—THE GUARANTEE LAW

A central question in the law of suretyship is: At what point may the surety properly be called upon to make good on the undertaking to guarantee? According to English law[381] and the *Mejelle,*[382] the creditor is entitled to proceed directly against the surety without first making demand upon the principal debtor. On the other hand, under the German Civil Code,[383] the Swiss Civil Code of 1941,[384] and the Nordic Draft Code of 1963,[385] the creditor must first obtain and levy execution on a judgment against the principal debtor; only after the execution has been returned unsatisfied may the creditor proceed against the surety. Under this approach, the creditor may look directly to the surety only when there is an express agreement

---

proach is contrary to English, German, and French law. However, surprisingly, he once again ignored the decisive influence of Jewish law on Sections 30 and 31.

380. For detailed discussion of these efforts, *see supra* pp. 1683–1684 and nn. 265–270. For an instructive example of the continuing development of Jewish law, *see* Nagar v. Nagar, 38(ii) *P.D.* 365, 402–407 (1984), discussed *infra* pp. 1794–1802, which deals with the fundamental and revolutionary change in the position taken by the halakhic authorities in recent generations regarding a woman's obligation to study the Oral Law—a change that led to the conclusion that a father and a mother jointly are obligated to educate their children, and to decide upon the nature of such education.

381. E. Jenks, *A Digest of English Civil Law* (3rd ed., 1938), I, p. 277, sec. 682.

382. *Mejelle,* secs. 643–644.

383. *Bürgerliches Gesetzbuch,* secs. 771, 773(1).

384. *Zivilgesetzbuch,* secs. 495, 496.

385. V. Kruse, *A Nordic Draft Code,* Copenhagen, 1963, p. 347, par. 1301.

between the creditor and the surety granting this right, or when special difficulties exist that prevent a claim from being made against the principal debtor.[386]

In Jewish law, this problem has undergone various stages of development, and its solution is identical with that of Swiss law, which is now one of the most modern suretyship laws. The basic principle that has held steadfast throughout every stage of Jewish law is that before making claim against a surety who has not explicitly otherwise agreed, the creditor must first obtain a judgment against the principal debtor and be unable to collect it. Logic also dictates this solution; one who undertakes as an accommodation to act as surety assumes that everything will be done to obtain payment from the principal debtor, and that only when the principal debtor cannot pay will the creditor make claim against the surety. It is also only fair that so long as the debt can be satisfied out of the assets of the principal debtor, who has received the loan proceeds, the surety should not be called upon to make good on his obligation.

However, in response to the needs of commerce and of an efficient system of credit, which often call for speedy and certain payment of debts, Jewish law has also provided that where at the outset the surety expressly so agrees, the creditor may proceed against him directly in the first instance because the surety has knowingly consented to such liability.[387] A creditor who wishes to assure that he will have this right must expressly so contract, so as to put the surety on notice of the nature and scope of the liability at the time the suretyship is created.[388]

In the Guarantee Bill submitted to the Knesset in 1964,[389] the problem was resolved in accordance with English law and the *Mejelle,* with one minor change: Before the creditor can require the surety to meet his obligation, he must first demand payment from the principal debtor and wait 48 hours, after which he is then free to proceed against the surety if payment has not been made. In the statute as enacted in 1967, this waiting period of

386. *E.g.,* when the principal debtor has become bankrupt or is abroad, and it is very difficult to proceed against him.

387. Another method by which the creditor obtains the right to proceed directly against the surety is by the surety's becoming an *arev kabbelan,* where the agreement makes no reference to suretyship, but instead the surety states, "Give to him and I shall give to you." *See* Sh. Ar. ḤM 129:15 *et seq.* This category also exists in the Swiss Code, sec. 496, where it is called *Solidarischer Bürger.*

388. *See* Maimonides, *MT,* Malveh ve-Loveh 25:1–5; *Tur* ḤM 129:8–20; Sh. Ar. ḤM 129:8–18. The rule of Swiss and Nordic law that when there are special difficulties in making claim against the principal debtor, the creditor may proceed against the surety in the first instance, also exists in Jewish law. *See* Maimonides, *op. cit.,* 25:3, 26:3; *Tur* ḤM 129:11–14; Sh. Ar. ḤM 129:10–12.

389. Bill No. 632, 1964, pp. 71–72, secs. 9–11.

48 hours (which really has no significance) was deleted and the text of the statute was amended to read:[390]

> The surety and debtor are jointly and severally liable to the creditor, but the creditor may not require the surety to fulfill his obligation as such unless demand has first been made on the debtor to satisfy the debt.

Thus, even in an ordinary suretyship, with no explicit agreement for direct liability of the surety, the creditor, as a practical matter, could proceed directly against the surety without first pursuing a claim against the principal debtor; a simple demand on the principal debtor to satisfy the debt was the only prerequisite. Even if the debtor could pay, the creditor did not have to attempt to levy against the principal debtor or even sue him. This provision was therefore completely contrary to the position of Jewish law.

This is an example of an important civil-law statute that, although according in substantial measure with the position of Jewish law, diverged from Jewish law and took a directly contrary position on a central issue. Adopting the position of Jewish law would have been consistent with current economic and social conditions, as demonstrated by the fact that it is the position adopted by the most modern legal systems. Was this not a good opportunity to base the Guarantee Law on this fundamental principle of Jewish law, rather than on a contrary principle of some other legal systems?[391]

On March 17, 1992, the Knesset enacted an amendment that brings the Guarantee Law closer to the Jewish law of suretyship. Section 17(c) of the Guarantee Law now provides that the creditor may not proceed against a noncorporate surety unless judgment has first been obtained against the principal debtor and reasonable efforts to execute on the judgment have been unsuccessful, or unless it is apparent that such efforts would be futile, as where the principal debtor is dead or has filed for bankruptcy.

The reason for the amendment is discussed in the Explanatory Notes to the bill (Bill No. 2072, July 16, 1991, p. 331): In recent years, accommodation guarantors of family members, friends, and fellow-workers have been subjected to serious hardship by being forced to pay creditors who, simply because it was more convenient to look to the guarantor in the first instance, made no effort to collect from the principal debtor.

Where the debt is to finance the purchase of the debtor's dwelling, the

390. *Laws of Israel,* 1967, No. 496, p. 46, sec. 8.

391. *See* M. Elon, "Ḥofesh ha-Hatna'ah be-Dinei Arvut ba-Mishpat ha-Ivri" [Freedom of Contract in the Jewish Law of Suretyship], *Proceedings of the Fourth International Congress of Jewish Studies,* I (1967), pp. 197–208. As to the Guarantee Law, 1967, *see* Kote v. Kote, 36(i) *P.D.* 236 (1981), *additional hearing,* 38(iii) *P.D.* 197 (1984).

amendment applies only where the guaranty is for no more than NIS (New Israeli Shekels) 250,000. Where the debt is incurred for any other purpose, the amendment applies only where the guaranty is for no more than NIS 40,000.

2. THE GIFT LAW

The Gift Law, 1968, is another puzzling example of refusal to accept the approach of Jewish law. The Explanatory Notes to the bill as introduced specifically emphasized that with regard to one of the central principles of the law of gifts, the Public Committee took into consideration

> the attitude of Jewish law and of English common law, according to which a person can bestow a gift upon another without the donee's knowledge, subject to the right of the donee to reject the gift after becoming aware of it. The Committee advised against the inclusion of such a provision in the bill. Instead, it has proposed that the silence of the donee should be regarded as consent unless the donee gives notice of rejection of the gift within a reasonable time.[392]

In this instance, the approach of Jewish law is the same as that of another modern and distinguished legal system, namely, English law, as well as of other legal systems, but the bill deliberately chose to accept the principle found in the legal systems that take a contrary approach. Indeed, when the Gift Law came up for its second and third readings in the Knesset, a number of amendments adopted, to some degree, principles of Jewish law, but no amendment made any change in regard to the essential nature of a gift.[393]

3. LIMITATION OF ACTIONS

In the two instances just discussed, the bills as originally introduced were not consonant with Jewish law. In other instances, legislation proposed by the Government was based on Jewish law, but the proposal was rejected in the later stages of the legislative process and a principle contrary to Jewish law was substituted. One example relates to limitation of actions, sometimes called "prescription."

The law of limitations, like other legal institutions in Jewish law, underwent a number of stages of development. In the Talmudic period,

392. Explanatory Notes to the Gift Bill, 1965 (Bill No. 669), p. 368; sec. 4, p. 369.

393. *See* Gift Law, 1968, secs. 2, 3. MK Klinghoffer's proposal to add a section adopting the principle of Jewish law that "a benefit may be conferred on a person in his absence" was rejected for reasons that are far from convincing. *See* the remarks of MKs Klinghoffer and Azanyah, 52 *DK* 2349–2351 (1968).

Jewish law, except in two cases,[394] did not recognize the principle of limitations at all; the principle was "the creditor may always collect."[395] From the thirteenth century on, Jewish law to some extent began to recognize the concept of limitations. Even while this was occurring, the law held fast to the principle that limitations did not extinguish the right; the new notion was that delay in making the claim could defeat the remedy by casting doubt on the credibility of the evidence offered to prove the claim. When a claim based on old documents was submitted for decision to Asheri, he wrote:[396]

> I am always very disturbed at the possibility of chicanery. Why have they been kept so long, if not to conceal the stratagem and cause it to be forgotten by the time the documents are produced? . . . Therefore, if the defendant pleads that he has discharged the debt or that it never existed, I inquire very carefully to get at the truth, and if the facts appear to me to establish that the claim is deceitful and untruthful, I say that no Jewish judge may undertake to try the case, and I deliver to the defendant a signed certification to this effect.

This view, however, did not immediately win general agreement; in the fourteenth century, Isaac b. Sheshet Perfet (Ribash) wrote that a plea of limitations was a "vain plea."[397] Nevertheless, over the course of time Asheri's view gained acceptance and was further refined. In the fifteenth century, Joseph Colon (Maharik) ruled that when a claim is stale, the claimant is suspected of deceit, and a particularly thorough investigation is required even when the promissory note itself states that "the defendant will not contest the document and accepts the obligation under solemn oath."[398] This ruling was later codified in the *Shulḥan Arukh.*[399]

In the sixteenth century, Samuel de Medina (Maharashdam) ruled that if there is no reasonable explanation for the delay in the assertion of the claim, the court must try to persuade the parties to arrive at a compromise settlement.[400] Isaac Adarbi, Maharashdam's contemporary, held that courts are required to compel the parties to accept a compromise of a stale claim.[401] Up to the beginning of the seventeenth century, there was no fixed

394. Namely, a claim for payment of a widow's *ketubbah* and a claim for her support from her husband's estate; TB Ketubbot 96a, 104a.

395. TJ Ketubbot 12:5, 67b (12:5, 35b); TB Ketubbot 104a/b.

396. *Resp. Asheri* 85:10, 68:20.

397. *Resp. Ribash* #404.

398. *Resp. Maharik* #190 (ed. Cracow, #186).

399. Sh. Ar. ḤM 61:9 (*see also* Rema's gloss), 98:1–2.

400. *Resp. Maharashdam,* ḤM #367.

401. *Resp. Divrei Rivot* #109.

period of limitations, and the court would carefully inquire into the circumstances of each case.

From the beginning of the seventeenth century, as the need increased for a clear legal rule with regard to the period during which the defendant could expect a claim to be made against him, Jewish law adopted, by way of legislation and custom, the principle that the mere staleness of a claim, without more, destroys the credibility of the proof offered to support it; a defendant who denies the existence of the debt may take an oath to the truth of his plea, and the claim is then dismissed. Even then, the principle persisted that limitations does not extinguish the right itself, and a defendant who did not deny his debt, and certainly a defendant who admitted it, was bound to pay even if the claim was long delayed. The period of limitations was generally three years, and in certain cases six years.[402]

This new stage in the Jewish law of limitations also did not win immediate acceptance by all the halakhic authorities. Abraham Ankawa, a *dayyan* of the Jewish community in Morocco in the mid-nineteenth century, wrote concerning this new rule adopted in the Polish and Lithuanian centers: "It is quite novel, and presumably they adopted an enactment for themselves for some reason that existed in their time, even though it is contrary to the law."[403] Even some of the authorities in Poland were still skeptical about this new development.[404] However, over the course of time, this new rule in the law of limitations became generally accepted, and a number of further elaborations and improvements were added, chiefly: (1) if the debtor becomes impoverished to the point where it is financially impossible to recover payment from him, the limitations period is tolled during his indigency; (2) limitations will not run during the minority of either the debtor or the creditor; and (3) where a debtor has unequivocally waived the plea of limitations in writing, proceedings can be instituted on the claim after the period of limitations has expired.[405]

In 1957, the Government introduced in the Knesset a bill on limitations[406] that accorded entirely in principle and also, for the most part, in detail, with the approach of Jewish law. The central principle in the bill was that limitations is a procedural and not a substantive matter, *i.e.*, it does not extinguish the right. This principle was not only implicit from a number

402. Dubnow, *supra* n. 198, Enactment #205 (1628), and others.

403. *Kerem Ḥemer*, Leghorn, 1869, ḤM #33.

404. *See Resp. Shevut Ya'akov*, III, ḤM #182; *Urim ve-Thummim* to Sh. Ar. ḤM ch. 61, Urim, subpar. 18.

405. Abraham David of Buczacz, *Kesef ha-Kodoshim* to Sh. Ar. ḤM 61:9. For further discussion of limitations in Jewish law, *see* M. Elon, "Ha-Hityashenut ba-Din ha-Ivri" [Limitations in Jewish Law], *Ha-Praklit*, XIV (1958), pp. 179–189, 243–279.

406. Bill No. 312, 1957, p. 280.

of sections in the bill,[407] but was also clearly and explicitly stated: "Staleness of a claim alone does not extinguish the [claimant's] right."[408] Another principle that followed Jewish law was also explicitly set forth in the bill: "A plea of limitations is not accepted if, after the claim has been filed . . . , the defendant, in any of the proceedings, has admitted the validity of the plaintiff's claim."[409] By adopting these two central principles, the bill conformed to the principles of limitations in Jewish law.

When the bill came up for second and third readings in the Knesset, there was a significant reduction in the extent of its conformity to the position of Jewish law. Although the provision that "staleness does not extinguish the right itself" remained undisturbed,[410] Section 3(b) of the bill was deleted; that section had provided that if during the course of the proceedings the defendant admits the validity of the claim, the defense of limitations is precluded. In addition, the statute as enacted specifically provides that the running of limitations is tolled by a defendant's admission of the validity of the claim only when the admission is unaccompanied by a plea of limitations.[411] The net result is that a defendant may admit that the debt exists and that he has not paid it, and at the same time assert that he is not willing to pay because the period of limitations has run. This approach is significantly contrary to that of Jewish law, and the courts have on more than one occasion requested the defendant to act *lifnim mi-shurat ha-din, i.e.,* more generously than the law requires, and pay to the plaintiff the amount of the debt.[412]

407. Sec. 2 (limitations is a defense to the claim only if the defendant raises it; if he does not, the court will not raise it on its own initiative); sec. 3(a) (the defendant must plead limitations at the first opportunity); sec. 20 (if the plaintiff holds a pledge or deposit as security for the loan, he may collect on his claim to the amount of the security, notwithstanding the expiration of the period of limitations).

408. Sec. 5.

409. Sec. 3(2).

410. Prescription Law, 1958 (*Laws of Israel,* 1958, No. 251, p. 112), at the end of sec. 2; all the other sections implying that limitations is only a procedural matter also remained.

411. Sec. 9.

412. *See* Boyer v. Shikkun Ovedim, 38(ii) *P.D.* 561 (1984). In its judgment, the Supreme Court requested the defendant to be more generous than the letter of the law required, and pay the plaintiff the money due to him. This request was based, *inter alia,* on Jewish law. In that case, the defendant admitted liability, but raised the defense of limitations. On the basis of that plea, the plaintiff's claim seeking restitution of a deposit made years previously, but at its much higher monetary value as of the time of trial, was dismissed. *See* the opinion in the *Boyer* case for additional cases cited there.

As to the weight to be given to legislative history recorded in *Divrei ha-Keneset* [Knesset Record] in interpreting statutes and as to the place of Jewish law in Knesset legislation, *see* (in addition to the citations *supra* in connection with the various statutes and to the discussion *infra*) *infra* pp. 1934–1935 and n. 104; A.M. Appelbaum, "Divrei ha-Keneset ki-Re'ayah le-Ferush ha-Ḥok" [The Knesset Record as Evidence in Statutory Interpretation],

E. Self-Sufficiency of the Law of the State of Israel

From the very beginning of the State of Israel, the desire was often expressed that the law of the independent Jewish state should be self-sustaining—should itself provide all the necessary means for its own interpretation—and should no longer be tied by Article 46 of the Palestine Order in Council as by an umbilical cord to English common law and equity. This self-sufficiency was achieved to a certain extent in 1957 as a result of decisions by the Supreme Court of Israel[413] that English decisions rendered after the establishment of the State of Israel in 1948 did not have the authoritative force of English decisions rendered before that time. Even the force of pre-1948 English decisions became progressively weakened. Beginning in 1965, a number of statutes (such as the Succession Law, 1965; the Land

---

Ha-Praklit, XXI (1965), pp. 411ff.; Y. Sussman, "Mikẓat Mat'amei Parshanut" [Some Choice Principles of Interpretation], *Pinḥas Rosen Jubilee Volume,* Jerusalem, 1962, pp. 147–161; U. Yadin, "Ḥok ha-Yerushah ke-Ḥelek me-ha-Ḥakikah ha-Ezraḥit be-Yisra'el" [The Succession Law as Part of Israeli Civil Legislation], *Iyyunei Mishpat,* III (1973), p. 26; *id.,* "Ve-Shuv al Perush Ḥukkei ha-Keneset" [More on the Interpretation of Knesset Legislation], *Ha-Praklit,* XXVI (1970), pp. 190–211, 358–377; S. Deutsch, "Gemirut Da'at be-Hitḥayyevuyot ba-Mishpat ha-Ivri" [Intention in Contractual Obligations under Jewish Law], *Dine Israel,* III (1972), pp. 207, 224–226; G. Tedeschi, "Ḥiyyuv ha-Mezonot be-Mishpateinu ha-Ezraḥi" [The Obligation of Support in Our Civil Law], *Mishpatim,* VI (1976), pp. 242–274; I. Shiloh, "Ḥok ha-Yerushah, 1965, bi-Re'i ha-Pesikah" [The Succession Law, 1965, as Reflected in Court Decisions], *Iyyunei Mishpat,* III (1973), pp. 34ff.; Z. Zeltner, "Dinei ha-Ḥozim be-Yisra'el be-Hitpatḥutam Meshekh Ḥaẓi ha-Yovel me-Az Kiyyum ha-Medinah" [The Development of Contract Law in Israel in the Quarter-Century of the State's Existence], *Ha-Praklit,* XXIX (1974), pp. 198, 229–230; the articles by Z. Falk, S. Agranat, M. Elon, N. Rakover, J. Goldsmidt, and A. Kirschenbaum in *Dine Israel,* V (1974), English Section, pp. VII–CXVI; H. Cohn, "Al ha-Mishpat ha-Ivri be-Ḥayyeinu" [On Jewish Law in Our Life], *Petaḥim,* II (32) (1975), pp. 43–47; M. Elon, "Ha-Mishpat ha-Ivri be-Mishpat ha-Medinah, Keiẓad?" [Jewish Law in the Legal System of the State—What Is the Way?], *De'ot,* X (1959), p. 15; *id.,* "Ha-Mishpat ha-Ivri be-Mishpat ha-Medinah, al ha-Maẓuy ve-al ha-Raẓuy" [Jewish Law in the Legal System of the State—Reality and Ideal], *Ha-Praklit,* XXV (1968), p. 27; *id., Ḥakikah, passim; id., Mi-Ba'ayot ha-Halakhah ve-ha-Mishpat bi-Medinat Yisra'el* [Problems of *Halakhah* and Law in the State of Israel], Publication of the Seminar on the Jewish People in the Diaspora held at the President's Residence, Institute for Contemporary Judaism, Hebrew University, Jerusalem, 1973, pp. 9–47; I.S. Ben-Meir, *Hashpa'at ha-Halakhah al Ḥukkei ha-Medinah* [The Influence of the *Halakhah* on the Laws of the State], Series on the People and the State, Tel Aviv, 1963, p. 141; M. Unna, *supra* n. 257; S. Shilo, "Le-Ma'amado Shel ha-Mishpat ha-Ivri ba-Medinah" [On the Position of Jewish Law in the State], *Dine Israel,* V (1974), pp. 255–258; Z. Falk, *Halakhah u-Ma'aseh bi-Medinat Yisra'el* [*Halakhah* and Its Practical Application in the State of Israel], Jerusalem, 1967; Elon, *supra* n. 11; E. Rackman, "Jewish Law in the State of Israel—Reflections from History," *Dine Israel,* VI (1975), English Section, pp. VII–XXIV; D. Friedmann, "Independent Development of Israeli Law," 10 *Israel L. Rev.* 515, 545–548, 555–562 (1975). *See also* Dan, Ltd. v. Attorney General, 20(iv) *P.D.* 253, 257–262 (1966) (resort to legislative history for statutory interpretation proper only when statute on its face is not clear).

413. The first such decision was Kokhavi v. Becker, 11 *P.D.* 225 (1957).

Law, 1969; the Contracts Law (Remedies for Breach of Contract), 1970; the Contracts Law (General Part), 1973; and the Contract for Services Law, 1974) provided that Article 46 did not apply to matters covered by those statutes.

On the other hand, other statutes, covering different areas of the law, did not include a similar provision severing the tie to English law.[414] This fact, and especially the fact that Article 46 continued to be generally applicable throughout Israeli law (except with regard to those statutes explicitly excluded from its coverage), produced a great deal of uncertainty, reflected in the decisions of the Supreme Court and in articles by scholars and jurists,[415] with regard to the extent to which the Israeli legal system was in fact self-sufficient. This uncertainty was resolved in the Foundations of Law Act, 1980, Section 2 of which expressly repealed Article 46 of the Palestine Order in Council.[416]

IV. JEWISH LAW IN ISRAELI JUDICIAL DECISIONS

Adjudication, especially Supreme Court adjudication, is the other channel through which Jewish law has influenced and enriched the Israeli legal system. Adjudication as a method of incorporating Jewish law has very

414. In March 1972, the Amendment of Law and Administration Ordinance Law (No. 14) was enacted, prescribing that "any provision in a statute to the effect that the statute, or any term used in the statute, shall be interpreted according to English law or according to English principles of legal interpretation is no longer binding" (*Laws of Israel,* 1972, p. 61). This amendment repealed express provisions in six ordinances dating from the British Mandate that required those ordinances to be interpreted according to English principles of legal interpretation (*e.g.,* Civil Wrongs Ordinance (New Version), 1968, sec. 1; Criminal Law Ordinance, 1963, sec. 4; etc.).

415. *See* Levontin and Goldwater, *Kelalei Bererat ha-Din be-Yisra'el ve-Siman 46 li-Devar ha-Melekh* [Israeli Choice-of-Law Principles and Article 46 of the Palestine Order in Council], Harry Sacher Institute for Research into Legislation and Comparative Law, Hebrew University, Jerusalem, 1974, p. 26; D. Friedmann, "Ha-Hora'ah bi-Devar Aẓma'ut ha-Ḥok u-Va'ayat ha-Lakunah ba-Ḥakikah ha-Yisra'elit ha-Ḥadashah" [The Provision Regarding Independence of the Law and the Problem of Lacunae in New Israeli Legislation], *Mishpatim,* V (1974), p. 91; A. Barak, "Ha-Hora'ah bi-Devar 'Aẓma'ut ha-Ḥok' u-Va'ayat ha-Lakunah ba-Ḥakikah ha-Yisra'elit ha-Ḥadashah" [same], *Mishpatim,* V (1974), p. 99; U. Yadin, "Keiẓad Yeforash Ḥok ha-Shomerim" [How Shall the Bailees Law Be Interpreted?], *Ha-Praklit,* XXIV (1968), p. 493; *id.,* "Ve-Shuv al Perush Ḥukkei ha-Keneset" [More on the Interpretation of Knesset Legislation], *Ha-Praklit,* XXVI (1970), p. 190; Z. Zeltner, "Haẓa'at Ḥok ha-Ḥozim (Terufot be-Shel Haforat Ḥozeh)" [The Contracts (Remedies for Breach of Contract) Bill], *Ha-Praklit,* XXVI (1970), p. 276; *id.,* "Hirhurim al Haẓa'at Ḥok ha-Ḥozim (Ḥelek Kelali)" [Reflections on the Contracts (General Part) Bill], *Iyyunei Mishpat,* III (1973), p. 121.

416. Subsec. 2(b) states that the repeal of Article 46 shall not "impair the effectiveness of the law that was accepted in this country before the effective date of this statute." For the meaning of "the law that was accepted in this country," *see infra* pp. 1829–1830, 1885–1894.

great practical importance: it confronts Jewish law with current legal problems, with the result that principles of Jewish law are classified according to a contemporary topical arrangement and formulated in modern legal terminology. In a host of Supreme Court decisions, whenever any of the sitting judges were knowledgeable in Jewish law, questions in all fields of law have been discussed in light of comparisons with Jewish law, which is sometimes the same and sometimes different from the law generally applicable in other legal systems. Jewish law is sometimes called upon for assistance in the interpretation of legal terms and definitions, and in not a few cases it has served as the principal source for the Supreme Court's decision.

Extensive use is made of Jewish law when the court must interpret and give content to value-laden legal terms, such as "public policy," "justice," "equity," "good faith," "self-defense," etc. A number of Supreme Court justices have stated that these terms must be construed in light of the fundamental notions of morality, culture, justice, and equity, as expressed in Jewish law and the Jewish literary sources. Especially in the second legislative period, the court turned increasingly to Jewish law; scores of decisions rendered during this period, covering all of the areas of the law—civil, criminal, administrative, evidence, and procedure—address the issues in the light of the sources of Jewish law.

It is indeed true that only a few judges have produced these decisions, which are therefore but a small part of the large outpouring of Supreme Court jurisprudence. However, this judicial *oeuvre* is sufficient to reveal the hidden treasures of Jewish law and demonstrate the great vitality of the Jewish legal sources, and the ability of this legal-cultural-spiritual system to evolve, develop, and grapple with the legal and social problems that constantly arise in the courts of the State.[417]

417. There is no need to discuss here these judgments of the Supreme Court in detail. These judgments are a suitable subject for study, although very little research has as yet been done. Some of the leading cases have already been discussed, and others will be discussed in this chapter and in later chapters. *See* the list of cases in the Index of Sources, *infra.* A partial listing of earlier cases can be found in M. Silberg, *Talmudic Law and the Modern State,* 1973, p. 150 n. 45. Other works in this area include: H. Cohn, *Jewish Law in Israeli Jurisprudence,* Louis Caplan Lecture on Jewish Law, 1968, Hebrew Union College Press, pp. 3–25; the surveys of S. Meron in *Dine Israel,* vols. 1–11 (the survey in vol. 3 is by M. Shapiro and the surveys in vols. 10–11 are by H. Kulin). These surveys also treat Jewish law in the decisions of the district and rabbinical courts. *See also* M. Elon, "Ha-Mishpat ha-Ivri be-Mishpat ha-Medinah, al ha-Maẓuy ve-al ha-Raẓuy," *supra* n. 412 at 34–35; *id.*, "Ashirim Hem ha-Mekorot Hallalu" [These Sources Are Indeed Rich], *Ḥok u-Mishpat,* XXII (1956), p. 5; *id.*, *Mi-Ba'ayot ha-Halakhah ve-ha-Mishpat bi-Medinat Yisra'el, supra* n. 412; *id.* "Le-Zikhro Shel Moshe Silberg" [In Memory of Moshe Silberg], *Shenaton,* II (1975), pp. 1, 5–13; *id.*, *Samkhut ve-Oẓmah,* pp. 7, 28–29.

For a partial listing of more recent decisions dealing with Jewish law, *see infra* n. 435.

V. JEWISH LAW IN THE INTERPRETATION OF ISRAELI LEGISLATION

As has been noted, the role of Jewish law in the interpretation of Israeli legislation was debated in the Knesset from the very beginning of the first legislative period. The issue has also been extensively discussed in the opinions of the Supreme Court. The debates in judicial opinions and in the legal literature have concerned not only the role of Jewish law but also the broader question of Israeli statutory interpretation generally. This subject took on added importance with the enactment of the Foundations of Law Act, 1980, which is the subject of chapter 44 of this work. In order to appreciate fully the divergent views concerning statutory interpretation expressed after the adoption of the Foundations of Law Act, it is important to understand the various approaches to statutory interpretation that were taken before that Act was adopted. We therefore start with a historical review of these approaches.

Additional cases include: Samuel Flato Sharon v. State of Israel, *supra* n. 92 (Dov Levin, J.); Ali v. Sasson, *supra* n. 305 (A. Sheinbaum, District Judge specially assigned to the Supreme Court); and the following opinions by District Judge Tirkel, specially assigned to the Supreme Court: Ben-Natan v. Negbi, 35(ii) *P.D.* 141, 147 (1980); Barazani v. Barazani, 35(ii) *P.D.* 317, 321, 322 (1981); Grätz Vertriebsgesellschaft v. Muhamad Ḥafez Dagoani, 35(ii) *P.D.* 351, 354 (1981); Mikkun Le-Matta, Ltd. v. Karnit, 35(ii) *P.D.* 383, 389 (1981); Baniel v. National Labor Court, 35(ii) *P.D.* 693, 696–697 (1981); Rosenberg v. Keren Ḥazzan, 35(ii) *P.D.* 742, 754–756 (1981); Ḥuli v. State of Israel, 35(iii) *P.D.* 477, 481 (1981); Inspector General of Police v. Baizer, 35(iv) *P.D.* 337, 353 (1981); State of Israel v. Grossman, 36(i) *P.D.* 405, 412–413 (1981); Sasi v. Kika'on, 36(i) *P.D.* 762, 767–768 (1981); Raviv v. Bet Jules, 37(i) *P.D.* 533, 564 (1982); United Dairies v. Dairy Council, 37(iv) *P.D.* 516, 524 (1983); Vatad v. Minister of Finance, 38(iii) *P.D.* 113, 119, 122–123 (1984).

In connection with the issue in Amidar v. Aharon, 32(ii) *P.D.* 337 (1978) (*see infra* n. 435), *see* Schonberg, "New Developments in the Israeli Law of Negligent Misrepresentation," 31 *Int. and Comp. L.Q.* 207–219 (1982).

From time to time, Jewish law is also discussed in the decisions of the Israeli district courts. The opinions are little known (*see* the surveys in *Dine Israel, supra*) and have not been the subject of research. The following are examples of such opinions: In Re Litvinsky Brothers Partnership, 18 *P.M.* 64 (1959) (Lamm, J.), discussed *infra* p. 1911 n. 38; the opinion by Judge Ḥarish quoted in Illit v. Eleko, 34(iv) *P.D.* 673, 685 (1980); the opinion by Judge Ibn Ari quoted in Petromilio v. State of Israel, 38(iv) *P.D.* 821, 824 (1984), and in Gali v. State of Israel, 40(iv) *P.D.* 169 (1986), and numerous opinions by Judge Tirkel in the Tel Aviv District Court (*e.g.*, Bilgah v. Estate of Taft, [1976] 2 P.M. 25, 31; Avner v. Mif'alei Rekhev Ashdod, [1977] 1 P.M. 444, 454; Estate of Hecht v. Vaknin, [1977] 2 P.M. 192, 200; Za'id v. Yardeniah Insurance Co., Ltd., [1978] 1 P.M. 163; Taviv v. Katz, [1978] 1 P.M. 366, 379). *See also infra* p. 1863 n. 164.

It would seem that a considerable number of district court judges have to a greater or lesser extent made use of Jewish law, and a study of such decisions would be extremely valuable. *See* S. Deutsch, "Ha-Mishpat ha-Ivri bi-Fesikat Battei ha-Mishpat" [Jewish Law in the Decisions of the General Courts], *Meḥkerei Mishpat,* VI (1988), p. 7.

A. Problems of Statutory Interpretation and Interpretive Approaches to Israeli Legislation

The interpretation of Israeli legislation has been a subject intensively and extensively debated from the time the codification of Israeli law began. On the one hand, the codification of the civil law, and especially the provisions repealing Article 46 of the Palestine Order in Council with respect to the matters covered by certain statutes, helped to sever the tie between Israeli and English law, and advanced the Israeli legal system on the road to independence and self-sufficiency. On the other hand, for several reasons, this very independence exacerbated a number of problems of Israeli statutory interpretation. First, the civil law was not codified all at once as a single comprehensive unitary code, such as, for example, the codes of the Continental legal systems; various factors stood in the way of an accomplishment of such magnitude. Thus, during a period of more than fifteen years, the Knesset passed statutes one by one in various areas of civil law. Each statute was generally drafted by a Public Committee, which included judges, law professors, and practicing lawyers; and the committees were constituted differently for each statute. Although each statute finally passed through the same process of debate in the Knesset and its Legislative Committee, the lack of coordination in the preparatory work of codification sometimes produced inconsistencies between different statutes and conflicting definitions of the same terms.

In addition, these statutes contain basic terms and refer to concepts for which no interpretive guidelines are provided, *e.g.*, the terms "legal (or juristic) act," "void," "voidable," and many others. These statutes also often contain terms which, because of their very nature, cannot be precisely defined by the Legislature, and must be given meaning by the courts, *e.g.*, "justification" for nonperformance of a contract; "good faith" in entering into or performing a contract or exercising rights under it; "reasonableness" of conduct; the duty of "loyalty" owed by a fiduciary; and many similar terms.

With regard to such provisions, the question is: What constitutes "justification"? What is "good faith"? What is "reasonable"? What is "loyalty"? The answers are especially difficult in the Israeli legal system, even apart from the fact that the legislation was enacted in stages. It is common knowledge that every judge and lawyer faces such doubts and problems in every legal system; statutory law, even a comprehensive code, constitutes only a small part of the entire system, and it is like "the tip of the iceberg which floats on the water, with nine-tenths of it hidden below."[418] Therefore, a

418. Z. Zeltner, *Dinei ha-Ḥozim Shel Medinat Yisra'el* [The Contract Law of the State of Israel], 1974, p. 12.

judge or lawyer necessarily turns for assistance, when in doubt, to the jurisprudence of his particular system, *i.e.*, the body of judicial decisions and works of legal scholarship built up over the course of many years, dealing with the meaning of the basic terms and primary concepts at the foundation of that system. Such jurisprudence, however, is almost non-existent in the Israeli legal system, which, relatively speaking, is still in its infancy; Israeli law therefore does not have the resources to provide the kind of assistance needed to deal with such problems.

Another recurrent problem, distinct from the question of the meaning of basic terms and inherently vague concepts, is the interpretation of ambiguous language in a particular statutory provision. In such a case, the judge seeks helpful analogies in the statute itself or elsewhere in the legal system, and also inquires into the essential thrust and purpose of the statute. He sometimes finds his answer in this way, but often finds in the law no more than a broad hint of what is needed to solve the problem. Finally, there is sometimes a lacuna in the law; the court can find in the law no solution either in precedents or analogy for the problem before it, so new ground must be broken.

Israeli jurists and scholars have suggested various ways of resolving these problems. Some take the view that a statute should be interpreted only "from within its four corners," supplemented by the use of analogy and custom.[419] Others believe that in every case it is proper for the court to look for guidance to the historical source from which a particular provision was taken. When a provision was influenced, for example, by German law, the court should turn to the German *Bürgerliches Gesetzbuch;* a provision whose source is in the Swiss *Zivilgesetzbuch* should induce the court to turn to that law; etc.[420] A third opinion is that even though recourse to English law is no longer obligatory, it is proper that the English legal system should continue to be the primary source of assistance for problems of statutory interpretation, except when the Knesset specifically provides otherwise.[421]

These approaches are flawed. The idea that the statute itself, with the assistance of analogy, provides the solution to every problem of its construc-

419. A. Barak, "Aẓma'utah Shel ha-Kodifikaẓyah ha-Ezraḥit ha-Ḥadashah—Sikkuyim ve-Sikkunim" [The Independence of the New Civil Codification—Prospects and Risks], *Mishpatim,* VII (1976), pp. 15, 28–30; *id.*, *Ḥok ha-Sheliḥut,* 1965 [The Agency Law, 1965], Jerusalem, 1975, p. 23; *id.*, "Likrat Kodifikaẓyah Shel ha-Mishpat ha-Ezraḥi" [Toward the Codification of the Civil Law], *Iyyunei Mishpat,* III (1973), pp. 5–25.

420. Z. Zeltner, "Hirhurim al Haẓa'at Ḥok ha-Ḥozim (Ḥelek Kelali)," *supra* n. 415 at 132; I. Sussman, "Tom Lev be-Dinei Ḥozim—Ha-Zikah la-Din ha-Germani" [Good Faith in Contract Law—The Link to German Law], *Iyyunei Mishpat,* VI (1979), p. 485.

421. D. Friedmann, "Od le-Farshanut ha-Ḥakikah ha-Yisra'elit ha-Ḥadashah" [More on the Interpretation of Modern Israeli Legislation], *Iyyunei Mishpat,* V (1977), pp. 463, 487–490 and n. 115.

tion is an illusion. Just as a pit cannot be perfectly refilled with the earth taken from it, the contours of a statute cannot be filled out by the statute's own provisions. The best proof of this is experience: when a problem arises that cannot be solved from within the statute itself, even with the help of analogy, the judge regularly seeks assistance from other legal systems or from the articles and books of their learned jurists and scholars. In these instances, the judge does not first reach his conclusion by applying his own reason and logic to what may be found "within the four corners" of the statute, and only then look for support in other legal systems. The actual process generally is the opposite: the judge comes to his conclusion because the solution suggested by some other legal system appears reasonable to him. Only after he has reached this point does he attempt to fit this solution into his own legal system. Sometimes this process is clearly apparent upon an examination of the judge's opinion, and at other times it is less so. But it is clear that in construing Israeli statutes there is no escape from the necessity to turn for direction and guidance to sources outside the Israeli legal system. The only question is, To what legal system should the judge turn?

The proposal to turn to the historical sources of the provision to be construed is gravely flawed. This approach would create serious dissonance and inconsistencies in the Israeli legal system: in one case, Israeli law would have a German, in another case a Swiss, and in a third case an English cast. In addition, under this approach the judge must first engage in extensive research to find out which legal system is the source of origin of a particular provision. Furthermore, what will be the law when, as is generally the case, the provision is not exactly the same in the other legal system, because the Israeli legislature has made certain modifications of its own? What should be done when a statutory provision has a counterpart in more than one legal system? To which system should the judge then look?[422] Perhaps most

422. For example, the Contracts Law (General Part), 1973, states (sec. 39): "A contractual obligation shall be performed and a right arising out of a contract shall be exercised in the usual and customary manner and in good faith (*tom lev*)." This section is new to Israeli contract law, and the questions naturally arise: What does *tom lev* mean? What is its scope? Concepts similar to *tom lev* exist in various Continental systems, such as Section 242 of the German *B.G.B.*, Section 1375 of the *Italian Civil Code*, Section 1134(3) of the *French Civil Code*, as well as in the *Swiss Civil Code*. According to which system should this concept in the Israeli Contract Law be interpreted? German civil law, for example, calls it *Treu und Glauben* (lit. trust and confidence); is that the same as the Israeli law's *tom lev?* Some believe that it is. Justice Sussman wrote (in his article, *supra* n. 420 at 485):

> It seems to me that since Section 242 of the German law is the source of Section 39 [of the Israeli Contracts Law], we cannot do better, for the purpose of interpretation, than to look to the German sources. This does not require blind obedience to the German sources, just as our decisions have never been subservient to English law, notwithstanding Article 46 of the Palestine Order in Council. However, a demand that

importantly, who is capable of accomplishing this task, in view of the difficulty of mastering the techniques of research in many different legal systems? Finally, what should the judge do when a particular provision is Israeli in origin?

The major argument of those who think that English law should guide Israeli statutory interpretation is that for more than fifty years, English law was the legal-cultural matrix of the Israeli legal system and was the background against which legislation was enacted; therefore, it is proper to make English law the primary source of reference in every instance of doubt or uncertainty. This argument, too, is unsound. Is a mere fifty years sufficient to establish the necessary legal and cultural environment, especially when the question relates to the legal system of a Jewish state whose people have had their own legal-cultural environment far longer than a mere half-century? Moreover, the statutory codification of Israeli civil law has been drawing less and less upon English law—as witness the principle of *"tom lev"* (good faith)—so what reason is there today, when the codification of the civil law has been largely completed, to see in English law the source for guidance and the legal-cultural background of Israeli law?

B. The Proper Method of Interpreting Israeli Legislation

What then is the proper method of interpreting Israeli legislation when the solution for the problem cannot be derived from the statute itself, and what legal system can and should serve as the source of guidance for the Israeli legal system in every such case? It is submitted that the proper and reasonable approach is that the primary source of guidance for Israeli statutory interpretation in such cases should be Jewish law.

---

we ignore the source of the law is ludicrous. Thus, the link to English law has been severed, but there remains another link, perhaps no less strong than its predecessor.

This method of interpretation is extremely questionable. Not only are the two terms *tom lev* and *Treu und Glauben* not identical as a matter of semantics and philology, but—and this is the main point—why should Israeli judges turn specifically to German law to give meaning to this concept? Why not Italian, French, or Swiss law—all of which have similar concepts? It is hardly likely that the purpose of severing the link to English law was to replace it with a link to German law. It would be very sad indeed if it should turn out that the Knesset labored to create an Israeli Contracts Law only in order to replace an orientation toward Britain with a dependence on Germany. This subject was discussed extensively in Roth v. Yeshufeh, 33(i) *P.D.* 617, 630 (1979) (Elon, J.), which argues that the term *tom lev* should be interpreted on the basis of Jewish law, where it is a synonym for "uprightness" or "full integrity" (*yosher lev*) and constitutes an element of the paramount Jewish norm "Do what is right and good," expressed in Deuteronomy 6:18. *See also* Laserson v. Shikkun Ovedim, 38(ii) *P.D.* 237 (1984); *supra* pp. 183–189.

1. VALUE-LADEN LEGAL TERMS

As has been indicated, a number of justices of the Supreme Court of Israel have from the very beginning looked to Jewish law for the interpretation of value-laden legal terms, such as "public policy"[423] and "justice,"[424] which must be interpreted "from the basic worldview that is deeply rooted in the Jewish consciousness, . . . and on the basis of our moral and cultural beliefs."[425] In a number of Supreme Court cases, the author of this work has used this approach to construe these terms,[426] as well as other similar value-laden legal terms. Thus, with regard to the term "*tom lev*" (good faith) in Sections 12 and 39 of the Contracts Law (General Part), 1973, and in a number of other statutes, it was stated:

> When we set out to interpret fundamental conceptual terms like those contained in the laws of the State of Israel, such as "good faith," which have a universal character and reflect legal and value judgments in every civilized legal system, we must examine the meaning of those terms primarily in the light of the principles of Jewish law and the Jewish heritage. A universal principle such as this [*i.e.*, good faith] manifests itself in the various legal systems of our own day, but its roots are embedded in the fundamental values which are humanity's heritage from ancient legal systems. Who knows precisely how such values influence the spirit of the law? Yet it is clear that they have somehow permeated the consciousness of all the generations up to the present juncture. And if this is so with respect to the legal systems of other nations, it certainly applies to the laws of the State of Israel, whose fundamental principles are rooted primarily in its ancient heritage, of which "the eye has not dimmed nor the vigor abated."[427]

Another relevant opinion deals with the question of whether defense of a third person will defeat a criminal prosecution to the same extent as self-defense under Section 22 of the Penal Law, 1977:

> The law relating to the defense of third persons involves concepts based on public policy, and a social and moral view of the duty to come to the aid of another who is in danger of physical attack. This conclusion is compelled by the logic and nature of civilized social life. We find this notion expressed by English and American legal scholars who see this as a matter of "public pol-

423. Zim v. Mazyar, 17 *P.D.* 1319, 1332 (1963) (Silberg, J.); Yekutiel v. Bergman, 29(ii) *P.D.* 757, 764–769 (1975) (H. Cohn and Kister, JJ.); Rothman v. United Mizraḥi Bank, 29(ii) *P.D.* 57, 59 (1975) (H. Cohn, J.).

424. Ben Shaḥar v. Maḥlev, 28(ii) *P.D.* 89, 98 (1974) (H. Cohn, J.).

425. Zim v. Mazyar, *supra* n. 423.

426. *See* Dicker v. Moch, 32(ii) *P.D.* 141, 149–152 (1978); *see also* the decisions cited *infra* nn. 427 and 429.

427. Roth v. Yeshufeh, *supra* n. 422 at 631ff, quoting Deuteronomy 34:7; *see also* Laserson v. Shikkun Ovedim, *supra* n. 422.

icy" and as "a peremptory response to injustice, ingrained in the good man." Last, and most important, this is the view reflected in the sources of Jewish law where the principle "do not stand idly by the blood of your fellow"[428] constitutes a basic principle of the world outlook of Judaism. In my opinion, fundamental concepts founded on moral attitudes and cultural values should be interpreted in the light of the moral and cultural heritage of Judaism.[429]

2. OTHER PROBLEMS OF STATUTORY CONSTRUCTION

The flaws in the other approaches to interpretation discussed above, together with a jurisprudential analysis of the codificatory methods and needs of Israeli law, compel the conclusion that primacy should be given to Jewish law also in the resolution of the other problems of interpretation in the Israeli legal system, such as the meaning of statutory terms and the construction of ambiguous language. As pointed out above, it was explicitly stated in the Explanatory Notes to the long array of bills codifying aspects of the civil law, as well as in the Knesset's debates when each bill was passed, that the legislation was based on research and analysis of other legal systems, with *special* attention given to Jewish law. When the drafters outlined the basis for their legislation, they stated that Jewish law was the primary source, and the other legal systems were subsidiary sources; and it is appropriate for the court to follow this pattern in interpreting legislation so drafted.

It is true that, even as a primary source, Jewish law is only persuasive, *i.e.*, not binding or decisive but only instructive and influential. However, just as those who proposed and drafted the statutes viewed Jewish law as providing the cultural-legal background of the Israeli legal system and therefore looked to it as the primary legal source, it is also appropriate that when the meaning of this legislation is uncertain and the statute itself does not point clearly to the proper interpretation, Jewish law should serve as the primary source—at least as the first among equals—to which the court should turn and by which its decision should be guided.

This approach would solve one of the difficult problems confronting the Israeli legal system, namely, the absence of its own jurisprudential base to which the court may turn when necessary. In other countries, codifications are normally the outgrowth of the existing jurisprudence, whereas in Israel codification came first, and the jurisprudence still awaits creation and development. One of the important functions of the Supreme Court is to create and develop this jurisprudence while engaged in the daily task of decision making. Making Jewish law the primary source for interpreting

428. Leviticus 19:16.
429. Afanjar v. State of Israel, 33(iii) *P.D.* 141, 155 (1979).

Israeli law, *i.e.,* the first legal system to be consulted in a doubtful case, would tend to create a uniform base for the development of a rich and homogeneous jurisprudence for the Israeli legal system. Israeli law, with no historical roots of its own, is "like a person without a shadow";[430] and if the primary source for interpreting Israeli law were Jewish law, and Jewish law would be examined with the careful analysis required in light of the needs of the times and the nature and substance of the law, that process might well provide Israeli law with historical roots of its own and develop a synthesis that is both necessary and appropriate for the legal system of the Jewish state. This subject will be further considered in the discussion below.[431]

Before concluding this discussion of the role of Jewish law as a source for judicial interpretation, an additional comment is in order. It was made in an opinion discussing the methods of interpretation of Israeli legislation:[432]

> Far be it from me to suggest that we not study and learn from the wisdom and judgments of the legal scholars and judges of other legal systems. Such study is fitting and proper for the broadening of horizons and the deepening of knowledge. Our halakhic authorities, too, in their broadmindedness and openness, acted in this way from ancient times. Permit me to quote what I wrote in this connection elsewhere:[433]
>
> > The halakhic authorities knew the law that was applied in the non-Jewish courts, and at times even recommended the acceptance of a foreign legal practice of which they approved. At times, the halakhic authorities recognized the particular social utility of non-Jewish law and even did not hesitate to praise the judicial system of the gentiles when it was administered better than the judicial system of the Jews.
>
> If this is so in a legal proceeding conducted entirely under Jewish law, it is certainly true when we set out to interpret the laws of the State of Israel in our time, for they derive their validity from the sovereign authority of the Knesset to legislate whatever it deems desirable and appropriate, and it is clear that the legislation was adopted after an examination of various legal systems in light of current social and economic needs.
>
> Consequently, it is certainly true that the legislation of the Knesset, and especially those statutes specifically providing for their independence and separation from the "umbilical cord" of Article 46 of the Palestine Order in

430. *See* M. Landau, "Halakhah ve-Shikkul Da'at ba-Asiyyat Mishpat" [Rule and Discretion in Judicial Decisionmaking], *Mishpatim,* I (1968), pp. 292ff. at p. 305.

431. *See* Hendeles v. Bank Kupat Am, 35(ii) *P.D.* 785 (1981), discussed *infra* pp. 1863–1871, 1927–1930.

432. Roth v. Yeshufeh, *supra* n. 422 at 632.

433. *Supra* pp. 63–64, and *see* accompanying notes.

Council, must be interpreted, in the apt expression of the late Justice Silberg, "from within . . . [their] four corners."[434] However, when this method fails to resolve our perplexities, we must look to the principles of Jewish law as the first and primary source for the solution to our problem.

3. *BANK KUPAT AM v. HENDELES*—THE FIRST HEARING

The approach to the interpretation of Israeli statutes outlined above has been discussed by the author of this work in a number of decisions, and the subject need not be further belabored here.[435] One example which illus-

434. *See* Ratner v. Palalum Ltd. (In Bankruptcy), 12(ii) *P.D.* 1465, 1471 (1958); *see also* Estate of Finkelstein v. Finkelstein, 22(i) *P.D.* 618 (1968).

435. In addition to the court decisions discussed in this and later chapters and those cited *supra* n. 417, Jewish law is discussed in many cases, of which the following are among the most important: Wertheim v. State of Israel, 32(ii) *P.D.* 225 (1978) (deliberate judgment [*halanat ha-din, hahmazat ha-din*] and unjustifiably delayed judgment [*innuy ha-din*]); State of Israel v. Rivkah Abukasis, 32(ii) *P.D.* 240 (1978) (pretrial detention of a suspect or an accused); Amidar v. Aharon, *supra* n. 417 (tort liability for negligent misrepresentation); Muberman v. Segal, 32(iii) *P.D.* 85 (1978) (possibility of conflict of interest in transaction by fiduciary); State of Israel v. Mishali, 32(iii) *P.D.* 245 (1978) (no appeal from acquittal); Zikit v. Eldit, 32(iii) *P.D.* 487 (1978) (relationship between a contract of sale and a contract to perform services); Feld v. State of Israel, 33(i) *P.D.* 540 (1979) (proof of death of decedent for purpose of inheritance); Kitan v. Weiss, 33(ii) *P.D.* 785 (1979) (law and *lifnim mi-shurat ha-din*); Azugi v. Azugi, 33(iii) *P.D.* 1 (1979) (joint ownership of property by spouses; statutory interpretation; contracting out of a Biblical norm; custom as overriding law; circumstantial evidence); Gutman v. Rabbinical Court, 34(i) *P.D.* 443 (1979) (law and religious commandment; law and morals); Goldberg v. Chairman of Ramat ha-Sharon Municipal Council, 34(iv) *P.D.* 85 (1980) (administrative law; delegation of authority); Illit v. Eleko, *supra* n. 417 (inequitable exploitation of financial distress or other disadvantage as possible criminal extortion or ground for rescission of contract); Alperowitz v. Mizrahi, 34(iv) *P.D.* 729 (1980) (construction of contracts); Jensen-Zohar v. Ashdod Rabbinical Court, 35(i) *P.D.* 1 (1980) (best interests of the child; laws of conversion to Judaism, generally and with particular reference to minors); Nagar v. State of Israel, 35(i) *P.D.* 113 (1980) (criminal law and procedure, evidence); Sharon v. Levi, 35(i) *P.D.* 736 (1980) (examination of body tissues to establish paternity; personal freedom—the right to bodily integrity; precluding suspicion of illegitimacy [*mamzerut*]); Rosen v. State of Israel, 35(ii) *P.D.* 821 (1981) (exemption of religious women from military service; definition of a religious way of life); Anonymous v. Anonymous, 35(iii) *P.D.* 57 (1981) (husband's right to be heard on the question of his wife's abortion; principles of natural justice); State of Israel v. Segal, 35(iv) *P.D.* 313 (1981) (protection of a prisoner's human dignity); Lieberman v. Lieberman, 35(iv) *P.D.* 359 (1981) (joint ownership of property by spouses; wife's right to compensation on divorce; the creative process in Jewish law; doing justice); Anonymous v. State of Israel, 35(iv) *P.D.* 438 (1981) (factors to be considered in sentencing; embezzlement of public funds); Hiram v. Minister of Defense, 35(iv) *P.D.* 505 (1981) (construction of contracts); Efrat v. State of Israel, 35(iv) *P.D.* 729 (1981) (interpreting a statute according to the ordinary meaning of its terms); Kokhavi v. State of Israel, 35(iv) *P.D.* 744 (1981) (methods of punishment; justice and mercy, law and clemency); State of Israel v. Lubaniov, 35(iv) *P.D.* 780 (1981) (pretrial detention in murder case; homicide); Ness v. Golda, 36(i) *P.D.* 204 (1981) (law and *lifnim mi-shurat ha-din*); Gabbai v. Valis, 36(i) *P.D.* 449 (1982) (measure of compensation due to widow for death of her husband upon whom she was dependent;

considerations for preventing women from becoming *agunot*); Yiẓḥak David v. Disciplinary Court of Israel Bar Association, 36(i) *P.D.* 779 (1982) (the term "deliver *into his hands*" as meaning to his dominion or control, and not to be taken literally in a physical sense); Minẓer v. Central Committee of Israel Bar Association, 36(ii) *P.D.* 1 (1982) (law and justice; standards and measures; a judgment that is truly correct—*din emet le-amito*); Lugasi v. Minister of Communications, 36(ii) *P.D.* 449 (1982) (good faith; "a scoundrel in the performance of public activity"; administrative law; law and *lifnim mi-shurat ha-din* in public affairs); Sedan v. Sedan, 36(iv) *P.D.* 169 (1982) (barring spouse's entry into jointly owned marital dwelling; injunction and judicial separation); Alon v. Government of Israel, 36(iv) *P.D.* 449 (1982) (legal truth and factual truth; justice and truth; "the oven of Akhnai"; disputes in *Halakhah*—"both views are the words of the living God"); Marcus v. State of Israel, 37(i) *P.D.* 225 (1983) ("A judge must be guided only by what his own eyes see, his own ears hear, and his own heart understands"); Krauss v. State of Israel, 37(i) *P.D.* 365 (1983) (pretrial detention; illegal sentence; judicial and legislative authority in Jewish law compared to other legal systems); Histadrut Po'alei Agudat Yisra'el v. Minister of Religions, 37(i) *P.D.* 813 (1983) (right to a hearing); Marcus v. Hammer, 37(ii) *P.D.* 337 (1983) (justice and law; law and *lifnim mi-shurat ha-din*); Ẓonan v. Stahl, 37(ii) *P.D.* 761 (1983) (private marriage; public welfare; judicial policy); Ali v. State of Israel, 37(iii) *P.D.* 169 (1983) (confessions in criminal proceedings; legal development in Jewish law); State of Israel v. Tamir, 37(iii) *P.D.* 201 (1983) (prisoner's right to free choice of medical treatment; human dignity of a prisoner); Rosenstein v. Solomon, 38(ii) *P.D.* 113 (1984) (self-help; judicial policy to prevent enmity); Boyer v. Shikkun Ovedim, *supra* n. 412 (law and *lifnim mi-shurat ha-din*, generally and in public affairs); Ḥadashot, Ltd. v. Minister of Defense, 38(ii) *P.D.* 447 (1984) (censorship; rule of law); Hokamah v. Minister of the Interior, 38(ii) *P.D.* 826 (1984) (rights of detainees and prisoners to vote in Knesset elections); Laserson v. Shikkun Ovedim, Ltd., *supra* n. 422 (good faith); Schein v. Minister of Defense, 38(iii) *P.D.* 393 (1984) (conscientious objection; civil disobedience); State of Israel v. Suisse, 38(iv) *P.D.* 701 (1984) (escape from lawful custody; interpretation in accordance with ordinary meaning, especially in criminal law); Omri v. Zouavi, 39(ii) *P.D.* 113 (1985) (distinction between substantive and procedural rules in Jewish law); Naiman v. Chairman, Central Elections Committee, 39(ii) *P.D.* 225 (1985) ("'You shall live by them'—and not die by them"; the Israeli Declaration of Independence and the principles of freedom, justice, equity, and peace of the Jewish heritage; different opinions in the realms of *Halakhah* and *Aggadah;* freedom of opinion and expression in Jewish law; judge should not act as prophet; rule of law and not rule of the legislator or judge; democratic and Jewish character of the State of Israel; equality and love of fellow man; attitude of the Jewish sources to ethnic minorities living under a Jewish government; destiny and image of the Jewish state); State of Israel v. Leviathan, 40(i) *P.D.* 544 (1986) (presumption of innocence; right to be free from detention; grounds for pretrial detention, length and delay of trial as factors favoring release from detention); State of Israel v. Avi Ẓur, 40(i) *P.D.* 706 (1986) (presumption of innocence extends to everyone until proof of guilt; right to be free from detention; grounds for pretrial detention); Tohami v. State of Israel, 40(i) *P.D.* 733 (1986) (theories of punishment; proportionality; Code of Hammurabi; law and clemency); Sagel v. State of Israel, 40(ii) *P.D.* 769 (1986) (justice and mercy); Gali v. State of Israel, *supra* n. 417 (origin and meaning of the term "*alimut*" ("violence"); difference between thief (*ganav*) and robber (*gazlan*); difference between theft and robbery; Foundations of Law Act); Zuckerman v. State of Israel, 40(iv) *P.D.* 209 (1986) (human dignity; prohibition against degrading treatment of criminal; after punishment, "he is like your brother"); Kahane v. Knesset Speaker, 40(iv) *P.D.* 393 (1986) (minority rights under the *Halakhah;* Jewish public law; duty of legislature to obey the law; relation between legislature and judiciary; importance of noting minority views); Miller v. Minister of the Interior (discussed and quoted *supra* n. 289); Aloni v. Minister of Justice, 41(ii) *P.D.* 1 (1987) ("The Nakash case"—legal standing; laws relating to the *agunah;* extradition; possible danger to life; the relation of Jewish law to non-Jewish law; Foundations of Law Act; the term

"Jewish heritage"); Dananashvili v. State of Israel, 41(ii) *P.D.* 281 (1987) (individual freedom—the foundation for freedom of expression and the right to demonstrate, and all other freedoms; principles of the Jewish heritage; no discrimination as between criminal defendants); Kleine-Bik v. Goldberg, 41(ii) *P.D.* 757 (1987) (will of *shekhiv me-ra;* language of the will; Foundations of Law Act; need for "spirit" of a legal system; good faith); Ẓemaḥ v. State of Israel, 41(iii) *P.D.* 17 (1987) (manslaughter; proportionality of punishment to severity of crime); Weil v. State of Israel, 41(iii) *P.D.* 477 (1987) (right of prisoner to dignity and physical and spiritual well-being; right to sexual relations is like any other basic right; right of prisoner to sexual relations and consortium with spouse; Foundations of Law Act; principles of freedom and equity in regard to prisoners; imprisonment according to principles applicable to cities of refuge [*see* Deuteronomy ch. 19]); Anonymous v. Attorney General, 41(iii) *P.D.* 544 (1987) (adoption; conduct in category of "it shall be neither yours nor mine; cut it in two!" [I Kings 3:26] is unreasonable); Miyari v. Knesset Speaker, 41(iv) *P.D.* 169 (1987) (right to present argument as a principle of natural justice in Jewish law; vexatious questions; separation of powers not a principle of Jewish governmental law, but concept of the rule of law as binding on the legislature is part of Jewish law); State of Israel v. Brown, 41(iv) *P.D.* 382 (1988) ("a judgment must do justice"—*yeẓe din ẓedek le-ẓidko*); Biazi v. Levi, 42(i) *P.D.* 446 (1988) (final resolution of disputes as a primary objective of adjudication; judgment that is completely and truly correct—*din emet le-amito;* legal truth and factual truth; compromise and settlement; Foundations of Law Act); Shakdiel v. Minister of Religions, 42(ii) *P.D.* 221 (1988) (halakhic adjudicatory policy; multiplicity of opinions in the *Halakhah;* custom as a determinant of law; the principle of equality; reciprocal influence of law and life; right of women to vote and hold public office; basic family values; protection of dignity of women, modesty, and moral values; study and teaching of Torah by women); Attorney General v. Anonymous, 42(ii) *P.D.* 661 (1988) (taking of kidney from retarded son for transplanting to father who has been devotedly caring for him; appointment and powers of guardian of person and property of persons under disability; duty of rescue; donation of organs generally and by persons under disability in particular; invasive procedures on a person under disability allowable on basis of benefit to the person under disability; inferences as to desire of person under disability; Foundations of Law Act); Minister of Justice v. Judge Arbel, 42(iii) *P.D.* 63 (1988) ("woe is the generation whose judges must be judged"; "take the mote from between your eyes"; "take the beam from between your eyes"; what is a mote in regard to a party is a beam in regard to the judge); Minister of Justice v. Judge Ḥarifai, 42(iii) *P.D.* 69 (1988) (to refrain from perverse speech is wise for everyone, but imperative for judges); Ravivo v. Chairman of the Local Council of Ofakim, 42(iii) *P.D.* 183 (1988) (no legislation should be imposed on the public unless the majority can conform to it); Adar v. Adar, 42(iii) *P.D.* 347 (1988) (support of children in accordance with station in life and not merely for necessities; support on basis of the law as to charity, in accordance with father's ability to pay); Amar v. Pereẓ, 42(iii) *P.D.* 485 (1988) ("nonperception is not proof of nonexistence"); Military Court of Appeals v. Vaknin, 42(iii) *P.D.* 837 (1988) (individual rights; right of privacy; protection of confidentiality; prohibition of spying and eavesdropping; Rabbenu Gershom's ban against reading correspondence of others; law against subversive incitement; prohibition of trespass on private property; protection of privacy of home and curtilage; injury caused by looking into someone's premises; legislative history of Foundations of Law Act); Avneri v. Shapiro, 42(iv) *P.D.* 20 (1988) (Jewish law as important source for interpreting the Defamation Law, as shown by the statute's legislative history and pursuant to Foundations of Law Act, 1980; prohibition of defamation in Jewish law; "Do not go about as a talebearer among your countrymen" [Leviticus 19:16] as basis for prohibition against defamation, and "Reprove your kinsman" [Leviticus 19:17] as basis for free public debate); State of Israel v. Albez, 42(iv) *P.D.* 385 (1988) (no appeal by the prosecution from judgment of acquittal); Rosenzweig v. Attorney General, 42(iv) *P.D.* 759 (1989) (no imprisonment of husband for disobedience to rabbinical court decision regarding divorce unless decision specifically compels divorce as distinguished from merely ruling that divorce should be given; hope expressed that after refusal of husband for nine years to give a divorce the rabbinical court will find a way to compel divorce, so that wife can be free to remarry); Moston v. Wiederman, 43(i) *P.D.* 278 (1989) (law of wills and inheritance; rights of remainderman upon sale by first legatee; advice to first legatee to sell frustrates intent of testator; relationship between law and morals as discussed by the halakhic authorities); Ḥermesh v. Bar Am, 43(i) *P.D.* 672 (1989) (cooperatives; governing principle is "Love truth and peace"); Zahav v. State of Israel, 43(i) *P.D.* 720 (1989) (no detention of accused except where *prima facie* proof of guilt; in case of serious crimes such as capital offenses, accused is detained throughout the judicial proceedings); State of Israel v. Lavan, 43(ii) *P.D.* 410 (1989) (ninth amendment [1988] to Criminal Procedures Law, balancing right to individual freedom against protection of public peace and security, on the basis of principles of Jewish law; everyone is presumed innocent; no detention except where *prima facie* proof of guilt or where crime is particularly serious or where there is reason to fear attempt to obstruct justice, and public peace and security are threatened; concept of creation of man in the image of God as basis for all freedoms; Foundations of Law Act); Masika v. State of Israel, 43(ii) *P.D.* 423 (1989) (equality and non-discriminatory treatment of co-defendants as implicit in principle of human freedom; "Beloved is man, for he was created in God's image"); State of Israel v. Benjamin, 43(ii) *P.D.* 430 (1989) (presumption of innocence persists until conviction; presumption attaches regardless of prominence of accused; defendant's position in the community may be a factor to be considered in sentencing, but not in regard to pretrial detention); State of Israel v. Maman, 43(ii) *P.D.* 441 (1989) (unjustified criticism of judges harms, and justified criticism benefits, the rule of law; judge's function is to render a completely and truly correct judgment (*din emet le-amito*), and he is commanded to fear no one, and to render judgment impartially); Ephraim v. State of Israel, 43(ii) *P.D.* 578 (1989) (rape—"this case is like that of a man attacking another and murdering him. For he came upon her in the open; though the . . . girl cried for help, there was no one to save her" [Deuteronomy 22:26–27]); Fund for the Movement of Progressive Judaism in Israel v. Minister of Religions, 43(ii) *P.D.* 661 (1989) (registration and performance of marriages have both administrative aspects subject to administrative authority, and substantive halakhic aspects requiring halakhic knowledge and expertise; consultation with expert, the Chief Rabbinate of Israel; compliance with legal requirements for effecting marriage does not infringe freedom of religion or conscience; the term "Law of the Torah"—*din Torah*—in the statute includes the entire *Halakhah;* attitude of the Reform movement to *Halakhah*); Organization of Torah-Observant Sephardim (Shas Movement) v. Kahana, Director of Population Registry of the Ministry of the Interior, discussed and quoted *supra* n. 289; State of Israel v. Shoradker, 43(iii) *P.D.* 1 (1989) (methods of punishment); Atias v. State of Israel, 43(iv) *P.D.* 170 (1989) (same); Meir Mizraḥi v. State of Israel, 43(iv) *P.D.* 388 (1989) (no *ex post facto* application of criminal statute except for repeal of offense or reduction of penalty; safeguarding rights of the accused); Shehino v. National Labor Court, 44(i) *P.D.* 143 (1989) (law and justice); One Heart and New Spirit Movement v. Knesset Speaker, 44(iii) *P.D.* 529 (1989) (interpretive methodologies); Manof Signal Financial and Investment, Ltd. v. Slayman, 44(iii) *P.D.* 758 (1989) (the nature of compromise); League for Civil Rights in Israel v. Commanding Officer, Southern Command, 44(iv) *P.D.* 626 (1990) (right to hearing; ancient origins of this right in the Jewish heritage); Deckel v. Minister of Finance, 45(i) *P.D.* 28 (1990) (political appointments of public servants); Konsalos v. Turgeman, 45(ii) *P.D.* 626 (1991) (principle of best interests of child in custody and adoption cases; child born out of wedlock; the meaning of *mamzer* in Jewish law; laws regarding conversion of minor to Judaism); State of Israel v. Darvish, 45(ii) *P.D.* 663 (1991) (fiduciary duty of public servant); Anonymous v. Attorney General, 45(iii) *P.D.* 460 (1991) (adoption); Ḥakak v. Ḥakak, 45(iv) *P.D.* 749 (1991) (amendment of Woman's Equal Rights Law permitting court, in fixing amount of maintenance and support by husband, to take into account wife's individual income from all sources); Haj Yiḥya v. State of Israel, 45(iv) *P.D.* 221 (1991) (defendant's right of cross-examination in criminal case; the force of prec-

trates the differences of opinion among the justices of the Supreme Court of Israel on the proper approach to Israeli statutory interpretation is *Bank Kupat Am v. Hendeles.*[436]

The facts of that case were as follows:[437] In a bank, on the floor of the main banking area, a man found an envelope containing bonds. The finder asked the bank manager whether the owner of the bonds could be identified. The manager replied in the negative and requested the finder to turn the bonds over to the bank to hold until the owner claimed them. The finder refused, and instead turned them over to the police. After the expiration of four months (the period designated in the Restoration of Lost Property Law, 1973, for the owner to appear and make claim) the finder requested the police to deliver the bonds to him pursuant to Section 4(a) of the statute, which provides that "if the identity of the owner is not ascertained within four months, he is considered to have abandoned [the property], and ownership becomes vested in the finder."

The bank, however, claimed that the bonds belonged to it. The bank contended that the applicable provision of the law was Section 3, which reads:

> If one finds a lost article in the *reshut* [the meaning of this term is the subject of the discussion which follows] of another person he must so inform the owner of the *reshut* and turn it [the article] over to him [the owner of the *reshut*] upon demand; if the owner of the *reshut* receives the lost article, he is to be considered the finder [*i.e.*, upon the expiration of the four-month period, the lost article belongs to the owner of the *reshut* even if he is not the actual finder].

The interpretation of Section 3 presented a number of problems. The phrase "in the *reshut* of another person" is ambiguous. *Reshut* can mean *ownership*, or *possession*, or *control*. The meaning in this case depends on an additional consideration: What was the objective of Section 3—what was it designed to accomplish? Was the purpose to provide only that if an article is lost in such a place, it may be assumed that the loser will inquire there for its return, and therefore the finder must turn it over to the owner of the

---

edent; the position of Jewish law). As to the judicial opinions in the area of Jewish law by the author of the present work, *see further Shenaton*, XIII (1987), ed. Rabello and Shilo, pp. 9–22.

436. 34(iii) *P.D.* 57 (1980). There was an additional proceeding in the *Hendeles* case, which once again dealt with the proper approach to Israeli statutory interpretation, this time in light of the Foundations of Law Act, 1980, which in the meantime had become law. *See infra* pp. 1863–1871.

437. 34(iii) *P.D.* at 59.

premises for safekeeping, with the section going on to provide that if the owner of the article fails to appear, the owner of the premises will then (and only then) become entitled as against the finder? Or, alternatively, was the purpose of Section 3 to establish that the owner of private premises acquires the article by virtue of his ownership of the premises, and therefore his claim is prior to that of the finder? The first approach takes the essential thrust of the section as being to designate a place where the owner of the lost article may inquire about his loss. According to the second approach, the essential thrust of the section is to establish that the owner of the premises acquires the article at the moment it is found, subject only to the right of the person who lost it to reclaim it within four months.

Each of these two approaches to the interpretation of the statute would produce a different result in the *Hendeles* case. The area where the bonds were found *belonged* to the bank, but was not under its *control*, since it was open to the public and many people came and went without any supervision or control over them being exercised by the bank. Justice Barak, with whom Justice Landau concurred, interpreted Section 3 as intending to establish an *address* where the owner of the lost article will likely inquire—not as providing that the owner of the premises is to be regarded as having possession of the article even before it has been found. On this theory, Section 3 applies even to premises completely open to the public, such as a bank or a supermarket. The finder must turn over the lost article to the owner of the premises where it was lost, even though the place is open to the public, because the owner of the article presumably will come to look for it there; if he fails to appear, the bonds will belong to the bank or supermarket, pursuant to Section 3. Justice Barak found support for this interpretation in articles by two American legal scholars.[438]

The dissenting opinion (Elon, J.) took the position that Section 3 should be interpreted as applying to articles found on premises in the *control* of another, in which case the right of the owner of the premises in the lost article is superior to the right of the finder—assuming, of course, that the owner of the lost article fails to appear. Since the bank allowed the public free access to the area where the bonds were found, the bank's right to the bonds was not superior to the right of the finder, and the general provisions of the law, contained in Sections 2 and 4, therefore applied. Under these sections, the bonds are to be given to the police, and if after the specified time period the owner has not been located, they belong to the finder and not to the bank.

438. Reisman, "Possession and the Law of Finders," 52 *Harv. L. Rev.* 1105 (1939); Mitchell, "Rights of Finders as Against the Owner of the Locus in Quo," 22 *Cornell L.Q.* 263 (1936).

This approach, it is submitted, best reflects the meaning and purpose of the statute, and also produces a fairer and more just result: the bonds should pass to the actual finder and not to the bank, which was not subjected to the temptation that the finder withstood and which did not take the trouble, as did the finder, to try to return them. This interpretation would also encourage the finder to disclose his find rather than yield to the temptation of taking it for himself. The issue was reviewed in detail in the dissenting opinion and need not be expanded upon here. As there pointed out, the dissenting view accords with the position taken by courts in England[439] and the United States[440] and particularly with the result reached in *Toledo Trust Co. v. Simmons,*[441] a very similar American case. Subsequent to the decision in *Hendeles,* an English court, on facts closely paralleling those in *Hendeles,* reached the same conclusion as the *Hendeles* dissent.[442]

However, the most decisive rationale for the conclusion reached by the dissent in *Hendeles* was the following:[443]

> Last and most important, I find in Jewish law the basis for this interpretation of the phrase "the *reshut* of another person" and for this reading of the purpose of Section 3. The Restoration of Lost Property Law, 1973, is an example of autonomous Israeli civil legislation, and a preeminent role was assigned to Jewish law in the interpretation of such legislation. I have extensively dealt with this important subject in *Roth v. Yeshufeh,*[444] to which the reader is referred. . . . Certainly, it goes without saying that interpretation of such autonomous legislation on the basis of Jewish law is improper when the content of the particular provision to be construed is clearly contrary to the position and objective of Jewish law on that subject. The judge should not "force" upon the statute or any of its sections an interpretive approach contrary to the

439. Two cases are particularly noteworthy: Bridges v. Hawkesworth, 15 Jur. 1079, 21 L.J.Q.B. 75, [1843–1860] All E.R. 122 (1851); Hannah v. Peel, [1945] 1 K.B. 509, 2 All E.R. 288. *See also* the *Hendeles* case, 34(iii) *P.D.* at 77–78 (Elon, J., dissenting).

440. *See* 34(iii) *P.D.* at 78–80.

441. 52 Ohio App. 373, 3 N.E.2d 61 (1935), discussed in detail, 34(iii) *P.D.* at 78–80.

442. Parker v. British Airways Board, [1982] 2 W.L.R. 503, 1 All E.R. 834. In this case, a passenger named Parker found a gold bracelet in an airport passenger lounge that was open to a particular category of passengers. The airline was the lessee of the lounge. The facts were thus similar to the *Hendeles* case, where the banking area was open only to business invitees (although it was shown that there was no close supervision and others did in fact enter). In fact, the banking area in the *Hendeles* case was more open to the public than the passenger lounge in the *Parker* case. Parker turned the bracelet over to an airline employee and left his address in case the owner of the bracelet did not claim it. The owner did not appear, and the airline sold the bracelet for £850 sterling, which it kept. Both the trial court and the appellate court held for Parker, and he was awarded £850 sterling as the bracelet's value and a further £50 sterling as interest. The judgment contains a comprehensive discussion of the issue, and its reasoning parallels that of the dissent in *Hendeles.*

443. 34(iii) *P.D.* at 80.

444. 33(i) *P.D.* at 632–633.

express provisions of the statute, and certainly should not combine things that do not belong together [*i.e.*, the judge should not inject incompatible elements into the statute under the guise of interpretation]. However, when this is not the case [*i.e.*, when there is no inconsistency between the statute and Jewish law] and a question arises for which the statute itself provides no conclusive resolution, we must resort primarily to the principles of Jewish law as the primary and preeminent source, which, although not binding, can provide guidance in solving the problem at hand.

When a question arose in the case before us as to the meaning of Section 3 of the statute and [particularly] of the phrase "the *reshut* of another person," and the question could not be resolved by reference to "the four corners of the statute," it was proper to turn to Jewish law to find the answer. This is certainly true where, as here, we know that the Restoration of Lost Property Law of the Knesset and the rules relating to the return of lost property in Jewish law have the same primary objective, *i.e.*, to ensure the return of lost articles to their owners, as we pointed out at the beginning of our opinion. In fact, the Knesset, during the second and third readings of the bill, saw fit to change the title from the "Care of Lost Property Law" to the "Restoration of Lost Property Law," because this is the purpose of the statute and this is the title given to this subject in Jewish law. Moreover, the concern to discover the owner of a lost article is so acute in Jewish law that certain lost articles with identifiable characteristics (which the owner therefore cannot be presumed to have abandoned hope of finding) never become the finder's property but are to be put aside "until the prophet Elijah comes," when their owners will be discovered.[445] While Jewish law originally provided that where the owner is presumed to have abandoned hope of finding a lost article the finder may take it for himself, it was established in Babylonia and Germany at the end of the tenth century that the finder must return even such a lost article to its owner when the owner so requests.[446]

Because of this basic objective of the law of return of lost property, together with other reasons, Jewish law resolved the particular problem here *sub judice* in the same way that we have interpreted Section 3 of the Restoration of Lost Property Law; and this problem, *inter alia*, was even discussed in Jewish law in connection with the subject of a lost article found on the premises of a "money changer," *i.e.*, the "banker" of those days.[447]

445. TB Bava Meẓi'a 30a; Maimonides, *MT*, Gezelah va-Avedah 13:10; Sh. Ar. ḤM 267:15.

446. *Resp. Rabbenu Gershom Me'or ha-Golah* #67 (ed. Eidelberg, pp. 154–158); *Teshuvot ha-Geonim Sha'arei Ẓedek*, IV, Sha'ar 1, #20; this rule was accepted in practice. *See also supra* pp. 686–688 and n. 32.

447. Jewish law on this subject in fact has a twofold objective: (a) to locate the owner of the article in order to restore it to him and (b) if the owner does not appear, to determine the right to the article as between the finder and the owner of the premises where the article was found. It is difficult to understand Justice Barak's argument that Jewish law does not concern itself with the issue before the court in *Hendeles*, and that the only concern of Jewish law is to determine superiority of right as between the finder and the owner of the premises

After examining the Restoration of Lost Property Law, 1973, from which it appears that many of its provisions and sections are based on the rules of Jewish law,[448] the dissenting opinion reviewed the Jewish law as to an article found in a shop, near a money changer, or in other places that belong to a private owner but are frequented by the public.[449] That review revealed that if the premises are "a guarded courtyard," *i.e.*, the owner of the premises has dominion and exercises control over it, he acquires the lost article before it is discovered by the finder; however, if an individual's premises consist of "an unguarded courtyard," *i.e.*, the owner of the premises does not exercise dominion and control over that place because it is frequented by members of the public, who regularly come and go, he does not acquire the lost article, and it belongs to its finder (all this, of course, again assuming that the owner of the article is unknown).

The dissent also pointed out that in the terminology of Jewish law and in Hebrew usage, the term *reshut* can properly be understood to connote "control and dominion,"[450] which is therefore a meaning well suited for "the *reshut* of another person" as that expression is used in Section 3. So construed, Section 3 gives the owner of the premises a right superior to that of the finder only when the owner of the premises exercises dominion and control over them, and they are not open to the public. The conclusion arrived at by turning to Jewish law for guidance in solving the problem in

---

(34(iii) *P.D.* at 65, 68). Jewish law is concerned with both problems and deals with them together; its concern for one is not less because of its concern for the other (*see* 34(iii) *P.D.* at 80–81), and the concern for the rights of the owner of the lost article weighs in favor of the conclusion reached by the dissent on the issue of the relative rights of the finder and the owner of the premises where the article was found.

448. The Restoration of Lost Property Law followed Jewish law in several respects. MK Bibi, who presented the bill for its second and third readings, had the following to say about the title of the law: "The expression *hashavat avedah* (restoration of lost property) is well known in Jewish law and most precisely expresses the purpose of the law." As to the obligation publicly to announce the finding of the article, *see* 34(iii) *P.D.* at 70; as to the presumption that "he [the owner of the lost article] has abandoned hope of finding it" (in sec. 4 of the statute), *see* the comments of MK Bibi: "Abandonment of hope of recovering a lost article is a factor that Jewish law also sees as sufficient to terminate the ownership of the previous owner of the article and vest ownership in the finder" (*see* 34(iii) *P.D.* at 84). The Explanatory Notes to the bill quote *in extenso* the verses on the return of lost property in Deuteronomy 22:1–3 (*see* 34(iii) *P.D.* at 69).

449. *See* TB Bava Meẓi'a 26b and commentaries, *ad loc.*; Maimonides, *MT*, Gezelah va-Avedah ch. 16; *Tur* and Sh. Ar. ḤM ch. 260, and other codes.

450. 34(iii) *P.D.* at 84. For example, TB Bava Kamma 70a states: "If an article is stolen and the owner does not abandon hope of recovering it, neither the thief nor the owner can consecrate the article; the thief, because it is not his, and the owner, because it is not in his *reshut* [*i.e.*, not under his control]." This is also the meaning of the term in ordinary Hebrew speech in various contexts, *e.g.*, "So-and-so stands in his own *reshut* [*i.e.*, controls his own affairs]."

the *Hendeles* case thus yields a result compatible with the accepted meaning in Jewish law of the term *reshut* used in Section 3.[451]

In the *Hendeles* decision, Justice Barak set forth his position on the role of Jewish law in the interpretation of Israeli legislation. He referred to the following statement in the lower court's opinion by Judge Judah Weiss, President of the District Court of Jerusalem:[452]

> The case before us deals with an Israeli statute enacted by the Knesset, and the terms which concern us, such as "the *reshut* of another person" and "the owner of the *reshut*," which appear in Section 3 of the statute, are, as stated, terms which are familiar to us from the *Halakhah*. Since this is so, there is good reason to examine what the *Halakhah* has to say on this subject and to learn from it whatever we can.

The district court concluded that under Jewish law the main banking area is in the category of an "unguarded courtyard," which does not acquire property for its owner, and the bonds therefore belonged to their finder.

As to this, Justice Barak stated:[453]

> The reference to Jewish law . . . with regard to the interpretation of the phrases "the *reshut* of another person" and "the owner of the *reshut*" is certainly permissible. At the same time, it is appropriate to mark out its limits. First, such reference is not obligatory but only discretionary. Second, Jewish law is consulted not as a normative system from which we seek a binding rule, but only as a storehouse of legal doctrine, from which we seek enlightenment. Jewish "law" is consulted in the cultural and not the normative sense of the term "law." In our case, we may look to Jewish law not to obtain from it the law relating to found property, but only so that it may shed some light that may help us find our own law.
>
> Third, when we discover the interpretation of a certain expression in our storehouse of cultural treasures, we must determine whether this interpretation, as one of a number of possible alternative interpretations, reflects

451. The dissent makes clear that the possibility of finding "dominion" or "control" as the meaning of the term *reshut* is not the reason for turning to Jewish law in *Hendeles*. Reference to Jewish law is justified not because the term *reshut* is a term of art peculiar to Jewish law, but by reason of the basic principle that when the meaning of a provision in a statute is doubtful and the ambiguity cannot be resolved on the basis of the text of the statute itself, the primary source for guidance should be Jewish law. This is especially true when various provisions in the statute are based on Jewish law, and Jewish law is compatible with the spirit and objective of the statute. The term *reshut* is accepted in current Hebrew legal terminology, but the fact that it is so used is not in itself sufficient reason to justify reference specifically to Jewish law. As to this point, *see* the opinions in the additional hearing in the *Hendeles* case by Cohn, J., 35(ii) *P.D.* at 789, and Elon, J., *id.* at 795.

452. The statement is quoted at 34(iii) *P.D.* 67.

453. 34(iii) *P.D.* at 67.

> the legislative purpose. It is for the purpose of determining the meaning of the phrase "the *reshut* of another person," and only for this purpose, that we are permitted to turn to Jewish law as one of a number of sources of possible enlightenment.
>
> As I have already mentioned, however, this is not the end of our journey but only the beginning. The duty of one who construes [a statute] is to select the appropriate alternative from among all those of which he is cognizant. This choice is not a technical act. It is a creative act. It is carried out in accordance with principles established in our law, the most important of which is that a statutory provision is to be interpreted to give effect to the objective of the legislation.

It is indeed true that recourse to Jewish law is only a search for guidance, and that Jewish law is not consulted in order to obtain a binding normative rule. However, it is submitted that, for the reasons above discussed, recourse to Jewish law—even if only for the purpose of enlightenment—should have precedence over recourse to other legal systems. It is also correct that resort to Jewish law is proper only if compatible with the objective of the statute being interpreted, but this was indeed the situation in *Hendeles*. As indicated above, the objective of the entire Restoration of Lost Property Law, and Section 3 in particular, is the same as that of the rules of Jewish law governing this subject.[454]

Justice Barak made an additional comment with regard to the method a court should employ in ascertaining the position of Jewish law on a matter *sub judice*. The district court, for the purpose of determining the Jewish law on the question before it, admitted in evidence the opinions of three well-known contemporary halakhic scholars. The court overruled an objection to the introduction of this evidence stating: "I do not fully understand . . . [the] objection. It is a daily occurrence for the court to obtain assistance from the responsa literature in the solution of problems *sub judice*. Why then is this improper when the halakhic authorities are contemporary?"[455]

On this point, Justice Barak stated:[456]

> With all due respect to the court below, responsa literature, which constitutes part of the system of Jewish law, is not the same as a specific answer to a specific question directly pertinent to a matter before the court. Jewish law on the issue before us is not "law" that is applicable in Israel, for our case is

454. The President of the Court, Justice Landau, was of the opinion that there should be no reference to Jewish law on the question before the court, because in his view it was not the purpose of Section 3 to establish whose right was superior as between the owner of the premises and the finder of the article. *See* 34(iii) *P.D.* at 86–87.

455. 34(iii) *P.D.* at 68, 83.

456. *Id.* at 68.

> governed not by Jewish law but by the Restoration of Lost Property Law. Jewish law is not even like a foreign legal system whose law [pursuant to Israeli rules of the conflict of laws] governs a particular case, and therefore must be proved as a fact by expert witnesses. Jewish law, so far as the issue before us is concerned, is a legal system which serves to enlighten us by way of comparative law. We learn about it from books that are open to the public. It does not seem to be proper, under these circumstances, to rely on the response to a question put to an expert which touches directly on the very point at issue and was prepared for this very case.

This rejection of the technique of submitting opinions by experts on Jewish law on the question at issue before the court seems completely unjustified. Why should a court be able to consult "books that are open to the public" to become enlightened on the position of Jewish law on an issue before it, yet not be able to obtain the assistance of experts on Jewish law in ascertaining the Jewish law on that very issue? Justice Barak's opinion does not attempt to answer this question. On this point, the dissent stated:[457]

> With all due respect, I do not agree with this qualification by my colleague. Mr. Schereschewsky made clear that the opinions were submitted in order to clarify the position of Jewish law and its sources on the basic question to be decided, and the learned trial judge also stated: "The submission will, of course, be accepted as legal matter, non-binding, in the nature of theoretical research" (see Record 73). Not only can no error be found in this procedure, but the procedure tends to make Jewish law more accessible to Israeli judges and thereby increase the likelihood of reference to that law. As is known, the study of Jewish law is sometimes laborious. Why not make this work of the judge easier by permitting opinions by scholars of Jewish law to clarify the position of Jewish law on the subject under discussion? About this, one may well say that all who add to "telling the story" of Jewish law by describing and explaining it are worthy to be praised.[458] These expert opinions will be of help to Israeli judges in investigating and deciding the legal issues before them, as indeed has been the case in the matter before us.[459]

457. *Id.* at 83.

458. This is an allusive echo of the passage in the Passover *Haggadah* that all who are expansive in "telling the story" of the Exodus from Egypt are worthy to be praised.

459. *See also infra* pp. 1929–1930. Justice Landau did not address this question at all. In the meantime, these opinions have been "rendered kosher" (*i.e.*, permissible for consultation by the courts), as a result of having been published. *See No'am, Shenaton le-Verur Ba'ayot ba-Halakhah* [*No'am*, Annual for the Clarification of Halakhic Questions], XXI (1979), Jerusalem, pp. 28–41 (opinions by Rabbis Moshe Feinstein, Ovadiah Yosef, M.N.N. Lemberger, and I.J. Fisher). These halakhic authorities reach the same conclusion as the dissenting opinion in *Hendeles*.

Differences of opinion with respect to the role of Jewish law in the interpretation of Israeli legislation resurfaced at the additional hearing in the *Hendeles* case, before an augmented panel of five judges. This additional hearing occurred after the Foundations of Law Act, 1980, had taken effect; and the majority of the judges at the additional hearing discussed these differences of opinion in the light of that statute. Their views will be examined in chapter 44, which deals with the Foundations of Law Act.

Chapter 43

THE LAW OF PERSONAL STATUS IN THE RABBINICAL AND GENERAL COURTS: ADDITIONAL ASPECTS OF THE PROBLEM OF THE STATUS OF JEWISH LAW IN THE LAW OF THE STATE OF ISRAEL

I. Adjudication in Matters of Personal Status
  A. Continuation of the Basic Allocation of Jurisdiction
  B. The Nature of the Problems Discussed in this Chapter
II. The Law Applied by the Rabbinical Courts in Matters of Personal Status
  A. Jewish Law
  B. Statutes Mandating Their Application by the Rabbinical Courts
III. Application of the Jewish Law of Personal Status by the General Courts
  A. Conflict of Laws
  B. Evidence and Procedure
  C. Privately Performed Marriages
    1. Marriage Between a *Kohen* and a Divorcée
    2. Marriages Permitted under the *Halakhah*
IV. The Weight Given by the General Courts to the Decisions of the Rabbinical Courts Interpreting Jewish Law
  A. The Earnings of a Wife from Her Employment
  B. The Rights and Obligations of Parents in the Education of Their Children
V. Legislation Contrary to Jewish Law—A Case Study of the Solution to a Problem
  A. The Obligation of a Husband to Support His Wife as Affected by Her Income from Employment and from Her Property
  B. Amendment of the Woman's Equal Rights Law
VI. Differing Trends in Regard to the Employment of Legislation in the Rabbinical System
  A. Decline in the Employment of Legislation as an Instrument of Halakhic Creativity
  B. The Rabbinical Court of Appeals—Accomplishments and Limitations
VII. Civil Law in the Rabbinical Courts
VIII. The Rabbinical Courts and the General Legal System of the State
  A. The *Wiloszni* Case
  B. The *Nagar* Case

I. ADJUDICATION IN MATTERS OF PERSONAL STATUS

A. Continuation of the Basic Allocation of Jurisdiction

Jurisdiction over matters of personal status continues to be allocated between the rabbinical courts and the general courts in essentially the same manner as it was when the State of Israel was established.[1] Starting in 1953, however, certain jurisdictional modifications have been made, and legislation has also been enacted concerning the authority of the rabbinical courts and the status of the rabbinical court judges.[2]

The law of personal status as adjudicated by the rabbinical and general courts constitutes a significant aspect of the general issue of the place of Jewish law in the State of Israel, and has given rise to an extensive literature.[3] Important contributions by the rabbinical court system to the development of Jewish law in the period preceding the establishment of the State have already been discussed. To some extent these occurred by way of judicial interpretation, but in the main they were the product of legislative enactments (*takkanot*) by the Chief Rabbinate relating to the judicial process and to personal status. These enactments dealt with such matters as the establishment of the Rabbinical Court of Appeals, rules of procedure, spousal maintenance, child support, the *ketubbah*, *ḥaliẓah*, levirate marriage, the ban of Rabbenu Gershom against bigamy, and the minimum age for marriage.[4]

Creative development of Jewish law through the adoption of rabbinic enactments continued during the early years of the State but gradually declined; and for over forty years, it has virtually ceased.[5] Since the establish-

1. *See supra* p. 1597 n. 52.

2. Rabbinical Courts Jurisdiction (Marriage and Divorce) Law, 1953, and various other statutes. *See, e.g.*, the discussion of the Capacity and Guardianship Law, 1962, *supra* p. 1671, and the Succession Law, 1965, *supra* p. 1688.

3. For a detailed discussion, *see* M. Silberg, *Ha-Ma'amad ha-Ishi be-Yisra'el* [Personal Status in Israel], Jerusalem, 1958; B. Schereschewsky, *Dinei Mishpaḥah* [Family Law], 3rd ed., 1984; Elon, *Ḥakikah;* M. Shava, *Ha-Din ha-Ishi be-Yisra'el* [Personal Law in Israel], 2nd ed., 1984; P. Schiffman, *Dinei Mishpaḥah be-Yisra'el* [Family Law in Israel], 1984; A. Rosen-Tzvi, *Yaḥasei Mamon Bein Benei Zug* [Financial Relationships between Spouses], Jerusalem, 1982; Z. Falk, *Tevi'at Gerushin mi-Ẓad ha-Ishah be-Dinei Yisra'el* [Jewish Law as to a Wife's Right to Obtain a Divorce], Jerusalem, 1973; *id.*, *Dinei Nissu'in ve-Gerushin* [Laws of Marriage and Divorce], Jerusalem, 1962.

4. *See supra* pp. 824–825, 1597–1599. *See also infra* pp. 1789–1787.

5. *See infra* pp. 1807–1809.

ment of the State, the major creativity of the rabbinical courts has been reflected in their judicial decisions. These decisions[6] reveal significant development in the area of family law,[7] but there is a growing tendency in this body of case law toward strictness.[8]

It is to be regretted that some urgent problems have not yet been solved, especially those relating to the *agunah.* These problems cry out for halakhic solutions through judicial expansion of the types of cases in which courts will compel a divorce,[9] and through appropriate halakhic legislation.

6. Since 1954, some of the decisions of the Rabbinical Court of Appeals and the district rabbinical courts have been published. To date, fifteen volumes have been published. In addition, Warhaftig, *Osef Piskei ha-Din* contains decisions of the Rabbinical Court of Appeals rendered before the State of Israel was established. *See supra* p. 826 n. 172, p. 1601.

7. For example, *see supra* p. 1600 n. 61 and accompanying text, discussing a wife's right to alimony *pendente lite* and to payment upon divorce of a sum appropriate to the circumstances of each case, in addition to the amount specified in her *ketubbah. See also infra* pp. 1784–1787, discussing a wife's right to retain her earnings from outside employment that is not exclusively "women's work." For further details, *see* the references cited *supra* n. 3.

8. For example, *see* In Re A.B., 7 *P.D.R.* 175 (1968) (quoted in Rodnitzky v. Rabbinical Court of Appeals, 24(i) *P.D.* 704, 709 (1970)), regarding the incompetence of a habitual violator of the sabbath to testify to the performance of a private marriage ceremony (between a *kohen* and a divorcée). The decision in *In Re A.B.* is contrary to that reached in the decision of the Rabbinical Court of Appeals in B. v. A. (1946), Warhaftig, *Osef Piskei ha-Din,* pp. 132, 137–138 (discussed *supra* pp. 1602–1603). It may be assumed, however, that the more stringent evidentiary ruling in the later case was influenced by the desire to avoid, at any cost, giving judicial sanction to the registration of a private marriage between a *kohen* and a divorcée. This aim is understandable, for the rabbinical court cannot be asked to distinguish between the *prohibition* of such a marriage and the *validity* of the marriage once it has been performed. Certainly, from the halakhic viewpoint, any such distinction could be criticized as rewarding rather than deterring transgression. (For a detailed discussion, *see infra* pp. 1772–1778.)

Nevertheless, these considerations cannot justify such a sweeping and far-reaching evidentiary ruling in direct conflict with the prior 1946 decision of the Rabbinical Court of Appeals, which the later decision did not even cite. The later decision is particularly questionable in that the disqualification of the witnesses was based solely on their own admission that they violated the sabbath. Moreover, an analysis of the decision indicates that the case could have been decided on other grounds, without reaching the issue of whether the witnesses were competent to testify. For a detailed discussion, *see* M. Elon, *Mi-Ba'ayot ha-Halakhah ve-ha-Mishpat bi-Medinat Yisra'el* [Problems of *Halakhah* and Law in the State of Israel], Ha-Makhon le-Yahadut Zemaneinu [Institute for Contemporary Judaism], 1973, pp. 22–28. *See also* the opinion of Justice Kister in the *Rodnitzky* case, *supra,* 24(i) *P.D.* at 727–728, attempting to reconcile these two decisions of the Rabbinical Court of Appeals; with all respect, his attempt seems less than successful.

9. Under Jewish law, divorce is effected not by judicial decree but rather by the husband's delivery of a *get* (bill of divorcement) to his wife, with her consent. The role of the court is to determine whether a divorce is justified or required under the circumstances. A husband's refusal to comply with a rabbinical court decree mandating a divorce and ordering him to deliver a *get* to his wife is punishable by imprisonment, pursuant to Section 6 of the Rabbinical Courts Jurisdiction (Marriage and Divorce) Law, 1953. However, the rabbinical courts rarely conclude that the facts are halakhically sufficient to warrant such an order. Instead, their decrees generally declare merely that the husband is under a legal obligation

It is true that for the past several centuries the majority of the halakhic authorities have abstained from enacting legislation providing for the annulment of marriages. However, the existence of the State of Israel, which has been reestablished as the center for the entire Jewish people, once again permits the resolution of the *agunah* problem through legislation. Such a solution—which is fully consonant with the outlook and methods of the *Halakhah*—is vital to the integrity and well-being of the halakhic system and, indeed, of the entire Jewish people, as has been previously discussed in greater detail in connection with the treatment of halakhic legislation, as well as in other contexts.[10]

The general courts, which apply Jewish law to a considerable portion of the matters of personal status, have also shown a great deal of creativity in their decisions; but as to some important questions, their decisions are

---

to divorce his wife, or even that it is a *mizvah* (religious or moral obligation) for him to do so, or simply that a divorce is appropriate. (For discussion of these various types of judgments in regard to divorce, *see* Gutman v. District Rabbinical Court, 34(i) *P.D.* 443 (1979), quoted *supra* pp. 121–122.) Under the statute, the sanction of imprisonment is not applicable to these latter types of decrees, because of concerns by the Chief Rabbinate that a divorce granted by a husband as a result of the imposition of a sanction in cases where the rabbinical court does not conclude that a divorce should be compelled would be invalid as a *get me'usseh* (divorce given as a result of improper compulsion). The only really effective sanction, namely, imprisonment, is thus unavailable in the vast majority of divorce cases.

However, according to Maimonides and other halakhic authorities who follow him, if a wife asserts, "I loathe him and I cannot willingly cohabit with him," her husband may be compelled to divorce her, "for she is not like a captive who can be required to cohabit with someone she loathes" (Maimonides, *MT,* Ishut 14:8). Many halakhic authorities, led by Rabbenu Tam, disagreed with Maimonides. In their view, such a feeling on the part of a wife is not a sufficient basis to compel her husband to divorce her (*see Tosafot,* Ketubbot 63b, s.v. Aval amrah). Application of Maimonides' view would solve a significant number of cases of *agunah* caused by the husband's recalcitrant refusal to divorce his wife. *See also* Z. Warhaftig, "Kefiyyat Get le-Halakhah u-le-Ma'aseh" [Compelling a Divorce—Theory and Practice], *Shenaton,* III–IV (1976–77), p. 153, and Warhaftig's conclusion, pp. 215–216; B.Z. Eliash, "Ethnic Pluralism or Melting Pot?," 18 *Israel L. Rev.* 348, 369ff. (1983); R. Arusi, "Ha-Gorem ha-Edati bi-Fesikat ha-Halakhah (Kefiyyat Get be-Moredet 'Ma'is Alai'—Ezel Yehudei Teiman)" [The Factor of Community in the Determination of the *Halakhah* (Compelling a Divorce among the Yemenite Jews in the Case of a *Moredet* Who Claims, "I Loathe Him")], *Dine Israel,* X–XI (1981–1983), p. 125. Arusi deals extensively with the subject.

10. For a detailed discussion, *see supra* pp. 846–879. In the Eastern communities, enactments concerning the annulment of marriages were promulgated as late as the eighteenth and nineteenth centuries. *See supra* pp. 874–878; Freimann, *Kiddushin ve-Nissu'in,* pp. 327ff.; Elon, *Yihudah Shel Halakhah,* pp. 15, 33–35.

Attempts have been made to promulgate enactments in other areas, but they have proved unsuccessful. *See supra* p. 1684 and n. 270 as to legislative proposals by the late Chief Rabbis of Israel, Isaac Herzog and Ben-Zion Uziel, with regard to inheritance by daughters—which were rejected by a majority of the rabbis. This rejection is to be regretted, especially in light of the important creativity demonstrated by the rabbinical court system in the area of legislation, beginning with the establishment of the Chief Rabbinate in 1921 and continuing through the early years of the State of Israel. *See supra* pp. 824–835, 1598–1599.

occasionally marked by a tendency to restrict narrowly both the application of Jewish law and the jurisdiction of the rabbinical courts.[11]

B. The Nature of the Problems Discussed in this Chapter

The exclusive jurisdiction of the rabbinical courts in certain matters of personal status, and the concurrent jurisdiction of the rabbinical and the general courts in other such matters, have given rise—particularly since the establishment of the State of Israel—to a number of highly significant questions concerning the place of Jewish law in the legal system of the State. The discussion here is not intended to present in detail the law of personal status as reflected in the decisions of the two court systems. This broad and interesting topic is discussed in works devoted entirely to that task,[12] and limitations of space do not permit going over the same ground. Neither does the present work treat the "jurisdictional competition" between the two court systems. This conflict in regard to jurisdiction is extensively discussed in the judgments of the courts of both systems, as well as in many books and articles; but it is neither relevant to the substance of Jewish law nor an appropriate subject for the present work. The appropriate questions for our discussion are those that relate directly to the way Jewish law is applied in the rabbinical courts and in the general courts, and to the relationship between these two court systems as it affects the application of Jewish law.

The problems in regard to the application of the Jewish law of marriage and divorce as well as spousal and child support differ substantially from the problems in regard to the application of other areas of Jewish law in the State of Israel, because the obligation to apply Jewish law and the method by which that law is incorporated into the legal system of the State are different for these legal areas than they are for all other areas, including other areas of the law of personal status. In regard to all branches of the law other than marriage, divorce, and spousal and child support, the Knes-

11. *See* Elon, *Ḥakikah,* pp. 68ff.; *id.*, "Ba'ayot u-Megamot be-Yaḥasei Halakhah u-Medinah" [Issues and Trends in the Relationship between *Halakhah* and State], *Ammudim,* 1974, pp. 202–207, 256–264. Justice Berinson took the view that the jurisdiction of the rabbinical courts, which are not part of the general judicial system, should be construed as strictly as possible. *See* Kahanof v. District Rabbinical Court of Tel Aviv, 29(i) *P.D.* 449, 453 (1974). *But cf.* Justice Berinson's opinion concerning the jurisdiction of the Druze religious courts, Ḥatar v. Druze Religious Court of Haifa, 27(i) *P.D.* 449 (1973). *See also* P. Schiffman's criticism of the *Kahanof* case, "Samkhut Bet Din Rabbani be-Nissu'in ve-Gerushin she-Ne'erkhu mi-Ḥuẓ le-Yisra'el [The Jurisdiction of the Rabbinical Courts over Marriages and Divorces Effected outside the State of Israel], *Mishpatim,* VI (1975), p. 372, and the article of the President of the Supreme Court, Justice Y. Kahan, "Shipput Rabbani ve-Shipput Ḥiloni" [Rabbinic Adjudication and Secular Adjudication], *Dine Israel,* VII (1977), pp. 205, 207–208. *See also* the further discussion in the present chapter.

12. Some of this literature is cited *supra* n. 3.

set's legislation itself explicitly selects and precisely prescribes the norms and principles of Jewish law to be applied. The previous chapter has pointed out that this method of selective incorporation of specific provisions of Jewish law is used in all areas of the law and is particularly prevalent with regard to those matters of personal status over which the general courts and the rabbinical courts have concurrent jurisdiction, such as legal capacity, guardianship, inheritance, and support of dependents other than a spouse or minor children. The problems presented by this direct and selective method of incorporation have already been considered to some extent and will be further discussed below.[13]

In contrast to this method of selective incorporation of specific provisions of Jewish law, the incorporation of Jewish law in matters of marriage, divorce, and spousal and child support has been accomplished through blanket incorporation by reference: The legislation provides generally that Jewish law governs these matters in all courts of the State of Israel; it does not spell out the specific provisions of Jewish law that must be applied. At first glance, it would seem that this method of blanket incorporation is clear and unambiguous; but, as the following discussion demonstrates, this method has its own difficulties, *e.g.*, how "complete" is the incorporation, and to what extent do the general courts—and even the rabbinical courts—need to look to Jewish law?

These questions have an important bearing on the issue of the place of Jewish law in the Jewish state; they involve further and different aspects than those presented when legislation by the Knesset directly incorporates specific provisions of Jewish law. Apart from these differences, however, there is an inescapable underlying problem inherent in any manner of attempt to apply Jewish law in the legal system of the State. This underlying problem results from the fact that the source of authority for the rabbinical courts in the State of Israel and for the application of Jewish law in the State, in matters of personal status as in all other areas of the law, is not the same source as that which has conferred binding authority on the *Halakhah* throughout the generations. The source of authority in the State of Israel is rather the authority of the Knesset, which is the basic norm (*Grundnorm*) for the entire legal system of the Jewish state. This difference in the basic norm has already been dealt with at some length in connection with the discussion of the early days of the Knesset.[14]

13. *See supra* pp. 1652–1683; *infra* pp. 1763, 1765. As to the distinction between selective incorporation of specific provisions of Jewish law and blanket incorporation by reference, *see supra* p. 1652.

14. *See* the discussion in the Knesset regarding the provisions of the Woman's Equal Rights Law applicable also to the religious courts, and Prime Minister Ben Gurion's views on this matter, *supra* pp. 1658–1659, as well as the discussion concerning the obligation to

II. THE LAW APPLIED BY THE RABBINICAL COURTS IN MATTERS OF PERSONAL STATUS

A. Jewish Law

When a rabbinical court deals with a matter of personal status within the jurisdiction conferred upon it by the law of the State, it decides according to its own jurisprudence, *i.e.*, Jewish law, unless a specific statute explicitly provides that statutory norms are controlling. This is the settled rule in the Supreme Court; it was summarized as follows in the seminal *Wiloszni* case.[15]

> As far as the legal system of the State is concerned, the jurisdiction of the rabbinical courts is conferred by the law of the State.[16] The power conferred by the law of the State upon the rabbinical courts in matters within their jurisdiction is the power to adjudicate according to the law applied by a rabbinical court, *i.e.*, Jewish law, except where there is a specific statute directed to the rabbinical courts that explicitly provides that they must apply the provisions of that statute. This is the case, for example, with regard to the provisions of the Woman's Equal Rights Law, 1951, which states (Section 7):
>
> > Every general court shall act in accordance with this statute; every religious court having jurisdiction to adjudicate matters of personal status shall also act in accordance with this statute.[17] . . .
>
> According to one view, whenever a rabbinical court fails to apply the provisions of such a statute, its decision is subject to review by the [Supreme Court sitting as the] High Court of Justice on the stated ground that in such a case, the rabbinical court has acted beyond its jurisdiction, and is subject to correction by the High Court of Justice pursuant to Section 7(b)(4) of the Courts Law, 1957.[18] According to another view, the rabbinical court has not exceeded its jurisdiction in such a case, but rather has committed an error of law, as to

---

respect one's parents, incorporated in the Capacity and Guardianship Law, *supra* pp. 1669–1670. *See also infra* pp. 1906–1909.

15. Wiloszni v. Rabbinical Court of Appeals, 36(ii) *P.D.* 733, 738–739 (1982) (Elon, Y. Kahan, and Levine, JJ.). Justice Elon wrote the opinion for the court, with Justice Levine reserving for further consideration only the question of whether rights under the Tenants Protection Law could be waived. *See* the discussion of this case, *infra* pp. 1820–1824.

16. *See* Bilat v. Rabbi Goren, 29(i) *P.D.* 98, 102 (1974), discussing the status and powers of the Chief Rabbinate, and its authority to advise on any matter on which it is consulted. In this connection, *see* the Chief Rabbinate of Israel Law, 1980, discussed in Fund of the Movement of Progressive Judaism in Israel v. Minister of Religions, 43(ii) *P.D.* 661, 671, 684ff. (1989).

17. For a discussion of the Woman's Equal Rights Law, *see supra* pp. 1656–1660. The extent to which the rabbinical courts defer to or disregard these particular provisions of the law is considered *infra* nn. 113, 118, and 120. *See also* Joseph v. Joseph, 24(i) *P.D.* 792, 809–810 (1970); Boronovsky v. Chief Rabbis of Israel, 25(i) *P.D.* 7, 15 (1971); Kahan, *supra* n. 11 at 210.

18. *See, e.g.,* Sidis v. Rabbinical Court of Appeals, 12 *P.D.* 1525 (1958).

which the basis of intervention by the High Court of Justice is the general provision in Section 7(a) of the Courts Law.[19] However, when is all this relevant? When the Legislature has specifically stated that a particular statute applies to the rabbinical courts. If this is not so stated, the rabbinical courts decide cases within their jurisdiction according to the *Halakhah*, and we do not intervene in such a case[20] unless there has been a violation of the principles of natural justice.[21]

19. *See* Sobol v. Goldman, 33(i) *P.D.* 789 (1979) (Ben Porat, J., pp. 793–794; Elon, J., p. 799); Nagar v. Nagar, 38(i) *P.D.* 365, 383 (1984). *See also* M. Shava, "Ha-Im Setiyyah o Hit'almut Shel Bet Din me-Hora'at Ḥok Ḥilonit ha-Mufnet elav bi-Meyuḥad, Kamoha ke-Ḥarigah mi-Samkhut?" [Does a Rabbinical Court's Departure from or Disregard of a Provision of a Secular (State) Law Specifically Directed to It Constitute Action in Excess of Jurisdiction?], *Ha-Praklit*, XXVIII (1972–1973), p. 299.

20. The High Court of Justice does not review the judgment of a rabbinical court for erroneous application of the rules of Jewish law nor does it have general appellate jurisdiction over the rabbinical courts. Note the following comments by Justice Haim Cohn in Streit v. Chief Rabbi of Israel, 18(i) *P.D.* 598, 608 (1964):

> The attorney for the petitioner argued to us that these judgments of the rabbinical courts are manifestly erroneous, and he labored diligently and found many cogent responsa of various halakhic authorities whose views and theories do not agree with the opinions stated in these rabbinical court judgments. However, it is the long-settled rule and established practice in this court that we do not hear appeals from religious courts. All their rulings are part of their religious law, and a civil court may not question their rulings as to the substantive content of that law. As Justice Silberg put it in his book *Ha-Ma'amad ha-Ishi be-Yisra'el* [Personal Status in Israel], p. 174: "Can we possibly describe the complexities and uncertainties that will result if, for example, the High Court of Justice were to consider a rabbinical court as having 'exceeded its jurisdiction' because it rules in a particular matter according to the view of Rashbeẓ rather than the contrary view of Ribash?" We have been commanded from ancient times to obey the judges of our time even if they appear to be ruling that right is left and left is right. (*Sifrei*, Deuteronomy 17:11.)

To the same effect is the opinion of Court President Olshan in the same case, 18(i) *P.D.* at 643. *See also* Joseph v. Joseph, *supra* n. 17, where Justice Kahan quoted the *Streit* opinion to support his position that the rulings of the rabbinical courts are binding on the general courts in matters such as support and maintenance, on which the general courts are required to rule in accordance with Jewish law. *See* 24(i) *P.D.* at 811. Justice Cohn did not agree with Justice Kahan in the *Joseph* case and apparently distinguished between the issue of Supreme Court review of the halakhic correctness of rabbinical court decisions and the issue of whether general courts are bound by rabbinical court decisions on matters of Jewish law. *See id.* at 808–810. For a detailed discussion, *see infra* pp. 1784–1794.

21. *See* Vicki Levy v. District Rabbinical Court of Tel Aviv-Jaffa, 13 *P.D.* 1182 (1959). "Violation of the principles of natural justice" refers to the violation of "fundamental principles of just adjudication," Shagav v. Rabbinical Court of Safed, 21(ii) *P.D.* 505, 512 (1967), such as the prohibition of bias, and the principle that both sides must be heard (*see infra*). *See also* Mossman v. Rabbinical Court, 18(iii) *P.D.* 502, 504 (1964). In the *Vicki Levy* case, *supra*, which involved a claim before a rabbinical court for divorce, the husband sought rescission of a prior order for the support of his wife, asserting that in the meantime she had left the marital home. The wife's attorney argued that she was forced to leave the home because the husband had beaten her. The attorney added that the husband's request to rescind the support order came as a surprise, and he therefore requested that the hearing be postponed in order to enable him to prove that the wife was justified in leaving the home.

B. Statutes Mandating Their Application by the Rabbinical Courts

During the period of the British Palestine Mandate, some legislative enactments required that they be applied by every court, whether general or religious, having jurisdiction over matters of personal status, even if the legislative provisions contravened the law of the particular religious community involved. For example, the distribution of the *miri* property of an estate was required to follow the schedule set forth in the Succession Ordinance, 1923, which provided for equality of sons and daughters, and of husbands and wives, in regard to rights of inheritance.

Similar statutes have been enacted by the Israeli Knesset, the prime example being the Woman's Equal Rights Law, 1951. We have already expressed the view that this statute is for the most part consistent with the position of Jewish law as it has developed, and that to the extent that particular provisions of the statute may not be consonant with existing Jewish law, the halakhic authorities have the power to enact appropriate *takkanot* that would respond to the contemporary social situation.[22] A number of such enactments were adopted by the Chief Rabbinate, but additional efforts in this direction, such as those proposed by Chief Rabbis Herzog and Uziel in the early days of the State, were successfully resisted by other halakhic authorities.[23] This resistance is also reflected in decisions of the rabbinical courts that have disregarded the provisions of the Woman's Equal Rights Law.[24]

The court refused the requested postponement and entered an immediate order terminating support for the wife.

In the Supreme Court, the attorney for the wife argued that the rabbinical court's procedure contravened the principles of natural justice, since the wife was not offered the opportunity to present her evidence. This, it was claimed, violated the principle of *audi alteram partem* ("hear the other side"). Finding merit in this claim, the Supreme Court vacated the order of the rabbinical court. Justice Silberg's opinion demonstrated that the procedure in the rabbinical court also fundamentally contravened Jewish law. The verse "Judge your neighbor fairly" (Leviticus 19:15) requires the court to treat "both parties impartially in all respects. One party should not be permitted to speak at length while the other is admonished to be brief. The judge should not speak softly and courteously to one party and harshly and irascibly to the other" (Maimonides, *MT,* Sanhedrin, 21:1–3, based on TB Shevu'ot 30a/b). To the same effect, *see Resp. Rema* #108; *supra* pp. 168–169. *See also* Histadrut Po'alei Agudat Yisra'el v. Minister of Religions, 37(i) *P.D.* 813 (1983). The Supreme Court is not authorized to intervene on the ground that the *content* of the religious decision contravenes natural justice. *See* Vicki Levy v. District Rabbinical Court of Tel Aviv-Jaffa, *supra,* 13 *P.D.* at 1193; Schlesinger v. Minister of the Interior, 17 *P.D.* 225, 231 (1963); Streit v. Chief Rabbi of Israel, *supra* n. 20 at 608, 611.

22. *See supra* pp. 1656–1657.

23. *See supra* p. 1494 and n. 124; p. 1687 n. 145; p. 1684 and n. 270.

24. *See infra* nn. 113, 118, 120; Joseph v. Joseph, and Boronovsky v. Chief Rabbis of Israel, *supra* n. 17. *See also* Kahan, *supra* n. 11 at 210.

A particularly instructive approach to the relationship between Israeli statutory law and Jewish law is taken by Rabbi Yosef Kafaḥ, a member of the Rabbinical Court of Appeals and a major halakhic authority in the State of Israel. Rabbi Kafaḥ's position is expressed in the leading case of *Nagar v. Nagar*,[25] discussed further below. In commenting on statements made by the district court as to the nature of statutory provisions expressly made applicable to the rabbinical courts as well as the general courts, he said:

> It would seem that these statements concerning "laws explicitly directed to them [the rabbinical courts]" are based on a perception that the Legislature has acted to require the rabbinical courts to reach decisions that are contrary to their religious beliefs. Indeed, many people share this perception, but their logic begs the question. They assume the premise that these laws require the rabbinical courts to reach decisions that are contrary to the laws of the Torah, and on the basis of that premise they conclude that the law "violates pure halakhic considerations." But this conclusion is not inevitable; rather, the law should be viewed according to its plain meaning.
>
> Section 1 of the Woman's Equal Rights Law provides: "The same law shall apply to women and men with regard to every legal transaction." Section 5 provides: "This law shall not affect the religious law in matters of marriage and divorce."[26]
>
> The plain meaning of these provisions is that the Legislature established a binding rule only with respect to monetary matters, in regard to which it perceived the existing law as discriminating against women. . . . The legislative mandate is manifestly based on the assumption that legislation as to monetary matters would not affect religious law, since the legislation is considered "a stipulation as to a monetary matter"; therefore, it is not a [prohibited] stipulation to contract out of a Biblical norm. Consequently, it may be assumed that the Legislature had no intention to interfere with anything that is not "a stipulation as to a monetary matter." This is an instance of an approach that can lead to a proper understanding of a number of statutes that have not been so understood.[27]

In other words, just as under Jewish law there is freedom of contract, *i.e.*, the parties to a legal transaction may agree on terms contrary to a particular halakhic rule, provided the agreement concerns a "monetary matter" (*mamon*) and not religious law (*issur*),[28] so a statute of the Knesset, enacted in the name of the people by their elected representatives, is in the nature of an agreement by the people to conduct their affairs in accordance with the legislative provisions. As long as the matter does not concern reli-

25. 38(i) *P.D.* 365 (1984).
26. *Id.* at 411.
27. *Id.* at 412.
28. *See supra* pp. 122–141.

gious law, such an agreement is fully effective even if it is contrary to a particular halakhic rule.[29] This interpretive approach by Rabbi Kafaḥ, which is particularly significant in that it is taken by a leading rabbinical court judge and important halakhic authority, is applicable not only to the particular question dealt with in the *Nagar* case but also, as explained more fully below, to the broader question of the relationship between the rabbinical courts and the general legal system of the State of Israel.[30]

Even when the Legislature explicitly requires the rabbinical courts to apply the provisions of a particular statute, a rabbinical court decision pursuant to the statutory mandate may nevertheless not reach the same result as a decision of a general court applying the same statute.[31] An instructive example is the judgment rendered by a special tribunal[32] in the *Nagar* case, which dealt with the question of the type of education the children of a separated or divorced couple should receive.[33] According to Section 3 of the Woman's Equal Rights Law, matters involving custody of children, including their education, are to be decided primarily on the basis of the principle of the "best interests of the child"; and the religious courts are explicitly directed to apply the provisions of this statute. It should be noted that, even

29. The boundary between "monetary matters" and "religious law" is not always clear and precise. A particular legal institution may contain elements of both. *See supra* pp. 132–137, and the discussion *infra* with regard to the principle of the best interests of the child.

30. *See infra* pp. 1824–1826.

31. One of the reasons why this is so is that, as has been mentioned, from the point of view of the *Halakhah,* a statute of the Knesset may be binding on the rabbinical courts only with regard to monetary matters and not with regard to religious law. *See* the further comments in Rabbi Kafaḥ's opinion in the *Nagar* case, *supra* n. 25 at 412. *See also* the opinion of Elon, J. in that case, *id.* at 408, quoted *infra.*

32. The jurisdiction of the special tribunal is defined at the end of Article 55 of the Palestine Order in Council, which provides: "Whenever a question arises as to whether or not a case is within the exclusive jurisdiction of a religious court, the matter shall be referred to a Special Tribunal, to be constituted as prescribed by Ordinance." Section 9 of the Courts Ordinance, 1940, provides that the Special Tribunal shall consist of three judges: two justices of the Supreme Court, and the president of the highest court of the particular religious community whose courts are claimed to have exclusive jurisdiction in the matter, or a judge designated by him.

33. The members of the Special Tribunal were: Justice Meir Shamgar, the President of the Supreme Court, Justice Menachem Elon, and Rabbi Yosef Kafaḥ of the Rabbinical Court of Appeals. The court's opinion was written by Justice Elon, with Rabbi Kafaḥ making some additional comments. The question was whether the education of the couple's children was within the exclusive jurisdiction of the rabbinical courts. The basis for the claim of exclusive jurisdiction by the rabbinical courts was that the husband and wife had agreed, both in the divorce agreement and in person before the rabbinical court, to the jurisdiction of the rabbinical court in matters concerning the education of their children. The dispute occurred when the wife changed her mind and brought the case before the general court, which ruled that the children should continue to attend a secular school. This ruling was contrary to the determination of the rabbinical court that the children should attend a religious school, as their father wished.

without this explicit directive, rabbinical courts decide matters involving custody according to the "best interests of the child," which has long been an important principle in Jewish law;[34] indeed, it was Jewish law that was the source from which this principle was introduced into Israeli law.[35]

The court in *Nagar* stated that a court's primary task when applying the principle of the "best interests of the child" is to examine carefully the factual circumstances of each case:

> The one and only guideline for the solution of a difficult and complex problem such as this, which touches the most sensitive aspect of the relation of parents and children, is the proper and wise application of the principle of the best interests of the children, which both the rabbinical courts and the general courts apply as they are directed to do. The application of this principle is fundamentally a matter of establishing the facts and circumstances: How will a change in educational orientation affect the children? How old are the children? What kind of school have they attended until now, and what kind of school is proposed for them in the future, etc.? In determining the answers to these questions, the courts will be aided by the opinions of experts.
>
> In the case before us, there are various conflicting opinions: Some point to the harm that will be caused to the children as a result of a change in the orientation of their education, particularly since they are in the custody of the mother, who does not follow a religious way of life. Others point to the positive aspects of their attending a religious school, where [not only is] the general atmosphere . . . consistent with the life-style of children of the same age in all types of schools, but in addition there is observance of the religious precepts, which will preserve the ties between the children and their father, who is careful about religious observance. In this way, they will not be deprived in their upbringing of the "image of the father," which is vital for a child's sound growth and rearing.[36]

Regarding the "best interests of the child," the court continued:[37]

> As stated, the first and primary inquiry in determining the best interests of the child is, What are the full factual circumstances of the particular case? However, there are relevant considerations beyond the facts, since the question of the best interests of the child requires value judgments involving personal philosophy and way of life. It has already been stated by this court:

34. *See, e.g., Resp. Rashba Attributed to Naḥmanides* #38; *Resp. Radbaz,* I, #123; *Resp. Mabit,* II, #62; Rema to Sh. Ar. EH 82:7 and *Pitḥei Teshuvah, ad loc. See also* Nagar v. Nagar, *supra* n. 25 at 393.

35. *See* Nagar v. Nagar, *supra* n. 25 at 392ff. *See also supra* p. 1666.

36. Nagar v. Nagar, *supra* n. 25 at 407.

37. *Id.* at 408–409.

> What are the best interests of the child? The answer to this question is one of the mysteries of the philosophy of education and lies in the recesses of psychology. . . . The Legislature did not define, nor could it define, what are the best interests of the child; it only listed the parents' duties, the essence and purpose of which are, of course, the best interests of the child. . . . The best interests of the child are the aggregate of physical needs and the needs of spiritual and cultural life: satisfaction of needs, preservation of assets, and training for a career, together with instruction and education that will make it possible for the child to participate in the spiritual and cultural life of the society of which he is a member.[38]

Thus, for example, in adoption proceedings and in other matters involving a child, the Legislature attributed special importance to the religious orientation of the child and his parents;[39] and the decisions of this court have often taken into consideration similar educational factors, such as the consideration that it is in the best interests of the child to grow up in the State of Israel.[40] It goes without saying that value judgments in light of one's worldview and way of life are regarded by Jewish law as factors to be considered in determining the question of the best interests of the child. The *Halakhah*, by its very nature, accords an honored place to these "extralegal" values, and these values are accorded great weight, particularly in "nonmonetary matters," *i.e.*, laws that are included, to a greater or lesser degree, within the category of "*issur*" (religious law).[41]

Because such value judgments are involved in applying the standard of the "best interests of the child," a general court and a rabbinical court may well reach different conclusions on the same set of facts. This is the inevitable result of the existence of two court systems that deal with matters of family law, the very nature of which makes them subject to differences of opinion based on differences in values and world outlook. This phenomenon—that the decision depends on who is the judge[42]—is not new; it has been experienced even within the same court system, among different general court judges, and different rabbinical court judges. When the Legislature vested the power of decision in human judges, and even more so when it gave that power to judges of two types of court systems known from the outset to have different value systems, the Legislature knew, understood, and anticipated that neither the judge nor the *dayyan* (rabbinical court judge) would disavow or disregard his own values. What the judicial office and intellectual honesty

38. Jensen-Zohar v. Zohar, 35(i) *P.D.* 1, 26–27 (1980); *see also id.* at 41.

39. Adoption of Children Law, 1981, sec. 5; Capacity and Guardianship Law, 1962, sec. 13(a); Jensen-Zohar v. Zohar, *supra* n. 38 at 25.

40. Amado v. Director of Immigrant Camp, 4 *P.D.* 4, 22ff. (1950); Anonymous v. Anonymous, 26(i) *P.D.* 85, 94ff. (1971); Jensen-Zohar v. Zohar, *supra* n. 38 at 25, and cases cited therein.

41. *See supra* pp. 122–141.

42. *See* Silberg, *supra* n. 3 at 6, quoted *infra* p. 1769.

require from both the *dayyan* and the judge is that when they reach a decision on the best interests of the child in the case before them, they give proper weight to the factual circumstances of the particular case, render their decision only after they have examined all of the factual circumstances, weigh every possible adverse consequence to the child that may result from each of the possible alternatives, and not give undue weight to value judgments that should not be persuasive in light of the totality of relevant considerations.

A case such as the one before us, in which the parents have not only parted as husband and wife but also have followed divergent life-styles, is a clear example of the difficult dilemma faced by both a judge and a *dayyan* in decisions concerning the education of children. The case may well be decided differently, depending on whether it is heard by a general court or a rabbinical court. So long as the basis of the decision is the "best interests of the child," and the weighing of the relevant factual and value-based considerations is not unreasonable, the decision is valid and appropriate, and will be affirmed by the Supreme Court if appealed.

III. APPLICATION OF THE JEWISH LAW OF PERSONAL STATUS BY THE GENERAL COURTS

Just as a rabbinical court that is required to apply a particular statute may reach a result different from that which the general courts would reach in the same case, the converse is also true when legislation directs the general courts to apply Jewish law. As noted above,[43] the Knesset has enacted detailed statutes on some aspects of family law—including support of family members (except for one's spouse and minor children), adoption, legal capacity, guardianship, and inheritance—the provisions of which are based in large part on Jewish law.[44] However, these provisions are construed on the basis of the statutory language; and the justices of the Supreme Court have disagreed as to whether, under what circumstances, and to what extent Jewish legal sources should be consulted.[45]

By contrast, the legislation on marriage and divorce, and on spousal and child support (which provides that even in the general courts the governing law is the personal law of the parties—*i.e.*, for Jews, Jewish law), does not set forth the specific provisions of Jewish law involved; rather, the statutes incorporate the Jewish law on the subject by general reference.[46]

43. *Supra* pp. 1652–1690.

44. *See id.*

45. *See supra* pp. 1662–1663, 1670–1671; *infra* pp. 1875–1884.

46. *See* Rabbinical Courts Jurisdiction (Marriage and Divorce) Law, 1953, sec. 2: "Marriage and divorce between Jews in Israel shall be effected according to Torah law (*din Torah*)." *See also supra* p. 1652. "Torah law" includes not only the Written Law but also the

Yet despite this general and apparently complete incorporation of Jewish law, decisions reached by a general court on any of these matters may differ from those reached by a rabbinical court on the very same facts, even though the legislation mandates that the governing law in both court systems shall be Jewish law. The following are several examples.

A. Conflict of Laws

The first example of such decisions results from the application by the general courts of the principles of the conflict of laws, which the civil courts deal with as a threshold question before reaching the issues involved in applying Jewish law. For instance, if a Jewish couple enter into a marriage in conformity with the law of their domicile outside the State of Israel, and they subsequently move to Israel, a general court will recognize the validity of their marriage, even if the marriage was not effected in accordance with the requirements of Jewish law, which is the law governing marriage for Jews in Israel. The recognition accorded such a marriage by the general courts is based on the rule of conflict of laws that one who acquires a status in a lawful manner in one country maintains that status wherever he goes, even in a country under whose law that status can be acquired only in a different manner.[47] A rabbinical court, however, would reach a contrary

---

entire *corpus juris* of the *Halakhah*. For a detailed discussion, *see* Fund of the Movement of Progressive Judaism in Israel v. Minister of Religions, *supra* n. 16 at 694ff.

It is interesting to note the response to an argument made during the period of the British Mandate with regard to the law to be applied by the general courts in adjudicating matters of personal status among Jews. Article 47 of the Palestine Order in Council provided that the general courts shall exercise their jurisdiction in matters of personal status "according to the personal law applicable." Section 64 explicitly provided that, in the case of a foreign citizen not a citizen of Palestine, the applicable personal law is his national law. The Order in Council did not state what was the personal law of a resident citizen of Palestine, but it was understood and accepted that the personal law of such a person was the law of his own religion. In a case heard by a general court involving a claim for support (both spouses being Jewish), it was contended that the personal law of a Jewish citizen of Palestine, then under the British mandate, was English law. This contention was rejected both by the district court and, on appeal, by the Supreme Court. The language of Justice Copeland's opinion for the Supreme Court (Shwalboim v. Shwalboim, 7 *P.L.R.* 20, 22 (1940)) is interesting:

> The learned president [of the district court] in his judgment declined to apply English law. . . . Mr. Bar-Shira, with much force and vigour, has tried to argue that this is a gross error and that the personal law is English law. This is an argument which no one would dream of advancing except to maintain a controversial position; it is an argument which really needs no reply. It is clear, and has been recognised as being clear for many many years, that in a case such as this the personal law is the Rabbinical law. It is said by Mr. Bar-Shira that he has been unable to find any such statement in the reported cases—he is now at any rate provided with one.

47. *See* Skornik v. Skornik, 8 *P.D.* 141 (1954).

decision: in determining the validity of such a marriage, it would apply substantive Jewish law and would not concern itself with conflict-of-laws questions.[48]

President Olshan of the Supreme Court stated the rationale for the general courts' circumscription of the application of Jewish law in this area as follows:[49]

> I concur with the view of the learned [district court] judge that without applying the rules of the conflict of laws, it is impossible to do justice to the parties. I also concur with his view that sound logic and policy argue for the application of the rules of the conflict of laws in conjunction with the religious law, particularly in a case such as this where the exclusive application of religious law involves the danger that the respondent will be denied a personal status that she previously acquired in a proper and legal manner. The problem is only whether a basis for reference to this sound reasoning and rational policy is also found in the legislation to which the courts in this country are subject.

Indeed, the justices of the Supreme Court found such a basis in their construction of the statutory language.

B. Evidence and Procedure

Another example of decisions by the general courts that differ from those of the rabbinical courts is the result of application of different rules of evidence and procedure. From the earliest days of the State, the Supreme Court held that a legislative mandate to a general court to apply Jewish law includes only the substantive Jewish law, not the Jewish law of evidence and procedure; even when substantive Jewish law is applied, evidence and procedure are governed by the law applicable in the general courts.[50] Justice

48. Justice Witkon has taken the far-reaching view, which has remained a minority opinion, that even the rabbinical courts are required to abide by the principles of the conflict of laws, since the jurisdiction of the rabbinical courts is conferred by the secular Legislature. *See* Skornik v. Skornik, *supra* n. 47 at 179–180. It should be noted that Jewish law has developed its own ramified system of rules governing the conflict of laws within Jewish law in cases where the law differs from place to place (*see supra* pp. 48, 677, 936), as well as rules governing the conflict between laws of the Jewish legal system and laws of other legal systems, to which the applicable principle is *dina de-malkhuta dina* ("the law of the land is law") (*see supra* pp. 78–79; M. Elon, EJ, V, pp. 882–890, s.v. Conflict of laws (reprinted in *Principles,* pp. 715–724)). The extent to which civil marriages are recognized under Jewish law has been extensively discussed in halakhic and scholarly literature, and need not be dwelt on here. *See also* Elon, *Ḥakikah,* pp. 169–172; Schereschewsky, *supra* n. 3 at 94–110.

49. Skornik v. Skornik, *supra* n. 47 at 155–156.

50. Kotik v. Wolfson, 5 *P.D.* 1341 (1951).

Silberg, in the first important case on this subject, provided an interesting explanation for this holding:[51]

> Concerning the additional question—or, more precisely, the threshold question—as to whether the general courts are required to decide this matter according to the rules of evidence of Jewish law, the attorney for the appellant answers: "Yes, they are most certainly required to do so! To decide a case according to Jewish law means to apply, without exception, the whole of Jewish law, including the law of evidence."
>
> When we asked the appellant's attorney whether, in his view, the judges of a general court dealing with the personal status of Jews in the Land of Israel must be "qualified to act as judges" under Jewish law (for the laws relating to judges are also part, and indeed the very first part, of the *Ḥoshen Mishpat*) he was unable to provide a clear answer. Apparently, he was unwilling to go that far, and this unwillingness laid bare the vulnerable point in his argument. . . .
>
> It is clear that when the general courts adjudicate matters of personal status involving an Israeli citizen who belongs to a particular recognized religious community they are not required to use the procedural and evidentiary rules of the religious court of that community. As to this proposition there is general consensus, which has never been questioned. Indeed, for example, the general courts have long accepted testimony from the parties themselves, even in matters concerning the personal status of Jews who are Israeli citizens, whereas Jewish [procedural] law clearly disqualifies a party as a witness.
>
> Moreover, as I have indicated, common reason compels this result. It is possible, in certain areas of the law, for a court to use a "relativistic" approach and apply different substantive law from that which it usually applies. But it is impossible to be so "discriminating" with regard to the judicial process itself, particularly with regard to the manner of determining the facts. If the proof in Reuben's case is regarded by the Legislature as sufficient to establish Reuben's claim, it will not do for the same proof to be considered insufficient in the case of Simeon.
>
> Why is personal status governed by the religious or "national" law of the parties? Because such questions cannot be resolved identically for everyone; these questions are interwoven with one's tradition and way of life, and they vary with the diverse personal philosophies of the parties in matters of religion, morals, culture, tradition, customs, etc. This rationale clearly has no application whatever when the question does not involve the rights and obligations of the parties, but the obligations and functions of the court. The determination of facts is not a "right" of the parties, but rather the obli-

51. *Id.* at 1344–1345.

gation of the court; and the court must fulfill this obligation in the manner prescribed for all litigants.[52]

The result of these two significant limitations on the application of Jewish law in the general courts, even when those courts are required by statute to apply Jewish law, has been summarized as follows:

> Jewish law as applied in the general courts differs from Jewish law as applied in the rabbinical courts. The approach is different, the litigation procedures are different, and at times even the actual results are different.[53] . . . This means that, in practice, in matters involving personal status, unlike in other branches of the law, there is no fixed substantive law; rather, what the law is depends on who is the judge. This is to say: It depends on the character—religious or secular—of the judicial tribunal which, perhaps by chance, has the first opportunity to deal with the question at issue. This is the "fly in the ointment" in matters of personal status, and the source of the difficulties and complications which the Legislature has not yet succeeded in overcoming.[54]

52. This limitation on the applicability of the Jewish law of evidence and procedure is also based on a construction of the term "personal law," which appears in Article 47 of the Palestine Order in Council with regard to religious law, and its parallel usage in Article 64 of the Order in Council with regard to the national law of a foreign citizen. This reasoning, however, is formalistic and not persuasive.

The distinction between the substantive part of Jewish law, on the one hand, and its evidentiary and procedural rules, on the other, often gives rise to difficulties. In certain instances, Jewish law treats matters of evidence as substantive or constitutive and not merely probative. For example, the witnesses to a marriage are essential to the validity of the marriage and do not serve merely an evidentiary function, inasmuch as under Jewish law "a marriage without witnesses . . . is invalid even if both parties admit that it took place" (Sh. Ar. EH 42:2). Thus, even a general court will not recognize the validity of a marriage if the two witnesses in whose presence it was performed are not competent witnesses under Jewish law (Cohen and Buslik v. Attorney General, 8 *P.D.* 4 (1954)). The line between the substantive and procedural parts of Jewish law is often very difficult to draw. *See* Elon, *Ḥakikah,* pp. 80–83. Omri v. Zouavi, 39(ii) *P.D.* 113 (1985), contains an extensive discussion of this problem. *See also* the detailed article by M. Shava on this case, "Al ha-Shipput be-Inyanei Mezonot Shel Muslemim ve-Noẓrim ve-al Middat Teḥulat ha-Hora'ah ha-Proẓeduralit she-be-Ḥok ha-Mezonot" [Concerning Adjudication in Matters of Support in Cases of Moslems and Christians, and the Extent to Which the Procedural Rules in the Maintenance Law Apply], *Ha-Praklit,* XXXVI (1986), pp. 464, 466ff., and sources cited, *id.* at 471.

53. Cohen and Buslik v. Attorney General, *supra* n. 52 at 19 (opinion of Justice Silberg).

54. Silberg, *supra* n. 3 at 6. For a detailed discussion of these two limitations on the application of the provisions of Jewish law in the rulings of the general courts, *see id.* at 211ff.; Elon, *Ḥakikah,* pp. 76–98; *id.*, "The Sources and Nature of Jewish Law and Its Application in the State of Israel," 3 *Israel L. Rev.* 416, 454ff. (1968); I. Englard, "Ma'amado Shel ha-Din ha-Dati ba-Mishpat ha-Yisra'eli" [The Status of Religious Law in the Israeli Legal System], Part 3, *Mishpatim,* VI (1975), pp. 5–22.

In the two examples just discussed, the Supreme Court limited the use of halakhic rules by an interpretation that precluded the application of Jewish law. In one example, under conflict-of-laws rules, the preclusion is complete: the law of the local jurisdiction, *i.e.*, Israeli law (which includes Jewish substantive law), is put aside in favor of the law of another country, which the court finds it preferable to apply. In the other example, the limitation is partial: the Jewish law of evidence and procedure is not applied for the reason, as the court has explained, that the Legislature never intended these areas of Jewish law to be applicable. In both instances, the general courts refrain, completely or in part, from applying Jewish law, and thus reach a decision different from that reached by the rabbinical courts. They do not, however, pick and choose from among the substantive rules of Jewish law or so modify those rules as to alter the form in which they appear in Jewish law.

However, in another instance, the general court did just that, and aroused a sharp dispute among the justices of the Supreme Court. The issue was the interpretation to be given to the prohibition of marriage between a *kohen* (priest) and a divorcée in light of Section 2 of the Rabbinical Courts Jurisdiction (Marriage and Divorce) Law, 1953, which provides that marriages and divorce in Israel are to be governed by Jewish law (*din Torah*). The issue arose against the background of the problems generated by privately performed marriages, which have been dealt with extensively by both the general courts and the rabbinical courts. The following discussion reviews the basic positions that have been taken on this problem.

C. Privately Performed Marriages

Privately performed marriages have raised problems in two types of cases: (1) where the marriage is entered into in private because, under the law, it could not take place in public with official sanction—*e.g.*, a marriage between a *kohen* and a divorcée; (2) where there is no legal impediment to the marriage, but because of conscientious scruples the couple do not wish to be married in a religious ceremony.

In a privately performed marriage, the man gives the woman a ring in the presence of two witnesses and declares to her: "Behold, you are betrothed unto me according to the law of Moses and Israel." In some cases, he may say: "You are my wife," or something similar. This manner of marriage is sometimes halakhically valid, and in any event the question of its validity is sufficiently substantial so that if one of the parties to such a marriage wishes to marry someone else, a divorce is required in order to remove any doubts. When a *kohen* marries a divorcée, Jewish law provides that even though the parties to such a marriage violate a prohibition, the marriage, once performed, is valid. However, Jewish law also provides that such a couple must be divorced and that they do not possess certain rights and are not subject to certain obligations ordinarily incident to the marital relationship.[55]

1. MARRIAGE BETWEEN A *KOHEN* AND A DIVORCÉE

The Israeli law as to the validity of a privately performed marriage between a *kohen* and a divorcée has passed through several stages in the course of a series of judicial decisions. In one case,[56] after the marriage was performed, the Ministry of the Interior refused to register the couple as married, whereupon the couple applied to the Supreme Court, sitting as the High Court of Justice. Various views on the question were expressed by the justices. Justice Silberg held that no relief should be given to such a couple; he reasoned that the legislation providing that Jewish law governs marriages and divorces of Jews in Israel fully incorporated the Jewish law regarding marriage between a *kohen* and a divorcée. His opinion states:[57]

> The above-mentioned Section 2 [of the Rabbinical Courts Jurisdiction (Marriage and Divorce) Law, 1953] states in mandatory and binding language that marriage and divorce between Jews in Israel shall be effected according to Jewish law. It is evident that the Legislature thereby introduced a very significant innovation, which was undoubtedly motivated by that great historical event, the establishment of the State of Israel and its organs of government. By this mandatory language, the Legislature provided that Jewish law should determine not only whether a marriage or divorce, having taken place, is valid *post factum,* but also whether a marriage or divorce may properly take place in the first instance. As a result, if a Jew, for example, marries his aunt or marries a woman who, under Jewish law, still has a husband (such as a woman previously married under Jewish law who was divorced only in a civil court), the marriage is both prohibited and invalid. The reason is that under Jewish law, a marriage that is prohibited under the penalty of *karet* ["extirpation" by divine act] is completely invalid. (A prohibited marriage that incurs the penalty of death by judicial decree is likewise invalid. Maimonides, *MT,* Issurei Bi'ah 1:1.)
>
> By contrast, if a *kohen* marries a divorcée or if a Jew who is not a *kohen* divorces his wife and then remarries her after she has been married to another man, a prohibition is transgressed [without the penalty of *karet,* Deuteron-

55. *See* Sh. Ar. EH ch. 116. These provisions are applicable *post factum,* if the marriage has already taken place. However, in the first instance, a marriage ceremony is to be performed in the presence of a quorum of ten men and under the direction of a rabbi. Other customs are also normally followed. With regard to the problem of secret marriages, *see supra* pp. 846–878. *See also* Schereschewsky, *supra* n. 3 at 33ff.

56. Gorfinkel and Ḥaklai v. Minister of the Interior, 17 *P.D.* 2048 (1963).

57. *Id.* at 2062–2063.

> omy 24:4], but the marriage is valid *post factum*. Valid as such marriages may be, they are nevertheless prohibited, even under the civil law, . . . for it is impossible to say that they were effected "according to Jewish law," and the Legislature has explicitly provided that marriages of Jews in Israel may not be effected except according to Jewish law. It is true that, with respect to a marriage that involves only the transgression of a prohibition [without the penalty of *karet*] (or a marriage to one who is within the secondary degree of consanguinity, which is only rabbinically prohibited), the law, from the *civil law* perspective, is of the type known by jurists as *lex imperfecta*, since it lacks all sanction either by way of invalidation or by way of punishment. Even such laws, however, are still laws, and citizens are obligated not to violate them.

It was Justice Silberg's position that inasmuch as the couple had violated the statute, the High Court of Justice should not grant their request to order the Ministry of the Interior to register them as married.

A different view was taken by Justice Landau. He held that Section 2 of the Rabbinical Courts Jurisdiction (Marriage and Divorce) Law, 1953, incorporates only the rule of Jewish law relating to the validity of the marriage between a *kohen* and a divorcée, but not the rule prohibiting such a marriage in the first instance.[58] In a subsequent case, he explained his view at length:[59]

> Section 2's establishment of the law of the Torah as the law governing the effectuation of marriages and divorces is not the same as the full incorporation of all the laws of the *Halakhah* relating to the subject of marriage and divorce. . . . Section 2 cannot be viewed as imposing a prohibition—exclusively religious in source and character—on all Jews in Israel, including those not motivated by religious faith to observance of religious prohibitions. In what way is the source of this prohibition religious? In that it is "based on the special position of the *kohen* in the religious life of the Jewish people. Since he is 'holy to his God,' he may not marry a divorcée" (Schereschewsky, *Dinei Mishpaḥah* [Family Law], p. 58). In what way is the character of the prohibition religious? In that the *Halakhah* itself makes a clear distinction between the legal consequences of a marriage between a *kohen* and a divorcée, on the one hand, and the prohibition against entering into such a marriage—a prohibition that is religious in origin—on the other. . . . We must therefore say that the couple have the *power* to marry each other, and thereby bring about an effective change in the legal relationship between them, although, due to the religious prohibition, they do not have the *right* to do so. Such a conceptual distinction is familiar in the *Halakhah*—for example, in the case of contracts entered into on the sabbath.[60]

58. *Id.* at 2068.

59. Rodnitzky v. Rabbinical Court of Appeals, 24(i) *P.D.* 704, 712 (1970).

60. As to a contract entered into on the sabbath in violation of religious law, *see supra* p. 129.

> As has been alluded to, . . . the 1953 law, including Section 2, was the product of a compromise. It was not intended to infringe upon the freedom of conscience guaranteed to every citizen in our country or to compel the non-religious community to fulfill religious commandments. In the *Yosipoff* case,[61] I remarked on the religious foundation of the entire Jewish legal system. Nevertheless, a distinction must be made between the principles that regulate human relationships and those that concern people's relationship to God. The prohibition against marriage between a *kohen* and a divorcée is religious in nature. . . . To a nonbeliever, this prohibition not only amounts to coercion in a matter of conscience, but also discriminates on religious grounds between a *kohen* and an ordinary Jew. As I said in the *Yosipoff* case:[62] "Religious coercion can exist only where religion commands or prohibits the performance of a particular act." We must so construe the 1953 law as to avoid such [coercion, which would amount to] an inconsistency with the fundamental principles of the law of the State.[63]

Justice Landau's opinion presents an interesting example of the interpretation of a statute against the background of the relationship between religion and state. He concluded that the prohibition of marriage between a *kohen* and a divorcée is made up of two components: a "religious" component—the prohibition against the *kohen*'s marriage to a divorcée, which is based on the religious life and holiness of the *kohen*—and a "legal" component—the question of the validity of the marriage, *i.e.*, the determination of the status of the couple. In his view, the Legislature adopted only the "legal" component—the rule that the marriage is valid—but not the "religious" component, which prohibits such a marriage in the first instance. The Legislature, in Justice Landau's view, did not adopt the religious component because to do so would infringe upon the freedom of conscience of nonbelievers and contravene the fundamental principles of the State.[64] Justice Landau's opinion continues:

61. Yosipoff v. Attorney General, 5 *P.D.* 481, 494 (1951).

62. *Id.*

63. *See also* Rodnitzky v. Rabbinical Court of Appeals, *supra* n. 59 at 711.

64. Justice Landau himself pointed to the difficulty involved in the distinction whereby the Knesset is held to have adopted only the legal component and not the religious component of Jewish law. Actually, the entire Jewish legal system rests on a religious foundation, and therefore the adoption of *any* law from the Jewish legal system, even if only the legal component is adopted, results in the adoption of a rule founded on religion. Justice Landau attempted to surmount this difficulty by making a further distinction between laws that regulate conduct between people and laws that deal with people's relation to God. This solution is unsatisfactory and cannot withstand analysis. The Legislature can reasonably be said to have derived from Jewish law the prohibition against a marriage between a *kohen* and a divorcée just as the Legislature, for example, could have expressly prohibited marriage between brother and sister—and no one would argue that the religious origin of that prohibition renders the prohibition invalid. Similarly, the Legislature has established that the sabbath and the Jewish festivals are the official days of rest for Jews, and that festivals of

> I can see no reason to criticize the conduct of the applicants in their use of the stratagem of effecting their marriage privately. Our country guarantees freedom of conscience to all its citizens. The applicants do not observe the religious precepts, and under the laws of the State they are free to so conduct themselves. They wish to live a family life and to raise children who will not be branded with the social stigma of being "born out of wedlock." They are faced with a religious prohibition that is entirely ritual in nature, being based on ancient concepts of the preferential status of the *kohen* in the divine service. It is difficult to reconcile the imposition of such a prohibition on a non-believer with the freedom of conscience and action that the prohibition infringes. . . . And, indeed, the religious law itself offers a way out of the dilemma in which they find themselves. Why should they be criticized if they take advantage of this way to extricate themselves from their dilemma?[65]

Justice Silberg viewed the actions of the couple entirely differently:[66]

> The first thing that comes to mind upon reading the petition in the instant case is the warning of King Yannai to his wife: "Do not fear the Pharisees or those who are not Pharisees, but fear only the hypocrites."[67] And "hypocrisy" is the word for this marriage, which, in the guise of a religious ceremony, violates [the precepts of] religion, and which the instant petition seeks to legitimize as acceptable conduct in Israeli society. . . . Are we, sitting as a High Court of Justice, required to nurture the growth of such a donkey-camel hybrid? I think not! Its parents will not be pleased with their unseemly legal progeny—neither the religious parent nor the secular parent. It will only turn all of Israeli family law into a laughingstock. If there is a hidden agenda behind the petition—and if indeed the real purpose "behind the curtain" is to do this—then most certainly we may not serve as the abettors of such a transparent and irresponsible scheme so disrespectful of the law.
>
> This court does not sit on Olympus, but in the midst of the people. We are well acquainted with the dispute that has broken out in Israel between those who would permit only a religious marriage ceremony and those who would turn marriage into a civil contract, and we neither close our eyes nor shut our ears to their mutual recriminations. But the problem is too serious, delicate, and multifaceted for the color-blind Daltonists who see everything in "black and white"—or "white and black"—ever to be able to solve it. For as to this problem, as with all the major social issues of our young country

---

other religious groups are the official days of rest of the members of those groups (*see supra* p. 1646). This provision is valid even though it is based on "the religious part" of the *Halakhah* and on the laws of other religions. With regard to the separation of the "legal" from the "religious" component of Jewish law, *see also supra* pp. 1590–1591 and *infra* pp. 1906–1914, 1927–1929.

65. Gorfinkel and Ḥaklai v. Minister of the Interior, *supra* n. 56 at 2068–2069.

66. *Id.* at 2060–2061, 2064.

67. TB Sotah 22b.

> and our ancient people, many different factors come into play: considerations of religion, morals, culture, manners, the reaction of the non-Jewish world, international solidarity and national responsibility, tradition and progress, people and state, diaspora and homeland. Only an all-seeing legislature, which can take account of all these amorphous values in a single sweeping survey, can mold them into legal forms. In any event, the problem will not be solved by clandestine partisan actions, nor will its sharp jagged edges be smoothed by legal legerdemain. . . . And if a citizen's conduct threatens to thwart the clear and firmly set legislative purpose, this court should not supply the implements to effect that result. . . .
>
> Inasmuch as the Israeli Legislature, after serious consideration and for weighty reasons, has prescribed that the rules of Jewish law govern the effectuation of a marriage, we must ensure that these rules are given effect *in toto*, and not enforced selectively on the basis of external, extralegal factors ("this law appeals to me, but this one does not"). If we are selective, the law will completely escape the authority of the Legislature, and will become like malleable clay in the hands of the individual judge sitting on the bench. We judges have never been accorded such a prerogative.

This trenchant statement sounds a well-founded warning that interpretation that does not preserve the spirit of a statute can drain the statute of all meaning. Justice Silberg concluded his opinion as follows:[68]

> Despite the earnest pleas of the applicant's attorney, I have not at all touched on the question of the nature and merits of the Rabbinical Courts Jurisdiction Law—whether it is desirable or [only] imposed, whether it is advantageous or injurious in the life of the Jewish citizen. I believe that as a judge of the State, sitting in judgment, I had best abstain from taking part in this ideological debate. For the purpose of this opinion, it is sufficient [to point out] that the provisions of the statute were adopted by the sovereign Legislature of the State of Israel, and woe to a country that permits any of its laws to be slighted, for the result will be anarchy and scorn for all of the country's laws.

The majority of the Supreme Court agreed with Justice Landau that a distinction should be made between the "religious" and the "legal" components of a marriage between a *kohen* and a divorcée. But the majority did not agree on who should instruct the Ministry of the Interior to register the couple as married. Justices Landau and Berinson held that the case should be remanded to the rabbinical court for that court to declare the marriage valid, and following such declaration, the couple should be registered as married. The hope was expressed that the rabbinical court would indeed act on remand in accordance with the mandate of the High Court of Justice, as it had done in a judgment rendered twenty-five years previously, in

68. 17 *P.D.* at 2067.

which the rabbinical court declared that a divorcée married to a *kohen* who subsequently died was his widow for purposes of inheritance.[69] According to Justices Witkon and Mani, the High Court of Justice itself should have instructed the Ministry of the Interior to register the applicants as married, for the proper registry of status is a matter of public concern, and the applicants were in fact married.[70]

When the case reached the rabbinical court, that court ruled that while each of the applicants was prohibited from remarrying without first obtaining a divorce, their status as married should not be certified, since they had transgressed a prohibition, and Jewish law forbids assisting transgressors and encouraging them to continue their transgression.[71] Nevertheless, the Ministry of the Interior registered the couple as married on the basis of the judgment of the rabbinical court that the parties were forbidden to remarry without a divorce.

Subsequently, a rabbinical court was again presented with a case of a privately performed marriage. This time, in light of what had taken place in the previous case, in which the Ministry of the Interior had registered the couple as married, the rabbinical court wrote in its decision: "Based on the evidence in this case, the court cannot certify the personal status of the applicants—or even, in the words of their attorney, 'some aspect' of their personal status—both because of the inconsistencies in the testimony of the witnesses [who testified to the marriage ceremony] and because of the question of their [the witnesses'] competency." It rejected the request that it declare that the parties were forbidden to marry anyone else without a divorce, since the purpose of the request was to circumvent the law and to enable the couple to be registered by the Ministry of the Interior as married.[72]

In light of these statements by the rabbinical court, the Ministry of the Interior refused to register the couple as married, and the couple petitioned the Supreme Court, sitting as the High Court of Justice. The majority of the Supreme Court decided, in an opinion by Justice Landau, that since the rabbinical court had not exercised its jurisdiction and had not declared that they were forbidden to marry anyone else without a divorce (which would have enabled them to be registered as a married couple), the Supreme Court was required to do so. The opinion further declared that since there was at least a doubt as to the validity of their marriage they were forbidden to marry anyone else without a divorce, and that the Ministry of the Interior was therefore required to register them as married. As for the statement

69. *Id.* at 2070–2072. *See also* Elon, *supra* n. 8 at 23ff.; *infra* n. 77.
70. 17 *P.D.* at 2057–2059.
71. A. v. B., 5 *P.D.R.* 219 (1964).
72. *See* Rodnitzky v. Rabbinical Court of Appeals, *supra* n. 59 at 709.

by the rabbinical court that one should not assist anyone to circumvent the law prohibiting the marriage of a *kohen* to a divorcée, the Supreme Court stated:[73]

> The Rabbinical Court of Appeals . . . acted in this manner with the aim of giving effect to the religious prohibition of marriage between a *kohen* and a divorcée. This is the rabbinical court's view of the public interest, a view nurtured by its strong religious beliefs. This court [the Supreme Court] has a different view of what the public interest requires in this matter, as has been explained in the *Ḥaklai*[74] and *Shagav*[75] cases—a view which rests on the law of the State, enacted by representatives of the entire population, both devout and irreligious, on behalf of the entire population.

Since, according to a majority of the Supreme Court, the statute does not incorporate the prohibition of marriage between a *kohen* and a divorcée, the public interest in having a public record of the marital status of the parties is preponderant.[76]

An opposite view was expressed in that case by Justice Kister.[77] He took the position that "as long as the laws governing marriages between Jews in Israel are the laws of the Torah, I do not believe that the courts may properly regard some prohibitions as less binding than others . . . ; and we ought not lend judicial assistance to a petitioner who does not come into court with clean hands." Moreover, in Justice Kister's view, the Supreme Court had no jurisdiction to determine whether the marriage was valid (or even whether it was of dubious validity), since that question was within the exclusive jurisdiction of the rabbinical courts.[78]

73. *Id.* at 715 (Landau, J.).

74. Gorfinkel and Ḥaklai v. Minister of the Interior, *supra* n. 56.

75. Shagav v. District Rabbinical Court of Safed, 21(ii) *P.D.* 505 (1967).

76. It should be noted that even the majority took pains to emphasize that "our decision is confined to the issue before us, namely, registration [of the marriage] in the population registry. We issue no directive to the rabbinical court; indeed, Section 40 of the Population Registry Law, 1965, provides that our decision on registration shall not affect questions of religious law . . . relating to marriage and divorce if such questions should come before the rabbinical court in the future." Rodnitzky v. Rabbinical Court of Appeals, *supra* n. 59 at 716 (Landau, J.).

77. *Id.* at 722, 725, 727. Justice Kister distinguished between the issue of judicial assistance to a *kohen* and a divorcée by a judgment sustaining the validity of their marriage—which the *Halakhah* prohibits—and other issues arising during the lifetime of the couple or after one of them has died, *e.g.*, a claim by the woman to inherit as the decedent's widow. As to the latter question, the Rabbinical Court of Appeals held, even before the establishment of the State, that the woman may inherit as widow, even though the decedent was a *kohen* and she was a divorcée when the marriage took place. *See* Elon, *Ḥakikah*, pp. 96–98; *id.*, *supra* n. 8 at 22–25.

78. Another Supreme Court decision regarding a privately performed marriage between a *kohen* and a divorcée, Cohen v. District Rabbinical Court, 26(i) *P.D.* 227 (1972),

The decisions on the issues raised by a privately performed marriage between a *kohen* and a divorcée illustrate the far-reaching effect of restrictive interpretation that is influenced by the personal philosophy of the judge. This influence is reflected in the artificial distinction, contrary to the plain meaning of the statute, between two aspects of the law relating to the marriage of a *kohen* and a divorcée, and in the conclusion that the statute incorporates only the "legal" and not the "religious" aspect of the law relating to such a marriage. This distinction was upheld by a majority of the justices, but two Supreme Court justices, who were more closely attuned to the Jewish legal system than the majority, strongly dissented.

The nature of the majority's restrictive interpretation is highlighted by the manner in which the principle of the "public interest" was used in these cases. The "public interest" from the standpoint of Jewish law as expressed by the Rabbinical Court of Appeals requires that transgressors should not be helped to violate the law. This is also recognized by the general legal system as an important public interest. The majority of the Supreme Court took the position that this interest is outweighed by the competing public interest in avoiding coercion in matters of conscience.

The important question, of course, is whether a statute clearly and explicitly adopting a rule of Jewish law that is rooted in a religious outlook and incorporated by the Legislature as a part of the laws of the State can properly be interpreted on the basis of a public interest premised on the denial of a religious outlook. Is such an interpretation not internally inconsistent? As noted, the public interest of the general legal system also requires that one should not assist those who violate the law; and consequently the general court is the guardian of the very same public interest as the rabbinical court that declined to render a decision regarding marriage between a *kohen* and a divorcée in order to avoid giving assistance to such a couple or extending recognition to such a marriage *post factum*.

---

also involved a denial by the rabbinical court of the parties' request to declare their marriage valid. In that case, the rabbinical court made two rulings: "(a) In light of the declarations of the petitioners, regardless of whether the declarations are true and correct, neither of the parties may marry anyone else, nor may they continue to live together—they are required to be divorced; and (b) the fact that petitioners may not marry anyone else does not in any way confer upon them the status of a married couple, and therefore they are not to be registered as married." In light of this ruling, the registry clerk in the Ministry of the Interior refused to register the couple as married. The Supreme Court, sitting as the High Court of Justice, held that inasmuch as the rabbinical court is presumed not to have intended to exceed its jurisdiction, the decision of the rabbinical court was intended solely to declare that according to the *Halakhah* the parties should not be registered as married, and not that such registration is forbidden by the law of the State. Since the requisites of the Population Registry Law, 1965, had been fulfilled, the Supreme Court ordered that the petitioners be registered as married.

Moreover, the determination of what constitutes the "public interest" of the Israeli population is itself a matter of dispute. Professor Englard has noted[79] that, according to Justice Silberg, "in truth and in fact, our religious marriage laws are not inconsistent with the outlook of the general Israeli population."[80] While this statement was made with regard to the prohibition of marriages between Jews and non-Jews, it can be argued that this prohibition, too, is discriminatory and infringes upon freedom of conscience. In addition, in defining the "public interest," it is hard to escape the fact that there are two "publics" in Israel. Englard states:

> The religious Jewish population of Israel, which accepts the religious laws as obligatory, far from viewing the solutions provided by religious law as infringing the fundamental rights of Israeli society, instead views the provisions of the religious law as an everlasting means to perfect the world under the sovereignty of God. It follows that the declaration by the general court that the content of the Jewish law is inconsistent with the public policy of the Jewish state cannot be accepted by the religious, who constitute a significant portion of the total population.[81]

The late Justice Yitzhak Kahan, President of the Supreme Court, after quoting these statements of Englard, cogently observed: "These statements sharply express the polarity between two court systems, rooted in opposing world outlooks."[82] Indeed, as we have seen also with regard to applying the principle of the "best interests of the child" in cases of custody and guardianship, it is clear that decisions in this sensitive area of marriage and divorce, and of family law in general, are influenced by the personal philosophy of each judge.[83]

It should be stressed, however, that these differences of opinion in the Supreme Court relate only to the question of registration of a marriage that has already taken place between a *kohen* and a divorcée. There is no dissent from the proposition that these decisions of the Supreme Court do not authorize performance of such a marriage in the first instance. This was the ruling of the Supreme Court in *Fund of the Movement of Progressive Judaism in Israel v. Minister of Religions*[84] in an opinion written by Deputy President Menachem Elon, speaking for all five justices constituting the panel in that case:[85]

79. Englard, *supra* n. 54, Part,2, *Mishpatim*, IV (1973), pp. 31, 40.
80. Schlesinger v. Minister of the Interior, 17 *P.D.* 225, 238 (1963).
81. Englard, *supra* n. 79 at 40.
82. Kahan, *supra* n. 11 at 207.
83. *See also* Englard, *supra* n. 54 at 34ff.
84. 43(ii) *P.D.* 661 (1989).
85. *Id.* at 698–700.

Whatever may be our opinion regarding the divergent views expressed in the *Gorfinkel*[86] and *Rodnitzky*[87] cases, even Justice Landau's opinion (which was the majority opinion in these cases) has no bearing on the question now *sub judice,* namely, What is the law pursuant to which one is required to perform marriages between Jews in Israel? In the view of all the justices of this court, without exception, this law is the law of the Torah, which encompasses the totality of all the provisions of the *Halakhah,* including [halakhic] legislation and interpretation, which have become part of this system in our own times.

Indeed, Justice Landau went on to say in the *Rodnitzky* case:[88]

> It must be clearly emphasized that our decision is confined to the issue before us, namely, registration [of the marriage] in the population registry. We issue no directive to the rabbinical court; indeed, Section 40 of the Population Registry Law, 1965, provides that our decision on registration shall not affect questions of religious law . . . relating to marriage and divorce if such questions should come before the rabbinical court in the future.

Even according to Justice Landau, the decision in the *Rodnitzky* case is applicable only to the particular issue decided in that case, *i.e.,* registration of the marriage in the population registry—that and no more. Just as that decision did not presume to direct the rabbinical court how to rule in a case involving a marriage between a *kohen* and a divorcée, it likewise cannot be read to require performance of a marriage between a *kohen* and a divorcée in the first instance. No one has ever suggested, or would ever suggest, that *Rodnitzky* is authority for the proposition that a *kohen* and a divorcée who wish to marry are entitled to a judicial decree ordering that the marriage be performed. On analysis, it is apparent that the sole thrust of that case was to assist a *kohen* and a divorcée who already were married, since, according to the *Halakhah,* their marriage, once entered into, is valid, and they are therefore entitled to have their personal status so entered in the population registry. The decision cannot be read to authorize the performance of the marriage in the first instance, in violation of a law of the Torah—however grave that transgression may or may not be—solely because such a marriage is valid *ex post.* Moreover, if any person authorized to perform marriages were to announce his willingness to perform a marriage ceremony for a couple between whom the *Halakhah* clearly forbids marriage, the Minister of Religions and the Chief Rabbinate would have the right to rescind his authority on the ground that the marriages he performs must conform with the legislative mandate, which is to follow the law of the Torah, *i.e.,* the currently accepted and customary law of the halakhic system. . . .

An additional important reason advanced by the justices who concluded that the Ministry of the Interior should be directed to register the mar-

86. Gorfinkel and Ḥaklai v. Minister of the Interior, *supra* n. 56.
87. Rodnitzky v. Rabbinical Court of Appeals, *supra* n. 59.
88. *Id.* at 716.

riage of a *kohen* and a divorcée who had been married in a private ceremony is that under the existing legal system there is no way the couple can marry without violating the prohibition against a *kohen*'s marrying a divorcée. On this point, Justice Agranat stated in *Shagav v. District Rabbinical Court of Safed*:[89]

> The law presents an insurmountable obstacle to the proper performance of a private marriage ceremony between a *kohen* and a divorcée, since the marriage violates two negative commandments of the Torah, notwithstanding that once performed, it is valid *ex post*. In view of this legal obstacle, I believe that in such a case the public, and not merely the parties immediately concerned, have a vital interest in obtaining an authoritative judicial ruling clarifying and defining the *ex post* effect of this marriage ceremony on their personal status, even if the ruling is limited to a declaration that the parties are prohibited from marrying anyone else until the bond of their marriage is severed by the delivery of a proper bill of divorcement.
>
> It cannot be overemphasized that the conclusion here reached is inescapable, notwithstanding the generally disfavored status of privately performed marriages. Our decision in no wise rests on the contention that the Biblical prohibition against marriage between a *kohen* and a divorcée is outmoded (see the views of Justice Landau in the *Gorfinkel* case[90]) and that it is therefore necessary for the current halakhic authorities to consider how to find, to the extent possible, a suitable halakhic solution to such problems, taking pains to enable such a couple to establish a normal Jewish family, and bearing in mind the approach indicated (albeit in a different context) by the learned [Professor] Freimann at the end of his great work, namely, [an approach based on] an "awareness of life's hardships, sensitivity to contemporary needs, and responsiveness to circumstances of time and place, [all of which were] exhibited by the legislation of our Rabbis in prior generations."
>
> What I wish to make clear is that, as long as this prohibition remains in effect, it is inconceivable, given the fact that a *kohen* and a divorcée have no way other than a privately performed marriage ceremony to enter into a binding marriage, that the personal status of the parties claiming to have been married in that manner should remain, *post factum*, unclear and undefined.

Thus, according to the reasoning of the majority, the determinative considerations are that the issue arises not *ex ante* but *ex post*, that the public as well as the parties has an interest in ascertaining the personal status of the couple in question, and that the law has made a proper and public marriage ceremony impossible for the parties. It is noteworthy that President Agranat stressed that, in his view, the argument that the prohibition of marriage be-

89. 21(ii) *P.D.* 505, 533–534 (1967).
90. 17 *P.D.* at 2069.

tween a *kohen* and a divorcée is outmoded in today's world is not a valid basis on which to ground the decision to issue the judgment declaring the personal status of the couple involved.

2. MARRIAGES PERMITTED UNDER THE *HALAKHAH*

The extent to which perceptions of the public interest may vary when the public interest is the determinative consideration in a sensitive area such as family law can be seen in the Supreme Court's treatment of the issue of whether a privately performed marriage is valid when Jewish law presents no impediment to the marriage, but the couple elect a private ceremony because they do not want a religious ceremony. A majority of the Supreme Court took the position that in such a case the couple should not be registered as married, because under Israeli law a marriage between Jews must be performed in accordance with Jewish law. The law of the State so provides, and it is in the public interest that marriages be performed publicly and registered, in order to prevent confusion and uncertainty.

However, this type of privately performed marriage, if effected in accordance with halakhic requirements, has an even stronger claim to *ex post* validity than a marriage between a *kohen* and a divorcée, because there is no halakhic impediment based on the identity of the parties, as there is in the case of the *kohen* and the divorcée. Nevertheless, the court did not grant the request of the couple for a judgment declaring them to be married and entitled to be so registered by the Ministry of the Interior. The court reasoned that a legally sanctioned ceremony was readily available for them, and the public interest in ensuring that marriages are effectuated in an orderly and proper manner takes precedence over the public interest in having the status of the parties clearly established. Recognizing that whether marriage ceremonies should be civil or religious is a controversial issue, Court President Agranat nevertheless stated:

> Once the Legislature in 1953 established a religious marriage ceremony as the exclusive method of effectuating marriage, this court is not the appropriate forum for waging the campaign for the above-mentioned reform.[91]

Justice Landau added:

> [While] the campaign to change the existing law is legitimate, it should not be conducted in an improper manner. The court must search for solutions within the framework of the existing law in order to reach a tolerable *modus vivendi;* and as long as the law remains unchanged, citizens must continue to obey it. This requires much tolerance on the part of both camps. But surely

91. Shagav v. District Rabbinical Court of Safed, *supra* n. 75 at 541.

> this nation, which has solidly united in order to defend its very existence, will be able to tread its path carefully through this minefield, while honoring one another's sensitivities and cooperating in the effort to solve rather than to exacerbate problems.[92]

Taking an approach contrary to the majority, one justice, dissenting, held that even such a privately performed marriage should be registered as valid in order that the status of the couple be accurately recorded. This conclusion, according to the dissent, follows *a fortiori* from the case of the *kohen* and the divorcée. "If the fact that a marriage between a *kohen* and a divorcée violates a religious prohibition is not cause for refusing to register a private marriage, . . . then *a fortiori* a marriage that does not violate a religious prohibition should be registered."[93]

The judicial policy underlying the court's refusal to confirm the validity of privately performed marriages in cases where the parties could have been married in a religious ceremony had they chosen to do so has been summarized as follows:[94]

> The judicial policy in regard to the invalidation of privately performed marriages is based on the fundamental principle of promoting the public welfare, sound administration, and the integrity of basic social institutions, for all of which the determination of marital status and the consequences of this status on a couple's relationship to each other and to society in general have particular importance. . . .
>
> After reviewing in detail the applicable Israeli law and the halakhic rulings and legislation throughout the history of Jewish law, the Supreme Court, in an opinion by President Agranat, summarized the matter as follows:
>
>> Anyone who participates in a privately performed marriage or assists in arranging such a marriage—whether or not such a marriage is valid *ex post*—is assuredly harming the public order as established by the statute relating to entry into the covenant of marriage by Jews in Israel. Moreover, such a person opens the door wide to all the many grave and baleful consequences that have previously resulted from secret marriages in their various forms, which the regulations established in this area by the law of the State were intended to prevent and eradicate. . . . The distinguished justices of this court have strongly deplored these marriages whenever a case involving a privately performed marriage has come before them. They have emphasized the resulting disorder in Israeli family life, and the chaos in matters of marriage and divorce gen-

92. *Id.* at 558.
93. *Id.* at 555 (Sussman, J.).
94. Ẓonan v. Stahl, 37(ii) *P.D.* 761, 766–767 (1983) (Elon, J.).

> erally, to which this devious manner of entry into the covenant of marital life is likely to lead.[95]

Indeed, judicial policy has been the basis of the judgments of the Supreme Court involving both categories of privately performed marriages—between a *kohen* and a divorcée, and between "ordinary" parties. We have previously reviewed this point:[96]

> We see here the nature of judicial policy. According to some of the justices of the Supreme Court, the statutory provision that the law governing marriage and divorce shall be the *Halakhah* plainly means the *Halakhah* in its totality, *i.e.*, that [all] prohibited marriages [that do not carry the penalty of *karet*] are forbidden *ex ante*, although valid *ex post*. However, according to the majority, the statute is directed only to the part [of Jewish law] relating to the *validity* of the marriage, and not the part relating to the *prohibition* of the marriage. Consequently, since the prohibition of a marriage between a *kohen* and a divorcée infringes upon freedom of conscience, the public interest requires that such marriages, even privately performed, should be registered by the Ministry of the Interior. However, privately performed marriages not involving a *kohen* and a divorcée should not be registered by the Ministry of the Interior, even though in these cases, too, the [prescribed] form of marriage ceremony is contrary to the conscience of those who choose not to be married in such a ceremony. The reason for the difference is that in the latter case the public interest in preserving the prescribed forms and the public character of marriage is paramount. According to a minority, even in such cases, the interest in correct registration of the couple's status outweighs the public interest in open and public marriage ceremonies.

IV. THE WEIGHT GIVEN BY THE GENERAL COURTS TO THE DECISIONS OF THE RABBINICAL COURTS INTERPRETING JEWISH LAW

The application of Jewish law by the general courts in matters of personal status can be considered from an additional perspective, namely, the bind-

95. The source of the quotation by Justice Agranat is Shagav v. District Rabbinical Court of Safed, *supra* n. 75 at 527. Justice Elon's opinion in *Ẓonan* states the view of four of the five justices who sat on that case. *See* 37(ii) *P.D.* at 766, 774. Justice Shelomo Levin, who expressed a minority view, made a distinction based on the nature of the assistance requested. He affirmed the refusal of a declaratory judgment on procedural grounds, and did not reach the merits of the question whether the marriage was valid. *See id.* at 772–773.

96. *See* Elon, *supra* n. 8 at 22. With regard to privately performed marriages, *see also* Schiffman, *supra* n. 3 at 226–242.

ing (or non-binding) force of the decisions of the rabbinical courts when the same issues are presented to the general courts. As previously pointed out,[97] it is fundamental that the Supreme Court does not review or become involved in the substantive content of the judgments of the rabbinical courts. The further question, whether the decisions of the rabbinical courts must be considered binding precedents in determining halakhic principles, was raised in the Supreme Court in a case involving the extent of the duty of a husband to support his wife when she is employed and earns her own living. Both the rabbinical courts and the general courts have dealt extensively with this issue against the background of the current situation in which women work outside their homes in various sectors of the economy. We first briefly examine one of the earliest rabbinical court cases on this point, a case notable for how it was resolved by an expansive and insightful interpretation.

A. The Earnings of a Wife from Her Employment

Jewish law requires a husband to support his wife (*i.e.*, to provide whatever is necessary for her maintenance, such as clothing, shelter, and medical care), and, correspondingly, entitles him to the benefit of his wife's "handiwork" (*ma'aseh yadeha, i.e.*, domestic services).[98] The wife may waive her right of support, in which case the husband is not entitled to her handiwork. However, the husband does not have a corresponding right to deprive his wife of her right to support by waiving his right to her handiwork.[99]

In *A. v. B.*,[100] after a brief period of marriage, the wife petitioned the rabbinical court for a divorce on grounds of incompatibility. After a hearing, the court granted the petition. One of the issues in the case was the ownership of the couple's furniture. Both parties stipulated that the wife had contributed from her own funds to the purchase of the furniture. The husband claimed that he had paid the balance of the purchase price, while the wife contended that she had paid the balance from wages she had earned as an office worker during the marriage. The husband countered that even if the wife's contention was correct, her earnings belonged to him because he supported her throughout the marriage, and consequently the furniture purchased with her earnings likewise belonged to him.

The issue thus presented was, Can a wife be deprived of furniture purchased with her own earnings? The rabbinical court resolved the issue by

97. *Supra* p. 1759 n. 20. *But see infra* n. 115.

98. TB Ketubbot 46b, 47b, 58b; Maimonides, *MT*, Ishut 12:1–4; Sh. Ar. EH 69:1–4. *See generally supra* pp. 571–572.

99. *See* sources cited *supra* n. 98.

100. 1 *P.D.R.* 81, 90–94 (1954).

going back to the Mishnaic rule entitling a husband to his wife's handiwork: "These are the types of work that a wife must perform for her husband: Grinding [corn], baking [bread], and washing clothes; cooking and nursing her children; making his bed and working with wool."[101] The court, relying on various sources in the responsa and codificatory literature, reasoned that a wife is required to perform only those types of "women's work" specified in the Mishnah, such as baking, spinning wool, etc., but not other types of work, even if in a particular place women do the other types of work as well. The court explained:

> A wife is not her husband's daily laborer such that we can say that in return for her husband's support her time belongs to him and she therefore spends "his" time when she does any type of work that is usual and customary in the[ir] locality. To the contrary, the enactment required the wife to perform only certain specified types of work, typically performed by women, in return for the support her husband is obligated to provide her.[102]

After establishing that a wife is required to perform only those types of work that are "typically performed by women," the court turned to the question: If a wife performs work she is not required to do for her husband, to whom do the earnings from that work belong? Does the principle that a wife's handiwork belongs to her husband apply only to "women's work," with the result that she may keep for herself her earnings from all other types of work even though she has received the benefit of support from her husband? The court, again relying on various views in the codificatory literature and on various interpretive approaches, concluded that such earnings do indeed belong to the wife and not to the husband.[103] Consequently, the rabbinical court held that the earnings of the wife from her employment belonged to her, and, it necessarily followed, so did the furniture purchased with her earnings.

This, however, did not fully dispose of the issue. The husband argued further that even if he was not entitled to all of his wife's earnings, he was entitled at least to the portion she earned when, because of her outside employment, she could not be home to perform her household duties (which, apparently, were in fact performed either by the husband himself or by special help hired by him for this purpose). Even this limited request of the husband was denied. The court reasoned that since the governing

101. M Ketubbot 5:5.

102. 1 *P.D.R.* at 90.

103. The halakhic authorities differ on this question, which was debated as early as in the Talmud. TB Ketubbot 66a considers whether a husband is entitled to the benefit of his wife's work over and above her normal household tasks, particularly if such work requires extraordinary effort. *See* Schereschewsky, *supra* n. 3 at 233ff.

principle is that "a wife is not her husband's daily laborer," she cannot be viewed as being "hired" for a specified time period in return for support, even though she is obligated to perform certain duties for him. If the conclusion were otherwise, it would follow that if she used for her own purposes the time necessary to fulfill her household obligations, she would have to pay her husband for the time so used, and that is not the law. As the rabbinical court said:[104]

> Her obligation is limited to the performance of the work itself. The fact that she receives support does not obligate her to work as a hired worker for any particular length of time. Thus, "if she wishes to remain idle and does not perform [the traditional wifely tasks], she is not required to pay [her husband for the time not spent on her household obligations]."

In short, a husband may require, in the first instance, that his wife devote her time to managing the household, and, if she works outside the home, that she arrange for someone else to perform the household tasks. If he does not so require, however, he may not later require his wife to account for the number of hours she failed to devote to the management of the household, as if, for example, he had hired her as a worker to perform these household tasks and she failed to do so. A wife is not a daily laborer; she is required to perform specified tasks, but her husband is not entitled to monetary compensation when she fails to perform them.

This disposed of the particular case under discussion. However, another issue later arose in this general subject area. If a wife who receives earnings from outside employment demands support from her husband, may he successfully claim that she should support herself from her own earnings, and that only if her earnings are insufficient should he be required to provide the necessary supplement? The answer given by the rabbinical courts is that although the husband has no right to his wife's earnings, and certainly cannot demand that she work to support herself, nevertheless, if she voluntarily chooses to become employed outside the home, he has the right to have his support obligation reduced by the amount of her earnings. Of course, the wife may stop working whenever she desires, and the husband will then be obligated to support her fully.[105]

The same subject was dealt with by the Supreme Court in a case in

104. 1 *P.D.R.* at 93.

105. The basis for this ruling was the husband's claim of *kim li, i.e.*, his assertion that he accepts the view of those halakhic authorities who rule that the husband is entitled to the benefit of the wife's work over and above the wife's normal household tasks, as well as her earnings from work other than typically "women's work." *See* A. v. B., 2 *P.D.R.* 220 (1957); Schereschewsky, *supra* n. 3 at 233–237. With regard to the claim of *kim li*, *see supra* p. 1282 n. 180 and accompanying text.

which a husband refused to support his wife on the ground that she was employed and earned enough to support herself. This case was first heard before a panel of three justices,[106] and subsequently reheard before a panel of five.[107] A majority of the panel of three, Justices Berinson and Mani, agreed with the husband's contention that since the wife was employed and earned enough to support herself, she was not entitled to spousal support. In reaching this result, they relied on Jewish law, as determined and applied by the rabbinical courts in the manner discussed above. Under the governing Israeli statute, the applicable law is Jewish law, since a claim for spousal support is determined by the personal law of the couple,[108] which for Jews is Jewish law. Justice Haim Cohn, dissenting, held that a husband may not require his wife to support herself from her own earnings even if she chooses to work outside the home; rather, she is entitled to retain all her earnings and her husband must support her. Justice Cohn also based his decision on Jewish law, as he was required to do under the Israeli statute; but in his view, Jewish law entitles a wife to receive support from her husband even though she is gainfully employed and entitled to retain her earnings.[109]

On rehearing, four of the justices followed the rulings of the rabbinical courts, while Justice Cohn adhered to his prior position. At the rehearing, the following question was raised: When a general court is required by statute to apply Jewish law, and the question before the court has already been decided by the rabbinical courts, is the general court bound to follow the ruling of the rabbinical courts as constituting the Jewish law on the issue, or is the general court free to examine afresh the question of Jewish law and reach a decision contrary to that of the rabbinical courts?

The views expressed on this question reflect three different approaches. Justice Kister, in an extensive discussion of the Jewish law and the decisions of the rabbinical courts on the point, took the position that

106. Joseph v. Joseph, 23(i) *P.D.* 804 (1969).

107. Joseph v. Joseph, 24(i) *P.D.* 792 (1970).

108. *See supra* p. 1660.

109. Justice Cohn's conclusion follows from his view that the wife as well as the husband can be said to have possession of the subject matter of the action (to be *muḥzak*) and therefore the husband cannot assert the claim of *kim li* (*see supra* n. 105). His primary reasoning, however, was that there was an existing Jewish custom that a wife's earnings from her employment belong to her even if she claims support from her husband. Justice Cohn based his conclusion as to the existence of this custom on Section 2 of the Woman's Equal Rights Law, 1951, which, in his view, applies to the earnings of a wife from her employment and entitles her to retain them even if she claims support from her husband. "Indeed, it is perfectly clear that the [secular] law, which is binding on all citizens of the State, accurately reflects the customs of the country, at least as long as no compelling proof is adduced to the contrary." 23(i) *P.D.* at 813; 24(i) *P.D.* at 809.

when a general court is required to apply Jewish law, it must accept the decisions of the rabbinical courts as definitive of Jewish law. He explained:

> The reason why we must follow the decisions of the rabbinical courts in these matters is to be found in the laws of the Torah, which provide that one must obey the decisions of the halakhic authorities of each generation, and "Jephthah in his generation is equal to Samuel in his generation." . . . The matter before us concerns halakhic enactments regarding monetary relationships between spouses, and the interpretation of these enactments. It is within the power of the rabbinical courts to adopt such enactments, as they have done at various times and places. . . . And it is certainly within their power to interpret the enactments of the Sages in a binding manner.[110]

110. 24(i) *P.D.* at 805. In Justice Kister's opinion, the Woman's Equal Rights Law was irrelevant to the issue before the court. According to that statute, a wife has full legal capacity to deal with her property as she pleases, to the same extent as if she were unmarried; thus, any property she purchases out of her own income belongs to her. However, in order for a claim for support—which is determined according to the personal law—to succeed, the prescribed requirements of that personal law must be met, and one such requirement is that the support she is owed by her husband is subject to reduction to the extent of her earnings. *See id.* at 807–808. In other words, Section 2 of the Woman's Equal Rights Law is intended to protect a wife's property rights, whereas the right of a husband to the earnings of his wife is contractual, and is conferred in consideration of his fulfillment of his obligation of support. The wife may elect to defeat her husband's entitlement to her earnings by relinquishing her claim to support and declaring: "I wish neither to receive support from you nor to work for you."

At the end of his opinion, Justice Kister considered the social and legal justification for the position taken by the rabbinical courts (24(i) *P.D.* at 808):

> One final comment. It is everywhere accepted that marriage imposes obligations on both spouses—reciprocal obligations toward each other and obligations toward their children—and also creates rights. No modern legislator would free wives from all obligations to their husbands and their families, and leave wives possessing only rights. The Woman's Equal Rights Law is a modern statute directed toward the goal of equality. Modern legal systems do not enumerate in detail the rights and obligations of each of the spouses. They do not assign certain specified functions to the husband and others to the wife. Modern codes do not refer specifically to the husband's obligation to support his wife or the obligation of the wife to run the household. Rather, the usual formulation is that each spouse must assist the other as needed, and that both spouses must exert their best efforts to ensure the continued existence and well-being of the family.
>
> Under the modern approach, even if the husband abandons his wife, she has no right to support from him except to the extent that she requires such support because her earnings are insufficient to sustain her, whether because the care of her children makes it impossible for her to work, or for other reasons. In today's world, in which women as well as men work and earn income in all professions, there is no basis for attributing to the Legislature an intent to permit a wife to make no effort to improve her family's economic situation or to assist her husband by obtaining gainful employment, but rather to sit idly or keep all her income for herself and yet have the right to support from her husband, however impoverished he may be. When, therefore, the applicable personal law gives the husband the right to require her to bear her share of the burden, we should not impute to the Legislature an intent to repeal this right.

Justice Cohn adhered to his position that under Jewish law—including existing custom[111]—a husband must support his wife even if she is gainfully employed, and may not require her to support herself from her earnings. To Justice Kister's argument that this view as to the position of Jewish law was inconsistent with the decisions of the rabbinical courts, Justice Cohn responded:[112]

> My distinguished colleague Justice Kister states that the view which I have expressed is inconsistent with the decisions of the rabbinical courts, and that in matters governed by Jewish law we must follow the rabbinical courts, because "one must obey the decisions of the halakhic authorities of each generation, and 'Jephthah in his generation is equal to Samuel in his generation.'"
>
> With all due respect, I agree that the fact that the generations have declined in stature does not diminish the power and authority of the rabbinical courts in our generation. However, the authority of the judge "of that time" (Deuteronomy 17:9) [*i.e.*, of every generation] applies not only to the rabbinical courts but to every judge in Israel. The proof is that three [judges] "of insubstantial quality"—Jerubaal, Bedan, and Jephthah—"are considered equal to three most outstanding [judges]—Moses, Aaron, and Samuel—to teach us that Jerubaal in his generation is equal to Moses in his generation, Bedan in his generation is equal to Aaron in his generation, and Jephthah in his generation is equal to Samuel in his generation. This means that even if the most insignificant person is chosen as a leader of the community, he should be considered the equal of the mightiest" (TB Rosh ha-Shanah 25b). And the Torah is not in heaven such that we should say: "We need a rabbinical court to go up to heaven and fetch it for us and impart it to us."[113]

111. *See supra* n. 109.
112. 24(i) *P.D.* at 809.
113. *Cf.* Deuteronomy 30:12. In further support of his position, Justice Cohn argued: Apart from all the considerations inherent in the nature of the Torah of Israel, it seems to me that there is another compelling reason why we cannot recognize the decisions of the rabbinical courts as binding: While the rabbinical courts adjudicate cases according to the law of the Torah, in which they are well versed, they completely ignore the laws of the State. Only in extremely rare instances can one find in the decisions of the rabbinical courts a reference to a law of the Knesset or a law from the period of the Mandate, and then only where a question has arisen regarding the jurisdiction of the rabbinical court in the case before it (*e.g.*, 1 *P.D.R.* at 355; 2 *P.D.R.* at 38, 285). I have searched in vain and found no instance in which they have relied on the laws of the State in deciding the merits of a case before them; for example, not a single reference can be found to the Woman's Equal Rights Law. How can we accept the decisions of the rabbinical courts as a guide . . . , [much less] as binding us on the law of women's rights and obligations, when they regard the statute passed by the Knesset on this subject as irrelevant? So long as they do not take account of the laws of the State, it is not proper for the general courts to follow them and accept their decisions as final and unchallengeable.

According to Justice Cohn, only a *takkanah* enacted by the Chief Rabbinate pursuant to its authority as "a legislative body by virtue of the law of the Torah" is binding on a general court as part of Jewish law.[114]

Justice Yitzhak Kahan agreed with Justice Kister that the decisions of the rabbinical courts on matters of Jewish law are binding on the general courts in cases where the general courts are required by statute to apply Jewish law. He argued that just as the Supreme Court, sitting as a High Court of Justice exercising supervisory authority over the rabbinical courts, does not review the halakhic correctness of rabbinical court decisions,[115] so the Supreme Court and other general courts, when required by statute to apply Jewish law, must accept rabbinical court decisions as the correct statements of Jewish law. As to the position taken by Justice Cohn, quoted above, Justice Kahan stated:[116]

> Another question that arises in this context is: Are the judges of a general court considered judges "of that time"? As to this question, it makes no difference whether we live in the generation of Samuel or in the generation of Jephthah.

After discussing the position of Jewish law that only one who accepts the "yoke" of its norms and feels bound by them is authorized to act as a decisionmaker in matters of Jewish law,[117] he continued:

114. Justice Cohn added the qualification that even legislation by the Chief Rabbinate "must not be inconsistent with any statute, particularly the Woman's Equal Rights Law. We will be happy to deal with that problem when it arises, but that time does not appear to have come." 24(i) *P.D.* at 810. It may be assumed that even in the view of Justice Cohn, this qualification would apply only when an issue of Jewish law arises in the general courts in a matter which the Legislature mandates that Jewish law govern. It would certainly not limit the authority of the Chief Rabbinate to promulgate such enactments as it considers appropriate; and should the rabbinical courts render a decision based on an enactment of the Chief Rabbinate that conflicts with a provision of the Woman's Equal Rights Law—which is binding on all rabbinical courts—this would be a ground for the intervention of the Supreme Court. *See supra* pp. 1758–1759.

115. Justice Cohn did not disagree with this proposition. Streit v. Chief Rabbi of Israel, 18(i) *P.D.* 598, 608 (1964); *see supra* p. 1759 and n. 20; Boronovsky v. Chief Rabbis of Israel, 25(i) *P.D.* 7, 15 (1971). At the beginning of his opinion, Justice Kahan discussed the views expressed in the Supreme Court regarding the authority of a general court to review the decisions of rabbinical courts for correctness as expressions of Jewish law. *See* 24(i) *P.D.* at 810. He was referring to Justice Witkon's opinion in Benjamin Gitiyah v. Chief Rabbinate, 22(i) *P.D.* 290, 297–298, 300 (1968). For a detailed discussion, *see* M. Shava, "Ta'ut bi-Kevi'at ha-Yahadut—Ha-Sholelet Samkhut?" [Does an Incorrect Determination of Jewish Identity Negate the Existence of Jurisdiction?], *Ha-Praklit,* XXV (1969), p. 617.

116. 24(i) *P.D.* at 811–812.

117. *See infra* pp. 1906–1909. The opinion quotes the critical comments of Professor I. Englard in "Shilluv ha-Din ha-Yehudi be-Ma'arekhet ha-Mishpat ha-Yisra'eli" [The Integration of Jewish Law into the Israeli Legal System], *Hagut ve-Halakhah,* Jerusalem, 1968, pp. 161, 166–167.

> Whoever maintains that the judges of a secular court, who do not submit to the "yoke" of the religious law, may assume the mantle of halakhic decision-maker must wrestle with the objections mentioned above and find an answer to them. There is the additional consideration that non-Jews also sit as judges of the general courts, and since we cannot discriminate between judges, the question arises whether the statement relied upon by my distinguished colleague Justice Cohn, that "Jephthah in his generation is equal to Samuel in his generation," applies even to a court which includes a non-Jewish judge.
>
> What I have said is not intended to be taken as a substantive position on the question alluded to, but only to demonstrate that the problem is not simple, that its ramifications are manifold and complex, and that it deserves profound and thorough consideration.[118]

In a third approach, Justice Berinson advanced a middle view:[119]

> As to the remarks of my distinguished colleague Justice Cohn regarding the question of the binding—or, more correctly, non-binding—force of religious court decisions on the secular courts, it stands to reason that a secular court, in reaching a decision on an issue that has been definitively determined by a religious court, will give that determination very great weight and will generally be guided by it. In my previous opinion in this case, I myself relied upon and followed the rabbinical courts.
>
> Nevertheless, it is clear to me that the decisions of the religious courts do not constrain or bind the general courts of the State in a matter within their jurisdiction, even if their decision must be based on the religious law. The *Halakhah* on any given point is often not settled beyond dispute, but is subject to differences of opinion, so that a decision on the matter must steer a course between the differing views. To the best of my knowledge, even in the rabbinical court system, one rabbinical court does not consider itself bound by a decision of another. Should not the same result follow *a fortiori* where the issue involves the relationship between a secular court and a religious court? Although, as stated, a secular court will give all due respect to a decision of a religious court in a matter over which it [the religious court] has

118. Justice Kahan also addressed the comments of Justices Cohn and Berinson (*see supra* n. 113 and *infra* n. 120) regarding the attitude of the rabbinical courts to laws of the State (24(i) *P.D.* at 812):

> My honorable colleagues' criticism of the approach of the rabbinical courts to the decisions of the general courts is completely irrelevant to the question posed above. Since both Justice Berinson and I concur with Justice Kister that in the case *sub judice* the rabbinical courts did not "err" in a matter of *Halakhah,* whatever we said with regard to the power of a general court to determine the *Halakhah* is mere *obiter dictum.* If I, too, have been drawn to comment on such matters of *dicta,* it is only to call attention to some of the problems involved.

119. 24(i) *P.D.* at 810. Justice Mani concurred in the opinion of Justice Berinson. *Id.*

jurisdiction, it [the secular court] is entitled to make its own independent determination according to the best of its knowledge and understanding.[120]

These differing opinions and approaches arise out of the unique pattern of the relationships between Jewish and Israeli law, and the resulting, and additional, relationship between the general and the rabbinical courts. It should be noted that the present discussion itself demonstrates the need for caution when using principles and terms that are appropriate to one legal system but not always correct in the context of another legal system. Thus, for example, one cannot reasonably assert that rabbinical court decisions should be binding precedents in the general courts, because there is no such thing as binding precedent in the Jewish legal system itself; the decision of one rabbinical court is never "binding" on another rabbinical court.[121]

The question of the duty of obedience to the decisions of the halakhic authorities in each generation is not identical or even related to the question of whether a decision is a binding precedent. Of course, a rabbinical court judge will very carefully examine prior decisions, with respect and reverence for the chain of halakhic authority, but he has the prerogative, if he finds "in the Talmud of Ravina and R. Ashi"[122] grounds for a contrary decision that are acceptable to his contemporaries, to render judgment according to his own opinion and understanding.[123]

However, it is not correct to say that judges who do not feel bound by religious persuasion to the halakhic system have the same authority to decide questions of Jewish law as judges who regard themselves as part of the halakhic system and bound by the *Halakhah*. To vest such authority in a nonreligious judge would be inconsistent with the basic tenets of Jewish law regarding the method by which Jewish law should be determined; it is the accepted and traditional view of all the authoritative decisionmakers of

120. In the course of his opinion, Justice Berinson alluded to the remarks of Justice Cohn (*see supra* n. 113) with regard to the attitude of the rabbinical courts to the laws of the State: "I only wish that, in matters coming before the rabbinical courts to which a statute of the State is applicable or concerning which there is a clear decision by an authorized general court, the rabbinical courts would accord them the respect and deference required by law."

121. *See supra* pp. 978–986. Thus, Justice Berinson was correct in concluding that in the rabbinical court system itself one court is not constrained by the decision of another court in the sense of being bound by the decision of the other court as a precedent.

122. The language follows Asheri in *Piskei ha-Rosh,* Sanhedrin, ch. 4, #6; *see supra* pp. 269, 985.

123. *See* Meiri, *Bet ha-Beḥirah,* Ketubbot 51b (ed. A. Sofer, p. 192). It certainly cannot be said that a judgment of the rabbinical courts is binding on the general courts on the basis of an obligation to obey the rulings of the halakhic authorities. From the point of view of the general courts, this obligation is not a legal, but rather a religious norm; how, then, for example, could this norm be applied to non-Jewish judges of the general court system?

the halakhic system that halakhic decision making, in its generally accepted sense, is the exclusive prerogative of the halakhic authorities. On the other hand, legal analysis or scholarly research that is not intended to render an authoritative halakhic ruling may arrive at a different conclusion on a particular point from the conclusion reached through the halakhic decision-making process.[124]

Nevertheless, even if the decisions of the rabbinical courts are not binding precedent, logic dictates that they be followed because of the expertise of the rabbinical courts on questions of Jewish law, and because following their decisions promotes good order, as well as the comity that is desirable between the two court systems.[125] Indeed, this is the approach that has been accepted by the overwhelming majority of the justices of the Supreme Court and has been followed by the lower general courts: the general courts do not reexamine the substantive halakhic correctness of rabbinical court decisions.

B. The Rights and Obligations of Parents in the Education of Their Children

Sometimes, on a particular point, the Supreme Court does express a view as to Jewish law that differs from the view expressed in a decision of a rabbinical court. It does so, however, not in order to set aside the judgment of the rabbinical court[126] but to engage in a halakhic discussion and make suggestions for consideration by the authorized halakhic tribunals. Of the several instances of such expressions,[127] we here examine once again the

124. For a detailed discussion, *see infra* pp. 1909–1911.

125. With regard to the obligation of comity between these two judicial systems, *see* Nagar v. Nagar, *supra* n. 25 at 397–400.

126. In the *Vicki Levy* case, *supra* n. 21, the High Court of Justice did vacate the judgment of the rabbinical court. It did so, however, on the broader ground that the judgment of the rabbinical court was contrary to the principles of natural justice. Justice Silberg demonstrated that the rabbinical court's judgment also violated the principles of natural justice embodied in Jewish law. *See supra* n. 21.

127. *See, e.g.,* Attorney General v. Yiḥya and Ora Abraham, 22(i) *P.D.* 29 (1968), where Justice Silberg expressed his views regarding the solution of the *agunah* problem when a recalcitrant husband refuses to divorce his wife. He proposed that every marriage contract include a clause whereby, upon the occurrence of a stipulated condition, the marital ties between the couple would be retroactively severed. *See supra* pp. 846–879; Freimann, *Kiddushin ve-Nissu'in,* p. 18.

Similarly, in Shakdiel v. Minister of Religions, 42(ii) *P.D.* 221 (1988), Deputy President Menachem Elon expressed the view that according to Jewish law as it has developed in modern times a woman has the right to serve as a member of a town's religious council. The Chief Rabbinate had expressed the view that such service by a woman is forbidden. Justice Elon stressed in his opinion that he was not presuming to make a halakhic ruling, but rather was expressing his view of Jewish law from a theoretical point of view, and that the Chief Rabbinate of Israel was the only institution authorized to make definitive halakhic

case of *Nagar v. Nagar,*[128] because it reflects recent and particularly significant developments in Jewish law relating to the rights and obligations of parents with regard to the education of their children.

The *Nagar* case involved a dispute between a divorced couple as to whether their children should attend a religious or secular school. When they married, neither party was religiously observant, but subsequently the father changed his outlook and began to follow a religious way of life. He desired that the children be educated in a religious school, but their mother did not agree. The question presented was difficult. The children had always attended a secular school. Under a judgment of the rabbinical court, the mother, who was not religious, had custody of the children. Social workers disagreed as to what would be in the "best interests of the children."

The rabbinical court decided that the children should be transferred from their secular school to a religious school. The sole reason given by the court—in an opinion of only six lines—was: "Since, according to Jewish law, it is the father who has the duty to educate his children, the court finds that he has the right to determine the nature of their education."[129]

When the matter reached the Supreme Court (or, more precisely, the Special Tribunal),[130] that court expressed its view that the rule that the father alone determines the nature of his children's education does not accord with current Jewish law. The court expressed the hope that when the question is presented to the Rabbinical Court of Appeals that court will decide that both parents have equal rights with regard to the education of their children. The portion of the court's opinion on this issue bears quotation at length because it is important not only for its substantive content but also for the methodology of its analysis:[131]

> With all respect, the categorical ruling of the rabbinical court to the effect that the education of children is the duty of their father alone and therefore he alone has the right to determine the nature of their education seems unlikely to be accepted by the Rabbinical Court of Appeals. Not only is the rabbinical court's decision inconsistent with the provision of the Woman's Equal Rights Law granting equal rights of custody to each parent—which implies equal rights to determine the nature of the children's education—but it also seems

---

rulings. He added that the Chief Rabbinate's view was possibly based on the erroneous assumption that one of the functions of a religious council is to render decisions on religious law. *See infra* pp. 1900–1903.

128. 38(i) *P.D.* 365 (1984); for the previous discussion of this case, *see supra* pp. 1761–1765.

129. The judgment of the rabbinical court was quoted "in full" in the opinion of the Special Tribunal, 38(i) *P.D.* at 400.

130. *See supra* n. 32.

131. 38(i) *P.D.* at 402–406.

to me, with all respect, that this decision is not consistent with the prevailing trend of contemporary *Halakhah*. . . .

According to various *rishonim*, [the Sages] R. Johanan and Resh Lakish disagreed on whether the duty to educate children to observe the religious precepts rests exclusively on the father or is shared by the mother,[132] and various *aharonim* also disagreed on this question.[133] Moreover, the main contribution to [children's] education is generally made by mothers, "who send their children to school, keep an eye on them to ensure that they study Torah, treat them kindly when they return from school, and encourage them in their devotion to Torah."[134] Mothers have a greater obligation than fathers to discipline their children, "since they are less occupied [with other tasks] and spend a greater amount of time at home."[135] Moreover, Scripture clearly states: "My son, heed the instruction of your father, and do not forsake the teaching of your mother."[136]

The right and the duty to educate one's children is a central factor in the question of custody. In this context, education, according to the *Halakhah*, includes not only training in Torah[137] and the necessary skills to earn a livelihood,[138] but also, first and foremost, the shaping of character. The rationale for the rule established by the Sages that ordinarily a daughter should live with her mother, and a son (after the age of six) with his father, is that "just as a mother will teach her daughter the proper behavior for daughters, so a father will teach his son what is appropriate for him,"[139] and also "teach him the way to study and the way to be a man."[140] For this reason, the Rabbinical Court of Appeals has held that the rule with regard to the custody of sons above the age of six applies even if the parents are not religious:

> Even if neither parent will educate the children in the study of Torah in the spirit of the statement of our Sages, of blessed memory, "in order to teach him Torah," nevertheless, a father owes to his son, and the son is entitled to receive from his father, a close and strong association whereby he can develop his son into an adult with manly personality and character.[141]

132. *See* TB Nazir 28b and Meiri, *Bet ha-Beḥirah, ad loc.*; Rashi, Ḥagigah 2a, s.v. Eizehu katan; *Tosafot*, Eruvin 82a, s.v. Katan ben shesh.

133. Abraham Danzig, *Ḥayyei Adam* 66:2, states: "A father is obligated to educate his sons and daughters, and some say that their mother also is obligated to educate them"; *see also* Jacob Ettlinger, *Arukh la-Ner* on TB Sukkah 2b.

134. Jonah Gerondi (thirteenth century, Spain), *Iggeret ha-Teshuvah*, sec. 72.

135. Isaiah Horowitz (sixteenth century, Germany), *Shenei Luḥot ha-Berit*, Sha'ar ha-Otiyyot, s.v. Derekh ereẓ.

136. Proverbs 1:8.

137. TB Kiddushin 29a; *see* 38(i) *P.D.* at 391ff.

138. TB Kiddushin 29a–30b; *Tosefta* Kiddushin 1:11 (S. Lieberman ed.); *Mekhilta* (Horowitz-Rabin ed.), Bo, sec. 18 (p. 73); TJ Kiddushin 1:7. *See also* 38(i) *P.D.* at 391ff.

139. Rabbenu Jeroham, *Toledot Adam ve-Ḥavvah*, Part Ḥavvah, path 23, sec. 3.

140. *Resp. Rashba Attributed to Naḥmanides* #38; *see also Resp. Radbaz*, I, #429.

141. A. v. B., 9 *P.D.R* 251, 259 (1974) (Kafaḥ, *Dayyan*).

Moreover, . . . "a father can teach his son those things that he is obligated to teach him, even if he does not live with him, such as [by] hiring a teacher for him or apprenticing him to a skilled craftsman."[142] This statement is particularly relevant in our day, when the education of children, in all of its forms and aspects, takes place by means of an extensive network of various types of educational institutions. In this connection, the Rabbinical Court of Appeals has stated . . . :[143]

> As to a son who studies Torah, Maimonides has written . . . that his teacher is to instruct him during the entire day and part of the night, in order to train him to study both during the day and at night. . . . This being so, there is no time remaining for his father to instruct him; rather, he would be in his father's custody only for eating and sleeping. In this respect, it can be fairly said that the father has no right to preference over the mother.[144]

While this statement was made with respect to a father's right to custody, it is directly relevant to the issue of whether a father has the superior right to determine the nature of his son's education.

Since sons are no longer educated by their fathers personally, but rather by teachers and rabbis, it stands to reason that they [the teachers and rabbis] should serve as the agents of both parents subject to the parents' joint authority.

It would seem that this conclusion is also the necessary consequence of the events and the halakhic decisions of recent generations. Under the *Halakhah* as set forth by the *tannaim* and *amoraim,* as mentioned above, a father, but not a mother, is obligated to teach their son Torah.[145] The Talmud states the reason for the rule as follows:[146]

> [The father is obligated] to teach him [his son] Torah. What is the source [of this rule]? Because it is written:[147] "You shall teach them to your sons. . . ." How do we know that she [the mother] has no obligation [to teach her son Torah]? Because it is written *"ve-limmadetem"* (you shall teach) [which can also be read as] *"u-lemadetem"* (you shall study) [since the unvocalized written form of the two words is identical in Hebrew]. [From this we learn that] whoever is commanded to study is

142. Responsum of Isaac de Molina, a contemporary of Joseph Caro (sixteenth century), published from ms. by Abraham David, *Kiryat Sefer,* XLIV (1969), p. 557, and quoted by E. Shochetman, "Le-Mahutam Shel Kelalei ha-Halakhah be-Sugyat Haḥzakat ha-Yeladim" [The Essential Nature of the Halakhic Principles Respecting Custody of Children], *Shenaton,* V (1978), 285, 301–302.

143. A. v. B., 7 *P.D.R.* 10, 17 (1967) (Avraham Shapira, *Dayyan*).

144. *See* Maimonides, *MT,* Ishut 21:17; *see also* Ovadiah Hadayah, *Resp. Yaskil Avdi,* II, Kunteres Aḥaron, EH #2; Ben-Zion Uziel, *Resp. Mishpetei Uziel,* Jerusalem, 1964, EH #91.

145. TB Kiddushin 29a (Mishnah and Gemara).

146. *Id.* 29b.

147. Deuteronomy 11:19.

> commanded to teach, and whoever is not commanded to study is not commanded to teach.
>
> And how do we know that she [the mother] is not obligated to study? Because it is written *"ve-limmadetem"* (you shall teach) [which can also be read as] *"u-lemadetem"* (you shall study). [From this we learn that] one whom others are commanded to teach is commanded to study, and one whom others are not commanded to teach is not commanded to study. [This is the converse of the above analogy.] And how do we know that others are not commanded to teach her? Because Scripture states: "You shall teach them to your sons"—not to your daughters.

The law is summarized by Maimonides as follows:

> Women . . . are exempt from the study of Torah; but a father is required to teach his minor son Torah, as it is stated: "You shall teach them to your sons. . . ." A woman is not required to teach her son, since [only] those who are obligated to study are also obligated to teach.[148]

As early as in the tannaitic period, differing views were expressed regarding this "triple" exemption of women—the exemption of a mother with respect to teaching her son, of a woman with respect to study, and of a daughter with respect to being taught. According to Ben Azzai, "One is obligated to teach his daughter Torah," while R. Eliezer b. Hyrcanus took the view that "Whoever teaches his daughter Torah is considered as if he taught her lewdness."[149] This dispute and R. Eliezer's acerbic remark have been explained in a number of ways; however, this is not the place for a full discussion of that subject.[150] Although various Talmudic and post-Talmudic sources have spoken in praise of wise and learned women who were astute expositors of Scripture,[151] the view of R. Eliezer came to be accepted as the law.[152]

With the passage of time, the law on this subject underwent a number

148. *MT,* Talmud Torah 1:1.

149. M Sotah 3:4.

150. For various explanations, *see* commentaries on M Sotah 3:4 and on TB Sotah 20a/b; Maimonides, *MT,* Talmud Torah 1:13; Sh. Ar. YD 246:6; *Torah Temimah* on Deuteronomy ch. 11, #48; TJ Sotah 3:4, 16a (3:4, 19a).

151. *See, e.g., Tosefta* Kelim (Zuckermandel ed.), first part, 4:17 ("His daughter's comments were more apt than his son's."); *Tosefta* Kelim (Zuckermandel ed.), middle part, 1:6 ("When they repeated the matter before Rabbi Judah, he said: 'Beruriah's comments are apt.'"); TB Bava Batra 119b ("The daughters of Zelophehad were wise and were insightful expositors [of Scripture]"). According to *Sibbuv ha-Rav Petaḥyah mi-Regensburg* [The Travels of R. Petaḥyah of Regensburg] (Kletter ed. 1912), p. 3b, the daughter of Samuel b. Eli Gaon, the head of the *yeshivah* of Baghdad in the second half of the twelfth century, was "proficient in Scripture and Talmud." *See also Resp. Tashbeẓ,* III, #76; *Resp. Maharshal* #29, *et al.*; Ḥida, *Shem ha-Gedolim,* Persons, s.v. Rabbanit.

152. *See* Maimonides, *MT,* Talmud Torah 1:13; Sh. Ar. YD 246:6. *See also Leḥem Mishneh* on *MT,* De'ot 6:7, regarding the acceptance of the view of R. Eliezer, who was an adherent of the School of Shammai.

of changes; the prohibition against teaching [Torah to women] became less broad both as to the subjects permitted to be taught (the Written Law and various laws with practical relevance) and as to how deeply the material should be taught; but, again, this is not the place to describe these changes in detail.[153]

In recent generations, there has been a profound change in attitude to this question, both in the *Halakhah* and in actual conduct, as a result of far-reaching social and ideological transformations. The halakhic authorities have explained this change in different ways, and the precise assessment of the nature and extent of the change follows from the particular explanation given. Israel Meir ha-Kohen of Radin (1838–1933), known as the Ḥafeẓ Ḥayyim, commented as follows on R. Eliezer's view that teaching Torah to one's daughter is prohibited:

> It would appear that this applies only to past generations . . . [when] there was a very strong tradition that everyone followed in the footsteps of our ancestors. . . . In such circumstances, it could be said that a daughter should not study Torah but rather should model her conduct on that of her righteous ancestors. Today, however, when because of our many sins our ancestral traditions have lost much of their hold . . . particularly among those [women] who learn how to write and speak the vernacular, it is certainly a great *miẓvah* to teach them the Pentateuch, and also the Prophets and Hagiographa and the ethical teachings of the Sages.[154]

This ruling was accepted throughout the Land of Israel, both before and after the establishment of the State. Thus, Rabbi Zalman Sorotzkin, one of the leading authorities in the *yeshivot,* has ruled:

> The statement that "whoever teaches his daughter Torah [is considered as if he taught her lewdness]" refers only to the intensive and dialectical study of the Oral Law. . . . Even as to the Oral Law, women may study the final conclusions without delving into the arguments and counter-arguments. . . . Recent times are not like earlier times: In earlier times, Jewish families lived according to the rules of the *Shulḥan Arukh,* and it was possible to learn the entire Torah from daily life at home. . . . But today . . . not only is it permitted to teach Torah and reverence for God to the daughters of our generation, but there is an absolute duty to do

153. For further discussion, *see* the excellent work of Dr. A. Ellinson, *Ha-Ishah ve-ha-Miẓvot* [Women and the Commandments], 2nd ed., I, pp. 147, 153–157; Y.Y. Neubert, *Ḥinnukh ha-Banim le-Miẓvot* [Education of Children to Observe the Commandments], Appendix to his book *Shemirat Shabbat ke-Hilkhatah,* Jerusalem, 1965, pp. 308–310.

154. *Likkutei Halakhot Shel ha-Ḥafeẓ Ḥayyim* [Collected Rulings of the Ḥafeẓ Ḥayyim], Sotah #21. *See also* Israel Meir ha-Kohen's responsum on this subject, dated Shevat 8, 5693 (1933), printed in A. Greenbaum, "Ha-Ḥinnukh ha-Dati li-Venot Yisra'el" [Religious Education for Jewish Women], in *Shevilei ha-Ḥinnukh* [Paths of Education], New York, 1966, pp. 24, 35.

> so, as we have explained; and it is a great *mizvah* to establish schools for girls to implant in their hearts a pure faith and [to teach them] . . . Torah and the commandments.[155]

Halakhic decision making, like decision making in all legal systems, does not break completely with, but rather limits, the preexisting *Halakhah*, and distinguishes between prior and newly developing *Halakhah*. Thus, the prohibition against teaching one's daughter Torah became limited so as to apply only to the study of the Oral Law through intensive study and dialectical argument. A significant number of the halakhic authorities of our time do not accept the prohibition even as so limited. Thus, Rabbi Ben-Zion Fierer, the Rabbi of Nir Galim, was asked, "Do the leaders of the religious education system act properly when they teach both the Written and the Oral Law to girls?" He responded unequivocally [in the affirmative], and distinguished between earlier periods and more recent times in which "a strong quest for the Tree of Knowledge has taken hold of all of humanity, men and women alike, and who can stop this mighty tide? . . . For it is inconceivable that the study of Torah and Judaism, in all its aspects, should be the very thing denied to girls." Rabbi Fierer took note of the current situation:

> Whether we like it or not, the fact is that the woman teacher has taken the place of the male teacher. The woman teacher teaches Torah to both boys and girls in the elementary schools. . . . Thus, . . . the performance of the religious precepts by boys [as well as girls] is dependent on her knowledge. Consequently, nowadays, all the laws—those that apply to her as a woman as well as those that apply to her as a teacher of boys—are equal[ly desirable for her to know]. Would that all Jewish women would study Torah![156]

The responsum of Rabbi Moshe Malka, formerly Rabbi of the Moroccan Jewish community and presently head of the Rabbinical Court of Petaḥ Tikva,[157] is instructive:

> Ben Azzai and R. Eliezer disagreed only with regard to their own times, when women's place was in the home, and when a woman never left the confines of her home and took no part in worldly affairs; her work and her skills were limited to the management of her household and to rearing and educating her children. . . . The situation is different now, when women play an important role in worldly affairs, plumb the depths of secular learning, occupy seats in the universities, manage of-

155. Z. Sorotzkin, *Moznayim la-Mishpat* [Scales of Justice], 1955, sec. 42. *See also* Ellinson, *supra* n. 153 at 158ff., and the responsum of Rabbi Kafaḥ, "Ḥinnukh ha-Bat le-Limmud Torah, le-Mussar u-le-Ezrat ha-Zulat" [Education of Daughters Concerning Torah, Ethical Teachings, and Helping Others], in *Ha-Ishah ve-Ḥinnukhah* [Women and Their Education], Kefar Saba, 1980, p. 31.

156. *Noam, Bamah le-Verur Ba'ayot ba-Halakhah* [*Noam:* A Forum for the Consideration of Halakhic Problems], Jerusalem, 1960, vol. 3, p. 134.

157. *Resp. Mikveh ha-Mayim,* III, YD #21.

fices, own businesses, and play a significant role in government and politics. . . .

R. Eliezer would certainly admit that it is not at all forbidden to teach a woman even the Oral Law, so that she may be able to take care to observe all the laws of the Torah that relate to her activities and her work. Indeed, it is our duty to educate her to the fullest extent possible.[158]

In the same vein is the following statement by Rabbi Aharon Lichtenstein, the head of Yeshivat Har Etzion at Alon Shevut in Gush Etzion:[159]

I believe that it is not merely permitted but desirable and [even] necessary to provide girls with an intensive education that includes the sources of the Oral Law. [This position is justified] either on the basis of the argument that when women engage in every field of endeavor, Torah should not be the one area in which they are denied an education, or on the basis of the arguments of the Ḥafeẓ Ḥayyim. . . . I believe that a practical religious training for girls requires far more than what is currently provided. We must strengthen the education of girls both quantitatively and qualitatively by providing instruction in every area of Torah. . . .

The study of the Oral Law must be intensified. From a practical point of view, it is appropriate to teach the Orders of *Zera'im, Mo'ed,* and *Nezikin,* together with those portions of the Orders of *Nashim, Kodashim,* and *Tohorot* that are currently applicable, and . . . these subjects should be taught in depth. . . . I have no objection to teaching girls Talmud . . . , and indeed this must be made an integral part of their school education, an actual Talmudic lecture (*shi'ur*). . . . This seems to me to be the preferable course for girls in our days.[160]

Following this detailed discussion of the Talmudic and post-Talmudic sources on the question of the obligation of a woman to study and to teach Torah, and of the change in the position of women in our time, when women study and teach equally with men—a change that led many halakhic authorities to take the view that, today, girls as well as boys are obligated to study Torah—the court concluded:[161]

158. *See also* Ḥayyim David ha-Levi (Chief Rabbi of Tel Aviv-Jaffa), *Resp. Aseh Lekha Rav,* II, #52.

159. "Ba'ayot Yesod be-Ḥinnukhah Shel ha-Ishah" [Fundamental Problems Concerning the Education of Women], in *Ha-Ishah ve-Ḥinnukhah, supra* n. 155 at 158–159. Rabbi Lichtenstein's comments were recorded in a question-and-answer session.

160. *See also* "Ha-Ishah bi-Mekorot ha-Yahadut" [Women in Jewish Sources], in *Hagut, Me'assef le-Maḥashavah Yehudit* [*Hagut:* An Anthology of Jewish Thought], published by the Department for Torah Culture, 1983, which contains various articles on the subject discussed by the court.

161. 38(i) *P.D.* at 406–407.

> As we have seen, the law that a father but not a mother is obligated to teach a son Torah is based on the rule that the father is required to study Torah himself whereas the mother is exempt from such study. The principle is that the responsibility for teaching rests on whoever is obligated to study.
>
> In view of the very significant change that has now taken place, when not only is there no prohibition against the study of Torah by women but it has been ruled that such study is obligatory, and when not only do women themselves study but they teach other people's children, it necessarily appears to follow that the obligation to teach a child Torah rests equally on both parents, on the basis of the principle that whoever is obligated to study also is obligated to teach. This is most certainly true when the obligation is fulfilled by selecting the school the child should attend.
>
> If I were not fearful [about making predictions], I would venture to say that the Rabbinical Court of Appeals, were it given an opportunity to rule on the issue of the obligation to educate children—both boys and girls—would conclude that both parents have equal rights and obligations, except, of course, in regard to the special contribution a father makes to a son and a mother makes to a daughter by virtue of the superior ability to understand and identify with children of one's own gender.

This kind of diffident and deferential venture by a general court into the jurisprudence of the rabbinical courts can help Jewish law to make progress in coping with current social and educational realities while carefully preserving the dignity and respect that should be accorded by each of the two judicial systems to the other. The *Nagar* case is particularly significant because the decision was rendered by a special tribunal composed of President Shamgar and Justice Elon (both representing the Supreme Court) and Rabbi Yosef Kafaḥ, a member of the Rabbinical Court of Appeals (representing the President of that court), and all three judges concurred in the decision that both parents have equal rights in regard to the education of their children.

V. LEGISLATION CONTRARY TO JEWISH LAW—A CASE STUDY OF THE SOLUTION TO A PROBLEM

A. The Obligation of a Husband to Support His Wife as Affected by Her Income from Employment and from Her Property

The previously discussed case that held that a husband may deduct from his required spousal support the amount of his wife's earnings from outside employment exacerbated a problem in regard to spousal support that had previously arisen under Section 2 of the Woman's Equal Rights Law, 1951. That section provides:

> A married woman has full legal capacity to acquire property and to engage in legal transactions as if she were single; the bond of marriage shall not impair her rights to property acquired by her before marriage.

The Supreme Court held in a series of cases that this section abolished the right of a husband to receive the income of his wife's *melog* property,[162] a right conferred upon him by Jewish law.[163] It soon became clear that this holding had a significant effect on the husband's obligation of support when his wife owns income-producing property. Under Jewish law, a wife's ownership of property does not affect her husband's obligation to support her; he must still support her, and she need not sell her property to sustain herself.[164] However, Jewish law also provides that if a wife receives income from her property, since this income belongs to the husband (it being derived from her *melog* property), the husband may require her to use this income for her support.[165]

Since the obligation of spousal support is determined by the personal law of the couple, *i.e.*, Jewish law, and since the Woman's Equal Rights Law establishes that the income from a wife's *melog* property belongs to the wife rather than to the husband, it follows that the support owed by the husband cannot be reduced by reason of such income to the wife, because, pursuant to the statute, the income no longer belongs to the husband but to the wife, and under the applicable Jewish law the fact that the wife has assets does not excuse the husband from his obligation to support her.[166]

The result is unfortunate, because the purpose and rationale of treating both spouses equally as to both rights and obligations requires that a wife who has income from her property should contribute toward the support

162. Sidis v. Rabbinical Court of Appeals, 12 *P.D.* 1525 (1958); Balaban v. Balaban, 14 *P.D.* 285 (1960); and other cases. The Supreme Court did not accept the view of Justice Schereschewsky to the contrary. *See* the *Sidis* case, 12 *P.D.* at 1535; Schereschewsky, *supra* n. 3 at 146 n. 31a and 213 n. 1a; Elon, *Ḥakikah,* pp. 38, 41. Similarly, the Spouses (Property Relations) Law, 1973, provides (sec. 4):

> Marriage or its dissolution does not, in and of itself, affect the assets of either spouse, transfer property rights from either spouse to the other, or render either spouse liable for the debts of the other.

As to the law of *melog* property, *see supra* pp. 568–569, 572.

163. TB Ketubbot 46b, 65b; Maimonides, *MT,* Ishut 12:3, 22:7; Sh. Ar. EH 69:3, 85:1.

164. *See Piskei ha-Rosh,* Ketubbot, ch. 4, #14; *Pitḥei Teshuvah* to EH ch. 85, subpar. 2 (at the end).

165. *See* A. v. B., 1 *P.D.R.* 239, 242 (1953); A. v. B., 2 *P.D.R.* 97, 98, 102 (1957).

166. Therefore, under Jewish law, if the wife acquires property from which the husband has no right to the income—for example, property acquired by gift conditioned upon the husband's having no rights to that property, in which case the income from the property would belong to the wife (TB Bava Batra 51b; Sh. Ar. EH 85:7,11)—the husband cannot claim that his obligation of spousal support should be reduced by the amount of income from this property, inasmuch as that income does not belong to him. A. v. B., 1 *P.D.R.* 97, 101–102 (1953).

of the household. The cause of the problem is the statute, which not only abrogated one rule of Jewish law governing the financial relationship between spouses (*i.e.,* the right of a husband to the income from his wife's *melog* property), but also indirectly affected another aspect of that relationship (*i.e.,* the husband's obligation to support his wife). That obligation, under other legislation, is governed by Jewish law, which requires a husband to support his wife even if she has her own property.

The rejection of one part of the Jewish law governing the financial relationship between spouses, coupled with incorporation of the Jewish law on other aspects of the relationship, including the husband's obligation to support his wife, upset the balance that had been maintained by Jewish law. Under Jewish law, a wife's *ownership* of property does not affect her husband's obligation to support her, but the *income* from such property is taken into account and reduces his obligation of support. On the other hand, by providing in the Woman's Equal Rights Law that the income from a wife's property belongs to her, the Legislature created a situation in which the husband's liability for support is not diminished even when the wife receives income from her property. This is an undesirable result, and it impelled the Supreme Court to request the Legislature to consider corrective action.[167]

The situation was exacerbated as a result of the decision of the Supreme Court in the *Joseph* case, discussed above. As mentioned, the Supreme Court, by a clear majority on both the original hearing and on the rehearing before five justices, held that a husband has the right to set off his wife's earnings from outside employment against the amount of her support. The consequence is that if a wife is wealthy and has income from her property, her right to support is not affected; but if she does not have property and only earns a wage from outside employment, she is not entitled to support from her husband as long as her salary is sufficient for her needs. This problem was discussed in *Cohen v. Cohen,*[168] where Justice Etzioni stated:[169]

167. Balaban v. Balaban, *supra* n. 162 at 292 (end of opinion of Olshan, J.). Justice Silberg took the position that despite the abrogation of the right of the husband to receive the income from his wife's *melog* property, the amount of that income may nevertheless be deducted from the amount of support she is entitled to receive from her husband. However, no other justice accepted this view. The three other justices concurred in Justice Olshan's opinion that the abrogation of the husband's right to receive the income of his wife's *melog* property destroyed the basis for permitting the reduction of his support obligation by the amount of the income from such property. Even Justice Silberg subsequently accepted the majority view as the law. *See* Rinat v. Rinat, 20(ii) *P.D.* 21, 24–25 (1966).

168. 25(ii) *P.D.* 327 (1971).

169. *Id.* at 332.

> In the matter of support, the decisions . . . and the existing legal situation have blatantly discriminated in favor of women who have substantial income-producing property and against working women whose income is derived from wages. In the first case, the court does not take a wife's income into account in setting the amount of support her husband is required to provide, while in the case of the working woman, the court does take her wages into account (her salary being considered her "handiwork"). This is an unacceptable state of affairs. The way to eliminate the inequality inherent in this state of affairs is either to treat a working woman the same as a woman who owns *melog* property in determining the amount of support (*i.e.*, the court will not take into account either the earnings from *melog* property or the income from outside employment) or—and this is the method I believe to be better suited for the situation of women in a society governed by the principle of gender equality—to apply to a woman who owns *melog* property the same rule that applies to a working woman.

President Agranat added:[170]

> The last ruling [*i.e.*, that a wife's support may be reduced by the amount of her wages], which comports with the modern aspiration to bring about equality between spouses in this area so that both will "exert their best efforts to ensure the continued existence and well-being of the family" (*Joseph* case, on rehearing, [24(i) *P.D.*] p. 808), strongly demonstrates the injustice of the first ruling [that the income of a wife from her *property* may not be set off against the support owed by her husband]. For a wife who has income only from her work outside the home will have her husband's support obligation reduced, but a wife with substantial property from which the income is more than ample to provide for her needs will not have her claim for support reduced. However . . . in order to assure that a wife's income from her property will be taken into account in determining the amount of support [owed by her husband], legislative intervention will, as stated, be required.

B. Amendment of the Woman's Equal Rights Law

The Supreme Court's recommendation to the Legislature that the statute be amended was followed:[171] in 1976, a new Section 2(a) was added. This section provides:

> Notwithstanding the provisions of the [Woman's] Equal Rights Law, 1951, in fixing the amount of support required to be paid to a spouse, the court may

170. *Id.* at 335.

171. Family Law Amendment (Maintenance) Bill (Amendment), 1975 (Bill No. 1168), p. 173; *see* Explanatory Notes, *id.* at 174.

take into account the income of the spouse from employment and from property and, if deemed appropriate, from any other source.

This amendment makes it possible for the court, in determining the amount of support, to take into account the income of the spouse, whether from employment or from property. As to income from employment, the amendment does not change the preexisting law, for the same conclusion had previously been reached by the Supreme Court,[172] applying Jewish law, based on decisions of the rabbinical courts. What the amendment does change is the law concerning income from property. Here the Legislature restored, in part (insofar as the wife's right to support is concerned), the rule of Jewish law that gives the husband the right to the income from his wife's *melog* property.[173] The amended statute establishes that the court may take into account the *income* from the property, but not the *property* itself. This, too, follows Jewish law, according to which, as previously discussed, a wife's ownership of property does not in itself affect the amount of support to which she is entitled from her husband.[174]

The enactment of Section 2(a) in 1976 as part of the Family Law Amendment (Maintenance) Law restored the balance in the law relating to a husband's obligation to support his wife, which had been upset twenty-five years previously as a result of the enactment of Section 2 of the Woman's Equal Rights Law in 1951, when that statute removed one piece of the total structure of spousal financial relationships established by Jewish law. The balance was restored when the statute was amended to incorporate the missing piece so as to achieve the result reached under Jewish law. This

172. Joseph v. Joseph, *supra* nn. 106–107.

173. *See also* Sporta v. Sporta, 32(ii) *P.D.* 709, 719 (1978) (Ben Porat, J.), regarding the effect of Section 2(a) in bringing the statute into conformity with the position of Jewish law.

174. Thus, the Explanatory Notes accompanying the bill (*supra* n. 171) stated: "It gives the court the right to take into account the income of the spouse from employment and from property, *as distinguished from taking into account the property itself*" (emphasis in original). The phrase "from any other source" in Section 2(a) was intended to include payments for damages and benefits (*see* Explanatory Notes, *id.*), and they were so interpreted in the *Sporta* case, *supra* n. 173 at 713. The amendment was extensively discussed in Ḥakak v. Ḥakak, 45(iv) *P.D.* 749 (1991). According to the decisions of the rabbinical courts, old-age pensions received from the National Insurance Foundation may not be taken into account in determining the amount of support. A. v. B., 11 *P.D.R.* 193, 196–197 (1976). *See also* Schereschewsky, *supra* n. 3 at 145 and nn. 30, 31a; 282ff. With regard to severance pay, *see* Shava, *supra* n. 3 at 245.

In the *Sporta* case, differing views were expressed regarding the scope of Section 2(a). In June 1980, the Family Law Amendment (Maintenance) Bill, 1980 (Amendment #2), was introduced. This bill was designed to amend Section 2(a) in order to resolve these differences.

See also Englard, *supra* n. 54 at 28–29; Rosen-Tzvi, *supra* n. 3 at 134–141; Shava, *supra* n. 3 at 242–251.

experience also demonstrates that when one provision is deleted from a complex structure of interrelated law on a particular subject, great care and thorough consideration are required to avoid untoward consequences that may result from the application of the related provisions that still remain part of the law.

VI. DIFFERING TRENDS IN REGARD TO THE EMPLOYMENT OF LEGISLATION IN THE RABBINICAL SYSTEM

A. Decline in the Employment of Legislation as an Instrument of Halakhic Creativity

An examination of the judgments of the rabbinical courts and the legislative activities of the rabbinate reveals much travail and vacillation with regard to the use of the creative methods of Jewish law even within the rabbinical legal system itself, notwithstanding that the rabbinate, within its own sphere, is free from the difficult problems discussed above arising from the friction between the general court system and the rabbinical court system.

A number of issues have been previously discussed, concerning which some of the rabbinical courts have been taking a more stringent position than heretofore and have not been sufficiently responsive to problems that Jewish law is capable of resolving;[175] indeed, the *Halakhah* calls for their resolution. This situation may to some extent be due to the tensions between the general court system and the rabbinical court system.[176] However, a more serious problem is the attitude of some rabbinical court judges in regard to the weight to be given to a significant portion of the legislation of the halakhic authorities themselves, namely, the enactments of the Chief Rabbinate.

As previously noted,[177] the Chief Rabbinate of the Land of Israel from the 1920s through the early years of the State enacted legislation in various areas of procedure and the law of personal status that were significant creative advances in Jewish law. The enactments included procedural rules for the rabbinical courts and provisions concerning such matters as the *ketub-*

175. *See supra* n. 8, discussing the question of the admissibility of the testimony of a person who habitually violates the sabbath; *supra* n. 9, noting the reluctance of the rabbinical courts, except in rare cases, to issue a decree compelling a husband to divorce his wife; *supra* n. 10, discussing the failure to adopt legislation needed to solve problems of the *agunah*.

176. This is the case, for example, with regard to the decision of the rabbinical court disqualifying as witnesses to a privately performed marriage between a *kohen* and a divorcée, persons who habitually violate the sabbath, and the Supreme Court decisions, accepting such witnesses and validating such marriages. *See supra* n. 8 and pp. 1778–1779.

177. *See supra* pp. 824–835, 1598–1599.

bah, the ban of Rabbenu Gershom against bigamy, levirate marriage and *halizah,* and the minimum age for marriage. These enactments, which were adopted after thorough discussion and formidable opposition on the part of some halakhic authorities,[178] were accepted at the time as binding and as an integral part of the *Halakhah,* to the same extent as the many thousands of enactments previously adopted throughout the generations in the diaspora.[179] However, since that time, there has been a continual decline in the employment of legislation as an instrument of halakhic creativity. Not only have the halakhic authorities virtually ceased to legislate since the earliest years of the State,[180] but even the recognition extended to the enactments of the Chief Rabbinate when they were adopted has been undercut by disregard of their provisions, by judicial limitations on their application, and even by explicit rejection.

Since the end of the eighteenth century and the decline, and eventual abolition, of Jewish juridical autonomy, the Jewish legal system's use of legislation (which by its very nature requires the existence of a functioning legal system) also declined.[181] With the expansion of the Jewish settlement in the Land of Israel and the establishment of the beginnings of a framework for Jewish governmental institutions, the late Chief Rabbi Kook foresaw and proclaimed, when the Chief Rabbinate was instituted in 1921, that "in our new national life in the Land of Israel, it will undoubtedly be vitally necessary for us, from time to time, to enact important *takkanot.*"[182] Chief Rabbis Herzog and Uziel, who initiated the adoption of the overwhelming majority of the enactments of the Chief Rabbinate in the 1940s and 1950s, continued on this same path.[183] But, as noted, since those years, this crea-

178. *See, e.g.,* the debates preceding the establishment of the Rabbinical Court of Appeals (*supra* pp. 824–825) and the enactment regarding the obligation of a father to support his children until they reach the age of fifteen (*supra* pp. 831–833). Also, as previously discussed, certain enactments proposed by the Chief Rabbis were not accepted because of the opposition of a majority of the members of the Council of the Chief Rabbinate. This occurred, for example, with regard to proposed enactments concerning inheritance by daughters (*see supra* p. 1684 and n. 270; p. 1755 and n. 10).

179. *See supra* p. 825, regarding the status of the enactment providing for a Rabbinical Court of Appeals as "a law of our Holy Torah"; and *supra* p. 832, regarding the enactment providing for the support of children up to the age of fifteen as having "full force and effect to the same extent as the enactments of 'Shum', Toledo, the Council of the Four Lands, etc."

180. *See supra* pp. 834–835, 1754–1755.

181. *See supra* pp. 1597–1598.

182. *See supra* p. 1338.

183. *See supra* pp. 826–834, 1599. *See also* B.Z. Eliash, "Ha-Ḥakikah ha-Rabbanit ba-Pesikah ha-Rabbanit—Hit'almut ve-Shivrah" [Disregard of Rabbinic Legislation in Rabbinical Court Decisions—The Harmful Results], *Dine Israel,* X–XI, pp. 137ff., at 211, with regard to the efforts of Chief Rabbi Herzog to promulgate additional enactments.

tive activity has again become stagnant to the point that it has virtually ceased.

The cessation of legislative activity has also had a negative influence on the attitude toward the enactments previously adopted. This regrettable trend is probably also due to the weakening of the position of the Chief Rabbinate of Israel as the supreme halakhic institution because of the refusal of a significant portion of the religious Jewish population to recognize it as such.[184] Additionally, the opposition to certain enactments results from the increasing tendency for the different "communities," such as the Ashkenazic and the Sephardic, to follow their own view of *Halakhah*.[185] This fragmentation along "community" lines itself appears to be a result of the weakening of the position of the Chief Rabbinate.

B. The Rabbinical Court of Appeals—Accomplishments and Limitations

Of particular interest, from the perspective of both the foregoing discussion and the interrelationship between Jewish law and other legal systems, are the developments that have occurred with respect to one of the most significant enactments of the Chief Rabbinate, adopted immediately upon its inception, namely, the *takkanah* establishing an appellate tribunal known as the Rabbinical Court of Appeals.

This appellate tribunal, established in 1921, was a halakhic innovation; Jewish law did not previously recognize the possibility that one court could reverse another court's decision.[186] At first, and for a considerable

184. *See supra* pp. 831–832 (statements made by Chief Rabbis Herzog and Uziel with regard to the enactment providing for the support of children up to the age of fifteen). These enactments were also given the force of communal enactments, but even that type of enactment has fallen into disuse. *See infra* pp. 1819–1824.

185. *See* the statements by Chief Rabbis Herzog and Uziel regarding the 1950 enactment that *ḥaliẓah*, rather than levirate marriage, is the primary obligation. This is an issue which has been disputed between Sephardic and Ashkenazic Jewry for many generations. The Chief Rabbis explained that "in order that the Torah not be as two separate Torahs, we hereby enact . . . a complete prohibition against the *miẓvah* of levirate marriage, so that *ḥaliẓah* is required." Ovadiah Yosef, who later served as the Chief Sephardic Rabbi of Israel, disagreed with the promulgation of this enactment, which mandates the Ashkenazic position for the Sephardic communities. He asserted that everyone is "required to take care to preserve the customs of his ancestors, in line with the verse [Proverbs 1:8] 'Do not forsake the instruction of your mother.'" *Resp. Yabi'a Omer*, VI, EH #14; this responsum sets forth at length Rabbi Yosef's approach, which differs from that of Rabbi Uziel, the earlier Sephardic Chief Rabbi, who initiated this enactment prohibiting levirate marriage. A similar situation has occurred with regard to the enactment concerning the ban of Rabbenu Gershom. *See also* Eliash, *supra* n. 183 at 190–211; B. v. A., 9 *P.D.R.* 152, 157–160 (1973) (Kafaḥ, *Dayyan*); *Resp. Yabi'a Omer*, V, EH #1.

186. *See supra* pp. 824–825.

period of time, this enactment was viewed as "an enactment of the halakhic authorities that has the status of a law of our Holy Torah, and whoever appears as a party in a case does so on that basis."[187] However, more recently, this important innovation in the Jewish legal system has shown some weakening; some district rabbinical courts have refused to accept the authority of the Rabbinical Court of Appeals.[188]

So extreme a position has been taken only by a small minority of the rabbinical court judges. However, there is another view, expressed by one prominent judge, that, while the enactment establishing the Rabbinical Court of Appeals effectively conferred on that court full authority to modify, and even to reverse, a judgment of a district rabbinical court, the Rabbinical Court of Appeals may not require any judge—even a judge of a district rabbinical court—to act contrary to his own opinion. This view is supported by the basic position of Jewish law according to which every duly authorized judge has the right to decide on the basis of his own understanding of the law and his own interpretation of the halakhic sources. According to this view, the appellate tribunal can set aside the lower court's judgment only insofar as the *parties* to that case are concerned. The lower court *judge*, however, has a duty to follow where his own conclusions lead him, and no authority can require him to act otherwise. The rationale for this view was fully set forth in a minority opinion in a case decided in 1968:[189]

> The judgment of the Rabbinical Court of Appeals states:
>
> > If the appellant deposits a bill of divorcement (*get*) with the district rabbinical court for the benefit of the respondent, the district rabbinical court shall rescind the order against the appellant contained in paragraph (b) of the above-mentioned judgment.
>
> In effect, the Rabbinical Court of Appeals seeks to require the district rabbinical court to render a judgment contrary to the district court's view of the law of the Torah—to write, sign, and stamp "permitted" on something that it believes is forbidden.

187. B. v. A. (1944), Warhaftig, *Osef Piskei ha-Din*, p. 71; *see supra* pp. 825–826; Elon, *Ḥakikah*, p. 160. *See also* the detailed discussion of the halakhic questions that have arisen with regard to the establishment of a Rabbinical Court of Appeals in Ovadiah Hadayah, *Resp. Yaskil Avdi*, EH #2, par. 1. These questions involve the principle that if one halakhic authority has ruled that a particular act is forbidden, no other halakhic authority may rule that it is permissible, and the principle that no court may upset the ruling of another court.

188. *See* the two examples discussed *infra* pp. 1815–1818, in which this matter is dealt with in opinions of the Supreme Court of Israel.

189. Case No. 520/1966 (unpublished). The judgment was rendered on September 20, 1968. The case was heard by a panel consisting of *Dayyanim* Y. Babliki, A. Shapira, and M. Eliyahu. The minority opinion appears to have been that of Rabbi Shapira, who subsequently served as Ashkenazic Chief Rabbi of Israel and President of the Rabbinical Court of Appeals. For some reason, the opinion has not been published.

This is a very strange ruling. In issuing it, the Rabbinical Court of Appeals is acting like the general appellate courts, which direct the lower courts to decide cases according to the law as determined by the appellate court rather than according to the views of the district judges. The Rabbinical Court of Appeals is equating itself to a general court.

With all respect, this equation is inappropriate. The general courts derive their authority from the laws of the State, and they reach their judgments according to the law of the land, as promulgated by the legislative body of the country. The same legislature that establishes the laws also authorizes the supreme appellate court to interpret those laws. Thus, while a district court judge [in the general court system] may believe that his interpretation of the law is correct, he must also admit that the law of the land provides that the appellate court's interpretation is as valid as if it had been explicitly enacted by the Legislature. It follows that no other interpretation of the law, even if it is intrinsically more reasonable, has any legal significance.

This is not the case with us Jewish judges of rabbinical courts. We render judgments only on the basis of the authority of the Torah over the entire Jewish people, and solely according to Jewish law, as is written:[190] "I [Moses] decide between one person and another, and I make known the laws and teachings of God." Since it is the laws of God with which we deal, the judge must follow only his own conscience and the truth in his heart, and nothing else. No one can presume to say: "I alone am the interpreter of the laws of God, and my interpretation is binding on all Jewish sages and judges." Therefore, no [rabbinical court] judge is subject to directives from any other halakhic authority, whoever he may be, as to how to decide a case under Jewish law. There is not the slightest possible warrant in the laws of the Torah for any halakhic authorities to assert that their decisions and interpretations of the Torah bind other halakhic authorities, and that the others must rule accordingly even if they do not concur. The rule that "you shall carry out the verdict that is announced to you" contained in the Torah portion of *Shofetim*[191] refers only to the [rulings of the] Great Sanhedrin of seventy-two Sages who were ordained in the chain of ordination going back to our teacher Moses, and who sat only in the Chamber of Hewn Stone near the altar in the Temple, and to the rulings arrived at jointly by all the halakhic authorities of the generation, as in the days of the Talmud. . . . All these matters are obvious, and it is distressing to [have to] discuss them.

But we have never seen or heard that a single one of all the leading rabbis throughout all the generations, who have studied the Torah [*i.e.*, the Talmud] of Ravina and Rav Ashi, the fathers of the Jewish people, ever presumed to claim that their rulings were binding on others. On the contrary, we have found and seen the opposite of this in their books, by the light of which we are enlightened.

190. Exodus 18:16.
191. Deuteronomy 17:10.

After correctly describing this basic approach of Jewish law (which, in fact, has never varied), the distinguished judge proceeded to discuss the procedural enactment adopted by the Chief Rabbinate for the rabbinical courts that provided for appellate review and established the Rabbinical Court of Appeals:

> It is true that, pursuant to statute and the procedural enactments of the Chief Rabbinate, as well as the customary practice in the State, the Rabbinical Court of Appeals has been established, to which parties litigant bring the decisions of the lower rabbinical courts for review, and the Rabbinical Court of Appeals may revise the [lower court's] judgment. This second judgment, under the law, is binding on the parties, since they litigated in the first instance on the understanding that their case was subject to review by the Rabbinical Court of Appeals, and they are in the same position as if they originally submitted their case to that court.
>
> This applies, however, only to the parties, but not to the judges; for a stipulation of the parties cannot change the law of the Torah as understood by the particular judge. If the same or a similar case comes before him again, he cannot and may not decide the case otherwise than according to his own opinion.
>
> Moreover, while the obligations assumed by the parties may be determinative in monetary matters or questions of support and the like, that is not the case in matters of religious prohibition (*issur*), such as the instant case. An obligation by a husband or wife undertaken pursuant to procedural enactments cannot at all change the substantive law. Therefore, if the majority of this court holds that this woman is a married woman and that the plaintiff is legally her husband for all purposes, no other halakhic authority or authorities have jurisdiction to determine that this court must render a judgment or take any action that is inconsistent with the judgment it has already entered.
>
> In addition, since, in the view of the majority of this court, the woman is clearly the plaintiff's wife, not only is there no obligation on his part to take any action with regard to a divorce against her will, but the stringent ban of Rabbenu Gershom prohibits such action. For if the plaintiff is legally her husband, the ban of Rabbenu Gershom prohibits him from divorcing her against her will. And the enactment of Rabbenu Gershom, as recorded in the *Kol Bo* and in [the writings of] Rabbi Meir of Rothenburg, explicitly provides that the ban is applicable not only to the husband but also to all who are his accessories, *i.e.*, the scribe, the witnesses, and the [husband's] agent. The rabbinical court judges are also in this category. The ban of Rabbenu Gershom thus means that the judges may not assist the husband to divorce his wife against her will. It is, therefore, forbidden for those members of this court who believe that the parties are legally married to act in any way to facilitate the divorce. . . .
>
> If the Rabbinical Court of Appeals disagrees with the district rabbinical

court, and it [the Rabbinical Court of Appeals] reaches a decision for the parties in accordance with Section 138 of the Procedural Enactments of the Chief Rabbinate of Israel of 1963, it [the Rabbinical Court of Appeals] may enter and execute its own judgment, but may not impose any obligation on the [lower] court.[192]

This is indeed a keen, interesting, and even persuasive halakhic analysis. As noted above,[193] this approach, stressing judicial independence and

192. *See also* the following further remarks in the same opinion:

> Moreover, according to Knesset legislation, bigamy is a criminal offense, and anyone who assists in its commission is considered an accomplice. As is known, the courts of the State have ruled that even a woman whose status as married is subject to some doubt is considered to be a married woman for purposes of all the rights provided by law. It is also well known that, at times, the courts of the State issue directives to the rabbinical courts, including the Rabbinical Court of Appeals, if, in their view, action was taken which violates the law. Thus, according to the bigamy statute, the woman is considered the wife of the petitioner even if her status as his wife is merely doubtful. And it may be assumed that a woman who has fought so tenaciously over the husband of her youthful years will not hesitate to petition the secular courts for an injunction to prevent the rabbinical courts from permitting her husband to marry another woman, thus causing great embarrassment [to the rabbinical courts].
>
> If, indeed, a rabbinical court believes that, in truth, the *Halakhah* permits the husband to marry another woman, its judges should let themselves be embarrassed for the sake of the Torah. For [the prophet] Ezekiel was called Ezekiel b. *Buzi* because he let himself be put to shame [*bizah azmo*] for the sake of the Torah. As stated in the *Sifrei*, it is with this understanding that rabbinical court judges are appointed. But if, in the view of the [district] rabbinical court, the husband is in fact prohibited from marrying another woman, and it is only the ruling of the Rabbinical Court of Appeals that permits him to marry, [then, if the district rabbinical court were required to change its judgment], the result would be that they [the judges of Rabbinical Court of Appeals] prescribe the outcome while others [the judges of the district rabbinical court] are the ones who are put to shame. This cannot be allowed.

193. *See supra* pp. 1061–1070. At the end of the minority opinion, there is a quotation of a relevant passage from a responsum of Ḥayyim Volozhiner that bears repetition here:

> The great Rabbi Ḥayyim of Volozhin wrote the following to the learned author of *Azei Arazim:*
>
> > In a case where it is doubtful whether the marriage has been consummated, Your Honor, in great modesty, has written that the view of our great master, may the Lord lengthen his days, should be relied upon. But I do not believe that the view of our master should be relied upon, and I adhere to my view, which is supported by many proofs from the Talmud and from worthy authorities. . . . The Torah contains the truth, and my interest is only in the truth, as it is stated: "You must love truth and peace" (Zechariah 8:19). Your Honor may not wish to contradict the view of our honored master for the sake of peace. But I, the lesser one, have attended our honored master when he was in our country, and am *a fortiori* obligated to honor and fear him as I fear Heaven. Nevertheless, I abide by the holy Talmud, which taught me in Chapter *Yesh Noḥalin* [TB Bava Batra 131a] that "a judge must be guided only by what his own eyes see." . . . Anyone who fears God would say: "How is it possible for me to rely on a ruling of this rabbi, when I have found many

freedom to decide, reflects a fundamental concept of Jewish law, which—within the framework of that law's principles and sources—provides halakhic decisionmakers with the opportunity for creativity and flexibility in solving the new problems that constantly arise. Indeed, we have seen that in the early days of the Chief Rabbinate, the institution of an appellate tribunal was accepted only after a sharp and mordant controversy between the proponents of the enactment and the opponents of such a court, who based their argument on the traditional view of Jewish law from earliest times.[194] Nevertheless, the halakhic authorities and the leaders of the Chief Rabbinate, who were responsible for establishing the rabbinical court system as an official judicial system of the state for all citizens, realized that an appellate tribunal was vitally necessary to strengthen the position of the rabbinical court system; and the Rabbinical Court of Appeals and the right of appeal to that court were established pursuant to an enactment "which has the status of a law of our Holy Torah."

The strengthening of the rabbinical court system was deemed to justify the limitations on the freedom of decision of the lower court judges resulting from the establishment of a judicial hierarchy and the acceptance of the authority of a higher court. It follows that a higher court should be able not only to modify or reverse the decisions of a lower court, but also to direct the lower court to act in accordance with the appellate mandate. The minority opinion previously quoted would limit the authority of the appellate court, but would not deprive it of the power to modify or reverse the lower court's judgment. Under that view, such a modification or reversal would be conclusive upon both the parties and the lower court judges, but it could not require a lower court judge to act contrary to his own view of the law.[195]

> difficulties with it?" I have already been warned of this by my teacher, the Holy One of Israel, our great and righteous rabbi, the Gaon of Vilna, [who cautioned me] not to be swayed by personal regard in rendering rulings.

These are the words of the great Rabbi Ḥayyim of Volozhin, of blessed memory. Strictly speaking, they do not constitute legal material, but many important rules can be learned from the holy golden tongue of this luminary of Israel, and they are directly applicable to the case at hand.

194. *See supra* pp. 824–826.

195. *See* A. v. B., 10 *P.D.R.* 168, 180 (1975) (Avraham Shapira, *Dayyan*):

> There are two bases for the authority of the Rabbinical Court of Appeals to set aside a decision of a district rabbinical court. The first is that the parties conduct their case pursuant to the procedural enactments [of the Chief Rabbinate], which provide that the Rabbinical Court of Appeals shall reexamine the matter and determine whether the [district rabbinical court's] decision is erroneous. Thus, the rule that "one court may not overturn the ruling of another court" does not apply; since the matter is considered anew, a new judgment is issued. The second is that since the evident pur-

As stated, there have in fact been a few instances in which a district rabbinical court completely refused to recognize the superior authority of the Rabbinical Court of Appeals. Two such cases came before the Supreme Court. The Supreme Court's opinions in those cases indicate its position with regard to the arguments made in the minority opinion above quoted. It is interesting to note that it was the judges of the Supreme Court of the general court system who came to the aid and upheld the honor and authority of the Rabbinical Court of Appeals.

In the first case,[196] the Rabbinical Court of Appeals directed the District Rabbinical Court of Jerusalem to transfer the case to the District Rabbinical Court of Tel Aviv. When the Jerusalem Rabbinical Court refused to comply, it was ordered to do so by the Supreme Court. The opinion by Justice Sussman begins: "This is an extraordinary and distressing dispute that has arisen between two levels of the rabbinical judicial tribunals."[197] The opinion concludes:[198]

> It goes without saying that in the existing judicial hierarchy a tribunal of first instance must obey the instructions of the appellate level. The dispute in which the first respondent [*i.e.*, the lower court] has engaged with the appellate court is an unbecoming spectacle, and it is inappropriate that this matter should require resort to this [Supreme] Court to compel the first respondent to follow the directives of the tribunal with appellate jurisdiction over it.[199]

---

pose of these enactments is to provide for the right of appeal, it follows that the [district] *rabbinical court* has understood that its decisions are conditional upon not being overturned by the Rabbinical Court of Appeals" (emphasis in original).

This statement by Rabbi Avraham Shapira himself implies that the Rabbinical Court of Appeals is authorized to reverse a decision of the district rabbinical court not only as it affects the litigants, but also insofar as it concerns the lower court judges whose decision was "conditional upon not being overturned by the Rabbinical Court of Appeals." However, while this statement provides support for the existence of power in the Rabbinical Court of Appeals to vacate or modify judgments of the district rabbinical courts, it does not obligate the district court judge who rendered the judgment to take action to implement the decision of the Rabbinical Court of Appeals. This is the only interpretation of Rabbi Shapira's opinion in this case that is consistent with the minority opinion in Case No. 520/1966, discussed *supra* pp. 1810–1814.

196. Kalir v. District Rabbinical Court, Jerusalem, 26(i) *P.D.* 757 (1972).

197. *Id.* at 758.

198. *Id.* at 759–760.

199. At the request of the petitioner, the Supreme Court ordered the judges who sat on the panel of the District Rabbinical Court of Jerusalem ("the Honorable *Dayyanim* Rabbi Avraham Kahana Shapira, Rabbi Aharon Katz, and Rabbi David Etaiya") to pay the petitioner's costs.

The second case[200] concerns a judgment handed down by the District Rabbinical Court of Jerusalem that determined that a certain woman was to be considered a *moredet* ("rebellious wife"). The Rabbinical Court of Appeals reversed the lower court's decision, and ruled that "we do not find that the woman should be adjudicated a *moredet.*"[201] The district rabbinical court rejected the ruling of the Rabbinical Court of Appeals, stating:[202]

> Since the Rabbinical Court of Appeals completely failed to understand the case . . . this court reaffirms its decision . . . that this woman is to be considered a *moredet.*

The Supreme Court, in an opinion by President Landau, stated:[203]

> Not only was the judgment of the court of first instance completely contrary to the ruling of the court above it, but the head of the [lower] court even permitted himself to announce that the appellate court "completely failed to understand the case." It should be added that none of the parties asked the district rabbinical court to reconsider the question of whether the appellant was a *moredet* after the Rabbinical Court of Appeals handed down its ruling. Rather, the district rabbinical court did so on its own initiative when both parties came to it with a joint request to remove a lien to permit the implementation of their agreement to divide their property. Furthermore, it is undisputed that between the time of the ruling of the Rabbinical Court of Appeals and the [second] judgment of the district rabbinical court . . . there was no change in circumstance relevant to the question whether the appellant is a *moredet.*

The Supreme Court vacated the "rebellious judgment" (as it was called in the Supreme Court's decision) of the district rabbinical court on the strength of the Rabbinical Court of Appeals' reversal of the previous judgment to the same effect. President Landau's comments in this regard are instructive:[204]

> The establishment of the Rabbinical Court of Appeals created a hierarchical structure in the rabbinical court system, and it follows that a lower court may not disobey an appellate court in the very case in which the appellate court has handed down its ruling. The same result clearly follows from Enactment #138 of the Procedural Enactments of the Rabbinical Courts. . . . In his book [*Ha-Mishpat ha-Ivri,* the Hebrew edition of the present work], . . . the learned

200. Fried v. Fried, 36(ii) *P.D.* 695 (1982).
201. *Id.* at 696.
202. *Id.* at 696–697.
203. *Id.* at 697.
204. *Id.* at 698–699.

> author describes the controversies that preceded the establishment of the Rabbinical Court of Appeals at the time of the British Mandate, and he notes on page 668[205] that despite the views of its opponents, "an appellate court was established, and thus an important new legal institution was purposefully introduced into Jewish law." He then quotes from a decision of the Rabbinical Court of Appeals (*B. v. A.* [1944], Warhaftig, *Osef Piskei ha-Din,* p. 71): "The matter of an appeal has been accepted as an enactment of the halakhic authorities that has the status of a law of our Holy Torah, and whoever appears as a party in a case does so on that basis."
>
> What is stated there [in *B. v. A., supra*] with respect to the parties [to that case], who litigated before a rabbinical court sitting as an arbitration tribunal, applies also—and perhaps even *a fortiori*—to a judge who sits on a lower court in the rabbinical court system. By his appointment to a state judicial tribunal subject to appellate supervision, he accepts the obligation to submit to the decisions of the appellate court, and it is on this basis that he is appointed. There is here no violation of the judge's conscience. He is not compelled to reach a decision contrary to his own view of the law, for once the appellate court has spoken, the authority of the lower court to make a decision has automatically terminated.

It is instructive to note the conceptual difference between Justice Landau's opinion and the minority opinion of the district rabbinical court, quoted earlier. The minority opinion distinguishes between the *parties,* who can undertake to obey the decision of the Rabbinical Court of Appeals, and the *judges,* who in principle cannot consent to decide a case contrary to their own understanding and conscience. Justice Landau's reasoning, however, is directly to the contrary: If the parties can undertake to obey the decision of an appellate court, it follows *a fortiori* that the judges must submit to the appellate decision, for the judge, "[b]y his appointment to a state judicial tribunal subject to appellate supervision, . . . accepts the obligation to submit to the decisions of the appellate court, and it is on this basis that he is appointed."

From the perspective of Jewish law, which encourages multiplicity of views and allows for wide freedom of decision as long as the decision is within the framework of the *Halakhah* and the decisionmaker accepts the *Halakhah* as binding, the minority decision is correct. However, the purpose of the enactment providing for an appellate tribunal was to limit this freedom of decision by conferring on the Rabbinical Court of Appeals a supervisory function that includes the power to require the lower court to take action to carry out the ruling of the appellate court even if this ruling is

205. *Supra* p. 825 in the present work.

contrary to the lower court's judgment. From this point of view, the decision and the reasoning of Justice Landau are correct.[206]

VII. CIVIL LAW IN THE RABBINICAL COURTS

It is interesting to note that the rabbinical courts have rendered a steadily increasing number of decisions covering a wide range of various areas of civil law in cases brought before them as arbitration tribunals.[207] Some illustrations of their creativity in the field of civil law have been noted in our discussion of the decisions of the rabbinical courts during the British Mandatory period,[208] and there has been a considerable expansion in this regard since the State of Israel was established. Of the fourteen volumes of rabbin-

206. With regard to the relationship between the district rabbinical courts and the Rabbinical Court of Appeals, *see* Z. Warhaftig, "Al ha-Takdim ba-Mishpat ha-Ivri" [On Precedent in Jewish Law], *Shenaton,* VI–VII (1979–1980), pp. 105, 131, arguing that a rabbinical court judge cannot be compelled by an appellate mandate to rule contrary to his conscience. Justice Landau in the *Fried* case, *supra* n. 200 at 698, rejected Warhaftig's approach, and rightly so, since Warhaftig's position is not consonant with the nature and purpose of an appellate tribunal and represents a regression from the original purpose for which appellate review was established in the rabbinical court system. The following opinion of Ovadiah Hadayah, who served as a member of the Rabbinical Court of Appeals in the early years of the State of Israel, in his book *Resp. Yaskil Avdi,* VI, EH #25, is instructive. That opinion, too, deals with the refusal of a district rabbinical court to obey an order of the Rabbinical Court of Appeals to transfer a case to another district rabbinical court. The opinion states:

> The Rabbinical Court of Appeals found no merit in the position of the first rabbinical court, and ruled differently. The first rabbinical court is required to conform to the ruling of the Rabbinical Court of Appeals, according to the secular law and according to the ruling of the *Shulḥan Arukh* [ḤM 14:1]. . . . Since the first rabbinical court did not obey the ruling of the Rabbinical Court of Appeals, it becomes the obligation of the Rabbinical Court of Appeals to vindicate its honor and to make every effort to implement its ruling under all circumstances. . . . It is therefore obligated to defend its honor, which is the honor of the entire Jewish people, so that this not become an obstacle and stumbling block in the future. . . . Since this relates to the defense of the honor of the Rabbinical Court of Appeals, this tribunal of the highest instance must defend its honor at any cost, and no one has the power to interfere with its efforts to do so.

207. The Arbitration Law, 1968, was enacted to replace the British Mandatory Arbitration Ordinance. Under the Mandatory Ordinance, as well as under Israeli law, a judgment issued by a rabbinical court sitting as an arbitration tribunal can be enforced only by the general courts. This requirement greatly reduces the likelihood that monetary disputes will be submitted to the rabbinical courts. For many years, bills have been introduced in the Knesset to confer jurisdiction in civil cases on the rabbinical courts when all parties consent. This would be similar to the concurrent jurisdiction of the rabbinical courts in certain matters involving personal status (for example, under the Succession Law, 1965). Such bills have not been enacted, and as a result, an important opportunity for employing Jewish law to solve actual problems arising in daily life has been unjustifiedly rendered unavailable.

208. *See supra* pp. 1600–1605.

ical court decisions that have been published up to 1992, approximately thirty percent of the decisions do not deal with matters of personal status, but rather with such matters as labor law, contracts, copyright, suretyship, bailments, partnerships, pledges, acquisitions, commercial transactions, and administrative law.

It is instructive to see how the concrete problems in these many diverse areas are solved under Jewish law. The rabbinical court judges sometimes employ a policy-oriented interpretation of the law, and also rely on custom and on the doctrine that "the law of the land is law" (*dina de-malkhuta dina*).[209] Although these decisions by the rabbinical courts are not part of the positive law of the State of Israel, they show how Jewish law deals with contemporary practical problems and how Jewish law can be applied to solve the problems that arise out of present-day economic and social life.[210]

VIII. THE RABBINICAL COURTS AND THE GENERAL LEGAL SYSTEM OF THE STATE

As has been noted, some Knesset statutes are addressed to the rabbinical courts and explicitly make their provisions applicable in those courts. Such statutes, however, are rare; ordinarily, the rabbinical courts apply only Jewish law. This situation gives rise to the question: What is the attitude of the rabbinical courts to the statutes of the general legal system that do not explicitly make their provisions applicable to the rabbinical courts? For example, in a case tried in a rabbinical court, an issue arises as to the validity of a contract entered into by the parties: If the contract is valid under the laws of the State but invalid under Jewish law, will the rabbinical court treat the contract as valid for purposes of the case before it, or will it rule the contract to be invalid pursuant to the provisions of Jewish law? This type of question can arise in the rabbinical courts in various ways; and it is important to analyze the approach of the rabbinical courts to this issue both

209. *See* the further discussion regarding the relationship between the rabbinical courts and the general legal system of the State, *infra* pp. 1800–1826.

210. *See* S. Shilo, "Dinei Mamonot be-Vattei Din ha-Rabbaniyyim" [Monetary Matters in the Rabbinical Courts], *Ha-Praklit,* XXVI (1970), pp. 524–542, XXVII (1971), pp. 254–260; *id.*, "Hassagot al Pesikat Battei Din Rabbaniyyim be-Inyan Hassagat Gevul Mis-ḥarit" [Critique of the Decisions of the Rabbinical Courts on Unfair Business Competition], *Mishpatim,* VI (1976), p. 530; A.H. Shaki, "Kavvei Yiḥud be-Sidrei Din ha-Rabbaniyyim" [Distinctive Characteristics of Rabbinical Court Proceedings], *Sefer Sanhedrai,* 1972, pp. 275–302; Elon, *Samkhut ve-Oẓmah,* pp. 28–31. It should be noted that, with rare exceptions, the reporting and arrangement of these decisions is very unsatisfactory, and their indexing does not attain even a minimal level of usefulness. As a result, the decisions are unfamiliar and often overlooked.

from the point of view of the general legal system and, most significantly, from the perspective of Jewish law itself.

A. The *Wiloszni* Case

The relation of the rabbinical courts to the general legal system of the State was dealt with at length by the Supreme Court in the *Wiloszni* case, previously discussed.[211] In connection with the divorce proceedings in that case, an issue arose as to the valuation of the couple's apartment. At the time of the proceedings, the apartment was occupied solely by the husband; the wife had left it because of the husband's violent behavior. The rabbinical court held that the value of the apartment should be divided equally between the parties and that the apartment should be considered vacant. The husband argued that under the Tenants Protection Law as interpreted by the Supreme Court, the apartment should be treated as occupied by the husband alone,[212] and its value in that situation—which was significantly less than the value of a vacant apartment or an apartment occupied by the couple—should be the sum to be divided between them. On the other hand, the wife argued that since she had been compelled to leave the apartment because of the husband's violence, the apartment should be treated as if it were still occupied jointly, and consequently should have the same valuation as a vacant apartment.

The Rabbinical Court of Appeals accepted the wife's argument on the basis of Jewish law. As we have seen, it acted properly in so doing, since the Legislature did not obligate the rabbinical courts to apply the Tenants Protection Law. However, in its decision, the rabbinical court added that "this matter [*i.e.*, its decision] does not contravene the Tenants Protection Law, which is given halakhic validity like any *sitomta* [*i.e.*, customary practice] or communal enactment; TB Bava Batra 9a."[213]

These remarks of the Rabbinical Court of Appeals induced the Supreme Court to discuss at length the question of the relation of Jewish law to the Israeli legal system, and it is worthwhile to take note of this discus-

211. Wiloszni v. Rabbinical Court of Appeals, 36(ii) *P.D.* 733 (1982); *see supra* pp. 1758–1759 .

212. 36(ii) *P.D.* at 735–738. The Supreme Court held that the result reached by the rabbinical court on this issue was the same as would be reached under the Tenants Protection Law. The decision of the Supreme Court on this point differed from the law as theretofore generally understood. The *Wiloszni* case formed the basis for a later decision of the Supreme Court, Anonymous v. Anonymous, 37(iv) *P.D.* 626 (1983).

213. 36(ii) *P.D.* at 737. The decision of the Rabbinical Court of Appeals was rendered by *Dayyanim* M. Eliahu, S. Mizraḥi, and J. Kafaḥ. The Hebrew translated as "communal enactment" is *lehassi'a al kiẓatan*. For a discussion of the meaning of this phrase, *see supra* p. 679 nn. 3–4.

sion of one of the central problems involved in the overall relationship between Jewish law and the law of the State. We can do no better than to quote the Supreme Court:[214]

> In this connection, it is appropriate to refer to an interesting, important, and relevant point made in the above-mentioned decision of the Rabbinical Court of Appeals. In part, it can be discerned in [other] decisions of the rabbinical courts; but in some respects this case involves a novel twist. It appears from the decision of the Rabbinical Court of Appeals that the parties presented this case on the assumption that the Tenants Protection Law (Consolidated Version) was applicable, and the court discussed the provisions of that statute in its decision and stated that its conclusion that the apartment should be considered vacant "does not contravene the Tenants Protection Law, *which is given halakhic validity like any* sitomta [*i.e.*, customary practice] *or communal enactment;* TB Bava Batra 9a" (emphasis added [by the Supreme Court]).
>
> The question of the relationship between Jewish law and another legal system within which it operates is an old one, and this is not the place to discuss it in detail.[215] However, it is appropriate to make a few extremely brief remarks to shed some light on the subject of the relationship of the decisions of the rabbinical courts to the general legal system, to which the Rabbinical Court of Appeals looked in its decision in the case before us.
>
> The well-known principle governing this broad subject is the doctrine of *dina de-malkhuta dina* ("the law of the land is law"), which was crystallized and so denominated by the *amora* Samuel in the third century C.E. during the Babylonian exile.[216] Divergent views have been expressed with regard to the applicability and scope of this doctrine, from the time of its origin to our own day, all of which need not be discussed here.[217] From time to time, the rabbinical courts have made use of the doctrine of *dina de-malkhuta dina* in their decisions in order to validate various legal transactions that are invalid under Jewish law.[218] Sometimes, they invalidated even a transaction that fulfilled the requirements of Jewish law but did not fulfill the requirements of the general law.[219] When the doctrine of *dina de-malkhuta dina* is applied, a rule

214. 36(ii) *P.D.* at 740–743.

215. *See supra* pp. 62–74.

216. *See* TB Nedarim 28a; Gittin 10b; Bava Kamma 113a/b; Bava Batra 54b–55a.

217. *See supra* pp. 64–74; S. Shilo, *Dina de-Malkhuta Dina*, Jerusalem, 1975.

218. *See, e.g.*, A. v. B., 5 *P.D.R.* 258, 264, 267–270 (1965) (with regard to a bank guaranty defective by reason of *asmakhta*—*cf. supra* p. 1604 n. 76); A. v. B., 10 *P.D.R.* 273, 288–289 (1975) (with regard to "legal personality," a concept of doubtful status in historical Jewish law); A. v. B., 6 *P.D.R.* 376, 380–382 (1967) (with regard to the registration of real property in the land registry).

219. *See, e.g.*, A. Building Co. v. Administration of Yeshiva C., 6 *P.D.R.* 249, 252 (1966) (with regard to the requirement of registration of real property in the land registry even though under Jewish law the agreement of the parties suffices to render the transfer effective).

of the general legal system is given binding effect but does not become a part of the Jewish legal system.

Sometimes, Jewish law not only recognizes the binding effect of a rule of another legal system but even incorporates that rule into the Jewish legal system itself. The legal source by means of which this is accomplished is custom. When the people conduct their activities according to a particular legal norm, this norm is recognized, under certain circumstances, as a part of Jewish law; and the norm is sometimes effective even if contrary to a specific rule of Jewish civil law. Just as two individuals may agree in a civil law matter to contract out of a law contained in the Torah, so, *a fortiori,* the public may stipulate by means of a custom to opt out of an existing halakhic rule in a matter of civil law.[220] This principle is expressed in the formulation "custom overrides the law,"[221] and I have already extensively dealt with this in connection with the incorporation of the law concerning joint ownership of property.[222]

Custom as a legal source[223] in Jewish law is known by the technical term *sitomta* (meaning "seal"), from the case discussed in the Talmud concerning the customary practice of purchasing wine by affixing a seal on the barrel; it was in connection with that practice that the principle of the creative power and binding force of custom was developed and elaborated.[224] Custom was the means by which various areas of Jewish law, and particularly the law of acquisitions and obligations, were extensively developed.[225] The rabbinical courts make broad use of custom, generally referred to as "the law of *sitomta,*" as a means for incorporating legal principles and rules from the general legal system into Jewish law.[226]

Besides judicial creativity, Jewish law has an additional and special method of developing the law: legislation directly enacted either by a Jewish

220. *See, e.g., Resp. Maharashdam,* ḤM #380.

221. TJ Bava Meẓi'a 7:1, 27b (7:1, 11b).

222. *See* Azugi v. Azugi, 33(iii) *P.D.* 1, 15–17 (1979); *supra* pp. 903–909.

223. As to the meaning of "legal source," *see supra* pp. 228–230.

224. *See* TB Bava Meẓi'a 74a.

225. *See* Rashba, Novellae to Bava Meẓi'a 74a (Devoritz ed.), s.v. Meshallem leih; Sh. Ar. ḤM 201:1–2. *See also supra* pp. 880–885, 913–920.

226. *See, e.g.,* Kraka Co., Ltd. v. Rothenburg and Partners, 4 *P.D.R.* 75, 81 (1961), (requirement of registration of real property in the land registry); A. v. B., 6 *P.D.R.* 376, 382–383 (1967) (same); A. v. B., 5 *P.D.R.* 258, 264–270 (1965) (validity of a bank guaranty); A. v. B., 10 *P.D.R.* 273, 288–289 (1975) (acceptance of the concept of "legal personality"); A. v. B., 7 *P.D.R.* 332, 336 (1969) (assignment of promissory notes); A. v. B., 4 *P.D.R.* 289 (1966) (method of obligating oneself to support a person whom one is not obligated to support under the law); Histadrut Po'alei Agudat Yisrael, Reḥovot Branch v. Histadrut Agudat Yisra'el, Reḥovot Branch, 6 *P.D.R.* 202, 203, 216 (1966) (signing of a contract between buyer and seller for both real and personal property); A. v. B., 4 *P.D.R.* 346, 349 (1962) (same); Nast v. Management Committee of Bet ha-Midrash ha-Merkazi, Haifa, 1 *P.D.R.* 330, 333 (1955) (obligation for severance pay); Kaiserman v. Direnfeld, 3 *P.D.R.* 272, 286–287 (1959) (same).

community having a minimal level of internal autonomy or by the representatives of such a community.[227] The first instances of such legislation are recorded in the *Tosefta*[228] and in the Talmud[229] in various commercial and social contexts: "The townspeople may fix [by means of legislation] market prices [of wheat and wine], weights and measures, and laborers' wages, and they may enforce their regulations." . . .

Over the course of time—and especially from the tenth century on, with the rise in power of local communities in the various diasporas—the scope of public legislative activity broadened to include different areas of civil, criminal, and public law. From then on, such legislation became known as communal enactments (*takkanot ha-kahal*). During the long history of Jewish law, various rules and limitations were established regarding such matters as the method of adopting such enactments, their subject matter,[230] and how to interpret them. This legislation became an integral part of, and greatly enriched, the Jewish legal system.[231]

Grounding the relationship between Jewish law and the general legal system of the State of Israel on the principle of the halakhic efficacy of public legislation has crucial significance. Under this principle, various rules of civil, criminal, and public law contained in the general law may be considered part and parcel of the Jewish legal system, because they came into being within the framework of that system in the broad sense of the term; they are not merely *recognized* by that system, like rules under the doctrine of *dina de-malkhuta dina*, or absorbed by it, like rules for which the source is custom.

As stated above, the rabbinical courts often utilize the doctrine of *dina de-malkhuta dina* or the law of *sitomta* (*i.e.*, custom) to give effect to or absorb a rule of the general legal system. The judgment before us is one of the few, and perhaps the only one (further research is required to determine which is the case), in which the provisions of the Tenants Protection Law are recognized as a part of the governing law in the rabbinical court, not only by virtue of the force of custom (*sitomta*), but also on the basis of the principle of the halakhic efficacy of communal legislation. The use of this principle by the Rabbinical Court of Appeals is, as stated, of great and far-reaching significance. It would seem that, by so doing, three distinguished judges of the Rabbinical Court of Appeals are continuing in the path of their predecessor

227. In the Talmud and in post-Talmudic literature, these representatives are often called *shiv'ah tovei ha-ir* (lit. "the seven good citizens of the town"). Other titles were used in various places in the diaspora, especially in the post-Talmudic period. *See supra* pp. 727–730.

228. *Tosefta* Bava Meẓi'a 11:23.

229. TB Bava Batra 8b–9a. The quotation in the text is from the *Tosefta, supra* n. 228. The Talmud is to the same effect with a slight difference in language. *See supra* p. 679 n. 3.

230. Thus, for example, such legislation was not enacted in the area of religious law (*issur ve-hetter*).

231. With regard to this creative method and its integration into the Jewish legal system, *see supra* pp. 678ff.

Ovadiah Hadayah, the distinguished *dayyan* of the Rabbinical Court of Appeals, who, in a detailed responsum,[232] dealt with the Tenants Protection Law from the perspective of Jewish law:

> We are not dealing here with foreign laws, but rather with laws that the government, like every other government, enacts for the welfare of the inhabitants of the State. The extensive discussion in Tractate *Bava Batra* 8b establishes that the townspeople may impose penalties for the violation of enactments they have adopted. . . . The purpose is to promote the public welfare; and to that end, the majority of the community or its leaders may certainly enact legislation and enforce it against the dissenting minority. . . .
>
> It is clear that the members of the Knesset in the State of Israel, chosen by all [the citizens of] the country, are no less empowered than the communal leaders to enact important legislation—even when it results in profit for some and loss for others—in order to promote the public welfare. The law regarding apartments certainly does not fall short in meeting the standard of promotion of the public welfare. It protects the people who suffer from a shortage of apartments, particularly during this period of increased immigration, when almost everyone suffers from a shortage of apartments. If such legislation were not enacted for the benefit of society, many persons would have to remain in the street because of the shortage of apartments and the high rentals. Not everyone can afford to rent an apartment for an extremely high rental. It was therefore found necessary to enact such legislation for the general welfare.

B. The *Nagar* Case

The question of the relation of the rabbinical courts to the general legal system of the State was also discussed in *Nagar v. Nagar,*[233] by Rabbi Yosef Kafaḥ, one of the three judges of the Rabbinical Court of Appeals who decided the *Wiloszni* case. His opinion in the *Nagar* case has been discussed above.[234] In this opinion, Rabbi Kafaḥ dealt with the important question of the significance and binding force, from the point of view of Jewish law, of a statute of the Knesset explicitly addressed to the rabbinical courts, such as the Woman's Equal Rights Law. According to Rabbi Kafaḥ, such a statute does not conflict with the *Halakhah,* since it concerns a monetary matter, as to which one may contract out of a law of the Torah. A statute of the Knesset is viewed as if all the people, through their representatives, agreed to follow a particular law on a given subject; under Jewish law, not only is

232. *Resp. Yaskil Avdi,* VI, ḤM #8. The responsum was issued in 1954.
233. 38(i) *P.D.* 365 (1984).
234. *See supra* pp. 1761–1765.

it permissible for the parties to apply such a law, but the law is binding on them.

The reasoning of Rabbi Kafaḥ is applicable *a fortiori* to other statutes enacted by the State which are not directly contrary to the provisions of Jewish law. These laws are certainly recognized by the *Halakhah* and are halakhically binding on the basis of the principle of Jewish law permitting freedom of contract in monetary matters. This reasoning is essentially similar to the reasoning in the *Wiloszni* case that the laws of the State are binding as customary law, for the principle that "custom overrides the law" is also based on the concept of freedom of contract in monetary matters.[235] However, from the point of view of the nature of the relationship of Jewish law to the general legal system, the straightforward rationale of freedom of contract provides a more direct basis for the efficacy, under Jewish law, of the statutes enacted by the Knesset. Under the rationale that one may contract out of a law of the Torah in a monetary matter, the statutes of the Knesset become an integral part of the Jewish legal system to a greater extent than under a theory of *dina de-malkhuta dina* or of the force of custom. Their status is the same as that of agreements between individuals to contract out of a law of the Torah; they are entered into according to the rules of the Jewish legal system and are integral to the system.

It is submitted that the different rationales found in the decisions of the rabbinical courts for the acknowledgement of Knesset legislation as a valid source of law from the perspective of the Jewish legal system have a significance beyond the question of statutory interpretation and efficacy. The different rationales also involve different conceptual frameworks for establishing a relationship between Jewish law as it has historically existed, and the legal system of a Jewish state whose laws, and the interpretation of those laws, are not the result of the traditionally accepted creative methods of the Jewish legal system. From the perspective of Jewish law, they were not derived from within the existing system but rather constitute an entirely new creation. This is a new phenomenon in Jewish history. Jewish law was always accustomed to mark out its relationship to other legal systems created by other nations, but it has never before faced the need to establish its relationship to another legal system created by its own people when the legislative and judicial institutions of that system do not recognize the *Halakhah* as binding.

To ground the halakhic validity of the laws of the Jewish state on *dina de-malkhuta dina,* or even on custom, is to view the legal system of the Jewish state as having no internal-creative link to Jewish law. On the other hand, to ground the halakhic validity of the laws of the Jewish state on the

235. *See* the discussion of the *Wiloszni* case, *supra* p. 1822.

authority of communal enactments is to consider the legal system of the Jewish state as a Jewish creation brought into being by means of one of the traditional methods historically accepted in the Jewish legal system.[236] As stated above, this latter approach is almost never taken in the decisions of the rabbinical courts, and has not been found in any rabbinical court decision other than the *Wiloszni* case.[237] This situation deserves serious consideration from the perspective of the rabbinical courts and especially from the perspective of the legal system of the State. We return to this subject later.[238]

236. The same can be said, to a certain extent, with regard to the additional reason given by Rabbi Kafaḥ in support of the validity of laws of the State even if they conflict with rules of Jewish law, namely, that in monetary matters one may contract out of a Biblical norm; *see supra* pp. 1824–1825.

237. *But cf.* the "freedom of contract" reasoning in the opinion of Rabbi Kafaḥ in the *Nagar* case. *See* the discussion *supra.*

238. *See infra* pp. 1906–1923, 1940–1946.

Chapter 44
THE FOUNDATIONS OF LAW ACT, 1980

I. The Purpose and Meaning of the Foundations of Law Act
  A. Repeal of Article 46 of the Palestine Order in Council
  B. The Principles of the Jewish Heritage as a Part of the Positive Law of the Israeli Legal System
  C. According Full Operative Force to the Fundamental Principles of the Israeli Declaration of Independence
  D. Legislation, Judicial Precedent, Analogy
  E. "A Legal Issue Requiring Decision"; Lacuna
  F. The Principles of Freedom, Justice, Equity, and Peace of the Jewish Heritage
  G. The Principles of the Jewish Heritage in the Decisions of the Courts
    1. The Fundamental Rights of Detainees and Prisoners
    2. Freedom from Detention
    3. Freedom of Thought and Speech
    4. Human Dignity and Equality
    5. Attitude toward National and Religious Minorities
    6. The Right of Privacy
    7. Other Court Decisions Discussing the Principles of the Jewish Heritage
    8. How the Sources of the Jewish Heritage Are to Be Used
II. The Interpretive Function of Jewish Law in the Israeli Legal System in Light of the Foundations of Law Act
  A. Uncertainty as to the Meaning of a Statute—The *Hendeles* Case, Additional Hearing
  B. The Interpretation of Value-Laden Legal Terms
  C. Terms and Expressions Unique to Jewish Law
  D. An Institution of Jewish Law Incorporated into Israeli Law—The *Koenig* Case, Additional Hearing
III. The Foundations of Law Act, 1980, and the Incorporation of the English Statute of Elizabeth, 1571
IV. Conclusion

I. THE PURPOSE AND MEANING OF THE FOUNDATIONS OF LAW ACT

In the foregoing discussion of Knesset legislation,[1] it was noted that the second legislative period—the period of civil codification—reached its cul-

1. *Supra* pp. 1624–1729.

mination with the enactment of the Foundations of Law Act, 1980.[2] The overwhelming majority of statutes relating to acquisitions and obligations were enacted prior to 1980, and thus the Foundations of Law Act, 1980, was the final step in the monumental effort to codify the civil law. The Foundations of Law Act was also the culmination in another and more fundamental sense: it established the independence of Israeli law from foreign legal systems.

The Foundations of Law Act had a twofold thrust: (1) it severed the Israeli legal system from the binding force of English common law and equity, and (2) it created a binding link with Jewish law, to which it gave official status as a complementary legal source, making Jewish law a part of Israeli positive law. The Foundations of Law Act thus constitutes, as the Supreme Court has put it, "one of the basic statutes establishing the foundation of the State of Israel."[3] By adopting it, the Knesset sought to enact "a fundamental law, whose place is at the eastern wall of the legal system of the State."[4] The following discussion examines how and to what extent this legislation severs the Israeli legal system from English law and links Israeli law to Jewish law, and to what degree the legislation has been implemented by the courts.

The Foundations of Law Act consists of two sections:

> 1. **Complementary Legal Sources.** Where a court finds that a legal issue requiring decision cannot be resolved by reference to legislation or judicial precedent, or by means of analogy, it shall reach its decision in the light of the principles of freedom, justice, equity, and peace of the Jewish heritage (*moreshet Yisra'el*).
>
> 2. **Repeal of Article 46 of the Palestine Order in Council, and Saving Clause.**
>
> a. Article 46 of the Palestine Order in Council, 1922–1947, is repealed.
>
> b. The provision of subsection (a) shall not impair the effectiveness of the law that was accepted in this country before the effective date of this statute.

A. Repeal of Article 46 of the Palestine Order in Council

The second section of the law, which repeals Article 46 of the Palestine Order in Council,[5] was designed to complete the severance of the Israeli

2. *See supra* p. 1624.

3. Naiman v. Chairman, Central Elections Committee, 39(ii) *P.D.* 225, 293 (1985).

4. Koenig v. Cohen, 36(iii) *P.D.* 701, 742 (1982); *see* the discussion of the *Naiman* and *Koenig* cases, *infra* pp. 1846–1856, 1875–1884. A seat at the eastern wall of the synagogue is a special honor and privilege for the congregant who possesses it.

5. With regard to Article 46, *see supra* pp. 1611–1612.

legal system from dependence on English law. The process of severance had begun in the 1950s in a decision by the Supreme Court,[6] and in a number of statutes which specifically provided that Article 46 did not apply to them.[7] With the passage of the Foundations of Law Act, the process was complete with respect to the entire Israeli legal system.

However, the repeal of Article 46 did not affect those provisions of Ottoman law that were in force when the State was established and that continued to be binding (by virtue of Section 11 of the Law and Administration Ordinance, 1948) to the extent that they had not been repealed by statutes enacted during the period of civil codification.[8] Several hundred sections of the *Mejelle* had not been explicitly repealed at this time, although they were not applied in practice.[9] These laws were at last formally excised from the Israeli statute books in June 1984 by the Repeal of *Mejelle* Law, 1984, the first section of which reads: "The *Mejelle* is repealed." (This section, consisting of only two words in Hebrew, is probably the briefest in Israeli legislation.) Section 2 of the Foundations of Law Act thus repealed the provision that created the link with English law, and Section 1 of the Repeal of *Mejelle* Law formalized the severance of Israeli law from Ottoman law.[10]

Section 2(b) of the Foundations of Law Act provides that the repeal of Article 46 does not "impair the effectiveness of the law that was accepted in this country" prior to the repeal of Article 46. This saving clause refers to those rules of English common law and equity that were actually incorporated into Israeli law through decisions of the Supreme Court prior to the effective date of the Foundations of Law Act. The Explanatory Note to this section[11] states that "the repeal of Article 46 shall not impair the effectiveness of any laws that have been derived from English law and have in the interim become incorporated into Israeli law [lit. "have become naturalized as Israeli laws"]."

Some legal commentators have suggested that Section 2(b) includes within its scope even those rules of English law that were not actually incorporated into Israeli law through the decisions of the Israeli Supreme Court, so long as they were appropriate for such incorporation prior to the

6. Kokhavi v. Becker, 11 *P.D.* 225 (1957).

7. *See supra* pp. 1672, 1728–1729.

8. *See* Explanatory Notes to Section 1 of Bill No. 1361, July 14, 1978.

9. *See* Repeal of *Mejelle* Bill, May 14, 1984 (Bill No. 1681).

10. Section 2 of the Repeal of *Mejelle* Law saves those provisions of the *Mejelle* that are specifically preserved by other statutes, and also makes clear that the repeal does not curtail the effectiveness of the *Shari'a* (Moslem religious law). Another statute which repeals Ottoman laws and British ordinances is the Obsolete Legislation (Repeal) Law, 1984.

11. Explanatory Notes to Bill No. 1361, *supra* n. 8.

effective date of the Foundations of Law Act.[12] This interpretation, however, cannot withstand critical analysis; it contravenes the plain meaning of Section 2(b). Moreover, this interpretation would drain virtually all meaning from the repeal of Article 46—and, indeed, from the entire Foundations of Law Act—since it would mean that Section 1 would apply only to a lacuna created after the repeal of Article 46, *i.e.*, as a result of legislation enacted after the Foundations of Law Act, 1980, became effective. This interpretation would also be in conflict with the provision of Section 1 that the lack of "judicial precedent" is one of the conditions for turning to the Jewish heritage as the complementary legal source.[13] The meaning of Section 2(b) will be discussed in greater detail later in this chapter.[14]

In an instructive decision, Yitzhak Kahan, the late President of the Supreme Court, expressed the view that, after the repeal of Article 46, it would be appropriate, in some circumstances, to establish new rules and even to change those rules which had actually been incorporated from English law. He stated:[15]

> The matter before us exemplifies the complications that confront us in deciding issues of administrative law. . . .
>
> This court's impressive development of the field of administrative law, which has become known as "Israeli common law," arose out of the need to fill the void resulting from the almost complete absence of legislation establishing norms binding on the government in conducting its many and varied activities. . . . In the natural course, and pursuant to Article 46 of the Palestine Order in Council, 1922, the court necessarily turned in this area to English common law and equity, from which it derived the basic rules for judicial supervision over public administrative activities. . . .

12. *See* D. Friedmann, *Dinei Asiyyat Osher ve-Lo ve-Mishpat* [The Law of Unjust Enrichment], 1982, p. 23 n. 52. *See also id.*, "Yesodot bve-Dinei Asiyyat Osher ve-Lo ve-Mishpat le-Or ha-Ḥakikah ha-Yisra'elit ha-Ḥadashah" [The Fundamentals of the Law of Unjust Enrichment in Light of Modern Israeli Legislation], *Iyyunei Mishpat,* VIII (1981), pp. 22, 34 n. 68; *id.*, "Od le-Farshanut ha-Ḥakikah ha-Yisra'elit ha-Ḥadashah" [More on the Interpretation of Modern Israeli Legislation], *Iyyunei Mishpat,* V (1976), p. 477; U. Procaccia, *Dinei Peshitat Regel ve-ha-Ḥakikah ha-Ezraḥit be-Yisra'el* [Bankruptcy Law and Civil Legislation in Israel], Jerusalem, 1984, pp. 17–18.

13. As to the meaning of the term "judicial precedent," *see* the discussion *infra.* pp. 1834–1835. *See also infra* pp. 1887–1888.

14. *Infra* pp. 1886–1887. This expansive interpretation of Section 2(b) is contrary to the view expressed in G. Tedeschi, "Bittul Siman 46 li-Devar ha-Melekh ve-Koaḥ Pe'ulato" [The Repeal of Article 46 of the Palestine Order in Council and Its Effect], *Mishpatim,* VIII (1977), pp. 180, 184; *id.*, "Heskemei ha-Minhal ha-Ẓibburi im ha-Perat" [Contracts of the Public Administration with Private Parties], *Mishpatim,* XII (1982), pp. 227, 237–239; and *id.*, "Sodot Iskiyyim" [Trade Secrets], *Ha-Praklit,* XXXV (1983), pp. 5, 10–11. My view accords with that of Prof. Tedeschi.

15. Shapira v. State of Israel, 36(i) *P.D.* 337, 357 (1981).

The problem is, however, that the adoption of the rules of English law has necessarily entangled us in the complications created by the decisions of the English courts. In this way, we have become involved in the intricate classification of defects in administrative action into defects that totally invalidate, defects that partially invalidate, and defects that do not invalidate but merely confer on the injured party the right to request the courts to set aside the administrative action. This system of classification has also greatly complicated the problem of the allocation of jurisdiction between the [Supreme Court sitting as the] High Court of Justice and the other general and religious courts.

At present, with the repeal of Article 46 of the Palestine Order in Council pursuant to Section 1 [the reference should be to Section 2] of the Foundations of Law Act, 1980, it seems to me that the time has come to consider making a fundamental change in the approach to judicial review of administrative action. If such a change is not forthcoming from the Legislature, it is appropriate for this court to attempt to establish new and clear rules that will untie the complicated knots that after many years we are now left to contend with in the area of administrative law.

B. The Principles of the Jewish Heritage as a Part of the Positive Law of the Israeli Legal System

The essence of the Foundations of Law Act—its "positive command"—is contained in Section 1. This section establishes "the principles of freedom, justice, equity, and peace of the Jewish heritage" as "complementary legal sources"[16] for the Israeli legal system (provided certain conditions exist, as will be discussed below) in lieu of Article 46, which is repealed by Section 2 of the Act. This represents the successful culmination of the untiring effort, which began even before the establishment of the State of Israel,[17] to accord the Jewish legal system, in one form or another, an official status in the legal system of the Jewish state.

Before this section was adopted, scholars and jurists expressed sharply conflicting views in articles and speeches;[18] and a series of proposed amendments to the bill, submitted by a number of Knesset members during its second and third reading, also reflected the same conflict. Some amendments would have expanded, and others would have curtailed, the obliga-

16. *See* the heading of Section 1.

17. *See supra* pp. 1612–1618.

18. *See, e.g.*, the excellent article by Dr. M. Cheshin, "Moreshet Yisra'el u-Mishpat ha-Medinah" [The Jewish Heritage and the Law of the State], in *Zekhuyyot Ezraḥ be-Yisra'el, Kovez̩ Ma'amarim li-Khevodo Shel Ḥayyim H. Cohn* [Civil Rights in Israel—Essays in Honor of Haim Cohn], Tel Aviv, 1982, pp. 47ff. This article is further discussed *infra* pp. 1921–1923.

tion to resort to Jewish law.[19] The Explanatory Notes to the bill commented as follows on the language that appears in the statute as enacted:

> This formulation was selected from among the different proposals so that the judge would be directed to look to the fundamental principles and ethical values of the Jewish heritage but would not be bound by all the provisions of Jewish law.

The Knesset thus placed on the judiciary the heavy and momentous responsibility of drawing upon the concepts and principles that have been the foundation of the Jewish legal system and of the Jewish cultural-spiritual worldview throughout Jewish history, up to and including the re-establishment of the Jewish state.

It is worthwhile, in view of the constitutional significance of the Foundations of Law Act, to take note of the changes made in the bill before it passed in its final form. In the bill as introduced, what is now Section 1 appeared as Section 2, and also as Section 33(a) of the Courts Law. The Explanatory Notes to the bill gave the following reason:

> The proposed provision is akin to the subject dealt with in Section 11 of the Law and Administration Ordinance; however, since it is essentially a general guideline for the courts rather than a substantive rule of law (such as the aforesaid Section 11), it is proposed to include it in the Courts Law, 1957, immediately after Section 33, which deals with judicial precedent.

The Knesset did not agree. It placed the section requiring resort to the principles of the Jewish heritage at the very beginning of the statute, where it stands as an independent substantive provision, a basic directive for the Israeli legal system, as indeed the very title of the statute emphasizes.

C. According Full Operative Force to the Fundamental Principles of the Israeli Declaration of Independence

The enactment of "the principles of freedom, justice, equity, and peace of the Jewish heritage" by the Foundations of Law Act as a part of the positive

19. *See* 89 *DK* 4099 (1980). Instead of the words "of the Jewish heritage (*moreshet Yisra'el*)," the following formulas were proposed by various members of the Knesset: M. Warshawsky—"and in the spirit of the [Israeli] Declaration of Independence"; S. Aloni—"in the spirit of the Declaration of Independence and Jewish law (*ha-mishpat ha-ivri*)"; T. Tuvi—"the universal heritage of all mankind"; M. Amar—"accepted in Israel." On the other hand, Z. Warhaftig, during the first reading of the bill, proposed to substitute "Jewish law (*mishpat ivri*)" for "the Jewish heritage" (88 *DK* 1821), MK Glass proposed "the principles of Jewish law" (*id.* at 1828), and M. Porush proposed a provision that would have made Jewish law the governing law (*id.* at 1836).

law of the State of Israel has important legal significance from another point of view. The Declaration of Independence of the State of Israel proclaims that the State "will be based on the principles of freedom, justice, and peace as illuminated by the visions of the prophets of Israel."

The Supreme Court early established that while the Declaration of Independence "expresses the vision and credo of the nation, it is not a constitution that sets forth positive law by which the validity of statutes or ordinances is to be measured."[20]

However, although the principles set forth in the Declaration of Independence have no direct legal effect, the court also stated:

> We are required to take account of its provisions when we interpret and give meaning to the laws of the State. . . . It is a well-known axiom that the law of a nation must be illuminated by the ordering of its national life.[21]

By taking account of the Declaration of Independence, the court introduced into the Israeli legal system "fundamental rights that are 'not set forth in writing' but rather flow directly from the character of our state as a democratic, freedom-loving state."[22]

With the enactment of the Foundations of Law Act, these fundamental rights became "set forth in writing." The Act, which forms a part of the statutory law of the State of Israel, now establishes that the principles of freedom, justice, equity, and peace of the Jewish heritage constitute part of the law of the Jewish state. As the court stated:[23]

> In 1980, the Knesset enacted the Foundations of Law Act, . . . which constitutes one of the basic laws establishing the foundation of the State of Israel. The fundamental principles referred to in the Declaration of Independence, "that the State of Israel will be based on the principles of freedom, justice, and peace as illuminated by the visions of the prophets of Israel," which had been only guidelines without the full force of positive law, have been transformed by the enactment of the Foundations of Law Act into fully operative principles of positive law. These "principles of freedom, justice, equity, and peace of the Jewish heritage" now serve as the basic principles—the foundation—of the entire legal system of the State.

20. Ẓevi Ziv v. Acting Commissioner of the Tel Aviv Municipal Area (Joshua Gobernik), 1 *P.D.* 85, 89 (1948).

21. Kol ha-Am v. Minister of the Interior, 7 *P.D.* 871, 884 (1953) (Agranat, President).

22. Ulpanei Hasratah v. Gerry, 16 *P.D.* 2407, 2415 (1962) (Landau, President). *See also* Shalom Cohen v. Minister of Defense, 16 *P.D.* 1023, 1027 (1962); Mercaz ha-Kabbelanim ve-ha-Bonim be-Yisra'el v. Government of Israel, 34(iii) *P.D.* 729, 755 (1979); Ḥadashot v. Minister of Defense, 38(ii) *P.D.* 477, 483 (1984).

23. Naiman v. Chairman, Central Elections Committee, 39(ii) *P.D.* 225, 293 (1985).

Thus, in various cases the court has elucidated the basic principles of human freedom—freedom of thought and expression, human dignity, and the rights of national and religious minorities to equal treatment and freedom from discrimination—as these fundamental principles have crystallized in the Jewish heritage.[24] From this time forward, the resort to the principles of freedom, justice, equity, and peace of the Jewish heritage is not simply a matter of "taking account of" the provisions of the Declaration of Independence or illumination of the law "by the ordering of [the] national life,"[25] as it was prior to the enactment of the Foundations of Law Act. The ordering of the national life, *i.e.*, the Jewish heritage, has become formally recognized by statute as a part of the legal system, and recourse to that heritage as a complementary legal source is a clear and positive legal obligation.[26]

D. Legislation, Judicial Precedent, Analogy

As stated, the duty of the court to turn to the principles of freedom, justice, equity, and peace of the Jewish heritage as a complementary legal source depends on the existence of a number of conditions. One condition is that the legal issue *sub judice* cannot be resolved on the basis of "legislation or judicial precedent, or by means of analogy." The meaning of "legislation" is clear. The term "judicial precedent" is found in Section 33 of the Courts Law, 1957, which provides that only a decision of the Supreme Court is binding on all courts (except for the Supreme Court itself), whereas a decision of any other court is entitled to respect by a lower court, but is only persuasive and not binding. Thus, for example, the magistrate's court is guided by the law declared by the district court but is not bound by it.

"Judicial precedent" in the Foundations of Law Act thus means binding case law, *i.e.*, law determined by the Supreme Court—and only that part of the Supreme Court's judgment which was the basis for the decision (the *ratio decidendi*), not *dicta* or a minority view.[27] It goes without saying that the provision of Section 33 of the Courts Law that the Supreme Court

24. *Id.* at 294ff.; Hokamah v. Minister of the Interior, 38(ii) *P.D.* 826 (1984); State of Israel v. Avi Ẓur, 40(i) *P.D.* 706 (1986). Each of these cases is discussed in detail *infra* pp. 1841–1856.

25. The quotation is from the opinion of Justice Agranat in Kol ha-Am v. Minister of the Interior, *supra* n. 21.

26. With regard to Jewish law as the national law of the Jewish people in the past and the present, *see* the opinion of Justice Agranat in Skornik v. Skornik, 8 *P.D.* 141, 176, 177 (1954). *See also supra* p. 5 n. 7 and *infra* pp. 1945–1946.

27. *See* the articles by Tedeschi, "Heskemei ha-Minhal ha-Ẓibburi im ha-Perat," and "Sodot Iskiyyim," *supra* n. 14.

is not bound by its own decisions is unaffected by the Foundations of Law Act.

The reference to "analogy" among the legal sources seems superfluous, since analogy is one of the methods of interpretation constituting the grist of the judicial mill in a court's daily task of deciding cases through interpretation of the law. The statute does not mention, for example, *interpretatio logica* or any other method of interpretation;[28] it is therefore difficult to perceive why the Legislature saw fit to single out for mention only analogy among all the methods of interpretation.[29] Likewise, it is surprising that the Act does not mention custom, which is one of the legal sources of Israeli as well as Jewish law.[30]

E. "A Legal Issue Requiring Decision"; Lacuna

A court is required to decide a case in light of the principles of the Jewish heritage when it is faced with "a legal issue requiring decision." The Supreme Court, in the additional hearing in *Hendeles v. Bank Kupat Am,*[31] con-

28. *See supra* ch. 9 as to the various methods of interpretation.

29. Prof. G. Tedeschi, in his work *Meḥkarim be-Mishpat Arẓeinu* [Studies in the Law of Our Land], 2nd ed., Jerusalem, 1959, pp. 132, 149–151, took the position that under the provisions of Article 46 of the Palestine Order in Council a lacuna was required to be filled not by means of analogy but by recourse to English common law. The courts did not adopt Prof. Tedeschi's view in their decisions interpreting Article 46. It would seem that the Foundations of Law Act can be said to have taken account of Prof. Tedeschi's position and explicitly provided that a court should first resort to analogy before turning to the principles of the Jewish heritage. It should be noted that a number of decisions of the district courts and the Supreme Court have cited the Foundations of Law Act as the basis for resorting to analogy. *See* Kashti v. Siani, [1982] 2 *P.M.* 263, 271; Insurance Corp. v. State of Israel, [1983] 1 *P.M.* 469, 476; Wertheimer v. Harari, 35(iii) *P.D.* 253, 270 (1981); Berkowitz v. Klimmer, 36(iv) *P.D.* 57, 64 (1982).

It is ironic that courts invoke the Foundations of Law Act to justify resorting to analogy to fill lacunae, when the use of analogy needs no statutory justification and the validation of analogy is only peripheral to the statute's central purpose, yet the courts hardly ever apply the Foundations of Law Act to give effect to its primary purpose and essential innovation, namely, to turn to the Jewish heritage as a complementary source of the Israeli legal system. This point is discussed further *infra* pp. 1921–1923, 1927ff.

30. *See supra* pp. 895–944. *See also* Wolfson v. Spinneys Co., Ltd., 5 *P.D.* 265 (1951); Hutman v. Sin-Moritz, 17 *P.D.* 1251 (1963); Explanatory Notes (end) to the Repeal of *Mejelle* Bill, 1984 (Bill No. 1681). With regard to the conditions found in the first section of the Act, *see also* M. Keshet, "Ḥok Yesodot ha-Mishpat, 5740—1980" [The Foundations of Law Act, 1980], *Ha-Praklit,* XXXIII (1981), p. 611; Y. Danziger, "Meḥvah Simlit she-Nizkah Rav mi-To'altah" [A Symbolic Gesture More Harmful than Helpful], *Ha-Praklit,* XXXIII (1981), p. 619; the articles by Tedeschi, "Heskemei ha-Minhal ha-Ẓibburi im ha-Perat" and "Sodot Iskiyyim," *supra* n. 14; U. Procaccia, "Ḥok Yesodot ha-Mishpat, 5740—1980" [The Foundations of Law Act, 1980], *Iyyunei Mishpat,* X (1984), p. 145.

31. 35(ii) *P.D.* 785, 793, 799 (1981).

strued the quoted language as referring only to a situation where the failure of the existing legal sources to provide the "solution to a particular legal issue" creates a lacuna; the court held that the statute does not apply "where there is no lacuna but rather an issue involving interpretation of a subsisting legal provision, a part of established law that is susceptible of differing interpretations, and the court is called upon to determine which interpretation is correct."[32]

Legal scholars and jurists disagree both as to whether a lacuna can exist at all in a legal system and, if so, as to just what is encompassed by the term.[33] Since the Foundations of Law Act addresses the situation where there is a lacuna, even if not explicitly so called, it is clear that Israeli law recognizes the possibility that a lacuna may exist. But what does it mean, when does it exist, and what situations does the term encompass? When is a particular question for which the terms of a statute provide no answer an instance of a lacuna, and when is it merely a question of statutory interpretation? There is consensus that when a particular legal subject is not dealt with at all in the Israeli legal system, a lacuna exists and Section 1 of the Foundations of Law Act applies. However, Section 1 of the statute clearly covers much more than this. On this point, the opinion I rendered in the additional hearing of the *Hendeles* case stated:[34]

> Distinguishing between whether there is a lacuna in the law or merely a question of construction of an ambiguous statute is not an easy task; there are no hard and fast rules. Scholars and jurists have pondered and debated the question, and this is not the place to expatiate upon it. I will give just one illustration. A number of justices of this court have decided more than once that legal terms that are prevalent in the Israeli legal system and are based on moral concepts and cultural values—such as "justice," "good faith," "public policy," etc.—must be interpreted according to the basic outlook of Jewish law, rooted in that law's moral and cultural values.[35] It appears that to give meaning to these value-laden terms which, except on the purely verbal level, have no substantive content, is a matter of filling a lacuna, particularly in the light of the provision of Section 2 [the reference should be to Section 1] of the Foundations of Law Act, which specifically refers to these value-laden

32. *Id.* at 793, 799. That was the situation in the *Hendeles* case, in which the construction of the phrase "the *reshut* of another person" in Section 3 of the Restoration of Lost Property Law was at issue. *See supra* pp. 1739–1751. With regard to whether the legislative intent was actually that the Act should apply only where there is a lacuna, *see infra* pp. 1936–1937, pointing out that the plain meaning of the Act is consistent with a broader interpretation, but such an interpretation would not be practical.

33. *See* Tedeschi, *supra* n. 29.

34. 35(ii) *P.D.* at 793.

35. *See* Dicker v. Moch, 32(ii) *P.D.* 141, 150 (1978); Roth v. Yeshufeh, 33(i) *P.D.* 617, 631 (1979); Afanjar v. State of Israel, 33(iii) *P.D.* 141, 155 (1979); and cases cited therein.

principles. Therefore, such "interpretation," used by these judges, involves more than merely interpretation; it constitutes the filling of a lacuna, and encompasses everything entailed in that process.[36]

Some scholars take the view that even the explication of general legal terms such as "negligence" also involves filling lacunae.[37] Thus, with regard to the general provision of the Unjust Enrichment Law concerning the obligation to make restitution or pay compensation upon the "unjust retention of a benefit," D. Friedmann has written:

> It has already been pointed out that if there is any distinction at all between the interpretation of a very general provision of this type and the filling of a lacuna, the distinction is extremely fine, and perhaps only semantic. It can also be said that whereas a lacuna in the usual sense of the term, arising from the silence of the Legislature, is concealed, [the use of statutory] language that is [so] general and vague "that [it] authorizes the court to legislate" is a declared and revealed lacuna.[38]

36. The same point was made with regard to the meaning of the term "good faith" in Laserson v. Shikkun Ovedim, 38(ii) *P.D.* 237, 265 (1984). President Sussman expressed the same view in his article "Mikẓat Mat'amei Parshanut" [Some Choice Principles of Interpretation], *Sefer ha-Yovel le-Pinḥas Rosen* [Jubilee Volume for Pinḥas Rosen], Jerusalem, 1962, pp. 147, 156, with regard to the term "justice" as used in Section 37 of the Tenants Protection Law, 1955: "The term 'justice,' found in Section 37, is an empty shell that the judge must fill with content; it is the judge who must determine what is 'justice.'" *See also* D. Friedmann, "Yesodot be-Dinei Asiyyat Osher ve-Lo ve-Mishpat le-Or ha-Ḥakikah ha-Yisra'elit ha-Ḥadashah," *supra* n. 12 at 32; *id.*, "Infusion of the Common Law into the Legal System of Israel," 10 *Israel L. Rev.* 324, 363 (1975).

37. *See* Friedmann, "Infusion of the Common Law into the Legal System of Israel," *supra* n. 36; Hendeles v. Bank Kupat Am, 35(ii) *P.D.* 785, 793 (1981). For additional examples, *see* Amidar v. Aharon, 32(ii) *P.D.* 337, 345, 348 (1978) (with regard to whether tort liability exists for negligent misrepresentation); Muberman v. Segal, 32(iii) *P.D.* 85, 97 (1978) (with regard to the fiduciary obligation of an administrator of an estate to refrain from purchasing assets of the estate). *See also infra* n. 38.

38. Friedmann, "Yesodot be-Dinei Asiyyat Osher ve-Lo ve-Mishpat le-Or ha-Ḥakikah ha-Yisra'elit ha-Ḥadashah," *supra* n. 12 at 32. *See also id.* at n. 54, where Friedmann explains the statement of President Sussman, quoted *supra* n. 36, that the term "justice" is an "empty shell":

> What is this void in the shell created by the Legislature, if not a lacuna? In the past, we may possibly have differentiated between the elucidation of such a term and a lacuna. Thus, if we had been dealing with an Ottoman law derived from a French source, we might have turned to French law in order to interpret the Ottoman law, whereas we would have turned to English law to fill a "lacuna." But this distinction is meaningless if in both instances we turn to the same source—which is, indeed, precisely what we do under modern Israeli legislation. In both instances—"interpretation" that in fact fills a lacuna, and a lacuna in the usual sense of the term—we turn to prior law (Section 2(b) of the Foundations of Law Act), and to judicial decisions, analogy, and the principles of freedom, justice, equity, and peace of the Jewish heritage (Section 1 of the Foundations of Law Act). Similarly, we have been directed to

Similarly, President Agranat listed among the "typical instances" of lacuna the situation where "the Legislature uses a key term without defining it."[39]

This view is persuasive. A broad interpretation of "lacuna," at least in the context of the Foundations of Law Act, derives additional support from the statutory language. The Knesset did not use the term "lacuna" or speak of a "gap," "unprovided for area," or "filling in a vacuum"; rather, Section 1 refers to "a legal issue requiring decision." This formulation includes not only the situation where the subject is not dealt with at all in the legal system, but also the situation where legislation employs general language that has no concrete meaning, as in the examples discussed above.[40]

According to Justice Barak, Section 1 of the Foundations of Law Act applies only when the legal system does not deal at all with a particular subject:

> When Israeli legislation uses basic terms such as "justice," "good faith," "public policy," and similar value-laden terms, the judicial function is to pour concrete meaning into these terms in accordance with the statutory purpose, taking into account the conditions, actual and ideal, of life in Israel. In these matters, the judge does not at all face an "unprovided for" area (lacuna), inasmuch as the Legislature has established an applicable norm. Therefore, I see no possibility in such a case of applying the provisions of the Foundations of Law Act, which contemplates only the filling of a vacuum.[41]

The three other justices on the panel in the additional hearing in the *Hendeles* case did not address this particular difference of opinion regarding the nature of the lacuna triggering the application of the Foundations of Law Act.

> turn to these sources both to imbue a general provision with content (which can be said to constitute "interpretation") and to fill another kind of lacuna because of the need, when all is said and done, to create a unified legal system.

See also supra pp. 1829–1830, where exception is taken to the portion of Friedmann's article concerning the extent of the applicability of prior law (the meaning of the words "the law that was accepted" in Israel in Section 2(b) of the Foundations of Law Act).

39. S. Agranat, "Terumatah Shel ha-Reshut ha-Shofetet le-Mif'al ha-Ḥakikah" [The Contribution of the Judiciary to Legislation, *Iyyunei Mishpat,* X (1984), pp. 233, 239. *See also id.* at 240 and n. 23.

40. The "plain meaning" of "a legal issue requiring decision" could also encompass the interpretation of an ambiguous statutory provision. *See* H. Gans, "Shikkul ha-Da'at Shipputi le-Aharon Barak" [Aharon Barak's View of Judicial Discretion], *Mishpatim,* XVIII, pp. 509, 525ff, which persuasively argues that "a legal issue requiring decision" can include a question as to the interpretation of a statutory provision as well as a lacuna. However, it is doubtful that the Legislature intended such a far-reaching result; such a broad reading of the statute would impose upon the courts a task that, given the present extent of their knowledge of Jewish law, they could not carry out. *See infra* pp. 1936–1937.

41. Hendeles v. Bank Kupat Am, 35(ii) *P.D.* at 797. With regard to these remarks of Justice Barak, *see infra* pp. 1872–1874.

F. The Principles of Freedom, Justice, Equity, and Peace of the Jewish Heritage

"Jewish heritage" (*moreshet Yisra'el*) is a novel term in Israeli legal terminology;[42] and since it has not yet been extensively used, it is not as well defined as the term "Jewish law" (*mishpat ivri*). Jewish religious sources use *morashah* to refer to the Torah[43] and also to the entire Oral Law.[44] It may be assumed that the ill-defined term *moreshet Yisra'el* was the result of a compromise between different legislative proposals.[45] However, it is clear that the core denotation of this term is Jewish law; this is confirmed by the Explanatory Notes to the bill which refer to "Jewish heritage" and "Jewish law" interchangeably.[46]

The courts will have to pour meaning into this term and determine what the term includes in addition to *mishpat ivri, e.g.,* what philosophical and intellectual currents of the historical Jewish heritage, and what cultural creations associated with the modern Jewish national renaissance. The courts should be conscious of the fact that the term being construed is part of a set of legal norms for practical application, and not merely an academic

42. The accepted term in legal literature, as well in the Explanatory Notes to various bills, is "Jewish law" (*mishpat ivri*). In Section 2 of the Rabbinical Courts Jurisdiction (Marriage and Divorce) Law, the term "Torah law" (*din Torah*) is used. *See also supra* p. 111 n. 84.

43. Deuteronomy 33:4 ("Moses charged us with the Torah as the heritage [*morashah*] of the congregation of Jacob"); TB Sanhedrin 91b ("Whoever withholds a *halakhah* from his student is considered as having robbed him of his ancestral inheritance, as it is written: 'Moses charged us with the Torah as the heritage of the congregation of Jacob'"). *See also* the *yoẓer* prayers in the morning service of *Rosh Ha-Shanah*: "I am in fear as I open my mouth to bring forth words [of prayer] . . . My Creator, make me understand how to acquire the heritage (*morashah*) [of Torah]." The term *morashah* is also used in the Torah to refer to the Land of Israel, in the sense of "ancestral possession": "I will bring you into the land which I swore to give to Abraham, Isaac, and Jacob, and I will give it to you for a possession (*morashah*), I the Lord" (Exodus 6:8).

44. *See supra* n. 19 with regard to the proposed alternatives for the term *moreshet Yisra'el*.

45. *See supra* pp. 1831–1832.

46. Clearly, one cannot attribute to this key phrase in one of the fundamental laws of the Israeli legal system such a vague and amorphous meaning—devoid of any real content—as "the sentiments of justice and equity that resonate in the hearts of present-day Israeli judges." *See* Cheshin, *supra* n. 18 at 58:

> If we were to say that the "Jewish heritage" is intended to refer to those sentiments of justice and equity which resonate in the hearts of our judges, who live and breathe and instruct present-day Israel, and if we were to conclude that the Legislature instructed Israeli judges to consult their wise hearts and inner feelings—all of which are included as part of the Jewish heritage—it might be difficult to arrive at a decision, but so far as we are concerned, such a situation would be acceptable.

From the context of these words and from the ensuing discussion, Cheshin appears to raise the possibility of this interpretation only for the sake of argument; the more reasonable interpretation, even according to his view, is that the "'Jewish heritage' includes Jewish law, and perhaps is even identical to it, if only in part."

abstraction. *Naiman v. Chairman, Central Elections Committee*[47] discussed the sources included in the term "Jewish heritage" and the use to be made of them; these questions are considered further below.[48]

The principles of freedom, justice, equity, and peace pervade the world of *Halakhah* and Judaism; nowhere in that world are they absent. These principles serve a dual role: (1) as legal principles in many different areas of the law, and (2) as metaprinciples for establishing legal and adjudicatory policy. Such metaprinciples as "they are My servants and not servants of servants,"[49] "do what is right and good,"[50] "judge your neighbor fairly,"[51] "justice, justice shall you pursue,"[52] "her ways are pleasant ways, and all her paths, peaceful,"[53] are prime examples of legal norms that establish policy in various areas of the law. In light of the policy so established, specific rules are derived on the basis of the principles of freedom, justice, equity, and peace. The same is true of a number of other similar metaprinciples. A vast amount of material may be found in the sources of the Jewish heritage concerning these metaprinciples and their application to various areas of the law, and these principles have been discussed in philosophical and scholarly literature. In the present work and elsewhere, these principles have been dealt with in connection with many diverse subjects.[54]

47. 39(ii) *P.D.* 225 (1985).

48. *See infra* pp. 1853–1854, 1861–1863.

49. TB Bava Meẓi'a 10a, 77a. This is derived from midrashic exegesis on the verse: "For it is to Me that the Israelites are servants: they are My servants, whom I freed from the land of Egypt, I the Lord your God" (Leviticus 25:55).

50. Deuteronomy 6:18.

51. Leviticus 19:15.

52. Deuteronomy 16:20.

53. Proverbs 3:17.

54. *With regard to freedom—see supra* pp. 587–591, 1635–1639; Elon, *Ḥerut, passim;* State of Israel v. Rivkah Abukasis, 32(ii) *P.D.* 240 (1978); State of Israel v. Lubaniov, 35(iv) *P.D.* 780 (1981); Sura v. State of Israel, 36(iv) *P.D.* 10 (1982); Krauss v. State of Israel, 37(i) *P.D.* 365 (1983); State of Israel v. Tamir, 37(iii) *P.D.* 201 (1984); Hokamah v. Minister of the Interior, 38(ii) *P.D.* 826 (1984); Naiman v. Chairman, Central Elections Committee, 39(ii) *P.D.* 225 (1985); State of Israel v. Avi Ẓur, 40(i) *P.D.* 706 (1986). With regard to the three cases last cited, *see* the discussion *infra* pp. 1841–1856.

With regard to equity—see supra pp. 167–189, 247–261, 623–628, 1736; *infra* pp. 1871–1874; Amsterdamer v. Moskovitz, 26(i) *P.D.* 793 (1972); Roth v. Yeshufeh, 33(i) *P.D.* 617 (1979); Kitan v. Weiss, 33(ii) *P.D.* 785 (1979); Ness v. Golda, 36(i) *P.D.* 204 (1982); Minẓer v. Central Committee of the Israel Bar Association, 36(ii) *P.D.* 1 (1982); Lugasi v. Minister of Communications, 36(ii) *P.D.* 449 (1982); Marcus v. Hammer, 37(ii) *P.D.* 337 (1984).

With regard to justice—see supra pp. 56–57, 72–73, 167–176, 247–261, 760–777, 942–944; Ben Shaḥar v. Maḥlev, 25(ii) *P.D.* 89 (1974); Roth v. Yeshufeh, 33(i) *P.D.* 617, 631 (1979); Lieberman v. Lieberman, 35(iv) *P.D.* 359 (1981); Minẓer v. Central Committee of the Israel Bar Association, 36(ii) *P.D.* 1 (1982); Hokamah v. Minister of the Interior, 38(ii) *P.D.* 826 (1984); Naiman v. Chairman, Central Elections Committee, 39(ii) *P.D.* 225 (1985). With regard to the two cases last cited, *see* the discussion *infra* pp. 1841–1842, 1846–1856.

G. The Principles of the Jewish Heritage in the Decisions of the Courts

In a number of cases, these metaprinciples have been applied in the context of the provisions of the Foundations of Law Act.

1. THE FUNDAMENTAL RIGHTS OF DETAINEES AND PRISONERS

The right of detainees and prisoners to vote in elections for the Knesset was considered by the Supreme Court in the case of *Hokamah v. Minister of the Interior.*[55] Under the Knesset Elections Law, voting is restricted to the polling place where a voter is registered to vote. As a result, thousands of prisoners and detainees, as a practical matter, have been disenfranchised. In the *Hokamah* case, the court required that all possible legal and administrative steps be taken to enable detainees and prisoners to exercise their right to vote, although in the *Hokamah* case itself the court did not grant the requested relief, since the case was brought to the court only about thirty days prior to the date of the election and there was insufficient time to comply with the statutory schedule for the preparation of voter lists.

The rationale of the decision to enable prisoners to exercise their right to vote was as follows:[56]

> There is an important principle that every human right is preserved even during detention or imprisonment; imprisonment alone cannot deprive anyone of any right, unless such deprivation is a necessary consequence of his confinement, or is explicitly required by statute.[57] The roots of this principle are found in the Jewish heritage from ancient times. [As pointed out in *State of Israel v. Tamir*:[58]]

With regard to peace—see supra pp. 387–390 (and *see* sources cited p. 387 n. 375), 504, 530 n. 153, 609 n. 269, 628–631; *Mafte'ah ha-She'elot ve-ha-Teshuvot Shel Hakhmei Sefarad u-Zefon Afrikah* [Digest of the Responsa Literature of Spain and North Africa], *Index of Sources,* vol. 1, p. XXV (an English translation of which appears in the *Legal Digest,* vol. 2, p. XLIII); Rosenstein v. Solomon, 38(ii) *P.D.* 113 (1984).

See also the cases cited *supra* p. 1739 n. 435.

55. 38(ii) *P.D.* 826 (1984).

56. *Id.* at 832–833.

57. *See* State of Israel v. Tamir, 37(iii) *P.D.* 201, 208 (1983). *See also* Weil v. State of Israel, 41(iii) *P.D.* 477 (1987), which extensively discusses the fundamental rights that are retained by prisoners, and the tension between the preservation of these rights and the deprivation of the freedom of movement to which a prisoner has been sentenced. The opinion in the *Weil* case established that a prisoner retains the fundamental right to continue marital relations with his or her spouse, subject only to the necessary constraints of status as a prisoner. The opinion discusses the concept of the punishment of imprisonment in Jewish law in light of the law regarding cities of refuge (Numbers 35:6–34) and the various laws dealing with the life to be led by the persons confined to those cities.

58. 37(iii) *P.D.* at 208.

> On the basis of the verse in Deuteronomy 25:3, "[He (a guilty party sentenced to flogging) may be given up to forty lashes, but not more] lest [being flogged further, to excess,] your brother be degraded before your eyes," the Sages established an important principle in Jewish penal law: "Once he [the guilty person] has been flogged, he is to be considered as your brother."[59] This important principle applies not only after his punishment but even while he is being punished, for he is your brother and fellowman, and his rights and his dignity as a human being are preserved and remain with him.

If this is true with respect to any right, it certainly applies to the right to vote for the Knesset, which is clearly a fundamental right in a democracy, explicitly secured by statute to every Israeli citizen who has reached the age of eighteen, so long as a court has not deprived him of that right pursuant to law. . . .[60]

It has also been stated in the decisions of this court that when a detainee or prisoner possesses any right, it may be asserted and exercised, provided that it does not conflict with the duty of the prison authorities to do what is necessary to control his movement and . . . to preserve security and order in the prison.

The *Hokamah* opinion goes on to state:[61]

> Since we are dealing with an issue for which the law makes no explicit provision, we are presented with a legal issue requiring decision, which cannot be answered by reference to legislation or judicial precedent, or by means of analogy, and which therefore must be decided "in the light of the principles of freedom, justice, equity, and peace of the Jewish heritage."[62] As noted above, Jewish law has established, on the basis of the principles of freedom and justice, that the rights and dignity of a prisoner as a human being are preserved and remain with him, and they must be respected in the same way as they are respected in the case of "your brother and fellowman." Pursuant to these principles, we must find a way to permit prisoners and detainees to exercise their right to vote, despite the technical difficulties involved.

2. FREEDOM FROM DETENTION

The decisions of the Israeli courts on the issue of pretrial detention of criminal defendants have gone through various stages. Section 34 of the Criminal Procedure Law (Consolidated Version), 1982, provides that a defendant may be detained until the completion of his trial when there is a reasonable suspicion that he has committed murder or a serious crime in-

59. M Makkot 3:15.
60. *See* Basic Law: The Knesset, secs. 4, 5.
61. 38(ii) *P.D.* at 834–835.
62. Foundations of Law Act, 1980, sec. 1.

volving the security of the State and punishable by life imprisonment. One accused of any other crime may not be detained, even when there is a *prima facie* case against him, unless (a) the nature and circumstances of the crime (*e.g.*, crimes involving rape, violence, or drugs) indicate that he would pose a danger to the public if allowed to go free; or (b) there is a substantial possibility that he will flee and not stand trial or will obstruct justice by intimidating witnesses, destroying evidence, etc.

These principles are accepted by all the justices of the Supreme Court. In the course of time, the Supreme Court decided that a public officeholder may be detained until the completion of his trial if there is *prima facie* evidence that he has accepted a substantial bribe or has committed a similar crime.[63] It also became accepted that the gravity of the crime alone (provided that there is *prima facie* evidence against the accused) may be sufficient to justify detention until the conclusion of the trial, even if the public would not be endangered by pretrial release and there is no reason to be concerned about the possibility of obstruction of justice.

It is the author's view that an accused, who is presumed to be innocent, may not be deprived of his freedom before judicial determination of his guilt merely because he holds a public office or because of the gravity of the alleged offense. However, in order to achieve unanimity among the justices hearing the case, including the author, it was agreed that a defendant holding a public office may be detained pending trial, provided that four conditions are met: (1) the alleged crime was committed against the public; (2) it was the defendant's public office that enabled him to commit the crime; (3) the crime involved large sums of money which the defendant received by virtue of his office; and (4) the defendant not only committed the crime himself but also caused his subordinates to commit many serious crimes.[64]

The enactment of the Foundations of Law Act, 1980, provides additional support for the view that the gravity of a crime is not in itself a justification for pretrial detention, and that a defendant's status as a public official does not justify treating him more severely than an ordinary citizen; rather, the law must treat them both alike. As stated in *State of Israel v. Avi Ẓur*:[65]

> I will not deny, and I acknowledge, that my hope and purpose in formulating this "four-part" test, each part of which is a necessary precondition, was that detention based solely on the gravity of a crime will disappear from our legal

63. Yadlin v. State of Israel, 31(i) *P.D.* 671 (1976); *see* State of Israel v. Avi Ẓur, 40(i) *P.D.* 706, 710–712 (1986).

64. State of Israel v. Avi Ẓur, *supra* n. 63 at 712.

65. *Id.* at 712–714.

scene, whether the accused is an "ordinary" or "important" person, and whether the amount involved is substantial or insignificant—except, of course, where there is a reasonable probability of obstruction of justice or danger to the public if the defendant is released.

With all respect, let us examine the nature of the rationale advanced in the above-mentioned *Yadlin* case,[66] namely, that the "public reaction to the release of the defendant who holds a [public] position" must be taken into account. Since when, with all due respect, do we take into consideration, in a case such as this, an argument such as "what will people say"? Can we, because of "what people will say," deprive an individual, on account of his importance and position, of the most fundamental of all human rights—the right to be unconfined by prison walls and iron bars? How carefully and apprehensively we avoid infringing, God forbid, any of the various freedoms—freedom of expression, freedom of opinion, freedom to demonstrate, etc.—even to the slightest extent! We take a strict position in any case in which these freedoms may be directly or even indirectly affected, and we very carefully strike a balance between the interests represented by these freedom-values and the countervailing fundamental values of security, public safety, etc. Yet the personal freedom of each human being is the very source and foundation of all of these other freedoms.

It is a fundamental principle in our legal system and in the worldview of Judaism that every person is presumed innocent until proved guilty and that every person is presumed to have acted properly—*every* person, even an important person! As we have said, a person's position, profession, or business may well be an important factor in the determination of his punishment if he is convicted, just as the Legislature has established that certain acts are crimes when committed by persons holding a given position. But prior to conviction, while a person is merely accused and awaiting trial, there is no basis or justification for discriminating between different defendants. Rather, a single set of laws and principles should be applied both to an "ordinary" defendant and to an "important" defendant.

There is a further ground for this conclusion. Since 1976, when the *Yadlin* case was decided, there has been a profound change in the Israeli legal system as a result of the enactment of the Foundations of Law Act, 1980. This statute "constitutes one of the basic statutes establishing the foundation of the State of Israel"; by virtue of the statute, the principles of freedom, justice, equity, and peace of the Jewish heritage (Section 1 of the Foundations of Law Act) constitute "the basic principles—the foundation—of the entire legal system of the State."[67] The right of personal freedom is a cornerstone of Jewish law, and one of the basic principles of freedom is that every person is presumed to have acted properly until the presumption is rebutted by proof to

66. Yadlin v. State of Israel, 31(i) *P.D.* 671 (1976).

67. The quotations are from Naiman v. Chairman, Central Elections Committee, 39(ii) *P.D.* 225, 293 (1985).

the contrary. Thus, we have seen that under Jewish law a defendant may not be detained unless he is accused of particularly serious offenses,[68] or unless there are grounds to conclude that he will obstruct justice.[69]

There is another basic principle in the Torah: "You shall not render an unfair decision: do not favor the poor or show deference to the rich; judge your kinsman fairly."[70] Just as this cardinal principle of Jewish law has been the basis for this court's decision that an "important" person may not be given special deference and treated more leniently with respect to release from prison after conviction,[71] so it should also be the basis for deciding that an "important" person may not be unfairly treated with greater severity than a "lesser" person with respect to detention before conviction. This verse was similarly interpreted in the following ruling by the "Great Eagle," Maimonides:[72]

> It is a positive commandment that a judge must judge fairly, as it is written: "Judge your neighbor fairly." What constitutes fair judging? Treating both parties equally in every respect.

This statement with respect to judicial procedure and the conduct of a trial is certainly applicable to a matter as fundamental as the deprivation of a person's freedom before trial.

On July 27, 1988, the Knesset enacted the Criminal Procedure Law (Amendment #9), 1988, amending the Criminal Procedure Law (Consolidated Version), 1982, to provide that the gravity of a crime is not in itself sufficient to justify the detention of a defendant pending the conclusion of his trial, unless the crime is punishable by death or life imprisonment or there are grounds to conclude that, if released, the defendant poses a danger to the public or threatens to obstruct justice. Even in the latter case (danger to the public or the possibility of obstruction of justice), the defendant should not be detained if the purpose of detention can be achieved by freeing the defendant on bond or by imposing any other condition that will be a lesser interference with his freedom than imprisonment. The statute thus adopted the position of Jewish law on the fundamental question of detention before trial.[73]

68. *Resp. Ribash* #236, with regard to the law regarding one suspected of murder or of being an informer.

69. *Id.*; *see* State of Israel v. Rivkah Abukasis, 32(ii) *P.D.* 240, 248ff. (1978); State of Israel v. Molcho, 37(i) *P.D.* 78, 83 (1983); Sura v. State of Israel, 36(iv) *P.D.* 10 (1982); Krauss v. State of Israel, 37(i) *P.D.* 365 (1983); State of Israel v. Leviathan, 40(i) *P.D.* 544 (1984).

70. Leviticus 19:15.

71. Rechtman v. State of Israel, 33(ii) *P.D.* 45, 48 (1979).

72. *MT*, Sanhedrin 21:1.

73. With regard to the 1988 amendment, *see* State of Israel v. Lavan, 43(ii) *P.D.* 410 (1989), which points out that the amendment resolved an ongoing dispute among the justices of the Supreme Court. *See also* Masika v. State of Israel, 43(ii) *P.D.* 423 (1989); State

3. FREEDOM OF THOUGHT AND SPEECH

Naiman v. Chairman, Central Elections Committee[74] (commonly known as the "Progressive List for Peace" case and the "Kach" party case) dealt with such fundamental questions as freedom of thought and expression, equality of treatment, and freedom from governmental discrimination against ethnic minorities. The Central Elections Committee had disqualified these two parties from competing in the elections for the Eleventh Knesset—the first, on the ground that its platform advocated the destruction of the State of Israel or the impairment of its territorial integrity, and the second, because its platform advocated the undermining of the democratic system of the country. The Supreme Court unanimously reversed the disqualification of these parties.

With regard to the "Progressive List for Peace," the court found that the grounds on which the Central Elections Committee disqualified the party had not been sufficiently proved. In the case of the "Kach" party (as to which the court held that the facts found by the Central Elections Committee were sufficiently supported by the evidence), the justices did not agree on the grounds for reversal. According to the majority of the five judges who sat on the case, neither the court nor certainly the Elections Committee could, under existing law, disqualify a party because of its platform, except where the party's goal is the destruction of the State's very existence or the impairment of its territorial integrity. When the exception is applicable, the government is duty-bound to prevent such a party from participating in elections for the Knesset on the basis of the right to self-preservation, as expressed by the fundamental principle of Judaism: "By the pursuit of them [*i.e.*, God's laws] 'you shall live'—not die."[75] The court recommended that the Knesset enact a statute that would clearly and explicitly specify the standards for disqualifying a party. Among the questions that such a statute should deal with are: (a) Which democratic principles are to be protected? (b) How strongly must those principles be assaulted,

---

of Israel v. Benjamin, 43(ii) *P.D.* 430 (1989). For a discussion of the law prior to the 1988 amendment, *see* Gindi v. State of Israel, 40(i) *P.D.* 449 (1986).

74. 39(ii) *P.D.* 225 (1985).

75. *Id.* at 291, alluding to TB Yoma 85b, which interprets Leviticus 18:5. In the view of Deputy President Ben Porat, there is no jurisdiction in any case to disqualify a party list by reason of the content of the party's platform unless a statute explicitly authorizes such action by the court or the Central Elections Committee. *See id.* at 280. In the view of Justice Barak, existing legislation grants such authority where the platform advocates undermining the foundation of Israeli democracy, but only if there is a reasonable possibility that this goal will be achieved. *See id.* at 304. The opinions contain various other differences in approach on the part of the five justices who heard the case.

and how imminently must they be threatened, before a party may be disqualified?[76]

The issues raised by the case were considered by the court, as required by the Foundations of Law Act, in light of "the principles of freedom, justice, equity, and peace of the Jewish heritage."[77] Thus, the decision contains an extensive discussion of the principles of freedom of thought and speech, human dignity and equality, and nondiscriminatory treatment of ethnic and religious minorities, as these principles have crystallized in the Jewish heritage. The court also clarified the scope of the term "Jewish heritage" as used in the Foundations of Law Act, delineated what this term includes beyond the distinctly legal norms of Jewish law, and outlined the method to be used for turning to the various, and sometimes conflicting, views contained in the sources of the Jewish heritage. A full understanding of these issues requires a close, even if somewhat lengthy, review of the decision.

The court's discussion of the principle of freedom of thought and speech stresses and exemplifies the great caution that courts must exercise in order not to restrict this freedom without explicit authorization from the Legislature. The following quotation describes the status and importance of this principle in the Jewish heritage:[78]

> The prophets of Israel and their prophecies have been and still are the prototype for sharp and uncompromising criticism of governments that abuse their power and of individuals or communities that act corruptly. The prophets raised a cry against injustice to the poor, oppression of widows, deprivation of individual and social rights, and deviations from both the letter and spirit of the Torah and the *Halakhah*. The steadfastness of the prophets of Israel in the face of fierce and angry opposition is a source of never-failing inspiration for the present-day struggle to achieve and preserve freedom of speech and enlightened democracy. These matters are common knowledge and need not be belabored; every student of political science and democracy is familiar with them.
>
> There is probably no more apt and incisive formulation of the principle of freedom of expression and the value of every opinion—even if held by only a single individual—than the formulation used by the Sages with regard to the differences of opinion between the schools of Shammai and Hillel, namely, that "both are the words of the living God."[79] For actual practice, the

76. *Id.* at 303–304 (Elon, J.). The justices differed as to whether to recommend the enactment of legislation and as to what any such legislation should provide.

77. Foundations of Law Act, 1980, sec. 1; 39(ii) *P.D.* at 293 (Elon, J.).

78. 39(ii) *P.D.* at 296–299.

79. TB Eruvin 13b; TJ Berakhot 1:4, 9b (1:7, 3b); TJ Yevamot 1:6, 9a (1:6, 3b).

view of the School of Hillel is the law, "because they were pleasant and tolerant";[80] but the view of the School of Shammai continues to constitute a legitimate and cogent opinion in the *Halakhah.* This approach [to minority opinions] has been an essential characteristic of the *Halakhah.*

The "rebellious elder" who disagreed with a decision of the Sanhedrin—the Supreme Court of the nation—could continue to maintain the correctness of his opinion and "to teach in the same way that he previously taught," so long as he did not rule that his view should be applied in deciding actual controversies.[81] Moreover, it was always contemplated that the minority view in any dispute could ultimately prevail and govern actual practice. R. Judah said: "The minority view is recorded [in the Mishnah] along with the majority view so that it is available to become the applicable law whenever the circumstances are appropriate."[82] . . . [As an important commentator explained]:[83]

> Although the minority opinion was not initially accepted, and had only few adherents, yet if another generation's majority will agree with its reasoning, it will become the law. For the entire Torah was given to Moses in this manner, with some indications for considering [an object] to be [ritually] impure and others for considering it to be pure. When the people said to Moses, "How long shall we take to clarify the matter?" he replied that the majority view is to be accepted, but both are the words of the living God.

The following pronouncement of Akavyah b. Mehalalel, who held an opinion contrary to that of the other Sages, his colleagues, still reverberates in our own time:

> Akavyah b. Mehalalel testified concerning four things. They [the Sages] said to him: "Akavyah, retract these four things you have said, and we will appoint you the head of the court for Israel." He said to them: "I would rather be called a fool for my entire life than to be deemed wicked before God for even one hour. People should not [have grounds to] say: 'He retracted for the sake of an office.'"[84]

A multiplicity of views is not harmful or disadvantageous; rather, it is essential to the outlook of the *Halakhah:* "[It] is not a deficiency, not does it imply that he has made the Torah into two Torahs, God forbid! On the contrary, such is the way of the Torah, and both . . . are the words of the living God."[85] Moreover, the multiplicity of views and approaches creates a type of harmony, and a unity fashioned from diversity. In the felicitous words of Jehiel

80. *See* Rashi, Eruvin 13b, s.v. Aluvin.

81. M Sanhedrin 11:2; TB Sanhedrin 86b.

82. *Tosefta* Eduyyot 1:4 (Zuckermandel ed.); *see* M Eduyyot 1:5.

83. Commentary of Samson of Sens on M Eduyyot 1:5.

84. M Eduyyot 5:6. *See also supra* pp. 1061–1072.

85. Ḥayyim b. Beẓalel, *Vikku'aḥ Mayim Ḥayyim,* Introduction. See the detailed discussion, *supra* pp. 1375–1379.

Michal Epstein, the most recent codifier of the *Halakhah,* [who wrote] at the beginning of the twentieth century:

> All the different points of view among the *tannaim,* the *amoraim,* the *geonim,* and the later authorities are, for those who truly understand, the words of the living God. All have a place in the *Halakhah,* and this indeed is the glory of our holy and pure Torah. The entire Torah is described as a song, and the beauty of a song is enhanced when the voices that sing it do not sound alike. This is the essence of its pleasantness.[86]

Indeed, this fundamental concept that "both are the words of the living God" had a decisive influence on the method and nature of the codification of the *Halakhah* throughout its history, and on the methods for determining the law to be applied in practice. . . . [This influence has been described in detail earlier in the present work.][87]

A multiplicity of views is an essential and welcome part of the life of a well-ordered society. The Sages even ordained a special blessing for the mystery at the core of this remarkable diversity of human opinion: "One who sees a large assemblage of people recites the blessing 'Blessed is He Who is the Master of Mysteries'; for their faces are all different and their opinions are not alike."[88] This is a fortunate circumstance for wisdom and creativity: "Just as the nature of creation even today is that each person's face is different , so too one must believe that the wisdom in the heart of each man is different."[89] The Midrash cogently states the respect that should be accorded by leaders and governments to diversity of opinion:[90]

> Just as [people's] faces are not identical, so too are their opinions diverse. Each person has his own view. Therefore, when Moses was about to die, he made this request of God: "Master of the Universe, the views of every person are well known to you, and the views of each of your children differ from one another. When I depart from them, please appoint a leader for them who will tolerate the respective opinions of each of them."

This is the teaching of the Jewish heritage in regard to leadership and government—that all persons and groups should be treated tolerantly, with respect for their views and world outlook. This is the great secret of tolerance and respect for the opinions of others, and the great power of the right of each individual and group to freedom of speech: not only are they essential to an orderly and enlightened government, but they are also essential for its generative power. In the world of nature, "two opposing elements join and create

86. *Arukh ha-Shulḥan,* ḤM, Introduction; *see supra* pp. 1451–1452.
87. *See supra* pp. 1061–1062 and references in n. 94.
88. *Tosefta* Berakhot 7:2 (Zuckermandel ed.). *See also* TB Berakhot 58a.
89. *Vikku'aḥ Mayim Ḥayyim, supra* n. 85.
90. *Midrash Rabbah,* Numbers, Pinḥas 21:2; *Midrash Tanḥuma,* Pinḥas #1.

something new; the same thing certainly happens in the realm of the spirit."[91]

4. HUMAN DIGNITY AND EQUALITY

As stated above, the Supreme Court of Israel decided in the *Naiman* case that, under the law as it then was, the court, and *a fortiori* the Elections Committee, could not disqualify a political party from competing in an election on the ground that its platform called for subversion of the Israeli democratic system. The court suggested that the Knesset enact legislation explicitly granting such power, and clearly specify the standards for such disqualification. The need for such a clear specification was explained as follows:[92]

> A general grant of authority by the Legislature to disqualify a party on the ground that its goal or its platform is contrary to the democratic principles upon which the State of Israel is founded or to the principles referred to in the Declaration of Independence, or any other similar vague and general standard, would be too uncertain for the court to apply. This is certainly true with regard to a body such as the Central Elections Committee, which (except for its chairman) is composed of members whose views and inclinations are clearly political. Democratic principles, including those referred to in the Declaration of Independence, are by their very nature susceptible of different interpretations; they reflect differing, and at times contradictory, viewpoints and approaches. This is generally true of enlightened democracies and particularly so of our society, where social, religious, economic, and political issues are legitimate points of dispute.

The principles that such legislation should seek to protect include respect for human dignity and equality, and freedom from governmental discrimination against ethnic and religious minorities. On this point, the opinion in *Naiman* stated:[93]

91. Rabbi Abraham Isaac ha-Kohen Kook, *Ha-Nir,* Jerusalem, 1909, p. 47; *id., Eder ha-Yekar,* 1967, pp. 13ff. The right of free speech must be balanced against the interests secured by the Prohibition of Defamation Law, 1965. *See supra* p. 1644 and n. 103. The Supreme Court confronted this problem in Avneri v. Shapiro, 42(iv) *P.D.* 20 (1988). In that case, a temporary injunction was sought against the publication of an allegedly libelous book. The opinion advanced two reasons for interpreting the statute in accordance with Jewish law: (1) the legislative history of the statute demonstrates that the statute was based on Jewish law, and (2) "the Foundations of Law Act, 1980, reinforced the importance of the Jewish heritage for the interpretation of the Prohibition of Defamation Law, 1965." 42(iv) *P.D.* at 26.

92. 39(ii) *P.D.* at 303.

93. *Id.* at 298.

The foundation of the worldview of Judaism is the concept of the creation of man in the image of God.[94] This is how the Torah begins, and from it the *Halakhah* derives fundamental principles concerning the worth of every human being—whoever he may be—and the right of every person to equal and loving treatment. "He [R. Akiva] would say: 'Beloved is man, for he was created in the image [of God]; but it was an act of greater love that it was made known to him that he was created in the image [of God], in that it is stated:[95] "God made man in His image."'"[96] The prohibition against murder enjoined upon the descendants of Noah even before the giving of the Torah is based on this latter verse.

The differing views of two of the leading *tannaim* as to what is the highest value in human relationships is instructive: "'Love your fellow as yourself';[97] R. Akiva says: 'This is a fundamental principle in the Torah.' Ben Azzai says: '"This is the record of Adam's line [When God created man, He made him in the likeness of God]";[98] this is a more fundamental principle.'"[99]

According to R. Akiva, the supreme value in human relationships is love for human beings; according to Ben Azzai, the supreme and superior value is human equality, since every person was created in God's image. These two values, human equality and love for human beings, have been melded in the thinking of the Jewish people; and both together have constituted the very foundation of Judaism throughout all of Jewish history. The following was said by way of amplification of this discussion:

> Ben Azzai says: "'This is the record of Adam's line'; this is a fundamental principle in the Torah." R. Akiva says: "'Love your fellow as yourself'; this is a more fundamental principle, so that you should not say: 'Since I have been disgraced, let my fellow be disgraced with me.'" . . . R. Tanḥuma said: "If you act in this manner, know Whom you are disgracing—'He made him in the likeness of God.'"[100]

The fundamental principle "Love your fellow as yourself" is not merely a theoretical matter, a matter of abstract love with no practical requirements. On the contrary, it expresses a way of life in the practical world. Hillel expressed this principle in the negative: "Whatever is hateful to you, do not do to your fellow."[101] Commentators on the Torah have noted that the statement of the principle in the negative form makes it more possible for human nature to comply with it: "For a human being simply cannot love his fellow as he loves himself. Moreover, R. Akiva himself had previously taught: 'One's own

94. Genesis 1:27.
95. Genesis 9:6.
96. M Avot 3:14.
97. Leviticus 19:18.
98. Genesis 5:1.
99. *Sifra,* Kedoshim 4:10.
100. *Genesis Rabbah* 24:7.
101. TB Shabbat 31a.

life takes precedence over the life of one's fellow.'"[102] R. Akiva who, as stated, declared that the primary principle is "love your fellow as yourself," also taught that in time of danger, to an individual or to the community, self-preservation takes precedence over preserving the life of one's fellow.[103]

The Jewish people must defend its own existence and defeat those who attack its independence and seek to drive it from its land. But even the enemy is accorded human value and dignity. When Jehoshaphat, King of Judah, triumphed over the Ammonites and the Moabites, the people sang: "Praise the Lord, for His steadfast love is eternal."[104] The Sages commented on this:

> Rabbi Johanan said: "Why does this praise of thanksgiving not include the words 'for He is good'?[105] Because the Holy One, Blessed be He, is not happy at the downfall of the wicked." Rabbi Johanan said further: "Why is it written: 'So that the one could not come near the other all through the night'?[106] When the ministering angels attempted to recite a song [of praise], the Holy One, Blessed be He, said: 'The works of My hand are drowning in the sea, and you wish to sing a song?'"[107]

The opinion then quotes the instructive words of Rabbi Abraham Isaac ha-Kohen Kook, the first Chief Rabbi of the Land of Israel, concerning love for human beings and God's creatures:

> Love for humankind must be alive in one's heart and soul—love for each individual separately, and love for all nations, [together with] desire for their advancement and for their spiritual and material progress—. . . an inner love from the depths of one's heart and soul, to be beneficent to all nations, to add to their material wealth, and to increase their happiness. . . .
>
> The highest form of love for all creatures is love for human beings, and it must include all people. Despite the many differences in opinions, religions, and beliefs, and despite the multiplicity of races and climates, one must attempt to achieve complete understanding of the various nations and groups, and to learn as much as possible about their traits and characteristics, in order to know how to base love for human beings on realistic foundations. For only when one is infused with love for God's creatures and all humankind can one elevate love of country to its most noble level, both spiritually and materially. Narrow-mindedness, which results in seeing everything outside the boundaries of one's own country—even if that country is Israel—as repulsive and

102. Naḥmanides, *Commentary on Leviticus* 19:18.

103. TB Bava Meẓi'a 62a.

104. II Chronicles 20:21.

105. As in Psalms 107:1, which reads: "Praise the Lord, for He is good; His steadfast love is eternal."

106. Exodus 14:20. The reference is to the Israelite and Egyptian camps on the Sea of Reeds.

107. TB Megillah 10b.

> unclean, is extremely contemptible; it leads to wide destruction of every valuable spiritual resource to which every decent person looks for enlightenment.[108]

Rabbi Kook's integration of the Jewish heritage with "natural ethics," the heritage of every cultured person of whatever background, is noteworthy. On this point it was stated in the *Naiman* case:[109]

> The views of Rabbi Kook on this subject, and on the worldview of Judaism in general, as to the relation between the "common natural ethics" of every cultured person and the ethical demands of Judaism, are particularly instructive:
>
>> Both from the perspective of the Torah and of common ethics, love for human beings must be carefully nurtured so that it may grow, as it should, beyond the superficial level that is as far as love can reach when it is not wholehearted. It is as if there is opposition or at least indifference to the love that should always fill all of the chambers of the soul.[110]
>
> In this training and education of a Jew, the Torah and natural ethics complement and reinforce each other:
>
>> The [religious] reverence for Heaven should not repress man's natural ethics, for then it is not true reverence for Heaven. True reverence for Heaven raises natural ethics, infixed in man's very nature, to greater heights than would be attainable by natural ethics alone. But "reverence for Heaven" such that more good would be done and greater benefits, both private and public, would accrue without it is not real reverence for Heaven.[111]
>
> In a later passage, he added:
>
>> Before the paths leading to the mystic higher ethics can be discovered, the manifest demands of natural ethics must be clearly perceived. Only by first putting in place the strong foundation [of natural ethics] can one build upon it the superstructure that reaches toward Heaven. The more the roots of a tree spread, deepen, and take hold, the more will its branches flourish and become strong and fruitful and its leaves remain verdant.[112]

108. *Middot ha-Re'iyah*, Ahavah, secs. 5, 10, in *Musar Avikha u-Middot ha-Re'iyah*, by Abraham Isaac ha-Kohen Kook, Jerusalem, 1971, 2nd ed., pp. 94, 96. The second passage from this book (sec. 10) is also quoted in the opinion of Justice Barak in the *Naiman* case, 39(ii) *P.D.* at 318. The beginning of this passage appears *infra* in the text accompanying n. 110.

109. 39(ii) *P.D.* at 299.

110. *Middot ha-Re'iyah*, *supra* n. 108, Ahavah, sec. 10. *See also* Abraham Isaac ha-Kohen Kook, *Orot ha-Kodesh* (David Cohen ed.), vol. 3, p. 218.

111. *Orot ha-Kodesh*, *supra* n. 110, vol. 3, preface to sec. 11, p. 27.

112. *Id.*, sec. 16, p. 32.

> Jewish ethics adds to and complements the requirements of moral conduct demanded in a cultured, advanced, and enlightened society; whoever disregards natural ethics is also lacking in Jewish ethics.

These instructive views of Rabbi Kook also shed light on what is encompassed by the term "Jewish heritage" in the Foundations of Law Act. This heritage does not negate the universal cultural heritage of natural ethics. It adds further demands and obligations to what is already required by the cultural heritage of "natural ethics" as accepted and customarily practiced among civilized nations.

5. ATTITUDE TOWARD NATIONAL AND RELIGIOUS MINORITIES

Elaborating on the principles of love for one's fellow human beings and of human equality, the *Naiman* opinion proceeded to outline the teachings of the Jewish heritage with regard to the treatment of national and religious minorities who live in a Jewish state:[113]

> This fundamental and basic worldview also determined the attitude taken in Jewish sources toward national minorities living under a Jewish government. The Torah explains a number of commandments basic to Judaism as commemorating historical events involving the nation's suffering as a minority under the rule of others: "For you were strangers in the land of Egypt."[114] The Torah goes even further: "You shall not abhor an Egyptian, for you were a stranger in his land."[115] Racism, with its numberless victims throughout human history up to our own days, is totally foreign to the outlook of Judaism, which absolutely rejects it. A non-Jew who joins the Jewish people is accepted as a fellow Jew, with all the rights and obligations of that status: "There shall be one law for you, whether stranger or citizen of the country";[116] "Let not the foreigner say, who has attached himself to the Lord, 'The Lord will keep me apart from His people' . . . for My House shall be called a house of prayer for all peoples."[117] This applies not only prospectively, but also retrospectively, as Maimonides said to Obadiah the Proselyte:
>
>> Whoever converts, in any generation, and whoever professes the unity of the Holy One, Blessed be He, as it is written in the Torah, is a disciple of our father Abraham, of blessed memory, and all [such proselytes] are members of his household. . . . There is no difference between us and you with respect to anything. . . . And do not disdain your lineage; if our pedigree ascends to Abraham, Isaac, and Jacob, yours ascends to Him-Who-Spoke-And-The-World-Came-Into-Being.[118]

113. 39(ii) *P.D.* at 300–302.
114. Leviticus 19:34; Exodus 22:20, 23:9; and other verses.
115. Deuteronomy 23:8.
116. Numbers 9:14.
117. Isaiah 56:3, 7.
118. *Resp. Maimonides,* ed. Freimann, #42; ed. Blau, #293.

The Jewish people does not actively seek to induce foreigners to join its ranks.[119] This fact reflects the protection accorded by Judaism to minorities wishing to live according to their own heritage and culture. The *Halakhah* has absolutely forbidden the practice—accepted in the ancient world and even later—of forcing minority groups to assimilate into the dominant majority of a country, on the basis of the principle of *cujus regio ejus religio* (*i.e.*, that the ruler determines the country's religion), pursuant to which members of minorities were persecuted until they accepted the religion of the dominant majority. Consequently, when the Jewish people won military victories, "the court did not accept proselytes during the entire period of David and Solomon: during the period of David, lest they may have converted because of fear; and during the period of Solomon, lest they may have converted because of the majesty, well-being, and greatness Israel enjoyed."[120]

According to the *Halakhah*, a member of a national minority is a "resident alien" (*ger toshav*). The only requisite demanded of him is to abide by the "Seven Noahide Laws"—the elementary rules viewed by the Sages as a type of universal natural law indispensable to a legal order and binding upon all civilized nations.[121] A national minority has all the civil and political rights enjoyed by the other residents of the country: "A *ger toshav*, let him live by your side."[122] "A *ger toshav* is to be treated with the same respect and kindness accorded a Jew, for we are obligated to sustain them . . . and since one is obligated to sustain a *ger toshav*, he must be given medical treatment without charge."[123] The Sages also said:[124] "One may not settle a *ger toshav* on the frontier or in an undesirable dwelling, but rather in a desirable dwelling in the center of the Land of Israel, where he may practice his trade, as it is written:[125] 'He shall live with you in any place he may choose among the settlements in your midst, wherever he pleases; you must not ill-treat him.'"

The principles governing the relationship of the Jewish state to all of its inhabitants are fundamental principles of the *Halakhah*, as instructively expressed by Maimonides: "For it is stated: 'The Lord is good to all, and His mercy is upon all His works.' And it is stated: 'Her ways are pleasant ways, and all her paths, peaceful.'"[126]

The foregoing discussion has touched on only a few of the rules of Jewish law on this important subject of the rights of minorities in a Jewish state, and this is not the place for an exhaustive dissertation. We conclude our comments with the following instructive quotation from Maimonides on the age-

119. *See* Micah 4:5; Maimonides, *MT*, Melakhim 8:10.

120. Maimonides, *MT*, Issurei Bi'ah 13:15.

121. *Id.* 14:7; TB Sanhedrin 56a; Naḥmanides, *Commentary on Genesis* 34:13. *See also supra* p. 194 and n. 18.

122. Leviticus 25:35.

123. Maimonides, *MT*, Melakhim 10:12; *id.*, Avodah Zarah 10:2.

124. M Gerim 3:4, based on Deuteronomy 23:17.

125. Deuteronomy 23:17.

126. Maimonides, *MT*, Melakhim 10:12, quoting Psalms 145:9 and Proverbs 3:17.

old yearning for the days of the Messiah, which, he states, "differ from the present world only with respect to servitude to [foreign] powers":[127]

> The Sages and prophets longed for the days of the Messiah, not to rule over the whole world, not to subjugate other nations, not to have other nations exalt them, and not to eat, drink, and rejoice, but rather to be free to study the Torah and its wisdom, and to be free from oppression, so that they can merit the life of the world to come, as we have explained in the Laws of Repentance. At that time, there will be neither hunger nor war, neither jealousy nor rivalry; for God's bounty will be abundant, all delicacies will be as plentiful as dust, and the only matter of concern to the world will be knowledge of God. Thus, the Jewish people will become great scholars, understand what is obscure, and learn to know their Creator to the limit of man's ability, as it is stated: "For the land shall be filled with knowledge of the Lord as water covers the sea."[128]

Jewish sovereignty and government do not exist to rule over the world or to subjugate other nations, but to prevent the oppression of the Jewish people and to permit them to study Torah and wisdom, so that the earth will be filled with knowledge and understanding. These noble sentiments expressed by a foremost Jewish sage encapsulate the mission and the character of the Jewish state.

6. THE RIGHT OF PRIVACY

One of the most significant statutes adopted by the Knesset is the Protection of Privacy Law, 1981, designed to protect the right of privacy and to prevent the personal and intimate details of a person's life from unjustifiably becoming matters of public knowledge. The approach to the interpretation of this statute generally, as well as to a particular aspect of it, was the subject of discussion by Deputy President Elon in the leading case of *Military Court of Appeals v. Vaknin:*[129]

> It would appear that the statute fails to deal with many questions, some of which are raised by the case at bar and others in discussions by scholars and jurists. . . .
>
> When the courts will be called upon to resolve the various questions involving this statute, it will be necessary, to a particularly great extent, to have recourse to the Jewish legal system. . . . First, a review of the legislative

127. Maimonides, *MT,* Melakhim 12:2, following the view of the *amora* Samuel in TB Sanhedrin 91b, 99a, *et al.*

128. Isaiah 11:9. The entire quotation is from Maimonides, *MT,* Melakhim 12:4–5.

129. 42(iii) *P.D.* 837 (1988).

history of the Protection of Privacy Law makes clear that the rules of Jewish law on this subject played a prominent and significant role.

The report of the Kahan Commission contains a chapter on the Jewish law governing the right of privacy.[130] The Introduction to this chapter states:[131]

> The Jewish legal sources very early recognized that the right of privacy was worthy of protection. The right to privacy is rooted in Scripture, and in the course of time this right was refined and crystallized into a legal right enforceable by civil and criminal penalties. The right to privacy was developed by interpretation of early sources as well as by adoption of legislation enacted when deemed necessary to reinforce and enhance the right.
>
> The protection of privacy took specific form in the protection of confidential communications, including correspondence and reading another's mail, and in protecting private life against unwarranted intrusion. One is not permitted to infringe privacy by entering the premises of another, or even by looking from outside the premises. The use of technical devices to eavesdrop on activities taking place on another's premises is clearly prohibited, even if the listening device is off the target premises. However, private premises cannot serve as a "city of refuge" for transgression and accomplishment of unlawful purposes. Thus, alongside the recognition of the right of privacy and its protection through appropriate sanctions, principles were established to protect society against the misuse of this right. . . . [132]

The requirement to seek guidance from Jewish law was strengthened with the adoption of the Foundations of Law Act, 1980; Section 1 of that Act requires that one who would interpret the Protection of Privacy Law must consult the principles of the Jewish heritage for assistance in this task.[133]

It is instructive to note the emphasis on privacy and the broad protection accorded to it by Jewish law, even in ancient times, in contrast to many other legal systems in which individual freedom and the right to privacy have only recently become the focus of attention. We here review some of the basic principles of Jewish law on this subject to bring them to the attention of the Israeli judges.

First, disclosing confidential information is as sinful as being a scoundrel: "A base fellow gives away secrets, but a trustworthy soul keeps a confi-

130. Ch. 3, pp. 5–8.

131. *Id.* at 5.

132. The Explanatory Notes to the Protection of Privacy Bill, Introduction (p. 206) contain substantially the same language. Various Jewish legal sources on the protection of privacy were quoted and discussed in the Knesset debates on the bill. *See, e.g.,* opening remarks of Minister of Justice S. Tamir, 89 *DK* 3487–3488 (1980), and the remarks of the following members of the Knesset who took part in the debates: MKs Shaḥal (89 *DK* 3494); J. Cohen (*id.* at 3509); S.Y. Gross (*id.* at 3510–3511); Shilansky (*id.* at 3512).

133. *See* Hendeles v. Bank Kupat Am, 35(ii) *P.D.* 785, 792ff. (1981); *supra* pp. 1835–1838.

dence."[134] Similarly, "When one tells something to another, it should not be disclosed [to a third person] unless he [who has told it] says to him [to whom he has told it]: 'You may divulge it.'"[135] The prohibition against revealing confidences gave rise to the principle that "it is forbidden to search out the secrets of one's fellow."[136] This is reflected in the enactment attributed to Rabbenu Gershom at the end of the tenth century C.E. that one who reads another's mail is subject to a ban.[137] Jewish law has treated with particular severity the reading of another's mail in order to steal trade secrets.[138] . . .

Jewish law has something valuable to teach concerning the protection of the privacy of one's home. It is proper conduct that "one may not enter another's home unless he [the homeowner] tells him [the visitor], 'Enter.'"[139] Beyond this, even members of the same family should respect one another's privacy. Thus, R. Akiva instructed his son, R. Joshua: "My son, . . . do not enter your own home, and certainly not the home of your fellow, without any forewarning."[140]

The broad scope of the legal protection of the privacy of one's home is exemplified by the Biblical injunction that a creditor may not enter the home of his debtor: "When you make a loan of any sort to your countryman, you must not enter his house to seize his pledge. You must remain outside, while the man to whom you made the loan brings the pledge out to you."[141]

One's privacy should be respected even when a creditor exercises the right to collect a debt. It was difficult to fulfill this idealistic requirement in the face of the demands of practical life, and various methods were devised in Talmudic and post-Talmudic law to facilitate the collection of debts, but always without infringing on the basic Biblical right to the protection of pri-

134. Proverbs 11:13.

135. TB Yoma 4b.

136. Jacob Ḥagiz, *Resp. Halakhot Ketannot,* I, #276.

137. *See* Enactments of Rabbenu Gershom Me'or ha-Golah, quoted in *Resp. Maharam of Rothenburg,* ed. Prague, p. 160a; B.Z. Dinur, *Yisra'el ba-Golah* [Israel in Diaspora], I(3), pp. 269–275; *supra* pp. 783–784 and n. 13.

138. Joseph David, *Resp. Bet David,* I, YD #158.

Sometimes there is a positive duty to attempt to discover confidential information, as where it is necessary to obtain evidence of a serious crime (*see* M Sanhedrin 7:10). Such an attempt has been held permissible in regard to any crime (*see* Joseph Babad, *Minḥat Ḥinnukh,* Commandment #462), but this conclusion appears to be contrary to M Sanhedrin 7:10, which states: "One may not spy on a person even for evidence of capital offenses, *except for this one* [*i.e.,* enticement to commit idolatry]" (emphasis supplied). Similarly, a letter may be opened when there is a reasonable belief that so doing will prevent an injury to business or property. *See* Ḥayyim Palache, *Resp. Ḥikekei Lev,* I, YD #49; Joseph Colon, *Resp. Maharik* #110; Rema to Sh. Ar. YD 228:33. *Cf.* Protection of Privacy Law, 1981, secs. 2(2), 2(5), 2(7), 2(8), and 2(9).

139. The Sages derived this rule by an inference *a fortiori* from the verses in Exodus 40:35 and Leviticus 1:1. *See Midrash Lekaḥ Tov,* also called *Pesikta Zutarta,* ed. Buber, Parashat Vayikra, p. 2.

140. TB Pesaḥim 112a. For detailed discussion, *see* Elon, *Ḥerut,* p. 32 n. 88.

141. Deuteronomy 24:10–11.

vacy. There were *tannaim* who held that the prohibition against entering the debtor's home applied only to the creditor personally and that the execution officer (in Talmudic terminology, the "court's agent") was privileged to enter the debtor's home to obtain the pledge.[142] For a long time this view was not accepted;[143] only in a later period did it become the law.[144] It must be stressed, however, that even then, when commercial necessity required the prohibition against entering the debtor's home to be relaxed to a certain extent, "the basic thrust of Jewish law as to the relation of creditor and debtor was preserved: if it was clear that the debtor was indigent, his home could not be entered [even by the court's agent], for such an entry would have no purpose except to oppress and shame."[145]

The invention of technological devices permitting eavesdropping and surveillance from a distance, and the rapid increase in number and density of population have made the need to protect privacy ever more acute.[146] Jewish law even from its earliest beginnings developed a remarkable body of doctrine around the concept of *hezzek re'iyyah* (injury caused by seeing).[147] This concept extends the right of privacy beyond protection of one's home against physical intrusion to include protection against surveillance or observation from outside.

This concept, like other basic concepts, has its origin in considerations of ethics and morality. The Book of Numbers[148] tells of Balaam, who sought to curse the Israelites, but in the end blessed them. Scripture states:[149] "Balaam . . . *saw* Israel encamped tribe by tribe" (emphasis supplied). He then blessed Israel, saying:[150] "How fair are your tents, O Jacob, Your dwellings, O Israel!" The Talmud comments on this: "What did he see? He saw that the entrances to their tents did not face each other, and this caused him to say: 'These [people] are worthy that the Divine Presence should abide with them.'"[151] The Israelites merited blessing because they set up their tents with the entrances not facing each other, so as to protect the privacy of the people.

This moral-ethical impulse toward the accommodation of privacy in the midst of community ultimately became a legal norm in Jewish law. The Mishnah states:[152] "No one may place an entrance . . . opposite the entrance [of

142. TB Bava Meẓi'a 113b.

143. *See* Maimonides, *MT*, Malveh ve-Loveh 2:2; Sh. Ar. ḤM 97:6.

144. *See* Meir ha-Levi Abulafia (twelfth century), quoted in *Tur* ḤM 96:26; Rabbenu Tam (twelfth century) and Asheri (thirteenth century), in *Sefer ha-Yashar le-Rabbenu Tam*, Ḥiddushim, ed. Schlesinger, 1959, #602, pp. 354–356; *Piskei ha-Rosh*, Bava Meẓi'a, ch. 9, ##46–47. For detailed discussion of this development in Jewish law, *see* Elon, *Ḥerut*, pp. 52–67.

145. Elon, *Ḥerut*, p. 67.

146. Explanatory Notes to Protection of Privacy Bill, *supra* n. 132.

147. *See supra* pp. 942–943.

148. Numbers 22–24.

149. Numbers 24:2.

150. Numbers 24:5.

151. TB Bava Batra 60a.

152. M Bava Batra 3:7.

another] . . . nor a window opposite [another's] window," and this rule was later codified.[153] Not only is a home so protected, but also a courtyard: "No one shall open up windows facing a jointly owned courtyard."[154] Thus, one co-owner of a courtyard may not place a window of his home where he can observe the courtyard, because this would infringe on the privacy of another co-owner while the other is in the courtyard. Of course, one certainly may not place a window where he can observe a courtyard of which he is not even a co-owner.[155]

The protection of privacy in Jewish law goes beyond prohibiting the observation of another's activities. There is a legal duty to prevent the possibility of observation that would infringe another's privacy; the mere existence of such a possibility inhibits the freedom of an individual to act as he wishes in his home or courtyard. Consequently, if one places a window where it overlooks the home or courtyard of a neighbor, the neighbor may obtain an injunction that not only prohibits being observed through the window, but also orders the window to be removed.[156] There were differences of opinion among the halakhic authorities as to whether and, if so, at what point, one who does not protest the placement of such a window has waived his rights.[157]

The foregoing material on the right of privacy in Jewish law, as well as many other references, can serve as a useful basis for the solution of manifold problems concerning the right of privacy—all within the context of the Protection of Privacy Law, the authors of which were aware and took account of the rules of Jewish law in this important and sensitive area.

7. OTHER COURT DECISIONS DISCUSSING THE PRINCIPLES OF THE JEWISH HERITAGE

A number of other cases have dealt with the principles of the Jewish heritage in the context of the provisions of the Foundations of Law Act. The following are the most important:

Attorney General v. Anonymous[158] presented the question whether the court should order that a kidney of a retarded adult son be transplanted to his father, who was devotedly caring for him. The Supreme Court refused to permit the taking of the kidney from the son, holding that on the partic-

153. Maimonides, *MT,* Shekhenim 5:6; Sh. Ar. ḤM 154:3.

154. M Bava Batra 3:7.

155. *See* TB Bava Batra 59b; Maimonides, *MT, supra* n. 153; Sh. Ar., *supra* n. 153.

156. Maimonides, *MT, supra* n. 153; Rema to Sh. Ar. ḤM 154:3, 7.

157. *See* TB Bava Batra 59a and Naḥmanides, *ad loc.*; Maimonides, *MT,* Shekhenim 7:6, 11:4; Sh. Ar. ḤM 142:3, 154:7. For discussion of this and other issues in the Jewish law of privacy, *see* Report of the Kahan Commission, pp. 5–8; N. Lamm, "The Fourth Amendment and Its Equivalent in the Halacha," 16 *Judaism* 300 (1965); N. Rakover, "Ha-Haganah Al Ẓin'at ha-Perat" [Protection of Individual Privacy], *Sidrat Meḥkarim u-Sekirot ba-Mishpat ha-Ivri* [Review of Research in Jewish Law], Ministry of Justice of Israel, 1970.

158. 42(ii) *P.D.* 661 (1988).

ular facts of the case the harm to the retarded person from such an operation was likely to be greater than the benefit he would receive. Among the subjects discussed in the light of the principles of the Jewish heritage were the powers of a guardian of the person and property of persons under disability; the duty to save the life of another person; the donation of organs generally and by persons under disability in particular; invasive medical procedures on a person under disability; and inferences as to the desire of a person under disability for such an invasive procedure.

Gali v. State of Israel[159] held that the seizure of a purse or other object from another's person on a public street is a violent act constituting robbery, even though the seizure is accomplished without any warning and without resistance by the victim. The result was reached under both Israeli statutory law and Jewish law, which distinguishes between *genevah* (theft of an object without the knowledge of the victim) and *gezelah* (robbery by force against the will of the victim).

Aloni v. Minister of Justice,[160] known as "the Nakash case," dealt with the request of the French Government to extradite a Jew named Nakash from Israel to France to stand trial for murder allegedly committed in France. The Supreme Court ordered that Nakash be extradited. An opinion by Justice Elon dealt in detail with the Jewish law relating to the extradition of a Jew to non-Jewish authorities, the problem of the wife of the person extradited becoming an *agunah* as a result of the extradition, the effect of the possible danger to the life of the extradited person as a result of the extradition, and the general relationship of Jewish law to non-Jewish law.[161]

8. HOW THE SOURCES OF THE JEWISH HERITAGE ARE TO BE USED

The following discussion of how the sources of the Jewish heritage are to be used pursuant to the Foundations of Law Act appears at the beginning of the *Naiman* decision:[162]

159. 40(iv) *P.D.* 169 (1986).

160. 41(ii) *P.D.* 1 (1987).

161. Additional cases in which the "principles of the Jewish heritage" were applied in the course of the interpretation and application of Israeli statutes include: Kleine-Bik v. Goldberg, 41(ii) *P.D.* 757 (1987) (testamentary law and the revocation of wills); Biazi v. Levi, 42(i) *P.D.* 446 (1988) (under Jewish law, compromise settlement is preferable to a decision based on the law, inasmuch as the primary objective of civil adjudication is the final resolution of disputes and this objective is better attained when accomplished by the parties themselves); Carmi v. State's Attorney, 44(i) *P.D.* 343 (1990) (interpretation of the Crime Register and Rehabilitation of Offenders Law, 1981, should be based primarily on Jewish law in view of both the legislative history of that statute and the Foundations of Law Act); *see supra* pp. 1707–1709).

162. Naiman v. Chairman, Central Elections Committee, 39(ii) *P.D.* 225, 293 (1985).

> It is well known that Jewish thought, throughout the generations, including even the halakhic system itself . . . , is replete with differing views and conflicting approaches. Each party to a dispute can easily find in the multifarious halakhic sources some support for his cause and his arguments. This is true with respect to all matters, including freedom of speech and of expression. . . .
>
> It goes without saying that all views and opinions have contributed to the depth and richness of Jewish thought throughout the generations. Nevertheless, the scholar and researcher must distinguish between statements made for a particular time only and statements intended for all times, and between statements reflecting the accepted view and those expressing aberrant views. Out of this vast and rich treasure, the researcher must extract the ample material to be applied so as to meet the needs of his time; and the new applications will then themselves be added to the storehouse of Jewish thought and the Jewish heritage. Such an approach and the making of such distinctions are essential to Jewish thought and to the *Halakhah*—as they are, because of their very nature, to every philosophical and theoretical system.

An example of the approach above suggested can be seen in the following quotation from the concluding portion of the opinion in "the Nakash case,"[163] which dealt with questions of the extradition of a Jew to non-Jewish authorities:

> Such an approach is illustrated instructively in the case before us. Many of the pertinent halakhic rules can be explained on the basis of the historical relationship between the Jewish community and the non-Jewish environment. Very often—too often—this was the relationship between a persecuted and barely tolerated minority and a powerful and dominant majority. This point was aptly and clearly expressed approximately a century ago by two leading halakhic authorities, the authors of *Arukh ha-Shulḥan* [Jehiel Michal Epstein] and *Keli Ḥemdah* [Meir Dan Plotzki], who explained some of the law pertaining to the subject under discussion, as well as a closely related subject, on the basis of the historical circumstances that existed in the Talmudic and post-Talmudic periods. They stated that circumstances had changed with the advent of the Emancipation and the adoption of more liberal policies by the European countries. If these leading halakhic authorities took such a view regarding the changes in Europe in the nineteenth century, then we must certainly take into consideration (in addition to the legal rules that are part of the Jewish heritage) the momentous and decisive change in Jewish history that occurred in our own generation with the reestablishment of Jewish national independence and sovereignty. This is a transformation that has a profound effect on the question of extradition. . . . This historical change is itself an integral and significant aspect of the Jewish heritage, and we must take

163. Aloni v. Minister of Justice, 41(ii) *P.D.* 1, 97–98 (1987).

careful account of it when we approach our task of applying the principles of the Jewish heritage as required by the Foundations of Law Act.

The above examples, taken from decisions of the Supreme Court, demonstrate how the principles of freedom, equity, justice, and peace of the Jewish heritage can be applied pursuant to the Foundations of Law Act; and they indicate the nature of the sources encompassed by the term "Jewish heritage."[164]

II. THE INTERPRETIVE FUNCTION OF JEWISH LAW IN THE ISRAELI LEGAL SYSTEM IN LIGHT OF THE FOUNDATIONS OF LAW ACT

Chapter 42[165] discussed the various problems that arose in connection with the interpretation of Israeli statutes, particularly since the beginning of the codification of civil law in the second legislative period, and the differing approaches to the solution of these problems reflected in the decisions of the Supreme Court and in scholarly literature.

What contribution do the provisions of the Foundations of Law Act make to the solution of these problems of interpretation? Does the Foundations of Law Act deal with all of the problems discussed or only with some of them? Can the desirable solution to those problems of interpretation that are not dealt with explicitly in the Foundations of Law Act be derived implicitly from the Act by means of analogy? The rest of the present chapter discusses the various views on these and related questions.

A. Uncertainty as to the Meaning of a Statute—The *Hendeles* Case, Additional Hearing

As has been pointed out, the Supreme Court justices unanimously agree that in the event of a lacuna in the law, the court is required to reach its decision on the basis of the principles of the Jewish heritage; however, there

164. *See also* Kook, *Eder ha-Yekar, supra* n. 91 at 13–20; M. Konvitz (ed.), *Judaism and Human Rights,* New York, 1972, Preface, p. 11. Several interesting recent decisions by the Israeli district courts have applied or discussed Jewish law in light of the Foundations of Law Act. *See* Lahav v. Lahav, [1982] 1 *P.M.* 39, 44 (I. Banai, J.); State of Israel, Ministry of Communications v. Briks, Ltd., [1985] 1 *P.M.* 228, 234–235 (H. Ben-Itto, J.); State of Israel v. Kurtam, [1985] 1 *P.M.* 45, 54 (I. Zahavi, J.); State of Israel v. Heimowitz, [1986] 1 *P.M.* 89, 99, 101 (H. Pizm and H. Ariel, JJ.). *See also* S. Deutsch, "Ha-Mishpat ha-Ivri bi-Fesikat Battei ha-Mishpat" [Jewish Law in the Decisions of the General Courts], *Meḥkerei Mishpat,* VI (1988), p. 7.

165. *Supra* pp. 1731–1751.

are differing views as to what constitutes a lacuna, and according to some, even the date on which the lacuna came into existence is a critical factor.[166] By contrast, there is disagreement among the justices on the basic issue of the role of Jewish law in interpreting Israeli legislation when there is no lacuna. This was the central question discussed in the additional hearing in the *Hendeles* case,[167] which occurred after the Foundations of Law Act took effect.

How should Israeli legislation be interpreted when there is no lacuna, but the meaning of a provision in the statute is uncertain and the provision can be variously construed? The author of the present work stated the following concerning this question[168] in the additional hearing in the *Hendeles* case:[169]

> What, then, should a judge do in a case such as this? What should be his methodology in interpreting the law? He should carefully examine the entire section of the statute involved, scrutinize the other sections, and try to draw analogies from the provisions of the other sections. These attempts may prove fruitful. In more general, but no less accurate terms, he searches for the essence and purpose of the law.
>
> In some cases, this may succeed in achieving the desired result; in others it will not, and the ambiguity will remain unresolved. It is well known that just as a hole in the ground cannot be perfectly refilled by the earth taken out of it, so a statute at times cannot be completely understood solely by studying its own sections. Frequently, a judge can derive from the text of the statute only hints as to how the question *sub judice* should be answered. In such a case, he draws the answer from other legal systems or from the works of legal scholars, sometimes consciously, openly, and explicitly, and sometimes without conscious deliberation or explicit awareness of the process.
>
> There are two situations when one turns to another legal system. One is when a court cannot find, either in the existing legal sources or by way of analogy, an answer to a particular question, so that there is a "lacuna." In such a case, since the repeal of Article 46 of the Palestine Order in Council, 1922, the Legislature has accorded "the principles of freedom, justice, equity, and peace of the Jewish heritage" the status of a complementary legal

166. Two justices of the Supreme Court differed as the breadth of the term "lacuna." *See supra* pp. 1835–1838. This matter is discussed further *infra* pp. 1871–1874. The view has also been expressed that the term "lacuna" refers only to a question arising as a result of legislation enacted after the effective date of the Foundations of Law Act. *See infra* pp. 1887, 1895.

167. Hendeles v. Bank Kupat Am, 35(ii) *P.D.* 785 (1981). For a discussion of the facts of this case and of the decision on the first hearing, *see supra* p. 1739–1751.

168. The nature of this problem and the various approaches proposed for its solution have been discussed *supra* pp. 1731–1739. The discussion *infra* should be read in the light of what has previously been said on this subject.

169. 35(ii) *P.D.* at 792–793.

> source. . . . The other situation is when the legal question does not involve a "lacuna," but a statutory provision is susceptible of more than one interpretation, so that the court is required to decide which interpretation is correct. An example of this latter situation is the question now before us, namely, how to interpret the provision of the above-mentioned Section 3, regarding "the *reshut* of another person." [170]
>
> There is an important difference between the two situations in regard to the status and authority of the other legal system to which the court turns. In a case of "lacuna," the above-mentioned principles of Jewish law have the status of a complementary legal source to the Israeli legal system, and the court is required to turn to these principles as a binding legal source. In the second instance, however, where there is uncertainty as to the interpretation of an existing statute, the other legal system is in the nature of a source of enlightenment—not binding but only persuasive, not decisive but only influential.

The foregoing propositions are not disputed by any of the justices of the Supreme Court. Beyond this, however, there is disagreement. My own opinion, although expressing a minority view, provides a suitable introduction to the subject and a helpful description of the issues:[171]

> When resort to another legal system is only for the purpose of enlightenment and the court must select the legal system to which to turn for this enlightenment, its first resort should be to the principles of Jewish law, as the primary and preeminent source for guidance. I have more than once characterized Jewish law as *primus inter pares* (first among equals) as a persuasive source; the most recent occasion was in my opinion on the original appeal in the instant case.[172]
>
> There are two basic reasons why Jewish law should be accorded this status. First, it necessarily follows from the legislative history of the statutes. Both in the Explanatory Notes to the bills and in the Knesset debates during the various stages of the legislative process, it was repeatedly stressed that, among the legal systems, the Jewish legal system served as the major source for the principles embodied in those statutes, and that particular attention was devoted to the incorporation of the principles of Jewish law into Israeli law.[173] The Restoration of Lost Property Law, which is the subject of the instant discussion, is a classic example.[174] It is undisputed that Jewish law was in the past and is today "part of the imperishable values of the culture [of the

170. *See supra* pp. 1743–1749 for a discussion of the decision on this point at the first hearing of the *Hendeles* case.

171. 35(ii) *P.D.* at 793–794.

172. Bank Kupat Am v. Hendeles, 34(iii) *P.D.* 57, 80 (1980).

173. *See, e.g.,* Muberman v. Segal, 32(iii) *P.D.* 85, 97 (1978); Roth v. Yeshufeh, 33(i) *P.D.* 617, 632–633 (1979); Howard v. Miarah, 35(ii) *P.D.* 505 (1981). *See also supra* p. 1626.

174. *See* Bank Kupat Am v. Hendeles, 34(iii) *P.D.* 57, 69–70, 80, 84 (1980).

> Jewish nation] . . . , the national law of the Jewish people."[175] It therefore follows that just as the draftsmen and legislative sponsors of the statute saw in Jewish law the primary source for Knesset legislation, so should the court look primarily to Jewish law, the legal system and the legal-cultural heritage of the Jewish people, for guidance in interpreting the law of the Jewish state.[176]
>
> The second reason is also of great significance. As is known, prior to the Israeli legislation, there was practically no system of Israeli jurisprudence to which a judge could turn when seeking, for example, to construe fundamental legal terms scattered throughout the legislation, or to reconcile contradictory sections of the statutes. One of the major tasks of a court in the course of everyday decision making is to fashion and develop such a jurisprudence. According preferred status to the Jewish legal system as a persuasive source for the interpretation of Israeli law, rather than referring to one legal system in regard to one issue and to a different legal system in regard to another issue, will make for more coherence and enhance the development of a rich and homogeneous jurisprudence in the Israeli legal system.

As was pointed out above in connection with the discussion of Israeli legislation,[177] in my view, these two reasons were sufficient to accord Jewish law the status of the primary persuasive source, first among equals, even before the adoption of the Foundations of Law Act. The adoption of the Foundations of Law Act reinforced these two reasons by adding two more. One was discussed in the additional hearing in the *Hendeles* case,[178] namely, that the first section of the Foundations of Law Act "indeed deals with the situation of a lacuna in the law, but it also implicitly indicates what legal system the Legislature prefers even as a source of enlightenment," namely, "the Jewish heritage," which basically means the Jewish legal system.[179]

This point illuminates and leads to still another reason, relating to the creation of a uniform base and homogeneous jurisprudence for the Israeli legal system. Since the effective date of the Foundations of Law Act, it has been unanimously agreed that, in a case of lacuna, "the Jewish heritage" is the binding complementary legal source. Is it not therefore desirable legal policy that the legal system to be utilized merely as a persuasive source for statutory interpretation should be the same legal system to which the judge is obligated to turn in a case of lacuna? Will this not promote to the fullest

175. Skornik v. Skornik, 8 *P.D.* 141, 177 (1954) (Agranat, J.). *See also supra* p. 5 n. 7 and *infra* pp. 1945–1946.

176. *See, e.g.*, Muberman v. Segal, 32(iii) *P.D.* 85, 97 (1978); Roth v. Yeshufeh, 33(i) *P.D.* 617, 632–633 (1979).

177. *Supra* pp. 1737–1739.

178. 35(ii) *P.D.* at 794. There, Section 1 of the Foundations of Law Act was erroneously referred to as Section 2.

179. *See supra* pp. 1840–1841.

extent possible the establishment of a coherent and homogeneous legal structure? Would not any other result necessarily create dissonance within the very same legal system and set the system at cross purposes with itself, in that in case of a lacuna, the Israeli judge would turn to "the Jewish heritage," as the law requires, while in case of doubt as to the interpretation of a statutory provision, the judge would turn to some other legal system? Why should different and conflicting approaches be deliberately introduced into the same legal system? Such a result is contrary to sound and desirable legal policy, and cannot have been intended by the Foundations of Law Act. To the contrary, the Legislature should be presumed to have sought to introduce order and logic into the legal system, not to have injected into the system a multitude of forces pulling against each other, each toward its own school of thought and its own legal sources.

In spite of these arguments, a majority of the justices in the additional hearing in the *Hendeles* case held that Jewish law should not be given preferred status even as a merely persuasive source when there is doubt as to the meaning of a particular statutory provision. Justice Barak stated:[180]

> When a legislative provision requires interpretation, and the task is difficult for a judge, it is wrong to conclude that interpretation must be guided primarily by the principles of Jewish law as the leading and preeminent source. It would be a mistake to substitute Jewish law for English law as the source for the interpretation of legislation. Legislation must be interpreted on the basis of its own content to accomplish its own objectives in the context of our own circumstances. If a particular legislative provision was influenced by a foreign legal system, we may turn to that system for interpretive enlightenment; this broadens our interpretive options. However, it should never be said that a particular system, however dear to us it may be, stands above the other systems and has the primary claim to interpretive inspiration. . . . In my view, not only is there no advantage in giving priority to Jewish law, but such priority runs counter to the essential nature of the interpretive process.

A similar rationale was expressed by Court President Landau:[181]

> In my opinion, we should not establish a hard-and-fast rule that would require us to turn primarily to the sources of Jewish law in order to resolve doubt as to the correct interpretation of a provision of Israeli legislation. I view the basic notion of obligating the interpreter to turn only to this source, and to no other, for the sole purpose of enlightenment (which is a matter properly in the realm of the interpreter's independent judgment), as self-contradictory, whether the obligation to follow Jewish law is absolute or whether Jewish law is only a "preferred persuasive authority."

180. 35(ii) *P.D.* at 797.
181. *Id.* at 798–799.

> In the Foundations of Law Act, the Israeli Legislature expressed its view on the relationship between Israeli legislation and Jewish law. It refrained from referring to Jewish law by name, instead choosing a term that until then had no legal definition: "the Jewish heritage." This term itself must still be given substantive content by means of interpretation, and the task will not be easy. And the Legislature directed us to do this only when a question cannot be answered by reference to legislation or judicial precedent or by means of analogy, *i.e.*, when there is a "blank area" (lacuna) in the law, as my colleague Justice Elon has well explained. It therefore follows that when, as in the case at bar, we do not face a "blank area," the Legislature did not wish our hands to be tied as we perform the task of interpretation—not even by requiring us to turn to the Jewish heritage—when the statutory language affords no basis for such a requirement.

The reasoning of Deputy President Haim Cohn is similar in some respects and different in others:[182]

> Just because an expression or a phrase taken from Jewish law must be interpreted according to the meaning given to it by Jewish law does not mean that the substantive provisions of Jewish law are to be applied as if they were statutory provisions enacted by our Legislature. Note what my distinguished colleague, Justice Elon, has done in the instant appeal with his great erudition and acuity: when he found that the term used by the Legislature, *reshut,* has a number of possible meanings, he did not search in Jewish law (or at all) for a definition of *reshut* or for a source-text that explains this term. Rather, he took the provision of the Mishnah setting forth the law relating to a lost article in the shop of a money changer, and he applied this provision to a lost article in a bank building, as if the provision of the Mishnah had been endowed with the force of a statute.
>
> It may be that the money changer of that time is the equivalent of the bank of today, and it is also possible that the money changer's shop is similar in all respects to a bank. It is even quite possible that the Mishnah's legal solution is better and more just than every other possible legislative solution. Nevertheless, the ambiguity of the term *reshut,* which our Legislature used, cannot justify incorporating the provision of the Mishnah into the body of the legislation concerning lost property, even if it could justify adopting the Jewish law's definition of *reshut*. . . . If the Legislature intended to make the law of the Mishnah or a similar law applicable to us, it could and should have so stated explicitly. . . . "If one finds a lost article in the *reshut* of another person," as stated in Section 3 of the law, means what it says: it refers to one who finds a lost article in a place that neither belongs to him nor is public domain. . . . I have no doubt that the bank building is the *reshut* of the bank, whether or not it is open to the public.

182. *Id.* at 790–791.

Justice Cohn thus supports his view with two arguments: (a) even if the meaning of the term *reshut* is uncertain, and even if the term *reshut* in the statute should be given the same meaning as it has in Jewish law, this would not justify applying the Jewish law concerning an article lost in the shop of a money changer to the *Hendeles* case, since the Legislature did not explicitly adopt the substantive rule relating to the money changer; and (b) there is no uncertainty as to the meaning of the term *reshut* in Section 3—the bank's premises are clearly included in the term "the *reshut* of another person."

At first blush, the first reason seems correct. It is actually the same rationale as that which underlies the approaches of Justices Landau and Barak, although Justice Cohn, characteristically, expressed it with striking clarity and cogency. However, with all due respect, one may well wonder that this argument was raised only with respect to Jewish law. The question arises: How is it that this argument was never raised, nor even mentioned, either orally or in writing, by Israeli judges when they freely and extensively made use of the substantive rules of all other legal systems for the purpose of interpreting Israeli legislation—and did so at a time when Israeli law did not explicitly provide that the laws of any of those legal systems should apply in any particular situation? For while it is a well-known truism that Article 46 of the Palestine Order in Council called for the application of English common law and equity only in case of a lacuna, it is also common knowledge—and quite evident from the hundreds of decisions of the Supreme Court—that recourse to English law went much further.[183] In fact, English law held sway over the entire Israeli legal system, except only as to part of family law, on which Jewish law had the major influence.

This being so, we also may express our own wonderment in the apt style of Justice Cohn: "Note what our distinguished colleagues, experienced and esteemed judges, with their great erudition and acuity, have done in almost every decision within their original or appellate jurisdiction. When they found that a particular term used by the Legislature was susceptible of more than one possible meaning, they did not search English, American, or Continental law—depending on the inclination of the particular judge, based on the judge's education and philosophical-jurisprudential predilections—for a definition of the term or for a source-text which would explain its meaning. Rather, they took the substantive rules of English, American,

183. Such recourse was by no means confined to cases involving ordinances prescribing that they are to be interpreted according to the principles of legal interpretation accepted in England, such as the Civil Wrongs Ordinance and the Criminal Law Ordinance. Moreover, these provisions requiring resort to English law were repealed in 1972, *see supra* pp. 1729 n. 414, but the courts continued even afterward to apply English law as if to do so were the natural course. *See infra* pp. 1920–1923.

or Continental law on the subject in connection with which the term was used by the Israeli Legislature, and they applied the foreign substantive law as if it had been endowed with the force of an Israeli statute. The particular foreign law's substantive rule may well have been fitting and appropriate, may have struck the right chord with the judge, and may even have been more just than every other possible legislative solution. Nevertheless, uncertainty as to the meaning of a particular term cannot justify incorporating a provision of English, American, or Continental law into the body of the legislation concerning the matter at issue, even if it could justify adopting the foreign law's definition of the particular term."

Indeed, we have cause for wonderment far more profound than Justice Cohn's. For what he was arguing against was precisely what all Israeli courts, led by the Supreme Court, did when they consulted foreign law, particularly English law, ever since the establishment of the State; and this is what the courts are still doing until this very day, despite the passage, beginning in the early 1960s, of the legislation codifying Israeli civil law. Moreover, the courts have held to this practice even throughout the not inconsiderable number of years that have passed since the Foundations of Law Act, 1980, came into force.

It is true that there has apparently been a certain decline, though not an especially significant one, in the recourse to English law; but, on the other hand, the tendency to look to American law appears to have been increasing. It goes without saying that no deprecation of the recourse to other legal systems is intended. Such recourse is salutary and beneficial; it widens horizons and deepens knowledge.[184] However, the argument against giving priority (not binding authority) to the adoption of a rule of Jewish law is untenable when such priority is routinely accorded to English and American law. There were serious and weighty reasons for giving such priority to Jewish law even before the Foundations of Law Act; these reasons became even stronger after that statute was enacted. Realities and practicalities have brought about substantial and significant recourse to English and American law, but they are not directly relevant to the present discussion and are the subject of the following chapter.

One might argue: Is not this comparison between the uses of English and Jewish law like a comparison between apples and oranges? For it has never been explicitly declared in so many words that English law is to be given preferential status as a source of enlightenment where there is no lacuna. By contrast, in the *Hendeles* case, there was an explicit statement of

184. This point is discussed *supra* pp. 62–64, 1738–1739, and in various judicial opinions. *See, e.g.*, Roth v. Yeshufeh, 33(i) *P.D.* 617 (1979).

our position that Jewish law should be accorded the preferred status of first among equals as a persuasive source for statutory interpretation.

The answer to this argument is that such a distinction, while perhaps valid from a strictly formal and technical point of view, has no substantial validity. The practice of Israeli judges and jurists to look to English law is well established, and everyone in the Israeli legal community has grown up with it and been educated by it. Consequently, the argument fails in either eventuality: If the practice of giving priority to English law when a question of statutory interpretation arises is improper and erroneous, why has no one ever objected to it (except, perhaps, in isolated instances), so as to correct the judges' error and to eliminate this impediment to proper statutory interpretation? And if the practice of giving priority to English law as a persuasive source for statutory interpretation is proper and correct, and the absence of objection to it is an implied admission of its correctness, why may the clear implication of the practice with regard to English law not be explicitly articulated with regard to Jewish law? Why the discrimination?

As to the second reason of Justice Cohn, it is true that if the term *reshut* were unambiguous and clearly included the bank's premises in the *Hendeles* case, then, as I stated in the additional hearing in that case:[185]

> There would be no justification for looking to any other legal system—Jewish law included—as persuasive authority for the explanation of the meaning of this section. A statute is to be interpreted, first and foremost, on the basis of its language, or, as the legal idiom puts it, "from within its own four corners." The problem is that, in the matter before us, the expression "the *reshut* of another person" is susceptible of different interpretations, as my distinguished colleague, Justice Barak, has shown, and as I too have pointed out.[186]

Since the expression "the *reshut* of another person" is thus susceptible of different interpretations, Justice Barak turned to articles by American legal scholars, and I turned to Jewish law which, in this particular case, reaches the same conclusion as the English and American decisions.

B. The Interpretation of Value-Laden Legal Terms

The previous discussion of the meaning of the term "lacuna" in the Foundations of Law Act noted that according to various legal scholars, interpreting value-laden legal terms such as "justice," "good faith," and "public policy" involves filling a lacuna, and also that our own view is that the phrase

185. 35(ii) *P.D.* at 792.
186. Bank Kupat Am v. Hendeles, 34(iii) *P.D.* 57, 61, 71 (1980).

"a legal question requiring decision" in Section 1 of the Foundations of Law Act includes questions as to the meaning of such value-laden terms.[187] It has previously also been pointed out that even before the enactment of the Foundations of Law Act, a number of justices of the Supreme Court had held that such value-laden terms should be interpreted according to the basic outlook of Jewish law—an outlook rooted in that law's moral and cultural values.[188] Thus, there is strong support for the view that value-laden terms such as "justice," "good faith," and "public policy" should be interpreted and fleshed out on the basis of the principles of the Jewish heritage.

As noted above, it is Justice Barak's view that a question as to the meaning of these value-laden terms is not the same thing as a lacuna. Consequently, in his opinion:

> When Israeli legislation uses basic terms such as "justice," "good faith," "public policy," and similar value-laden terms, the judicial function is to pour concrete meaning into these terms in accordance with the statutory purpose, taking into account the conditions, actual and ideal, of life in Israel. . . . Therefore, I see no possibility in such a case of applying the provisions of the Foundations of Law Act, which contemplates only the filling of a vacuum.[189]

How will the court carry out this difficult task of pouring "concrete meaning into these terms in accordance with the statutory purpose, taking into account the conditions, actual and ideal, of life in Israel"? What is the nature of this guideline? As noted above,[190] it is well known that in order to perform this task, judges often need to seek enlightenment by consulting some other legal system; they do not spin out justice and equity from within themselves.[191] It is also self-evident that it is almost impossible to determine in advance how a judge, when engaged in giving meaning to such value-laden terms, is to achieve the proper balance among the different interests involved. With regard to this point, Justice Barak has stated:[192]

> There are some who maintain that the judge should seek the same balance as the Legislature would have arrived at if it had considered the matter. As Professor Atiyah has correctly pointed out, this is only a fiction—the fiction of "the reasonable legislator," who is none other than the judge himself. It

187. *See supra* pp. 1835–1838.
188. *See supra* pp. 1729–1730, 1736–1737.
189. Hendeles v. Bank Kupat Am, 35(ii) *P.D.* 785, 797 (1981); *see supra* p. 1838.
190. *See supra* pp. 1733–1734.
191. *See* Cheshin, *supra* n. 18 at 79.
192. A Barak, "Al ha-Shofet ke-Farshan" [On the Judge as Interpreter], *Mishpatim*, XII (1982), pp. 248ff., at 254–255.

> seems to me that we would do better to admit that a judge performs the balancing according to his own judgment; that judgment, however, is not subjective, but rather the judge's objective view of the needs of society. Of course, a pure objective approach is difficult to achieve, and objectivity is most often colored by much subjectivity—the subjectivity involved in the application of an objective test. All that can be said is that a judge who construes a statute must strive for the greatest possible objectivity, even while we recognize that full attainment of this goal is impossible. . . . [193]
>
> This approach sheds light on the question that has arisen a number of times in the Supreme Court as to whether such elastic terms in Israeli legislation as "good faith" and "public policy" should be interpreted according to their meaning in Jewish law. See *Roth v. Yeshufeh,* 33(i) *P.D.* 617. Such reference to Jewish law is certainly not sanctioned by the Foundations of Law Act, 1980, since we are not dealing with filling a lacuna, but only with interpretation. Such interpretation must be governed, as we have seen, by the judge's objective perception of our current social needs, and there is therefore no basis for turning to another legal system that reflects only the balance achieved at a different time. Of course, light can be sought for the interpretive process from these and other sources, but the final balance must be struck by the judge in accordance with his understanding of the needs of his own society.[194]

As stated, I concur with those who hold that such value-laden terms as "good faith" and "justice" involve lacunae; consequently, in my view, the Foundations of Law Act requires the judge to interpret these terms in the light of the principles of the Jewish heritage. However, even admitting, for the sake of argument, that this is not mandatory, it is difficult to understand the argument that because the term "good faith" must be interpreted according to "the judge's objective perception of our current social needs," there is no basis and no "sanction" for turning to Jewish law to interpret the term inasmuch as Jewish law "reflects only the balance achieved at a different time." In the additional hearing in the *Hendeles* case, I emphasized that recourse to Jewish law for enlightenment must be carried out "with appropriate deliberation, necessary care, and due consideration of the needs of the time and the purpose of the law."[195] How is the objective-subjective balance produced by consulting a different legal system—for a judge does not spin out justice and equity from within himself—superior

193. On this subject, *see* the instructive work of the late Prof. B. Akzin, *Sugyot be-Mishpat u-vi-Medina'ut* [Topics in Law and Statesmanship], Jerusalem, 1966, pp. 144–157; Elon, *Ḥakikah,* pp. 69–76.

194. Barak, *supra* n. 192 at 255 n. 49.

195. 35(ii) *P.D.* at 795.

to or more reliable than the balance derived from looking to Jewish law while taking into consideration the "needs of the time"?[196]

C. Terms and Expressions Unique to Jewish Law

Another question discussed in the additional hearing in the *Hendeles* case is how to interpret a term used by a statute, when that term has a commonly accepted meaning in the Jewish legal system. On this question, Deputy President Cohn stated:[197]

> The learned district court judge regarded the term *reshut* as having been taken by the Legislature from Jewish law and, therefore, to be interpreted according to its meaning in Jewish law. I do not dispute the basic premise that when the Legislature has chosen an expression or phrase unique to Jewish law, it must be interpreted according to its meaning (or one of its meanings) in Jewish law, and this court has interpreted statutes in this manner many times. I do, however, dispute the proposition that the term *reshut* was taken by the Legislature from Jewish law. This is a common term in our ordinary everyday legal language, and it is neither necessary nor proper to seek it out in Jewish law and borrow it [for our own]. The late Justice Cheshin has noted that the Israeli Legislature, from the nature of things, uses many legal terms that are also used by Jewish law, such as *shetar ḥov* (promissory note), *milvah* (loan), *shi'bud* (lien), *shutafut* (partnership), etc.[198] But this cannot justify, and certainly cannot require, interpreting these terms according to Jewish law.
>
> A statute is to be interpreted according to the presumed intent of the Legislature. If the Legislature has expressed an intent that a statute should be interpreted according to Jewish law, *e.g.*, by opting to use an expression or a phrase that is unique to Jewish law and not ordinarily used by lawyers today, then the court will attempt to give effect to the intent of the Legislature and draw upon Jewish legal sources to construe the statute. However, the court will not take that course when the Legislature has chosen to use common legal terms that are in everyday use. In such a case, the presumed intent is that the language should be interpreted according to its plain meaning, using the generally accepted rules of statutory interpretation as they have always been employed in our courts. This simple approach has not been affected by the enactment of the Foundations of Law Act, 1980. The need to consult the legal sources that are part of the Jewish heritage simply does not arise so long as it is possible to search out and find in "legislation or judicial precedent, or by means of analogy" a solution to the legal question requiring decision. We must first look to the statute itself for the solution to our problem and should

196. *See also* A. Barak, *Ḥakikah Shipputit* [Judicial Legislation], *Mishpatim,* XIII (1983), pp. 25ff., at p. 40 and n. 90. Justice Barak's position has yet to be fully clarified.

197. 35(ii) *P.D.* at 789.

198. Mitoba v. Kazam, 6 *P.D.* 4 (1952).

interpret the statute in accordance with the rules of interpretation that have been settled by judicial precedent.

Justice Cohn's distinction between terms unique to Jewish law and terms in everyday use is convincing.[199] An example of a term unique to Jewish law is *gemirut da'at* (*i.e.*, a deliberate and final intention to take certain action), found in the Contracts Law (General Part), 1973.[200] This term originated with Jewish law and is unique to it; and it cannot be adequately translated into any other language. It should therefore be interpreted according to Jewish law.[201]

D. An Institution of Jewish Law Incorporated into Israeli Law—The *Koenig* Case, Additional Hearing

In his opinion in the *Hendeles* case, Justice Cohn indicated that when a statute not only uses a particular term but incorporates a legal institution of Jewish law, the court must resolve questions that arise in connection with that institution by turning to Jewish law (so long, of course, as there is no statutory provision explicitly negating such recourse).[202] Indeed, shortly thereafter, the Supreme Court, again in an additional hearing before a panel of five justices, was faced with a problem of interpretation where a legal institution, and not merely a legal term, had been explicitly incorporated into Israeli legislation.

The case, *Koenig v. Cohen*,[203] involved a young woman who committed suicide, leaving a will written in her own hand just prior to her death. Section 19 of the Succession Law, 1965, provides that "a holographic will

199. *See* Hendeles v. Bank Kupat Am, 35(ii) *P.D.* 785, 798 (1981), where Justice Landau expressed his concurrence with the opinion of Justice Cohn. However, the view that accords the broadest scope to the Foundations of Law Act has no need for the distinction. *See infra* pp. 1894–1897.

200. The term appears in Section 5 of the statute, with regard to *gemirut da'at* in entering into a contract. *See also* S. Deutsch, "Gemirut Da'at ve-ha-Kavvanah le-Yiẓẓur Yaḥasim Mishpatiyyim be-Dinei Ḥozim ba-Mishpat ha-Ivri, ha-Angli ve-ha-Yisra'eli" [*Gemirut Da'at* and the Intent to Create Legal Relationships in Jewish, English, and Israeli Contract Law], *Shenaton*, VI–VII (1979–1980), p. 71.

201. It would seem that this distinction between terms commonly used in daily Hebrew and terms unique to Jewish law is a valid basis for limiting the scope of Mitoba v. Kazam, *supra* n. 198, which asserted that there is no obligation to give Hebrew terms in a statute the same meaning they have in the literary sources of Jewish law. The rule announced in *Mitoba* applies only when the term had been commonly used in ordinary legal language before it was incorporated into Israeli legislation. The term *gemirut da'at* was derived from Jewish law and was not part of Israeli legal usage until legislation introduced it as a new legal term in Israeli law.

202. *See* the opinion of Justice Cohn, quoted *supra* p. 1868.

203. 36(iii) *P.D.* 701 (1982).

shall be entirely in the handwriting of the testator, who shall also date and sign it." There was no doubt that the will in the *Koenig* case was written shortly before the suicide and was entirely in the decedent's handwriting, but it was neither dated nor signed. Accordingly, it did not qualify for probate under Section 19, and was required to comply with the formalities of an ordinary will, including signature and witnesses, unless saved by Section 25, which permitted probate of a will despite certain defects, including a defect in the signature, if the court is convinced of the will's authenticity. A majority of the justices on the panel decided that Section 25 did not apply when a will is defective for total lack of a signature.[204]

According to the majority, the term "defect in the signature" in Section 25 did not include the total absence of a signature, and there was therefore no basis for permitting the will in the *Koenig* case to be probated. As to the provision of Section 25 that allows for disregarding defective compliance with procedural requirements, only Sections 20–23 (and not Section 19) were included among the procedural sections listed there. Justice Barak, dissenting, argued that when there is no doubt as to the authenticity of a holographic will, the will can be probated even if it is not signed by the testator. It was his view that the absence of a signature on a will is a defect that may be cured pursuant to Section 25 of the statute. It was my opinion that although the will could not be probated as a holographic will pursuant to Section 19, because it was not signed by the testatrix, it could be probated pursuant to Section 23(a) of the Succession Law, which provides:

204. When the *Koenig* case was decided, Section 25 read as follows:

> If the court has no doubt as to the authenticity of a will, it may admit the will to probate even if there is a defect in the signatures of the testator or the witnesses, in the date of the will, in compliance with the procedures set forth in Sections 20 to 23, or in the competence of the witnesses.

In 1985 (three years after the *Koenig* case), Section 25 was amended by the addition of the following subsection:

> If the court has no doubt as to the authenticity of a holographic will and as to the testamentary intent (*gemirut da'at*) of the testator, it may, in special circumstances, admit the will to probate even if the signature or date required by Section 19 is lacking.

The marginal heading to Section 25, which previously read "Probate of a Will despite Formal Defects," was amended to read "Probate of a Will despite Formal Defects or Lack of Compliance with Formal Requirements."

The amendment was enacted as a result of the decision of the majority in the *Koenig* case that the absence of a signature or date cannot be considered a "defect" within the meaning of Section 25. In order not to do an injustice to a beneficiary of the will by disregard of the obvious intention of the testator, the statute now contains an explicit provision "that makes it possible for the court, even in the absence of a signature and a date, to probate the will as written if the court has no doubt as to the authenticity of the document and as to the testamentary intent of the testator, and there are special circumstances justifying such action." Explanatory Note to Bill No. 1653 of 1984, p. 94.

> A person on his deathbed (*shekhiv me-ra*) or one who, under the circumstances, reasonably apprehends imminent death may make an oral will in the presence of two witnesses who understand his language.[205]

My opinion stated:[206]

> Before discussing the nature of the provisions of this section and what they require in light of . . . Section 25, it is appropriate to discuss the character of such a will in Jewish law, since it is recognized that Jewish law is the source of the section of the Succession Law that provides for this type of will. The principles of Jewish law should therefore guide us, so long as they are consistent with the language and purpose of the statute. This was explicitly stated in the Explanatory Notes to the Draft Succession Bill,[207] and has been repeatedly confirmed in the decisions of this court.[208] This conclusion now holds with even greater force, in view of the provisions of the Foundations of Law Act.

Under Jewish law, a will executed by a person in good health and under normal circumstances (such a will is known as *mattenat bari*—the gift of a healthy person) must be accompanied by an act of acquisition (*kinyan*), which signifies the deliberate and final intent of the donor (*gemirut da'at*) to dispose of his property in accordance with the will. The situation is different when the will is executed by a person who is so severely ill as to be properly considered a *shekhiv me-ra* (facing imminent death from illness),[209] or by a person who, though in good health, otherwise faces imminent danger of death. In such instances, the will is valid even if not accompanied by a *kinyan*. The opinion discusses in detail the Jewish law regarding the will of a *shekhiv me-ra* or of one who is otherwise in imminent danger of death,[210] and states:[211]

205. On *shekhiv me-ra, see supra* pp. 580 n. 148, 1682–1683, and *infra* n. 209 and accompanying text. Section 23 of the Succession Law continues:

> (b) The testator's declaration, with a notation of the date and the circumstances under which the will was made, shall be recorded in a memorandum, which the two witnesses shall sign and file with a district court; the memorandum shall be made, signed, and filed as soon as practicable.
>
> (c) An oral will becomes void one month after the circumstances that warranted its making have ceased to exist, provided the testator is still alive.

206. 36(iii) *P.D.* at 733.

207. Draft Succession Bill, published by the Israel Ministry of Justice, 1952, pp. 71–72.

208. *See, e.g.*, Rosenthal v. Tomashevski, 25(i) *P.D.* 488 (1971).

209. The Aramaic word *me-ra* refers to a sick person or an illness. Thus, the verse in II Kings 13:14, "Elisha had been stricken with the illness of which he was to die," is translated into Aramaic by *Targum Yonatan b. Uzziel* using the words "*me-ra yas mar'ay,*" meaning "stricken with the illness."

210. 36(iii) *P.D.* at 733–736.

211. *Id.* at 734–735.

> In sum, when presented with the will of a *shekhiv me-ra* or of one who apprehends imminent death, our task is to determine the authenticity of the will, *i.e.*, whether the testator did in fact make the statements or write the document. But this will need not be accompanied by a *kinyan*. Although a *kinyan* is necessary for the will of a person in good health to show that the testator had the necessary testamentary intent, in the case of a *shekhiv me-ra* or of one who apprehends imminent death, the presumption arises from the circumstances in which the will was made that it was done with such intent.
>
> This is so because in these circumstances a person clearly wishes his instructions to be carried out and would be tormented "by the anguish of knowing that his children will not carry out his will,"[212] and also because what is said in this moment of truth is said seriously and with a deliberate intent, for "no one mocks when about to meet his Maker." We are thus necessarily brought to one further conclusion. The sole function of the witnesses needed for the will of a *shekhiv me-ra* is to prove the content of the will and that it was made by a *shekhiv me-ra*. Such testimony, however, is not a constitutive requirement for the basic validity and efficacy of the will.

Consequently:[213]

> The will of a *shekhiv me-ra* may be made either orally or in writing. Indeed, a written will is better evidence of its content than an oral will, the proof of which depends on how accurately it was heard and how correctly it was testified to by the witnesses who heard the statements. . . . The written will of a *shekhiv me-ra* is valid and subsisting from the moment it is written.[214]

The foregoing is a brief description of the will of a *shekhiv me-ra* in Jewish law, and a summary of the basic laws with regard to it that are relevant to our discussion.

In Section 23 of the Succession Law, to which reference has been made, the Israeli Legislature adopted the Jewish law relating to the will of a *shekhiv me-ra*. In this connection, my opinion in the *Koenig* case stated:[215]

> An examination of the provisions of this section [23] reveals that in it the Legislature, with only a few insignificant changes, adopted the provisions of Jewish law with regard to the nature, elements, and principles relating to the will of a *shekhiv me-ra*. Subsection (a) alludes to a *shekhiv me-ra* and to one who apprehends imminent death, and the principle is that the statement of a *shekhiv me-ra* has the same legal force as if it had been in writing and delivered. Subsection (c) provides that the will of a *shekhiv me-ra* is automatically

212. Rashbam, Bava Batra 147b, s.v. Mattenat shekhiv me-ra.

213. 36(iii) *P.D.* at 736.

214. *See* Maimonides, *MT*, Zekhiyyah u-Mattanah 5:2; *Tur* ḤM 250:1; Sh. Ar. ḤM 250:21, and *Sema, ad loc.*, subpar. 8.

215. 36(iii) *P.D.* at 736.

> void once the circumstances justifying its making have changed—which is also the rule in Jewish law—and the subsection sets up a predetermined period of one month so as to reduce the uncertainty as to [when the will becomes invalid after the] change of circumstances. Another addition, which is also not a fundamental change in the character of the will, is found in subsection (b), which provides for the filing of a memorandum of the terms of the will with the district court.
>
> As in Jewish law, the necessary testamentary intent of the testator who is a *shekhiv me-ra* is presumed from the fact that the will was made in the special circumstances of mortal illness or imminent death. Thus, in order for an ordinary will made in the presence of witnesses under Section 20 to be valid, the testator must declare in the presence of witnesses that the instrument is his will, and the witnesses must contemporaneously confirm by their signatures that the testator has so declared in their presence. The purpose of this requirement is "to impress upon both the testator and the witnesses the solemnity of the document and of the occasion."[216] However, there is no such requirement for a will of a *shekhiv me-ra;* the particular circumstances in which the *shekhiv me-ra* or one who believes himself to be facing death finds himself are themselves sufficient to assure the solemnity of the occasion and the deliberateness and finality of the testator's intent—"no one mocks when about to meet his Maker." The sole purpose of the witnesses to such a will is to provide evidence as to what the testator actually said.[217]

Subsequently in the opinion, it was pointed out that the provisions of Section 25 of the Succession Law are explicitly made applicable to the will of a *shekhiv me-ra* for which provision is made in Section 23, and that a prior decision of the Supreme Court[218] had established that even if a will is completely lacking in any of the legal requirements prescribed in Sections 20 to 23 of the Succession Law, the defect is to be considered merely procedural, so long as such a will contains the "distinguishing features essential to a will."[219] In light of these considerations, the following conclusion is warranted:

> There are two distinguishing features essential to the will of a *shekhiv me-ra:* (a) the testator must be mortally ill or believe himself to be facing imminent death; (b) there must be no doubt as to the contents and the authenticity of the will. In contrast to these, the requirement [of Section 23 of the Succession Law] that the will be made orally and the additional requirement—which necessarily follows from the requirement that the will be made orally—that

216. Sharabi v. Sobri, 25(i) *P.D.* 429, 431–432 (1971).

217. *See also* Rosenthal v. Tomashevski, 25(i) *P.D.* 488 (1971).

218. Brill v. Attorney General, 32(i) *P.D.* 98 (1977).

219. *Id.* at 101. Thus, for example, the absence of a date in a will which is witnessed is a procedural defect that may be corrected despite the fact that Section 20 of the statute explicitly requires that the will be dated.

> the *shekhiv me-ra* must declare his intent in the presence of two witnesses who are to make a memorandum of his statement and duly file it, are merely procedural rules. It is with respect to such rules that Section 25 provides that as long as there is no doubt of the authenticity of the will, the court may admit it to probate even where these requirements have not been fulfilled. An example of such a case is that of a will in the handwriting of a *shekhiv me-ra* or of one who believes himself to be facing imminent death, where the court is convinced that the handwriting is genuine and that the will is authentic and accurate. . . .[220]
>
> Certainly, if only Section 23 were before us, we would have to conclude that the Legislature decreed that the will of a *shekhiv me-ra* must be oral and must be made in the presence of witnesses. However, since the Legislature provided in Section 25 that the court may probate the will of a *shekhiv me-ra* even if compliance with the procedure outlined in Section 23 is defective (and "procedural defect" has been interpreted to include even complete noncompliance with the particular procedural requirement), we may probate a holographic will made by a *shekhiv me-ra* or by one who believes himself to be facing imminent death when we are convinced that the will is authentic and was written by the testator.[221]

For all these reasons I came to the conclusion that the decedent's will should be held valid under Sections 23 and 25, because it was made by one who believed, reasonably under the circumstances, that she was facing imminent death, and we had no doubt that the will was authentic and that it was in the decedent's handwriting.[222]

Court President Landau and Justice Shelomo Levin disagreed. According to Justice Levin, holding an unwitnessed will written by a *shekhiv me-ra* to be legally equivalent to a will made orally and in the presence of two witnesses is "an encroachment upon the prerogative of the Legislature," and the provisions of Section 25 do not apply to such a case. This, in substance, was also the view of Justice Landau. Justice Landau's opinion also discusses the question whether the Foundations of Law Act has any bearing

220. 36(iii) *P.D.* at 737.

221. *Id.* at 738.

222. Similarly, the rabbinical courts have ruled that in the case of a will written by a person who subsequently commits suicide, if it is clear that the will was written in contemplation of imminent suicide—"there can be no clearer example of a will made in contemplation of death, and it is valid even without any *kinyan.* [The will in] such a case is certainly no less [valid] than the will of a testator setting out on a sea voyage or a journey over land, or about to be put to death, [all of] which are instances specifically mentioned in the Mishnah and the Talmud." A. v. B., (1943), Warhaftig *Osef Piskei ha-Din,* p. 20. The same ruling can be found in *Resp. Yaskil Avdi,* VI, ḤM #17 (by Rabbi Ovadiah Hadayah, who served as a member of the Rabbinical Court of Appeals). *See also* Koenig v. Cohen, 36(iii) *P.D.* 701, 739 (1982).

on how Israeli legislation should be interpreted in a case like *Koenig v. Cohen:*[223]

> In *Rosenthal v. Tomashevski,*[224] which my colleague Justice Elon cited, I stated (at page 492) that the term *shekhiv me-ra,* which appears in Section 23 of the Succession Law, is not defined in the statute, but was adopted from Jewish law, and we may therefore have recourse to the general principles of the *Halakhah* on this subject as closely as we can perceive their thrust. I then quoted the definition of the term *shekhiv me-ra* from the *Shulḥan Arukh.* It is not a fair conclusion from this that we can resort to the rules of Jewish law to interpret Section 23 as a whole, since it is clear from the language of the section that the Israeli Legislature established a statutory regime that differs from Jewish law. When the Legislature explicitly refers to an oral will in that section, we cannot rely on the halakhic sources to say that an oral will also means a written will.
>
> We must interpret the sections of the statute as they stand, and give effect to the fundamental differences between the rules of Jewish law and the statute that the Legislature desired to enact. The Foundations of Law Act is irrelevant here because the statute itself provides an unambiguous answer. I therefore cannot agree with my distinguished colleague when he states that an examination of the provisions of Section 23 reveals that in this section the Legislature adopted the provisions of Jewish law with regard to the nature, elements, and principles relating to the will of a *shekhiv me-ra,* with only a few insignificant changes.
>
> My distinguished colleague has enlightened me that I did not reflect the views of the halakhic authorities, when, in the *Rosenthal* case, I equated the two witnesses required by Section 23 with *edei kiyyum* (constitutive witnesses) under Jewish law. This, of course, I must accept. But it still seems to me that a testator's oral declaration in the presence of two witnesses to his statement is the constitutive basis for an oral will under Section 23.

Justice Landau's disagreement with my conclusion thus stems from his view that the provision in Section 23 for two witnesses (not required by Jewish law) to a will of a *shekhiv me-ra* is a constitutive requirement that the Israeli Legislature explicitly prescribed, and therefore an unwitnessed written will of a *shekhiv me-ra* cannot be validated under the statute, even though such a will is valid under Jewish law. As stated in my opinion, I believe that this is not the correct interpretation of the provision for witnesses under Section 23. Had I thought that this is the correct interpretation of Section 23, I too would have concurred with Justice Landau, for it cannot be disputed that when the Legislature explicitly declares that it does not

223. 36(iii) *P.D.* at 744–745.
224. 25(i) *P.D.* 488 (1971).

accept a particular rule of the Jewish law of *shekhiv me-ra,* that declaration is the law for the Israeli legal system.

Justice Landau conceded that since the term *shekhiv me-ra* was adopted from Jewish law, we may have recourse to the general principles of the *Halakhah* on this subject, as closely as we can perceive their thrust, except where "it is clear from the language of the section that the Israeli Legislature established a statutory regime that differs from Jewish law." The logic of this interpretive approach is compelling, both as to the general rule and the exception. This approach has also been mandated by every possible correct standard of sound and desirable legal policy since the time of the enactment of the Succession Law in 1965, in view of the fact that the Succession Law incorporated the *shekhiv me-ra*'s will as a legal institution from the Jewish legal system. As discussed above, it is certainly the correct and requisite interpretive approach at the present time, in light of the Foundations of Law Act, which took effect in 1980.

As has been noted, this approach is also indicated in the opinion of Justice Cohn in the additional hearing in the *Hendeles* case. According to Justice Cohn, there is no requirement to look to the content of Jewish law relating to a particular legal institution when the Legislature has used only a term or expression taken from Jewish law, but recourse to the content of Jewish law would be required when the Legislature has incorporated a general principle or an entire legal institution from Jewish law.[225]

Justice Barak did not reach the question of the interpretation of Section 23 of the Succession Law. Since the parties had not raised this issue, he preferred to leave the issue open.[226] However, he expressed the general view that even if an Israeli statute incorporates a legal institution from Jewish law, the rules of Jewish law should not be used as either a binding source or even a primary persuasive source for the interpretation of that legal institution. Justice Barak stated:[227]

> My distinguished colleague, Justice Elon, states that in the light of the provisions of the Foundations of Law Act, 1980, we are directed to turn to Jewish law to interpret the provisions of Section 23 of the Succession Law. In view of my basic approach, I wish to abstain from any discussion of this subject. It is sufficient for me to refer to what I stated in the *Hendeles* case[228]—that the Foundations of Law Act deals with the filling of a void in the law, *i.e.,* the creation of a new law where the existing law is silent and its silence is not a mandate for a negative. Here, however, we are concerned with the interpre-

225. *See supra* p. 1875; *see* 35(ii) *P.D.* at 790.
226. 36(iii) *P.D.* at 725.
227. *Id.* at 725–726.
228. 35(ii) *P.D.* at 787.

> tation of a legal norm, *i.e.*, the contours of a statutory provision which answers our question. The Foundations of Law Act is therefore inapplicable.
>
> As to interpreting the provisions of the statute in light of Jewish law, from which it was taken, it suffices for me to reiterate that what the Israeli Legislature incorporated from Jewish law is a concept, not a legal rule. The concept became law only by action of the Israeli Legislature; but this action did not incorporate Jewish law. Therefore, we need not find in the Israeli statute a provision that negates or is inconsistent with Jewish law, in order for Jewish law to be inapplicable. The reason Jewish law does not apply is that Jewish law was not incorporated.
>
> At the same time, it is proper and desirable for Jewish law, which was the inspiration for the enactment of the provision of the law, to be a source for interpretive enlightenment, *i.e.*, for expanding the judge's horizons and field of vision, so as to produce additional depth of interpretive creativity. Nevertheless, the decision as to the choice among the various possibilities is for us, to be made unfettered by any system outside our own and without primacy or priority accorded to any other system, no matter how dear to us it may be.

Under this approach, even when Israeli legislation incorporates an institution from Jewish law, it incorporates "a concept, not a legal rule." Therefore, "Jewish law does not apply" because it "was not incorporated"; and consequently—contrary to what was said by Presiding Justice Landau—"we need not find in the Israeli statute a provision that negates or is inconsistent with Jewish law, in order for Jewish law to be inapplicable."

I responded to Justice Barak's approach as follows:[229]

> Upon reading the additional remarks of my distinguished colleague, Justice Barak, which in part deal with the interpretation of the Foundations of Law Act, I again considered the interdependence between the intent of the interpreter and the intent of the legislator, and the care necessary to prevent the legislator's intent from being submerged by the interpreter's intent. The judgment in the case before us has been concluded, and it is inappropriate that I should add any further comment on this statute. I dealt with it in the *Hendeles* case,[230] and at the proper time, I shall again discuss this matter further.
>
> At this opportune moment, I will say only the following: It is accepted that one of the basic rules of interpretation is that the Legislature does not use superfluous verbiage, and that the words it uses are to be given meaning. This rule has particular force when a new and comprehensive statute is involved, and utmost force when the statute is a basic statute that occupies an extremely important place in the legal system of the State. With regard to the

229. 36(iii) *P.D.* at 742–743.
230. 35(ii) *P.D.* at 792.

> question before us, it is clear that the Legislature incorporated from the Jewish legal system the essential features of the will of a *shekhiv me-ra* or of a person who believes himself to be facing imminent death, and there is nothing in the language or objective of the law to rule out the logical consequences of this incorporation. All this being so, if the Foundations of Law Act nevertheless does not suffice to endow Jewish law with any higher status than the persuasiveness possessed by every other legal system, what is the purpose of Section 2 [the reference should be to Section 1] of this statute, which not only constitutes half of the statutory text but is the statute's "affirmative commandment," and what change does the statute's enactment effectuate?
>
> Even before this statute became part of the Israeli legal system, the court could engage in the venerable task of turning to Jewish law for the purpose of "expanding the judge's horizons and field of vision, so as to produce additional depth of interpretive creativity." What change, then, has now been introduced by the enactment of the statute entitled the "Foundations of Law" Act? If the response is that Jewish law will have its day when there is a lacuna, and if we define lacuna as my distinguished colleague did in the *Hendeles* case, and if a lacuna does not include what he said it does not include, I would very much like to know when and how it will be possible to find a lacuna totally unaddressed by the law in "legislation or judicial precedent, or by means of analogy." Is it indeed possible to interpret a statute so that the Legislature's words have even less legal meaning than the [dried] "fig of Rabbi Ẓadok"?[231] Were all the debates that took place and all the versions that were drafted (by the members of the Knesset in particular and the legal community in general) before the enactment of this basic statute solely for the purpose of addressing the problem of a lacuna which has never yet nor will ever likely occur, and which, if and when it does occur, will more than likely encounter the refusal of a majority of the court to acknowledge its existence? I wonder.

Since 1982, when these words were written, my wonderment has not abated.[232]

231. *See* TB Gittin 56a. The expression refers to a dried fig from which all the juice has been squeezed. With regard to the incorporation of the will of a *shekhiv me-ra* in the Succession Law, 1965, *see also supra* pp. 1682–1683.

232. These words have indeed proved almost prophetic. During the course of publication of the present translation, the Supreme Court of Israel decided one of its most important cases. In that case, Jerczewski v. Prime Minister Yitzhak Shamir, 45(i) *P.D.* 749 (1991), Justice Barak formulated a theory he called "development of the law (*pittu'aḥ ha-mishpat*)," according to which the existence of a lacuna in the Israeli legal system is virtually impossible. The discussion that the case merits would be too extensive to be undertaken here; this note merely sketches one of the highlights. It is hoped that a full discussion can be published in the near future and incorporated into later editions of the present work.

Jerczewski is one of the leading constitutional and public law cases in Israeli jurisprudence. At issue was the legal effect of a typical agreement between political parties for a coalition looking to the formation of a government acceptable to a majority of the Knesset.

III. THE FOUNDATIONS OF LAW ACT, 1980, AND THE INCORPORATION OF THE ENGLISH STATUTE OF ELIZABETH, 1571

The strange and puzzling heading of this section may well startle the reader. What connection is there between the Foundations of Law Act, enacted by the Israeli Knesset in 1980 for the purpose of integrating the principles of the Jewish heritage into the Israeli legal system, and a British statute enacted over four hundred years ago? But so wondrous are the ways of statutory interpretation and legal scholarship that the creation of this strange amalgam of the laws of the Jewish state in the second half of the twentieth century and the laws of Great Britain in the second half of the sixteenth century is not beyond their power. We learn of this strange combination from a book by Professor Uriel Procaccia that appeared in 1984 on the subject of the Israeli law of bankruptcy.[233]

It is general knowledge that statutory interpretation is the province not only of the courts but also of legal scholars in their respective fields. Al-

---

The issue had never before been adjudicated, and Israeli law offered no analogies. If ever there was a case of a lacuna, it was this one.

Justice Barak and I agreed that, with certain limitations not relevant here, such political agreements are legally binding, but our reasons were sharply divergent. In my view, there was a lacuna, and we were therefore obligated to look to the sources of the Jewish heritage, *i.e.*, the responsa literature and the current rulings of the rabbinical courts affirming the binding effect of such agreements. According to Justice Barak, however, there was no lacuna and therefore no obligation to look to the sources of the Jewish heritage. He grounded the binding force of political agreements on a postulated premise of Israeli public law to the effect that a public official is bound to serve faithfully, reasonably, and fairly. On this basis, he concluded that one who undertakes to serve the public has a legal duty to perform his political agreements. Justice Barak calls the novel legal device that yields this conclusion "development of the law," which he explains as follows:

> This activity is neither judicial interpretation nor the filling of a lacuna. This is judicial activity in the "development of the law." . . . It is the mechanism by which we determine new rights and obligations.

In the opinion I wrote in this case, I expressed my wonderment at how it was possible to derive from these *general principles* of the Israeli legal system the conclusion that political agreements are *legally* binding, but that is not the point here. The critical question here is: How, if we accept this theory of "development of the law," will it ever be possible for a lacuna to exist or for the Foundations of Law Act ever to require judges to look to the principles of the Jewish heritage? It is submitted that to adopt the theory that legal questions for which the existing legal order provides no answer can be resolved by "basic principles" of the legal system is to negate completely any possibility of a lacuna as well as any requirement of the Foundations of Law Act ever to look to the principles of the Jewish heritage. Justice Barak's opinion (in which no other justice joined) would turn the Foundations of Law Act into a dead letter. *See further* Jerczewski v. Prime Minister Yitzhak Shamir, *supra* at 776–785 and 822–834 (Elon, J.), and at 838–844 and 858–860 (Barak, J.).

233. U. Procaccia, *Dinei Peshitat ha-Regel ve-ha-Ḥakikah ha-Ezraḥit be-Yisra'el* [Bankruptcy Law and Civil Legislation in Israel], Jerusalem, 1984.

though such academic interpretation is purely theoretical and, unlike judicial interpretation, creates no enforceable obligations, both the judge and the academic scholar wrestle with the same problematics of the interrelationship between the desires of the interpreter and the intent of the legislator that were previously discussed in connection with the additional hearing in the *Koenig* case. It is therefore appropriate to consider the views of legal academicians on this issue as bearing on the interpretation of the Foundations of Law Act.

The beginning of this chapter[234] dealt with the divergent views regarding the interpretation of the expression "the law that was accepted in this country" in Section 2 of the Foundations of Law Act. As was stated, in my view, this expression refers to those rules of English common law and equity that were *actually* incorporated into Israeli law through decisions of the Supreme Court. An opposing view holds that the phrase refers to those laws which could have been incorporated into Israeli law even if no judicial decision had actually done so. According to this latter view, the provision of Article 46 of the Palestine Order in Council of 1922 to the effect that in case of a lacuna the gap should be filled by English common law and equity was "self-executing,"[235] *i.e.,* English law was automatically incorporated whenever there was a lacuna, and such incorporation did not require a decision by any court.

However, if one holds, as I do, that Article 46 was enabling legislation (*i.e.,* it authorized the court to use English law in case of a lacuna, but so long as the court had not applied a rule of English law in an actual case, the rule did not become part of the Israeli legal system), it follows that if a case involving a lacuna first arises after the repeal of Article 46, then even if the lacuna in the law existed before Article 46 was repealed, the lacuna should no longer be filled by English law, but rather by the principles of the Jewish heritage, as provided in the Foundations of Law Act.

Professor Procaccia, who is a proponent of the view that Article 46 was self-executing, contends that "the repeal of Article 46 of the Palestine Order in Council leaves in full effect all the legal rules that constituted a part of our law in force before the repeal, despite the fact that only some of these English laws were explicitly 'adopted' by an Israeli court."[236] He does not see in this any inconsistency with "the goal of the Foundations of Law Act, which was to weaken the link [of Israeli law] . . . with English law."

234. *Supra* pp. 1828–1829.

235. *See* Tedeschi, "Bittul Siman 46 li-Devar ha-Melekh ve-Ko'aḥ Pe'ulato," *supra* n. 14. This article by Tedeschi uses the terms "self-executing legislation" and "enabling legislation."

236. Procaccia, *supra* n. 233 at 17. This is also the view of Prof. Friedmann. *See supra* pp. 1828–1829.

He argues that although at first glance the Act seems to require "sever[ing] the ties between our legal system and all those rules of the common law that had not yet been explicitly adopted in a domestic decision [*i.e.*, a decision by a court of competent jurisdiction in the Land of Israel]," nevertheless, he considers the goal of the Act to be accomplished because the repeal of Article 46 will operate in cases of lacuna that will arise in the Israeli legal system in connection with legislation enacted *after* the effective date of the Foundations of Law Act. He contends that "this, therefore, is the normative expression of the weakening of the link between our system and English law. Thus, the Legislature's words were not rendered devoid of meaning."[237]

Professor Procaccia addresses an additional difficulty in his position, namely, the requirement in Section 1 of the Foundations of Law Act that in order for a lacuna to exist there must be no "judicial precedent" on the question requiring decision by the court. In his own words:[238]

> The question now arises: Under our view, what is the "judicial precedent" that is the source for a legal rule whose existence will prevent the occurrence of a lacuna? Some have expressed the view that "judicial precedent" refers to legal rules found in Israeli court judgments, including decisions that have applied rules of common law and equity; however, if there is no such decision, the lacuna should no longer be filled by English law but by "the principles of freedom, justice, equity, and peace of the Jewish heritage." According to this view, the Legislature that enacted the Foundations of Law Act viewed Article 46 as an enabling act and denied normative status to all the rules of English common law and equity not expressly adopted by a decision of an Israeli court.

Professor Procaccia, differing with the approach just described, responds as follows to the problem he raised:

> This approach can be justified only if the term "judicial precedent" is interpreted narrowly, as including only the judgments of the domestic [*i.e.*, Israeli] courts. I see no reason to resort to such a narrow interpretation. Common law and equity are also "judicial precedent," and, pursuant to Section 1 of the Interpretation Ordinance, acquired official sanction as "law" from the Legislature. Thus, such judicial precedent differs from legal rules contained in the judgments of foreign legal systems, such as the United States of America, which, with all their persuasive value, do not have formal status as "law."

237. Procaccia, *supra* n. 233 at 17. In the view of Prof. Tedeschi, Article 46 itself should be considered as self-executing; however, he takes the position that Section 2(b) of the Foundations of Law Act preserves only those laws that were in fact expressly incorporated by judicial decision, not those that were merely appropriate for such incorporation. *See* his article on the repeal of Article 46 (*supra* n. 235) and his other articles cited in n. 14 *supra*.

238. Procaccia, *supra* n. 233 at 17–18.

> Only an *a priori* rejection of the theory that the law [Article 46] was self-executing (with the consequence that before a common-law rule is judicially adopted in Israel, it is not yet "law") can justify the narrow interpretation of the term "judicial precedent" in Section 1 of the Foundations of Law Act. However, since the question before us is whether to accept the "self-executing" theory or the "enabling legislation" theory, it is obvious that the question cannot be answered by adopting a construction that assumes the *a priori* rejection of the "self-executing" theory.

Professor Procaccia therefore concludes:[239]

> In sum, the situation appears to be as follows: Article 46 of the Order in Council, when in force, incorporated the rules of the common law and equity as a part of our law in all instances of lacuna. Such incorporation required no explicit pronouncement by a domestic court in order to achieve normative efficacy. The repeal of Article 46 cannot, therefore, abrogate the efficacy of all the laws that were incorporated in this manner. The effect of the repeal of this Article is to prevent the incorporation of the rules of English common law and equity to fill new lacunae that will be created from time to time in our system. From now on, these new lacunae will be filled "in the light of the principles of freedom, justice, equity, and peace of the Jewish heritage."

To exemplify his approach, Professor Procaccia points to a lacuna in the Israeli law of insolvency—the case of a non-bankrupt debtor who transfers his assets without consideration in order to put them beyond the reach of his creditors.[240]

Section 96 of the Israeli Bankruptcy Ordinance (New Version), 1980, states:

> a. A gratuitous transfer of assets made within two years prior to bankruptcy is void as to the trustee.
>
> b. Unless the transferee establishes that, at the time of the transfer, the transferor had sufficient resources, exclusive of the assets transferred, to pay all his debts, a gratuitous transfer of assets made more than two years but less than ten years before bankruptcy is void as to the trustee, and the transferor's rights in the asset thereupon vest in the trustee.

Professor Procaccia points to a number of difficulties in applying the provisions of Section 96 to solve the problems of a debtor's conveyance of assets in fraud of creditors. One such problem is that the section does not

239. *Id.*

240. *Id.* at 13 n. 16. Incidentally, Professor Procaccia deserves commendation for actually pointing to an instance of a lacuna in the Israeli legal system. It must be observed, however, that the Bankruptcy Ordinance quoted immediately below can be read as a ten-year statute of limitations, which would preclude any lacuna.

provide for setting aside such a conveyance except where the conveyance has been made within certain fixed time periods.[241] He therefore proposes to fill the lacuna as to the invalidation of fraudulent conveyances by recourse to the English "Statute of Elizabeth," enacted in 1571. He argues:[242]

> The direct way [to fill this lacuna] is by recognizing that the laws generally known as the "Statute of Elizabeth" apply in Israel. The Statute of Elizabeth is an English statute of 1571, which was codified more than 350 years later as part of the English Property Act. Under Section 1 of the Statute of Elizabeth, fraudulent gifts, as defined in that statute, may be set aside without any limitation as to time. Thus, this law is decidedly more favorable to creditors than the provisions of Section 96 of the Bankruptcy Ordinance, which authorizes the trustee to set aside transfers made within specified periods of time.

The problem is: How can the Statute of Elizabeth of 1571, which was never recognized as controlling by the decisions of the Israeli courts, be binding in the Israeli legal system? This was an apt question even before the repeal of Article 46 by the Foundations of Law Act, since what is involved here is an English *statute* which is not one of the prescribed sources for filling a lacuna, even under the provisions of Article 46. The question is even more apt since the repeal of Article 46 by the Foundations of Law Act.

To this problem, Professor Procaccia responds:[243]

> It seems to me that, prior to the Knesset's enactment of the Foundations of Law Act, there could be no real doubt that the Statute of Elizabeth was binding in our legal system. It is, of course, true that Article 46 of the Palestine Order in Council effected the incorporation of common-law but not statutory rules. However, [the provisions of] this particular statute, in spite of the statute's antiquity, were not the product of the British legislature, but merely codified the preexisting common law, which the courts continued to develop organically even after the statute was enacted. The problem is that prior to the adoption of the Foundations of Law Act, no Israeli court had occasion to address the question and explicitly incorporate the general principles of the Statute of Elizabeth into our legal system. As a result, the status of this law in Israel today depends on how the person construing [Article 46 and the Foundations of Law Act] views the present relationship between our positive law and English common law.
>
> In the first part of this work, I argued that the preferable interpretation of the Foundations of Law Act was that the "inventory" [of laws] incorporated from English law into our [legal] system became frozen as of the day the Act was adopted by the Knesset. This "freezing of the inventory," together

241. *Id.* at 119.
242. *Id.* at 119–120.
243. *Id.*

> with the preference for the "self-executing" theory over the "enabling legislation" theory, compels the conclusion that the provisions of the Statute of Elizabeth are still a part of our binding law in Israel. The rejection of the "self-executing theory" approach, and the adoption of the principle that, after [the enactment of] the Foundations of Law Act, common-law rules not yet adopted by explicit adjudication have no normative significance in Israel, would lead to the opposite conclusion, namely, that the Statute of Elizabeth is not a part of the law in force in our country.

Professor Procaccia thus clearly maintains that Article 46 still has life and vigor, even after the enactment of the Foundations of Law Act, as to every lacuna that might possibly have become manifest before the adoption of the Foundations of Law Act, even if the issue never arose in an actual case and no Israeli court ever addressed it. Indeed, he even goes so far as to assert that pursuant to Article 46 not only English common law and equity, which are referred to in Article 46, but even an English statute must be looked to in order to fill the lacuna. He justifies this conclusion on the basis of the "history" of the Statute of Elizabeth. Historically, it is argued, this was not a statute whose provisions originated with the British Parliament but rather one that "merely codified the preexisting common law, which the courts continued to develop organically even after the statute was enacted." In other words, a four-hundred-year-old statute, because it was inspired by the judgments of the English courts, is not a statute for purposes of Article 46, but rather is "common law" within the meaning of this Article, and it is therefore a legitimate part of the Israeli legal system even after Article 46 was repealed by the Foundations of Law Act. All this is premised on the theory that Article 46 was self-executing and therefore the term "judicial precedent" in Section 1 of the Foundations of Law Act is so broad as to include even judgments of English courts rendered prior to 1571.

Our Sages have said that "the gates of tears are not closed."[244] It would also seem, paraphrasing this statement, that "the gates of interpretation are not closed," and the acuity and inventiveness of the interpreter have no bounds. There is no need to belabor further the point that Professor Procaccia's approach is contrary to the plain and clear meaning of the Foundations of Law Act and would render the Act virtually devoid of any practical significance.

What is particularly ironic is that it is precisely by the simple and reasonable interpretation of the Act according to its plain meaning that any lacuna in the Israeli law of insolvency can be appropriately filled. Under that interpretation, a lacuna previously neither addressed nor resolved by

244. TB Berakhot 32b.

the Supreme Court of Israel must be filled by consulting the principles of the Jewish heritage that are specified in the Act; and, indeed, the question of fraudulent conveyances has already been clearly and unequivocally resolved by "the principles of justice and equity" that are part of "the Jewish heritage."

The subject of fraudulent conveyances by a debtor to place assets out of the reach of his creditors is extensively discussed in Jewish law.[245] Here, it will suffice to examine the rulings of two leading halakhic authorities concerning this problem and to note the method by which they arrived at their conclusions. A number of responsa of Rashba and his contemporary Asheri, who lived in Spain in the second half of the thirteenth century and the beginning of the fourteenth century, discuss various common fraudulent practices by debtors of their time to place assets beyond the reach of their creditors. The fraud took various forms, *e.g.*, the debtor would transfer his assets to his wife or minor children, or would admit owing some relative a type of debt having preference over the debt owed to the creditor he was attempting to defraud.

In one responsum,[246] Rashba took the position that while such transactions might be valid as a matter of strict law, they should nevertheless be set aside, because "whoever judges in such a case must render a judgment that is completely and truly correct, for our Torah is truth, and it totally rejects evildoers, as R. Ḥisda said to Mari b. Isak: 'This is how I judge you and all your violent friends.'"[247] In another responsum,[248] Rashba added the following rationale: "It is proper for a court to take action, since these are stratagems by those who act improperly.[249] . . . As he had done, so should it be done to him; his conduct should be requited.[250] . . . And in any case, the community may establish safeguards against wrongdoers so that [others] will be deterred; and the court has authority [to do this], for the court has power to expropriate property (*hefker bet din hefker*)."

The book of Asheri's responsa includes an entire section devoted to the problem of fraudulent conveyances by a debtor.[251] This section contains four extensive responsa which give a detailed description of such practices

245. *See* Elon, *Ḥerut,* pp. 118–126.

246. *Resp. Rashba,* II, #283.

247. TB Ketubbot 27b. In that case, the burden of proof was shifted to the defendant, who was known as a violent hoodlum, against whom the witnesses were afraid to testify. *See supra* pp. 248, 1715.

248. *Resp. Rashba,* II, #360.

249. *See* TB Yevamot 110a: "He acted improperly; therefore the Rabbis treat him 'improperly.'"

250. *See* TB Gittin 40a; Bava Meẓi'a 101b; *cf.* Obadiah 1:15.

251. *Resp. Asheri,* Principle 78.

at the end of the thirteenth century in Spain. One responsum states:[252] "You have posed this situation: Reuben was obligated to Simeon on an oral loan, and he [Reuben] gave all his property to Levi in order to defeat Simeon's claim." Asheri responded that the facts conclusively showed that the transfer to Levi was a sham, and on the basis of such a determination, the Sages have invalidated various types of legal transactions: "There is no clearer proof than this—[the fact that] a person gives all his assets to others. Will he go begging from door to door? Rather, his intention is to defraud, to deprive Simeon of the money he lent; but his scheme will not succeed, and his trickery will not help him." After citing a number of Talmudic references where various fraudulent transactions were set aside, Asheri concluded:

> We see from all these instances that whenever anyone sought to scheme against his fellow, the Sages of the Talmud stood against him to frustrate his plan. And we shall draw inferences and reach conclusions by analogy from one case to another [*i.e.*, from the action taken by the Sages], for the Sages of the Talmud were not able to specify everything that would happen in the future. In this case, our decision is certainly based on clear law, for there can be no case with stronger proof than this one.

The other responsa in Asheri's section on fraudulent conveyances give explicit, minutely detailed descriptions of different types of crafty fraudulent transfers, together with Asheri's decision setting the transfers aside. One of these responsa is particularly instructive in a number of respects: its size and scope, its marshaling of the proof supporting its conclusion that the fraudulent transfer must be set aside, and its discussion of the overarching principles of justice and equity upon which its conclusion is based. Several passages in this responsum directly relevant to the subject bear quotation.[253] The responsum begins:[254]

> The Holy One, Blessed be He, gave to His people, Israel, through Moses, of blessed memory, a Torah of truth, good laws, and just rules. Its ways are pleasant ways, and all its paths, peaceful.[255] The righteous will follow them, but the Sages of Israel must frustrate the plans and nullify the schemes of the

252. *Resp. Asheri* 78:1. For a discussion of the views expressed by Asheri in this and related responsa with regard to the principle of good faith, *see supra* p. 186, and with regard to the methodology of interpretation of the *Halakhah, see supra* pp. 416–418.

253. This responsum is discussed in detail in Elon, *Ḥerut,* pp. 125–126.

254. *Resp. Asheri* 78:3.

255. Proverbs 3:17. The Sages viewed this verse as an overarching principle in halakhic decision making. *See supra* pp. 387–389; p. 530 n. 153; p. 1005 n. 62; p. 1193; *Digest of the Responsa Literature of Spain and North Africa, supra* n. 54.

evildoers, who deal deceitfully and pervert honesty in order to amass wealth through false scales.[256] Concerning this it is said:[257] "Justice, justice shall you pursue," and our Sages have stated:[258] "[This refers to] a completely and truly correct judgment that rejects deceit." I have seen some people who transfer their assets to Jews or gentiles and afterwards borrow money, and when the creditor comes to collect the debt from his [the debtor's] assets, he produces the document [of transfer] and claims that his assets belong to others.

Asheri then described at length the particular case submitted to him, including the conditions in the deed of "gift" to facilitate the fraud, and he continued:

> My goal is to break the teeth of evil, to frustrate the schemes of the cunning, and to thwart their plan. I make plain and declare that there is no substance to this gift, because the facts clearly establish that he [the debtor] did not intend to transfer his assets, but intended to conceal them from his creditor. He would borrow and live on the money of others, and nothing would be found from which to make good his debts.

Asheri substantiated this position with many proofs, some of which had been cited in his prior responsa. He then stressed the severe consequences such fraud would have for the entire economic system:

> Everyone would engage in this conspiracy and trickery, would transfer assets to friends, and would hold the deed [of transfer] to produce whenever he wishes. No one would feel safe in lending money to another, the door will be closed to borrowers, and commerce will be stifled. No one would be able to buy land, because he could not rely on the seller's undertaking to indemnify him [if the land is taken by a creditor of the seller], since the [prospective] buyer would be afraid that the seller has conveyed all his assets to someone else.

After Asheri established that both the law and the needs of the time required the invalidation of these transfers, he concluded:

> All legal instruments executed up to this time to effectuate fraudulent conveyances must be voided; and when they are brought before a court, they should be destroyed. An enactment should be adopted in Toledo that no scribe or witness should write or sign a deed of gift if it appears to be a scheme or trick; instead, they should bring the matter to the town authorities, and

256. *Cf.* Hosea 14:10.
257. Deuteronomy 16:20.
258. TB Shabbat 10a; Sanhedrin 7a; *Tosafot,* Megillah 15b, s.v. Zeh ha-dan din emet le-amito; *Tosafot,* Bava Batra 8b, s.v. Din emet le-amito.

follow their instructions. Violation of the enactment should result in removal from their positions.[259]

It is clear that the Jewish heritage fills the lacuna dealt with by Professor Procaccia. The halakhic authorities and codifiers extensively and comprehensively dealt with both the legal and social aspects of the problem. Rashba and Asheri, some two hundred years before the enactment of the Statute of Elizabeth, voided such fraudulent transfers and based their decisions on the principles of justice and equity, on the obligation of the judge to render a judgment that is completely and truly correct, and on the overarching principle of the *Halakhah* that "all its ways are pleasant ways, and all its paths, peaceful." This is an example of the full use of those principles in the Jewish heritage that the Legislature directed the courts to apply in order to resolve a question for which no answer is provided by legislation, judicial precedent, or analogy.

Asheri's emphasis on the overarching nature of these basic principles and their ability to solve problems such as the one under discussion, which are created by ever-changing circumstances, is instructive: "The Sages of the Talmud were not able to specify everything that would happen in the future," but they established, on the strength of the metaprinciples of justice, equity, truth, and peace, that those who intend to defraud must be blocked and their chicanery thwarted, and therefore we, in every generation, must "draw inferences and reach conclusions by analogy from one case to another."

Considerations of rational interpretation, consistency with the statutory purpose, and sound legal policy all lead to the conclusion that the Foundations of Law Act should be interpreted to mean what it says, and that the laws of the Jewish heritage should be the source of the solution the statute so clearly and instructively provides. Is this interpretive approach not preferable to strained constructions and legal gymnastics, which may perhaps be useful for sharpening the mind, but have no relevance to the true meaning or purpose of the Foundations of Law Act, and which lead, at the end of a tortuous road, not to the principles of equity and justice of the Jewish heritage, but to a statute enacted in 1571, when Queen Elizabeth ruled Britannia and Britannia ruled the waves?

IV. CONCLUSION

The Foundations of Law Act, 1980, was the culmination of a long and arduous gestation, and its birth pangs were accompanied by both great ex-

259. It would seem that this was an important decision that Asheri circulated to the judges and scribes, in order to put a stop to the plague of fraudulent conveyances.

pectations and great apprehension. Finally, the Legislature had its say, and the statute was "delivered." While it was still in its infancy, government spokesmen took the position that above and beyond its specific provisions the Act had the overall objective of integrating the Jewish legal system into the Israeli legal system.[260] The judicial branch then began to examine this infant, and developed differing views as to how it should be treated.[261]

Some advocate an extremely narrow interpretation. According to this view, "a legal issue requiring decision [that] cannot be resolved" exists only in the rare situation where the legal system had never dealt at all with the subject in issue, either directly or indirectly. According to those who would construe the Act most strictly, the only lacuna to which the Act applies is a lacuna that did not exist until after the Act took effect in 1980. The narrow view holds that, with only very rare exceptions, the Act does not accord any special status to Jewish law, either as binding or as first among equals, even where the Israeli Legislature deliberately and expressly incorporated an entire legal institution, and not merely a term or expression, from the Jewish legal system. According to this approach, the infant has no hope for a future of normal growth, but is condemned forever to remain stunted. This approach renders the Foundations of Law Act completely ineffectual and turns the "foundations (*yesodot*)" of the law into the "secrets (*sodot*)" of the law, so well hidden that they will never see the light of day.

A second and different approach, espoused by a significant number of judges and legal scholars, views the Foundations of Law Act as making certain positive changes in regard to recourse to Jewish law. Some who take this approach hold that a "lacuna" exists not only in cases where there is a complete void in the Israeli legal system, but also where the Legislature has used value-laden legal terms, such as "justice," "good faith," and "public policy," or very general abstract terms, such as "negligence," whose substantive content is essentially elastic. This approach has fortified the position of those Supreme Court justices who had long held that such value-

260. *See* the views expressed by Minister of Justice M. Nissim, in his survey of the work of the Ministry of Justice, *DK*, 10th Knesset, 2d Sess., 99th meeting, p. 2775 (1982):

> In 1980, the Knesset enacted the Foundations of Law Act, 1980, which severs the link between Israeli law and English law, and instead establishes a new link to "the principles of freedom, justice, equity, and peace of the Jewish heritage." With the enactment of this statute, the sources of Jewish law have become a part of the law of the State of Israel, and the Ministry of Justice has participated in preparing the legal community for this change by providing advice, offering programs of continuing legal education, compiling legal studies, and preparing guidebooks. It goes without saying that we will now be particularly diligent in our efforts to integrate the legal principles of Jewish law into both previous and future Israeli legislation.

261. As noted *supra*, academicians and lawyers have also taken differing views on how the Act should be interpreted.

laden terms as "justice," "good faith," and "public policy" must be interpreted to accord with the cultural and ethical values of the Jewish heritage.

Another application of the second approach holds that statutory terms or expressions not commonly used in ordinary legal language but peculiar to Jewish law should be so interpreted as to accord them their original meaning in Jewish law; and when the Israeli Legislature has incorporated not only a term or expression but an entire legal institution from Jewish law, such as the will of a *shekhiv me-ra,* Israeli law concerning that institution should be so interpreted as to accord with the applicable principles under Jewish law, unless there is an explicit statutory provision on the particular point that is inconsistent with the corresponding provision of Jewish law.

Under this second approach, the Foundations of Law Act accords no special status to Jewish law except in the instances above enumerated. In all other cases, constituting the majority of the daily run of litigation in which an Israeli statute is ambiguous or uncertain, the second approach does not regard Jewish law as even "first among equals." According to this view, the Foundations of Law Act does not even counsel, let alone require, that a judge should look first to Jewish law when he cannot resolve the question "from within the four corners" of the statute and seeks guidance from another legal system. Rather, every non-Israeli legal system has equal status as a possible source of enlightenment.[262]

The third approach, advocated here, holds that Jewish law governs in the instances where the second approach would apply it, but also asserts that the Foundations of Law Act establishes Jewish law as the primary persuasive source, the "first among equals," in every case where an Israeli statute is ambiguous or uncertain, except only where the Israeli statute explicitly differs from Jewish law. It is submitted that Jewish law had this preferred status even before the enactment of the Foundations of Law Act. However, the enactment of this statute has reinforced the requirement to turn to Jewish law as the primary complementary source of enlightenment—duly taking into account, of course, "the needs of the time and the purpose of the law."[263]

Divergence of interpretations such as has occurred with respect to the

262. Clearly, from an official-formal point of view, no non-Israeli legal system has any preferential status as a source of enlightenment. During the second codificatory period and before the enactment of the Foundations of Law Act, some scholars had advocated a different approach. Professor Zeltner urged that the historical source from which a particular legal provision was derived should be looked to for guidance in interpreting the provision, and Professor Friedmann advocated the English legal system as the primary source for interpretive enlightenment. *See supra* p. 1733. *See also* the discussion *infra.* For a criticism of the approaches of Prof. Zeltner and Prof. Friedmann, *see* Gans, *supra* n. 40 at 525ff.

263. Quoting from Hendeles v. Bank Kupat Am, 35(ii) *P.D.* 785, 795 (1981).

Foundations of Law Act is not unusual in the law. Jurists routinely interpret legislation in different ways on the basis of different approaches, with different interpreters advancing different theories and reaching different conclusions. It is no secret that statutory interpretation involves much more and cuts much deeper than technical-legal application of rules of interpretation. The previous discussion of the relationship between the legislator's intent and the interpreter's desires makes this abundantly clear.[264] If this is true with regard to statutory interpretation in general, it is *a fortiori* true with regard to a statute with the nature, content, and background of the Foundations of Law Act.

Furthermore, while it is true that according to the first two approaches to the interpretation of the Act, every non-Israeli legal system has equal status as a source of enlightenment when the meaning of an Israeli statute is uncertain, this equality, as has been shown in this and in the preceding chapters,[265] is only theoretical, formal, and ceremonial. Unofficially, the vast majority of the adherents of either of these approaches in fact accord clear preference to one or another non-Israeli legal system—American, English, and sometimes Continental. According primary, and almost exclusive, persuasive authority to one of these systems is a daily occurrence as a matter of course. By contrast, Jewish law is consulted by adherents of the first two approaches only in the rarest of instances. The professed equality of all legal systems as sources of enlightenment for the interpretation of Israeli legislation is meaningless in light of the actual practice of the vast majority of those who profess to adhere to either of these two approaches.

What are the forces at work that have caused this situation? What is it that "involves much more and cuts much deeper" in regard to this complex issue of the status of Jewish law in the Israeli legal system, and the role of Jewish law in the interpretation of Israeli legislation? The next and final chapter of this work is an attempt to answer these questions.

264. *See supra* pp. 1872–1873, and source cited in n. 193. *See also* M. Elon, "Od le-Inyan Ḥok Yesodot ha-Mishpat" [More about the Foundations of Law Act], *Shenaton,* XIII (1987), pp. 227–256. This article was written in response to an article by Justice Barak, "Ḥok Yesodot ha-Mishpat u-Moreshet Yisra'el" [The Foundations of Law Act and the Jewish Heritage], *Shenaton,* XIII (1987), pp. 265–283.

265. *See supra* pp. 1731–1735; *infra* pp. 1920–1923.

Chapter 45

THE RELIGIOUS AND CULTURAL ASPECTS OF THE QUESTION OF THE STATUS OF JEWISH LAW IN THE JEWISH STATE

I. In General
II. Jewish Law in the Independent Israeli Legal System from the Perspective of the Traditional Jewish Legal System
   A. The Nature of the State's Incorporation of Jewish Law
   B. The Prohibition Against Litigating in Non-Jewish Courts
   C. The Problems When Jewish Legislation and Adjudication Are Not Based on Jewish Law
III. Jewish Law in the Independent Israeli Legal System from the Perspective of the Law of the State
   A. The Legislature
   B. The Courts
IV. Subjective and Objective Factors Affecting Recourse to Jewish Law
   A. Subjective Factors
   B. Objective Factors
   C. Observations Concerning Fears and the Fearful
V. Concluding Reflections

I. IN GENERAL

To base a viable legal system of a sovereign state in the twentieth century on Jewish law is no easy task; it calls for great intellectual effort, creativity, and boldness. As seen in the previous chapters, Jewish law continued throughout the Jewish diaspora to be applied in everyday life, and consequently to develop creatively, until the end of the eighteenth century. However, the Emancipation virtually ended this process of development. Except for the North African and Middle Eastern countries, Jewish juridical autonomy was brought to an end by the general governments, and Jews in increasing numbers no longer felt bound to adjudicate their disputes according to Jewish law. Practical application of most areas of Jewish law therefore gradually diminished to the point that the law ceased to respond creatively to the needs of the times.

All this occurred during the nineteenth century, when momentous industrial, social, and economic developments were working their changes in the legal systems of other nations.[1] The creation of a legal system for the new State of Israel required solution of the many problems arising out of the social and economic conditions of the twentieth century; preexisting legal institutions needed to be changed, and new ones needed to be created.[2] This was obviously a difficult and onerous task that would certainly be expected to occasion many significant differences of opinion as to how best to accomplish it.

From time immemorial, the Jewish legal system has had well-accepted methods for solving such problems. Jewish law has always confronted social, spiritual, and economic changes occurring in one or another era or diaspora. The problems generated by such changes have been solved by means of the creative legal sources—interpretation, legislation, custom, *ma'aseh,* and legal reasoning—which are at the very heart of the halakhic system; indeed, a major part of the present work has been devoted to the study of this creative process. The Jewish legal system was also positioned to undertake this task at a time of historic opportunity offered by the renewal of Jewish sovereignty and juridical autonomy. This undoubtedly would have been a protracted process, accompanied by sharp debates between widely different views, as had previously been the case during the long history of the Jewish law. But this process would have resulted in a Jewish legal system based on and nurtured by the past, yet responsive to the needs of the present, and looking forward to and developing with the future.

Examples of the operation of the halakhic process in the present day can be found in the application of Jewish law in Israeli rabbinical courts. As has been seen, the rabbinical courts have either exclusive or concurrent jurisdiction over matters of personal status. The fact that this part of Jewish law is once again being applied in practice has inevitably engendered legal creativity in the use of interpretation and legislation to supplement or modify the existing law. Thus, the rabbinical courts have utilized interpretation to reach the conclusion that they may award compensation to a wife at the time of divorce and require support from her husband during temporary separation; and the Chief Rabbinate has adopted legislation providing for the establishment of an appellate rabbinical court and the imposition of an

1. *See supra* pp. 1577–1578, 1586–1588.
2. *See supra* pp. 1598–1599, 1608–1618.

obligation on parents to support children until the age of fifteen. There has been, and there continues to be, much debate regarding rabbinic legislation. The view has been urged that enactments already adopted should be weakened and that additional legislation should not be enacted. There has also occasionally been a tendency towards a stringency in judicial decisions that is hardly responsive to the needs of the times.[3] These eddies and crosscurrents may in part be the result of certain social tensions and the particular sensitivity of issues of family law. They do not, however, bedim the luster of the overall contribution of the rabbinical court system to the creative development of Jewish law by means of the time-honored methods for attaining that end.

A striking illustration of the operation of the halakhic process is the debate during the past few years on the question of membership of women on the local religious councils in the State of Israel. These councils finance and supervise the provision of religious services to the general population. The question of whether a woman may serve as a member of such a council was thoroughly considered by the Supreme Court in *Shakdiel v. Minister of Religions.*[4] In that case, the court held that a woman is qualified for service on a religious council; and our opinion expressed the view, contrary to that of the Chief Rabbinate, that this decision was in accord with Jewish law. The opinion states:[5]

> The divergent views on the question before us are characteristic of the *Halakhah.* Indeed, such disputes are an essential part of the process of deliberation and final determination of legal issues, in accordance with the basic guideline laid down with reference to the disputes between the schools of Hillel and Shammai: "Both are the words of the living God."[6] . . . The rules of the *Halakhah* in the early sources are stated anonymously and categorically. The decisions of the Sanhedrin, reached by majority vote, were rendered in the name of the entire Sanhedrin. With the end of the period of the *Zugot* at the beginning of the first century C.E., disputes increased in all areas of the *Halakhah,* in both theory and practice; each school of thought had its own practices.[7] As a result of both external political conditions and internal factors (*e.g.,* the conflict between the Pharisees and the Sadducees, and the controversies among the Pharisees themselves, such as those between the schools

3. *See supra* pp. 824–835, 1599, 1753–1755, 1784–1787, 1807–1826; Elon, *Ḥakikah,* pp. 157ff.; *id., Mi-Ba'ayot ha-Halakhah ve-ha-Mishpat bi-Medinat Yisra'el* [Problems of *Halakhah* and Law in the State of Israel], Jerusalem, 1973, 7th pamphlet, pp. 9–47; *id.,* "Ba'ayot u-Megamot be-Yaḥasei Halakhah u-Medinah" [Problems and Trends in the Relation between *Halakhah* and State], *Ammudim* (Publication of the Kibbutz ha-Dati), 1974.

4. 42(ii) *P.D.* 222 (1988).

5. *Id.* at 263–265.

6. TB Eruvin 13b. *See supra* p. 1067.

7. *See supra* pp. 1061–1069. As to the *Zugot, see supra* p. 1043.

of Hillel and Shammai), the *Halakhah* became fragmented and lost its ability to arrive at binding decisions: "From the time when there was an increase in the number of students of Shammai and Hillel who did not serve [their teachers] sufficiently [*i.e.*, did not follow a sufficiently long course of apprenticeship, or did not study enough], disputes in Israel multiplied and the Torah became as two Torahs."[8]

These disputes introduced into the *Halakhah* the phenomenon of pluralism with regard to the law applied in practical life. In the beginning, and for some time, this situation was tolerable.[9] However, this "pluralism" with regard to rules governing practical conduct could not possibly continue. The disputes concerning various questions of family law, and of ritual purity and impurity, brought on acrimonious arguments, and threatened national disintegration.[10]

A generation after the destruction of the Temple, at the beginning of the second century C.E., with the establishment of the new center at Yavneh under the patriarchate of Rabban Gamaliel II, uniformity of halakhic practice was restored. The Talmud records that in Yavneh, "a voice from heaven emerged and declared: 'The words of both are the words of the living God, but the law is in accordance with the School of Hillel.'" Thus, while it was unequivocally determined that the *Halakhah* could not tolerate pluralism in practice, the important principle was also established that in the realm of ideas, for the purpose of debate and study, "the words of both are the words of the living God." In regard to practical application, "Why did the School of Hillel merit having the law established in accordance with their opinions? Because they were pleasant and tolerant."[11]

I am not a halakhic decisionmaker and have no pretensions to that status. However, it is a question of Torah and it is incumbent upon us to learn. I have put my thoughts on paper in a halakhic discussion only for the purpose of acquiring knowledge and drawing from the springs of our halakhic authorities from whose waters we drink and by whose words we live. If it were possible, I would do the same as Chief Rabbi Uziel, of blessed memory, and publish my opinion only much later, at an opportune time. However, the choice is not mine, inasmuch as the very sensitive and complex issue before us involves a halakhic analysis and a clarification of the views of our halakhic authorities. The issue is a recurring one. It is therefore not the time to keep one's thoughts secret.

How wise were the words of Rabbi Jehiel Weinberg, the author of *Resp. Seridei Esh*, who said concerning the differences of opinion on this subject, "Let time take its course and render the decision." And time has indeed rendered its decision. Three of the outstanding halakhic authorities of the pre-

8. TB Sanhedrin 88b. In TJ Sanhedrin 1:4, 8b (1:4, 19c), the reading is: "who did not serve their teachers as they should have."

9. *See Tosefta* Yevamot 1:10–11; M Yevamot 1:4; M Eduyyot 4:8.

10. *See supra* pp. 1065–1066.

11. *See supra* pp. 1066–1067.

vious generation held that women may not vote in elections. These authorities were the Chief Rabbi of the Land of Israel, Abraham Isaac Kook; the leading respondent in the diaspora, Ḥayyim Ozer Grodzinski; and the most important halakhic decisionmaker (*posek*) of the generation—Israel Meir ha-Kohen, author of *Mishnah Berurah*. In addition, many other rabbis agreed with them. But time took its course and decreed otherwise: in the entire religious community, without exception—Hasidic and anti-Hasidic, Zionist and non-Zionist—women of all groups and subgroups vote in all Israeli elections, national and local. This has been the practice for many years, and during this time we have heard of no halakhic authority who has directed religious women not go to the polls. Voting by women is a practice no one now questions; the controlling principle is: "Go and see what the people are doing."

Rabbi Jehiel Weinberg's statement that time will decide related also to the question of women's election to public office. On this question, too, time has rendered its decision for the majority of the religious community: religious women have served as members of the Knesset, and have served, and are serving, on local councils and in various other positions of public service. As noted above, they do this with the approval of outstanding halakhic scholars and authorities. It is true that the women of a particular segment of the religious community do not serve as members of local councils or other public bodies. However, on what basis can a religious woman who desires to comply with the view of the law held by the eminent halakhic authorities who have no objection to the election of women to public office be prevented from following the example of the many hundreds of other religious women who are serving in many types of public positions? Can one really contend today that membership in the Knesset or a local council or kibbutz secretariat is inconsistent with the modesty that is proper for a Jewish woman? . . .

The petitioner in this case seeks to be a member of the Religious Council of Yeroḥam. The local council, *i.e.*, the public, selected and proposed her for this position. As noted, the religious council has no jurisdiction over halakhic issues and makes no halakhic decisions. Even if its membership were entirely male, it might not even be *qualified* to decide halakhic questions, for the primary qualifications for making halakhic rulings are knowledge of the Talmud and the codes, and the requisite intellectual capacity. The task of the religious council is only to assure that religious services are provided—to oversee the construction and maintenance of ritual baths, the public teaching of Torah and Judaism, and the provision of kosher food. Can it be seriously contended that although a religious woman may be an inspector for kosher food products, as Rabbi Moses Feinstein has ruled, the petitioner is forbidden to administer the budget and ensure that there is adequate kosher food supervision in Yeroḥam?

I am not unmindful of the opinion of the Council of the Chief Rabbinate that women may not be permanent members of religious councils. All of us must have the greatest respect and esteem for this highest halakhic body of

> the State, whose leaders are the two Chief Rabbis of the State of Israel, and whose members are scholars of Torah and *Halakhah*. I stated above that I write only to enlighten myself and to engage in a halakhic discussion. This discussion has cited the views of leading halakhic scholars, a Chief Rabbi of the Land of Israel and other halakhic authorities, to the effect that a woman may hold a public office to which she is elected. At first glance, it would seem that the Chief Rabbinate does not agree with those halakhic authorities. However, were I bold enough, I would venture the suggestion that the Chief Rabbinate Council does not really disagree with those who hold that a woman may occupy a public office, but rather is under the mistaken impression that the religious councils deal with the halakhic aspects of the religious services that are provided. I find support for this suggestion in the fact the Ministerial Committee was also under the same mistaken impression when it reached its decision. . . . If this is so and there is merit to my suggestion, the Chief Rabbinate Council may wish to review again the question of the petitioner's membership in the Religious Council of Yeroḥam.

The problems incident to the incorporation of Jewish law into the legal system of a modern Jewish state are not due to any lack of ability of Jewish law to respond to present-day needs, but rather to much more general causes related to the social conditions and the spiritual temper of the times. These general conditions have to some extent affected the course taken by Jewish law, both in the general and in the rabbinical court systems, even in regard to matters of personal status, as to which the Israeli legal system has incorporated by reference the entire body of Jewish law. Thus, the Knesset, a non-halakhic legislative body, has made certain statutes binding even on the religious courts, and the general court system has been sparing in the use it has made of the rules of Jewish law. These and similar effects of the changed conditions of life on the law of personal status have been previously discussed.[12]

The problems encountered in the incorporation of Jewish law into the legal system of the State are related not primarily to the law of personal status but to other areas of the law where the incorporation of Jewish law has been accomplished, or has been attempted, either by direct Knesset legislation or by decisions of the general courts. This chapter is devoted to a discussion of the problems involved in the relationship between Israeli law and Jewish law in those areas.

The problems that have arisen in those areas are not intrinsic to the halakhic system. They do not involve the question of how to make use of the creative sources of Jewish law to solve the problems arising in the latter part of the twentieth century. Rather, these problems are rooted in the un-

12. *See supra* pp. 1758–1770.

precedented historical situation in which the Jewish state, into whose legal system Jewish law is proposed to be incorporated, does not regard the *Halakhah* as binding. The essential question today is not, as it has always been in the past, how to use the creative sources of Jewish law to meet contemporary needs, but *whether* it is proper and desirable at all to integrate Jewish law into the legal system of a state that neither aspires to continue the historical halakhic system nor derives its legitimacy from the traditional sources of authority of Jewish law—and, if such integration is proper and desirable, how it should be accomplished.

This question must be faced both by those who adhere to the traditional religious view of the authority of Jewish law and those who view Jewish law as a national and cultural asset that must be preserved. The debate over these questions by the religious traditionalists began with the establishment of the State, but the seeds of the debate were planted much earlier by those who viewed the issue in national-cultural terms. At the beginning of the twentieth century, as the dream of establishing the Jewish state was beginning to take form, those who wished to base the legal system of the future Jewish state on Jewish law because of its cultural value and national importance spoke of the need to continue with the "process of separating law from ethics and religion . . . and [to] prepare Jewish law to exist as a secular legal system."[13] This "process," however, has not been completed; indeed its success is in great doubt. It would seem to be now generally recognized that, to the Jewish people and to Judaism, the connection between religion, on the one hand, and nationality, law, and all other fundamental values, on the other, is so integral and organic that while boundaries may possibly be marked between them, the connection cannot be completely severed. This interconnection is inherent in the very nature of Jewish law. Nevertheless, one of the central problems in regard to the relationship between Jewish law and the legal system of the State of Israel is whether this process of converting "Jewish law" into a "secular legal system" can be successfully carried out. This subject has been discussed previously and will be dealt with further below.[14]

Those who insist on the "independence" of the Israeli legal system have pondered this problem at length: Is "independence" of the legal sys-

13. The quoted language is from the Introduction to the first issue of the periodical *Ha-Mishpat ha-Ivri,* Moscow, 1918. *See supra* p. 1590.

14. *See, e.g., supra* pp. 1772–1775, reviewing the Supreme Court's extensive discussion of separating the "religious" and "legal" components of the law as to marriage between a *kohen* and a divorcée. The Jewish law on that subject was incorporated into the Israeli legal system by the Rabbinical Courts Jurisdiction (Marriage and Divorce) Law, 1953, sec. 2. *See also* Yosipoff v. Attorney General, 5 *P.D.* 481, 494 (1951); *infra* pp. 1928–1929.

tem of the State, in the sense not merely of independence from external and foreign legal systems, but also from the traditional Jewish legal system, compatible with the creation of special "relationships" with the traditional system and, if so, what is the nature and extent of these relationships? Or should there be any relationship at all between the Israeli legal system and traditional Jewish law?

The debate as to the proper role of Jewish law in the Israeli legal system involves both ideological and pragmatic arguments. Conflicting, and sometimes even bizarre, ideas have been expressed. Many of the arguments are based on fact, but some are not. Some adherents of traditional Jewish law contend that no attempt should be made to incorporate Jewish law into a legal system that "rebels" against its past; these "Guardians of the Walls" fear all innovation. On the other side, among the theorists of the new jurisprudence, one finds hypersensitivity and inordinate suspicion, and even a significant degree of arrogance, as they mass their troops behind the barricade of "legal independence," like young revolutionaries fighting their past and the source of their own strength.

The discussion up to this point has noted differing views of legislators, judges, jurists, and legal scholars, which have exposed some of the problems and reflected various approaches in regard to the role of Jewish law in the law of the State of Israel. Most of these views have appeared in legal writings, including judicial opinions and legal studies concerning the interpretation of a statute or other legal norm. Rarely has the issue been dealt with on a philosophical level such as was attained in the debates of the Knesset on various bills in the first legislative period,[15] or as is exhibited by a limited number of Supreme Court opinions.[16]

The relative paucity of fundamental philosophical analysis of the issue is unfortunate because the status of Jewish law in the legal system of the Jewish state is more than merely a legal, professional, or technical problem. If the interpretation of a statute reflects, to one degree or another, the personal philosophy and world outlook of the interpreter,[17] the status of Jewish law in the legal system of a Jewish state that is not bound by the *Halakhah* is by its very nature even more deeply enmeshed in a web of philosophic considerations, worldviews, historical perceptions, social

15. *See supra* pp. 1655–1656, 1658–1659, 1669–1670, *et al.*

16. *See, e.g.,* Rodnitzky v. Rabbinical Court of Appeals, 24(i) *P.D.* 704 (1970) (concerning the problem mentioned *supra* n. 14); Sidis v. Chief Execution Officer, 8 *P.D.* 1020 (1954) (whether the Knesset can abrogate a religious norm, or can only instruct the general courts not to follow that norm in their decisions). *See also supra* p. 1660 and n. 154; Elon, *Ḥakikah*, pp. 37–41.

17. *See, e.g., supra* pp. 1762–1765, 1770–1784, 1883–1884, 1890.

mores, matters of faith, and concepts of justice and morality, as well as—to a not inconsiderable extent—considerations of convenience and utility. These and other similar considerations, some quasi-legal and others non-legal, suffuse and motivate, consciously or subconsciously, the differing views as to the proper status of Jewish law in the State of Israel. As is usual with problems of cultural, social, and historical dimensions, there are on both sides yea-sayers and nay-sayers, as well as those who view the issue broadly and those who take a narrower view. The following discussion treats the fundamental aspects of the question, beginning with the viewpoint of the adherents of the traditional Jewish legal system.

II. JEWISH LAW IN THE INDEPENDENT ISRAELI LEGAL SYSTEM FROM THE PERSPECTIVE OF THE TRADITIONAL JEWISH LEGAL SYSTEM

A. The Nature of the State's Incorporation of Jewish Law

Some champions of the *Halakhah* argue that the incorporation of Jewish law into the legal system of a Jewish state that does not accept the binding authority of the *Halakhah* as a religious mandate—even if the incorporation is orderly and complete[18]—is contrary to the spirit of Jewish law and amounts to a "secularization of the *Halakhah.*" This argument is based on the fact that the State's incorporation of principles of Jewish law is not the result of a religious mandate to recognize their binding authority, but rather of considerations based on human, national, or other interests. It is also argued that neither the Knesset nor the courts meet the qualifications required by the halakhic system for making binding rulings on halakhic questions.[19]

This attitude is illustrated by an argument made by one of the religious members of the Knesset in the course of the debate on a section of the

18. Chapters 42 and 43 of the present work have discussed in some detail the legal and practical problems that arise from the *method* of incorporation of Jewish law into Knesset legislation (direct incorporation of a rule of Jewish law versus general incorporation by reference such as the statutes concerning marriage, divorce, and spousal and child support) and the *extent* of incorporation (selective incorporation, severance of the law from its original sources, etc.). These problems, too, are fraught with many philosophical difficulties. Here, we do not attempt to deal with the details of how the incorporation is accomplished but with the basic problem posed by the integration of two legal systems, Jewish law and the law of the State of Israel, which differ so fundamentally in their spirit and philosophy.

19. *See* Y. Leibowitz, "Ha-Torah ke-Mishpat Yisra'el" [The Torah as the Law of Israel], *Sura*, III, pp. 496–497; I. Englard, "The Problem of Jewish Law in a Jewish State," 3 *Israel L. Rev.* 254 (1968).

Capacity and Guardianship Bill. Section 20 of the bill provided that a minor must obey his parents in every matter for which they have been made responsible, and that the parents may take all proper steps for the minor's upbringing. Several members of the Knesset opposed this section on the ground that the Knesset should not legislate in regard to personal relations between parents and children, and therefore the statute should not provide that children must obey their parents. One member supported this position with the following argument:[20]

> A well-known story has it that a certain community once copied the Ten Commandments into its communal register. They were asked: "Why are you copying the Ten Commandments into your register?" They answered: "The people do not obey what is written in the Torah. Maybe they will obey what is written in the communal register."
>
> Do you wish to put the Ten Commandments into the communal register? Will that assure that they will be obeyed? . . . There are things that do not require legislation. With regard to them, we have the Ten Commandments. I would understand if you proposed a sanction—for example, that a child who does not obey his parents will be imprisoned until he obeys. If you do not and cannot propose a sanction, why repeat the Ten Commandments and, thereby, if you will forgive me [for saying this], reduce this eternal commandment from its lofty height to the level of a transient statute?

This argument, and others advanced by those who view the incorporation of Jewish law into the law of the State as being contrary to the spirit of Jewish law,[21] cannot be lightly dismissed.[22] However, the argument has two flaws: it misapprehends the worldview of the *Halakhah*, and it misconceives the nature and significance of the incorporation of Jewish law into the law of the State. There is no halakhic reason why the sanctity and religious nature of a principle of Jewish law should be diminished by reason of

20. Remarks of MK Warhaftig, 32 *DK* 56 (1962). This passage was quoted *supra* pp. 1669–1670. It bears repetition here because it well illustrates the nature of the problem inherent in the change in the source of the binding force of a rule of Jewish law when that rule is incorporated into the law of the State of Israel.

21. *See* Leibowitz and Englard, *supra* n. 19.

22. *See also* the comments of Rabbi Shaul Yisraeli opposing the incorporation of particular provisions of Jewish law into Knesset statutes that in the main conflict with Jewish law, in *Da'atenu* [Our Opinion], a bi-monthly periodical of social and political commentary published by the Youth Commission of Mafdal [National Religious Party], No. 2–3, Iyyar-Tammuz 1965, pp. 4–6. This publication also contains the views of Justices Agranat, Silberg, Kister, and Elon, and MKs Ben-Meir, Unna, and Warhaftig. For a discussion of these differing views, *see* M. Unna, "Mashma'utah Shel ha-Hashpa'ah ha-Hilkhatit Shel ha-Ḥakikah" [The Significance of the Influence of the *Halakhah* on Legislation], *Hagut ve-Halakhah,* 1968, pp. 147–160.

the fact that the general law regards the *Grundnorm* and source of the binding authority of the principle as changed when the principle is incorporated into Knesset legislation. The entire change in the hierarchy of norms is of consequence solely within the legal system of the State; the *Halakhah,* from its own perspective, cannot be adversely affected or reduced in sanctity in the slightest degree because of the new *Grundnorm.*[23] Strong evidence of the correctness of this proposition is the fact that the overwhelming majority of religious thinkers and Knesset members (including those of the Agudat Israel party) have repeatedly called for all civil and criminal statutes on the Knesset agenda to be based on Jewish law.[24] This was, for example, also the program advocated by Rabbi Isaac Herzog, the Chief Rabbi of the State of Israel, when he addressed this issue at the time the State was established.[25] It is hardly likely that halakhic authorities and religious leaders would advocate and strive to accomplish the "secularization of the *Halakhah.*"

The argument made in the Knesset against enacting the provision that a child must obey his parents, namely, that the provision would be like "copying the Ten Commandments into the communal register" (an analogy notably less than apt), amounts to an assertion that the very act of incorporating a principle of Jewish law into Israeli legislation is undesirable, because the change in the basic norm reduces the level of the principle from divine precept to human enactment. Many Knesset members strongly opposed this argument, pointing out that as a practical matter the argument sweeps too broadly: it would render the incorporation of Jewish law into Knesset legislation totally impossible. One Knesset member rejected the argument precisely because of his religious outlook, and urged that the precept of obedience to parents be enacted as a statutory provision. Indeed, he advocated including a specific statutory reference to the commandment to honor one's father and mother as contained in the Ten Commandments, in order to "express a link with the commandment to honor one's parents. . . . This link should be explicit in the statute to indicate the ancient and hallowed source of the provision in Jewish thought. . . . In short, we should identify the basis on which we have rested this law and its provisions."[26]

23. As to the basic norm (*Grundnorm*) of the *Halakhah, see supra* pp. 232–234.

24. *See supra* pp. 1627ff. for the detailed discussion of this subject in the debate on bills before the Knesset. MK Warhaftig also favored the incorporation of Jewish law into Knesset legislation. His reservations with regard to the proposed statutory provision that a minor must obey his parents were expressed in connection with his demand that the statute's formal link with English law be severed and that the statute should be linked instead to the principles of Jewish law. *See supra* pp. 1669–1671 *et seq.* and n. 207.

25. *See supra* pp. 1614–1616 and *infra* n. 46.

26. Remarks of MK Unna, 34 *DK* 3078, 3086 (1962).

The section, as adopted, reads: "A minor, duly honoring his father and mother, shall obey his parents in all matters within the scope of their parental responsibilities."[27]

The second flaw in the approach of those who would reject on halakhic grounds the incorporation of Jewish law into the law of the State is that they fail to appreciate the distinction between the incorporation of a law by the Knesset and the courts, on the one hand, and the rendering of a halakhic decision by a halakhic authority, on the other. When the Knesset or the courts incorporate a principle of Jewish law, they do not, and cannot, pretend to be making a halakhic ruling, as that term is understood in the halakhic system. Neither the Knesset nor the courts can pretend to have the authority conferred by the halakhic system to determine the *Halakhah*.[28] However, when were study and research of Jewish law and performance of its precepts confined exclusively to the halakhic authorities? It is a commonplace that the world of the *Halakhah* encompasses students as well as decisionmakers, and their views and conclusions are often different and even contradictory.

There can be no doubt that a research scholar and a decisionmaker approach their tasks differently. A halakhic decisionmaker, such as a *dayyan,* decides halakhic questions in the same manner as a judge in any legal system decides legal questions: he studies and ascertains the law as it stands in his time. By contrast, the scholar makes an analytical-historical investigation of the subject in all of its stages in the various periods of the law, in order to seek out the core common to all these periods, *e.g.*, that in general a witness is admonished, but not sworn, to tell the truth, but the court has discretion to require that the witness be sworn;[29] that a creditor must pursue his remedies against the principal debtor before he can proceed against the surety, unless the parties have specifically otherwise agreed;[30] etc.[31]

27. Capacity and Guardianship Law, 1962, sec. 16. The connection to the fifth commandment is signified by the statutory language *mi-tokh kibbud av va-em* ("duly honoring his father and mother"); the Hebrew tracks the language of the fifth commandment, *kabbed et avikha ve-et immekha* ("honor your father and your mother").

28. *See* the difference of opinion regarding this question between Justices Haim Cohn and Yitzhak Kahan in Joseph v. Joseph, 24(i) *P.D.* 792, 809, 811–812 (1970); their views are discussed in detail *supra* pp. 1790–1792. A similar disagreement arose in the Knesset as to whether the Knesset has the power—or desire—to abrogate a rule of the *Halakhah,* or whether it may only instruct the courts of the State, including the rabbinical courts, not to apply the rule. Differing views on this question have also been expressed in the decisions of the Supreme Court. *See supra* p. 1660 n. 154.

29. *See supra* pp. 1697–1702.

30. *See supra* p. 1722.

31. *See supra* pp. 90–91, 1627ff.

In the course of a detailed discussion of this subject,[32] the author of the present work stated the following:[33]

> It is clear that the difference between study and adjudication . . . is substantial and significant. The difference between scholarly research and adjudication is even more so. The student's endeavor is to obtain a basic understanding of the subject; his main interest is to analyze the issues and to study the various views and methodologies of the *rishonim* and *aḥaronim*—all through the filter of his own method of study.[34] On the other hand, the main interest of the decisionmaker is to make a ruling on the particular problem brought before him, be it a real or threatened controversy, a request for advice, or a hypothetical question. The decisionmaker therefore does not need to examine all the sources marking the historical development of various schools of thought on the subject, or to delve—even if he sometimes does so—into the more theoretical aspects of the topic and the details of its treatment by the *rishonim* and *aḥaronim;* his main concern is with the present *Halakhah* on his subject, as reflected in the codes and the responsa.
>
> Frequently, the conclusion that a student reaches when he "solves" a problem in the Talmud and Maimonides will be quite different from the one reached by the decisionmaker's method of dealing with the subject and the relevant literature. Indeed, a number of rules have been developed that recognize such differences, *e.g.*, that Rashi's commentary is intended only to explain and not to make halakhic rulings, and that decisions in responsa have greater weight than other types of halakhic literature because they reflect actual practice.[35] One need hardly point out that both the student and the

32. M. Elon, "Od le-Inyan Meḥkaro Shel ha-Mishpat ha-Ivri" [More about Research into Jewish Law], *Mishpatim*, VIII (1977), pp. 116–120, 127–130, translated into English in *Modern Research in Jewish Law* (ed. B.S. Jackson), Leiden, 1980, pp. 66ff., 86–91, 99–102. The quotation in our text is our own translation of the Hebrew.

33. Elon, *supra* n. 32 at 118–120.

34. As to this method of study, as pursued in the *yeshivot* of Lithuania in recent generations, *see* G. Alon, "Yeshivot Lita" [The *Yeshivot* of Lithuania], *Meḥkarim be-Toledot Yisrael* [Studies in Jewish History], I, pp. 1, 3–5, and M. Elon, "Le-Zikhro Shel Moshe Zilberg" [In Memory of Moshe Silberg], *Shenaton*, II (1975), pp. 1, 2–3.

35. *See* the detailed discussion *supra* pp. 960–968, 975–978, 1457–1459. A story is told in the *yeshivot* that, even if it may be only apocryphal, can illustrate our point. Rabbi Ḥayyim of Brisk had a practical question that required an answer. He wrote to the recognized authority of his generation, Yiẓḥak Elhanan of Kovno: "This is what happened and this is my question. Please answer in one line only—kosher or non-kosher, guilty or innocent—without giving any reasons." When Rabbi Ḥayyim was asked why he had requested that no reasons be given, he answered: "I am bound by a decision of R. Elhanan, since he is the authority of the generation; therefore, he must tell me his conclusion. But he should not give his reasoning, for my approach to the study and understanding of the Talmud differs from his. If he gives his reasoning, I may find that he erred in his understanding of the Talmud and I will doubt his decision. Therefore, it is best that I should not be told his reasons." This story makes clear the distinction between a student or scholar and his methodology, on one hand, and a decisionmaker and his authority, on the other.

> decisionmaker, in spite of their different methods and even though they might reach significantly different conclusions, are an integral, legitimate, and organic part of the halakhic system.
>
> If there is such a substantial difference between the student and the decisionmaker . . . , the difference between the scientific scholar and the decisionmaker is even greater. The scholar must be more exhaustive than the student. He must review the entire Talmudic literature on the subject, including sources not ordinarily available to the general run of students. He must examine variant texts according to different manuscripts to a far greater extent than is typical for the student. He must review all the various opinions, without exception, on the subject at hand, and acquaint himself with the historical and social background of the law. Finally, he must, consistent with his own methodology, review the development of his subject throughout the various periods of Jewish law and identify the legal sources through which this development took place.[36]
>
> It is therefore not surprising that the scholar, even more so than the student, may well reach conclusions that differ substantially from the conclusions of the decisionmaker; and this too is perfectly permissible, acceptable, and even desirable from the halakhic point of view, so long as the scholar does not purport to act as judge or decisionmaker but contents himself with scholarly inquiry designed to achieve a deeper understanding of the *Halakhah*.[37]
>
> This kind of inquiry has great importance not only for the contribution that scientific research makes to the clarity and coherence of Jewish law, but also for the nature and character of the integration of Jewish law into the legal system of the State.

When the State, by statute or judicial decision, incorporates a principle of Jewish law, it does not do so in order to add another rule to the religious obligations mandated by the *Shulḥan Arukh;* it does so in order to integrate the concept taken from Jewish law into the legal system of the State, which imposes legal obligations on all its citizens. Such an incorporation of Jewish law is fitting, proper, and desirable, even though it does not constitute a halakhic determination in the religious sense.[38] It is clear that from the per-

36. *See supra* pp. 80–91.

37. Leading halakhic authorities have often distinguished between their views as scholars and their rulings as decisionmakers. *See, e.g.*, Rashbam, *Commentary on Genesis* 37:2, regarding the *dictum* that a Biblical text can never completely escape beyond its plain meaning, and the views of Maimonides and Yom Tov Lipmann Heller, author of *Tosafot Yom Tov*, regarding the plain meaning of the Mishnah, *supra* p. 1107 n. 10.

38. Professor I. Englard does not support this approach to the incorporation of Jewish law into Israeli law. However, an example he cites to support his own position reinforces the correctness of the approach taken here. In *In re Litvinski Brothers Partnership*, 18 *P.M.* 64 (1959), certain property was to be divided between two equal partners. The question arose: Should the allocation be made by drawing lots, or should one of the partners be allowed to choose that part of the property which for personal reasons had particular value only to

spective of the *Halakhah* it is desirable and preferable for a dispute to be resolved in accordance with the substantive rules and the concepts of justice in the *Shulḥan Arukh* rather than by rules of some other legal system.[39]

---

him? The late Judge Lamm of the district court decided not to follow English law, which denies the right to such a choice, and instead relied on Jewish law, which, according to one view, grants the right to choose and asserts that "refusal to allow such a choice is characteristic of the practices of Sodom" (Maimonides, *MT,* Shekhenim 12:1; Sh. Ar. ḤM 174:1). Although there is a contrary position in Jewish law to the effect that even where no monetary loss is involved, the partner who prefers a particular part of the partnership property must compensate the other partner, the court, on reflection, preferred the view that such a choice is permitted and no compensation need be paid.

The court stated: "It does not seem right to me that the partition should be implemented in a way that precludes a person who contributed to the expansion and prosperity of the enterprise from choosing the part he prefers, when it is undisputed that both parts are of equal value" (18 *P.M.* at 68). Englard criticized this decision, stating: "The judge thus chose between the opposing opinions of the authorities (in favour of the one partner) according to his own considerations and extended the rule beyond the case of abutting lands. Is this halakhic innovation authoritative and effective?" (Englard, *supra* n. 19 at 272).

The answer to Englard's question is quite simple. Judge Lamm's innovation is fitting and proper. It adapts the Jewish legal principle that "we apply the force of the law against the traits of Sodom (*kofin al middat Sedom*)" and also the principle that we should "do what is right and good," which is the basis of the halakhic legislation concerning adjoining landowners, as well as of other areas of Jewish law, particularly the law of partnership; *see supra* pp. 623–628. Judge Lamm should be commended for rejecting the results reached by the English equity courts when those results do not conform to the conditions of life in the State of Israel, and for applying the Jewish sources of justice and equity in light of the economic and social situation of the State of Israel. This is the same approach used by Rabbi Jacob Reischer who, in a similar situation, refused to follow the principle that *kol de-alim gaver* ("whoever is stronger will prevail"), since "there is considerable doubt as to whether this principle . . . should be applied in these times." *Resp. Shevut Ya'akov,* II, ḤM #167. *See* the extensive discussion of this question and of the views of Jacob Reischer in Rosenstein v. Solomon, 38(ii) *P.D.* 113 (1984), quoted *supra* pp. 1715–1716. To apply Jewish law as Judge Lamm did is not only proper but desirable, even though the decision has no religious status as a halakhic ruling, and the judge never pretended to be a halakhic authority. *See also* M. Elon, "Ha-Mishpat ha-Ivri be-Mishpat ha-Medinah, Keiẓad?" [Jewish Law in the Legal System of the State—What Is the Way?], *De'ot,* X (1959), pp. 15ff.

39. Although relating to a fundamentally different situation, the statement of Israel Isserlein concerning the development of tax law in the medieval Jewish community provides some support for this conclusion. Over a long period of time, beginning particularly with the twelfth century, the halakhic authorities and communal leaders developed a comprehensive system of tax law, much of which did not accord with Talmudic law. These laws were introduced into the *Halakhah* by means of legislation (mainly communal enactments) and custom (*see supra* pp. 745–751, 920–923). With regard to the tax law used by the Jewish community, Israel Isserlein stated (*Terumat ha-Deshen* #342):

> All actions taken by the public collectively are governed by the customs and arrangements they institute to meet their needs and circumstances. If you require them to follow the law of the Torah in all matters, there will always be strife among them. . . . It would seem, however, that even though we have previously mentioned that in tax matters custom overrides the law, it is always appropriate and correct to consider carefully whether it is possible to reconcile all customs with the law of the Torah. Even

The negative attitude toward the incorporation of Jewish law into the law of the State appears to be only one aspect of a much broader rejection of all spiritual ties between the two segments into which the Jewish people divided after the Emancipation—one that has retained a religious perspective and regards the *Halakhah* as binding, and one that has developed a secular outlook and does not recognize the authority of the *Halakhah*. This negative attitude is based on the farfetched argument that the *Halakhah* does not recognize the "Jewish" status of a Jewish state which does not accept the binding character of the *Halakhah*, and which depends for its legitimacy only upon the authority of its government.[40]

It is true that after the onset of the Emancipation, which changed the previous completely traditional character of Jewish society, sharp controversies arose in the religious community concerning the relationship of the *Halakhah* to various aspects of the movement of national reawakening that were not based on the acceptance of the Torah as binding. There were even times (and how far away they now seem!) when a part of religious Jewry viewed the use of the Hebrew language in ordinary daily life, and the development and adaptation of Hebrew to the needs of modern society, as a profanation of the "holy tongue." There was also a time when they viewed the settlement of the Holy Land by those who did not adhere to the religious precepts as an offense to the sacred values of the nation. This opposition, and the conclusions to which it led with regard to the revival of the Hebrew language and the settlement of the Land of Israel, in its time had a much more reasonable basis than does the opposition to the incorporation of Jewish law into the law of the State. Nevertheless, the attitude of those religious Jews who perceived in the revival of the Holy Land and the "holy tongue" the manifestation of the divine will ultimately prevailed after strenuous struggles, and was accepted as correct and legitimate by the overwhelming and decisive majority of religious Jewry; and this is the attitude today of the overwhelming majority of religious Jewry with regard to Jewish life in the State of Israel.

> if this cannot be done completely, it is highly desirable to find reinforcement and support in the words of the halakhic authorities and buttress them [the practices] with good reason and logic.

The conditions of those times often required the promulgation of various tax laws that did not fully accord with Talmudic law. Although, according to Jewish law, such laws are valid, it is desirable to link these laws, to the extent possible—"even if this cannot be done completely"—with the law of the Torah, and to find reinforcement and a rationale for them in the rulings of the halakhic authorities. This, indeed, was the practice of the halakhic authorities whenever they dealt with any matter in this broad area. *See supra* pp. 745–751, 920–923; M. Elon, EJ, XV, pp. 840ff., s.v. Taxation (reprinted in *Principles*, pp. 662, 669).

40. *See* Leibowitz, *supra* n. 19 at 500; Englard, *supra* n. 19 at 274–277.

Why should we revive today, with regard to the renewal of Jewish law among all segments of the people of the State of Israel, an argument that has proved to be without substance? The incorporation of Jewish law into the legal system of the State cannot "damage" Jewish law, and cannot "secularize" the *Halakhah*. Jewish law will not be strengthened by isolation, no matter how "pure" and "protected" in its isolation it may be. To the contrary: The primary method of reviving Jewish law and restoring it to practical life is through its renewal by incorporation into the legal system of the Jewish state. Only in this way will Jewish law again be able to grapple with contemporary problems and thereby attain renewed vigor and creativity.[41]

B. The Prohibition Against Litigating in Non-Jewish Courts

Another argument sometimes raised during discussions on the place of Jewish law in the law of the Jewish state is worthy of comment. It is argued that the rule forbidding recourse to non-Jewish courts (*arka'ot*) applies to litigation in a court where the judges are Jewish but do not judge according to Jewish law.[42] In light of the previous detailed discussion of this rule,[43] the argument, for both halakhic and historical reasons, seems more than passing strange. The entire subject of litigation before a court where the judges are Jewish but do not judge according to the *Halakhah* is found in chapter 8 of *Shulḥan Arukh Ḥoshen Mishpat*. It is treated separately from the prohibition against resorting to non-Jewish courts, which is dealt with in all its aspects (including detailed stringencies, prohibitions, and exceptions) in chapter 26 of *Shulḥan Arukh Ḥoshen Mishpat*.

As previously noted, all the halakhic sources have emphasized the close connection between the prohibition against litigating in non-Jewish courts and the danger of undermining Jewish juridical autonomy.[44] It is true

41. As to this aspect of the problem of incorporating Jewish law into the law of the State, *see* Elon, *supra* n. 32 at 134–137; M. Unna, *Bi-Derakhim Nifradot—Hamiflagot ha-Datiyyot be-Yisra'el* [With Diverse Approaches—the Religious Parties in Israel], 1984, pp. 335ff.

42. *See* J. Segal, "Al ha-Mishpat ha-Ḥiloni ba-Areẓ" [On Secular Law in the Land of Israel], *Ha-Torah ve-ha-Medinah*, VII–VIII, pp. 74ff. *See also* the statement of the editor, *id.*, disagreeing with the conclusion reached by the author. Englard, *supra* n. 19 at 271 n. 48, expresses no categorical conclusion as to the position of Jewish law on this issue.

43. *See supra* pp. 13–18.

44. This point is emphasized in an interesting manner by Shabbetai ha-Kohen (*Shakh* to Sh. Ar. ḤM ch. 22, subpar. 15, discussed *supra* pp. 17–18), who held that an agreement to litigate before non-Jewish courts is invalid only if it provides for "appearance before non-Jewish courts generally." If, however, the parties agree to litigate before a particular named non-Jewish judge, the agreement is binding because "this gentile is trustworthy in their eyes and they have confidence in him, and it is effective in the same way as if they agreed on one who is a relative or is otherwise disqualified." Thus, litigating before a non-Jewish judge

that this distinction between Jewish and non-Jewish courts was made when the generality of Jewish society viewed the *Halakhah* as the supreme and binding norm. Therefore, even the Jewish lay tribunals that did not judge according to the *Halakhah* did not ordinarily use a different legal system, but followed their own judgment and the principles of justice and equity. By contrast, the courts of the State of Israel, which do not judge according to Jewish law, do judge according to a different legal system, which has been set up by the authorized and elected institutions of the State. Nevertheless, the fact is that even before the Emancipation there were Jewish lay tribunals that judged according to other systems of laws and customs;[45] and the change in the spiritual climate of the Jewish people after the Emancipation cannot weaken the fundamental distinction made throughout the entire course of the *Halakhah* between Jewish judicial tribunals which do not apply the *Halakhah*, on the one hand, and judicial tribunals of a non-Jewish government, on the other: only the latter are included in the law prohibiting litigation before non-Jewish courts.[46]

---

does not violate the prohibition against resorting to non-Jewish courts (and therefore such an agreement is valid) as long as the parties do not submit themselves generally to non-Jewish adjudication. It would seem, therefore, that litigation before a non-Jewish judge appointed by a Jewish government would be permissible, and the parties could agree to have such a judge hear their case.

45. *See, e.g.*, the comments of Meiri on *arka'ot she-be-Suria* ("the courts in Syria"), *supra* p. 24 n. 80, and the enactment of the community of Leghorn, *supra* pp. 28–29.

46. *Ḥazon Ish*, Sanhedrin 15:4 (end), stated with regard to this issue:

> There is also the case in a place where no one is a *gamir* [*i.e.*, no one has learned rules and laws from scholars and judges], where those who have not studied any Torah at all, and who will adjudicate according to ordinary human intelligence, are appointed as judges in order to prevent resort to *arka'ot* (non-Jewish courts). This is done for the public welfare. All this is explained in the responsum of Rashba (quoted in *Bet Yosef* ch. 8), concerning the courts known as *arka'ot she-be-Suria* ("the courts in Syria"). There is some slight support for the view that the *dayyan she-be-Suria* mentioned in the Talmud refers to a judge who does not apply the laws of the Torah at all; however, it appears from the Talmud that he is a judge who rules according to the laws of the Torah, but is disqualified because of the paucity of his knowledge of the Torah and his propensity to err. (The proof for this is that arbitration, in which each party chooses one arbitrator [and the two arbitrators choose a third], is conducted according to the law of the Torah, yet the Sages ruled that if a party chooses an arbitrator from among the judges of the *arka'ot she-be-Suria*, the judge cannot be disqualified, since he was appointed by the public. We thus see that he is supposed to judge according to the laws of the Torah.) Possibly Rashba concluded that inasmuch as the judge's authority rests on his appointment by the public, he is qualified even if he is entirely ignorant of the laws of the Torah, as it is all for the public welfare.
>
> Despite the fact that there is no one among them who can judge according to the rules of the Torah, and they are compelled to appoint a person of intelligence [who will judge] according to human ethical notions, [they] may not take upon them-

The argument based on the halakhic prohibition against litigating in non-Jewish courts is also surprising in view of the fact that since the abro-

---

> selves the laws of [other] nations or enact legislation. When a judge rules solely according to his own sense of justice, he acts as an arbitrator, and thus does not give rise to a perception that he has forsaken the Fount of Living Waters to hew broken cisterns [*cf.* Jeremiah 2:13]. But if judges establish their own system of laws, they desecrate the Torah. Concerning them, it is said: "'You shall set before them' [Exodus 21:1] . . . but not before *hedyotot.*" This is explained in [*Bet Yosef*] ch. 26.
>
> It makes no difference whether a case is brought before non-Jews or before Jews who judge according to false laws. Indeed, it [*i.e.,* bringing a case before such Jewish judges] is the more discreditable, since they have abandoned the rules of the Torah in favor of false rules. If the townspeople should agree to do so, their agreement is invalid, and if they enforce such an agreement, their judgments amount to theft and extortion, and they raise their hand against the Torah of Moses.

In the interest of arriving at the truth of the matter, the statement of the *Ḥazon Ish* must perforce be examined in the spirit of a student questioning his teacher. His conclusion seems surprising. It has already been noted (*supra* p. 24 n. 80) that many *rishonim* held the view that the judges of the *arka'ot she-be-Suria* were completely ignorant of Torah law, and did not base their decisions on it. It was also noted that in the view of Meiri, the judges of those courts judged not only on the basis of their personal estimate of the case but also on the basis of established rules and usages, *i.e.,* they accepted upon themselves a foreign system of laws. Moreover, the principle "'before them' but not before *hedyotot*" (the term *hedyotot* is used here to mean unlearned judges rather than judges who are learned but not ordained—the latter being the meaning in TB Gittin, the original source of the expression) is discussed in Sh. Ar. ḤM ch. 8, and is not mentioned at all in ch. 26. Thus, the rule set forth in ch. 26—that litigation may not be brought before non-Jewish courts even with the consent of the litigants—is inapplicable to litigation before *hedyotot,* even if that term is used to mean unlearned judges. Indeed, ch. 8 specifically states that litigation may be brought before *hedyotot* with the consent of the parties, and it does not use the expression "they raise their hand against the Torah of Moses," which is applied (in ch. 26) only to those who litigate before non-Jewish courts.

Chief Rabbi Herzog had the following to say on this question (*Ha-Torah ve-ha-Medinah* [The Torah and the State], VII, pp. 9–12): "In my view, for the Jewish people as an entity in its own land to adjudicate its disputes according to foreign laws is a thousand times worse than for individuals or groups of Jews to litigate before non-Jewish courts." These words point to the great spiritual danger involved in the application of non-Jewish law, but they do not represent a legal determination that resort to Jewish courts in the State of Israel that do not apply Jewish law comes within the prohibition of litigation before *arka'ot.* Indeed, in his further remarks, Rabbi Herzog proposed that Jewish law be prepared in

> an organized manner, in a form likely to be accepted by jurists. . . . If we should prepare such a book, it seems likely that they [the jurists] will not completely disregard the laws of the Torah, but will adopt various portions of it. While the Torah will still gird itself in sackcloth over such a compromise, the desecration of the name of God will nevertheless not be so great.

This is what the Knesset has in fact done, often incorporating the principles of Jewish law into its legislation. If the *halakhic* prohibition of resorting to *arka'ot* were applicable, how could such a compromise be accepted? *See also* Segal, *supra* n. 42 at 74–85, and the comments of Rabbi Shaul Yisraeli, in his notes, *id.* at 75–78. It should also be reiterated that the responsa of Rashba quoted by *Bet Yosef* at the end of ḤM ch. 26 deal with litigation before non-Jewish courts, and not with litigation before unlearned Jewish judges (*hedyotot*), and there is nothing in these responsa at variance with the views expressed here.

gation of Jewish juridical autonomy, the prohibition has all but lost its effectiveness. Not only has resort to the general courts greatly increased throughout the Jewish diaspora since the end of Jewish juridical autonomy, but the halakhic authorities have reconciled themselves to litigation by Jews in non-Jewish courts and have given the prohibition an entirely different interpretation from that maintained by the halakhic authorities during all prior periods.[47] Today, even the most strictly observant Jews throughout the diaspora turn to the courts of the countries in which they reside. It is thus particularly ironic that the prohibition against "resorting to non-Jewish courts" is invoked precisely with regard to the Jewish courts of a Jewish state in which Jewish law is a "member of the family"—or at least a frequent guest. The prevalence of litigation by Jews in non-Jewish courts throughout the diaspora and the incorporation of a significant portion of Jewish law into the legal system of the Jewish state are facts that cannot be ignored.

C. The Problems When Jewish Legislation and Adjudication Are Not Based on Jewish Law

The existence of a Jewish legislative and judicial system that is not based on Jewish law is a troublesome situation for Judaism generally and for Jewish law in particular. The fact that the prohibition against litigation in non-Jewish courts does not extend to courts composed of Jewish judges who do not judge according to Jewish law does not diminish the seriousness of the problems presented by a Jewish legal system not based on Jewish law, or the seriousness of the implications of such a situation for Jewish law. The problem is not one of formal prohibition against applying non-halakhic rules in Jewish life; the *Halakhah* itself provides mechanisms for the application of such rules.[48] The difficulty is the disheartening severance of the legal system of the sovereign Jewish state from the magnificently rich legal and cultural treasure produced by generation after generation of Jews without a sovereign state of their own who nevertheless ceaselessly struggled to maintain their juridical autonomy. This difficulty is not, and cannot be, remedied by any kind of formal dispensation.

47. *See supra* pp. 1582–1584 and nn., *ad loc.*

48. *See supra* pp. 678ff. and the summary at pp. 778–779. *See also supra* pp. 19–36, 123–127, 903–909; and the comments of Rashbeẓ and Shimon Shkop, *supra* pp. 135–137.

III. JEWISH LAW IN THE INDEPENDENT ISRAELI LEGAL SYSTEM FROM THE PERSPECTIVE OF THE LAW OF THE STATE

A. The Legislature

We have previously discussed the twofold approach taken by the Knesset with regard to the Israeli legal system.[49] On the one hand, the Knesset for a long time opposed the establishment of an official link between Israeli law and Jewish law until the enactment of the Foundations of Law Act in 1980 established an official, if modest, connection between Israeli law and the principles of Jewish law and the Jewish heritage. On the other hand, from the very beginning of its legislative activity, the Knesset based a considerable number of the institutions and laws of the Israeli legal system on the principles of Jewish law. What motivated the Knesset to make use of Jewish law as the legal system upon which to base much of its legislation? The answer is indicated in the following statement of legislative policy by those who drafted and sponsored various bills for the codification of civil law in the early years of the State:[50]

> It might have been thought desirable to take one of the foreign legal systems and translate it into Hebrew, with slight adaptations, as the Turks did with Swiss law, and the Japanese with German law. Taking this course, however, would not in our view be doing our duty. Such a mechanical incorporation of foreign law would not only have prevented the revival of Jewish law but also would not have satisfied the requirements of an independent Israeli culture.

The late Professor Zeltner understood this point well, even though, as we shall see, he himself did not agree:

> In the present situation of law and, especially, jurisprudence, the Legislature actually had only two reasonable options: One was the adoption of the entire *corpus juris* of another state, excepting only such provisions as were not appropriate for the particular conditions in the country.
>
> This was the course taken by great nations with ancient cultures, such as China, which accepted the German Civil Code, and Turkey, which adopted the Law of Obligations of the Swiss Code. The other approach was to leave the law . . . in its present state, to remove the remnants of Islamic and Otto-

49. *See supra* pp. 1621ff.

50. Draft Succession Bill, July 1952, Introduction, p. 7, published by the Ministry of Justice.

man law, and, to the extent necessary, modify the remaining English law. Our Legislature, with great ambition, went its own way.[51]

For reasons founded on fundamental conceptions of the nature, function, and purpose of a legal system, the Israeli Knesset decided not to follow in the lead of the Chinese, the Japanese, or the Turks. Concerning the course of action taken by the Knesset, Professor Zeltner clearly and candidly commented as follows:[52]

> One who sees the law as an expression of the totality of the national character will reach different conclusions from those reached by one who sees law only as a technical discipline. The former will more easily recognize the urgent necessity of giving the Jewish people in its homeland its "own" law, just as he will see the necessity for the Hebrew language to take root and flourish. . . . One who sees law, as the present writer does, as no more than an instrument whereby to achieve certain social objectives (except, perhaps, in limited areas, such as family and succession law), or one who in the final analysis seeks through law the furtherance of the general security, the achievement of practical social goals, and the shaping of the future rather than discovery and perpetuation of the past, will harbor more and greater doubts. . . . The primary task of the Legislature is, therefore, to be concerned with the anticipated consequences of transactions that have legal significance. The testator must know the consequences of his will, and one who enters into an agreement must know the consequences, under the law of contracts, of the contract he makes. It is true that no law will fully achieve certainty in this regard. Life is too complex, and technical and social developments are too rapid, for the law to capture in its net all possible future situations. The question, however, is one of degree. The Legislature must attempt to come as close as possible to achieving this goal.[53]

The Israeli Legislature correctly believed that the legal system is one of the most significant manifestations of a nation's culture. It reveals a society's conception of law and equity, justice and compassion, individual rights and social obligations.[54] For these reasons, the Israeli Legislature undertook to

51. Z. Zeltner, "Dinei ha-Ḥozim be-Hitpatḥutam Meshekh Ḥaẓi ha-Yovel me-Az Kum ha-Medinah" [The Law of Contracts as Developed during the Quarter-Century since the Establishment of the State], *Ha-Praklit,* XXIX (1975), pp. 198, 231.

52. *Id.* at 229–230.

53. Differences of opinion regarding the appropriate method of codification in the Jewish state—based on these and other arguments—had arisen at the beginning of this century, when the Ha-Mishpat Ha-Ivri Society was founded in Moscow in 1918. *See supra* p. 1589 n. 26 as to the interesting debate that took place on this question.

54. *See* G.W. Paton, *Jurisprudence,* Oxford, 4th ed., 1972, pp. 19–21, 188ff., 194ff.; W.N. Hibbert, *Jurisprudence,* London, 1932.

prepare its own codification. This task was performed in stages and extended over a long period. The codification was based on the principles of various legal systems, but Jewish law was the primary source because it "is one of our national cultural treasures that we must renew and carry forward."[55] Even the severance of the Israeli legal system from English law was accomplished only gradually. For a long period of time—far longer than necessary or reasonable—the Knesset was reluctant to link the legal system of the Jewish state formally and officially to Jewish law, until in 1980, as discussed in detail in the previous chapter,[56] it summoned up its courage, repealed the requirement to look to English law, and recognized "the principles of justice, freedom, equity, and peace of the Jewish heritage" as a complementary and binding source of Israeli law.

B. The Courts

The progress of the Israeli Legislature toward its goal of strengthened ties between the Israeli legal system and the Jewish legal system did not evoke from the courts the response it merited. Although some ten years after the establishment of the State, the Israeli Supreme Court held that English cases decided after the creation of the State did not have the binding force possessed by pre-1948 English cases,[57] this decision had no practical effect on the extent to which Israeli courts looked to English law and English judicial decisions. Certainly, there have always been individual Supreme Court justices, as well as judges of other courts, who also looked to Jewish law, at first only for purposes of comparison and in connection with the interpretation of value-laden legal principles, but eventually also as a source for decision. However, this is not the way by which the vast majority of Israeli judges arrive at their judgments.

English law—and, recently, also American law—have been routinely consulted almost as though the value of this practice were self-evident in the very nature of things. All the judicial pronouncements that every question of statutory interpretation must be decided from within the four corners of the statute, and that the Israeli legal system is fully independent of every other legal system, are merely ceremonial; they have virtually no significance in day-to-day adjudication. Certainly, no Israeli judge will say that he is required to look to the law of other countries, but in fact he does look to English (and American) law in every case involving a question of statutory interpretation for which the statute itself provides no clear answer.

55. Draft Succession Bill, *supra* n. 50 at 6; *see supra* pp. 1626–1627.
56. *See supra* pp. 1827ff.
57. Kokhavi v. Becker, 11 *P.D.* 225 (1957); *see supra* pp. 1728, 1829.

These two non-Israeli legal systems constitute, as a practical matter, the basic foundation of Israeli jurisprudence and the grist of the Israeli judicial mill. This strange and puzzling state of affairs, which has continued even after the enactment of the Foundations of Law Act, is evident from the overwhelming proportion of the decisions of the Supreme Court and the district courts taken up with the analysis of English and American cases.[58]

The situation was well described by the legal scholar Mishael Cheshin in his comments on the Foundations of Law Bill:[59]

> In this connection, let us briefly consider the place of English law in the Israeli legal system. At the beginning, before the establishment of the State and after the national awakening, we drew to the full from English law and never said, "Enough!" We went so far as to fill in the *Mejelle* with the substance of English law. Indeed, if a stranger had studied how English law fared in our country he would have found, to his amazement, that "the whole land . . . [was] full of its glory"—much more so than analysis of the pertinent legal sources could justify. This was the case in days gone by; but in recent years, as close observation will reveal, we have distanced ourselves from English law. [It was as if] after having regularly orbited the sun year after year, the earth began to work its way out of its orbit until it worked itself free from the sun's gravitational pull and began its own journey through space.
>
> But behold . . . we suddenly notice from the corner of our eye an unusual phenomenon incongruous with the new setting we have built. We pause for a moment, move closer, and stand astonished and amazed: Is this real or only an illusion? And this is what we see: When they are required to construe new statutes enacted by the Knesset, the courts, all the while proclaiming the independence we have attained, make extensive use of foreign—particularly English—decisions. On festivals and holidays we wave the banner of independence, but on workdays, it is business as usual. Even on holidays, once we have waved the flag, we read from the holy scriptures of others. Given the path that we followed, and especially in light of the progress—an organic progress—that has been achieved, it is very strange that even as we wave the banner of independence, we look to the rules of English law as if they were relevant to Knesset legislation, even where the particular statute involved has not been shown to have been based particularly on English law.
>
> Sometimes, the rules of English law enter the process of interpretation of Knesset legislation in the manner of one entering one's own home, and the

58. *See supra* pp. 1869–1871. *See also supra* p. 1863 n. 164, regarding the trend in the district courts to make greater use of Jewish law.

59. M. Cheshin, "Moreshet Yisra'el u-Mishpat ha-Medinah" [The Jewish Heritage and the Law of the State], in *Zekhuyyot Ezraḥ be-Yisra'el, Koveẓ Ma'amarim li-Khevodo Shel Ḥayyim H. Cohn* [Civil Rights in Israel—Essays in Honor of Haim Cohn], Tel Aviv, 1982, pp. 47, 77–78.

courts rely on them without so much as stopping to question. Sometimes, when the courts do perceive the paradox in what they are doing, and feel some slight embarrassment at their conduct, they reflect upon the matter and tell us that recourse to foreign law (primarily the rules of English law) is for the purpose of widening horizons and receiving enlightenment; it is proper for us to examine the laws of civilized and enlightened nations and study the experience and accumulated wisdom of others in order to learn what is best for ourselves.

This is what happened: At the beginning, we held that the precedents of English law were binding. Later, we established that they were only persuasive. Years passed, and we said that we were working on a domestic enterprise and that foreign precedents in our hands are only the raw material for our own product. [Finally,] today, to broaden our vision, we go squinting at foreign legal systems. Why all this? Have we not retrogressed and returned to times past? How can we reconcile independence—political independence, independence the Legislature explicitly proclaimed, independence which the courts have stressed, the development and severance which have occurred—with the present state of affairs?

What caused this puzzling development in the decisions of the courts? Cheshin went on to list a number of reasons. First, long-ingrained habits and inertia. Second, the desire of the courts to enhance (*leyappot*) their image by visiting "the tents of Japheth (*Yafet*)." Third and, according to Cheshin, most important, is the following:[60]

Judges have a deep inner need to find support in a legal system that is faithful to its professed principles and is complete and homogeneous. . . . Knesset legislation, as well as judicially created rules not grounded in statutes, . . . are all . . . [like] trees planted on streams of water, islands in the sea, saplings in a hothouse. One who is responsible for making legal rulings must immerse himself in the stream, swim in the sea, breathe in the atmosphere of the hothouse. . . . This is the way of the man of law, wherever he may be. Even if you tell him to do what is good and right as he sees fit, even then, consciously or subconsciously, he will seek to channel justice and equity along some well-worn path. He will feel the need for neutral principles, as it were, and will not create justice and equity on his own. It is the nature of justice and equity to seek out their place within the framework of law.

We have no streams of water of our own,[61] and it will be many years before we will have sufficient water from our own springs and will be capable of building a hothouse of our own. . . . Therefore, it is as if we have silently

60. *Id.* at 78–80.
61. *See infra* pp. 1932–1934 regarding "our own streams of water."

> come to the conclusion that we go to English law; it is part of us and we are part of it. Our thoughts are its thoughts, and its language comes familiarly to our tongues. This is so for English law, as well as—albeit to a lesser extent—for other legal systems that have lighted our way.

The words quoted above were written during the debate on the bill which became the Foundations of Law Act, and their purpose was to *prevent* the enactment of that statute. Cheshin stated his principal reasons for his opposition to the Foundations of Law Act: (1) the many difficulties involved in finding and understanding Jewish law, (2) Jewish law's many and divergent views and subtle nuances, (3) the lack of sufficient preparation for the incorporation of Jewish law into the law of the State, (4) the absence of a literature suitable and adequate for ready study and understanding, and (5) the great concern that the overwhelming majority of lawyers and judges do not have even a minimal knowledge of Jewish law or the skills necessary to navigate in the sea of the Talmud or to find their way in the codificatory and responsa literature. The point that the great majority of Israeli judges and lawyers are ignorant of Jewish law has considerable force; we shall therefore discuss it further below. For now, it suffices to say that time has made clear that the learned author of the foregoing quotation could well have spared himself his fears about the consequences of the Foundations of Law Act.

The statute was adopted, and a number of years have passed; yet the great majority of the judges still refer neither to the statute nor to Jewish law. The law and the judges are doing business as usual. English law and other legal systems continue to be grist for the mill of most Israeli judges. If this occasions surprise and disbelief, the discussion in the previous chapter provides a ready explanation of how this situation came to be. There are many ways to interpret a statute, and a court has considerable latitude for expansive or restrictive interpretation. Thanks to these techniques, there has been no "earthquake" in the Israeli legal system as a result of the adoption of the Foundations of Law Act, 1980. Except for a tiny tremor no more violent than the prick of a needle, one can discern no meaningful change in the decisions of most Israeli judges under the influence of the "foundations" and the "law" referred to in that statute.

IV. SUBJECTIVE AND OBJECTIVE FACTORS AFFECTING RECOURSE TO JEWISH LAW

A number of factors have led to the situation described above. Some are subjective; they are based on emotional and irrational reactions, inordinate suspicion, inexplicable apprehensiveness, and lack of proper intellectual and emotional appreciation of the place of Jewish law in the spirit and culture of the Jewish people. Others are objective, and will require much reflection, effort, and astuteness to overcome them. Court decisions exemplify both types.

A. Subjective Factors

Afanjar v. State of Israel[62] illuminates the subjective factors. There is a principle in criminal law which, with limitations not pertinent here, permits the wounding of a person who unlawfully attacks another, when the intent of the wounding is to repel the attack. Such defense can be either self-defense, as when the victim defends himself by resisting the aggressor, or it can be the defense of a third person.[63] The *Afanjar* case concerned the scope of this principle under the Penal Law, 1977, when defense of a third person is involved. The issue was whether the right to defend a third person is limited to the defense of relatives or of persons to whom the defender owes a duty based on a special relationship, or whether the right extends to the defense of anyone under attack.

My opinion in the above case was that the principle extends to the defense of anyone, even a stranger, and I therefore voted to reverse the appellant's conviction. I relied primarily on the rules of Jewish law concerning the rescue of a victim from an attacker.[64] According to Jewish law, there is a duty to rescue any person by wounding and, when necessary, even killing the attacker. The source of this obligation is the verse: "Do not stand idly by the blood of your fellow."[65] I mentioned in my opinion that this is also the rule in English and American law as well as in some Continental systems.[66] My reason for looking particularly to Jewish law was based on the following aspect of the obligation to defend another:

> This concerns concepts rooted in public policy and in the socio-moral outlook on life as it affects the rescue of another person who is in danger of bodily injury. . . . In my opinion, it is appropriate to interpret basic concepts rooted

62. 33(iii) *P.D.* 141 (1979).

63. Penal Law, 1977, sec. 22.

64. TB Sanhedrin 73a *et al.*

65. Leviticus 19:16. Another source is Deuteronomy 25:12: "Show no pity." *See* the detailed discussion in Maimonides, *MT,* Roẓe'aḥ u-Shemirat ha-Nefesh 1:6–16; Afanjar v. State of Israel, *supra* n. 62 at 150–155.

66. *See* Afanjar v. State of Israel, *supra* n. 62 at 149–150, 155; A. Enker, *Ha-Koraḥ ve ha-Ẓorekh be-Dinei Onshin* [Duress and Necessity in Penal Law], Ramat-Gan, 1977, pp. 97ff.

> in moral standards and cultural values in the light of the moral and cultural heritage of Judaism.[67]

The late Court President Sussman agreed that appellant's conviction should be reversed, but he reached this conclusion by a different route. He determined that the case involved the appellant's own self-defense and left open the question of how far beyond self-defense the principle in question extended. At the beginning of his opinion, Justice Sussman wrote:[68]

> With all due respect, I join in the conclusion reached by my distinguished colleague, Justice Elon. However, since I arrived at it by a different route than my distinguished colleague, I must put my reasoning on the record. The sole question before us is whether the defense of necessity under Section 18 of the Criminal Code Ordinance, 1936, is available to the appellant.[69] In answer to this question, I may not turn for assistance to Jewish law. Jewish law is undoubtedly a valuable cultural asset of our people, from which both the Legislature and the courts may draw inspiration. But we are dealing here with a specific provision of a criminal statute which has a different origin and has nothing to do with Jewish sources. I also venture to doubt whether the application of Jewish criminal law would really be acceptable to the Israeli public. For example, would the Israeli public be ready, in 1979, on the basis of the rules of Jewish law, to put an adulterous woman to death by stoning, or, if she was the daughter of a *kohen,* by burning?

It is extremely difficult to understand the pertinence of these last remarks. What possible relevance can punishment of an adulterous woman have to the question of the right to come to the defense of another person? The first argument of Justice Sussman—that since the principle of self-defense in Israeli criminal law is not derived from Jewish law, the principle should be interpreted not in accordance with Jewish law but in accordance with the law from which it was derived[70]—is understandable, although, it is submitted, unsound, as previously pointed out.[71] In particular, the argument is unsatisfactory when it concerns a value-laden legal principle that

67. Afanjar v. State of Israel, *supra* n. 62 at 155. *See also supra* pp. 1730, 1736–1737, 1836–1838, with regard to the use of Jewish law by various justices of the Supreme Court interpreting value-laden legal terms.

68. Afanjar v. State of Israel, *supra* n. 62 at 160.

69. Criminal Law Ordinance, 1936, sec. 18, which was still in force at the time *Afanjar* was decided, recognized "necessity" as a defense. *See* Afanjar v. State of Israel, *supra* n. 62 at 146.

70. Justice Sussman made a similar argument in connection with the interpretation of "good faith" in Israeli legislation. He contended that the interpretation should be based on Section 242 of the *German Civil Code,* which, in his view, is the historical source of the principle of good faith in the Israeli legal system. *See supra* p. 1734 n. 422.

71. *Supra* p. 1734 n. 422.

in the view of a number of Supreme Court justices should be interpreted according to the moral and cultural principles of Jewish law.[72] But why should this recourse to Jewish law be rejected in every case because of the presence of one rule in Jewish law that today's public would find unacceptable? Even on substantive grounds, President Sussman's argument is untenable because the four types of capital punishment in Jewish law were abrogated when the Sanhedrin went into exile,[73] and death sentences by Jewish courts were abolished about two thousand years ago, except for serious cases against informers, who endangered the very existence of the Jewish community.[74]

However, that is not the main reason the argument is puzzling. What is involved here is a provision of Jewish law requiring rescue of a victim from his attacker—the principle of Jewish law that commands: "Do not stand idly by the blood of your fellow." What is the relevance of the law regarding an adulterous woman to this? A comparison with English criminal law exposes the flaw in the argument. Until the first half of the nineteenth century, English criminal law had the "distinction" of being in the first rank for barbaric and brutal execution of death sentences, which the English law of the time imposed for various offenses (over two hundred in number!) such as theft, forgery, robbery, and many other similar offenses, in addition to murder, treason, rape, etc.[75] The descriptions by Radzinowich and Holdsworth of these gruesome executions—some by hanging, some by burning (a method reserved mainly for women), some accompanied by brutal abuse at the time of death and some by abuse of the corpse after execution—are hair-raising to the point that it would be in bad taste to repeat them here.[76] It is enough to note that even minors seven and ten years old were sentenced to death and executed.[77] According to Holdsworth, the situation on the European continent was even worse.[78] Yet, we have never heard that a court should not have recourse to English or Continental criminal law on any matter because of the barbarity and brutality

72. *See supra* pp. 1730, 1736–1737, 1836–1838.

73. TB Ketubbot 30a/b; *see supra* p. 6 n. 10 and accompanying text.

74. *See supra* p. 11 n. 25, pp. 801–803.

75. *See* L. Radzinowich, *A History of English Criminal Law and its Administration from 1750,* London, 1948, I, pp. 3–227; W. Holdsworth, *A History of English Law,* XI, pp. 556–586; XV, pp. 163–167.

76. The interested reader may find the gory details in the sources cited *supra* n. 75. *See also* Manby v. Scott, 1 Mod. 124, 132, 86 Eng. Rep. 781, 786 (Exch. 1663) (stating that prison authorities were not obligated to provide even minimal food to a person imprisoned for failure to pay a debt; rather, "let him die in the name of God, says the law; and so say I"). This language was quoted in State of Israel v. Tamir, 37(iii) *P.D.* 201, 208 (1983).

77. *See* Radzinowich, *supra* n. 75 at 12ff.

78. *See* Holdsworth, *supra* n. 75 at XI, 580–581.

with which these legal systems actually operated until about 140 years ago. Raising such an irrelevant argument solely with respect to Jewish law indicates that emotional factors which, with all respect, are not understood by those who are prey to them are strongly at work.

Inapposite arguments, or rather emotional reactions, like the one just discussed,[79] are very rarely raised, although they do appear from time to time.[80] A different type of argument is more frequent. As has been seen, Justice Sussman, in his opinion in the *Afanjar* case, began with words of praise for Jewish law as "a valuable cultural asset of our people" from which we may "draw inspiration." Similar words of affection and esteem are showered on Jewish law by many others who praise its wisdom, culture, justice, and morality.[81] Their words, however, are only lip service not translated into action in any form or manner. Jewish law finds no place in their judgments, either as a primary source of guidance or even as a source of illumination on a par with others. Pronouncements and practice bear no relation to each other; Jewish law is commended but not consulted. Why should this be?

In the additional hearing in the *Hendeles* case, I expressed the view that when there is a question as to the meaning of an Israeli statute that cannot be resolved by existing Israeli law, and the judge turns to another legal system for the light it sheds on the problem, it is appropriate for Jewish law to be the primary source to which he should turn.[82] I quoted the following statement by Justice Landau:[83]

79. It should be noted that the Penal Law (General Part) Bill adopted the view advocated in the author's opinion in the *Afanjar* case. Section 35 of the bill, published in *Mishpatim,* X (1980), p. 203 states: "Action taken in order to repel an imminent, unlawful attack on his own or another's life, freedom, person, or property shall not give rise to criminal responsibility." The Explanatory Notes to the bill stated: "The main departure from the existing law is that a distinction is no longer made between the legitimacy of self-defense and the legitimacy of defense of another person. There was no actual justification for this distinction" (*id.* at 224). The same point was made in the New Penal Law (Preliminary and General Parts) Bill, and Summary Explanation, published in *Mishpatim,* XIV (1984), p. 127, sec. 43 (at p. 145).

80. *See* S.Z. Feller, "Le-Ittui ha-Hashlamah Shel Averat ha-Genevah" [Concerning the Time when the Crime of Theft is Consummated], *Mishpatim,* X (1980), pp. 121, 145–148; *id.*, "Pesak Din Tamu'ah" [A Surprising Decision], *Mishpatim,* X (1980), pp. 339, 347. In both of these articles, Prof. Feller relies on the arguments raised in Justice Sussman's opinion in Afanjar v. State of Israel, *supra* n. 62.

81. *See, e.g.,* Hendeles v. Bank Kupat Am, 35(ii) *P.D.* 785, 798–799 (1981) (Landau, J.); Koenig v. Cohen, 36(iii) *P.D.* 701, 726 (1982) (Barak, J.).

82. Hendeles v. Bank Kupat Am, *supra* n. 81 at 793; *see* the detailed discussion, *supra* pp. 1863–1876.

83. M. Landau, "Halakhah ve-Shikkul Da'at ba-Asiyyat Mishpat" [Rule and Discretion in Judicial Decision Making], *Mishpatim,* I (1969), pp. 292ff. at p. 305.

> Secular Israeli law is a law that has no historical roots. It is like a person without a shadow. It is made up of different layers, each one having its own historical source. But the history is not ours. . . . This is the great problem of modern Israeli law, and many of us, even the secularists among us, are pained that until now no way has been found to synthesize Jewish law, our national cultural treasure, with the needs of a modern society such as ours.

I then added the following:[84]

> Looking to Jewish law as the primary source of assistance in the interpretation of Israeli law, if done with appropriate deliberation, necessary care, and due consideration of the needs of the time and the purpose of the law, will give Israeli law its own historical roots and develop this synthesis [referred to by Justice Landau] between Jewish law and the legal system of the Jewish state.

As noted in the preceding chapter, Justice Landau, in the additional hearing in the *Hendeles* case, was of the opinion that Jewish law should not be accorded any preference over other systems even as only persuasive rather than binding authority.[85] In his opinion in that case, he commented on his statement quoted above regarding the need to develop a synthesis between Israeli law and Jewish law:

> In my recently published article on "Rule and Discretion in Judicial Decision Making," I spoke of the desirable synthesis—not yet achieved—between Jewish law, as a national cultural treasure, and the requirement of a modern society such as ours. I do not believe that this synthesis will be achieved by trying to fit the needs of our society into the fixed framework of the Jewish legal system, because Jewish law is basically a legal system that demands absolute and unqualified acknowledgement of its authority.[86]

With all due respect, it is impossible to fathom Justice Landau's meaning. What is the connection between the nature of Jewish law, with its demand for absolute acceptance, and the view that Jewish law should be accorded a preferential, persuasive (but not binding) status as a source of enlightenment in matters of statutory interpretation? I wrote in the *Hendeles* case that recourse to Jewish law as persuasive authority should be undertaken "with appropriate deliberation, necessary care, and due consideration of the needs of the time and the purpose of the law," and that this will be carried out by Israeli judges, who are subject to appellate review by the justices of the Supreme Court. What, therefore, is this mysterious fear of "a legal system that demands absolute and unqualified acknowledgment of its

84. Hendeles v. Bank Kupat Am, *supra* n. 81 at 795.
85. *Id.* at 798–799, quoted *supra* pp. 1867–1868.
86. Hendeles v. Bank Kupat Am, *supra* n. 81 at 799.

authority," which, with all due respect, has no relevance to the proposition that Jewish law should have priority as persuasive authority.

Indeed, there is no better, more convenient, or more effective way to create a synthesis between Jewish law, as a national cultural treasure, and the needs of a modern society such as ours, than to search out the solutions offered by Jewish law to problems of interpretation that cannot be resolved under existing law, and to accept this solution when the judge concludes that it accords with the needs of the time and the purpose of the law. It is difficult to conceive of a better and more logical method to create this synthesis: the creators of this synthesis would be judges, the problems would be contemporary, and the synthesis would be created step by step, depending on the frequency with which problems arise that cannot be resolved by the existing law. It is difficult to find a rational justification for the excessive apprehensiveness exhibited in these judicial comments.[87]

Another example of a subjective factor is the opinion of Justice Barak that in determining the position of Jewish law on a particular question a court may consult only "books that are open to the public" but may not "rely on the response to a question put to an expert which touches directly on the very point at issue and was prepared for this very case." According to Justice Barak, this stricture is to apply even when judges look to Jewish law solely for its instructive value and are careful to regard the response as non-binding, like any other scholarly research helpful in the judicial process.[88] In the *Hendeles* case, I took issue with this view of Justice Barak,[89] which remains the view of only a single justice. With all due respect, what rational justification can be offered for this stricture? What basis is there for the distinction between "books that are open to the public," which may be consulted by the court, and a responsum on point by an expert halakhic authority, which, although not yet published, is readily available to any interested person? If, as may be supposed, the concern is that the judge, although explicitly stressing that the responsum is not binding and that it is

87. It is interesting to compare the statement of forebodings quoted *supra* by Justice Landau p. 1928 with his opinion in Rodnitzky v. Rabbinical Court of Appeals, 24(i) *P.D.* 704, 712 (1970), discussed *supra* pp. 1772–1773. That case concerned the marriage of a *kohen* and a divorcée, which, under the Rabbinical Courts Jurisdiction (Marriage and Divorce) Law, 1953, sec. 2, is governed by Jewish law. Justice Landau took the view that the statute incorporated only the "legal" part of Jewish law (pursuant to which the marriage is valid) but not the "religious" part of Jewish law (the prohibition against performing such a marriage). If such a distinction can be made when the law specifically directs the application of Jewish law, as it does with respect to a marriage between a *kohen* and a divorcée, what reason is there to fear that such a distinction will not also be made when Jewish law is not binding but is only a source of enlightenment, and the reference to Jewish law is made with due consideration of the needs of the time and the requirements of each case?

88. Bank Kupat Am v. Hendeles, 34(iii) *P.D.* 57, 68 (1980).

89. *Id.* at 83.

being received only for the value to which its reasoning entitles it, may nevertheless consider it binding and thus constrict the decisional process, is this not irrationally excessive fearfulness?[90]

Another subjective factor, never mentioned in court decisions, has surfaced from time to time in Knesset debates and in writings of legal scholars. It has been contended that recourse to the Jewish heritage pursuant to the requirement of the Foundations of Law Act is "the first step in an invasion of the heretofore secular legal system by religious law . . . and from there the religious influence will spread."[91] One learned author goes even further. According to Professor Ruth Gavison, not only may the Foundations of Law Act be the start down the slippery slope to religious coercion, but it may even threaten civil rights in general:[92]

> The Foundations of Law Act raises concerns about two forms of religious and cultural coercion: coercion of nonreligious Jews, and coercion of non-Jews. In a society that consists of members of at least two nationalities and includes the nonreligious as well as the religious, the legal system that is maintained by the power of the state in which all these individuals are citizens should not adopt as its own the principles of the religion or national heritage of only a portion of the population to the exclusion of [the principles of] the others.

Professor Gavison is quick to concede that hers are not legal arguments. Rather, "these arguments against the solution adopted in the Foundations of Law Act are nonlegal arguments, based on a conception of the ideal rights of citizens. . . . The arguments for the enactment of this statute were not of a strictly legal nature, nor were many of the arguments against the statute. Since the statute expresses a particular political credo, it cannot be interpreted without addressing that credo." This subjective approach,[93]

90. *See also* the comments of Elon, J., *id.*, quoted *supra* p. 1750.

91. *See* the comments of MK Avneri in the debate on the Foundations of Law Act, 88 *DK* 2146 (1980):

> What we are confronted with here is the first step in the religious legal system's invasion of the previously secular legal system. This starts with a small incursion; the Minister of Justice can say that *in toto* we are speaking of lacunae which may appear [only] here and there in the law. However, this is only the first foothold. From there the religious influence will spread, since, in this matter, the religious camp has no sense of restraint, or willingness to be content with small gains. . . . If we adopt this bill, we are opening the door a little. The religious "foot" will be allowed to insert itself, and we will no longer be able to close the door. It will be able only to be opened wider and wider.

See also id. at 2342ff. and MK Avneri's comments on the third reading of the bill, 89 *DK* 4030 (1980).

92. *Zekhuyyot Ezraḥ be-Yisra'el, Kovez̩ Ma'amarim li-Khevodo Shel Ḥayyim H. Cohn, supra* n. 59, Introduction, pp. 33–34.

93. This approach brings to mind the factor that caused the influence of Jewish law over the internal life of the Jewish public to wane after the onset of the Emancipation.

based on a political ideology, can subconsciously influence the legal interpretation of the statute, at least by those who share the approach.

A final argument reflecting subjective concerns is sometimes raised to justify the failure to incorporate Jewish law into the law of the State of Israel. The argument is that the halakhic authorities have not adequately met the need to solve the various legal problems that have arisen in contemporary society. The present work has discussed in several connections the need for the halakhic authorities to solve certain current problems, and has reviewed the complexities of this task,[94] but what relevance does this argument have to the issue under discussion? The issue concerns the use by the general court system of the principles of Jewish law. It is the general court judges who would decide when and how to use the principles of Jewish law as they understand Jewish law to be. Why should these judges be prevented from utilizing Jewish law because of the failure of the halakhic authorities to take action to solve one or another particular problem? Israeli judges do not need the permission of the halakhic authorities to apply the rules of Jewish law; the general court system has exclusive jurisdiction of all civil legal matters. It is hardly fair to argue that the failure of the general court system to utilize Jewish law is justified by the failure of the halakhic authorities to solve certain problems at a time when consideration of most of those problems by the halakhic authorities was only theoretical and did not involve adjudication of actual cases.

B. Objective Factors

In addition to the various subjective factors that operate, consciously or subconsciously, to induce restrictive interpretation and reluctance to utilize the rules of Jewish law, there are also objective factors that merit serious consideration.

The troublesome factors that pose formidable obstacles to the utilization of Jewish law by the courts are the ignorance of Jewish law on the part of judges and lawyers, and the great difficulty they have in finding their way in the Jewish legal sources. This difficult and worrisome situation is only one aspect of the more general and more serious problem of ignorance of

---

Yeḥezkel Kaufmann described this factor as the "secular outlook on life and culture in this period." (*See* the detailed discussion, *supra* pp. 1577–1579.) But nowadays this "fear" has no rational or objective basis, for the *extent* and *method* of resort to Jewish law are entrusted to the legislative and judicial authorities of the State. Why are the principles of justice, freedom, and peace of the Jewish heritage any less sound merely because their origin is religious?

94. As to the law of personal status, *see supra* pp. 1753–1756 and nn., *ad loc.*; as to other areas of the law, *see supra* pp. 1898–1900 and nn., *ad loc.*

Judaism generally, which is the unfortunate result of deficiencies in the curricula and instruction offered by the Israeli educational system during the latter half of the twentieth century. To a considerable proportion of the nation's leaders—its writers, thinkers, professionals, men of affairs, and many, many others—the cultural treasures of Judaism are almost a closed book. Not only are these leading citizens unable to make use of the book, but they often do not even know that it exists. It is to be hoped—and there are signs it may come to pass—that this serious general situation will be remedied in the future, and that the remedy will also improve the position of Jewish law. In the interim, the situation is especially difficult for the judges and jurists called upon to study an issue of Jewish law. Jewish law is an important subject of study for jurists, not only for the gratification that comes from familiarity with a spiritual treasure but also as a legal area to be mastered by the techniques generally employed in studying any legal problem.

This ignorance, along with the attendant fear of the unknown, is probably the main reason for the tendency, whether conscious or unconscious, to restrict within the narrowest possible limits any need to utilize a legal system in which neither judges nor lawyers feel themselves competent. It is on this account that the Jewish legal system has been denied primacy as persuasive authority and that the Foundations of Law Act, 1980, has been construed so restrictively, in contravention of the statute's clear purpose.

As Mishael Cheshin, the learned author quoted above, rightly said: "We have no streams of water of our own, and it will be many years before we will have sufficient water from our own springs and will be capable of building a hothouse of our own. We are a people wise in the ways of the law; it is in our blood. Yet we are also a small people with only a small body of law."[95] The context makes clear that Cheshin was referring to the absence of a jurisprudential foundation for fashioning and developing *Israeli* law during the period since the State of Israel was established in 1948. He did not advert to the mighty waters of Jewish law, probably because of the daunting difficulty involved in finding one's way among the sources, mastering the many nuances, sorting out the plethora of conflicting opinions, and overcoming similar obstacles.[96] It is extremely disheartening that outstanding jurists and scholars are brought to such a view not by their conscious will, but on account of the limitations of their training and experience. For we indeed have flowing and surging streams of our own and a large and formidable hothouse, which in the course of a long history has

95. Cheshin, *supra* n. 59 at 79–80.
96. *See id.* at 67–76.

nurtured a highly sophisticated body of law and sustained us for thousands of years.

The fact is that the law "is in our blood," apparently more so than is the case for any other nation. Where else can one find school children, beginning with the age of seven and eight, studying legal rules governing the return of lost property like those contained in chapter *Ellu Meẓi'ot* and the laws of bailees and bailments found in chapter *Ha-Mafkid* of Tractate *Bava Meẓi'a* in the Babylonian Talmud? And as the young students of Jewish law study these chapters, they also encounter the legal rules relating to ownership and abandonment of property, modes of acquisition, obligations, evidence and oaths, interpretive methods, and the enactment of legislation—all of which, along with many other subjects, are discussed in those chapters. This was the schooling of generations upon generations of seven-and-eight-year-olds who continued to study and increase knowledge and wisdom until they were "mature" students at the ages of ten to thirteen, and full-fledged scholars of Jewish law when they grew older. Is it then any wonder that law is truly in our blood, even when it is now the law of the Continental codes and the common law rather than the law debated by the *amoraim* Abbaye and Rava that is the focus of our study?

Notwithstanding the difficulty of the struggle, we must not yield to our ignorance. We cannot afford to relinquish the law that is our great national cultural asset cherished as a heritage throughout the generations, especially when we have been directed by the Foundations of Law Act, 1980, to preserve and maintain it. Even if the struggle is at the cost of physical and spiritual pain, we should not shirk. The Jewish people won back its land and its language in a struggle tenfold more difficult than the effort to educate its people about its law.

Indeed, the argument based on the claim of ignorance is overdrawn; as a result of strenuous effort, progress is slowly being made. Research studies being published in all areas of Jewish law by jurists and authors now make it much easier to find and understand the riches of Jewish law. A substantial number of judicial opinions, especially by the Supreme Court of Israel, covering almost every type of legal issue, rely on Jewish law as a basis for decision or at least discuss Jewish law for comparative purposes. The rabbinical courts have decided numerous civil-law matters on the basis of Jewish law, and these decisions are published in the reports of the rabbinical court decisions. Law schools in English-speaking countries as well as in Israel are offering substantial programs in Jewish law, some of which include required courses as well as electives; and there is increasing participation in conferences and seminars on Jewish law. Much more must be done to find ways to increase the number of people who are knowledgeable about Jewish law and familiar with its sources. We must improve the way we teach it and promote its study.[97] We must encourage the publication of scholarly articles as well as analytical commentaries on the statutes that have codified Israeli civil law, so that the position of Jewish law with regard to the matters covered in each statutory provision can be clearly set forth in terms understandable to contemporary lawyers. We must, in short, do everything possible to bring the entire Jewish legal system within the reach of judges, lawyers, and academic legal scholars, particularly in Israel.[98]

We may learn, by analogy, from a familiar situation with which Israeli lawyers have had personal experience. The Israeli law of marriage and divorce, as well as family law in general, currently requires substantial knowledge of Jewish law; even in matters of family law regulated directly by statutes of the Knesset, such as support and guardianship of children, lawyers quite frequently look to Jewish law for solutions. An examination of judicial decisions on every level relating to any of these family-law matters reveals that the Israeli judges, most of whom cannot be counted as particularly knowledgeable in Jewish law, discuss and utilize the rules and principles of Jewish law because Israeli law to a significant extent *requires* the courts to apply the rules of Jewish law in these cases. The courts, being obligated to apply Jewish law, do what they must to fulfill their obligation. Courts and lawyers could also familiarize themselves with the Jewish law in other legal fields if they felt obligated to do so.

Indeed, this obligation is precisely what the Foundations of Law Act plainly establishes, as the preceding chapter's analysis of the specific provisions of the Act has shown. The general purpose of the statute also strongly reinforces this conclusion. It is fundamental that a statute is to be interpreted in accordance with its purpose: "A statute is a means to achieve the legislative purpose, and therefore should be interpreted accordingly";[99]

97. As to the teaching of Jewish law, *see* M. Elon, "Im ha-Shenaton" [On the Appearance of the *Shenaton*], *Shenaton*, I (1974), pp. 7, 10–12.

98. The Institute for Research in Jewish Law of the Hebrew University is presently heavily engaged in preparing meticulous indexes to the vast responsa literature. These indexes are very useful not only in facilitating research into the legal material in the responsa, but also in establishing a contemporary system of classification and terminology for Jewish law. *See supra* pp. 90–91, 1525–1528. To date, five volumes of the *Digest of the Responsa Literature of Spain and North Africa* (from the eleventh to fifteenth centuries) have been published. The *Legal Digest* consists of two volumes, the *Index of Sources* one volume, and the *Historical Digest* two volumes. The Institute is now beginning to prepare related studies in various branches of the law. The Shema Project at Bar-Ilan University provides important assistance in locating Jewish legal sources through a computer data base containing the text of many responsa and codificatory works. The Israeli Ministry of Justice has published a significant number of pamphlets, both in the early years of the State and particularly in recent years, which discuss the position of Jewish law on the various legal subjects concerning which legislation has been introduced into the Knesset.

99. Rosenberg v. Shtesal, 29(i) *P.D.* 505, 516 (1974) (Sussman, J.).

"underlying the language of the Legislature is always the legislative purpose, and when we discover it, it sets the tone of the legislation and enables us to determine the statutory meaning."[100] It has also been said that "the cardinal rule of statutory interpretation is to discover the legislative purpose underlying the enactment."[101] The goal of interpretation is to achieve "the basic objective of the statute"[102]—"its purpose."[103] Legislative history (the proceedings of the Knesset and other sources that throw light on the history of a statute) also plays an important role in statutory interpretation by helping to reveal the statutory objective:

> A statute is to be interpreted in accordance with its purpose, which sometimes is to be revealed not only . . . by reading all of its sections, but also by examining the legislative history in order to understand what mischief the Legislature was attempting to prevent or eliminate by enacting the statute, and what remedy it [the Legislature] established for this purpose.[104]

The language of the Foundations of Law Act, the lengthy and protracted debates before the statute was drafted and during its course through the Knesset committees and the Knesset itself, and the remarks of both the proponents and the opponents of its enactment all compel the conclusion that the objectives of this statute were: (1) that it should constitute the cornerstone of the independence of the Israeli legal system, and (2) that it should establish a formal and binding link between the Israeli legal system and Jewish law. These interconnected and complementary objectives should point the way to proper interpretation and application of the Act. The interpretation of the statute should not be distorted because of the problems stemming from ignorance of Jewish law or because of personal disagreement with the Act's underlying objectives.[105]

100. Baḥan v. Rosenzweig, 22(i) *P.D.* 569, 577 (1968) (Sussman, J.).

101. Ashdod Metals Refinery v. State of Israel, 34(ii) *P.D.* 182, 186 (1979) (Ben Porat, J.).

102. Mizraḥi v. State of Israel, 35(iv) *P.D.* 421, 427 (1980) (Barak, J.).

103. Of ha-Emek Agricultural Society v. Ramat Yishai Local Council, 40(i) *P.D.* 113, 141 (1986) (Barak, J.).

104. S. Agranat, "Terumatah Shel ha-Reshut ha-Shofetet le-Mif'al ha-Ḥakikah" [The Contribution of the Judiciary to Legislation], *Iyyunei Mishpat,* X (1984), pp. 233, 241. *See* Kibbutz Ḥaẓor v. Income Tax Assessor of Rehovot, 39(ii) *P.D.* 70, 74 (1985); A. Barak, "Al ha-Shofet ke-Farshan" [On the Judge as Interpreter], *Mishpatim,* XII (1982), pp. 248ff. at p. 253. *See also* the difference of opinion between Justice Barak, who strongly relies on legislative history, and Justice Shelomo Levin in Of ha-Emek Agricultural Society v. Ramat Yishai Local Council, *supra* n. 103, with regard to the extent of reliance on Knesset debates in interpreting legislation; *see further* the discussion of this issue, *supra* p. 1727 and n. 412.

105. *See* the comments of Justice Barak in his article "Ḥakikah Shipputit" [Judicial Legislation], *Mishpatim,* XIII (1983), pp. 25ff. at p. 77:

The proper judicial policy points to the [appropriate] course of action—active or pas-

As stated in the previous chapter, the Foundations of Law Act mandates recourse to Jewish law only when there is a lacuna. This much is undisputed, although there is disagreement about what "lacuna" means.[106] I did not come easily to this narrow interpretation of the statute, because the ordinary meaning of the language of Section 1 of the statute does not necessarily require such an interpretation. The section speaks of "a legal question requiring decision"; this language could include not only a lacuna[107] but any uncertainty as to the interpretation of a statutory provision (such as the doubt that arose in the *Hendeles* case regarding the meaning of the term "the *reshut* of another person").[108] During the additional hearing in the *Hendeles* case, when the question of the interpretation of Section 1 of the Foundations of Law Act arose for the first time, I had great difficulty deciding whether to read "a legal question requiring decision" expansively to include every instance where the meaning of a statute is ambiguous or uncertain or to limit the meaning so that the Act would apply only to a lacuna. I came to the conclusion that the restrictive interpretation was correct, because the statute imposes a *duty* to look to Jewish law, and if such a requirement were to apply to every case of uncertainty as to the meaning of a statute (and such cases are very frequent) it would be a duty that the courts in the present state of their knowledge of Jewish law would be incapable of performing. An important halakhic principle states that a legislative enactment should not be adopted unless a majority of the public

---

> sive, as the particular matter requires—unaffected by our personal view of the substantive merits of the legislation. It is not proper to contend that judicial activism is desirable in order to reach the result I personally prefer, and that judicial passivism is desirable where there is reason to think that the result I believe to be correct will not be accepted. The criteria for proper judicial policy forbid giving weight to such considerations. The legitimate criteria apply whether or not we agree with the legislative solution to the particular problem involved. We may not discourage the judge from engaging in judicial activism merely because we do not agree with his solution. We may not discourage the judge from engaging in judicial passivism even if the result of inaction may maintain a *status quo* that we oppose. It would be unthinkable to create a judicial policy which would be appropriate to apply when we approve of the result reached by the court, but would be inappropriate to apply when we disapprove. From this perspective, we must aspire to the greatest possible objectivity.

These observations are sound, and they have particular significance with regard to the interpretation of the Foundations of Law Act.

106. *See supra* pp. 1835–1838.

107. Although the Explanatory Notes to the bill refer to a "lacuna," it is accepted that the Explanatory Notes to a bill do not have binding force. Explanatory Notes may help determine legislative intent when a statute is unclear or ambiguous, but they cannot prevail over the plain meaning of a clear and unambiguous statute which, as is the case here, is inconsistent with the Explanatory Notes. *See* Of ha-Emek Agricultural Society v. Ramat Yishai Local Council, *supra* n. 103, and the cases cited there.

108. *See supra* pp. 1743–1744, 1864–1865.

is able to conform to it;[109] the same principle also applies to statutory interpretation, so that it may be assumed that the Legislature did not intend such an expansive interpretation.

Recourse to Jewish law in a case not of lacuna but of uncertainty as to the interpretation of a statutory provision is thus discretionary and not obligatory; but even in such a case, when Jewish law is only a persuasive source, it should be first among equals. Of course, the judge should also examine the views and approaches of other legal systems. The halakhic authorities of earlier generations, whose rulings strictly adhered to Jewish law, did not close their minds to the lessons to be learned from the legal systems of other nations; in certain instances, they even found a rule of another system preferable.[110] The practice should certainly be no different with regard to the interpretation of a statute of the Knesset, which derives its force from the authority of the Knesset and is enacted after examining not only Jewish law but also other legal systems in the context of contemporary social and economic needs.[111] However, it is the Jewish legal system that should constitute the substratum, the jurisprudential basis, of the Israeli legal system, whether as a binding complementary source in the case of lacuna, or as the primary persuasive source in cases involving other types of uncertainty.

In the past, during the debates on the proper role for Jewish law, the argument was raised that Jewish law is not capable of solving the many problems that face a contemporary legal system.[112] Today, this argument is hardly ever advanced, and for good reason. Certainly, the suitable preparation of the rules and institutions of Jewish law to serve modern-day needs is indispensable. But this can be accomplished by thorough study and research into the legal materials and by filling gaps in the law through interpretation and legislation.[113] The Jewish legal system has coped with such problems throughout its history, and its ability to continue to do so in the contemporary world has been demonstrated through a long and continuing series of halakhic rulings, judicial opinions, and scholarly works.[114] Even if

109. *See supra* pp. 531–541.

110. *See supra* pp. 63–64.

111. *See* Roth v. Yeshufeh, 33(i) *P.D.* 617, 632 (1979), *supra* quoted pp. 1738–1739. *See also* State of Israel v. Kedar, 36(i) *P.D.* 492, 497–498 (1982) (Landau, President), to the effect that even after the enactment of the Foundations of Law Act "we do not blindfold ourselves to prevent us from looking at what is done around us in other countries, to increase our wisdom and broaden the perspective of our analysis and discussions."

112. *See supra* p. 1622.

113. *See supra* pp. 1589–1591, 1608–1611, 1898–1900.

114. *See supra* pp. 1525–1528, 1554–1556, 1562–1564, 1569–1572, 1729–1730 and n. 417, 1739 n. 435, 1818–1819. *See also* Bibliography, *infra*. As to the expected results of the Foundations of Law Act, the factors leading to its enactment, and the factors that oper-

such efforts are not always fully satisfactory, the problem is not the *ability* of Jewish law to confront contemporary issues, but rather the substantive choices made in the formulation and execution of judicial policy and scholarly projects.

C. Observations Concerning Fears and the Fearful

As has been pointed out, the incorporation of Jewish law into the Israeli legal system is neither a ruling by a halakhic authority in the Jewish legal system nor an impairment of the sovereign legislative power of the Knesset in the Israeli legal system. Decisions of courts that look to Jewish law as persuasive authority incorporate certain principles of law, equity, and justice, as well as an attitude toward the disadvantaged and the powerful in society, and basic concepts such as those in the law of ownership and acquisition. All of these are drawn from a cultural heritage and legal philosophy created and developed by the Jewish people over many generations, of which our generation is only one link, important but small, in a long and magnificent chain of hundreds and thousands of years of creativity. It would seem that the time has come for us to free ourselves from the overwrought emotionalism and baseless apprehensiveness toward the religious aspect of Jewish law that find expression in the examples previously discussed.

When the debate was taking place on the question of what the policy should be with regard to incorporation of Jewish law into the Knesset's legislation, I wrote:[115]

> The principle established in the first years of the State—that Jewish law should serve as the primary source for legislation to the extent that practical conditions permit—must be carried out in accordance with its obvious spirit. When we apply the principle in this manner, the first conclusion that follows is that wherever a principle of Jewish law is found to be applied in a currently accepted legal system, we should incorporate the principle into our own legal system for one reason only—that the principle is our own, a part of the heritage of Jewish legal thought. Can anyone fairly argue that the principle that a claim should not be made in the first instance against a surety unless an express agreement so provides is inappropriate for us, especially when this

---

ated after the statute was enacted, *see* A. Kirschenbaum, *Ḥok Yesodot ha-Mishpat—Meẓi'ut ve-Ẓippiyyot* [The Foundations of Law Act—Reality and Expectations], *Iyyunei Mishpat,* XI (1986), pp. 117ff.

115. M. Elon, "Ha-Mishpat ha-Ivri be-Mishpat ha-Medinah, al ha-Maẓuy ve-al ha-Raẓuy" [Jewish Law in the Legal System of the State—Reality and Ideal], *Ha-Praklit,* XXV (1968), pp. 27, 44–50; *id.*, *Ha-Mishpat ha-Ivri* [Jewish Law], 1st and 2nd eds., pp. 123–125.

same principle has been accepted in Swiss law since 1941 and in the 1963 draft code of the North European countries?[116] Will anyone argue that we should not adopt the principle that a benefit may be conferred on a person even in his absence when such a principle exists in many other legal systems?[117] The same is true with regard to other illustrations which pass "the test of confronting practical circumstances." Can it be sincerely and honestly argued by anyone who appears daily in the courts and observes the rote and even disrespectful recitation of the oath automatically required of every witness, that it would not be better to admonish every witness [as was the practice in Jewish law], and administer an oath only to those whose veracity appears to the judge to be suspect?[118] And are we really honest with ourselves when we permit a person to admit that he has not paid his debt, yet permit him to escape payment by pleading that the period of limitations has expired?[119]

One may ask: If we incorporate the principles of Jewish law only after concluding that they are suitable for us, what is the special significance of such incorporation? For example, with regard to suretyship, we could say that we incorporated a principle from Swiss law and, with regard to conferring benefits on a person in his absence, a principle of English law. The answer is that the premise of the question is false. Individuals and the public (and perhaps especially the public) both prefer something that is their own. Law is a national cultural creation, which every nation imbues with its own perceptions of justice, its own approach to morality, and its own intellectual and spiritual strengths. If this is so with regard to every nation, it is even more so with regard to the relation between the Jewish people and Jewish law. Moreover, each incorporation of a principle of Jewish law adds another link to the chain of continuity with the . . . past. This continuity is not only abstract and spiritual; it involves study and analysis of the literary sources . . . in which the principle is found and explicated. Does the generation that lived through the [Israeli] War of Independence and the Six-Day War and has discovered its past within itself, the generation that clings to every physical remnant of its ancient culture that is uncovered in the depths of the soil of its homeland, still require an explanation for these feelings and associations?

These words were written in the 1960s, at the beginning of the second legislative period, at the outset of the period of civil codification. Legislative codification has now come to an end. Not all the hopes for the incorpora-

116. *See supra* pp. 1721–1723.

117. *See supra* p. 1724.

118. *See supra* pp. 605–606, 1705–1706. The position taken here was later adopted in the Rules of Evidence Amendment (Warning of Witnesses and Abolition of Oath) Law, 1980; *see supra* pp. 1706–1707.

119. *See supra* pp. 1724–1727.

tion of Jewish law have been fulfilled, but some of these aspirations have been realized. Israeli law severed its ties to English law and achieved independence, and the Foundations of Law Act declared that the principles of the Jewish heritage constitute the complementary source for the Israeli legal system. The Legislature completed its work; since then, responsibility for incorporating Jewish law into the Israeli legal system has rested mainly on the courts as they go about interpreting the statutes and adjudicating the daily run of litigation.

The policy reasons for incorporation, discussed above in connection with legislation, are also fully applicable to judicial decisions, subject to one obvious and basic limitation: If a statute indicates an intent to adopt a rule or principle contrary to Jewish law, the judge has no choice but to follow the legislative mandate. Except for this limitation, however, when the courts are uncertain as to how to interpret a statute, they should look first and foremost to Jewish law for light in their search for a solution to their problem. The logic of Israeli legislation requires this course, both because Jewish law has been the major source for the legislation and because Israeli law needs its own homogeneous jurisprudential base. History calls upon us to continue the pattern of Jewish legal thought and analysis that has been preserved and taught for thousands of years and was the basis of the legal system that governed day-to-day life in every Jewish diaspora. It is inconceivable that now that the Jewish people has regained its own sovereignty, this magnificent heritage should be rejected as a foundation for the legal system of the Jewish state.

V. CONCLUDING REFLECTIONS

At the beginning of this chapter, it was argued that not only is it important for the legal system of the Jewish state that it be based on Jewish law, but it is also important for Jewish law itself that it be the basis of the law of the State, because Jewish law will thereby be connected again to practical life, and the day-by-day creativity of Jewish law will be restored. However, notwithstanding the significance of this benefit, the continuation and vitality of the Jewish legal system are not in doubt, regardless of whether Jewish law is incorporated into the legal system of the Jewish state. The sources and principles of Jewish law are presently being studied, pondered, and discussed every hour of every day by many thousands of students, young and old. The teachings of R. Akiva and R. Ishmael; the disputes of Abbaye and Rava; the codes and rulings of Alfasi, Maimonides, Joseph Caro, and Moses Isserles; the commentaries of Rashi, the Tosafists, Naḥmanides, and

Meiri; the responsa and legal studies of Rashba, Ritba, Ezekiel Landau, and Moses Sofer; the novellae of Samuel Edels, Jacob Falk, the Gaon of Vilna, and the Ḥazon Ish—all of these, and many, many similar works, are still alive and have been studied over the years no less than when they first appeared, some of them many hundreds of years ago. This intensive study has continued even after the Emancipation, when Jewish law ceased to be applied to practical problems as a result of the abrogation of Jewish juridical autonomy at the end of the eighteenth century. Such a situation appears to be unique—without parallel in any other legal system.

Moreover, it is a fundamental principle of Jewish law that the teachings and rulings of the more recent halakhic authorities, even when they involve important innovations, do not render obsolete the views of the previous authorities; rather, they add to and are integrated with them. Ezekiel Landau in the eighteenth century did not replace Rashba, who lived in the thirteenth century, nor did Moses Sofer in the nineteenth century replace Ritba, who lived in the fourteenth century; and, certainly, none of these reduced the importance of the teachings of R. Akiva, of the second century, or the views of Rava, of the fourth century. The doctrines of all of them, spanning many generations, are eagerly studied in great depth just as when first spoken and written.

Continuous creativity founded upon the past is characteristic of all Jewish culture. There is no better example of such creativity than the revival of the Hebrew language in our own day. This revival is the outcome of tireless efforts to create new terms and expressions, and a fresh style and syntax, that in large measure were derived from the resources accumulated over the years in the storehouse of the language: Talmudic and post-Talmudic works, ethical writings, and poetic compositions written throughout the generations. These efforts had a twofold objective: (1) to respond to the constantly evolving needs of a contemporary, modern language, and (2) to preserve the link between the "holy tongue," thousands of years old, and the national language of our time. It is this continuity that has enabled modern Hebrew to become an essential and integral component of historical Jewish creativity.

The example of the Hebrew language provides reason for hope that Jewish law will be integrated into the legal system of the Jewish state and that the legal system of the State will thus take its place in the historical record of Jewish creativity. In the past, we have offered some thoughts on this subject, and now, in light of the changes and events that have occurred since then, some additional remarks seem appropriate.

During the intense debate among jurists and scholars as to whether, in addition to repealing Article 46, the Knesset should enact legislation requiring that Jewish law replace English law as a complementary source, one view was that as a matter of principle it was wrong to establish *any* complementary source for the Israeli legal system:[120]

> Article 46 declared and established that there can be no Israeli law without English law to supplement it. Now that the State has been established, must we still hold to the idea that we must be dependent on an external legal system, notwithstanding that English law would be replaced by Jewish law?

The learned author of that view had an unequivocal answer: Israeli law "no longer needs a complementary legal system—neither English, nor even Jewish law."[121]

Our experience since these words were written at the beginning of the period of civil codification has taught us that this view is erroneous. The Israeli legal system greatly needs much enlightenment from outside sources. It has many inconsistencies and problems, and it is far from being fully self-contained and self-sustaining. It was for this reason that the Knesset enacted the Foundations of Law Act, 1980. However, even after the adoption of the Foundations of Law Act, we are still faced with a much more fundamental problem, which goes to the root of our present cultural and spiritual existence—the problem of the relation between the Israeli legal system, in its present state, and historic Jewish law.

There have been times in the history of Jewish law when another legal system has functioned in parallel with the judicial and legislative system of the halakhic authorities. The basis in Jewish law for this parallel governance is the authority that Jewish law confers on the king's law in the legislative, judicial, and administrative areas,[122] and on various forms of government, both central and local.[123] In both the Talmudic and post-Talmudic periods, for hundreds of years in the various Jewish centers, judgments were rendered by courts composed of public lay leaders,[124] and legislation was enacted by communal leaders and representatives.[125]

In many respects, these judgments and enactments deviated from the rules of Jewish law; but the halakhic system, with characteristic resilience, developed a series of principles and guidelines for absorbing the judgments

120. U. Yadin, "Keiẓad Yeforash Ḥok ha-Shomerim?" [How Should the Bailees Law Be Interpreted?], *Ha-Praklit,* XXIV (1968), p. 493.

121. *Id.* at 495.

122. *See supra* pp. 55–57.

123. *See supra* pp. 58–61. *See also* the statement of Chief Rabbi Abraham Isaac Kook, quoted *supra* p. 59, to the effect that the autonomous institutions of the Jewish community in the Land of Israel in his time were vested with the authority possessed by the king's law. These comments apply *a fortiori* at present to the government of the State of Israel.

124. *See supra* pp. 19–36.

125. *See supra* pp. 678ff.

and enactments of the public and its representatives as an essential and integral part of the *Halakhah*.[126] In Jewish society before the Emancipation, such an interrelationship was natural and well understood; it was a society in which both the public and the halakhic authorities recognized a single and supreme guiding and ultimate value—the supremacy of the Torah and, consequently, the authority of the *Halakhah*. The public leadership did not view their judgments and legislation as impairing or evading the authority of the *Halakhah;* to the contrary, they saw their actions as a way, distinctly suited to the needs of the place and the time, of basing communal and individual life upon the principles, objectives, and spirit of the *Halakhah*.[127]

This character of Jewish society has fundamentally changed today: Jews are no longer united in outlook, and the legislative and judicial institutions of the Jewish state do not recognize the authority of the *Halakhah* as the supreme guiding value. Given this situation, is it still possible for us to find some alternative whereby Israeli law, now in the process of development, may conceivably be melded with historic Jewish law into a single structure?

This question was posed in an article published in 1968,[128] and again in the previous editions of the present work.[129] It was suggested that a possible and hopefully realistic solution might be the enactment of a statute that would establish Jewish law as a complementary source for Israeli law in the event of a lacuna:[130]

> Is it not possible that such an official and fundamental connection, slight and modest as it may be, between the Israeli legal system and historic Jewish law may enable us to create the connecting link, and perhaps even the halakhic basis, for such a development in the future? Is dependence of Israeli law on the principles of Jewish law in the event of a lacuna really dependence on an outside legal system, as was the case when English law was the complementary source? Can it really be said that such a bond between the law of the sovereign Jewish state and the legal system which, for hundreds and thousands of years, was the expression of Jewish autonomy, constitutes a link to a foreign system? In the final analysis, we are connecting ourselves to ourselves; we are linking our current legal doctrine with the legal doctrine of all our prior generations.

126. *See supra* pp. 57, 751–779.

127. *See supra* pp. 778–779.

128. Elon, "Ha-Mishpat ha-Ivri be-Mishpat ha-Medinah, al ha-Maẓuy ve-al ha-Raẓuy," *supra* n. 115 at 27.

129. M. Elon, *Ha-Mishpat ha-Ivri* [Jewish Law], 1st ed. (1973), 2nd ed. (1978).

130. Elon, "Ha-Mishpat ha-Ivri be-Mishpat ha-Medinah, al ha-Maẓuy ve-al ha-Raẓuy," *supra* n. 115 at 52–53; Elon, *supra* n. 129 at 128. On a comparable matter, *see Kitvei B. Katznelson* [The Writings of B. Katznelson], 12 vols. (1945–1950), VI, pp. 365–367, 385–393.

> Clearly, linking modern Israeli law with historic Jewish law in this way will fill a large gap in the Israeli legal system. It may be true that, in the formal sense, "Israeli law no longer needs a complementary legal system." However, both in theory and practice, the Israeli courts eagerly consult many other legal systems, even if only "as persuasive authority" to help them with many important problems. Undoubtedly, this enriches legal research and broadens the perspective of decision making, but this is not how a legal system perfects its distinctive character. Just as a nation's language requires a foundation and a history—and who knows better than we who have experienced the miracle of the revival of the Hebrew language?—a nation's law also, and, it may be said, even more so, needs roots and a past on which it can draw for its sustenance. The law taking form in the Jewish state needs its own roots and past, which it will find only if it learns how to tap into the roots of the historic Jewish legal system.
>
> It serves no purpose to prophesy concerning the future course of Jewish spiritual history. This future, for one who holds faith higher than reason, is part of the mystery of faith, and, for one who holds reason higher than faith, will be revealed only as history unfolds. But perhaps one may express the hope, based on various other spiritual and social developments in current Jewish society, that if we use an appropriate and consistent method of incorporating the principles of Jewish law into our legal system and we look to Jewish law when gaps in our system need to be filled, then some day the unity and integrity, and consequently the continuity, of the Jewish legal system as a prime cultural and spiritual asset of Judaism will be restored.

Since these words were written, the Knesset passed the Foundations of Law Act, 1980, creating "an official and fundamental connection, slight and modest as it may be, between the Israeli legal system and historic Jewish law." However, as indicated in this and the preceding chapter, the way in which this connection has been used to the time of this writing does not herald the creation of "the connecting link, and perhaps even the halakhic basis, for such a development in the future."

The *Wiloszni* case[131] dealt with the relationship between the halakhic system and Knesset legislation from the perspective of the decisions of the rabbinical courts. The rabbinical courts recognize the binding halakhic validity of many provisions of the laws of the State, generally on the basis of the doctrine of *dina de-malkhuta dina* ("the law of the land is law") or on the basis of custom, and in rare instances on the theory that a statute of the Knesset constitutes a communal enactment.[132] A determination that the legislation of the Jewish state is halakhically valid on either of the first two bases involves a recognition by the halakhic system of the binding nature

131. Wiloszni v. Rabbinical Court of Appeals, 36(ii) *P.D.* 733 (1982).
132. *See supra* pp. 1820ff.

of these statutes, but in each case the legal system of the Jewish state is viewed as a legal system "having no internal-creative link to Jewish law."[133]

By contrast, "to ground the halakhic validity of the laws of the Jewish state on the authority of communal enactments is to consider the legal system of the Jewish state as a Jewish creation brought into being by means of one of the traditional methods historically accepted in the Jewish legal system."[134] Unfortunately, however, such halakhic validation of Knesset legislation, for reasons whose explanation is beyond the scope of the present work, is extremely rare.

From the halakhic point of view, the acknowledgement of the laws of the Jewish state as "communal enactments" or as instances of the "king's law" is undoubtedly the classic method of integrating Israeli law and historic Jewish law into a uniform system. However, the judicial rejection of any special status for Jewish law in the Israeli legal system even as primary *persuasive* authority and, even more so, the almost total preclusion of the Jewish heritage as a complementary source to fill a lacuna, do not inspire much hope of progress toward such integration.

The crucial link between the Israeli legal system and historic Jewish law created by the Foundations of Law Act must be strengthened through constant and dedicated efforts. Success in these efforts will require an appreciation of how vital this link is to the Israeli legal system, and a faith that some day the unity and integrity of the Jewish legal system will be restored. The goal can be achieved only if there is a strong desire to attain it, and that desire can arise only where there is broad and penetrating historical vision.

An opinion in one of the Supreme Court's earliest cases by Justice Agranat, a distinguished President of the Court, exhibits such vision:[135]

> In these days, it is almost superfluous to explain what should now be obvious to all: The Jews, even after they were exiled from their land, never thought of themselves solely as a religious group; they never stopped considering themselves a nation—like the other nations of the world—whose loss of its land, to which its members faithfully preserved their tie, was only temporary. It was a nation that carried with it, in all the lands of its dispersion and during all the periods of its exile, its inalienable cultural treasures, its national assets, of which Jewish law is one.
>
> When we acknowledge, as we must, the continued existence of the Jews in all the generations and in all the lands of their dispersion as a separate nation, we must in turn examine the character of Jewish law according to the

133. *See supra* p. 1825. *See also* Wiloszni v. Rabbinical Court of Appeals, *supra* n. 131 at 742.

134. *See supra* pp. 1825–1826. *See also* Wiloszni v. Rabbinical Court of Appeals, *supra* n. 131 at 742.

135. Skornik v. Skornik, 8 *P.D.* 141, 176–177 (1954) (Agranat, President).

> Jewish nation's historical attitude to it. Then we will perforce conclude that the Jewish nation has, indeed, in all eras and in all the lands of its dispersion, treated Jewish law as its special possession, as part of the imperishable values of its culture. In other words, this law served in the past as the national law of the Jewish people, and to this day it bears this national character for Jews wherever they may be.

These words were not mere rhetoric, but were the basis for a decision in an actual case.[136]

President Agranat's words, written in the seventh year of the State of Israel, very soon after Jewish legal sovereignty was regained, have not had from the great majority of Israeli judges the resounding echo they deserve. There is reason to fear that today, when the State of Israel has passed its fourth decade, the reverberations of these words have been stilled, and the passion that suffused them has considerably waned. The judicial system of the Jewish state has made but little use of the invaluable legal heritage that is our national cultural treasure.[137] Is this likely to change for the better in the future? Will the Jewish state be able to create a uniquely Jewish legal system? Will the principles of freedom, equity, justice, and law of the State of Israel become integrated with and carry forward the essential nature of these fundamental principles of the historic Jewish legal heritage? The courts have yet to render their final verdict.

136. In the *Skornik* case, a collateral issue arose as to the validity of a marriage entered into under Jewish law by a Jewish couple in a country whose laws did not recognize such a marriage. Premised on this description of the nature of Jewish law, Justice Agranat concluded:

> [For] the limited purpose of according legitimacy to such a marriage, the national law, which was then, and continues to be, their law to this day, namely, Jewish law, should override the foreign national law (*lex patriae*) that applied to the parties at the time of their marriage and recognizes only marriages celebrated pursuant to a prescribed civil form.

Id. at 178. *See also supra* p. 5 n. 7.

137. For an extensive critique, *see* M. Elon, "Od le-Inyan Ḥok Yesodot ha-Mishpat" [More about the Foundations of Law Act], *Shenaton,* XIII (1987), pp. 227–256, responding to A. Barak, "Ḥok Yesodot ha-Mishpat u-Moreshet Yisra'el" [The Foundations of Law Act and the Jewish Heritage], *Shenaton, id.*, pp. 265–283.

Appendixes, Glossary, Bibliography, and Indexes

APPENDIX A
CROSS-REFERENCE TABLE—MAIMONIDES' *MISHNEH TORAH* AND THE *SHULḤAN ARUKH*

The purpose of this Appendix is to facilitate finding parallel references in the *Mishneh Torah* and the *Shulḥan Arukh.* In general, parallel references to the *Mishneh Torah* in *Sefer ha-Turim* will be identical with those given for references in the *Shulḥan Arukh.* A horizontal line opposite an entry for the *Mishneh Torah* or the *Shulḥan Arukh* indicates that the matter referred to has no parallel references in the other code. The cross-references in these tables are intended to designate the location of broad subject areas, not individual laws. These tables also highlight the respective approaches of Maimonides and Joseph Caro to various aspects of codification discussed in the appropriate chapters in the text.

CROSS-REFERENCES FROM THE *MISHNEH TORAH* TO THE *SHULḤAN ARUKH*

MISHNEH TORAH	*SHULḤAN ARUKH*
Sefer ha-Madda [The Book of Knowledge]	
Hilkhot Yesodei ha-Torah [Laws of the Fundamentals of the Torah]	
Chapters 1–4	———
Chapter 5	YD (Avodat Elilim [Idol Worship]) chs. 155, 157
Chapter 6	YD (Sefer Torah [The Torah Scroll]) ch. 276
Chapters 7–10	———
Hilkhot De'ot [Laws of Ethical Principles]	OḤ (Hanhagat Adam ba-Boker [Conduct upon Arising in the Morning], etc.) chs. 2–3, 157, 231, 240
Hilkhot Talmud Torah [Laws of Study of Torah]	
Chapters 1–5	YD (Kevod Rabbo ve-Talmid Ḥakham [Honor Due to One's Teacher and to a Scholar]) chs. 242–246; OḤ chs. 155–156, 238
Chapter 6	YD chs. 243–244, 334
Chapter 7	YD (Niddui va-Ḥerem [Ban and Excommunication]) ch. 334

MISHNEH TORAH	*SHULḤAN ARUKH*
Hilkhot Avodat Kokhavim ve-Ḥukkoteihem [Laws Relating to Idol Worship]	
Chapters 1–10	YD (Avodat Elilim [Laws of Idol Worship]) chs. 139–154, 158
Chapters 11–12	YD (Ḥukkot Amamin [Laws of the Non-Jews], etc.) chs. 156, 178–182
Hilkhot Teshuvah [Laws of Repentance]	OḤ (Rosh ha-Shanah, Yom ha-Kippurim [Rosh Ha-Shanah, Day of Atonement]) chs. 603, 606–607
Sefer Ahavah *[The Book of Love (of God)]*	
Hilkhot Keri'at Shema [Laws of the Recitation of the Shema]	OḤ (Keri'at Shema u-Virkhotehah [Recitation of the Shema and Its Blessings], etc.) chs. 58–88, 235–236
Hilkhot Tefillah u-Virkat Kohanim [Laws of Prayer and the Priestly Blessing]	
Chapters 1–10	OḤ chs. 1, 4–7, 46–47, 51–57, 89–127, 131–134, 232–237, 239, 267–268, 286, 290, 292, 294, 422–423, 425, 487–488, 490, 557, 565, 581–582, 591, 599, 604, 622–624, 663, 668, 682, 693
Chapter 11	OḤ (Bet ha-Keneset [Synagogue]) chs. 150–154
Chapters 12–13	OḤ chs. 135–149, 282–285, 292, 423, 425, 428, 488, 494, 559, 566, 584, 601, 621–622, 659, 662–663, 668–669, 684–685, 693
Chapters 14–15	OḤ (Nesi'at Kappayim [Priestly Blessing], etc.) chs. 128–129, 566, 622
Hilkhot Tefillin u-Mezuzah ve-Sefer Torah [Laws of Phylacteries, *Mezuzah*, and the Torah Scroll]	
Chapters 1–4	OḤ (Tefillin [Phylacteries]) chs. 25–45
Chapters 5–6	YD (Mezuzah) chs. 285–291
Chapters 7–10	YD (Sefer Torah [The Torah Scroll]) chs. 270–284
Hilkhot Ẓiẓit [Laws of the Fringes]	OḤ (Ẓiẓit [Fringes]) chs. 8–24
Hilkhot Berakhot [Laws of Benedictions]	OḤ (Netilat Yadayim [Washing of the Hands], etc.) chs. 158–230, 424, 426
Hilkhot Milah [Laws of Circumcision]	YD (Milah, Avadim, Gerim [Circumcision, Slaves, Proselytes]) chs. 260–269; OḤ ch. 331
Seder ha-Tefillot [Order of Prayers]	OḤ chs. 51, 114–118, 187–189, 267–268, 281, 284, 294, 422, 425, 428, 487, 490, 494, 557, 565, 582, 591, 623, 663, 668, 682, 693

MISHNEH TORAH	***SHULḤAN ARUKH***
Sefer Zemanim *[The Book of Seasons]*	
Hilkhot Shabbat [Laws of the Sabbath]	
Chapter 1–Chapter 12, Paragraph 7	OḤ (Shabbat [Sabbath]) chs. 243–247, 252–259, 261, 263–266, 275–278, 293, 306, 308, 313–321, 325–326, 328–331, 334, 336–337, 340, 344
Chapter 12, Paragraph 7–Chapter 17	OḤ (Shabbat [Sabbath]) chs. 345–365
Chapters 18–26	OḤ (Shabbat [Sabbath]) chs. 243–247, 252–259, 261, 265–266, 279, 287, 301–324, 326–328, 330, 332–343
Chapters 27–28	OḤ (Teḥumim [Boundaries]) chs. 396–407
Chapter 29	OḤ (Shabbat [Sabbath], etc.) chs. 269, 271–273, 289, 296–299, 473, 490–491, 600–601, 619, 624, 643, 661, 668–669
Chapter 30	OḤ (Shabbat [Sabbath]) chs. 242, 249–250, 260, 262, 274, 280, 288–289, 291, 300
Hilkhot Eruvin [Laws of *Eruv*]	
Chapters 1–5	OḤ (Shabbat [Sabbath]) chs. 366–395
Chapters 6–8	OḤ (Eruvei Teḥumim [Merging of Boundaries]) chs. 408–416
Hilkhot Shevitat Asor [Laws of Cessation from Work on the Tenth (of Tishrei, *i.e.*, the Day of Atonement)]	OḤ (Yom ha-Kippurim [Day of Atonement]) chs. 608–618
Hilkhot Shevitat Yom Tov [Laws of Cessation from Work on Festivals]	
Chapters 1–6	OḤ (Yom Tov [Festivals]) chs. 495–529
Chapters 7–8	OḤ (Ḥol ha-Mo'ed [Intermediate Days of Festivals]) chs. 530–548
Hilkhot Ḥameẓ u-Maẓẓah [Laws of Leavened Foods and Unleavened Bread]	OḤ (Pesaḥ [Passover]) chs. 431–486
Hilkhot Shofar ve-Sukkah ve-Lulav [Laws of the *Shofar*, the Tabernacle, and the Palm Branch]	
Chapters 1–3	OḤ (Rosh Ha-Shanah) chs. 585–596
Chapters 4–6	OḤ (Sukkah [Tabernacle]) chs. 625–643, 666–667
Chapters 7–8	OḤ (Lulav [Palm Branch]) 644–658, 660, 664–665
Hilkhot Shekalim [Laws of the *Shekalim* (Levy for the Temple)]	———
Hilkhot Kiddush ha-Hodesh [Laws of Sanctification of the New Moon]	
Chapters 1–4	———
Chapter 5	OḤ (Yom Tov [Festivals], etc.) chs. 496, 601
Chapters 6–10	OḤ (Rosh Hodesh [New Moon]) chs. 427–428
Chapters 11–19	———

MISHNEH TORAH	*SHULḤAN ARUKH*
Hilkhot Ta'aniyyot [Laws of Fasts]	OḤ (Tish'a be-Av u-She'ar Ta'aniyyot [The Ninth Day of Av and Other Fasts], etc.) chs. 418, 549–555, 560–564, 566–579, 597, 602, 686
Hilkhot Megillah ve-Ḥanukkah [Laws of the Scroll of Esther and of Hanukkah]	
Chapters 1–2	OḤ (Megillah [Scroll of Esther]) chs. 687–692, 694–697
Chapters 3–4	OḤ (Ḥanukkah, etc.) chs. 422, 488, 584, 644, 670–683, 693
***Sefer Nashim** [The Book of Women]*	
Hilkhot Ishut [Laws of Personal Status]	
Chapter 1	EH (Ishut [Personal Status]) ch. 15
Chapter 2	EH (Kiddushin [Betrothal and Marriage], etc.) chs. 44, 155, 172
Chapters 3–10	EH (Ishut [Personal Status], Kiddushin [Betrothal and Marriage]) chs. 17–18, 26–49, 55–56, 61–62, 64, 66–67
Chapters 11–14	EH (Ketubbot [Marriage Contracts]) chs. 67–79, 89
Chapters 15–25	EH chs. 1, 6–7, 11, 39, 51–54, 57–58, 66, 80–86, 88, 90–96, 98–105, 111–117, 154, 160, 168
Hilkhot Gerushin [Laws of Divorce]	
Chapters 1–10	EH (Gittin [Divorces], etc.) chs. 12, 119–153
Chapter 11	EH chs. 10–11, 13, 155, 178
Chapters 12–13	EH chs. 17, 152
Hilkhot Yibbum va-Ḥaliẓah [Laws of Levirate Marriage and Release Therefrom]	
Chapters 1–3	EH (Yibbum [Levirate Marriage]) chs. 156–168
Chapter 4	EH (Ḥaliẓah [Release from Levirate Marriage]) ch. 169
Chapters 5–7	EH (Ḥaliẓah ve-Yibbum [Levirate Marriage and Release Therefrom]) chs. 170–176
Hilkhot Na'arah Betulah [Laws of a Virgin Maiden]	EH (Ones u-Mefatteh [Rape and Seduction]) ch. 177
Hilkhot Sotah [Laws of the Suspected Wife]	
Chapters 1–2	EH (Sotah [Suspected Wife], etc.) chs. 11, 178
Chapter 3	————
Chapter 4	EH (Sotah [Suspected Wife]) ch. 178
***Sefer Kedushah** [The Book of Holiness]*	
Hilkhot Issurei Bi'ah [Laws of Prohibited Sexual Intercourse]	
Chapters 1–2	EH (Ishut [Personal Status]) chs. 15, 19–20
Chapter 3	————

MISHNEH TORAH	*SHULḤAN ARUKH*
Chapters 4–11	YD (Niddah [Menstruant Woman]) chs. 183–197; EH ch. 63
Chapter 12	EH chs. 4, 6, 8, 16
Chapters 13–14	YD (Avadim [Slaves]) ch. 267; (Gerim [Proselytes]) chs. 268–269
Chapters 15–22	EH chs. 1–9, 19–25; OḤ ch. 240
Hilkhot Ma'akhalot Asurot [Laws of Prohibited Foods]	
Chapters 1–2	YD (Terefot [Animals Unfit for Food]) chs. 79–80, 82–85
Chapter 3	YD (Terefot [Animals Unfit for Food], etc.) chs. 81, 86, 115, 119
Chapter 4	YD (Sheḥitah [Ritual Slaughter], etc.) chs. 17, 28, 62, 116
Chapter 5	YD (Terefot [Animals Unfit for Food]) ch. 62
Chapter 6	YD (Terefot [Animals Unfit for Food]) chs. 66–78
Chapter 7	YD (Terefot [Animals Unfit for Food]) chs. 64–65
Chapter 8	YD (Terefot [Animals Unfit for Food], etc.) chs. 63, 65, 117–118
Chapter 9	YD (Basar be-Ḥalav [(Mixture of) Meat and Milk]) chs. 87–97
Chapter 10	YD (Ḥadash [New Grain Ripening after Passover]) ch. 293; (Orlah)* ch. 294; (Kil'ei ha-Kerem [Hybrid Plants in a Vineyard]) ch. 296
Chapters 11–13	YD (Yein Nesekh [Libation Wine], Kelei ha-Yayin [Wine Vessels], etc.) chs. 118–119, 123–138
Chapter 14	YD 98:6, ch. 155; OḤ chs. 617–618
Chapters 15–16	YD (Ta'arovot [Admixtures], etc.) chs. 98–110, 122
Chapter 17	YD (Pat u-Shelakot ve-Ḥalav u-Gevinah Shel Amamin [Bread, Boiled Foods, Milk, and Cheese of Non-Jews]) chs. 112–114, 120–121
Hilkhot Sheḥitah [Laws of Ritual Slaughter]	
Chapters 1–4	YD (Sheḥitah [Ritual Slaughter]) chs. 1–15, 18–27
Chapters 5–11	YD (Terefot [Animals Unfit for Food]) chs. 29–60
Chapter 12	YD (Sheḥitah [Ritual Slaughter]) ch. 16
Chapter 13	YD (Shilu'aḥ ha-Ken)† ch. 292
Chapter 14	YD (Sheḥitah [Ritual Slaughter]) ch. 28

*Fruit of a tree in the first three years from its planting. *See* Leviticus 19:23.

†Lit. "sending from the nest," referring to the duty to drive the mother bird from her nest before taking her fledglings or eggs. *See* Deuteronomy 22:6.

MISHNEH TORAH	*SHULḤAN ARUKH*
Sefer Hafla'ah [Book of Asseveration]	
Hilkhot Shevu'ot [Laws of Oaths]	
Chapters 1–10	YD (Shevu'ot [Oaths]) chs. 236–239
Chapter 11	ḤM ch. 87
Chapter 12	YD (Shevu'ot [Oaths]) ch. 237
Hilkhot Nedarim (Laws of Vows]	YD (Nedarim [Vows]) chs. 203–235
Hilkhot Nezirut [Laws of the Nazirite]	———
Hilkhot Arakhin va-Ḥaramim [Laws of Votive Gifts to the Temple]	———
Sefer Zera'im [The Book of Seeds]	
Hilkhot Kilayim [Laws of Hybrids]	
Chapters 1–9	YD (Kil'ei Ilan, Kil'ei ha-Kerem, Kil'ei Zera'im, Kil'ei Behemah [Hybrid Trees, Vines, Seeds, Animals]) chs. 295–297
Chapter 10	YD (Kil'ei Begadim [Hybridized Clothing]) chs. 298–304
Hilkhot Mattenot Aniyyim [Laws of Gifts to the Poor]	
Chapters 1–5	YD (Terumot [Priestly Tithes], etc., Mattenot Aniyyim [Gifts to the Poor]) ch. 332
Chapter 6	YD (Terumot u-Ma'asrot [Priestly and Other Tithes]) ch. 331
Chapters 7–10	YD (Ẓedakah [Charity]) chs. 247–259
Hilkhot Terumot [Laws of the Priestly Tithes]	YD (Terumot u-Ma'asrot [Priestly and Other Tithes]) ch. 331
Hilkhot Ma'aser [Laws of Tithes]	YD (Terumot u-Ma'asrot [Priestly and Other Tithes]) ch. 331
Hilkhot Ma'aser Sheni ve-Neta Reva'i [Laws of the Second Tithe and Plantings in Their Fourth Year]	
Chapters 1–8	YD (Terumot u-Ma'asrot [Priestly and Other Tithes]) ch. 331
Chapters 9–10	YD (Orlah)* ch. 294
Chapter 11	YD (Terumot u-Ma'asrot [Priestly and Other Tithes]) ch. 331
Hilkhot Bekhorim im She'ar Mattenot Kehunah she-bi-Gevulin [Laws of Firstlings and the Other Gifts to the Priests Within the Boundaries (of the Land of Israel)]	
Chapters 1–4	———
Chapters 5–8	YD (Ḥallah [Dough Offering]) chs. 322–330
Chapter 9	YD (Terefot [Animals Unfit for Food]) ch. 61
Chapter 10	YD (Terumot [Priestly Tithes], etc., Reshit ha-Gez [The First Shearing]) ch. 333

*Fruit of a tree in the first three years from its planting. *See* Leviticus 19:23.

MISHNEH TORAH	*SHULḤAN ARUKH*
Chapter 11	YD (Pidyon Bekhor [Redemption of the First-Born]) ch. 305
Chapter 12	YD (Peter Ḥamor [Firstlings of Donkeys]) ch. 321
Hilkhot Shemittah ve-Yovel [Laws of the Sabbatical and Jubilee Years]	
Chapters 1–8	———
Chapter 9	ḤM (Halva'ot [Loans]) ch. 67
Chapters 10–13	———
Sefer Avodah [The Book of Temple Service]	
Hilkhot Bet Ha-Beḥirah [Laws of the Chosen House (The Temple)]	———
Hilkhot Kelei ha-Mikdash ve-ha-Ovdim Bo [Laws of the Temple Utensils and Those Who Served in the Temple]	———
Hilkhot Bi'at ha-Mikdash [Laws of Entering the Temple]	———
Hilkhot Issurei Mizbe'aḥ [Laws of Things (Animals) Forbidden to Be Brought on the Altar]	———
Hilkhot Ma'aseh ha-Korbanot [Laws of the Sacrificial Service]	———
Hilkhot Temidin u-Musafin [Laws of the Daily and Additional Offerings]	
Chapters 1–6	———
Chapter 7	OH (Pesaḥ [Passover]) ch. 489
Chapters 8–10	———
Hilkhot Pesulei ha-Mukdashin [Laws of Unfit Consecrated (Animals)]	———
Hilkhot Avodat Yom ha-Kippurim [Laws of the Service of the Day of Atonement]	———
Hilkhot Me'ilah [Laws of Sacrilege]	
Chapter 1	YD (Hilkhot Bekhor Behemah Tehorah [Laws of Firstlings of Ritually Clean Animals]) ch. 308
Chapters 2–8	———
Sefer Korbanot [The Book of Sacrifices]	
Hilkhot Korban Pesaḥ [Laws of the Paschal Sacrifice]	———
Hilkhot Ḥagigah [Laws of the Festive Offering]	———
Hilkhot Bekhorot [Laws of Firstlings]	
Chapters 1–5	YD (Hilkhot Bekhor Behemah Tehorah [Laws of Firstlings of Ritually Clean Animals]) chs. 306–320
Chapters 6–8	———
Hilkhot Shegagot [Laws of Sacrifices for Unintentional Sins]	———

MISHNEH TORAH	*SHULḤAN ARUKH*
Hilkhot Meḥusrei Kapparah [Laws of Those Who Are Lacking (Complete) Atonement]	———
Hilkhot Temurah [Laws of Substitution of Sacrificial Offerings]	———
Sefer Tohorah [The Book of Purity]	
Hilkhot Tum'at Met [Laws of Ritual Impurity of a Dead Body]	YD (Avelut [Mourning]) chs. 369–372
Hilkhot Parah Adummah [Laws of the Red Heifer]	———
Hilkhot Tum'at Ẓara'at [Laws of the Ritual Impurity of Leprosy]	———
Hilkhot Metammei Mishkav u-Moshav [Laws Concerning Those Who Render Beds and Seats Ritually Impure]	———
Hilkhot She'ar Avot ha-Tum'ot [Laws of the Other Primary Sources of Ritual Impurity]	———
Hilkhot Tum'ot Okhlin [Laws of Ritual Impurity of Foods]	———
Hilkhot Kelim [Laws of Utensils]	———
Hilkhot Mikva'ot [Laws of Ritual Baths]	YD (Niddah [Menstruant Woman]) chs. 198–202
Sefer Nezikin [The Book of Damages]	
Hilkhot Nizkei Mamon [Laws of Damages Caused by Property]	ḤM (Nizkei Mamon [Damages Caused by Property]) chs. 389–419
Hilkhot Genevah [Laws of Theft]	
Chapters 1–6	ḤM (Genevah [Theft]) chs. 348–358
Chapters 7–8	ḤM (Ona'ah u-Mikaḥ Ta'ut [Overreaching and Transactions Resulting from Mistake]) ch. 231
Chapter 9	ḤM (Ḥovel be-Ḥavero [Wounding One's Fellow]) ch. 425
Hilkhot Gezelah va-Avedah [Laws of Robbery and Lost Property]	
Chapters 1–10	ḤM (Gezelah [Robbery], etc.) chs. 90, 136, 292, 359–377
Chapters 11–17	ḤM (Avedah u-Meẓi'ah [Lost and Found Objects]) chs. 259–271
Chapter 18	ḤM (Halva'ot [Loans]) ch. 65
Hilkhot Ḥovel u-Mazzik [Laws of Wounding and Damaging]	
Chapters 1–5	ḤM (To'en ve-Nit'an [Plaintiff and Defendant]) ch. 90; (Ḥovel ba-Ḥavero [Wounding One's Fellow]) chs. 420–426
Chapters 6–8	ḤM (Nezikin [Damages], Me'abbed Mamon Ḥavero be-Yadayim u-Moser u-

MISHNEH TORAH	*SHULḤAN ARUKH*
	Malshin [Directly Destroying the Property of One's Fellow, Traducers, Informers], etc.) chs. 128, 378–388
Hilkhot Roẓe'aḥ u-Shemirat ha-Nefesh [Laws of Homicide and Preservation of Life]	
Chapters 1–10	———
Chapter 11	ḤM (Miẓvat Aseh Lehasir Kol Mikhshol [The Positive Commandment to Remove Any Obstacle]) ch. 427; YD ch. 116
Chapter 12	YD (Avodat Elilim [Idol Worship], etc.) chs. 116, 151, 153, 155–156
Chapter 13	ḤM (Perikah u-Te'inah ve-Din Holkhei Derakhim [Unloading and Reloading (Overloaded Animals); Laws of Travelers]) ch. 272
Sefer Kinyan [The Book of Acquisitions]	
Hilkhot Mekhirah [Laws of Sales]	
Chapters 1–11	ḤM (Mikaḥ u-Mimkar [Purchase and Sale], etc.) chs. 66, 126, 190–207
Chapters 12–18	ḤM (Ona'ah u-Mikaḥ Ta'ut [Overreaching and Transactions Resulting from Mistake]) chs. 227–234
Chapters 19–28	ḤM (Mikaḥ u-Mimkar [Purchase and Sale], etc.) chs. 91, 209–226
Chapters 29–30	ḤM ch. 235; EH ch. 90
Hilkhot Zekhiyyah u-Mattanah [Laws of Entitlement and Gifts]	
Chapters 1–2	ḤM (Mikaḥ u-Mimkar [Purchase and Sale]) ch. 194; (Hefker ve-Nikhsei ha-Ger [Ownerless Property and Property of Proselytes]) chs. 273–275
Chapters 3–5	ḤM (Mattanah [Gifts]) chs. 241–245, 249
Chapter 6	ḤM (Mattanah [Gifts]) chs. 246–247; EH (Kiddushin [Betrothal and Marriage]) chs. 50–51, 59, 106–107
Chapter 7	EH (Kiddushin [Betrothal and Marriage]) ch. 60
Chapters 8–12	ḤM (Mattenat Shekhiv Me-ra [Gifts of a Person Dangerously Ill or Otherwise Reasonably Apprehending Imminent Death], etc.) chs. 125, 248–258
Hilkhot Shekhenim [Laws of Neighbors]	
Chapter 1–Chapter 12, Paragraph 3	ḤM (Nizkei Shekhenim [Damages to Neighbors]) chs. 153–156; (Shutafim be-Karka [Concurrent Owners of Land]) chs. 157–170; (Ḥalukat Shutafut [Dissolution of Partnership]) chs. 171–175:4

MISHNEH TORAH	*SHULḤAN ARUKH*
Chapter 12, Paragraph 4–Chapter 14	ḤM (Miẓranut [Adjoining Landowners]) 175:5-end
Hilkhot Sheluḥin ve-Shutafin [Laws of Agency and Partnership]	
Chapters 1–3	ḤM (Ha-Oseh Shali'aḥ Ligbot Ḥov, Harsha'ah [Appointment of an Agent to Collect a Debt; Power of Attorney]) chs. 121–123; (Sheluḥin [Agency]) chs. 182–188
Chapters 4–5	ḤM (Shutafin [Partnership]) chs. 176–179
Chapters 6–8	YD (Ribbit [Interest and Usury]) ch. 177
Chapters 9–10	ḤM (To'en ve-Nit'an [Plaintiff and Defendant]) chs. 93–94
Hilkhot Avadim [Laws of Slaves]	
Chapters 1–4	————
Chapters 5–9	YD (Avadim [Slaves]) ch. 267
Sefer Mishpatim [The Book of Civil Laws]	
Hilkhot Sekhirut [Laws of Leasing and Hiring]	
Chapters 1–3	ḤM (Shomer Sakhar [Paid Bailee], etc.) chs. 125, 291, 301–305
Chapters 4–7	ḤM (Sokher [Hirer]) chs. 307–319
Chapter 8	ḤM (Ḥakirut ve-Kabbelanut [Sharecropping]) chs. 320–330
Chapter 9	ḤM (Sekhirut Po'alim [Hiring of Laborers]) chs. 331–336
Chapter 10	ḤM (Umanim [Artisans], etc.) chs. 305–306
Chapters 11–13	ḤM (To'en ve-Nit'an [Plaintiff and Defendant]) ch. 89; (Sekhirut Po'alim [Hiring of Laborers]) chs. 337–339
Hilkhot She'elah u-Fikkadon [Laws of Borrowing and Pledges]	
Chapters 1–3	ḤM (She'elah [Borrowing]) chs. 340–346
Chapters 4–8	ḤM (To'en ve-Nit'an [Plaintiff and Defendant]) ch. 90; (Pikkadon [Pledges]) chs. 291–301
Hilkhot Malveh ve-Loveh [Laws of Creditor and Debtor]	
Chapters 1–3	ḤM (Geviyyat Milvah [Collection of a Loan], etc.) chs. 86, 97–99, 101, 127
Chapters 4–10	YD (Ribbit [Interest and Usury]) chs. 159–176
Chapters 11–24	ḤM (Halva'ot [Loans], etc.) chs. 39–41, 43, 45–46, 48–54, 56–58, 60, 64–65, 69–75, 82–85, 91, 98–120, 125–126
Chapters 25–26	ḤM (Arev [Suretyship], etc.) chs. 76–77, 96, 128–132
Chapter 27	ḤM (Halva'ot [Loans]) chs. 42, 44–46, 68

MISHNEH TORAH	***SHULḤAN ARUKH***
Hilkhot To'en ve-Nit'an [Laws of Plaintiff and Defendant]	
Chapters 1–7	ḤM (To'en ve-Nit'an [Plaintiff and Defendant], etc.) chs. 72, 75, 79–82, 87–89, 91–92, 94–96
Chapters 8–10	ḤM (Ḥezkat Metaltelin [Possession of Personal Property]) chs. 133–139
Chapters 11–16	ḤM (Ḥezkat Karka'ot [Possession of Land]) chs. 140–152
Hilkhot Naḥalot [Laws of Inheritance]	
Chapters 1–9	ḤM (Naḥalot [Inheritance]) chs. 276–287
Chapters 10–11	ḤM (Naḥalot [Inheritance], Apotropos [Guardian, Administrator, Trustee]) chs. 288–290
Sefer Shofetim *[The Book of Judges]*	
Hilkhot ha-Sanhedrin ve-ha-Onshin ha-Mesurin Lahem [Laws of the Sanhedrin and Its Penal Jurisdiction]	
Chapters 1–8	ḤM (Dayyanim [Judges]) chs. 1, 3–5, 7–8, 13–14, 18, 20–22, 25
Chapters 9–10	————
Chapter 11	ḤM (Dayyanim [Judges]) chs. 3, 5, 7, 18
Chapters 12–19	————
Chapter 20–23	ḤM (Dayyanim [Judges]) chs. 6–7, 9–10, 12, 15, 17, 19
Chapter 24	ḤM (Dayyanim [Judges]) chs. 2, 15; YD (Niddui va-Ḥerem [Ban and Excommunication]) ch. 334
Chapters 25–26	ḤM (Dayyanim [Judges]) chs. 5, 8, 11, 19, 26–27
Hilkhot Edut [Laws of Evidence]	ḤM (Edut [Evidence]) chs. 28–38; (Halva'ot [Loans]) chs. 45–46, 51
Hilkhot Mamrim [Laws of Rebels]	
Chapters 1–4	————
Chapters 5–6	YD (Kibbud Av va-Em [Honoring One's Parents]) chs. 240–241
Chapter 7	————
Hilkhot Evel [Laws of Mourning]	OḤ chs. 420, 548; YD (Bikkur Ḥolim [Visiting the Sick], Keri'ah [Tearing (of Garments)], Avelut [Mourning]) chs. 335–403; EH (Ishut [Personal Status]) ch. 14
Hilkhot Melakhim u-Milḥamoteihem [Laws of Kings and Their Wars]	————

CROSS-REFERENCES FROM THE *SHULḤAN ARUKH* TO THE *MISHNEH TORAH*

Shulḥan Arukh Oraḥ Ḥayyim

SHULḤAN ARUKH ORAḤ ḤAYYIM	*MISHNEH TORAH*
Hilkhot Hanhagat Adam ba-Boker [Laws of Conduct upon Arising in the Morning]	
Chapter 1	Hilkhot Tefillah u-Virkat Kohanim [Laws of Prayer and the Priestly Blessing] ch. 7
Chapters 2–3	Hilkhot De'ot [Laws of Ethical Principles] ch. 5
Hilkhot Netilat Yadayim, Berakhot [Laws of Washing of Hands, Blessings]	
Chapters 4–7	Hilkhot Tefillah u-Virkat Kohanim [Laws of Prayer and the Priestly Blessing] chs. 4, 7, 10
Hilkhot Ẓiẓit [Laws of the Fringes]	
Chapters 8–24	Hilkhot Ẓiẓit [Laws of the Fringes]
Hilkhot Tefillin [Laws of the Phylacteries]	
Chapters 25–45	Hilkhot Tefillin u-Mezuzah ve-Sefer Torah [Laws of Phylacteries, *Mezuzah*, and the Torah Scroll] chs. 1–4
Hilkhot Birkhot ha-Shaḥar u-She'ar Berakhot [Laws of the Preliminary Blessings Recited in the Morning, and Other Blessings]	
Chapters 46–57	Hilkhot Tefillah u-Virkat Kohanim [Laws of Prayer and the Priestly Blessing] chs. 7–9; Seder ha-Tefillot [Order of Prayers] at the end of *Sefer Ahavah*
Hilkhot Keri'at Shema u-Virkhotehah [Laws of the Recitation of the Shema and Its Blessings]	
Chapters 58–88	Hilkhot Keri'at Shema [Laws of the Recitation of the Shema]
Hilkhot Tefillah [Laws of Prayer]	
Chapters 89–127	Hilkhot Tefillah u-Virkat Kohanim [Laws of Prayer and the Priestly Blessing] chs. 1–6, 8–10; Seder ha-Tefillot [Order of Prayers] at the end of *Sefer Ahavah*
Hilkhot Nesi'at Kappayim [Laws of the Priestly Blessing]	
Chapters 128–129	Hilkhot Tefillah u-Virkat Kohanim [Laws of Prayer and the Priestly Blessing] chs. 14–15
Chapter 130	———
Hilkhot Nefilat Appayim, Tefillah [Laws of Falling on the Face (a form of prostration during the *Taḥanun* prayer), Laws of Prayer]	

SHULḤAN ARUKH ORAḤ ḤAYYIM	***MISHNEH TORAH***
Chapters 131–134	Hilkhot Tefillah u-Virkat Kohanim [Laws of Prayer and the Priestly Blessing] chs. 5, 7, 9
Hilkhot Keri'at Sefer Torah [Laws of Reading of the Torah Scroll] Chapters 135–149	Hilkhot Tefillah u-Virkat Kohanim [Laws of Prayer and the Priestly Blessing] chs. 12–13
Hilkhot Bet ha-Keneset [Laws of the Synagogue] Chapters 150–154	Hilkhot Tefillah u-Virkat Kohanim [Laws of Prayer and the Priestly Blessing] ch. 11
Chapters 155–156	Hilkhot Talmud Torah [Laws of Study of Torah] chs. 1, 3
Hilkhot Netilat Yadayim [Laws of Washing of the Hands] Chapter 157	Hilkhot De'ot [Laws of Ethical Principles] ch. 4
Chapters 158–165	Hilkhot Berakhot [Laws of Blessings] ch. 6
Hilkhot Beẓi'at ha-Pat [Laws of Breaking Bread] Chapters 166–168	Hilkhot Berakhot [Laws of Blessings] chs. 4, 7
Hilkhot Se'udah [Laws of the Meal] Chapters 169–181	Hilkhot Berakhot [Laws of Blessings] chs. 4, 6–7
Hilkhot Birkat ha-Mazon [Laws of Grace after Meals] Chapters 182–201	Hilkhot Berakhot [Laws of Blessings] chs. 1–5, 7; Text of *Birkat ha-Mazon* [Grace after Meals] at the end of *Sefer Ahavah*
Hilkhot Berakhot [Laws of Blessings] Chapters 202–230	Hilkhot Berakhot [Laws of Blessings] chs. 1, 3, 8–11
Chapter 231	Hilkhot De'ot [Laws of Ethical Principles] chs. 3–4
Hilkhot Tefillat ha-Minḥah [Laws of the Afternoon Prayer] Chapters 232–234	Hilkhot Tefillah u-Virkat Kohanim [Laws of Prayer and the Priestly Blessing] chs. 1, 3, 6–7, 9
Hilkhot Keri'at Shema u-Tefillah Shel Arvit [Laws of the Recitation of the Shema and the Evening Prayer] Chapters 235–237	Hilkhot Keri'at Shema [Laws of the Recitation of the Shema] ch. 1; Hilkhot Tefillah u-Virkat Kohanim [Laws of Prayer and the Priestly Blessing] chs. 1, 3, 5–7, 9

SHULḤAN ARUKH ORAḤ ḤAYYIM	***MISHNEH TORAH***
Chapter 238	Hilkhot Talmud Torah [Laws of Study of Torah] chs. 1, 3
Chapter 239	Hilkhot Tefillah u-Virkat Kohanim [Laws of Prayer and the Priestly Blessing] ch. 7
Hilkhot Ẓeni'ut [Laws of Modesty] Chapters 240–241	Hilkhot De'ot [Laws of Ethical Principles] chs. 4–5; Hilkhot Issurei Bi'ah [Laws of Prohibited Sexual Intercourse] ch. 21
Hilkhot Shabbat [Laws of the Sabbath] Chapters 242–266	Hilkhot Shabbat [Laws of the Sabbath] chs. 3–6, 9, 19–25, 30; Hilkhot Shevitat Yom Tov [Laws of Cessation from Work on Festivals] ch. 8
Chapters 267–268	Hilkhot Tefillah u-Virkat Kohanim [Laws of Prayer and the Priestly Blessing] chs. 3, 5, 9–10; Seder ha-Tefillot [Order of Prayers] at the end of *Sefer Ahavah*
Chapters 269–280	Hilkhot Shabbat [Laws of the Sabbath] chs. 2, 5–6, 25, 29–30
Chapter 281	Seder ha-Tefillot [Order of Prayers] at the end of *Sefer Ahavah*
Chapters 282–285	Hilkhot Tefillah u-Virkat Kohanim [Laws of Prayer and the Priestly Blessing] chs. 12–13; Seder ha-Tefillot [Order of Prayers] at the end of *Sefer Ahavah*
Chapter 286	Hilkhot Tefillah u-Virkat Kohanim [Laws of Prayer and the Priestly Blessing] chs. 1–3
Chapters 287–291	Hilkhot Tefillah u-Virkat Kohanim [Laws of Prayer and the Priestly Blessing] ch. 7; Hilkhot Shabbat [Laws of the Sabbath] chs. 24, 29–30
Chapter 292	Hilkhot Tefillah u-Virkat Kohanim [Laws of Prayer and the Priestly Blessing] chs. 9, 12–13
Chapter 293	Hilkhot Shabbat [Laws of the Sabbath] ch. 5
Chapter 294	Hilkhot Tefillah u-Virkat Kohanim [Laws of Prayer and the Priestly Blessing] ch. 2; Seder ha-Tefillot [Order of Prayers] at the end of *Sefer Ahavah*
Chapter 295	Hilkhot Tefillah u-Virkat Kohanim [Laws of Prayer and the Priestly Blessing] ch. 9
Chapters 296–344	Hilkhot Milah [Laws of Circumcision] ch. 2; Hilkhot Shabbat [Laws of the Sabbath] chs. 1–2, 6–12, 18–26, 29–30
Chapters 345–365	Hilkhot Shabbat [Laws of the Sabbath] chs. 12–17
Chapters 366–395	Hilkhot Eruvin [Laws of *Eruv*] chs. 1–5

SHULḤAN ARUKH ORAḤ ḤAYYIM	*MISHNEH TORAH*
Hilkhot Teḥumim [Laws of Boundaries] Chapters 396–407	Hilkhot Shabbat [Laws of the Sabbath] chs. 27–28
Hilkhot Eruvei Teḥumim [Laws of Merging of Boundaries] Chapters 408–416	Hilkhot Eruvin [Laws of *Eruv*] chs. 6–8
Hilkhot Rosh Ḥodesh [Laws of the New Moon]	
Chapter 417	———
Chapter 418	Hilkhot Ta'aniyyot [Laws of Fasts] ch. 1
Chapter 419	———
Chapter 420	Hilkhot Evel [Laws of Mourning] ch. 11
Chapters 421–423	Hilkhot Tefillah u-Virkat Kohanim [Laws of Prayer and the Priestly Blessing] chs. 1–2, 9,12–13; Seder ha-Tefillot [Order of Prayers] at the end of *Sefer Ahavah*; Hilkhot Megillah ve-Ḥanukkah [Laws of the Scroll of Esther and of Hanukkah] ch. 3
Chapter 424	Hilkhot Berakhot [Laws of Blessings] ch. 2
Chapter 425	Hilkhot Tefillah u-Virkat Kohanim [Laws of Prayer and the Priestly Blessing] chs. 2, 13; Seder ha-Tefillot [Order of Prayers] at the end of *Sefer Ahavah*
Chapter 426	Hilkhot Berakhot [Laws of Blessings] ch. 10
Chapters 427–428	Hilkhot Tefillah u-Virkat Kohanim [Laws of Prayer and the Priestly Blessing] ch. 13; Seder ha-Tefillot [Order of Prayers] at the end of *Sefer Ahavah*; Hilkhot Kiddush ha-Ḥodesh [Laws of Sanctification of the New Moon] chs. 6–10
Hilkhot Pesaḥ [Laws of Passover]	
Chapters 429–430	———
Chapters 431–486	Hilkhot Ḥameẓ u-Maẓẓah [Laws of Leavened Foods and Unleavened Bread]
Chapters 487–488	Hilkhot Tefillah u-Virkat Kohanim [Laws of Prayer and the Priestly Blessing] chs. 1–2, 9, 12–13; Seder ha-Tefillot [Order of Prayers] at the end of *Sefer Ahavah*; Hilkhot Megillah ve-Ḥanukkah [Laws of the Scroll of Esther and of Hanukkah] ch. 3
Chapter 489	Hilkhot Temidin u-Musafin [Laws of the Daily and Additional Offerings] ch. 7
Chapter 490	Hilkhot Tefillah u-Virkat Kohanim [Laws of Prayer and the Priestly Blessing] chs. 1–2, 9; Seder ha-Tefillot [Order of Prayers] at the end of *Sefer Ahavah*; Hilkhot Shabbat [Laws of the Sabbath] ch. 29

SHULḤAN ARUKH ORAḤ ḤAYYIM	***MISHNEH TORAH***
Chapter 491	Hilkhot Shabbat [Laws of the Sabbath] ch. 29
Chapters 492–493	———
Chapter 494	Hilkhot Tefillah u-Virkat Kohanim [Laws of Prayer and the Priestly Blessing] chs. 12–13; Seder ha-Tefillot [Order of Prayers] at the end of *Sefer Ahavah;* Hilkhot Megillah ve-Ḥanukkah [Laws of the Scroll of Esther and of Hanukkah] ch. 3
Hilkhot Yom Tov [Laws of Festivals]	
Chapters 495–529	Hilkhot Shevitat Yom Tov [Laws of Cessation from Work on Festivals] chs. 1–6; Hilkhot Kiddush ha-Ḥodesh [Laws of Sanctification of the New Moon] ch. 5
Hilkhot Ḥol ha-Mo'ed [Laws of Intermediate Days of Festivals]	
Chapters 530–547	Hilkhot Shevitat Yom Tov [Laws of Cessation from Work on Festivals] chs. 6–8
Chapter 548	Hilkhot Evel [Laws of Mourning] ch. 10
Hilkhot Tish'a be-Av u-She'ar Ta'aniyyot [Laws of the Ninth Day of Av and Other Fasts]	
Chapters 549–555	Hilkhot Ta'aniyyot [Laws of Fasts] ch. 5
Chapter 556	———
Chapter 557	Hilkhot Tefillah u-Virkat Kohanim [Laws of Prayer and the Priestly Blessing] ch. 2; Seder ha-Tefillot [Order of Prayers] at the end of *Sefer Ahavah*
Chapter 558	———
Chapter 559	Hilkhot Tefillah u-Virkat Kohanim [Laws of Prayer and the Priestly Blessing] chs. 12–13; Hilkhot Ta'aniyyot [Laws of Fasts] ch. 5
Chapters 560–564	Hilkhot Ta'aniyyot [Laws of Fasts] chs. 1, 5
Chapter 565	Hilkhot Tefillah u-Virkat Kohanim [Laws of Prayer and the Priestly Blessing] ch. 2; Seder ha-Tefillot [Order of Prayers] at the end of *Sefer Ahavah*
Chapter 566	Hilkhot Tefillah u-Virkat Kohanim [Laws of Prayer and the Priestly Blessing] chs. 12–14
Chapters 567–579	Hilkhot Ta'aniyyot [Laws of Fasts] chs. 1–4
Chapter 580	———
Hilkhot Rosh ha-Shanah [Laws of Rosh Ha-Shanah]	
Chapter 581	Hilkhot Tefillah u-Virkat Kohanim [Laws of Prayer and the Priestly Blessing] ch. 5
Chapter 582	Hilkhot Tefillah u-Virkat Kohanim [Laws of Prayer and the Priestly Blessing] chs. 2,

SHULḤAN ARUKH ORAḤ ḤAYYIM	*MISHNEH TORAH*
	10; Seder ha-Tefillot [Order of Prayers] at the end of *Sefer Ahavah*
Chapter 583	————
Chapter 584	Hilkhot Tefillah u-Virkat Kohanim [Laws of Prayer and the Priestly Blessing] chs. 12–13; Hilkhot Megillah ve-Ḥanukkah [Laws of the Scroll of Esther and of Hanukkah] ch. 3
Chapter 585–590	Hilkhot Shofar ve-Sukkah ve-Lulav [Laws of the *Shofar*, the Tabernacle, and the Palm Branch] chs. 1–3
Chapters 591–596	Hilkhot Shofar ve-Sukkah ve-Lulav [Laws of the *Shofar*, the Tabernacle, and the Palm Branch] ch. 3
Chapter 597	Hilkhot Ta'aniyyot [Laws of Fasts] ch. 1
Chapter 598	————
Chapter 599	Hilkhot Tefillah u-Virkat Kohanim [Laws of Prayer and the Priestly Blessing] ch. 2
Chapter 600	Hilkhot Shabbat [Laws of the Sabbath] ch. 29
Chapter 601	Hilkhot Tefillah u-Virkat Kohanim [Laws of Prayer and the Priestly Blessing] ch. 13; Hilkhot Shabbat [Laws of the Sabbath] ch. 29; Hilkhot Kiddush ha-Ḥodesh [Laws of Sanctification of the New Moon] ch. 5
Chapter 602	Hilkhot Ta'aniyyot [Laws of Fasts] ch. 5
Chapter 603	Hilkhot Teshuvah [Laws of Repentance] ch. 2
Hilkhot Yom ha-Kippurim [Laws of the Day of Atonement]	
Chapter 604	Hilkhot Tefillah u-Virkat Kohanim [Laws of Prayer and the Priestly Blessing] ch. 5; Hilkhot Nedarim [Laws of Vows] ch. 3
Chapter 605	————
Chapters 606–607	Hilkhot Teshuvah [Laws of Repentance]
Chapters 608–618	Hilkhot Shevitat Asor [Laws of Cessation from Work on the Tenth (of Tishrei, *i.e.*, the Day of Atonement)]
Chapter 619	Hilkhot Shabbat [Laws of the Sabbath] ch. 29
Chapter 620	————
Chapters 621–624	Hilkhot Tefillah u-Virkat Kohanim [Laws of Prayer and the Priestly Blessing] chs. 1–2, 12–14; Seder ha-Tefillot [Order of Prayers] at the end of *Sefer Ahavah*; Hilkhot Shabbat [Laws of the Sabbath] ch. 29
Hilkhot Sukkah [Laws of the Tabernacle]	
Chapters 625–642	Hilkhot Shofar ve-Sukkah ve-Lulav [Laws

SHULḤAN ARUKH ORAḤ ḤAYYIM	***MISHNEH TORAH***
	of the *Shofar*, the Tabernacle, and the Palm Branch] chs. 4–6
Chapter 643	Hilkhot Shabbat [Laws of the Sabbath] ch. 29; Hilkhot Shofar ve-Sukkah ve-Lulav [Laws of the *Shofar*, the Tabernacle, and the Palm Branch] ch. 6
Chapter 644	Hilkhot Shofar ve-Sukkah ve-Lulav [Laws of the *Shofar*, the Tabernacle, and the Palm Branch] ch. 7; Hilkhot Megillah ve-Ḥanukkah [Laws of the Scroll of Esther and of Hanukkah] ch. 3
Hilkhot Lulav [Laws of the Palm Branch]	
Chapters 645–658	Hilkhot Shofar ve-Sukkah ve-Lulav [Laws of the *Shofar*, the Tabernacle, and the Palm Branch] chs. 7–8
Chapter 659	Hilkhot Tefillah u-Virkat Kohanim [Laws of Prayer and the Priestly Blessing] ch. 13
Chapter 660	Hilkhot Shofar ve-Sukkah ve-Lulav [Laws of the *Shofar*, the Tabernacle, and the Palm Branch] ch. 7
Chapter 661	Hilkhot Shabbat [Laws of the Sabbath] ch. 29
Chapter 662	Hilkhot Tefillah u-Virkat Kohanim [Laws of Prayer and the Priestly Blessing] ch. 13
Chapter 663	Hilkhot Tefillah u-Virkat Kohanim [Laws of Prayer and the Priestly Blessing] chs. 2, 12–13; Seder ha-Tefillot [Order of Prayers] at the end of *Sefer Ahavah*
Chapters 664–665	Hilkhot Shofar ve-Sukkah ve-Lulav [Laws of the *Shofar*, the Tabernacle, and the Palm Branch] ch. 7
Chapter 666–667	Hilkhot Shofar ve-Sukkah ve-Lulav [Laws of the *Shofar*, the Tabernacle, and the Palm Branch ch. 6
Chapters 668–669	Hilkhot Tefillah u-Virkat Kohanim [Laws of Prayer and the Priestly Blessing] chs. 2, 13; Seder ha-Tefillot [Order of Prayers] at the end of *Sefer Ahavah*; Hilkhot Shabbat [Laws of the Sabbath] ch. 29
Hilkhot Ḥanukkah [Laws of Hanukkah]	
Chapters 670–683	Hilkhot Tefillah u-Virkat Kohanim [Laws of Prayer and the Priestly Blessing] ch. 1; Seder ha-Tefillot [Order of Prayers] at the end of *Sefer Ahavah*; Hilkhot Megillah ve-Ḥanukkah [Laws of the Scroll of Esther and of Hanukkah] chs. 3–4
Chapters 684–685	Hilkhot Tefillah u-Virkat Kohanim [Laws of Prayer and the Priestly Blessing] chs. 12–13

SHULḤAN ARUKH ORAḤ ḤAYYIM	*MISHNEH TORAH*
Hilkhot Megillah [Laws of the Scroll of Esther]	
Chapter 686	Hilkhot Ta'aniyyot [Laws of Fasts] ch. 5
Chapters 687–692	Hilkhot Megillah ve-Ḥanukkah [Laws of the Scroll of Esther and of Hanukkah] chs. 1–2
Chapter 693	Hilkhot Tefillah u-Virkat Kohanim [Laws of Prayer and the Priestly Blessing] chs. 2, 13; Seder ha-Tefillot [Order of Prayers] at the end of *Sefer Ahavah;* Hilkhot Megillah ve-Ḥanukkah [Laws of the Scroll of Esther and of Hanukkah] ch. 3
Chapters 694–697	Hilkhot Megillah ve-Ḥanukkah [Laws of the Scroll of Esther and of Hanukkah] ch. 2

Shulḥan Arukh Yoreh De'ah

SHULḤAN ARUKH YOREH DE'AH	*MISHNEH TORAH*
Hilkhot Sheḥitah [Laws of Ritual Slaughter]	
Chapters 1–15	Hilkhot Sheḥitah [Laws of Ritual Slaughter] chs. 1–2, 4
Chapter 16	Hilkhot Sheḥitah [Laws of Ritual Slaughter] ch. 12
Chapter 17	Hilkhot Ma'akhalot Asurot [Laws of Prohibited Foods] ch. 4
Chapters 18–27	Hilkhot Sheḥitah [Laws of Ritual Slaughter] chs. 1–3
Chapter 28	Hilkhot Sheḥitah [Laws of Ritual Slaughter] ch. 12; Hilkhot Ma'akhalot Asurot [Laws of Prohibited Foods] ch. 4
Hilkhot Terefot [Laws of Animals Unfit for Food]	
Chapters 29–60	Hilkhot Sheḥitah [Laws of Ritual Slaughter] chs. 5–11
Chapter 61	Hilkhot Bekhorim im She'ar Mattenot Kehunah she-bi-Gevulin [Laws of Firstlings and Other Gifts to the Priests within the Boundaries (of the Land of Israel)] ch. 9
Chapter 62	Hilkhot Ma'akhalot Asurot [Laws of Prohibited Foods] chs. 4–5
Chapter 63	Hilkhot Ma'akhalot Asurot [Laws of Prohibited Foods] ch. 8
Chapter 64	Hilkhot Ma'akhalot Asurot [Laws of Prohibited Foods] ch. 7

SHULḤAN ARUKH YOREH DE'AH	*MISHNEH TORAH*
Chapter 65	Hilkhot Ma'akhalot Asurot [Laws of Prohibited Foods] chs. 7–8
Chapters 66–78	Hilkhot Ma'akhalot Asurot [Laws of Prohibited Foods] ch. 6
Chapters 79–80	Hilkhot Ma'akhalot Asurot [Laws of Prohibited Foods] ch. 1
Chapter 81	Hilkhot Ma'akhalot Asurot [Laws of Prohibited Foods] ch.3
Chapters 82–85	Hilkhot Ma'akhalot Asurot [Laws of Prohibited Foods] chs. 1–2
Chapter 86	Hilkhot Ma'akhalot Asurot [Laws of Prohibited Foods] ch. 3
Hilkhot Basar be-Ḥalav [Laws of (Mixture of) Meat and Milk]	
Chapters 87–97	Hilkhot Ma'akhalot Asurot [Laws of Prohibited Foods] ch. 9
Hilkhot Ta'arovot [Laws of Admixtures (of Forbidden and Permitted Foods)]	
Chapters 98–110	Hilkhot Ma'akhalot Asurot [Laws of Prohibited Foods] chs. 15–16
Chapter 111	———
Hilkhot Pat u-Shelakot ve-Ḥalav u-Gevinah Shel Amamin [Laws of Bread, Boiled Foods, Milk, and Cheese of Non-Jews]	
Chapters 112–114	Hilkhot Ma'akhalot Asurot [Laws of Prohibited Foods] ch. 17
Chapter 115	Hilkhot Ma'akhalot Asurot [Laws of Prohibited Foods] ch. 3
Chapter 116	Hilkhot Ma'akhalot Asurot [Laws of Prohibited Foods] ch. 4; Hilkhot Roẓe'aḥ u-Shemirat ha-Nefesh [Laws of Homicide and Preservation of Life] chs. 11–12
Chapter 117	Hilkhot Ma'akhalot Asurot [Laws of Prohibited Foods] ch. 8
Chapter 118	Hilkhot Ma'akhalot Asurot [Laws of Prohibited Foods] chs. 8, 13
Chapter 119	Hilkhot Ma'akhalot Asurot [Laws of Prohibited Foods] chs. 3, 11; Hilkhot Ma'aser [Laws of Tithes] chs. 10–12
Chapters 120–121	Hilkhot Ma'akhalot Asurot [Laws of Prohibited Foods] ch. 17
Chapter 122	Hilkhot Ma'akhalot Asurot [Laws of Prohibited Foods] ch. 15
Hilkhot Yein Nesekh, Kelei ha-Yayin [Laws of Libation Wine, Wine Vessels]	
Chapters 123–138	Hilkhot Ma'akhalot Asurot [Laws of Prohibited Foods] chs. 11–13
Hilkhot Avodat Elilim [Laws of Idol Worship]	
Chapters 139–150	Hilkhot Avodat Kokhavim ve-Ḥukkoteihem

SHULḤAN ARUKH YOREH DE'AH	***MISHNEH TORAH***
	[Laws Relating to Idol Worship] chs. 1–10
Chapters 151–154	Hilkhot Avodat Kokhavim ve-Ḥukkoteihem [Laws Relating to Idol Worship] chs. 9–10; Hilkhot Roẓe'aḥ u-Shemirat ha-Nefesh [Laws of Homicide and Preservation of Life] ch. 12
Chapter 155	Hilkhot Yesodei ha-Torah [Laws of the Fundamentals of the Torah] ch. 5; Hilkhot Ma'akhalot Asurot [Laws of Prohibited Foods] ch. 14; Hilkhot Roẓe'aḥ u-Shemirat ha-Nefesh [Laws of Homicide and Preservation of Life] ch. 12
Chapter 156	Hilkhot Avodat Kokhavim ve-Ḥukkoteihem [Laws Relating to Idol Worship] ch. 11; Hilkhot Roẓe'aḥ u-Shemirat ha-Nefesh [Laws of Homicide and Preservation of Life] ch. 12
Chapter 157	Hilkhot Yesodei ha-Torah [Laws of the Fundamentals of the Torah] ch. 5
Chapter 158	Hilkhot Avodat Kokhavim ve-Ḥukkoteihem [Laws Relating to Idol Worship] ch. 10; Hilkhot Roẓe'aḥ u-Shemirat ha-Nefesh [Laws of Homicide and Preservation of Life] ch. 4
Hilkhot Ribbit [Laws of Interest and Usury]	
Chapters 159–176	Hilkhot Malveh ve-Loveh [Laws of Creditor and Debtor] chs. 4–10
Chapter 177	Hilkhot Sheluḥin ve-Shutafin [Laws of Agency and Partnership] chs. 6–8
Ḥukkot Amamin [Laws of the Nations]	
Chapters 178–182	Hilkhot Avodat Kokhavim ve-Ḥukkoteihem [Laws Relating to Idol Worship] chs. 11–12
Hilkhot Niddah [Laws of the Menstruant Woman]	
Chapters 183–197	Hilkhot Issurei Bi'ah [Laws of Prohibited Sexual Intercourse] chs. 4–11
Chapters 198–202	Hilkhot Mikva'ot [Laws of Ritual Baths]
Hilkhot Nedarim [Laws of Vows]	
Chapters 203–235	Hilkhot Nedarim [Laws of Vows]
Chapters 236–239	Hilkhot Shevu'ot [Laws of Oaths] chs. 1–10, 12
Hilkhot Kibbud Av va-Em [Laws of Honoring One's Parents]	
Chapters 240–241	Hilkhot Mamrim [Laws of Rebels] chs. 5–6
Hilkhot Kevod Rabbo ve-Talmid Ḥakham [Laws of Honor Due to One's Teacher and to a Scholar]	

SHULḤAN ARUKH YOREH DE'AH	*MISHNEH TORAH*
Chapters 242–246	Hilkhot Talmud Torah [Laws of Study of Torah] chs. 1–6
Hilkhot Ẓedakah [Laws of Charity] Chapters 247–259	Hilkhot Mattenot Aniyyim [Laws of Gifts to the Poor] chs. 7–10
Hilkhot Milah (Laws of Circumcision] Chapters 260–266	Hilkhot Milah [Laws of Circumcision]
Hilkhot Avadim [Laws of Slaves] Chapter 267	Hilkhot Milah [Laws of Circumcision]; Hilkhot Issurei Bi'ah [Laws of Prohibited Sexual Intercourse] chs. 13–14; Hilkhot Avadim [Laws of Slaves] chs. 5–9
Hilkhot Gerim [Laws of Proselytes] Chapters 268–269	Hilkhot Milah [Laws of Circumcision]; Hilkhot Issurei Bi'ah [Laws of Prohibited Sexual Intercourse] chs. 13–14
Hilkhot Sefer Torah [Laws of the Torah Scroll] Chapters 270–284	Hilkhot Yesodei ha-Torah [Laws of the Fundamentals of the Torah] ch. 6; Hilkhot Tefillin u-Mezuzah ve-Sefer Torah [Laws of Phylacteries, *Mezuzah*, and the Torah Scroll] chs. 7–10
Hilkhot Mezuzah [Laws of the *Mezuzah*] Chapters 285–291	Hilkhot Tefillin u-Mezuzah ve-Sefer Torah [Laws of Phylacteries, *Mezuzah*, and the Torah Scroll] chs. 5–6
Hilkhot Shilu'aḥ ha-Ken [Laws of *Shilu'aḥ ha-Ken*]* Chapter 292	Hilkhot Sheḥitah [Laws of Ritual Slaughter] ch. 13
Hilkhot Ḥadash [Laws Relating to New Grain Ripening after Passover] Chapter 293	Hilkhot Ma'akhalot Asurot [Laws of Prohibited Foods] ch. 10
Hilkhot Orlah [Laws of *Orlah*]† Chapter 294	Hilkhot Ma'akhalot Asurot [Laws of Prohibited Foods] ch. 10; Hilkhot Ma'aser Sheni ve-Neta Reva'i [Laws of the Second Tithe and Plantings in Their Fourth Year] chs. 9–10
Hilkhot Kil'ei Ilan [Laws of Hybrid Trees] Chapter 295	Hilkhot Kilayim [Laws of Hybrid Mixtures] chs. 1, 3, 6

*Lit. "sending from the nest," referring to the duty to drive the mother bird from her nest before taking her fledglings or eggs. *See* Deuteronomy 22:6.

†Fruit of a tree in the first three years from its planting. *See* Leviticus 19:23.

SHULḤAN ARUKH YOREH DE'AH	*MISHNEH TORAH*
Hilkhot Kil'ei ha-Kerem [Laws of Hybrid Plants in a Vineyard] Chapter 296	Hilkhot Kilayim [Laws of Hybrid Mixtures] chs. 5–8; Hilkhot Ma'akhalot Asurot [Laws of Prohibited Foods] ch. 10
Hilkhot Kil'ei Zera'im, Kil'ei Behemah [Laws of Hybrid Seeds and Hybrid Animals] Chapter 297	Hilkhot Kilayim [Laws of Hybrid Mixtures] chs. 1–4, 9
Hilkhot Kil'ei Begadim [Laws of Hybridized Clothing] Chapters 298–304	Hilkhot Kilayim [Laws of Hybrid Mixtures] ch. 10
Hilkhot Pidyon Bekhor [Laws of Redemption of the First-Born] Chapter 305	Hilkhot Bekhorim im She'ar Mattenot Kehunah she-bi-Gevulin [Laws of Firstlings and Other Gifts to the Priests within the Boundaries (of the Land of Israel)] ch. 11
Hilkhot Bekhor Behemah Tehorah [Laws of Firstlings of Ritually Clean Animals] Chapters 306–320	Hilkhot Me'ilah [Laws of Sacrilege] ch. 1; Hilkhot Bekhorot [Laws of Firstlings] chs. 1–5
Hilkhot Peter Ḥamor [Laws of Firstlings of Donkeys] Chapter 321	Hilkhot Bekhorim im She'ar Mattenot Kehunah she-bi-Gevulin [Laws of Firstlings and Other Gifts to the Priests within the Boundaries (of the Land of Israel)] ch. 12
Hilkhot Ḥallah [Laws of the Dough Offering] Chapters 322–330	Hilkhot Bekhorim im She'ar Mattenot Kehunah she-bi-Gevulin [Laws of Firstlings and Other Gifts to the Priests within the Boundaries (of the Land of Israel)] chs. 5–8
Hilkhot Terumot u-Ma'asrot u-Mattenot Aniyyim ve-Reshit ha-Gez [Laws of Priestly and Other Tithes, Gifts to the Poor, and the First Shearing] Chapter 331	Hilkhot Mattenot Aniyyim [Laws of Gifts to the Poor] ch. 6; Hilkhot Terumot [Laws of the Priestly Tithes]; Hilkhot Ma'aser [Laws of Tithes]; Hilkhot Ma'aser Sheni ve-Neta Reva'i [Laws of the Sec-

SHULḤAN ARUKH YOREH DE'AH	*MISHNEH TORAH*
	ond Tithe and Plantings in Their Fourth Year] chs. 1–8, 11
Chapter 332	Hilkhot Mattenot Aniyyim [Laws of Gifts to the Poor] chs. 1–5
Chapter 333	Hilkhot Bekhorim im She'ar Mattenot Kehunah she-bi-Gevulin [Laws of Firstlings and Other Gifts to the Priests within the Boundaries (of the Land of Israel)] ch. 10
Hilkhot Niddui va-Ḥerem [Laws of Ban and Excommunication]	
Chapter 334	Hilkhot Talmud Torah [Laws of Study of Torah] chs. 6–7; Hilkhot ha-Sanhedrin ve-ha-Onshin ha-Mesurin Lahem [Laws of the Sanhedrin and Its Penal Jurisdiction] ch. 24
Hilkhot Bikkur Ḥolim u-Refuah ve-Noteh Lamut ve-Goses, Keri'ah, Avelut [Laws of Visiting the Sick, Medicine, the Terminally Ill, Persons *in Extremis*, Tearing (of Garments), and Mourning]	
Chapters 335–403	Hilkhot Tum'at ha-Met [Laws of Ritual Impurity of a Dead Body]; Hilkhot Evel [Laws of Mourning]

Shulḥan Arukh Even ha-Ezer

SHULḤAN ARUKH EVEN HA-EZER	*MISHNEH TORAH*
Hilkhot Periyyah u-Reviyyah [Laws of Procreation]	
Chapters 1–6	Hilkhot Ishut [Laws of Personal Status] chs. 15, 24; Hilkhot Issurei Bi'ah [Laws of Prohibited Sexual Intercourse] chs. 12, 15–21
Hilkhot Ishut [Laws of Personal Status]	
Chapters 7–9	Hilkhot Ishut [Laws of Personal Status] ch. 24; Hilkhot Issurei Bi'ah [Laws of Prohibited Sexual Intercourse] chs. 12, 17–19, 21
Chapters 10–13	Hilkhot Ishut [Laws of Personal Status] ch. 24; Hilkhot Gerushin [Laws of Divorce] chs. 10–11; Hilkhot Sotah [Laws of the Suspected Wife] ch. 2
Chapter 14	Hilkhot Evel [Laws of Mourning] ch. 6
Chapter 15	Hilkhot Ishut [Laws of Personal Status] ch. 1; Hilkhot Issurei Bi'ah [Laws of Prohibited Sexual Intercourse] chs. 1, 2

SHULḤAN ARUKH EVEN HA-EZER	*MISHNEH TORAH*
Chapter 16	Hilkhot Issurei Bi'ah [Laws of Prohibited Sexual Intercourse] ch. 12
Chapters 17–18	Hilkhot Ishut [Laws of Personal Status] ch. 4; Hilkhot Gerushin [Laws of Divorce] chs. 12–13
Chapters 19–25	Hilkhot Issurei Bi'ah [Laws of Prohibited Sexual Intercourse] chs. 1, 21–22
Hilkhot Kiddushin [Laws of Betrothal and Marriage]	
Chapters 26–65	Hilkhot Ishut [Laws of Personal Status] chs. 1–10, 20, 23; Hilkhot Zekhiyyah u-Mattanah [Laws of Entitlement and Gifts] chs. 6–7
Hilkhot Ketubbot [Laws of Marriage Contracts]	
Chapters 66–117	Hilkhot Ishut [Laws of Personal Status] chs. 10–14, 16–25; Hilkhot Gezelah va-Avedah [Laws of Robbery and Lost Property] ch. 18; Hilkhot Mekhirah [Laws of Sales] ch. 30; Hilkhot Zekhiyyah u-Mattanah [Laws of Entitlement and Gifts] chs. 6, 11; Hilkhot Sheluḥin ve-Shutafin [Laws of Agency and Partnership] ch. 9; Hilkhot She'elah u-Fikkadon [Laws of Borrowing and Bailment] ch. 7; Hilkhot Malveh ve-Loveh [Laws of Creditor and Debtor] ch. 24; Hilkhot To'en ve-Nit'an [Laws of Plaintiff and Defendant] chs. 13–14
Chapter 118	————
Hilkhot Gittin [Laws of Divorce]	
Chapters 119–153, and the Order of the Bill of Divorcement (following Chapter 154)	Hilkhot Gerushin [Laws of Divorce] chs. 1–10, 12
Chapter 154	Hilkhot Ishut [Laws of Personal Status] chs. 15, 25
Hilkhot Me'un [Laws of Disaffirmance]	
Chapter 155	Hilkhot Ishut [Laws of Personal Status] ch. 2; Hilkhot Gerushin [Laws of Divorce] ch. 11
Hilkhot Yibbum [Laws of Levirate Marriage]	
Chapters 156–168	Hilkhot Ishut [Laws of Personal Status] ch. 22; Hilkhot Yibbum va-Ḥaliẓah [Laws of Levirate Marriage and Release Therefrom] chs. 1–3
Hilkhot Ḥaliẓah [Laws of Release from Levirate Marriage]	

SHULḤAN ARUKH EVEN HA-EZER	*MISHNEH TORAH*
Chapter 169; Overview of Ḥaliẓah Procedure	Hilkhot Yibbum va-Ḥaliẓah [Laws of Levirate Marriage and Release Therefrom] ch. 4
Hilkhot Ḥaliẓah ve-Yibbum [Laws of Levirate Marriage and Release Therefrom] Chapters 170–176	Hilkhot Ishut [Laws of Personal Status] ch. 2; Hilkhot Yibbum va-Ḥaliẓah [Laws of Levirate Marriage and Release Therefrom] chs. 5–7
Hilkhot Ones u-Mefatteh [Laws of Rape and Seduction] Chapter 177	Hilkhot Na'arah Betulah [Laws of a Virgin Maiden]
Hilkhot Sotah [Laws of the Suspected Wife] Chapter 178	Hilkhot Gerushin [Laws of Divorce] ch. 11; Hilkhot Sotah [Laws of the Suspected Wife] chs. 1–2, 4

Shulḥan Arukh Ḥoshen Mishpat

SHULḤAN ARUKH ḤOSHEN MISHPAT	*MISHNEH TORAH*
Hilkhot Dayyanim [Laws of Judges] Chapters 1–27	Hilkhot ha-Sanhedrin ve-ha-Onshin ha-Mesurin Lahem [Laws of the Sanhedrin and Its Penal Jurisdiction] chs. 1–8, 11, 20–26
Hilkhot Edut [Laws of Evidence] Chapters 28–38	Hilkhot Edut [Laws of Evidence]
Hilkhot Halva'ot [Laws of Loans] Chapters 39–74	Hilkhot Shemittah ve-Yovel [Laws of the Sabbatical and Jubilee Years] ch. 9; Hilkhot Gezelah va-Avedah [Laws of Robbery and Lost Property] ch. 18; Hilkhot Mekhirah [Laws of Sales] ch. 6; Hilkhot Malveh ve-Loveh [Laws of Creditor and Debtor] chs. 11, 13–20, 22, 24, 27; Hilkhot To'en ve-Nit'an [Laws of Plaintiff and Defendant] chs. 4, 8; Hilkhot Edut [Laws of Evidence] chs. 3, 5–8, 14
Hilkhot To'en ve-Nit'an [Laws of Plaintiff and Defendant] Chapters 75–96	Hilkhot Shevu'ot [Laws of Oaths] ch. 11; Hilkhot Gezelah va-Avedah [Laws of Robbery and Lost Property] ch. 4; Hilkhot Ḥovel u-Mazzik [Laws of Wounding and Damaging] ch. 5; Hilkhot

SHULḤAN ARUKH ḤOSHEN MISHPAT	*MISHNEH TORAH*
	Mekhirah [Laws of Sales] ch. 20; Hilkhot Sheluḥin ve-Shutafin [Laws of Agency and Partnership] chs. 9–10; Hilkhot Sekhirut [Laws of Leasing and Hiring] ch. 11; Hilkhot Malveh ve-Loveh [Laws of Creditor and Debtor] chs. 2, 13–14, 16–17, 24–25; Hilkhot To'en ve-Nit'an [Laws of Plaintiff and Defendant] chs. 1–7
Hilkhot Geviyyat Milvah [Laws of Collection of a Loan]	
Chapters 97–106	Hilkhot Malveh ve-Loveh [Laws of Creditor and Debtor] chs. 1–3, 11, 13, 19–20, 22
Hilkhot Geviyyat Ḥov me-ha-Yetomim [Laws of Collection of Debt from Orphans] Chapters 107–110	Hilkhot Malveh ve-Loveh [Laws of Creditor and Debtor] chs. 11–12, 17–18
Hilkhot Geviyyat Ḥov mi-Neḥasim Meshu'badim [Laws of Collection of Debt from Encumbered Property] Chapters 111–116	Hilkhot Malveh ve-Loveh [Laws of Creditor and Debtor] chs. 11, 14, 18–19, 21
Hilkhot Apoteki [Laws of Mortgages] Chapters 117–120	Hilkhot Malveh ve-Loveh [Laws of Creditor and Debtor] chs. 16, 18–19
Hilkhot ha-Oseh Shali'aḥ Ligbot Ḥov [Laws of Appointment of an Agent to Collect a Debt] Chapter 121	Hilkhot Sheluḥin ve-Shutafin [Laws of Agency and Partnership] chs. 1–3
Hilkhot Harsha'ah [Laws of Powers of Attorney] Chapters 122–128	Hilkhot Ḥovel u-Mazzik [Laws of Wounding and Damaging] ch. 8; Hilkhot Mekhirah [Laws of Sales] ch. 6; Hilkhot Zekhiyyah u-Mattanah [Laws of Entitlement and Gifts] ch. 10; Hilkhot Sheluḥin ve-Shutafin [Laws of Agency and Partnership] ch. 3; Hilkhot Sekhirut [Laws of Leasing and Hiring] ch. 1; Hilkhot Malveh ve-Loveh [Laws of Creditor and Debtor] chs. 2, 16, 26
Hilkhot Arev [Laws of Suretyship] Chapters 129–132	Hilkhot Malveh ve-Loveh [Laws of Creditor and Debtor] chs. 25–26
Hilkhot Ḥezkat Metaltelin [Laws of Possession of Personal Property]	

SHULḤAN ARUKH ḤOSHEN MISHPAT	*MISHNEH TORAH*
Chapters 133–139	Hilkhot Gezelah va-Avedah [Laws of Robbery and Lost Property] ch. 6; Hilkhot To'en ve-Nit'an [Laws of Plaintiff and Defendant] chs. 8–10
Hilkhot Ḥezkat Karka'ot [Laws of Possession of Land] Chapters 140–152	Hilkhot To'en ve-Nit'an [Laws of Plaintiff and Defendant] chs. 11–16
Hilkhot Nizkei Shekhenim [Laws of Damages by Neighbors] Chapters 153–156	Hilkhot Shekhenim [Laws of Neighbors] chs. 5, 7–11
Hilkhot Shutafim be-Karka [Laws of Concurrent Owners of Land] Chapters 157–170	Hilkhot Shekhenim [Laws of Neighbors] chs. 1–6
Hilkhot Ḥalukat Shutafut [Laws of Dissolution of Partnership] Chapter 171–Chapter 175, Paragraph 4	Hilkhot Shekhenim [Laws of Neighbors] chs. 1–2, 12 (to paragraph 3)
Hilkhot Miẓranut [Laws of Adjoining Landowners] Chapter 175 (from paragraph 5 on)	Hilkhot Shekhenim [Laws of Neighbors] chs. 12 (from paragraph 4 on) to 14
Hilkhot Shutafin [Laws of Partnership] Chapters 176–179	Hilkhot Sheluḥin ve-Shutafin [Laws of Agency and Partnership] chs. 4–5
Chapter 180	Hilkhot Nedarim [Laws of Vows] ch. 7
Chapter 181	Hilkhot Gezelah va-Avedah [Laws of Robbery and Lost Property] ch. 12
Hilkhot Sheluḥin [Laws of Agency] Chapters 182–188	Hilkhot Sheluḥin ve-Shutafin [Laws of Agency and Partnership] chs. 1–3
Hilkhot Mikaḥ u-Mimkar [Laws of Purchase and Sale] Chapters 189–226	Hilkhot Mekhirah [Laws of Sales] chs. 1–11, 19–28; Hilkhot Zekhiyyah u-Mattanah [Laws of Entitlement and Gifts] ch. 1
Hilkhot Ona'ah u-Mikaḥ Ta'ut [Laws of Overreaching and Transactions Resulting from Mistake] Chapters 227–240	Hilkhot Genevah [Laws of Theft] chs. 7–8; Hilkhot Mekhirah [Laws of Sales] chs. 12–18, 29–30
Hilkhot Mattanah [Laws of Gifts] Chapters 241–249	Hilkhot Zekhiyyah u-Mattanah [Laws of Entitlement and Gifts] ch. 3–6, 11–12
Hilkhot Mattenat Shekhiv Me-ra [Laws of Gifts of a Person Dangerously Ill or	

SHULḤAN ARUKH ḤOSHEN MISHPAT	*MISHNEH TORAH*
Otherwise Reasonably Apprehending Imminent Death] Chapters 250–258	Hilkhot Zekhiyyah u-Mattanah [Laws of Entitlement and Gifts] chs. 8–12
Hilkhot Avedah u-Meẓi'ah [Laws of Lost and Found Objects] Chapters 259–271	Hilkhot Gezelah va-Avedah [Laws of Robbery and Lost Property] chs. 11–17
Hilkhot Perikah u-Te'inah ve-Din Holkhei Derakhim [Laws of Unloading and Reloading (Overloaded Animals); Laws of Travelers] Chapter 272	Hilkhot Roẓe'aḥ u-Shemirat ha-Nefesh [Laws of Homicide and Preservation of Life] ch. 13
Hilkhot Hefker ve-Nikhsei ha-Ger [Laws of Ownerless Property and Property of Proselytes] Chapters 273–275	Hilkhot Zekhiyyah u-Mattanah [Laws of Entitlement and Gifts] chs. 1–2
Hilkhot Naḥalot [Laws of Inheritance] Chapters 276–289	Hilkhot Naḥalot [Laws of Inheritance] chs. 1–10
Hilkhot Apotropos [Laws of the Guardian, Administrator, and Trustee] Chapter 290	Hilkhot Naḥalot [Laws of Inheritance] chs. 10–11
Hilkhot Pikkadon [Laws of Pledges] Chapters 291–302	Hilkhot Gezelah va-Avedah [Laws of Robbery and Lost Property] ch. 3; Hilkhot Sekhirut [Laws of Leasing and Hiring] chs. 2–3; Hilkhot She'elah u-Fikkadon [Laws of Borrowing and Pledges] chs. 4–8
Hilkhot Shomer Sakhar [Laws of the Paid Bailee] Chapters 303–305	Hilkhot Sekhirut [Laws of Leasing and Hiring] chs. 1–3, 10
Hilkhot Umanim [Laws of Craftsmen] Chapter 306	Hilkhot Sekhirut [Laws of Leasing and Hiring] ch. 10
Hilkhot Sokher [Laws of the Hirer (Lessee)] Chapters 307–319	Hilkhot Sekhirut [Laws of Leasing and Hiring] chs. 4–7
Hilkhot Ḥakirut ve-Kabbelanut [Laws of Sharecropping] Chapters 320–330	Hilkhot Sekhirut [Laws of Leasing and Hiring] ch. 8
Hilkhot Sekhirut Po'alim [Laws of Hiring of Laborers]	

SHULḤAN ARUKH ḤOSHEN MISHPAT	*MISHNEH TORAH*
Chapters 331–339	Hilkhot Sekhirut [Laws of Leasing and Hiring] chs. 9, 11–13
Hilkhot She'elah [Laws of Borrowing] Chapters 340–346	Hilkhot She'elah u-Fikkadon [Laws of Borrowing and Pledges] chs. 1–3
Chapter 347	Hilkhot Nizkei Mamon [Laws of Damages Caused by Property] ch. 4
Hilkhot Genevah [Laws of Theft] Chapters 348–358	Hilkhot Genevah [Laws of Theft] chs. 1–6
Hilkhot Gezelah [Laws of Robbery] Chapters 359–377	Hilkhot Gezelah va-Avedah [Laws of Robbery and Lost Property] chs. 1–10
Hilkhot Nezikin [Laws of Damages] Chapters 378–387	Hilkhot Ḥovel u-Mazzik [Laws of Wounding and Damaging] chs. 6–8
Hilkhot Me'abbed Mamon Ḥavero be-Yadayim u-Moser u-Malshin [Laws of Directly Destroying the Property of One's Fellow and of Traducers and Informers] Chapter 388	Hilkhot Ḥovel u-Mazzik [Laws of Wounding and Damaging] chs. 6–8
Hilkhot Nizkei Mamon [Laws of Damages Caused by Property] Chapters 389–419	Hilkhot Nizkei Mamon [Laws of Damages Caused by Property]
Hilkhot Ḥovel ba-Ḥavero [Laws of Wounding One's Fellow] Chapters 420–426	Hilkhot Ḥovel u-Mazzik [Laws of Wounding and Damaging] chs. 1–5
[Hilkhot] Miẓvat Aseh Lehasir Kol Mikhshol she-Yesh Bo Sakkanat Nefashot ve-Asiyyat Ma'akeh le-Gaggo [(Laws of) the Positive Commandment to Remove Any Obstacle Posing a Danger to Life and to Erect a Parapet on One's Roof] Chapter 427	Hilkhot Roẓe'aḥ u-Shemirat ha-Nefesh [Laws of Homicide and Preservation of Life] ch. 11

APPENDIX B
ADDITIONAL EXAMPLES[1] COMPARING THE LANGUAGE AND STYLE OF MAIMONIDES' *MISHNEH TORAH*, THE *TURIM*, AND THE *SHULḤAN ARUKH*

EXAMPLE 1

MISHNEH TORAH[2]

9. A person steals from one of five [people], but it is unknown who the victim was, and each one of them makes a claim against him and states, "You stole from me," [then] even though there are no witnesses to the theft, each of them [the claimants] takes an oath that the defendant stole from him, and he [the defendant] pays the [amount of] the theft to each one [of

TURIM[3]

A person steals from one of five [people], but he does not know[4] who the victim was, and each one [of them] states, "It was from me that he stole,"[5] [then] each one takes an oath and recovers [the value of the stolen object]. Maimonides has written that [this law applies] even though there are no witnesses to the theft. The same applies if he stole from two [people], a hundred

SHULḤAN ARUKH[6]

1. A person steals from one of five [people], but he does not know[7] from which one he stole, [and] each of them states, "It was me from that he stole," [then] even though there are no witnesses to the theft, each of them [the claimants] takes an oath that the defendant stole from him, and he [the defendant] pays [the amount] of the theft to each of them.

1. For four other examples, *see supra* pp. 1327–1340.

2. Maimonides, *MT*, Gezelah va-Avedah 4:9–10. This same passage is also quoted *supra* pp. 148–149. The translation here differs in some respects from the translation there, since here it is necessary to provide a more literal translation in order to appreciate the stylistic differences between the three codes.

3. *Tur* ḤM 365:9–10.

4. Maimonides uses the expression "it is unknown," which is more accurate. In M Yevamot, both versions ("it is unknown" and "he does not know") are found; *see* the textual variants *ad loc. Tur* ed. Cremona, 1558, and ed. Sabbioneta, 1559, have the reading which appears in our text.

5. This is the reading in ed. Sabbioneta, 1559. In ed. Cremona, 1558, the reading is: "and each one states that the theft was from him."

6. Sh. Ar. ḤM 365:1–2.

7. This is the reading in eds. Venice 1565, 1567, and 1574. It also is the reading in the *Turim; see* n. 4 *supra.*

MISHNEH TORAH

them]. This too[8] is a penalty imposed by the Sages because he transgressed and stole; under Biblical law, however, he is not required to pay, because of the uncertainty.[9]

10. [If] he says to two [people]: "I stole from one of you or from the father of one of you, and I do not know [from] which [one]," if he wishes to fulfill his duty in the sight of Heaven, he must pay to each one the [full amount] stolen. However, his legal obligation is to restore only the amount stolen, and they divide it between themselves, as neither was aware that anything of his had been stolen; rather, it was this one [the thief] who volunteered the information. The Sages did not impose any penalty in this case, inasmuch as no claim was made against him.[10]

TURIM

[coins] from one and two hundred from the other, and he does not know to whom the two hundred [coins] belong, and each of them says: "They were mine." [In such a case], each one takes an oath and recovers (two hundred).[11] When is this rule applicable? If claims are made against him. However, if no claims are made against him but he himself says, "I have stolen from one of you but I do not know [from] which one," or "[I do not know] to whom the two hundred [coins] belonged"—[in such a case] the court cannot hold him liable, but if he wishes to fulfill his duty in the sight of Heaven, he must pay each one.

SHULḤAN ARUKH

2. [If] he says to two [people], "I stole from one of you and I do not know [from] which [one]," he need make only one payment, and they divide [it] between them, since they would not have been aware that anything of theirs had been stolen if he had not informed them. Nevertheless, if he wishes to fulfill his duty in the sight of Heaven, he must pay to each one the entire [amount] stolen. But if two [persons] make claim against one [person], and each of them says to him, "You have stolen one hundred [coins] from me," and he responds, "It is true that I stole one hundred [coins] from one of you, but I do not know from which one," he [the defendant] must pay one hundred [coins] to each of them.

A comparison of the different versions of this law in the *Mishneh Torah*, the *Turim* and the *Shulḥan Arukh* reveals interesting features of the style of each of these three codes. Again in this example, the *Mishneh Torah* has the most detail, but, unlike the other examples,[12] the *Turim* is the briefest. The *Turim* omits the statement at the end of paragraph 9 in the *Mishneh Torah* that the legal source of this law is an enactment of the Sages, and that under the strict law the transgressor should have been exempt because the claimant has the burden of proof and cannot meet it. Indeed, there was no reason to make any point about the legal source of this law, for hundreds of laws in the *Mishneh Torah*, the *Turim*, and the *Shulḥan Arukh* are

8. The word "too" relates to *MT*, Gezelah va-Avedah 4:1, which sets forth the enactment by the Sages that one who is the victim of a theft may take an oath and recover the amount due him. The word *kenas* (penalty) here is used to mean "enactment," as it is in paragraph 1, where nearly identical terminology is found in regard to the Sages' enactment of the "Mishnaic oath." *See supra* pp. 615–616.

9. The source of this law is M Yevamot 15:7 and TB Yevamot 118b.

10. The source of this law is M Bava Meẓi'a 3:3 and TB Bava Meẓi'a 37a.

11. In current printed eds., the words "two hundred" appear in parentheses. In ed. Sabbioneta, 1559, they appear without parentheses; in ed. Cremona, 1558, they do not appear at all. The source of this additional law is analogy from the law of bailments; *see* M and TB Bava Meẓi'a, *supra* n. 10, and *Be'ur ha-Gra* to Sh. Ar. ḤM 365, subpar. 5.

12. *See supra* pp. 1327–1340.

derived from enactments of the Sages, yet ordinarily their derivation is not pointed out. Similarly, the *Turim* omits the example given by Maimonides of a theft from "the father of one of you." This example, which is derived from M and TB *Bava Meẓi'a*, was included by Maimonides in keeping with his policy of not omitting any concrete example included in the Talmudic sources, even if the example adds nothing new.[13]

The *Shulḥan Arukh* follows the *Turim* with regard to these omissions. The *Turim* includes several other instances of a more terse style. Thus, it has "each one takes an oath and recovers" instead of the longer version found in the *Mishneh Torah*—"each of them [the claimants] takes an oath that the defendant stole from him, and he [the defendant] pays the [amount of] the theft to each one [of them]." Moreover, the *Turim* does not include Maimonides' statement of the rationale: ". . . as neither was aware that anything of his had been stolen; rather, it was the thief who volunteered the information. The Sages did not impose any penalty in this case, inasmuch as no claim was made against him." And, whereas Maimonides states that to fulfill the thief's duty in the sight of Heaven, "he must pay to each one the [full amount] stolen," the *Turim* adopts an abbreviated formulation: "He must pay each one."

Most of these abbreviated formulations and omissions were not conformed to by Caro, who chose to follow Maimonides (except that even he did not include a portion of Maimonides' reasoning, *i.e.*, the statement that "the Sages did not impose any penalty in this case, inasmuch as no claim was made against him"). However, even where Caro accepted Maimonides' version, he introduced a number of stylistic changes. For example, the *Mishneh Torah* (and the *Turim*) state that "it is unknown" or "he does not know" who the victim was, while the *Shulḥan Arukh* adopts the formulation "but he does not know from which one he stole." Similarly, the *Mishneh Torah* states, "as neither was aware that anything of his had been stolen; rather, it was the thief who volunteered the information," whereas the *Shulḥan Arukh* reads: "since they would not have been aware that anything of theirs had been stolen if he had not informed them." What is the reason for this stylistic change, which does not result in a more concise statement of the law (except, perhaps, in the second example)? As will be seen below, this kind of redrafting by Caro is not infrequent, and further study is necessary in order to clarify the reasons for it.

In one instance, the *Mishneh Torah* and the *Shulḥan Arukh* are more concise than the *Turim*. The *Turim* includes the case, omitted from the *Mishneh Torah* and *Shulḥan Arukh*, of the thief who steals one hundred coins from one person and two hundred coins from another.[14] In another instance, however, it is the *Shulḥan Arukh* that adds an example which appears to be unnecessary. The last part of the

13. *See supra* pp. 1211–1214.

14. This case is included in the glosses of Rema to Sh. Ar., *ad loc.* Similarly, Caro's formulation "even though there are no witnesses to the theft" is briefer than that of the *Turim*: "Maimonides has written that [this law applies] even though there are no witnesses to the theft." The *Turim*, as it generally does, reviews the various opinions, while the *Shulḥan Arukh*, in general, cites only the view in accordance with which it rules. Here, the style of the *Shulḥan Arukh* follows Maimonides.

second paragraph in the *Shulḥan Arukh* ("But if two [persons] make claim against one [person] . . .) does not appear to add anything new,[15] and it is not found in either the *Mishneh Torah* or the *Turim*.

EXAMPLE 2

MISHNEH TORAH[16]

12. [If] one leases a field from his fellow[17] and it was not productive,[18] [then] if it has the capability of producing enough to yield [the value of] two *seahs* after expenses, the lessee is obligated to work it, for he writes as follows to the owner of the land: "I will arise and plow, sow, reap, sheave, thresh, winnow, and place heaps before you, and you will take half of it (or whatever [share] they agree to), and I will take the re-

TURIM[19]

[If] one leases a field from his fellow and desires to rescind because it [the field] is of poor quality, [then] if it is capable of yielding [the value of] two *seahs* after all expenses, he may not rescind, but if not, he may rescind.[20] . . . [If] he did not work it, but let it lie fallow, an estimate is made of how much it could have yielded if he had worked it, and he pays him according to their agreement, for he writes as follows to him: "If I let it lie

SHULḤAN ARUKH[21]

1. [If] one leases a field from his fellow and it was not productive, [then] if it has the capability of producing enough to yield [the value of] two *seahs* after expenses, the lessee is obligated to work it, for he writes as follows to the owner of the land: "I will arise and sow, etc., and place heaps before you, and you will take your share, etc."[22]

2. [If] he did not work it but let it lie fallow, in whole or in part, an estimate is

15. *See* Sema to Sh. Ar., *ad loc.*, subpar. 5: "This is not in the *Tur* or the *Mishneh Torah*. . . . It is a redundancy, for he [Caro] already included this law in paragraph 1." *See also Be'ur ha-Gra, ad loc.*, subpar. 4. It should be noted that the current printed eds. are identical to eds. Venice 1565, 1567, and 1574 (both printings).

For a further discussion of the law in this example, and its implications for the relationship between law and morals in the Jewish legal system, *see supra* pp. 148–149.

16. *MT*, Sekhirut 8:12–13.

17. The reference here is to a sharecropping arrangement, whereby the lessee works the field and obligates himself to give a portion of the produce (*i.e*, one-half, one-third, or one-quarter) to the owner. This differs from an ordinary lease, pursuant to which the lessee pays the lessor a fixed sum as rent. The rules contained in these quoted passages all relate solely to sharecropping agreements, for in ordinary lease agreements, the owner of the land always receives the fixed sum agreed upon by both parties. The sources of paragraph 12 are M Bava Meẓi'a 9:5 and TB Bava Meẓi'a 105a; *see* Rashi to M Bava Meẓi'a, *ad loc.*

18. *I.e.*, the yield was low, and the sharecropper did not want to harvest it.

19. *Tur* ḤM ch. 328.

20. The quoted passage continues: "This rule applies only in the case of a sharecropping arrangement, but in the case of an ordinary lease, even if the field is entirely unproductive, he [the lessee] must pay the rent." This is based on Rashi, Bava Meẓi'a 105a. Maimonides undoubtedly accepted this proviso (*see supra* n. 17), but simply saw no need to make a point of it.

21. Sh. Ar. ḤM 328:1–2.

22. Rema adds in his glosses: "Even if he did not write such a provision, it is considered as if he had done so." This is the view of many *rishonim*, and from the end of the discussions of the subject by Maimonides, the *Turim*, and the *Shulḥan Arukh*, it can be inferred that they too would apply this principle to the second rule.

MISHNEH TORAH

mainder as payment for my work and expenses."

13. [If] one leases a field from his fellow, and after he acquired it[23] he lets it lie fallow,[24] an estimate is made of how much it could have yielded, and he [the lessee] gives him [the lessor] the share to which he was entitled, for he writes as follows to the owner of the land: "If I let it lie fallow and do not work it, I will pay according to its choicest yield."[25] The same rule applies if he let [only] a portion of the land lie fallow. Why is he liable to pay? Because he did not undertake to pay a sum certain that [was large enough so that it] could be said to be equivalent to *asmakhta* [*i.e.*, lacking deliberate and unqualified intent to be bound];[26] rather, he agreed to pay according to the choicest yield of the field and therefore had deliberate and unqualified intent, and entered into a binding obligation. How-

TURIM

fallow and do not work it, I will pay you[27] according to its choicest yield." However, if he wrote him, "If I let it lie fallow and do not work it, I will pay you 1,000 *zuzim*," it is *asmakhta* and is ineffective; it is as if he had not written him [such an undertaking], and he pays him [his share] based on the productive capability [of the land].

SHULḤAN ARUKH

made of how much it could have yielded, and he [the lessee] gives him [the lessor] the share to which he [the lessor] was entitled. However, if he agreed with him: "If I let it lie fallow and do not work it,[28] I will pay 1,000 *zuz*," this is *asmakhta* and he is not obligated to pay [the stipulated amount]; rather, he [the lessor] gives [the owner of the land] only [an amount] based on the productive capability [of the land].

23. *I.e.*, the sharecropping agreement was formalized by an act of acquisition (*kinyan*). The sources of paragraph 13 are M Bava Meẓi'a 9:3 and TB Bava Meẓi'a 104a/b.

24. The owner, who was supposed to receive a portion of the produce as rent, would therefore suffer a loss, since he would not be paid anything.

25. In ed. Rome, 1480, the Aramaic word for "according to its choicest yield," *be-meitvah*, ends with the letter *he*, rather than with an *aleph*, as it appears in other eds. *See also Dikdukei Soferim*, Bava Meẓi'a 104a/b, Letter *pe*.

26. If he had agreed to pay a definite, disproportionately high sum, bearing no relationship to the extent of the actual damage to the owner of the field, the agreement would be impaired by *asmakhta*, *i.e.*, a lack of deliberate and unqualified intent to be bound. (The lessee would have been confident that the condition set forth in the agreement—his failure to work the field—would not occur; he therefore was prepared to say that he would pay any sum requested, without seriously contemplating the consequence of his undertaking.)

27. In eds. Cremona, 1558 and Sabbioneta, 1559, the reading is *lo* ("him") rather than *lakh* ("you").

28. In eds. Venice 1565, 1567, and 1574, the term used for "work it" is *e'evod* (rather than *a'avid*, which appears in other eds.). Except for this variant reading (and the one mentioned *supra* n. 27), eds. Venice 1565, 1567, and 1574 are identical to the current printed versions.

MISHNEH TORAH	*TURIM*	*SHULḤAN ARUKH*
ever, if he said, "If I let it lie fallow and do not work it, I will give you one hundred *dinarim*," this is *asmakhta* and he is not obligated to pay [the stipulated amount]; rather, he need give [the owner of the land] only [his share] based on the productive capability [of the land].		

This example also has a number of interesting aspects. The version of Maimonides is taken, with stylistic changes, from its sources in the Mishnah, the *baraita*, and the Talmud.[29] In this example, Maimonides—contrary to his general practice—leaves part of the agreement in the original Aramaic rather than translating the entire agreement into Hebrew.[30] The version of the *Turim* is very different from that of the *Mishneh Torah*. Instead of the original Hebrew phrase (found in the Mishnah and the *baraita* and adopted by Maimonides) "and it was not productive," the *Turim* substitutes its own lengthier expression: "and desires to rescind because it is of poor quality." Similarly, the *Turim* continues, "if it is capable of yielding [the value of] two *seahs* after all expenses, he may not rescind, but if not, he may rescind," while Maimonides reads more succinctly: "if it has the capability of producing enough to yield [the value of] two *seahs* after expenses, the lessee is obligated to work it." Maimonides' formulation follows the version of the Mishnah and the *baraita*. On the other hand, the *Turim* is more terse in omitting the explanation "I will arise and plow, etc." in the first rule (although it does include the explanation "If I let it lie fallow, etc." in its formulation of the second rule!).[31] The *Turim* is also more succinct at the beginning of the second rule in that, unlike Maimonides, it does not repeat the introductory phrase, "[if] one leases a field from his fellow." Rather, the *Turim* begins by saying directly: "[If] he did not work it, but let it lie fallow . . . ." Moreover, the *Turim* omits entirely the passage in

29. *See supra* nn. 17, 23.

30. Maimonides' practice in this regard is not uniform. Maimonides states in Aramaic the condition "if I let it lie fallow and do not work it, I will pay according to its choicest yield" (the term for "work it" should, apparently, be *a'avid* [which is Aramaic] rather than *e'evod* [which is Hebrew]; ed. Rome, 1480, has *a'avid*). The Aramaic text of this condition had become accepted by the people; apparently, therefore, it was included in the Mishnah in its original Aramaic version. This may possibly explain why Maimonides also stated it in Aramaic. By contrast, the condition set forth in paragraph 12 has been translated into Hebrew, based on the Aramaic version which appears in the *baraita* quoted in TB Bava Meẓi'a 105a (it appears that the condition is part of the *baraita*, not an addition by the *amoraim*). However, even here, the first word of the condition, "I," is retained by Maimonides in the original Aramaic (*ana*). Another example where Maimonides retained a word in the original Aramaic is *MT*, Malveh ve-Loveh 25:9. The matter of the use of Aramaic in the *Mishneh Torah* requires further study and research.

31. Actually, the explanation is not needed. The point is not that such a condition was actually included in the agreement in the particular case; rather, this condition was customary and accepted, so that it implicitly became part of the agreement even if not stated explicitly. *See supra* n. 22 and commentators, *ad loc.*

middle of paragraph 13 of the *Mishneh Torah*—"Why is he liable to pay? Because he . . . had deliberate and unqualified intent, and entered into a binding obligation"—since this passage does not prescribe a legal rule but merely provides the reason for the law.[32]

In the second rule, the *Turim* states the hypothetical case of an agreement to pay 1,000 *zuzim*, which was the sum stated in the case discussed in the Talmud.[33] By contrast, Maimonides speaks of 100 *dinarim*, an amount not mentioned in the Talmud.

In general, Caro adopts the style of Maimonides rather than that of the *Turim*, *e.g.*, "it was not productive,"[34] "if it is has the capability of producing enough[35] to yield [the value of] two *seahs* after expenses, the lessee is obligated to work it," etc. In the first rule, Caro includes Maimonides' explanation "for he writes as follows to the owner of the land," although he quotes only the introductory words, apparently relying on the full text set forth in the *Mishneh Torah*.[36] (In the second rule, Caro completely omits the explanation "for he writes as follows to the owner of the land," although the *Turim* includes it and Caro himself includes it in his formulation of the first rule. The reason for this has not been ascertained.) In the interest of brevity, Caro, like the *Turim*, omits the beginning of Maimonides' second rule ("[If] one leases a field from his fellow") and the passage in the middle of that rule ("Why is he liable to pay?").

It is also interesting how Caro retained the substance of the law in the *Mishneh Torah* that "the same rule applies if he let a portion of the land lie fallow." Caro nicely incorporated this rule, which is based on the incident related in the Talmud, into the beginning of the second rule: "[If] he did not work it but let it lie fallow, in whole or in part." Similarly, Caro, like the *Turim*, states the hypothetical amount of 1,000 *zuzim*—the amount set forth in the Talmudic discussion—rather than one hundred *dinarim*, given by Maimonides. However, the *Turim* sets forth the amount in Aramaic (*alfa zuzei*), whereas Caro gives it in Hebrew (*elef zuz*).[37]

32. The *Turim* also omits the statement of the *Mishneh Torah* that "the same rule applies if he let [only] a portion of the land lie fallow," apparently on the theory that this was obvious and did not add anything. Maimonides included the statement because the issue was mentioned in the Talmudic discussion between Rava and the Nehardeans in TB Bava Meẓi'a 104b. For Caro's approach to this issue, *see infra*.

33. TB Bava Meẓi'a 104b.

34. The heading of Sh. Ar. ḤM ch. 328 reflects the language of the *Turim*: "The Law of a Sharecropper Who Desires to Rescind Because of the Poor Quality of the Field."

35. The *Shulḥan Arukh* (printed eds., and also eds. Venice 1565, 1567, and 1574) uses the phrase *kedei lehoẓi* (lit., "the capability of producing"); in the Mishneh Torah, the phrase *kedei she-toẓi* (lit., "a capability such that it will produce") appears. Why did Caro make this type of small change? This matter requires comprehensive study. *See also infra* Example 3.

36. The reliance must be on the *Mishneh Torah*, for the *Turim* does not include this condition at all. It is possible that this abbreviated version of the condition, ending with "etc.," was added by the printer, not by Caro. The matter requires further study and clarification.

37. Similarly, Caro omits the clause "it is as if he had not written him [such an undertaking]." This clause states nothing more than what is obvious without it. *See also supra* n. 22.

EXAMPLE 3

***MISHNEH TORAH*[38]**

1. [If] one lends money to his fellow, and after the loan was made, a person said to him, "I stand surety"; or if he sued the borrower in court, and another person said to him, "Leave [him alone], and I [will] stand surety"; or if he was strangling his fellow in the marketplace to make him pay his debt, and he said to him, "Leave [him alone], and I [will] stand surety," the surety has no liability whatever. [This is so] even if he said "I [will] stand surety" in the presence of a court. But if there was a formal act of acquisition signifying his acceptance of suretyship for this debt, then [in] all of these circumstances—whether the act took place before a court or between the surety and the lender—he is legally bound.

2. [If] he said to him at the time the money was transferred, "Lend to him, and I [will] stand surety," then the surety is legally bound, and no *kinyan* [formal act of acquisition] is required. Similarly, if he was made a surety by the court, he is legally bound even if there was no formal act of acquisition. For example, if the court desired to collect [the debt] from the debtor, and he said to them, "Leave him alone, and I [will] stand surety [for him] to you,"

***TURIM*[39]**

One who stands surety for his fellow is bound by Torah law, even in the absence of a *kinyan*. When is this so? When he agrees to become a surety at the time that the money is transferred. [In such a case], even if he bound himself with language of *asmakhta* [*i.e.*, that did not signify a deliberate and unqualified intent to become a surety, such as] "if so-and-so will not pay you, I will pay you," he is obligated: because of the benefit he derives from the fact that he [the lender] trusted him, he [the surety] had a deliberate and unqualified intent and agreed to be bound, even if the debtor has no assets.[40] But if, after he lent him the money, he said, "I stand surety"; or if someone was strangling his fellow to make him pay his debt, and he said to him [the creditor], "Leave him alone, and I will give it to you"; or if the creditor demanded that the debtor pay his debt, and he [the person undertaking to be a surety] said to him, "Leave him alone, and I [will] stand surety to you"—in all these cases, he becomes bound only by a *kinyan*. But a surety of a court does not require a *kinyan*. It would seem that the term "a surety of a court" refers to someone who undertakes to become a surety in the pres-

***SHULḤAN ARUKH*[41]**

1. [If] one lends money to his fellow, and after the loan was made, another person said to him, "I stand surety"; or if he sued the borrower in court, and another person said to him, "Leave [him alone], and I [will] stand surety"; or if he was strangling his fellow in the marketplace to make him pay his debt, and he said to him, "Leave [him alone], and I [will] stand surety," the surety has no liability whatever. [This is so] even if he said in the presence of a court, "I [will] stand surety." But if there was a formal act of acquisition signifying his acceptance of suretyship for this debt, whether the act took place before a court or between the surety and the lender, he is legally bound.

2. [If] he said to them at the time the money was transferred, "Lend to him, and I [will] stand surety," then the surety is legally bound, and no *kinyan* [formal act of acquisition] is required. Similarly, if he was made a surety by the court, he is legally bound even if there was no formal act of acquisition. For example, if the court desired to collect [the debt] from the debtor, and he said to them, "Leave him alone, and I [will] stand surety [for him] to you," then since he derives benefit

38. *MT*, Malveh ve-Loveh 25:1–2.
39. *Tur* ḤM ch. 129.
40. *See* TB Bava Batra 173b.
41. Sh. Ar. ḤM 129:1–2.

MISHNEH TORAH	*TURIM*	*SHULḤAN ARUKH*
then since he derives benefit from the fact that he was trusted by the court, he became legally bound by reason of that benefit.	ence of the court. But Maimonides has written that even if he states in the presence of a court "I stand surety," he does not become bound unless the court desired to collect [the debt] from the debtor, and he said to them, "Leave him alone, and I will give it to them or be responsible to you." [In such a case], since he derives benefit from the fact that he was trusted by the court, he becomes legally bound by reason of that benefit.	from the fact that he was trusted by the court, he became legally bound by reason of that benefit.

In this example, the *Turim* sets forth the same laws contained in the *Mishneh Torah* concerning the distinction between suretyship created at the time of the loan and suretyship created at a later time, with regard to the requirement of a *kinyan* (formal act of acquisition), and the matter of "a surety in the presence of the court" or "a surety for the court."[42] The style of the *Turim*, however, is completely different. The *Turim* adds clarifications and rationales concerning the concept of *asmakhta* and, in a discursive style, cites an alternate view by name ("It would seem that . . . But Maimonides has written . . . ").

Caro sets forth the same laws, but returns to the clear and plain style of the *Mishneh Torah*, which he quotes with insignificant stylistic variances.[43] The *Mishneh Torah* states "and after the loan was made, *a person* said to him," while the *Shulḥan Arukh* instead reads "*another person* said to him."[44] The *Mishneh Torah* states "even if he said 'I [will] stand surety' in the presence of a court," whereas the *Shulḥan Arukh* reverses the order: "even if he said in the presence of a court, 'I [will] stand surety.'" The *Mishneh Torah* includes the phrase "then [in] all of these circumstances," whereas the *Shulḥan Arukh* does not contain this phrase. At the end of the second paragraph, Maimonides uses the word *haniyyah* (instead of the more common word *hana'ah*) to signify "benefit," whereas the *Shulḥan Arukh* uses *hana'ah*.[45] What is the reason for these stylistic changes that have no substantive significance? Caro obviously modeled his version of these two laws on the *Mishneh*

42. *See* TB Bava Batra 173b, 176a/b.

43. These stylistic variances are found even in eds. Venice 1565, 1567, 1574, etc.

44. This particular variance can easily be explained as a copyist's or printer's error. In the Hebrew, the *Mishneh Torah* reads *eḥad* ("one [person]"), whereas the *Shulḥan Arukh* reads *aḥer* ("another"). The only difference between the two words in the unvocalized Hebrew is that the last letter changes from a *dalet* to a *resh*, and both letters are very similarly shaped.

45. Both the *Mishneh Torah* (including ed. Rome, 1480) and the *Shulḥan Arukh* do, however, use the word *hana'ah* in the previous clause, "since he derives benefit."

Torah; why, then, did he deliberately introduce these changes, as well as similar changes in other instances, of which there are more than a few?[46] Perhaps they may be explained by changes in Hebrew style that took place during the four centuries between Maimonides and Caro. The question requires further study and clarification. Indeed, the entire subject of the stylistic similarities and differences between the three central codificatory works of Jewish law—the *Mishneh Torah*, the *Turim*, and the *Shulḥan Arukh*—still awaits thorough analysis.

46. *See* the two previous examples in Appendix B, and the examples set forth *supra* pp. 1327–1340.

APPENDIX C[1]
A LISTING OF THE SOME OF THE BEST-KNOWN COLLECTIONS OF RESPONSA

INTRODUCTION

For the convenience of the interested reader, we include here a list of some of the best-known collections of responsa. The present work has frequently cited or quoted responsa from these important collections, which are widely used in research into Jewish law.[2] The list begins with the most significant collections from the geonic period, and continues with collections of responsa of the *rishonim* and the *aḥaronim*, classified according to the geographical center and the century in which the particular respondent's activity was primarily concentrated.[3] It should always be borne in mind that many halakhic authorities were active in different geographical centers during various periods in their lives. The list includes the name of the collection and of the author and, if the collection is divided into parts, the list will often indicate the number of parts or volumes in the collection.[4]

For additional details regarding the authors and their works, the chapters in which the responsa are discussed should be consulted.[5] It should also be noted that

1. This appendix relates to Chapter 39 *supra*.

2. For a discussion of *Kunteres ha-Teshuvot*, a listing of compilations of responsa by Boaz Cohen, *see supra* pp. 1524, 1562.

3. The Institute for Research in Jewish Law of the Hebrew University in Jerusalem has undertaken the preparation of digests to the responsa literature of the period of the *rishonim* (the eleventh to the sixteenth centuries), organized according to the geographical areas of the respondents. The first digest to appear was the *Digest of the Responsa Literature of Spain and North Africa*, which will consist of seven volumes, of which five have been published to date: two volumes of the *Legal Digest* (1986); two volumes of the *Historical Digest* (1981, 1986); and one volume of the *Index of Sources* (1981). The Institute is now engaged in the preparation of a digest of the responsa originating in Germany, Provence, Italy, and the other centers of the Jewish diaspora. For a detailed discussion of these digests, *see supra* pp. 1525–1528.

4. Sometimes, a collection will print as a single responsum several responsa that were sent together in answer to a group of questions. Thus, there may be more responsa actually contained in a given collection than are indicated by the numbering in the book.

5. *See* the Subject Index *infra*, under the name of the author and the name of the book. In general, the list in this Appendix does not set forth the various editions, the dates

the collections often do not include all of the author's responsa, many of which may be scattered in other works of his contemporaries or of later authorities. Moreover, a significant number of responsa by some halakhic authorities have been lost and are no longer extant. On the other hand, the presence of a particular responsum in a certain collection does not establish that the responsum was actually written by the halakhic authority to whom the collection attributes it. Often, collections include responsa by other halakhic authorities, whether or not they are identified as the authors of those responsa. For a detailed discussion, *see* Chapter 39 *supra*.[6]

THE GEONIC PERIOD

1. *Halakhot Pesukot min ha-Geonim [Halakhic Rulings of the* Geonim*]*. This earliest printed collection of geonic responsa was first published in 1516 in Constantinople. It was reprinted in 1893 by Joel Müller, together with a commentary and index, and a facsimile copy of the 1893 edition was published in Jerusalem in 1967.
2. *She'elot u-Teshuvot ha-Geonim [Geonic Responsa]*. This volume was first published in Constantinople in 1575, and was reprinted in Vilna in 1884 with a commentary by Mordecai Eliyahu Rabinowitz. A facsimile copy of the Vilna edition was published in Jerusalem in 1960.
3. *Sha'arei Ẓedek [Gates of Righteousness]*. First published in 1792 by Ḥayyim Moda'i; reprinted, Jerusalem, 1966.
4. *Teshuvot ha-Geonim Sha'arei Teshuvah [Geonic Responsa Gates of Response]*. These volumes were first published in Salonika in 1802, with notes by David Luria. They were reprinted in Leipzig in 1858, and a facsimile copy of this second printing was published in Jerusalem (undated), with notes by Zev Wolf Leiter (New York, 1946). I.M. Ḥazzan wrote a commentary on vol. 1 of this collection, entitled *Iyyei ha-Yam* [Islands of the Sea] (Leghorn, 1869).
5. *Teshuvot Geonim Kadmonim [Responsa of Early* Geonim*]*. These responsa were arranged by Joseph Tov Elem, and were published by David Cassel (Berlin, 1848). They were reprinted in Tel Aviv (undated).
6. *Ḥemdah Genuzah [Hidden Treasure]*. Printed in Jerusalem, 1863; reprinted, 1967.
7. *Teshuvot ha-Geonim [Geonic Responsa]*. Published by Jacob Musaphia (Lyck, 1864); reprinted in Jerusalem, 1967.

---

of publication, etc. These may be found in the various bibliographical works; *see supra* pp. 1560–1564. The names of the editors and the places of publication have been included when this information is customarily used to identify the particular book. This is often the case with regard to the geonic responsa, as well as sometimes with regard to responsa from later periods, especially when the book has been edited relatively recently, with an introduction and explanatory notes.

6. *See supra* pp. 1453–1528; in particular, pp. 1501–1523.

8. *Teshuvot ha-Geonim [Geonic Responsa]*. Published by Nahman Nathan Koronel (Vienna, 1871); reprinted in Jerusalem, 1967.
9. *Toratan Shel Rishonim [The Teachings of the Early Sages]* (two volumes), published by Chaim Meir Horovitz, Frankfurt-am-Main, 1882. This work also includes geonic responsa.
10. *Teshuvot ha-Geonim [Geonic Responsa]*. Published by Avraham Eliyahu Harkavy (as part of *Zikkaron la-Rishonim* [In Memory of the Early Ones], Berlin, 1887). Reprinted in Jerusalem, 1966 (*see also infra*: The Eleventh Century—*Resp. Alfasi*).
11. *Teshuvot Ge'onei Mizraḥ u-Ma'arav [Responsa of* Geonim *from the East and the West]*. Published by Joel Müller, Berlin, 1888. Reprinted in Jerusalem, 1967, together with *Halakhot Pesukot min ha-Geonim*.
12. *Ginzei Yerushalayim [The Treasures of Jerusalem]*. Published by Solomon Aaron Wertheimer, Jerusalem, 1896.
13. *Kohelet Shelomo [The Collection of Solomon]*. Published by Solomon Aaron Wertheimer, Jerusalem, 1899.
14. *She'elot u-Teshuvot ha-Geonim min ha-Genizah [Geonica]*. Published by Louis Ginzberg, New York, 1909.
15. *Sefer Ge'on ha-Geonim*. Published by Solomon Aaron Wertheimer, Jerusalem, 1925.
16. *Teshuvot ha-Geonim [Geonic Responsa], I,* published by Simḥah Assaf (in *Kovez̩ Madda'ei ha-Yahadut*, II), Jerusalem, 1927.
17. *Teshuvot ha-Geonim, II,* published by Simḥah Assaf, Jerusalem, 1929.
18. *Teshuvot ha-Geonim,* published by Abraham Marmorstein in the periodical *Oz̩ar ha-Ḥayyim*, 1928; reprinted, Jerusalem, 1968.
19. *Ginzei Schechter [Schechter's* Genizah *Manuscripts],* vol. II, published by Louis Ginzberg, New York, 1929.
20. *Mi-Sifrut ha-Geonim [Selections from the Geonic Literature],* published by Simḥah Assaf, Jerusalem, 1933.
21. *Teshuvot ha-Geonim min ha-Genizah [Geonic Responsa from the* Genizah*],* published by Simḥah Assaf, Jerusalem, 1942; reprinted, Jerusalem, 1971.

Mafte'aḥ li-Teshuvot ha-Geonim [Index to Geonic Responsa], by Joel Müller, Berlin, 1891, includes an index to the first eleven collections of responsa listed above. The index is arranged by subject matter and names of the respondents. With regard to *Oz̩ar ha-Geonim* [A Geonic Treasury], which contains a large number of geonic responsa, *see supra* pp. 1114, 1472–1473.

THE ELEVENTH CENTURY

Germany

1. *Resp. Rabbenu Gershom Me'or ha-Golah,* published by Solomon Eidelberg, New York, 1956.

France

2. *Resp. Rashi,* published by I.S. Elfenbein, New York, 1943; reprinted, Jerusalem, 1967 (two volumes).
3. *Resp. Ḥakhmei Ẓarfat ve-Lutir [Responsa of the Halakhic Authorities of France and Lotharingia (Lorraine)],* published by Joel Müller, Vienna, 1881; reprinted, Jerusalem, 1967 (this work includes responsa from the early halakhic authorities of Germany and France).
4. *Ma'aseh ha-Geonim [The Work of the Great Halakhic Authorities],* published by Abraham Epstein, Berlin, 1910. This work includes responsa of Rashi and of the halakhic authorities of the communities of "Shum" (Speyer, Worms, and Mainz).

Spain

5. *Die Responsen der Spanischen Lehrer des 10 Jahrhunderts, R. Mose, R. Chanoch, R. Joseph ibn Abitur* [*The Responsa of the Spanish Teachers of the Tenth Century, Rabbi Moses, Rabbi Hanokh, and Rabbi Joseph b. Abitur*], *Siebenter Bericht über die Lehranstalt für die Wissenschaft des Judentums in Berlin* [*Seventh Report of the Berlin Institute for the Science of Judaism*], published by Joel Müller, Berlin, 1889, s. 3–37. *See also Teshuvot Ge'onei Mizraḥ u-Ma'arav [Responsa of* Geonim *from the East and the West],* published by Joel Müller, Berlin, 1888, sections 163 *et seq.*
6. The most important compilations of the responsa of Isaac (b. Jacob) ha-Kohen Alfasi (Rif, or Alfasi) are:
   a. *Resp. Alfasi,* Leghorn, 1781; reprinted, Pittsburgh, 1955, with notes by Zev Wolf Leiter. This compilation includes some of Alfasi's responsa which are also found in the Harkavy and Bilgoraj compilations (see below). *See also* the v.l. to Alfasi's responsa included as an appendix to *Teshuvot Ḥakhmei Provinẓiyah* [Responsa of the Halakhic Authorities of Provence], *infra* (Thirteenth Century).
   b. *Teshuvot ha-Geonim [Geonic Responsa].* Published by Avraham Eliyahu Harkavy (*see supra,* The Geonic Period, No. 10). This collection includes nearly 200 responsa of Alfasi, some of which are also found in the Leiter and Bilgoraj compilations.
   c. *Resp. Alfasi,* published by Ze'ev Byednowitz, Bilgoraj, 1925. The responsa included in this collection are also found in the Leiter and Harkavy compilations.

Responsa of Alfasi may also be found in *Ḥemdah Genuzah* [Hidden Treasure] (*supra,* The Geonic Period, No. 6), sections 144–159; and in various sections of *Koveẓ Teshuvot ha-Rambam* [Resp. Maimonides], Leipzig, 1859.

THE TWELFTH CENTURY

Germany

1. ***Sefer Even ha-Ezer, by Raban*** (Eliezer [b. Nathan] of Mainz). This book, which includes novellae, halakhic rulings, and responsa, is also known as *Ẓofenat Pa'ane'aḥ* [Revealer of Secrets]. A scientific edition of this book was published by Shalom Albeck (Warsaw, 1905), up to section 337 (the end of the laws of *niddah;* also included is a ruling on the subject of *kilayim*). Sections 318 *et seq.* were published by Aryeh Leib Raskas, Jerusalem, 1913–1915, with explanations and notes. The book was also published together with the commentary *Even Shelomo* by Solomon Zalman Ehrenreich in Simluel-Silvaniei, Romania in 1926. This edition was recently reprinted in facsimile (*see also supra* p. 1179).
2. ***Sefer ha-Raviah,*** by Eliezer (b. Joel) ha-Levi. This book likewise includes novellae, halakhic rulings, and responsa (*see also supra* pp. 1238–1239 regarding Raviah's responsa).

France

3. ***Sefer ha-Yashar,*** by Rabbenu Tam (Jacob [b. Meir] Tam). The first part of this book contains novellae, and the second, responsa. The second part was published in Germany, 1898, by S.P. Rosenthal.
4. ***Resp. Rabi Av Bet Din,*** by Abraham (b. Isaac), who headed the rabbinic court in Narbonne in southern France, and is also known as Rabad II (R. Abraham, Av Bet Din). Some of his responsa were published by Simḥah Assaf in his *Sifran Shel Rishonim,* Jerusalem, 1935. A more comprehensive collection of his responsa was published by Joseph Kafaḥ, Jerusalem, 1962.
5. ***Sefer Temim De'im,*** by Rabad (Abraham [b. David] of Posquières in Provence), the author of the critical glosses on Maimonides' *Mishneh Torah.* The edition published in 1812 is complete; the edition of 1896 is missing a number of the responsa. The most recent compilation of Rabad's responsa is *Rabad, Teshuvot u-Pesakim* [Rabad: Responsa and Halakhic Rulings], published by Joseph Kafaḥ, Jerusalem, 1964.

Spain

6. ***Resp. Ri Migash,*** by Joseph (b. Meir) ha-Levi ibn Migash. Responsa of Ri Migash may also be found in various sections of *Resp. Maimonides,* Leipzig, 1859.
7. ***Resp. Maimonides,*** by Moses b. Maimon. Various editions of Maimonides' responsa have been published; two are noted here:
   a. ***Resp. Maimonides,*** ed. A.H. Freimann, Jerusalem, 1934.
   b. ***Resp. Maimonides,*** ed. J. Blau, 3 vols., Jerusalem, 1958–1961. This edition is the most complete available, and includes virtually all of Maimonides' extant responsa.

THE THIRTEENTH CENTURY

Germany

1. ***Resp. Maharam of Rothenburg,*** by Meir (b. Baruch) of Rothenburg. There are five compilations of Maharam of Rothenburg's responsa. Each compilation contains different responsa (a few responsa appear in more than one compilation). In order to differentiate between the compilations, each one is referred to by the name of the city where it was first published (or, occasionally, by the name of the editor), as follows:
   a. ***Resp. Maharam of Rothenburg,*** ed. Cremona, 1557.
   b. ***Resp. Maharam of Rothenburg,*** ed. Prague, 1608.
   c. ***Resp. Maraham of Rothenburg,*** ed. Lemberg, 1860 (ed. R.N.N. Rabinowitz).
   d. ***Resp. Maharam of Rothenburg,*** ed. Berlin, 1891 (ed. M.A. Bloch).
   e. ***Resp. Or Zaru'a and Maharam of Rothenburg,*** ed. I.Z. Kahane, *Sinai,* vols. 8–13 (reprinted separately, Jerusalem, 1943).

   The first four volumes have been reprinted in facsimile.

   Three volumes of a scientific edition of the responsa of Maharam of Rothenburg, entitled *Teshuvot, Pesakim u-Minhagim* [Responsa, Halakhic Rulings, and Customs], were published in 1957–1963 by Mosad ha-Rav Kook (ed. I.Z. Kahane). Since Kahane's death, the work has remained unfinished. This edition is arranged according to the order of the *Shulḥan Arukh*. The three volumes which have appeared deal with the matters covered in the *Oraḥ Ḥayyim* and *Yoreh De'ah* sections.
2. ***Teshuvot Ba'alei ha-Tosafot [Responsa of the Tosafists],*** ed. I.A. Agus, New York, 1954. The Tosafists wrote many responsa in the twelfth and thirteenth centuries. Many of these responsa are scattered throughout various books; some are still in manuscript; and others have been lost altogether. Agus's book includes 135 responsa by the Tosafists.
3. ***Resp. Or Zaru'a and Maharam of Rothenburg*** (*see* No. 1(e) *supra*). This volume includes the responsa of Isaac b. Moses, author of *Or Zaru'a*. His responsa are also found in his book *Or Zaru'a,* which includes novellae, halakhic rulings, and responsa (*see supra* p. 1241).
4. ***Resp. Maharaḥ Or Zaru'a,*** by Ḥayyim b. Isaac Or Zaru'a, son of the author of *Or Zaru'a*.

Spain

5. ***Or Ẓadikkim*** [***Light of the Righteous***], which includes responsa by Meir (b. Todros ha-Levi) Abulafia (Ramah). Sixty-nine of Ramah's extant responsa (#240–#308) are found in *Or Ẓaddikim,* which also includes halakhic and aggadic material from other halakhic authorities.
6. ***Sifran Shel Rishonim,*** published by Simḥah Assaf, Jerusalem, 1935, which contains responsa of Naḥmanides (Moses b. Naḥman). Only a few of Naḥmanides' responsa are extant (the responsa contained in *Resp. Attributed to Naḥ-*

manides are largely those of Rashba). Some of Naḥmanides' responsa are also found in *Sefer ha-Terumot* by Samuel Sardi.

7. ***Resp. Rashba,*** by Solomon (b. Abraham) Adret. *Resp. Rashba* have been published in seven parts; each part is separately numbered (the second part is also known as *Toledot Adam*). In addition, most of the responsa in *Resp. Attributed to Naḥmanides* are those of Rashba.

Germany—Spain

8. ***Resp. Asheri,*** by Asher b. Jehiel. The book is divided into 108 *kelalim* (principles), each of which contains responsa dealing with the same general area of the law. *Ḥazeh ha-Tenufah* by Moses Brosilis includes an abridgement of 64 additional responsa of Asheri. *Resp. Asheri* was reprinted in Jerusalem, 1971. *See also* E.E. Urbach, "She'elot u-Teshuvot ha-Rosh be-Kitvei Yad u-vi-Defusim" [Responsa of Asheri in Manuscript and in Print], *Shenaton*, II (1975), pp. 1ff.

Italy

9. ***Resp. Rid,*** by Isaiah (b. Mali) of Trani I (also known as the Elder, to distinguish him from his grandson Riaz, also known as Isaiah the Latter), published by Abraham Joseph Wertheimer, Jerusalem, 1967.

Egypt

10. ***Resp. Avraham b. ha-Rambam,*** published by A.H. Freimann, Jerusalem, 1938. Another compilation of the responsa of Abraham son of Maimonides, entitled *Birkat Avraham,* was published in Lyck, 1870.

France

11. ***Teshuvot Ḥakhmei Provinẓiyah*** *[Responsa of the Halakhic Authorities of Provence],* by Abraham Sofer, Jerusalem, 1967.

THE FOURTEENTH CENTURY

Spain

1. ***Resp. Ritba,*** by Yom Tov (b. Abraham) Ishbili, published by Joseph Kafaḥ, Jerusalem, 1959.
2. ***Resp. Zikhron Yehudah,*** by Judah (b. Asher), son of Asheri.
3. ***Resp. Ran,*** by Nissim (b. Reuben) Gerondi.

4. *Resp. Ribash,* by Isaac (b. Sheshet) Perfet. In 1901, David Fraenkel published a book entitled *Resp. Ribash ha-Ḥadashot* [The New Responsa of Ribash]; however, it appears that most of the responsa included in this book are not those of Ribash.

Italy

5. *Piskei ve-Shut Recanati [Halakhic Rulings and Responsa of Recanati],* by Menahem (b. Benjamin) of Recanati.

Egypt—Syria

6. *Resp. Yehoshua (b. Avraham) ha-Nagid,* a descendant of Maimonides, published by A.H. Freimann, *Kovez̤ al Yad,* New Series, vol. 3 (13), 1940; reprinted, Jerusalem, 1971.

THE FIFTEENTH CENTURY

Germany

1. *Resp. Maharil* (also known as *Resp. Mahari Segal*), by Jacob (b. Moses) ha-Levi Moellin. *Resp. Maharil* was published by Isaac Satz, Makhon Yerushalayim, 1980, based on manuscripts and printed sources. Earlier, in 1977, Satz had published *Resp. Maharil ha-Ḥadashot* [The New Responsa of Maharil].
2. *Terumat ha-Deshen,* by Israel (b. Petaḥiah) Isserlein, also known as Maharya or Maharai. This work consists of two parts: the first contains 354 responsa (the numerical value [*gematria*] of 354 is the same as that of the word *deshen*; hence, the name *Terumat ha-Deshen*); the second contains 267 responsa, and is known as *Pesakim u-Khetavim.* The responsa of Israel Isserlein are also found in *Leket Yosher* (by Joseph [b. Moses], a student of Isserlein), which contains Isserlein's customs, halakhic rulings, and responsa. *Leket Yosher,* which consists of two parts—*Oraḥ Ḥayyim* and *Yoreh De'ah*—was published by Jacob Freimann, Berlin, 1903–1904.
3. *Resp. Maharyu,* by Jacob (b. Judah) Weil.
4. *Resp. Mahari mi-Bruna,* by Israel (b. Ḥayyim) Bruna (of Brünn, Moravia).
5. *Resp. Maharam Mintz,* by Moses (b. Isaac) Mintz.

Italy

6. *Resp. Maharik,* by Joseph (b. Solomon) Colon. In 1970, in Jerusalem, Eliyahu Pines published *Shut u-Fiskei Maharik ha-Ḥadashim* [The New Responsa and Halakhic Rulings of Maharik].

7. *Resp. Mahari Minẓ,* by Judah (b. Eliezer) ha-Levi Minẓ. Most of Mahari's responsa were burnt during wars, and only a few have been preserved. These were published with the responsa of his son's son-in-law, Maharam of Padua (*see infra,* The Sixteenth Century).

North Africa

8. *Resp. Tashbeẓ,* by Simeon (b. Ẓemaḥ) Duran, of Spain and Algeria. (The acronym *Tashbeẓ* comes from the initial letters of *Teshuvot Shim'on b. Ẓemaḥ* [Responsa of Simeon b. Ẓemaḥ].) The work is divided into three parts. Printed versions of *Sefer Tashbeẓ* also contain a fourth part, entitled *Ha-Ḥut ha-Meshullash,* which contains responsa of three other halakhic authorities. "The First Row" [*Ha-Tur ha-Rishon*] of this part includes the responsa of Solomon (b. Ẓemaḥ) Duran ("the Latter Rashbeẓ"), a halakhic authority in Algeria in the second half of the sixteenth century, who was of the sixth generation down the line from Simeon b. Ẓemaḥ Duran. "The Second Row" [*Ha-Tur ha-Sheni*] contains responsa by Solomon Ẓeror; and "The Third Row" [*Ha-Tur ha-Shelishi*] contains responsa by Abraham (b. Jacob) ibn Tava. Ẓeror and Tava were also halakhic authorities in Algiers and Tunis in the second half of the sixteenth century (*see* H.Z. Hirschberg, *Toledot ha-Yehudim be-Afrikah ha-Ẓefonit* [The History of the Jews in North Africa], II, pp. 44, 155–156).
9. *Resp. Rashbash,* by Solomon (b. Simeon) Duran, son of Rashbeẓ.
10. *Yakhin u-Vo'az,* by Ẓemaḥ (b. Solomon) Duran, son of Rashbash. This book also contains the responsa of Ẓemaḥ's brother Simeon (b. Solomon) Duran.

THE SIXTEENTH CENTURY

The Land of Israel

1. *Resp. Mahari Berab,* by Jacob (b. Moses) Berab.
2. *Resp. Maharalbaḥ,* by Levi (b. Jacob) ibn Ḥabib.
3. *Resp. Bet Yosef,* by Joseph (b. Ephraim) Caro; this collection includes responsa on matters covered in *Even ha-Ezer.* Another collection of Caro's responsa is *Avkat Rokhel,* which includes responsa covering all areas of Jewish law, including *mishpat ivri.*
4. *Resp. Mabit,* by Moses (b. Joseph) of Trani. The book is divided into two parts (in various editions, the second part is subdivided into two sections).
5. *Resp. Maraham Alshekh (Resp. R. Moshe Alshekh),* by Moses (b. Ḥayyim) Alshekh.
6. *Resp. R. Yom Tov Ẓahalon,* by Yom Tov (b. Akiva) Ẓahalon. In 1951, Ẓahalon's responsa to the community of Eana were published by Meir Benayahu in Jerusalem. In 1980–1981, two volumes entitled *Resp. Maharit Ẓahalon ha-*

Ḥadashot [The New Responsa of R. Yom Tom Ẓahalon] were published by Makhon Yerushalayim.

Egypt

7. *Resp. R. Beẓalel Ashkenazi,* by Beẓalel (b. Abraham) Ashkenazi.
8. *Resp. Maharam Alashkar,* by Moses (b. Isaac) Alashkar.
9. *Resp. Radbaz,* by David (b. Solomon) ibn Zimra (seven parts).
10. *Resp. Oholei Ya'akov,* by Jacob (b. Abraham) Castro (known as Maharikash).
11. *Resp. Maharam Gavison,* by Meir Gavison; published by Makhon Yerushalayim, Jerusalem, 1985 (ed. Eliav Shochetman).

Turkey and the Balkan Countries

There were many important respondents in Turkey and the Balkan countries; therefore, the respondents are listed according to the place of their primary activity (some respondents were active in more than one place):

CONSTANTINOPLE

12. *Resp. Elijah Mizraḥi (Resp. Re'em),* by Elijah (b. Abraham) Mizraḥi. This collection includes only Mizraḥi's responsa. Another collection, entitled *Resp. Mayim Amukkim,* includes both Mizraḥi's responsa and, in a separate section, the responsa of Ranaḥ (*see infra* No. 14).
13. *Resp. Maharibal,* by Joseph (b. David) ibn Lev. This collection is divided into four parts. The first comprises ten principles (*kelalim*); each principle includes various responsa to questions in the same general legal area.
14. *Resp. Ranaḥ,* by Elijah b. Ḥayyim. Additional responsa of Ranaḥ are included in *Resp. Mayim Amukkim,* the first part of which contains responsa of Elijah Mizraḥi (*supra* No. 12), and the second, the responsa of Ranaḥ.

SALONIKA

15. *Resp. Maharashdam,* by Samuel (b. Moses) de Medina (these responsa are organized according to the order of the *Turim*).
16. *Resp. Maharshakh,* by Solomon (b. Abraham) Cohen (four parts).
17. *Resp. Divrei Rivot,* by Isaac (b. Samuel) Adarbi.
18. *Resp. Torat Emet,* by Aaron (b. Joseph) Sasson (Mahara Sasson).
19. *Resp. Leḥem Rav,* by Abraham (b. Moses) di Boton.
20. *Resp. Mekor Barukh,* by Baruch (b. Solomon) Kalai.
21. *Resp. Benei Shemu'el,* by Samuel (b. Isaac) Ḥayon.

GREECE

22. ***Resp. Binyamin Ze'ev,*** by Benjamin Ze'ev (b. Mattityahu), who served as head of the religious court and the *yeshivah* in Arta, Greece. The book is divided into 28 parts, each dealing with a particular subject area.

CORFU

23. ***Resp. Radakh,*** by David (b. Ḥayyim) ha-Kohen (also known as Mahardakh). This book is divided into 30 sections, called *battim* (lit., "houses"), each of which is subdivided into *ḥadarim* (lit., "rooms").

Italy

24. ***Resp. Maharam of Padua,*** by Meir (b. Isaac) Katzenellenbogen. These responsa are printed together with those of the father of his father-in-law, Mahari Minẓ (*see supra,* The Fifteenth Century, No. 7).
25. ***Resp. Rama of Fano,*** by Menahem Azariah (b. Isaac Berakhiah) de Fano, of Mantua.
26. ***Resp. R. Yiẓḥak (b. Emanuel) mi-Litash,*** by Isaac (b. Emanuel) de Lattes, of Bologna and Ferrara.

North Africa

27. ***Ha-Ḥut ha-Meshullash,*** by Solomon (b. Ẓemaḥ) Duran (sixth generation after Rashbeẓ), Solomon Ẓeror, and Abraham (b. Jacob) ibn Tava. The book is printed together with *Resp. Tashbeẓ* (*see supra,* The Fifteenth Century, No. 8, regarding *Resp. Tashbeẓ*).

Poland

28. ***Resp. Rema,*** by Moses (b. Israel) Isserles. A new edition was published in 1971 by Asher Siev.
29. ***Resp. Maharshal,*** by Solomon (b. Jehiel) Luria.
30. ***Resp. Maharam mi-Lublin*** **(also known as *Manhir Einei Ḥakhamim*),** by Meir (b. Gedaliah) of Lublin.
31. ***Resp. She'erit Yosef,*** by Joseph (b. Mordecai Gershon) Katz.
32. ***Resp. Ge'onei Vatra'ei,*** which includes responsa by Joshua Falk (b. Alexander) Katz. *See also infra,* The Seventeenth Century, No. 1.
33. ***Resp. Massat Binyamin,*** by Benjamin Aaron (b. Abraham) Slonik.

THE SEVENTEENTH CENTURY

Poland and Germany

1. ***Resp. Baḥ; Resp. Baḥ ha-Ḥadashot*** (two collections), by Joel (b. Samuel Jaffe) Sirkes (known as Baḥ after the initials of *Bayit Ḥadash,* his commentary on the *Turim*). Some of Sirkes's responsa are included in *Resp. Ge'onei Vatra'ei* (*see supra,* The Sixteenth Century, No. 32).
2. ***Resp. Ẓemaḥ Ẓedek,*** by Menahem Mendel (b. Abraham) Krochmal.
3. ***Resp. Emunat Shemu'el,*** by Aaron Samuel (b. Israel) Koidenover (Maharshak).
4. ***Resp. Keneset Yeḥezkel,*** by Ezekiel (b. Abraham) Katzenellenbogen.
5. ***Resp. Avodat ha-Gershuni,*** by Gershon (b. Isaac) Ashkenazi.
6. ***Resp. Penei Yehoshu'a,*** by Joshua (b. Joseph) of Cracow. (This book is to be distinguished from the book of novellae on the Talmud, also known as *Penei Yehoshu'a,* written by the grandson of Joshua of Cracow's daughter, and also from another work entitled *Resp. Penei Yehoshu'a* written in the seventeenth century by a halakhic authority in Salonika, *see infra* Nos. 28–29.)
7. ***Resp. Eitan ha-Ezraḥi,*** by Abraham (b. Israel Jehiel) ha-Kohen Rapaport.
8. ***Resp. Ḥavvot Ya'ir,*** by Jair Ḥayyim (b. Moses Samson) Bacharach. Additional responsa of Bacharach are found in *Ḥut ha-Shani,* which also contains responsa by his father and grandfather.
9. ***Resp. Ḥakham Ẓevi,*** by Ẓevi (b. Jacob) Ashkenazi. This book was so named because Ashkenazi also studied with the Sephardic halakhic authorities in Salonika and Constantinople, and received the honorary title *Ḥakham,* the Sephardic equivalent of "Rabbi."
10. ***Resp. Me'il Ẓedakah,*** by Jonah (b. Elijah) Landsofer.

Turkey and the Balkan Countries

CONSTANTINOPLE

11. ***Resp. Ri (R. Jehiel) Basan,*** by Jehiel (b. Ḥayyim) Bassan.
12. ***Resp. Maharit* (also known as *Maharimet*),** by Joseph (b. Moses) Trani. The book is divided into two parts (three, in some editions), and the responsa are numbered separately for each of the four *Turim* according to which the responsa are grouped. In 1978, a new edition, entitled *Teshuvot u-Fiskei Maharit ha-Ḥadashim* [The New Responsa and Rulings of Maharit], was published by Makhon Yerushalayim, Jerusalem.
13. ***Resp. Penei Moshe,*** by Moses (b. Nissim) Benveniste (three parts).
14. ***Resp. Lev Same'aḥ* (vol. 2),** by Abraham (b. Solomon) Alegre.
15. ***Resp. Muẓal me-Esh,*** by Jacob (b. Ḥayyim) Alfandari. This collection was edited by the author's nephew Ḥayyim (b. Isaac Raphael) Alfandari, and is printed together with *Esh Dat* by Ḥayyim Alfandari (which is also printed separately).

IZMIR (SMYRNA)

16. ***Resp. Mahari Escapa,*** by Joseph (b. Saul) Escapa.
17. ***Resp. Ba'ei Ḥayyei,*** by Ḥayyim (b. Israel) Benveniste.
18. ***Resp. Benei Aharon,*** by Aaron (b. Isaac) Lapapa.

SALONIKA

19. ***Resp. Torat Ḥayyim,*** by Ḥayyim Shabbetai. The book consists of three parts which deal, respectively, with matters covered in *Oraḥ Ḥayyim, Yoreh De'ah* and *Ḥoshen Mishpat*. Responsa on matters of family law are contained in another book, entitled *Sefer She'elot u-Teshuvot be-Dinei Tur Even ha-Ezer* [The Book of Responsa on Matters Dealt with in *Tur Even ha-Ezer*] (*see also infra* No. 31 with regard to the book *Kerem Shelomo*).
20. ***Resp. Magen Gibborim,*** by Daniel Estrosa.
21. ***Resp. Bet Shelomo,*** by Solomon (b. Aaron) ibn Ḥason (*see also* No. 22 *infra*).
22. ***Resp. Mishpatim Yesharim,*** which includes additional responsa by Solomon ibn Ḥason, as well as responsa by Samuel (b. Eli) Gaon.
23. ***Resp. Shai la-Mora,*** by Shabbetai (b. Jonah) ha-Kohen.
24. ***Resp. Mahari ha-Levi,*** by Jacob (b. Israel) of the House of Levi.
25. ***Resp. Barukh Angil,*** by Baruch Angel.
26. ***Resp. Paraḥ Matteh Aharon,*** by Aaron (b. Ḥayyim) Peraḥiah ha-Kohen.
27. ***Resp. Torat Ḥesed,*** by Ḥasdei (b. Samuel) Peraḥiah ha-Kohen.

28 and 29. ***Resp. Shenei ha-Me'orot ha-Gedolim [Responsa of the Two Great Luminaries],*** which contains two parts. The first, entitled *Aderet Eliyahu,* contains responsa by Elijah (b. Judah) Covo (Kovo); the second, entitled *Penei Yehoshu'a,* contains responsa by Joshua (b. Joseph) Handali.

30. ***Resp. Sam Ḥayyai,*** by Ḥayyim (b. Benjamin) Asael. Some of the author's responsa are found in *Zera Avraham,* by Abraham Yiẓḥaki (*see infra* No. 35).
31. ***Resp. Kerem Shelomo,*** by Solomon (b. Joseph) Amarillo. Additional responsa by Amarillo are included at the end of the third part of *Torat Ḥayyim,* by Ḥayyim Shabbetai (*see supra* No. 19).
32. ***Resp. Giv'ot Olam,*** by Joseph (b. Shemaiah) Covo (Kovo).

Land of Israel

33. ***Resp. Halakhot Ketannot,*** by Israel Jacob (b. Samuel) Ḥagiz (two parts).
34. ***Resp. Kol Gadol; Resp. Devar Sha'ul,*** by Moses (b. Solomon) ibn Ḥabib, whose book *Get Pashut* is arranged according to the laws relating to divorces in the *Shulḥan Arukh*.
35. ***Resp. Zera Avraham,*** by Abraham (b. David) Yiẓḥaki (two parts).

Egypt

36. *Resp. Darkhei No'am,* by Mordecai (b. Judah) ha-Levi.
37. *Resp. Ginat Veradim,* by Abraham (b. Mordecai) ha-Levi.
38. *Resp. Matteh Yosef,* by Joseph (b. Moses) ha-Levi Nazir (two parts).

North Africa

39. *Resp. Ohel Ya'akov,* by Jacob (b. Aaron) Sasportas, who was the rabbi of various communities in Algeria and Morocco. Because of persecution by the secular authorities, he left North Africa and became the Rabbi of Amsterdam, and of other communities in Europe.

Italy

40. *Resp. ha-Ramaz,* by Moses (b. Mordecai) Zacuto.
41. *Resp. Ziknei Yehudah,* by Judah Aryeh (b. Isaac) Modena; the book was published in 1956 by S. Simonson in Jerusalem.
42. *Resp. Devar Shemu'el,* by Samuel (b. Abraham) Aboab.
43. *Resp. Be'er Sheva,* by Issachar Ber (b. Israel Leizer) Parnas.

THE EIGHTEENTH CENTURY

Germany and Poland

1. *Resp. Shevut Ya'akov,* by Jacob (b. Joseph) Reicher (three parts).
2. *Resp. Panim Me'irot,* by Meir (b. Isaac) Eisenstadt (three parts).
3. *Resp. She'elat Ya'veẓ,* by Jacob (b. Ẓevi) Emden (two parts).
4. *Resp. Noda bi-Yehudah,* by Ezekiel (b. Judah ha-Levi) Landau. *Resp. Noda bi-Yehudah* is extant in two "versions"—*Mahadura Kamma* (the first version) and *Mahadura Tinyana* (the second version). Each "version" contains different responsa (the term "*mahadura*" is not used here in its currently accepted sense of "edition").
5. *Resp. Zikhron Yosef,* by Joseph (b. Menahem) Steinhardt.
6. *Resp. Or Yisra'el,* by Israel (b. Eliezer) Lipschuetz.
7. *Resp. Nish'al David,* by David Oppenheim, published in three parts by Makhon Ḥatam Sofer, Jerusalem, 1975.

Land of Israel

8. *Resp. Neḥpeh be-Khesef,* by Jonah (b. Ḥanun) Navon (two parts).
9. *Resp. Shetei ha-Lehem,* by Moses (b. Jacob) Ḥagiz (known as Mani'aḥ).

10. *Resp. Ḥayyim le-Olam,* by Ḥayyim Modai.
11. *Resp. Admat Kodesh,* by Moses (b. Joseph) Mizraḥi.
12. *Resp. Sedeh ha-Areẓ,* by Abraham (b. Samuel) Meyuḥas.
13. *Resp. Simḥat Yom Tov,* by Yom Tov (b. Israel Jacob) Algazi.
14. *Resp. Maharam ben Ḥabib,* by Moses ben Ḥabib.

Italy

15. *Resp. Shemesh Ẓedakah,* by Samson (b. Joshua Moses) Morpurgo.
16. *Resp. Mayim Rabbim,* by Raphael (b. Eleazar) Meldola.
17. *Resp. Mikhtam le-David,* by David (b. Jacob) Pardo (Radaf).
18. *Resp. Torat Shelamim,* by Isaiah (b. Israel Hezekiah) Bassano. The book is published in two parts; the second part is known as *Laḥmei Todah.*

Land of Israel—Italy

19. *Resp. Ḥayyim Sha'al; Resp. Yosef Omeẓ; Resp. Tov Ayin,* by Ḥayyim Joseph David (b. Isaac Zeraḥiah) Azulai (Ḥida).

Turkey and the Balkan Countries

SALONIKA

20. *Resp. Matteh Asher,* by Asher (b. Emanuel) Shalem.
21. *Resp. Devar Moshe,* by Moses (b. Solomon) Amarillo.
22. *Resp. Bet David,* by Joseph David.
23. *Resp. Be'erot ha-Mayim,* by Isaac (b. Elijah) Shanji.
24. *Resp. Rosh Mashbir,* by Joseph Samuel Modigliano.
25. *Resp. Tal Orot,* by Joseph ibn Goya.

CONSTANTINOPLE

26. *Resp. Divrei Emet,* by Isaac Bekhor b. David.
27. *Resp. Maḥaneh Efrayim,* by Ephraim (b. Aaron) Navon.

IZMIR (SMYRNA)

28. *Battei Kehunah,* by Isaac (b. Judah) ha-Kohen Rapaport; a section of this book is known as *Bet Din.*
29. *Resp. Ḥikrei Lev,* by Raphael Joseph (b. Ḥayyim) Ḥazzan (seven parts).

Rhodes

30. *Resp. Massat Moshe,* by Moses (b. Abraham) Israel (three parts).
31. *Resp. Kol Eliyahu; Resp. Uggat Eliyahu,* by Elijah (b. Moses) Israel.

Babylonia

32. *Resp. Ẓedakah u-Mishpat,* by Ẓedakah (b. Saadiah) Ḥoẓin.

North Africa

33. *Resp. Bet Yehudah; Resp. Benei Yehuda* **(vol. 2),** by Judah (b. Isaac) Ayash.
34. *Resp. Mishpat u-Ẓedakah be-Ya'akov,* by Jacob (b. Reuben) ibn Ẓur.
35. *Resp. Mishpatim Yesharim; Resp. Torot Emet,* by Raphael (b. Mordecai) Birdugo.

Yemen

36. *Resp. Pe'ullat Ẓaddik,* by Yeḥaiah (b. Joseph) Ẓalaḥ (Saliḥ) (known as Mahariẓ). The first part was published in 1947; parts 2 and 3 were published in 1965.
37. *Resp. Revid ha-Zahav*—up to chapter 26, by David (b. Solomon) Misraki (Mizraḥi); published in Tel Aviv, 1955; chapter 26 *et seq.*, by Yeḥaiah (b. David) Misraki (Mizraḥi).

THE NINETEENTH CENTURY

Germany

1. *Resp. Teshuvah me-Ahavah,* by Eliezer (b. David) Fleckeles (three parts).
2. *Resp. Har ha-Mor; Resp. Parashat Mordekhai,* by Mordecai (b. Abraham) Banet.
3. *Resp. R. Akiva Eger,* by Akiva (b. Moses) Eger. Other collections of Eger's responsa which have been published include *Teshuvot Rabbi Akiva Eger Mahadura Tinyana* [Responsa of R. Akiva Eger, Second Edition]; *Teshuvot ve-Ḥiddushei Rabbi Akiva Eger he-Ḥadash* [The New Responsa and Novellae of R. Akiva Eger]; and *Teshuvot Rabbi Akiva Eger mi-Khetav Yad* [Responsa of R. Akiva Eger from Manuscript].
4. *Resp. R. Azriel,* by Azriel (b. Aryeh Leib) Hildesheimer (published in Tel Aviv, 1969).
5. *Resp. Matteh Levi,* by Mordecai Horowitz (two parts).
6. *Resp. Yad ha-Levi,* by Isaac Dov ha-Levi Bamberger (published in Jerusalem, 1965).
7. *Resp. Binyan Ẓiyyon,* by Jacob Ettlinger.

Hungary

8. *Resp. Ḥatam Sofer,* by Moses (b. Samuel) Sofer (Schreiber) (six parts). Other responsa of Sofer are contained in *Likkutei Teshuvot Ḥatam Sofer* [Collected Responsa of Ḥatam Sofer].

9. *Resp. Ketav Sofer,* by Abraham Samuel Benjamin (b. Moses) Sofer.
10. *Resp. Yehudah Ya'aleh,* by Judah (b. Israel) Aszod (Aszud) (two parts).
11. *Resp. Ḥatan Sofer,* by Samuel (b. David Ẓevi) Ehrenfeld.
12. *Resp. Maharam Schick,* by Moses Schick (two volumes).
13. *Resp. Maḥaneh Ḥayyim,* by Ḥayyim Sofer (eight parts).

Galicia

14. *Resp. Bet Efrayim,* by Ephraim Zalman (b. Menahem Mannes) Margolis (Margolioth).
15. *Resp. Shenot Ḥayyim* (2 vols.); *Resp. Ha-Elef Lekha Shelomo; Resp. Tuv Ta'am ve-Da'at; Resp. Kin'at Soferim,* by Solomon (b. Judah Aaron) Kluger.
16. *Resp. Sho'el u-Meshiv,* by Joseph Saul (b. Aryeh Leibush) Nathanson; the book contains six "editions" (*i.e.,* parts); each "edition" contains different responsa.
17. *Resp. Divrei Ḥayyim,* by Ḥayyim (b. Aryeh Leibush) Halberstamm (the Hasidic Rebbi of Zanz).
18. *Resp. Bet Yiẓḥak,* by Isaac Judah (b. Ḥayyim Samuel) Schmelkes (seven parts).
19. *Resp. Maharsham,* by Shalom Mordecai (b. Moses) ha-Kohen Schwadron (six parts).
20. *Resp. Yeshu'ot Ya'akov,* by Jacob Meshullam (b. Mordecai Ze'ev) Ornstein.
21. *Resp. Maharaẓ Chajes,* by Ẓevi Hirsch (b. Meir) Chajes.

(Russian) Poland and Lithuania

22. *Resp. ha-Rim,* by Isaac Meir (b. Israel) Alter (the Hasidic Rebbi of Gur).
23. *Resp. Avnei Nezer,* by Abraham (b. Ze'ev Nahum) Bornstein (the Hasidic Rebbi of Sochaczew) (seven parts).
24. *Resp. Meshiv Davar,* by Naftali Ẓevi Judah (b. Jacob) Berlin (Neẓiv) (two parts).
25. *Resp. Ẓemaḥ Ẓedek,* by Menahem Mendel (b. Sholom Shakhna) Schneerson (the Lubavitcher Rebbi) (four parts).
26. *Resp. Be'er Yiẓḥak; Resp. Ein Yiẓḥak* (2 vols.), by Isaac Elhanan (b. Israel Isser) Spektor.
27. *Ḥikrei Halakhah u-She'elot u-Teshuvot.* The book contains responsa by Samuel (b. Judah) Mohilewer.
28. *Resp. Aderet Eliyahu,* by Elijah Gutmacher (published in Jerusalem, 1984, two volumes).

Turkey and the Balkan Countries

IZMIR (SMYRNA)

29. *Resp. Ḥayyim ve-Shalom* (2 vols.); *Resp. Ḥikekei Lev* (3 parts); *Resp. Ḥukkot ha-Ḥayyim; Resp. Semikhah le-Ḥayyim; Resp. Ḥayyim be-Yad; Resp. Lev Ḥayyim,* by Ḥayyim (b. Jacob) Palache.

30. *Resp. Nediv Lev,* by Ḥayyim David (b. Joseph) Ḥazzan (two parts). Ḥazzan immigrated to the Land of Israel, where he was chosen as *ḥakham bashi* (the title of the Chief Rabbi in the Ottoman period).

SALONIKA

31. *Resp. Be'er ha-Mayim,* by Raphael Jacob (b. Abraham) Manasseh.
32. *Resp. Sha'ar Asher,* by Raphael Asher (b. Jacob) Covo (Kovo) (two parts).
33. *Resp. Ẓel ha-Kesef,* by Abraham Ḥayyim Benveniste Gatigno.
34. *Resp. Divrei Shemuel,* by Raphael Samuel Arditi.

Land of Israel

35. *Resp. Kappei Aharon,* by Aaron (b. Conforte) Azriel.
36. *Resp. Yisa Ish; Resp. Sha'al ha-Ish; Resp. Moshe ha-Ish; Resp. Ma'aseh ha-Ish; Resp. Olat Ish; Resp. Simḥah la-Ish,* by Jacob Saul (b. Eliezer Jeroham) Elyashar (the acronym "Yisa" stands for Ya'akov Sha'ul Elyashar; the acronym "Ish" stands for Elyashar Ya'akov Sha'ul).
37. *Resp. ha-Ridbaz,* by Jacob David (b. Ze'ev) Willowksi.
38. *Resp. Zayit Ra'anan,* by Moses Judah Leib (b. Benjamin) Zilberberg (two parts).
39. *Resp. Maharil Diskin,* by Moses Joshua Judah (b. Benjamin) Diskin.

Egypt

40. *Resp. Ta'alumot ha-Lev,* by Elijah (b. Abraham) Ḥazzan (four parts).
41. *Resp. U-Maẓor Devash,* by Raphael Aaron b. Simeon.

North Africa

42. *Resp. Kerem Ḥemer,* by Abraham (b. Mordecai) Ankawa (two parts).
43. *Resp. Le-Yiẓḥak Rei'aḥ,* by Isaac (b. Samuel) Abendanan.

Iraq (Babylonia)

44. *Resp. Rav Pa'alim,* by Joseph Ḥayyim (four volumes).

Yemen

45. *Resp. Ḥayyei Shalom,* by Yeḥaiah b. Shalom ha-Kohen, (published in manuscript form, Jerusalem, 1982). The book is published as an appendix to *Keẓ ha-Mizbe'aḥ* by Ḥayyim Kasaer.
46. *Resp. Ḥen Tov,* by Yeḥaiah Badache (published in Jerusalem, 1970).
47. *Resp. Shoshanat ha-Melekh,* by Shalom Ḥabshush. This book is an abridgment

of *Resp. Pe'ullat Ẓaddik* (*see supra,* The Eighteenth Century, No. 36); it was published by S. Geridi, Jerusalem, 1967.

48. *Resp. R. Yeḥaiah Kafaḥ,* a compilation of his responsa from manuscript by his grandson, Joseph Kafaḥ.

THE TWENTIETH CENTURY

Galicia

1. *Resp. Maharash Engel,* by Samuel (b. Ze'ev Wolf) Engel (eight parts).
2. *Resp. Radad,* by David Dov (b. Aryeh Judah Jacob) Meisels (two parts).
3. *Resp. Ḥedvat Ya'akov,* by Aryeh Judah Jacob (b. David Dov) Meisels.
4. *Resp. Ẓevi la-Ẓaddik,* by Ẓevi Elimelech (b. David) Shapira.
5. *Resp. Maḥazeh Avraham,* by Abraham Menahem (b. Meir) ha-Levi Steinberg (two parts).
6. *Resp. Harei Besamim,* by Aryeh Loeb (b. Isaac) ha-Levi Ish-Horowitz (three volumes).
7. *Resp. Imrei Yosher,* by Meir (b. Aaron Judah) Arik (two parts).
8. *Resp. Dovev Meisharim,* by Dov Berish (b. Jacob) Weidenfeld (three parts).

Russia, Poland, Lithuania, Romania, and Germany

9. *Resp. Edut be-Ya'akov,* by Isaac Jacob (b. Solomon Naphtali) Reines.
10. *Resp. Aḥi'ezer,* by Ḥayyim Ozer (b. Solomon) Grodzinski (three parts).
11. *Resp. Ẓafenat Pa'ane'aḥ,* by Joseph (b. Ephraim Fishel) Rosen (the Rogachover) (three parts).
12. *Resp. Gevul Yehudah; Resp. Aẓei ha-Levanon; Resp. Lev Yehudah,* by Judah (b. Moses Ḥayyim) Ẓirelson.
13. *Resp. Minḥat Eleazar,* by Eleazar (b. Ẓevi Hirsch) Shapiro (three parts).
14. *Resp. Or ha-Me'ir,* by Judah Meir (b. Jacob Samson) Shapiro.
15. *Resp. Abir Ya'akov,* by Jacob (b. Abraham Issachar Ber) Avigdor.
16. *Resp. Malamed Leho'il,* by David Ẓevi Hoffmann (three parts).
17. *Resp. Divrei Malki'el,* by Malkiel Tannenbaum (seven parts).
18. *Resp. Levush Mordekhai,* by Mordecai Winkler (three parts).

The Balkan Countries

19. *Resp. Ḥoshen ha-Efod,* by David (b. Abraham) Pipano.

North Africa

20. *Resp. To'afot Re'em,* by Raphael (b. Mordecai) Ankawa.

Western Europe (after the Holocaust) and Responsa from the Holocaust

21. *Resp. Seridei Esh,* by Jehiel Jacob (b. Moses) Weinberg (four parts).
22. *Resp. Ḥelkat Ya'akov,* by Mordecai Jacob (b. Ḥayyim) Breisch (two parts).
23. *Resp. Ohel Moshe,* by Moses Jonah (b. Meir) ha-Levi Zweig (two parts).
24. *Resp. Minḥat Yiẓḥak,* by Isaac Jacob (b. Joseph Judah) Weiss; as of 1986, nine parts were published.
25. *Resp. Me-Emek ha-Bakha; Resp. Mi-Gei ha-Haregah,* by Simeon (b. Yekutiel) Ephrati.
26. *Resp. Mi-Ma'amakkim,* by Ephraim (b. Dov) Oshry.

United States

27. *Resp. Iggerot Moshe,* by Moses (b. David) Feinstein (seven parts).

Land of Israel and State of Israel

28. *Resp. Mishpat Kohen; Resp. Da'at Kohen; Resp. Ezrat Kohen; Resp. Oraḥ Mishpat,* by Abraham Isaac (b. Solomon Zalman) ha-Kohen Kook.
29. *Resp. She'erit Yisra'el,* by Israel Ze'ev Mintzberg.
30. *Resp. Har Ẓevi,* by Ẓevi Pesaḥ (b. Judah Leib) Frank (three parts).
31. *Resp. Mishpetei Uziel,* by Ben Zion Meir Ḥai (b. Joseph Raphael) Uziel (six parts).
32. *Resp. Heikhal Yiẓḥak,* by Isaac (b. Joel Aryeh) Halevi Herzog (three parts).
33. *Resp. Yaskil Avdi,* by Ovadiah Hadayah (eight parts).
34. *Resp. Bet Zevul,* by Jacob Moses (b. Zevulun) Charlap (five parts).
35. *Resp. Kol Mevasser,* by Meshullam (b. Simeon) Rath (two parts).
36. *Resp. Ẓiẓ Eliezer,* by Eliezer Judah (b. Jacob Gedaliah) Waldenberg (fifteen parts).
37. *Resp. Yabi'a Omer* (six parts); *Resp. Yeḥavveh Da'at* (six parts), by Ovadiah (b. Jacob) Yosef.
38. *Resp. Devar Yehoshu'a,* by Joshua Menahem (b. Isaac Aryeh) Ehrenberg.
39. *Resp. Bet Mordekhai,* by Mordecai (b. Menahem Nahum) Fogelman.
40. *Resp. Mekor Ḥayyim,* by Ḥayyim David (b. Moses) Halevi (three parts).
41. *Resp. Divrei Ḥakhamim,* by Shalom Y. ha-Levi (Jerusalem, 1972).
42. *Resp. Dover Shalom,* by Solomon Tovim (Yihud, 1973).
43. *Resp. Ha-Ḥayyim ve-ha-Shalom,* by Ḥayyim Kasaer (Jerusalem, 1982) (published as an appendix to *Keẓ ha-Mizbe'aḥ* by the same author).
44. *Resp. Zikhronei Ish,* by Abraham Nidaf (part 2 of *Anaf ha-Ḥayyim*) (Jerusalem, 1981).
45. *Resp. le-R. Shalom Z.I. Avigad [Responsa of Shalom Z.I. Avigad],* on the laws of *eruvin* (1968–1970).
46. *Resp. le-R. Ḥozeh Saadiah ben Yefet [Responsa of Hozeh Saadiah b. Japheth], Sefer Toledot R. Shalom Shabazi,* Jerusalem, 1973, pp. 147–176.

GLOSSARY

aggadah ("telling") the non-halakhic, non-normative portion of the *Torah she-be-al peh* consisting of historical, philosophical, allegorical, and ethical rabbinic teachings

aginut the state of being an *agunah*

agoria, *pl.* **agoriot** non-Jewish court

agunah ("anchored" or "bound") a woman unable to remarry because she is "bound," *e.g.*, to a husband who has disappeared and cannot be legally proved dead or who has abandoned her or who refuses to divorce her

aḥarei rabbim le-hattot "follow the majority" of a court or of legislative representatives

aḥaronim ("later ones") later halakhic authorities, generally referring to those from the sixteenth century onward. *See also rishonim*

am ha'areẓ ("people of the land") (1) national council; (2) hoi polloi; (3) ignorant, unlearned person; (4) a person not punctilious in observance, opposite of *ḥaver* and *ḥasid;* (5) the assembled public

amora, *pl.* **amoraim** (1) rabbis of the Talmudic period (220 C.E. to end of the fifth century C.E.); (2) *meturgeman,* which *see*

Anshei Keneset ha-Gedolah ("Men of the Great Assembly") Ezra, Nehemiah, and those who entered with them into the covenant to observe the laws of the Torah after the return of the Babylonian exiles. The Great Assembly was the supreme institution of the Jewish people during the time it was active, from the latter half of the fifth century B.C.E.

arba'ah shomerim ("four bailees") the four types of bailees in Jewish law—the unpaid bailee (*shomer ḥinam),* the borrower (*sho'el*), the paid bailee (*shomer sakhar*) and the hirer (*sokher*)

arev kabbelan one who has undertaken to be a surety by a declaration that entitles the creditor to look to him for payment without first pursuing a claim against the principal debtor

arka'ot (shel goyim) non-Jewish courts

arvit evening prayer

asharta judicial "certification" that a legal document has been properly authenticated

asmakhta ("something to lean on," "supportive device") (1) an action or transaction without an unqualified and deliberate intention to take the action or enter into the transaction; (2) a transaction involving a penalty or forfeiture; (3) exegesis identified by the Sages as integrative, not creative; (4) according to some, a strained and far-fetched (symbolic and figurative) exegesis that is necessarily only integrative

avak ribbit ("dust of interest") any form of benefit (other than actual stipulated interest) received by a lender that exceeds the value of the money or property lent; it is not expressly prohibited by the Torah, but is rabbinically proscribed because it partakes of the nature of interest

av bet din ("father of the court") (1) one of the two national leaders during the period of the *Zugot;* (2) presiding judge

avot nezikin ("fathers of damages") primary categories of causes of damage, namely, "ox" "pit," "grazing animal," and "fire." *See bor, mav'eh,* and *shor*

Bagaẓ acronym for *Bet Din Gavo'ah le-Ẓedek,* which *see*

bal tigra ("you shall not take away") the prohibition (Deut. 4:2, 13:1) against taking away from any commandments (*miẓvot*) set forth in the Torah; antonym of *bal tosif*

bal tosif ("you shall not add") the prohibition (Deut. 4:2, 13:1) against adding to the commandments (*miẓvot*) set forth in the Torah

baraita, ***pl.*** **baraitot** tannaitic *dictum* not included in the Mishnah (capitalized if referred to collectively)

be-di-avad ("after the fact," ***ex post*****)** usually employed in connection with the question whether an act in violation of a prohibition is not only a transgression but also without legal effect. *See also le-khateḥillah*

bein adam la-Makom ("between man and God") (1) involving human relationships with God; (2) pertaining to "religious" law as distinguished from civil law; (3) pertaining to matters of private conscience

bein adam le-ḥavero ("between a person and his fellow") (1) involving relationships between people; (2) pertaining to civil as distinguished from "religious" law

berurim ("selected ones," "arbiters") (1) members of the community council; (2) representatives for enacting legislation; (3) arbitrators selected by the parties; (4) lay judges; (5) communal leaders

bet din, ***pl.*** **battei din ("house of law")** (1) a court or panel of judges who adjudicate in accordance with the *Halakhah;* (2) a Jewish arbitral tribunal

Bet Din Gavo'ah le-Ẓedek "The High Court of Justice," the capacity in which the Supreme Court of Israel sits as a court of original jurisdiction to review administrative or governmental action claimed to be arbitrary or in excess of jurisdiction

bet din shel hedyotot ("a court of ordinary people") (1) a court lacking a rabbinic judge who is ordained; (2) a court composed entirely of laymen not knowledgeable in the law

Corpus Juris (Civile) ("Body of the [Civil] Law") (1) The Code of Justinian; (2) a comprehensive legal code that has achieved ultimate authoritative status

corpus juris the total body of law in a given legal system

darkhei shalom ("the ways of peace") the social and religious interest in peace and tranquillity

darshan (1) "exegete"; (2) preacher, homilist

dat (1) religious faith; (2) law, particularly law based on custom; (3) established practice

dayyan ("judge") a judge according to the *Halakhah;* a judge of a rabbinical court

de-oraita "Biblical"; the precise contours of this concept cannot be indicated in a glossary. *See* vol. 1, pp. 207ff.

de-rabbanan "rabbinic"; for the precise contours of this concept, *see* vol. 1, pp. 207ff.

derishah va-ḥakirah ("inquiry and examination") thorough interrogation of witnesses by the *dayyanim* of a *bet din*

din, *pl.* **dinim ("law")** (1) law generally; (2) "interpretation," particularly analogical or syllogistic interpretation or *a fortiori* reasoning; (3) sometimes, law included in the Order of *Nezikin;* (4) law based on a source other than custom or legislation

din Torah (1) Jewish law generally; (2) a case before a rabbinical court

dinei issur ve-hetter ("laws of prohibition and permissibility") laws governing religious and ritual matters, *i.e.*, matters involving relationships with God

dinei kenasot ("law of fines") (1) laws in civil cases pursuant to which the prescribed payment is not equivalent to actual loss suffered; (2) in modern usage, also a criminal fine or civil penalty

dinei malkot or **makkot ("laws of flogging")** laws relating to offenses punishable by flogging

dinei mamonot ("monetary laws") the body of Jewish law generally, but not completely, corresponding to civil law in contemporary legal systems

dinei nefashot ("law of souls") the body of Jewish law involving (a) capital crimes, (b) crimes punishable by corporal punishment, or (c) criminal law

din emet le-amito ("a judgment that is completely and truly correct") a judgment that combines principled decisionmaking with individualized fairness and equity based on thorough understanding of the particular circumstances as well as the law and the general background

divrei kabbalah ("matters of tradition") (1) the writings of the Prophets and the Hagiographa; (2) teaching transmitted orally by teacher to disciple, from one generation to the next; (3) Jewish mysticism (a much later meaning)

divrei soferim ("words of the Scribes") (1) equivalent to *de-rabbanan;* (2) matters essentially rooted in the written Torah but explained by the Oral Law; (3) enactments of the Scribes

divrei Torah ("words of the Torah") equivalent to *de-oraita* ("Biblical")

ed sheker "false witness"

edim zomemim ("scheming witnesses") witnesses who conspire to testify falsely

ein li ("I have nothing") an oath by a debtor attesting inability to pay the debt and undertaking to fulfill certain stringent requirements as to future earnings

erusin ("betrothal") (1) synonym for *kiddushin;* creates the personal status of husband and wife *vis-à-vis* the whole world, but marital rights between the couple do not arise until after *nissu'in, i.e.,* entry under the *ḥuppah* (marital canopy); (2) (in modern Hebrew) engagement

eruv ("merging") a method or device to (a) extend the boundaries within which one may walk or carry on the sabbath, or (b) permit food to be cooked on a festival for consumption on the sabbath immediately following

Even ha-Ezer one of the four principal divisions of the *Sefer ha-Turim* and the *Shulḥan Arukh,* dealing mainly with family law

exilarch the head of the internal Jewish government in the Babylonian diaspora

gabbai, *pl.* **gabba'im** (1) collector of dues, charitable contributions, or assessments; (2) director of a craft guild; (3) manager or director of a synagogue, with particular reference to the religious service

gaon, *pl.* **geonim** *see geonim*

garmi (geramei, gerama) (1) indirect causation; (2) harm other than by direct physical impact

GeFeT Hebrew acronym for "Gemara, Ferush, and Tosafot," *i.e.,* Talmud, Rashi, and Tosafot

Gemara ("completion" or "study" or "tradition") that part of the Talmud that contains discussion of the Mishnah

gematria a method of reaching or supporting conclusions on the basis of the numerical equivalents of letters of key words

gemirut da'at serious, deliberate, and final intent, without reservation, to enter into a legal transaction or perform a juristic act

geonic pertaining to the *geonim* or the gaonate

geonim heads of Talmudical academies (*yeshivot),* (the most famous being Sura and Pumbedita in Babylonia), from the end of the sixth or middle of the seventh century C.E. to the middle of the eleventh century C.E. in the west and the thirteenth century in the east

get bill of divorcement

get me'usseh ("a compelled divorce") a divorce that is invalid because given not voluntarily but rather as a result of improper compulsion

gezel mi-divreihem ("robbery by their words") theft under rabbinic law, *i.e.,* acts designated by the Rabbis as theft, although they do not constitute theft under Biblical law and were not prohibited by the Bible at all

gezerah ("decree") legislative enactment by the halakhic authorities; in the technical sense, as used by some authorities, limited to an enactment that extends or adds prohibitions beyond preexisting *Halakhah,* as distinguished from *takkanah,* an enactment prescribing performance of designated acts

gezerah shavah ("[comparison with] similar matter") inference from similarity of words or phrases. One of the thirteen canons of Biblical interpretation

guda ("wall") a ban

ha'anakah ("bonus," or "gratuity") a sum given to a Hebrew slave upon attaining freedom after six or more years of service; *see* Deuteronomy 15:11–18

haftarah, *pl.* **haftarot** prophetic reading that supplements the weekly Torah portions read during the synagogue service on sabbaths and other holy days

ḥakham, *pl.* **ḥakhamim ("sage")** (1) through the Talmudic period, rabbinic Sage; (2) in subsequent periods, halakhic authority, Talmudic scholar

halakhah le-ma'aseh a legal norm intended to be applied in practice, as distinguished from a theoretical or academic statement

Halakhah the generic term for the entire body of Jewish law, religious as well as civil

halakhah, *pl.* **halakhot ("the law")** (1) a binding decision or ruling on a contested legal issue; (2) a statement of a legal rule not expressly based on a Biblical verse, made in a prescriptive form; (3) in the plural, a collection of any particular category of rules

halakhah le-Moshe mi-Sinai ("law given to Moses at Sinai") (1) a law specifically given to Moses at Sinai, not indicated by or deducible from the Biblical text; (2) a law unanimously accepted by the Sages, having a tenuous connection with the Biblical text, given the designation to emphasize the law's authority; (3) a law so well settled that it is as authoritative as if it had explicitly been given to Moses at Sinai

halanat ha-din ("deferring judgment") deliberation in judgment

ḥaliẓah ("removal," "pulling off") release from levirate marriage by a rite whose central feature is removal of a sandal from a foot of the *levir. See* Deuteronomy 25:7–10. *See also levir*

ḥasid (1) pious; (2) equitable, more generous than the law requires; (3) punctilious in observance; synonym for *ḥaver*

haskamah, *pl.* **haskamot** (1) "agreement"; (2) (as the term was used by Spanish halakhic authorities) enactment

hassagat gevul (1) "removing a landmark" [*i.e.*, boundary marker]; (2) copyright infringement; (3) unfair competition; (4) unfair interference with contract or economic advantage

ḥaver (1) "friend," "comrade, "fellow"; (2) one punctilious in observance of the laws of ritual purity, (3) generally a halakhic scholar

ḥazakah (from *ḥazak*, "strong") (1) a mode of acquisition of property; (2) a legal presumption; (3) possession; (4) the rule that possession of real property for three years under claim of right is equivalent to a deed as proof of ownership; (5) an act of dominion such as putting up a fence or locking the premises

hedyot ("ordinary") (1) pertaining to mundane affairs, as distinguished from matters of Torah; (2) layman; (3) one untutored in the law

hefker bet din hefker ("ownerless [declared by] a *bet din* is ownerless") a halakhic court has the authority to expropriate property; the principle was later used as authority to legislate

hefker ẓibbur hefker ("ownerless" [declared by] the community is ownerless") the community has the authority to expropriate property and legislate

hekkesh ("analogy") analogical reasoning, a method of Biblical interpretation

hekkesh ha-katuv ("Scriptural analogy") analogy made by the Bible itself

henpek same as *asharta,* which *see*

ḥerem, *pl.* **ḥaramim ("ban")** (1) a ban as a sanction for transgression; (2) in its most severe form, total excommunication, an enforced exclusion from communal Jewish religious, social, and civic life; (3) oath; (4) sanctification

ḥerem ha-yishuv ("ban with respect to settlement") an enactment prohibiting settlement in a town without the consent of the townspeople, and providing penalties for violation

ḥezkat kashrut "presumption of propriety," *i.e.*, the presumption that persons behave correctly and that what should have been done has been properly done

ḥezkat shanim "possession for [a specified number of] years," which may serve as a substitute for proof of ownership

ḥiddushim, *sing.* **hiddush ("innovations")** novellae, *i.e.*, new legal interpretations and insights

hilkheta Aramaic for *halakhah*

hilkheta gemiri (1) "a determined [settled and accepted] rule"; (2) a rule handed down by tradition; (3) equivalent of *halakhah le-Moshe mi-Sinai*

hilkheta ke-vatra'ei "the law is in accordance with [the view of] the later authorities"

ḥiyyuv (1) contract; (2) obligation; (3) debt

ḥok (1) law; (2) statute; (3) regulation

hora'at sha'ah ("a directive for the hour") a temporary legislative measure permitting conduct forbidden by the Torah when such legislation is a necessary precaution to restore people to the observance of the faith; some legislation originally adopted or justified as a temporary measure has become an established part of Jewish law

Ḥoshen Mishpat one of the four principal divisions of the *Sefer ha-Turim* and the *Shulḥan Arukh*, dealing mainly with matters of *mishpat ivri*

ḥuppah the nuptial "canopy," under which bride and groom join in the concluding phase (*nissu'in*) of the marriage rite

innuy ha-din ("torture of the law") delay of justice, the law's delays

issur, also **issura ("prohibition")** and **issur ve-hetter ("prohibition and permission")** "religious" or ritual law; laws other than *dinei mamonot*

Jerusalem Talmud the Talmud of the *amoraim* of the Land of Israel

jus cogens ("compelling law") a mandatory legal norm not subject to variance or modification by agreement of the parties affected

jus dispositivum ("displaceable law") a legal rule that can be varied by agreement, as distinguished from *jus cogens*, which may not be varied by agreement

jus naturale ("natural law") law whose source is "in nature" and which is therefore common to all humanity; sometimes called "higher law," superior to law pronounced or enacted by human agency. *Cf.* Noahide laws

jus non scriptum ("unwritten law") in Roman law, law not reduced to writing, *e.g.*, custom. Not synonymous with the Jewish Oral Law

jus scriptum ("written law") in Roman law, law that has been reduced to writing. Not synonymous with the Jewish Written Law

kabbalah ("tradition") *See divrei kabbalah*

kabbalat kinyan assumption of an obligation made binding by exchange of a symbolic object (*sudar*) as "consideration" for the obligation

kallah (1) semiannual assembly of scholars and teachers at a *yeshivah;* (2) bride; (3) daughter-in-law

kal va-ḥomer ("easy and hard," "minor and major") inference *a fortiori* (one of the thirteen canons of Biblical interpretation)

karet, *pl.* **keritot** or **keretot ("extirpation"** or **"excision")** premature death by divine action as punishment for sin

kasher ("fit") (1) kosher; (2) competent (as applied to a witness)

kashrut ("fitness") dietary laws as to permissible and forbidden foods and food preparation. *See also ḥezkat kashrut*

kehillah the organized Jewish community, especially when possessed of juridical autonomy

kelalei ha-Talmud ("principles of the Talmud") methodology and rules of halakhic decision making

kerem be-Yavneh ("the vineyard in Yavneh") the academy of the Sages in Yavneh (also called Jabneh and Jamnia)

ketubbah, *pl.* **ketubbot ("writing")** marriage contract prescribing a wife's economic entitlements during the marriage and in the event of divorce or the husband's death, in addition to such other provisions as may be agreed by the parties

Ketuvim ("writings") the Hagiographa; *i.e.*, the third division of the Hebrew Bible, the other two being the Torah (Pentateuch) and the Prophets

kim li ("it is established for me") a plea that the defendant's position is supported by a halakhic authority, and that therefore the defendant is not liable. The plea lost its effectiveness with the acceptance of the *Shulḥan Arukh* as the authoritative code of Jewish law

king's law (*mishpat ha-melekh*) the legal authority of the Jewish king (later extended to other forms of Jewish governance), which includes the power to temper the *Halakhah* to meet social needs

kinyan ("acquisition") (1) a formal mode of acquiring or conveying property or creating an obligation; (2) ownership; (3) contract; (4) abbreviation of *kinyan sudar*

kinyan agav karka ("acquisition incident to land"); also **kinyan agav** a conveyance of land in which chattels are incidentally transferred without limitation as to quantity, kind, location, or value

kinyan ha-guf ownership or acquisition of property as distinguished from the right to income

kinyan ḥalifin ("acquisition by barter") exchange of one chattel for another, in which each party acquires the other's chattel

kinyan meshikhah ("acquisition by pulling") a mode of acquisition created by an enactment pursuant to which ownership is not acquired upon payment of the purchase money (which is sufficient under Biblical law to transfer ownership to the buyer) but is acquired only when actual possession is taken

kinyan perot (1) the right to income; (2) acquisition of the right to income

kinyan sudar ("acquisition by kerchief") symbolic barter. The transferee gives the transferor a symbolic object such as a *sudar* (kerchief) in exchange for the object that is the subject of the transaction. The *sudar* is returned to the transferee upon completion of the transaction. This mode of acquisition is also used to create a contractual obligation

kiyyum shetarot ("validation of legal instruments") judicial authentication and certification of legal instruments

Knesset the Israeli parliament

kohen "priest," a member of the tribe of Levi descended from the branch of the tribe authorized to perform the Temple service and other sacred duties

kol de-alim gaver ("whoever is the stronger [of claimants to property] prevails") whoever obtains possession by self-help when self-help is permissible may retain the property

kol di-mekaddesh ada'ata de-rabbanan mekaddesh ("all who marry do so subject to the conditions laid down by the Rabbis") a principle upon which the Rabbis were empowered to annul marriages

kum va-aseh ("arise and do") a category of legislation permitting the performance of an act prohibited by the Torah

laẓeit yedei shamayim ("to fulfill a duty in the sight of Heaven") fulfilling a moral, but not legal, obligation

le-hatnot al mah she-katuv ba-Torah ("to contract out of a law contained in the Torah") by agreement between the parties, varying or rendering inapplicable a rule of the Torah

le-khateḥillah ("in the beginning") *ex ante,* in the first instance. *See also be-di-avad*

le-ma'aseh ("for action") in actual practice, or for practical application, as distinguished from "*le-halakhah*" ("for law," *i.e.*, as theoretical doctrine, not practical application)

le-migdar milta ("to safeguard the matter") the principle that authorizes the halakhic authorities, as a protective measure, to adopt enactments in the field of criminal law that prescribe action the Torah prohibits

lefi sha'ah ("temporarily") a principle authorizing legislation permitting conduct contrary to the Torah as a temporary measure under exigent circumstances

leshon benei adam ("colloquial usage of the people") (1) the principle that terms in a legal document should be construed according to their colloquial meaning, not in the sense used in Scripture or by the Sages; (2) according to R. Ishmael, the principle that the Torah speaks as people speak, and therefore there are redundancies in the Torah and not every word has midrashic significance

letakken olam ("to improve [or mend] the world") to promote the public welfare

levir brother-in-law of the widow of a man who has died leaving no children; he must marry the widow unless the rite of *ḥaliẓah* is performed (Deut. 25:5–10). *See also ḥaliẓah*

lifnim mi-shurat ha-din ("on the inside of the line of the law") acting more generously than the law requires

ma'amad sheloshtan ("a meeting of the three") a method of assignment of property rights or obligations: the creditor-assignor, in the presence of the debtor and the assignee, states that the ownership of the property or obligation is assigned to the assignee

ma'aseh, *pl.* **ma'asim** "act," "incident," "event," or "case" that is the source of a new halakhic norm or declarative of a preexisting norm

ma'aseh adif ("a *ma'aseh* takes precedence") a *ma'aseh* is entitled to particular deference

ma'aseh ha-ba ba-averah a transaction involving illegality

ma'aseh rav "a *ma'aseh* is [of] great [significance]"

ma'aseh yadeha "her [a wife's] handiwork," *i.e.*, the domestic services to which a husband is entitled from his wife in consideration of his obligation to support her

mah lo leshakker ("why should he lie") *see migo*

makkot mardut disciplinary flogging

malkot flogging; stripes

malshinut (1) "slander"; (2) informing, betrayal, *i.e.*, a slanderous accusation against a Jew of a kind that, if heard by a non-Jew, would likely cause harm to the person accused

mamon; also **mamona** "money" matters, *i.e.*, civil-law matters, as distinguished from religious-law matters

mamzer ("misbegotten") offspring of an incestuous or adulterous union that is subject to capital punishment by a court or extirpation (*karet*) by God; often mistranslated as "bastard," in the sense of one born out of wedlock

Mappah ("Tablecloth") the title of the commentary by Moses Isserles (Rema) on Joseph Caro's *Shulḥan Arukh* ("Set Table")

mattenat bari ("gift of a healthy person") a form of disposition of property essentially equivalent to a will, whereby the donor "gives" property to his beneficiaries but retains possession and control during his lifetime

mattenat shekhiv me-ra ("gift of one facing imminent death") gift in contemplation of death made by a *shekhiv me-ra*, or the last will and testament of a *shekhiv me-ra*, for which the usual formal requirements are relaxed

me-aḥar ("since") *see migo*

Megillah "scroll," usually referring to the Book of Esther

meḥusar amanah ("lacking in trustworthiness") a description applied by a court as a sanction to a person who reneges on a transaction as to which there is only an unenforceable oral agreement

me'ilah ("sacrilege") unlawful use of consecrated property

Mejelle the Ottoman code of civil law, based on Mohammedan principles and formally repealed in the State of Israel in 1984

melog, also **nikhsei melog ("plucked [usufruct] property")** property belonging to a wife, of which the income belongs to the husband and the principal remains the wife's; the husband is not responsible for loss or diminution in value of *melog* property as he is for *ẓon barzel* property

memrah, *pl.* **memrot ("statement")** a law originated by the *amoraim*

meshikhah ("pulling") *see kinyan meshikhah*

meturgeman (1) spokesman; (2) one who repeated aloud the words of a speaker to a large audience for whom it would be difficult to hear the speaker directly; (3) interpreter

me'un ("refusal") disaffirmance by a woman of a marriage entered into when she was a minor

meẓavveh meḥamat mitah "a testator on the brink of death," for whose will the usual formal requirements are relaxed

mezuzah (1) parchment scroll containing Deuteronomy 6:4–9 and 11:13–21, affixed to the right doorpost in a wooden, metal, or other case; (2) doorpost

mi-de-oraita *see de-oraita*

mi-de-rabbanan *see de-rabbanan*

middah, *pl.* **middot** (1) canon of interpretation; (2) desirable quality of character

middat ḥasidut ("the quality of piety or benevolence") pious or altruistic behavior

mi-divrei soferim ("from the words of the Scribes") *see divrei soferim*

midrash (1) interpretation of Scripture and *Halakhah;* (2) exegesis; (3) a particular midrashic text (when used in this sense in this work, *midrash* is italicized)

midrash ha-Halakhah interpretation of *Halakhah*

midrash mekayyem ("confirming exegesis") integrative exegesis, by which existing law is "integrated" or connected with a Biblical text

midrash yoẓer ("creative exegesis") exegesis that is the legal source of new law

migo ("since," "because" [Aramaic]) a procedural rule to the effect that a claim, despite insufficiency of proof, is deemed valid "since" (or "because") if the claimant had desired to lie, he could have stated a more plausible case that would have been accepted as true, and therefore the weaker claim actually made should also be accepted; also called *me-aḥar* and *mah lo leshakker*

mikveh ("collection of water") ritual bath

minhag (1) "custom" (in modern Hebrew, custom operating as an independent legal norm), *cf. nohag;* (2) legislative enactment (*takkanah*); (3) prescribed practice, *i.e.*, a legal rule for which the Torah itself is the source

minhag garu'a ("bad custom") custom deemed undesirable, which some halakhic authorities held for that reason legally ineffective

minhag ha-medinah ("custom of the region") local custom

minhag le-dorot ("a prescribed practice for the generations") a law for all time

minhag mevattel halakhah ("custom overrides the law") the principle that in monetary matters, custom controls even if contrary to the *Halakhah*

minḥah afternoon prayer

minyan ("number") a quorum of ten, the minimum number for public congregational prayer

mi she-para ("He Who punished . . .") an imprecation by the court addressed to a party who has violated a moral obligation for which there is no legal sanction

Mishnah the code of R. Judah Ha-Nasi, redacted about 200 C.E., which is the basis of the Gemara

mishnah, *pl.* **mishnayot** the smallest division of the Mishnah; the Mishnah is divided into Orders, tractates, chapters, and mishnayot (paragraphs)

mishnat ḥasidim ("standard of the pious") a higher ethical and personal standard than the law requires

Mishneh Torah Maimonides' Code, also called *Yad ha-Ḥazakah*

mishpat (1) adjudication, the act of judging; (2) decision; (3) justice; (4) a system of laws; (5) a legal right; (6) custom, usage, or practice

mishpat ha-melekh *see* "king's law"

mishpat ivri ("Jewish law") that part of the *Halakhah* corresponding to what generally is included in the *corpus juris* of other contemporary legal systems, namely, laws that govern relationships in human society

mishum eivah ("because of enmity") a principle of legislation to the effect that laws should be designed to prevent strife and enmity

miẓvah, *pl.* **miẓvot ("commandment")** (1) religious obligation; (2) good deed

miẓvah ha-teluyah ba-areẓ ("precept dependent upon the land") a precept directly relating to the Land of Israel, *e.g.*, the sabbatical year and the law of the firstfruits

mored a "rebellious" husband who refuses to cohabit with his wife

moredet a "rebellious" wife who refuses to cohabit with her husband

mu'ad ("forewarned") having given notice of propensity for causing harm. Opposite of *tam;* if the cause of harm is *mu'ad,* damages are higher than if the cause is *tam*

na'arah ("girl") a female minor, *i.e.*, a girl who is more than twelve years and one day old but has not reached the age of twelve years, six months, and one day

na'arut ("girlhood") the legal status of a *na'arah*

nasi, *pl.* **nesi'im ("patriarch")** president of the Sanhedrin

naval bi-reshut ha-Torah ("scoundrel within the bounds of the Torah") one who keeps within the letter but violates the spirit of the Torah

nekhasim benei ḥorin ("free [*i.e.*, unencumbered] property") property fully subject to execution of a judgment against the owner

nekhasim meshu'badim ("encumbered property"); nekhasim she-yesh lahem aḥarayut ("property bearing responsibility") real estate, which is responsible for and secures the owner's contractual obligations by virtue of an automatic lien created by entry into the contract

nekhasim she-ein lahem aḥarayut ("property bearing no responsibility") personal property, as to which no lien arises upon the creation of a contractual obligation

Nevi'im the Prophets, *i.e.*, the second division of the Hebrew Bible, the other two being the Torah and the Ketuvim (Hagiographa)

nezikin (1) damages; (2) torts; (3) injuries

niddui ("banning") semi-ostracism, a less severe ban than total excommunication

nikhsei melog *see melog*

niksei ẓon barzel *see ẓon barzel*

nissu'in ("marriage") joinder under the *ḥuppah* (wedding canopy). *See also erusin*

nohag (1) "usage," "conventional custom"; (2) in modern Hebrew, custom given operative effect not as an independent legal norm but because parties are presumed to have acted pursuant to it. *Cf. minhag*

nos'ei kelim ("armor bearers") commentaries and glosses to a legal code

novellae *see ḥiddushim*

ona'ah ("overreaching") taking unfair advantage, as by fraud or deception, in a legal transaction (Lev. 25:14)

ones, pronounced **o-nes ("force")** (1) coercion; (2) duress; (3) act of God (*vis major*); (4) rape

Oraḥ Ḥayyim ("The Way of Life") one of the four principal divisions of the *Sefer ha-Turim* and the *Shulḥan Arukh,* generally dealing with ritual and religious matters outside the scope of *mishpat ivri*

Oral Law (Torah she-be-al peh) all of Jewish law except the part explicitly written in Scripture

parshanut ("explanation") (1) commentary; (2) synonym for midrash

pasul unfit; opposite of *kasher*

pe'ah, *pl.* **pe'ot** "corner" of a field, where a portion of the crop must be left for the poor by the reapers

perat u-khelal ("specification and generalization," "particular and general") inference from a specification followed by a generalization. One of the thirteen canons of Biblical interpretation

peri eẓ hadar ("product of hadar trees") the *etrog* (citron)

perushim "commentaries"

pesak, *pl.* **pesakim** (1) legal ruling; (2) judgment in a litigated case

pesharah "compromise," "settlement"

peshat "plain meaning," as distinguished from midrash

pilpul a method of halakhic study characterized by subtle dialectics and finespun distinctions

piskei ba'alei battim ("judgments of householders") lay judgments

posek, *pl.* **posekim** (1) authoritative decisionmaker, decisor; (2) codifier

praesumptio juris a legal presumption whereby the law assumes the existence of a fact or condition unless the presumption is rebutted by proof to the contrary

prosbul a legal formula authorized by an enactment of Hillel whereby a debt would not be released by the sabbatical year, notwithstanding Deuteronomy 15:1–12, which prescribes such release

rabbinic period the period following the *geonim* to the present time. There are three subperiods: (a) the period of the *rishonim* (eleventh to sixteenth century C.E.), (b) the period of the *aḥaronim* (sixteenth century to the beginnings of the Jewish Emancipation in the late eighteenth century), and (c) the post-Emancipation period

regi'ah ("rest," "allocation of time [rega]" an agreement in restraint of trade allocating time for work and rest (*margo'a*)

resh galuta exilarch

rishonim (1) in prior historical periods, "earlier" halakhic authorities who lived longer ago than in the then recent past; (2) in contemporary usage, halakhic authorities from the eleventh to the sixteenth century. *See also aḥaronim*

rosh yeshivah head of a talmudical academy

Sanhedrin (1) the assembly of 71 ordained scholars constituting the supreme legislative and judicial authority of the Jews during the period of the Second Temple and some time thereafter; (2) the name of a tractate of the Talmud

savoraim ("reasoners") rabbinic Sages from the end of the fifth to the beginning of the sixth or middle of the seventh century C.E.

seder, *pl.*, sedarim ("order") (1) one of the six major divisions of the Mishnah; (2) the ritual meal on the first night of Passover

sefer halakhot a code that includes a discussion of the range of views of the various authorities

Sefer ha-Turim the code of Jewish law written by Jacob b. Asher

sefer keritut "bill of divorcement"; *see also get*

sefer pesakim a code written in prescriptive terms, without discussion of legal theory or conflicting opinions

semikhah ("laying on of hands") rabbinic ordination

sevarah "legal reasoning"

shali'aḥ "agent"

she'elot u-teshuvot ("questions and answers") responsa

Shekhinah Divine Presence, the "immanent" or "indwelling" aspect of God

shekhiv me-ra one who is dangerously ill and faces or otherwise reasonably apprehends imminent death

Shema three Biblical passages recited twice daily, beginning with "Hear (shema) O Israel" (Deut. 6:4), constituting the confession of the Jewish faith

shetar, *pl.* shetarot (1) legal document; (2) contract; (3) deed

shev ve-al ta'aseh ("sit and do not do") a category of legislation directing that an affirmative precept, obligatory according to Biblical law, not be performed

shevi'it ("seventh [year]") the sabbatical year

shevu'at ha-edut ("witness's oath") an oath by one formally called upon to bear witness, to the effect that the affiant has no knowledge of the matter about which he is called to testify

shevut ("[sabbath] rest") (1) work rabbinically forbidden on the sabbath; (2) the rabbinical prohibition of such work

shi'bud nekhasim ("encumbrance of property") (1) lien, security interest; (2) the general lien on the real estate of an obligor that arises automatically upon creation of the obligation

shi'buda de-oraita "Biblical lien"

shiddukhin an agreement to enter into marriage

shikkul ha-da'at (1) [judicial] "discretion"; (2) decision on a moot point of law; (3) the zone of permissible latitude of a *dayyan* to disagree with other authorities

shimmush (1) "service" to the Torah; (2) attendance upon a halakhic scholar; (3) apprenticeship to a halakhic authority

shi'ur (1) prescribed measure; (2) "lesson," talmudic lecture

sho'el ("borrower") a bailee in possession of property as a result of borrowing it from another

shofet (1) "judge"; (2) magistrate, ruler

shomer ḥinam "an unpaid bailee," *i.e.,* one who undertakes without compensation to preserve property of another

shomer sakhar a "paid bailee" who is compensated for his service in connection with the bailment

shufra de-shetara ("adornment of the *shetar*") clauses designed to enhance the effectiveness of a legal document, *e.g.,* waiver of certain defenses otherwise available

Shulḥan Arukh (the "Set Table") the code of Jewish law written by Joseph Caro in the sixteenth century; the most authoritative of the Jewish legal codes

sitomta ("seal") mark placed on a barrel or other large container identifying the owner; placing the mark was recognized as a mode of acquisition

sofer, *pl.* **soferim ("counter," "scribe")** (1) a halakhic authority of the period of Ezra the Scribe; (2) a scholar of the Talmudic period. *See divrei soferim*

sof hora'ah ("the end of instruction") the completion of the Talmud

sokher ("hirer") a bailee or lessee who pays for the right to possession of the bailed or leased property

sudar ("kerchief") the instrument used in the most widespread mode of acquisition in Jewish law. *See kinyan sudar*

sugyah, *pl.* **sugyot** (1) passage; (2) discussion; (3) issue; a Talmudic subject or area

sukkah "booth" or "tabernacle" erected for the festival of *Sukkot*

supercommentary a commentary on a commentary

takkanah, *pl.* **takkanot ("improvement," "repair")** legislative enactment by halakhic or communal authorities. *See also gezerah*

takkanah kevu'ah ("established enactment") legislation permanently in effect, as distinguished from a temporary measure. *See also hora'at sha'ah*

takkanat ha-kahal "communal enactment"

takkanat ha-shavim ("enactment for the encouragement of penitents") a category of enactments to encourage penitence and rehabilitation, *e.g.,* an enactment providing that a thief may be relieved of the obligation to return stolen property and may pay its value instead, when the property has been incorporated into a building and would be very expensive to retrieve

takkanat ha-shuk ("enactment for the market") an enactment to promote the security of transactions in the open market ("market overt") by protecting the purchaser from a thief at such a market against claims by the owner of the stolen property

takkanat medinah "a regional enactment," intended to be applicable to many Jewish communities (*kehillot*)

talmid ḥakham ("wise scholar") (1) halakhic scholar; (2) learned and pious person

Talmud the Mishnah and the discussion of the Mishnah by the *amoraim* of Babylonia (comprising the Babylonian Talmud) and the *amoraim* of the Land of Israel (comprising the Jerusalem Talmud)

talmud ("learning") (1) academic study; (2) midrash; (3) the colloquy between *tannaim* on a specific law

Talmud Bavli Babylonian Talmud

talmud lomar ("the text teaches") a statement introducing a conclusion derived by implication through exegesis

Talmud Yerushalmi Jerusalem Talmud

tam ("innocuous") not chargeable with notice of propensity to cause harm (opposite of *mu'ad*); if the cause of harm is *tam,* damages are less than if the cause is *mu'ad*

tanna, ***pl.*** **tannaim** rabbi of the Mishnaic period (first century to approximately 220 C.E.)

tanna kamma ("the first ***tanna*****")** a *tanna* whose opinion is stated first, without attribution, in a *mishnah*

tenai, ***pl.*** **tena'im** (1) "condition"; (2) legislative enactment (*takkanah*); (3) in plural, (a) marriage contract, (b) formal betrothal contract

tenai bet din ("stipulation [or requirement] imposed by the court") a legislative enactment (*takkanah*); the term indicates that the legislation is based on prior private agreements that have become more or less standard

terumah ("contribution") (1) priestly tithe, which only priests and their families are permitted to eat; (2) in modern Hebrew, a donation

teshuvah (1) responsum; (2) "return," or repentance; (3) refutation

tikkun (ha-)olam ("improvement [or mending] of the world") promotion of the public welfare; the verb form, "to promote the public welfare," is *letakken olam*

tofes ("template") the main body of a legal document, containing basic and generally standard provisions relating to the type of transaction involved

tom lev ("purity of heart") (1) good faith; (2) wholeheartedness; (3) integrity; (4) sincerity

Torah ("teaching") (1) the five books of Moses (Pentateuch); (2) the entire Hebrew Bible; (3) doctrine; (4) custom; (5) the prescribed procedure; (6) divine revelation; (7) all Jewish study, the entire religious and ethical and cultural literature of Judaism

Torah min ha-shamayim ("Torah from Heaven") divine revelation, the article of Jewish faith that the Torah was given by God to the Jewish people

Torah she-be-al-peh ("Oral Law") (1) all Jewish law that is not set forth in Scripture; (2) the entire Teaching of Judaism, including *aggadah*

Torah she-bi-khetav "Written Law," *i.e.,* the law explicitly set forth in the text of the Torah

toref ("blank") the parts of a legal document relating to the individual aspects of the transaction, filled in as to the details of the particular transaction

Tosafot ("additions") critical and explanatory glosses on the Babylonian Talmud written by a school of scholars in France and Germany in the twelfth and thirteenth centuries

tosefet ketubbah ("addition to the ***ketubbah*****")** an optional supplement to the mandatory minimum amount of the *ketubbah*

Tosefta ("additions") a collection of tannaitic statements supplementing the Mishnah

tovei ha-ir ("the good citizens of the town") lay judges or communal officials. Sometimes called "the seven *tovei ha-ir;*" they were the political and economic heads of the community

uvda Aramaic for *ma'aseh*—an act, incident, event, or case that gives rise to new law or is declarative of an existing norm

Va'ad Arba (ha-)Araẓot ("Council of the Four Lands") the central institution of Jewish self-government in Poland and Lithuania from the sixteenth to the eighteenth century

Written Law law explicitly set forth in Scripture

Yad ha-Ḥazakah the *Mishneh Torah,* Maimonides' Code

Yavneh (Jabneh, Jamnia) a town in Judea where R. Johanan b. Zakkai established an academy for teaching and studying the law after the destruction of the Temple in 70 C.E. *See kerem be-Yavneh*

yeshivah ("a place of sitting") academy for Talmudic study

yeẓe din ẓedek le-ẓidko ("let a righteous judgment justly issue") a judgment must do justice, let justice be done

Yom Tov ("good day") festival, holiday

Yoreh De'ah ("it will teach knowledge") one of the four principal divisions of *Sefer ha-Turim* and the *Shulḥan Arukh*

zaken mamre ("rebellious elder") a rabbi who adjudicates contrary to the ruling of the Sanhedrin

zav, *pl.* zavim ("bodily issue") *Zavim* is the title of a tractate of the Talmud in the Order of *Tohorot*

ẓavva'at shekhiv me-ra a deathbed will, or a will of one who apprehends imminent death. *See shekhiv me-ra*

ẓon barzel ("iron flock") assets of a wife over which a husband has almost complete dominion; he is responsible for any loss or diminution in value of these assets, as distinguished from *melog* property, since he has undertaken to preserve "like iron" the value of the *ẓon barzel* property at the time of the marriage

Zug, *pl.* Zugot ("pair") the *Zugot* consisted of the *nasi* and the *Av Bet Din,* who were the acknowledged leaders of the Jewish people from 160 B.C.E. to the beginning of the common era

BIBLIOGRAPHY

This bibliography lists the scholarly articles and books cited or quoted in this work. Citations to the traditional halakhic sources (including Scripture, Mishnah, Talmud, commentaries, codes, responsa, enactments, and reference works) and to legislative materials, statutes, and cases are set forth in the Index of Sources, which immediately follows this bibliography. In addition, most of the materials (reference works, bibliographies, etc.) discussed in Chapter 40 (pp. 1540–1572) and not cited elsewhere in the work have not been included in this bibliography; these materials are referenced in the general index. Editors' introductions to Talmudic and post-Talmudic works are generally not included in this bibliography; they are referenced in the Index of Sources and in the Subject Index (under the name of the work).

I. Abrahams and H.P. Stokes, *Starrs and Jewish Charters Preserved in the British Museum*, London, 1930–1932, *1538*

Y. Abramsky, *Dinei Mamonot*, London, 1939, *111*

S. Abramson, *Ba-Merkazim u-va-Tefuẓot bi-Tekufat ha-Geonim* [In the Centers and the Diasporas in the Geonic Period], Jerusalem, 1965, *1468*

S. Abramson, "Ha-Genizah she-be-Tokh ha-Genizah" [The *Genizah* within the *Genizah*], *Proceedings of the Rabbinical Assembly of America*, XV (1951), pp. 227–228, *1161–1162*

S. Abramson, *Inyanot be-Sifrut ha-Geonim* [Studies in Geonic Literature], 1974, *1159, 1165, 1472, 1515*

S. Abramson, *Kelalei ha-Talmud be-Divrei ha-Ramban* [Talmudic Principles in the Works of Naḥmanides], Jerusalem, 1971, *1124*

S. Abramson, "Pashtut" [Simplicity, Plain Meaning], *Leshonenu* [Our Language], XVI (1949), pp. 164–168, *58*

S. Abramson, "Min ha-Makor ha-Aravi Shel Sefer ha-Mikaḥ ve-ha-Mimkar le-Rav Hai Gaon" [From the Arabic Original of Rabbi Hai Gaon's *Book of Purchase and Sale*], *Jubilee Volume for J.N. Epstein*, Jerusalem, 1950, pp. 296ff., *1165*

S. Abramson, *Rav Nissim Gaon, Ḥamishah Sefarim* [R. Nissim Gaon, Five Books], Jerusalem, 1965, *1115, 1131, 1183*

S. Abramson, "Sifrei Halakhot Shel ha-Ra'avad" [Rabad's Books of *Halakhot*], *Tarbiẓ*, XXXVI (1967), pp. 158–179, *1224*

N.M. Adler, *Netinah la-Ger*, *1045–1046*

S.Y. Agnon, *Me-Aẓmi el Aẓmi* [From Myself to Myself], Tel Aviv, 1976, *1593–1594*

S. Agranat, "Terumatah Shel ha-Reshut ha-Shofetet le-Mif'al ha-Ḥakikah" [The

Contribution of the Judiciary to Legislation], *Iyyunei Mishpat*, X (1984), pp. 233ff., *1838, 1935*

I.A. Agus, "Ha-Shilton ha-Aẓma'i Shel ha-Kehillah ha-Yehudit bi-Mei ha-Beinayim" [The Autonomy of the Jewish Community in the Middle Ages], *Talpiot*, V (1951–1952), pp. 176–195, 637–648; VI (1953–1955), pp. 305–320, *685, 716, 718*

B. Akzin, *Sugyot be-Mishpat u-vi-Medina'ut* [Topics in Law and Statesmanship], Jerusalem, 1966, *1873*

B. Akzin, *Torat ha-Mishtarim* [Theories of Government], Jerusalem, 1969, *231–232, 278, 537*

H. Albeck, *Commentary on Mishnah* and *Hashlamot*, *21, 112, 192, 233, 341–342, 351, 408, 486, 492, 501, 503, 508, 512, 516, 525, 543, 560, 569, 585, 885–886, 907, 934, 936, 952, 958, 1034, 1055, 1059, 1065, 1073, 1295, 1697*

H. Albeck, *Das Buch der Jubiläen und die Halacha* [The Book of Jubilees and the *Halakhah*], Berlin, 1930, *1034, 1037*

H. Albeck, "Ha-Sanhedrin u-Nesi'ah" [The Sanhedrin and Its Patriarch], *Zion*, VIII (1943), p. 169, *486*

H. Albeck, *Mavo la-Mishnah* [Introduction to the Mishnah], Jerusalem, 1959, *192, 203, 205, 208, 210, 224–225, 227, 285, 287–289, 297, 303, 383–384, 400, 404, 492, 549–550, 1043–1044, 1050–1053, 1056–1057, 1061, 1063, 1072, 1106–1110*

H. Albeck, *Mavo la-Talmudim* [Introduction to the Talmuds], Tel Aviv, 1969, *967, 1040, 1044, 1048–1049, 1081, 1084–1085, 1087–1088, 1090, 1092, 1456*

H. Albeck, *Meḥkarim ba-Baraita u-va-Tosefta ve-Yaḥasan la-Talmud* [Studies in the *Baraita* and the *Tosefta* and Their Relation to the Talmud], Jerusalem, 1944, *1080, 1550*

H. Albeck, "Sof ha-Hora'ah ve-Siyyum ha-Talmud" [The End of Instruction and the Completion of the Talmud], *Sinai*, Jubilee Volume, 1958, pp. 73–79, *1093*

S. Albeck, *Mavo le-Even ha-Ezer me'et ha-Raban* [Introduction to *Even ha-Ezer* by Raban], Warsaw, 1905, *1179*

S. Albeck, "Sof ha-Hora'ah ve-Aḥaronei ha-Amoraim" [The End of Instruction and the Last *Amoraim*], *Sinai*, Jubilee Volume, 1958, pp. 57–73, *1093*

S. Albeck, "Yaḥaso Shel Rabbenu Tam le-Va'ayot Zemano" [Rabbenu Tam's Attitude Toward the Problems of His Time], *Zion*, XIX (1954), pp. 104–141, *685, 717*

S. Albeck, "Yesodot Mishtar ha-Kehillot bi-Sefarad ad ha-Ramah" [The Foundations of Communal Government in Spain until Ramah], *Zion*, XXV (1960), pp. 85–121, *685*

C.K. Allen, *Law in the Making*, 7th ed., Oxford, 1964, *179, 230, 234–235, 263, 478–479, 537, 903, 980*

G. Alon, *Meḥkarim be-Toledot Yisra'el bi-Mei Bayit Sheni u-vi-Tekufat ha-Mishnah ve-ha-Talmud* [Studies in Jewish History in the Days of the Second Temple and in the Mishnaic and Talmudic Period], Tel Aviv, 1957–1958, *19, 21, 25, 236, 279, 301, 485, 516, 885, 908*

G. Alon, "On Philo's Halakhah," in *Jews, Judaism and the Classical World*, Jerusalem, 1977, ***1037***

G. Alon, *Toledot ha-Yehudim be-Ereẓ Yisra'el bi-Tekufat ha-Mishnah ve-ha-Talmud* [History of the Jews in the Land of Israel during the Period of the Mishnah and the Talmud], 3d ed., Tel Aviv, 1959, ***6–7, 13, 19, 21–22, 525, 555, 558, 1088***

G. Alon, "Yeshivot Lita" [The *Yeshivot* of Lithuania], *Meḥkarim be-Toledot Yisra'el* [Studies in Jewish History], I, pp. 1ff., ***1910***

M.A. Amiel, *Middot le-Ḥeker ha-Halakhah* [Principles of Halakhic Research], ***137***

A.M. Appelbaum, "Divrei ha-Keneset ki-Re'ayah le-Ferush ha-Ḥok" [The Knesset Record as Evidence of Statutory Meaning], *Ha-Praklit*, XXI (1965), pp. 411ff., ***462, 1727–1728***

A.V. Aptowitzer, "Emdat ha-Ubar be-Dinei ha-Onshin Shel Yisra'el" [The Status of the Fetus in Jewish Criminal Law], *Sinai*, XI (1942), pp. 9–32, ***200***

A.V. Aptowitzer, *Mavo le-Raviah* [Introduction to Raviah], Jerusalem, 1938, ***1168, 1179, 1511***

R. Arusi, "Ha-Gorem ha-Edati bi-Fesikat ha-Halakhah (Kefiyyat Get be-Moredet 'Ma'is Alai' Eẓel Yehudei Teiman)" [The Communal Factor in Halakhic Decision Making (The Practice of the Jews of Yemen to Compel Divorce in the Case of a *Moredet* for Incompatibility)], *Dine Israel*, X–XI (1981–1983), pp. 125–175, ***1374, 1755***

R. Arusi, "Yiḥudo Shel Tarlal Mashta (le-Ḥeker ha-Olam ha-Ruḥani Shel Yahadut Shar'ab me-ha-Me'ah ha-17)" [The Distinctiveness of Tarlal Mashta (A Study of the Spiritual World of the Jews of Shar'ab from the Seventeenth Century)], printed as the Introduction to *Tarlal Mashta Shabazi*, 1986, ***1374***

S. Assaf, Remarks on Commentary by Saadiah b. David Adani (al-Adani) on *MT*, *Kiryat Sefer*, XXII (1945), pp. 240–244, ***1232***

S. Assaf, Remarks on the Book *Musar ha-Dayyanim*, *Tarbiẓ*, VII (1936), p. 217, ***983***

S. Assaf, "Al Kitvei Yad Shonim" [On Various Manuscripts], *Kiryat Sefer*, XI (1934–1935), pp. 492–498, ***1538***

S. Assaf, *Battei ha-Din ve-Sidreihem Aḥar Ḥatimat ha-Talmud* [Courts and Their Procedures after the Completion of the Talmud], Jerusalem, 1924, ***10, 12, 19, 28, 34–35, 51, 83, 743, 794, 801, 825, 827, 1576, 1594***

S. Assaf, "Bavel ve-Ereẓ Yisra'el bi-Tekufat ha-Geonim" [Babylonia and the Land of Israel in the Geonic Period], *Ha-Shilo'aḥ*, XXXIV (1918), pp. 286–295, ***1456***

S. Assaf, *Be-Oholei Ya'akov, Avadim u-Seḥar Avadim Eẓel ha-Yehudim bi-mei ha-Beinayim* [In the Tents of Jacob—Slavery and the Slave Trade among Jews in the Middle Ages], ***1337***

S. Assaf, "Bittulah Shel Ketubbat Benin Dikhrin" [The Abrogation of the *Ketubbah* Clause Concerning the Wife's Sons], *Ve-Zot li-Yehudah* [Jubilee Volume in Honor of Y.A. Blau], 1926, pp. 18–30, ***577, 656***

S. Assaf, *Ha-Onshin Aḥarei Ḥatimat ha-Talmud* [Penal Law after the Completion of the Talmud], Jerusalem, 1922, ***10, 12, 47, 64, 83, 518, 692, 1476, 1596***

S. Assaf, "Ha-Takkanot ve-ha-Minhagim ha-Shonim bi-Yerushat ha-Ba'al et Ishto" [The Various Enactments and Customs in Regard to the Husband's Right to Inherit from His Wife], *Madda'ei ha-Yahadut*, I (1926), pp. 79–94, ***787, 806, 836, 838–839***

S. Assaf, "Le-Sidrei Vattei ha-Din be-Ashkenaz" [On Proceedings before Jewish Courts in Germany], *Ha-Mishpat ha-Ivri*, I, pp. 105–120, ***17***

S. Assaf, "Le-Toledot ha-Yehudim bi-Sefarad" [On the History of the Jews in Spain], *Mekorot u-Meḥkarim* [Sources and Studies], 1946, pp. 100–103, ***1536***

S. Assaf, "Li-She'elat ha-Yerushah Shel ha-Bat" [On the Question of Inheritance by a Daughter], *Jacob Freimann Jubilee Volume*, 1937, pp. 8–11, ***846***

S. Assaf, "Mafte'aḥ li-She'elot u-Teshuvot ha-Geonim ha-Muva'ot be-Sefer ha-Ittur" [An Index of the Geonic Responsa Cited in *Sefer ha-Ittur*], *Ha-Ẓofeh le-Ḥokhmat Yisra'el*, VI (1922), pp. 289–309, ***1269***

S. Assaf, "Mashehu le-Toledot Maharshal" [A Brief Biography of Maharshal], *Jubilee Volume in Honor of Louis Ginzberg*, New York, 1950, Hebrew sec., pp. 45–63, ***1385***

S. Assaf, *Mekorot le-Toledot ha-Ḥinnukh be-Yisra'el* [Sources for the History of Jewish Education], 2d ed., Tel Aviv, 1948, ***1380***

S. Assaf, *Mekorot u-Meḥkarim* [Sources and Studies], Jerusalem, 1946, ***1476***

S. Assaf, *Mi-Sifrut ha-Geonim* [From the Geonic Literature], ***625***

S. Assaf, *Sifran Shel Rishonim*, Jerusalem, 1935, ***11, 47, 145, 1513***

S. Assaf, "Talyanim Yehudim" [Jewish Hangmen], *Mekorot u-Meḥkarim* [Sources and Studies], pp. 252ff. (also printed in *Tarbiẓ*, V [1934], pp. 224–226), ***11***

S. Assaf, *Tekufat ha-Geonim ve-Sifrutah* [The Geonic Period and Its Literature], Jerusalem, 1955, ***7, 34, 643–646, 1099, 1113–1114, 1150, 1153–1157, 1159–1160, 1162, 1164–1165, 1170, 1471–1472, 1541–1542, 1550***

S. Atlas, *Keta'im mi-Sefer Yad ha-Ḥazakah la-Rambam* [Excerpts from Maimonides' *MT*], London, 1940, ***1215***

L. Auerbach, *Das jüdische Obligationenrecht nach den Quellen und mit besonderer Berücksichtigung des römischen und deutschen Rechts, systematisch dargestellt* [The Jewish Law of Obligations Systematically Presented According to the Sources, with Special Regard to Roman and German Law], Berlin, 1870, and ed. A.M. Fuss, 1976, ***82, 595, 1540***

M. Avi-Yonah, *The Jews under Roman and Byzantine Rule*, Magnes Press, 1984, ***1088***

S. Avitzur, "Ẓefat Merkaz le-Ta'asiyat Arigei Ẓemer ba-Me'ah ha-Ḥamesh Esreh" [Safed, A Center of the Wool Weaving Industry in the Fifteenth Century], *Sefer Ẓefat*, I, Jerusalem, 1962, pp. 41ff., ***1133, 1311***

W. Bacher, "Die Agada in Maimunis Werken" [Aggadic Material in Maimonides' Works], *Sefer ha-Yovel la-Rambam* [Jubilee Volume in Honor of Maimonides], Leipzig, 1914, ***95***

W. Bacher, *Erkhei Midrash* [Midrashic Terminology], Tel Aviv, 1923, ***94, 203, 318, 347, 1042, 1053, 1084–1085, 1090, 1208, 1553, 1566***

W. Bacher, "Zum Sprachlichen Charakter des Mischna Tora" [On the Linguistic Character of the *Mishneh Torah*], in *Moses Ben Maimon, Sein Leben, Seine Werke und Sein Einfluss* [Maimonides: His Life, Works, and Influence], Leipzig, 1914, II, pp. 280–305, *1208*

M. Baer, *Rashut ha-Golah be-Vavel bi-Mei ha-Mishnah ve-ha-Talmud* [The Exilarchy in Babylonia in the Period of the Mishnah and the Talmud], *58*

Y. Baer, "L. Finkelstein: Jewish Self-Government in the Middle Ages," *MGWJ*, LXXI (1927), pp. 392–397; LXXIV (1930), pp. 31–34, *784*

Y. Baer, *Die Juden im Christlichen Spanien, Urkunden und Regesten* [The Jews in Christian Spain: Documents and Government Records], Berlin, 1929–1936, *705, 798, 1532–1533, 1538*

Y. Baer, "Ha-Yesodot ha-Historiyyim Shel ha-Halakhah" [The Historical Foundations of the *Halakhah*], *Zion*, XVII (1952), pp. 1–55, 173; XXVII (1962), pp. 117–155, *62, 205, 225, 236, 488, 681, 894, 1074*

Y. Baer, "Ha-Yesodot ve-ha-Hatḥalot Shel Irgun ha-Kehillah ha-Yehudit bi-Mei ha-Beinayim" [The Foundations and Beginnings of Jewish Communal Organization in the Middle Ages], *Zion*, XV (1950), pp. 1–41, *667–668, 683, 685, 716–718, 784*

Y. Baer, *A History of the Jews in Christian Spain*, *9, 37, 796–798, 804, 1253, 1476, 1533, 1538*

Y. Baer, *Yisra'el ba-Ammim* [Israel among the Nations], Jerusalem, 1955, *62, 236*

M. Balaban, *Bet Yisra'el be-Folin* [The Jews in Poland], ed. Halpern, Jerusalem, 1948, *9, 37, 823, 1345–1346*

A. Barak, "Al ha-Shofet ke-Farshan" [On the Judge as Interpreter], *Mishpatim*, XII (1982), pp. 248–256, *1872–1873, 1935*

A. Barak, "Aẓma'utah Shel ha-Kodifikaẓyah ha-Ezraḥit ha-Ḥadashah—Sikkuyim ve-Sikkunim" [The Independence of the New Civil Legislation—Prospects and Risks], *Mishpatim*, VII (1976), pp. 15ff., *1733*

A. Barak, "Ha-Hora'ah bi-Devar 'Aẓma'ut ha-Ḥok' u-Va'ayat ha-Lakunah ba-Ḥakikah ha-Yisra'elit ha-Ḥadashah" [The Provision Regarding Independence of the Law and the Problem of Lacunae in New Israeli Legislation], *Mishpatim*, V (1974), pp. 99ff., *1729*

A. Barak, "Ḥakikah Shipputit" [Judicial Legislation], *Mishpatim*, XIII (1983), pp. 25–80, *1874, 1935–1936*

A. Barak, *Ḥok ha-Sheliḥut, 1965* [The Agency Law, 1965], Jerusalem, 1975, *1733*

A. Barak, "Ḥok Yesodot ha-Mishpat u-Moreshet Yisra'el" [The Foundations of Law Act and the Jewish Heritage], *Shenaton*, XIII (1987), pp. 265–283, *1897, 1946*

A. Barak, "Likrat Kodifikaẓyah Shel ha-Mishpat ha-Ezraḥi" [Toward the Codification of the Civil Law], *Iyyunei Mishpat*, III (1973), pp. 5ff., *1733*

A. Barak, "Overruling Precedent," 21 *Israel L. Rev.* 269 (1986), *980*

M. Bar-Ilan (Berlin), "Ḥok u-Mishpat bi-Medinateinu" [Statute and Law in Our State], *Yavneh, Kovez Akadema'i Dati*, 1949, p. 29, *1606, 1616–1617*

S.W. Baron, *A Social and Religious History of the Jews*, *7, 62*

S.W. Baron, *The Jewish Community*, Philadelphia, 1942, *26, 37, 1576*

E. Bashan, "Shemot Arei Ereẓ Yisra'el ke-Khinnuyim le-Arim be-Ḥuẓ la-Areẓ be-

Sifrut ha-She'elot u-Teshuvot Shel ha-Tekufah ha-Ottomanit" [Names of Towns in the Land of Israel as Designations of Diaspora Towns in the Responsa Literature of the Ottoman Period], *Sefer ha-Shanah le-Madda'ei ha-Yahadut ve-ha-Ru'aḥ Shel Universitat Bar Ilan* [Bar Ilan University Annual for Judaic Studies and Humanities], XII (1974), pp. 137–165, *1515*

J. Bassfreund, "Zur Redaktion der Mischna" [On the Redaction of the Mishnah], *MGWJ*, LI (1907), pp. 429–444, *1057*

A. Bein, *Im Megillat ha-Aẓma'ut Shel Medinat Yisra'el* [On the Declaration of Independence of the State of Israel], Jerusalem, 1949, *1650*

S. Belkin, *Philo and the Oral Law*, 1940, *1037*

M. Benayahu, "Ḥiddushah Shel ha-Semikhah bi-Ẓefat" [The Reinstitution of Ordination in Safed], *Sefer Yovel Likhevod Yiẓḥak Baer* [Jubilee Volume in Honor of Yiẓḥak Baer], Jerusalem, 1961, pp. 248–269, *1310*

M. Benayahu, *Rabbi Ḥayyim Yosef David Azulai*, Jerusalem, 1959, *1112, 1439*

M. Benayahu, "Sifrei Takkanot u-Minhagim Shel Yerushalayim" [Books of Enactments and Customs of Jerusalem], *Kiryat Sefer*, XXII (1945–1946), pp. 262–265, *1532*

M. Benayahu, "Takkanot Tiryah" [The Enactments of Tyre], *Koveẓ al Yad*, IV/XIV (1946), pp. 195–228, *1532*

B.Z. Benedikt, "He'arot le-Toledot ha-Rif" [Notes on the Life of Alfasi], *Kiryat Sefer*, XXVII (1951), pp. 119–120, *1168, 1171*

B.Z. Benedikt, "Le-Darko Shel ha-Rambam be-Ta'amo Shel Din" [On Maimonides' Methodology in Regard to Rationales for Legal Rules], *Koveẓ Torah she-be-al Peh* [Collected Essays on the Oral Law], Mosad ha-Rav Kook, 1964, pp. 87ff., *1193*

B.Z. Benedikt, "Le-Toledotav Shel Merkaz ha-Torah be-Provenẓ" [On the History of the Center for the Study of Torah in Provence], *Tarbiẓ*, XXII (1951), pp. 85–109, *1171*

B.Z. Benedikt, "Tchernowitz, Chaim, *Toledot ha-Posekim*," *Kiryat Sefer*, XXV (1949), pp. 164–176, *1176*

I. Benjacob, *Oẓar ha-Sefarim* [A Treasury of Books], Vilna, 1877–1880, *1411, 1561*

I.S. Ben-Meir, *Hashpa'at ha-Halakhah al Ḥukkei ha-Medinah* [The Influence of the *Halakhah* on the Laws of the State], Series on the People and the State, Tel Aviv, 1963, pp. 141ff., *1728*

N. Ben Menahem, "Ha-Defusim ha-Rishonim Shel ha-Shulḥan Arukh" [The First Printed Editions of the *Shulḥan Arukh*], *Koveẓ Rabbi Yosef Caro* [The Rabbi Joseph Caro Anthology], ed. I. Raphael, Jerusalem, 1969, pp. 101–120, *1344*

H.H. Ben-Sasson, *Hagut ve-Hanhagah* [Concept and Conduct], Jerusalem, 1959, *28, 1380*

H.H. Ben-Sasson, *Perakim be-Toledot ha-Yehudim bi-Mei ha-Beinayim* [Chapters in the History of the Jews in the Middle Ages], Tel Aviv, 1969, *37, 84, 1157*

H.H. Ben-Sasson, "Toledot Yisra'el bi-Mei ha-Beinayim" [A History of the Jews in the Middle Ages], in *Toledot Am Yisra'el* [History of the Jewish People], II, Tel Aviv, 1969, *37, 66, 1310*

M. Ben-Sasson, "Seridim mi-Sefer ha-Edut ve-ha-Shetarot le-Rav Saadiah Gaon"

[Surviving Fragments of the Book of Evidence and Legal Instruments by Rabbi Saadiah Gaon], *Shenaton*, XI–XII (1984–1986), pp. 135–280, ***1535–1536***

A. Berger, *Encyclopedic Dictionary of Roman Law*, Philadelphia, 1953, ***980***

E. Berkovitz, *Tenai be-Nissu'in u-ve-Get* [Contractual Conditions Regarding Marriage and Divorce], Jerusalem, 1967, ***879***

A. Berliner, "Rabbi Israel Isserlein," *MGWJ*, XVIII (1869), pp. 269–277, ***1517***

A. Berliner, *Targum Onkelos*, Berlin, 1884, 2 vols., ***1045–1046***

W.M. Best, *The Principles of the Law of Evidence* (12th ed.), London, 1922, ***1700***

S. Bialoblotzky, "Rav Saadiah Gaon," reprinted in Bialoblotzky, *Em la-Masoret: Meḥkarim u-Ma'amarim*, Ramat Gan, 1971, pp. 127–206, ***1161***

Black's Law Dictionary, 5th ed., 1979, ***790***

H. Black, *Handbook on the Constitution and Interpretation of the Laws*, 1986, ***291***

2 Blackstone, *Commentaries* 241–242, ***1673***

L. Blau, "Das Gesetzbuch des Maimonides Historisch Betrachtet" [A Historical View of Maimonides' Code], in *Moses Ben Maimon, Sein Leben, Seine Werke und Sein Einfluss* [Maimonides: His Life, Works, and Influence], Leipzig, 1914, II, pp. 331–358, ***1057, 1099, 1183, 1221, 1223***

L. Blau, *MGWJ*, LXIII (1919), ***562***

M. Blau, "Yesodot ha-Ḥukkah ba-Medinah ha-Yehudit" [The Constitutional Foundations of the Jewish State], *Yavneh, Koveẓ Akadema'i Dati*, 1949, pp. 33–40, ***1614***

Y.A. Blau, "Hashva'ot Bein ha-Mishpat ha-Ivri le-Hellenisti-Miẓri" [Comparative Study of Jewish and Hellenistic-Egyptian Law], *Ha-Mishpat ha-Ivri*, V (1936), pp. 13–31, ***13***

M. Bloch, *Das mosaisch-talmudisch Besitzrecht* [The Mosaic-Talmudic Law of Possession], Budapest, 1897, ***82***

M. Bloch, *Das mosaisch-talmudisch Erbrecht* [The Mosaic-Talmudic Law of Succession], Budapest, 1890, ***82***

M. Bloch, *Das mosaisch-talmudische Polizeirecht* [Mosaic-Talmudic Criminal Law], Budapest, 1879, ***82***

M. Bloch, *Das mosaisch-talmudische Strafgerichtsverfahren* [Mosaic-Talmudic Criminal Proceedings], Budapest, 1901, ***82***

M. Bloch, *Der Vertrag nach mosaische-talmudischen Rechte* [The Mosaic-Talmudic Law of Contract], Budapest (Leipzig), 1893, ***82***

M. Bloch, *Die Vormundschaft nach mosaisch-talmudischen Recht* [Fiduciary Relations in Mosaic-Talmudic Law], Budapest, 1882, ***82***

M.A. Bloch, *Sha'arei Torat ha-Takkanot* [On Legislative Enactments], Vienna-Budapest, 1879–1906, ***490, 492, 540–541, 549–550, 555, 559, 561, 566, 568–569, 612, 614, 622, 629***

I. Breitowitz, "The Plight of the *Agunah*: A Study in *Halacha*, Contract, and the First Amendment," 51 *Md. L. Rev.* 312 (1992), ***879***

I. Breuer, "Tokhnit la-Ḥukkah ba-Medinah ha-Yehudit" [A Constitutional Program for the Jewish State], *Yavneh, Koveẓ Akadema'i Dati*, 1949, pp. 33–40, ***1613***

N. Brüll, "Die Entstehungsgeschichte des babylonischen Talmuds als Schriftwerkes" [The History of the Writing of the Babylonian Talmud], *Jahrbücher für Jüdische Geschichte und Literatur* [Jewish History and Literature Annual], II (1876), pp. 1–123, ***1456***

P. Buchholz, "Historischer Überblick über die Mannigfachen Codificationen des Halachastoffes, von ihren Ersten Anfängen bis zu ihrem Letzten Abschlusse" [A Historical Overview of the Manifold Codifications of the Corpus of the *Halakhah*, from Their First Beginnings to Their Final Conclusion], *MGWJ*, XIII (1864), pp. 201–217, 241–259, ***1264***

G. Calabresi, *A Common Law for the Age of Statutes* (1982), ***291***

B. Cardozo, "Law and Literature," in *Law and Literature and Other Essays* 10 (1931), ***291***

M.D. Cassuto, "Al Mah Neḥleku Rav Saadiah Gaon u-Ven-Meir?" [What Was the Dispute between Rabbi Saadiah Gaon and Ben-Meir?], *Sefer Rav Saadiah Gaon* [Rabbi Saadiah Gaon Volume], Jerusalem, 1943, pp. 333–364, ***1159***

C. Chavel, *Rabbenu Moshe ben Naḥman*, Jerusalem, 1967, ***1124***

M. Cheshin, "Moreshet Yisra'el u-Mishpat ha-Medinah" [The Jewish Heritage and the Law of the State], in *Zekhuyyot Ezraḥ be-Yisra'el, Kovez̩ Ma'amarim li-Khevodo Shel Ḥayyim H. Cohn* [Civil Rights in Israel—Essays in Honor of Haim Cohn], Tel Aviv, 1982, pp. 47ff., ***1831, 1839, 1921, 1932***

Chitty on Contracts, 21st ed., ***328***

A. Cohen, *Oz̩erot Teiman*, Bene-Berak, 1985, ***1501***

A.S. Cohen, "R. Mordekhai b. Hillel Ashkenazi, Parashat Ḥayyav, Ketavav" [The Life and Works of Mordecai b. Hillel ha-Kohen], *Sinai*, IX to XVI, ***1250***

B. Cohen, *Jewish and Roman Law*, New York, 1966, ***62, 81***

B. Cohen, *Kunteres ha-Teshuvot* [A Bibliography of Responsa], Budapest, 1930; facsimile ed., Jerusalem, 1970, ***89, 1477, 1513, 1524–1525, 1528, 1562***

B. Cohen, *Law and Tradition in Judaism*, New York, 1959, ***292***

B. Cohen, "Mazkeret Meḥabberei ha-Teshuvot be-Sefer Paḥad Yiz̩ḥak" [A Record of the Authors of the Responsa in *Paḥad Yiz̩ḥak*], *Alexander Marx Jubilee Volume*, ed. D. Frankel, New York, 1943, pp. 41–57, ***1551, 1554***

P.Y. Cohen, *Oz̩ar ha-Be'urim ve-ha-Perushim*, ***1411***

H. Cohn, "Al ha-Mishpat ha-Ivri be-Ḥayyeinu" [On Jewish Law in Our Life], *Petaḥim*, II (32) (1975), pp. 43–47, ***1728***

H. Cohn, "De'agah le-Yom Maḥar" [Concern for the Future], *Ha-Praklit*, III (1946), pp. 38ff., ***88, 1613***

H. Cohn, "De'agah Shel Yom Etmol" [Concern for the Past], *Sura*, 1957–1958, pp. 745ff., ***1613***

H. Cohn, "Hefker Bet Din: Le-Shittatam Shel R. Yiz̩ḥak ve-Shel R. Eleazar" [The Power of the Court to Expropriate: According to the Views of R. Isaac and R. Eleazar], *Proceedings of the Fourth International Congress of Jewish Studies*, 1967, pp. 185–188, ***508***

H. Cohn, *Jewish Law in Israeli Jurisprudence*, Louis Caplan Lecture on Jewish Law, 1968, Hebrew Union College Press, ***1730***

H. Cohn, *The Trial and Death of Jesus*, Ktav, 1977, ***6***

M. Corinaldi, "Sa'ad ha-Hafradah ha-Zemanit Bein ha-Ba'al ve-ha-Ishah ve-Hitpatḥuto bi-Fesikat Battei ha-Din ha-Rabbaniyyim be-Yisra'el" [Alimony *Pendente Lite* between Husband and Wife and Its Development in the Decisions of the Rabbinical Courts in Israel], *Shenaton*, I (1974), pp. 184–218, ***1600***

M. Corinaldi, "Shomer she-Masar le-Shomer ba-Mishpat ha-Ivri u-ve-Ḥok ha-Shomerim, 5727–1967" [A Bailee Who Delegates to Another Bailee, in Jewish Law and in the Bailees Law, 1967], *Shenaton*, II (1975), pp. 383–453, ***1694***

Cox, "Judge Learned Hand and the Interpretation of Statutes," 60 *Harv. L. Rev.* 370 (1947), ***291***

R. Cross, *Precedent in English Law*, 1961 & 3d ed., Oxford, 1977, ***230, 961, 980***

Curtis, "A Better Theory of Legal Interpretation," 3 *Vand. L. Rev.* 407 (1950), ***230***

Y. Danziger, "Meḥvah Simlit she-Nizkah Rav mi-To'altah" [A Symbolic Gesture More Harmful than Helpful], *Ha-Praklit*, XXXIII (1981), pp. 619–623, ***1835***

D. Daube, Book Review, "F. Schulz, *History of Roman Legal Science*," *Journal of Roman Studies*, XXXVIII (1948), pp. 113ff., ***292***

D. Daube, "On the Third Chapter of the Lex Aquilia," 52 *L.Q.R.* 253 (1936), ***292***

D. Daube, "Rabbinic Methods of Interpretation and Hellenistic Rhetoric," *HUCA*, XXII (1949), pp. 239–264, ***292***

M.D. David, *Hebrew Deeds of English Jews before 1290*, London, 1888, ***1538***

H. Dernburg, *Pandekten*, 5th ed., Berlin, 1896, ***291***

S. Deutsch, "Gemirut Da'at be-Hitḥayyevuyot ba-Mishpat ha-Ivri" [Intention in Contractual Obligations under Jewish Law], *Dine Israel*, III (1972), pp. 207–226, ***1728***

S. Deutsch, "Gemirut Da'at ve-ha-Kavvanah le-Yiẓẓur Yaḥasim Mishpatiyyim be-Dinei Ḥozim ba-Mishpat ha-Ivri, ha-Angli ve-ha-Yisra'eli" [*Gemirut Da'at* and the Intent to Create Legal Relationships in Jewish, English, and Israeli Contract Law], *Shenaton*, VI-VII (1979–1980), pp. 71–104, ***1873***

S. Deutsch, "Ha-Mishpat ha-Ivri bi-Fesikat Battei ha-Mishpat" [Jewish Law in the Decisions of the General Courts], *Meḥkerei Mishpat*, VI (1988), pp. 7ff., ***1729, 1863***

B. De Vries, *Toledot ha-Halakhah ha-Talmudit* [A History of Talmudic *Halakhah*], Jerusalem, 1969, ***208, 384, 492, 891, 906, 908, 1090***

J.J. Dienstag, "Le-Yaḥas Maran el Mishpat ha-Rambam" [On the Attitude of Rabbi (Kook) to Maimonides' Teaching], *Sinai*, LIX (1966), pp. 54–75, ***1208***

P. Dikstein (Dykan), "Aẓma'ut Medinit ve-Aẓma'ut Mishpatit" [Political Independence and Juridical Independence], *Ha-Praklit*, V (1948), pp. 107–113, ***1617***

P. Dikstein (Dykan), "Hakhrazah al ha-Mishpat ha-Ivri" [A Declaration Regarding Jewish Law], *Ha-Praklit*, V (1948), pp. 3–8, ***1617***

P. Dikstein (Dykan), "Le-Zekher Dr. Avraham Ḥayyim Freimann z"l" [Dr. A.H. Freimann: In Memoriam], *Ha-Praklit*, V (1948), pp. 67–70, ***1618***

P. Dikstein (Dykan), "Lo Titakhein Medinah Ivrit le-Lo Mishpat Ivri" [A Jewish State Is Inconceivable without Jewish Law], *Ha-Praklit*, IV (1947), pp. 328–330, ***1617***

H. Dimitrovsky, "Al Derekh ha-Pilpul" [On the Pilpulistic Method], *Jubilee Volume in Honor of Salo W. Baron*, Jerusalem, 1975, Hebrew sec., pp. 111–181, *1381*

H. Dimitrovsky, "Vikku'aḥ she-Avar bein Maran Rabbi Yosef Caro ve-ha-Mabit" [A Dispute between Our Master, Rabbi Joseph Caro, and Mabit], *Sefer Ẓefat*, Jerusalem, 1969, I, pp. 82ff., *1317*

I. Dinari, "Ha-Minhag ve-ha-Halakhah bi-Teshuvot Ḥakhmei Ashkenaz be-Me'ah ha-Tet-Vav" [Custom and Law in the Responsa of the Halakhic Authorities of Germany in the Fifteenth Century], *B. De Vries Memorial Volume*, 1969, pp. 168–198, *900, 911*

I. Dinari, *Ḥakhmei ha-Halakhah be-Ashkenaz be-Shilhei Yemei ha-Beinayim* [The Halakhic Authorities in Germany at the End of the Middle Ages], Jerusalem, 1987, pp. 302ff., *1517*

B.Z. Dinur, "Le-Mashma'utah Shel Massekhet Avot ke-Makor Histori" [On the Significance of Tractate *Avot* as a Historical Source], *Zion*, XXXV (1970), pp. 1ff., *550*

B.Z. Dinur, *Yisra'el ba-Golah* [Israel in Diaspora], 2d ed., Tel Aviv, 1959, *37, 688, 784–785, 1468, 1858*

W.O. Douglas, "Stare Decisis," 49 *Colum. L. Rev.* 735 (1949), *980*

M. Drori, "Shegagah ba-Mishpat ha-Ivri: Ta'ut be-Din ve-Ta'ut be-Uvdah" [Error in Jewish Law: Mistake of Law and Mistake of Fact], *Shenaton*, I (1974), pp. 72ff., *399, 1323*

P. Dykan (Dikstein), *Mishpat ha-Shalom ha-Ivri, She'elotav le-Halakhah u-le-Ma'aseh* [The Jewish Court of Arbitration—Its Theoretical and Practical Problems], 1925, *1589, 1592–1595*

P. Dykan (Dikstein), *Toledot Mishpat ha-Shalom ha-Ivri* [History of the Jewish Court of Arbitration], Tel Aviv, 1964, *1589, 1592–1596, 1633*

A. Ehrlich, *Mikra ki-Feshuto*, *996*

S. Eidelberg, Review of P. Tishbi, "Ha-im ha-Takkanah she-Lo Laset Shetei Nashim mi-Rabbenu Gershom Hi?" [Is the Enactment Prohibiting Polygamy That of Rabbenu Gershom?], *Tarbiẓ*, XXXIV (1965), pp. 287–288, *784*

S. Eidelberg, "Ḥukkim Germaniyyim be-Aḥat ha-Teshuvot Shel Rabbenu Gershom Me'or ha-Golah" [German Law in a Responsum of Rabbenu Gershom, the Light of the Exile], *Zion*, XVIII (1953), pp. 83–87, *63*

S. Eidelberg, "Matbe'ot Lashon ba-Ivrit Shel Yehudei Ashkenaz be-Shilhei Yemei ha-Beinayim" [Hebrew Idioms and Expressions of the Jews of Germany at the End of the Middle Ages], *Sinai*, LXX (1972), pp. 225–230, *1511*

S. Eisenstadt, "Al Hora'at ha-Mishpat ha-Ivri be-Vet ha-Sefer le-Mishpat Shel Memshelet Ereẓ Yisra'el" [On Teaching Jewish Law in the Law School of the Palestine Government], *Ha-Mishpat*, II (1927), pp. 209–216, *87*

S. Eisenstadt, *Ein Mishpat* [A Bibliography of Jewish Law], Jerusalem, 1931, *62, 81, 1540, 1562*

S. Eisenstadt, *Ha-Mishpat ha-Roma'i* [Roman Law], 2d ed., Tel Aviv, 1962, *93, 292*

S. Eisenstadt, "Medinah u-Mishpat" [State and Law], *Ha-Praklit*, V (1948), p. 113, *1613*

S. Eisenstadt, *Ẓiyyon be-Mishpat* [Zion with Justice], Tel Aviv, 1967, *83, 1588, 1595*

I.S. Elfenbein, "Minhagim Shel Kol ha-Shanah me-Ashkenaz le-Rabbenu Yiẓḥak mi-Dura" [Customs for the Entire Year from Ashkenaz by R. Isaac of Düren], *Ḥorev*, X (1948), pp. 129–184, ***1249***

B.Z. Eliash, "Ethnic Pluralism or Melting Pot?," 18 *Israel L. Rev.* 348 (1983), ***1755***

B.Z. Eliash, "Ha-Ḥakikah ha-Rabbanit ba-Pesikah ha-Rabbanit—Hit'almut ve-Shivrah" [Disregard of Rabbinic Legislation in Rabbinical Court Decisions—The Harmful Results], *Dine Israel*, X–XI, pp. 177–215, ***1808–1809***

A. Ellinson, *Ha-Ishah ve-ha-Mizvot* [Women and the Commandments], 2nd ed., Jerusalem, 1982, ***1799–1800***

P. Elman, "The Basic Law: The Government," 4 *Israel L. Rev.* 242 (1969), ***1651***

M. Elon, "Ashirim Hem ha-Mekorot Hallalu" [These Sources Are Indeed Rich], *Ḥok u-Mishpat*, XXII (1956), pp. 6–8, ***1730***

M. Elon, "Ba'ayot u-Megamot be-Yaḥasei Halakhah u-Medinah" [Problems and Trends in the Relationship between *Halakhah* and State], *Ammudim* (Publication of the Kibbutz ha-Dati), 1974, pp. 202–207, 256–264, ***1756, 1900***

M. Elon, "Darkhei ha-Yeẓirah ha-Hilkhatit be-Fitronan Shel Ba'ayot Ḥevrah u-Mishpat ba-Kehillah" [The Methodology of Halakhic Creativity in Solving Social and Legal Problems in the Jewish Community], *Yiẓḥak Baer Memorial Volume* (*Zion*, XLIV [1979]), pp. 241–264, ***96, 707, 779, 1007***

M. Elon, "Ekronot Musariyyim ke-Normah Hilkhatit" [Moral Principles as Halakhic Norm], *De'ot*, XX (1962), pp. 62–67, ***158, 387***

M. Elon, "Ha-Halakhah ve-ha-Refu'ah ha-Ḥadishah" [*Halakhah* and Modern Medicine], *Molad* (New Series) XXI (1971), pp. 228–236, ***147, 970, 1243***

M. Elon, "Ha-Hityashenut ba-Din ha-Ivri" [Limitation of Actions in Jewish Law], *Ha-Praklit*, XIV (1958), pp. 179–189, 243–279, ***744, 1013, 1726***

M. Elon, *Ḥakikah Datit be-Ḥukkei Medinat Yisra'el u-vi-Shefitah Shel Battei ha-Mishpat u-Vattei ha-Din ha-Rabbaniyyim* [Religious Legislation in the Statutes of the State of Israel and in the Decisions of the General and the Rabbinical Courts], Tel Aviv, 1968, ***105, 230, 235, 572, 786, 828, 831, 879, 1293, 1486, 1600, 1610, 1647, 1651, 1653, 1657, 1660, 1662, 1664, 1671, 1685, 1689, 1728, 1753, 1756, 1767, 1769, 1777, 1803, 1873, 1900, 1905***

M. Elon, "Ha-Ma'asar ba-Mishpat ha-Ivri" [Imprisonment in Jewish Law], *Jubilee Volume for Pinḥas Rosen*, Jerusalem, 1962, pp. 171–201, ***9, 28, 47, 64, 207, 517–518, 692, 821***

M. Elon, *Ha-Mishpat ha-Ivri* [Jewish Law], 1st and 2nd eds., ***1938, 1943***

M. Elon, "Ha-Mishpat ha-Ivri be-Mishpat ha-Medinah, al ha-Maẓuy ve-al ha-Raẓuy" [Jewish Law in the Legal System of the State—Reality and Ideal], *Ha-Praklit*, XXV (1968), pp. 27–53, ***1728, 1730, 1938, 1943–1944***

M. Elon, "Ha-Mishpat ha-Ivri be-Mishpat ha-Medinah, Keiẓad?" [Jewish Law in the Legal System of the State—What Is the Way?], *De'ot*, X (1959), pp. 15–22, ***91, 1728, 1912***

M. Elon, "Ha-Yesh li-Menahel ha-Izavon Kinyan Bo" [Does the Administrator Have a Property Right in the Assets of the Estate?], *Ha-Praklit*, XI (1955), pp. 205–209, ***1674***

M. Elon, *Ḥerut ha-Perat be-Darkhei Geviyyat Ḥov ba-Mishpat ha-Ivri* [Individual Freedom and the Methods of Enforcing Payment of Debts in Jewish Law], Jerusalem, 1964, *11, 28, 48–49, 62, 64, 70, 80, 91, 118–119, 127, 186, 310–311, 399, 414, 416–417, 588–590, 644, 646, 652–654, 709–710, 748, 750, 808–809, 821, 823, 925, 975, 1014, 1027, 1245, 1461, 1466–1467, 1534–1535, 1584, 1586, 1629, 1635–1637, 1639, 1858–1859, 1891–1892*

M. Elon, "He-Arev, ha-Ḥayyav ha-Ikkari ve-Ekron Ḥofesh ha-Hatna'ah be-Dinei Arvut ba-Mishpat ha-Ivri" [The Surety, the Principal Debtor, and the Principle of Freedom of Contract in the Jewish Law of Suretyship], *Proceedings of the Fourth International Congress of Jewish Studies*, I (1967), pp. 197–208, *127, 1090, 1097, 1215, 1246, 1723*

M. Elon, "Im ha-Shenaton" [On the Appearance of the *Shenaton*], *Shenaton*, I (1974), pp. 7–13, *91, 1934*

M. Elon, "In Memory of Asher Gulak," *Shenaton*, IX-X (1982–1983), pp. 3–10, *83*

M. Elon, "Le-Mahutan Shel Takkanot ha-Kahal ba-Mishpat ha-Ivri" [On the Nature of Communal Enactments in Jewish Law], *Meḥkerei Mishpat le-Zekher Avraham Rosenthal* [Legal Studies in Memory of Abraham Rosenthal], Magnes Press, Jerusalem, 1964, pp. 1–54, *685*

M. Elon, "Le-Zikhro Shel Moshe Zilberg" [In Memory of Moshe Silberg], *Shenaton*, II (1975), pp. 1–13, *1730, 1910*

M. Elon (ed.), *Mafte'aḥ ha-She'elot ve-ha-Teshuvot* [Digest of Responsa Literature], *Responsa of Asheri*, Institute for Research in Jewish Law, Jerusalem, 1965, *12, 63, 80*

M. Elon (ed.), *Mafte'aḥ ha-She'elot ve-ha-Teshuvot Shel Ḥakhmei Sefarad u-Ẓefon Afrikah* [Digest of the Responsa Literature of Spain and North Africa], Institute for Research in Jewish Law, Hebrew University, Jerusalem, 1981–1986, *12, 63, 80, 158, 174, 387, 443, 646, 783, 823, 1463, 1520, 1522, 1525–1528, 1531, 1540, 1841, 1892, 1934*

M. Elon, "Meni'im ve-Ekronot be-Kodifikaẓiyah Shel ha-Halakhah" [Motive Forces and Principles in the Codification of the *Halakhah*], *Hagut ve-Halakhah*, XII (1968), pp. 75–119 (*Gevilin*, 1967, pp. 71–85), *1147*

M. Elon, *Mi-Ba'ayot ha-Halakhah ve-ha-Mishpat bi-Medinat Yisra'el* [On the Problems of *Halakhah* and Law in the State of Israel], Publication of the Seminar on the Jewish People in the Diaspora held at the President's Residence, Ha-Makhon le-Yahadut Zemaneinu [Institute for Contemporary Judaism], Hebrew University, Jerusalem, 1973, Sixth Series, Seventh Pamphlet, pp. 9–47, *1587, 1606, 1728, 1730, 1754, 1784, 1900*

M. Elon, "Od le-Inyan Ḥok Yesodot ha-Mishpat" [More about the Foundations of Law Act], *Shenaton*, XIII (1987), pp. 227–256, *1897, 1946*

M. Elon, "Od le-Inyan Meḥkaro Shel ha-Mishpat ha-Ivri" [More About Research into Jewish Law], *Mishpatim*, VIII (1977), pp. 99–137, translated into English in *Modern Research in Jewish Law* (ed. B.S. Jackson), Leiden, 1980, pp. 66–111, *83, 91, 111, 1910, 1914*

M. Elon, "Samkhut ve-Oẓmah ba-Kehillah ha-Yehudit; Perek ba-Mishpat ha-Ẓibburi ha-Ivri" [Authority and Power in the Jewish Community: A Chapter in Jewish Public Law], *Shenaton*, III–IV (1976–1977), pp. 7–34, *96, 387, 702–703, 718, 779, 1007, 1730, 1819*

M. Elon, "The Sources and Nature of Jewish Law and Its Application in the State of Israel" (Part III), 3 *Israel L. Rev.* 416 (1968), *1600, 1613, 1627, 1657, 1769*

M. Elon, "The Sources and Nature of Jewish Law and Its Application in the State of Israel" (Part IV), 4 *Israel L. Rev.* 80 (1969), *575, 587, 605, 607, 829, 1626–1627, 1684, 1728*

M. Elon, "Yiḥudah Shel Halakhah ve-Ḥevrah be-Yahadut Ẓefon Afrika mi-le-Aḥar Gerush Sefarad ve-ad Yameinu" [The Exceptional Character of *Halakhah* and Society in North African Jewry from the Spanish Expulsion to the Present], *Halakhah u-Petiḥut, Ḥakhmei Marokko ke-Fosekim le-Doreinu* [*Halakhah* and Open-Mindedness: The Halakhic Authorities of Morocco as Authorities for Our Own Time], ed. Moshe Bar Yuda, Histadrut Center for Culture and Education, 1985, pp. 15–38, *153, 808–809, 1539, 1584, 1586, 1672, 1755*

Encyclopaedia Brittanica, 1966, *1140*

Encyclopaedia of the Social Sciences, 1949, *1140–1141*

Encyclopedia of Islam, *1466*

Encyclopedia Judaica, Jerusalem, 1971, *1554–1556, 1560*

II, pp. 98–101, s.v. Abortion (by M. Elon), *604*

III, pp. 294–300, s.v. Arbitration (by M. Elon), *20*

V, pp. 857–859, s.v. Compromise (by M. Elon), *20, 175*

V, pp. 882–890, s.v. Conflict of laws (by M. Elon), *10, 38, 48, 79, 213, 677, 878, 936, 1007, 1484, 1767*

V, pp. 923–933, s.v. Contract (by M. Elon), *77, 127, 581, 590–591, 706, 913, 917*

VI, pp. 51–55, s.v. Dina de-malkhuta dina (by S. Shilo), *65*

VI, pp. 1007–1020, s.v. Execution (civil) (by M. Elon), *627, 652–653*

VII, pp. 1003–1007, s.v. Ha'anakah (by M. Elon), *924, 1632*

VII, pp. 1460–1466, s.v. Hassagat gevul (by M. Elon), *395–396, 883*

VII, pp. 1516–1522, s.v. Ḥazakah (by M. Elon), *998, 1201, 1332*

VIII, pp. 279–287, s.v. Hekdesh (by M. Elon), *10, 48, 78, 684–685, 751*

VIII, pp. 1303–1309, s.v. Imprisonment for debt (by M. Elon) *9, 652*

XI, pp. 122–131, s.v. Levirate marriage and *ḥaliẓah* (by M. Elon), *788, 833*

XI, pp. 227–232, s.v. Lien (by M. Elon), *77, 590–591, 596, 648*

XI, pp. 251–254, s.v. Limitation of actions (by M. Elon), *1013*

XI, pp. 565–566, s.v. Lunel, *1240*

XII, pp. 109–151, s.v. Mishpat ivri (by M. Elon), *47, 1555*

XII, pp. 1310–1316, s.v. Obligations, law of (by M. Elon), *77, 109, 588, 596, 706, 1245*

XIII, pp. 636–644, s.v. Pledge (by M. Elon), *590*

XIII, pp. 709ff., s.v. Poland (by H.H. Ben-Sasson), *1346–1347*

XIII, pp. 1351–1359, s.v. Public authority (by M. Elon), *10, 48, 78, 704, 707, 735, 751*

XIV, p. 1145, s.v. Semikhah, *1401*

XIV, pp. 1385–1390, s.v. Shetar (by A. Fuss), *1535*

XV, pp. 524–529, s.v. Suretyship (by M. Elon), *705*

XV, pp. 837–873, s.v. Taxation (by M. Elon), *10, 48, 78, 446, 450, 683, 685, 703, 722, 745–748, 750, 767, 770, 775–776, 921, 923, 942, 1289, 1444, 1913*

XVI, p. 388, s.v. Weights and measures (by D. Sperber), *1073*

Encyclopedia Judaica, Berlin, 1927–1936, *525, 1560*

I. Englard, "The Example of Medicine in Law and Equity on a Methodological Analogy in Classical and Jewish Thought," 5 *Oxford Journal of Legal Studies* 238 (1985), *181*

I. Englard, "Ma'amado Shel ha-Din ha-Dati ba-Mishpat ha-Yisra'eli" [The Status of Religious Law in the Israeli Legal System], *Mishpatim*, II (1970), pp. 268–316, 510–522; IV (1972), pp. 31–62; VI (1975), pp. 5ff., *1653, 1769, 1779, 1806*

I. Englard, "The Problem of Jewish Law in a Jewish State," 3 *Israel L. Rev.* 254 (1968), *1906, 1911–1914*

I. Englard, *Religious Law in the Israel Legal System*, Jerusalem, 1975, *1653*

I. Englard, "Research in Jewish Law: Its Nature and Function," *Modern Research in Jewish Law* (ed. B.S. Jackson), Leiden, 1980, pp. 21–65, *91, 111*

I. Englard, "Shilluv ha-Din ha-Yehudi be-Ma'arekhet ha-Mishpat ha-Yisra'eli" [The Integration of Jewish Law into the Israeli Legal System], *Hagut ve-Halakhah*, XII (1968), pp. 161–198, *1789*

I. Englard, "Tannuro Shel Akhnai—Perushah Shel Aggadah" [Akhnai's Oven—An Interpretation of an *Aggadah*], *Shenaton*, I (1974), pp. 45–56, *263*

A. Enker, *Ha-Koraḥ ve-ha-Ẓorekh be-Dinei Onshin* [Duress and Necessity in Penal Law], Ramat-Gan, 1977, *1922*

A. Enker, "Self-Incrimination in Jewish Law, A Review Essay," *Dine Israel*, 1973, p. cvii (English section), *691*

Ha-Enẓiklopedyah ha-Ivrit [The Hebrew Encyclopedia], Jerusalem, 1949–1981, *232, 604, 1154–1156, 1553, 1555, 1560, 1608, 1632*

Enẓiklopedyah Mikra'it [Encyclopaedia Biblica], Jerusalem, 1950–1982, *93, 167, 1036, 1555*

Enẓiklopedyah Talmudit [Talmudic Encyclopedia], Jerusalem, 1947– , *21, 23, 65–66, 70, 73, 94, 109, 146, 194, 203–204, 208, 210, 212, 271, 305, 322–323, 331, 334, 343–344, 347, 350, 355, 360, 372, 415, 510, 514, 518, 583–584, 1422, 1554, 1604*

A. Epstein, "Al Sefer Halakhot Gedolot" [On the Book *Halakhot Gedolot*], *Ha-Goren*, III (1902), p. 46, *1155*

A. Epstein, *Kadmoniyyot ha-Yehudim* [Early History of the Jews], *1155*

I. Epstein, *The Responsa of Rabbi Simon b. Ẓemaḥ Duran*, 1930 (Jews' College Publications, No. 13), *133, 806–807*

J.N. Epstein, "Ma'asim li-Venei Ereẓ Yisra'el," *Tarbiẓ*, I, book 2 (1930), pp. 33–42, *126*

J.N. Epstein, *Mavo le-Nusaḥ ha-Mishnah* [Introduction to the Text of the Mishnah], 2d ed., Jerusalem, 1964, *224–225, 227, 1042, 1052, 1088, 1109, 1155, 1550*

J.N. Epstein, *Mevo'ot le-Sifrut ha-Amoraim* [Introductions to Amoraic Literature], Jerusalem, 1962, *679, 1008, 1091, 1543, 1550*

J.N. Epstein, *Mevo'ot le-Sifrut ha-Tanna'im* [Introductions to Tannaitic Literature],

Jerusalem, 1957, *276–277, 284–285, 312, 314–315, 378–379, 428, 1029, 1048–1050, 1052, 1057–1059, 1061, 1069, 1080–1081, 1110, 1550*

J.N. Epstein, "Shetar Mattanah le-Ḥud ve-ha-Ẓedak" [The Deed of Special Gift and the *Ẓedak*], *Ha-Mishpat ha-Ivri*, IV (1933), pp. 125–134, *805*

J.N. Epstein, "Tashlum Perush ha-Geonim le-Tohorot" [Supplement to the Geonic Commentary on *Tohorot*], *Tarbiẓ*, XVI (1945), pp. 71–134, *1106*

S. Ettinger, "Toledot Yisra'el ba-Et ha-Ḥadashah" [History of the Jews in the Modern Period], in H.H. Ben-Sasson, *Toledot Am Yisra'el* [History of the Jewish People], Tel Aviv, 1970, III, pp. 17–137, *1576*

D. Even, "Samkhuto ha-Tevu'ah shel Bet ha-Mishpat: Makor le-Sa'adei Yosher" [The Inherent Authority of the Court: A Source for Equitable Relief], *Mishpatim*, VII (1976), pp. 490ff., *177*

Falk, *De'ot*, IX (Passover, 1959) and XI (Sukkot, 1959), *73*

Z. Falk, *Halakhah u-Ma'aseh bi-Medinat Yisra'el* [*Halakhah* and Its Practical Application in the State of Israel], Jerusalem, 1967, *1728*

Z. Falk, *Introduction to Jewish Law of the Second Commonwealth*, Leiden, 1972, *1037*

Z. Falk, *Nissu'in ve-Gerushin* [Marriage and Divorce], Jerusalem, 1962, *786, 1753*

Z. Falk, *Tevi'at Gerushin mi-Ẓad ha-Ishah be-Dinei Yisra'el* [Jewish Law as to a Wife's Right to Obtain a Divorce], Jerusalem, 1973, *1753*

H. Fassel, *Das Mosaisch-Rabbinische Strafgesetz und strafrechtliche Gerichts-Verfahren* [Mosaic Rabbinic Penal Law and Criminal Proceedings], Gross-Kanisza, 1870, *82*

N. Fayyumi, *Gan ha-Sekhalim*, Halikhot Am Yisra'el, Kiryat Ono, 1984, *1464*

S. Federbush, *Bi-Netivot ha-Talmud* [In the Pathways of the Talmud], 1957, *355*

S. Federbush, *Ha-Musar ve-ha-Mishpat be-Yisra'el* [Jewish Law and Morals], Jerusalem, 1950, *154*

S. Federbush, *Mishpat ha-Melukhah be-Yisra'el* [Jewish Governmental Law], Jerusalem, 1952, *56*

S.Z. Feller, "Le-Ittui ha-Hashlamah Shel Averat ha-Genevah" [Concerning the Time when the Crime of Theft Is Consummated], *Mishpatim*, X (1980), pp. 121–149, *1927*

S.Z. Feller, "Pesak Din Tamu'ah" [A Surprising Decision], *Mishpatim*, X (1980), pp. 339–358, *1927*

M. Findling, *Teḥukat ha-Avodah . . . Lefi Dinei ha-Torah . . .* [Labor Law . . . According to the Torah . . .], Jerusalem, 1945, *158, 926*

H. Finkelscherer, "Zur Frage fremder Einflüsse auf das rabbinische Recht" [On the Question of Foreign Influences on Rabbinic Law], *MGWJ*, LXXIX (1935), pp. 38–83, *62*

A.A. Finkelstein, "Midrash, Halakhot ve-Haggadot" [Midrash, Laws, and Aggadot], *Sefer Yovel li-Khevod Yiẓḥak Baer* [Jubilee Volume in Honor of Yiẓḥak Baer], Jerusalem, 1961, pp. 28–47, *277*

L. Finkelstein, *Ha-Perushim ve-Anshei ha-Keneset ha-Gedolah* [The Pharisees and the Men of the Great Assembly], 1950, *555*

L. Finkelstein, *Jewish Self-Government in the Middle Ages*, New York, 1924, *10, 17, 37, 715, 782, 784–792, 794, 796–798, 811, 813– 814, 816–817, 872, 1532*

S.J. Finn, *Kiryah Ne'emanah* [The Faithful City], Vilna, 1915, *308, 1559*

J.L. Fishman (Maimon), "Ha-Minhag be-Sifrut ha-Geonim" [Custom in Geonic Literature], *B.M. Lewin Jubilee Volume*, Jerusalem, 1940, pp. 132–159, *900*

Frank, *Kehillot Ashkenaz u-Vattei Dineihem* [Jewish Communities of Germany and Their Courts], Tel Aviv, 1938, *20*

Z. Frankel, *Darkhei ha-Mishnah* [The Methodology of the Mishnah], ed. Berlin, 1923; ed. Sinai, 1959, *94, 110, 205, 236, 377, 379–380, 399, 401, 547, 1021, 1044, 1046, 1052, 1057, 1106–1108, 1110, 1549*

Z. Frankel, *Der gerichtliche Beweis nach mosaisch-talmudischen Rechte: Ein Beitrag zur Kenntniss des mosaisch-talmudischen Criminal und Civilrechts* [Legal Proof in Mosaic-Talmudic Law: A Contribution to Knowledge of Mosaic-Talmudic Criminal and Civil Law], Berlin, 1846, *82, 1021, 1037*

Z. Frankel, *Entwurf Einer Geschichte d. Literatur d. Nachtalmudischen Responsen* [Outline of the History of the Post-Talmudic Responsa Literature], Breslau, 1865, *1455*

Z. Frankel, *Mevo ha-Yerushalmi* [Introduction to the Jerusalem Talmud], Breslau, 1870, *52, 1091–1092, 1094, 1097–1098, 1549*

Z. Frankel, "Über manches Polizeiliche des talmudischen Rechts" [On Various Talmudic Police (Criminal) Laws], *MGWJ*, I (1851–1852), pp. 243–261, *82*

Frankfurter, "Some Reflections on the Reading of Statutes," 47 *Colum. L. Rev.* 527 (1947), *291*

S. Freehof, Supplement to B. Cohen, *Kunteres ha-Teshuvot*, in *Studies in Bibliography and Booklore*, V (1961), Cincinnati, *1524*

S. Freehof, *The Responsa Literature*, JPS, Philadelphia, 1959, *1442, 1506*

A.H. Freimann, Critique of S. Atlas' Edition of Rabad's Commentary on *Bava Kamma*, *Kiryat Sefer*, XX (1943–1944), pp. 25–28, *1124*

A.H. Freimann, "Ascher Ben Jechiel, Sein Leben und Wirken" [Asher b. Jehiel, His Life and Works], *JJLG*, XII (1918), pp. 237– 317, *1252–1253, 1272, 1519*

A.H. Freimann, "Darkhei ha-Ḥakikah be-Yisra'el" [The Methodology of Jewish Legislation], *Yavneh*, I (1946), 2–3, pp. 41– 44, *1100*

A.H. Freimann, "Die Ascheriden" [The Descendants of Asheri], *JJLG*, XIII (1919), pp. 142–254, *1223, 1253, 1277–1278, 1282, 1301*

A.H. Freimann, "Dinei Yisra'el be-Ereẓ Yisra'el" [Jewish Law in the Land of Israel], *Lu'aḥ ha-Areẓ*, 1946, pp. 110–125, *88, 1576, 1584, 1596, 1601, 1613*

A.H. Freimann, "Ha-Takkanot ha-Ḥadashot Shel ha-Rabbanut ha-Rashit le-Ereẓ Yisra'el be-Dinei Ishut" [The New Enactments of the Chief Rabbinate of Israel on Family Law], *Sinai*, XIV (1944), pp. 254–263, *823*

A.H. Freimann, "Mezonot Shel Yeled she-Nolad she-Lo be-Nissu'im al pi Dinei Yisra'el" [Maintenance of a Child Born out of Wedlock, According to Jewish Law], *Ha-Praklit*, II (1945), pp. 163ff. (reprinted in *Ha-Praklit*, XXV (1968), pp. 163–173), *30*

A.H. Freimann, "Rov u-Mi'ut ba-Ẓibbur" [Majority and Minority in the Community], *Yavneh*, II, Tishri 1948, pp. 1–6, *683, 685, 717*

A.H. Freimann, *Seder Kiddushin ve-Nissu'in Aḥarei Ḥatimat ha-Talmud, Meḥkar Histori-Dogmati be-Dinei Yisra'el* [Law of Betrothal and Marriage after the Completion of the Talmud: A Historical-Dogmatic Study in Jewish Law], Mosad ha-Rav Kook, Jerusalem, 1945, *11, 83, 642, 657–658, 795, 810, 847, 864, 870–872, 875–876, 879, 1506, 1582, 1584, 1755, 1794*

J. Freimann, *Leket Yosher le-Rabbenu Yosef b. R. Moshe, z.l.* [*Leket Yosher* by Rabbenu Joseph b. Moses, of Blessed Memory], Berlin, 1903–1904, *1517*

E. Freund, *Legislative Regulation*, New York, 1932, *1140*

H.D. Friedberg, *Bet Eked Sefarim*, 2d ed., Tel Aviv, 1951–1956, *1411, 1561*

D. Friedmann, "Consequences of Illegality under the Israeli Contracts Law (General Part), 1973," 33 *Int. and Comp. L.Q.* 81 (1984), *1720*

D. Friedmann, *Dinei Assiyat Osher ve-Lo ve-Mishpat* [The Laws of Unjust Enrichment], 1982, *1696, 1830*

D. Friedmann, "Ha-Hora'ah bi-Devar Aẓma'ut ha-Ḥok u-Va'ayat ha-Lakunah ba-Ḥakikah ha-Yisra'elit ha-Ḥadashah" [The Provision Regarding Independence of the Law and the Problem of Lacunae in New Israeli Legislation], *Mishpatim*, V (1973), pp. 91–98, *1729*

D. Friedmann, "Independent Development of Israeli Law," 10 *Israel L. Rev.* 515 (1975), *1728*

D. Friedmann, "Infusion of the Common Law into the Legal System of Israel," 10 *Israel L. Rev.* 324 (1975), *1837*

D. Friedmann, "Od le-Farshanut ha-Ḥakikah ha-Yisra'elit ha-Ḥadashah" [More on the Interpretation of Modern Israeli Legislation], *Iyyunei Mishpat*, V (1977), pp. 463ff., *1733, 1830*

D. Friedmann, "Toẓa'ot I-Ḥukkiyyot ba-Din ha-Yisra'eli le-Or Hora'ot Se'ifim 30–31 le-Ḥok ha-Ḥozim (Ḥelek Kelali)" [The Consequences of Illegality in Israeli Law in the Light of the Provisions of Sections 30–31 of the Contracts Law (General Part)], *Iyyunei Mishpat*, V (1976–1977), pp. 618ff., *1717*

D. Friedmann, "Yesodot be-Dinei Assiyat Osher ve-Lo ve-Mishpat le-Or ha-Ḥakikah ha-Yisra'elit ha-Ḥadashah" [The Fundamentals of the Law of Unjust Enrichment in Light of Modern Israeli Legislation], *Iyyunei Mishpat*, VIII (1981), pp. 22ff., *1696, 1830, 1837–1838*

A.L. Frumkin, *Toledot Ḥakhmei Yerushalayim* [Biographies of the Scholars of Jerusalem], Jerusalem, 1928–1930, *1112*

G. Frumkin, *Derekh Shofet bi-Yerushalayim* [The Way of a Judge in Jerusalem], Tel Aviv, 1955, *1591–1592*

E. Gans, "Die Grundzüge des mosaisch-talmudischen Erbrechts" [Basic Elements of the Mosaic-Talmudic Law of Succession], *Zeitschrift für die Wiss. des Jud.* (Zunz), B.I. (1823), *81*

H. Gans, "Shikkul ha-Da'at Shipputi le-Aharon Barak" [Aharon Barak's View of Judicial Discretion], *Mishpatim*, XVIII (1988), pp. 509–529, *1838, 1896*

Ben-Zion Gat, *Ha-Yishuv ha-Yehudi be-Ereẓ Yisra'el bi-Shenot 5600–5641* [The Jewish Community in the Land of Israel, 1840–1881], Jerusalem, 1963, *1584*

R. Gavison, Introduction to *Zekhuyyot Ezraḥ be-Yisra'el, Koveẓ Ma'amarim li-Khevodo Shel Hayyim H. Cohn* [Civil Rights in Israel—Essays in Honor of Haim Cohn], Tel Aviv, 1982, *1930*

M. Gavra, *Le-Derekh Mahariẓ ba-Halakhah* [On Mahariẓ's Halakhic Methodology] (unpublished thesis, Bar-Ilan University, 1986), *1374*

Gerstein, *Ohel Mo'ed*, 1928, *73*

Y.D. Gilat, "Shetei Bakkashot le-R. Moshe mi-Kuẓi" [Two Requests of R. Moses of Coucy], *Tarbiẓ*, XXVIII (1959), pp. 54–58, *1261*

Y.D. Gilat, "Bet Din Matnin La'akor Davar min ha-Torah" [The Court May Legislate to Uproot a Biblical Law], *Bar Ilan Annual*, 1969–1970, pp. 117–132, *506, 632, 635*

I.M. Ginsberg, *Mishpatim le-Yisra'el* [Laws for Israel], Jerusalem, 1956, *47, 517, 536*

L. Ginzberg, "Al ha-Shittah ha-Madda'it be-Ḥakirat ha-Mishpat ha-Ivri" [On the Scientific Method of Research in Jewish Law], *Ha-Mishpat ha-Ivri*, IV (1933), pp. 208–212, *1037*

L. Ginzberg, *Geonica*, New York, 1909, *268, 1099, 1153*

L. Ginzberg, "Keta'im mi-Kitvei ha-Geonim min ha-Genizah she-be-Miẓrayim" [Fragments from the Geonic Writings from the *Genizah* in Egypt], *Ginzei Schechter*, II, New York, 1929, pp. 47ff., *1460*

L. Ginzberg, *Perushim ve-Ḥiddushim ba-Yerushalmi* [A Commentary on the Palestinian Talmud], *261, 555, 716, 935, 1065, 1098, 1128, 1130–1134, 1136*

Ginzei Schechter, New York, 1929, *16, 113, 766, 1472*

A.L. Globus, "Al Bet Din Ivri" [Concerning the Jewish Court], *Ha-Praklit*, IV (1947), p. 111, *1613*

S.D. Goitein, *Sidrei Ḥinnukh bi-Mei ha-Geonim u-Bet ha-Rambam* [Educational Systems from the Geonic Period to Maimonides], Jerusalem, 1962, *42, 53, 1166–1167, 1183*

S.D. Goitein and A. Ben Shemesh, *Ha-Mishpat ha-Muslemi bi-Medinat Yisra'el* [Moslem Law in the State of Israel], Jerusalem, 1957, *93, 292, 1466*

A. Goldberg, *Kiryat Sefer*, XLII (1967), pp. 460ff., *1150*

Goldstein, *Precedent in Law*, Oxford, Clarendon Press, 1988, *980*

Goodhart, "Determining the Ratio Decedendi of a Case," 40 *Yale L.J.* 161 (1930), *961*

S. Goren, "Leḥimah be-Shabbat le-Or ha-Mekorot" [Warfare on the Sabbath in Light of the Sources], *Sinai*, Jubilee Volume, Jerusalem, 1958, *1036*

H. Graetz, *Divrei Yemei Yisra'el* [History of the Jews], Hebrew trans. S.P. Rabinowitz, Warsaw, 1900, *1224*

H. Graetz, *History of the Jews*, JPS, Philadelphia, 1894, *1094, 1224*

A. Greenbaum, "Ha-Ḥinnukh ha-Dati li-Venot Yisra'el" [Religious Education for Jewish Women], in *Shevilei ha-Ḥinnukh* [Paths of Education], New York, 1966, pp. 24ff., *1799*

Y. Gross, "Haganat Sekhar Ha-Oved" [Wage Protection for the Laborer], *Ha-Praklit*, XVI (1960), pp. 72–86, 153–178, *1630*

A. Grossman, "Yaḥasam Shel Ḥakhmei Ashkenaz ha-Rishonim el Shilton ha-Kahal" [The Relationship of the Early Ashkenazic Halakhic Authorities to Communal Government], *Shenaton*, II (1975), pp. 175–199, *686, 779*

Z. Grunner, "Le-Ẓuratan ha-Mekorit Shel Ḥamishah Kuntresei Teshuvot" [On the

Original Form of Five Compilations of Responsa], *Alei Sefer*, II (1976), p. 5, *1471*

I. Grunwald, *Ha-Rav R. Yosef Caro u-Zemano* [Rabbi Joseph Caro and His Times], New York, 1954, *1373*

A. Gulak, *Das Urkundenwesen im Talmud* [The Nature of Legal Instruments in the Talmud], Jerusalem, 1935, *1028, 1540*

A. Gulak, *Ha-Ḥiyyuv ve-Shi'budav* [Obligations and Their Liens], *627*

A. Gulak, "Hashva'ah Kelalit bein Ru'aḥ Dinei Mamonot ha-Ivriyyim ve-Ru'aḥ Dinei Mamonot ha-Roma'im" [A General Comparison of the Spirit of Jewish Civil Law with That of Roman Civil Law], *Madda'ei ha-Yahadut*, I (1926), pp. 45–50, *76*

A. Gulak, *Le-Ḥeker Toledot ha-Mishpat ha-Ivri bi-Tekufat ha-Talmud* [Studies in the History of Jewish Law in the Talmudic Period], Ha-Sifriyyah ha-Mishpatit, Jerusalem, 1929, *81*

A. Gulak, "Le-Siddur Ḥayyeinu ha-Mishpatiyyim ba-Areẓ" [On the Organization of Our Legal System in the Land of Israel], *Ha-Toren*, New York, 1921, *1592*

A. Gulak, *Oẓar ha-Shetarot ha-Nehugim be-Yisra'el* [A Treasury of the Legal Instruments Used by Jews], Jerusalem, 1926, *513, 1533–1534, 1537, 1539–1540, 1665*

A. Gulak, "Shetar Erusin u-Devarim ha-Niknim be-Amirah be-Dinei ha-Talmud" [The Document of Betrothal and Things that Can Be Acquired by Oral Statements According to Talmudic Law], *Tarbiẓ*, III (1932), pp. 361–376, *424*

A. Gulak, "Tokhnit le-Avodat Ḥevrat Ha-Mishpat Ha-Ivri" [A Program for the Ha-Mishpat Ha-Ivri Society], *Ha-Mishpat ha-Ivri*, II (1927), pp. 195–204, *86*

A. Gulak, *Toledot ha-Mishpat be-Yisra'el bi-Tekufat ha-Talmud, ha-Ḥiyyuv ve-Shi'budav* [A History of Jewish Law in the Talmudic Period: Obligations and Their Associated Liens], Jerusalem, 1939, *81*

A. Gulak, *Yesodei ha-Mishpat ha-Ivri* [The Foundations of Jewish Law], Jerusalem, 1923, *7, 19, 21, 25, 58, 69, 75–76, 80, 82– 83, 120, 146, 219–220, 222, 301, 492, 510, 513, 543, 547, 566, 568, 580, 583–584, 614, 636, 649, 841, 982, 995, 1200, 1534–1535, 1604, 1665, 1667, 1673–1674, 1676, 1679, 1694*

A. Gumaini, *Ḥadirat ha-Shulḥan Arukh le-Teiman* [The *Shulḥan Arukh*'s Penetration into Yemen], 1986, *1374*

I.M. Guttmann, *Mafte'aḥ ha-Talmud* [Key to the Talmud], Budapest-Breslau, 1906–1930, *301, 303, 306–307, 1084*

I.M. Guttmann, *Zur Einleitung in die Halacha* [An Introduction to the *Halakhah*], *94*

A.M. Haberman, *Ha-Genizah ve-ha-Genizot*, Jerusalem, 1971, *1469*

"Ha-Ishah bi-Mekorot ha-Yahadut" [Women in Jewish Sources], in *Hagut, Me'assef le-Maḥashavah Yehudit* [*Hagut*: An Anthology of Jewish Thought], published by the Department of Torah Culture, 1983, *1801*

M. ha-Kohen, "Le-Toledot Mishpat ha-Shalom ha-Ivri be-Ereẓ Yisra'el" [On the History of the Jewish Court of Arbitration in the Land of Israel], in P. Dykan (Dikstein), *Mishpat ha-Shalom ha-Ivri, She'elotav le-Halakhah u-le-Ma'aseh*

[The Jewish Court of Arbitration—Its Theoretical and Practical Problems], Tel Aviv, 1925, pp. 3–4, *1592–1594*

P.I. ha-Kohen, *Oẓar ha-Be'urim ve-ha-Perushim* [A Thesaurus of Explanations and Commentaries], London, 1952, *1110, 1541, 1562*

D. Halaḥmi, *Ḥakhmei Yisra'el* [The Sages of Israel, Rabbinical Biographies], 1980, *171*

I. Fauer ha-Levi, "Yaḥas Ḥakhmei ha-Sefardim le-Samkhut Maran ke-Posek" [The Attitude of the Sephardic Rabbis to Our Master's (Caro's) Authority as an Authoritative Decisionmaker], *Koveẓ R. Yosef Caro* [The Rabbi Joseph Caro Anthology], ed. I. Raphael, Jerusalem, 1969, pp. 189–197, *1373*

S. ha-Levi, "Sippur Shevaḥav Shel Niftar Talmid Ḥakham be-Fanav be-Yom Tov Sheni" [Eulogizing a Deceased Halakhic Scholar on the Second Day of a Festival], *Koveẓ Har'el*, ed. Y. Ratzhabi and Y. Shavtiel, Tel Aviv, 1962, pp. 98–198, *1501*

I. Halevy, *Dorot ha-Rishonim* [lit. "The Early Generations"—A History of the Oral Law to the *Geonim*], Frankfurt-am-Main, 1897–1906, *52, 486, 1092, 1094, 1155*

D. Ha-Livni, *Mekorot u-Masorot le-Seder Nashim* [Sources and Traditions Pertinent to the Order of *Nashim*], Tel Aviv, 1969, *565, 632*

A.A. Harkavy, *Ha-Peles*, year 2, 1902, p. 75, *894*

Ha-Tor, 1921, *824–825*

M. Havaẓelet, "Yaḥas ha-Rambam le-Takkanot ha-Geonim" [Maimonides' Attitude to Geonic Enactments], *Talpiot*, VII (1958), pp. 99–125, *646*

S.Z. Havlin, "Mishneh Torah le-Rambam—Sof Ge'onut" [Maimonides' *Mishneh Torah*—The End of the Geonate], *Ha-Ma'ayan* (Isaac Breuer Institute), V (1965), pp. 41–59, *1221*

S.Z. Havlin, "Takkanot Rabbenu Gershom Me'or ha-Golah be-Inyanei Ishut bi-Teḥumei Sefarad u-Provenẓ" [The Enactments of Rabbenu Gershom Concerning Marital Status in the Regions of Spain and Provence], *Shenaton*, II (1975), pp. 200–257, *785*

S.Z. Havlin, "Teshuvot Ḥadashot le-Rashba" [New Responsa of Rashba], *Moriah*, 1st annual, III–IV, pp. 58–67, *785*

I. Heinemann, *Philons Griechische und Jüdische Bildung* [Philo's Greek and Jewish Education], Breslau, 1932, *1037*

M.D. Herr, "Le Va'ayat Hilkhot Milḥamah be-Shabbat bi-Mei Bayit Sheni u-vi-Tekufat ha-Mishnah ve-ha-Talmud" [On the Question of the Laws of War on the Sabbath in the Second Commonwealth and the Mishnaic and Talmudic Periods], *Tarbiẓ*, XXX (1961), pp. 242–256, 341–356, *1036*

T. Herzl, *The Jewish State*, in L. Lewisohn, *Theodore Herzl, A Portrait for This Age*, World Publishing Co., 1953, *1607*

Hertz, *Pentateuch and Haftorahs* (2d ed., 1977), *195*

I. Herzog, "Ha-Teḥikkah ve-ha-Mishpat ba-Medinah ha-Yehudit" [Legislation and Law in the Jewish State], *Yavneh, Koveẓ Akadema'i Dati*, 1949, pp. 9–13, *1614–1615*

I. Herzog, "Gedarim be-Din Malkhut," *Ha-Torah ve-ha-Medinah*, VII–VIII (1955–1957), pp. 9–12, ***1916***

I. Herzog, "Haẓa'at Takkanot bi-Yerushot" [Proposed Enactments on Inheritance], *Talpiot*, VI (Nissan 1953), pp. 36–50, ***1494, 1684***

I. Herzog, *The Main Institutions of Jewish Law*, 2d ed., London, 1965–1967, ***66, 83, 154, 208, 1053, 1694***

I. Herzog, "Mashehu al Yosef ben Mattityahu" [A Note on Josephus], *Sinai*, XXV (1949), pp. 8–11, ***1037***

W.N. Hibbert, *Jurisprudence*, London, 1932, ***1919***

M. Higger, *Oẓar ha-Baraitot* [A Treasury of the *Baraitot*], New York, 1938–1948, ***1040***

H.Z. Hirschberg, *Toledot ha-Yehudim be-Afrikah ha-Ẓefonit* [History of the Jews in North Africa], Jerusalem, 1962, ***37, 804, 807, 859, 1168***

H. Hirschfeld, "Arabic Portion of Cairo *Genizah* at Cambridge," *JQR* [Old Series], XVI (1904), pp. 290–299, ***1161***

A. Hirschmann, *Rabbi Yiẓḥak bar Sheshet (ha-Ribash), Derekh Ḥayyav u-Tekufato* [Rabbi Isaac b. Sheshet, His Life and Times], Jerusalem, 1956, ***133, 1253***

S.B. Hoenig, *The Great Sanhedrin*, 1953, ***558***

D.Z. Hoffmann, *Der Oberste Gerichtshof* [The Supreme Tribunal], Berlin, 1878, ***244, 558***

D.Z. Hoffmann, *Die Erste Mischna und die Controversen der Tannaim* [The Early Mishnah and the Tannaitic Disputes] (translated into Hebrew as *Ha-Mishnah ha-Rishonah u-Felugta de-Tanna'i* by S. Greenberg, Berlin, 1914), ***1050***

W. Holdsworth, *A History of English Law*, ***1926***

O.W. Holmes, *The Common Law*, Harvard U. Press, 1963, ***1711***

O.W. Holmes, "Theory of Legal Interpretation," in *Collected Legal Papers* 207 (1921), ***291***

S.A. Horodezky, *Kerem Shelomo*, 1897, ***1385, 1388***

M. Horovitz, *Die Frankfurter Rabbinerversammlung von Jahre 1603* [The Frankfurt Rabbinical Synod of 1603], ***794–795***

M. Horovitz, *Rabbanei Frankfurt* [Frankfurt's Rabbis], Heb. trans., Jerusalem, 1972, ***794***

A.H. Hyman, *Toledot Tannaim va-Amoraim* [A History of the *Tannaim* and *Amoraim*], London, 1910, ***567, 1044, 1088, 1588***

C. Ilbert, *The Mechanics of Law Making*, New York, 1914, ***1140***

International Encyclopaedia of Social Sciences, 1968, ***1140, 1144***

N. Isaacs, "Influence of Judaism on Western Law," in *Legacy of Israel*, Oxford, 1927, pp. 377–406, ***63***

M. Ish-Shalom, *Hakdamah la-Mekhilta* [Introduction to the *Mekhilta*], Vienna, 1870, ***94, 891, 1048***

Jackson, "Decisional Law and Stare Decisis," 30 *A.B.A.J.* 334 (1944), ***980***

Jackson, "The Meaning of Statutes: What Congress Says or What the Court Says," 34 *A.B.A.J.* 535 (1948), ***291***

M. Jastrow, *A Dictionary of the Targumim, the Talmud Babli and Yerushalmi, and the Midrashic Literature*, Philadelphia, 1903 (New York, 1950), ***338, 946, 1566***

H. Jaulus, "R. Simeon ben Zemach Duran," *MGWJ*, XXIV (1875), pp. 160–178, ***1474***

I. Jeiteles, "Fremdes Recht in Talmud" [Foreign Law in the Talmud], *JJLG*, XXI (1930), pp. 109–128, ***62***

A. Jellinek, *Kunteres ha-Kelalim*, Vienna, 1878; facsimile ed., Jerusalem, 1970, ***1541***

E. Jenks, *A Digest of English Civil Law* (3rd ed., 1938), ***1721***

H.F. Jolowicz, *Historical Introduction to the Study of Roman Law*, 2d ed., Cambridge, 1952, ***191, 1466***

J.P.D., "Le-Darkhei ha-Ḥakikah bi-Medinateinu" [On Approaches to Legislation in Our State], *Ha-Praklit*, VI (1949), pp. 144ff., ***1613***

J. Kafaḥ, *Halikhot Teiman* [The Practices of Yemen], 1961, ***1499–1501***

J. Kafaḥ, "Ḥinnukh ha-Bat le-Limmud Torah, le-Mussar u-le-Ezrat ha-Zulat" [Education of Daughters Concerning Torah, Ethical Teachings, and Helping Others], in *Ha-Ishah ve-Ḥinnukhah* [Women and Their Education], Kefar Saba, 1980, ***1800***

J. Kafaḥ, "Kesharehah Shel Yahadut Teiman im Merkazei ha-Yahadut" [The Ties between the Jews of Yemen and the Centers of Jewish Life], *Yahadut Teiman—Pirkei Meḥkar ve-Iyyun* [Research Studies on the Jews of Yemen], Jerusalem, 1976, pp. 43ff., ***1500***

J. Kafaḥ, "Sheliḥim Niskarim le-Teiman" [Paid Solicitors for Charity in Yemen], in *Meḥkerei Ereẓ Yisra'el*, Book 2/5, Jerusalem, 1955, pp. 297–300, ***1501***

K. Kahana Kagan, *The Case for Jewish Civil Law in the Jewish State*, London, 1960, ***168***

K. Kahana Kagan, *Three Great Systems of Jurisprudence*, London, 1955, ***168***

Y. Kahan, "Shipput Rabbani ve-Shipput Ḥiloni" [Rabbinic Adjudication and Secular Adjudication], *Dine Israel*, VII (1977), pp. 205–213, ***1756, 1758, 1760, 1779***

I.Z. Kahane, "Halakhah u-Minhag" [Law and Custom], *Mazkeret le-Rav Herzog z.l.* [A Memorial to Rabbi Herzog], Jerusalem, 1962, pp. 554–564, ***899–900, 903, 908, 911***

I.Z. Kahane, "Ha-Pesak ve-ha-Teshuvah" [The Codificatory Ruling and the Responsum], *Sefer ha-Shanah le-Madda'ei ha-Yahadut ve-ha-Ru'aḥ Shel Universitat Bar Ilan* [Bar Ilan University Annual for Judaic Studies and Humanities], I (1963), pp. 270–281, ***1459***

I.Z. Kahane, "Ha-Pulmus mi-Saviv Kevi'at ha-Hakhra'ah ke-ha-Rambam" [The Controversy Concerning Determination of the Law in Accordance with the Views of Maimonides], *Sinai*, XXXVI (1956), pp. 391–411, ***705, 1223, 1230, 1323***

I.Z. Kahane, *Le-Takkanat Agunot* [On Solving the Problems of *Agunot*], Jerusalem, 1947, ***529***

I.Z. Kahane, *Maharam me-Rothenburg, Teshuvot, Pesakim u-Minhagim* [Maharam of Rothenburg, Responsa, Rulings, and Customs], ***1520***

I.Z. Kahane, *Meḥkarim be-Sifrut ha-Teshuvot* [Studies in the Responsa Literature], JPS, Philadelphia, 1959, *1454*

I.Z. Kahane, *Sefer ha-Agunot*, Jerusalem, 1954, *524, 529–530*

A.A. Kaplan, *Be-Ikvot ha-Yir'ah*, Jerusalem, 1960, *83*

J. Kaplan, *The Redaction of the Babylonian Talmud*, New York, 1933, *1092, 1094*

A. Karlin, *Sinai*, XXIX (1951), pp. 141–145, *204*

A. Karlin, "Dinei Mekhirah Lefi Tokhnit Sefer ha-Mikaḥ ve-ha-Mimkar Shel Rav Hai Gaon" [Laws of Sale according to *Sefer ha-Mikaḥ ve-ha-Mimkar* of Rabbi Hai Gaon], *Divrei Mishpat*, IV (1956), *1166*

A. Karlin, "Ha-Halakhah ve-ha-Mishpat be-Torato Shel Rabbenu Saadiah Gaon Zal" [*Halakhah* and Law in the Teachings of Rabbenu Saadiah Gaon, of Blessed Memory], *Sefer Rav Saadiah Gaon: Kovez̧ Torani-Madda'i* [Rabbi Saadiah Gaon: A Religious and Scientific Anthology], Mosad ha-Rav Kook, Jerusalem, 1943, pp. 428–441, *1161*

A. Karlin, "Midrash Halakhah," *Sinai*, XXXI (1952), pp. 163–176, *322*

M. Kasher, *Ha-Rambam ve-ha-Mekhilta de-R. Shim'on bar Yoḥai* [Maimonides and the *Mekhilta* of R. Simeon bar Yoḥai], New York, 1943, *391, 1205*

M. Kasher, *Sarei ha-Elef*, New York, 1959, *1111, 1472, 1477, 1561–1562*

J. Katz, "Af Al Pi She-Ḥata Yisra'el Hu" [A Jew, Notwithstanding He Has Sinned, Remains a Jew], *Tarbiz̧*, XXVII (1958), pp. 203–217, *103*

J. Katz, *Exclusiveness and Tolerance*, *37–38, 66, 70, 1584*

J. Katz, "Ma'ariv bi-Zemano ve-she-Lo bi-Zemano" [The Evening Prayer Within and Outside of Its Appointed Time], *Zion*, XXXV (1970), pp. 35–60, *911*

J. Katz, "Maḥloket ha-Semikhah bein Rabbi Ya'akov Beirav ve-ha-Ralbaḥ" [The Dispute over Ordination between Rabbi Jacob Berab and Ralbaḥ (Rabbi Levi b. Ḥabib)], *Zion*, XVI (1951), pp. 28–45, *1310*

J. Katz, *Tradition and Crisis*, 1961, *28, 37, 756, 1380, 1576*

Kitvei B. Katznelson [The Writings of B. Katznelson], 1945–1950, *1943*

Y. Kaufmann, *Commentary on the Book of Judges*, 1962, *1054*

Y. Kaufmann, *Golah ve-Nekhar* [Exile and Estrangement], 1962, *38–39, 1576–1578*

Y. Kaufmann, *Toledot ha-Emunah ha-Yisra'elit* [History of the Jewish Religion], 2d ed., Jerusalem, 1954, *41*

R. Keeton, *Venturing to Do Justice* (1969), *291*

H. Kelsen, "On the Pure Theory of Law," 1 *Israel L. Rev.* 1 (1966), *142*

I. Kena'ani, "Ha-Ḥayyim ha-Kalkaliyyim bi-Z̧efat u-Sevivotehah ba-Me'ah ha-Shesh Esreh va-Ḥaz̧i ha-Me'ah ha-Sheva Esreh" [The Economic Life of Safed and its Environs in the Sixteenth and the First Half of the Seventeenth Centuries], *Zion* (Me'asef), VI (1934), Jerusalem, pp. 172–217, *1133*

Kerem Ḥemed, 1839, *1088, 1217, 1230–1231*

M. Keshet, "Ḥok Yesodot ha-Mishpat, 5740—1980" [The Foundations of Law Act, 1980], *Ha-Praklit*, XXXIII (1981), pp. 611– 618, *1835*

A. Kimmelman, "Luaḥ Ezer le-Ferushim mi-Tekufat ha-Geonim (me-Erez̧ Yisra'el, Bavel, ve-Kairouan)" [Citator to the Commentaries of the Geonic Period (in the Land of Israel, Babylonia, and Kairouan)], *Shenaton*, XI–XII (1984–1986), pp. 463–564, *1114*

A. Kirschenbaum, "Dinei ha-Yosher ba-Mishpat ha-Ivri" [The Laws of Equity in Jewish Law], *Da'at*, Bar-Ilan University, 1984, pp. 43ff., *177, 253*

A. Kirschenbaum, *Ḥok Yesodot ha-Mishpat—Meẓi'ut ve-Ẓippiyyot* [The Foundations of Law Act—Reality and Expectations], *Iyyunei Mishpat*, XI (1986), pp. 117ff., *1938*

A. Kirschenbaum, *Self-Incrimination in Jewish Law*, New York, 1970, *691*

G. Kisch, *Jewry-Law in Medieval Germany*, 1949, *37–38*

I. Kister, "Dinei Ẓedakah ve-Shimmusham ba-Mishpat be-Yisra'el" [The Laws of Charity and Their Application in Israeli Law], *Ha-Praklit*, XXIV (1968), pp. 168–177, *1661*

S. Klein, *Toledot ha-Yishuv ha-Yehudi be-Ereẓ Yisra'el me-Ḥatimat ha-Talmud ad Tenu'at Yishuv Ereẓ Yisra'el* [A History of Jewish Settlement in the Land of Israel from the Completion of the Talmud until the Movement for the Resettlement of the Land of Israel], Tel Aviv, 1928, pp. 126ff., *1132*

S. Klein, "Zur Ortsnamenkunde Palastinas" [On the Study of Palestinian Place Names], *MGWJ*, 1920, pp. 181–196, *525*

A.P. Kleinberger, *Ha-Maḥashavah ha-Pedagogit Shel ha-Maharal mi-Prag* [The Educational Philosophy of Maharal of Prague], Jerusalem, 1962, *1380*

H. Klinghoffer, "Die Entstehung des Staates Israel" [The Birth of the State of Israel], *Jahrbuch des Offentlichen Rechts der Gegenwart*, Neue Folge, X (1961), pp. 439–484, *231*

H. Klinghoffer, *Mishpat Minhali* [Administrative Law], Jerusalem, 1957, *142*

Kokourek and Koven, "Renovation of the Common Law Through Stare Decisis," 29 *Ill. L. Rev.* 971 (1935), *980*

M. Konvitz (ed.), *Judaism and Human Rights*, New York, 1972, *1863*

S.H. Kook, *Iyyunim u-Meḥkarim*, Jerusalem, 1959, *1265*

Koveẓ R. Yosef Caro [The Rabbi Joseph Caro Anthology], ed. I. Raphael, Jerusalem, 1969, *1371*

Nachman Krochmal, *Moreh Nevukhei ha-Zeman* [A Guide for the Perplexed of the Time], ed. S. Rawidowicz, Berlin, 1924, *41, 193, 205, 1070, 1549*

Kitvei Reb Naḥman Krochmal [The Collected Writings of Nachman Krochmal], ed. S. Rawidowicz, Berlin, 1924, *556*

N. Lamm, "The Fourth Amendment and Its Equivalent in the Halacha," 16 *Judaism* 300 (1965), *1860*

M. Landau, "Halakhah ve-Shikkul Da'at ba-Asiyyat Mishpat" [Rule and Discretion in Judicial Decision Making], *Mishpatim*, I (1969), pp. 292–307, *1738, 1927*

M. Landau, "Legislative Trends in the Land Code Bill, 1964," *Scripta Hierosolymitana*, 1966, pp. 136ff., *1710*

Landes and Posner, "Legal Precedent: A Theoretical and Empirical Analysis," 19 *J. Law and Economics* 249 (1976), *980*

Landis, "Statutes and the Sources of Law," in *Harvard Legal Essays* 213 (1934) (reprinted in 2 *Harv. J. on Legis.* 7 [1965]), *291–292*

Landis, "A Note on 'Statutory Interpretation,'" 43 *Harv. L. Rev.* 886 (1930), *292*

M.E. Lang, *Codification in the British Empire and America*, Amsterdam, 1924, *1140*

Leach, "Revisionism in the House of Lords: The Bastion of Rigid Stare Decisis Falls," 80 *Harv. L. Rev.* 797 (1967), ***980***

R.W. Lee, *The Elements of Roman Law*, London, 1946, ***191***

R. Leflar, *Appellate Judicial Opinions* (1974), ***292***

Lehman, "How to Interpret a Difficult Statute," 1979 *Wis. L. Rev.* 489, ***292***

N. Leibowitz, *Studies in Bereshit* (Genesis), 3d rev. ed., 1976, ***196***

Y. Leibowitz, "Ha-Torah ke-Mishpat Yisra'el" [The Torah as the Law of Israel], *Sura*, III (1957), pp. 495–509, ***1906, 1913***

"Le-Toledot Ḥevrat ha-Mishpat ha-Ivri" [History of the Ha-Mishpat Ha-Ivri Society], *Ha-Mishpat*, II (1927), pp. 220–222, ***1588–1589***

B. Levine, "On Translating a Key Passage," 1 *S'vara* 71 (1990), ***970***

J. Levinger, *Darkhei ha-Maḥashavah ha-Hilkhatit Shel ha-Rambam* [Methodology of Maimonides' Halakhic Thought], Jerusalem, 1965, ***204–205, 208–209, 1193, 1197, 1205, 1208***

Levontin and Goldwater, *Kelalei Bererat ha-Din be-Yisra'el ve-Siman 46 li-Devar ha-Melekh* [Israeli Choice-of-Law Principles and Article 46 of the Palestine Order in Council], Harry Sacher Institute for Research into Legislation and Comparative Law, Hebrew University, Jerusalem, 1974, ***1729***

J. Levy, *Wörterbuch über die Talmudim und Midraschim* [Talmudic and Midrashic Dictionary], 2d ed., Berlin, 1924, ***13, 388, 572, 680, 946, 991, 1053–1054, 1565–1566***

B.M. Lewin, "Mi-Seridei ha-Genizah" [Some *Genizah* Fragments], *Tarbiẓ*, II (1931), pp. 383–410, ***1157***

B.M. Lewin, *Oẓar Ḥilluf Minhagim bein Benei Ereẓ Yisra'el u-vein Benei Vavel* [Compendium of Differences in Customs between the Residents of the Land of Israel and the Residents of Babylonia], Jerusalem, 1942, ***1361***

B.M. Lewin, "Rabbanan Savora'i ve-Talmudam" [The Savoraic Rabbis and Their Talmud], *Rabbi Kook Memorial Volume*, IV, pp. 148ff., ***1093–1094, 1456***

L. Lewin, *Die Landessynode der Grosspolnischen Judenschaft* [The National Synod of Greater Polish Jewry], Frankfurt-am-Main, 1926, ***820***

A. Lichtenstein, "Ba'ayot Yesod be-Ḥinnukhah Shel ha-Ishah" [Fundamental Problems Concerning the Education of Women], in *Ha-Ishah ve-Ḥinnukhah* [Women and Their Education], Kefar Saba, 1980, ***1801***

H. Lichtenstein, "Die Fastenrolle, Eine Untersuchung zur Jüdisch-hellenistischen Geschichte" [The Scroll of Fasts—An Inquiry in Jewish-Hellenistic History], *HUCA*, VIII–IX (1931–1932), pp. 257–351, ***516, 1040***

S. Lieberman, *Ha-Yerushalmi ki-Feshuto* [TJ According to Its Plain Meaning], Jerusalem, 1935, ***940, 1066, 1136***

S. Lieberman, *Greek in Jewish Palestine*, New York, 1942, ***588***

S. Lieberman, *Hellenism in Jewish Palestine*, 1950, ***94, 224, 227, 276, 306–307, 312–313, 315, 351, 1051–1052***

S. Lieberman, *Hilkhot ha-Yerushalmi le-Rabbenu Moshe ben Maimon* ["Laws of the Jerusalem Talmud" by Maimonides], New York, 1948, ***96, 1107, 1187, 1215***

S. Lieberman, "Mashehu al Mefarshim Kadmonim la-Yerushalmi" [On Early

Commentators on the Jerusalem Talmud], *Alexander Marx Jubilee Volume*, New York, 1950, Hebrew section, pp. 287–301, ***1130, 1132***

S. Lieberman, *Talmudah Shel Keisarin* [The Talmud of Caesaria], Jerusalem, 1931 (published in *Tarbiẓ* [supplement], II, book 4 [1931], pp. 1–108), ***1097***

S. Lieberman, "Tikkunei Yerushalmi" [Emendations in TJ], *Tarbiẓ*, V (1934), pp. 97–110, ***517***

S. Lieberman, *Tosefet Rishonim*, Jerusalem, 1937–1939, ***364, 680***

S. Lieberman, *Tosefta ki-Feshutah*, New York, 1955–1967, ***213, 303, 425, 428, 503, 508, 540, 557, 559, 561, 624, 681, 716, 885, 888, 902, 949, 969, 970, 972, 993, 1036, 1059, 1065–1066, 1110, 1281***

B. Lifshitz, "Ma'amadah ha-Mishpati Shel Sifrut ha-She'elot ve-ha-Teshuvot" [The Legal Status of the Responsa Literature], *Shenaton*, IX–X (1982–1983), pp. 265–300, ***1460, 1503***

E.M. Lipschuetz, *R. Shelemo Yiẓḥaki (Rashi)* (in E.M. Lipschuetz, *Ketavim*, I (1947), and republished as a separate volume by Mosad ha-Rav Kook, Jerusalem, 1966), ***975, 1116, 1132***

B. Lipkin, "Arikhat Din be-Mishpat ha-Torah" [Advocacy under the Law of the Torah], *Sinai*, XXX (1952), pp. 46–61; XXXI (1952), pp. 265–283, ***1505***

B. Lipkin, "Hatna'at ha-Goremim bi-Devarim she-be-Mamon" [Stipulation by the Parties in Monetary Matters], *Sinai*, XXXV (1954), pp. 111–126, ***127***

B. Lipkin, "Samkhut ha-Ḥakikah Shel ha-Ẓibbur" [The Legislative Authority of the Public], *Sinai*, XXV (1949), pp. 233–253, ***493, 713***

B. Lipkin, "Shittot ha-Rishonim be-Takkanot ha-Kahal" [The Approach of the *Rishonim* to Communal Enactments], *Ha-Torah ve-ha-Medinah* [Torah and State], II (1950), pp. 41–54, ***717***

B.Z. Luria, *Megillat Ta'anit*, Jerusalem, 1964, ***1040***

S.D. Luzzatto, *Ohev Ger*, 2nd ed., Cracow, 1895, ***1045***

Maḥanayim, LIX (1961), p. 36, ***1036***

J.L. Maimon, "Shulḥan Arukh ve-Nos'ei Kelov" [The *Shulḥan Arukh* and Its Commentaries], *Koveẓ R. Yosef Caro* [The Rabbi Joseph Caro Anthology], ed. I. Raphael, Jerusalem, 1969, pp. 42–63, ***1411***

J. Mann, "The Responsa of the Babylonian *Geonim* as a Source of Jewish History," *JQR* (N.S.), VII (1916–1917), p. 460, ***1513***

J. Mann, "Sekirah Historit le-Dinei Nefashot ba-Zeman ha-Zeh" [Historical Survey of Contemporary Law on Capital Cases], *Ha-Ẓofeh le-Ḥokhmat Yisra'el*, X (1926), pp. 200–208, ***37***

H.D. Mantel, *Studies in the History of the Sanhedrin*, Cambridge, Mass., 1965, ***486, 525, 558, 566, 1043***

A. Marcus, *Ha-Ḥasidut* [Hasidism], Tel Aviv, 1954, ***1580***

S. Marcus, "Korot Shalshelet ha-Rabbanim le-Mishpaḥat Bekemoharar" [A History of the Rabbinic Dynasty of the Bekemoharar Family], *Mizraḥ u-Ma'arav*, V (1930), pp. 173–184, ***1439***

S. Marcus, "Toledot ha-Yehudim be-Khene'a ba-I Kretim" [History of the Jews of Candia on the Island of Crete], *Tarbiẓ*, XXXVIII (1969), pp. 161–174, ***11***

M. Margaliot, *Ha-Ḥillukim she-bein Anshei Mizraḥ u-Venei Ereẓ Yisra'el* [The Differences between the People of the East and the Residents of the Land of Israel], Jerusalem, 1938, *933, 1098, 1131, 1361–1362*

M. Margaliot, *Sefer Hilkhot ha-Nagid* [The Book of Laws of the Nagid], Jerusalem, 1962, *1115, 1468, 1477, 1543*

R. Margaliot, "Defusei ha-Shulḥan Arukh ha-Rishonim" [The First Printed Editions of the *Shulḥan Arukh*], *Kovez̤ Rabbi Yosef Caro* [The Rabbi Joseph Caro Anthology], ed. I. Raphael, Jerusalem, 1969, pp. 89–100, *1344*

R. Margaliot, "Ha-Rambam ve-ha-Ra'avad" [Maimonides and Rabad], *Sinai*, XXXVI (1954), pp. 387–390, *1224*

R. Margaliot, *Toledot Adam, Korot Yemei Ḥayyei ha-Maharsha* [The Story of a Man: A Biography of Maharsha], Lemberg, 1911, *1128*

P.B. Maxwell, *On the Interpretation of Statutes*, 12th ed., Bombay, 1969, *292*

S. Mayer, *Die Rechte der Israeliten, Athener und Römer, mit Rücksicht auf die neuen Gesetzgebungen* [Israelite, Athenian, and Roman Law in the Light of Modern Legislation], Leipzig, 1865–1868, *81*

E.Z. Melamed, "Ha-Ma'aseh ba-Mishnah ki-Mekor le-Halakhah" [*Ma'aseh* in the Mishnah as a Source of *Halakhah*], *Sinai*, XLVI (1960), pp. 152–156, *948, 951*

E.Z. Melamed, "Keniyyat Me'arat ha-Makhpelah" [The Purchase of the Cave of Machpelah], *Tarbiz̤*, XIV (1943), pp. 11–18, *196*

E.Z. Melamed, *Midreshei Halakhah Shel ha-Tannaim ba-Talmud ha-Bavli* [The Halakhic *Midrashim* of the *Tannaim* in the Babylonian Talmud], Jerusalem, 1943, *1048*

I. Meron, "Nekudot Magga Bein ha-Mishpat ha-Ivri le-Vein ha-Mishpat ha-Muslemi" [Points of Contact between Jewish and Moslem Law], *Shenaton*, II (1975), pp. 343–359

J.D. Michaelis, *Abhandlungen von dem Ehegesetzen Mosis, welche die Heyrathen in die nahe Freundschaft untersagen* [Studies in Mosaic Marriage Laws Forbidding Incestuous Marriages], Goettingen, 1768, *81*

J.D. Michaelis, *Mosaisches Recht* [Mosaic Law], 2nd ed., Reutlingen, 1785–1793, *81*

J.D. Michaelis, *Mosaisches Peinliches Recht nebst einer Vergleichung des heutigen Peinlichen Rechtes mit demselben* [A Comparative Study of Mosaic and Contemporary Penal Law], Braunschweig u. Hildesheim, 1778, *81*

M. Mielziner, *Mavo la-Talmud* [An Introduction to the Talmud], 4th ed., New York, 1968, *52*

Millon Ben Yehudah [Ben Yehudah's Hebrew Dictionary], Tel Aviv, 1959, *107, 203*

Mitchell, "Rights of Finders as Against the Owner of the Locus in Quo," 22 *Cornell L.Q.* 263 (1936), *1744*

M. Molkho, "Toledot Yehudei Saloniki" [A History of the Jews of Salonika], in *Saloniki, Ir va-Em be-Yisra'el* [Salonika, A Major Jewish City], Jerusalem-Tel Aviv, 1967, pp. 5–37, *865*

S. Morag, "Hai-Ḥayyim (le-Mahut Shemo Shel ha-Rav Hai Gaon)" [Hai-Ḥayyim (On the Nature of the Name of Hai Gaon)], *Tarbiz̤*, XXXI (1962), pp. 188–190, *1164*

D.H. Müller, "Die Gesetze Hammurabis und ihr Verhältnis zur mosaischen Gesetzgebung sowie zu den XII Tafeln" [The Laws of Hammurabi and their Relationship to Mosaic Legislation and the Twelve Tables], *Jahresbericht der Israelitisch-Theologischen Lehranstalt* [Jewish Theological Seminary Annual], Vienna, X (1903), pp. 16–17, 92, ***197, 1013***

J. Müller, "Briefe und Responsen in der Vorgeonaischen Jüdischen Literatur" [Epsitles and Responsa in Pre-Geonic Jewish Literature], *Vierter Bericht über die Lehranstalt fur die Wissenschaft des Judenthums in Berlin* [Fourth Report of the Berlin Institute for the Science of Judaism], Berlin, 1886, ***1455***

J. Müller, *Mafte'aḥ li-Teshuvot ha-Geonim* [Index to Responsa of the *Geonim*], Berlin, 1891, ***1178***

A. Naḥlon, "Samkhut ha-Ẓibbur le-Hatkin Takkanot Lefi ha-Tashbeẓ: Ha-Guf ha-Matkin Takkanot" [The View of Tashbeẓ on the Authority of the Community to Enact Legislation: The Legislative Body], *Shenaton*, I (1974), pp. 142–178, ***778***

A. Naḥlon, "Samkhut ha-Ẓibbur le-Hatkin Takkanot Lefi ha-Tashbeẓ: Mahutan ha-Mishpatit Shel Takkanot ha-Kahal" [The View of Tashbeẓ on the Authority of the Community to Enact Legislation: The Legal Nature of Communal Enactments], *Shenaton*, III–IV (1976–1977), pp. 271–326, ***778–779***

Y.L. Nahum, "Avelut be-Furim" [Mourning on *Purim*], *Sinai*, XCII (1983), pp. 254–265, ***1374***

Y.L. Nahum, "Birkhat Hadlakat Ner Shel Yom Tov" [Benediction on Lighting the Festival Candles], *Sinai*, LXXXV (1979), pp. 55–91, ***1374***

Y.L. Nahum, *Ḥasifat Genuzim mi-Teiman* [Laying Bare the Archives of Yemen], Holon, 1981, ***1464***

Y.L. Nahum, "Keri'at Targum ha-Torah ve-Haftarah be-Ẓibbur" [Public Reading of the Torah and Haftarah in Aramaic Translation], *Sinai*, LXXXVIII (1981), pp. 219–238, ***1374***

Y.L. Nahum, *Ẓohar le-Ḥasifat Ginzei Teiman* [Light on the Discovery of the Archives of Yemen], Tel Aviv, 1986, ***1232, 1374, 1496, 1501***

B. Netanyahu, *Don Isaac Abravanel: Statesman and Philosopher*, Philadelphia (2d ed., 1968), ***253***

J. Neubauer, "Halakhah u-Midrash Halakhah" [*Halakhah* and Halakhic Midrash], *Sinai*, XXII (1948), pp. 49–80, ***286***

J. Neubauer, *Ha-Rambam al Divrei Soferim* [Maimonides on *Divrei Soferim*], Jerusalem, 1957, ***208, 286***

Y.Y. Neubert, *Ḥinnukh ha-Banim le-Miẓvot* [Education of Children to Observe the Commandments], Appendix to *Shemirat Shabbat ke-Hilkhatah*, Jerusalem, 1965, pp. 308–310, ***1799***

H.S. Neuhausen, *Torah Or le-ha-Rambam* [Scriptural Index for Maimonides], Baltimore, 1942, ***1198***

J. Neusner, *A History of the Jews in Babylonia*, Leiden, 1965–1970, ***525***

R.A. Newman, *Equity and Law: A Comparative Study*, New York, 1961, ***177***

R.A. Newman, "Equity in Comparative Law," 17 *Int. and Comp. L.Q.* 807 (1968), ***177***

R.A. Newman, "The Hidden Equity," 19 *Hastings L.J.* 147 (1967), ***177***

I. Nissim, "Haggahot ha-Rema al ha-Shulḥan Arukh" [Rema's Glosses to the *Shulḥan Arukh*], *Sinai*, Jubilee Volume, 1958, pp. 29–39, ***1357, 1361, 1363***

I. Nissim, "Haggahoteihem Shel Rabbi Ya'akov Castro ve-Rabbi Ya'akov Ẓemaḥ al Shulḥan Arukh" [The Glosses of Rabbi Jacob Castro and Rabbi Jacob Ẓemaḥ to the *Shulḥan Arukh*], *Sefunot*, II (1958), pp. 89–102, ***1371***

Note, "Intent, Clear Statements, and the Common Law: Statutory Interpretation in the Supreme Court," 95 *Harv. L. Rev.* 892 (1982), ***292***

Note, "Oaths in Judicial Proceedings and Their Effect upon the Competency of Witnesses," 51 *Amer. L. Reg.* 373 (1903), ***1700***

C.E. Odgers, *The Construction of Deeds and Statutes*, 4th ed., London, 1956, ***328***

R.S. Offenstein, *Sefer ha-Yovel la-Rambam, 700 Shanah le-Mitato* [Maimonides' Jubilee Volume: The Seven Hundredth Anniversary of His Death], 1908, ***198***

M. Ostrowsky, *Mavo la-Talmud* [Introduction to the Talmud], Tel Aviv, 1935, ***331, 355***

J. Parkes, *The Jews in the Medieval Community*, London, 1938, ***37***

G.W. Paton, *Jurisprudence*, 3rd ed., 1964; 4th ed., Oxford, 1972, ***1459, 1919***

H. Perlman, *Al ha-Ẓedek* [On Justice], Jerusalem, 1962, ***168, 177***

A. Perls, "Der Minhag im Talmud" [Custom in the Talmud], *Tiferet Yisra'el (Israel Lewy Jubilee Volume)*, 1911, German Section, pp. 66–75, ***885, 888, 932***

I. Pokrovsky, *Toledot ha-Mishpat ha-Roma'i* [A History of Roman Law], Jerusalem, 1925, ***93, 103, 312***

I. Pokrovsky, *Ha-Problemot ha-Yesodiyyot Shel ha-Mishpat ha-Ezraḥi* [The Fundamental Problems of Civil Law] (Hebrew trans., A. Litai), Jerusalem, 1922, ***1140–1141***

I. Polotzki, "Ha-Te'udot ha-Yevaniyyot mi-Me'arat ha-Iggerot" [Greek Documents from the Cave of the Documents], *Yedi'ot be-Ḥakirat Ereẓ Yisra'el ve-Atikotehah* [Recent Developments in the Archeology of Ancient Israel], 1962, pp. 237–241, ***1036***

R. Powell, "Good Faith in Contracts," 9 *Current Legal Problems* 16 (1956), ***188***

"Practice Statement (Judicial Precedent)," [1966] 1 *Weekly L.R.* 1234, ***980***

U. Procaccia, *Dinei Peshitat Regel ve-ha-Ḥakikah ha-Ezraḥit be-Yisra'el* [Bankruptcy Law and Civil Legislation in Israel], Jerusalem, 1984, ***1830, 1885–1890***

U. Procaccia, "Ḥok Yesodot ha-Mishpat, 5740—1980" [The Foundations of Law Act, 1980], *Iyyunei Mishpat*, X (1984), pp. 145ff., ***1835***

Annotation, "Prospective or Retroactive Operation of Overruling Decisions," 10 *A.L.R.3d* 1371 (1968), ***980***

J.J. Rabinowitz, *Jewish Law, Its Influence on the Development of Legal Institutions*, New York, 1956, ***62, 1540***

R.N.N. Rabinowitz, *Ma'amar al Hadpasat ha-Talmud* [Essay on the Printing of the Talmud], ed. A.M. Haberman, Jerusalem, 1952, ***1176, 1254***

E. Rackman, "Jewish Law in the State of Israel—Reflections from History," *Dine Israel*, VI (1975), English section, pp. VII–XXIV, ***1728***

L. Radzinowich, *A History of English Criminal Law and its Administration from 1750*, London, 1948, ***1926***

N. Rakover, "Al Leshon ha-Ra ve-al ha-Anishah Alehah ba-Mishpat ha-Ivri" [On Defamation and Its Penalties in Jewish Law], *Sinai*, LI (1962), pp. 197–209, 326–345, ***1644***

N. Rakover, "Ha-Haganah al Ẓin'at ha-Perat" [Protection of Individual Privacy], *Sidrat Meḥkarim u-Sekirot ba-Mishpat ha-Ivri* [Review of Research in Jewish Law], Ministry of Justice of Israel, 1970, ***1860***

N. Rakover, "Mekorot ha-Mishpat ha-Ivri le-Ḥok ha-Shomerim" [The Jewish Law Sources of the Bailees Law], *Ha-Praklit*, XXIV (1968), pp. 208ff., ***1694***

M.W. Rapaport, *Der Talmud und sein Recht* [The Talmud and Its Law], Berlin, 1912

M.W. Rapaport, "Ha-Mishpat ha-Ivri be-Sifrut Yisra'el" [Jewish Law in Jewish Literature], *Ha-Shilo'aḥ*, XXIX (1913), pp. 293–305, ***110***

H.Z. Reines, *Torah u-Musar* [Torah and Morals], Jerusalem, 1954, ***142***

Reisman, "Possession and the Law of Finders," 52 *Harv. L. Rev.* 1105 (1939), ***1744***

Report of the Kahan Commission, ***1858***

Restatement in the Courts, Permanent Edition, 1945, ***1144***

Restatement of the Law, Conflict of Laws, 1934, ***1144***

I. Rivkind, Review of *Le-Toledot ha-Defus ha-Ivri be-Folin* [Studies in the History of Hebrew Printing in Poland], *Kiryat Sefer*, XI (1934–1935), pp. 95–104, ***1521***

S. Rosenberg, "Ve-Shuv al Derekh ha-Rov" [More About the Way of the Majority], *Sefer Manhigut Ruḥanit be-Yisra'el, Morashah ve-Ya'ad* [The Book of Spiritual Leadership in Israel—Tradition and Objective], ed. A. Belfor, 1982, pp. 87ff., ***177, 253***

E.S. Rosenthal, "Al Derekh ha-Rov" [On the Way of the Majority], *Perakim* (The Annual of the Schocken Institute for Judaic Research), Jerusalem, I (1967–1968), pp. 183ff., ***177, 253, 500, 624, 1193***

S. Rosenthal, "Shinnuyei Nusḥa'ot be-Sefer ha-Mordekhai" [Textual Variances in *Sefer ha-Mordekhai*], *Shanah be-Shanah* (Heichal Shelomo Annual), 1968, pp. 234–243, ***1250***

A. Rosen-Tzvi, *Yaḥasei Mamon Bein Benei Zug* [Financial Relationships between Spouses], Jerusalem, 1982, ***1753, 1806***

A. Ross, *On Law and Justice*, London, 1958, ***177***

Z. Rubashov (Shazar), "Yiddishe Gevi'us Eidus in die Shailes u-Teshuvos" [Testimony in Yiddish in the Responsa], *Yivo, Historishe Shriften* [Yivo, Historical Studies], I, Warsaw, 1929, pp. 116–195, ***1507***

J.L. Saalschütz, *Das Mosaisches Recht mit Berücksichtingung des spätern Jüdischen* [Mosaic Law in the Light of Later Jewish Law], Berlin, 1846–1848, ***81***

J.W. Salmond, *Jurisprudence*, 12th ed., London, 1966, ***106, 191, 229–232, 292, 328, 478–479, 903, 930, 979–980, 1018***

J. Salvdor, *Histoire des Institutions de Moïse et du Peuple Hébreu* [A History of Mosaic and Hebrew Institutions], Paris, 1828, ***81***

M. Samet, *Kiryat Sefer*, XLIII (1968), pp. 429–441, ***1242***

Sanders and Wade, "Legal Writings on Statutory Construction," 3 *Vand. L. Rev.* 569 (1950), ***292***

Schaefer, "Precedent and Policy," 34 *U. Chi. L. Rev.* 3 (1966), ***980***

S. Schechter, "A Hoard of Hebrew Manuscripts," *Studies in Judaism* (Second Series), JPS, 1908, ***1469***

I. Schepansky, "Takkanot ha-Geonim" [Geonic Enactments], *Ha-Darom*, XXIV (1967), pp. 135–197, ***646***

I. Schepansky, "Takkanot ha-Rishonim" [Enactments of the *Rishonim*], *Ha-Darom*, XXVIII (1969), pp. 145–159, ***782, 787–788, 810***

I. Schepansky, "Takkanot Rabbenu Gershom Me'or ha-Golah" [Enactments of Rabbenu Gershom, the Light of the Exile], *Ha-Darom*, XXII (1966), pp. 103–120, ***782, 784–785***

I. Schepansky, "Takkanot Shum" [The Enactments of "Shum"], *Ha-Darom*, XXVI (1968), pp. 173–197, ***782, 788, 836***

J.E. Scherer, *Die Rechtsverhältnisse der Juden in der Deutsch-Österreichischen Ländern* [Legal Relationships of the Jews in the German-Austrian States], Leipzig, 1901, ***37–38***

B.Z. Schereschewsky, *Dinei Mishpaḥah* [Family Law], 3rd ed., Jerusalem, 1984, ***572, 786, 790, 829, 1657, 1753, 1767, 1771, 1786–1787, 1803***

B. Schieber, "The Albeck System in Talmudic Research," *Modern Research in Jewish Law* (ed. B.S. Jackson), Leiden, 1980, pp. 112–122, ***91***

P. Schiffman, *Dinei Mishpaḥah be-Yisra'el* [Family Law in Israel], 1984, ***1753, 1784***

P. Schiffman, *Samkhut Bet Din Rabbani be-Nissu'in ve-Gerushin she-Ne'erkhu mi-Ḥuẓ le-Yisra'el* [The Jurisdiction of the Rabbinical Courts over Marriages and Divorces Effected outside the State of Israel], *Mishpatim*, VI (1975), pp. 372ff., ***1756***

D. Schonberg, "New Developments in the Israeli Law of Negligent Misrepresentation," 31 *Int. and Comp. L.Q.* 207 (1982), ***156, 1729***

R. Schroeder, *Lehrbuch der Deutschen Rechtsgeschichte* [Textbook on the History of German Law], 6th ed., Berlin, 1922, ***37***

F. Schulz, *History of Roman Legal Science*, Oxford, 1951, ***93, 191***

J. Segal, "Al ha-Mishpat ha-Ḥiloni ba-Areẓ" [On Secular Law in the Land of Israel], *Ha-Torah ve-ha-Medinah*, VII–VIII (1955–1957), pp. 74–95, ***1914, 1916***

M.Z. Segal, "Derash, Midrash, Bet Midrash," *Tarbiẓ*, XVII (1946), pp. 194–196, ***276***

M.Z. Segal, *Sefer ha-Zikkaron le-A. Gulak u-le-S. Klein* [Memorial Volume for A. Gulak and S. Klein], Jerusalem, 1942, ***198, 1024***

A.H. Shaki, "Ba'ayat ha-Ḥozeh le-Tovat Ẓad Shelishi" [The Problem of Third-Party-Beneficiary Contracts], *Sugyot Nivḥarot ba-Mishpat* [Selected Subjects in Law], Jerusalem, 1958, I, pp. 470–508, ***113***

A.H. Shaki, "Kavvei Yiḥud be-Sidrei Din ha-Rabbaniyyim" [Distinctive Characteristics of Rabbinical Court Proceedings], *Sefer Sanhedrai*, 1971, pp. 275–302, ***1819***

A.H. Shaki, *Mi-Hu Yehudi be-Dinei Medinat Yisra'el* [Who Is a Jew According to the Laws of the State of Israel], Jerusalem, 1977, ***1688–1689***

G. Shalev, *Tenayot Petor be-Ḥozim* [Exculpatory Clauses in Contracts], Harry Sacher Institute for Research into Legislation and Comparative Law, Hebrew University, Jerusalem, 1974, ***184***

Shapiro, "Toward a Theory of Stare Decisis," 1 *J. Legal Studies* 125 (1972), *980*

N. Shapiro, "Ha-Lashon ha-Tekhnit ba-Sifrut ha-Rabbanit" [Tehcnical Language in Rabbinic Literature], *Leshonenu*, XXVI (1962), pp. 209–216, *1511*

M. Shava, "Al ha-Shipput be-Inyanei Mezonot Shel Muslemim ve-Nozrim ve-al Middat Teḥulat ha-Hora'ot ha-Prozeduraliot she-be-Ḥok ha-Mezonot" [Concerning Adjudication in Matters of Support in Cases of Moslems and Christians, and the Extent to Which the Procedural Rules in the Maintenance Law Apply], *Ha-Praklit*, XXXVI (1985), pp. 464–477, *1769*

M. Shava, "Comments on the Law of Return (Who Is a Jew)," 3 *Tel Aviv University Studies in Law* 140 (1977), *1689*

M. Shava, *Ha-Din ha-Ishi be-Yisra'el* [Personal Law in Israel], 2nd ed., 1984, *1753, 1806*

M. Shava, "Ha-im Setiyyah o Hit'almut Shel Bet Din me-Hora'at Ḥok Ḥilonit ha-Mufnet elav bi-Meyuḥad, Kamoha ke-Ḥarigah mi-Samkhut?" [Does a Rabbinic Court's Departure from or Disregard of a Provision of a Secular (State) Law Specifically Directed to It Constitute Action in Excess of Jurisdiction?], *Ha-Praklit*, XXVIII (1972–1973), pp. 299ff., *1759*

M. Shava, "Ta'ut bi-Kevi'at ha-Yahadut—Ha-Sholelet Samkhut?" [Does an Incorrect Determination of Jewish Identity Negate the Existence of Jurisdiction?], *Ha-Praklit*, XXV (1969), pp. 617–641, *1789*

H.J. Sheftel, *Erekh Millin, le-Shi'urei Torah she-bi-Khetav ve-she-be-al Peh, le-Matbe'ot, Middot* . . . [On Units of Measurement in the Written and Oral Law for Coins, Measures, etc.], Berdichev, 1904; reprinted, Tel Aviv, 1969, *1073*

H. Shein, "Al Derekh ha-Rov—Maḥaloket Medummah?" [On the Way of the Majority—A Pseudo-Controversy?], *Da'at*, 1984, pp. 55ff., *177, 253*

S. Shilo, *Dina de-Malkhuta Dina*, Jerusalem, 1975, *70, 1819*

S. Shilo, "Dinei Mamonot be-Vattei ha-Din ha-Rabbaniyyim" [Civil Law in the Rabbinical Courts], *Ha-Praklit*, XXVI (1970), pp. 523–542; XXVII (1971), pp. 254–260, *155, 158, 1819*

S. Shilo, "Ha-Bissus ha-Mishpati la-Kelal Dina de-Malkhuta Dina" [The Legal Basis for the Doctrine of *Dina de-Malkhuta Dina*], *Mishpatim*, II (1970), pp. 329–344, *66*

S. Shilo, "Hassagot al Pesikat Battei ha-Din ha-Rabbaniyyim be-Inyan Hassagat Gevul Misḥarit" [Critique of the Decisions of the Rabbinical Courts on the Question of Unfair Business Competition], *Mishpatim*, VI (1975), pp. 530ff., *155, 158, 1819*

S. Shilo, "Le-Ma'amado Shel ha-Mishpat ha-Ivri ba-Medinah" [On the Position of Jewish Law in the State], *Dine Israel*, V (1974), pp. 255–258, *1728*

I. Shiloh, "Ḥok ha-Yerushah, 1965, bi-Re'i ha-Pesikah" [The Succession Law, 1965, as Reflected in Court Decisions], *Iyyunei Mishpat*, III (1973), pp. 34ff., *1728*

Shimon Shkop, *Sha'arei Yosher*, *137*

E. Shochetman, "Ḥovat ha-Hanmakah ba-Mishpat ha-Ivri" [The Obligation to

State Reasons for Legal Decisions in Jewish Law], *Shenaton*, VI–VII (1979–1980), pp. 319–397, *1468, 1503*

E. Shochetman, "Le-Mahutam Shel Kelalei ha-Halakhah be-Sugyat Haḥzakat ha-Yeladim" [The Essential Nature of the Halakhic Principles Respecting Custody of Children], *Shenaton*, V (1978), pp. 285–320, *1797*

E. Shochetman, *Ma'aseh ha-Ba be-Averah* [Transactions Involving Illegality], Jerusalem, 1981, *130*

D.M. Shohet, *The Jewish Court in the Middle Ages*, New York, 1931, *62*

Shur, *Kadmoniyyot ha-Yehudim* [Antiquities of the Jews], *1032*

Shuraki, *Korot ha-Yehudim bi-Ẓefon Afrikah* [History of the Jews of North Africa], Tel Aviv, 1975, *1583*

A. Siev, *Ha-Rema*, Jerusalem, 1957, *1346, 1349, 1356–1357*

M. Silberg, *Ha-Ma'amad ha-Ishi be-Yisra'el* [Personal Status in Israel], 4th ed., Jerusalem, 1958, *6, 786, 1681, 1753, 1759, 1764, 1769*

M. Silberg, "Li-She'elat Arikhat Kodex Ivri" [On the Question of Preparing a Jewish Legal Code], *Ha-Praklit*, IV (1947), pp. 262–265, *1612–1613*

M. Silberg, *Talmudic Law and the Modern State*, New York, 1973, *88, 111, 128–129, 154, 181–183, 263, 512, 626, 628, 1612, 1730*

Rudolph Sohm, *Institutionen, Geschichte und System des Römischen Privatrechts* [Institutions, History, and System of Roman Private Law], 17th ed., Berlin, 1949, *2, 290–291*

Z. Sorotzkin, *Moznayim la-Mishpat* [Scales of Justice], 1955, *1800*

A. Sperber, *Kitvei ha-Kodesh be-Aramit al Yesod Kitvei Yad u-Sefarim Atikim* [The Holy Scriptures in Aramaic on the Basis of Manuscripts and Ancient Books], 4 vols., 1959–1968, *1045*

Sprecher, "The Development of the Doctrine of Stare Decisis and the Extent to Which It Should Be Applied," 31 *A.B.A.J.* 501 (1945), *980*

I.S. Spiegel, "Sefer Maggid Mishneh she-al Mishneh Torah le-Rambam" [The Book *Maggid Mishneh* on Maimonides' *Mishneh Torah*], *Kiryat Sefer*, XLVI (1970), pp. 554–579, *1233*

"Status of the Rule of Judicial Precedent (Cincinnati Conference on Judicial Precedent)," 14 *U. Cinn. L. Rev.* 203 (1940), *980*

H.N. Steinschneider, *Ir Vilna, Zikhronot Adat Yisra'el ve-Toledot Ḥayyei Gedolehah* [Vilna, A History of the Jewish Community and Biographies of Its Leading Halakhic Authorities], Vilna, 1900, *1558–1559*

S.M. Stern, "Ḥalifat ha-Mikhtavim Bein ha-Rambam ve-Ḥakhmei Provinẓa" [The Correspondence between Maimonides and the Scholars of Provence], *Zion*, XVI (1951), pp. 18–29, *1185*

M. Sternberg, "Ha-Normah ha-Basisit Shel ha-Mishpat be-Yisra'el" [The Basic Norm of the Law in Israel], *Ha-Praklit*, IX (1953), pp. 129–143, *231*

Otto Stobble, *Die Juden in Deutschland während des Mittelalters* [The Jews in Germany during the Middle Ages], 3rd ed., Berlin, 1923, *37*

J. Stone, *Precedent and Law: Dynamics of Common Law Growth*, Sydney, Australia, Butterworth, 1985, *980*

H. Strack, *Introduction to the Talmud and Midrash*, Athenaeum, New York, 1974, *94, 407, 1053, 1084–1085*

Sunstein, "Interpreting Statutes in the Regulatory State," 103 *Harv. L. Rev.* 405 (1989), *292*

I. Sussman, "Tom Lev be-Dinei Ḥozim—Ha-Zikah la-Din ha-Germani" [Good Faith in Contract Law—The Link to German Law], *Iyyunei Mishpat*, VI (1979), pp. 485ff., *1733–1735*

Y. Sussman, "Mikẓat Mat'amei Parshanut" [Some Choice Principles of Interpretation], *Sefer ha-Yovel le-Pinḥas Rosen* [Jubilee Volume for Pinḥas Rosen], Jerusalem, 1962, pp. 146–161, *1728, 1837*

Sykes, "A Modest Proposal for a Change in Maryland's Statutes Quo," 43 *Md. L. Rev.* 647 (1984), *292*

S. Tal, "Ha-Get mi-Klivah" [The Bill of Divorcement from Cleves], *Sinai*, XXIV (1949), pp. 152–167, 214–230, *1506*

D. Tamar, Review of R.J.Z. Werblowski, *Joseph Karo, Lawyer and Mystic*, in *Kiryat Sefer*, XL (1965), pp. 65–71, *1316*

D. Tamar, *Meḥkarim be-Toledot ha-Yehudim be-Ereẓ Yisra'el u-ve-Italyah* [Studies in the History of the Jews in the Land of Israel and in Italy], Jerusalem, 1970, *1310*

D. Tamar, "Le-Verur Shenat Petiratam Shel Gedolei Ḥakhmei Ereẓ Yisra'el ve-Turkiyah" [On the Clarification of the Date of Death of Leading Scholars of the Land of Israel and of Turkey], *Sinai*, LXX (1972), pp. 231ff., *1234*

Tanakh, Jewish Publication Society, 1985, *139, 276, 302, 309, 341, 346, 368, 388, 509, 553, 907, 970, 997, 1065, 1120, 1297, 1643*

I. Ta-Shema, "Al Sefer Issur ve-Hetter Shel R. Yeruḥam ve-al R. Yiẓḥak mi-Dura" [On *Sefer Issur ve-Hetter* of R. Jeroham and on R. Isaac of Düren], *Sinai*, LXIV (1969), pp. 254–257, *1249*

I. Ta-Shema, "Yeẓirato ha-Sifruti Shel Rabbenu Yosef ha-Levi ibn Migash" [The Literary Works of R. Joseph ha-Levi ibn Migash], *Kiryat Sefer*, XLVI (1971), pp. 541–553, *1183*

V.A. Tcherikover and A. Fuchs, *Corpus Papyrorum Judaicorum*, vols. I–III, Jerusalem-Cambridge, Mass., 1957–1964, *1028*

Ch. Tchernowitz (Rav Ẓa'ir), *Toledot ha-Halakhah* [History of the *Halakhah*], 2d ed., New York, 1945, *64, 193, 205, 236, 301, 884, 1550*

Ch. Tchernowitz (Rav Ẓa'ir), *Toledot ha-Posekim* [History of the *Posekim*], New York, 1946–1948, *96, 1155, 1157, 1170–1171, 1221, 1269, 1304, 1316, 1342, 1347, 1356, 1363, 1376, 1388, 1550*

G. Tedeschi, "Ba'ayat ha-Likkuyim be-Ḥok ve-Siman 46 li-Devar ha-Melekh be-Mo'aẓato" [The Problem of Lacunae in the Law, and Article 46 of the Palestine Order in Council], in *Meḥkarim be-Mishpat Arẓeinu* [Studies in the Law of Our Land], 2nd ed., 1959, pp. 132ff., *1622–1623*

G. Tedeschi, "Bittul Siman 46 li-Devar ha-Melekh ve-Ko'aḥ Pe'ulato" [The Repeal of Article 46 of the Palestine Order in Council and Its Effect], *Mishpatim*, VIII (1977), pp. 180–185, *1830, 1886–1887*

G. Tedeschi, "Heskemei ha-Minhal ha-Ẓibburi im ha-Perat" [Contracts of the Public Administration with Private Parties], *Mishpatim*, XII (1982), pp. 227–247, *1830, 1834–1835*

G. Tedeschi, "Ḥiyyuv ha-Mezonot be-Mishpateinu ha-Ezraḥi" [The Obligation of Support in Our Civil Law], *Mishpatim*, VI (1976), pp. 242–274, *1728*

G. Tedeschi, "Mashber ha-Mishpaḥah va-Ḥasidei ha-Masoret" [The Crisis in Family Life and the Devotees of Tradition], *Studies in Memory of Avraham Rosenthal*, Jerusalem, 1964, pp. 282ff., *1670–1671*

G. Tedeschi, *Meḥkarim be-Mishpat Arẓeinu* [Studies in the Law of Our Land], 2nd ed., Jerusalem, 1959, *1835–1836*

G. Tedeschi, "Sodot Iskiyyim" [Trade Secrets], *Ha-Praklit*, XXXV (1983), pp. 5–34, *1830, 1834–1835*

I. Tishbi, "Iggerot R. Ya'akov Sasportas Neged Parnesei Livorno mi-Shenat 5441" [Letters of R. Jacob Sasportas against the Communal Leaders of Leghorn in 1681], *Koveẓ al Yad*, XIV, Mekiẓei Nirdamim, Jerusalem, 1946, pp. 145–159, *34*

I. Tishbi, *Mishnat ha-Zohar*, 2d ed., Jerusalem, 1957, *1316*

P. Tishbi, "Ha-im ha-Takkanah she-Lo Laset Shetei Nashim mi-Rabbenu Gershom Hi?" [Is the Enactment Prohibiting Polygamy That of Rabbenu Gershom?], *Tarbiẓ*, XXXIV (1965), pp. 49–55, *784*

S. Toaff, "Maḥaloket R. Ya'akov Sasportas u-Farnesei Livorno al ha-Shipput ha-Otonomi 'ba-Umah ha-Yehudit' be-Livorno bi-Shenat 5441" [Controversy between R. Jacob Sasportas and the Communal Leaders of Leghorn Concerning Juridical Autonomy in the "Jewish Nation" in Leghorn in 1681], *Sefunot*, IX (1965), pp. 167–191, *28, 34*

J. Tobi, *Iyyunim bi-Megillot Teiman* [Studies in Yemenite Documents], Jerusalem, 1986, *1500*

I.M. Toledano, "Matai u-ve-eillu Mekomot Nitkabbel ha-Shulḥan Arukh le-Halakhah Pesukah" [When and Where the *Shulḥan Arukh* Was Accepted as the Authoritative Law], *Koveẓ R. Yosef Caro* [The Rabbi Joseph Caro Anthology], ed. I. Raphael, 1969, pp. 184–188, *1373, 1422*

I.M. Toledano, *Ner ha-Ma'arav, Toledot Yisra'el be-Marokko* [The Light of the West: A History of the Jews in Morocco], Jerusalem, 1911, *807, 1168, 1539*

Tushnet, "Following the Rules Laid Down: A Critique of Interpretivism and Neutral Principles," 96 *Harv. L. Rev.* 781 (1983), *292*

I. Tuvi (ed.), *The Yemenite Manuscripts in the Ben-Zvi Institute*, Ben-Zvi Institute, Jerusalem, 1982, *1232*

I. Twersky, "Al Hassagot ha-Ra'avad le-Mishneh Torah" [On Rabad's Critical Glosses to the *Mishneh Torah*], *Harry Wolfson Jubilee Volume*, New York, 1965, Hebrew section, pp. 169–186, *1216, 1224*

I. Twersky, "The Beginnings of *Mishneh Torah* Criticism," *Biblical and Other Studies*, ed. A. Altmann, Cambridge, Mass., 1963, pp. 161–182, *1216*

I. Twersky, *Rabad of Posquières*, JPS, 1980, *1111, 1123–1124, 1216, 1224*

H. Tykocinski, *Die Gaonäischen Verordnungen*, Berlin, 1929, *646*

H. Tykocinski, *Takkanot ha-Geonim* [Geonic Enactments], Jerusalem, 1970, *646–647, 650–653, 656–657, 659–660*

M. Unna, *Bi-Derakhim Nifradot—Ha-Miflagot ha-Datiyyot be-Yisra'el* [With Diverse Approaches—The Religious Parties in Israel], 1984, ***1606, 1914***

M. Unna, *Ha-Mishpat ha-Ivri be-Ḥakikat ha-Keneset* [Jewish Law in Knesset Legislation], Lecture delivered at Bar-Ilan University (undated), ***1681, 1728***

M. Unna, "Mashma'utah Shel ha-Hashpa'ah ha-Hilkhatit Shel ha-Ḥakikah" [The Signficance of the Influence of the *Halakhah* on Legislation], *Hagut ve-Halakhah*, 1968, pp. 147–160, ***1907***

Y. Unna, *Rav Moshe ben Naḥman (Ha-Ramban), Ḥayyav u-Pe'ulato* [Naḥmanides—His Life and Work], Jerusalem, 1954 (2d expanded ed.), ***1124***

E.E. Urbach, *Ba'alei ha-Tosafot, Toledoteihem, Ḥibbureihem ve-Shittatam* [The Tosafists: Their History, Writings, and Methodology], Jerusalem, 1956, ***718, 766, 911, 1117–1119, 1121–1123, 1132, 1179, 1235, 1239–1240, 1242, 1253, 1259, 1263, 1285, 1545, 1550***

E.E. Urbach, "Ha-Derashah ki-Yesod ha-Halakhah u-Va'ayat ha-Soferim" [Exegesis as the Foundation of the *Halakhah* and the Problem of the *Soferim*], *Tarbiẓ*, XXVII (1958), pp. 166–182, ***41, 276, 286, 288, 312, 547, 891***

E.E. Urbach, "Ha-Halakhah ve-ha-Nevu'ah" [*Halakhah* and Prophecy], *Tarbiẓ*, XVIII (1947), pp. 1–27, ***204, 264***

E.E. Urbach, "Hilkhot Avadim ki-Mekor la-Historyah ha-Ḥevratit bi-Mei ha-Bayit ha-Sheni u-vi-Tekufat ha-Mishnah ve-ha-Talmud" [The Laws of Slavery as a Source for the Social History of the Second Temple, Mishnaic, and Talmudic Periods], *Zion*, XXV (1960), pp. 141– 189, ***1632***

E.E. Urbach, "Mi-Darkhei ha-Kodifikaẓyah—Al Sefer ha-Turim le-Rav Ya'akov b. Rav Asher" [On Codificatory Methodology—The *Turim* of Rabbi Jacob b. Rabbi Asher], *Jubilee Volume*, American Academy of Jewish Studies, XLVI–XLVII (1979–1980), pp. 1ff., ***1326***

E.E. Urbach, *The Sages, Their Concepts and Beliefs*, I. Abrahams trans., Jerusalem, 1975, ***94, 118, 154, 156–157, 191, 193, 225, 242, 264, 624, 894***

E.E. Urbach, "She'elot u-Teshuvot ha-Rosh be-Kitvei Yad u-vi-Defusim" [Responsa of Asheri in Manuscript and in Print], *Shenaton*, II (1975), pp. 1ff., ***1995***

Ben-Zion Uziel, "Ha-Ishah be-Naḥalat Ba'alah" [Inheritance by Women from Their Husbands], *Ha-Torah ve-ha-Medinah*, II (1946), pp. 9–17, ***1684***

Ben-Zion Uziel, "Mishpetei Yerushat ha-Bat" [The Law Relating to Inheritance by a Daughter], *Talpiot*, V (1952), pp. 451–474; VI (1953), pp. 51–64, ***1684***

Ben-Zion Uziel, "Takkanot Ḥakhamim bi-Yerushat ha-Ishah" [Legislation by the Halakhic Authorities on Inheritance by Women], *Or ha-Mizraḥ*, I (1957), pp. 2–8, ***1684***

M. Vager and P. Dykan (Dikstein), *Piẓẓuyei Pitturin, Perek be-Hitpatḥut Dinei Avodah ba-Yishuv ha-Ivri bi-Zemaneinu* [Severance Pay: A Chapter in the Development of Labor Law in the Contemporary Jewish *Yishuv*], Jerusalem, 1940, ***1633***

Z. Vilnay, *Ariel, An Encyclopaedia of the Land of Israel*, ***169***

P. Vinogradoff, *Roman Law in Medieval Europe*, 2nd ed., Oxford, 1929, *2*

S. Warhaftig, *Dinei Avodah ba-Mishpat ha-Ivri* [Labor Law in Jewish Law], Tel Aviv, 1969, *614, 620, 1630, 1632*

Warhaftig, "Dinei Borerut ba-Mishpat ha-Ivri" [Arbitration in Jewish Law], *Mazkeret, A Torah Collection in Memory of Rabbi Herzog*, Jerusalem, 1962, pp. 507–529, *19–20*

Z. Warhaftig, "Al ha-Takdim ba-Mishpat ha-Ivri" [On Precedent in Jewish Law], *Shenaton*, VI–VII (1979–1980), pp. 105ff., *1818*

Z. Warhaftig, *Ha-Ḥazakah ba-Mishpat ha-Ivri* [*Ḥazakah* in Jewish Law], Jerusalem, 1964, *601, 1201*

Z. Warhaftig, "Kefiyyat Get le-Halakhah u-le-Ma'aseh" [Compelling a Divorce—Theory and Practice], *Shenaton*, III–IV (1976–1977), pp. 153–216, *1755*

M. Weinfeld, *Mishpat u-Ẓedakah be-Yisra'el u-va-Ammim* [Law and Equity in Israel and among Other Peoples], Jerusalem, 1985, *167*

S. ha-Kohen Weingarten, "Teshuvot she-Nignezu" [Responsa That Were Suppressed], *Sinai*, XXIX (1951), pp. 90–99, *1521*

A. Weiss, *Hithavut ha-Talmud bi-Shelemuto* [The Formulation of the Full Text of the Talmud], New York, 1947, *1092*

A. Weiss, *Le-Ḥeker ha-Talmud* [On Research of the Talmud], New York, 1955, *565, 632, 635, 967–968, 1092*

I.H. Weiss (ed.), *Bet Talmud*, Vienna, 1881–1889, *1183, 1541, 1545*

I.H. Weiss, *Dor Dor ve-Doreshav* [lit. "The Generations and Their Interpreters"—A History of the Oral Law], 6th ed., Vilna, 1915, *52, 94–95, 193, 200, 205, 236, 399, 407, 541–542, 646, 884, 937, 951, 1057, 1094, 1155, 1550*

I.H. Weiss, "Toledot ha-Rav Rabbenu Moshe b. Maimon" [A Biography of Maimonides], *Bet Talmud*, I (1881), pp. 225–236, *1188*

R.J.Z. Werblowski, *Joseph Karo, Lawyer and Mystic*, London, 1962, *1316*

Wigmore on Evidence (J. Chadbourne rev. 1976), *1700, 1702*

G. Williams, "Husband and Wife," 10 *Modern L. Rev.* 16 (1947), *629*

G. Williams, *The Proof of Guilt*, London, 3rd ed., 1963, *694*

H.J. Wolff, *Roman Law*, 1951, *2*

U. Yadin, "Keiẓad Yeforash Ḥok ha-Shomerim" [How Should the Bailees Law Be Interpreted?], *Ha-Praklit*, XXIV (1968), pp. 493–495, *1729, 1942*

U. Yadin, "Ḥok ha-Yerushah ke-Ḥelek me-ha-Halakhah ha-Ezraḥit be-Yisra'el" [The Succession Law as Part of Israeli Civil Legislation], *Iyyunei Mishpat*, III (1973), pp. 26ff., *1728*

U. Yadin, "The Law of Succession and Other Steps toward a Civil Code," *Scripta Hierosolymitana*, XVI (1966), pp. 115ff., *1681*

U. Yadin, "The Principle of Good Faith in the New Legislation," *Proceedings of Judges' Seminar*, Jerusalem, 1975, pp. 30ff., *186*

U. Yadin, "Ve-Shuv al Perush Ḥukkei ha-Keneset" [More on the Interpretation of Knesset Legislation], *Ha-Praklit*, XXVI (1970), pp. 190–211, 358–377, *1728–1729*

Y. Yadin, *Ha-Ḥippusim Aḥar Bar Kokhba* [In Search of Bar Kokhba], Jerusalem, 1971, *1036*

Y. Yadin, "Maḥaneh D—Me'arat ha-Iggerot" [Camp D—The Cave of the Documents], *Yedi'ot be-Ḥakirat Ereẓ Yisra'el ve-Atikotehah* [Recent Developments in the Archeology of Ancient Israel], 1962, pp. 204–236, ***1036***

R. Yaron, *Gifts in Contemplation of Death in Jewish and Roman Law*, Oxford, 1960, ***1540***

R. Yaron, *Ha-Mishpat Shel Mismekhei Yev* [Law in the Elephantine Papyri], Jerusalem, 1962, ***1028, 1540***

Z. Yavetz, *Toledot Yisra'el* [History of the Jewish People], rev. ed., Tel Aviv, 1955–1963, ***1456***

S. Yavne'eli, *Masa le-Teiman* [Journey to Yemen], Tel Aviv, 1952, pp. 185–200, ***1497***

S. Yisraeli, Comments in *Da'atenu*, Youth Commission of Mafdal [National Religious Party], No. 2–3, Iyyar-Tammuz 1965, pp. 4–6, ***1907***

Z. Zeltner, "Dinei ha-Ḥozim be-Yisra'el be-Hitpatḥutam Meshekh Ḥaẓi ha-Yovel me-Az Kum ha-Medinah" [The Development of Contract Law in Israel during the Quarter-Century Since the Establishment of the State], *Ha-Praklit*, XXIX (1974), pp. 198ff., ***1728, 1919***

Z. Zeltner, *Dinei ha-Ḥozim Shel Medinat Yisra'el* [The Contract Law of the State of Israel], 1974, ***1732***

Z. Zeltner, "Haẓa'at Ḥok ha-Ḥozim (Terufot be-Shel Haforat Ḥozeh)" [The Contracts (Remedies for Breach of Contract) Bill], *Ha-Praklit*, XXVI (1970), pp. 276ff., ***1729***

Z. Zeltner, "Hirhurim al Haẓa'at Ḥok ha-Ḥozim (Ḥelek Kelali)" [Reflections on the Contracts (General Part) Bill], *Iyyunei Mishpat*, III (1973), pp. 121ff., ***1729, 1733***

M. Zena, "Le-Toledot Kehillat Bologna bi-Teḥillat ha-Me'ah ha-Shesh-Esreh" [Studies in the History of the Jewish Community of Bologna in the Early Sixteenth Century], *HUCA*, XVI (1941), Hebrew sec., pp. 35–98, ***1504***

B. Ziemlich, "Plan und Anlage des Mischne Tora" [Plan and Design of the *Mishneh Torah*], in *Moses Ben Maimon, Sein Leben, Seine Werke und Sein Einfluss* [Maimonides: His Life, Works, and Influence], Leipzig, 1908, I, pp. 254–256, ***1217, 1221***

M.M. Zlotkin, *Shemot ha-Seforim ha-Ivrim, Lefi Sugeihem ha-Shonim, Tekhunatam u-Te'udatam* [The Names of Hebrew Books, According to Their Respective Categories, Characteristics, and Purposes], Neufchatel (Switzerland), 1940, ***1486***

J.L. Zunz, *Ha-Derashot be-Yisra'el ve-Hishtalshelutan ha-Historit* [Midrashic Literature and Its Historical Evolution], ed. H. Albeck, Jerusalem, 1954, ***1045***

J.S. Ẓuri, *Mishpat ha-Talmud* [Talmudic Law], Warsaw, 1921–1922, ***80***

J.S. Ẓuri, *Toledot ha-Mishpat ha-Ẓibburi ha-Ivri, Shilton ha-Nesi'ut ve-ha-Va'ad* [A History of Jewish Public Law, The Rule of the Patriarchate and the Council], Paris, 1931, ***81***

INDEX OF SOURCES

TABLE OF CONTENTS TO INDEX OF SOURCES

Scripture, *2063*
Mishnah, *2068*
Tosefta, *2071*
Halakhic Midrashim, *2072*
Targumim, *2073*
Apocrypha and Related Sources, *2073*
Jerusalem Talmud, *2074*
Babylonian Talmud, *2076*
Minor Tractates, *2082*
Aggadic Midrashim, *2082*
Scriptural Commentaries, *2082*
Commentaries on Mishnah, *2083*
Commentaries on Tosefta, *2084*
Commentaries on Halakhic Midrashim, *2084*
Commentaries on Jerusalem Talmud, *2084*
Commentaries on Babylonian Talmud, *2084*
Codificatory Works, *2092*
  Alfasi, Sefer ha-Halakhot, *2092*
  Commentaries on Alfasi, *2092*
  Maimonides, Mishneh Torah, *2092*
  Commentaries on Mishneh Torah, *2095*
  Turim, *2096*
  Commentaries on Turim, *2097*
  Shulḥan Arukh, *2097*
  Commentaries on Shulḥan Arukh, *2099*
  Other Codificatory Works, *2101*
  Commentaries on Other Codificatory Works, *2103*
Responsa, *2104*
Books of Ethics, Philosophy, Homilies, etc., *2113*
Enactments, *2114*
Reference Works, *2115*
Legislation—State of Israel, *2117*
  Statutes, *2117*
  Bills, *2118*
  Draft Proposals for Israeli Legislation, *2119*
British Mandatory Legislation, *2119*
Ottoman Legislation, *2119*
Other Legislation, *2119*
Divrei ha-Keneset [Knesset Record], *2119*
Cases, *2121*

INDEX OF SOURCES

SCRIPTURE

Genesis
1:27, *1851*
2:14, *1290*
2:18, *1291*
2:20, *1291*
2:24, *629–630, 873*
3:5, *250*
4:10, *1699*
5:1, *1851*
6:9, *94*
6:13, *1151, 1297*
9:6, *1851*
9:7, *437*
11:4, *1395*
14:24, *554*
17:1, *94*
17:13, *234*
18:19, *195, 1241, 1297*
18:21, *872*
18:25, *73, 175*
20:5–6, *183*
23:3–20, *195*
23:10–12, *195*
23:16–18, *1023*
23:17, *196, 394*
25:27, *1120*
26:5, *195, 234*
28:11, *337*
28:22, *393*
29:3, *1436*
31:1ff., *196*
31:13, *393*
31:30, *372*
31:39, *196*
31:50, *571*
32:32–33, *233*
33:11, *1387–1388*
34:7, *873*
37:17, *1395*
38:6–26, *197*
38:8, *198*
38:17–18, *1026*

Genesis *continued*
38:20, *1026*
38:24, *198*
38:26, *198*
40:13, *106*
40:15, *372*
41:24, *1247*
43:9, *1026, 1151*
43:12, *1232*
44:8, *347*
46:12, *1513*
47:22, *106*
49:10, *1580*

Exodus
6:8, *1839*
6:12, *347*
6:14, *1513*
9:29, *650*
12:2, *202*
12:3, *342*
12:6, *112, 342*
12:19, *115*
13:2, *329*
13:7, *115*
13:16, *1046*
13:19, *1356*
14:20, *1852*
15:25, *14, 106–107, 553*
16:22, *1232*
16:22–26, *202*
16:29, *202, 1154*
16:29–30, *202*
18:14–16, *278*
18:16, *1811*
18:18, *1390*
18:20, *94, 155*
18:21–26, *6*
18:23–24, *1297*
18:26, *139*
19:5, *650*
20–23, *1020*
20:1–14, *5, 138*
20:7, *1697*
20:8–11, *202*
20:9–10, *331–332*
20:10, *202*
20:13, *142, 334, 356*
20:16, *1697*
21–22, *358*
21:1, *13, 20, 106–107, 135, 138, 322–323, 1916*
21:2, *200, 320*
21:3, *200, 472*
21:6, *250, 377, 1031*
21:7, *201*
21:9, *93, 201*
21:10, *125, 571*
21:14, *199*
21:16, *334–335*
21:20, *1034*
21:20–21, *338*
21:26–27, *356*
21:28–32, *359*
21:33, *403*
21:33–34, *341, 359*
21:35, *108*
21:35–36, *359, 1009*
21:37, *108*
22:2, *589*
22:3, *108, 326, 403*
22:4, *301–302, 359*
22:5, *359*
22:6–8, *326*
22:6–14, *348, 1695*
22:7, *1029*
22:7–8, *250*
22:8, *326, 1029–1030*
22:9, *325, 352*
22:9ff., *325*
22:9–12, *196–197*
22:13, *348, 352*
22:20, *1854*
22:24, *652*
22:24–26, *589, 651*
23:1, *1502*
23:2, *262, 383, 683, 717–718, 997, 1068*
23:3, *143*
23:4, *337, 403*
23:5, *337*
23:6, *143*
23:7, *1046*
23:9, *1690. 1854*
23:10ff., *107*
23:12, *202*
23:19, *500*
24:12–13, *992*
24:14, *385, 460, 992–993*
26:32, *1260*
28:15–30, *1288*
28:30, *1292*
31:12–17, *202*
31:15ff., *234*
31:18, *241*
32:18, *1395*
33:11, *947*
34:21, *202*
34:27, *193, 224–225, 234*
35:3, *202, 332*
40:35, *1858*

Leviticus
1:1, *1858*
1:2, *324, 328*
1:9, *97*
1:17, *97*
2:1, *97*
2:2, *97*
5, *1020*
5:1, *283–285, 1001–1002, 1047, 1699*
5:23, *601*
6:11, *106*
7:12, *382*
7:23, *998*
10:16, *1357*
13:2, *347*
13:14, *346*
13:47, *381*
13:49, *808*
14:1–32, *377*
14:9, *377–378*
14:34ff., *334*
15:1–15, *369*
17:10–14, *377*
17:13, *377–378*
18, *373, 483, 557*
18–21, *1020*
18:5, *519, 990, 1846*
18:6, *334, 571*
18:7ff., *334*
18:30, *107, 483, 485, 490, 699*
19:2, *159*
19:3, *323*
19:11, *335, 1151*
19:13, *335–336, 1629*
19:14, *5, 1640*
19:15, *105, 140, 143, 168, 1299, 1760, 1840, 1845*
19:16, *970, 1643–1644, 1737, 1741, 1924*
19:17, *1644, 1741*
19:18, *142, 1851*
19:19, *507, 887*
19:20, *372*
19:23, *887*
19:24, *902*

19:32, *5*
19:34, *1854*
19:35–36, *5*
19:36, *118, 1209*
20, *557*
20:9, *321, 440*
20:10–21, *373*
21:9, *379*
21:14, *381*
22:7, *1059*
23:14, *480, 887*
23:34, *4*
23:39–43, *4*
23:40, *114, 205, 286, 387*
24, *1020*
24:10–16, *237*
24:10–23, *951*
24:22, *605*
25, *1020*
25:4, *320*
25:14, *298*
25:23, *1651*
25:29–30, *562, 1652*
25:35, *1855*
25:39, *589*
25:41, *200–201*
25:53, *996*
25:55, *415, 925, 1634, 1840*
26:20, *836*
26:25, *1034*
26:46, *193*
27, *1020*
27:29, *487*
27:34, *243*

Numbers
5:12–31, *1193*
5:13, *356*
6:22–27, *531*
6:26, *531*
9:1 *et seq.*, *901*
9:1–14, *237*
9:6–14, *951*
9:14, *1854*
11:16, *482*
12:14, *350*
15:15, *252*
15:32–34, *202*
15:32–36, *237, 951*
16:22, *73*
19:2, *1247*
21:26, *376*
22–24, *1859*
24:2, *943, 1859*
27, *1020*
27:1–11, *951*
27:3–4, *237*
27:5, *106, 237*
27:6–11, *237*
27:8, *152, 574, 1672*
27:8–11, *289, 841*
27:11, *289*
30:2–17, *952*
30:3, *394, 934, 1700*
31:27, *554*
32:22, *623*
35, *357, 1020*
35:9–34, *608*
35:16–18, *357*
35:19, *358*
35:21, *358*
35:22–25, *358*
35:30, *1034*
36, *1020*
36:5–9, *237*

Deuteronomy
1, *1020*
1:11, *496*
1:16, *1299*
1:17, *105–106, 108, 1299*
4, *1020*
4:2, *496, 1100*
4:7, *501*
4:8, *106*
4:33, *1580*
5, *1020*
5:11, *1697*
5:17, *334, 1697*
5:30, *94*
6:4–7, *320*
6:7, *309, 1321*
6:8, *1046*
6:9, *1046*
6:13, *372*
6:17–18, *185, 623*
6:18, *160, 182, 184, 624, 1735, 1840*
7:12, *107*
8:3, *104, 571, 1379*
8:8, *208*
10:12, *98*
10:19, *1690*
10:20, *372*
11:16, *1329*
11:18, *1046*
11:19, *1797*
11:20, *1046*
11:22, *104*
11:31–32, *1648*
11:32, *279*
12:4, *368*
12:13–14, *520*
12:28, *624*
13:1, *480, 496, 501, 1100*
13:2, *243*
13:5, *94*
13:9, *108*
13:15, *275, 284, 606*
13:13–17, *367–368*
14:1, *890, 935*
14:4–5, *324*
15:1–2, *511*
15:3, *513*
15:9, *512*
15:9–10, *511*
15:12–14, *1631*
15:13–14, *924*
15:14, *1633*
15:17, *377*
15:18, *925, 1631*
15:19, *329*
16–17, *1020*
16:18, *6, 1299*
16:18–19, *1640*
16:19, *14, 106, 1641*
16:20, *14, 169, 654, 1840, 1893*
16:21, *14*
17, *484*
17:4, *275*
17:6, *323, 613, 1354*
17:8, *108, 279, 485, 1281*
17:8 *et seq.*, *181*
17:8–9, *266, 701*
17:8–11, *237, 279, 482, 499*
17:8–13, *249, 1460*
17:9, *59, 139, 243, 486, 973, 1790*
17:10, *288, 1811*
17:11, *159, 238, 243, 256, 263, 279, 482–483, 485, 498, 501, 1284, 1296*
17:12, *250, 288, 1068*
17:14–20, *55, 486, 1024*
17:16, *1212*
18:15, *520*
18:22, *108*
19–25, *1020*

Deuteronomy *continued*
19:6, *106*
19:10, *61*
19:13, *107*
19:14, *394, 688, 894, 1300*
19:15, *149, 356, 522, 527, 610, 1001, 1698*
19:19, *398*
20:20, *1036*
21:5, *346*
21:17, *106*
21:18–21, *365*
21:21, *107, 516*
21:22, *323*
22:1–3, *332, 956, 1747*
22:2, *299, 548, 654*
22:9, *507, 887*
22:10, *322, 440*
22:11, *322*
22:16, *386, 995*
22:18, *1029*
22:19, *109*
22:23–24, *340*
22:23–27, *1030*
22:25–27, *339–340, 344*
22:26, *344*
22:26–27, *1742*
22:27, *1030*
22:29, *109*
23:3, *353*
23:4, *353, 363*
23:4–7, *361*
23:8, *1854*
23:13–15, *294*
23:17, *1855*
23:18, *1046*
23:25, *886*
24, *295*
24:1, *292–293, 375, 377, 469, 535, 1533*
24:1–2, *785*
24:1–4, *201*
24:3, *375*
24:6, *340, 589, 651*
24:7, *334–335*
24:10–11, *399, 1858*
24:10–13, *310, 589, 651*
24:11, *595*
24:12–13, *295*
24:14–15, *336*
24:15, *98, 1629*
24:16, *73, 303, 1026*
24:17, *295*
25:1–3, *201*
25:3, *1842*
25:5, *198–199, 389, 1029*
25:5–6, *125*
25:5–10, *198, 1002*
25:7–9, *199*
25:9, *907*
25:12, *1924*
26:1–11, *113*
27:17, *394*
27:25, *1640*
28:49, *1353*
29:11, *234*
29:13–14, *234*
29:28, *480*
30:12, *242, 245, 262, 480, 1790*
31:9, *192*
31:10–13, *408*
31:21, *356, 1067*
31:27, *347*
32:2, *104*
32:4, *248–249, 251*
32:7, *482, 484–486*
32:31, *14, 1580*
33:4, *309, 1839*
33:10, *242*
34:7, *1736*
34:12, *1197*

Joshua
1:1, *910*
1:8, *309*
1:18, *55, 60*
2:21, *873*
6:15, *107*
6:26, *735*
7, *103*
7:11, *103*
10:11, *169*
11:6, *532*
15:35, *41, 1043*
15:48, *41, 1043*
16:3–5, *169*
18:13–14, *169*
19:51, *509–510, 687*
20:1, *687*
24:25, *55, 553, 1297*

Judges
3:10, *105*
4:4, *105*
4:5, *106*
5:2, *872*
5:8, *872*
5:10, *872*
5:15–16, *1395*
11–12, *487*
16:13, *1054*
18:7, *107*
21:1, *733*

I Samuel
1, *1515*
2:23–24, *872*
4:18, *105*
7:12, *1291*
7:15–16, *1297*
8, *55, 67, 486*
8:11–17, *1024*
12:11, *687*
14:1, *1173*
14:7, *1173*
14:12, *1173*
14:13, *1173*
14:24–45, *670*
14:44, *487*
15:1–3, *1205*
16:13, *363*
17:11, *1043*
17:25, *363*
17:55, *362*
17:58, *362*
21:8ff., *362*
22:2, *310*
22:9ff., *362*
25:29, *1395*
30, *554*
30:24, *554*
30:24–25, *55, 1027*
30:25, *554*
30:27 *et seq.*, *554*

II Samuel
6:1, *96*
7:19, *1243*
8:15, *1298*
13:12–13, *873*
20, *970*
20:21–22, *970*
20:22, *970–971*

I Kings
2:5, *199*
2:28, *199*
2:32, *199–200*

3:3, *1298*
3:9, *1298*
3:10, *1298*
3:12, *1298*
3:16ff., *55*
3:26, *1741*
3:28, *106, 1298*
9:4, *183*
12:33, *497*
16:9–10, *1515*
16:34, *735*
18:19–46, *257, 520*
18:28, *107*
21, *55, 60, 1025*
21:2, *1025*
21:3, *1025*
21:13, *1025*
21:15–16, *1025*
21:18, *1025*
21:19, *1677*

II Kings
2:12, *482*
4:1, *310, 589*
9:31, *1515*
13:14, *1877*
14:6, *73, 304, 1025–1026*
15:5, *55*
18:14, *938*
23:25, *1298*

Isaiah
1:17, *1299*
1:18, *1299*
1:21, *1298*
1:23, *1299, 1640*
1:24, *1299*
1:27, *1299, 1571–1572*
2:3, *1649*
8:12, *768*
10:13, *364*
11:4, *1298*
11:9, *1856*
12:3, *1378*
28:9, *1290*
28:15, *80*
29:14, *1311*
33:6, *98, 1344*
34:16, *1191*
42:21, *1157*
48:1, *812*
50:1, *310, 589*
52:15, *585*
54:13, *530*
56:1, *1299*
56:3, *1854*
56:7, *1854*
58:13, *1021*
59:21, *1344*
62:1, *1240*

Jeremiah
2:13, *1916*
17:11, *1696*
17:21–22, *1022*
21:12, *55, 107*
22:3, *107*
22:13, *106*
22:16, *139*
29:1, *1011*
29:4, *1087*
29:5, *1011*
29:6, *577*
29:10, *1011*
29:31, *1087*
32, *1010*
32:7, *1024*
32:7–8, *106*
32:9–12, *1022*
32:12, *469, 1023*
32:14, *469, 1012, 1533*
32:44, *203–204, 1010–1011, 1023*
49:6, *364*

Ezekiel
1:1, *1087*
3:11, *1087*
3:15, *1087*
14:5, *1329*
36:20, *18*
44:23–24, *242*

Hosea
4:12, *1281*
5:10, *394*
8:12, *225*
8:14, *100–101*
14:10, *1893*

Joel
2:13, *203*

Amos
2:6, *589*
3:12, *197*
8:4–6, *589*
8:5, *1022*
8:11–12, *1067*
8:12, *1280*
9:14, *364*

Obadiah
1:15, *1891*

Micah
3:3, *571*
3:11, *1640*
4:5, *1855*
6:6, *1344*

Habakkuk
3:6, *94*

Zephaniah
3:13, *918*

Zechariah
8:16, *172, 258*
8:19, *388, 1065, 1813*
9:12, *1232*

Malachi
2:1–7, *309*
2:7, *242, 309*
2:8–9, *309*
3:9, *763, 768*
3:22, *265*

Psalms
19:8, *1321*
25:14, *225*
29:11, *530*
33:15, *250*
34:13–14, *1643*
37:21, *1245*
52, *362*
78:72, *183*
80:9, *679*
82:3, *144*
82:5, *250*
82:6–7, *1387*
97:11, *1241*
99:4, *1271*
101:2, *183*
102:15, *1240, 1650*
104:22–23, *905*
107:1, *1852*
107:42, *585*
116:16, *363*
117:2, *1344*
118:22, *84*
119:99, *1344*
119:121, *1298*

Psalms *continued*
119:126, *226, 257, 503, 520, 534*
145:9, *1855*
145:17, *248*
147:19, *263*

Proverbs
1:8, *733, 894, 1796, 1809*
1:11, *1265*
1:13, *1265*
2:20, *156, 158, 162, 766, 925, 929, 1634*
3:4, *624*
3:17, *61, 387, 702, 724, 1005, 1193, 1840, 1855, 1892*
3:27, *552*
3:28, *1629*
5:15, *947*
6:1–3, *1163*
6:1–5, *916, 1026, 1163*
7:4, *1321*
7:26, *1493*
8:22, *1295*
9:1–2, *1322*
10:22, *837*
11:10, *1699*
11:13, *1858*
11:15, *916, 1027, 1163*
16:2, *1065*
17:18, *916, 1027*
20:16, *1027*
21:2, *1065*
21:3, *1299*
21:30, *910*
22:6, *1266*
22:26–27, *916, 1027, 1162*
22:28, *394, 893–894*
23:10, *394*
23:20, *366*
23:22, *893*
25:11, *1349*
27:13, *1027*
29:24, *600*

Job
5:16, *585*
11:9, *241*
17:3, *916, 1027*
20:12, *1398*
22:28, *263*
24:2, *394*
37:23, *763*

Song of Songs
1:2, *160*

Ruth
1:1, *105*
3:10, *1395*
3:12, *1024*
4:4, *1024*
4:7, *221, 582, 1022*
4:9, *1023*

Ecclesiastes
1:11, *268*
2:14, *1064*
2:25, *837*
4:9, *1434*
7:10, *266*
7:20, *1357*
8:1, *276*
12:12, *1389*

Esther
1:14, *728*
2:14, *1135*
2:15, *1352*
8:15–16, *1400*
10:3, *1232*

Ezra
1:3, *1650*
7:6, *312*
7:10, *275–276, 313*
7:12, *312*
7:25, *556*
10, *554*
10:8, *204, 508, 679, 685–686, 700, 764, 851–852*
10:19, *916*

Nehemiah
5:1–13, *310, 589*
5:3, *1026*
5:9, *311*
8, *554*
8:1–8, *312–313*
8:8, *556*
9:1, *313*
9:37, *65*
10, *554*
10:32, *1022*
13:15–19, *1022*

I Chronicles
2:28, *1043*
11:8, *1298*

II Chronicles
17:6, *1298*
19:6, *139, 258, 1298*
19:8, *55*
19:11, *139*
20:21, *1852*
26:21, *55*
28:18, *316, 1044*
36:23, *1650*

MISHNAH

Berakhot
1:1, *1059–1060*
1:2, *1060*
1:3, *320, 1064*
5:5, *113*
6:8, *407–408, 898*
9:5, *503–504*

Pe'ah
2:6, *1050*
3:7, *583*

Shevi'it
4:1, *550*
4:2, *550*
4:10, *1107*
10:1, *1058*
10:3, *561*
10:3–4, *504, 512*
10:9, *151, 705*

Terumot
1:1–2, *585*
1:4, *635*
1:10, *635*
8:12, *970*

Ma'aser Sheni
5:1 *et seq.*, *902*
5:2, *542–543*
5:4, *902*

Orlah
3:9, *887*

Bikkurim
3:3, *681*
3:12, *588*

Shabbat
1:4, *1063*
2:5, *472*
24:5, *958*

Eruvin
1:6, *898*
7:11, *113*
8:5, *679*
10:10, *933, 937*

Pesaḥim
1:6–7, *961*
4:1, *935*
4:1–5, *933*
6:1, *901*

Shekalim
1:1, *507*
1:2, *507–508*
3:2, *623–624*

Yoma
8:2, *999*

Sukkah
2:7, *959*
3:11, *933*

Beẓah
2:6, *1064*
3:5, *1455*
5:2, *516*

Rosh ha-Shanah
1:4, *570*
2:1, *504*
2:9, *245*
3:1, *1169*
4:1, *493, 950*

Ta'anit
2:1, *203*

Megillah
1:4–11, *1056*

Ḥagigah
1:8, *108*
2, *41*
2:2, *41, 1043, 1062*

Yevamot
1:4, *1065, 1068, 1901*
2:4, *208, 557*
5:6, *407*
8:3, *361*
12:1, *907*
13:12, *997*
14:1, *785*
15:1, *402, 524*
15:1–2, *426, 523, 957*
15:1–3, *131*
15:2, *402, 523–524*
15:3, *123, 426–427*
15:7, *148, 1980*
16:4, *1014*
16:5, *528*
16:6, *528, 1014*
16:7, *504, 525–526, 528, 610, 1014*

Ketubbot
1:1, *1264*
1:2, *560, 792*
1:5, *933*
2:2, *993*
2:5, *369, 385–386, 994*
4:4, *628*
4:6, *403, 427, 1081*
4:7, *492, 561, 569*
4:9, *145*
4:10, *573, 575–576*
4:11, *575, 1672*
4:12, *492, 573, 933*
5:1, *215, 560*
5:5, *1786*
5:7, *659*
6:3–4, *912*
6:4, *933*
7:6, *885*
7:8, *996*
7:10, *659*
9:1, *124*
9:4, *630*
9:9, *549*
10:4, *919*
11:2, *20*
11:5, *565*
13:1, *492*
13:3, *404, 575, 1672, 1679*
13:11, *213*

Nedarim
2:2, *708*
9:5, *952*

Nazir
5:4, *1087*
5:5, *1107*

Sotah
3:4, *1798*

Gittin
2:5, *951*
2:5–6, *1076*
3:3, *996*
4, *1056*
4:1, *564*
4:1–2, *631*
4:2, *491, 563, 1056*
4:2–3, *526*
4:2–7, *504*
4:2–5:3, *621*
5, *1056*
5:1, *588, 592*
5:2, *591*
5:3, *504, 592*
5:4, *603*
5:5, *602, 1708*
5:6, *569*
5:7, *585, 1664*
5:8, *586, 1715*
5:8–9, *504, 621, 628, 1056*
6:3, *404–405*
6:6, *472*
8:1, *375*
8:3, *588*
9:10, *293, 785*

Kiddushin
1:1, *535, 1055*
1:2–6, *1055*
1:5, *297, 583, 590–591*
1:6, *423, 582*
1:7, *408*
1:9, *886*
2:4, *405*
3:1, *641*

Bava Kamma
1:1, *359*
1:2, *1076*
1:3, *1079*
2:5, *1084*
2:6, *602*
3:1, *411*
3:6, *1059*
5:7, *403*
6:4, *146*
7:7, *549*
10:3, *597*
10:9, *1212*

Bava Meẓi'a
1:1, *1210*
1:5, *409, 628*
1:6, *590*
2:3, *956*
2:5, *333*

Bava Meẓi'a *continued*
2:6, *549*
2:7, *299, 548–549*
3:3, *148, 1980*
3:6, *1080*
3:10, *1695*
3:11, *405*
4:2, *148, 297, 581*
4:7–8, *1056*
4:12, *395*
5:5, *931*
5:7, *560*
7:1, *905, 909, 931, 933*
7:2 *et seq.*, *886*
7:8, *886, 1695*
7:10, *126*
7:11, *124*
9:1, *930, 933*
9:3, *429, 1983*
9:5, *1982*
9:13, *295, 340*

Bava Batra
1:1, *933, 941*
1:1–2, *931*
1:5, *776, 921*
1:6, *1075*
2:1, *1073–1074*
3:1, *1008, 1075, 1331–1334*
3:2, *1013*
3:3, *1008*
3:5, *1334*
3:7, *943, 1859–1860*
5:10, *1035*
6:3, *1080*
6:7, *749*
8:1, *289, 573*
8:1–2, *841*
8:2, *152, 574, 1672*
8:5, *99, 124, 126, 150, 961, 1673, 1675*
9:1, *404, 575, 930, 1679*
10:1, *912, 933*
10:1–2, *433*
10:2, *433–434, 467*
10:6, *588*
10:7, *954*
10:8, *594, 953–954*

Sanhedrin
1:1, *19*
1:2, *728*
1:5, *1460*
1:6, *1646*
3:1, *19*
3:1–2, *19*
3:2, *742*
3:7, *882*
4:1, *605*
4:5, *606, 1699*
5:1, *517, 691*
5:1–2, *606*
5:5, *719*
7:2, *972*
7:3, *1033*
7:10, *1858*
8:1, *365*
8:2, *365–366*
8:4, *365–366*
8:5, *258*
9:1, *1033*
9:5, *517*
11:2, *287–288, 977, 1067, 1460, 1848*

Makkot
1:10, *692–693*
3:7–8, *1213*
3:15, *1052, 1842*

Shevu'ot
1:1, *1056*
3:8, *708, 713*
6:5–6, *1330*
7, *620*
7:1, *615–616*
7:1–2, *149*
8:1, *1692*

Eduyyot
1:1–3, *1062*
1:4, *1054*
1:4–6, *1218*
1:5, *259, 541, 983, 1089, 1848*
1:5–6, *1071*
1:6, *541*
1:12, *123, 131, 504, 523–524*
2:3, *952*
4:8, *1065, 1068, 1901*
5:6, *540, 1848*
6:1, *526*
8:4, *206*
8:5, *526*
8:7, *206*

Avodah Zarah
2:6, *670, 1052*
4:10, *408*

Avot
1, *41*
1:1, *192, 239, 555*
1:2, *1295*
1:2–3, *41*
1:3, *1043*
1:4–15, *1043*
1:5, *527*
1:8, *31, 800, 1503*
1:11, *1216*
1:18, *172, 1295*
2:2, *1052*
3:2, *1296*
3:14, *1851*
4:7, *1493*
4:8, *1646*
4:12, *373*
4:13, *276, 1084*
5:8, *1298*
5:14, *1008*
5:17, *1066*
5:21, *1084*
6:5, *947*

Menaḥot
13:11, *97*

Ḥullin
7:6, *233*
8:3, *1058*
8:4, *500*

Bekhorot
4:6, *827*
5:5, *21*

Arakhin
8:5, *1058*
9:4, *562*

Keritut
1:7, *370*

Me'ilah
6:5, *406*

Kelim
5:10, *261*
21:1, *1054*

Oholot
8:4, *1054*

Niddah
5:3 *et seq.*, *585*

Zavim
2:2, *369–370*

Yadayim
4:3, *206*, *1084*
4:4, *363–364*, *998*
4:6, *1056*
4:7, *1056*
4:8, *1056*

TOSEFTA*

Berakhot
1:1, *1059*
1:2, *969*
1:4, *949*
2:6, *969*
6:23–24, *503*
7:2, *1849*

Pe'ah
3:1, *628*

Demai
5:24, *949*

Terumot
7:20, *970–971*

Shevi'it
3:8–9, *550*
3:10, *550*
3:11, *540*
3:13, *540*, *549*
4:21, *566*
8:3, *1053*

Ma'aser Sheni
1:9, *550*

Shabbat
1:16, *1063*, *1066*
13(14):1, *424*

*For the Orders of Zera'im and Mo'ed, and the Tractates of Yevamot, Ketubbot, Nedarim, and Nazir in the Order of Nashim, the citations are to ed. Lieberman; for all other Orders and tractates, the citations are to ed. Zuckermandel.

Eruvin
3(4):6, *504*
3(4):7, *1036*
11:24 (8:23), *108*

Pesaḥim
3(2):14, *892*
4:13–14, *901*
4:14, *902*

Shekalim
1:3, *507*
2:2, *623–624*

Rosh ha-Shanah
2(1):3, *266*
2:9, *493*
2(4):11, *933*

Sukkah
4:6, *681*

Megillah
3(4):15, *932*

Mo'ed
2:14–15, *884–885*

Ḥagigah
1:9, *108*
2:9, *1063–1064*, *1281*
2:11, *1062*

Yevamot
1:8–10, *1043*
1:9–10, *1066*
1:10, *1064*
1:10–11, *1065*, *1901*
1:11, *1068*
1:13, *1064*
3:1, *557*
4:4, *641*
12:8, *997*
12:11, *908*
14:7, *528*

Ketubbot
1:4, *888*, *933*
2:2, *593*
3:3, *132*
4:7, *679*
4:9, *424*, *632*
4:9 *et seq.*, *423*, *932*
4:9–13, *1081*
4:10, *428–429*
6:5–6, *912*
7:7, *885*
9:6, *549*
12:1, *493*, *559*
12:2, *301–302*
12(13):6, *213*

Sotah
14:9, *1064*
15:10, *540*

Gittin
4(3), *621*
4:1, *565*
4(3):5, *603*
4(3):6, *146*
4(3):6–7, *604*
5(3):4–5, *621*

Kiddushin
1:11, *1796*
3:7, *125*
3:7–8, *125–126*
3:8, *122*
5:4, *364*

Bava Kamma
1:2–3, *1079–1080*
2:10, *169–170*
2:11, *1059*
4:2, *110*
6:16–17, *146*
6:17, *146*, *605*
8:14, *455*
9:11, *146*, *604*
10:27, *551*

Bava Meẓi'a
2:16, *549*
2:17, *549*
3:7, *1080*
3:8, *1080–1081*
5:6, *933*
5:6–7, *931*
5:7, *933*
5:23, *933*
7:13, *926*
7:14, *927*
10:11, *341*
11:8, *551*
11:18, *419*, *921*
11:23, *419*, *667*, *679–680*, *755*, *921*, *1074*, *1823*
11:23–25, *741*
11:23–26, *487*, *753*
11:24–25, *867*
11:24–26, *680–681*

Bava Batra
6:5, *1080*
9:1, *1087*
11, *433*
11:3, *213*
11:13, *423, 431*
11:15, *72*

Sanhedrin
2:13, *540*
5:5, *1000*
7:1, *1063–1064*
7:7, *360*
7:11, *315*
9:1, *288–289*
11:6, *366*
14:1, *368–369*

Makkot
2:5, *146*

Shevu'ot
1:7, *316*
3:5, *374*
3:8, *284, 314, 356, 1047*

Eduyyot
1:1, *1067, 1069, 1280*
1:4, *1848*
1:6, *523*

Avodah Zarah
8(9):4, *108*

Ḥullin
8:6, *1058*
10:13, *628*

Bekhorot
3:8, *108*

Kelim
First Part, 4:17, *1798*
Middle Part, 1:6, *1798*

Niddah
9:18, *550*

Zavim
1:5, *1051*
2:5, *369*

Yadayim
2:17–18, *363, 998*
2:18, *364*

HALAKHIC MIDRASHIM

Mekhilta de-R. Ishmael*
BO, TRACTATE DE-PISḤA
sec. 3 (p. 11), *342*
sec. 5 (p. 17), *342*
Bo, sec. 18 (p. 73), *1796*
BE-SHALLAḤ, TRACTATE DE-VA-YASSA
sec. 1 (p. 156), *107*
sec. 1 (p. 158), *151*
YITRO, TRACTATE DE-AMALEK
sec. 2 (pp. 196–197), *278*
sec. 2 (p. 198), *155*
YITRO, TRACTATE DE-BA-ḤODESH
sec. 8 (p. 233), *334*
sec. 8 (pp. 233–234), *335*
MISHPATIM, TRACTATE DE-NEZIKIN
sec. 1 (p. 246), *108, 1322*
sec. 1 (p. 249), *320*
sec. 1 (p. 250), *200–201*
sec. 2 (p. 253), *377*
sec. 2 (p. 254), *1031*
sec. 7 (p. 274), *339*
sec. 9 (pp. 279–280), *357*
sec. 11 (p. 289), *341–342*
sec. 15 (p. 300), *1029–1030*
sec. (p. 302), *1030*
MISHPATIM, TRACTATE DE-KASPA
sec. 18 (p.), *1690*
sec. 20 (p. 321), *403*
sec. 20 (pp. 321–322), *1502*
sec. 20 (pp. 323–324), *338*
sec. 20 (p. 325), *338*
sec. 20 (p. 328), *1046*
KI TISSA, TRACTATE DE-SHABBATA
sec. 1 (p. 341), *1022*
sec. 1 (p. 347), *332*

*The citations are to ed. H.S. Horowitz-Y.A. Rabin, Frankfurt, 1931. The numbers in parentheses refer to the pages in this edition.

Mekhilta de-R. Shim'on bar Yohai
ed. Hoffman, p. 117, *13*
ed. Epstein-Melamed, p. 161, *391*

Baraita de-R. Ishmael, Foreword (Petiḥta) to Torat Kohanim†
p. 1a, *318*
p. 1a/b, *350*
p. 2a, *325*
p. 2a/b, *329*
p. 2b, *331*
p. 2b–3a, *334*
p. 3a, *315*

Sifra (Torat Kohanim), Leviticus‡
VA-YIKRA, DIBBURAH DE-NEDAVAH
4:5 (p. 6a), *382*
ẒAV
sec. 5, 11:6 (pp. 34b–35a), *382*
TAZRIA
13:2 (p. 68a), *381–382*
AḤAREI MOT
11:10 (p. 84b), *378*
13:22 (p. 86b), *483, 485*
KEDOSHIM
sec. 1 (p. 86b), *323*
4:2 (p. 89a), *143*
4:10, *1851*
4:12 (p. 89a), *142*
ch. 8 (p. 91a), *1209*
9:5 (p. 91b), *322*
chs. 10–11 (pp. 92b–93a), *373*
EMOR
17:5–8 (p. 103a), *886*
BEHAR
8:8 (p. 110a), *996*

†The *Baraita de-R. Ishmael* is printed at the beginning of *Sifra*; the page citations are to ed. I.H. Weiss, Vienna, 1862.

‡The citations are to ed. I.H. Weiss, Vienna, 1862. The numbers in parentheses refer to the pages in this edition.

BEḤUKKOTAI
5:3 (p. 111b), *836*
sec. 2, 8:12 (p. 112b), *193*
13:7 (p. 115b), *243*

Sifrei, Numbers§
secs. 7, 161, *356*
BE-HA'ALOTEKHA
sec. 75 (p. 70), *382*
sec. 106 (p. 105), *350*
SHELAḤ
sec. 112 (p. 121), *371*
PINḤAS
sec. 134 (p. 179), *290*
sec. 136 (p. 182), *1322*
MAS'EI
sec. 160 (p. 218), *358*

Sifrei, Deuteronomy‖
DEVARIM
sec. 15 (p. 25), *1299*
VA-ETḤANAN
sec. 34 (p. 60), *1321*
EKEV
sec. 41 (pp. 84–86), *1084*
sec. 48 (p. 113), *104, 1067*
RE'EH
sec. 58 (p. 124), *279*
sec. 79 (p. 145), *160, 624*
sec. 80 (p. 146), *1648*
sec. 82 (p. 148), *496*
sec. 92 (p. 153), *367*
sec. 92 (p. 154), *368*
sec. 93 (p. 154), *368–369*
sec. 116 (pp. 174–175), *117*
sec. 119 (p. 178), *1631*
sec. 120 (p. 179), *1632*
sec. 122 (p. 180), *378*
sec. 144 (p. 197), *1640*
SHOFETIM
sec. 152 (p. 205), *279*
sec. 153 (p. 206), *139, 242, 266, 1759*
sec. 154 (p. 207), *244, 249*

§The citations are to ed. H.S. Horowitz, Leipzig, 1917. The numbers in parentheses refer to the pages in this edition.

‖The citations are to ed. A.A. Finkelstein-Horowitz, Berlin-New York, 1940. The numbers in parentheses refer to the pages in this edition.

sec. 175 (p. 221), *257, 520*
sec. 188 (p. 227), *397*
sec. 188 (p. 228), *527*
sec. 203 (p. 238), *1036*
sec. 204 (p. 240), *1036*
sec. 208 (p. 243), *346*
KI TEẒE
sec. 214 (p. 247), *145*
sec. 218 (pp. 250–251), *365*
sec. 219 (p. 252), *366*
sec. 221 (p. 253), *517–518, 694*
sec. 223 (p. 256), *299*
sec. 238 (p. 270), *1029*
sec. 243 (p. 273), *340, 1031*
sec. 247 (p. 276), *94*
sec. 249 (pp. 275–276), *354*
sec. 249 (p. 277), *361*
sec. 269 (pp. 288–290), *1043*
sec. 269 (p. 289), *378*
sec. 269 (p. 290), *375–376*
sec. 272 (p. 292), *340*
sec. 279 (p. 296), *337*
sec. 280 (p. 297), *304*
sec. 288 (p. 306), *1029*
HA'AZINU
sec. 306 (pp. 328–343), *104*
sec. 310 (p. 351), *482*

Midrash Tannaim, Deuteronomy¶
13:13 (p. 66), *367*
16:19 (p. 96), *14*
17:11 (pp. 102–103), *244*
17:11 (p. 103), *482*
19:15 (p. 115), *526–527*
23:15 (p. 148), *294*
24:1 (p. 154), *377*
25:5 (p. 165), *1029*

TARGUMIM

Onkelos
Genesis 20:5–6, *183*
Exodus 21:9, *93*
Exodus 23:7, *1046*
Numbers 19:2, *1247*

¶The citations are to ed. D.Z. Hoffmann, Berlin, 1909. The numbers in parentheses refer to the pages in this edition.

Deuteronomy 6:8, *1046*
Deuteronomy 6:9, *1046*
I Kings 9:4, *183*
Psalms 78:72, *183*
Psalms 101:2, *183*

Jonathan b. Uzziel*
Genesis 38:18, *914*
Exodus 22:8, *681*
Deuteronomy 24:16, *304*
II Kings 13:14, *1877*

APOCRYPHA AND RELATED SOURCES

Letter of Aristeas
158–159 (ed. Kahana, II, p. 49), *1036*

Aristotle
Ethics 5:13, *248*

Ben Sira
8:16–17 (ed. Segal; ed. Kahana 8:12–13), *1035*
29:17 (ed. Segal; ed. Kahana 29:14), *1035*
29:18–22 (ed. Segal; ed. Kahana 29:15–19), *1035*
29:23 (ed. Segal; ed. Kahana 29:20), *1035*
39:1–3, *314*
42:4 (ed. Kahana, II, p. 515), *1034–1035*

Flavius Josephus
THE ANTIQUITIES OF THE JEWS
Book IV
8:4, *1032, 1055*
8:12, *4*
8:14, *243, 727*
8:28, *1031*
8:34, *1032*
Book XI
5:2, *1087*

*The citations are to M. Ginzburger, *Targum Yonatan ben Uzziel al ha-Torah, Ne'etak mi-Khetav Yad London* [Jonathan b. Uzziel's Translation of the Torah, Copied from the London Manuscript], Berlin, 1903.

Flavius Josephus *continued*
Book XII
1:1, *1035*
6:2, *1036*
Book XV
3:1, *1087*
Book XX
11:2, *4*
CONTRA APIONEM
I, sec. 22, *1035*
II, sec. 18, *4*

Jubilees
4:31–32 (ed. Kahana, p. 34), *1033–1034*

Maccabees
I, 2:32ff. (ed. Kahana, II, p. 107), *1035*
II, 3:10, *562*
II, 3:22–24, *562*

Philo
De Specialibus Legibus, III, pp. 77–78, *1030*

Septuagint
Exodus 22:7, *1029*
Deuteronomy 22:18, *1029*
Deuteronomy 25:5, *1029*

Megillat Ta'anit (ed. Lichtenstein)
pp. 278–279, 319, 334, *1040*

Tobit
7:12 (ed. Kahana, II, p. 331), *1034*

JERUSALEM TALMUD*

Berakhot
1:1, 4b (1:1, 2c), *946*
1:4 (3b), *243*
1:4, 8b (1:8, 3b), *160*
1:4, 9a, *259*
1:4, 9a (1:4, 3b/c), *1067*
1:4, 9a (1:7, 3b), *264, 279, 1847*
2:4, 17a (2:4, 4d), *555*
7:3, 55a (7:4, 10c), *891*

Pe'ah
1:4, 4a (1:1, 15d), *117*
2:4, *95*
2:4, 13a (2:6, 17a), *40, 964*
3:9, 18a (3:9, 17d), *946*
5:1, 25a (5:1, 18d), *508*
7:5, 34b (7:6, 20c), *882, 898, 902*
8:9, 21a, *100*

Kilayim
2:8, *967*

Shevi'it
1:1, 1a (1:1, 33a), *541*
4:2, 10b (4:2, 35b), *540, 542*
5:1, 13a (5:1, 35d), *891, 900*
10:1–2, 29a/b (10:2–3, 39c), *513*
10:2, 29b (10:3, 39c), *301*
10:4, *705*

Terumot
1:8, 7a *et seq.* (1:8, 40d *et seq.*), *635*
8:4, 44a (8:10, 46b), *154*
8:10, 47a (8:10, 46b), *971–972*

Ma'aserot
2:4, 12a (4:7, 50a), *886*

Ma'aser Sheni
5:2, 30a (5:3, 56b), *882, 898, 902*

Orlah
1:1, *967*
1:3, *967*
3:7, 20a (3:8, 63b), *887*

Bikkurim
1:5, 3b (1:5, 64a), *932*

Shabbat
1:4, 9a (1:8, 3c), *556, 1063, 1066*
1:4, 10b (1:8, 3d), *541*
2:1, 25b (1:1, 4c), *542*
6:2, 34a (6:2, 8a), *541– 542*
16:1, 79b (16:1, 15c), *424*
19:1, 87a (19:1, 17a), *883*
19:2, 87b (19:2, 17a), *371*

Eruvin
3:2, 20b (3:3, 20d), *387*
7:9, 49b (7:10, 24c), *387*

Pesaḥim
4:1, *731*
4:1, 25b (4:1, 30c/d), *932, 940*
4:1, 25b (4:1, 30d), *885, 939–940*
4:1, 25b–26a (4:1, 30d), *933*
4:1, 26a (4:1, 30d), *933, 935, 941*
4:3, 27a (4:3, 30d), *888*
4:6, 28b (4:6, 31a), *890*
6:1, 39a (6:1, 33a), *344, 354–355*
6:1, 39a/b (6:1, 32a), *901*

Shekalim
1:1, 2b (1:1, 46a), *109, 890*
1:2, 3a/b (1:2, 46a), *508*
5:1, 21a (5:1, 48c), *1051*
5:1, 21a (5:1, 48d), *1056*
5:6, 49b, *100*

Beẓah
2:1, 10a (2:1, 61b), *964*
5:2, 20a (5:2, 63a), *516*

Ta'anit
1:6, 6a (1:6, 64c), *933, 940*

Megillah
1:5, 6b (1:7, 70d), *555*
1:5, 7b (1:7, 71a), *890*
3:2, *704, 1427*

*The Jerusalem Talmud is cited by chapter and paragraph (*halakhah*), and by page and folio. The citation to the current printed editions (with commentaries) is followed by a citation (in parentheses) to ed. Venice. For example, TJ Shevi'it 1:1, 1a (1:1, 33a) means that the cited material appears in chapter 1, *halakhah* 1, on page 1a of the current printed editions, and in chapter 1, *halakhah* 1, on page 33a of ed. Venice.

3:2, 24a (3:2, 74a), *727–728*
3:6, 26a (3:7, 74b), *172*
4:1, 29a/b (4:1, 75a), *556*

Ḥagigah
1:1, 3a (1:1, 76a), *336*
1:8, *95*
2:2, *694*
2:2, 10b (2:2, 77d), *1062, 1064*
2:2, 11b (2:2, 78a), *515–518*
2:3, 12a (2:3, 78a), *1062*

Mo'ed Katan
3:1, 10b (3:1, 81d), *242, 261*

Yevamot
1:6, 9a (1:6, 3b), *1064–1067, 1847*
2:4, 11b (2:4, 3d) *et seq.*, *557*
2:4, 12a (2:4, 3d), *557*
4:11, 28a (4:11, 6b), *1052, 1061*
7:3, 40a (7:2, 8a), *882, 898, 903*
11:1, 62a (11:1, 11d), *374*
12:1, 66a (12:1, 12c), *907*
13:3, 78a (13:3, 14d), *932*
15:1, 77a (15:1, 14d), *523*
15:3, 78a (15:3, 14d), *423–424, 427–428*
15:3, 78b (15:3, 14d), *428*
16:7, 84b (16:8, 15c), *526*
16:7, 84b (16:7, 16a), *529, 610*

Sotah
3:4, 16a (3:4, 19a), *1798*
3:6, 17b (3:6, 19b), *1061*
5:5, 25b (5:7, 20c), *316*
9:1, 40a (9:1, 23b), *367*

Ketubbot
1:1, 2b–3a (1:1, 25a), *888*
1:5, 5b (1:5, 25c), *493*
4:8, 29a (4:8, 28d), *423, 427*
4:8, 29a (4:8, 28d–29a), *424, 632*
4:8, 29a/b (4:8, 28d–29a), *932*
4:8, 29a (4:8, 29a), *427–429*
4:8, 29b (4:8, 29a), *428*
4:10, 30a (4:11, 29a), *1503, 1505*
4:14, 31a (4:15, 29b), *574*
5:8, 38a (5:10, 30b), *126*
6:3, 39b–40a (6:3, 30c/d), *912*
6:4, 40a/b (6:4, 30d), *679*
8:11, 50b (8:11, 32b), *559*
8:11, 50b (8:11, 32b/c), *559–560*
8:11, 50b (8:11, 32c), *559–560*
9:1, 51a *et seq.* (9:1, 32c *et seq.*), *124, 126*
9:1, 52b (9:1, 32d), *125*
9:1, 53b (9:1, 33a), *126, 836*
9:4, 52b (9:4, 33a), *630, 1715*
12:5, 67b (12:5, 35b), *1725*
13:1, 68a, *1087*
13:11, 72a (13:11, 36b), *211, 214, 560*

Nedarim
9:4, 30b (10:3, 41c), *142*

Gittin
4:2, 20b (4:2, 45c), *565, 634–635*
5:1, 26b (5:1, 46c), *301–302*
5:3, 28b (5:3, 46d), *882, 912*
8:1, 44a (8:1, 49b), *375–376*
8:3, *629*

Kiddushin
1:1, 1a (1:1, 58b), *1209*
1:1, 4b (1:1, 58d), *264*
1:7, *1796*
1:2, 11b (1:2, 59d), *377–378*
1:5, 16a/b (1:5, 60c), *582, 1023–1024*
2:1, 23a (2:1, 62a), *342*
3:12, 40b–41a (3:14, 64d), *1455*
4:6, 46a (4:6, 66a), *888, 932*

Bava Kamma
3:1, 12a (3:1, 3c), *1715*
8:8, 37a (8:11, 6c), *127*
10:1, 42a (10:1, 7b), *596*
10:3, 43b (10:3, 7c), *598*

Bava Meẓi'a
1:6, 4b (1:6, 8a), *596*
2:4, 7a (2:4, 8c), *956–957*
5:4, 21b (5:6, 10b), *931*
6:4, 27a (6:4, 11a), *926*
6:6, 27a/b (6:8, 11a), *156*
7:1, 27b (7:1, 11b), *906, 1822*
7:7, 29a (7:10, 11c), *125*

Bava Batra
1:2, 1b (1:2, 12d), *931*
3:1, 7b (3:1, 13d), *1008–1009, 1013*
5:1, 15b (5:1, 15a), *551*
5:1, 15b *et seq.* (5:1,15a), *551*
8:5, 24a (8:6, 16b), *126*
8:8, 26b (8:10, 16c), *126*
9:4, 28b (9:6, 17a), *1503, 1505*
10:1–3, 30b–31b (10:1–3, 17c), *433*
10:8, 33a (10:14, 17d), *1090, 1097*

Sanhedrin
1:1, *13, 175*
1:1, 1b (1:1, 18a), *6–7*
1:4, 8b (1:4, 19c), *1063–1064, 1901*
3:1, 13b (10:1, 21a), *19*
3:2, 14a (3:2, 21a), *25*
4:2, 21a/b (11:2, 22a), *259, 383*
7:2, *7, 13*
7:2, 31a/b (14:2, 24b), *6*
7:3, 31b (7:3, 24b), *1034*
10:2, 52b (17:2, 29a), *96*

Shevu'ot
4:1, 19a/b (4:1, 35b/c), *356*
5:5, *967*
7:1, 33b (7:1, 37c), *618*

Avodah Zarah
2:7, 15a (2:8, 41c), *160*
2:8, 16a (2:9, 41d), *540–541*

Avodah Zarah *continued*
5:12, 36b (5:12, 45b), *374*

Horayot
1:1, 2b (1:1, 45d), *244*

Niddah
3:1, 9a (3:1, 50c), *890*

BABYLONIAN TALMUD

Berakhot
2b, *1059*
7b, *947*
10b, *969*
11a, *886, 949, 1064*
17a, *366*
19b, *131, 238, 482, 518*
20a, *1090*
22a, *899*
24a, *964*
26b, *550*
27b–28a, *363*
28a, *363, 998*
30a, *1648*
31a, *891*
32b, *1890*
33a, *555*
33b, *98*
38b, *1321*
41b, *300*
45a, *881, 898*
50a, *891*
52a, *264, 891*
52b, *900*
58a, *1849*
63a, *503*

Shabbat
3b, *1054*
6b, *224*
10a, *159, 250, 1296, 1893*
14a–15b, *622*
14b, *491, 493, 559–560*
15a, *6, 501, 1062–1063*
15b, *491, 566*
16b, *493, 559–560*
17a, *1066*
18b, *514*
19a, *1036*
21a, *946, 1441, 1457*
21a–23b, *481–482*
21b, *481, 504*
23a, *139*
29b, *472*
31a, *142–143, 151, 191, 1053, 1085, 1851*
54a, *964*
56a, *1297*
56b, *1298*
60a, *504, 523*
63a, *988*
64a, *352*
70a, *332*
88a, *234*
104a, *1296*
116b, *424*
119b, *366*
123b, *550*
128b, *532*
138b, *1067*
139a, *1298*

Eruvin
4a, *208*
4b, *300–301*
6b, *1064, 1087*
13b, *259, 264, 1067, 1847, 1900*
14b, *898*
17a, *492, 551*
17a/b, *551*
21b, *501, 557, 947*
31b, *996*
32a, *996*
32b, *504, 1085*
45a, *504*
46b, *899, 1089*
49a, *492*
50b, *268*
53a, *267*
62b, *891–892, 900*
71b–72a, *892*
72a, *891, 900*
82a, *408*

Pesaḥim
6b, *115*
22b, *372–373*
25b, *991*
39a, *388*
48b, *932*
49b, *726*
50b, *733, 735, 894, 933, 938*
50b–51a, *934, 1318*
51a, *885, 934–936*
51b, *936*
54a, *881, 898*
66a, *355, 360, 882–884, 901*
68b, *1321*
70b, *315, 1043*
91a, *918*
99a, *527*
103a, *891, 900*
104a, *891*
112a, *1858*
113b, *73*
114a, *264*

Yoma
4b, *1858*
9b, *267*
11a, *1087*
14b, *1050*
16a, *1050*
18a, *369*
18b, *810*
69a, *503*
74a, *998*
81a, *373*
82a, *991*
85b, *504, 519, 990*

Sukkah
20a, *311, 1087, 1347*
28a, *300–301, 1090*
29a, *988*
31a, *602*
32a, *388*
32b, *388*
35a, *205, 286*
41b, *114*
43a/b, *886*
44a, *208, 549, 889*
44b, *889–890*
51b, *681, 1212*

Beẓah
3b, *212*
4b, *493, 498*
5a/b, *542*
20a, *1062*
20b, *349*
25b, *885*
38b, *131*

Rosh ha-Shanah
6a, *679*
15b, *891, 900*
16a/b, *497*
18b, *543*
21b, *570*

22a, *529*
23b, *1087*
25a/b, *687*
25b, *266, 1790*
28b, *496, 498*
29b, *950*

Ta'anit
21a, *1044*
26b, *891, 898, 900*

Megillah
2a, *541, 555*
3a, *1045*
10b, *1852*
17b, *555*
19b, *40, 192*
26a, *704, 727*
28b, *93–94, 1042*
29a, *1240*

Mo'ed Katan
3b, *541–542*
5a, *61, 483*
14b, *109*
28a, *1321*

Ḥagigah
3b, *256–257, 1067*
15b, *313*
18a, *245*
22a, *628, 726, 1715*

Yevamot
13b, *550, 890*
13b–14a, *935*
14a, *1065–1066*
14b, *1065–1066*
15a, *530, 1064*
16a, *1062, 1064*
20a, *160, 208, 557*
21a, *483, 490, 557, 699*
21a/b, *557*
22a, *224, 960*
25a, *527*
25b, *691, 695*
27a, *550*
27b, *550*
31b, *611*
35b, *1002–1004*
37b, *810*
42b–43a, *1061*
46a/b, *955*
46b, *954–955*
52a, *535*
62a/b, *437*
62b, *447, 790, 830*
64b, *561*
65a, *785*
68b, *372*
76b, *361–362*
76b–77a, *362*
77a, *361–363, 964*
79a, *503–504*
87b, *389–390, 527, 530*
88a, *527*
89a/b, *636*
89a–90b, *506, 531*
89b, *204, 509, 530, 532, 687, 689, 844, 851, 853*
90a/b, *506*
90b, *248, 250, 255, 257, 515–516, 520, 532–534, 536, 565, 631, 690, 694, 697, 853, 871*
91a, *132*
93b, *527*
102a, *908*
109a, *1163*
109b, *1493*
110a, *521, 632, 637–638, 849–850, 852–853, 858, 862, 871, 1891*
112b, *509*
115a, *525, 527*
116b, *402, 504, 523–524, 527, 1014*
118b, *113, 148, 1980*
122b, *530, 609*

Ketubbot
2b–3a, *633*
3a, *634, 642, 853, 858, 862–863*
10a, *211, 389, 560*
12a, *888, 933*
13a, *985*
15a, *1544*
17a, *1415*
18b, *611*
21a–22a, *613*
21b, *612*
22a, *386, 913, 994–995, 1004*
22b, *528*
24a, *132*
27b, *248, 1715, 1891*
28a, *612*
30a/b, *1926*
32b, *691*
37b, *142*
40b, *131*
45b, *1029*
46a, *1029*
46b, *131, 1785, 1803*
47a, *628, 1715*
47b, *211, 570, 572, 1785*
49a, *116*
49b, *116, 161, 224, 567, 1455, 1661*
50a, *568, 657, 827*
51a, *647, 882, 912*
52b, *575–577, 579, 655, 800, 837, 840, 1503, 1505, 1679*
53b, *575*
54a, *573*
56a, *125, 215–216*
56a/b, *127*
58b, *571–572, 628, 1715, 1785*
58b–59a, *570*
61b, *810*
62b, *873*
63a *et seq.*, *659*
63a–64a, *660*
64a, *660–661*
65b, *116, 1803*
66a, *1786*
67a, *648, 882*
68a, *578–579*
68b, *985*
69a, *224, 579*
69a/b, *967*
69b, *647, 882, 912*
70b, *572*
73b, *132, 860*
75b, *996*
77a *et seq.*, *659*
79a, *967*
79b, *572*
80a/b, *572*
82b, *492–493, 559, 570, 590*
83a, *840*
83a *et seq.*, *211*
83a/b, *572*
83b, *433*
83b–84a, *124, 126, 573*
84a, *215*
84b–86a, *1089*
85a, *1212–1213*

Ketubbot *continued*
86a, *117–118, 214, 219, 654, 800*
88a, *650*
92a, *591*
94a, *722*
94b, *985*
95b, *985*
96a, *1725*
97b, *573*
99b, *706*
102b, *583*
103b, *1053*
104a, *179, 1725*
104a/b, *1725*
104b, *967*
105a, *1087, 1641*
106a, *1084*
110b, *211, 213–214, 560*
112a/b, *1650*

Nedarim
8a, *1697*
15a, *934*
25a, *234*
27a/b, *704*
28a, *65, 68, 139, 1821*
49a, *447*
50a, *873*
51b, *437*
60a/b, *438*
62a, *387*
63a/b, *437*
78b, *21*
86a, *679*

Nazir
12a, *996*
28b, *1796*
34b, *327*

Sotah
2a/b, *356*
16a, *377*
20a/b, *1798*
21a, *366*
22a, *948, 1042, 1352, 1381, 1405, 1416*
22b, *1774*
27a, *997*
34a, *1209*
37a, *203*
39b, *988*
41b, *108*
47b, *108, 1064*
48b, *907*
49b, *523*

Gittin
2b, *131, 522*
3a, *131, 611–612*
6b, *259, 263, 988*
10a, *469*
10b, *65, 68, 469, 1821*
13a, *220*
13b, *589*
13b–14a, *584*
14b, *584*
19a, *860, 949*
33a, *565, 631–633, 642, 858, 860, 862*
33b–34a, *635*
34a, *131–132*
34b, *564, 1454*
35a, *1091*
36a, *203–204, 469, 491–492, 513, 613, 704*
36a/b, *514*
36b, *204, 512, 541, 642, 700, 734, 853, 866*
37a, *860, 949, 1667*
38b, *504*
39b, *132*
40a, *1891*
44a, *110*
45a, *600*
46a, *704*
47b, *114*
47b–48b, *114*
48b–49b, *303*
49b, *303, 589*
50b, *593*
53a, *603*
55a, *601*
55a/b, *510*
56a, *1884*
59a, *585–586, 1664, 1884*
59b, *387*
60a, *226*
60b, *193, 224, 234, 534, 1296*
61a, *219*
63b, *132*
64a, *996*
64b–65a, *214–215*
66a, *472*
66b, *469, 1455*
67a, *1240, 1245*
71a, *610*
73a, *634, 642*
74b–75a, *562*
77a, *375–376*
86a, *469*
86b, *469*
88b, *13, 20–23, 110, 660–662, 679*

Kiddushin
2a, *196*
3a, *196*
3b, *131*
4b, *535*
5a/b, *469*
9a, *300–301*
9b, *535, 988*
11b, *196*
12b, *535*
15a, *1031, 1631–1632*
16b, *1631–1632*
17a/b, *1632–1633*
17b, *491*
21b, *378, 1711*
22b, *925*
24b, *357*
25a, *357*
26a, *583, 1649*
27b–28a, *132*
28b, *510*
29a, *1666, 1796–1797*
29a–30b, *1796*
29b, *1797–1798*
30a, *313, 1321*
30b, *323*
34a, *408*
35a, *108, 344*
38b, *887*
38b–39a, *889*
39b, *1329*
40a, *1329*
40b, *1084*
41b, *112, 342*
42b, *1364*
48a, *337, 584*
49a, *912*
49b, *1327*
52a, *857*
58b, *641*
59a, *153, 395*
59b, *985*
63a, *628, 1715*

63b, *408*
66b, *1689*
68b, *1689*
71b, *873*
74a, *1208*
78b, *888, 932*

Bava Kamma
2b, *204*
3b, *207*
8a, *592*
9a, *408*
10a/b, *1077*
11b, *591, 966*
14b, *21*
15a, *108–109, 323, 1009*
15a/b, *108*
15b, *207*
17b, *207*
25a, *350*
27b, *131, 411–413, 1096, 1715*
27b–28a, *408*
28b, *764*
29b, *115*
30a, *413*
32a, *629, 1059*
40b, *589*
41b, *372–373*
46a/b, *131, 906*
46b, *249, 385, 460, 992–993*
55b–56a, *146*
62a, *636*
62b, *327*
66a, *601*
70a, *1747*
70b, *129, 1210*
79b, *540*
80a, *455*
80b, *492, 551*
80b–81b, *551*
81a, *552*
81b, *551–553*
82a, *556, 1264*
82b, *367–368, 523*
87a, *108*
89a/b, *629*
92a, *1171*
92b, *15–16, 96*
93a, *127, 1171*
94b, *602*
95a, *650*
96b, *985*
99b, *156*
99b–100a, *155*
103b, *492*
113a, *69–70, 110*
113a/b, *65, 68, 1821*
113b, *68, 134*
114b, *551*
115a, *597–600*
116b, *138, 415, 680–681, 926–927*
117a, *680*
118b, *1212*

Bava Meẓi'a
2b, *249*
10a, *415, 628–629, 1635, 1715, 1840*
10b, *1364*
12a, *113, 409*
12b, *410, 588, 628, 1715*
16b, *627*
20b, *131*
22b, *687*
24a, *96*
24b, *156*
25b, *956*
26b, *1747*
27a *et seq.*, *211*
27a/b, *298–299*
27b, *132, 299–300, 688*
28a, *299, 654*
28b, *549*
30a, *132, 957, 1746*
30b, *155, 159, 165, 250, 253, 957*
31b, *117*
32a, *20, 1209*
32b, *628*
35a, *627*
35a/b, *627*
35b, *165, 628*
36a, *964–965*
36b, *966*
37a, *1980*
37a/b, *148*
39b, *248, 1715*
43a, *406, 1695*
44a, *148*
47a, *581, 1022*
47b, *211, 297, 492, 989*
48a, *917*
48b, *148*
49a, *118, 151, 581, 705*
51a/b, *126*
57b, *325*
59a/b, *242*
59b, *261–262, 1068–1069, 1690*
60a/b, *395*
61a, *128*
62a, *1852*
63b *et seq.*, *222*
65a, *128*
66a, *985*
67b, *679*
67b–68a, *931*
68b, *931*
69b, *931*
69b–70a, *909*
70a, *946, 966–967*
71a, *117*
71b, *110*
72a, *129*
72b, *560*
73b, *748–749, 767, 1340*
74a, *914, 1822*
75b, *154*
77a, *415, 1840*
83a, *144, 156, 165, 766, 925, 931, 1634*
83a/b, *905*
83b, *905, 1634*
85b, *1053*
86a, *263, 661, 932, 1092*
87a, *932*
88a, *173*
92a, *224*
94a, *125–126, 581, 583, 589*
94b, *352–353, 1695*
94b–95a, *322*
95a, *348–349*
99a, *581*
101b, *1891*
102a, *628*
103b, *931*
104a, *423–424, 428–429, 432, 932*
104a/b, *1983*
104b, *1985*
105a, *1982, 1984*
108a, *625*
108a/b, *417*
108b, *626*
110a, *985*
110b, *337*

Bava Meẓi'a *continued*
112b, *617–618*
112b–113a, *620*
113b, *1859*
114a, *1455*
115a, *295–296*
116b, *1627*
119a, *132*

Bava Batra
2a–3a, *941*
3a, *583*
4a, *931, 941*
5a/b, *249, 996*
7b–8a, *921*
8a, *776*
8b, *116, 487, 667, 679, 686, 689, 703, 714–715, 732, 745, 765, 767, 794, 853, 865, 1074, 1824*
8b–9a, *1823*
9a, *679, 681, 704, 716, 752–753, 755–757, 759, 853, 867, 1820–1821*
12a, *1076*
15a, *555*
21b, *395, 683*
23b, *179*
24b, *749–750*
28a, *1010*
28a *et seq.*, *1007*
28a–29a, *1008–1010*
29a, *985*
29b, *1334–1335*
29b–31a, *1089*
30b, *744*
31b, *996*
32b–34b, *1089*
33b, *985*
34b, *1208*
36a, *1213*
36b, *1010, 1332, 1455*
41b, *596, 1455*
43a, *737, 840*
47b–48b, *636*
48a, *852*
48b, *521, 632, 637, 853, 858, 862*
51b, *1803*
53b–54a, *959*
54a, *960*
54b–55a, *65, 68, 1821*
55a, *748, 767, 769*
56b, *1210*
57a/b, *132*
58a, *96*
59a, *1860*
59b, *1860*
60a, *943, 1859*
60b, *540*
65a, *985*
68a, *1334*
69a/b, *196*
76a, *220*
83a, *946, 1457*
87a, *1330*
90b–91a, *1300*
92a/b, *131, 906*
99b, *750*
99b–100a, *749*
100a, *749, 764–765*
100b, *933*
108b, *290*
109a, *290, 1029*
109b, *573, 964*
111a, *350*
111b, *573*
115b, *844*
115b–116a, *844*
116a, *844*
119b, *1798*
121a, *733*
126b, *124, 126*
127a, *1455*
127a/b, *1455*
130b, *95, 947, 961–964, 976–977, 983, 1229, 1457*
130b–131a, *982–983*
131a, *416, 840, 1813*
131b, *404*
133b, *99, 150, 152*
134a, *1090*
136a–137b, *114*
137a, *154*
137b, *114*
139b, *569*
143b, *437, 446–448*
144b, *892*
145a, *892–893*
147a/b, *580*
149a, *220, 1200*
155a, *1665*
155a–156a, *587*
160a, *433, 469, 1024*
165a, *912*
166a, *433*
166b, *435, 932, 1340*
166b–167a, *434*
167a, *433*
171b, *837*
173a, *469*
173b, *916, 985, 1026, 1090, 1097, 1151, 1986–1987*
173b–174a, *1163*
174a, *117, 590, 1209*
174b, *154*
175a, *596*
175b, *510, 589, 594*
176a/b, *1987*

Sanhedrin
2a–3b, *683*
2b, *109*
3a, *22–23, 1646*
5a, *58, 607, 985, 1645–1646*
5b, *948*
6a, *23*
6b, *180, 250*
7a, *159, 180, 1893*
7b, *23, 859, 1183, 1299, 1321, 1493, 1507*
10b, *728*
13b–14a, *7*
14a, *96*
16b, *368–369*
17a, *257*
19a, *556*
19b, *827*
20b, *67, 69, 486, 1024, 1205*
21b–22a, *311*
23a, *19, 24–25, 883*
24a, *738, 1259*
24b, *742*
27b, *304*
29a, *1455, 1698–1699*
30a, *356, 387, 882, 933, 1000–1002*
31a, *982*
31b, *686, 825, 1460*
32a, *510*
32a/b, *606–608*
32b, *169–170, 654, 1087, 1460*
33a, *269, 876, 982, 984, 1420*
33b, *1046*
34b, *346*
36a, *109*

37a, *1698*
40a/b, *691*
40b, *253*
41a, *254, 517*
44a, *103*
45a, *142*
45b, *518*
46a, *31, 57, 323, 515, 690, 694, 696–697, 1326*
48b, *486, 1025*
49a, *55, 1298*
51b, *289, 372, 380*
52a, *972*
52b, *142, 972–973*
53a, *207*
56a, *108, 138, 194, 1855*
57b, *110*
64b, *371*
66a, *322*
67b, *94*
68b, *365*
69a, *365*
71a, *366, 368–369*
72a, *258*
72b, *970*
73a, *344–345, 360, 970, 1924*
74a, *345, 374, 504, 970, 990–991*
76b, *358*
81a, *395*
82b, *207*
84b, *143*
86a, *334–335, 1052*
86b, *1848*
87a, *279*
87a/b, *109*
88a, *244*
88b, *207, 496, 1063–1064, 1281, 1901*
91b, *1839, 1856*
99a, *1856*
108a, *1297*
109b, *872*
111b, *368–369*
113a, *368*

Makkot
3b, *127*
5b, *373–374*
7a, *692*
17b, *374*
23b, *234*
24a, *395*

Shevu'ot
4a, *1061*
22b, *1004*
26a, *316–317*
26b, *452*
27a/b, *322, 440*
30a, *168*
30a *et seq.*, *1698*
30a/b, *1760*
30b, *132*
36a/b, *132*
41a, *218*
42b, *1330*
44b, *149*
45a, *492, 616–619*
45b, *620*
48b–49a, *620*
49a, *620*

Avodah Zarah
7a, *212*
7b, *1087*
9a, *436*
13a, *532*
14b, *890*
19b, *1493*
26a, *628*
27b, *991*
35b *et seq.*, *670, 762*
35b–36b, *622*
36a, *539, 541, 670, 683, 763, 765, 794, 907*
36a/b, *763, 768*
41b, *996*
50a, *891*
58b, *447*

Horayot
2b, *245*
3b, *763, 1493, 1507*

Zevaḥim
34a, *324*
44b–45a, *52*
48a, *360*
49b, *319, 344*
106b, *373–374*

Menaḥot
29b, *206–207, 382*
31b–32a, *909*
35b, *903*
99a/b, *503*
104b, *97*
110a, *97*

Ḥullin
6b–7a, *937–938*
9a, *1267*
10b, *131, 997*
11a, *683, 997*
11a–12a, *997*
59b, *1455–1456*
63a, *909*
85a, *1060*
93b, *894*
95b, *1455*
113a, *500*
114a–116a, *351*
115b, *500*
134a, *132, 144*
137b, *447*

Bekhorot
13b, *110*
19a, *329*
26b, *245*
28b, *606–607, 1645*
29a, *827*
37a, *22*
49b, *132, 593*
52b, *211, 573*

Arakhin
16b, *1584*
22a, *110, 117*
31b–32a, *562*
32b, *1632*

Temurah
2b, *323*
14a/b, *1455*
14b, *224, 226, 503, 534*
16a, *242–243, 947*

Keritot
11a, *371*

Niddah
19b, *355*
22b, *352*
24b, *132*
25a, *132, 203*
32a/b, *300–301*
66a, *890–891*
68a, *1455*

MINOR TRACTATES

Gerim
3:4, *1855*

Derekh Ereẓ Rabbah
ch. 1, *380*
3:6 (ed. Higger, p. 267), *380*

Soferim
1:7 (ed. Higger, pp. 100–105), *1037*
ch. 14, (ed. Higger, p. 271), *883*

Semaḥot (ed. Zlotnick)
Introduction, *1150*

AGGADIC MIDRASHIM

Avot de-R. Nathan
1:1, *239*
1st version, ch. 3 (p. 16), *948*
1st version, ch. 15 (p. 31a), *191, 193*
1st version, ch. 18 (pp. 34a, 73a), *1051*
1st version, ch. 37 (p. 110), *315*
2nd version, ch. 26, *142*

Midrash Aseret ha-Dibberot
Ḥeder Rishon, p. 72, *1705*

Midrash Lekaḥ Tov
Vayikra, p. 2, *1858*
Deuteronomy 4:2, *497*
Shofetim 17:11, *244*

Midrash Mishlei
22:28, *885, 893*

Midrash Tehillim
12:4 (pp. 107–108), *383*

Midrash Rabbah
Genesis Rabbah
19, *250*
24:7, *1851*
43:14, *554*
58:11, *196*
85:6, *198*
92:7, *347, 350*
Exodus Rabbah
28:4, *242*
30:23, *519*
41:6, *241*
Leviticus Rabbah
6:3, *654, 1705*
30:15, *205*
Numbers Rabbah
19:17, *487*
21:2, *1849*
Shir ha-Shirim (Song of Songs) Rabbah
1, *160*
1 (third), par. 2, *244*
6:10, *1053*
6:14, *1054*
Ruth Rabbah
7:11, *1024*
Kohelet Rabbah
1:4, *266*

Pesikta Rabbati
sec. 3, *263, 482*
sec. 6, *101*

Tanḥuma
Va-Yera, sec. 5, *225*
Va-Yeshev, sec. 2, *263*
Mishpatim, sec. 3 (p. 98), *14*
Mishpatim, sec. 6 (p. 100), *13, 20*
Yitro, sec. 11, *242*
Ki Tissa, sec. 34, *225*
Naso, sec. 29, *263, 482*
Ḥukkat, sec. 16, *276*
Pinḥas, sec. 1, *1849*
Mattot, sec. 1, *1705*

Sefer Ve-Hizhir
Mishpatim 38:1, *762*

Yalkut Shim'oni
Emor 631:75, *380–381*
Shofetim 911, *244*

SCRIPTURAL COMMENTARIES

Abravanel
on Deuteronomy 17:8–11, *246, 253–254*

Akedat Yiẓḥak
Exodus, Yitro, gate 43, *247–251*

Cassuto
on Exodus 21:14, *199*
on Exodus 22:12, *197*

Divrei David
on Deuteronomy 17:11, *244*

Elijah, Gaon of Vilna
on Proverbs 6:4, *180, 1296*

Gur Aryeh
on Deuteronomy 4:2, *496–497, 502*
on Deuteronomy 17:11, *245*

Hoffmann
on Leviticus, pp. 3–8, *203*
on Deuteronomy 13:13, *367–368*
on Deuteronomy 17:8–11, *6, 55, 108, 309, 558*
on Deuteronomy 17:11, *244*
on Deuteronomy 21:15–17, *203*

Ibn Ezra
on Exodus 18:19, *1297*
on Exodus 21:10, *571*
on Leviticus 5:1, *284*
on Deuteronomy 17:8–11, *237*

Keli Ḥemdah
Mishpatim #1, *15–16, 1583*

Keli Yakar
on Deuteronomy 17:11, *256–258*

Malbim
Ayyelet ha-Shaḥar (Introduction), *308*

Meiri
on Psalms 119:126, *503*

Meẓudat David
on Isaiah 8:12, *769*

Naḥmanides
on Genesis 34:13, *194, 1855*
on Genesis 38:8, *198*
on Exodus 15:25, *55, 553*
on Exodus 21:1, *13–15, 25*
on Exodus 21:10, *571*
on Leviticus 5:1, *284*
on Leviticus 19:2, *185*

on Leviticus 19:18, *1851–1852*
on Leviticus 23:24, *1022*
on Leviticus 25:29, *562*
on Leviticus 27:29, *487*
on Deuteronomy 4:2, *497, 501–502*
on Deuteronomy 6:18, *185, 625*
on Deuteronomy 7:12, *107–108*
on Deuteronomy 12:28, *185, 625*
on Deuteronomy 17:8–11, *237*
on Deuteronomy 17:11, *245– 246, 279*

Obadiah Seforno
on Numbers 31:27, *554*
on Psalms 119:126, *503*

Or ha-Ḥayyim
on Deuteronomy 1:16, *168*

Ralbag
on II Kings 14:6, *304*

Rashbam
on Genesis 26:5, *195, 234*
on Genesis 37:2, *1911*
on Exodus 18:13, *195*

Rashi
on Genesis 14:24, s.v. Hane'arim, *554*
on Exodus 21:1, s.v. Lifneihem, *14–15*
on Leviticus 2:1, *97*
on Leviticus 24:11, *1515*
on Numbers 35:16, *358*
on Deuteronomy 13:1, s.v. Lo tosef alav, *496*
on Deuteronomy 16:18, *1299*
on Deuteronomy 17:8–11, *237*
on Deuteronomy 19:15, s.v. Al pi shenei edim, *610*
on Deuteronomy 21:11, *1711*
on Isaiah 8:12, *768*
on Amos 8:5, *1022*
on Psalms 119:126, *503*
on Proverbs 7:26, *1493*

Redak
on I Kings 21:10, *1025*
on II Kings 14:6, *304*
on Amos 8:5, *1022*

M.Z. Segal
on Amos 8:5, *1022*

Torah Shelemah
XVII, pp. 9–11, *13*

Torah Temimah
Genesis, Introduction, ch. 2, par. 9 (p. 15), *391*
on Exodus 22:9, *325*
on Deuteronomy ch. 11, #48, *1798*
on Deuteronomy 24:1, *376*

Turim
on Exodus 18:19, *1297*

COMMENTARIES ON MISHNAH

Asheri
to Yadayim 4:3, *206*

Gilyon R. Akiva Eger
to Berakhot 5:4, *95*

Obadiah Bertinoro
to Berakhot 1:1, *1059*
to Yevamot 16:7, *525*
to Avot 1:1, *143*
to Me'ilah 6:5, *406*
to Zavim 2:2, *370*

Derekh Ḥayyim
to Avot 1:1, *140*
to Avot 6:6, *1380*

Eliyahu Rabbah
to Kelim 5:10, *261*

Magen Avot
Introduction, *894*

Maimonides
Introduction, *202, 205, 239, 243, 265, 286, 490–493, 500–501, 882, 1053–1055, 1092–1093, 1106–1107, 1171, 1184, 1187, 1543*
to Shevi'it 4:10, *1107*
to Shabbat 7:21, *142*
to Gittin 5:2, *592*
to Gittin 5:7, *585*
to Kiddushin 1:7, *408*
Introduction to Chapter Ḥelek, Sandhedrin, *507*
to Sanhedrin 3:7, *882*
to Sanhedrin 11:2, *288*
to Makkot 1:5, *1515*
to Eduyyot 1:5, *541*
to Eduyyot 8:7, *206*
Introduction to Shemonah Perakim, *1190*
to Avot 1:1, *555*
to Avot 1:8, *800*
to Ḥullin 7:6, *233–234*
to Bekhorot 4:4, *58*
to Tamid 5:1, *1187*
to Kelim 17:12, *208*
to Zavim 2:2, *370*
to Ukẓin (end), *1187*

Melekhet Shelomo
to Yevamot 16:7, *525*

Rabad
to Eduyyot 1:5, *541*

Rabbenu Jonah
to Avot 1:2, *1295–1296*

Samson of Sens
to Yadayim 4:3, *206*
to Eduyyot 1:5, *259, 541, 1848*

Tiferet Yisra'el
to Bava Batra 10:8, *140*

Tosafot R. Akiva Eger
Gittin, ch. 4, #35, *533*

Tosafot Yom Tov
Introduction, *1108–1109*
to Berakhot 5:4, *95*
to Shevi'it 4:10, *1107*
to Ma'aser Sheni 5:2, *542–543*
to Nazir 5:5, *1107*
to Avot 1:8, *1503*
to Arakhin 9:4, *562*

COMMENTARIES ON TOSEFTA

Ḥazon Yeḥezkel
to Kiddushin 3:9, *125*

Minḥat Bikkurim
to Kiddushin 3:9, *125*

Miẓpeh Shemu'el
to Kiddushin 3:9, letter *lamed*, *125*

COMMENTARIES ON HALAKHIC MIDRASHIM

Masoret ha-Talmud
on Baraita de-R. Ishmael, Foreword to Torat Kohanim, p. 3a, letter *ẓadi*, *315*

Rabad on Sifra
on Baraita de-R. Ishmael, Foreword to Torat Kohanim, p. 1a, *318*
on Baraita de-R. Ishmael, Foreword to Torat Kohanim, p. 1b, *336*
on Baraita de-R. Ishmael, Foreword to Torat Kohanim, p. 3a, *315*, *334*
on Sifra, Tazria 13:2 (p. 68a), *382*

Rabbenu Hillel
on Sifrei, Deuteronomy Re'eh, sec. 92, *368*

COMMENTARIES ON JERUSALEM TALMUD

Ahavat Ẓiyyon vi-Yerushalayim
to Pe'ah 8:9 (p. 80), *100*
to Shekalim 8:6 (pp. 34–35), *100*
to Shabbat 6:2 (p. 73), *542*

Korban ha-Edah
to Pesaḥim 4:1, *935*
to Mo'ed Katan 3:1, *261*
to Gittin 8:1, *376*
to Sanhedrin 1:1, *7*

Mar'eh Panim
to Shekalim 5:1, *1051*
to Shevu'ot 7:6, *1135–1136*

Penei Moshe
to Kilayim 2:8, *967*
to Pesaḥim 4:1, *935*
to Gittin 8:1, *376*
to Bava Kamma 10:3, *598*
to Bava Meẓi'a 2:4, *957*
to Bava Batra 3:1, *1010*

Sha'ar Yosef
to Horayot 1:1, *244*

Sha'arei Torat Ereẓ Yisra'el
to Pe'ah 8:9, *100*

Sheyarei Korban
to Sanhedrin 1:1, s.v. Bimei Shim'on b. Shataḥ, *7*

COMMENTARIES ON BABYLONIAN TALMUD

Zechariah Agamati
to Bava Meẓi'a 104a, *423–424*

Arukh la-Ner
to Sukkah 2b, *1796*

Bet ha-Beḥirah (Meiri)
Preface, *53*
Berakhot, Introduction (ed. Dickman, 1960)
p. 28, *976*
p. 32, *53*, *1293*
p. 33, *1293*
to Pesaḥim 51a, *939*
to Beẓah 5a, *542*
to Yevamot 87b, *528*
to Yevamot 90b, *520*
to Yevamot 105a (ed. Dickman, p. 375), *908*
to Yevamot 110a (ed. Dickman, pp. 414–415), *639*
to Ketubbot 3a (ed. Sofer, p. 14), *639*, *642*
to Ketubbot 9a (ed. Sofer, p. 45), *264*
to Ketubbot 51a, *145*
to Ketubbot 51b (ed. Sofer, p. 192), *1793*
to Ketubbot 66a (ed. Sofer, pp. 284–285), *913*
to Ketubbot 86a (ed. Sofer, pp. 384–385), *118*
to Nazir 28b, *1796*
to Gittin 34b (ed. Schlesinger, p. 144), *563*
to Gittin 36b (ed. Schlesinger, p. 159), *542*
to Gittin 59a (ed. Schlesinger, pp. 244–245), *585*
to Kiddushin 15a, *1631*
to Kiddushin 21b, *1711*
to Bava Kamma 14b, *21*
to Bava Kamma 56a (ed. Sofer, pp. 171–172), *147*
to Bava Kamma 84b (ed. Schlesinger, pp. 246–247), *692*
to Bava Kamma 113a, *66*
to Bava Kamma 113b (ed. Schlesinger, pp. 331–332), *66*, *69–70*
to Bava Meẓi'a 32a (ed. Sofer, p. 116), *21*
to Bava Meẓi'a 69b (ed. Schlesinger, p. 262), *909*
to Bava Meẓi'a 83a (ed. Schlesinger, pp. 321–322), *906*
to Bava Meẓi'a 112b (ed. Schlesinger, p. 418), *617*
to Bava Batra 2a (ed. Sofer, p. 6), *941*
to Bava Batra 8b (ed. Sofer, pp. 59–60), *752*, *754*
to Bava Batra 9a, *702*
to Bava Batra 48b (ed. Sofer, p. 267), *636*, *638*
to Bava Batra 55a, *70*
to Bava Batra 126b, *127*
to Bava Batra 130b, *963*, *983*
to Bava Batra 175b (ed. Sofer, p. 726), *590–591*
to Sanhedrin 23a (ed. Sofer, pp. 78–79), *25*
to Sanhedrin 32b, *170–171*

to Sanhedrin 52b (ed. Sofer, p. 212), *58–59, 518*
to Sanhedrin 72b (ed. Sofer, p. 270), *972*
to Avodah Zarah 16a, *70*
to Avot, Introduction (ed. Jerusalem, 1944)
pp. 64–65, *1153, 1166*
p. 67, *1177*
p. 68, *1177*

Z.H. Chajes
to Bava Meẓi'a 96b, *486*

Gilyon ha-Shas
Yevamot 88a, s.v. Tosafot s.v. Mi-tokh, *533*

Ḥazon Ish
Bava Kamma 23:2, *73*
Bava Batra 4:8, *702–703*
Bava Batra 4:10, *703*
Bava Batra 5:1, *726*
Sanhedrin 15:4, *25*

Ḥokhmat Shelomo
Eruvin 61a, s.v. Kulei hai, *1392*
Yevamot 87b, *390*
Sanhedrin 38b, s.v. Gemara, U-le-mikẓeh hashamayim ad keẓeh hashamayim, *1392*
Sanhedrin 52b, s.v. Ta'ah bi-de-Rav Mattnah, *973*

Maharsha
Shabbat 31a, s.v. Pilpalta be-ḥokhmah, *1383*
Shabbat 63a, s.v. Al tikri, *1383*
Yevamot 122b (end), *390, 530–531, 610*
Sotah 22a, s.v. Yere et hashem beni, *1383–1384, 1422*
Bava Meẓi'a 85a, s.v. Delishtakaḥ, *1383*
Bava Batra 28b, s.v. Be-oto dibbur ve-od, *1011*
Bava Batra 73b, s.v. Ḥazinan, *1383*
Sanhedrin 71a, *366*

Mar'eh Kohen
to Yevamot 90b, *632*

Margoliot ha-Yam
to Sanhedrin 32b, *172*

Masoret ha-Shas
Introduction, *1176*
Yevamot 22b, *1004*
Ketubbot 49b, *567*
Bava Batra 173b, *1151*

Middot le-Ḥeker ha-Halakhah [Principles of Halakhic Research]
Middah 11, Meẓi'ut ve-Din, *137*

Mishpat Shalom
#231, Kunteres Tikkun Olam, *719, 756*

Naḥalat Ya'akov
to Derekh Ereẓ Rabbah, ch. 1, *381*

Naḥmanides
Yevamot 90b, *520*
Ketubbot 63b, s.v. U-maẓinu bi-Yerushalmi, *662*
Ketubbot 64a, *660*
Gittin 59a, *586*
Bava Meẓi'a 104a, s.v. Rabbi Meir hayah doresh leshon hedyot, *423, 428*
Bava Meẓi'a 104a, s.v. U-mah she-feresh, *425, 430*
Bava Batra 2a, s.v. Matnitin, *941*
Bava Batra 9a, s.v. Ha de-amrinan be-hanhu bei trei tabḥei, *680, 717, 752–753*
Bava Batra 55a, s.v. Im ken bittalta yerushat beno ha-bekhor, *70*
Bava Batra 59a, *1860*
Bava Batra 111a, *350*
Bava Batra 126b, s.v. Harei zu mekuddeshet u-tena'o batel, *127*
Bava Batra 144b, s.v. Ha de-amrinan, *884*

Penei Yehoshu'a
Gittin 36b, s.v. Gemara ella i amret, *514*

Raban
to Bava Kamma 55b, *147*
to Bava Meẓi'a, ch. 2 (beginning), *688*

Rabbenu Gershom
Bava Batra 8b, s.v U-lehassia al kiẓatan, *679*

Ran
Nedarim 28a, s.v. Bemokhes ha-omed me-elav, *65–66*
Bava Meẓi'a 112b, s.v. Akaruha rabbanan, *617–619*
Bava Batra 9a, *753, 759*
Bava Batra 130b–131a, s.v. Ve-i la hadrana bei, *983*
Sanhedrin 2b, s.v. U-ve-din hu de-liba'ei mumḥin, *23*
Sanhedrin 3a, s.v. I efshar de-leika, *22*
Sanhedrin 5a, *1645*
Sanhedrin 23a, *25*
Sanhedrin 46a, s.v. Bet din makkin ve-onshin, *517*
Shevu'ot 45a, s.v. Akaruhah rabbanan, *617*

Rashba
Shabbat 18b, s.v. Gigit ner u-kederah, *514*
Rosh ha-Shanah 16a, s.v. Lamah tok'in u-meri'in, *497*
Yevamot 88a, s.v. Ha de-amrinan ella sevarah hi, *527*
Yevamot 90b, *520*
Ketubbot 66a, s.v. Keneged ha-shum, *913*
Nedarim 28a, s.v. Bemokhes, *65*
Nedarim 90b, s.v. Ḥazru lomar, *499*
Gittin 33a, s.v. Kol dimekaddesh, *641*
Gittin 36b, s.v. Rava amar

Rashba *continued*
hefker bet din hefker, *509, 513*
Kiddushin 58b, s.v. Ve-halakh ve-kiddeshah, *641*
Bava Kamma 12a, s.v. Me-ha de-amrinan, *583*
Bava Kamma 15a, s.v. Hishvah ha-katuv, *323*
Bava Meẓi'a 74a, s.v. Me-shallem leih, *915, 1822*
Bava Batra 28a, s.v. Sedeh ha-ba'al, *1008*
Bava Batra 48b, s.v. De-ha ishah, *638*
Bava Batra 175b, s.v. Amar Rava, *590*

Rashbam
Bava Batra 36b, s.v. De-amar Rav Yehudah amar Shemuel zo divrei R. Yishmael ve-R. Akiva, *1010*
Bava Batra 48b, s.v. Teinaḥ de-kaddesh be-khaspa, *513–514*
Bava Batra 48b, s.v. Mar bar Rav Ashi amar, *637*
Bava Batra 54a, s.v. De-rav lo kana le-ginta de-vei Rav, *960*
Bava Batra 54b, s.v. Ve-ha-amar Shemuel dina de-malkhuta dina, *66, 133*
Bava Batra 57a, *1334*
Bava Batra 100a, s.v. U-metamhinan atu rabbim gazlanin ninhu, *765*
Bava Batra 100a, s.v. Ki-she-avdah lahen derekh be-otah sadeh, *765*
Bava Batra 109a, s.v. Ben u-vat ki hadadi ninhu, *1029*
Bava Batra 126b, s.v. Be-davar shel mamon, *125*
Bava Batra 126b, s.v. Ha-tam, *126*
Bava Batra 130b, *962–964, 977*
Bava Batra 131a, *982–983*
Bava Batra 132b, s.v. U-mikulei ketubbah shanu kan, *214*
Bava Batra 133b, s.v. Ein ru'aḥ ḥakhamim, *150*
Bava Batra 137b, s.v. Ve-im lav lo yaẓa, *114*
Bava Batra 143b, s.v. Muttar bi-venei vanim, *437*
Bava Batra 144b, s.v. Makom she-nahagu le-haḥazir kiddushin, *892*
Bava Batra 145a, s.v. Amar R. Joseph, *892*
Bava Batra 145a, s.v. Gezerah shemma yomru, *893*
Bava Batra 147b, s.v. Mattenat shekhiv me-ra, *1878*
Bava Batra 155b, s.v. Hashta u-mah zevini de-ka-shakil zuzi, *587*
Bava Batra 167a, s.v. Yad ba'al ha-shetar al ha-taḥtonah, *434*
Bava Batra 170a, s.v. Ein ẓarikh le-kayyemo, *611–612*
Bava Batra 174a, s.v. Rav Huna bereih de-Rav Yehoshu'a amar, *648*
Bava Batra 174b, s.v. Ei-zehu rasha arom, *154*
Bava Batra 175b, s.v. Shi'buda de-oraita, *595*

Rashi
Berakhot 2a, *1059*
Berakhot 19b, s.v. Mamona, *131*
Berakhot 31a, s.v. Asur be-hana'ah u-mo'alin bah, *891*
Berakhot 47b, s.v. She-lo shimmesh talmid ḥakham, *988*
Shabbat 6b, s.v. Megillat setarim, *224*
Shabbat 14b, s.v. Tikken ketubbah, *561*
Shabbat 18b, s.v. Gigit, *514*
Shabbat 21a, *1457*
Shabbat 30b, s.v. Dishe'ilna kadameikhon, *1152*
Shabbat 31a, s.v. Da-alakh senei le-ḥavrakh la ta'aveid, *142*
Shabbat 85b, s.v. Be-noteh shurah le-khan ve-shurah le-khan, *784*
Shabbat 113b, s.v. She-lo, *1022*
Shabbat 145b, s.v. Le-edut ishah, *528*
Eruvin 13b, s.v. Aluvin, *1848*
Eruvin 14b, s.v. Ama devar, *898*
Pesaḥim 22b, s.v. Et lo dareish, *373*
Pesaḥim 22b, s.v. Lerabbot talmidei ḥakhamim, *373*
Pesaḥim 66a, s.v. Ve-khi me'aḥar de-gamiri, *360*
Pesaḥim 99a, s.v. Mi-kan amru, *527*
Yoma 11a, *1087*
Yoma 69a, s.v. Et la'asot, *503*
Sukkah 11b, s.v. Lo yalfeinan, *355*
Sukkah 20a, *1087*
Sukkah 20a, s.v. Hareini kapparat, *1347*
Sukkah 28a, s.v. Gemara, *988*
Sukkah 28b, s.v. U-meshannen ba-sukkah, *988*
Sukkah 31a, s.v. Lo makshinan, *355*
Sukkah 32b, s.v. Dolba, *388*
Sukkah 32b, s.v. Hirduf, *388*
Sukkah 32b, s.v. Derakheha darkhei no'am, *388*
Sukkah 32b, s.v. Ha-emet ve-ha-shalom ehavu, *388*
Sukkah 44a, s.v. Minhag, *889–890*

Sukkah 44b, s.v. Minhag nevi'im hu, *890*
Rosh ha-Shanah 16b, s.v. Kedei le'arbev, *497*
Beẓah 5a, s.v. Mina amina lah, *542*
Beẓah 25b, s.v. Dateihen shel ellu, *885*
Beẓah 27b, s.v. Ein posekin, *1022*
Beẓah 37a, s.v. Mishum mikaḥ u-mimkar, *1022*
Beẓah 38b, s.v. Amar lo, *131*
Megillah 27b, s.v. Ḥaver ir, *715*
Megillah 28b, *1042*
Hagigah 2a, s.v. Eizehu katan, *1796*
Hagigah 3b, s.v. Kullon el eḥad amaran, *1067*
Yevamot 14a, s.v. Ḥayyavei keritut, *1065*
Yevamot 14a, s.v. De-modai le-hu, *1066*
Yevamot 15a, s.v. Mah na'aseh, *1066*
Yevamot 42b, *1061*
Yevamot 46b, s.v. Uvda hava, *955*
Yevamot 46b, s.v. Ve-rav Safra matnei, *955*
Yevamot 46b, s.v. Dilma de-ikle'u, *955*
Yevamot 87b, s.v. Derakheha darkhei no'am, *390*
Yevamot 89b, s.v. Mi-deoraita avuha yareit lah, *509*
Yevamot 89b, s.v. Hefker bet din hayah hefker, *510*
Yevamot 90a, s.v. Shev veal ta'aseh, *506*
Yevamot 90b, s.v. Kegon Eliyahu be-har ha-Carmel, *520*
Yevamot 109b, s.v. Vegamar halakhah, *1493*
Yevamot 110a, s.v. Ve-ka afke'inhu le-kiddushin mineih, *639*
Yevamot 110a, s.v. Shavyuha li-ve'ilato be'ilat zenut, *639*
Ketubbot 10a, s.v. Asvuhu kofri, *388*
Ketubbot 22a, s.v. Natati leish asrah, *386*
Ketubbot 49b, s.v. Ke-shehen ketannin, *568*
Ketubbot 52b, *577*
Ketubbot 56a, s.v. Be-davar she-be-mamon, *125*
Ketubbot 56a, s.v. Aval al peh, *216*
Ketubbot 57a, s.v. Ha kamashma lan, *259, 408*
Ketubbot 67a, s.v. Asmakhtaihu alaihu, *648*
Ketubbot 69a, *579*
Ketubbot 72a, s.v. Dat yehudit, *885*
Ketubbot 82b, *559*
Ketubbot 83b, s.v. Yad ba'al ha-shetar al hataḥtonah, *433*
Ketubbot 86a, s.v. Peri'at ba'al ḥov mizvah, *118, 589*
Ketubbot 106a, *1084*
Sotah 19a, s.v. Ve-Rabbi Yehudah, *245*
Sotah 22a, *1381*
Sotah 47b, s.v. Zeḥoḥei halev, *1064*
Gittin 3a, s.v. Na'asah kemi she-neḥkerah edutan bi-vet din, *611*
Gittin 9b, s.v. Kesherin, *194*
Gittin 9b, s.v. Huẓ mi-gittei nashim, *67, 194*
Gittin 14a, s.v. Ke-hilkheta be-lo ta'ama, *584*
Gittin 14a, s.v. Epitropia, *584*
Gittin 19a, s.v. Ve-khi mipenei she-anu medammin, *949*
Gittin 33a, s.v. Ada'ata derabbanan mekaddesh, *632*
Gittin 34a, s.v. Hakha mamona, *131*
Gittin 34a, s.v. Hakha issura, *131*
Gittin 36a, s.v. Ba-shevi'it ba-zeman ha-zeh, *513*
Gittin 36b, s.v. Rava amar, *510*
Gittin 37a, s.v. Medammin, *949*
Gittin 55a, s.v. Mipenei takkanat ha-shavim, *602*
Gittin 59a, s.v. Mishum kedei ḥayyav, *586*
Gittin 59a, s.v. Ka mashma lan, *585*
Gittin 59a, s.v. Kefiẓah, *585*
Gittin 60a, s.v. Et la'asot lashem, *534*
Gittin 60a, s.v. Keivan de-lo efshar, *534*
Gittin 67a, s.v. Oẓar balum, *1051*
Gittin 71a, *611*
Gittin 77a, s.v. Talmud lomar ve-natan mi-kol makom, *376*
Gittin 88b, s.v. Lifneihem, *14*
Kiddushin 11b, s.v. U-tenan shevu'at ha-dayyanim, *245*
Kiddushin 29a, *1666*
Kiddushin 59a, s.v. Ani hamehapekh be-ḥararah, *154*
Kiddushin 59a, s.v. Nikra rasha, *154*
Kiddushin 63a, s.v. Mishum eivah, *628*
Bava Kamma 2b, s.v. Divrei kabbalah, *203*
Bava Kamma 3b, s.v. Be-ḥaẓi nezek ẓerorot, *207*
Bava Kamma 9a, s.v. Urevi'a be-ma'ot, *408*
Bava Kamma 14b, s.v. Ella, *21*
Bava Kamma 48b, s.v. Ḥayyavim, *1059*
Bava Kamma 81a, s.v. Bateḥillah, *552*
Bava Kamma 88b, s.v. Be-Usha hitkinu, *569*

Rashi *continued*
Bava Kamma 94b, *602*
Bava Kamma 115a, s.v. Takkanat ha-shuk, *598*
Bava Kamma 116b, s.v. Bekhusya, *681*
Bava Kamma 116b, s.v. Meḥashvin lefi masui, *927*
Bava Meẓi'a 12a, s.v. A-de-rabbi Ḥiyya bar Abba, *410*
Bava Meẓi'a 25b, s.v. Safek hinu'aḥ, *957*
Bava Meẓi'a 35a, s.v. Ada'ata de-ar'a neḥut, *628*
Bava Meẓi'a 37b, s.v. Ve-ha amar R. Abba bar Zavda safek hinu'aḥ, *957*
Bava Meẓi'a 49a, s.v. Ella she-yehei hen shelekha, *151*
Bava Meẓi'a 65a, s.v. Gelima lo mafkinan mineih, *128*
Bava Meẓi'a 70a, s.v. Attu be-minhaga tayla milta, *909*
Bava Meẓi'a 74a, s.v. Sitomta, *914*
Bava Meẓi'a 83a, s.v. Bederekh tovim, *156*
Bava Meẓi'a 86a, s.v. Sof hora'ah, *1092*
Bava Meẓi'a 87a, s.v. Meshamnin beineihem, *932*
Bava Meẓi'a 96b, s.v. Nim'alu bet din, *486*
Bava Meẓi'a 104a, s.v. Ketubbot iman, *425*
Bava Meẓi'a 104a, s.v. Doresh leshon hedyot, *431*
Bava Meẓi'a 105a, s.v. Ḥayyav letappel bah, *1982*
Bava Meẓi'a 108a, s.v. Lo mesalkinan leih, *626*
Bava Meẓi'a 108a, s.v. Vaasita ha-yashar ve-hatov, *626*
Bava Meẓi'a 108b, Le-ishah u-le-yatmei u-le-shutafei, *626*
Bava Meẓi'a 110b, s.v. Sekhirut eina mishtalemet, *337*
Bava Meẓi'a 112b, s.v. Hani halakhah ninhu, *617*
Bava Meẓi'a 112b, s.v. Takkanot kevu'ot, *617, 620*
Bava Meẓi'a 112b, s.v. Sheneihem roẓim behakafah, *619*
Bava Batra 8b, s.v. Lehassi'a al kiẓatam, *672, 679–680*
Bava Batra 8b, s.v. Mipenei she-hu ke-dinei mamonot, *703*
Bava Batra 9a, s.v. Lav kol ke-minaihu de-matnu, *757*
Bava Batra 23b, *179*
Bava Batra 28a, s.v. Sedeh bet ha-ba'al, *1008*
Bava Batra 28b, s.v. Le-rabbanan mai, *1010*
Sanhedrin 3a, s.v. Degamir, *22*
Sanhedrin 5a, s.v. Savirna, *22*
Sanhedrin 5a, s.v. Shevet, *58*
Sanhedrin 6b, s.v. Ella, *180*
Sanhedrin 16a, s.v. Davar davar, *355*
Sanhedrin 23a, s.v. Bearka'ot she-be-Suria, *24*
Sanhedrin 30a, *1000*
Sanhedrin 31b, *686*
Sanhedrin 32b, s.v. Beẓedek tishpot, *169*
Sanhedrin 32b, s.v. Aval kera'ei, *170–171*
Sanhedrin 44a, s.v. Ḥata Yisra'el, *103*
Sanhedrin 45b, s.v. Ein danin shenayim beyom eḥad, *518*
Sanhedrin 46a, s.v. She-bet din, *515*
Sanhedrin 46a, *516*
Sanhedrin 66a, s.v. Aviv she-lo immo, *322*
Sanhedrin 66a, s.v. R. Yonatan omer, *322*
Sanhedrin 71a, s.v. Vaafillu mezuzah aḥat, *368*
Sanhedrin 73a, s.v. Hekkeisha hu, *344, 355, 360*
Sanhedrin 73a, s.v. Ve-khi mah lamadnu miroẓe'aḥ, *345*
Sanhedrin 74a, s.v. Sevara hu, *991*
Sanhedrin 74a, s.v. Mari Dorai, *991*
Sanhedrin 74a, s.v. Mai ḥazit, *991*
Sanhedrin 81b, s.v. Veheikha remiza, *207*
Sanhedrin 84b, s.v. Veahavta le-re'akha kamokha, *143*
Sanhedrin 87a, s.v. Lamishpat, *279*
Avodah Zarah 19b, *1493*
Shevu'ot 7b, s.v. Mi-tum'ot ve-lo kol tum'ot, *245*
Shevu'ot 45a, s.v. Hani hilkhata ninhu, *617*
Shevu'ot 45a, s.v. Ki heikhi di-litaggeru leih po'alim, *618*
Shevu'ot 45a, s.v. Ki heikhi di-litaggerei ba'al habayit, *618*
Shevu'ot 45b, s.v. Sheneihem roẓim behakafah, *619*
Makkot 4b, s.v. Le-didi mefarsha li, *127*
Makkot 7a, s.v. Af, *693*
Zevaḥim 45a, s.v. Hilkheta le-meshiḥa, *52*
Zevaḥim 45a, s.v. Amar leih hakha ka amina, *52*
Menaḥot 35b, s.v. Ve-ailah le-tefirah le-gev, *903*
Menaḥot 35b, s.v. Mai ama devar, *903*
Ḥullin 6b, s.v. Et Bet She'an kullah, *938*

Ḥullin 7a, s.v. Mi-kan, *938*
Ḥullin 7a, s.v. Ein maziḥin, *938*
Ḥullin 95b, *1455*
Ḥullin 134a, *144*
Bekhorot 19a, s.v. Kelal ha-ẓarikh li-ferat, *329*
Bekhorot 26b, s.v. Lo mesarekha ha-katuv ella la-ḥakhamim, *245*
Keritot 8a, s.v. Nikhnas le-vet din lilmod, *370*
Niddah 19b, s.v. Ein adam, *355*

Ri Migash
Bava Batra 54b, s.v. Dina di-malkhuta dina, *72*
Bava Batra 160a, s.v. Katav mi-lema'alah, *433*
Shevu'ot 45a, s.v. Hani nishba'in ve-notelin, *617*

Ritba
Pesaḥim 51a, *909*
Yevamot 88a, s.v. Mi-tokh ḥomer she-heḥemarta aleha be-sofah, *527–528*
Yevamot 90b, *520*
Yevamot 90b, s.v. Ve-nigmar mineih, *514*
Yevamot 91b, s.v. Ve-nigmar mineih, *521*
Ketubbot 51a, *145*
Ketubbot 56a, s.v. Amar Rabbi, *216*
Ketubbot 100a, *744–745, 911*
Kiddushin 13b, *590*
Bava Meẓi'a 74a, s.v. Hai sitomta kanya, *911*
Bava Meẓi'a 74a, s.v. Satimta kanya, *915*
Bava Batra 8b, s.v. Lehassia al kiẓatan, *679, 700*
Bava Batra 9a, s.v. Hanhu (bei trei) tabḥei, *753*
Bava Batra 9a, s.v. Va-asikna de-hani mili, *759*
Bava Batra 28b, s.v. Le-rabbanan mai, *1008, 1010*
Bava Batra 28b, s.v. U-mihu kasheh, *1011*
Bava Batra 36a, s.v. Matnitin, *1008*
Bava Batra 55a, s.v. Hanei telat millei, *66–67*
Bava Batra 115a, s.v. Kol ha-omer tirash, *845*
Bava Batra 130b, s.v. Mar savar, *963*
Bava Batra 130b, s.v. U-mar savar, *963*
Bava Batra 130b, *983*
Bava Batra 147b, s.v. Shema titaref da'ato, *580*
Avodah Zarah 35a, s.v. Mikhlal de-ikka man de-shari, *541*
Avodah Zarah 36b, s.v. Katuv be-shem ha-rav Rabbenu Yonah, *715–716, 756, 771*

Sefer ha-Yashar le-Rabbenu Tam
Introduction (ed. Schlesinger, p. 9), *1117*
sec. 140 (ed. Schlesinger, p. 105), *787*
sec. 315 (ed. Schlesinger, p. 197), *1119*
sec. 602 (ed. Schlesinger, pp. 354–356), *1859*
sec. 788 (ed. Schlesinger, pp. 465–466), *787, 836–837*

Sha'arei Yosher
5:1, *119, 136–137*

Shittah Mekubbeẓet
Ketubbot 3a, *638, 641–642*
Ketubbot 3a, s.v. Ve-ha-Rashba z.l. katav, *528, 642*
Ketubbot 3a, s.v. U-ve-shittah katuv, *641*
Ketubbot 3a, s.v. Ve-khen katav ha-Ra'ah z.l. talmido, *370*
Ketubbot 3a, s.v. Ha-teinaḥ de-kaddesh be-khaspa, *632*
Ketubbot 3a, s.v. Od katav, *632*
Ketubbot 51a, *145*
Ketubbot 56a, s.v. Ve-zeh leshon ha-Ritba z"l, *216*
Ketubbot 56a, s.v. Ta'ama de-katvah leih, *216*
Ketubbot 56a, s.v. Aval al peh lo, *216*
Ketubbot 64a, *122*
Ketubbot 66b, s.v. Ve-zeh leshon ha-Re'ah z.l., *913*
Ketubbot 78b, s.v. Ve-khen pershu talmidei Rabbenu Yonah, *569*
Ketubbot 80a, s.v. Iba'ya lehu, *572*
Ketubbot 100a, s.v. Ve-zeh leshon ha-Ritba, *911*
Ketubbot 100a, s.v. Ve-katav rabbenu ha-Ramban z.l. bi-teshuvat she'elah, *911*
Nedarim 28a, *66*
Bava Kamma 2b, s.v. Mi-divrei kabbalah, *203*
Bava Kamma 96b, s.v. Katav ha-Rif z.l., *515*
Bava Kamma 96b, s.v. Ve-zeh leshon ha-Ram mi-Sarkeseta z.l., *515*
Bava Meẓi'a 12a, s.v. Ve-talmid ha-Rap, *410*
Bava Meẓi'a 32a, *20–21*
Bava Meẓi'a 47b, s.v. Devar torah ma'ot konot, *989*
Bava Meẓi'a 74a, s.v. Hai sitomta kanya, *915*
Bava Meẓi'a 74a, s.v. Ve-ha-Ra'avad peresh, *915*
Bava Meẓi'a 83a, s.v. Ha-sokher et ha-po'alim, *906*
Bava Meẓi'a 104a, s.v. Ve-zeh leshon ha-Ramban, *423*
Bava Meẓi'a 104a, s.v. Ve-zeh leshon ha-Rashba, *425*
Bava Meẓi'a 108a, s.v. I

Shittah Mekubbeẓet
continued
mishum dina de-bar meẓra, *626*
Bava Batra 9a, s.v. Heikha de-ikka adam ḥashuv, *759*
Bava Batra 28a, s.v. Sedeh ha-ba'al, *1008*
Bava Batra 126b, s.v. Hatam, *126*
Bekhorot 19a, letter *tet*, *329*
Temurah 14b, subpar. 5, *503*

Torat Ḥayyim
Sanhedrin 32b, s.v. Eḥad le-din ve-eḥad lifesharah, *171–172*

Tosafot
Berakhot 48a, s.v. Ve-leit hilkheta ke-khol hanei shematata ella ki ha katan ha-yode'a, *939*
Shabbat 14b, s.v. Ve-illu Shammai ve-Hillel, *1066*
Shabbat 18b, s.v. Demafkar lehu afkorei, *514*
Shabbat 88a, Kafah aleihem har ke-gigit, *234*
Shabbat 88a, Moda'a rabbah le-oraita, *234*
Eruvin 82a, s.v. Katan ben shesh, *1796*
Eruvin 101b, s.v. Rabbi Yose omer issur nahagu bo ve-hittiru lahem, *937*
Yoma 74a, s.v. Keivan deḥazei le-iẓtarufei issura ka akhil, *1000*
Sukkah 31a, s.v. Ve-Ri savar lo makshinan, *355*
Beẓah 5a, s.v. Kol davar she-be-minyan ẓarikh minyan aḥer le-hattiro, *542*
Rosh ha-Shanah 16b, s.v. Ve-tok'in u-meri'in keshe-hen omdin, *497*
Megillah 15b, s.v. Zeh hadan din emet la-amito, *1893*
Yevamot 21a, s.v. Rav Yehudah amar, *557*
Yevamot 31b, s.v. De-ḥazu be-khetava ve-atu umesahadi, *610*
Yevamot 35b, s.v. Ve-ha leit leih, *1003*
Yevamot 46b, s.v. Shema minah de-ger ẓarikh sheloshah, *955*
Yevamot 79b, s.v. Bi-mei Rabbi bikshu lehattir netinim, *514*
Yevamot 88a, s.v. Mi-tokh ḥomer she-heḥemarta aleha be-sofah, *527–528, 533*
Yevamot 89b, s.v. Keivan de-la yartei lah karyah ve-la anu lah, *528*
Yevamot 90b, s.v. Ve-ligmar mineih, *520*
Yevamot 110a, s.v. Lefikhakh asu lo she-lo kehogen ve-afke'inhu lekiddushei mineih, *639*
Yevamot 116b, s.v. Be-otah sha'ah amru ha-ishah she-amrah met ba'ali, *524*
Yevamot 117a, s.v. Bet Hillel, *427*
Ketubbot 22a, s.v. Minayin she-ha-peh she-asar, *385*
Ketubbot 47a, s.v. Katav lah perot kesut vekhelim, *787, 838*
Ketubbot 48a, s.v. R. Eliezer b. Ya'akov omer, *570*
Ketubbot 49b, s.v. Ke-shehem ketannim, *568*
Ketubbot 51a, s.v. Mimekarke'ei ve-lo mimetaltelei bein limezonot u-vein lefarnasah, *912*
Ketubbot 53a, s.v. She-ein ani kore bah, *427*
Ketubbot 63b, s.v. Aval amrah, *1755*
Ketubbot 65b, s.v. Aval zan ketanei ketannim, *116, 568*
Ketubbot 67a, s.v. Gemalim shel aravya ishah govah parna mehem, *648, 882*
Ketubbot 69a, s.v. Ve-ishtik, *580*
Keutbbot 81a, s.v. Man sham'et lei, *427*
Ketubbot 82b, s.v. Avit shel neḥoshet garsinan, *559*
Ketubbot 82b, s.v. Bateḥillah hayu kotevim la-betulah matayim, *560*
Ketubbot 92b, s.v. Dina hu de-azil Reuven umafẓei leih,
Nazir 35b, s.v. Ikka, *328*
Nazir 43b, s.v. Ve-hai met miẓvah hu, *528, 533*
Gittin 14a, s.v. Ke-hilkheta be-lo ta'am, *584*
Gittin 33a, s.v. Kol dimekaddesh ada'ata derabbanan mekaddesh, *632*
Gittin 33a, s.v. Ve-afke'inhu rabbanan le-kiddushin mineih, *641*
Gittin 34b, s.v. Ve-khol shum she-yesh lo, *563*
Gittin 36b, s.v. Ella, *1066*
Gittin 88b, s.v. Lifneihem ve-lo lifnei hedyotot, *14*
Kiddushin 2b, s.v. Litni sheloshah, *322*
Kiddushin 5a, s.v. She-ken podin bo hekdeishot uma'aser, *583*
Kiddushin 30a, s.v. Al tegamgem ve-tomar lo, *1321*
Kiddushin 43b, s.v. Vehashta di-tikkun rabbanan shevu'at hesset, *399, 1698*
Kiddushin 45b, s.v. Havah uvda, *270*
Kiddushin 58b, s.v. Haomer ve-halakh ve-

kiddeshah le-aẓmo mekuddeshet, *641*
Bava Kamma 8a, s.v. Kullan nikhnesu taḥat ha-ba'alim, *593*
Bava Kamma 12a, s.v. Ana matnita yada'na, *583*
Bava Kamma 14b, s.v. Perat le-vet din hedyotot, *21*
Bava Kamma 15a, s.v. Hishvah ha-katuv, *323*
Bava Kamma 25a, s.v. Kal va-ḥomer la-shekhinah, *350*
Bava Kamma 27b, s.v. Ka mashma lan de-ein holkhin be-mamon aḥar ha-rov, *131*
Bava Kamma 27b, s.v. Amai patur iba'i leih le-iyyuni, *412*
Bava Kamma 48b, s.v. U-sheneihem, *1059*
Bava Kamma 70a, s.v. Ametaltelin de-kafreih, *649*
Bava Kamma 82b, s.v. Ata ihu ve-tikken afillu le-divrei Torah, *542*
Bava Kamma 94b, s.v. Bimei rabbi nishneit mishnah zu, *602*
Bava Kamma 100a, s.v. Lifnim mi-shurat ha-din, *156*
Bava Kamma 104b, s.v. Agav asipa de-veiteih, *583*
Bava Kamma 116b, s.v. Ve-rasha'im ha-ḥamarim lehatnot beineihem, *679*
Bava Meẓi'a 20b, s.v. Issura mi-mamona, *131*
Bava Meẓi'a 24b, s.v. Lifnim mi-shurat ha-din, *156*
Bava Meẓi'a 25b, s.v. Ve-im natal lo yaḥazir, *957*
Bava Meẓi'a 59b, s.v. Lo va-shamayim hi, *1068*
Bava Meẓi'a 59b, s.v. Zeh tannur shel akhnai, *261*
Bava Meẓi'a 83a, s.v. Ha-sokher et ha-po'alim ve-amar lahem le-hashkim u-le-ha'ariv, *906*
Bava Meẓi'a 104a, s.v. Hayah doresh leshon hedyot, *429–430*
Bava Meẓi'a 108a, s.v. Hai man de-aḥazik be-rakta de-nehara, *626*
Bava Meẓi'a 112b, s.v. Mi-kelal de-ikka ketannot, *617*
Bava Meẓi'a 112b, s.v. Shekaluha rabbanan li-shevu'ah mi-ba'al ha-bayit ve-shadyuha asakhir, *617*
Bava Meẓi'a 112b, s.v. I hakhi neitav leih be-lo shevu'ah, *618*
Bava Batra 2a, s.v. Ba-gevil zeh noten sheloshah tefaḥim, *941*
Bava Batra 8b, s.v. Din emet le-amito, *1893*
Bava Batra 28b, s.v. Ella me-atah ḥazakah she-ein imah ta'anah, *1010*
Bava Batra 28b, s.v. Ve-dilma eẓah tovah ka mashma lan, *1011*
Bava Batra 44b, s.v. De-lo havah leih ar'a me-olam, *651*
Bava Batra 48b, s.v. Teinaḥ de-kaddesh be-khaspa, *514, 632, 637*
Bava Batra 115b, s.v. Afillu nasi she-be-Yisra'el, *845*
Bava Batra 167a, s.v. U-mashvei leih zuzei, *434*
Bava Batra 175b, s.v. Devar torah ba'al ḥov dino be-zibburit, *590*
Sanhedrin 5a, s.v. Dan afilu yeḥidi, *23*
Sanhedrin 5a, s.v. De-hakha, *59*
Sanhedrin 66a, s.v. Ad she-yefaret, *322*
Sanhedrin 74b, s.v. Ve-ha Ester parhesia havai, *345*
Sanhedrin 89b, s.v. Eliyahu be-har ha-Carmel, *520*
Makkot 3b, s.v. Al menat she-ein bo ona'ah, *127*
Makkot 7a, s.v. Dilma, *693*
Shevu'ot 22b, s.v. Iba'it eima kera, *1004*
Shevu'ot 45a, s.v. Gedolot mi-kelal de-ikka ketannot, *492, 617*
Shevu'ot 45a, s.v. Akaruha rabbanan shevu'ah mi-ba'al ha-bayit, *617*
Shevu'ot 45a, s.v. Ba'al ha-bayit tarud be-fo'alav, *618*
Shevu'ot 45a, s.v. Ve-neitav leih be-lo shevu'ah, *618*
Avodah Zarah 13a, s.v. Amar Abbaye amar kera, *532*
Avodah Zarah 27b, s.v. Yakhol afillu, *990*
Avodah Zarah 36a, s.v. Asher, *1052*

Tosafot Rid

Pesaḥim 66a, s.v. Le-maḥar, *902*
Gittin 9b, *67*
Gittin 14a, *584*
Gittin 59a, *585*

Tosafot Yeshanim

Yevamot 88a, *527*
Yevamot 90b, s.v. Shav-yuhu rabbanan li-ve'ilato be'ilat zenut, *641*

Yad Ramah

Bava Batra 8b, #91, s.v. Tashlum baraita, *679, 700*
Bava Batra 9b, #103, s.v. Hanhu tabḥei de-atnu be-hadi hadadi, *752, 759*
Bava Batra 28b, #20, s.v.

Yad Ramah *continued*
Ve-daikinan le-rabbanan mai, *1011*
Bava Batra 35b, #67, s.v. U-mi-de-kametam-hinan mi metakkenei rabbanan milta de-ati bah li-dei peseida, *769*
Bava Batra 126b, #100, s.v. Beram, *126*
Bava Batra 130b, #132, *963*
Bava Batra 130b, #133, *947*
Bava Batra 169a, #89, *1537*
Sanhedrin 23a, *25*
Sanhedrin 32b, s.v. Tanya ẓedek ẓedek tirdof, *170–171, 173–174*
Sanhedrin 33a, *983*
Sanhedrin 73a, s.v. Matnitin ve-eillu she-maẓẓilin otan, *345*
Sanhedrin 74a, s.v. Arayot u-shefikhut damim, *345*

CODIFICATORY WORKS

Alfasi, Sefer ha-Halakhot
to Shabbat 21b (Hilkhot Ḥanukkah), *1192*
to Eruvin 104b (#687), *1098, 1131, 1170, 1354*
to Ketubbot 63a (p. 27a), *660, 663*
to Kiddushin 39b, *1329*
to Bava Kamma 92a (#167), *1171*
to Bava Kamma 116b, *927*
to Bava Batra 9a, *752, 755*
to Sanhedrin 5a, *1645*
to Shevu'ot 41b (#1156), *1189*

Commentaries on Alfasi
SEFER HA-MA'OR
Introduction, *1173*
NIMMUKEI YOSEF
Yevamot 90b, *514*
Yevamot 91b, s.v. Tanya amar R. Eliezer b. Jacob, *521*
Nedarim 28a, s.v. Ve-ha-amar Shemuel dina de-malkhuta dina, *65*
Bava Kamma 83b, *391*
Bava Meẓi'a 47b (p. 28b), *989*
Bava Meẓi'a 74a, s.v. U-ve-atra de-kani, *915*
Bava Meẓi'a 108a, s.v. Lo mesalkinan leih (p. 64a), *626*
Bava Meẓi'a 114a, s.v. Aval lo le-ishto u-vanav (p. 69b), *218*
Bava Batra 8b, s.v. U-lehas-si'a al kiẓatan (p. 6b), *679–680*
Bava Batra 9a, s.v. Aval heikha de-ikka adam ḥashuv (p. 6b), *717*
Bava Batra 55a, s.v. U-ferush dina de-malkhuta dina, *70*
Bava Batra 115b, s.v. Kol ha-omer tirash bat, *845*
Bava Batra 144b, s.v. Bi-mefaresh (p. 67b), *911*
Sanhedrin 4b, *27*
RAN
Ketubbot 85b, s.v. Ha-mokher shetar ḥov (p. 44), *590*
Gittin 10b, s.v. U-de-amri-nan dina de-malkhuta dina, *70*
Kiddushin 58b, s.v. Ha-omer le-ḥavero (p. 23b), *641*
Bava Batra 55a, s.v. Im ken bittalta yerushat beno ha-bekhor, *70*
Shevu'ot 41b, s.v. Amar Rav Yehuda amar Rav Assi, *1189*
Shevu'ot 49a, s.v. Lifto'aḥ, *620*
SHILTEI GIBBORIM
to Ketubbot 64a, *662*

Maimonides, Mishneh Torah
Introduction, *39, 279, 286, 484, 490, 501, 534, 645–646, 668, 1069, 1145, 1148, 1184–1186, 1188, 1195, 1202, 1204, 1228–1229, 1235, 1255, 1339, 1437, 1471*
SEFER HA-MADDA
HILKHOT YESODEI HA-TORAH
5:1, *990*
5:2 *et seq.*, *991*
5:5, *971*
5:7, *991*
9:1, *264, 480, 535*
9:2, *265*
9:3, *520*
9:4, *242, 264–265*
HILKHOT DE'OT
4, *1243*
6:4, *1690*
7:1, *1643*
HILKHOT TALMUD TORAH
1:1, *1798*
1:13, *1798*
HILKHOT AVODAT KOKHAVIM VE-ḤUKKOTEIHEM (AVODAH ZARAH)
1, *1193*
2:6, *1197*
10:2, *1855*
SEFER AHAVAH
HILKHOT KERI'AT SHEMA
1:5 *et seq.*, *969*
2:5, *969*
HILKHOT TEFILLAH
1:3ff., *1193*
5:3, *1648*
SEFER ZEMANIM
HILKHOT SHABBAT
2, *519*
2:3, *519*
23:12, *1022*
HILKHOT ERUVIN
1:20, *113*
6:18, *113*
HILKHOT SHEVITAT ASOR
2:1, *999*
3:3, *910*
HILKHOT YOM TOV
2:12, *936, 1189*
8:20, *936*
HILKHOT ḤAMEẒ U-MAẒẒAH
5:20, *669*
HILKHOT LULAV
8:10–11, *115*

HILKHOT SHEKALIM
2:5, *623*
2:10, *624*
HILKHOT KIDDUSH HA-ḤODESH
1:8, *1649*
11:2–3, *1190*
11:16, *1188*
17:24, *1190*
19:16, *1190–1191*
HILKHOT MEGILLAH VE-ḤANUKKAH
3:1–3, *1191–1192*
4:12–14, *1192–1193*
4:14, *1715*
SEFER NASHIM
HILKHOT ISHUT
1:1, *1193*
1:2, *208, 1209–1210, 1331*
1:6, *557*
2, *585, 1200*
2:1–2, *567*
3:20–21, *535*
3:21, *535*
5:17, *584*
6:9–10, *125*
8:4–5, *1327–1329*
10:9, *1198*
11:13, *1189*
12:1–4, *1785*
12:2, *571*
12:3, *573, 1803*
12:4, *572*
12:7–9, *127*
12:9, *573*
14, *659*
14:2, *810*
14:8, *1755*
14:14, *645, 661*
15:19, *790*
16:7, *648*
16:7–9, *645, 648, 928*
16:9, *560–561, 648*
17:5–6, *648*
19:17, *575*
19:17–18, *648*
20:5, *912*
21:9, *630–631, 1715*
21:17, *1797*
22:7, *569, 1803*
23:12, *928*
HILKHOT GERUSHIN
4, *334*
8:21, *562*
9:8, *633–634*
9:27, *469*
13:28, *609*
13:29, *529, 610*
SEFER KEDUSHAH
HILKHOT ISSUREI BI'AH
1:1, *1771*
1–3, *1290*
12, *1290*
12:13, *1046*
12:18, *363*
12:25, *364, 998*
13–14, *1689*
13:15, *1855*
14–16, *1290*
14:7, *1855*
14:11–13, *960*
15:20, *997*
21:14, *534*
21:29, *810*
22:21, *1193*
HILKHOT MA'AKHALOT ASUROT
7:1, *998*
9:4, *501*
HILKHOT SHEḤITAH
14:11, *377*
14:16, *1193*
SEFER HAFLA'AH
HILKHOT SHEVU'OT
1:12, *1698*
9 *et seq.*, *1698*
11:8, *620*
11:12, *620*
HILKHOT NEDARIM
3:9, *532*
8:13, *455*
9, *437*
9:1, *437*
9:13, *437*
HILKHOT NEZIRUT
5:10, *1213*
5:13, *1213*
5:16, *1213*
HILKHOT ARAKHIN VA-ḤARAMIN
1:1 393, 6:26, *392*
6:31–32, *392–393*
6:33, *393*
SEFER ZERA'IM
HILKHOT MATTENOT ANIYYIM
7:10, *116*
HILKHOT BIKKURIM
4:6, *114*
HILKHOT SHEMITTAH VE-YOVEL
9, *1290*
9:10, *127*
10:4, *1188*
10:5, *946*
10:6, *946*
12:7, *562*
SEFER AVODAH
HILKHOT ME'ILAH
8:8, *1193*
SEFER TOHORAH
HILKHOT TUM'AT ẒARA'AT
11:1, *378*
16:10, *1193*
SEFER NEZIKIN
HILKHOT NIZKEI MAMON
2:3, *207*
2:7, *207*
4:2, *146*
5, *553*
5:3, *551–553*
5:4, *552*
5:5, *553*
8:12, *648*
12:9, *414*
13:15, *553*
14:14, *146*
HILKHOT GENEVAH
5:1–3, *599–601*
6:1–2, *1212*
7:11, *395*
8:1, *1209*
8:20, *1209*
HILKHOT GEZELAH VA-AVEDAH
1:1, *118*
1:3, *218*
1:5, *602*
1:13, *602*
4:1, *1980*
4:1–2, *149*
4:9, *149*
4:9–10, *148–149, 1979–1980*
5:6, *648*
5:9ff., *56*
5:9–14, *70*
5:9–18, *486–487*
5:14, *72, 175, 772*
5:16, *1340*
5:17, *68*
5:18, *66*
6:7–16, *218*
6:10, *218*

Maimonides, Mishneh Torah *continued*
6:16, *218–219*
11:7, *160*
13:10, *1746*
13:14, *927*
16, *1747*
17:8–9, *629*
17:12, *586*
HILKHOT ḤOVEL U-MAZZIK
1:6, *207*
1:11, *602*
4:16–18, *629*
7:1–3, *603–604*
7:7–12, *219*
HILKHOT ROẒE'AḤ U-SHEMIRAT HA-NEFESH
1:6–16, *1924*
2:4, *56*, *486*
2:4–5, *695*
10:8, *1205*
11, *1326*
13:14, *1193*
SEFER KINYAN
HILKHOT MEKHIRAH, *1324*
1:1, *917*
1:1–2, *917*
1:17, *1330*
3:17–18, *1330*
4:5, *1209*
5:5, *583*
6:8, *584*
7:1, *148*
7:8, *150*
7:9, *705*
10:1, *636*
13:3–4, *127*
14:4, *1300*
14:8, *1300*
14:11, *759*
22, *392*
22:15, *393–394*
29:1, *586*, *1665*
29:2, *585*
29:4, *586*
29:5, *586*
29:6, *586*
29:12, *585*
29:12–13, *587*
29:13, *1665*
30:7, *129*, *1022*, *1603*
HILKHOT ZEKHIYYAH U-MATTANAH
1:15, *132*
3:3, *584*
3:9, *115*
5:2, *1878*
5:6, *1208*
6:18, *893*
8–12, *1673*
8:2, *1682*
8:24, *1682*
8:25–26, *1682*
9:10, *101*
11:1, *437*
HILKHOT SHEKHENIM
2:14, *941*
2:15, *941*
5:6, *1860*
7:6, *1860*
11:4, *1860*
12:1, *1912*
12:5, *184*, *625–626*
12:13–14, *626*
HILKHOT SHELUḤIN VE-SHUTAFIN
1:1, *1364*
3:1–7, *649*
3:3, *722*
3:7, *645*, *649–651*
4:1 *et seq.*, *919*
5:1, *931*
6–8, *1290*
8:4, *931*
HILKHOT AVADIM
1:8, *1340*
2:12, *391*
SEFER MISHPATIM
HILKHOT SEKHIRUT
1, *1695*
1:1, *1695*
1:2, *1695*
8:6, *931*
8:12–13, *1982–1984*
11:6, *619–620*
11:9, *620*
13:7, *1630*
HILKHOT MALVEH VE-LOVEH
1:7, *652*
1:8, *218*
2:1, *652*, *1635*
2:2, *652–653*, *1859*
2:4, *653–654*
4–6, *222*
4–10, *1246*, *1290*, *1294*
4:6, *129*, *1603*
6:5, *1603*
7:2–3, *931*
11:4, *590*, *596*
11:11, *648*
15:1–2, *1188–1189*
15:2, *1006*, *1189*
21:1, *593*
22:16, *627*
25:1–2, *1207*, *1986–1987*
25:1–5, *1722*
25:3, *1722*
25:3–4, *1363*
25:4, *1215*
25:5, *1209*
25:9, *1984*
25:10, *72*
26:3, *1722*
27:14, *433*, *435*
27:14–17, *433*
27:15, *434*, *932*, *1340*
27:16, *433*
HILKHOT TO'EN VE-NIT'AN
1:12, *621*
5:4, *1330*
9:7, *1210*
9:7–8, *1211*
10:4, *1332*
10:6, *1208*
11:1 *et seq.*, *1332*
12:1, *1331–1333*
12:5, *1335–1336*
12:15, *1213*
HILKHOT NAḤALOT
1:3, *1673*
1:6, *1672*
1:7, *1674*
1:8, *573*
5:5–9, *1680*
6:1, *127*, *1672*
6:12, *1674*
SEFER SHOFETIM
HILKHOT SANHEDRIN
2:10–11, *1646*
4:7, *96*
4:13, *58*
5:1, *1460*
6:1, *982*
6:1–2, *607*, *1645*
6:6, *686*
6:6–9, *1460*
7, *19*
7:6–8, *982*
12:1–3, *254*

12:3, *1699*
14:1, *207*
14:2, *56, 486*
16, *608*
16:4, *691*
16:12, *517, 790*
18:6, *56, 486, 691, 695, 699*
20:7–8, *1493*
21:1, *1845*
21:1–3, *168, 1760*
22:9, *882*
22:10, *883*
23, *1640*
23:1, *1641*
23:2, *1640*
23:3, *1640*
23:6, *168–169*
24:1, *1212–1213*
24:4, *533*
24:4–9, *518*
24:4–10, *47, 835*
24:10, *518–519*
26:7, *15–16, 20*
HILKHOT EDUT
3:1–2, *608*
3:4, *613*
3:12, *1715*
4:2–3, *1001*
4:7, *1210*
5:1–3, *529*
6, *612*
6:1, *614*
9:2, *323*
11:6, *134*
13:15, *304*
17:2, *1698*
17:7, *146*
HILKHOT MAMRIM
1:1–2, *238–239, 484–485*
1:2, *203, 279, 286, 492– 493*
1:2–3, *882*
1:4, *288*
2:1, *542, 1499*
2:2, *541, 543, 882*
2:4, *503, 519, 533, 543*
2:5, *492*
2:5–7, *540–541*
2:9, *255, 499–500, 533, 535*
5–7, *1290*
6:3, *117*
7:5–6, *365*
7:7, *365*
7:9, *365*
7:10, *1677*
7:14, *1677*
HILKHOT EVEL
Introductory Caption, *1197, 1202*
3:14, *518*
HILKHOT MELAKHIM
1:2, *1205*
3, *486*
3:1, *55*
3:6, *487*
3:10, *56*
4, *56, 486*
5:1–3, *56, 486*
5:7, *1212*
5:10, *1650*
8:10, *1855*
9:14, *194*
10:12, *1855*
12:2, *1856*
12:4–5, *1856*

Commentaries on Mishneh Torah

EVEN HA-EZEL
to Nizkei Mamon 8:5, *67*
HAGGAHOT MAIMUNIYYOT
to Tefillah 13, subpar. 2, *910*
to Ishut 14, subpar. 30, *789*
to Mekhirah 14, subpar. 3, *754*
to Shekhenim 2, subpar. 20, *941*
to Roẓe'aḥ u-Shemirat ha-Nefesh 10:8, *1205*
KESEF MISHNEH
to MT, Introduction, *1320*
to Ishut 1:2, *208*
to Ishut 12:2, *571*
to Nedarim 3:9, *532–533, 536*
to Mekhirah 14:11, *754*
to Sheluḥin ve-Shutafin 3:7, *651*
to Naḥalot 1:8, *573*
to Edut 9:2, *322–323*
to Mamrim 2:1, *1099*
to Mamrim 2:4, *515*
to Mamrim 2:9, *500*
to Melakhim 1:2, *1205*
to Melakhim 5:7, *1212*
KIRYAT SEFER
to Sanhedrin 26:7, *20*
to Mamrim 1:1–2, *238*
LEḤEM MISHNEH
to De'ot 6:7, *1798*
to Tefillah 11:15, *1234*
to Gerushin 13:29, *529, 610*
to Malveh ve-Loveh 1:8, *218*
to Malveh ve-Loveh 2:4, *654*
to Edut 3:4, *613*
to Mamrim 1:1–2, *238*
to Mamrim 2:9, *500*
to Melakhim 1:2, *1205*
MIGDAL OZ
to Yom Tov 2:12, *1189*
MAGGID MISHNEH
to Ḥameẓ u-Maẓẓah 5:20, *669*
to Megillah ve-Ḥanukkah 3:1–3, *1192*
to Ishut 1:2, *208*
to Ishut 11:12, *1189*
to Ishut 12:2, *571*
to Ishut 17:13, *21*
to Mekhirah 7:6, *915*
to Mekhirah 14:10, *680*
to Mekhirah 14:11, *759*
to Shekhenim 14:5, *142, 159–160, 625*
to Sekhirut 8:13, *1363*
to Malveh ve-Loveh 2:4, *654*
to Malveh ve-Loveh 25:3, *268*
to Malveh ve-Loveh 25:10, *72*
to Malveh ve-Loveh 27:1, *70*
to Naḥalot 1:8, *573*
to Zekhiyyah u-Mattanah 9:10, *102*
MISHNEH LA-MELEKH
Introduction, *1234*
to Zekhiyyah u-Mattanah 9:10, *102*
RABAD
to MT, Introduction, *1205, 1228*
to Arakhin va-Ḥaramin 6:33, *393*
to Kilayim 6:2, *1194–1195*
to Ma'aser Sheni ve-Neta Reva'i 1:3, *910*

Commentaries on Mishneh Torah *continued*
to Mekhirah 22:15, *394*
to Mekhirah 29:2, *585*
to Malveh ve-Loveh 25:10, *72*
to Naḥalot 1:8, *573*
to Mamrim 2:2, *542*
to Mamrim 2:9, *500, 520*
RADBAZ
to Sanhedrin 22:9, *882–883*
to Sanhedrin 26:7, *16*
to Edut 17:2, *1698*
to Mamrim 2:4, *517, 519*
to Mamrim 2:9, *500*
to Mamrim 7:14, *1677*
to Melakhim 1:2, *1205*

Turim
ORAḤ ḤAYYIM (OḤ)
Introduction, *1280, 1284, 1286, 1289, 1520*
1 (Preface), *1299*
95:1, *1648*
156, *1697, 1705–1706*
158 *et seq.*, *1389*
242, *1299*
625, *1299*
670, *1192*
678, *1193*
YOREH DE'AH (YD)
Introduction, *1280, 1284, 1286–1287, 1290, 1293*
116, *1323*
157, *1389*
159–177, *1289, 1294*
228, *1289*
240–241, *1289*
243, *1289*
256:10, *715*
267:32–33, *1340*
268–269, *1689*
334, *1289*
335, *1243*
EVEN HA-EZER (EH)
Introduction, *1291*
1 (Preface), *1299*
1–25, *1290*
17, *1290*
25:20, *535*
26–65, *1290*
26:7, *535*
38, *1327–1329*
38:12–13, *127*
50, *1290*
51, *1290*
55, *1290*
66–118, *1290*
68, *889*
71, *1289*
77, *659*
118, *796, 839, 841*
119–154, *1291*
154, *786*
155, *1291*
156–168, *1291*
163:4–8, *1680*
169–176, *1291*
177, *1291*
178, *1291*
ḤOSHEN MISHPAT (ḤM)
Introduction, *1251, 1281, 1284, 1286–1287, 1289–1291, 1293*
1 (Preface), *1295–1299*
1–2, *1307*
1–27, *1292*
1:1–2, *108*
2, *47, 518, 697, 1326*
3, *1646*
3:1, *22–23*
3:2, *23*
7:18, *740*
8:5–8, *1493*
9, *1640*
10:2–6, *1493*
12, *1307*
13, *19*
19:1, *883*
25, *982*
25:1, *23*
26:1, *15*
26:5, *15*
26:6–7, *15*
28–38, *1292*
33, *737*
37, *737*
37:12, *739*
39–66, *1293*
39–74, *1324*
39–347, *1292*
42, *433, 1340*
42:8, *435*
42:14–15, *436*
42:16, *434*
42:21, *432*
61, *433*
61:1, *596*
61:9–13, *1534*
67, *1290*
67:12, *127*
68, *1293–1294*
69, *1294*
70, *1294*
71, *1294*
72, *1459*
72–74, *1294*
75–86, *1295*
87–96, *1295*
96:26, *1859*
97–106, *1294*
107–110, *1294*
111–116, *1294*
117–119, *1294*
119:4, *593*
120, *1294*
121:12, *1363*
129, *1363, 1986–1987*
129:8–20, *1722*
129:11–14, *1722*
129–132, *1294*
131:5, *145*
133–139, *1295*
135, *1334*
140–152, *1295*
141, *1331–1335*
144, *1335–1338*
153–156, *1294*
157:16, *941*
157–175, *1294, 1325*
163, *1289, 1444*
175, *1294*
182:1–3, *1326*
182:4, *1364*
190 *et seq.*, *1294, 1324*
190–226, *1324*
193, *1330–1331*
227:24–26, *127*
231:26–30, *1300*
231:30, *756, 759*
241–249, *1673*
250–258, *1673*
250:1, *1878*
260, *1747*
272:17, *927*
274, *553, 1327*
274:1, *552*
274:6, *552*

276–289, *1673*
280:10–12, *1680*
303–306, *1294, 1325*
307–319, *1294*
320–330, *1294*
328, *1982–1983*
331–339, *1294*
348–358, *1292*
353:5, *601*
356:4, *600*
356:5, *601*
359–377, *1292*
365:9–10, *1979–1980*
368, *894*
369:13, *1340*
369:14, *72*
376:1, *1300*
378–388, *1292*
389–419, *1292*
409, *543*
420–426, *1292*
425, *697, 1326*

Commentaries on *Turim*

BAYIT ḤADASH (BAḤ)
ORAḤ ḤAYYIM (OḤ)
214, *1347*
242, *1299*
356:2, *1252*
625, *1299*
682, *1250*
YOREH DE'AH (YD)
142:16, *1252*
196, *1517*
EVEN HA-EZER (EH)
1, *1299*
ḤOSHEN MISHPAT (ḤM)
Introduction, *1416*
1 (Preface), *1296*
12:4, *157, 167, 925*
17:1, *168*
97:28, *710*
131, *1363*
201:2, *916*
274:1, *553*
BET YOSEF
ORAḤ ḤAYYIM (OḤ)
Introduction, *901, 1172, 1253, 1272, 1288, 1302, 1311–1319, 1339, 1362, 1392, 1520*
25, *1316*
31, *1316*
141, *1316*
YOREH DE'AH (YD)
157 (Bedek ha-Bayit), *1389*
168–169, *1459*
201, *1459*
228, *719*
341, *1459*
EVEN HA-EZER (EH)
28, *871*
ḤOSHEN MISHPAT (ḤM)
1 (Preface), *1296*
7:18, *740*
8, *1915*
13:9, *465, 719*
26, *15, 1916*
26:7, *70*
37:12, *738*
42:21, *431, 928*
104:15, *218*
119:4, *593*
163, *1444*
231:30, *717*
278:1, *1674*
353:5, *601*
368:6, *911*
388, Meḥudashot sec. 8, *1476*
BIRKEI YOSEF
OḤ #470, par. 3, *1361*
ḤM #26, piska 3, *15, 17*
DARKHEI MOSHE
Introduction, *1350–1356*
ḤM 4, subpar. 3, *750*
ḤM 7, subpar. 7, *740*
ḤM 163, *1444*
DARKHEI MOSHE HA-AROKH
Printer's Introduction, *1361*
OḤ, Introduction, *1350–1356*
YD, Introduction, *1350–1356*
DERISHAH
YD 168–169, subpar. 14, *1459*
ḤM 1, subpar. 2, *157, 159, 167, 180–182, 251, 1296*
HAR ẒEVI
ḤM 409, *543*
ḤIDDUSHEI HAGGAHOT
ḤM 1, letter *dalet* (ed. Koenigsberg, letter *he*), *1297*
KENESET HA-GEDOLAH
OḤ, Introduction, *1435–1437*
OḤ #462, Haggahot Bet Yosef, subpar. 5, *1323*
EH #28, Haggahot Bet Yosef, #36, *854*
EH #118, Haggahot ha-Tur, subpar. 47, *796–797*
EH #118, Haggahot ha-Tur, subpar. 48, *797*
EH #119, Haggahot ha-Tur, subpar. 9, *786*
ḤM, Introduction, *1436*
ḤM 7:53, *740*
ḤM #13, Haggahot Bet Yosef, letter *kaf et seq.*, *719*
ḤM 13:39, Haggahot Bet Yosef, *720*
ḤM #17, Haggahot ha-Tur, Mahadura Kamma, #19, *1505*
ḤM ch. 25, Haggahot Bet Yosef, pars. 6–19, *1283*
ḤM 37, Mahadura Kamma and Mahadura Batra, *738*
Sheyarei Keneset ha-Gedolah, OḤ, Introduction, *1437*
MATTEH SHIM'ON
Introduction, *1439–1440*
PANIM ḤADASHOT
Introduction, *1409*
PERISHAH
ḤM 1, *1296*
ḤM 72:35, *1459*
ḤM 272:18, *170*
YAD AHARON
OḤ, Introduction, *1438*
EH, Introduction, *1438–1439*
EH 17, *1438*

Shulḥan Arukh

Introduction, *1320–1322, 1343*
ORAḤ ḤAYYIM (OḤ)
1–88, *1321*
88, *1321*

Shulḥan Arukh *continued*
89–169, *1321*
95:1, *1648*
156, *1697, 1705–1706*
165:2, *1327*
166:1, *1339*
170–259, *1321*
260–317, *1321*
263, *1360*
318–372, *1321*
373–467, *1321*
468–544, *1321*
545–684, *1321*
612:9, *999*
658:4–9, *115*
685–697, *1321*
670ff., *1192*
678, *1193*
End, *1343*
YOREH DE'AH (YD)
1–61, *1321*
62–124, *1321*
125–182, *1321*
160 *et seq.*, *222*
161:1–11, *1603*
161:11, *129*
183–220, *1321*
217:1, *437*
221–259, *1321*
228:33, *699, 713*
240:5, *110*
240:9, *1347*
242:28, *1347*
246:6, *1798*
247–251, *1661*
249:16, *100–101*
251, *1661*
251:3, *101, 117*
251:11, *1327*
256:3, *703*
260–297, *1321*
267:16, *1340*
268–269, *1689*
269:10, *960*
298–342, *1321*
336, *1243*
336:1, *146*
343–403, *1321*
End, *1343*
EVEN HA-EZER (EH)
1–12, *1321*
1:8, *1430*
1:9, *1430*
2:4, *1430*
4:10, *364, 998*
4:15, *997*
13–66, *1321*
15, *557*
17, *1290, 1442*
18:1, *1602*
25:4, *535*
26:4, *535*
38:5, *127*
38:20, *1327–1329*
38:27–32, *1327–1329*
42:2, *1602, 1769*
67–118, *1321*
68:2, *889*
69:1–4, *1785*
69:3, *1803*
69:4, *572*
71:1, *117*
77, *659*
83:2, *629*
85, *572*
85:1, *1803*
85:7, *1803*
85:11, *1803*
90:9, *569*
93–94, *1679*
93:2, *1674*
93:3, *1680*
112, *1679*
112:10, *1680*
112:11, *1679*
116, *1771*
119–153, *1321*
130:18, *469*
143:4, *562*
154–173, *1321*
154, *1354*
154:22, *787*
163:2, *788*
163:4–8, *1680*
165:4, *788*
169, *1354*
174–178, *1321*
End, *1344*
ḤOSHEN MISHPAT (ḤM)
1–43, *1321*
2, *47, 518, 698, 1326*
3, *1646*
3:1, *23, 27*
7:7, *134*
7:12, *740*
8, *27, 35, 1916*
8:1, *26*
9, *1640*
9:1, *1640–1641*
9:3–5, *827*
12:2, *175*
13, *19*
14, *825*
14:1, *1818*
14:1–3, *1460*
17, *169*
17:1, *168*
18:6, *883*
19:1, *883*
20, *982*
22:1, *27*
22:2, *18*
25, *607, 1645*
25:1–2, *982*
25:2, *271*
25:3, *23, 982*
26, *35, 1916*
26:1, *15*
26:2, *16*
26:3, *15*
26:4, *16*
28:7, *1699*
30:6–8, *1001*
32:1, *130*
32:2, *146*
33, *737*
34:2, *1602*
34:2–3, *1602*
34:24, *1602*
37, *737*
37:18 *et seq.*, *737*
37:22, *739*
39–74, *1323*
39–96, *1323*
42, *433*
42:5, *433, 435*
42:6, *433*
42:8, *433*
42:9, *436*
42:12, *433*
42:15, *432, 434, 1340*
43:29, *1321*
44–74, *1321*
46:3, *613*
52:1, *129*
60:6, *394*
61, *433, 442*
61:9, *1725*
61:15–16, *442*

66, *220*
67:9, *127*
75–96, *1323–1324*
75–102, *1321*
87:14–15, *620*
97–106, *588*
97:6, *1859*
97:26, *654*
98:1–2, *1725*
99:2, *1327*
103–141, *1321*
103:9, *627–628*
104:2, *745*
107:1, *596*
111, *590*
113:2, *651*
126, *220*
129, *120*
129:1–2, *1986–1987*
129:4, *1339*
129:5, *120, 1323*
129:8–18, *1722*
129:10–12, *1722*
129:14, *1363*
129:15 *et seq.*, *1722*
131:4, *1339, 1363*
131:5, *145*
135:2, *1334*
140:7, *1334*
141:1, *1331–1335*
142–175, *1321*
144:1, *1335–1338*
154:3, *1860*
156, *151*
156:1, *683*
157–170, *1325*
157–175, *1325*
163, *1444*
171–175:2, *1325*
174:1, *1912*
175, *626*
176–224, *1321*
176:1–2, *919*
182, *1326, 1364*
182:1, *1364*
189–226, *1324*
189–240, *1324*
189:1, *917*
193:1, *1330–1331*
195:11, *129*
201:1, *1323*
201:1–2, *120, 916, 1822*
201:2, *1027*
204:1, *148*
204:4, *148*
204:8, *705*
204:9, *705*
205:1, *636*
207:19, *120, 916*
208:1, *129*
212:7, *394*
225–263, *1321*
227–240, *1324*
227:21, *127*
231:23, *1300*
231:26, *1300*
231:28, *753, 757, 759*
235:1, *1665*
235:9, *1665*
235:28, *129, 1324*
237ff., *1324*
241–249, *1673*
241:6, *115*
246:5, *1674*
247:3, *437*
250–258, *1673*
250:1, *1682*
250:2, *1682*
250:5, *1682*
250:8, *1682*
250:21, *1878*
251:2, *1674*
253:2, *1673*
259:5, *160*
260, *1747*
264–311, *1321*
267:15, *1746*
270:1, *586*
272:17, *927*
276–289, *1673*
276:1, *1673*
276:4, *1672*
276:6, *1674*
280:10–12, *1680*
281:1, *1672*
281:7, *1673*
283:2, *1674*
290:24, *1668*
291:1, *1695*
303–305, *1325*
303:2–3, *1695*
306, *1325*
312–388, *1321*
320:4–5, *931*
328:1–2, *1982–1983*
328:2, *1363*
340:1, *1695*
356:2, *599*
360:1, *602*
365:1, *149*
365:1–2, *149, 1979–1980*
365:2, *149*
366:1, *602*
368:1, *73*
369:4–11, *70*
369:8, *72*
369:11, *1340*
370:2–3, *218*
375, *432*
376:1, *395, 397*
386, *219*
386:1, *1327*
389–427, *1321*
396:4, *146*
404:2, *553*
410:29, *414*
418:11, *146*
421:3, *602*
421:12, *629*
424:10–11, *629*
425, *1326*
427, *1323, 1325–1326*
427:9, *1323*
End, *1344*

Commentaries on Shulḥan Arukh

ATERET ẒEVI
to ḤM 32, subpar. 1, *130*
BE'ER HA-GOLAH
Introduction, *1426*
BET SHEMU'EL
EH, Introduction, *1419, 1430*
to EH 1, subpar. 16, *1430*
to EH 1, subpar. 22, *1430*
to EH 2, subpar. 11, *1430*
to EH 85, subpar. 38, *572*
to EH 130, subpar. 20, *1517*
BE'UR HA-GRA
to OḤ 70, subpar. 4, *969*
to YD 160, subpar. 35, *1427*
to YD 228, subpar. 93, *699*
to YD 228, subpar. 94, *713*
to YD 249, subpar. 20, *101*
to YD 251, subpar. 1, *1248*
to EH 28, subpar. 57, *871*
to ḤM 28, subpar. 56, *613*
to ḤM 46, subpar. 13, *613*

Commentaries on Shulḥan Arukh *continued*
to ḤM 87, subpar. 113, *654*
to ḤM 163, subpar. 103, *1427*
to ḤM 204, subpar. 11, *705*
to ḤM 365, subpar. 4, *1982*
to ḤM 365, subpar. 5, *1980*
BIRKEI YOSEF
OḤ, Introduction, *1439*
OḤ #188, par. 12, *1373*
ḤM #25, par. 29, *1370*
ḤM #26, piska 3, *17*
HALAKHAH PESUKAH
Preface, *1443*
ḤELKAT MEḤOKEK
to EH 80, subpar. 29, *630*
KESEF HA-KODASHIM
to ḤM 26, *17*
to ḤM 61:9, *1726*
to ḤM 201:1, *212, 919–920*
KEẒOT HA-ḤOSHEN
ḤM, Preface, *265*
to ḤM 32, subpar. 1, *147*
to ḤM 201, subpar. 1, *917*
to ḤM 259, subpar. 3, *73*
LEKET HA-KEMAḤ
OḤ, Introduction, *1438*
LEKET YOSHER
OḤ, p. 58, *1512*
OḤ, pp. 63–64, *1511–1512*
OḤ, p. 104, *1512*
OḤ, p. 105, *1512*
YD, pp. 19–20, *1512*
YD, pp. 77–79, *794*
MAGEN AVRAHAM
OḤ 9, subpar. 7, *543*
OḤ 128, subpar. 29, *95*
OḤ 588, subpar. 4, *533*
MAḤAZIK BERAKHAH
YD #47, par. 4, *1373*
MISHNAH BERURAH
to OḤ 139, *1192*
MISHPAT SHALOM
#231, Kunteres Tikkun Olam, *719*
NAḤAL YIẒḤAK
Part 1, Introduction, *265*
NETIVOT HA-MISHPAT
ḤM 9, Be'urim, subpar. 1, *130*
ḤM 25, Laws of Self-Help, rule 20, *1420*
ḤM 25, subpar. 20, *271*
Novellae, ḤM 26, subpar. 2, *17*
ḤM 201, subpar. 5, *917*
PANIM ḤADASHOT
Introduction, *1434*
PERI ḤADASH
to OḤ 468, *936*
to OḤ 496, *936*
to OḤ 588:5, *533*
PERI MEGADIM
YD, Introduction, *1378, 1419*
YD, Introduction, Rules for Decision Making in Matters of *Issur ve-Hetter*, par. 9, *1279, 1516*
PITḤEI TESHUVAH
YD
Introduction, *1441*
to 242, subpar. 8, *1422*
EH
Introduction, *1441*
to 82, subpar. 7, *1667, 1763*
to 85, subpar. 2, *1803*
ḤM
to 7, subpars. 26–29, *740*
to 17, subpar. 11, *1503*
to 25, subpar. 2, *1420*
to 25, subpar. 8, *269, 271*
to 32, subpar. 1, *130*
to 34, subpar. 1, *1604*
to 37, subpar. 14, *739*
to 163, subpar. 16, *944*
to 328, subpar. 2, *1363*
to 333, subpar. 3, *165*
REMA
Introduction, *901, 1359, 1361–1362, 1366*
YD
160:16, *1427–1428*
160:18, *901*
228:33, *1858*
EH
28:21, *871*
70:12, *790*
82:7, *1667, 1763*
90:1, *846*
119:6, *786*
154:3, *791*
163:2, *788*
ḤM
2, *723*
2:1, *700*
3:1, *27*
8:1, *26–27*
12:2, *157, 167, 925*
17:5, *1503*
22:1, *27*
25:2, *268, 271*
25:3, *982*
28:2, *64, 605, 1702*
37:22, *703, 740*
42:9, *437*
42:15, *671*
46:4, *913*
61:9, *1725*
81:1, *705–706*
87:14–15, *620*
107:2, *975*
121:9, *1363*
129:5, *1027*
129:14, *1363*
131:4, *1363*
141:1, *1335*
142:3, *1860*
154:3, *1860*
154:7, *1860*
157:4, *941*
163, *1444*
163:3, *772, 928, 942*
163:6, *705, 1427*
182:1, *1364–1365*
192:1, *1331*
208:1, *129*
209:4, *120*
212:7, *394*
231:28, *717, 753–754, 756*
259:7, *73*
274, *553, 1327*
282:1, *1673*
283:2, *1674*
328:1, *1363, 1982*
328:2, *1363*
331:1, *928*
356:2, *600*
356:7, *73, 597, 601, 688*
365:1, *1981*
366:1, *602*
369:11, *70*
383:2, *414*
425:1, *698*
SEFER MAYIM ḤAYYIM
OH 128, subpar. 20, *95*

SEFER ME'IRAT EINAYIM (SEMA)
Introduction, *226, 1207, 1251, 1279–1280, 1286, 1288, 1303, 1325, 1361, 1365–1366, 1408–1414*
ḤM
3, subpar. 2, *22*
8, subpar. 1, *26*
25, subpar. 19, *271*
26, subpar. 11, *17*
34, subpar. 5, *1603*
42, subpar. 10, *435*
42, subpar. 32, *433*
43, subpar. 53, *1321*
60, subpar. 18, *394*
86, subpar. 2, *1631*
111, subpar. 1, *590*
121, subpar. 20, *1363*
129, subpar. 16, *120*
131, subpar. 4, *1363*
156, subpar. 6, *683*
163, subpar. 13, *726*
182, subpar. 1, *1326*
182, subpar. 2, *1365*
201, subpar. 2, *915*
201, subpar. 6, *917*
204, subpar. 14, *706*
231, subpar. 42, *1300*
231, subpar. 44, *1300*
231, subpar. 45, *754, 756*
250, subpar. 8, *1878*
274, subpar. 2, *553*
278, subpar. 27, *1674*
365, subpar. 5, *149, 1982*
410, subpar. 44, *414*
427, subpar. 1, *1326*

SHA'AREI TESHUVAH
Author's Introduction, *1440*
Introduction of Ephraim Zalman Margolioth, *1440–1441, 1458*

SIFTEI KOHEN (SHAKH)
YD
Introduction, *1419*
160, subpar. 27, *901*
196, subpar. 20, *1516–1517*
ḤM
3, subpar. 3, *27*
17, subpar. 1, *168*
22, subpar. 15, *18, 1914*
25, subpar. 15, *27*
25, subpar. 21, *271*
33, subpar. 1, *210*
42, subpar. 27, *433*
42, subpar. 36, *432*
46, subpar. 8, *913*
46, subpar. 9, *612, 1520*
73, subpar. 36, *70*
73, subpar. 39, *73*
86, subpar. 3, *1631*
131, subpar. 4, *1363*
201, subpar. 1, *917*
231, *758*
231, subpar. 4, *753, 756*
356, subpar. 4, *598*
356, subpar. 10, *73, 601, 688*

TOKFO KOHEN
#93–95, *1283*

TUREI ZAHAV (TAZ)
YD, Introduction, *1419*
on YD 328, subpar. 2, *1516–1517*
on ḤM 26:3, *17*

URIM VE-THUMMIM
to ḤM ch. 25, subpar. 123–124, *1421*
to ḤM ch. 25, subpar. 125, *1420*
Abridgment of *Tokfo Kohen* #124 (ḤM, following ch. 25), *1283*
to ḤM ch. 26, Thummim, subpar. 2, *17*
to ḤM ch. 28, Urim, subpar. 3, *1603*
to ḤM ch. 28, Urim, subpar. 10, *1704*
to ḤM ch. 61, Urim, subpar. 18, *1726*
to ḤM 97, subpar. 13, *710*

Other Codificatory Works

ABUDARHAM, BOOK OF DAILY PRAYERS
Commentary on the Thirteen Canons, *334*

ARUKH HA-SHULḤAN
ḤM, Introduction, *1448–1449, 1452, 1849*
ḤM 7:22, *740*
ḤM 123:3, *650*
ḤM 131:6, *145*
ḤM 304:11, *144*
ḤM 356:2, *598*
Arukh ha-Shulḥan he-Atid, Editor's Introduction, *1449*

HA-ESHKOL
ed. Albeck, I, pp. 157–158, Hilkhot Sefer Torah, *95*
ed. Auerbach, II, Laws of the Torah Scroll, p. 50, *1158*

HALAKHOT GEDOLOT (BY SIMEON KAYYARA)
Laws of Megillah (ed. Hildesheimer, p. 198), *894*

ḤAYYEI ADAM
66:2, *1796*

ḤAZON ISH
Bava Batra 4:8, *702–703*
Bava Batra 4:10, *703*
Bava Batra 5:1, *726*
Sanhedrin 15:4, *25*

HILKHOT BEKHOROT VE-ḤALLAH (BY NAḤMANIDES)
Introduction, *1242*

HILKHOT NIDDAH (BY NAḤMANIDES)
Introduction, *1242–1243*

ḤUKKAT MISHPAT
Laws of Sales 30:12, Be'urim u-Mekorot (pp. 255–256), *130*

KIẒẒUR SHULKḤAN ARUKH
ch. 139, *1192*
chs. 179–189, *1448*

KOL BO
#116, *719, 785*
#142, *718–719*

LEVUSHIM
Introduction, *227, 1365, 1394–1402*
Levush ha-Tekhelet, Laws of Birkat ha-Mazon 193:6, *940*

LIKKUTEI HALAKHOT SHEL HA-ḤAFEẒ ḤAYYIM [COLLECTED RULINGS OF THE ḤAFEẒ ḤAYYIM]
Sotah #21, *1799*

MAḤZOR VITRY
#380 (p. 442), *784*
#424 (p. 462), *203*

Other Codificatory Works *continued*
#469 (p. 588), *974*
MASSA ḤAYYIM
Introduction, *1447*
MASSA MELEKH
Introduction, *923, 1445*
V, gate 1, law 3, *720*
MINHAGEI MAHARIL
Laws of Marriage, #318 (p. 87b), *792*
MISHPAT HA-ḤEREM (BY NAḤMANIDES)
End of *Sefer Kol Bo* (p. 16c/d), *729, 733, 735*
MORDEKHAI
Shabbat #472–473, *917*
Ketubbot #154, *1283*
Bava Kamma #179, *716*
Bava Meẓi'a #257, *157, 182, 925*
Bava Meẓi'a #334, *705*
Bava Meẓi'a #366, *883, 941*
Bava Meẓi'a #457–458, *704– 705*
Bava Batra #477, *749, 922*
Bava Batra #480, *716, 729*
Bava Batra #481, *716*
Bava Batra #482, *716*
Bava Batra #522, *748–749*
Bava Batra #656, *773*
Shevu'ot #755, *713*
OR ZARU'A
Preface, *1241*
I, Laws of Charity, #30, *901*
III, Piskei Bava Kamma, #145, *1716*
III, Piskei Bava Batra, #112–114, *95*
III, Piskei Bava Batra, #199 (p. 30a), *975*
PISKEI HA-ROSH
BERAKHOT
ch. 1, #16, *668*
SHABBAT
ch. 2, #15, *668*
ch. 23, #1, *268*
BEẒAH
ch. 5, #2, *129*
YEVAMOT
ch. 4, #33, *955*
KETUBBOT
ch. 1, #25, *888*
ch. 4, #14, *1803*
ch. 4, #24, *655*
ch. 5, #35, *660*
GITTIN
ch. 4, #13, *514*
KIDDUSHIN
ch. 2, #7–8, *268*
BAVA KAMMA
ch. 10, #18, *600*
BAVA MEẒI'A
ch. 3, #10, *268*
ch. 4, #19, *268*
ch. 4, #21, *268*
ch. 5, #19, *128*
ch. 5, #72, *916*
ch. 9, #20, *626*
ch. 9, #24, *625*
ch. 9, #46–47, *1859*
BAVA BATRA
ch. 1, #5, *941*
ch. 1, #29, *37, 746, 921*
ch. 1, #33, *755–756, 759*
ch. 2, #11, *683*
SANHEDRIN
ch. 1, #1, *23*
ch. 1, #2, *23*
ch. 4, #6, *269, 271, 668, 984, 1228, 1793*
HILKHOT MIKVA'OT, *206*
SEDER RAV AMRAM
p. 38, *1157*
SEFER EẒ ḤAYYIM
Introduction, *1255–1256, 1261*
III, p. 159, *1256*
SEFER HA-AGUR
Introduction, *1305–1306*
SEFER HA-ARVUT VE-HA-KABBELANUT (BY SAMUEL B. ḤOPHNI GAON)
Introduction, *1162–1163*
SEFER HA-HASHLAMAH
Introduction, *1244*
SEFER HA-ḤINNUKH
Author's Letter, *1265–1266*
Commandment #329, *1266*
Commandment #420, *1266*
Commandment #450, *924, 1632*
Commandment #508, *245*
Commandment #606, *1266*
SEFER HA-ITTUR
Introduction, *1267–1268*
Book II, gate II (pp. 29d *et seq.*), *1269*
p. 50b, #54, *1268*
p. 121b, #143, *1268*
Conclusion (p. 77c/d), *1267*
SEFER HA-MAHARIL
Hilkhot Tefillah, p. 61b, *1302*
SEFER HA-MANHIG
Introduction, *1240–1241*
SEFER HA-MIẒVOT (BY MAIMONIDES)
Introduction, *1078, 1184, 1186–1187, 1191, 1206*
Shoresh 1, *484*
Second Principle, *209*
Affirmative Commandment #153, *1649*
Affirmative Commandment #173, *60*
Negative Commandment #199, *1189*
Negative Commandment #287, *304*
Negative Commandment #290, *693*
Negative Commandment #300, *517*
SEFER HA-ORAH
II, ch. 12, *974*
SEFER HA-PARDES
p. 353, *910*
SEFER HA-RABAN
EH, II, p. 47b, *848*
Bava Meẓi'a, ch. 2 (beginning), *688*
SEFER HA-SHE'ILTOT (BY AḤA OF SHABḤA) (ED. MIRSKY)
she'ilta 1, *1152*
she'ilta 2, *13, 1715*
she'ilta 4, *1151*
she'ilta 16, *1151*
she'ilta 17, *1151*
she'ilta 20, *1151*
she'ilta 33, *1026, 1151–1152*
she'ilta 76, *894*
SEFER HA-SHETAROT (BY SAADIAH GAON)
Introduction, *1161*
SEFER HA-TERUMAH
Introduction, *1239–1240*

Introduction to Laws of the Land of Israel, *1240*
SEFER HA-TERUMOT
Introduction, *1245–1246*
gate 35, ch. 1, par. 27, *144*
gate 35, ch. 1, par. 28, *1246*
gate 46, ch. 8, par. 5, *69, 132*
SEFER HA-YERUSHOT (BY SAADIAH GAON)
Introduction, *1160*
pp. 9, 20–21, *1159–1160*
SEFER ḤUKKOT HA-DAYYANIM
chs. 20–21, *1307*
SEFER MEISHARIM
Introduction, *1251, 1270–1271*
Path 8, *1272*
Path 9, *1272*
Path 10, *1272*
Path 11, *1272*
Path 23, *791*
Path 31, *1272*
SEFER MINHAGIM (BY ISAAC TIRNAU)
Minhag of Purim, Glosses, subpar. 2, *1302*
SEFER MIẒVOT GADOL (SEMAG)
Introduction, *1261–1263*
SEFER MIẒVOT KATAN (SEMAK)
Author's Letter, *1263–1264*
Table of Contents, *1264–1265*
SEFER ORḤOT ḤAYYIM
Introduction, *1257*
SEFER SHIBBOLEI HA-LEKET
Introduction, *1247*
ch. 263 (ed. Buber, p. 252), *1247*
II, #75 (ed. Ḥasida, pp. 147–148), *1476*
SEFER TASHBEẒ (BY SAMSON B. ẒADOK)
pars. 1, 7, 18–23, *973–974*
par. 533, *100*
SEFER YERE'IM
Introduction, *1259–1260*
TOLEDOT ADAM VE-ḤAVVAH
Introduction, *1270–1271*
Part Ḥavvah, path 22, sec. 4, *855–856*
Part Ḥavvah, path 23, sec. 3, *1796*
TORAT HA-ADAM (BY NAḤMANIDES)
pp. 42ff. (ed Chavel, II), *143, 147*
TORAT HA-BAYIT
Introduction, *1273–1274, 1322*
Introduction to Bet ha-Nashim, *1224*
YAM SHEL SHELOMO
BEẒAH
ch. 1, #9, *542*
YEVAMOT
ch. 4, #16, *1388*
ch. 4, #18, *788, 792*
ch. 10, #1, *527*
ch. 10, #19, *510*
KETUBBOT
ch. 4, #14, *788, 838*
KIDDUSHIN
ch. 1, #22, *925*
BAVA KAMMA
Introduction, *984, 1228, 1251, 1282–1283, 1384–1387*
Title page (ed. Prague, 1616), *1390*
ch. 2, #5, *1386*
ch. 3, #5, *1716*
ch. 5, #36, *917*
ch. 6, #6, *147*
ch. 8, #58, *1391*
ch. 8, #59, *1389*
ch. 8, #65, *15–16*
ch. 10, #11, *913*
ḤULLIN
First Introduction, *1387–1388*
Second Introduction, *1389–1392*
ch. 8, #14–42, *1389*
ẒEIDAH LA-DEREKH
Introduction, *1172, 1307–1308*
Essay 3, rule 3, ch. 1, *1308*

Commentaries on Other Codificatory Works

BEDEK HA-BAYIT (ON TORAT HA-BAYIT)
Introduction, *1276, 1343*
DIVREI ḤAMUDOT (ON PISKEI HA-ROSH)
Ḥullin, ch. 8, #185, *1323*
ELIYAHU ZUTA (ON LEVUSHIM)
Introduction, *1403*
HA'AMEK SHE'ELAH
she'ilta 58, par. 14, *533*
Kidmat ha-Emek (Preface of Neziv), ch. 1, subpars. 1–3, *207*
HAGGAHOT ASHERI (ON PISKEI HA-ROSH)
Ketubbot, ch. 5, #35, *660*
Kiddushin, ch. 3, #16, *789*
Bava Batra, ch. 1, #5, *941*
Bava Batra, ch. 9, #32, *975*
HAGGAHOT HA-BAḤ (ON HAGGAHOT ASHERI)
Bava Batra, ch. 1, #5, gloss #9, *941*
HAGGAHOT HA-GRIP (ON PISKEI HA-ROSH)
Bava Meẓi'a, ch. 4, #19, *268*
ḤAGURAT SHEMU'EL (ON LEVUSHIM)
Introduction, *1402*
KATUV SHAM (RABAD'S CRITIQUE OF THE *MA'OR*)
Sukkah 14a (p. 3), *1172*
KORBAN NETANEL (ON PISKEI HA-ROSH)
Shabbat, ch. 23, #1, subpar. 4, *268*
Beẓah, ch. 5, #2, subpars. 80, 90, *129*
Ketubbot, ch. 1, #25, subpar. 10, *889*
Gittin, ch. 4, #13, subpar. 4, *514*
MARGANITA TAVA (ON SEFER HA-MIẒVOT BY MAIMONIDES)
Second Principle, *210*
MEGILLAT ESTHER (ON SEFER HA-MIẒVOT BY MAIMONIDES)
Second Principle, *210*

ḤAGURAT SHEMU'EL (ON LEVUSHIM)
Introduction, *1402, 1418*
MINḤAT ḤINNUKH (ON SEFER HA-ḤINNUKH)
Commandment #59, *1695*
Commandment #462, *1858*
MISHMERET HA-BAYIT (ON TORAT HA-BAYIT)
Introduction, *1277*
NAḤMANIDES' CRITICAL COMMENTARY (HASSAGOT) ON *SEFER HA-MIẒVOT* BY MAIMONIDES
Shoresh Rishon (First-Principle), *238, 245*
Shoresh 2 (Second Principle), *209–211, 355*
PILPULA ḤARIFTA (ON PISKEI HA-ROSH)
Bava Meẓi'a, ch. 5, #38, subpar. 2, *710*
SHILTEI HA-GIBBORIM (ON MORDEKHAI)
Gittin #444, *939*
TIFERET SHEMU'EL (ON PISKEI HA-ROSH)
Ketubbot, ch. 1, #25, subpar. 12, *889*
VIKKU'AḤ MAYIM ḤAYYIM (ON TORAT ḤATTAT)
Introduction, *1347–1348, 1375–1379, 1420, 1848–1849*

RESPONSA

Resp. Anaf Ḥayyim
II, pp. 169–172, *1496*

Resp. Alfasi
#13 (ed. Leiter), *715, 883*
#14 (ed. Leiter), *1098*
#156, *63*

Resp. Asefat Geonim, *1518*

Resp. Aseh Lekha Rav
II, #52, *1801*

Resp. Asheri
Table of Contents, *1413*
1:8, *1283*
2:19, *1511*
4:10, *1518*
5:2, *1511*
5:4, *738–739*
5:6, *1507*
6:5, *683, 717, 729, 1005*
6:7, *718, 1005*
6:8, *458*
6:15, *739*
6:19, *705*
6:21, *705, 739*
7:3, *98–99, 725–726*
7:11, *28*
12:3, *918, 943*
13:20, *739, 1509, 1518*
14, *1518*
15:3, *1518*
17:1, *11, 802, 1501, 1511*
17:8, *11*
17:10, *1502, 1504*
18:4–5, *1511*
18:5, *1511*
18:13, *28, 518*
18:16, *73, 745*
19:6, *1509*
20:20, *1512*
23:9(2), *1512*
29:1, *1518*
31:9, *1226–1227*
32:11, *1515*
32:14(2), *1518*
35, *1522*
35:1, *851–852*
35:2, *850–851*
35:5, *1509*
35:6, *1522*
42:1, *786*
43:8, *662–665, 674*
43:9(2), *1511*
43:12, *1227*
47–49, *1518*
50:10, *452*
51:2(49:1), *1518*
55:1, *840–841*
55:1–3, *796*
55:5, *796*
55:7, *452, 465, 841*
55:7–8, *796, 841*
55:9, *270, 471, 1228, 1673*
55:10, *884, 903, 909–910, 940*
57:2, *1515*
58:3, *739*
64:3, *1509*
64:4, *904*
67:2, *1283*
68:14, *435–436*
68:20, *1725*
74:4, *1512*
78, *1891*
78:1, *417, 1892*
78:3, *417–418, 1502, 1892–1894*
79:4, *928*
79:11(2), *1507*
80:4, *1507*
84:2, *399*
84:3, *1251, 1283*
84:4, *1510*
85:5, *1501*
85:10, *1725*
85:11, *1283*
86:15, *1509*
94:5, *1227–1228, 1386*
97:1, *1501, 1508*
100:1, *1512*
100:2, *1228*
101:1, *692*
101:3, *414*
104:5, *1519*
107:6, *96*
107:6(1), *1502*
108:11, *1281*

Resp. Avkat Rokhel
#32, *713, 1311*
#80, *917, 1483, 1505–1507*
#81, *1502, 1505–1507*
#201, *1317, 1520*

Resp. Avraham b. ha-Rambam
#78, *625*
#89, *940*
#97, *63, 416, 968*
#102–104, *443*
#106, *810*

Resp. Ba'alei ha-Tosafot (ed. Agus)
pp. 57–58, *939*
#12 (p. 58), *65*
#12 (p. 60), *67*

Resp. Ba'ei Ḥayyai
ḤM, ch. 81, *707*
ḤM, II, #1, *18*
ḤM, II, #158, *18*

Resp. Baḥ ha-Ḥadashot
#42, *1415–1416*
#43, *757*

Resp. Baḥ ha-Yeshanot
#43, *1521*
#80, *1415*
#136, *1415*

Resp. Berekh Moshe
#33, *874*

Resp. Bet David
I, YD #158, *1858*

Resp. Bet Yiẓḥak
YD, II, #75, *74*

Resp. Bet Yosef
#6, *870–871, 875*
Dinei Kiddushin, #10, *658, 1506*

Resp. Binyamin Ze'ev
Introduction, *1522*
#1, *524*
#64, *788*
#282, *18*
#290, *717*
#293, *923, 927*
#295, *748, 784*
#296, *717*
#298–300, *717*

Devar Avraham
I, #11, par. 7 (p. 59), *700*

Sefer Devar Halakhah
p. 9, *524*

Resp. Devar Shemu'el
#255, *1371*

Resp. Devar Yehoshu'a
II, #19, *1521*

Resp. Divrei Rivot
#56, *865*
#68, *724*
#109, *1725*
#216, *1506*
#217, *1506*
#218, *1506*
#244, *724*
#292, *1006*

Resp. Divrei Yosef
#27, *907–909*

Resp. Ein Yiẓḥak
II, *1583–1584*

Resp. Eitan ha-Ezraḥi
#43–44, *697*
#45, *11, 697*

Resp. Elijah Mizraḥi
#53, *700–701, 727*
#57, *701–702, 717, 724, 727*
#66, *1284*

Resp. Ge'onei Vatra'ei, *1518*

Resp. Ginat Veradim
II, ḤM 6:1, *1531*

Ginzei Schechter
II, p. 118, *16*
II, pp. 127–128, *16, 766*
II, pp. 416–420, *1472*
II, p. 548, *113*

Resp. Ha-Elef Lekha Shelomo
HM #2, *1584*

Resp. Ḥakham Ẓevi
#93, *1516*

Resp. Ḥakhmei Ẓarfat ve-Lutir
#24, *713*

Resp. Halakhot Ketannot
I, #276, *1858*

Resp. Ḥatam Sofer
EH, #1, *785*
ḤM, #21, *883*
ḤM, #22, *1584*
ḤM, #41, *669, 673–674, 676*
ḤM, #79, *673, 676*
ḤM, #116, *719–723, 758*
ḤM, #162, *1698*
ḤM, #207, *1698*
OḤ, #208, *61–62, 194, 264, 715*
Likkutim #57, *673–674, 676*

Resp. Ḥavvot Ya'ir
#70, *471*
#81, *772*
#136, *35*
#146, *11*
#163, *127*
#165, *1420–1421, 1426*
#168, *1363*
#192, *205*

Resp. Ḥayyim Sha'al
#48, *1323*
II, #38, sec. 51, *1361*

Resp. Ḥayyim ve-Shalom
II, #102, *30*

Resp. Ḥikekei Lev
I, YD, #49, *1858*
II, ḤM, #5, *1586*

Resp. Ḥikrei Lev
ḤM, #23, *739*

Resp. Ḥut ha-Meshullash
#8, *978, 1494*

Resp. Ḥut ha-Shani, *1518*

Kerem Ḥemer
ḤM #33, *1726*
II, pp. 2–43, *807–809, 1531*

Resp. Kol Mevasser
I, #3, *540*
I, #13, *669, 674*

Resp. Leḥem Rav
#2, *725*
#87, *175*
#216, *717*

Leket Yosher
OḤ, p. 58, *1512*
OḤ, pp. 63–64, *1511–1512*
OḤ, p. 104, *1512*
OḤ, p. 105, *1512*
YD, pp. 19–20, *1512*
YD, pp. 77–79, *794*

Resp. Lev Nishbar
#3, *876–877*

Resp. Lev Same'aḥ
ḤM, #5, *720*

Ma'arkhei Lev
Responsa, ḤM, #113, *130*

Resp. Mabit
Introduction, *1514*
I, #84, *727, 729–730*
I, #264, *719*
II, #62, *1763*
II, #138, *1519–1520*
III, #21, *1505*
III, #188, *1510*
III, #228, *706, 1510*

Resp. Maharaḥ Or Zaru'a
#25, *17*
#65, *728–729*
#69, *789*
#126, *789*
#142, *17*
#191, *789*
#222, *144, 716, 734, 756, 763–766, 769, 1512*
#226, *775*

Resp. Maharalbaḥ
#99, *756–757, 759*

Resp. Maharam Alashkar
#48, *633, 854, 864–868, 1507*
#49, *734, 754*
#83–85, *1506*

Resp. Maharam Alshekh
#39, *271*

Resp. Maharam Mintz
Introduction to Table of Contents, *1513–1514*
#6, *756*
#10, *792*
#21, *1507*
#47, *846*
#63, *794*
#102, *784–786*

Resp. Maharam of Lublin
#11, *1384*
#94, *1384*
#100, *1502*
#102, *1384*
#118, *1385*
#126, *1384*
#135, *1384*
#138, *11, 697, 973, 1521*

Resp. Maharam of Padua
#14, *785*
#40, *1501, 1504*
#43, *25*

Resp. Maharam of Rothenburg
ED. BERLIN
#25, *1283*
#220, *690*
#238, *745*
#290, *789*
#337–339, *661*
#386, *900*
#865, *716, 725*
ED. CREMONA
#72, *787*
#78, *17, 786*
#146, *590*
#159, *1283*
#230, *716*
#232, *11*
#291, *790*
ED. LEMBERG
#136, *661*
#213, *750*
#247, *11*
#248, *11*
#371, *748–749*
#423, *672, 688–690, 760, 1515*
ED. PRAGUE
#38, *705*
#72, *415*
#81, *791*
#85, *415, 925*
#106, *748–749, 769, 922*
#153, *785, 788*
#345, *910*
#383, *690*
#485, *11*
#692, *100*
#770, *688*
#865, *661*
#915, *748–749*
#927, *791, 1513*
#934, *787*
#940–941, *1444*
#941, *142–143*
#968, *716*
#995, *749, 922*
#1022, *788–789*
p. 159c, *784, 786*
p. 160a, *1858*

Resp. Maharash le-Vet ha-Levi
OḤ #9, *1323*

Resp. Maharashdam
EH, #48, *441–442*
EH, #123, *1666*
ḤM, #1, *1317*
ḤM, #12, *865*
ḤM, #29, *1283*
ḤM, #33, *929*
ḤM, #40, *1506*
ḤM, #61, *1283*
ḤM, #99, *929*
ḤM, #109, *1503*
ḤM, #128, *1505*
ḤM, #154, *1283*
ḤM, #218, *1505*
ḤM, #327, *1007, 1483*
ḤM, #327–332, *1506–1507*
ḤM, #328, *71–72*
ḤM, #360, *16*
ḤM, #367, *1725*
ḤM, #369, *923*
ḤM, #380, *904, 930, 1822*
ḤM, #398, *719*
ḤM, #404, *923*
ḤM, #406, *719*
ḤM, #421, *724*
ḤM, #436, *928*
ḤM, #447, *700*
OḤ, #37, *702, 724*
YD, #82, *719*
YD, #117, *718–719*
YD, #151, *719*

Resp. Mahari Bruna
#28, *1512*
#92, *1510*
#132, *63*
#265, *11*

Resp. Mahari Minẓ
#7, *418–421, 717, 725, 772*
#15, *1302, 1358*

Resp. Mahari Weil
#36, *10*
#66, *671*
#101, *671, 793*
#114, *11*
#146, *30*

Resp. Maharibal
I, #75(73), *712–713, 1283*
I, #115, *719*
I, #122, *719*
I, #126, *719*
II, #23, *1506*
III, #72, *865*

Resp. Maharik
#8, *910*
#9, *910*
#10, *433, 439–440*
#17, *748–784*
#54, *909–910*
#74, *1520*
#84, *268–270*
#94, *271, 436–437, 1520*
#101, *785*
#102, *927*
#110, *1858*
#128, *100*
#137, *1459, 1521–1522*
#149, *1283*
#161, *1459*
#171, *899*
#177, *719–720*
#179, *679, 702, 719–720, 752, 1520*
#181, *679, 702, 752*
#182, *1283*
#186, *1512*
#187, *70*
#190, *1725*
#210, *271*

Resp. Maharil
#37, *901*
#70, *1501–1502, 1504, 1510*
#72, *90, 976–977, 1458*
#74, *1507*
#75, *1501*
#76, *1502, 1507*
#77, *1501*
#80, *1501*
#82, *63*
#88, *846*
#100, *1510*
#121, *671*
#151, *1512*
#192 (following), *1516*

Resp. Maharit
I, #58, *719*
I, #68, *719*
I, #69, *725*
I, #70, *1513–1514*
I, #95, *719*
II, ḤM #7, *1459*

Resp. Maharitaẓ
#67, *1372*
#129, *1506, 1514*
#259, *1372*

Resp. Maharif
#61, *1283, 1373*

Resp. Maharshakh
I, #44, *415, 1505*
II, #81, *1283*
II, #95, *725*
II, #109, *719*
III, #64, *1506*
III, #65, *1506*
III, #66, *1506*
III, #76, *725*

Resp. Maharshal
#4, *30*
#29, *1798*
#33, *30*
#35, *1386*
#89, *396*
#93, *28, 30*

Resp. Maharsham
III, #18, *920*

Resp. Maharyu
#29, *1501*
#40, *1509*
#70, *1510*
#80, *1501, 1507–1508*
#89, *1509*
#124, *1507*
#147, *1507, 1511*
#151, *1501*
#170, *1501*

Maimonides, Koveẓ Teshuvot ha-Rambam ve-Iggerotav [Compilation of Responsa and Epistles of Maimonides]
I, #49, *1188*
I, #140 (pp. 25–26), *50, 1197, 1205, 1216–1221, 1287*
II, p. 8, *1223*
II, p. 15, *1208*
II, p. 24ff., *1190*
II, pp. 24–25, *1223*
II, p. 26a/b, *1194*
II, p. 30, *1214–1215, 1222*

Resp. Maimonides
ED. J. BLAU
I
#5, *63*
#9, *63*
#14, *1477*
#32, *63*
#52, *63*
#64, *63*
#69, *63*
#90, *63*
#93, *63*
II
#192, *63*
#194, *63*
#210, *63*
#242, *810*
#251, *1171*
#252, *1193*
#258, *810*
#293, *1854*
#310, *1229*
#347, *810*
#348, *810*
#350, *609*
#364, *1477*
#391, *1477*
#407, *1477*
#410, *63*
#412, *1477*
#435, *1477*
ED. A.H. FREIMANN
Introduction, p. LXI, *1185*
#42, *1854*
#69, *1223*
#152, *1465*

Resp. Maimuniyyot
Ishut, #9, *1506*
Kinyan, #2, *73*
Kinyan, #27, *716*
Shofetim, #10, *716*

Resp. Matteh Levi
#19, *1506*

Resp. Mayim Amukkim, *1518*
#1, *1301*
#63, *705–707, 1510*

Resp. Mayim Ḥayyim
ḤM, #6, *165*

Resp. Meshiv Davar
I, #24, *90, 977–978, 1458*
III, #10, *172–173*

Resp. Mikveh ha-Mayim
III, YD #21, *1800*

Mishpat Kohen
#144, *59*

Resp. Mishpat u-Ẓedakah be-Ya'akov
Introduction, *1539*
#33, *920*
II, #5, *1373*

Resp. Mishpat Ẓedek
II, #4, *719*
II, #35, *719*

Resp. Mishpatim Yesharim, *1518*

Resp. Mishpetei Uziel
EH #91, *1797*
III, ḤM, #13, *1698*

Resp. Moharam of Rothenburg ha-Aḥaronim
ḤM, #20, *942, 944*

Resp. Naḥalah li-Yehoshu'a
#12, *1506–1507*

Resp. Naḥalat Shiv'ah
#27, *719*

Resp. Naḥalat Ya'akov
#57, *872–874*

Resp. Naḥmanides
#3, *415*
#7, *883*
#63, *16*
#75, *1509*

Resp. Nediv Lev
II, EH, #8, *876–877*

Resp. Ne'eman Shemuel
#84, *18*

Resp. Neḥpah ba-Kesef
II, EH #27, *1458*

Resp. Noda bi-Yehudah
MAHADURA KAMMA
Introduction, *1508*
EH, #31, *1507*
EH, #72, *1521*
ḤM, #20, *1503, 1505*
MAHADURA TINYANA
EH, #129, *786*
ḤM, #40, *770, 923*
YD, #161, *95*

Ohel Moshe
II, #138, *920*

Resp. Oholei Ya'akov
#20, *1371*
#45, *1506*

Resp. Or ha-Yashar, *1506*

Resp. Or Yisra'el
#1–33, *1506*

Oẓar ha-Geonim (ed. B.M. Lewin), Responsa Section
PESAḤIM
p. 6, *493*
MEGILLAH
p. 49, *894*
KETUBBOT
pp. 18–19, *657*
p. 89, *1157*
p. 138, *655*
pp. 139–140, *655*
p. 168, *125*
p. 191, *790*
pp. 191–192, *659–660*
pp. 191–193, *660*
p. 210, *647–648*
pp. 210–213, *647*
p. 212, *648*
NEDARIM
p. 15, *713*
KIDDUSHIN
p. 60, *650–651*
pp. 60–63, *1647*
p. 62, *650*
p. 63, *651*
BAVA KAMMA
p. 69, *15*
p. 100, *16*

Oẓar ha-Geonim to Tractate Sanhedrin (ed. Taubes)
p. 171, #358, *740*

Resp. Penei Moshe
I, #12, *1458*

Resp. Penei Yehoshua
II, YD, #18, *1403*
II, EH, #52, *1407, 1417*

Resp. Penei Yiẓḥak
EH, #13, *875–876*
EH, #16, *874–875*

Resp. Pe'ullat Ẓaddik
I, Introduction, *1500*

Resp. Raban
EH, III, p. 47b (ed. Jerusalem), *848, 1506*

Resp. Rabbenu Beẓalel Ashkenazi
#22, *1285*

Resp. Rabbenu Gershom Me'or ha-Golah
#67, *73, 686–687, 1746*

Resp. Rabi Av Bet Din (ed. Kafah)
#124, *145*
#149, *11, 47, 1513*

Resp. Radakh
II, #10, *1283*

Resp. Radbaz
I, #65, *759*
I, #123, *1666, 1673*
I, #263, *1667*
I, #278, *918*
I, #360, *1667*
I, #380, *919*
I, #429, *1796*
I, #503, *219–222*
II, #647, *95*
II, #796, *810, 1521*
II, #825, *1283*
III, #1049, *398–399*
III, #1052, *1005*

IV, #1165, *674–675, 810*
IV, #1187 (#116), *1283*

Resp. Rama of Fano
#89, *791*

Resp. Ramah
#242, *1509*
#251, *1508*
#255, *1507*
#259, *1512*
#271, *1510*
#273, *1509*
#285, *1510*
#290, *1510*
#292, *1510, 1515*
#293, *1515*
#296, *1508*
#298, *838*
#305, *1510*

Resp. Ran
#2, *746*
#38, *63*
#54, *430*
#62, *711, 1223, 1475*
#67, *1512*
#72, *1501*
#73, *17*

Resp. Ranaḥ
#10, *1373*
I, #46, *1459*
#58, *18*
#63, *18*
#93, *1502, 1505*
#109 (second responsum), *1373*

Resp. Rashba
I
#166, *1512*
#181, *11*
#253, *713, 1223, 1281*
#335, *95*
#366, *1476*
#494, *1275*
#551, *712, 854–855, 868*
#562, *1484*
#571, *1476*
#573, *664*
#590, *471*
#617, *727–728*
#662, *429–430*
#664, *922*
#680, *738*
#729, *699, 742–743*
#769, *700*
#778, *430*
#781, *670*
#788, *766–767*
#811, *738*
#893, *745*
#894, *745*
#895, *70*
#1010, *30*
#1069, *1534*
#1129, *63*
#1146, *975*
#1148, *17, 1502*
#1162, *852*
#1166, *1520*
#1185, *304, 641, 852*
#1192, *664*
#1206, *700, 755, 758, 853–854, 1465*
#1235, *664*
II
#14, *415*
#96, *1509*
#104, *721*
#107, *738, 744*
#111, *743–744*
#182, *1507–1508*
#223, *430*
#233, *439*
#237, *441*
#261, *443*
#268, *886, 943*
#269, *434*
#276, *664*
#279, *717, 761–763*
#283, *1891*
#290, *23–24, 28*
#305, *434*
#339, *465*
#360, *700, 1891*
III
#7, *1476*
#17, *425, 429–430*
#22, *1507*
#65, *394*
#95, *1507*
#98, *1509*
#109, *70*
#138, *1508*
#153, *63*
#160, *63*
#166, *1508*
#203–204, *443*
#206, *441*
#208, *443*
#210, *430*
#213, *1507*
#218, *63*
#304, *719*
#307, *443*
#318, *692*
#330, *471*
#335, *323*
#386, *465–467*
#387, *468*
#393, *28, 47, 694*
#394, *717*
#396, *471*
#397, *464–465*
#398, *747–748, 922*
#403, *465*
#406, *448, 747*
#407, *461*
#408, *461*
#409, *445, 449, 459*
#410, *774*
#411, *668–671, 700, 707–708, 731, 763, 774, 796*
#412, *773–775*
#417, *700*
#421, *63*
#422–425, *471*
#426, *1508*
#427, *462*
#431, *465, 745*
#433, *429–430*
#436, *922*
#438, *742–743*
#443, *728*
IV
#35, *63*
#57, *1507*
#59, *1507*
#61, *1510, 1518*
#111, *63*
#125, *430–432*
#142, *488, 515, 700, 745*
#152, *1476*
#161, *439*
#172, *1507*
#177, *922*
#181, *443*
#185, *714, 717, 754–755, 758*

Resp. Rashba *continued*
#186, *425, 430*
#199, *744*
#213, *443*
#215, *1508*
#240, *1507*
#258, *1508*
#260, *747, 773, 922*
#268, *449–450*
#269, *459, 1507–1508*
#271, *946*
#294, *443*
#308, *457*
#309, *774*
#311, *28, 691–692, 694–695*
#312, *471*
#313, *471*
#320, *1507*
#330, *1510*
V
#95, *664*
#125, *683, 730, 758–759*
#126, *471, 488, 515, 699–700, 717*
#139, *1507–1508*
#166, *1508*
#167, *63, 430*
#168, *1507–1508*
#178, *766–767, 771*
#179, *773*
#180, *922*
#183, *63*
#184, *738*
#220, *1507–1508*
#221, *445, 471*
#222, *459–460*
#238, *519*
#242, *717*
#245, *758*
#247, *457*
#253, *672, 728*
#260, *440–441*
#263, *922*
#266, *441*
#270, *37, 717, 746, 921–922*
#273, *738*
#277, *471*
#279, *471, 1502, 1507*
#280, *459*
#281, *459, 464*
#282, *450–452*
#283, *471*
#284, *471, 1507–1508*
#285, *471*
#286, *737–738*
#287, *462, 761, 943*
#288, *471*
#289, *445*
#290, *11, 471*
VI
#1, *1508*
#5, *443*
#7, *471, 738, 740, 744*
#62, *1510*
#92, *63*
#149, *63*
#151, *438–439, 443*
#176, *1508*
#254, *15, 63, 70*
VII
#108, *758, 760–762, 943*
#244, *707*
#340, *761*
#490, *700*

Resp. Rashba Attributed to Naḥmanides
#13, *1508*
#14, *430*
#16, *63*
#22, *63*
#38, *1763, 1796*
#59, *745*
#65, *25, 63, 717, 738, 741–742, 759*
#93, *323*
#108, *434, 439*
#112, *1473*
#125, *304, 852*
#133, *63*
#134, *669*
#142, *852*
#222, *1473, 1475*
#223, *63*
#240, *11*
#268, *439*
#279, *28, 518, 691, 698*
#280, *683, 717, 758*

Resp. Rashbash
#78, *806*
#112, *706–707*
#211, *708, 738*
#230, *1505*
#419, *910*
#562, *911*
#566, *702, 706*

Resp. Rashi (ed. Elfenbein)
#70, *784*
#74, *1502, 1504*
#248, *786*

Resp. Rema
#10, *61*
#25, *1347*
#33, *28, 30*
#35, *1360*
#40, *1349, 1512*
#48, *1351*
#57, *791*
#67, *1263*
#73, *723*
#81, *1349, 1512*
#100, *1250*
#108, *1760*
#109, *17*
#124, *1521*
#131, *1360*

Resp. Reshakh
I, #134, *1369–1370*

Resp. Ri Migash
#106, *63*
#114, *25, 1181–1182, 1471, 1512*
#118, *63*

Resp. Ribash
#5, *791, 1501–1502, 1505*
#21, *711*
#40, *1512*
#43, *63*
#44, *1230*
#46, *1513*
#46–52, *1007, 1506*
#47, *1512*
#52, *1513*
#58, *1510, 1513*
#66, *1512*
#79, *1502*
#80, *1502*
#94, *63*
#97, *63*
#101, *1505*
#105, *711, 797, 884*
#106, *656*

#107, *806*
#110, *652*
#119, *542*
#120, *1506*
#124, *975*
#127, *1505*
#128, *1513*
#130, *63*
#146, *940, 1506*
#153, *1512*
#157, *1512*
#159, *1507*
#168, *1509*
#170, *248, 605, 1507, 1700, 1715*
#175, *1502–1503, 1508–1509*
#177, *1508*
#178, *707*
#179, *1503*
#185, *707*
#193, *1476, 1512*
#194, *1512*
#195, *928*
#214, *797*
#228, *704, 797, 1475*
#234, *63, 695, 1509*
#236, *1845*
#238, *63*
#239, *63*
#249, *435, 471, 716–717, 729*
#251, *11, 694–695*
#257, *443*
#262, *1512*
#266, *63*
#268, *1476*
#269, *1476*
#270, *1476*
#271, *133, 668–669, 1381, 1476*
#272, *1477*
#277, *1512*
#299, *63*
#304, *468–471*
#305, *63, 708*
#309, *1502*
#311, *740*
#322, *63*
#328, *200, 1520*
#331, *462–464*
#345, *435, 711, 884, 917*
#362, *464*
#375–376, *1701*
#377, *859*
#378, *859*
#388, *745*
#390, *745*
#399, *639–640, 700, 712, 732–735, 753–754, 856–859, 864, 866–867, 871, 1005–1006, 1507*
#404, *1725*
#427, *63*
#467, *707*
#473, *1502*
#475, *776, 928–929, 1507*
#475–477, *738, 740*
#476, *705–706, 738, 740, 776*
#477, *768, 773–777, 1507, 1512*
#478, *711*
#480, *436*
#484, *119, 127, 709–710, 1461, 1534*
#490, *17, 1502*
#493, *711*
#510, *1502*

Resp. Ribash ha-Ḥadashot
#9, *65, 73, 175*

Resp. Ritba
#11, *439*
#50, *471*
#53, *430*
#82, *459, 1507*
#100, *1507*
#111, *1507*
#120, *459*
#131, *11, 17, 47, 692, 738*
#134, *445–448*
#146, *63*
#156, *1507*
#157, *465*
#164, *1509*
#180, *514*
#182 (220), *1508*
#190, *21*
#203, *439*

Resp. Seridei Esh
III, #41, *111*

Resp. Sha'ar Ephraim
#42, *1516–1517*

Resp. Sha'ot de-Rabbannan
#14, *707*

Resp. She'elat Ya'veẓ
II, #82, *1516*

She'elot u-Teshuvot min ha-Shamayim, *1517*

Resp. Shenei ha-Me'orim ha-Gedolim, *1518*

Sheva Einayim
pp. 60ff., *884*

Resp. Shevut Ya'akov
I, #145, *130, 1717*
II, ḤM #167, *1716, 1912*
III, ḤM #182, *1726*

Resp. Sho'el u-Meshiv
Mahadura Kamma, Part I, #44, *74*

Resp. Tashbeẓ
I
#1, *1505*
#15, *1536*
#21, *1505*
#23, *1507*
#50, *1506*
#51, *1506*
#56, *1509*
#58, *1505–1506*
#58–61, *1007*
#61, *865, 1005*
#62, *1508*
#72, *1225, 1465*
#73–80, *1509*
#81, *1005, 1509*
#85, *1475*
#93, *1508, 1515*
#94, *1508, 1510*
#95, *1510*
#96, *1510*
#100, *1507*
#123, *1005–1006, 1521*
#124, *1502*
#131, *861*
#133, *471, 700, 861–862*
#152, *1502, 1518*
#154, *862, 940*

Resp. Tashbeẓ *continued*
#158, *15, 71, 73, 133–135, 1521*
#158–162, *133*
#159, *714, 736*
#162, *1521*
#163, *1464*
#164, *1464*
#165, *1464*
#166, *1464*
#172, *1464*
II
#5, *471, 700, 859–861, 1465, 1473*
#15, *913*
#61, *454–456, 865*
#63, *708, 714, 737*
#83, *859*
#96, *1501*
#97, *1501*
#98, *713*
#103, *805*
#117, *1515*
#119, *1516*
#132, *707, 710, 734–735*
#153, *713*
#176, *63*
#196, *711*
#239, *707*
#256, *711*
#265, *806*
#290, *14*
#292, *1516, 1531*
#292, *tikkun* 3, *840*
#292, *tikkun* 7, *806*
#292, *tikkun* 8, *806*
#292, *tikkun* 9, *777, 806*
#292, *tikkun* 11, *777, 806*
#292, *tikkun* 12, *805*
III
#5, *63*
#8, *1518*
#13, *1701*
#15, *64, 605, 1701*
#18, *1518*
#24, *1515*
#73, *806*
#76, *1798*
#82, *146, 604–605*
#106, *1006*
#168, *96*
#190, *99–102, 120, 152–153, 1672*
#257, *1301*
#303, *806*
#325, *1518*
#327, *1301*

Temim De'im
#50, *71*
#61–62, *1471*
#203, *531*
#238, *1172–1174*

Terumat ha-Deshen
#195, *1521*
#196, *1521*
#218, *791*
#220, *788*
#281, *714*
#332, *913*
#338, *63*
#342, *778, 786, 923, 928–929, 942, 944*
#344, *703, 726, 749–750*
#345, *750*
#346, *750*
PESAKIM U-KHETAVIM
#19–21, *1510*
#40, *1519*
#42, *1519*
#47, *1507*
#55, *1507*
#60, *1511–1512*
#61, *1519*
#62, *791, 1502, 1504, 1519*
#63, *10*
#65, *10*
#67, *1507*
#73, *1509*
#83, *63, 1507*
#89, *1501*
#102, *1515*
#104, *63, 1515*
#124, *1511*
#128, *1501*
#130, *1507*
#138, *1501*
#161, *1507, 1511, 1519*
#175, *1501*
#214, *703, 791, 1501, 1505*
#220, *1507*
#221, *1510, 1519*
#222, *1507*
#232, *1519*
#252, *10, 671, 793*
#253, *671, 793*
#257, *1513–1514*
#260, *1504*
#261, *1502, 1504*
#262–264, *788*

Teshuvot ha-Geonim
ED. ASSAF
#105 (p. 95), *650*
#113 (p. 101), *657*
#158 (p. 81), *1158*
p. 75, *65*
pp. 125–126, *1098, 1131*
ED. HARKAVY
#9, *95*
#349, *1098*
#353, *95*
#434, *1098*
#594, *1471*

Teshuvot ha-Geonim, Ḥemdah Genuzah
#62, *647*
#65, *647–648*
#110, *1158*
#124, *95*

Teshuvot ha-Geonim, Sha'arei Teshuvah
#307, *889*

Teshuvot ha-Geonim, Sha'arei Ẓedek
Part IV, Sha'ar 1, #20, *73, 688, 894, 1746*
Part IV, Sha'ar 4, #15, *659*
Part IV, Sha'ar 4, #16, *685–686, 771*
Part IV, Sha'ar 4, #17, *655*

Teshuvot Ḥakhmei Provence (ed. Sofer)
pp. 419–420, *70*
pp. 420ff., *69*
p. 421, *68*
pp. 426–427, *70*
p. 427, *65, 67*

Teshuvot u-Fesakim Shel ha-Rabad
#131 (ed. Kafaḥ, p. 176), *71*

Teshuvot u-Fesakim le-Rabbenu Avraham b. David
#141, *171*

Resp. Torat Emet
#207, *1283*

Resp. Torat Ḥayyim, *1458*

Tum'at Yesharim
#173, *796–797*

Resp. Ve-Shav ha-Kohen
#92, *756*

Resp. Yabi'a Omer
V, EH #1, *1809*
VI, EH #14, *1809*
VI, EH #25, *1818*

Resp. Yad ha-Levi, *977*

Resp. Yakhin u-Vo'az
I, #6, *14*
II, #12, *806*
II, #20, *863–864*
II, #46, *864*

Yam Gadol
#22, *925*

Sefer ha-Yashar le-Rabbenu Tam, Responsa Section
#24, *661*
#43–50, *910*
#45, par. 5, *786*
#46, par. 4, *1476*
#101, *1098*

Resp. Yaskil Avdi
II, Kunteres Aharon, EH #2, *1797*
VI, ḤM #8, *1824*

Resp. Yismaḥ Lev
EH, #15, *876*

Resp. Zekan Aharon
#2–4, *1506*

Resp. Ẓemaḥ Ẓedek
#2, *96–99, 725–727, 1715*
#9, *1420*
#28, *371*
#37, *928, 1501–1502, 1510*

Resp. Zera Anashim, *1518*

Resp. Zikhron Yehudah
#15, *1459, 1465*
#49, *1281*
#54, *1253*
#58, *11, 28, 47, 696*
#78, *777, 806*
#79, *11, 518, 698*
(end), *768*

Zikkaron la-Rishonim (Harkavy)
#182, *652*

Resp. Ziknei Yehudah (ed. Simonson)
#78, *814*

BOOKS OF ETHICS, PHILOSOPHY, HOMILIES, ETC.

Ahavat Ḥesed
beginning of ch. 9, *1630*

Derushei ha-Ẓelaḥ
Sermon #3, par. 12–14, *32–33*
Sermon #8, par. 10, *33*
Homily #8, par. 14, *1579*
Homily #22, par. 24, *1579*

Derashot ha-Ran
#7, *245, 263, 265*
#11, *56–58, 60, 64, 245–246, 265*

Diwan Shemu'el ha-Nagid, Ben Tehillim
p. 235, *43, 1164*

Eder ha-Yekar
pp. 13ff., *260, 1850*
pp. 31ff., *1100*
pp. 42ff., *203*

Edut bi-Yehosef
pp. 36–37, *1582*

Guide for the Perplexed (Moreh Nevukhim)
Part I, ch. 71, *226*
Part II, ch. 8, *1190*
Part III, ch. 12, *252*
Part III, ch. 34, *252*
Part III, ch. 41, *501*
Part III, ch. 49, *251*

Ḥafeẓ Ḥayyim
10:12, *1643*
II, 9:1, *1709*

Kuzari
Essay (Ma'amar), *3*
pars. 35ff., *202–203*
pars. 39–41, *265*

Ha-Nir (by Rabbi A.I. Kook)
p. 47, *1849–1850*

Ḥovot ha-Levavot
"Love of God" section, ch. 6, *1705*

Iggeret ha-Teshuvah
sec. 72, *1796*

Iggerot ha-Re'iyah
I, #103, *96, 265*

Keneh Ḥokhmah
Sermon on *Dayyanim*, pp. 25–26, *31–32*

Middot ha-Re'iyah
Ahavah, secs. 5, 10, *1852–1853*

Netivot Olam
Netiv ha-Torah, ch. 15, *1381*

Or ha-Shem (by Ḥasdai Crescas)
Introduction, p. 2, *1230*
p. 2a, *1123*

Orot ha-Kodesh
Vol 3, p. 318, *1853*
Vol. 3, preface to sec. 11, p. 27, *1853*
Vol. 3, sec. 16, p. 32, *1853*

Sefer ha-Ikkarim
3:14, *498*
3:23, *225–226, 241*

Sefer ha-Mikneh (by Joseph Rosheim)
pp. 7–9, 24–29, *11*

Sefer Ḥasidim
#1301, *64*

Sefer ha-Zikhronot (by Samuel Aboab)
Zikkaron 10:3, *14–15, 28, 34, 51*

Sefer Hazkarat Neshamot [Memorial Book] of the Community of Worms
Kovez al Yad, III, p. 1, *784*

Shenei Luḥot ha-Berit
SHA'AR HA-OTIYYOT
letter *kuf*, Kedushah 1393, s.v. Derekh erez, *1796*

Zekher Ẓaddik [Remembrance of a Righteous Man] (by Eliezer Katzenellenbogen)
SECTION MA'ALELEI ISH
p. 4ff., *1579*
pp. 7–9 ("Ẓiyyon be-Mishpat" sermon), *1579–1582*
p. 17, *1579*
p. 18, *1580*

ENACTMENTS

Book of Enactments of the Jewish Community of Cracow (ed. M. Balaban), in *Jahrbuch d. Jüdisch Literarischen Gesellschaft* [Jewish Literary Society Annual], X, pp. 296–360, XI, pp. 88–114, *821*

Pinkas ha-Medinah o Pinkas Va'ad ha-Kehillot ha-Rashiyyot bi-Medinat Lita [The Record Book of the Land or the Record Book of the Council of the Principal Jewish Communities of Lithuania] (ed. S. Dubnow)
Introduction, *819*
Enactment #37, *1668*
Enactment #205, *1726*
Enactment #364, *28*
Enactment #753, *445*
Enactment #758, *445*

Pinkas Hekhsherim Shel Kehillat Pozna [The Record Book of Kosher Food Certification of Posen] (ed. D. Evron), *823*

Pinkas Va'ad Arba Arazot [The Record Book of the Council of the Four Lands] (ed. I. Halpern)
Introduction, *818*
Preface, *818*
Enactment #125, *1665*

Sefer Takkanot Nikolsburg [The Book of the Enactments of Nikolsburg] (ed. Roth)
Introduction, *823*

Takkanot Candia ve-Zikhronotehah [The Enactments and Annals of Candia] (ed. A.S. Artom and D.A. Cassuto), *811–812*

Takkanot Medinat Mehrin [The Enactments of the Community of Moravia] (ed. I. Halpern)
Introduction, *820*
Enactment #176, *673, 756*
Enactment #265, *16*
Enactment #286, *756*
Enactment #292, *445*
Enactment #335, *756*

Enactments of Algeria (Algiers), *804–806, 839–840, 1531*
Enactments of Aragon, *797–798*
Enactments of Barcelona, *669, 748, 797*
Enactments of Bingen, *793–794*
Enactments of Boskowitz, *823*
Enactments of Candia (Crete), *811–813, 1240*
Enactment of Casalli, *872*
Enactments of the Council of Four Lands (*Va'ad Arba Arazot*), *818, 1665*
Enactments of Corfu, *817, 872*
Enactments of Cracow, *821–822*
Enactments of Damascus, *839, 874–877*
Enactments of Egypt, *809–810*
Enactments of Ferrara, *813, 816–817*
Enactments of Fez, *806–809, 845–846, 869–870, 1531*
Enactments of Florence, *816*
Enactments of Forli, *813–816*
Enactments of Frankfurt, *794–796*
Enactment of Ḥamah, *870*
Enactments of Helishuh, *823*
Enactments of Kremzir, *823*
Enactments of Leghorn (Livorno), *28–29*
Enactment of Lerida, *745*
Enactments of Lithuania, *28, 445, 818–819, 1668*
Enactment of Lucena, *743–744*
Enactments of Lvov, *823*
Enactments of Mainz, *793*
Enactments of Molina, *796–797, 839–842, 1531*
Enactments of Moravia, *445, 756, 819–820*
Enactments of Narbonne, *787, 836*
Enactments of Nikolsburg, *823*
Enactments of Nuremberg, *793*
Enactments of Posen, *823*

Enactment of Salonika, *865–869*
Enactment of Saragossa, *709, 745*
Enactments of "Shum" (Speyer, Worms, and Mainz), *788–789, 838, 1531*
Enactments of Spain, *838–839*
Enactments of Titkin, *823*
Enactment of Tlemcen, *862–863*
Enactments of Toledo, *796–797, 839–842, 1531*
Enactment of Tortosa, *856–859*
Enactments of Tribich, *823*
Enactments of Troyes, *786–788, 836–838*
Enactment of Tudela, *711, 745*
Enactments of Usha, *116–117, 486, 566–569*
Enactments of Valladolid, *8–9, 25–26, 798–804, 842–845*

Enactment of [King] David, *554*
Enactments of David b. Kalonymus, *788*
Enactments of Ezra, *556*
Enactment of Ḥayyim Or Zaru'a, *791*
Enactments of Hillel the Elder, *561–562*
Enactments of Joshua, *551–554*
Enactments of Maharam of Rothenburg, *789–790*
Enactments of Maimonides, *809–810*
Enactments of Rabban Gamaliel the Elder, *525–526, 563–566*
Enactments of Rabban Gamaliel of Yavneh, *566*
Enactments of Rabban Johanan b. Zakkai, *566, 570*
Enactments of Rabbenu Gershom Me'or ha-Golah, *293, 663–664, 674–675, 783–786, 811, 1858*
Enactments of Rabbenu Pereẓ of Corbeil, *789–791*
Enactments of Rabbenu Tam, *10, 17, 671, 786–788, 836–838*
Enactments of Rashi, *671, 786*
Enactments of Simeon b. Shataḥ, *559–561, 569–570*

Enactments of the Chief Rabbinate of the Land of Israel, *117, 801, 825–835, 1596–1601, 1609–1610, 1654–1655, 1807–1809*
Enactments of 1921, *801, 824–826, 1598–1599*
Enactments of 1944, *117, 828–833, 1599, 1609–1610,*
Enactments of 1950, *833–834, 1599, 1654–1655*
Procedural Enactments of 1943, *826–829, 834, 1599*

REFERENCE WORKS

Arukh ha-Shalem

s.vv. Agor, Agori, *13*
s.v. Amar (I, p. 128), *1088*
s.v. Halakh (III, p. 208), *93*
s.v. Hassi'a, Hassi'ah (III, p. 227; V, p. 355), *679*
s.v. Henpek, *613*

Works of Z.H. Chajes

DARKHEI HA-HORA'AH [METHODOLOGY OF DECISION MAKING], *1549*
II (Collected Writings of Maharaẓ Chajes, I, pp. 250–252), *95*
DARKHEI MOSHE [THE WAYS OF MOSES], *1231*
IMREI BINAH
#1, *95*
#10, *492*
MAVO HA-TALMUD [THE STUDENT'S GUIDE THROUGH THE TALMUD]
ch. 3 (pp. 21–28), *193*
ch. 4 (p. 29), *989*
ch. 12 (pp. 101–102), *492*
ch. 13 (pp. 105ff.), *533*
ch. 15 (pp. 120–125), *992, 997–998*
ch. 15 (p. 125), *991*
TIFERET LE-MOSHE [THE GLORY OF MOSES], *1231*
TORAT HA-NEVI'IM
ch. 1, "Elleh ha-Miẓvot," *264*
ch. 4, Ma'amar Torah She-be-al Peh [Essay on the Oral Law], *205, 208*
HORA'AT SHA'AH
p. 24b, *504*
pp. 40ff., *533, 536*
CH. 7, "DIN MELEKH YISRA'EL" [THE LAW OF THE KING OF ISRAEL]
pp. 43–49, *487*
pp. 46b–47a, *60*
BAL TOSIF *97–498*
ch. 2, *502*
I, p. 79, *498*
I, p. 96, *498*
LO TASUR (pp. 97–111) *486*

Dor De'ah [An Enlightened Generation]

pp. 81–86, *1579, 1582*

Iggeret Rav Sherira Gaon [Epistle of Rabbi Sherira Gaon] (ed. B.M. Lewin)

p. 39, *1047*
p. 40, *1087*
p. 41, *1087*
pp. 69–71, *1094*
p. 70, *1093*
p. 95, *1093*
p. 97, *1093*
p. 103, *1150*

Kehillat Ya'akov (by Israel Jacob Algazi)
II, "Leshon Benei Adam", *442*
II, Ma'aneh Lashon, Leshon Ḥakhamim, letters *alef* to *tav*, *408, 415*

Korei ha-Dorot (by David Conforte, ed. Kassel)
p. 41a, *1371*

Likkutim mi-Divrei Yosef le-R. Yosef b. Yiẓḥak Sambari [Selections from *Divrei Yosef* by Joseph b. Isaac Sambari], in A. Neubauer, Seder ha-Ḥakhamim ve-Korot ha-Yamim [Medieval Jewish Chronicles], I
pp. 115–162, *1557*
p. 124, *1224*
p. 156, *1543*

M.H. Luzzatto, Ma'amar ha-Ikkarim [Essay on Basic Principles]
"On the Question of the Oral Law and the Talmud," *502*

Malmad ha-Talmidim [A Goad to Scholars]
Mishpatim, pp. 71b–72b, *138–139*

Or ha-Ḥayyim (by H. Michael)
pp. 143–144, *1258*
p. 224, *1306*
pp. 259–260, *1459*
p. 262, *1285*
p. 488, *1285*
p. 489ff., *1302–1303*
pp. 506–507, *1520*
p. 579, *1277*

Sedeh Ḥemed
Divrei Ḥakhamim #81 (V, p. 404), *1022*
VI, Rules for Decision Making #2, subpars. 9, 12, 13 (p. 60b *et seq.*), *1316*
VI, Rules of the *Posekim*, par. 10:3, *1275*
Kelalei ha-Posekim #14, Kelalei ha-Rema, subpar. 4 (VI, p. 99), *1361*
Rules of Decision, ch. 15, par. 36 (VI, p. 108b), *1265*

Seder Ḥakhamim ve-Korot ha-Yamim [Medieval Jewish Chronicles] (by A. Neubauer)
I, p. 59, *1100*
I, p. 73, *43*
I, p. 78, *43*
I, pp. 115–162, *1557*
I, p. 124, *1224*
I, p. 156, *1543*
I, p. 178, *1156*
II, p. 88, *1469*

Seder Olam Zuta, in A. Neubauer, Seder ha-Ḥakhamim ve-Korot ha-Yamim [Medieval Jewish Chronicles]
I, p. 178, *1156*

Seder Yuḥasin ha-Shalem (by Abraham Zacuto)
p. 225, *804*
end, *1541*

Sefer ha-Kabbalah (by Abraham Ibn Daud)
SEFER HA-QABALLAH, TRANS. AND ED. G. COHEN
p. 45, *1094*
pp. 47–48, *1150, 1152–1153*
pp. 58–59, *1164–1165*
p. 84, *1171*
IN A. NEUBAUER, SEDER HA-ḤAKHAMIM VE-KOROT HA-YAMIM [MEDIEVAL JEWISH CHRONICLES], I
p. 59, *1100*
p. 73, *43*
p. 78, *43*

Sefer ha-Keritut (by Samson of Chinon)
ch. "Netivot Olam," *317*

Shalshelet Rabbanei Saloniki [The Rabbinical Line of Salonika] (by David Pipano), at the end of his book *Ḥagor ha-Efod*
p. 3a, par. 11, *865*
p. 4b, par. 15, *865*

Shem ha-Gedolim (by Ḥayyim Joseph David Azulai)
BOOKS
Letter *aleph*, #16, *1306*
Letter *bet*, #31, *1373*
Letter *bet*, #59, *1312, 1369–1370*
Letter *vav*, #3–4, *1304*
Letter *zayin*, #23, *1321*
Letter *tet*, #12, *1344*
Letter *lamed*, #12, *1403*
Letter *mem*, #165, *1254*
Letter *ayin*, #32, *1267, 1269*
Letter *pe*, #120, *1285*
Letter *pe*, #137, *1431*
Letter *ẓadi*, #4, *1308*
Letter *ẓadi*, #32, *1307*
Letter *ẓadi*, #37, *1307*
Letter *shin*, #27, *1248*
Letter *shin*, #75, *1371–1372*
PERSONS
Letter *aleph*, #130, *1258*
Letter *ḥet*, #3, *1431*
Letter *ḥet*, #20, *1307*
Letter *yod*, #165, *1344*
Letter *yod*, #208, *1285*
Letter *yod*, #382, *1272*
Letter *yod*, #402, *1516*
Letter *mem*, #49, *1308*
Letter *mem*, #98, *1393*
Letter *mem*, #102, *1302*
Letter *shin*, #19, *1277*
s.v. Rabbanit, *1798*

Yad Malakhi
I, KELALEI HA-ALEF
#17, *269*
#72, *95*

I, KELALEI HA-DALET
#144, *315, 391*
#169, *269*
II, KELALEI HA-RAMBAM [PRINCIPLES OF MAIMONIDES]
#4, *1205*
II, KELALEI RASHI VE-TOSAFOT VE-HA-ROSH [PRINCIPLES OF RASHI, TOSAFOT, AND ASHERI]
#32, *1252*
#36, *1253*
II, KELALEI HA-RIBAH U-MOHARIKA [PRINCIPLES OF THE *TURIM* AND CARO]
#5–10, 13, 23, 27, 30, *1286*
#21, *1285*
#42, *1546*
II, KELALEI HA-SHULHAN ARUKH U-REMA [PRINCIPLES OF THE *SHULḤAN ARUKH* AND REMA]
#1, *1409*
#2, *1371–1373*
#9–17, *1339*
II, KELALEI SHE'AR HA-MEḤABBERIM VE-HA-MEFORSHIM [PRINCIPLES OF THE OTHER AUTHORS AND COMMENTATORS]
#19, *1272*

LEGISLATION—STATE OF ISRAEL

Statutes

Adoption of Children Law, 1960, *1663, 1664, 1671*
Adoption of Children Law, 1981, *828, 1671, 1764*
Agency Law, 1965, *1691, 1692*
Amendment of Evidence Ordinance Law, 1955, *1703*
Amendment of Law and Administration Ordinance Law (No. 14) 1972, *1729*
Arbitration Law, 1968, *1704, 1818*
Bailees Law, 1967, *1692, 1693, 1694, 1695, 1696*
Bankruptcy Ordinance (New Version), 1980, *1888*
Basic Law, Israel Lands, 1960, *1651, 1842*
Basic Law: The Knesset, *1842*
Capacity and Guardianship Law, 1962, *1622, 1625, 1663, 1665, 1666, 1667, 1668, 1669, 1670, 1753, 1764, 1909*
Citizenship Law, 1952, *1690*
Chief Rabbinate of Israel Law, 1980, *1758*
Civil Procedure (Amendments) Law, 1963, *1703*
Civil Wrongs Ordinance (Amendment No. 3) 1959, *1645*
Civil Wrongs Ordinance (New Version), 1968, *629, 1665, 1729*
Consumer Protection Law, 1981, *1691*
Continuity of Debate Law, 1964, *1636*
Contract for Services Law, 1974, *1692, 1729*
Contracts Law (General Part), 1973, *166, 1692, 1716, 1717, 1719, 1720, 1729, 1734, 1736, 1875*
Contracts Law (Remedies for Breach of Contract) 1970, *166, 1729*
Cooperative Houses Law, 1952, *1627*
Copyright Ordinance, *1692*
Courts Law, 1957, *1646, 1758, 1759, 1832, 1834*
Courts Law (Consolidated Version), 1984, *1646, 1691*
Crime Register and Rehabilitation of Offenders Law, 1981, *1707, 1708, 1861*
Criminal Law Ordinance, 1963, *1729, 1868*
Criminal Procedure Law, 1965, *1704, 1705, 1845*
Criminal Procedure Law (Consolidated Version) 1982, *1707, 1742, 1842, 1845*
Defamation Law, 1962, *1642*
Defective Products (Liability) Law, 1980, *1691*
Development Authority (Transfer of Property) Law, 1950, *1652*
Evidence Ordinance (New Version), 1971, *1691*
Execution [of Judgments] Law, 1967, *1638*
Family Law Amendment (Maintenance) Law, 1959, *833, 1625, 1653, 1660, 1662–1663, 1669*
Family Law Amendment (Maintenance) Law, 1976, *1806*
Fiduciary Law, 1975, *1691*
Foundations of Law Act, 1980, *1624, 1627, 1707, 1729, 1731, 1740–1743, 1751, 1828–1838, 1841–1844, 1847, 1854, 1857, 1860, 1861, 1863, 1864, 1866, 1867, 1868, 1870, 1871–1875, 1877, 1880–1890, 1894–1897, 1918, 1921, 1923, 1931, 1932, 1934–1938, 1940, 1942, 1944, 1946*
Gift Law, 1968, *1641, 1724*
Guarantee Law, 1967, *1691, 1721, 1723*
Hire and Loan Law, 1971, *183, 1691*
Interpretation Law, 1981, *276, 323, 442*
Interpretation Ordinance (New Version), 1974, *276, 323, 442*
Judges Law, 1953, *1645*
Key-Money Law, 1958, *1622*
Kosher Food for Soldiers Ordinance, 1949, *1647*

Statutes *continued*
Land Law, 1969, *166, 1628, 1709–1712, 1714, 1729*
Law and Administration Ordinance, 1948, *232, 538, 1143, 1620–1622, 1646, 1656, 1832*
Law of Return, 1950, *1647–1651*
Law of Return (Amendment No. 2), 1970, *1688*
Litigation between Spouses (Regulation) Law, 1969, *629–630*
Marriage Age Law, 1950, *834, 1653–1655, 1657, 1660, 1665*
Marriage Age (Amendment) Law, 1960, *834, 1654*
Military Justice Law, 1955, *1707*
Names Law, 1956, *1685*
Obsolete Legislation (Repeal) Law, 1984, *1829*
Penal Law, 1977, *1706, 1736, 1924,*
Penal Law Revision (Abolition of the Death Penalty for Murder) Law, 1954, *1615*
Penal Law Revision (Bribery) Law, 1950, *1640–1642*
Penal Law Revision (Bribery) Law, 1952, *1642*
Pig-Raising Prohibition Law, 1962, *1647*
Pledges Law, 1967, *1691*
Population Registry Law, 1965, *1689, 1690, 1777, 1778*
Prescription [Statute of Limitations] Law, 1958, *1727*
Procedural Enactments for the Rabbinical Courts of the Land of Israel, 1943, *826ff., 846*
Procedural Enactments for the Rabbinical Courts of Israel, 1960, *834*
Prohibition of Defamation Law, 1965, *1630, 1644, 1850*
Protection of Privacy Law, 1981, *1691, 1856, 1857, 1858*
Public Lands (Removal of Squatters) Law, 1981, *1712*
Rabbinical Courts Jurisdiction (Marriage and Divorce) Law, 1953, *111, 120, 831, 1616, 1652, 1753, 1754, 1758, 1765, 1770–1772, 1775, 1839, 1904, 1929*
Repeal of Mejelle Law, 1984, *1829*
Restoration of Lost Property Law, 1973, *1743, 1745, 1746, 1747, 1749, 1750, 1836, 1865*
Rules of Evidence Amendment (Warning of Witnesses and Abolition of Oath) Law, 1980, *1697, 1706, 1707, 1939*
Rules of Evidence Amendment (Warning of Witnesses and Abolition of Oath) Law, 1984, *1707*
Safekeeping of Property Law, 1965, *1692, 1693*
Sale Law, 1968, *183, 1693*
Severance Pay Law, 1963, *1633, 1694*
Spouses (Property Relations) Law, 1973, *1803*
State Property Law, 1951, *1652*
Succession Law, 1965, *829, 1671, 1674, 1678, 1679, 1681–1683, 1685, 1687, 1688, 1692, 1728, 1753, 1818, 1876–1879, 1881, 1882*
Tenants Protection Law (Consolidated Version), 1972, *166, 1758, 1820, 1821, 1823, 1824, 1837*
Transfer of Obligations Law, 1969, *1691*
Unjust Enrichment Law, 1979, *1696, 1837*
Wage Delay Prohibition Law, 1955, *1629, 1630, 1694*
Wage Protection Law, 1958, *1629, 1694*
Woman's Equal Rights Law, *1653, 1656, 1657, 1660, 1665–1667, 1671, 1684, 1743, 1757, 1758, 1760–1762, 1788–1791, 1795, 1802–1806, 1824*

Bills
Application of Principles of Jewish Law Bill, 1958, *1622*
Capacity and Guardianship Bill (No. 456), 1961, *1664, 1907*
Civil Wrongs Ordinance (Amendment No. 3) Bill (No. 380, 1955), *1645*
Contracts Bill (General Part), 1970, *1718, 1719*
Cooperative Houses Bill, 1952, *1627–1628*
Copyright Ordinance (Amendment No. 4) Bill (No. 1517, 1981), *1691*
Courts Bill, 1955, *1646*
Courts Law (Amendment No. 13) Bill (No. 1478, 1980), *1691*
Crime Register and Rehabilitation of Offenders Bill (No. 1514, 1981), *1708*
Criminal Code Ordinance (Amendment) Bill (No. 31, 1950), *1654*
Defamation Bill, (No. 504, 1962), *1642, 1643*
Defamation (Amendment) Bill (No. 693, 1966), *1644*
Execution of Judgments (Bill No. 659, 1965), *1638*

Family Law Amendment (Maintenance) Bill (Amendment) (No. 1168, 1975), *1638*
Family Law Amendment (Maintenance) Bill (Amendment) (No. 267, 1956), *1660*
Family Law Amendment (Maintenance) Bill (Amendment) (Amendment #2) 1980, *1806*
Foundations of Law Bill, 1980, *1921*
Gift Bill, (No. 669, 1965), *1724*
Guarantee Bill (No. 632, 1964), *1722*
Labor Contracts Bill (No. 1718, 1985), *1635*
Land Code Bill, 1964, *1709*
Law of Return Bill (No. 48, 1950), *1647*
Limitations Bill (No. 312, 1957), *1724–1726*
Penal Law (General Part) Bill, 1980, *1927*
Penal Law Revision (Bribery and Rewards) Bill, 1950, *1640–1642*
Protection of Privacy Bill, 1980, *1857, 1859*
Repeal of Mejelle Bill (No. 1681, 1984), *1829*
Safekeeping of Property Bill (No. 676, 1965), *1692*
Severance Pay Bill, (No. 493, 1962), *1633*
Succession Law Bill (No. 334, 1958), *1672, 1675, 1676, 1679, 1680*
Unjust Enrichment Bill, (No. 1353, 1978), *1696*
Wage Delay Prohibition Bill, 1955, *1629*
Wage Protection Bill, (No. 280, 1957), *1629*
Woman's Equal Rights Bill, (No. 75, 1951), *1658*

Draft Proposals for Israeli Legislation

Draft Constitution, 1949, *1621–1622*
Draft Evidence Bill, 1952, *1625, 1702*
Draft Individual and Family Bill, 1955, *1625, 1660*
Draft Succession Bill, 1952, *1625, 1626, 1674, 1675, 1677, 1678, 1679, 1680, 1683, 1686, 1877, 1920*

BRITISH MANDATORY LEGISLATION

Arbitration Ordinance, 1926, *1593, 1818*
Palestine Order-in-Council, 1922,
  Article 46, *1611, 1617, 1621, 1622, 1623, 1624, 1662, 1669, 1672, 1728, 1729, 1732, 1734, 1738–39, 1828–1831, 1864, 1869, 1886, 1887, 1888, 1889, 1941*
  Articles 47, 51–57, 64–65, *827, 1612, 1762, 1766, 1769*
Civil Wrongs Ordinance, 1944–1947, *628, 1612, 1617–1618, 1642, 1869*
Courts Ordinance, 1940, *1762*
Criminal Law Ordinance, 1936, *1617, 1642, 1702, 1729, 1869, 1925*
Imprisonment for Debt Ordinance, *1636*
Succession Ordinance, 1923, *827, 828, 829, 1399, 1684, 1688, 1760*
  Second Supplement (Enactment #182, Procedural Enactments of the Chief Rabbinate), *829*

OTTOMAN LEGISLATION

Civil Procedure Code, 1879, *1612*
Land Law, 1858, *1709, 1710, 1712, 1714, 1918*
Mejelle, *1612, 1721, 1722, 1829*

OTHER LEGISLATION

Assyrian Code, *310*
Code of Hammurabi (Babylonia), *197, 310, 1013*
Code Napoleon, *1141*
French Civil Code, *1734*
German Bürgerliches Gesetzbuch, *1721, 1733, 1734, 1735, 1918, 1925*
25 Hen. VIII (Eng.) c. 22, *235*
Italian Civil Code, *1675, 1734*
Lex Aquilia (Rome), *292*
Model Probate Code (U.S.), *1681*
Nordic Draft Code, 1963, *1721–1722, 1939*
Prussian Code (late 18th century), *1141*
Statute of Elizabeth, 1571 [Fraudulent Conveyances], *1885***ff.**
Swiss Zivilgesetzbuch, 1941, *1721, 1722, 1734, 1918, 1939*
Twelve Tables (Rome), *290, 292, 310*
Uniform Simultaneous Death Act (U.S.), *1681*

DIVREI HA-KENESET [KNESSET RECORD]

4 DK (1950),
  p. 638, *1655*
  p. 639, *1654, 1655*
  p. 655, *1654*
  p. 659, *1656*
  p. 661, *1654*
  pp. 665–666, *1656*
  p. 667, *1656*

DIVREI HA-KENESET [KNESSET RECORD] *continued*
5 DK (1950),
p. 1705, *1654*
p. 1726, *1654*
p. 1740, *1654*
p. 1832, *1654*
6 DK 1207ff., 2035ff. (1950), *1647*
7 DK 354, 361 (1951), *1634*
8 DK (1951),
p. 761, *1627*
p. 765, *1622, 1628*
p. 766, *1628*
p. 771, *1628*
pp. 771–775, *1628*
p. 775, *1622*
p. 1201, *1634*
8A DK (1951),
p. 802, *1640*
p. 803, *1641*
p. 815, *1641*
p. 817, *1641*
p. 818, *1641*
p. 819, *1642*
9 DK (1951),
p. 2007, *1658*
p. 2090, *1658*
p. 2100, *1656*
p. 2102, *1658*
pp. 2105–2106, *1657*
pp. 2116–2117, *1658*
p. 2118, *1656*
p. 2124, *1656*
pp. 2125–2126, *1658*
p. 2129, *1656*
p. 2132, *1658*
p. 2168, *1660*
p. 2187, *1658–1660*
p. 2193, *1658*
p. 2196, *1659*
11B DK 1413 (1952), *1642*
12 DK 2786 (1952), *1622*
13 DK 266–267, *1622*
15 DK 823 (1954), *1647*
17 DK 1712 (1955), *1646*
18 DK 1659–1660, 1672 (1955), *1629*
19 DK 886–889 (1956), *1629*
20 DK (1956),
p. 1079, *1634*
pp. 1933–1934, *1661*
p. 1934, *1661*
p. 1942, *1661*
p. 1944, *1662*
p. 1945, *1661*
p. 1947, *1662*
pp. 1968–1969, *1661*
p. 1974, *1661*
21 DK (1957),
p. 373, *1629, 1630*
p. 376, *1629, 1630*
p. 380, *1630*
p. 385, *1630*
p. 390, *1630*
p. 398, *1630*
P. 400, *1630*
P. 404, *1630*
P. 406, *1630*
P. 1082, *1634*
22 DK 1623 (1957), *1634*
23 DK (1958),
pp. 93, 100–101, 130, 131, 257, 259, *1635*
p. 1234, *1630*
24 DK (1958),
p. 2105, *1675*
p. 2106, *1679*
p. 2140, *1688*
p. 2141, *1686*
p. 2181, *1683*
p. 2182, *1683*
p. 2192, *1680*
p. 2357, *1679*
p. 2358, *1686*
p. 2478, *1622*
p. 2513, *2514*
25 DK 231, 232 (1958), *1622*
26 DK (1959),
pp. 1123–1124, *1670*
pp. 1126–1127, *1662*
p. 1138, *1662*
p. 1147, *1661, 1663*
28 DK (1960),
p. 9, *1654*
p. 10, *1654–1655*
p. 23, *1654–1655*
p. 24, *1654–1655*
p. 26, *1654–1655*
p. 29, *1654–1655*
p. 356, *1679*
p. 435, *1688*
p. 441, *1677*
p. 442, *1680*
p. 465, *1684*
p. 466, *1676*
p. 478, *1677*
p. 569, *1686*
pp. 643–644, *1645*
p. 645, *1646*
p. 711, *1646*
29 DK (1960),
pp. 1781, 1783, 1784, 1786, 1789, 1827, 1833, 1836, 1862, 1863, *1636*
pp. 1916–1917, *1651*
p. 2111, *1637*
32 DK (1961),
pp. 46–47, *1665*
p. 48, *1666, 1667*
p. 49, *1668*
p. 51, *1669*
p. 54, *1669*
p. 55, *1669*
pp. 56–57, *1622, 1669*
p. 156, *1670*
pp. 158–159, *1670*
pp. 160, *1670*
p. 173, *1671*
p. 190, *1671*
pp. 292–293, *1670*
p. 407, *1669*
p. 413, *1670*
p. 552, *1671*
p. 959, *1677*
p. 960, *1688*
p. 962, *1680, 1683*
p. 966, *1688*
33 DK (1962),
p. 1050, *1633*
p. 1066, *1688*
p. 1068, *1686*
p. 1070, *1634*
pp. 1081–1082, *1634*
p. 1160, *1634*
pp. 1161–1163, *1634*
p. 1300, *1634*
p. 1303, *1634*
34 DK (1962),
p. 3078, *1670, 1908*
p. 3081, *1665*
p. 3086, *1670, 1908*
pp. 3095, 3096, 3140, *1671*
37 DK (1962–1963),

pp. 2401, 2402, 2404, ***1643***
p. 2454, ***1644***
p. 2460, ***1644***
p. 2462, ***1630***
p. 2572, ***1644***
p. 2581, ***1644***
40 DK 2131, 2278, 2282, 2342 (1964), ***1709***
41 DK 475–477, 477–478, 479–480, 664, 667–669, 669–670 (1965), ***1691***
42 DK (1965),
p. 952, ***1687***
p. 953, ***1681***
p. 954, ***1675***
p. 958, ***1683***
p. 964, ***1676***
p. 970, ***1683***
p. 972, ***1676***
p. 974, ***1676***
p. 997, ***1683***
p. 1005, ***1680, 1683***
pp. 1007–1008, ***1686, 1687***
p. 1008, ***1687***
p. 1031, ***1688***
p. 1115, ***1687***
p. 1116, ***1688***
43 DK (1965),
p. 2370, ***1704***
p. 2434, ***1704***
p. 2435, ***1704***
pp. 2525–2526, ***1691***
pp. 2528, 2567, 2568, ***1638***
44 DK (1966),
p. 38, ***1691***
pp. 215–218, 324–327, ***1693***
46 DK (1966),
p. 1707, ***1622***
p. 2451, ***1644***
48 DK 1730 (1967), ***1644***
49 DK (1967),
p. 2148, ***1693***
p. 2149, ***1693***
pp. 2926–2927, ***1639***
52 DK 2349–2351 (1968), ***1724***
55 DK (1969),
p. 3759, ***1713***
pp. 3811–3812, ***1714***
p. 3831, ***1691***
59 DK 273–275, 280–282, 288–289, 528–530 (1971), ***1691***
73 DK 2896 (1985), ***1691***
83 DK 3917 (1978), ***1696***
84 DK 1113 (1979), ***1696***
85 DK 1303 (1979), ***1691***
88 DK (1980),
p. 1821, ***1832***
p. 1828, ***1832***
p. 1836, ***1832***
p. 2146, ***1930***
p. 2342, ***1930***
89 DK (1980),
p. 3487, ***1691***
pp. 3487–3488, ***1857***
p. 3494, ***1857***
p. 4030, ***1930***
p. 4099, ***1832***
90 DK (1981),
p. 48, ***1691***
pp. 310–313, ***1691***
p. 319, ***1691***
91 DK (1981),
p. 1892, ***1708***
p. 2153, ***1691***
DK 10th Knesset, 2d Session (1982),
83rd Sitting, p. 2319, ***1709***
99th Sitting, p. 2775, ***1627, 1895***

CASES

A. v. B. (1943), Warhaftig, Osef Piskei ha-Din, p. 20, ***1880***
A. v. B. (1945), Warhaftig, Osef Piskei ha-Din, p. 63, ***1604***
A. v. B. (1945), Warhaftig, Osef Piskei ha-Din, p. 86, ***1604***
A. v. B. (1945), Warhaftig, Osef Piskei ha-Din, p. 110, ***926***
A. v. B. (1947), Warhaftig, Osef Piskei ha-Din, p. 148, ***832***
A. v. B., 1 P.D.R. 65 (1954), ***982***
A. v. B., 1 P.D.R. 81 (1954), ***1785, 1786, 1787***
A. v. B., 1 P.D.R. 239 (1953), ***1803***
A. v. B., 2 P.D.R. 65 (1956), ***833***
A. v. B., 2 P.D.R. 97 (1957), ***1803***
A. v. B., 2 P.D.R. 220 (1957), ***1787***
A. & B. v. C., 3 P.D.R. 179 (1959), ***833***
A. v. B., 4 P.D.R. 3 (1959), ***833***
A. v. B., 4 P.D.R. 289 (1966), ***1822***
A. v. B., 4 P.D.R. 346 (1962), ***920, 1822***
A. v. B., 5 P.D.R. 132 (1962), ***158***
A. v. B., 5 P.D.R. 219 (1964), ***1776***
A. v. B., 5 P.D.R. 258 (1965), ***1821, 1822***
A. v. B., 6 P.D.R. 376 (1967), ***1821, 1822***
A. v. B., 7 P.D.R. 10 (1967), ***1797***
A. v. B., 7 P.D.R. 332 (1969), ***1822***
A. v. B., 9 P.D.R. 251 (1974), ***1796***
A. v. B., 10 P.D.R. 168 (1975), ***1814, 1821***
A. v. B., 10 P.D.R. 273 (1975), ***1822***
A. v. B., 11 P.D.R. 193 (1976), ***1806***
A. v. Management of the General Old Age Home, Jerusalem, 4 P.D.R. 126 (1960), ***926***
In re A.B., 7 P.D.R. 175 (1968), ***1754***
A. Building Co. v. Administration of Yeshiva C., 6 P.D.R. 249 (1966), ***1821***
Adar v. Adar, 42(iii) P.D. 347 (1988), ***1741***

CASES *continued*
Administration of Yeshivah B. v. Trustees of Endowment A. (1944), Warhaftig, Osef Piskei ha-Din, p. 33, ***1604***
Afanjar v. State of Israel, 33(iii) P.D. 141 (1979), ***1737, 1836, 1924, 1925, 1927***
Agudat Yisra'el v. Mafdal, Rehovot Branch, 6 P.D.R. 166 (1966), ***707***
Al Baḥiri v. State of Israel, 37(iii) P.D. 169 (1983), ***698***
Ali v. Sasson, 36(iii) P.D. 281 (1982), ***1696, 1731***
Ali v. State of Israel, 37(iii) P.D. 169 (1983), ***1740***
Alon v. Government of Israel, 36(iv) P.D. 449 (1982), ***262–263, 1740***
Aloni v. Minister of Justice, 41(ii) P.D. 1 (1987), ***1740, 1861, 1862***
Alperowitz v. Mizraḥi, 34(iv) P.D. 729 (1980), ***436, 1739***
Altegar v. Mayor and Local Council of Ramat Gan, 20(i) P.D. 29 (1966), ***704***
Amado v. Director of Immigrant Camp, 4 P.D. 4 (1950), ***1764***
Amar v. Perez, 42(iii) P.D. 485 (1988), ***1741***
Amidar v. Aharon, 32(ii) P.D. 337 (1978), ***156, 1731, 1739, 1837***
Amrani v. Rabbinical Court of Appeals, 37(ii) P.D. 1 (1982), ***184***
Amsterdamer v. Moskovitz, 26(i) P.D. 793 (1972), ***1840***
Anderson v. Sorrell, 481 A.2d 766 (D.C. App. 1984), ***158***
Anonymous v. Anonymous, 26(i) P.D. 85 (1971), ***1764***
Anonymous v. Anonymous, 35(iii) P.D. 57 (1981), ***1739***
Anonymous v. Anonymous, 37(iv) P.D. 626 (1983), ***1820***
Anonymous v. Attorney General, 41(iii) P.D. 544 (1987), ***1741***
Anonymous v. Attorney General, 45(iii) P.D. 460 (1991), ***1742***
Anonymous v. State of Israel, 35(iv) P.D. 438 (1981), ***1739***
Ashdod Metals Refinery v. State of Israel, 34(ii) P.D. 182 (1979), ***1935***
Atias v. State of Israel, 43(iv) P.D. 170 (1989), ***1742***
Attorney General v. Anonymous, 42(ii) P.D. 661 (1988), ***1741, 1860***
Attorney General v. Yiḥya and Ora Abraham, 22(i) P.D. 29 (1968), ***1794***
Avner v. Mif'alei Rekhev Ashdod, [1977] 1 P.M. 444, ***1731***
Avneri v. Shapiro, 42(iv) P.D. 20 (1988), ***1645, 1741, 1850***
Azugi v. Azugi, 33(iii) P.D. 1 (1979), ***128, 1739, 1822***
B. v. A. (1944), Warhaftig, Osef Piskei ha-Din, p. 41, ***1604***
B. v. A. (1944), Warhaftig, Osef Piskei ha-Din, p. 71, ***826, 1810***
B. v. A. (1946), Warhaftig, Osef Piskei ha-Din, p. 132, ***1602–1603, 1754***
B. v. A., 9 P.D.R. 152 (1973), ***1809***
Bahan v. Rosenzweig, 22(i) P.D. 569 (1968), ***1935***
Balaban v. Balaban, 14 P.D. 285 (1960), ***1804***
Bank Kupat Am v. Hendeles, 34(iii) P.D. 57 (1980), ***6, 1692, 1743, 1745, 1746, 1748, 1749, 1865, 1871, 1929***
Baniel v. National Labor Court, 35(ii) P.D. 693 (1981), ***1731***
Barazani v. Barazani, 35(ii) P.D. 317 (1981), ***1731***
Barnet v. Barnet, 12(i) P.D. 565 (1957), ***630***
Becker v. Judge Hayyim Eilat, 32(iii) P.D. 370 (1978), ***64, 1704ff.***
Ben-Natan v. Negbi, 35(ii) P.D. 141 (1980), ***1731***
Ben Shaḥar v. Maḥlev, 27(ii) P.D. 449 (1973), 28(ii) P.D. 89 (1974), ***178, 1736, 1840***
Ben Shalom v. Central Elections Committee, 43(iv) P.D. 221, 264 (1989), ***1648–1651***
Beresford v. Minister of the Interior, 43(iv) P.D. 793 (1989), ***1690***
Berkowitz v. Klimmer, 36(iv) P.D. 57 (1982), ***1835***
Biazi v. Levi, 41(i) P.D. 446 (1988), ***1741, 1861***
Bilat v. Rabbi Goren, 29(i) P.D. 98 (1974), ***1758***
Bilgah v. Estate of Taft, [1976] 2 P.M. 25, ***1731***
Biton v. Halamish, 36(ii) P.D. 706 (1982), ***165***
Board of Trustees of Bank Leumi of Israel, Ltd. v. Director of Estate Taxation, 32(ii) P.D. 202 (1978), ***443***
Boehm v. Mayor of Tel Aviv, 3 P.M. 98 (1948), ***328***
Boronovsky v. Chief Rabbis of Israel, 25(i) P.D. 7 (1971), ***1758, 1760, 1791***
Boyer v. Shikkun Ovedim, 38(ii) P.D. 561 (1984), ***164, 1727, 1740***

Bridges v. Hawkesworth, 15 Jur. 1079, 21 L.J.Q.B. 75 (1851), [1853–1860] All E.R. 122, *1745*
Brill v. Attorney General, 32(i) P.D. 98 (1977), *1879*
Brook v. B., [1861] 9 H.L.C. 193, *235*
Carmi v. State's Attorney, 44(i) P.D. 353 (1990), *1709, 1861*
Clark v. Minister of the Interior, 27(iii) P.D. 148 (1973), *1647*
S. Cohen and Company v. Capun, 7 P.L.R. 80, 1 I.S.C.J. 63, 7 C.L.R. 61 (1940), *1633*
Cohen v. Cohen, 25(ii) P.D. 327 (1971), *1804*
Cohen v. District Rabbinical Court, 26(i) P.D. 227 (1972), *1777, 1778*
Cohen v. Minister of Defense, 16 P.D. 1023 (1962), *1833*
Cohen and Buslik v. Attorney General, 8 P.D. 4 (1954), *1769*
Custodian of Abandoned Property v. Na'im and Khalil Abud, 16 P.D. 2649 (1962), *628*
Dan, Ltd. v. Attorney General, 20(iv) P.D. 253 (1966), *462, 1728*
Dananashvili v. State of Israel, 41(ii) P.D. 281 (1987), *1741*
David v. Disciplinary Court of Israel Bar Association, 36(i) P.D. 779 (1982), *1740*
Deckel v. Minister of Finance, 45(i) P.D. 28 (1990), *1742*
De Nicols v. Curlier, [1900] A.C. 21, *1483*
Dicker v. Moch, 32(ii) P.D. 141 (1978), *1736, 1836*
Edrei v. Gedalyahu, 36(iv) P.D. 281 (1982), *1720*
Efrat v. State of Israel, 35(iv) P.D. 729 (1981), *1739*
Ephraim v. State of Israel, 43(ii) P.D. 578 (1989), *1742*
Epstein v. Aharoni, 15 P.D. 682 (1960), *629, 630*
Feld v. State of Israel, 33(i) P.D. 540 (1979), *1692, 1739*
Estate of Finkelstein v. Finkelstein, 22(i) P.D. 618 (1968), *1739*
Flato-Sharon v. State of Israel, 38(ii) P.D. 757 (1984), *1642, 1731*
Frank v. Belelius, 1 P.D.R. 353 (1955), *1790*
Fried v. Fried, 36(ii) P.D. 695 (1982), *1816, 1818*
Friedman v. Savorai, 4 P.D.R. 391 (1962), *158*
Fund for the Movement of Progressive Judaism in Israel v. Minister of Religions, 43(ii) P.D. 661 (1989), *1742, 1758, 1766, 1779*
Gabbai v. Valis, 36(i) P.D. 449 (1982), *1739*
Gali v. State of Israel, 40(iv) P.D. 169 (1986), *1731, 1740, 1861*
Gindi v. State of Israel, 40(i) P.D. 449 (1986), *1846*
Gitiyah v. Chief Rabbinate of Israel, 22(i) P.D. 290 (1968), *1791*
Goldberg v. Chairman of Ramat ha-Sharon Municipal Council, 34(iv) P.D. 85 (1980), *707, 1739*
Goldstein v. Neuman, 5 P.M. 329 (1950), *1633*
Gorfinkel and Ḥaklai v. Minister of the Interior, 17 P.D. 2048 (1963), *111, 1771, 1774, 1775, 1776, 1777, 1780*
Gottliffe v. Edelston, [1930] 2 K.B. 378, *629*
Grätz Vertriebsgesellschaft v. Muhamad Ḥafez Dagoani, 35(ii) P.D. 351 (1981), *1731*
Gutman v. District Rabbinical Court, Tel Aviv-Jaffa, 34(i) P.D. 443 (1979), *121, 1739, 1755*
Haber v. Rabbinical Court of Appeals, 32(iii) P.D. 324 (1978), *121*
Ḥadashot, Ltd. v. Minister of Defense, 38(ii) P.D. 447 (1984), *1740, 1833*
Haj Yiḥya v. State of Israel, 45(v) P.D. 221 (1991), *1742*
Ḥakak v. Ḥakak, 45(iv) P.D. 749 (1991), *1806*
Ḥaliḥal v. State of Israel, 23(i) P.D. 733 (1969), *692*
Hananiah v. Friedman, 18(iii) P.D. 25 (1964), *630*
Hannah v. Peel, [1945] 1 K.B. 509, 2 All E.R. 288, *1745*
Ḥatar v. Druze Religious Court of Haifa, 27(i) P.D. 449 (1973), *1756*
Estate of Hecht v. Vaknin, [1977] 2 P.M. 192, *1731*
Hendeles v. Bank Kupat Am, 35(ii) P.D. 785 (1981), *6, 1692, 1710, 1738, 1836–1838, 1857, 1864–1867, 1871–1875, 1882–1884, 1898, 1927, 1928, 1936*
Ḥermesh v. Bar Am, 43(i) P.D. 672 (1989), *1742*
Hiram v. Minister of Defense, 35(iv) P.D. 505 (1981), *436, 1739*
Histadrut Po'alei Agudat Yisrael, Reḥovot Branch v. Histadrut

CASES *continued*
Agudat Yisra'el, Reḥovot Branch, 6 P.D.R. 202 (1966), ***920, 1822***
Histadrut Po'alei Agudat Yisra'el v. Minister of Religions, 37(i) P.D. 813 (1983), ***1740, 1760***
Hokamah v. Minister of the Interior, 38(ii) P.D. 826 (1984), ***1740, 1834, 1840–1842***
Howard v. Miarah, 35(ii) P.D. 505 (1980), ***1692, 1717–1720, 1865***
Ḥuli v. State of Israel, 35(iii) P.D. 477 (1981), ***1731***
Hutman v. Sin-Moritz, 17 P.D. 1251 (1963), ***1835***
Idah v. Sasson, 11 P.D. 1100 (1957), ***276***
Illit v. Eleko, 34(iv) P.D. 673 (1980), ***1692, 1731, 1739***
Inspector General of Police v. Baizer, 35(iv) P.D. 337 (1981), ***1731***
Insurance Corp. v. State of Israel, [1983] 1 P.M. 469, ***1835***
Jabotinski v. Weizmann, 5 P.D. 801 (1951), ***1078***
Jacobs v. Kartoz, 9 P.D. 1401 (1955), ***128, 1718***
Jensen-Zohar v. Ashdod Rabbinical Court, 35(i) P.D. 1 (1980), ***1739, 1764***
Jensen-Zohar v. Zohar, 35(i) P.D. 1 (1980), ***1764***
Jerczewski v. Prime Minister Yitzhak Shamir, 45(i) P.D. 749 (1991), ***1884, 1885***
Joseph v. Joseph, 23(i) P.D. 804 (1969), ***1788, 1806***
Joseph v. Joseph, 24(i) P.D. 792 (1970), ***1758, 1759, 1760, 1788, 1789, 1790, 1791, 1792, 1806, 1909***
Kahane v. Knesset Speaker, 40(iv) P.D. 393(1986), ***1740***
Kahanof v. District Rabbinical Court of Tel Aviv, 29(i) P.D. 449 (1974), ***1756***
Kaiserman v. Direnfeld, 3 P.D.R. 272 (1959), ***925, 926, 1633, 1822***
Kalir v. District Rabbinical Court, Jerusalem, 26(i) P.D. 757 (1972), ***1815***
Kashti v. Siani, [1982] 2 P.M. 263, ***1835***
Katebi v. Libby, Chairman of the Kiryat Ekron Council, 20(ii) P.D. 102 (1966), ***704***
Kibbutz Ḥaẓor v. Income Tax Assessor of Reḥovot, 39(ii) P.D. 70 (1985), ***1935***
Kitan v. Weiss, 33(ii) P.D. 785 (1979), ***161ff., 165, 167, 1739, 1840***
Kleine-Bik v. Goldberg, 41(ii) P.D. 757 (1987), ***1741, 1861***
Koenig v. Cohen, 36(iii) P.D. 701 (1982), ***1671, 1828, 1875, 1876, 1877, 1878, 1880, 1881, 1882, 1883, 1927***
Kokhavi v. Becker, 11 P.D. 225 (1957), ***1728, 1829, 1920***
Kokhavi v. State of Israel, 35(iv) P.D. 744 (1981), ***1739***
Kol ha-Am v. Minister of the Interior, 7 P.D. 871 (1953), ***1833, 1834***
Konsalos v. Turgeman, 45(ii) P.D. 626 (1991), ***1742***
Kote v. Kote, 36(i) P.D. 236 (1981), additional hearing 38(iii) P.D. 197 (1984), ***1723***
Kotik v. Wolfson, 5 P.D. 1341 (1951), ***1767***
Kraka Co., Ltd. v. Assaf Rothenburg and Partners, 4 P.D.R. 75 (1961), ***920, 1822***
Krauss v. State of Israel, 37(i) P.D. 365 (1983), ***1740, 1840, 1845***
Lahav v. Lahav, [1982] 1 P.M. 39, ***1863***
Landsman v. Ha-Va'adah le-Har Ẓiyyon, 1 P.D.R. 169 (1954), ***72***
Lansky v. Minister of the Interior, 26(ii) P.D. 337 (1972), ***1647***
Laserson v. Shikkun Ovedim, 38(ii) P.D. 237 (1984), ***187, 188, 1735, 1736, 1740, 1837***
Lazarowitz v. Supervisor of Food Products, 10 P.D. 40 (1956), ***328***
League for Civil Rights in Israel v. Commanding Officer, Southern Command, 44(iv) P.D. 626 (1990), ***1742***
Lev v. Siegel, 3 P.D.R. 91 (1958), ***165***
Levy v. District Rabbinical Court of Tel Aviv-Jaffa, 13 P.D. 1182 (1959), ***1759, 1760, 1794***
Lieberman v. Lieberman, 35(iv) P.D. 359 (1981), ***1600, 1739, 1840***
In re Litvinski Brothers Partnership, 18 P.M. 64 (1959), ***1731, 1911***
Lugasi v. Minister of Communications, 36(ii) P.D. 449 (1982), ***48, 707, 1740, 1840***
Mafdal of Reḥovot v. Agudat Yisra'el of Reḥovot, 6 P.D.R. 173 (1966), ***1822***
Malka v. Oved Seri Levi, 20(i) P.D. 651 (1966), ***704***
Manby v. Smith, 1 Mod. 124, 86 Eng. Rep. 781 (Exch. 1663), ***1926***
Manof Signal Financial and Investment, Ltd. v.

Slayman, 44(iii) P.D. 758 (1989), *1742*
Marcus v. Hammer, 37(ii) P.D. 337 (1983), *166, 167, 1740, 1840*
Marcus v. State of Israel, 37(i) P.D. 225 (1983), *1740*
Masika v. State of Israel, 43(ii) P.D. 423 (1989), *1742, 1845*
Merkaz ha-Kabbelanim veha-Bonim be-Yisra'el v. Government of Israel, 34(iii) P.D. 729 (1979), *1833*
Mikkun Le-Matta, Ltd. v. Karnit, 35(ii) P.D. 383 (1981), *1731*
Military Court of Appeals v. Vaknin, 42(iii) P.D. 837 (1988), *1741, 1856*
Miller v. Miller, 5 P.D. 1301 (1949), *574, 1483*
Miller v. Minister of the Interior, 40(iv) P.D. 436 (1986), *1690, 1740*
Minister of Justice v. Judge Arbel, 42(iii) P.D. 63 (1988), *1741*
Minister of Justice v. Judge Ḥarifai, 42(iii) P.D. 69 (1988), *1741*
Minẓer v. Central Committee of Israel Bar Association, 36(ii) P.D. 1 (1982), *178ff., 1740, 1840*
Mitoba v. Kazam, 6 P.D. 4 (1952), *1874, 1875*
Miyari v. Knesset Speaker, 41(iv) P.D. 169 (1987), *1741*
Mizraḥi v. State of Israel, 35(iv) P.D. 421 (1980), *1935*
Mizraḥi v. State of Israel, 43(iv) P.D. 388 (1989), *1742*
Mossman v. Rabbinical Court, 18(iii) P.D. 502 (1964), *1759*
Moston v. Wiederman, 43(i) P.D. 278 (1989), *1742*
Muberman v. Segal, 32(iii) P.D. 85 (1978), *6, 1692, 1739, 1837, 1865, 1866*
Nagar v. Nagar, 38(i) P.D. 365 (1981), *1664, 1666, 1667, 1759, 1762, 1763, 1794, 1795, 1802, 1824, 1826*
Nagar v. State of Israel, 35(i) P.D. 113 (1980), *47, 692, 1739*
Naiman v. Chairman, Central Elections Committee, 39(ii) P.D. 225 (1985), *1740, 1828, 1833, 1840, 1844, 1850, 1853, 1854, 1861*
Nast v. Management Committee Bet ha-Midrash ha-Merkazi, Haifa, 1 P.D.R. 330 (1955), *926, 1634, 1822*
Ness v. Golda, 36(i) P.D. 204 (1981), *164, 165, 1739, 1840*
Nili v. Shelomi, 30(ii) P.D. 3 (1976), *1719*
Nir v. Nir, 35(i) P.D. 518 (1980), *1666*
Of ha-Emek Agricultural Society v. Ramat Yishai Local Council, 40(i) P.D. 113 (1986), *1935, 1936*
Omri v. Zouavi, 39(ii) P.D. 113 (1985), *1671, 1740, 1769*
Omychund v. Barker, 1 Atk. 22, 26 Eng. Rep. 15 (1744), *1700*
One Heart and New Spirit Movement v. Knesset Speaker, 44(iii) P.D. 529 (1989), *1742*
Parker v. British Airways Board, 2 W.L.R. 503, 1 All E.R. 834 (1982), *1745*
Petromilio v. State of Israel, 38(iv) P.D. 821 (1984), *1731*
Ports Authority v. Ararat, Ltd., 31(i) P.D. 533 (1976), *985*
Proper v. General Custodian, 35(ii) P.D. 561 (1984), *164*
Ratner v. Palalum, Ltd., 12(ii) P.D. 1465 (1958), *1739*
Raviv v. Bet Jules, Ltd., 37(i) P.D. 533 (1982), *1731*
Ravivo v. Chairman of the Local Council of Ofakim, 42(iii) P.D. 183 (1988), *1741*
Rechtman v. State of Israel, 33(ii) P.D. 45 (1979), *1845*
Rinat v. Rinat, 20(ii) P.D. 21 (1966), *1804*
Rodnitzky v. Rabbinical Court of Appeals, 24(i) P.D. 704 (1970), *1754, 1772, 1773, 1776, 1777, 1780, 1905, 1929*
Rosen v. State of Israel, 35(ii) P.D. 821 (1981), *1739*
Rosenberg v. Keren Ḥazzan, 35(ii) P.D. 742 (1981), *1731*
Rosenberg v. Shtesal, 29(i) P.D. 505 (1974), *1934*
Rosenstein v. Solomon, 38(ii) P.D. 113 (1984), *1692, 1710, 1711, 1712, 1714, 1715, 1740, 1841, 1912*
Rosenthal v. Tomashevski, 25(i) P.D. 488 (1971), *1877, 1879, 1881*
Rosenzweig v. Attorney General, 42(iv) P.D. 759 (1989), *1741*
Roth v. Yeshufeh, 33(i) P.D. 617 (1979), *6, 184, 185, 188, 1692, 1718, 1735, 1736, 1738, 1836, 1840, 1865, 1866, 1870, 1873, 1937*

CASES *continued*

Rothman v. United Mizraḥi Bank, 29(ii) P.D. 57 (1975), *1736*
Rufeisen v. Minister of the Interior, 16 P.D. 2428 (1962), *1647*
Sagel v. State of Israel, 40(ii) P.D. 769 (1986), *1740*
Salem v. Minister of the Interior, 21(i) P.D. 59 (1967), *704*
Sasi v. Kika'on, 36(i) P.D. 762 (1981), *1731*
Savitzky v. Minister of Finance, 19(ii) P.D. 369 (1965), *462*
Schein v. Minister of Defense, 38(iii) P.D. 393 (1984), *1740*
Schlesinger v. Minister of the Interior, 17 P.D. 225 (1963), *1760, 1779*
Sedan v. Sedan, 36(iv) P.D. 169 (1982), *1740*
Shagav v. Rabbinical Court of Safed, 21(ii) P.D. 505 (1967), *1759, 1777, 1781, 1782*
Shakdiel v. Ministry of Religions, 42(ii) P.D. 221 (1988), *1656, 1741, 1794, 1900*
Shalit v. Minister of the Interior, 23(ii) P.D. 477 (1970), *1649*
Shapira v. State of Israel, 36(i) P.D. 337 (1981), *1830*
Sharabi v. Sobri, 25(i) P.D. 429 (1971), *1879*
Sharon v. Levi, 35(i) P.D. 736 (1980), *128, 143, 1739*
Shehino v. National Labor Court, 44(i) P.D. 143 (1989), *1742*
Shoresh v. Ha'avarah, 3 Ha-Mishpat 71 (1948), *1697*
Shwalboim v. Shwalboim, 7 P.L.R. 20 (1940), *1766*
Sidis v. Chief Execution Officer, 8 P.D. 1020 (1954), *1905*
Sidis v. Rabbinical Court of Appeals, 12 P.D. 1525 (1958), *1758, 1803*
Skornik v. Skornik, 8 P.D. 141 (1954), *5, 1766, 1767, 1834, 1866, 1945, 1946*
Sobol v. Goldman, 33(i) P.D. 789 (1979), *20, 175, 1759*
Sporta v. Sporta, 32(ii) P.D. 709 (1978), *1806*
State of Israel v. Abukasis, 32(ii) P.D. 240 (1978), *128, 1739, 1840, 1845*
State of Israel v. Albez, 42(iv) P.D. 385 (1988), *1741*
State of Israel v. Avi Ẓur, 40(i) P.D. 706 (1986), *1740, 1834, 1840, 1843*
State of Israel v. Benjamin, 43(ii) P.D. 430 (1989), *1742, 1846*
State of Israel v. Brown, 41(iv) P.D. 382 (1988), *1741*
State of Israel v. Darvish, 45(ii) P.D. 663 (1991), *1742*
State of Israel v. Grossman, 36(i) P.D. 405 (1981), *1731*
State of Israel v. Heimowitz [1986] 1 P.M. 89, *1863*
State of Israel v. Kedar, 36(i) P.D. 492 (1982), *1937*
State of Israel v. Kurtam [1985] 1 P.M. 45, *1863*
State of Israel v. Lavan, 43(ii) P.D. 410 (1989), *1742*
State of Israel v. Leviathan, 40(i) P.D. 544 (1986), *1740, 1845*
State of Israel v. Lubaniov, 35(iv) P.D. 780 (1981), *1739, 1840*
State of Israel v. Maman, 43(ii) P.D. 441 (1989), *1742*
State of Israel v. Mishali, 32(iii) P.D. 245 (1978), *1739*
State of Israel v. Molcho, 37(i) P.D. 78 (1983), *1845*
State of Israel v. Pesler, 16 P.D. 102 (1962), *1685*
State of Israel v. Segal, 35(iv) P.D. 313 (1981), *1739*
State of Israel v. Shoradker, 43 (iii) P.D. 1 (1988), *1742*
State of Israel v. Suisse, 38(iv) P.D. 701(1984), *1740*
State of Israel v. Tamir, 37(iii) P.D. 201 (1983), *128, 142, 1639, 1740, 1840, 1841, 1926*
State of Israel, Ministry of Communications v. Briks, Ltd. [1985] 1 P.M. 228, *1863*
Steiner v. Attorney General, 9 P.D. 241 (1954), *1666*
Streit v. Chief Rabbi of Israel, 18(i) P.D. 598 (1964), *1759, 1760, 1791*
Sura v. State of Israel, 36(iv) P.D. 10 (1982), *1840, 1845*
Taviv v. Katz, [1978] 1 P.M. 366, *1731*
Tohami v. State of Israel, 40(i) P.D. 733 (1986), *1740*
Toledo Trust Co. v. Simmons, 52 Ohio App. 373, 3 N.E.2d 61 (1935), *1745*
Ulpanei Hasratah v. Gerry, 16 P.D. 2407 (1962), *1833*
United Dairies, Ltd. v. Dairy Council, 37(iv) P.D. 516 (1983), *1731*
Vatad v. Minister of Fi-

nance, 38(iii) P.D. 113 (1984), *1731*
Weil v. State of Israel, 41(iii) P.D. 477 (1987), *1841*
Wertheim v. State of Israel, 32(ii) P.D. 225 (1978), *1739*
Wertheimer v. Harari, 35(iii) P.D. 253 (1981), *1835*
Wiloszni v. Rabbinical Court of Appeals, 36(ii) P.D. 733 (1982), *74, 924, 1601, 1758, 1820, 1821, 1824–1826, 1944, 1945*
Wolfsohn v. Spinneys Co., Ltd., 5 P.D. 265 (1951), *1633, 1835*
Yadlin v. State of Israel, 31(i) P.D. 671 (1976), *1843, 1844*
Yeager v. Palevitz, 20(iii) P.D. 244 (1966), *1685*
Yeinot Eliaz Co. v. Eshkolot Anavim Co., 1 P.D.R. 178 (1953), *1695*
Yekutiel v. Bergman, 29(ii) P.D. 757 (1975), *1736*
Yosipoff v. Attorney General of the State of Israel, 5 P.D. 481 (1951), *6, 1773, 1904*
Zahav v. State of Israel, 43(i) P.D. 720 (1989), *1742*
Za'id v. Yardeniah Insurance Co., Ltd. [1978] 1 P.M. 163, *1731*
Ẓemaḥ v. State of Israel, 41(iii) P.D. 17 (1987), *1741*
Zikit v. Eldit, 32(iii) P.D. 487 (1978), *1692, 1739*
Zim v. Mazyar, 17 P.D. 1319 (1963), *1736*
Ziv v. Acting Commissioner of the Tel Aviv Municipal Area, 1 P.D. 85 (1948), *1833*
Ẓonan v. Stahl, 37(ii) P.D. 761 (1983), *1740, 1783*
Zuckerman v. State of Israel, 40(iv) P.D. 209 (1986), *1740*

SUBJECT INDEX

A
Aaron b. Jacob ha-Kohen of Lunel, *1257–1258*
Aaron b. Meir, dispute with Saadiah Gaon, *1159–1161*
Aaron ha-Levi, glosses on *Torat ha-Bayit*, *1276*
Abba, Joseph b. (R.), Sages' opposition as changing, *892n.53*
Abba, (R.), on the force of *ma'aseh*, *962*
Abbasid dynasty
  limited contacts with Jews, *43*
  authority of Babylonian Talmud enhanced by, *1131*
Abbaye (R.), justification of Hillel's authority re *prosbul* enactment and, *513*
abduction, before marriage, as basis for annulment legislation, *637–638*
Abin, R., on custom based on error, *939*
Aboab, Isaac, commentaries, *1302n.276*, *1315n.17*
Aboab, Samuel
  on contradictions between *Bet Yosef* and *Shulhan Arukh*, *1371*
  on decline of Jewish legal creativity, *50*
  on juridical autonomy, *34–36*
  responsa literature of, *1489*
abortion, tort liability for, *604–605*
Abrabanel, Isaac, *246–247*
Abrabanel, Don Samuel, civil law commentaries, *1308*
Abraham (patriarch), negotiations with Hittites, *195–197*
Abraham ibn Daud. *See* Rabad.
Abramsky, Y., commentaries of, *1113n.45*
Abulafia, Isaac, power to annul marriages contravening Rabbinic enactments, *874–875*
Abulafia, Meir ha-Levi. *See* Ramah
"acceptance," as basis of binding effect of communal enactments, *732*
acquisition (*kinyan*)
  agav karka, *583–584*
  by barter, actual (*kinyan halifin*) and symbolic (*kinyan sudar*), *581–583*
  communal enactments, *704–706*, *716*, *736n.221*
  custom as source of, *919*
  legal capacity (mental competence), *585–587*
  legislative enactments, *301n.51*, *580–587*
  "law of the land is law," 68n.61
  laws on, in Books of Jeremiah and Ruth, *1022–1024*
  mattenat bari (gift of a healthy person) as requiring, *1682*
  meaning of, in Jewish law, *80*
  "meeting of three" (*ma'amad sheloshtan*) enactment, *584*
  meshikhah (pulling). *See kinyan meshikhah*
  in *Mishneh Torah*, *1200*
  moral-religious sanctions and, *151*
  of personal property (*kinyan agav karka*), *583–584*
  sitomta, *See sitomta*
  tannaitic legislation, *580–587*
  will of *shekhiv me-ra* and, *1877–1884*
  See also property law
Adarbi, Isaac
  definition of majority, for purpose of communal enactments, *724*
  limitation of actions legislation, *1725–1726*
Adeni, Solomon, commentaries of, *1109*
ad de-tinasevan le-guvrin, *575*
"additional soul" (*neshamah yeterah*), good faith (*tom lev*), *187*
adjoining landowner's preemptive right (*din bar mezra*), *625–626*
adjudication
  "judge your neighbor fairly," 169
  legal standards (*ma'aseh*), *179–182*, *945–946*

Administration Ordinance, *1729n.414*
administrative law
  classification of, *77–78*
  communal enactments equated with court legislation, *707n.112*
  juridical autonomy and, *48*
  king's law and, *56*
  validity of legislative delegation, *730*
Admonition in Place of Oath provision, *1706*
admonition of witnesses
  commentaries on, *1697–1707*
  modern legislation, *1706*
adoption, laws regarding
  Adoption of Children Law, *827n.178*, *1663n.171*
  jurisdiction of rabbinical courts over, *1671n.211*
  procedural enactments of Rabbinical courts, *827*
adversary litigation, ambiguity of communal enactments and, *464–468*
Afanjar v. State of Israel, *1924*, *1927*
affirmation. *See* oaths
a fortiori inference (*kal va-homer*), 328n.147, *343*, *347–351*
  conclusion and premise in, *349–351*
  criticism of, *380–383*
  in fraudulent conveyances laws, *417–418*
  fraudulent marriages, enactments regarding, *847–848*
  justification for custom overriding Halakhah, *1822–1824*
  from leniency to stringency, *348–349*
  limitations on use, *327–328*, *360*, *389–390*
  in post-Talmudic halakhic interpretation, *415–416*
  from stringency to leniency, *349*
  validity of privately performed marriages, *1783–1784*
  Wiloszni case and, *1822–1824*
Africa, communal legislation in, *804–809*
Agatharchides, *1035*
agency, law of, *342–343*
Agency Law, *1625*
Aggadah
  in Alfasi's *Sefer ha-Halakhot*, *1170–1172*
  as basis for legal decisions, *102–103*
  military law, *554n.36*
  relationship to *Halakhah*, *94–104*, *152*
  responsa as source for, *1464*
  Sefer ha-She'iltot and, *1152*
Agnon, S. Y., *1593n.33*
Agranat, Court President, *1781–1782*, *1945–1946*
  on the nature of lacuna, *1838*
  on wife's income from employment and property, *1804n.167*
agricultural law. *See* specific agricultural laws, e.g. livestock, laws concerning
Agudat Halikhot Am Yisrael, *1232n.145*
Agudat Israel, *1613–1614*
agudot (separate factions), and validity of local custom, *935*
agunah (*agunot*)
  in amoraic era, *526–528*
  contemporary halakhic legislation concerning, *878–879*
  explicit enactments concerning annulment of marriage, *850*
  fraudulent marriages, enactments regarding, *847–848*
  Gamaliel the elder's legislation on, *522–526*, *566*
  Gamaliel II on, *526*
  halakhic solutions to problem of, *402*, *1754–1756*
  halizah ceremony, *530n.153*, *830–831*
  historical background, *504*
  hora'at sha'ah, *634*
  legislation as remedy for, *834–835*, *1014*, *1807n.175*
  mamzerim and, *527–528*
  Moroccan enactments concerning, *808*
  procedural enactments of Israeli Chief Rabbinate concerning, *830–831*
  Rabbi Judah's view on, *523–524*
  relaxation of rules of evidence to permit remarriage, *528–530*, *609n.269*
  School of Hillel and, *402*, *524–525*
  in *Sefer ha-Turim*, *1290–1291*
  witnesses, inquiry and examination procedures, *609n.269*
  Women's Equal Rights Law and, *1658*
  Yad Aharon responsa on, *1438–1439*
Aha of Shabha, *Sefer ha-She'iltot* of, *1150–1153*
Ahab (King), Naboth the Jezreelite and, *1025*
Ahai of Bei-Hittim, R., *10*
aharei rabbim le-hattot ("follow the majority").
  See majority rule.
aharonim
  authority of, *267–272*

commentaries on *Tosefta*, *1111–1113*
historical period of, *44*
on justice as supplement to law, *171–172*
legal interpretations of, *44, 277–278*
literary legal sources of, *1101–1102*
ma'aseh authoritativeness
as compared to code, *977–978*
meanings of term, *44, 268n.102*
novellae, *1127–1129*
responsa literature, *1482–1491*
use of non-Jewish courts, attitude to, *17*

Ahavat Hesed, *1630n.27*

Ahavat Ziyyon vi-Yerushalayim, *1137*

Akavyah b. Mahalalel, *1044, 1848*

Akedat Yizhak
commentaries on Deuteronomy, *253*
law and equity discussed in, *247–251*

Akhnai, oven of, *261–263, 1068*

akhilat perot, liability of encumbered property for, *592n.210*

Akiva, R., *6*
absolution of vows, *953*
agunot legislation, *525–526*
on *asmakhta*, *302*
on death penalty, *692–694*
development and redaction of Mishnah, *1051–1052*
on divorce law, *294–295*
"do what is right and good", *624–625*
expansion of laws by interpretation, as encouraging codification, *1069*
interpretation of Torah by, *316–317*
interpretive methodology, *371–383*
"love your fellow as yourself," *1851–1852*
ma'aseh, relation to codified law, *948, 953*
metaphorical and symbolic interpretations by, *375–376*
midrashic compilations, *1048–1049*
mishnayot compilations, *1051–1052*
recitation of *shema*, *969*
right of privacy, *1858*
"set table" metaphor used by, *1322n.36*
in third tannaitic generation, *1044*
on tithing of vegetables, *949n.19*
witnesses, inquiry and examination procedures, *609*

Alashkar, Moses (Maharam), 859, abstention from exercising legislative powers, *864–869, 877–878*

Al-Bargeloni, Isaac b. Reuben, *1165*

Al-Bargeloni, Judah, *1177–1178*
Sefer ha-Shetarot of, *1536–1537*

Albeck, Hanokh, *1110*
guidebook on Mishnah, Talmud, Baraita, and Tosefta, *1550*
on nature of Mishnah, *1057, 1072n.147*

Albo, Joseph, on comprehensiveness of Torah, *241–242*

Alegre, Abraham, majority rule and communal enactments, *720*

Alexandria, observance of Jewish law of betrothal, *424–426*

Alfandari, Aaron, *1438–1439*

Alfasi, Isaac b. Jacob ha-Kohen of Fez (Rif), *53, 715*
acceptance of, in Europe and North Africa, *1179n.114*
on Babylonian Talmud, *1095, 1131*
commentaries on, *1315n.19, 1406–1407*
Heller's view's on codificatory method of, *1406–1407*
index to laws of, *1172n.84*
influence of, on halakhic authorities, *1172*
Jacob b. Asher's codification, relation to, *1284*
on Jerusalem Talmud, *1132*
Maimonides and, *1145–1146*
Meshullam b. Moses supplement to, *1244*
Nahmanides influenced by, *1242*
opinions of, in *Sefer ha-Ittur*, *1269n.142*
rulings used in *Sefer ha-Hinnukh*, *1265*
Sefer ha-Halakhot of, *1139–1140, 1167–1176*
Yemenites' preservation of code of, *1500n.131*

Alfual, Abraham b., *858*

Algazi, Solomon, *1547*

Algazi, Yom Tov, *1242n.23, 1490*

Algeria, Jewish community in
communal enactments in, *804–805*
equal inheritance rights for sons and daughters, enactments for, *845n.243*
Fez enactments of 1494 and 1592, *869–870*
husband's inheritance rights, enactments restricting, *838–840*
juridical autonomy in, *1585–1586*

"all her ways are pleasant ways and all her paths peaceful," as guideline for legislation and adjudication
communal enactments, *702n.92*
fraudulent conveyances, *1894*
halizah requirement and, *389–390*
legal reasoning (*sevarah*) and, *989, 1000–1004*

Algeria *continued*
national and religious minorities, *1855–1856*
"all who marry do so subject to conditions laid down by the Rabbis, and the Rabbis annul this marriage," relation to legislation
abduction before marriage, *637–638*
annulment legislation, *858–859*
betrothal laws, *641n.64*
civil laws, *635n.53*
coerced marriages, *638–642*
commentaries on, *631, 634*
communal enactments and, *633n.48*
force majeure, *633n.49*
geonic annulment enactments, *658n.61*
get (bill of divorcement) and, *631, 640*
Hananel discussion of, *638*
hefker bet din hefker, *635n.53*
issur (religious) legislation, *635n.53*
Jerusalem Talmud and, *634–636, 640*
legislation, *631–642*
mamzerim and, *631, 641n.65*
Sages' commentaries on, *631–635, 640*
See also annulment of marriage
Almosnino, Moses, *Tikkun Soferim* of, *1538*
Alon, Gedaliah, on lay tribunals, *22*
Aloni, S., on Foundations of Law Act, *1832n.19*
Aloni v. Minister of Justice, *1861–1863*
Amar, M., on Foundations of Law Act, *1832n.19*
Amaziah, King, *1025–1026*
ambiguities in law, resolution against obligee for, *433–436*
Ameimar
on betrothal laws, *893n.53*
"one-tenth of the estate" legislation (*isur nekhasim*), *579–580*
Amendment of Copyright Ordinance Bill, *1691n.290*
Amendment of Courts Law Bill
Jewish law as source for, *1691n.290*
severing of ties to English law, *1729n.414*
Amendment of Evidence Ordinance Bill, *1691n.290*
American Digest system, *1526n.244*
American law
application of, with lacuna, *1870*
Israeli courts' reliance on, *1920–1923*
American Law Institute, *1144n.7*
Ammi, R., abstention from exercising legislative powers, *866n.303*
Ammonites
gezerah shavah canon regarding, *354–355*
prohibition of marriage with, *361–364*
Ammudei Golah Hem Shiv'ah Ammudei Olam, *1264n.119*
amora, defined, *1083–1084*
amoraic era
adjoining landowner's preemptive right (*din bar mezra*) legislation, *625–626*
agunot legislation and, *527–528*
"all who marry do so subject to conditions laid down by the Rabbis and the Rabbis annul this marriage" legislation, *631–642*
authoritative character of Mishnah in, *1061*
Babylonian Talmud contents and teachings, *1088–1092*
Biblical vs. rabbinical law in, *211–212*
court authority regarding legislation, *506, 542–544*
custom as legal source of law and, *881–882*
daughters' right to inheritance, *575*
deceased proselyte, assets of, laws concerning, *959–960*
"do what is right and good," *623–629*
exegetical interpretation during, *383–390*
family law under, *676*
Gamaliel the elder's bill of divorcement, *564–566*
halakhic interpretation during, *267–268, 407–414, 889–892*
hefker bet din hefker, *508–510*
on hybrid casuistic-normative style of Mishnah, *1076*
integrative interpretations of, *297–300*
issur-mamon distinction in *Halakhah* and, *126, 131–132*
Jerusalem Talmud compilation, *1095–1098*
kum va-Aseh circumvented by, *521*
labor legislation, *619–620*
"law of the land is law," *65*
lay tribunals in, *22*
leading generations of, *1085–1086*
legal literature during, *42*
legal reasoning (*sevarah*), *998–1004*
legislation to prevent strife and enmity (*mi-shum eivah*), *629–631*

legislative guidelines, *491–492, 505n.50, 515–519*
literary legal sources in, *1083–1100*
ma'aseh legislation and, *954–957*
market overt legislation, *598–600*
"one-tenth of the estate" legislation (*isur nekhasim*), *579– 580*
oral vs. documented debt, encumbered property and, *594–595*
payment of debt as religious obligation, *117–119*
property lien legislation and, *593*
prosbul enactment and, *512–513*
reduction of Oral Law to writing and, *224–227*
religious law (*issur*), custom and, *909–910*
responsa in Talmudic sources and, *1454–1456*
Sages' authority regarding annulment, *846–847*
Schools of Hillel and Shammai, alliance of, *1065–1066*
shuma hadra (return of appraised property) legislation, *627–628*
spousal support legislation, *570–571*
survival of Jewish law during, *2*
Talmudic research and, *42*
tanna and, *1042*
tannaitic legislation classification, *547*
tort law interpretations, *411–413*
Yom Kippur laws, custom as source, *899–900*
Amos, Book of, sabbath law in, *1022n.8*
amputations, laws regarding, legal reasoning
(*sevarah*) and, *1005n.62*
analogic interpretation
in post-Talmudic halakhah, *415–416, 418*
in the Talmud, *401*
of Torah, *343–360*
analogical reasoning, limitations on, *964n.72*
Foundations of Law Act and, *1834–1835*
legal reasoning (*sevarah*) and, *1009–1010*
Anan b. David, *1156–1157*
law of interest and, *966–967*
Anatoly, Jacob, *138–139*
ancestral customs, as legislative source, *497–499*
See also custom (*minhag*)
ancillary oath (*gilgul shevu'ah*)
use of, in labor legislation, *620n.307*
See also oaths
Ankawa, Abraham, *807–808, 1539*
limitation of actions legislation, *1726*
responsa literature of, *1495*
Ankawa, Raphael, responsa literature of, *1496*
annulment of marriage, laws regarding
abstention from exercising legislative powers, *864–869*
a fortiori inference regarding legislation, *876–877*
authority to annul
"all who marry do so subject to conditions laid down by the Rabbis and the Rabbis annul this marriage," *641–642*
"approval of all halakhic authorities of region," requirement of, *856–859*
power of halakhic authorities to abrogate Biblical law, *521–522*
circumvention of *kum va-Aseh* and, *522–530*
controversy between authorities of Mainz and authorities of Worms and Speyer, *848–850*
course of legislation concerning, *846–879*
court authority regarding, *506n.58*
eastern countries, eighteenth and nineteenth century enactments, *874–878*
explicit enactments, views of Asheri, Rashba and Jeroham, *850–856*
Fez enactments of 1494 and 1592, *869–870*
fraudulent marriages, *847–848*
geonic betrothal legislation, *657–658*
modern legislative enactments, *1755n.10*
sixteenth and seventeenth century enactments concerning, *872–874*
theory vs. practice in legislation in, *859–864*
"anonymous" form of law, Mishnah compared with cognate sources, *1060*
anpilin, halizah rules, *907–908*
Anshei Keneset ha-Gedolah. See Great Assembly
Anshei Shem, Toledot Rabbanei Lvov, 1558
Antiochus Epiphanes, *1043n.7*
Antigonus of Sokho, *41, 192, 1043*
Antiquities of the Jews, The, 1031–1033
Apocrypha
as literary source of law, *1019, 1033–1036*

Apocrypha *continued*
suretyship law in, *1027n.35*
apotiki, law of obligations, *590n.198*
appeal, right of, Valladolid enactments regarding, *800–801*
"approval of all halakhic authorities of region," regarding annulments, *856–859*
Arabanel, Isaac, commentaries on Deuteronomy, *253–256*
Arabic language
Maimonides' rejection of, *1208*
monographs written in, *1158–1167, 1207–1208*
Aragonian enactments, *797–798*
Arak, Meir, responsa literature of, *1496*
Arama, Isaac
on justice and equity, *255–256*
on law and equity, *247–252*
Aramaic language
Maimonides' translation of, *1207–1210*
in responsa, *1507–1512*
in *Shulhan Arukh*, *1340*
translations of Scripture in, *1095–1096*
Aramaic Papyri of Elephantine. *See* Elephantine papyri
Arazi, MK, Land Law legislation and, *1713–1714*
arba'ah shomerim (categories of bailees), *1693–1694*
Arba'ah Turim. *See Sefer ha-Turim*
arbitration, Jewish juridical authority over, *19*
Arbitration Law, rabbinical courts and, *1818n.207*
arev kabbelan
Jerusalem Talmud and, *1096n.63*
suretyship law and, *1722n.387*
Aristeas, Letter of, *1036*
Aristotle's *Book of Ethics*, *248*
arka'ot she-be-Suria, *24n.80*
Arka'ot Shel Goyim. *See* non-Jewish tribunals
Arta, Greece, use of non-Jewish courts in, *18n.54*
Arukh, concept of *Halakhah* in, *93*
Arukh ha-Shalem, *1565*
Arukh ha-Shulhan he-Atid, *1449*
Arukh ha-Shulhan
extradition laws and, *1862*
as legal source, *1448–1450*
Arukh la-Ner, *1129n.104*
Aryeh Leib b. Joseph Heller
Even ha-Ezer commentaries of, *1431*
Kezot ha-Hoshen commentaries of, *1428*
Asefat Zekenim, *1126–1127*
asharta, authentication of witnesses' testimony, *613*
Asher, Judah b., criminal communal enactments and, *696–698*
Asher Shalem, responsa literature of, *1490*
Asheri (Asher b. Jehiel [Rosh])
abstention from exercising legislative powers, *866–867*
annulment of marriage, enactments concerning, *850–856*
class-related issues on voting rights, *98n.27*
code of, *54*
codificatory methodology of, *1278–1280*
on circumstantial evidence, *96n.14*
competency of witnesses, *738–739*
criticism of *Mishneh Torah* by, *1226–1229*
custom as source of law, *904n.29, 919*
custom based on error, *939–940*
digest of responsa of, *1526n.242*
"distinguished person's" approval, *755–756*
on fraudulent conveyances laws, *417, 1891–1894*
good faith (*tom lev*), *186–187*
on halakhic authority, *269–270, 1121n.71*
Heller's commentary on, *1406–1407*
hilkheta ke-vatra'ei, *1284–1285*
husband's inheritance rights, enactments restricting, *839n.218*
on inheritance law, *1673n.218*
interpretation of communal enactments by, *452–453*
on lay tribunals, *28*
majority rule and communal enactments, *717–718*
moredet legislation, *662–665*
Piskei ha-Rosh of, *1251–1255*
Piskei ha-Tosafot, *1122*
precedent in Jewish law and, *984–985*
on resolution against obligee, *435–436*
responsa as source for legal terminology, 12, *80*
responsa questions submitted by, *1476, 1478*
Asheri, Jacob, *1253*
on "scribal errors" in communal enactments, *458–459*
on Valladolid enactments, *802–803*
Ashi, R.
amoraic view of Mishnah and, *1061*
Babylonian Talmud redaction, *1092, 1097*

on betrothal law, *893n.53*
on burden of proof, *992–993*
on local custom as law, *934n.171*
precedent in Jewish law and, *984*
Ashishot, 1254
Ashkenazi, Abraham, *1307*
Ashkenazi, Bezalel, *1126–1127*
Kelalei ha-Talmud of, *1547*
Ashkenazi, Joseph, *1109*
Ashkenazi, Samuel Jaffe, *1133n.119*
Ashkenazic communities, *89n.49*
annulment, enactments concerning, *871n.316*
Asheri's leadership of, *1226–1229*
commentaries on *Sefer ha-Turim, 1302–1304*
communal representatives, communal enactments by, *728n.195*
custom as law regarding *Yom Kippur, 900n.14*
halakhic interpretation of legislation in, *1809*
halakhot of, *1305–1306*
hilkheta ke-vatra'ei, 1284–1287, 1357–1366
novellae of Tosafists, *1118–1123*
Rema's listing of authorities, in *Darkhei Moshe, 1353–1354*
responsa literature from, *1490–1494*
Asiyat Osher ve-Lo be Mishpat, Unjust Enrichment Law and, *1696n.307*
asmakhta (supportive interpretation)
Babylonian Talmud and, *1091*
Biblical vs. rabbinical law and, *210–211*
communal enactments, *683n.16, 706, 707n.111*
history of legislative activity, *549n.12*
interpretation of Torah and, *285–286*
Jerusalem Talmud and, *302–303*
on legislative power of halakhic authorities, *483n.34*
liability law and, *303–304*
in midrash, *300–305*
religious-legal obligations and, *120*
as support for custom, *918n.84*
suretyship law and, *1096n.63*
Assaf, Simhah, *83*
Assault and battery cases, use of non-Jewish courts for, *17*
assets, concealment of
issur vs. communal enactments and, *710n.133*
property lien legislation and, *591–592*
Assi, R., abstention from exercising legislative powers, *866n.303*
Assyrian Code, debtors' laws in, *310*
Atlas Ez Hayyim, 1559
Attachment of property, as enforcement of judicial decisions, *10*
attestation. *See* testimony; witnesses.
Attorney General v. Anonymous, 1860–1861
audi alteram partem ("hear the other side,") *1760n.21*
Auerbach, Leopold, *82*
Auerbach, Meir, responsa literature of, *1495*
Augustus, Sigismund, *9n.20*
avak ribbit ("dust of interest"), *221n.149*
Av Bet Din, 1178n.106
defined, *41*
Avia, R., legislative power of halakhic authorities, *482–485*
Avnei Millu'im, commentaries on *Even ha-Ezer, 1431*
Avneri v. Shapira, 1850n.91
Avodat Massa, 1446
Avot Tractate, *1054*
legislative enactments of Great Assembly and, *555*
as literary legal source, *1043–1044*
on origins of Oral Law, *192*
Avtalyon, as part of *Zugot, 1043*
Azariah, Eleazar b. (R.), recitation of *shema, 969*
Azikri, Eleazar, commentary of, *1133n.119*

B

Ba'alei ha-Nefesh, 1243n.26
Ba'alei ha-Tosafot, Toleodteihem, Hibbureihem ve-Shittatam, 1550
ba'al hov, law of obligations and, *588*
"Ba'ayot u-Megamot be-Yahasei Halakhah u-Medinah," *1756n.11*
Babad, Joseph, *1695n.300*
Babliki, Y., *1810n.189*
Babylonian Jewish community (*golah*)
communal enactments in, *683–684*
debate with Israel on responsa, *1455–1456*
geonic legislative enactments during diaspora, *643–646, 650–651*
literary legal sources in, *1087–1088*
responsa literature from, *1490*
spiritual hegemony of, *666–668*
ties with Israel and legislative authority, *525n.132*

Babylonian Talmud
Alfasi's *Sefer ha-Halakhot* and, *1170*
amoraic teachings and, *1088–1091*
annulment of marriage, enactments regarding, *849*
Babylonian diaspora and, *1087–1088*
contents of, *1091*
custom as source of legislation, *891–892*
divrei kabbalah and, *204*
geonic commentaries on, *656, 1113–1114*
"law of the land is law," *69*
as literary legal source, *1087–1095*
ketubbah obligations in, *213–214*
ma'aseh concerning lost or stolen property, *956–957*
Maimonides' compilation and reworking of halakhic material, *1187, 1207*
Mishnah as resource for, *52*
Mishnah tractates in, *1094–1095*
novellae on, *1118–1129*
precedent in Jewish law and, *984*
production of, during *amoraim* era, *42*
Rabbenu Gershom Me'or ha-Golah and students' commentary on, *1115–1116*
Rabbenu Hananel's commentary on, *1114–1115*
Rashi's commentary on, *1116–1117*
redaction and completion of, *1091–1093*
role of public in legislation, *539*
savoraim and, *1093–1094*
Sefer ha-Ittur and, *1269*
Sefer ha-Mordekhai included in, *1250n.60*
as source of Jewish law, *2–3*
teachings of *amoraim* of Israel, *1090*
Tosafists and, *1119–1120*
translations of, *1129n.105*
Babylonian Talmud, Translated into English with Notes, Glossary and Indices under the Editorship of Dr. I. Epstein, 1130n.105
Der Babylonische Talmud ... übersetzt ... von Lazarus Goldschmidt, 1130n.105
Bacharach, Jair Hayyim
equal application of communal enactments, *772*
responsa literature of, *1420, 1489*
Bacher, Wilhelm, *1553*
"bad custom" (*minhag garu'a*), *941–942*
Baer, Yitzhak, rise of *kehillah* and, *667*
Baghdad Caliphate, *645*
bailees (*shomerim*), laws regarding
categories of, in modern bailees law, *1693–1696*
Jewish law as source for modern legislation, *1692–1696*
liability of, in modern legislation, *1695–1696*
Bailees Law of 1967, *1692–1696*
oath as defense to, *615*
tort liability of, *630n.39*
bailments, law of
distinguishing process and, *964–966*
Jewish law as source for modern legislation, *1694–1696*
in *Mishneh Torah, 1200–1201*
Septuagint as source for, *1029*
Balfour Declaration, *Ha-Mishpat Ha-Ivri* (Jewish Law) Society and, *1588–1591*
Balkans
Jewish diaspora in, *1482*
responsa literature from, *1489–1490, 1495*
Bamberger, Isaac Dov, responsa literature and *ma'aseh, 977*
Bamberger, Moses Aryeh
responsa literature and *ma'aseh, 977*
sources of Jewish law and, *1458n.16*
ban (*herem*)
"distinguished person's" approval, *757n.293*
as enforcement method, *11–12*
issur vs. communal enactments, *708n.114*
legal vs. religious obligations and, *119–120*
of Rabbenu Gershom, *785*
as source for *Halakhah, 40, 93–94*
dates for compilation of, *42*
Banet, Mordecai, *673n.30*
bankruptcy laws
English statutes incorporated in, *1885–1894*
Israeli Bankruptcy Ordinance, *1888–1889*
suretyship law and, *1722n.386*
Barak, Aharon (Justice)
on authenticity of will, *1876–1884*
freedom of thought and speech, *1846n.75*
on *Hendeles* case, *1744, 1746n.447, 1748–1751*
lacuna interpreted by, *1838*
pittu'ah ha-mishpat theory, *1884n.232*
subjective factors affecting recourse to Jewish law, *1929–1931*
uncertainty of statutory interpretation and, *1867, 1869, 1871*

value-laden legal terms and lacuna, *1872–1874*
Basic Law: Israel Lands, *1651–1652*
Bar-Ilan, Rabbi Meir, *1606n.82*
role of Jewish law in Zionist movement, *1616–1617*
Bar Kokhba rebellion, *13n.33*
juridical autonomy, and, *19*
legal documents from, *1036*
legislative enactments during, *567*
Baraita de-R. Ishmael, *1048*
baraitot
contents of Babylonian Talmud and, *1088*
law of Mishnah compared with cognate sources, *1058–1059*
as literary source for law, *1040*
Maimonides codification of, *1333n.83*
R. Ishmael's compilations of, *1048*
tanna and, *1042*
Barcelona, diaspora in, territorial scope of legislation, *669–670*
Bar Mezera. *See* adjoining landowners' preemptive rights.
Bartenura. *See* Obadiah of Bertinoro
bartering, laws regarding
kinyan halifin and symbolic barter (*kinyan sudar*), *581–582*
rabbinic laws, *221*
Baruch b. Isaac Ashkenazi, *811n.120, 812n.123, 1239–1240, 1245n.37*
Baruch b. Samuel of Mainz, *788*
bat kol, *agunot* legislation and, *528n.148*
Bava, Judah b. (R.), *96n.14*
Bava Batra
structure of, *1054–1055*
theoretical study of, *1586*
Bava Kamma
juridical autonomy in, *1586*
public domain law in, *1096n.63*
redaction of, *1097*
structure of, *1054–1055*
Bava Mezi'a
juridical autonomy in, *1586*
redaction of, *1097*
structure of, *1054–1055*
Bayit Hadash (Bah), *1417*
commentary on *Sefer ha-Turim*, *1303–1304*
Becker v. Judge Hayyim Eilat, *1704–1706*
Bedek ha-Bayit (Repair of the House), *1276–1277, 1343, 1371, 1373n.18*
Be'er ha-Golah
Even ha-Ezer commentaries in, *1430*
Hoshen Mishpat commentaries in, *1426*
on *Orah Hayyim* and *Yoreh De'ah*, *1431*
Be'er Heitev, *1437*
Bein, Dr. Alex, *1650*
bein adam la-makom concept, *93*
"be killed rather than transgress," legal reasoning (*sevarah*) and, *990–991*
ben (offspring), laws regarding, *1029*
Ben Gurion, David (Prime Minister), *1757n.14*
on Law of Return, *1647n.113*
Women's Equal Rights Law and, *1658–1660*
Ben Shalom v. Central Elections Commission, *1647–1651*
Ben Sira, Book of, death penalty and, *1034–1035*
Bentwich, Norman, establishment of Chief Rabbinate, *1597–1598*
Benveniste, Abraham (Don), *8, 798*
Benveniste, Hayyim, *1304*
Keneset ha-Gedolah of, *1434–1437*
responsa literature of, *1489, 1523–1524*
Benveniste, Joshua, Jerusalem Talmud commentary of, *1134*
Benveniste, Moses, *1458n.18*
Berab, Jacob. *See* Ri Berab
Berakhot Tractate, *52*
class-related issues on giving in, *98*
Berdugo, Raphael, enactments of, *808n.100*
bererah, Babylonian Talmud and, *1091*
Beresford v. Minister of the Interior, *1690n.289*
Berinson, Justice
earnings of wife from her employment, rabbinical court decisions regarding, *1788, 1792–1793*
marriage between *kohen* and divorcee, Jewish law incorporated in state legislation, *1775–1776*
role of Jewish law in State legislation, *1756n.11*
Berlin, Naftal: Zevi Judah. *See* Neziv
Berlin-Pick, Isaiah, glosses on *Sefer ha-Hinnukh*, *1267n.134*
Berokah, Johanan b. (R.), on distinguishing process, *962*
Bertinoro Obadiah, *See* Obadiah of Bertinoro
"best interests of the child," *1763–1765*
bet din shel hedyotot. *See* Lay tribunals
Bet Eked Sefarim, *1561*
Bet ha-Behirah, *53*

Bet ha-Behirah, 1126, 1543
  commentary on *Sefer ha-She'iltot, 1153*
  duty to obey halakhic authorities in, *1793n.123*
Bet Horon village, *169n.315*
betrothal laws (*kiddushin, erusin*)
  "all who marry do so subject to conditions laid down by the Rabbis and the Rabbis annul this marriage" legislation, *641n.64*
  Corfu enactments regarding, *817*
  custom as source of law on, *892n.53*
  geonic enactment concerning, *656–658*
  Hillel's interpretation of *ketubbah* and, *425–426*
  legislative authority regarding, *507n.58*
  ma'aseh combining halakhic authority and judicial decision, *974–975*
  mi-shum eivah (prevention of strife and enmity) legislation, *628n.31*
  theory vs. practice in legislation in, *861–863*
  See also divorce law; family law; *huppah* (nuptial ceremony); *ketubbah*; marriage law
Bet Shemu'el, 1419, 1516–1517
  commentaries on *Even ha-Ezer, 1430*
Bet Yisra'el, commentary on *Sefer ha-Turim, 1303*
Bet Yosef, 1231
  Alfasi's influence on, *1172*
  codification methodology in, *1313–1322, 1342–1343*
  commentaries listed in, *1315–1316*
  contradictions with *Shulhan Arukh, 1370–1372*
  Darkhei Moshe linked with, *1392–1394*
  Falk's commentaries on, *1408–1414*
  Gamaliel on, *41*
  historical conditions of Jewish law in, *1311–1312*
  Jaffe's attempts at abridgement of, *1396–1397*
  Joel Sirkes' commentary on, *1416*
  Maharam of Lublin's commentaries on, *1384–1385*
  Maharibal's commentary on, *1368–1369*
  Maharshal's commentary on, *1385–1394*
  prohibition against litigation in non-Jewish courts and, *1916n.46*
  responsa compilations, *1304, 1433, 1486*
  Sefer ha-Ittur quoted in, *1269*
  Sefer ha-Turim discussed in, *1253, 1288n.200, 1302n.276, 1303*
  Sephardic authorities' acceptance of, *1373*
  supersedes *Darkhei Moshe* codification, *1351–1356*
  tax law compilations, *1444–1445*
Be'ur ha-Gra
  annulment enactments in, *871n.316*
  Even ha-Ezer commentaries in, *1430*
  Hoshen Mishpat commentaries in, *1427*
  on *Orah Hayyim* and *Yoreh De'ah, 1432*
Be'urim. See Netivot ha-Mishpat
Bibi, MK, *1747n.448*
Biblical interpretation
  amoraic halakhic interpretation and, *409*
  vs. halakhic interpretation, *401*
Biblical law (*de-oraita*)
  affirmative and negative commandments, *505–506*
  classification of, *208–212*
  enumeration of, in codificatory literature, *1259–1267*
  exegesis of, *278–280*
  inheritance rights for sons and daughters, enactments for, *844–845*
  legal reasoning (*sevarah*) and, *989, 1000–1004*
  legislation and, *477–478*
  as modification of earlier law, *197–200*
  nullification of, with criminal punishment, *515–519*
  Oral Law and, *207–223*
  Sages' law and, *214–217*
  "you shall not add or take away," *496–502*
Biblical period
  legal research into, *81*
Bibliographic Guide to Mishpat Ivri: Books and Articles in English, The, 1564
Bibliographies of halakhic works, *1560–1564*
bigamy, laws regarding
  limitations and accomplishments of Rabbinical Court of Appeals and, *1813n.192*
  Woman's Equal Rights Law and, *1656–1657*
Bingen, enactments of, *793–794*
Birkei Yosef, 1373n.18, 1439
Black Death, *1345*
  decline of Jewish population during, *1310*

persecution of Jews during, *792, 797–798*
responsa literature declines during, *1479*
blanket incorporation by reference of Jewish law
debate over, with Capacity and Guardianship Law, *1666–1671*
in State legislation, *1757*
statutory incorporation as, *1652–1653*
Blau, L.
content of Mishnah and, *1057*
on legal role of Talmud, *1099*
Blau, Moshe, *1614*
Bloch, Moses, *82*
history of legislative activity, *548n.10*
bodily harm, freedom of contract and, *127n.145*
Boleslav the Pious, *1345*
bondmen, laws regarding, *1031–1033*
Bonstrok, Isaac, *805*
Book of the Commandments (*Sefer ha-Mizvot*), *209–210*
Book of Enactments of the Jewish Community of Cracow, *821–822*
"books that are open to the public," statutory incorporation of Jewish law, *1750–1751*
borei nefashot rabbot ("who creates many living things"), *898*
borrowing laws. *See* lending, laws regarding
Boskowitz, enactments of, *823*
Boton, Abraham di
commentaries of, *1233–1234*
definition of majority, in communal enactments, *724–725*
Braun, A., *1305n.291*
"breach fences and spoil what is good," communal enactments and, *760–762*
Breuer, Dr. Isaac, *1613*
bribery, laws regarding
in Ottoman law, *1641*
Penal Law Revision (Bribery) Law, *1640–1642*
verbal bribery, *1640n.70*
British Mandatory law
Amendment of Copyright Ordinance, *1691n.290*
Amendment of Evidence Ordinance, *1691n.290*
Administration Ordinance, *1729n.414*
Arbitration Ordinance, *1818n.207*
Israeli Bankruptcy Ordinance, *1888–1889*
Civil Wrongs Ordinance (Amendment No. 3), *1645*
Criminal Law Ordinance, *1869n.183*
establishment of Chief Rabbinate, *1597–1598*
general courts' incorporation of Jewish law in personal status legislation, *1766n.46*
Hebrew language and, *1612*
immunity of judges in, *1646n.110*
Interpretation Ordinance and, *276n.7*
Israeli legal system and, *1611–1612*
Kosher Food for Soldiers Ordinance, *1647*
land laws, *1709–1710*
Law and Administration Ordinance of 1948, *537–538, 1143n.6, 1620, 1646–1647*
Law and Administration Ordinance of 1948
legal system of, *231–232, 235n.24*
Mishpat Ha-Shalom Ha-Ivri (Jewish Court of Arbitration) and, *1593*
rabbinical courts' jurisdiction and, *1760–1765, 1818n.207*
severance pay legislation, *1633*
Torts Ordinance, *1869n.183*
Bruna, R., "all who marry do so subject to conditions laid down by the Rabbis and the Rabbis annul this marriage" legislation, *638*
Buber, Solomon, *1247n.47*
"build fences and tend to improve,"
communal enactments in consonance with, *760–762*
custom as source of law, *943n.208*
building laws
Israeli state legislation regarding, *1627–1629*
burden of proof
on claimant, legal reasoning (*sevarah*) and, *992–993*
communal tax enactments, *747*
issur-mamon dichotomy and, *131–132*
Bürgerliches Gesetzbuch, *1733–1735*
burning, as means of capital punishment, *972n.100*
business law. *See* commercial law
Byzantine Empire, *2n.1*

C

Candia (Crete), communal enactments of, *811–813*
Canon law, compared with Jewish law, *5*
Canons of Biblical Interpretation, *315–316*

Canons of Biblical Interpretation *continued*
seven canons (Hillel), *315–317*
thirteen canons (*middot*) of Ishmael, *318–399*
See also specific canons
Capacity and Guardianship Law, *1663–1671*
passage of, *1625*
secularization of halakhic concepts, *1906–1908*
capital crimes, context as basis of explanation in, *335*
capital punishment (death penalty)
abrogation of, in State of Israel, *1615n.102*
subjective factors affecting recourse to Jewish law and, *1926–1931*
"Care of Lost Property Law." *See* Restoration of Lost Property Law
Carmi v. State's Attorney, expunction of criminal records and, *1709*
Caro, Joseph, *1072*
admonition of witnesses by, *1699*
annulment enactments, *870–872, 875–876*
circumvention of *kum va-Aseh* and, *532n.156*
codification methodology of, *1309–1344*
criminal communal enactments, *698*
decision making endorsed by two hundred rabbis, *1369–1370*
dual codification methodology of, *1312–1313*
early life, *1310*
halakhic competence of witnesses, *739*
Hayyim b. Bezalel's critique of, *1376*
Heller's commentary on, *1404–1407*
idolatry laws codification, *1327–1329*
Jeroham's work criticized by, *1272*
Joshua's property enactments and, *553n.34*
Kelalei ha-Gemara of, *1545–1546*
Kesef Mishneh of, *1233*
language and style compared with Maimonides and Jacob b. Asher, *1327–1340*
le-migdar milta, *536n.177*
Maharshal's commentary on, *1385–1394*
Maimonides' influence on, *1206–1208, 1221n.115*
Mishneh Torah commentaries of, *1226n.130, 1233–1234*
omissions in Babylonian Talmud and, *1095n.61*
pesakim of Asheri compared with responsa, *1459n.19*
on *Piskei ha-Rosh*, *1253*
possession (*hazakah*) law codification, *1331–1335*
property laws codification, *1330–1331*
Rashba's influence on, *1277*
responsa literature of, *1481–1482, 1486, 1520n.213*
Sefer ha-Turim commentary, *1288n.200, 1302n.276, 1303*
on *Semag* authority, *1263*
Shulhan Arukh codification, *1319–1322*
Talmudic research and, *44*
"three pillars of instruction," *1172*
cartels, formation of, Moroccan enactments concerning, *808–809*
case or incident (*ma'aseh*), as legal source of Jewish law, *239, 945–1014*
Castro, Jacob, *1371*
casuistic style
defined, *1072–1073*
halakhic studies and, *1049n.45*
Mishnah's legal style, *1073–1074*
Mishnah's literary style, *1049n.45*
Maimonides' use of, *1211–1214*
Cave of Machpelah example, of early legal practices, *195–196*
Cazimir the Great, *1345*
censorship
Ferrara enactments regarding, *816–817*
of responsa, *1466n.39, 1520–1523*
Chajes, Z. H., history of legislative activity, *548n.10*
Chamber of Hewn Stone, criminal communal enactments and, *696*
"chain of tradition," in *Mishneh Torah*, *1186*
Chaldäisches Wörterbuch Über die Targumim, *1565*
"change in the natural order," *911*
charity
class-related values and, *97–99*
legal-moral reciprocity and, *117, 143*
loan of monies owned by, *900n.14*
rules of precedence in, *100–102*
See also tithes
"charity can be compelled," in
Family Law Amendment (Maintenance) Law, *1661–1663*

Charters of Privileges, *8, 1345*
juridical autonomy and, in non-Jewish countries, *37n.108*
in Polish diaspora, *9n.20*
chattels. *See* personal property
Cheshin, Mishael, *1921–1923*
on objective factors affecting recourse to Jewish law, *1932–1938*
unique terminology of Jewish law and, *1874–1875*
Unjust Enrichment Law and, *1696n.307*
Chief Rabbinate of the Land of Israel
Aggadic-Halakhic reciprocity and, *152n.250*
child support laws, *832–833*
earnings of wife from her employment, *1791n.114*
establishment of, *1593–1594, 1596–1598*
halakhic decision-making by, *1899–1902*
powers of, in rabbinical courts, *1758n.16, 1807–1809*
Procedural Enactments of, *846n.244*
takkanah on marriage age, *1654–1656*
Women's Equal Rights Law and, *1657–1658, 1760–1765*
child support laws
Family Law Amendment (Maintenance) Law, *1660–1663*
religious vs. legal obligations in, *116–117, 120n.121*
children, laws regarding
Capacity and Guardianship Law, *1662–1671*
educational routine of, *4*
illegitimate children, enactments concerning, *827n.178*
laws regarding, as literary source, *1025–1026*
liability of, for parents, *303–304*
property legislation concerning, *585–586*
restrictive interpretations of Torah regarding, *365–366*
support laws, procedural enactments concerning, *831–833*
Usha's legislative enactments, *567–568*
See also custody of children
Christian judges, reciprocity with Jewish legal system, *63n.40*
Christianity, Oral Law's relation to, *225*
circumcision, required by conversion to Judaism, *955–956*
cities of refuge imprisonment law and, *1841n.57*
civil law (noncriminal)
incremental codification of, *1732, 1827–1828*
Israeli legislative policy and, *1625–1627, 1639*
rabbinical courts and, *1600–1605, 1818–1819*
civil law (Roman and Continental)
Cooperative Houses Law, *1627–1629*
Imprisonment for Debt law, *1635–1639*
juridical autonomy and, *34n.104, 47–48*
Labor law, *1629–1634*
lay tribunals and, *24–26*
suretyship law and, *1723–1727*
civil law (noncriminal) (*mamon*)
"all who marry do so subject to conditions laid down by the Rabbis and the Rabbis annul this marriage" legislation, *635n.53*
communal enactments and, *685–688*
community groups' legislative authority, *488–490*
creative power of custom in, *903–905*
custom and usage regarding, *911n.56, 931–932*
dinei mamonot and, *109*
distinction with "ritual law" in *Halakhah*, *111n.82*
halakhot on, *1306–1308*
"I have nothing" oath, *651–654*
issur vs. communal enactments and, *708n.117, 710*
Jacob b. Asher's codification, *1280–1281*
juridical autonomy and, *34n.104, 47–48*
"law of the land is law" and, *65n.47, 68–70*
laws derived from custom vs. laws derived from legal sources, *888–889*
lay tribunals and, *24–26*
legal reasoning (*sevarah*) and, *992*
legislative authority of community groups and, *488–490*
legislative terminology and, *492n.72*
ma'aseh and, *975–978*
in *Mishneh Torah*, *1199, 1292–1302*
Rabbinical Court of Appeals, rulings, *825–826*
religious vs. legal obligations and, *122–123*
responsa literature and, *1492–1494*

civil law (noncriminal) *continued*
Valladolid enactments regarding, *799–801*
Civil Procedure (Amendments) Law, *1703–1704*
civil rights, vs. religious coercion, in Jewish law, *1930–1931*
Civil Wrongs Ordinance (Amendment No. 3), *1645*
class issues in law
lay tribunals and, *33*
voting rights as, *96–97*
classification of Jewish law, *75–79*
conflict of laws, *78–79*
law of obligations, *76–77*
public and administrative law, *77–78*
Code of Hammurabi
debtors' laws in, *310*
liability law in, *197*
codification methodology
alternatives to *Shulhan Arukh*, *1385–1407*
in common-law countries, *1142–1144*
in continental Europe, *1141–1142*
crystallization of, following *Shulhan Arukh*, *1341–1344*
current problems in, *1451–1452*
in *Darkhei Moshe*, *1350–1356*
decline of, during diaspora, *1309–1312*, *1450–1451*
defined, *1140–1141*, *1143–1144*
"dual" methodology, *1273–1276*, *1312–1313*
Heller's methods, *1403–1407*
historical context of, *1343–1344*
Jaffe's discussion of, *1394–1403*
in Jewish law, *1144–1148*
kim li plea and, *1282–1283*
in *Mappah*, *1359–1365*
objectives of, *1141–1142*
opposition to, without alternatives, *1375–1385*
of Pollack and Shakhna, *1345–1348*
in *Shulhan Arukh*, *1319–1322*, *1327–1340*
tendency toward, during rabbinic era, *1181–1184*
topical arrangement of material, *1341n.116*
in *Torat Hattat*, *1357–1359*
codificatory literature
after *Shulhan Arukh*, *1424–1452*, *1443–1452*
after Maimonides, *1237–1238*
Aggadah and, *95n.13*
Bet Yosef, *1313–1319*
Caro's codificatory methods, *1309–1344*
classification of, *1139–1140*
commentary and novellae in, *1105*
current problems in, *1451–1452*
earnings of wife from her employment, rabbinical court decisions regarding, *1786*
Eastern countries' reaction to, *1368–1373*
enumeration of Biblical commandments as organizational technique, *1259–1267*
following the order of the Talmud, *1238–1258*
from France and Germany, *1178–1179*
in geonic period, *1150–1167*
Habiba's commentaries on, *1176*
of Hai Gaon, *1164–1166*
halakhic monographs, geonic era, *1158–1167*
Halakhot Gedolot, *1155–1156*
Halakhot Pesukot of Yehudai Gaon, *1153–1155*
historic origins of, *43–44*
Hoshen Mishpat commentaries, *1424–1429*
idiosyncratic organization of, *1267–1273*
on *issur* (religious law), *1447–1448*
Jacob b. Asher's methodology of, *1277–1287*
Jonathan of Lunel's commentaries on, *1175*
Joshua Boaz's commentaries on, *1176*
as legal source, *1102–1103*
limited access to multiple opinions in, *1377–1379*
Nahmanides (Ramban)'s commentaries, *1174–1175*
neglect of study as result of, *1377–1379*
in non-Jewish legal systems, *1140–1144*
power of, vs. responsa, *1460n.20*
Rabad's commentaries on, *1173–1174*
Ran's (Nissim Gerondi) commentaries on, *1176–1177*
Rashba's "dual" methodology, *1273–1277*
relationship to commentaries, novellae and response, *1138–1139*
of Rema (Moses Isserles), *1345–1366*
responsa compared with, *1456–1457*
Rezah's commentaries on, *1173*
of Saadiah Gaon, *1159–1161*
of Samuel b. Hophni, *1161–1164*
Sefer ha-Halakhot of Alfasi, *1167–1176*
Sefer ha-She'iltot of Aha of Shabha, *1150–1153*

Sefer ha-Turim commentaries, *1302–1308*
Sefer ha-Turim as primary source, *1277–1302*
Shulhan Arukh, *1319–1340*, *1365–1366*
from Spain, *1177–1178*
Talmudic sources, *1122n.72*
tax law compilations, *1444–1447*
coerced marriage
"all who marry do so subject to conditions laid down by the Rabbis and the Rabbis annul this marriage" legislation, *636–642*
Valladolid enactments regarding, *801–802*
cohabitation, modern Succession Law and, *1685–1688*
Cohen, Boaz, *81*, *1524*
Cohen v. Cohen case, *1804–1805*
Cohen v. District Rabbinical Court, *1777n.78*
Cohn, Haim (Justice), *1759n,20*
earnings of wife from her employment, decisions regarding, *1788*, *1790–1791*, *1793n.120*
Koenig v. Cohen case and, *1875*
tort liability of spouses, *630n.37*
uncertainty of statutory interpretation and, *1868–1871*
unique terminology of Jewish law and, *1874–1875*
collective punishment, "law of the land is law" and, *72–73*
colloquial usage. *See leshon benei adam*
Colon, Joseph
on force of communal enactment, *702n.92*
on halakhic authority, *270–271*
leshon benei adam, *439–440*
commentaries
on Alfasi's work, *1269n.142*
on Babylonian Talmud, *1113–1117*
Caro's list of, in *Bet Yosef*, *1315–1316*
characteristics of, *1105*
codificatory literature and, *1138–1139*
on *Even ha-Ezer*, *1429–1431*
geonic commentaries, *1113–1114*
R. Gershom Me'or ha-Golah and his students, *1115–1116*
on halakhic *midrashim*, *1110–1111*
Hananel's commentary, *1114–1115*
Hillel's commentary on the *Sifra* and *Sifrei*, *1111*
as historical source, *43–44*, *1462n.28*
on *Hoshen Mishpat*, *1424–1429*
on Jeroham's codifications, *1272*
on Jerusalem Talmud, *1130–1137*
Lieberman's *Tosefta Ki-Feshutah* commentary, *1112–1113*
as literary source, *1102–1103*
of Maimonides, *1106–1110*
on *Mishneh Torah*, *1231–1237*
on *Orah Hayyim* and *Yoreh De'ah*, *1431–1432*
Pardo's *Hasdei David*, *1112*
on *Piskei ha-Rosh*, *1253–1255*
Rabad's commentary on the *Sifra*, *1110–1111*
Rashi's commentary on the Talmud, *1116–1117*
of *rishonim*, *1474–1475*
scientific legal research and, *89–90*
on *Sefer ha-Halakhot*, *1173–1176*
on *Sefer ha-Hinnukh*, *1266–1267*
on *Sefer ha-Turim*, *1302–1304*
Sephardic commentaries, *1123–1127*
on *Shulhan Arukh*, *1407–1419*
on *Tosefta*, *1111–1113*
See also glosses; *midrash*; responsa
Commentary on the Mishnah, Maimonides introduction to, *1543*
commercial law
custom as source of, *913–920*
individual rights, in communal enactments, *769–771*
"law of the land is law" and, *68n.59*
power of attorney legislation, *649–651*
common law
codification in, *1142–1144*
king's law and, *57*
precedent in Jewish law and, *980–981*
responsa compared with, *1467*
vs. statutes, *1460n.20*
tort liability of spouses, *629n.37*
"commonly reputed spouse" concept, Succession Law and, *1685– 1688*
"commorientes." *See* simultaneous death
communal agreements (haskamot ha-kahal). *See* communal enactments (*takkanot ha-kahal*)
communal council (*berurim*), halakhic competence of witnesses, *738n.227*
communal enactments (*takkanot ha-kahal*)
abrogation of juridical autonomy and, *1587n.23*
"all who marry do so subject to conditions laid down by the Rabbis and the

communal enactments *continued*
Rabbis annul this marriage" legislation, *633n.48*
ambiguity, interpretation in cases of, *464–468*
applicability to minors, future generations and subsequent community members, *731–735*
attempts to revive lay courts, *1610*
authority to interpret, *445–448*
Biblical sources for, *699n.84*
binding force of, *713–714*
civil law and, *685–688*
commentaries of Elijah, Gaon of Vilna, *1427n.15*
by communal representatives, *727–730*
compilations of, *1531–1532*
competence of judges, *739–740*
competence of witnesses, *737–739*
condemnation of overnice technical interpretations, *461*
consonance with equity and justice, *760–777*
constitution of majority, *723–727*
countrywide legislation, *797*
court and community standing equated, *699–707*
criminal law, *688–698*
custom as influence on, *896n.2*
deviation from Jewish law, *1942–1945*
doreshin leshon hedyot, *429n.31, 430–432*
enactments of 1950, *833–834*
equal application of, to total community, *771–772*
equated with court legislation, *705n.99*
explanatory remarks as interpretive source, *462–464*
good public order, *462*
halakhic authorities and, *60–61, 777–778*
hefker bet din hefker and, *514*
inheritance law interpretations, *452–453*
interpretation of, *277–278, 444–473*
issur ("religious" law), *707–712*
Kezot ha-Hoshen commentaries on, *1428*
king's law and, *57*
Israeli statutes as, *1611–1612, 1621–1629, 1721–1751, 1899– 1906*
landlord/tenant law interpretations, *453–456*
language of enactment as basis for interpretation, *449–459*
"law of the land is law," *67n.53*
lay community equal to court standing, *699–707*
legal reasoning (*sevarah*) and, *1005–1006*
legislative authority and, *487–489, 538–541*
limits of, *287*
lost property law and, *299n.45*
majority rule and, *683n.16, 715–723, 762–763*
Marriage Age Law and, *1656n.143*
marriage dowries, taxation of, *446–447*
minors, persons yet unborn, and persons joining subsequent to adoption, *731–735*
mishnayot as, *1074n.151*
ownership claims, limitation period on, *744–745*
preamble as interpretive source, *462*
prejudice of minority rights prohibited, *763–771*
prospective vs. retroactive application, *772–777*
"scribal errors" in text, *458–459*
signatures, town scribe vs. witnesses' signature, *741–744*
source of authority and legal effectiveness, *685–714*
as subordinate legislation, *479n.9*
tax law, *450–452, 745–751*
territorial scope of, *668–675*
text of enactment as limit on interpretation, *457–458*
textual inconsistencies and ambiguities, *464–468*
townspeople and community, *679–685*
universally agreed intent in, *459–460*
Wiloszni case and, *1823*
See also specific enactments.
communal legislation. *See* communal enactments
communal institutions, in Polish diaspora, *1346*
communal representatives (*shiv'ah tovei ha-ir*)
communal enactments, *727–730*
modern legislation, *1823n.227*
community (*kehillah*)
halakhic-aggadic reciprocity in, *96–99*
halakhic influence on, *54n.14, 272n.117*
Jewish court system and, *6*
juridical autonomy and, *48*
public and administrative law and, *77–78*

competition, limits to freedom of, *395–397*
"compromises" (*pesharot*)
adjoining landowner's preemptive right (*din bar mezra*), *625n.16*
good faith (*tom lev*), *185–186*
justice as supplement to law and, *171–174, 175n.336*
Maharshal's commentaries on, *1390–1391*
Concordances to halakhic literature, *1568*
confidentiality, criminal evidence and, *1858n.138*
conflict of interest
competence of judges and, *739–740*
halakhic competence of witnesses and, *737–739*
conflict of laws
applicability of, in evidence and procedure, *1770*
as category of Jewish law, *78–79*
custom and, *936*
general courts' incorporation of Jewish law and, *1766–1767*
halakhic disqualification of signature, on communal enactments, *743n.241*
local legislation and, *677*
and Polish diaspora, *10n.20*
conjugal rights, issur-mamon dichotomy and, *125n.138*
conjunctive terminology, in explicative exegesis, *321–323*
consanguinity, laws regarding
Ezra's legislative enactments and, *556–558*
halakhic competence of witnesses and, *737–739*
See also incestuous relationships
conscription, king's law and, *56n.22*
consecration of property, post-Talmudic exegetical interpretation, *392–394*
Constantinople, responsa literature from, *1486–1487, 1489–1490*
Constitutional law, legal norms and, *232n.10*
"constructive desertion" doctrine, *790n.42*
context, as explanation, in thirteen canons, *334–335*
Continental law
application of, with lacuna, *1870*
interpretive approaches to Israeli legislation and, *1732*
Land Law legislation and, *1710, 1714–1716*
continuity of generations, in modern Succession Law, *1674–1683*
contra legem, custom as contrary to, *903*
contract law
civil procedure and, *1603–1605*
good faith (*tom lev*), *183, 187–188*
illegal contract legislation, *1716–1720*
king's law and, *59n.32*
law of obligations and, *76–77, 587–591*
"law of the land is law," *66*
lifenim mi-shurat ha-din, *164–166*
moral-religious sanctions and, *119–120, 149–154*
property lien legislation and, *591n.203*
terminology for, in Jewish law, *80*
See also freedom of contract; illegal contracts
Contracts Law (General Part)
gemirut da'at in, *1875*
illegal contract legislation, *1716–1720*
interpretive approaches to, *1734n.422*
Remedies for Breach of Contract section, *1729*
severing of ties to English law, *1729*
value-laden legal terms, *1736–1737*
contradictory passages in Torah, explicative exegesis regarding, *335–339*
conversos, responsa literature and, *1478, 1481*
conversion to Judaism
laws regarding assets of deceased proselyte, *959–960*
ma'aseh legislation regarding, *954–956*
status, *1688–1690*
copyists' errors
Caro's correction of, *1315n.17*
codification methodology and, *1181n.3*
in *Mishneh Torah*, *1215n.101, 1227n.135*
in Rema's codification literature, *1363*
in responsa literature, *1507–1512*
copyright law
"law of the land is law," *74n.87*
territorial scope of communal enactments and, *676n.36*
See also intellectual property law; printing; publishing
Corfu, enactments of, *817*
corporal punishment
as enforcement of judicial decisions, *10*

corporal punishment *continued*
incorporation of non-Jewish provisions, *64n.44*
legislative authority not prescribed in Torah, *515–519*
written legislation and, *534–536*
corporative state, existence of, in Jewish law, *1576–1577*
corpus juris
content of Mishnah and, *1057*
literary form of Mishnah and, *1050*
literary sources of Jewish law and, *1018–1019*
sources of custom (*ma'aseh*) legislation, *1050*
corrigenda of Caro, *1371*
Council of Four Lands (*Va'ad Arba ha-Arazot*)
codificatory literature and, *1108n.17*, *1346*
"distinguished person's" approval, *757*
enactments of, *818*
legal capacity of children, *1665*
Council of Lithuania
Capacity and Guardianship Law linked with enactments of, *1668*
codificatory literature and, *1346*
enactments of, *818–819*
Council of the Chief Rabbinate
halakhic decision-making, *1902*
procedural enactments adopted by, *1599–1600*
countrywide enactments, *797*. *See also* **specific countries**
Court of the fairs (Poland), *9n.20*
Court of the Four Lands (Poland), *9n.20*
court system
communal enactments equated with, *699–707*, *735n.218*
costs, payment of, *826–827*
criminal communal enactments and, *690–691*
differences with lay tribunals and, *30n.95*
enactments regarding proceedings of, *793*
Ezra's legislative enactments and, *556*
geonic legislative enactments in, *648n.17*
Jewish heritage (*moreshet Yisra'el*) and decisions by, *1841–1863*
juridical autonomy of, *6–10*
laws regarding, in *Mishneh Torah*, *1201–1203*
legislative authority of, *486–490*
limitation period for ownership claims, *744n.245*
majority rule and communal enactments, *719–720*
number of judges in, laws concerning, *1646n.110*
non-Jewish sources of law in, *1917*
overturning of legislation and, *541–544*
prohibition against litigation in non-Jewish courts, *1914–1917*
shev ve-Al Ta'aseh regarding, *505–506*
statutory incorporation of Jewish law and, *1739–1743n.435*, *1745–1751*, *1920–1923*
territorial scope of legislation and, *671*
tort liability of agents, *604–605*
See also general courts; Rabbinical courts; Supreme Court (Israel)
Courts Law
immunity of judges in, *1646n.110*
Section 33, judicial precedent defined, *1834–1835*
Cracow, communal enactments in, *756n.292*, *821–822*
craftsmen's guilds
communal enactments regarding, *681*, *823*
majority rule and communal enactments, *717n.157*
cravon (pledge), suretyship law and, *1026n.28*
creative interpretation (*midrash yozer*)
defined, *285–286*
vs. explicative exegesis, *374–384*
literary forms for, *305–307*
credibility, of testimony, *995n.25*
credit, laws regarding. *See* debt.
creditors
limitation of actions regarding, *1725–1727*
right of privacy and, *1858–1860*
suretyship law and, *1721–1727*
Crescas, Hasdai, *1230n.139*
Crime Register and Rehabilition of Offenders Law, *1707–1709*
criminal law
abrogation of English sources, in State of Israel, *1617n.110*
circumvention of *kum va-Aseh* and, *531–533*
codification methodology regarding, *1326–1327*
communal enactments and, *688–698*

crime register and rehabilitation of offenders law, *1707*
Defamation Law, *1642–1644*
dinei nefashot and, *109*
expunction of criminal records and, *1708–1709*
freedom from detention, *1842–1845*
immunity of Judges, *1645–1646*
incorporation of non-Jewish provisions, *64n.44*
judges interpretation of law and, *288–289*
juridical autonomy in, *34n.104, 47–48*
justice and equity in, *254–255*
king's law and, *56*
lay tribunals and, *24–26, 28*
legislative authority and, *515–519*
minimum age of criminal responsibility, *1665n.182*
modern Israeli legislation, *1639–1652*
Penal Law Revision (Bribery) law, *1640–1642*
in *Shulhan Arukh, 1326*
subjective factors affecting, *1924–1931*
tannaitic legislation, *605*
Valladolid enactments regarding, *799–801*
Criminal Law Ordinance, *1869n.183*
Criminal Procedure Law, *1707n.336*
Amendment #9, *1845*
freedom from detention, *1842–1845*
witnesses' oaths or affirmations and, *1704–1705*
criminal records, expunction of, *1708–1709*
cujus regio ejus religio, 1855
"cunning rogue,"
in estate law, *102n.38*
"sages are displeased" concept and, *154n.255*
currency, laws regarding
ketubbah obligations and, *213–214*
"law of the land is law," *69n.66*
use of non-Jewish courts for, *17*
custody of children, rabbinical courts' jurisdiction over, *1762–1765*
custom (*minhag*)
anonymous origin for, *890n.48*
ascendancy over law (*minhag mevattel halakhah*), *223n.151*
"bad custom" (*minhag garu'a*), *940–942*
binding force of, scriptural support, *893–894*
Caro's codification of, *1311n.4*
change to existing law with, *903–911*
civil procedure and, *1601–1602*
communal enactments, binding force of, *731–735*
conflict of laws and, *936*
creative force of, *911–927*
debt, recovery of, laws regarding, *912–913*
defined, *880*
determination of law, *898–900*
doreshin leshon hedyot, 431–432
equity and justice, *942–944*
error as basis of, *937–940*
extent and efficacy of, *883–885*
financial relations between husband and wife, *912–913*
Foundations of Law Act and, *1835*
functions of, *896*
general custom, *934–935*
halakhic authorities control of, *937–944*
halakhot written on, *1305–1306*
as historical source of law, *880–881*
husband's inheritance rights, enactments regarding, *838n.216*
interchangeable use of, with *takkanah* and *halakhah, 888*
issur (religious law) and, *903–905, 909–911*
issur-mamon distinction in *Halakhah* and, *130, 903–905*
Johanan on custom as law, *889, 891, 894, 935*
legal documents, laws regarding, *912–913*
as legal source of Jewish law, *239, 881–882, 888–893, 902*
literary sources for, *1050*
local custom, *935*
mamon (civil law) and, *903–905*
meaning of, *885–888*
mishpat as, *106–107*
modes of acquisition and creation of obligations, *913–920*
proof of, *927–929*
Rema's codification literature, *1362n.189*
responsa compared with, *1457–1459*
severance pay, laws regarding, *924–926*
as supplement to law, *901–903*
in tax law, *920–923*
terminology of, *492–493, 885–888*
unreasonable or illogical custom, *940*
usage and, *896–897, 930–932*
See also ma'aseh; local custom
"custom overrides the law" (*minhag mevattel halakhah*),

"custom overrides the law" *continued*
codificatory literature and, *896, 903–911, 905–909*
Jerusalem Talmud and, *906*
labor law, *906n.38*
Cutheans, *949n.19*

D
dahuk, property laws, protection of minority rights in, *766n.325*
Damascus enactments (*ke-minhag Damesek*), *930n.218*
darkhei shalom (public order), historical background for, *504*
darosh, defined, *275*
darshan, interpretation of Torah by, *315*
Da Silva, Hezekiah, *1431*
daily life, laws regarding codification of, in *Tur Orah Hayyim*, *1289*
Danzig, Abraham, codificatory literature of, *1447*
Darkhei ha-Mishnah, *1549*
Darkhei Hora'ah, *1549*
Darkhei Moshe
codificatory methodology of, *1350–1356*
commentary on *Sefer ha-Turim*, *1303*
Darkhei Moshe ha-Arokh, *1356*
Darkhei Moshe ha-Kazar, *1356*
Falk's commentaries on, *1408–1414*
links with *Bet Yosef*, *1392–1394*
"quotations" in *ad kan leshono*, *1352n.159*
tax law compilations, *1444*
Darkhei Teshuvah, *1442*
dat (*dat yehudit*) (Jewish custom)
meaning of, *885*
See also custom (*minhag*)
daughters' inheritance rights of, *152n.250, 828–829, 842–846*
hefker bet din hefker, *509n.67*
one-tenth of estate legislation, *578–580*
rabbinical court rulings on, *1755n.10*
Succession Law Bill, *1672n.215*
See also ketubbah
davar she-Hayah bi-Khelal ve-Yaza canons, *330–333*
David (King)
military legislation of, *554*
Moabite ancestors of, *362*
David b. Joseph Abudarham, *1305*
David b. Judah, *1402n.114*
commentaries on Caro and Rema, *1420n.168*
Jaffe's *Levushim* criticized by, *1418n.161*
David b. Samuel ha-Levi, *1419*
commentaries on *Even ha-Ezer*, *1429*
commentaries on *Hoshen Mishpat*, *1425*
on *Orah Hayyim* and *Yoreh De'ah*, *1431*
David b. Solomon Mashraki, responsa literature of, *1491*
Day of Atonement. *See Yom Kippur*
dayyan (rabbinical court judge)
immunity of, *1644–1646*
limitations and accomplishments of, *1810–1818*
witnesses' oaths or affirmations, *1703–1704*
dayyo la-ba min ha-din liheyot ka-nidon, *350–351*
Dead Sea Scrolls, as source for legal material, *1036n.85*
deaf mutes, property legislation concerning, *585–586*
death penalty
in Book of Jubilees, *1033–1034*
courts' administration of, *11*
criminal communal enactments and, *695–696*
Flavius Josephus' interpretation of, *1032–1033*
Jewish juridical autonomy regarding, *8*
king's law and, *55–56, 56n.23, 61n.37*
legal-moral reciprocity and, *142n.206*
legislative authority not prescribed in Torah, *515–519*
ma'aseh legislation, *971–972*
scriptural analogy canon (*hekkesh ha-Katuv*), *345n.195*
debt, laws regarding
authorized entry on property and, *399n.418*
Biblical vs. rabbinic laws regarding, *218n.130*
burial of debtor and, *975n.105*
communal, prospective vs. retroactive enactments, *774–777*
creditor's rights, in property liens, *595n.219*
custom as legal source of law on, *882n.8, 912–913*
fraudulent conveyances laws, *416–418*
"I have nothing" oath to enforce civil judgments, *651–654*
illegal contracts and, *128–130*
imprisonment. *See* imprisonment for debt.
interpretive differences in, *295–297*

issur (religious law) vs. communal enactments, 709–710 in *Mishneh Torah*, *1213n.98*
law of obligations and, *76–77, 588–591*
"law of the land is law," *72n.77*
logical interpretation of Torah and, *340–341*
ma'aseh concerning suretyship, *953–954*
oral vs. documented, encumbered property and, *593–596*
partial claims, oaths required for, *615*
property equalization for debt satisfaction, *646–648*
property lien legislation and, *591–597*
prosbul enactment and, *512–513*
as religious obligation, *117–119*
right of privacy and, *1858–1860*
servitude as penalty for, *310–311*
unliquidated, encumbered property and, *592–593*
See also fraudulent conveyances; imprisonment for debt
decision-making, *95–96*
abrogation of juridical autonomy and, *1587n.23*
abstention from, *1475n.69*
Alfasi's *Sefer ha-Halakhot* and, *1170–1171*
anonymous source of law and, *1060n.90*
Caro's method of, *1226n.134, 1311n.4, 1317–1319, 1369–1370*
Darkhei Moshe codification and, *1350–1356*
development of Babylonian Talmud and, *1089–1091*
halakhic authorities' approach to, *1251n.65*
hilkheta ke-vatra'ei, *267–271, 1345–1348*
Heller's commentaries on, *1109n.22*
issur-mamon distinction in *Halakhah* and, 131–132 judicial, *416*
mishpat as, *106*
vs. research activities, *1909–1914*
See also halakhic decision making
"deed of half a male" (*shetar hazi zakhar*), *846n.244*
Defamation Law (*Hok Leshon ha-Ra*), *1642–1644, 1645n.103*
civil procedure and, *1604–1605*
defendant, plaintiff's power of attorney against, *649–651*
de Medina, Samuel, documentary interpretation of, *441–443*
De'ot (Ethical Principles), *1198*
Derekh Hayyim, criticism of *pilpul* in, *1381n.39*
Derekh Shofet bi-Yerushalayim, *1591n.28*
derishah va-hakirah, witnesses, inquiry and examination procedures, *605–609*
Derush ve-Hiddush, *1129n.104*
destruction of the Temple, revival of court system and, *6–7*
detention, freedom from, Foundations of Law Act and, *1842–1845*
Deuteronomy, Book of
Chapter 17, legislative power of Halakhic authorities, *484–485*
exegetical interpretation of, *279–280*
influence of Oral Law on, *201–202*
interpretation of legal rules and, *292–293*
legal sources of Jewish law and, *236–237*
as literary source for law, *1024–1025, 1029*
Maimonides' reliance on, *1210*
Mishneh Torah and, *1197*
on personal freedom of debtors, *310*
Development Authority, Basic Law: Israel Lands and, *1651–1652*
development of the law
overview, *46–50*
pittu'ah ha-mishpat theory, *1884n.232*
diaspora
abrogation of juridical autonomy and, *1579–1588*
appeals courts of, *825n.171*
communal legislation during, *488–490*
conflict of laws and, *78–79*
decline of codification during, *1310–1312*
history of legislative activity, *547–548*
issur vs. communal enactments during, *710*
Jewish Government in, *58–59*
juridical autonomy during, *2–3, 7–8, 15–16, 46–48*
Law of Return and, *1648–1651*
"law of the land is law," *65*
lay tribunals during, *27–29*
responsa literature generated by, *1477*
rise of *kehillah* and, *666–670*
scientific legal research about, *85–86, 88n.49*
sukkah laws and, *498n.10*
tax laws, communal enactments in, *745–751*
See also specific countries.
Dictionary of Jewish-Palestinian Aramaic, *1566*

Dictionary of Talmud Babli, Yerushalmi, Midrashic Literature and Targumim, *1566*
dietary laws
integrative interpretation of, *377n.335*
kelal u-ferat canon regarding, *324–325*
power of custom and, *909n.49*
restrictive interpretations of Torah and, *369–370*
See also fasting, laws regarding.
Digest of Responsa Literature, *1525–1528, 1540*
Digest of the Responsa Literature of Spain and North Africa, *443n.87, 1526n.244, 1934n.98*
Dikdukei Soferim, *1567*
Dikdukei Soferim ha-Shalem, *1567*
dilma. *See ma'aseh*
din, terminology of, *238n.38, 350n.212*
dina de-malkhuta dina. *See* "law of the land is law"
din bar mezera. *See* adjoining landowners' preemptive right
dinei kenasot, law of fines, *108n.73*
dinei mamonot
in civil law, *109*
in criminal law, *109*
justice and equity and, *257–258*
in *Mishneh Torah*, *1212n.98*
dinei nefashot (laws of souls), *108–109*
"Dinei Yisra'el be-Erez Yisra'el" (Jewish Law in the Land of Israel), *110, 1613*
din emet le-amito
justice and equity as basis for, *250–251*
tax law compilations, *1446n.78*
Dine Israel, *1570–1571*
dinim, terminology and classification, *108–109*
disaffirmance, laws regarding, *1291*
discipline, role of, in Jewish society, *1576–1577*
disinheritance of heirs. *See* Inheritance law
disjunctive terminology, in explicative exegesis, *321–323*
"distinguished person's" approval
Asheri's commentaries on, *755–756*
ban (*herem*), *757n.293*
communal enactments integrated into halakhic system, *751–759*
Council of Four Lands approval, *757*
enforcement of communal enactments by, *684n.19, 702n.92, 714n.144*
halakhic scholar (*talmid hakham*), as," *755–759*
majority rule and communal enactments, *715n.150*
distinguishing process in Jewish law
bailments and, *964–966*
law of interest and, *966–968*
ma'aseh and, *960–964*
District Rabbinical Court (Israel), *707n.112*
influence of Jewish law in, *1731n.417*
Rabbinical Court of Appeals and, *1817–1818*
Divine revelation, supreme vs. subordinate legislation, *479–480*
divorce law
abstention from exercising legislative powers, *864–869*
arrangement of laws in Mishnah, *1056*
blanket incorporation of Jewish law, in modern legislation, *1652*
consent of wife required, *785–786*
decline in legislation affecting validity, *846–879*
desertion by wife, enactments regarding, *790n.42*
differences in interpretation in, *293–297*
din Torah and, *111n.84*
earnings of wife from her employment, *1785–1794*
enactments prohibiting challenges to validity of, *787*
Gamaliel the elder's legislative enactments, *563–566*
get me'usseh (improper coercion), *851*
geonic legislation, *656–665*
halakhic religious-legal interactions in, *120–122*
indirect halakhic interpretation, *404–405*
integrative interpretation and, *375–376*
ketubbah obligations and, *213–214*
law of pleadings and, *385–386*
law of principal and agent and, *113n.91*
"law of the land is law," *67n.59*
legal vs. moral obligations in, *145n.214*
moredet legislation, *658–665*
Oral Law influence on, *200–202*
practice of, during Diaspora, *1605–1606*
prolonged separation, enactments regarding, *787–788*
rabbinical court rulings on, *1754n.9, 1759n.21*
reliance on Jewish law in, *1934*
Sages' legislative authority and, *522n.122*
sectarian disputes about, *1065*
Sefer ha-Turim codification of, *1291*

Wiloszni case and, *1820*
Women's Equal Rights Law and, *1656–1660*
See also family law; *get* (bill of divorcement); marriage law
divrei kabbalah (matters/words of tradition)
halakhic classification and, *208*
as literary source, *1021n.3*
Oral Law and, *203–204*
Divrei ha-Keneset, 1727n.412
Divrei Yemei Yisra'el be-Togarma, 1559
"Doctrine of Worthier Title," inheritance law and, *1673n.219*
documentary interpretation
ambiguities resolved against obligee, *433–436*
communal enactments and, *467–468*
dominance of later clause, *433–436*
doreshin leshon hedyot, 422–432
guidelines for, *432–443*
leshon benei adam, 437–443
vav (Hebrew letter) conjunction and disjunction, *440–441*
Doeg the Edomite, *362*
Donin, Nicholas, codificatory literature and, *1263*
"Do not stand idly by the blood of your fellow," 1924–1931
Dor Dor ve-Doreshav, 1550
doreshin leshon hedyot
"ascertaining lay usage" with, *429–432*
custom and usage, *932*
documentary interpretation, *422–432*
interpretation of *ketubbah* with, *422–428*
sharecropping lease laws and, *428–429*
Dorot ha-Rishonim, 1550
dough-tithe, Rashba's codificatory literature on, *1276n.160*
"do what is right and good"
adjoining landowner's preemptive right, (*din bar mezra*), *625–626*
amoraic legislation based on, *623–629*
shuma hadra (return of appraised property) legislation, *627–628*
Draft Evidence Bill, passage of, *1625*
Draft Individual and Family Bill, *1660n.156, 1625*
Draft Land Bill, *1709–1710*
Draft Succession Bill, adoption of, *1626, 1671–1672*
Dubnow, Simon, *819*
"dust of the earth," illegal contract legislation, *1720*
"duty in the sight of heaven," (*lazeit yedei shamayim*)
good faith (*tom lev*), *183*
legal vs. moral obligations, *148–149*
Dykan, Prof. P. (Dikstein)
Mishpat Ha-Shalom Ha-Ivri and, *1595–1596*
on proposals requiring recourse to Jewish law, *1617–1618*

E

economic conditions
enforcement of communal enactments, *684n.20, 726n.187*
Jewish community and government and, *36–37*
lay tribunals and, *27–28*
Edels, Samuel, restrictive interpretations of Torah, *366n.281*
Eduyyot Tractate, legal development of rules, *1069*
ma'aseh regarding legal instruments, *952*
education of children
divorced couples' responsibility regarding, *1762–1765*
lack of curricula and instruction on Judaism in, *1931–1933*
parents' rights and obligations, *1794–1802*
Valladolid enactments, *799*
Effect of Admonition provision, *1706*
Efrati, Simon, responsa literature of, *1408*
Egypt, Jewish community in
Maimonides' enactments and, *809–810*
prohibition against returning to, in *Mishneh Torah*, *1212n.98*
Ehrenberg, Joshua Menahem, responsa literature of, *1499*
Eina, R., *1094*
Einleitung in Talmud und Midrash, 1549
Ein Mishpat, 1562–1563
Ein Mishpat-Ner Mizvah, 1176n.99
Eisenstadt, Abraham Zevi Hirsch, *1441*
ejusdem generis canon, *328n.149*
Eleazar b. Judah, *1239*
Elephantine papyri, as literary source for Jewish law, *1028, 1037*
Elhanan, Yizhak, *1910n.35*
Eliezer b. Hyrcanus
on concessions to suprahuman influence, *264–265*
as halakhic authority, *261–262*
on literary legal sources, *1044, 1068*

Eliezer b. Jacob, R.
on anonymous law, *1060n.89*
codification methodology of, *505n.50, 1326n.54*
criminal communal enactments, *694*
development and redaction of Mishnah, *1050–1052*
legislative authority not prescribed in Torah, *515–516*
ma'aseh and, *948*
tractates of, *1050*
Eliezer b. Joseph, responsa questions submitted by, *1476*
Eliezer Ben Yehuda
on responsa literature, *1511n.175*
Eliezer ben Yehudah, *1608*
Elijah (prophet), halakhic authority of, *261–263*
Elijah b. Benjamin Wolff Shapiro of Prague, *1403*
Elijah of Fulda, commentary and novellae of, *1134–1135*
Elijah b. Shelomo Zalman, Gaon of Vilna, commentaries of
on *Even ha-Ezer*, *1430*
on *Hoshen Mishpat*, *1427*
on Jerusalem Talmud, *1136–1137*
on *Orah Hayyim* and *Yoreh De'ah*, *1432*
on *Tur Hoshen Mishpat*, *1296n.232*
Elishar, Jacob Saul, responsa literature of, *1495*
Eliyahu, M., *1810n.189*
Eliyahu Rabba, *1403n.115*
elohim, Septuagint interpretation of, *1029*
Elon, Menachem
Defamation Law and, *1645n.103*
dissenting opinion on *Hendeles* case, *1742–1745*
distinction between study and adjudication, *1910–1911*
education of children, parents' rights and responsibilities, *1794n.127, 1802*
extradition cases, *1861*
Fund of the Movement of Progressive Judaism in Israel v. Minister of Religions, *1779–1782*
Law of Return, *1647–1648*
Nagar case, *1762n.33*
right of privacy, *1856–1860*
status of converted Jews, *1689n.289*
Wiloszni case, *1758–1759, 1820–1824, 1944–1945*
Emancipation, era of
abrogation of juridical autonomy during, *1582–1588*
attitudes toward Jewish law in, *1578–1579*
changes in Hebrew language during, *1577–1578*
communal enactments following, *490, 824*
halakhic authorities' warnings regarding changes, *1579–1582*
impact on character of Jewish society, *1913–1914*
internal-spiritual and external-political changes, *1576–1577*
juridical authority and, *3*
responsa literature of, *1491–1495*
Emden, Jacob (Ya'vez)
commentaries of, *1426n.13*
responsa literature of, *1490*
emergency regulations, legislative authority and, *538n.183*
eminent domain, "law of the land is law" and, *68*
Encyclopaedia Judaica
alphabetic arrangement of *mishpat ivri*, *1554–1556*
German and English versions, *1560*
Encyclopedias of halakhic literature, *1551–1556*
alphabetical arrangement of, *1554–1556*
biographical articles in, *1560*
Enziklopedyah Talmudit, *1554*
Die Exegetische Terminologie der Jüdischen, *1553*
Mafte'ah ha-Talmud, *1553–1554*
Pahad Yizhak, *1551–1552*
Sedei Hemed, *1552–1553*
enforcement methods for Jewish judicial decisions, *10–13*
Engel, Samuel, responsa literature of, *1496*
Englard, Professor I., *1911n.38*
English and Empire Digest, The, *1526n.244*
English Jews, legal instrument compilations of, *1537–1538*
English law
application of, with lacuna, *1870–1871*
developmental changes in, *49*
"Doctrine of Worthier Title" in, *1673n.219*
ejusdem generis, *328n.149*
divine law as source for, *235n.24, 263n.85*

Foundations of Law Act and, *1828, 1890–1894*
illegal contracts in, *128*
Israeli courts' reliance on, *1920–1923*
Israeli legislation linked with, *1621–1623, 1728–1729, 1766n.46*
king's law in, *57*
legal norms and, *231–232*
precedent in Jewish law and, *980*
repeal of Article 46 and, *1828*
severing of tie with Israeli law, *1617n.110, 1670–1671, 1732– 1735*
Succession Law influenced by, *1673n.219, 1674nn.225–226*
suretyship law and, *1721–1722*
English statute of Elizabeth of 1571, *1885–1894*
Enlightenment (*Haskalah*)
history of legislative activity, *548*
decline of *kehillah* and, *667*
enumeration of Biblical commandments, codificatory literature on, *1259–1267*
Enziklopedyah le Hakhmei ha-Talmud ve-ha-Geonim, 1560
Enziklopedyah Talmudit, 1554
Enziklopedyah le-Toledot Gedolei Yisra'el Mi-Sof Tekufat ha-Geonim Ad ha-Me'ah ha-Tesha-Esreh, 1560
Ephraim of Luntshits, *1418n.161*
Ephraim Zalman Margolioth of Brody, *1432, 1440–1441*
Epstein, Jehiel Michal
codificatory literature, *1448–1450*
on competence of judges, *740*
on freedom of thought and speech, *1848–1849*
Epstein, J. N.
development and redaction of Mishnah and, *1052*
interpretation of Torah and, *285*
equality
halakhic-aggadic reciprocity on, *97–99*
in inheritance rights for sons and daughters, *575–578, 828–829, 842–846*
composition of majority, in communal enactments, *724*
of sexes, in modern Succession Law, *1683–1688*
equity (*yashar*)
Akedat Yizhak, discussion of, *247–251*
Arama's discussion of, *247–252, 255–256*
communal enactments consonance with, *760–777*
criminal law and, *254–255*
custom (*minhag*) and, *942–944*
din emet le-amito and, *250–251*
dinei mamonot and, *257–258*
Foundations of Law Act and, *1839–1840*
justice and, *248–251*
king's law and, *57*
"law of the land is law," *72*
lifenim mi-shurat ha-din, 167–182
literary sources on, *1840n.54*
rule and discretion and, *176–182*
Erekh Lehem, 1371
Ergas, Joseph, on power of custom, *908n.46*
Erkenntnisquellen des Rechts, 235n.25. See also literary sources of Jewish law
Erkhei Midrash, 1553
erusin (betrothal), *424n.8*
ervat davar, differences in interpretation in, *293–295*
eruv hazerot, and *eruv tehumin*, law of principal and agent and, *113n.91*
Escapa, Joseph, *1446*
estates, and wills
daughters' inheritance rights in, *152–153*
disinheritance in place of charity, *99–102*
issur-mamon distinction in *Halakhah* and, *124–125*
freedom of contract and, *126n.140*
laws regarding, *1200–1201*
modern Succession Law and, *1681–1683*
"oral will," modern Succession Law and, *1682–1683*
"quasi will" provision, *1687–1688*
in suicide cases, *1875–1884*
support of daughters out of father's estate, *574–575*
Torah's provisions for, *152n.250*
validity of, *99–102, 1875–1884*
See also inheritance law; wills and estates
estoppel, "I have nothing" oath to enforce civil judgments, *651n.29*
et, Biblical use of word, *372–374*
ethical grounding of rules, Maimonides' compilation of, *1193*
Etzioni, Justice, *1804–1805*
etrog, taking of, religious-legal obligations and, *114n.97*
Et Sofer, 1539
European law, codification in, *1141–1142*
Even ha-Ezel, 1129n.104
Even ha-Ezer
as codificatory literature, *1179*

Even ha-Ezer continued
commentaries on, *1429–1431*
contents and organization of, *12*
David b. Samuel ha-Levi's commentaries on, *1425*
as legislative source, *105*
modern responsa to, *1498–1499*
Ozar ha-Posekim on, *1442*
responsa literature and, *1492*
Rivkes' commentaries on, *1426*
Yad Aharon responsa on, *1438–1439*
eviction law, *lifenim mi-shurat ha-din*, *167n.305*
evidence, laws of
civil procedure and, *1602–1603*
Criminal Procedure Law and, *1707n.337*
general courts' circumspection of Jewish law in, *1767–1770*
halakhic-aggadic reciprocity on, *96n.14*
issur-mamon distinction and, *131n.167*
"law of the land is law," *70n.73*
in *Mishneh Torah*, *1201–1202, 1292n.216*
rabbinical courts' ruling on, *1754n.8*
state laws regarding, Jewish law as source for, *1691n.290*
tannaitic legislation concerning, *605–614*
See also witnesses
excavations, laws regarding, casuistic style of Mishnah and, *1073–1074*
Execution Law, imprisonment for debt legislation, *1638–1639*
exegetical interpretation
in amoraic period, *383–390*
analogical exegesis, *343–360*
antiquity of, *308–309*
Biblical vs. rabbinical law and, *210–211*
decline in use of, *383–384*
explicative exegesis, *319–339*
Ezra the Scribe and, *309–314*
methods of Akiva and Ishmael, *316–317, 371–383*
in post-Talmudic period, *391–399*
thirteen canons of (*middot*), *318–319*
in*Zugot* period, *314–315*
See also logical interpretation; restrictive interpretation
Die Exegetische Terminologie der Jüdischen, *1553*
exilarch
influence of, *645*
territorial scope of legislation and, *671*
ex nihilo, illegal contract legislation, *1720*
Exodus, Book of, *elohim* interpreted in, *1029*
ex parte decisions, enactment of Hayyim or Zaru'a, *791*
expert testimony, statutory interpretation, according
to Jewish law, *1750–1751*
explicative exegesis
classification of, *319*
conjunctive, disjunctive, masculine and feminine terms, *321–323*
contextual explanations and, *333–335*
contradictory passages, *335–339*
vs. creative and integrative interpretation, *374–384*
defined, *319*
generalization and specification in, *323–333*
terminology of, *320–321*
See also specific generalization/specification canons
explicit analogy, scriptural analogy canon and (*hekkesh ha-Katuv*), *344–345*
extradition laws, Jewish heritage and, *1861–1863*
extravagance in dress
Forli enactments regarding, *814–815*
Valladolid enactments concerning, *803–804*
Eybeschütz, David Solomon, *1432*
Eybeschütz, Jonathan, *1421n.173*
on *Orah Hayyim* and *Yoreh De'ah*, *1432*
Urim ve-Thummim of, *1426–1427*
on witnesses' oaths or affirmations and, *1704n.330*
"eye for an eye," *halakhah le-Moshe mi-Sinai* concept and, *207n.86*
Ezekiel, Book of, laws of idolatry in, *1329n.63*
Ez Hayyim, *1300n.269*
Ezra, Book of
communal enactments and, *686*
court's authority to expropriate in, *510n.73*
hefker bet din hefker, *508*
legislative enactments and, *554–558*
Ezra the Scribe, exegetical interpretation from, *309–314*

F

Falk, Joshua, commentaries of, *1207n.74*
criticism of Jaffe's commentary, *1403*

on *Hoshen Mishpat*, *1424–1425*
legal research of, *159, 167*
legislative enactments, *1129*
on *Sefer ha-Turim*, *1303*
on *Shulhan Arukh*, *1408–1414*
false testimony, modern legislation on, *1697–1707*
Family Bill, *1625*
family law
Capacity and Guardianship Law, *1663–1671*
contraction in scope of during post-geonic period, *676–677*
Corfu enactments regarding, *817*
daughter's support out of father's estate, *574–575*
distinguishing process and, *961–962*
earnings of wife from her employment, *1785–1794*
enactments of 1944 regarding, *829–833*
Family Law Amendment (Maintenance) Law, *1660–1663*
financial aspects of, full legislative authority over, *835–846*
general courts' application to personal status legislation, *1765–1784*
halakhot on, *1306–1308*
husband's right of inheritance, *573–574*
inheritance rights, *575–578*
Israeli legislation on, *1652–1690*
"jurisdictional competition" in, *1756–1757*
legislative enactments concerning, *570–580*
in Maimonides' *Sefer Nashim*, *1198–1199*
Marriage Age law, *1653–1656*
melog property usufruct, *572*
mi-shum eivah (prevention of strife and enmity) legislation, *629–631*
"one-tenth of the estate" enactment, *578–580*
Orah Hayyim and *Yoreh De'ah* commentaries, *1431–1432*
Rabbenu Gershom's enactments concerning, *785–786*
Rabbinical jurisdiction over, *1753–1765*
reliance on Jewish law in, *1934*
rights to wife's handiwork, *571–572*
in *Sefer Ez Hayyim*, *1256n.88*
Sefer ha-Turim codification of, *1290–1291*
spousal support enactments, *570–571*
widow's right to maintenance, *573–574*
Women's Equal Rights Law and, *1656–1660*
See also children, laws regarding; divorce law;
inheritance law; marriage law; wife-beating
Family Law Amendment (Maintenance) Law, *1653, 1660–1663*
adoption of, *1625*
amendment of Woman's Equal Rights Law and, *1806–1807*
linked with Capacity and Guardianship Law, *1669*
"family provision" allowance, in inheritance law, *1678–1679*
Fas ve-Hakhameha, *1559*
Fassel, Hirsch, *82*
fasting, laws regarding, *le-migdar milta*, *536n.177*
Fatwa of Moslem law, responsa compared with, *1466–1468*
Feinstein, Moses (Rabbi), halakhic decision making, *1902*
"fence around the Torah," and criminal communal enactments, *692–696*
Ferrara, Italy, enactments adopted in, *813, 816–817*
festivals
halakhot on, *1305*
Rashba's codificatory literature on, *1275n.160*
as subject of *Sefer ha-Ittur*, *1268*
festive banquets
Forli enactments regarding, *814–815*
Valladolid enactments concerning, *803–804*
Fez, Jewish community in
differences between 1494 and 1592 enactments, *869–870*
husband's inheritance rights, enactments, *838–840*
enactments of, *806–809*
equal inheritance rights for sons and daughters,
enactments for, *845–846*
fictions, religious-legal obligations and, *115*
fictitious names and places, use of, in responsa, *1512–1515*
Fierer, Ben-Zion (Rabbi), *1800*
Fifth Commandment, Capacity and Guardianship Law and, *1670–1671*
Figo, Azariah b. Ephraim, *1246*

Figo, Azariah b. Ephraim *continued*
findings of fact, civil procedure and, *1604–1605*
First Amendment to U.S. Constitution, *105n.52*
firstborn, generalization and specification in canons regarding, *329–330*
First fruits (*bikkurim*)
  mishpat, *107*
  religious-legal obligations and, *114*
flogging (*ve-yisru*) law
  influence of Oral Law on, *201–202*
  Septuagint as source for, *1029*
  See corporal punishment
Florence, enactments of, *816*
"follow the majority," 717–718.
  See also majority rule
"follow the way of the good," 156n.264, *158n.272*
force majeure, bailee's liability and, *1695–1696*
foreign law, recognition of, in Jewish courts, *1583n.17*
  See also specific law, e.g., English law; American law, etc.
"forever" (*le-olam*), Flavius Josephus' interpretation of, *1031–1032*
forgery, laws regarding
  authentication and certification of legal instruments, *611–614*
  by heirs, inheritance rights of, *1677n.242*
Forli, enactments adopted in, *813–816*
"for the sake of his livelihood," labor legislation, *519–520*
Foundations of Law Act (1980)
  complementary legal sources and, *1828, 1942*
  constitutional significance of, *1832*
  court decisions and, *1841–1863, 1895–1897*
  English law linked with, *1921–1923*
  English statute of Elizabeth incorporated in, *1885–1894*
  freedom from detention, *1842–1845*
  freedom of thought and speech, *1846–1850*
  fundamental rights of detainees and prisoners under, *1841–1842*
  human and dignity and equality, *1850–1854*
  Israeli Declaration of Independence and, *1832–1834*
  Jewish heritage (*moreshet Yisra'el*) and, *1839–1840, 1861–1863*
  lacunae and, *1835–1838*
  "legal issues requiring decision" and, *1835–1838*
  legislation, judicial precedent and analogy in, *1834–1835*
  link between Jewish law and Israeli legal system, 1731–1732, *1743n.436, 1751, 1863–1884, 1934–1938, 1945– 1946*
  national and religious minorities, attitudes toward, *1854–1856*
  origins of, *1624–1627*
  Palestine Order in Council Article 46 repeal and, *1828–1832*
  "positive command" section, *1831–1832*
  right of privacy under, *1856–1860*
  Section 2(b), *1829–1831*
"four cubits in the Land of Israel," 649–651
force majeure
  "all who marry do so subject to conditions laid down by the Rabbis and the Rabbis annul this marriage" legislation, *633n.49*
  Biblical oaths and, *615*
  protection of minority rights, in communal enactments, *764*
  theory vs. practice in legislation in, *862*
Fraenkel, David, commentary and novellae of, *1135*
France, Jewish community in
  codificatory literature from, *1178–1179*
  Jewish expulsion from, *1478*
  legislative enactments by, *783–796*
  proliferation of *halakhot* in, *1279*
Frank, Zevi Pesah,
  responsa literature of, *1499*
Frankel, Zacharias, *82*
  on Josephus' literary work, *1032–1033*
  on tannaitic legislation, *546–547*
Frankfurt, enactments of, *794–796*
fraudulent conveyances
  Jewish law concerning, *1891–1894*
  post-Talmudic halakhic resourcefulness in combating, *416–418*
fraudulent marriages. *See* annulment of marriage
freedom of contract
  halakhic religious-legal distinctions and, *123–127*
  inheritance matters and, *126n.140*
  invalidation of contracts and personal freedom, *127n.146*

religious-legal obligations and, *123–127*
See also contract law
freedom, principles of
Foundations of Law Act and, *1839–1840*
literary sources on, *1840n.54*
Freimann, Abraham Haim, *83, 88*
on Asheri's *Piskei ha-Rosh*, *1252n.66*
on Jewish law in Land of Israel, *1613*
on *kim li* plea, *1282n.179*
as literary source, *1519n.207 1552n.90*
Freimann, Jacob
as literary source, *1552n.90*
on overruling of legislation, *543n.202*
Friedmann, D. (Prof.), *1896n.262*
illegal contract legislation, *1717–1718*
on lacuna, *1837*
"from within its four corners," interpretive approaches to Israeli legislation, *1733–1735*
fruit, rules forbidding eating of untithed, custom based on error regarding, *938–939*
Frumkin, Gad, *1591n.28*
"fulfillment of duty in the sight of heaven" (*lazeit yedei shamayim*), *148–149*
"full integrity" (*yosher lev*), statutory incorporation of Jewish law in legislation, *1735n.422*
Fund of the Movement of Progressive Judaism in Israel v. Minister of Religions, *1779–1782*
future generations, communal enactments, binding force of, *731– 735*

G

Gagin, Hayyim Abraham, commentaries of, *1305n.286*
Gagin, Shalom Moses Hai
annulment enactments, *876–878*
commentaries of, *1305n.286*
Galante, Mordecai, annulment enactments, *874*
Gali v. State of Israel, extradition laws and, *1861*
Galileans, interpretation of*ketubbah* by, *806n.93*
Galipapa, Elijah, history of legislative activity, *548n.10*
gam, Biblical use of word, *372–374*
Gamaliel the Elder, Rabban, *41*
agunot legislation and, *526*
"all who marry do so subject to conditions laid down by the Rabbis and the Rabbis annul this marriage" legislation, *40, 631–35, 640*
arrangement of laws in Mishnah, *1056*
legislative enactments of, *563–566*
as major *tannai*, *1043–1044*
moredet legislation, *663n.82*
responsa in Talmudic literature, *1454–1455*
Gamaliel II, Rabban
agunot legislation and, *526*
halakhic pluralistic disputes and, *1068–1069*
Yavneh center established, *1066–1067*
in second tannaitic generation, *1044*
Gamaliel, Simeon b. (Rabban)
on *Bet Yosef*, *41*
on inheritance law, *1674*
issur-mamon distinction in *Halakhah* and, *125–126*
on *ketubbah* obligations, *214*
writings of, *6, 1901*
Gamaliel of Yavneh, Rabban. *See* Gamaliel II, Rabban
gambling
imprisonment for, Cracow enactments concerning, *821–822*
Forli enactments regarding, *814*
rabbinic law regarding, *218–219*
gamir, lay tribunals and, *22–23*
Gans, Eduard, writings of, *81*
Ganzfried, Solomon, codificatory literature of, *1447–1448*
garmi concept, rabbinic law regarding, *219–220*
"gates of influence," Moroccan enactments and, *809*
"gates of tears are not closed,"
Foundations of Law Act and, *1890–1891*
Gavison, Professor Ruth, on statutory interpretation, *1930*
Gedolei Saloniki le-Dorotam, *1559*
Gemara
Halihkhot Olam as guide to, *1545*
Mishneh Torah and, *1226–1227*
overview of, *1084–1085*
gemirut da'at (legal binding)
communal enactments equated with courts, *706*
contract law, *1875, 1876n.204*
custom regarding, *943–944*
modes of acquisition and, *917*
validity of wills and, *1877–1884*

gender-discrimination laws, incorporation of Jewish law and, *1721*
gender-specific terminology, explicative exegesis and, *322–323*
General Archive for Jewish History, *1532n.5*
general courts
  conflict of laws, *1766–1767*
  evidence and procedure legislation, *1767–1770*
  personal status legislation and, *1755–1756, 1765–1784*
  rabbinical courts' decisions on, *1784–1802*
  recognition of foreign law in, *1583n.17*
general literature, as literary source for Jewish law, *1027– 1036*
general principle canon (*binyan av*)
  a fortiori inference and, *328*
  analogical interpretation of, *343, 355–360*
  for documentary interpretation, *432–443*
  overview of, *330–333*
  priority of, *360*
generalization, in thirteen canons
  in addition to specification, *330–333*
  explicative exegesis, *323–330*
  literal application of discouraged, *408n.23, 439–440*
  post-Talmudic halakhic interpretations and, *418–421*
  relationship to other canons, *327–328*
  requiring a specification, *328–330*
  specification required by, *328–329*
  See also specification, in thirteen canons
genevah, distinction from *gezelah*, *1861*
Genizah of Cairo
  fragments of Samuel b. Hophni Gaon's works, *1161*
  halakhic monographs and, *1166n.62*
  responsa buried in, *1469, 1472*
geonic period (*geonim*)
  codificatory works in, *1150–1167*
  commentaries and novellae in Mishnah during, *1106*
  commentaries on Babylonian Talmud in, *1113–1114*
  communal legislation during, *489–490*
  debates over codification during, *1156–1158*
  doreshin leshon hedyot, *423*
  exegetical interpretation by, *391*
  halakhic-aggadic reciprocity in, *96n.14*
  halakhic authority in, *53–54, 268*
  history of legislation during, *643–646*
  "I have nothing" oath to enforce civil judgments, *651–654*
  legal interpretations of, *277–278*
  literary legal sources of, *1101–1102*
  Maharshal's commentaries and, *1388n/62*
  marriage and divorce legislation, *656–665*
  midrashic compilations, *1047*
  power of attorney legislation, *649–651*
  property equalization for debt satisfaction, *646–648*
  resolution of conflicts between Babylonian and Jerusalem Talmud, *1131–1132*
  responsa literature in, *1468–1472*
  survival of Jewish law during, *2*
  Talmudic research during, *42–43*
  tannaitic legislation classification, *547, 1042*
  territorial scope of legislation during, *667–668*
  transformation of Babylonian Talmud by, *1099–1100*
  See also specific *geonim*; specific works
German law
  Civil Code, suretyship law and, *1721*
  interpretive approaches to Israeli legislation and, *1733–1735*
Germany, Jewish community in
  codificatory literature from, *1178–1179*
  decline of codificatory literature in, *1309–1312*
  Emancipation in, *1491–1494*
  halakhot produced in, *1305–1306*
  Jewish diaspora in, *1484–1486*
  legislative enactments in, *783–796*
  proliferation of *halakhot* in, *1279*
  responsa literature from, *1478–1479, 1492, 1495, 1500n.131*
  restriction on marriage and divorce legislation, *846n.244, 847*
Gerondi, Jonah, *halakhot* literature, *1305n.291*
Gerondi, Nissim (Rabbenu, Ran)
  admonition of witnesses and, *1701n.323*
  commentaries of, *1315n.19*
  on death penalty, *56–57*
  halakhic authorities and, *245–246*
  on king's law, *247n.26*
  precedent and judgment in Jewish law, *1093*

as possible commentator on *Mishneh Torah*, *1314n.16*
on *Sefer ha-Halakhot*, *1176–1177*
Gershom Me'or Ha-Golah ("Light of the Exile"), Rabbenu
civil law, communal enactments in, *686–688*
commentaries of, *1115–1116, 1258*
dispute over attribution of enactments, *784n.14*
enactments regarding tenants' law, *811*
legislative enactments against polygamy and divorce, *783–786*
moredet legislation, *663*
on Torah as source of communal enactments, *736*
territorial scope of legislation and, *674–675*
get (bill of divorcement)
"all who marry do so subject to conditions laid down by the Rabbis and the Rabbis annul this marriage" legislation, *631, 640*
arrangement of laws in Mishnah, *1056*
betrothal law and, *893n.53*
communal enactment interpretation and, *468–471*
Gamaliel the elder's legislative enactments, *563–566*
legal presumptions and, *996n.28*
lost property law and, *299n.45*
ma'aseh regarding, *951–952*
rabbinical court rulings on, *1754n.9*
sectarian disputes about, *1065*
get me'us-seh, rabbinical court rulings on, *1755n.9*
Gevurat Ari, *1129n.104*
gezel mi-divreihem, rabbinic law and, *218–220, 223n.152*
gezelah, distinction from *genevah*, *1861*
gezerah (*gezerot*)
as codification, *1140–1141*
hora'at sha'ah and, *635*
laws regarding, in *Mishneh Torah*, *1202*
legislative power of halakhic authorities over, *483–485*
role of public in legislation, *540*
terminology of, *490–492*
gezerah atu, terminology of, *491n.71*
gezerah shavah canon, *351–355*
Ammonites and, *354–355*
death penalty and, *1034*
halakhah le-Moshe mi-Sinai, *355n.229*
halakhic interpretation and, *401n.3*
mamzerim and, *353–354*
priority of, *360*
gezerah shema, terminology of, *491n.71*
gezerot tah ve-tat, *1420*
Gibeah, concubine of, communal enactments and, *732–733*
Giddulei Terumah, *1246*
Gift Law
bribery law influenced by, *1641n.89*
legislation contrary to Jewish law and, *1724*
gift, laws regarding
deed of gift as fraudulent conveyance, *1893–1894*
modern Succession Law and, *1681–1683*
Gilyon ha-Shas, *1128n.100*
gimmel benei ha-keneset (three-member panel), *21n.69*
Ginzburg, Jacob Meshullam, codificatory literature, *1443*
Gittin, (Tractate)
arrangement of laws in Mishnah, *1056*
Tractate, on *ma'aseh* regarding legal instruments, *951–952*
Glass, MK, Foundations of Law Act, *1832n.19*
glosses (*haggahot* or *he'arot*)
contents of, *1128n.100*
on *Mishneh Torah*, *1366*
multiplicity of opinions in, *1379n.36*
on *Sefer ha-Halakhot*, *1173–1176*
on *Sefer ha-Hinnukh*, *1266–1267*
on *Shulhan Arukh*, *1359–1365*
on *Torat Hattat*, *1347n.138*
golah (Babylonian diaspora). *See* Babylonian Jewish community
good faith (*tom lev*), *183–189*
"additional soul" concept and, *187*
Asheri's commentaries on, *186–187*
"compromises" (*pesharot*) and, *185–186*
in contract law, *183, 187–188*
"duty in the sight of heaven," (*lazeit yedei shamayim*), *183*
interpretive approaches to Israeli legislation and, *1734–1736*
lacuna and, *1837n.36*
good public order, communal enactments as promotion of, *462*
Goren, Shlomo, responsa literature of, *1499*

goyim (non-Jews)
courts, exclusion of Jewish disputes from, *806n.94*
relations with, enactments concerning, *786*
sacrifice of one life to save others, laws regarding, *971–972*
Valladolid enactments concerning, *802–803*
See also conversion to Judaism
gratuity, laws concerning, *1631–1632*
Great Assembly (*Anshei Keneset ha-Gedolah*)
legislative enactments and, *486–490, 554–558*
Talmudic research, *41*
Gregory IX (Pope), codificatory literature and, *1263*
Grodzinski, Hayyim Ozer
halakhic decision-making, *1902*
responsa literature of, *1496*
group defamation, Defamation Law and, *1643n.98*
Grundnorm
incorporation of Jewish law in State legislation, *1670–1671, 1757*
secularization of *Halakhah* and, *1908–1914*
terminology of, *230–232*
Guarantee Law, legislation contrary to Jewish law and, *1721–1724*
"Guardians of the Walls," incorporation of Jewish law into Israeli legal system and, *1905*
guardianship law, Jewish heritage (*moreshet Yisra'el*), *1861*
Gufei Halakhot, 1547
Guide for the Perplexed, 252n.56
Guidebooks to Jewish law
Bet ha-Behirah, 1543
Commentary on the Mishnah as, *1543*
Halikhot Olam, 1545
Iggeret Rav Sherira Gaon, 1542
Kelalei ha-Gemara, 1545–1546
Kelalei ha-Talmud, 1547
Mevo ha-Talmud, 1543
overview of, *1541–1551*
scientific study of Judaism and, *1548–1551*
Seder Tannaim va-Amoraim, 1541–1542
Sefer keritut, 1544–1545
She'erit Yosef, 1545
Yad Malakhi, 1547–1548
Yavin Shemu'ah, 1547
See also Bibliographies; Biographies; Encyclopedias;
guilds. *See* craftsmen, guilds of
Gulak, Asher
on arbitration procedures, *19*
on creativity of Jewish law, *88n.47*
legal research, *81*
Ozar ha-Shetarot of, *1539–1540*
Gumbiner, Abraham Abele
commentaries, *1419*
on *Orah Hayyim* and *Yoreh De'ah, 1431*
Guttmann, I. M.
on *asmakhta, 301–305*
on literary forms of interpretation, *306–307*
Guttmann, Jehiel Michal
legal sources of, *1553–1554*
scientific legal research of, *82–83*
tannaitic legislation classification, *547*

H

Ha'amek Davar, as literary source, *1102n.6*
Habad (Lubavitch) Hassidic movement, *1447*
Habiba, Joseph, commentaries on *Sefer ha-Halakhot, 1176*
habitual violators of sabbath, competency of, as witnesses, *1754n.8, 1776–1783, 1807n.175*
hadash, custom as source of law, *887–888*
Hadayah, Ovadiah, responsa literature of, *1499*
Hadrian, Emperor, *7*
child support laws, *831*
legislative enactments under, *567*
Ha-Enziklopedyah ha-Ivrit, 1560
Hafez Hayyim (Israel Meir Ha-Kohen of Radin)
Defamation Law and, *1643*
exemption of women from studying Torah, *1799*
on expunction of criminal records, *1709–1710*
on labor law, *1630–1631*
on legislative sources, *1448*
on voting by women, *1902*
Haftarah, power of custom and, *910–911*
Haggadah (Passover), *1750n.458*
See also Aggadah
Haggahot Asheri, 1253–1254
Haggahot Maimuniyyot (Maimonidean Glosses), *1234–1235*

Hagigah Tractate, *Zugot* mentioned in, *1043*
Hagiographa (*Ketuvim*)
Aramaic translation of, *1045*
on debtors' personal freedom, *310*
on *divrei kabbalah*, *203–204*
inheritance rights of wife's sons (*ketubbat benin dikhrin*) and, *577n.141*
as literary source of law, *1021*
suretyship law in, *1026–1027*
Hagiz, Moses (Mani'ah)
literary sources of Jewish law and, *1437–1438*
responsa literature of, *1490*
Hagurat Shemu'el, *1402n.114*
ha-Horani, Johanan b. (R.), laws regarding *sukkah*, *959*
Hai b. Sherira Gaon
on Aha of Shabha, *1150*
Arabic monographs of, *1207n.75*
as authority on Jewish law, *43*
on Babylonian Talmud redaction, *1093*
betrothal legislation, *657*
custom as legal source, *894*
doreshin leshon hedyot, *431n.37*
Iggeret Rav Sherira Gaon, *1542*
"I have nothing" oath, *652*, *654n.50*
on Jerusalem Talmud, *1131*
legal research, *43*
on local custom as law, *935*
midrashic compilations of, *1047–1049*
monographs of, *1164–1166*
moredet legislation, *659–660*
precedent and judgment in Jewish law, *983n.132*
responsa literature and, *1470–1472*
on *savoraim*, *1094*
Sefer ha-Shetarot of, *1536*
on *Sifra* and *Sifrei* compilations, *1047*
ha-Kala'i. *See* Alfasi, Isaac b. Jacob ha-Kohen
hakhmei ha-Halakhah, tannaitic legislation classification, *546–547*
Hakhmei ha-Talmud, *1558*
Hakhmei Yisra'el be-Djerba u-ve Tunis, *1559*
ha-Kohen, Judah, *750*
Halihal v. State of Israel, *692*
Halakhah
binding authority of, in Israeli legal system, *1899–1906*, *1943–1946*
child support laws, religious-legal obligations, *116–117*
civil-ritual matters in, *111n.82*
collection and arrangement of legal rules, *1069–1070*
communal enactments equated with, *736–778*
competence of witnesses, requirements for, *737–739*
concept of, *93–94*
courts' adherence to, *1793–1794*
creativity in, *51–54*
critical research on, *84*
custom as source of, *886–887*
debt payment as religious obligation, *117–119*
declining utility of, *1582–1584*, *1670n.207*, *1807–1809*
Defamation Law, influence on, *1644*
difficulties of literature in, *85–86*
"distinguished person", approval by, *751–759*
division regarding authority of, *1493*
freedom of thought and speech, *1848–1849*
interchangeable use of, with *minhag* and *takkanah*, *888*
issur-mamon dichotomy, *122–141*
Jewish government and, *10*, *58–59*
Jewish heritage (*moreshet Yisra'el*), *1840*
Jewish vs. non-Jewish law and, *62–74*
king's law and, *55–57*
"law of the land is law" (*dina de-malkhuta dina*), *64–74*
lay tribunals and, *24–26*, *30–33*, *35n.105*, *61*
legal and religious terminology in, *107*, *111–112*
legal-moral reciprocity in, *4–5*, *111–114*, *141–149*
literary form of, in Mishnah, *1049–1050*
local Jewish self-government and, *60–61*
major literary sources for, *1038–1039*, *1102–1103*
Marriage Age Law and, *1655–1656*
mishnaic literary form compared with *midrashim*, *1049–1050*, *1070–1072*
national and religious minorities and, *1855–1856*
non-Jewish courts, prohibition against litigation in, *1915–1917*
obligations by vow, ban, or oath in, *119–120*
Oral Law and. *See* Oral law (*Torah she-be-al-peh*)

Halakhah continued
payment of debt as religious obligation, *117–119*
public leadership as creative factor in, *54–61*
privately performed marriages under, *1782–1784*
Rabbinical Court of Appeals' limitations and, *1810–1818*
reciprocity with *Aggadah*, *94–104*, *152*
redaction of Talmud and, *1038–1039*
responsa as source for, *1464*
schism in, *1063–1070*
scientific research on, *80–91*
secularization of, *1579–1582*, *1906–1914*
Sefer ha-She'iltot and, *1152*
statutory incorporation in Israeli legal system, *1721–1727*, *1762n.31*
Talmudic and post-Talmudic divisions in, *39–40*
tax enactments, *746–751*
terminology of *Mishpat Ivri* in, *105–111*
women, teaching of Torah to, *1800–1802*
halakhah le-ma'aseh, distinguishing process and, *963*
halakhah le-Moshe mi-Sinai, *204–207*
aggadic interpretations, *382–383*
custom as source of law and, *887*
gezerah shavah canon and, *355n.229*
halakhic classification and, *208*
terminology, *206n.83*
See also Sinaitic Revelation
Halakhah Pesukah, *1443*
halakhic decision making
absence of suprahuman authority in, *242–265*
agunot legislation, *401*
on Alfasi's *Sefer ha-Halakhot*, *1171–1172*
in amoraic period, *407–414*
authorization of prophets, *242–243*
background to, *400–401*
bailments laws, *405–407*
vs. Biblical interpretation, *401*
biographies of, *1556–1560*
on bodily issues, *370n.300*
Caro's list of, in *Bet Yosef*, *1315–1316*
codification seen as limitation on, *1375–1379*
communal enactment interpretation by, *445–448*, *685*, *777–778*
concessions to suprahuman powers, *264–265*
conduct of, law of interest and, *966–968*
control over custom, *937–944*
criticism of lay tribunals, *30–33*
custom based on error, rulings regarding, *937–940*
divinity of Torah and, *240–242*
divorce law, *404–405*
fraudulent conveyance laws, *416–418*
generational differences in, *266–267*
hilkheta ke-vatra'ei, *267–272*
indirect evidence, *404–407*
inheritance law, *403–404*
integration of modern and ancient decisions, *1940–1941*
Israeli legal system and, *1899–1906*
judicial guidelines, *416*
law and equity for, *247–261*
legislation and, *477–478*, *495*
ma'aseh and, *947–950*, *958–960*
minors' legal capacity in law of finders, *409–411*
nineteenth century ideological split in, *1493–1494*
oven of Akhnai and, *261–263*
plain meaning vs. nonliteral interpretation, *409–411*
in post-Talmudic period, *414–421*
responsa and, *1461*
search for legal sources for rules, *1007–1014*
vs. statutory incorporation, *1909–1914*
in tannaic era, *402–407*
tannaic vs. amoraic interpretations, *407–409*
territorial scope of legislation and, *671–675*
Torah as source of authority, *243–247*, *481–485*
tort law, *411–414*
traditional canons, use of, *418–421*
halakhic literature
abbreviations in, *1566–1567*
alphabetic arrangement, in encyclopedias, *1554*
bibliographies of, *1560–1564*
as codification source, *1158*
concordances, *1568*
lexicons on, *1564–1566*
objectives of, *1166–1167*
responsa as source for, *1464–1465*
source references, sayings and aphorisms, *1568–1569*

as summaries of law, *1158*
textual variants, *1567*
topical arrangement and classification of, *1196–1197*
See also specific works and authors
halakhic scholar (*talmid hakham*), as "distinguished person," 755–759
halakhot
as codificatory literature, *1139–1140*
commentary and novellae in, *1105n.2*
of geonic era, *1150*
literary forms of, after Maimonides, *1237–1238*
modification of codification methodology and, *1183–1184*
proliferation of, *1279–1280*
Sefer ha-Terumot as example of, *1245–1246*
See also communal enactments
Halakhot Gedolot, *1155–1156*
as model for Alfasi's *Sefer ha-Halakhot*, *1168*
topical arrangement and classification in, *1196*
Halakhot Kelulot (Comprehensive *Halakhot*), *1177*
Halakhot Ketannot (Alfasi), *1155*, *1169*, *1253n.69*
halakhot keti'ot, *1157*
Halakhot Ketu'ot, *1155*
Halakhot Kezuvot Meyuhas le-Rav Yehudai Gaon, *1155*, *1156n.24*, *1203n.63*
Halakhot Pesukot, *1153–1155*, *1300*
Maimonides' compilation of, *1191*
topical arrangement and classification in, *1196*
halakhot, in labor law, *617*
halikhah (going or walking), concept of, *94n.7*
Halikhot Eli, *1547*
Halikhot Olam, *1545*
halizah ceremony
agunot legislation and, *530n.153*
contemporary legislation concerning, *878–879*
"custom overrides the law," *907–908*
enactments of 1950 regarding, *833–834*
enactments of David b. Kalonymus, *788*
guidelines for, *389–390*
halakhic interpretation and, *1809n.185*
Jerusalem Talmud and, *907–908*
Johanan's commentaries on, *1003–1004*
judicial procedure and law of personal status, *1599–1600*
legal reasoning (*sevarah*) and, *1002–1004*
legislative enactments regarding, *834–835*
levirate marriage and, *199*
procedural enactments concerning, *830–831*
Women's Equal Rights Law and, *1658*
half-measures, Biblical prohibition of legal reasoning (*sevarah*) and, *998–999*
Halpern, Israel, *818*
Ha-Ma'amad ha-Ishi be-Yisra'el, *1681n.256*
Hamah, Jewish community in, annulment enactments in, *870–872*
Ha-Ma'or ha-Gadol (The Great Luminary), *1173*
Ha-Ma'or ha-Katan (The Lesser Luminary), *1173*
hamas, in *Sefer ha-She'iltot*, *1151*
hamez (leaven)
laws regarding search for, *1268n.139*
prohibition against, religious vs. legal obligations and, *115*
Ha-Mishpat (periodical), *86*
Ha-Mishpat Ha-Ivri (periodical), *86*
Ha-Mishpat Ha-Ivri (Jewish Law) Society, *86*
draft documents of, *1591n.28*
National Awakening and, *1588–1591*
ha-mishpat ha-ivri (spirit of Jewish law)
Foundations of Law Act and, *1832n.19*
legislative enactments, *1571–1572*
See also mishpat ivri
Hammurabi, Code of, *1013n.85*
Hanan the Scoundrel, market overt legislation, *599*
Hananel R. (amora)
"all who marry do so subject to conditions laid down by the Rabbis and the Rabbis annul this marriage" legislation, *638*
Hananel b. Hushiel (Rabbenu)
commentary of, *1114–1115*, *1168*
on custom regarding modes of acquisition, *916n.71*
on Jerusalem Talmud, *1132*
yeshivot of, *1168*
Hananiah b. Judah Gaon
on communal enactments, *685–686*, *771*
wife's sons inheritance rights (*ketubbat benin dikhrin*), *655–656*
Ha-Nasi, Judah (R.), *41–42*

Ha-Nasi, Judah (R.) *continued*
edits Mishnah, *52*
halakhic interpretation of, *407*
justice and equity discussed by, *259–260*
reduction of Talmudic literature to writing, *227*
"handiwork" (*ma'aseh yadeha*)
rabbinical court decisions regarding, *1785–1794*
rights to wife's handiwork, *571–572*
handshake ritual (*toke'im*)
as seal of contract, *916–917*
suretyship law and, *1027*
hangmen, in Jewish legal system, *11n.26*
Haninah, R., witnesses' inquiry and examination procedures, *606–607*
Hanina Segan ha-Kohanim, as major *tannaim*, *1044*
Hanukkah
binding force of custom during, *731–732*
halakhic authorities legislative power over, *481–483*
historical background for, *504*
laws regarding, Maimonides' compilation of, *1191–1193*
rituals for kindling lights, *890*
Hasadim, on *issur* (religious law), *1239n.5*
Hasdei David commentary, *1112*
hashavat avedah (restoration of lost property). *See* lost or stolen property.
Hasifat Genuzim mi-Teman, *1464n.34*
haskamot. *See* communal enactments
hassagat gevul ("moving a landmark"), *673n.30*
"Ha-Tehikkah ve-ha-Mishpat be-Medinah ha-Yehudit," *1614–1615*
Ha-Torah ve-ha-Medinah, *1916n.46*
havayot, Babylonian Talmud and, *1090–1091*
haver, definition of, *504n.43*
Haviva, R., on *sitomta*, *914*
Ha-Yarhi, Abraham b. Nathan, *1240–1241*
Ha-Yerushalmi ha-Meforash, *1137*
Ha-Yerushalmi ke-Feshuto, *1137*
hayu soferim, practice of, *313*
hayyav, law of obligations and, *588*
Hayyei Adam (The Life of Man), *1447*
Hayyim b. Atar, on *Orah Hayyim* and *Yoreh De'ah*, *1431*
Hayyim b. Bezalel, *1347n.138*
commentaries on Caro and Rema, *1420n.168*
rejection of codification by, *1375–1379*
Hayyim of Brisk (Rabbi), *1910n.35*
Hayyim David Hazzan, responsa literature of, *1495*
Hayyim Mordecai Margolioth, *1440–1441*
Hayyim Or Zaru'a, *1241n.21*
enactments of, *791*
responsa questions submitted by, *1476*
Hayyim Palache, responsa literature of, *1495*
Hayyim b. Samuel, *1307*
Hayyim of Volozhin, *1813n.193*
Hayyim Zevi Taubes, *1472*
Haza'at Takkanot bi-Yerushot, *1494n.124*
hazakah (legal presumption), *See* possession, laws regarding
hazmanah milta, *1091*
ha-zokheh biyerushah, inheritance law and, *1673n.218*
Hazon Ish
codificatory literature and, *1129n.104*
historical background of, *702*
prohibition against litigation in non-Jewish courts and, *1916n.46*
Hazon Yehezkel commentary, *1113n.45*
Hazzan, Elijah, responsa literature of, *1495*
Hazzan, Jacob
legal categories used by, *108n.70*
responsa literature of, *1300n.269*
Hazzan, Rahamim Elijah, responsa literature of, *1442*
Hazzan, Raphael Joseph, responsa literature of, *1490*
He-Arukh, *1564–1565*
Hebrew language
British Mandatory legal system and, *1612*
changes in, during Emancipation period, *1577–1578*
in *Mishneh Torah*, *1207–1210*
official position of, in State of Israel, *1620–1624*
in responsa, *1507–1512*
restoration of, as language of daily life, *1607–1608, 1913–1914, 1941–1942*
hedyot. *See* Lay tribunals
hefker bet din hefker
"all who marry do subject to conditions laid down by the Rabbis and the Rabbis annul this marriage," *635n.53*
annulment enactments, *852–856, 874–876*
civil law, communal enactments in, *686–688*

communal enactments and, *514, 679n.3, 686–690, 706*
communal property legislation, *700n.88*
court authority regarding, *507–515, 706*
criminal communal enactments, *689–690*
divrei kabbalah and, *204*
equal inheritance rights for sons and daughters, enactments for, *844*
fraudulent conveyances law and, *1891*
inheritance law and, *509–510*
initial stages of, *507–508*
legislative authority and, *488–489, 508–510*
legislation containing, *507–515*
le-migdar milta and, *533n.158*
litigation and court cost procedures, *827*
minority rights, communal enactments protecting, *764n.318*
property legislation, *700n.88*
prosbul enactment, *511–513*
scope of application, *510–511*
theory vs. practice in legislation in, *860–861*
Heilprin, Jacob, annulment enactments, *872–874*
Helishuh, enactments of, *823*
Helkat Mehokek, 1419
commentaries on *Even ha-Ezer, 1429–1430*
Heller, Yom Tov Lipmann
Alfasi, views on codificatory methodology of, *1406–1407*
codification methodology of, *1403–1407*
commentaries generally, *1254, 1382n.43, 1448n.89*
communal enactments on matters of *issur* and, *710n.133*
Piskei ha-Rosh commentary, *1385*
Tosafot Yom Tov commentary of, *1108–1109*
Hendeles v. Bank Kupat Am
disputes over terminology in, *1936*
statutory intercorporation of Jewish law in Israeli legislation, *1739–1751, 1863–1871*
"legal issue requiring decision," *1835–1838*
subjective factors affecting recourse to Jewish law and, *1927–1931*
unique terminology of Jewish law and, *1874–1875*
value-laden legal terms and lacuna, *1873–1874*
will of *shekhiv me-ra* and, *1882–1884*
henpek, authentication of witnesses' testimony, *613*
herem ha-shiddukhim, territorial scope of legislation and, *674n.30*
herem ha-yishuv, territorial scope of legislation and, *674n.30*
Hershler, M., *1305n.292*
Herzl, Theodor, *1607–1608*
Herzog, Isaac ha-Levi, R., *83*,
on civil procedure, *1601*
commentaries of, *1442, 1494n.124*
equality of inheritance rights among sexes and, *1684*
prohibition against litigation in non-Jewish courts and, *1916n.46*
responsa literature of, *1499*
on role of Jewish law in State of Israel, *1614–1615, 1808–1809*
secularization of *Halakhah* and, *1908*
Woman's Equal Rights Law, jurisdiction over, *1760–1761*
Herzog, I., *83*
Hevrat Shikkun Ovedim (Workers Housing Authority), *164*
"he who punishes" imperative (*mi she-para*), *148, 150–151*
Hezekiah, on latent damage legislation, *603n.247*
hezkat shanim, legal sources for rules regarding, *1007–1008*
hezzek re'iyyah (injury caused by seeing), *1859–1860*
Hida (Hayyim Joseph David Azulai)
commentaries of, *1239n.5*
contradictions between *Bet Yosef* and *Shulhan Arukh, 1373n.18*
on prohibition against studying *Bet Yosef, 1369–1370*
responsa literature of, *1439, 1490*
Hiddushei ha-Ramban, 1124
Hiddushei ha-Ritba ha-Hadashim, 1125n.90
Hiddushei Halakhot, 1128, 1383–1385
Hiddushei Halakhot Maharam Schiff, 1129n.104
Hiddushei ha-Rim, 1129n.104
Hiddushei Hattam Sofer, 1129n.104
Hiddushei Rabbenu Hayyim ha-Levi, 1129n.104
Hiddushim. See Netivot ha-Mishpat
High Court of Justice
marriage between *kohen* and divorcee,

High Court of Justice *continued*
Jewish law incorporated in state legislation, *1775–1776*
rabbinical court adjudication and, *1759n.20*
Hildesheimer, Azriel, responsa literature of, *1495*
Hilkhata Gavrata, 1178n.107
hilkheta be-lo ta'ama, "meeting of three" (*ma'amad sheloshtan*) legislation, *584, 649n.20*
hilkheta gemirei lah, halakhah le-Moshe mi-Sinai concept and, *207n.86*
hilkheta ke-vatra'ei concept
Alfasi's *Sefer ha-Halakhot* and, *1170*
Ashkenazic authorities embrace of, *1360–1366*
in *Darkhei Moshe, 1354–1356*
endorsement of, by two hundred Eastern rabbis, *1369–1370*
guidelines contained in, *267–272*
Jacob b. Asher's codification on, *1284–1287*
Maharshal's commentaries and, *1389–1394*
precedent in Jewish law and, *984–985*
resistance to codificatory works in Polish diaspora and, *1345–1348*
responsa literature on, *1504–1506*
Hilkhot Avadim (Laws of Slaves), *1200*
Hilkhot Bekhorot ve-Hallah, 1242n.23
Hilkhot De'ot, 1243n.29
Hilkhot Edut (Laws of Evidence), *1201–1202, 1288n.200*
Hilkhot Evel (Laws of Mourning), *1201–1202*
Hilkhot Genevah (Laws of Theft), *1199*
Hilkhot Gerushin (Laws of Divorce), *1199*
Hilkhot Gezelah va-Avedah (Laws of Robbery and Lost Property), *1199*
Hilkhot Halva'ot (Laws of Loans), *1288n.200*
Hilkhot ha-Rosh. See Piskei ha-Rosh
Hilkhot ha-Sanhedrin va-ha-Onshin ha-Mesurin Lahem (Laws of the Sanhedrin and its Penal Jurisdiction), *1201–1202*
Hilkhot ha-Yerushalmi (le-ha-Rambam), *1137, 1187*
Hilkhot Hovel u-Mazzik (Laws of Wounding and Damaging), *1199*
Hilkhot Ishut (Laws of Personal Status), *1198n.51, 1199*
Sefer ha-Turim codification compared with, *1291*
Hilkhot Ketubbot, 1291
Hilkhot Kiddush ha-Hodesh, 1188n.22
Hilkhot Kiddushin, 1291
Hilkhot Malveh ve-Loveh (Laws of Creditor and Debtor), 1200–1201, *1246n.42*
Maimonides' codification methodology, *1294*
Hilkhot Mamrim (Laws of Rebels), *1201–1202*
Hilkhot Mekhirah (Laws of Sales), *1200*
Hilkhot Melakhim u-Milhamoteihem, 1201–1202
Hilkhot Na'arah Betulah (Laws of a Virgin Maiden), *1199*
Hilkhot Nahalot (Laws of Inheritance)
as codificatory literature, *1200–1201*
succession law in, *1673n.218*
Hilkhot Nedarim, 1242n.24
Hilkhot Niddah (The Laws of the Menstruant Women), *1242–1243*
Hilkhot Nizkei Mamon (Laws of Damages Caused by Property), *1199*
Hilkhot Re'u. See Halakhot Pesukot
Hilkhot Roze'ah u-Shemirat ha-Nefesh (Laws of Homicide and Preservation of Life), *1199, 1220–1221*
language and style compared with *Hoshen Mishpat, 1326*
Hilkhot Sekhirut (Laws of Leasing and Hiring), *1200*
Tur Hoshen Mishpat compared with, *1294*
Hilkhot She'elah u-Fikkadon (Laws of Borrowing and Bailment), *1200*
Hilkhot Shekhenim (Laws of Neighbors), *1200*
Tur Hoshen Mishpat compared with, *1294*
Hilkhot Sheluhin ve-Shutafin (Laws of Agency and Partnership), *1200*
Rema's glosses to, *1364*
Hilkhot Shemittah ve-Yovel, 1188n.22
Hilkhot Sotah (Laws of the Suspected Wife), *1199*
Hilkhot Tefillah, 1234
Hilkhot Tikkun Shetarot, 1536–1537
Hilkhot To'en ve-Nit'an (Laws of Plaintiff and Defendant), *1200–1201*
Hilkhot Yibbum va-Halizah (Laws of Levirate Marriage and Release Therefrom), *1199*
Hilkhot Yom Tov, 1242n.23
Hilkhot Zekhiyyah u-Mattanah (Laws of Entitlement and Gifts)
as codificatory literature, *1200–1201*
succession law in, *1673n.218*
Hillel the Elder, *41*

Babylonian diaspora and, *1087–1088*
custom as legal source of law, *882*
interpretation of *ketubbah* by, *424–426*
legislative enactments of, *561–562*
on paschal sacrifice, *901–902*
as part of *Zugot*, *1043*
Hillel b. Eliakim, Rabbenu
commentary on the *Sifra* and *Sifrei*, *1111*
Hillel, School of
agunot legislation and, *402*, *524–525*
civil law, communal enactments in, *687*
on collection of *ketubbah*, *426–427*
custom as source of law, *891n.50*
on divorce law, *293–295*
halakhic decision making and, *1900–1901*
interpretation of Torah by, *315–317*
issur-mamon distinction, *123*
justice and equity in, *258–259*
"laying on of hands", laws regarding, *1062–1063*
laws regarding *olah*, *349*
laws regarding *sukkah*, *959*
multiple opinions in Mishnah and, *1071–1072*
on local custom as law, *935*
Oral Law terminology and, *191–192*
penitence and rehabilitation (*takkanat ha-shavim*) legislation, *602*
prosbul enactment and, *512–513*
recitation of *Shema*, *321*
sectarian disputes and, *1064–1070*
tannaitic legislation classification, *546–547*
hillukim system
as legislative source, *1345*
rishonim responsa and, *1485*
hinhig, meaning of, *885–886*
Hire and Loan Law, good faith (*tom lev*), *183*
Hisda, R.
bailments and, *965*
court authority regarding legislation, *506*
on fraudulent conveyances law, *1891*
hora'at sha'ah (temporary measures), *520n.117*
on local custom as law, *934n.171*
Historical Digest,
as literary source, *1526–1527*, *1540*
modern Israeli legislation and, *1934n.98*
historical-dogmatic research in Jewish law, *80–91*
classification of, *236*
defined, *228–230*
literary interpretation of Torah and, *307*
historical sources of law
custom as, *881–882*
responsa as, *1465–1466*
A History of Jews in Christian Spain, *1532n.17*, *1538*
Hiyya b. Abba, R., *410–411*
Hiyya Rabbah (R. Hiyya "the Great")
on anonymous law, *1060*
as major *tannai*, *1044*
Tosefta redaction and, *1081n.176*
hiyyuv, law of obligations and, *588*
Hokamah v. Minister of the Interior, *1841–1842*
Hokhmat Adam (The Wisdom of Man), *1447*
Hokhmat Sheomo, *1129n.104*
Hokhmat Yisra'el jüdische Wissenschaft, *1548–1549*
Hok Issur Leshon ha-Ra (Prohibition of Defamation Law), *1644*
hok u-mishpat, Joshua's property enactments and, *553*
Holdsworth, W., *1926*
holkhei Usha, *1008n.73*
Holmes, Justice Oliver Wendell, Land Law legislation and, *1711*
Holocaust
adoption laws following, *827*
communal enactments and, *674n.30*
responsa literature from, *1496–1499*
hora'at sha'ah. *See* temporary measures (*hora'at sha'ah*)
Horayot Tractate, *1055n.68*
Horowitz, Isaiah, *1393n.78*, *1418n.161*
Hoshen Mishpat (*Shulhan Arukh*)
as codificatory literature, *12*
commentaries on, *1424–1429*
compared with *Tur Hoshen Mishpat*, *1326–1340*
contents of, *1323–1327*
evidence and procedure legislation and, *1767–1768*
Falk's commentaries on, *1414*
juridical autonomy and, *1586*
as legislative source, *105*, *1283n.180*, *1443*
modern responsa to, *1498–1499*
Mishpat Ha-Shalom Ha-Ivri and, *1594–1596*
prohibition against litigation in non-Jewish courts, *1914–1917*
Rema's glosses to, *1364*

Hoshen Mishpat continued
responsa literature and, *1436n.38, 1491–1492*
See also Tur Hoshen Mishpat
House of Study (*holkhei le-vet ha-midrash*), *1008n.73*
hov, origin of word, *588n.185*
Howard v. Miarah, illegal contract legislation and, *1717–1720*
Hubarah, J., *1464n.34*
Hullin Tractate, *54*
human dignity and equality, Jewish heritage (*moreshet Yisra'el*)and , *1850–1854*
huppah (nuptial ceremony)
Corfu enactments regarding, *817*
enactments of 1950, *833–834*
legislative authority regarding, *507n.58*
theory vs. practice in legislation in, *861–863*
validity of marriage without, *1602n.69*
See also betrothal; marriage law.
Huzin, Zedakah, responsa literature of, *1491*
hybrid casuistic-normative legal style
defined, *1073–1074*
of specific laws, *1074–1076*
hypothetical cases, responsa literature on, *1516–1517*

I

Ibn Migash, Joseph. *See* Ri Migash
identification marks, lost property law and, *300*
idolatry
circumvention of *kum va-Aseh*, *532n.156*
codificatory literature on, *1327–1329*
restrictive interpretations of Torah, *367–369*
iggeret kelaf ("document on parchment"), *823n.164*
Iggeret Rav Sherira Gaon, *1542*
"I have nothing" oath, *651–654*
"ikka de-amri" (there are some who say), custom as source of law and, *884n.12*
illegal contracts, *issur-mamon* distinction and, *128–130*
Immi, R., "custom overrides the law," *906*
immigration to Israel, Law of Return and, *1647–1651*
Immunity of Judges law, *1645–1646*
Imrei Binah, *1495*
imprisonment provisions, incorporation of non-Jewish law and, *64n.44*
imprisonment for debt
enslavement for, *652n.35, 1014n.87*
Execution Law, *1638–1639*
modern legislation on, *1635–1639*
incest, laws regarding
agunot legislation and, *527–528*
Ezra's legislative enactments and, *556–558*
judges' interpretation of, *289*
legislative power of halakhic authorities over, *483–485*
rabbinic law and, *208n.88*
See also consanguinity; family law
inconsistency, in communal enactments, *464–468*
indemnification agreement (*shetar hazzalah*), halakhic competence of witnesses, *738n.227*
Index of Sources, *1526–1527, 1934n.98*
individual rights
communal enactments, *766–771*
tax enactments, *749–751*
inference, in thirteen canons
generalization followed by specification (*kelal u-ferat*), *324–325*
generalization followed by specification followed by generalization (*kelal u-ferat u-khelal*), *326–327*
similarity of words and phrases, *343*
specification followed by generalization (*perat u-khelal*), *325*
See also a fortiori inference
infidelity, general principle canon and, *356n.236*
informers (*malshinim*), Valladolid enactments regarding, *801–803*
inheritance law
communal enactments interpretation and, *452–453*
convicted murderers prohibited from inheriting from victim, *1677–1678*
daughters' right to inherit, rabbinical court rulings on, 1657n. 145, *1672n.215, 1755n.10*
determination of heirs under simultaneous death, *1680–1683*
equal inheritance rights for sons and daughters, *575–578, 828–829, 842–846, 1657n.145*
financial aspects of, *835–846*
halakhic interpretation of, *403*
hefker bet din hefker, *509–510*
heirs of decedent, defined in Jewish law, *1672–1674*

husband's rights, legislation concerning, *573–574, 787, 835– 840*
illegitimate heirs and heirs from prohibited marriages, *1674–1675*
interpretation of *ketubbah* and, *427–428*
leshon benei adam (colloquial usage) and, *437–438*
in *Mishneh Torah, 1200–1201*
Moroccan enactments concerning, *808*
mother's right to inherit, *840–841, 1672n.216*
"one-tenth of the estate" legislation, *578–580*
provisions contrary to Jewish law, *1683–1688*
Rabbenu Tam's enactments, *836–838*
"reserved portion" of estate under, *1678–1681*
"Shum" enactments restricting husband's rights, *836–838*
Succession Law Bill, *1672–1683, 1683–1688*
support of daughters out of father's estate, *574–575*
widow's right to maintenance, *573–574*
wife's property, communal enactments concerning, *796–797*
wife's sons, rights of (*ketubbat benin* dikhrin), *575–578, 655–656*
See also estates; wills
innocence, presumption of, legal reasoning (*sevarah*) and, *996n.29*
In re Litwinski Bros. Partnership, 1911n.38
Institute for Research in Jewish Law (Jerusalem), *90, 1525, 1934n.98*
integrative interpretation (*midrash mekayyem*), *285–286*
decline in use of, *384–386*
expansion of, *374–384*
guidelines for, *297–300*
of Johanan, *297–298*
literary forms for, *305–307*
intellectual property law, Jewish law as source for, *1691n.290*
See also copyright law
interest. *See* conflict of interest
interest, on loans
codificatory literature on, *1290n.206*
distinguishing technique and, *966–968*
in *Hilkhot Malveh ve-Loveh, 1246n.42*
rabbinic law and, *221–222*
internal factor of Jewish law, *4–5*
International Congress of Jewish Studies Jewish Law Section, *1613n.95*
International Labor Organization, *1629–1630*
international law, Law of Return and, *1650–1651*
interpretatio authentica, 313
interpretatio doctrinalis, 313
interpretatio logica, 1835
interpretation (*midrash*)
asmakhta in, *300–305*
as creative source, *286–290*
communal enactments, *452–459*
creative and integrative interpretation, *285–286*
of documents, *422–443, 467–468*
differences in methods for, *292–297*
general guidelines for, *387–390*
of *Halakhah, 445–448*
halakhic authority and, *256*
ketubbah, 424–428
as legal source of Jewish law, *239*
literary forms for, *305–307*
in Roman law, *290–292*
scriptural authority for, *278–280*
See also specific types of interpretation, e.g. codificatory interpretation.
Interpretation Ordinance (*Pekudat ha-Parshanut*), *276n.7*
inter vivos gift, inheritance laws regarding disposition of, *1673–1674*
intestate succession
modern Succession Law and, *1675n.228, 1676*
role of family in laws regarding, *1686n.280*
Isaac b. Abba Mari of Marseilles, *1267–1269*
codificatory works of, *1179n.113*
responsa questions submitted by, *1476*
Sefer ha-Ittur of, *1537*
Isaac b. Joseph Caro, *1371n.13*
Isaac b. Joseph of Corbeil, *1263–1265*
Isaac b. Judah, *1116–1117*
Isaac b. Judah ibn Ghayyat, *1168*
Isaac b. Meir of Düren, *1248–1249*
Isaac b. Moses of Vienna, Land Law legislation and, *1715–1716*
Isaac b. Samuel of Dampier. *See* Ri.
Isaac b. Simeon of Spain, *1158n.31*
Isaac ha-Levi ("Segan Leviyyah"), *1116n.54*
Isaac ibn Danan, *1495*
Isaac the Elder, on Alfasi's *Sefer ha-Halakhot, 1171–1172*

Isaac ibn Ezra, Joseph b., custom as source of tax law, *923n.108*
Isaiah b. Elijah de Trani ("Later Isaiah") (Riaz), *1176, 1241n.16, 1258n.98*
Isaiah b. Mali of Trani, the Elder (Rid), *1258n.98*
Isaiah, Book of, as literary source for law, *1021–1022*
Ishmael, R., *6*
  canonical interpretations by, *374–384*
  caution regarding *ma'aseh*, *949*
  exegetical interpretation of Torah by, *316–317*
  halakhic interpretation techniques of, *371–383*
  legal development of rules by, *1069*
  midrashic compilations of, *1048*
  thirteen canons of interpretation (*middot*), *318–399*
Ishmael b. Elisha, R., *1044*
Israel b. Joseph, *1303n.278*
Israel of Bruna, *63n.40*
Israel of Krems, *1242n.21, 1253–1254*
Israel, Elijah, responsa literature of, *1491*
Israel, Moses, responsa literature of, *1491*
Israel, Land of. *See* Land of Israel
Israel, State of
  courts and Jewish law in, *1920–1923*
  Defense Forces, responsa literature of, *1499*
  Hebrew language in, *1608*
  Jewish Government in, *58–59*
  Jewish law as foundation for legal system in, *1592n.29, 1611–1617, 1620–1729, 1731–1751, 1756–1757, 1918–1920*
  Law and Administration Ordinance, *1143n.6*
  Law of Return and, *1647–1651*
  legal norms of legal system in, *231–232, 235n.24*
  legislature, *lifenim mi-shurat ha-din* and, *166*
  mishpat ivri in legal system, *137n.184*
  modern-day use of Halakhic literature, *54n.13*
  proposals requiring recourse to Jewish law in, *1617–1618*
  responsa literature from, *1496–1499*
Israeli Bankruptcy Ordinance, *1888–1889*
Israeli Declaration of Independence
  fundamental concepts, *1832–1834*
  Law of Return and, *1650*
Isserlein, Israel
  codificatory literature of, *703, 778n.363*
  on custom as source of tax law, *922–923*
  on halakhic decision making, *1912n.39*
  hypothetical responsa of, *1516–1517*
  "reinforcement and support" of customs, *942*
  responsa of, *1253, 1479, 1486n.96, 1510n.169*
Isserles, Moses (Rema)
  admonition of witnesses, *1702, 1707*
  annulment, enactments for, *870–872*
  codificatory literature of, *1345–1366, 1349–1365*
  commentary on *Sefer ha-Turim*, *1303*
  enactments of Hayyim Or Zaru'a against, *791*
  Falk's commentaries on, *1412–1414*
  financial relations between husband and wife, source of, *913*
  on halakhic authorities, *271*
  Hayyim b. Bezalel's critique of, *1375–1376*
  individual rights, in communal enactments, *769–771*
  on "law of the land is law," *70*
  on lay tribunals, *26–27*
  majority rule in communal enactments, *723n.177*
  responsa literature of, *1488*
  Sefer ha-Mordekhai commentary, *1250*
  source references omitted by, *1360n.186*
  Talmudic research and, *44*
issur (religious and ritual law)
  Alfasi's *Sefer ha-Halakhot* and, *1169–1170*
  "all who marry do so subject to conditions laid down by the Rabbis and the Rabbis annul this marriage" legislation, *635n.53*
  annulment of marriage, enactments, *851–852*
  applicability of, in modern Succession Law, *1688*
  asharta, *613n.280*
  Candia, enactments of, *811*
  Capacity and Guardianship Law linked with, *1669–1671*
  circumvention of *kum va-Aseh* and, *532n.156*
  codificatory literature on, *1447–1448*
  communal enactments and, *707–714*
  creative power of custom in, *903–905*

custom as source of, *884–885, 896, 900, 909–910*
dichotomy with "legal" laws, *93, 111–122*
halizah and, *1002–1004*
laws derived from custom vs. laws derived from legal sources, *888–893*
legal reasoning (*sevarah*) and, *992, 1002–1004*
legal research on, *4–5, 107*
legislation incorporating tenets of, *1646–1647*
legislative terminology and, *492n.72*
le-migdar milta, 536n.177
ma'aseh and, *975–978*
majority rule, in communal enactments, *725*
minors and future generations, enactments for, *731*
"mouth that has prohibited is the mouth that has permitted," *994–995*
multiplicity of opinions in, *1379n.36*
Onkelos' translations as source for, *1046*
personal status legislation and, *1768–1679*
practice of, during Diaspora, *1605–1606*
purity laws, in *Mishneh Torah, 1213n.98*
rabbinical courts' jurisdiction over, *1761–1762, 1764*
religious vs. legal obligations and, *122–123*
responsa literature and, *975–978, 1492*
scriptual analogy canon, *346*
in *Sefer ha-Roke'ah, 1239*
in *Sefer Yere'im* (Book of the God-Fearing), *1259–1261*
in *Sha'arei Dura, 1248–1249, 1357–1358*
on slaughter, Saadiah Gaon's monograph on, *1159*
in *Torat ha-Bayit, 1273–1275*
in *Torat Hattat, 1357–1359*
Tur Yoreh De'ah codification, *1289–1290*
witnesses' oaths or affirmations and, *1704–1706*
Women's Equal Rights Law and, *1657–1660*
"yoke of" regarding earnings of wife from her employment, *1791–1793*
"you shall add or take away," *500–502*
Italy, Jewish community in
connections to Israel, *1132n.114*
countrywide enactments, *813–817, 872–874*
decline of legal creativity among, *51*
responsa literature of, *1479–1480*
See also specific Italian cities.
Ittur Soferim. See Sefer ha-Ittur
Ivri, terminology of, *110–111*
Iyash, Judah, responsa literature of, *1490*
Izmir, responsa literature from, *1489–1490*

J

Jacob b. Asher, *1272*
codification methodology of, *1277–1287, 1341*
early life, *1278–1279*
Heller's commentary on, *1404–1407*
hilkheta ke-vatra'ei, 1359n.182
idolatry laws, codification of, *1327–1329*
language and style compared with Maimonides and Caro, *1327– 1340*
Piskei ha-Tosafot, 1122
possession (*hazakah*) laws, codification, *1331–1335*
property laws, codification of, *1330–1331*
responsa literature and, *1481, 1489*
Sefer ha-Turim of, *1277–1303*
See also Sefer ha-Turim
Jacob b. Judah Hazzan, *1255–1256*
Jacob b. Korshai, R.
development and redaction of Mishnah and, *1051–1052*
mishnayot compilations, *1051–1052*
Jacob b. Nissim, *Iggeret Rav Sherira Gaon, 1542*
Jacob b. Yakar, commentaries of, *1116–1117*
Jacob ibn Habib, *1315n.17*
table metaphor used by, *1311n.36*
Jacob ibn Zur
Et Sofer of, *1539*
responsa literature of, *1490*
Jaffe, Mordecai, *940*
Jaffe, Mordecai b. Abraham
commentaries on codification by, *1394–1403*
Falk's commentaries on, *1410n.137*
Jaffe, Samuel, *Tikkun Soferim* of, *1538*
jails and imprisonment, Cracow enactments concerning, *821*
Jannai, Alexander, *1043n.8*
Jehiel, Nathan b., *93*
Jehiel of Paris, *811n.120*
Jerczewski v. Prime Minister Yitzhak Shamir, 1884n.232

Jeremiah, Book of
as literary source for law, *1022–1024*
ownership laws in, *1010–1012*
Jeroham b. Meshullam, Rabbenu
annulment of marriage, enactments concerning, *850–856*
"approval of all halakhic authorities of the region," *858n.277*
as literary source, *1251n.64, 1269–1272*
Jerusalem Talmud
Alfasi's *Sefer ha-Halakhot* and, *1170*
"all who marry do so subject to conditions laid down by the Rabbis and the Rabbis annul this marriage" legislation, *634–636, 640*
asmakhta (supportive interpretation) and, *302–303*
Benveniste's commentary on, *1134*
commentaries and novellae on, *54n.13, 1130–1137*
current resettlement of Israel and, *1133n.118*
"custom overrides the law," *906*
custom as source of law, *902*
on death penalty, *972*
differences with Babylonian Talmud, *1095–1097*
Elijah of Fulda's commentary and novellae, *1134–1135*
Fraenkel's commentary and novellae on, *1135*
Gaon of Vilna's commentary on, *1136–1137*
halizah rules and, *907–908*
ketubbah interpretation in, *427*
as literary legal source, *1095–1098*
Maimonides' compilation of halakhic material and, *1187, 1207*
Margoliot's commentary and novellae, *1135–1136*
market overt legislation, *598*
morality of charity and, *101*
on death penalty for murder, *1034*
Order of *Zera'im* and, *52*
precedent in Jewish law and, *984*
production of, during *amoraic* era, *42*
Rabbenu Hananel's commentary on, *1115*
redaction of, *1097–1098*
role of public in legislation, *540*
Sefer ha-Ittur source, *1269*
Sirillo's commentary on, *1132–1133*
teachings of, in Babylonian Talmud, *1090*
Yavneh center established, *1067*
Jesurun, Isaac, *1304*
Panim Hadashot of, *1433–1434*
Jewish Encyclopedia, The, *1560*
Jewish Enlightenment (*Haskalah*), *1549*
responsa literature and, *1492*
Jewish Government, in Israel and Diaspora, *58–59*
Jewish heritage (*moreshet Yisra'el*)
analogous reasoning, *1835n.29*
court decisions and, *1841–1863*
Foundations of Law Act and, *1828, 1839–1840, 1895n.260*
freedom from detention, *1843–1845*
freedom of thought and speech, *1846–1850*
human dignity and equality and, *1850–1854*
as part of Israeli legal system, *1831–1832*
privacy, right of, *1856–1860*
sources of, *1861–1863*
uncertainty of statutory interpretation and, *1867–1871*
Jewish law. *See mishpat ivri* (Jewish law)
Jewish Law Annual, The, *1564, 1571*
Jewish Law: Bibliography of Sources and Scholarship in English, *1564*
Jewish National Fund, Basic Law: Israel Lands and, *1651–1652*
Jews for Jesus, *1690n.289*
Joash, King, *1025–1026*
Johanan b. Meir Kremnitzer, *1361n.186*
Johanan ha-Sandelar, R., *1044*
Johanan b. Zakkai, R.
legislative enactments of, *566*
as literary source, *1044*
Johanan, R.
amoraic view of Mishnah and, *1061*
on anonymous law, *1060*
bailments and, *965*
custom as law, *889, 891,894, 935*
on half-measure prohibition, *998–999*
halizah and, *1003–1004*
integrative interpretations of, *297–298*
latent damage legislation, *603n.247*
on legal capacity of children, *1664–1665*
legal reasoning (*sevarah*) and, *989n.5, 1003–1004*
on "love your fellow as yourself," *1852*
plain meaning vs. nonliteral halakhic interpretation, *410–411*
responsa questions submitted by, *1476*
on responsa in Talmudic sources, *1455–1456*

tort law interpretations, *412–414*
Yom Kippur, custom as law regarding, *899–900*
joint property ownership, freedom of contract and, *128n.146*
joint tenancy, modern Succession Law and simultaneous death, *1681n.256*
Jonah, Meir, glosses on *Sefer ha-Ittur*, *1269n.143*
Jonah, Rabbenu, commentary in *Tur Hoshen Mishpat* on, *1295–1299*
Jonathan ha-Kohen of Lunel
commentaries on *Sefer ha-Halakhot*, *1175*
Maimonides' correspondence with, *1175*, *1185n.9*
Joseph b. Judah ibn Aknin, Maimonides' correspondence with, *1214–1215*, *1222–1223*
Joseph b. Judah ibn Simeon, *1222n.117*
Joseph ibn Ezra, *1445–1446*
Joseph ibn Verga, *Sher'erit Yosef* of, *1545*
Joseph, Dov (Minister of Justice), *1671n.211*
Joseph, R., on local custom as law, *934n.171*
Joshua, Rabbi
amoraic view of Mishnah and, *1061*
early enactments of, *551–553*
on halakhic authority, *261–263*
ma'aseh and, *948*
"mouth that has prohibited is the mouth that has permitted," *993–994*
Joseph Tov Elem, tax law compilations, *1444*
Josephus, Flavius
arrangement of laws in Mishnah, *1055n.72*
as literary source of law, *1019*, *1031–1033*, *1037*
on laws regarding war on sabbath, *1035*
Joshua, enactments of, *550–553*
Joshua Abraham Judah, *1446*
Joshua b. Hananiah, *1044*
Joshua b. Joseph of Cracow, *1403n.117*
on authority of *Shulhan Arukh*, *1417n.161*
Joshua b. Perahyah, as part of *Zugot*, *1043*
Joshua Boaz b. Simon Baruch, *1250n.63*
commentaries on *Sefer ha-Halakhot*, *1176*
Joshua ha-Levi, *Halihkhot Olam* of, *1545*
Joshua, R.
halakhic pluralism and, *1068*
on anonymous law, *1060n.89*
Jubilees, Book of, as literary source of law, *1033–1034*
Judah b. Bathyra, R., *1077–1078*
Babylonian diaspora and, *1087*
in second tannaitic generation, *1044*
Judah b. Bava, *agunot* legislation and, *526*
Judah b. Ilai, *1044*
Judah b. Nathan (Riban), commentary of, *1117n.57*
Judah b. Shimon Ashkenazi, *1437*
Judah b. Tabbai, as part of *Zugot*, *1043*
Judah Gaon, betrothal legislation, *656–657*
Judah Halevi, *1168*
Judah Ha-Nasi, R. (Gamaliel III)
"all who marry do so subject to conditions laid down by the Rabbis and the Rabbis annul this marriage" legislation, *631*, *634*
arrangement of laws in Mishnah, *1056*
Babylonian Talmud redaction and, *1092*
codification methodology of, *1343*
compilation of Jerusalem Talmud and, *1095–1097*
content of Mishnah and, *1057–1062*
custom based on error, rulings regarding, *938–939*
development and redaction of Mishnah and, *1051–1053*
on distinguishing process, *962*
as fifth tannaitic generation, *1044*
Gamaliel the elder's bill of divorcement, *565–566*
influence on codificatory methodology, *1286–1287*
as major *tannai*, *1044*
Maimonides comments on, *1218–1219*
Mishnah redaction of, *1049–1050*, *1052*, *1148*
mi-shum eivah (prevention of strife and enmity) legislation, *628n.31*
multiple opinions in Mishnah and, *1070–1072*
stolen property legislation, *602n.243*
Judah, R.
agunot legislation and, *523–524*
custom as source of legislation, *891*
development and redaction of Mishnah and, *1051*
freedom of thought and speech, *1848*
holkhei Usha, *1008n.73*
king's law and, *55–56*
labor law, *617*
on levirate marriage, *197–199*

Judah, R. *continued*
mishnayot compilations, *1051*
recitation of *shema*, *969*
restrictive interpretations of Torah by, *365–366*
on sacrifice of life to save another, *970–971*
Yom Kippur, custom as law regarding, *899*
Judaism, conversion to. *See* conversion to Judaism.
Judeans, interpretation of*ketubbah* by, *806n.93*
"judge not alone, for none may judge alone save One," *1646n.110*
"judge your neighbor fairly"
freedom from detention based on, *1845*
justice and equity in, *168–169*
justice as supplement to law, *173n.334, 174*
in Leviticus (19:15), *1760n.21*
judges
arka'ot she-be-Suria and, *25n.80*
authority of, *242–243*
communal leaders equated with, *704n.97*
competence of, in communal enactments, *739–740*
decision-making, post-Talmudic halakhic interpretations, *416*
Foundations of Law Act interpretations, *1895–1897*
intrepretation methods of, *288–289*
in Jewish court system, *6*
legal-moral reciprocity and, *144n.214*
legal standards for, *179–182*
liability of, regarding witnesses, *606n.264*
responsibilities of, under Foundations of Law Act, *1832*
Valladolid enactments regarding, *799–801*
See also dayyan (rabbinical court judge)
judgment
mishpat and, *105–106*
precedent in Jewish law and, *981–982*
"judicial benches" concept of Caro, *1318–1319*
judicial precedent, Foundations of Law Act and, *1834–1835, 1887–1888*
judicial procedure, personal status law and, *1598–1600*
juridical autonomy
abrogation of, during Emancipation, *2–3, 44, 1578–1588, 1898–1899*
codificatory literature and, *1374–1375*
conflict of laws and, *78–79*
custom as source of law in, *920*
decline of, in non-Jewish countries, *13–18, 36–37, 50–51, 1428*
disputes between Jew and non-Jew and, *37n.109*
economic-social relationships and, *36–37*
equity and, *182n.360*
hilkheta ke-vatra'ei, 1345–1348
Jewish court system and, *6–10*
law and equity and, *182n.360*
"law of the land is law," *69–72*
lay tribunals as protection of, *23–29, 33*
legislation as instrument of halakhic authority, *1808–1809*
loss of, during Emancipation, *2–3, 44*
majority rule and communal enactments, *720–722*
in *Mishneh Torah*, *1201–1202*
Rabbinical Court of Appeals and, *1813–1818*
record books of, responsa compared with, *1466n.42*
renewal of, in Israeli legal system, *1899*
responsa literature and, *1460–1461, 1467nn.42, 45, 1475–1476, 1491–1494*
rise of *kehillah* and, *666–668*
rishonim responsa, *1480–1481*
scientific legal research and, *84–86, 89n.49*
Shulhan Arukh and, *1419–1422*
vs. statutes, *1459n.20*
survival of Jewish state and, *38–39*
"jurisdictional competition," role of, in State legislation, *1756–1757*
jurisprudence
interpretive approaches to Israeli legislation and, *1732–1735*
Jewish law as primary guidance, *1737–1739*
jus cogens
freedom of contract law, *123*
in religious law of Torah, *904*
jus dispositivum
in Biblical civil law, *904*
freedom of contract law, *123*
jus naturale, legal norms and, *234*
jus non scriptum, *191*
jus scriptum, *191*
justice (*zedek*)
commentary in *Tur Hoshen Mishpat* on, *1295–1300*

communal enactments' consonance with, *760–777*
in criminal law, *254–255*
custom (*minhag*) and, *942–944*
dinei mamonot, 257–258
din emet le-amito as basis for, *250–251*
equity and, *248–251*
Foundations of Law Act and, *1839–1840*
vs. king's justice, *56–57*
"law of the land is law," *72*
as legal norm, *175–176*
lifenim mi-shurat ha-din, 167–182
literary sources on, *1840n.54*
morals and equity and, *181n.360*
Ramah (Abulafia) on, *170–171, 174*
as supplement to law, *169–175*
See also equity
"justice, justice shall you pursue," 173n.334, *174*
Justinian (Roman Emperor), *2n.1*

K

kabbalah.
literature, *1316n.23*
terminology of, *203n.65*
See also tradition
"Kach" party case. *See Naiman v. Chairman, Central Elections Committee*
kadesh/kadesha, laws regarding, Onkelos' translations as source for, *1046n.28*
Kadsheff, Jacob Ibn, *23*
ka-din ve-she-lo ka-din, 248
Kafah, Yosef (Rabbi), *1232n.145, 1500n.131*
education of children, parents' rights regarding, *1802*
interaction of statutory law and Jewish law, *1761–1762*
rabbinical courts and, *1824–1826*
Kahan Commission, *1857*
Kahan, Yitzhak (Justice), *1779*
earnings of wife from her employment, decisions regarding, *1791–1792*
on repeal of Article 46, *1830–1831*
on Streit v. Chief Rabbi of Israel, *1759n.20*
Kahana, R., *1061*
Kahana, K., Women's Equal Rights Law and, *1658n.151*
Kalonymus, David b., enactments of, *788*
kal va-homer. See a fortiori inference
Kaplan, Abraham Elijah, *819n.147*
Karaism
codification debate and, *1156–1157*
encyclopedic sources on, *1553n.91*
Maimonides' codificatory methodology, *1220–1221, 1287n.194*
responsa literature on, *1486n.98*
Saadiah Gaon and, *1159*
Karelitz, Abraham Isaiah, communal enactments equated with courts, *702*
karet
half-measure prohibition and, *999*
punishment, *1065–1066*
kashrut, practice of, during Diaspora, *1605–1606*
Kasovsky, Chayim Yehoshua, *1568*
Katz, J., on power of custom, *911n.54*
Kaufmann, Yehezkel, *1577–1578, 1931n.93*
Kayyara, Simeon
Halakhot Gedolot, 1170
literary sources of Jewish law and, *1155–1156*
kehillah (Jewish community)
custom as source of law in, *920*
"distinguished person" approval, *752n.272*
enforcement of communal enactments, *681–682*
spiritual hegemony and, *666–668*
kelal ha-rov (probabilities), "custom overrides the law," *906*
kelal u-ferat canon, explicative exegesis, *324–325*
kelal u-ferat u-khelal canon, explicative exegesis, *326–327*
Kelalei ha-Gemara, 1545–1546
Kelalei ha-Talmud, 1547
guidebooks and, *1541*
Kelei Yakar, 1418n.161
Keli Hemdah, extradition laws and, *1862*
Kelsen, *Grundnorm* theory of, *230–232*
Keneset ha-Gedolah (Great Assembly), *1304, 1615n.101*
questioning methods in responsa and, *1505n.150*
responsa literature and, *1434–1437, 1489, 1523–1524*
Kerem Hemer, 1539
Kesef Mishneh, 1233
ketubbah (marriage contract)
Algerian enactments concerning, *805–806*
"all who marry do so subject to conditions laid down by the Rabbis and the

ketubbah continued
Rabbis annul this marriage" legislation, *639n.63*
arrangement of laws in Mishnah, *1056*
betrothal legislation, *657*
Biblical vs. rabbinical law and, *211–212*
Book of Tobit as source on, *1034*
collection of, according to wife's testimony, *426–427*
doreshin leshon hedyot, *423–428*
equalization of property for debt satisfaction, *647–648*
financial relations between husband and wife, custom as source of, *912–913*
inheritance laws and, *427–428, 575–578*
interpretation of communal enactments and, *452–453*
issur-mamon distinction and, *131n.166*
in Jerusalem Talmud, *427*
Joshua's property enactments and, *551n.28*
judicial procedure and law of personal status, *1599–1600*
as legal document, *277–278*
legal vs. moral imperative and, *145n.214*
legislative terminology concerning, *491–492*
leniency regarding rabbinic law and, *213–214*
liability law and, *561n.68*
ma'aseh regarding, *952–953, 974–975*
Maharam of Rothenburg's enactments, *789n.37*
Mainz enactments regarding, *792*
miminum amounts, enactments concerning, *830*
moredet legislation, *659–660*
Moroccan enactments concerning, *808*
Rabbenu Gershom's enactments concerning, *785*
rabbinical court decisions regarding, *1754n.7*
rabbinic law supersedes Biblical law, *215–217*
Sefer ha-Ittur codification of, *1268*
Sefer ha-Turim codification of, *1290–1291*
Simeon b. Shatah, enactment of, *559–561*
Tosefta legal rules regarding, *1081*
widow's right to maintenance, *573–574*
widow's right to recover, *841–842*
ketubbat benin dikhrin (wife's sons, rights of)
inheritance law and, *575–578, 655–656*
Keren Kayemet le-Yisra'el (Jewish National Fund), *164*
Kezot ha-Hoshen, commentaries on *Hoshen Mishpat* in, *1428*
kiddush ha-hodesh (sanctification of the New Moon), *1188–1190*
Kiddushin Tractate, *1055–1056*
kidnapping, laws regarding
context as basis of explanation in, *335*
fraudulent marriages, enactments regarding, *847n.248*
melog property legislation, *572n.120*
kidney transplants, Jewish heritage, laws regarding, *1860–1861*
kilayim
custom as source of law, *887–888*
hefker bet din hefker, *507, 508n.61*
kim li
earnings of wife from her employment, rabbinical court decisions regarding, *1787n.105, 1788n.109*
Jacob b. Asher's codification, *1282–1283*
Maharshal's commentary on, *1386*
multiplicity of opinions in, *1379n.36*
responsa literature on, *1504*
king's law
communal enactments and, *679n.1*
deviation from Jewish law, *1942–1946*
as discriminatory law, *72–73*
equity and, *247n.26*
halakhic authorities and, *55–57*
issur-mamon distinction and, *133n.174*
vs. Jewish government, in Israel and diaspora, *58–59*
"law of the land is law," *65n.46, 66n.51, 67n.53*
legislative authority and, *486–490*
as literary source for law, *1024–1025*
in *Mishneh Torah*, *1202*
property law and, *454–456*
territorial scope of legislation and, *671*
Kings, Book of, as literary source for law, *1025*
kinyan agav karka
Law of Return and, *1647–1651*
legislative enactments, *583–585*
kinyan meshikhah (pulling)
acquisition, legislative enactments, *581*
Biblical vs. rabbinical law and, *211–212*
custom as source for law, *915–916*
hefker bet din hefker, *511*
integrative interpretations as basis for, *297–298*

legal norms as basis for, *233*
legal reasoning (*sevarah*) as basis for, *989n.5*
legislation as basis for, *297–298*
kinyan. *See* acquisition (*kinyan*)
Kiryat Sefer, *1563*
Kister, Justice
earnings of wife from her employment, decisions regarding, *1788–1790*
marriage between *kohen* and divorcee, decisions on, *1777–1778*
kiyyum bet din, *issur* vs. communal enactments, *709*
kizah, enforcement of communal enactments and, *679n.4*
Kizzur ha-Mordekhai, *1250n.63*
Kizzur Shulhan Arukh (The Abridged *Shulhan Arukh*), *1447–1448*
Klausner, Abraham, *1305*
Klinghoffer, MK, *1671n.211*, *1724n.393*
Kluger, Solomon, *1584n.18*
Knesset
Adoption of Children Law, *827n.178*
Contracts Law passed by, *130n.161*
Elections Law, *1841–1842*
first legislative period, *1627–1690*
Foundations of Law Act, *1624*
halakhic decision making and, *1903–1914*
imprisonment for debt legislation, *1636–1639*
incorporation of Jewish law by, *1627–1720*, *1756–1757*, *1918–1920*, *1938–1940*
Jewish law as *din Torah* in, *111n.84*
lacuna interpreted by, *1836–1838*
Land Law legislation, *1710–1716*
legal norms in, *234n.24*
Legislative Committee interpretations of law, *1732*
legislation passed by, *478–479*
Public Committee interpretations of law, *1732*
second legislative period, *1690–1720*, *1827–1828*
severance pay legislation, *1633–1634*
ultra vires and, *537–538*
See also legislative law.
Kobo, Raphael Asher, responsa literature of, *1495*
Kodashim law (Consecrated Things), abrogation of, *1583–1584*
Kodashim Order
history of Jewish law and, *52n.10*, *54*
in Mishnah, *1054*
omission of, in Babylonian Talmud, *1095*
responsa literature and, *1491*
as source of Jewish law, *1253n.69*
Koenig v. Cohen, *1875–1884*
kohen, marriage to divorcee by
general court decisions regarding, *1770–1782*, *1929n.87*
Jewish law as basis for rulings, *1602–1603*, *1655n.139*
rabbinical court decisions regarding, *1754n.8*
"religious" vs. "legal" components of, *1770–1782*, *1904n.14*
kol di-mekaddesh ada'ata de-rabbanan mekaddesh, betrothal annulment and, *507n.58*
Kolin, Samuel ha-Levi, *1432*
Kook, Abraham Isaac ha-Kohen (Rabbi)
codificatory literature and, *824*, *826*
establishment of Chief Rabbinate, *1597–1598*
history of Jewish law and, *59*
integration of Jewish heritage and "natural ethics," *1852–1854*
on juridical autonomy, *1808–1809*
on sources of Jewish law, *1496n.127*, *1499*
on state legislation, *1902*
Korban ha-Edah, *1135*
Korban Nethanel, *1255*
Korei ha-Dorot, *1558*
Korha, Joshua b. (R.), *112*
legal reasoning (*sevarah*) pertaining to witnesses, *1000–1001*
Korot ha-Yehudim be-Turkiyah u-ve-Arzot ha-Kedem, *1559*
Kosher Food for Soldiers Ordinance, *1647*
Kovez ha-Rambam
Maimonides' discussion in, *1215n.100*
as source of Jewish law, *1190n.28*, *1194n.40*
kunteres (notebooks)
Kremzir, enactments of, *823*
Kreti u-Peleti, *1432*
Krochmal, Menahem Mendel
on halakhic-aggadic reciprocity, *96–99*
majority rule, in communal enactments, *725–726*
proof of custom, *928n.131*
responsa literature of, *1510n.167*
source of Jewish law and, *1420*
Krochmal, Nachman, Ezra's legislative enactments and, *556*

kum va-Aseh, court authority regarding, *506, 521–533*
Kunteres ha-Agunot, *1458n.15*
Kunteres ha-Teshuvot, *1524, 1562*
Kunteres Ozar Mefarshei Mishneh Torah, *1232n.145*
Kupat ha-Rokhelim, *1177n.102*
kupot, "do what is right and good," *623*

L

la'alot, right of, *1647–1651*
labor law
  contradictory passages in Torah regarding, *336–337*
  "custom overrides the law," *906n.38*
  custom and usage regarding, *909n.48, 931–932*
  Israeli legislative policy regarding, *1629–1634*
  modern contract legislation on, *1634n.51*
  severance pay, custom as source of law, *924–926*
  tannaitic legislation, *614–621*
lacunae
  Capacity and Guardianship Law as example, *1668–1671*
  disputes over definition of, *1936–1938*
  English statute of Elizabeth, 1571, incorporation of, *1889–1894*
  Foundations of Law Act and, *1835–1838*
  in *Hendeles* case, additional hearing, *1863–1871*
  interpretive approaches to Israeli legislation and, 1732–1735, *1895–1897*
  Jewish law as complementary source in, *1943–1944*
  pittu'ah ha-mishpat theory, *1884n.232*
  repeal of Article 46 and, *1830–1831*
  value-laden legal terms and, *1871–1874*
Lagos, Ptolemy, *1035*
Lakish, Resh (Simeon b. Lakish)
  on Babylonian diaspora, *1087n.16*
  on half-measure prohibition, *998–999*
  labor law, in tannaitic era, *614n.287*
  legal reasoning (*sevarah*) and *halizah*, *1003–1004*
  on local custom as law, *935*
  on Mishnaic "Orders," 1053n.62
Lamm (Judge), *1912n.38*
Lampronti, Isaac, *1551–1552*
Landau, Ezekiel, *32–33*
Land Law
  self-help and, *1709–1716*
  severing of ties to English law, *1728–1729*
landlord/tenant agreements, laws regarding, *453–456*
Land of Israel
  Babylonian diaspora and, *1087–1088*
  Chief Rabbinate of, enactments of, *824–833*
  Crusaders' destruction of, *1132n.113*
  current remigration to, *1133n.118*
  debate with Babylonia on responsa, *1455–1456*
  Joshua's property enactments and, *553n.34*
  "language war" in, *1608*
  legislation in, vs. other legal systems, *478–481*
  rabbinical courts of, procedural enactments, *826–829*
  rishonim responsa from, *1486–1490, 1495*
  Southern Italy and, *1132n.114*
  tort liability of spouses, *629n.37*
  ultra vires, and legislation, *537–538*
  See also Israel, State of
Landau, Ezekiel
  codificatory literature, *770n.343*
Landau, Jacob, *1305*
Landau, Moshe (Justice)
  on district courts, *1818n.206*
  on *Hendeles* case, *1744, 1749n.454*
  on land laws, *1709–1710*
  limitations and accomplishments of Rabbinical Court of Appeals and, *1816–1817*
  marriage between *kohen* and divorcee, Jewish law incorporated in state legislation, *1772–1774, 1776, 1782–1784*
  statutory incorporation and, *1579–1580*
  on subjective factors affecting recourse to Jewish law, 1928–1931
  uncertainty of statutory interpretation and, *1867–1869*
  will of *shekhiv me-ra* and, *1880–1884*
Landau, Jacob, *1305*
Laserson v. Shikkun Ovedim, good faith in, *1837n.36*
le'assot kizatan (enforcement), of communal enactments, *679n.3, 680n.6*
latent damage legislation, *603n.247*
  tort liability and, *602–604*
Law and Administration Ordinance of 1948
  Jewish law incorporated in, *1646–1647*

Section 9, *537–538*
Section 11, *1620*
law, as concept
as English translation of *Torah*, *191n.2*
English and German definitions of, *106n.62*
law of agency, indirect halakhic interpretation, *404–405*
law of obligations
classification of, *76–77*
debtors' rights vs. creditors' rights, *589n.197*
legislation concerning, *587–601*
personal aspect of, *589n.197*
law of pleadings, integrative interpretation and, *385–386*
law of principal and agent, *112–113*
Law of Return, *1647–1651*, *1689–1690n.289*
"law of the land is law" (*dina de-malkhuta dina*)
abrogation during Emancipation and, *1583–1584*
acquisition (*kinyan*), and, *68n.61*
"all her ways are pleasant ways and all her paths are peaceful," 989, *1000–1004*
in amoraic era, *65*
in Babylonian Talmud, *69*
Biblical law and and, *1005n.62*
civil law (noncriminal) and, *65n.47*, *68–70*
collective punishment and, *72–73*
commercial law and, *68n.59*
communal enactments and, *514*, *688n.35*
conflict of laws and, *79*, *677n.44*, *1767n.48*
contract law and, *66*
copyright law and, *74n.87*
currency laws and, *69n.66*
custom as source of law and, *921–922*
debt laws and, *72n.77*
divorce law and, *67n.59*
during diaspora, *65*
eminent domain and, *68*
equal application of communal enactments, *772n.347*
equity and, *72*
evidence laws and, *70n.73*
Halakhah as source of, *64–74*
halakhic authorities and, *64–74*, *1944–1945*
issur-mamon distinction and, *132–137*, *139*
juridical autonomy and, *15–18*, *69–72*
justice as legal norm and, *72*, *175–176*
king's law and, *60n.32*
legal documents and, *68n.62*
lifenim mi-shurat ha-din, *164–166*
market overt issue, *601n.237*
Nagar case and, *1825–1826*
rabbinical courts and, *1819*
tax enactments, *749*
Wiloszni case and, *1823–1824*
Law Reports (English Law), responsa compared with, *1467*
"laws currently applicable," in *Bet Yosef*, *1313–1316*
"laws of fines" (*dinei kenasot*), *108n.73*
"Laws of the Land of Israel," in *Sefer ha-Terumah*, *1240n.9*
"laws that are not practiced at the present time," responsa literature and, *1491–1492*
lay courts, Mishpat Ha-Shalom Ha-Ivri and, *1594n.43*
lay tribunals (*battei din shel hedyotot*)
criticism of, by Halakhic authorities, *30–33*
halakhic authorities and, *61*
judgments (*piskei ba'alei battim*), *31*
cross reference piskei ba'alei battim to judgment
enforcement of communal enactments, *682n.14*
juridical autonomy and, *20–29*
public acceptance of, *25n.80*, *27n.83*
terminology for, in different countries, *27n.84*
lay usage and practice, in *doreshin leshon hedyot*, *429–432*
leadership, king's law and, *57–58n.27*
leasing, laws regarding, *1268n.139*
lefi sha'ah, legislation and, *533–536*
legal capacity,
Capacity and Guardianship Law, *1664–1671*
See also mental competency
legal consequences, Biblical or rabbinic law classification and, *212–223*
Legal Digest of Spanish and North African Responsa, *12n.30*, *1526–1527*, *1934n.98*
legal education, reliance on Jewish law in, *1932–1934*

"legal" *Halakhah*, vs. "religious" *Halakhah*, *111–122*
terminology of, *107*
legal instruments (documents) (*shetarot*)
authentication and certification, tannaitic legislation, *610–614*
in Christian Spain, Jews' compilations of, *1538*
communal enactments and, *468–471*, *736n.221*
compilations of, *1531–1541*
custom as factor in preparation of, *912–913*
encumbered property, legislation concerning, *593n.213*
English Jews' compilations, *1537–1538*
in *Et Sofer*, *1539*
"law of the land is law," *68n.62*
as literary source, *1102–1103*
ma'aseh regarding, *951–952*
Mahzor Vitry compilation of, *1537*
in *Nahalat Shiv'ah*, *1539*
in *Ozar ha-Shetarot*, *1539–1540*
protection of deeds, during exile, *1011–1014*
Sefer ha-Ittur, *1267–1269*, *1537*
Sefer ha-Shetarot of Hai b. Sherira Gaon, *1536*
Sefer ha-Shetarot of Judah al-Bargeloni, *1536–1537*
Sefer ha-Shetarot of Lucena, Spain, *1536*
Sefer ha-Shetarot of Saadiah Gaon, *1535–1536*
shufra de-shetara (adornments of the shetar), *1534*
Spanish and North African compilations, *1540*
Tikkun Shetarot, *1538*
Tikkun Soferim of Moses Almosnino and Samuel Jaffe, *1538*
Tikkun Soferim of Rashbash, *1538*
tofes (template) and *toref* (blank) sections of, *1533–1534*
Yad Ramah compilations of, *1537*
"legal issue requiring decision,"
Foundations of Law Act and, *1835–1838*
"legal" laws
vs. moral imperatives, in Jewish legal system, *141–189*
vs. "religious", *93*, *107*, *111–122*
legal literature, as literary source for Jewish law, *1027–1036*
legal norms
custom as legal source of law, *882*
decline of Jewish law and, *1609*
Grundnorm concept, *230–232*
justice as, *175–176*
legal-moral reciprocity and, *144*
lifenim mi-shurat ha-din and, *157–160*
ma'aseh and, *946–948*
morashah concept and, *1839–1840*
rule and discretion in, *176–180*
sources of law and, *228–230*
Torah as basic norm, *232–234*
"legal order", concept of, Noahide laws and, *194*
legal presumption (*hazakah*), legal reasoning *sevarah* and, *995–998*
legal reasoning (*sevarah*)
in amoraic era, *998–1004*
amputations, laws regarding, *1005n.62*
analogous reasoning and, *1009–1010*
"be killed rather than transgress," *990–991*
Biblical verse and, *1000–1004*
burden of proof and, *992–993*
in codificatory literature, *989n.5*, *1003–1004*
communal enactments and, *1005–1006*
definition as legal source, *987–990*
halakhic-aggadic reciprocity and, *104*
halakhic authorities' search for rules, *1007–1014*
half-measures, Biblical prohibition of, *998–999*
halizah and, *1002–1004*
innocence, presumption of, *996n.29*
issur (religious law) and, *992*, *1002–1004*
"law of the land is law" and, *139*
as legal source of Jewish law, *239*
ma'aseh and, *988*
mamon law and, *137–141*
"the mouth that has prohibited is the mouth that has permitted," *993–995*
pertaining to witnesses, *1000–1001*
in post-talmudic era, *1004–1006*
reliance on majority, *995–998*
as source for legal ideas, *992–998*
witnesses, laws pertaining to, *1000–1002*
See also "law of the land is law"
legal rights, *mishpat* as, *106*
legal sources of Jewish law
classification of, *236–239*
custom as, *881–885*
defined, *229–230*
role of, in Israeli legal system, *1899*

legal system (Jewish)
legislation in, vs. other legal systems, *478–481*
mishpat as, *106*
norms of, *230–232*
terminology in, *79–80*
Leghorn, Italy, Jewish community in
juridical autonomy in, *34–36*
lay tribunals and, *28–29*
legis actio permanus iniectionem, *589*
legislation (*takkanah and gezrah*)
acquisition legislation (*kinyan*), in tannaitic era, *580–587*
acts prohibited by Torah (*kum va-Aseh*), *521–533*
agunah, legal source for, *1014n.87*
anonymous, *579–601*, *895–896*
authority of competent bodies and, *486–490*
conflict of laws and, *79*, *677*
contraction in scope of, *676–677*
during era of Ezra and Great Assembly, *554–558*
early history of, *546–554*
Foundations of Law Act and, *1834–1835*
Gamaliel the Elder's enactments, *563–566*
guidelines for, *505–533*
halakhic authorities, Torah as source of, *481–485*
hefker bet din hefker, *507–515*
Hillel, enactments of, *561–562*
included in Oral Law, *191*
influence of Jewish law on, *1624–1729*, *1731–1751*, *1863–1871*
issur-mamon distinction in *Halakhah* and, *130*
Jewish legal system and, *478–481*
Joshua's property enactments, *551–553*
as legal source of Jewish law, *239*
literary interpretation of Torah and, *307*
midrash and, *477–478*
military legislation of David, *554*
non-Jewish sources of, *1917*
personal status legislation, *1753–1756*
power of, vs. responsa, *1460n.20*
punishment not prescribed in Torah and, *515–519*
"religious" or "ritual" issues in, *105n.52*
role of public in, *538–541*
Sanhedrin as legislative body, *558–559*
scientific legal research and, *85*
scope of halkhic authorities' activity, *495*
shev ve-Al Ta'aseh (court's authority), *505–506*
Simeon b. Shatah's enactments concerning *ketubbah*, *559–561*
in tannaitic period, anonymous enactments, *569–601*
temporary measures (*hor'at sha'ah*), *519–520*
termination of activity, *834–835*
terminology of, *490–492*
territorial scope of, *668–675*
theory vs. practice in, *859–864*
Torah, preservation of, *503–505*
Usha, enactments of, *566–569*
"you shall not add or take away," *496–502*
See also specific types of legislation, e.g. communal enactments; halakhot; statutory incorporation of Jewish law
Legislature. *See* Knesset
lehassi'a al kizatan, enforcement of communal enactments and, *679n.3*, *680n.6*
Lehem Hamudot, *1254*
Lehem Mishneh, *1233–1234*
le-kiddushin, enactments of Frankfurt and, *795n.59*
Leib ha-Kohen, Aryeh, *265*
Leket ha-Kemah, *1437–1438*, *1490*
le-ma'aseh, caution of halakhic authorities and, *949–950*
le-migdar milta, legislation and, *515–516*, *533–536*
lending laws
in *Mishneh Torah*, *1187–1189*, *1200–1201*
in *Hilkhot Malveh ve-Loveh* and, *1246n.42*
Sefer ha-Terumot discussion of, *1245–1246*
leniency
post-Talmudic halakhic interpretation, *415n.41*
rabbinic law and, *212–214*
Sages' laws vs. Biblical law regarding, *214–217*
Lerida enactment, *745n.246*
leshon benei adam (colloquial usage)
Colon's commentary on, *439–440*
documentary interpretation, *429n.31*, *430–432*, *437–443*
inheritance law and, *437–438*
leshon ha-ra ("language of evil"), Defamation Law and, *1642–1644*
Levi, Joshua b. (R.), legal source for *lulav* prohibition, *889*

Levin, Shelomo (Justice), *1880–1884, 1935n.104*
levirate marriage
agunot legislation and, *523–524, 530n.153*
David b. Kalonymus, enactments of, *788*
early legal practices and, *197–199*
halakhic interpretation and legislative enactments, *1809n.185*
halizah ceremony, *389–390*
issur-mamon distinction in *Halakhah* and, *125, 127*
judicial procedure and law of personal status, *1599–1600*
law of principal and agent and, *113n.91*
Mainz enactments regarding, *792*
Moroccan enactments concerning, *808*
presumption of majority in, *997n.36*
procedural enactments concerning, *830–831*
sectarian disputes about, *1065*
Septuagint as source for, *1029*
Leviticus, Book of
Defamation Law influenced by, *1643–1644*
freedom of thought and speech, *1846n.75*
"judge your neighbor fairly," (19:15), *1760n.21*
Maimonides' reliance on, *1209*
Levites
authority of, *242–243*
interpretation of Torah by, *309–310*
Levush ha-Ateret Zahav Gedolah (The Robe of Magnificent Crown of Gold), *1401*
Levush ha-Hur (The White Robe), *1401, 1402n.113*
Levush ha-Tekhelet (The Blue Robe), *1400–1401, 1402n.113*
Levush Ir Shushan (The Robe of the City of Shushan), *1401*
Levush Malkhut, 1394–1403
Levush Mordekhai, 1129n.104
Levush Takhrikh Buz ve-Argaman (The Robe of Fine Linen and Purple Wool), *1401*
Levushei Serad, 1432
Levushim, 1394–1403
Maharam of Lublin's commentaries on, *1384*
Lewin, Benjamin Menashe, *1472*
geonic commentaries collected by, *1114*
Iggeret Rav Sherira Gaon, 1542
lexicons on halakhic literature, *1564–1566*
Lex Poetelia, *589*
liability law
asmakhta (supportive interpretation) and, *303–304*
general principle canon and, *358–359*
ketubbah legislation and, *561n.68*
law of Mishnah compared with cognate sources, *1059n.87*
legal commands vs. moral imperative, *146–147*
lifenim mi-shurat ha-din, 156n.259, 161–164
"religious" and "legal" aspects of *Halakhah* and, *115*
of paid bailee, *196–197*
rabbinic law regarding, *218–220*
See also tort law
licensed concessions, legal protection of, *395–397*
Lichtenstein, Aharon (Rabbi), *1801–1802*
lidrosh, defined, *275–276*
Lieberman, Saul, *1112–1113*
liens, on property
law of obligation and, *590–591*
legislative terminology and, *492n.74*
tannaitic legislation concerning, *591–597*
wife's property exempted, *654n.46*
life insurance, inheritance of, in simultaneous death, *1681n.256*
lifnim mi-shurat ha-din
adjoining landowner's preemptive right (*din bar mezra*), *625n.16*
contract law, *164–166*
custom as source of law regarding severance pay, *925–962*
equity and, *167–182*
eviction law, and, *167n.305*
good faith (*tom lev*), *183–189*
Israeli legislature and, *166*
justice and, *167–182*
law and equity and, *182n.360, 251*
liability law, *156n.259, 161–164*
limitation of actions legislation, *1727*
moral-legal sanctions and, *155–167*
statutory incorporation of legislation, *1634n.51*
Lik, 1178n.107
Lima, Moses, *1419*
commentaries on *Even ha-Ezer, 1429–1430*
limitation of actions, legislation contrary to Jewish law and, *1724–1727*
linen (*argaman*), Valladolid enactments concerning, *803–804*
Lipschutz, Israel, *140–141, 1109–1110*

literary sources of Jewish law
acquisition laws as, *1022–1024*
Apocrypha, *1033–1036*
classification of, *235–236*
defined, *228*
Flavius Josephus, *1031–1033*
general sources, *1017*
Hagiographa (*Ketuvim*), *1021*
King's law, *1024–1025*
legal and general literature, *1018–1019, 1027–1036*
nonauthoritative sources, *1019*
official publications, *1017–1018*
papyri sources, *1028*
Philo of Alexandria, *1030–1031*
Prophets (*Nevi'im*), *1021*
Sabbath laws, *1021–1022*
Septuagint, *1029*
in Sinaitic Revelation era, *1020–1040*
suretyship law, *1026–1027*
in tannaitic period, *1038–1082*
transgression laws, *1025–1026*
translation issues regarding, *1037*
types of sources, overview, *1039–1040*
Written Law, *1020–1027*
See also specific sources; reference works
Lithuania, Jewish community in
enactments by, *818–819*
Jewish diaspora in, *1484–1486*
responsa from, *1495*
litigation
between spouses, tort liability of, *629n.37*
procedural enactments of Rabbinical courts and, *826–827*
livestock, laws regarding, overruling of legislation concerning, *543n.202*
See also agricultural law
local custom (*minhag ha-medinah*)
examples of, *933–936*
general custom and, *897, 932–936*
overrides general law, *926–927*
Loew, Judah of Prague (Maharal), *1108–1109*
logical interpretation of Torah
agency law, *342–343*
mamon law and, *137–141*
thirteen canons of Ishmael and, *339–343*
logic, *mamon* law and, *137–141*
Lorbeerbaum, Jacob, *1429*
"Lord is good to all, and His mercy is upon all His works," *1855–1856*
lost or stolen property
civil law, communal enactments in, *686–688*
custom as legal source of law, *894n.61*
general and specific rules regarding, *332–333*
general principle canon and, *358–359*
integrative interpretations of, *298–300*
logical interpretation of Torah and, *341–342*
ma'aseh concerning, *956–957*
market overt legislation and, *597–601*
statutory incorporation of legislation, *1746n.447*
use of, in religious matters, *602n.242*
see also property law; theft, laws regarding
lo titgodedu ("you shall not gash yourselves"), custom and, *890n.48, 935*
loveh, law of obligations and, *588*
"love your fellow as yourself,"
human dignity and equality, *1851–1854*
Luah ha-Arez, *1613n.95*
lulav ritual
affirmative commandments regarding, *505–506*
customs (*minhag*) regarding, *886*
legal source for prohibition on Sabbath, *889*
legislation regarding, *499n.16*
as religious-legal obligation, *118*
Luria, Isaac (Ari), *1316n.23*
Luzzatto, S. D.
criticism of Maimonides, *1230n.141*
on Maimonides' correspondence with Phinehas b. Meshullam, *1217n.106*
Lvov, enactments of, *823*

M
Ma'adanei Melekh, *1254*
ma'aseh
assets of deceased proselytes, *959–960*
civil law and, *975–978*
conversion to Judaism and, *954–956*
debt suretyship, *953–954*
distinguishing process and, *960–964*
judicial decision making, *950–957*
legal instruments and, *951–952*
legal norms and, *946–948*
legal reasoning (*sevarah*) and, *988*
as legal source, *944–946, 1014*
lost property, return of, *956–957*
in post-Talmudic period, *968–978, 973–975*

ma'aseh continued
precedent in Jewish law and, *980–981*
responsa literature and, *975–978*
sabbath laws and, *958*
sukkah, ritual laws of, *959*
vows, release from, *952–953*
Ma'aseh adif, *946*
Ma'aseh rav, *946*
Mabit (Moses b. Joseph Trani)
legislative enactment, *729–730*
responsa of, *1486n.98*
Maccabees, Book of, as literary source for law, *1035–1036*
Machpelah cave transaction, as literary source for law, *1023n.14*
Mafte'ah ha-Talmud, *1553–1554*
Magen Avot, *1258n.98*
Magen Avraham
commentaries on, *1432*
on *Orah Hayyim* and *Yoreh De'ah*, *1431*
as literary source, *1419*
Maggid Meisharim, *1316n.23*
Maggid Mishneh
commentary on *Mishneh Torah*, *1314n.16*
as literary source, *1232–1233*
Maharai. *See* Isserlein, Israel
Maharal of Prague (Judah Loew b. Bezalel)
Jaffe's contradiction of, *1400n.103*
rejection of codification by, *1375*, *1379–1382*
as source of Jewish law, *140*
"you shall not add or take away," *496n.4*
Maharam Alashkar (Moses b. Isaac Alashkar), *1302n.276*
Maharam of Lublin (Meir b. Gedaliah), *1383–1385*
Maharam of Padua (Meir Katzenellenbogen)
codificatory literature and, *816–817*
as literary source, *1487*
on questioning methods in responsa, *1504*
Maharam of Rothenburg
Asheri's *Piskei ha-Rosh*, *1251–1253*
criminal enactments, *690–691*
on custom as source of law, *900n.14*
enactments of, *704*, *789–791*
as halakhic authority, *101n.36*
imprisonment, *811n.120*
as literary source, *1305*
post-Talmudic halakhic interpretations, *415n.41*, *418–420*
protection of minority rights, *769*
responsa of, *1279*, *1476*, *1478*
tax enactments, *748–750*, *922*
Yom Kippur, custom as law, *899n.14*
Maharashdam (Samuel de Medina)
composition of majority, in communal enactments, *724*
on guardianship of children, *1666*
legal reasoning (*sevarah*) and, *1007n.65*
limitation of actions legislation, *1725–1726*
proof of custom, *929*
on questioning methods in responsa, *1503*
responsa literature of, *1487*
Maharaz Chajes (Zevi Hirsch Chajes)
as literary source, *1549*
responsa literature of, *1495*
Mahardakh (David ha-Kohen), responsa literature of, *1487*
Maharhash (Hayyim Shabbetai)
as literary source, *1458n.15*
responsa literature and, *1489*
Maharibal (Joseph ibn Lev),
on *issur* vs. communal enactments, *712*
prohibition against studying *Bet Yosef*, *1368–1369*
Maharik, Joseph Colon, limitation of actions legislation, *1725*
Maharikash. *See* Castro, Joseph
Maharil (Jacob b. Moses ha-Levi Moellin)
custom as law regarding *Yom Kippur*, *899n.14*
as literary source, *1305*
on loan of orphans' money, *900n.14*
ma'aseh, *792*, *976–977*
territorial scope of legislation and, *671*
Maharit (Joseph Trani)
responsa literature of, *1489*
on use of fictitious names and places, *1514n.187*
Maharsha (Samuel Eliezer Edels)
agunot legislation and, *530n.153*
on authority of *Shulhan Arukh*, *1419–1422*
codification rejected by, *1383–1385*
nomenclature of Rema (Moses Isserles) and, *1349n.142*
novellae of, *1128*
Maharshal (Solomon Luria)
alternatives to *Shulhan Arukh* from, *1385–1394*

on capital punishment, *973n.100*
on *kim li* plea, *1282n.179*
Land Law legislation and, *1716*
as literary source, *1121n.68*
on licensed concessions, *396–397*
on *Mishneh Torah*, *1228n.137*
"pleasant ways," 390
responsa literature of, *1488*
mah ha-zad canon, *355n.232*
Mahazik Berakhah
contradictions between *Bet Yosef* and *Shulhan Arukh*, *1373n.18*
as literary source, *1439*
Mahazit ha-Shekel, *1432*
mah mazinu canon, *355n.232*
mah lo leshakker, *995n.27*
Mahzor Vitry, *1179*, *1537*
Maimonides
adjoining landowner's preemptive right (*din bar mezra*), *626*
admonition of witnesses by, *1698*
agunot legislation and, *529–530*
on Alfasi's *Sefer ha-Halakhot*, *1171–1172*
Asheri's reaction to, *1226–1229*
assessment of *Mishneh Torah's* impact, *1235*
authentication of witnesses' testimony, *613–614*
on Babylonian Talmud, *1092*, *1099–1100*
on "bad custom" (*minhag garu'a*), *941n.197*
"be killed rather than transgress," *990n.10*
on Biblical law, *209–210*
Caro compared with, *1323n.39*, *1327–1340*
casuistic style of Mishnah and, *1077–1078*
categorical statements of legal rules, *1203–1206*
circumvention of *kum va-Aseh* and, *532n.156*
Code of (*Mishneh Torah*), *54*, *76*
codification methodology of, *1184–1215*, *1215–1231*, *1278*, *1341*
codificatory literature of, *1139–1140*
commentaries on Joshua, *55n.20*
commentaries on *Mishneh Torah* of, *1231–1235*
commentary on Mishnah (*Sefer ha-Ma'or*), *1106–1107*
compilation and reworking of halakhic material, *1186–1195*
on consecration of property, *392–394*
continuous correction and perfection of work by, *1215n.101*
criminal communal enactments, *693–694*
custom as legal source of law, *882n.6*, *917n.77*
on death penalty, *972*
on decline of legal creativity, *50*
disagreements with Alfasi, *1284*
on divorce law, *1755n.9*
Egyptian enactments of, *809–810*
exegetical interpretation of Deuteronomy, *279–280*
on exemption of women from studying Torah, *1798–1799*
factual-casuistic formulations of, *1211–1215*
on finality of post-Talmudic rulings, *1228n.138*
geonic legislative sources, *648n.17*, *1471n.55*
on *halakhah le-Moshe mi-Sinai* concept, *205–206*
on halakhic authorities, *243*
Hanukkah laws, compilation of, *1191–1193*
Heller's commentary on, *1405–1407*
"he who punishes," *150*
on *hora'at sha'ah* (temporary measures), *519–520*
"I have nothing" oath to enforce civil judgments, *652–653*
imprisonment for debt legislation, *1635–1636*
on inheritance and law of succession, *1677n.241*
interim summaries of, *1229–1231*
issur vs. communal enactments, *713n.138*
Jacob b. Asher compared with, *1292–1302*, *1327–1340*
on Jerusalem Talmud, *1132*
Jonathan of Lunel's correspondence with, *1175*
Joseph ibn Aknin's correspondence with, *1222–1223*
Joshua's enactments concerning property law, *551–552*
"judge your neighbor fairly," *168–169*
on justice and equity, *252n.56*
labor legislation, *620–621*
latent damage legislation, *603–604*
on *lazeit yedei shamayim*, *148–149*

Maimonides *continued*
legal capacity legislation and, *587*
on legal norms as binding source, *233–234, 238*
on legal order in Noahide laws, *194n.17*
legislative authority, *483–485, 518*
on literary style of Mishnah, *1078*
on *ma'aseh*, *946*
market overt legislation, *600–601*
mathematical astronomy and, *1189–1191*
"meeting of three" (*ma'amad sheloshtan*) legislation, *584*
on *mi-divrei soferim* terminology, *208n.88*
Mishneh Torah of. *See* Mishneh Torah
mi-shum eivah (prevention of strife and enmity) legislation, *629–631*
Moses of Coucy influenced by, *1261–1262*
on national and religious minorities, *1854–1856*
on Onkelos' translations, *1046n.28*
on ordained judges, *20n.64*
overruling of court legislation, *543–544*
Phinehas of Alexandria's correspondence with, *1145–1146, 1194, 1197, 1216–1221, 1286–1287, 1312–1313*
possession (*hazakah*) laws codification, *1331–1335*
power of attorney legislation, *651*
practical application of law and, *181n.355*
preeminence of, among Yemeni Jews, *1373*
on prohibition of work on Sabbath, *202n.63*
proof of custom, *927–929*
property laws' codification, *1330–1331*
property lien legislation and, *592*
on quality of Jewish law, *1145–1146*
Rabad's critical glosses of, *1223–1225*
responsa literature of, *1215n.101, 1477n.80, 1478, 1508n.159, 1519n.207*
on Ri Migash, *1123*
on role of prophets, *264–265*
role of public in legislation, *540–541*
rulings used in *Sefer ha-Hinnukh*, *1265*
Saadiah Gaon's influence on, *1160*
on sacrifice of life to save another, *971*
sedeh bet ha-shelahin codification, *1333–1334*
on sequential order of tractates, *1054n.68*
style and draftsmanship of *Mishneh Torah*, *1206–1210*
on *takkanah* and *gezerah*, *490–491*
Talmudic sources cited by, *1336–1340*
topical arrangement and classification methods, *1195–1203*
Tosafists' disagreement with, *1279–1280*
use of aggadic material, *95n.13*
on use of fictitious names and places, *1515n.189*
witnesses, inquiry and examination procedures, *608*
Yemenite Jews influenced by, *1432, 1499n.131*
on "you shall not add or take away," *499–502*
maintenance concept, Jewish law in modern Succession Law regarding, *1679–1680*
Mainz, Jewish community in
annulment of marriage, enactments regarding, *848–850*
enactments of, *792*
protection of minority rights, enactments for, *763–766*
majority rule (*aharei rabbim le-hattot*)
communal enactments and, *683n.16, 715–724, 762–763*
composition of, for communal enactments, *723–727*
conformity with enactments by, *762–763*
halakhic-aggadic reciprocity on, *96–99*
halakhic disqualification of signature and, *742–743*
issur-mamon distinction in *Halakhah* and, *131n.167*
legal presumption, basis for, *997–998*
legal reasoning (*sevarah*) and, *992n.18, 1005–1006*
in quality and number (*rov binyan ve-rov minyan*), *725–726*
Makhon Moshe, *1232n.145*
makkot mardut, written legislation and, *534–536*
Makkot Tractate, *1054*
Malachi (prophet), *309–310*
Malachi ha-Kohen, *Yad Malakhi* of, *1546–1548*
Malbim, Meir Leibush
commentaries of, *1111n.35*
legal research on, *308*
Malka, Moshe (Rabbi), on women's study of Torah, *1800–1801*
Malkhei Rabbanan, *1559*
malshinut. *See* informers.
malveh, law of obligations and, *588*

mamon (civil law and procedure). *See* civil law (noncriminal)
mamon gavo'ah, doreshin leshon hedyot, 423n.6
mamon hedyot, doreshin leshon hedyot principle, *423n.6*
mamzer (*mamzerim*)
agunot legislation and, *527–528*
"all who marry do so subject to conditions laid down by the Rabbis and the Rabbis annul this marriage" legislation, *631, 641n.65*
enactments concerning, *827n.178*
Gamaliel the elder's bill of divorcement, *563–565*
gezerah shavah canon and, *353–354*
Hillel's interpretation of *ketubbah* and, *424–426*
inheritance law and, *1674*
legal presumptions and, *997n.36*
moredet legislation, *661*
responsa literature on, *1486n.98*
Schools of Hillel and Shammai and, *1065–1066*
"Shum" enactments, *789*
man'al, and *halizah* rules, *907–908*
Manny, Justice
earnings of wife from her employment, decisions regarding, *1788, 1972n.119*
marriage between *kohen* and divorcee, decisions regarding, *1775–1776*
Manyumi, Joseph b. (R.), *20n.65*
Mappah
codification methodology and, *1359–1365*
Falk's commentaries on, *1409–1410*
legal research and, *44*
Mar'eh ha-Panim, 1135–1136
Margoliot, Moses, commentary and novellae of, *1135–1136*
Margolioth, Ephraim Zalman, responsa literature of, *1495*
Margolioth, Jacob, *1345*
Mar Joseph, *1208*
marital property, law of, judicial procedure, *1600n.61*
market overt legislation, and stolen property, *596–601*
Marranos, legal reasoning (*sevarah*) and, *1007n.65*
Marriage Age (Amendment) Law, *1654n.138*
Marriage Age Law, *1653–1656*
marriage laws
abstention from exercising legislative powers, *864–869*
"all who marry do so subject to conditions laid down by the Rabbis and the Rabbis annul this marriage" legislation, *631–642*
blanket incorporation of Jewish law in modern legislation, 1652
ceremonies, enactments regarding, *786*
circumvention of *kum va-Aseh* and, *521–530*
contemporary legislation concerning, *878–879*
Corfu enactments regarding, *817*
decline in employment of legislation as instrument of halakhic authority, *1807–1809*
differences in interpretation in, *293–297*
doreshin leshon hedyot, 430–432
dowry provisions, interpretation of, *445–447*
during Diaspora, *1605–1606*
effected by sexual intercourse, *535n.172*
enactments of 1950, *833–834*
Ezra's legislative enactments and, *556–558*
financial relations between husband and wife, custom as source of, *912–913*
fraudulent marriages, enactments regarding, *847–848*
freedom of contract and, *126n.140*
geonic legislation, *656–665*
halakhic interpretation of, *1782–1784*
Hillel's interpretation of *ketubbah* and, *424–426*
indirect halakhic interpretation, *404–405*
influence of *din Torah* on, *111n.84*
influence of Oral Law and, *200–202*
issur vs. communal enactments and, *711–712*
kohen's marriage to a divorcee, *1602–1603, 1655n.139, 1754n.8, 1770–1784*
law of place of marriage, *1483n.93*
legislative power of halakhic authorities over, *483–485*
ma'aseh combining halakhic authority and judicial decision, *974–975*
Maimonides' Egyptian enactments on, *810*
marital property and, *1660n.61*
mi-divrei soferim terminology and, *208n.88*

marriage laws *continued*
Mishnaic arrangement of, *1055–1056*
in *Mishneh Torah*, *1290n.206*
Moroccan enactments concerning, *808*
prohibition of marriage with national groups, *361–364*
prosbul enactment and, *513–514*
Rabbenu Gershom's enactments concerning, *785*
reliance on Jewish law in, *1770–1784, 1934*
"religious" vs. "legal" components of, *1773–1774*
Sefer ha-Turim codification of, *1290–1291*
subsequent expression as explanation in, *334*
termination of enactments about, *834–835*
Valladolid enactments regarding coerced marriage, *801–802*
validity of, in non-Jewish systems, *5n.7, 846–879*
Women's Equal Rights Law and, *1656–1660*
See also ketubbah; levirate marriage
See also betrothal; divorce law; family law;
huppah (nuptial ceremony); *ketubbah*; levirate marriage
Marx, A., *Kelalei ha-Talmud* and, *1547*
Mashber ha-Mishpahah va-Hasidei ha-Masoret, *1670n.207*
mashkon, law of obligations, *590n.198*
Mashraki, David, *1432*
Masoret ha-Shas, *1176n.99*
Massa Hayyim, *1447*
Massa Melekh,
on custom as source of tax law, *923n.108*
as literary source, *1445–1446*
"Masters of *Takkanot*, Moravian enactments, *820*
mathematical literature
Maimonides' interest in, *1189–1191*
responsa as source for, *1464n.34*
matrilineal descent, as determination of Jewishness, *1689n.289*
Mattathias Gaon, *655*
Mattathias, the Hasmonean, on laws regarding fighting on the sabbath, *1035–1036*
Mattathias, Jonathan b., *133n.172*
Matteh Shim'on, *1439–1440*
mattenat bari (gift of a healthy person), *1682, 1877*
mattenat shekhiv me-ra, *1682*
Mavo la-Mishnah, *1550*
Mavo la-Raviah, *1239n.4*
Mavo la-Talmudim, *1550*
Mavo le-Nusah ha-Mishnah, *1550*
Mawza, Jewish expulsion from, *1500n.131*
Mayer, Samuel, *81*
Mazli'ah, Asheri's dispute with, *1226–1227*
Me'ah She'arim, *1269n.142*. *See also Sha'arei Simhah*
me-ahar. *See* "mouth that has prohibited is the mouth that has permitted"
medicine, laws regarding, in *Torat ha-Adam*, *1243*
Medini, Hayyim Hezekiah, *1552–1553*
"meeting of three" (*ma'amad sheloshtan*)
halakhic sources on, *220n.139*
legislative enactments, *584, 649n.20*
Megillah, customs regarding reading of, *733*
Megillat Ta'anit (The Scroll of Fasts), *1040n.5*
Meginei Shelomo, *1129n.104*
Mehkarim ba-Varaita ve-Tosefta ve-Yahasan la-Talmud, *1550*
me'ilah, law of, indirect halakhic interpretation of, *406–407*
Me'ir Einayim, *1563*
Me'ir Einei Hakhamim, *1129n.104, 1384*
Meir ha-Kohen of Rothenburg, *Haggahot Maimuniyyot* (Maimonidean Glosses) of, *1234–1235*
Meir, Jacob (Rabbi). *See* Tam, Rabbenu
Meir ha-Levi Abulafia. *See* Ramah
Me'ir Nativ, *1128n.100*
Meir, R.
"all who marry do so subject to conditions laid down by the Rabbis and the Rabbis annul this marriage" legislation, *639n.63*
amoraic view of Mishnah and, *1061*
development and redaction of Mishnah and, *1051–1052*
as fourth generation tannaim, *1044*
law of Mishnah compared with cognate sources, *1059*
mishnayot compilations, *1051–1052*
Meiri, Menahem, *41, 53*
on codificatory literature, *1153, 1258n.98*
commentaries of, *1126*

on halakhic monographs, *1166*
introduction to *Bet ha-Behirah*, *1543*
on Judah al-Bargeloni's work, *1177*
legal research and, *41*, *53*
Mejelle
British Mandatory legal system and, *1612*, *1921*
repeal of Article 46 and, *1829*
suretyship law and, *1721–1722*
Mekhilta
commentaries on, *1110–1111*
explicative exegesis terminology explained in, *320–321*
logical interpretation of Torah and, *341–342*
Onkelos' translations as source for, *1046*
Mekhilta de-R. Ishmael
English translation of, *1111n.36*
as literary source, *1048*
Mekhilta de-R. Simeon b. Yohai, *1048*
mekorot rishumiyyim. *See* literary sources of Jewish law
Melekhet Shelomo (Work of Solomon), *1109*
melog property
amendment of Woman's Equal Rights Law and, *1806–1807*
legislative enactments concerning, *486n.44*, *568–569*
usufruct legislation, *572*
wife's income from employment and property and, *1803–1805*
Meltzer, Isser Zalman, R., *1442*
Menahem, as part of *Zugot*, *1043*
Menahem b. Aaron ibn Zerah, *1307–1308*
Menahem of Merseburg, *1444*
Menasseh, Raphael Jacob, *1495*
menstruant women, custom as source of ritual law, *891n.48*
See also mikveh (ritual bath)
mental competency, legislative enactments concerning, *585–587*
Me'orei Galiziah, Enziklopedyah le-Hakhmei Galiziah, *1559*
Meshovev Netivot, *1429*
Meshullam, Asher b., *kum va-Aseh*, circumvention of, *531–533*
Meshullam b. Moses of Beziers, *1243–1244*
Messianic Jews, Succession Laws regarding, *1690n.289*
metakkenei takkanot ve-gozrei gezerot, *546–547*
met mizvah, Joshua's property enactments and, *553*
metaprinciples, and Jewish heritage (*moreshet Yisra'el*), *1840*
meturgeman, defined, *1084*
Mevo ha-Mishnah, *1549*
Mevo ha-Talmud (Chajes), *1549*
Mevo ha-Talmud (Samuel ha-Nagid), *1543*
Mevo ha-Yerushalmi, *1549*
Mevo'ot le-Sifrut ha-Amoraim, *1550*
Mevo'ot le-Sifrut ha-Tannaim, *1550*
mezuzah, laws regarding
literary sources for, *1036*
Onkelos' translations as source for, *1046*
mezavveh mehamat mitah, modern Succession Law and, *1682*
Michaelis, Johann David, *81*
Middle Ages, responsa literature during, *1477–1480*
mi-divrei soferim (scribal law)
authentication of witnesses' testimony, *613–614*
classification of, *478*
latent damage legislation, *603–604*
terminology of, *207–208n.88*
"you shall not add or take away," *501–502*
midrash (midrashim)
Babylonian Talmud and, *1088–1091*
commentaries and novellae on, *1110–1111*
creative function of, *286–290*
dates for compilation of, *42*
development of, *308–317*
early anonymous works, *1150n.1*
establishment of Chief Rabbinate, *1598*
halakhic interpretation, *401*
legislation and, *477–478*
literary interpretation of Torah and, *307–308*
multiplicity of views in, *1849–1850*
as source for *Halakhah*, *40*, *1040*
Talmud as, *1084n.5*
tannaitic compilations, *1047–1049*
terminology of, *275–277*
See also interpretation
midrash ketubbah terminology, in sharecropping lease laws, *428n.26*
Midrash Tannaim, on halakhic authorities, *244n.17*
Migash, Joseph ibn. *See* Ri Migash
Migdal David, commentaries, *1402n.114*, *1418n.161*
Migdal Oz, *1232*

migo, *995n.27*
Mi Hu Yehudi be-Dinei Medinat Yisra'el, *1688n.288*
Mikhlol ha-Ma'amarim ve-ha-Pitgamim, *1569*
mikveh (ritual bath)
  Maimonides' Egyptian enactments on, *810*
  Rashba's codificatory literature on, *1276n.160*
  required by conversion to Judaism, *955–956*
Milhamot ha-Shem (The Wars of the Lord), *1174*
Military Court of Appeals v. Vaknin, *1856–1860*
military legislation, *554*
Miller v. Minister of the Interior, Succession Laws and, *1690n.289*
Milli, Eliezer, *Tikkun Shetarot* of, *1538*
Millon Shimushi la-Talmud, la-Midrash ve-la-Targum, *1566*
milvah (loan), *1874*
minhag. *See* custom (*minhag*)
minhag le-dorot, definition, *886*
minhag mevattel halakhah. *See* custom overrides the law
minhah (afternoon prayer), custom as law regarding, *898–899*
Minhat Hinnukh
  commentary on bailees' law and, *1695n.300*
  glosses on *Sefer ha-Hinnukh*, *1267n.134*
minimum age laws
  Capacity and Guardianship Law, *1662–1671*
  Marriage Age Law and, *1654–1656*
Minister of Interior (Israel), "distinguished person's" approval, *752n.272*
minority, rights of, protection of, in communal enactments, *763–771*
"minor tractates," *1150n.1*
minors
  communal enactments, binding force of, *731–735*
  legal capacity of, halakhic interpretation, *409–411*
  legal reasoning (*sevarah*) and, *1006n.65*
  Moroccan enactments concerning, *808*
miri property
  inheritance laws and, *828–829*
  rabbinical courts' jurisdiction and, *1760–1765*
Mintz, Moses, *793–794*
minyan, custom based on error regarding, *939*
Minz, Judah, halakhic interpretations of, *418–420*
mi-penei darkhei shalom, *586n.180*
mi-sevarat ha-keres, *1390*
mi she-para. *See* "he who punishes imperative"
Mishmeret ha-Bayit (Defense of the House), *1276–1277*
Mishnah
  Adeni's *Melekhet Shelomo*, *1109*
  admonition of witnesses in, *1698*
  agunot legislation and, *514–515*
  Albeck's commentary on, *1110*
  amoraic view of, *1061*
  arrangement of laws in, *1055–1056*
  Babylonian Talmud omission of, *1094–1095*
  casuistic style of, *1073–1074*
  children's rights in, *1662*
  class-related issues in giving, *98*
  codificatory methodology of, *1057–1078*, *1286–1287*, *1382n.43*
  cognate sources compared with, *1058–1059*
  commentaries and novellae on, *1106–1110*
  content of, *1057–1072*
  custom as source of law, *886–887*, *898*
  "custom overrides the law," *905–906*
  dates for compilation of, *42*
  development and reduction to writing of, *1050–1052*
  diversity and uniformity of Jewish law in, *1061–1070*
  earnings of wife from her employment, decisions regarding, *1786*
  etymology of, *1052–1053*
  geonic commentaries and novellae on, *1106*
  hefker bet din hefker, *507*
  halakhic literary form in, *1049–1050*
  halizah rules, *907–908*
  Heller's *Tosafot Yom Tov*, *1108–1109*
  Hillel's legislative enactments, *562*
  historical context of, *1343*
  hybrid casuistic-normative style, *1074–1076*
  issur-mamon distinction and, *124–125*, *140–141*
  lay tribunals and, *21n.67*

on legal capacity (mental competency), ***585–587***
legal style of, ***1072–1078***
Lipschutz's *Tiferet Yisra'el,* ***1109–1110***
as literary source, ***1040***
literary structure of, ***52, 1040, 1052–1056, 1078***
Maimonides commentary on, ***1106–1107***
multiple opinions in, ***1070–1072***
normative style, ***1076–1078***
Obadiah of Bertinoro's commentary, ***1108***
"Orders" (*sedarim*) of, ***1053–1055***
on paschal sacrifice, ***901***
prosbul enactment and, ***512***
right to privacy and, ***1859–1860***
"sages are displeased with him" sanction in, ***150***
Sefer ha-Turim compared with, ***1286–1287***
sharecropping, custom and usage regarding, ***930–931***
as source for *Halakhah,* ***40***
stolen property, market overt legislation, ***597–601***
witnesses, inquiry and examination procedures, ***606***
Talmud as replacement for, ***1099–1100***
tannaitic compilations of, ***408n.23***
terminology of, ***288n.17***
topical arrangement and classification in, ***1195–1196***
tort law in, ***411–414***
Tosefta as supplement to, ***1078–1081***
translations of, ***1110n.29***
Mishnah Berurah
as literary source, ***1448***
statutory incorporation and, ***1902***
mishnah rishonah, development and redaction of, ***1050–1052***
"Mishnaic Oath," in labor law, ***616***
Mishnaic Order of Tohorot, ***369–370***
mishnayot
development and redaction of, ***1050–1052***
legal rules in, ***1074n.151***
Mishnah development and redaction, ***1050–1052***
tanna and, ***1042***
Mishneh le-Melekh
glosses on *Sefer ha-Hinnukh,* ***1267n.134***
as literary source, ***1234, 1234n.157***
will of *shekhiv me-ra* and, ***102n.38***
Mishneh Torah,
Alfasi's influence on, ***1172***
bibliography of commentaries on, ***1232n.145***
Caro's commentaries on, ***1314n.14***
codification methodology, ***1145–1148, 1181–1184, 1286–1287, 1340–1341***
commentaries on, ***1231–1237.*** *See also* **specific commentaries**
factual-casuistic formulation in, ***1211–1214***
glosses to, ***1366***
goals of, ***1184–1186***
Hanukkah laws compilation in, ***1192n.34***
Heller's commentary on, ***1405–1406***
inconsistencies in *Sefer ha-Ma'or* and, ***1107n.11***
inheritance laws in, ***1200–1201***
interest and usury laws in, ***1290n.206***
juxtaposition of laws in, ***1202–1203***
lack of reference to sources in, ***1204–1206***
language and style compared with *Turim* and *Shulhan Arukh,* ***1327–1340***
as legal code for the people, ***1214–1215***
legal research on, ***76, 82***
lending laws in, ***1187–1189***
as literary source, ***1072***
mishpat ivri laws in, ***1290n.206, 1293–1302***
Moses ha-Kohen's critical glosses on, ***1225n.130***
omission of names of Sages in, ***1218–1219***
on finality of post-Talmudic rulings, ***1228n.138***
opposition to methodology of, ***1237–1238***
as *pesakim,* ***1139–1140***
Piskei ha-Rosh compared with, ***1253***
possession (*hazakah*) codification, ***1331–1335***
property laws codification, ***1330–1331***
prosbul laws in, ***1290n.206***
Rabad's criticism of, ***1223–1225, 1320***
Saadiah Gaon's influence on, ***1160***
sections of, ***1197–1203***
Sefer ha-Mordekhai modeled on, ***1250n.63***
Sefer ha-Turim compared with, ***1300–1302***
Sefer Meisharim compared with, ***1272n.151***
Semag organization modeled after, ***1262***
Shulhan Arukh codification as departure from, ***1323–1340***
starting dates for composition of, ***1188n.22***
style and draftsmanship of, ***1206–1210***

Mishneh Torah continued
succession law in, *1673n.218*
tax law compilations, *1444*
To'en ve-Nit'an (laws of plaintiff and defendant) in, *1293n.217*
topical arrangement and classification, *1195–1203*
Tur Hoshen Mishpat codification influenced by, *1292–1302*
ultimate achievement of, *1235*
Yemeni acceptance of, *1374n.20*
"you shall not add or take away," *499–502*
See also specific Books, e.g. *Sefer Nashim*, and sections, e.g. *Hilkhot Ishut*
mishpat, definitions and terminology of, *105–107*
mishpat ha-edah (communal court), *21n.69*
Mishpat ha-Herem, communal enactments and, *733*
Mishpat ha-Kohanim. See Netivot ha-Mishpat
Mishpat Ha-Shalom Ha-Ivri (The Jewish Court of Arbitration), *1592–1596*
attempts to revive lay courts, *1609–1611*
civil law and, *1600–1605*
severance pay legislation, *1632–1634*
Mishpat ha-Urim. See Netivot ha-Mishpat
mishpat ivri (Jewish law)
abrogation during Emancipation and, *1583–1584*
alphabetic arrangement, in encyclopedias, *1554–1556*
bibliographies of, *1562–1564*
Bingen enactments and, *794*
Candia enactments and, *811*
communal enactments, enforcement, *682*
custom (*minhag*) and, *897, 944*
decline of, during National Awakening, *1608–1611*
dominance of, in responsa, *1462–1463*
Foundations of Law Act and, *1828, 1832n.19, 1839–1840*
Frankfurt enactments, *794–796*
general courts influenced by, *1784–1802*
Great Assembly, enactments of, *555*
Hai Gaon's monographs on, *1165–1166*
halakhah le-Moshe mi-Sinai concept and, *207n.86*
Hillel's legislative enactments, *561–562*
history of legislative activity, *547–548*
incorporation of, in Israeli legislation, *1612–1617, 1690–1692, 1731–1751, 1756–1757, 1898–1946*
Jacob b. Asher's codification, *1280–1281*
journals and periodicals, *1570–1572*
judicial decisions and, *1729–1730*
Law and Administration Ordinance, Section 11, *1620*
legal enforcement of rabbinic law, *217–223*
legislation contrary to, *1721–1727, 1802–1807*
leniency regarding rabbinic law and, *212–214*
limits of applicability of, *1621–1623, 1769n.52, 1937–1938*
Lithuanian enactments, *819*
Mishneh Torah codification, *1199, 1290n.206, 1293–1302*
monographs on, *1158*
objective factors affecting recourse to, *1931–1938*
official position of, in State of Israel, *1620–1624*
Orah Mishpat compilation, *1442*
parallel function of, with other legal systems, *1942–1943*
personal status matters, *1758–1759, 1765–1784*
rabbinical court influenced by, *1758–1759, 1784–1802*
"religious" vs. "legal" components of, *1773–1774, 1778*
Samuel b. Hophni Gaon's works on, *1161–1164*
Sanhedrin's legislative enactments, *558*
scholarly research on, *1569–1570*
self-help guidelines in, *1714–1716*
Sefer ha-Turim codification and, *1300–1302*
Sephardic commentaries on, *1124–1125*
seventeenth and eighteenth century enactments on, *820*
Succession Law and, *1677–1683*
subjective factors affecting recourse to, *1924–1931*
terminology of, *105–111, 1874–1875*
terminology unique to, *1874–1875*
Tur Yoreh De'ah codification, *1289–1290*
Woman's Equal Rights Law and, *1806–1807*
mishum eivah (prevention of strife and enmity)
amoraic legislation for, *629–631*
Land Law and, *1715–1716*
legislation, *628n.31*

Mitoba v. Kazam, 1875
Mizrahi, Elijah
commentaries of, *700–702*
communal representatives, communal enactments by, *730n.205*
composition of majority, in communal enactments, *724*
mizvah (good deeds)
communal enactments and, *713–714*
custom as source of law regarding, *901n.14*
divorce law and, *1755n.9*
halakhic religious-legal interactions in, *121–122*
laws regarding adoption, *827*
in *Mishneh Torah, 1202–1203*
teaching Torah to women as, *1799*
Moabites, *gezerah shavah* canon regarding, *354–355*
modes of acquisition. *See* acquisition (*kinyan*)
Mo'ed Order
legal research and, *53*
in Mishnah, *1053*
Sefer Avi ha-Ezri and *Sefer Avi'asaf* and, *1238–1239*
Molina, Jewish community in
communal enactments in, *796–797*
equal inheritance rights for sons and daughters, *843–844*
husband's inheritance rights, restriction of, *838–840*
monetary law (*dinei mamonot*), *108–109*
fines as enforcement of judicial decisions, *10*
halakhah le-Moshe mi-Sinai concept and, *207n.86*
rabbinical courts' jurisdiction over, *1761–1762*
religious-legal aspects of, *118n.115*
scriptural analogy canon (*hekkesh ha-Katuv*), *346*
moneylending, during Babylonian diaspora, *644*
monopolies, formation of, Moroccan enactments concerning, *808–809*
moral-legal sanctions in Jewish law, *141–189*
lifenim mi-shurat ha-din, 155–167
moral-religious sanctions
"fulfillment of duty in the sight of heaven" (*lazeit yedei shamayim*), *148–149*
"he who punished" (*mi she-para*), *148, 150–151*
"lacking in trustworthiness" (*mehusar amanah*), *151*
"sages are displeased with him," *149–154*
morashah, 1839
Moravia, enactments of, *756n.291, 819–820*
on gambling, *822*
Mordecai ha-Levi, *1489*
Mordecai b. Hillel ha-Kohen,
codificatory literature and, *1249–1250*
statutory incorporation and, *1593n.33*
Mordekhai. See Sefer ha-Mordekhai
moredet legislation
explicit enactments concerning annulment of marriage, *851*
geonic enactments concerning, *658–665*
mamzerim and, *661*
Moroccan enactments concerning, *808*
"Shum" enactments, *789n.37*
Moreh Nevukhei ha-Zeman, 1549
morenu (teacher), *1401n.110*
mores civitatis, custom and, *897*
Moroccan Council of Rabbis, *153n.250*
Morocco, Jewish community in, enactments of, *807–808*
Moses, prerogatives of halakhic authorities and, *242*
Moses of Coucy
codificatory methodology of, *1279*
as literary source, *1256, 1261–1263*
Moses b. Jacob (Gaon), equalization of property for debt satisfaction, *647–648*
Moses ha-Kohen of Lunel (Remakh), *1225n.130*
Moses ibn Habib, responsa literature of, *1489*
Moslem countries, Jewish communal enactments in, *675*
Moslem law
compared with Jewish law, *5*
religious/legal dichotomy in, *93n.2*
"mouth that has prohibited is the mouth that has permitted," commentaries on, *993–995*
"moving a landmark" (*hassagat gevul*), *394–397*
mukademin, criminal communal enactments and, *695*
Multi-Language Bibliography of Jewish Law, The, 1564

multiplicity of opinions
codification as limitation on, *1064–1072, 1378–1379*
freedom of thought and speech and, *1848–1850*
in Mishnah, *1071–1072, 1378–1379*
sectarian disputes regarding, *1064–1070*
See also pluralism
murder, laws regarding
"be killed rather than transgress," *990–991*
criminal communal enactments and, *692–696*
early legal practices regarding, *199–200*
general principle canon and, *357–358*
inheritance by convicted murderers prohibited under, *1677–1678*
judges interpretation of law and, *289*
penalty for, in Book of Jubilees, *1033–1034*
"a person shall be put to death only for his own crime," *1025–1026*
scriptural analogy canon (*hekkesh ha-Katuv*), *345n.195*
musaf (additional prayer), custom as law regarding, *898–899*
"my father is acceptable to me," and waiver regarding witnesses' signatures, *742–743*
mysticism, *divrei kabbalah* and, *203n.65*

N
na'al (shoe), *halizah* rules, *907–908*
na'aseh ma'aseh, caution of halakhic authorities and, *949–950*
Naboth the Jezreelite, *1025*
Naftali Zevi Judah Berlin (Neziv), *1111n.35*
Nagar v. Nagar
interaction of statutory law and Jewish law in, *1761–1765, 1795–1802*
legislation contrary to Jewish law and, *1721n.380*
rabbinical courts and general legal system of state, *1824–1826*
Nagar v. State of Israel, *692*
Nahalat Shiv'ah, *1539*
Nahman, R.
adjoining landowner's preemptive right (*din bar mezra*), *626n.19*
law of interest, *966*
moredet legislation, *661*
Nahmani, Judah b., *224–225*
Nahmani, Samuel b. (R.), on burden of proof, *992–993*
Nahmanides (Ramban)
adjoining landowner's preemptive right (*din bar mezra*), *625n.16*
on Biblical law, *209–210*
binding force of communal enactments and, *733*
codificatory works of, *1242–1243*
commentaries of, *1124*
communal representatives, communal enactments by, *729–730*
"distinguished person's" approval, *753n.278*
efficacy of custom as source of law and, *884n.12*
exegetical interpretation of Deuteronomy, *279–280*
good faith (*tom lev*), *185*
on halakhic authorities, *244–245*
on Jerusalem Talmud, *1132*
on liability of physicians, *147n.220*
legislative authority of king, *487*
legislative power of halakhic authorities, *483–485*
migration to Holy Land, *811n.120*
moredet legislation, *662, 665*
novellae of, *1315n.19*
post-Talmudic halakhic interpretations and, *415n.41*
responsa literature of, *1279, 1478*
rulings used in *Sefer ha-Hinnukh*, *1265*
on Sardi's *Sefer ha-Terumot*, *1246n.44*
Sefer ha-Halakhot, *1174–1175*
on terminology of *mishpat*, *107n.70*
on use of non-Jewish courts, *16*
"you shall not add or take away," *497n.4*
Nahum of Gimzo
codificatory literature, *1044*
exegetical interpretation of Torah by, *316*
halakhic interpretation and, *371*
metaphorical and symbolic interpretations by, *375–376*
Nahum the Mede, *1087*
Nahum, Y. S., *1232n.145*
Naiman v. Chairman, Central Elections Committee
freedom of thought and speech, *1846–1850*
human dignity and equality and, *1850–1854*
Jewish heritage (*moreshet Yisra'el*), *1840, 1861–1863*

national and religious minorities, *1854–1856*
"Nakash case." *See Aloni v. Minister of Justice*
Names Law, modern Succession Law and, *1685*
Napoleonic Code
abrogation of Jewish law and, *1582nn.14–15*
codificatory literature, *1141–1142*
Narbonne, Jewish community in, husband's inheritance rights, restriction, *836–837*
Nashim, Order of
legal research, *53*
in Mishnah, *1053*
in *Sefer Avi ha-Ezri* and *Sefer Avi'asaf* and, *1239*
nasi
defined, *41*
lay tribunals and, *22*
territorial scope of legislation and, *671*
theory vs. practice in legislation in, *862*
Nathan Av ha-Yeshivah, Rabbenu, *1087, 1106n.5*
Nathan b. Jehiel, and Jerusalem Talmud, *1132n.114*
Nathan ha-Bavli, *1469–1470*
Nathanson, Joseph Saul, *1376n.26*
responsa literature of, *1495*
National Awakening
era of, *1588–1611*
Ha-Mishpat ha-Ivri Society and, *1588–1591*
Hebrew language during, *1607–1611*
Mishpat Ha-Shalom Ha-Ivri (Jewish Court of Arbitration), *1592–1596*
Rabbinical Courts in the Land of Israel, *1596–1605*
religious leadership on Jewish law during, *1605–1606*
responsa literature from, *1496*
National Jewish Law Review, *1571*
national legal system, Jewish law as, *4–5*
national and religious minorities, Jewish heritage regarding, *1854–1856*
national security, *lifenim mi-shurat ha-din* and, *158n.272*
nationalism, in Jewish law, *1578–1579*
Natronoi Kahana, *1150*
"natural ethics," integration of Jewish heritage with, *1853–1854*
"natural justice," violation of, *1759, 1794n.126*
Navon, Ephraim, responsa literature of, *1490*
Navon, Joseph, on weight and significance of responsa, *1458n.15*
Nazirite prohibitions, in *Mishneh Torah*, *1213n.98*
Nedarim Tractate, Ritba's commentary on, *1126*
negligence (*peshi'ah*)
bailee's liability for, *1695–1696*
lacunae and, *1837–1838*
laws concerning, *681–682*
lifenim mi-shurat ha-din, *156n.259, 161–162*
See also liability law
Nehemiah
condemnation of slavery for debt, *310–311, 589*
as member of Great Assembly, *554*
Nehemiah, R.
custom as source of *issur* law, *900n.13*
development and redaction of Mishnah and, *1051*
as fourth tannaitic generation, *1044*
halakhic authorities power, *482–485*
interpretation of Torah, *310–311*
law of obligations and, *589–590*
Nehunya b. ha-Kanah, R
codificatory literature, *1044*
exegetical interpretation of Torah by, *316*
halakhic interpretation and, *371*
ne'ilah (closing prayer), custom as law regarding, *898–899*
Ne'ilat She'arim, *1446*
nekhasim benei horin, property lien legislation, *591–592*
nekhasim meshu'badim, property lien legislation, *591–592*
Neofiti I, *1045*
neshamah yeterah. *See* additional soul
neta reva'i rule, custom as source of law on, *902*
Netiv Hayyim, *1432*
Netivot ha-Mishpat, *1429*
Netivot Mishpat, *1272*
Netivot Yerushalayim, *1137*
Neubauer, J., on midrash, *286*
Nezikin, Order of, *53, 1053–1054*
Neziv, Naphtali Zevi Judah Berlin,
legal research, *171–174*
on legislation, *977*
nikhsei melog, *melog* property legislation, *572n.118*

nikhsei zon barzel, melog property legislation, *572n.118*
Nikolsburg, enactments of, *823*
Nimmukei Yosef (The Argumentations of Joseph)
legal reasoning (*sevarah*) and, *989n.5*
as source of Jewish law, *1176, 1315n.19*
Nimmukim, tax law compilations, *1444*
Nir, MK, *1671n.211*
Nissim b. Jacob (Nissim Gaon)
commentary of, *1115*
on Jerusalem Talmud, *1132*
yeshivot of, *1168*
Nissim, Moshe (Minister of Justice),
statutory incorporation, *1691n.290*
on expunction of criminal records and, *1708n.342*
Nittai ha-Arbeli, as part of *Zugot*, *1043*
Noahide laws
"law of the land is law," *67–68*
national and religious minorities and, *1855–1856*
as source of Oral Law, *194*
No'am Yerushalayim, *1137*
Nofet Zufim, *1254*
nohag. *See* "usage"
noncorporate surety, Guarantee Law provisions for, *1723–1724*
nondiscrimination, "law of the land is law" and, *72n.80*
non-Jewish courts (*arka'ct*)
halakhic-aggadic reciprocity on, *96n.14*
Jewish use of, *50–51*
lay tribunals as alternative to, *24–29*
prohibition against litigation in, *1914–1917*
various forms of Jewish adjudication and, *34–36*
non-Jewish law
aid to Jewish authorities from, *11*
economic-social relationship with Jewish community and, *36–37*
forms of incorporation into Jewish law, *64n.44*
reciprocity with Jewish law, *62–74*
responsa as source for, *1463*
non-Jewish Tribunals (*Arka'ot Shel Goyim*), *13–18*
non-Jews. *See goyim*
Nordic Draft Code, suretyship law and, *1721*
normative rules, custom as legal source of law, *882*
normative style
defined, *1072*
Maimonides' use of, *1211–1214*
of Mishnah legal rules, *1076–1078*
normative rules. *See* legal norms
North Africa, Jewish communities in
admonition of witnesses in, *1700*
compilation of legal instruments in, *1540*
juridical autonomy in, *1584–1586*
legal activity, *89n.49*
responsa literature from, *1478–1479, 1490–1492, 1495*
Torah centers in, *43*
nos'ei kelim ("armor bearers"), *1231n.144*
See also glosses
notarikon, *1566*
notebooks (*kunteresim*)
commentaries recorded in, *1117*
See also specific *Kunteres*
novellae
of *aharonim*, *1127–1129*
Ashkenazic novellae, *1118–1123*
on Babylonian Talmud, *1118–1129*
characteristics of, *1105*
codificatory literature and, *1138–1139*
on halakhic *midrashim*, *1110–1111*
as historical source, *43–44, 1462n.28*
Kezot ha-Hoshen as, *1428*
as literary source, *1102–1103*
on Jerusalem Talmud, *1130–1137*
on Mishnah, *1106–1110*
scientific legal research and, *89–90*
Sephardic commentaries and novellae, *1123–1127*
Numbers, Book of, right to privacy and, *1859–1860*
nuptial ceremony. *See huppah* (nuptial ceremony)
Nuremberg, Jewish community in
enactments regarding court proceedings, *793*
marriage enactments, *789n.37*

O

oaths
administration of, nonJewish institutions, *64n.44*
admonition instead of, *1697–1707*
affirmation in lieu of, *1700n.320, 1704–1707*
bailee's defense to liability, *615*
Biblical vs. rabbinic laws regarding, *218n.130*

codification of, in *Tur Yoreh De'ah*, *1289n.202*
"I have nothing" oath (*she-vu'at ein li*), *651–654*
individual rights, in communal enactments, *770n.343*
issur vs. communal enactments, *708n.114*
labor law, in tannaitic era, *614–621*
legal reasoning (*sevarah*) and, *1002n.51*
modern legislation on admonition of witnesses and, *1697–1707*
"oath of suspicion" (*shevu'at ha-hashad*), *652*
by order of court, *1706*
for partial claims, *615*
on testimony of single witness, *615*
witnesses, inquiry and examination procedures, *605–606*
Obadiah of Bertinoro, commentaries on Mishnah, *1108*
obedience to halakhic authorities, duty to, *1793–1794*
obiter dictum, distinguishing process and, *961n.63*
obligations, law of
asmakhta (supportive interpretation) and, *301n.51*
custom as source of, *913–920*
legislation concerning, during tannaitic era, *587–601*
personal and real character of, *587–591*
rabbinic law and, *222–223*
"obligatory precept," vs. "optional precept," 118n.115
occupational groups, legislative authority of, *488–490*
See also craftsmen, guilds of; tradesmens' associations.
olah, *a fortiori* inference canon regarding, *349*
Olshan, Court President
general courts' circumspection of Jewish law, *1767*
on Streit v. Chief Rabbi of Israel, *1759n.20*
wife's income from employment and property and, *1804n.167*
Omayyad caliphs, academic disputes of, *43*
onah, spousal support legislation, *571*
"one court may not overturn the ruling of another court," limitations of Rabbinical Court of Appeals and, *1814n.195*
o'nes, meaning of, in Jewish law, *80*
"one-tenth of the estate" enactment
family law and, *578–580*
inheritance law and, *578–580*
Onkelos' translation of Torah, *1045–1046*
Oppenheim, Seligmann, *793–794*
"optional precept," vs. "obligatory precept," *118n.115*
Orah Hayyim
commentaries on, *1431–1432*
contents and organization of, *12, 105*
David b. Samuel ha-Levi's commentaries on, *1425*
Pithei Teshuvah on, *1441*
responsa and, *1462, 1491–1492*
Sha-arei Teshuvah on, *1441*
Yad Aharon responsa on, *1438–1439*
Orah Mishpat, *1442*
oral contracts
custom as source of law on, *916–918*
encumbered property, lien legislation and, *593–596*
oral law (*Torah she-be-al peh*)
antiquity of, *192–203*
Biblical and Rabbinic law and, *197–200, 207–223*
codification of, *1148, 1157*
defined, *190–192*
divrei kabbalah ("matters of tradition"), *203–204*
during patriarchical period, *195–197*
expansion of, *307–308*
Halakhah-Aggadah reciprocity and, *95–96*
Halakhah as portion of, *93*
halakhic literature and, *1038–1039*
legal consequences of, *212–223*
lifenim mi-shurat ha-din, *158–159*
literary interpretation as bridge with Written Law, *307*
Mishnah and, *1049–1050*
Noahide laws, *194*
prohibition against reduction to writing, *224–226*
reduction of Talmudic literature to writing, *227*
Sinaitic revelation and, *204–207*
as supplement to Written Law, *200–203*
Talmud and, *39–40, 1038–1039*
woman's obligation to study, *1721n.380, 1799–1802*
written legislation and, *534–536*
"you shall not add or take away," *500*
"Oral Will," modern Succession Law and, *1682–1683*

orandi, defined, *28n.91*
Order of *Zera'im*, *52*
"Orders" of the Mishnah
  Babylonian Talmud compilation and, *1094–1095*
  commentaries on, *1106–1110*
  Jerusalem Talmud compilation and, *1098*
  mnemonic for, *1054n.65*
  Ritba's commentaries on, *1125n.90*
  structure and division of, *1053–1055*
  vowel points to text, *1110n.28*
"Orders" of the Talmud
  Alfasi's *Sefer ha-Halakhot* and, *1169–1170*
  Maimonides' compilation and reworking of, *1187–1195*, *1292–1293*
  Sefer ha-Turim codification influenced by, *1293n.217*
  See also specific orders
ordination of judges (*semikhah*), *20*
Organization of Torah-Observant Sephardim (Shas Movement) v. Kahana, *1689n.289*
Or ha-Hayyim, *1266n.131*, *1561*
orkhata, defined, *1471n.56*
orlah
  custom as source of law, *887–888*
  legal source for prohibition of, *889*
Or Same'ah, *1129n.104*
Or Zaru'a, *1241*
  commentary on *Piskei ha-Rosh*, *1254*
Osef Piskei ha-Din, *1754n.6*
oseh sehorah be-farato shel havero, *1696*
Oshry, Ephraim, responsa literature of, *1408*
ostracism (*niddui*)
  of debtors, *653*, *654n.50*
  "distinguished person" approval, *757n.293*
Ottolenghi, Joseph, *1250n.63*
Ottoman Empire, responsa literature from, *1490–1492*
Ottoman law
  bribery law influenced by, *1641*
  British Mandatory government and, *1611–1612*
  imprisonment for debt legislation, *1635*
  Land Law of 1858, *1709*, *1714–1716*
  Mishpat Ha-Shalom Ha-Ivri and, *1593*
  repeal of Article 46 and, *1829*
Ovadiah Hadaya, Tenants Protection Law, *1824*
Oven of Akhnai, halakhic authorities and, *261–263*
ownership, concept of. *See* Property law
ox-goring, laws regarding, *1009–1010*
Ozar Divrei Hakhamim u-Fitgameihem, *1569*
Ozar ha-Aggadah, *1569*
Ozar ha-Be'urim ve-ha-Perushim, *1562*
Ozar ha-Geonim
  codificatory literature, *1114*, *1472*
  compilations of responsa, *1525n.240*
Ozar ha-Mishpat, *1563–1564*
Ozar ha-Posekim, *1442*
Ozar ha-Sefarim, *1561*
Ozar ha-Shetarot, *1539–1540*
Ozar ha-Targum, *1568*
Ozar Imrei Avot, *1569*
Ozar Leshon ha-Mishnah, *1568*
Ozar Leshon ha-Talmud, *1568*
Ozar Leshon ha-Tannaim
  on *Mekhilta de-R. Ishmael*, *1568*
  on *Sifra-Torat Kohanim*, *1568*
  on *Sifrei*, *1568*
Ozar Leshon ha-Tosefta, *1568*
Ozar Leshon Talmud Yerushalmi, *1568*
Ozar Ma'amarei Halakhah, *1569*
Ozar Roshei Teivot be-Lashon u-ve-Sifrut mi-Mei Kedem ad Yameinu, *1567*

P

Pahad Yizhak, *1551–1552*
"pairs." *See Zugot*
Palache, Hayyim, *1447*
  sources of law and, *1447*
  statutory incorporation and, *1582n.22*
Palestine Order in Council of 1922
  Article 46, *1611–1612*, *1617–1618*, *1624–1625*, *1662*, *1669*, *1728–1729*, *1732*, *1828*
  Article 47, *1766n.46*, *1767n.52*
  Article 51, *827*
  Article 55, *1762n.32*
  Article 64, *1767n.52*
  lacunae in, *1835n.29*
  Saving Clause, *1828*
Paltoi b. Abbaye (Gaon)
  legal research, *15*
  literary sources of Jewish law, *1157–1158*
  on primacy of Talmudic sources, *1230*
  reaction to *Shulhan Arukh*, *1369*
Panim Hadashot
  codificatory literature of, *1304*, *1433–1434*, *1436*, *1438*
  responsa literature of, *1524*
Papa, R.
  on betrothal laws, *893n.53*
  market overt legislation, *598–599*

oral vs. documented debt, encumbered property and, *596*
witnesses, inquiry and examination procedures, *607–609*
Papi, R., on laws regarding *sitomta*, *914*
papyri, as literary source for Jewish law, *1028*
See also Elephantine papyri
Pardo, David b. Jacob
commentaries of, *1112*
responsa literature of, *1490*
parents
Capacity and Guardianship Law and, *1665–1671*
commandment to honor (*kibbud av va-em*), *1908–1914*
laws of respect due to, *1290n.206*
restrictive interpretations of Torah regarding, *365–366*
See also children, laws regarding; custody of children
Parker v. British Airways Board, *1745n.442*
Parnas, Moses, *1255*
parshanut, terminology of, *275–277*
partnership, laws regarding
codificatory literature and, *1326n.52*, *1364–1365*
communal enactments and, *683n.17*
halakhic decision making in, *1912n.38*
majority rule and communal enactments, *722n.176*
paschal sacrifice
custom as supplement to law regarding, *901–903*
logical interpretation of Torah and, *342–343*
Passover, laws regarding
local custom as law, *933–936*
responsa concerning, *1500n.131*
paternity suits, lay tribunals and, *30n.97*
"paths" to law, *1271–1272*
patriarchal era
hassagat gevul, *394–395*
legal practices during, *195–197*
Patriarchs (*nesi'im*)
as source of early legislation, *550*
legislative authority of, *486–490*
"peace and tranquility" enactments
Foundations of Law Act and, *1839–1840*
Land Law legislation and, *1715–1716*
pe'ah laws, *1053*
in *Arukh ha-Shulhan*, *1449*
Peel Commission, role of Jewish law in Jewish state, *1613*
penal code, codification methodology regarding, *1326–1327*
Penal Law Revision (Bribery) Law, *1640–1642*
abrogation of, in State of Israel, *1615n.102*
fundamental rights of detainees and prisoners, Jewish heritage and, *1841–1842*
subjective factors affecting, *1924*, *1927n.79*
value-laden legal terms, *1736–1737*
penalties (*kenas*), by lay tribunals, *21n.67*
pendente lite
judicial procedure, *1600n.61*
Land Law legislation and, *1714–1716*
rabbinical court decisions regarding, *1754n.7*
Penei Moshe, *1135–1136*, *1458n.18*
Penei Yehoshu'a, *1129*, *1403n.117*
on authority of *Shulhan Arukh*, *1417n.161*
penitence and rehabilitation (*takkanat ha-shavim*), *601–602*
Pentateuch
Aramaic translation of, *1045*
Rashi's commentary on, *1302n.275*
Perahiah b. Meshullam, *1464n.34*
perat u-khelal, explicative exegesis, *325*
Peratei Peratin, *1124*
Perez b. Elijah of Corbeil, Rabbenu
codificatory literature, *1255n.78*
enactments of, *789–791*
Peri Hadash, *1431*
Peri Megadim
literary sources of Jewish law and, *1413n.143*, *1429n.20*
on *Orah Hayyim* and *Yoreh De'ah*, *1432*
Peri To'ar, *1431*
personal freedom, freedom of contract and, *127nn.145–146*
personal property
hefker bet din hefker, *510–511*
ketubbah enactment of Simeon b. Shatah, *559–561*
legislative enactments concerning, *583–585*
See also lost or stolen property; property law
personal status, laws regarding
basic allocation of jurisdiction over, *1753–1756*
definition of a Jew in, *1688–1690*

personal status *continued*
incorporation of Jewish law in, *1765–1784*
Israeli legislation on, *1652–1690*
judicial procedure and, *1598–1600*
rabbinical courts and, *1753–1765*
Succession Law and, *1678–1683*
Women's Equal Rights Law and, *1656–1660*
Perushim ve-Hiddushim ba-Yerushalmi, *1137*
Pesahim Tractate,
as literary source, *1169–1170*
local custom as law, *935–936*
pesakim
as codificatory literature, *1139–1140*
commentary and novellae in, *1105n.2*
Maharal's rejection of, *1380*
Maimonides' compilation of, *1191*
Sefer ha-Turim as example of, *1285–1287*
Semak regarded as work of, *1265*
Shulhan Arukh as, *1319–1322*
on weight and significance of responsa, *1459n.19*
Pharisees, interpretation of Torah, *314–315*
Philo of Alexandria, as literary source of law, *1019, 1030–1031, 1037*
phylacteries, power of custom and, *909n.47*
physicians
legal-moral reciprocity and, *143n.206*
liability and legal vs. moral imperative, *146–147*
pikpeku (resist), role of public in legislation, *540n.190*
Phinehas b. Meshullam of Alexandria
Maimonides' correspondence with, *1145–1146, 1194, 1197, 1216–1221, 1286–1287, 1312–1313*
responsa literature and, *1477n.80*
Phoebus, Samuel
commentaries on *Even ha-Ezer*, *1430*
hypothetical responsa of, *1516–1517*
"piecemeal adoption procedures," *1710–1716*
Pig-Raising Prohibition Law, *1647*
pilpul, *1345*
limitations of, *1380*
novellae of *aharonim* and, *1127–1129*
resistance to, *1383*
responsa of aharonim and, *1485*
Pilpula Harifta, *1254*
Pinkas ha-Kehillot (Record Book of the Communities), *1532n.5*
Pinkas Va'ad Arba Arazot, *818*
pious behavior (*middat hasidut*), *1005n.62*
Pipano, David, responsa literature of, *1496*
pirkha (refutation)
a fortiori inference and, *351*
defined, *1084*
Piskei ha-Ri'az, *1258n.98*
Piskei ha-Rid, *1258n.98*
Piskei ha-Rosh
Alfasi's influence on, *1172*
codificatory methodology of, *1278–1280*
commentaries on, *1253–1255*
compilation and organization, *1251–1253*
Heller's commentary on, *1404–1407*
Mishneh Torah criticized in, *1228n.137*
on weight and significance of responsa, *1459n.19*
Piskei ha-Tosafot, *1122*
Piskei Hallah, *1276n.160*
Pithei Teshuvah, *1441*
pittu'ah ha-mishpat theory, *1884n.232*
plaintiff, power of attorney against defendant, *649–651*
pluralism of Jewish law
multiple opinions in Mishnah and, *1071–1072, 1378–1379*
sectarian disputes regarding, *1064–1070*
See also multiplicity of opinions
Plotzki, Meir Dan
legal research, *16n.45*
statutory incorporation, *1583n.18*
pogroms, impact of, on communal enactments, *792, 797–798*
See also Holocaust.
Pohovitzer, Judah Leib, *31–32*
Poitou, Rabbenu Tam's enactments regarding, *836n.205*
Poland, Jewish community in
codification methodology of, *1345–1348*
Council of the Four Lands enactments, *818*
Emancipation in, *1491–1494*
Jewish juridical autonomy in, *9–10*
legal creativity of, *51*
persecution of, *1345*
rejection of codification in, *1374–1375*
responsa literature in, *1487–1488, 1492*
political systems
"law of the land is law," *66*
loss of, survival of Jewish law and, *2–3*
Pollack, Jacob
codification methodology of, *1345–1348, 1355, 1362*
pilpul method and, *1380*

rejection of codification by, *1374*
responsa literature of, *1487–1488*
polygamy
inheritance rights of wife's sons (*ketubbat benin dikhrin*), and, *576n.138*
Moroccan enactments concerning, *808*
territorial scope of legislation and, *674–675*
Population Registry Law
converted Jews under, *1689–1690n.289*
marriage and divorce issues in, *1777n.76*
Porat, Ben (Deputy President), *1846n.75*
Porush, M., *1832n.19*
posekim, literary guidebooks and, *1548n.79*
possession, laws regarding (*hazakah*)
codificatory literature, *1331–1340*
Israeli statutory interpretation and, *1743–1751*
legal sources for rules regarding, *1007–1008, 1010n.76*
meaning of, in Jewish law, *79–80*
in Mishnah, *1074–1075*
in *Mishneh Torah*, *1200–1201*
real property possession, *1075*
uncertainty of statutory interpretation and, *1864–1871*
See also property law
post factum applications
privately performed marriages, Jewish law incorporated in state legislation, *1770n.55, 1778–1779, 1781–1782*
post-Talmudic period
exegetical interpretation during, *391–399*
Halakhah-Aggadah reciprocity in, *95–96*
halakhic interpretation, *414–421*
legal reasoning (*sevarah*) in, *1004–1006*
legal research during, *82–84*
legal rulings in, Maimonides' discussion of, *1228n.138*
literary legal sources of, *1101–1103*
ma'aseh in, *968–978*
practical application of law, *3–4*
creation of *Halakhah* and, *52–54*
creativity as reflection of, *51–54*
decline in, during Diaspora, *1605–1606*
developmental changes and, *46–50*
Ha-Mishpat Ha-Ivri (Jewish Law) Society and, *1589–1591*
interpretation of Torah and, *310*
law and equity and, *182n.360*
Mishpat Ha-Shalom Ha-Ivri and, *1593–1596*
scientific legal research and, *84–88*
"practice of the people," vs. custom, *891–892*
prayer (*amidah*)
custom as law regarding, *898–899*
"custom overrides the law," *903n.27*
Maimonides' Egyptian enactments on, *810*
See also specific prayers
precedent, in Jewish law, *978–985*
"case" and precedent in other legal systems, *978–980*
decision-making, *983–985*
judgment and, *981–982*
ma'aseh and precedent in common law, *980–981*
Prescription Law, limitation of actions legislation, *1727n.410*
press, freedom of, Defamation Law as limitation on, *1643–1644*
pretrial detention, freedom from detention issues, *1843–1845*
"prevent strife and enmity". *See mi-shum eivah*
priests
authority of, *242–243*
failure of, to interpret Torah, *309–312*
married daughters of, laws regarding, *379–380*
scriptual analogy canon (*hekkesh ha-Katuv*) regarding tasks, *346–347*
prima facie evidence, freedom from detention issues, *1843–1845*
primogeniture, in modern Succession Law, *1683–1688*
See also inheritance law
primus inter pares ("first among equals")
interpretation of Foundations of Law Act and, *1896–1897*
uncertainty of statutory interpretation and, *1865–1866*
Principles of Jewish Law, *1556*
printing, laws regarding
Ferrara enactments regarding, *816–817*
territorial scope of legislation and, *673n.30*
See also copyright; publishing.
prison law
incorporation of non-Jewish provisions for, *64n.44*
as part of legal system, *11*
See also imprisonment for debt; penal code

privacy, right of, Jewish heritage regarding, *1856–1860*
privately performed marriages
halakhic interpretation of, *1782–1784*
Jewish law incorporated in state legislation, *1770–1782*
Procaccia, Uriel, *1885–1894*
procedural enactments
limitations and accomplishments of Rabbinical Court of Appeals and, *1812–1814*
modern enactments, *829n.181*
vs. substantive law, *1008n.69*
tannaitic legislation, *605–614*
Women's Equal Rights Law and inheritance laws, *1657n.145*
procedure, legal, general courts' circumspection of Jewish law in, *1767–1770*
"Progressive List for Peace" case. *See Naiman v. Chairman, Central Elections Committee*
promissory notes
"I have nothing" oath and, *652*
legal capacity of children regarding, *1665*
rabbinic law and, *220n.141*
statutory incorporation and, *1874*
use of non-Jewish courts for, *17*
"property bearing no responsibility" (*nekhasim she-ein lahem aharayut*), *591*
"property bearing responsibility." *See* "responsibility of property."
property law
asmakhta (supportive interpretation) and, *302–305*
Basic Law: Israel Lands, *1651–1652*
building of partition, custom as law regarding, *941–943*
burden of proof, *131n.166*
casuistic style of Mishnah and, *1073–1074*
Cave of Machpelah example of, *195–196*
communal enactments and, *450–452, 686–688, 700n.88, 706n.110*
comparisons of codification methodology, *1330–1331*
contradictory passages in Torah regarding, *337–338*
court expropriation authority, *507–515*
courts equated with communal enactments, *700n.88, 706n.110*
custom as source of, *894n.61, 913–920*
daughters' share of father's property, *152n.250*
division of commonly owned property, *1075–1076*
divrei kabbalah and, *204*
earnings of wife from her employment, rabbinical court decisions regarding, *1789n.110*
equalization of property for debt satisfaction, *646–648*
halakhic decision making in, *1912n.38*
halakhic disqualification of signature, on communal enactments, *742–744*
history of legislative activity, *549–550*
hybrid casuistic-normative style, *1075*
inheritance laws regarding disposition of, *1673–1674*
integrative interpretations of, *297–300*
Joshua's enactments concerning, *551–553*
kelal u-ferat u-khelal canon and, *326–327*
king's law and, *56n.22*
Land Law legislation and, *1711–1716*
"law of the land is law," 66–67, *71–72*
legal reasoning (*sevarah*) and, *1008–1014*
legal sources for rules regarding, *1007–1008*
lifenim mi-shurat ha-din, 160n.281
limitation period on, in communal enactments, *744–745*
as literary source for law, *1023–1024*
"mouth that has prohibited is the mouth that has permitted," 993–995
in *Mishneh Torah, 1199–1201, 1213n.98*
normative style of Mishnah and, *1077–1078*
ownership claims, limitation period on, in communal enactments, *744–745*
partition of, reciprocity regarding, *1628n.15*
post-Talmudic exegetical interpretation, *392–394*
"property bearing responsibility" (*nekhasim she-yesh lahem aharayut*), *590–591*
prosbul enactment and, *511–513*
protection of minority rights, in communal enactments, 763–771
rabbinic law regarding, *219–223*
Rabbinical Court of Appeals rulings and, *154n.256*
religious-legal obligations and, *114*
responsa literature on, *1484n.93*
sale of, lien legislation and, *596n.223*
shi'bud nekhasim legislation, *587–601*
statutory interpretation and, *1743–1751*

tax laws regarding, *450–452, 745n.246, 766–768*
use of non-Jewish courts for, *17*
wife's income from employment and property and, *1802–1805*
See also acquisition; *melog* property; liens, on property for debt; lost or stolen property; military law for spoils of war; personal property; possession;

Prophets (*Nevi'im*)
Aramaic translation of, *1045*
authority of, *242–243, 260–261*
concessions to authority of, *264–265*
on *divrei kabbalah, 203–204*
inheritance rights of wife's sons (*ketubbat benin dikhrin*) and, *577n.141*
legislative authority of, *520n.117*
as literary source of law, *1021*
rebuke priests for failing to interpret Torah, *309–311*
as source of early legislation, *550*

prosbul enactments
"all who marry do so subject to conditions laid down by the Rabbis and the Rabbis annul this marriage" legislation, *642n.66*
arrangement of laws in Mishnah, *1056*
binding force of, on future generations, *734n.216*
hefker bet din hefker, 511–513
Hillel's legislative enactments, *561–562*
historical background for, *504, 548n.10*
in *Mishneh Torah, 1290n.206*
in *Sefer Avi ha-Ezri* and *Sefer Avi'asaf* and, *1238–1239*

proselytes, deceased, laws regarding assets of, *959–960*

prospective communal enactments, *772–777*

Protection of Privacy Law, Jewish heritage and, *1856–1860*

Proverbs, Book of
as literary source for Jewish law, *1027–1028*
table metaphor used in, *1311n.36*

Provisional Council of State, legal norms of legal system in, *231*

Prussian Code, *1141–1142*

public debate, Defamation Law as limitation on, *1643–1644*

"public interest," marriage and divorce issues in, *1778–1782*

public law
classification of, *77–78*
communal enactments as form of, *684*
incorporating of Jewish heritage in, *1646–1647*
Israeli lands, *1651–1652*
Jewish legal system and, *10*
juridical autonomy and, *48*
Law of Return, *1647–1651*
in *Mishneh Torah, 1201–1202*
modern Israeli legislation, *1639–1652*
See also civil law (noncriminal)

public leadership, as creative factor in Jewish law, *54–61*

public officeholders, freedom from detention issues, *1843–1845*

public premises, laws regarding possession on, *1742–1745*

public welfare (*mipenei tikkun ha-olam*), lien legislation and, *591–593*

publishing legislation, communal enactments and, *675n.36*

"pulling". *See kinyan meshikhah*

Pumbedita academy (Babylonia), *43*
influence of, *645*

Purim, binding force of custom during, *731–732*

Q

"Quasi-Will" provision of Succession Law, *1687–1688*

R

Rabad (Abraham b. David of Posquières)
agunot legislation and, *530*
on Alfasi's *Sefer ha-Halakhot, 1172–1174*
books of *halakhot* by, *1224n.127*
commentary on *Sifra, 1110–1111*
criticism of Maimonides, *1194–1195, 1205–1206, 1223–1225, 1232n.146, 1320*
legal research, *71, 72n.77*
novellae/commentaries of, *1123–1124*

Rabad II, codificatory works of, *1179n.113*

Raban (Eliezer b. Nathan of Mainz)
annulment of marriage, enactments regarding, *848–849*
civil communal enactments, *688n.35*
codificatory works of, *1179*
legal reasoning (*sevarah*) and, *1001–1002*
responsa literature and, *1486n.96, 1518–1519*

Rabbah
on court authority regarding legislation, *506*
hora'at sha'ah (temporary measures), *520n.117*
oral vs. documented debt, encumbered property and, *595*
Rabba, Hiyya (R.), *42*
Rabbanei Frankfurt, *1559*
Rabbenu Hillel of Greece and Rumania. *See* Hillel b. Eliakim
rabbinic era
codificatory tendencies during, *1181–1184*
legal research, *2*, *43–44*
See also specific subperiods
Rabbinic law (*de-rabbanan*)
authority over Biblical law, *214–217*
classification of, *208–212*
legal enforcement regarding, *217–223*
leniency regarding, *212–214*
Oral Law and, *207–223*
Rabbinic legislation (*mi-de-rabbanan*)
classification of, *478*
legal reasoning (*sevarah*) and, *988–989*
nullification of, *541–544*
Rabbinical Court of Appeals of Israel
accomplishments and limitations, *1809–1818*
on Capacity and Guardianship Law, *1667*
on civil procedure, *1601–1605*
education of children, parents' rights and responsibilities, *1795–1796*
employment of legislation as instrument of halakhic authority, *1808n.179*
establishment of, *824–826*
illegal contracts, *130n.160*
legislation, *707n.112*
lifenim mi-shurat ha-din, *158n.272*
moral-legal reciprocity in property law and, *154n.256*
personal status legislation, *1753–1756*
procedural enactments of, *826–829*
published decisions of, *1754n.6*
responsa compared with, *1467n.42*
rulings on evidentiary matters, *1754n.8*
Wiloszni case and, *1820–1824*
rabbinical courts
adjudication in personal status laws, *1753–1757*
application of law in personal status suits, *1758–1765*
chief rabbinate established, *1596–1598*
civil law in, *1600–1605*, *1818–1819*
earnings of wife from her employment, decisions regarding, 1785–1794
general state legal system, *1819–1826*
halakhic process in, *1899–1900*
influence on general courts of, *1784–1802*
judicial procedure and law of personal status, *1598–1600*
jurisdiction, religious-legal interactions in, *121–122*
legislation employed by, *1807–1818*
marriage and divorce law, *1616n.104*
marriage between *kohen* and divorcee, Jewish law incorporated in state legislation, *1770–1782*
relationship with general courts, *1793–1794*
statutes mandating application by, *1760–1765*
will of *shekhiv me-ra* and, *1880n.222*
Rabinowitz, A. Z., *1553*
racism, Jewish heritage regarding, *1854–1856*
Radbaz (David Ibn Zimra)
custom as source of oral contract agreements, *918–919*
on guardianship of children, *1666*
on inheritance and law of succession, *1677n.241*
legal enforcement of rabbinic law and, *218–220*
legislative authority not prescribed in Torah, *517–519*
responsa of, *1486*
scheming witness, *397–399*
territorial scope of communal enactments, *675n.34*
Yekar Tiferet of, *1233*
Radzinowich, L., *1926*
Rahumi, R., as one of *savoraim*, *1093*
Ralbah (Levi ibn Habib), *1486*
Ramah (Meir ha-Levi Abulafia)
commentaries of, *1124*
husband's inheritance rights, restriction of, *838–839*
justice in law and, *170–171*, *174*
property laws, protection of minority rights in, *768–769*
responsa of, *1279*
Yad Ramah of, *1537*
Ramban. *See* Nahmanides
Ran. *See* Gerondi, Nissim (Ran)
Rapaport, Mordecai, *82*

rape
laws regarding, logical interpretation of Torah and, *339–340*
location as basis in, *1030–1031*
Philo of Alexandria as source of, *1030–1031*
Raphael ha-Kohen, on abrogation of Jewish law, *1579–1582*
Rash (Samson b. Abraham) of Sens
on fraudulent conveyances law, *1891–1894*
on Jerusalem Talmud, *1132*
as leading Tosafist, *1121*
prohibition against litigation in non-Jewish courts, *1915n.46*
Rashba (Solomon b. Adret)
abstention from exercising legislative powers, *866–867*
"all who marry do so subject to conditions laid down by the Rabbis and the Rabbis annul this marriage" legislation, *638n.61*
annulment of marriage, enactments concerning, *850, 852–856*
classification of two types of lay tribunals, *30n.95*
codificatory methodology of, *1273–1277, 1341*
commentaries, *1124–1125*
communal representatives, enactments by, *727–728, 730n.205*
competence of judges, *740*
courts equated with communal legislation, *699–700*
criminal enactments, *691*
on custom as law, *922, 943*
"distinguished person's" approval, *754–755, 758, 759n.296*
doreshin leshon hedyot, *431–432*
"dual" methodology of, *1273–1276, 1313*
equal application of communal enactments, *771*
halakhic competence of witnesses and, *737–738*
interpretation of communal enactments by, *449–450*
justice and equity in communal enactments, *760–7621*
on "law of the land is law," 70
on lay tribunals, *23–26*
limitation period for ownership claims, *744–745*
Maimonides' influence on, *1221n.115*
majority rule and communal enactments, *717n.156*
minority rights, in communal enactments, *766–768*
minors, future generations, and subsequent community members, enactments for, *731–732*
novellae of, *1315n.19*
prospective vs. retroactive communal enactments, *773–777*
responsa of, *1279, 1315n.22, 1476, 1478, 1481*
on scope of authority to interpret communal enactments, *457–458*
signature of town scribe vs. witness' signature, *741–744*
table metaphor used by, *1311n.36*
tax enactments, *747–748, 922*
territorial scope of communal legislation, *669–670*
on universally agreed intent, *459–460*
"you shall not add or take away," *497–498*
Rashbam (Samuel b. Meir)
commentary of, *1117n.57*
on distinguishing process, *962*
enactments of, *786*
as leading Tosafist, *1120*
legal research and, *17*
Rashbash (Simeon b. Solomon Duran)
binding force of communal enactments and, *714*
as literary source, *1538*
power of custom and, *911*
theory vs. practice in legislation, *859–864*
Rashbez, Simeon b. Zemah Duran
abstention from exercise of legislative powers, *871–872*
on admonition of witnesses, *1700–1702, 1707*
custom based on error, *940*
enactments restricting husband's inheritance rights, *840*
as exile leader, *1482*
on halakhic religious-legal interactions, *119n.115*
on hypothetical responsa, *1516*
on landlord/tenant agreements, *453–456*
"law of the land is law," *132–136*
legal research, *99–102*
on liability of physicians, *147n.220*
as literary source, *1315n.21*
on mathematics in responsa, *1464n.34*

Rashbez, Simeon b. Zemah Duran *continued*
migration to Algeria, *805*
on questioning methods in responsa, *1502n.136*
responsa literature of, *1478, 1519n.211*
on Sages' moral-religious sanctions, *151–152*
theory vs. practice in legislation, *859–864*
Rashi (Solomon b. Isaac (Solomon Yizhaki))
commentaries of, *1108, 1116–1119, 1302n.275, 1315n.19*
enactments of, *786*
on Jerusalem Talmud, *1132*
Mishnaic commentaries, *1108*
on questioning methods in responsa, *1502–1503*
School of, codificatory literature from, *1178–1179*
Talmudic commentaries of, *1118–1119*
Rath, Meshullam
legislative enactments, *674n.30*
literary sources of Jewish law, *1499*
ratio decidendi
distinguishing process and, *961n.63, 962–964*
precedent in Jewish law and, *985*
Rav
Babylonian diaspora and, *1088*
Babylonian Talmud, *1088–1091, 1455*
bailments and, *965*
on King's law, *1024n.20*
ma'aseh concerning lost or stolen property, *956–957*
Rava
custom as source of legislation, *891*
force majeure, *634n.49*
prosbul enactment and, *513*
witnesses, inquiry and examination procedures, *607*
Raviah (Eliezer b. Joel ha-levi)
on legislation, *788*
as literary source, *1238–1239*
majority rule and communal enactments, *716*
Ravina, Babylonian Talmud redaction and, *1092*
Ravina II, Babylonian Talmud redaction and, *1093*
Re'ah (Aaron ha-Levi), precedent and judgment in Jewish law, *983n.131*
real estate matters. *See* property law
"rebellious elder" (*zaken mamre*)
creative function of midrash and, *287–288*
freedom of thought and speech, *1848*
literary sources, *1202*
reciprocity
between law and morals, *142–144*
Jewish and non-Jewish law, *62–64*
protection of minority rights, in communal enactments, *766*
wife's handiwork legislation (*ma'aseh yadehah*), *571–572*
"recognized laws" (*ha-mizvot ha-nikarot*), *234n.22*
Re'em (Eliezer b. Samuel), as literary source, *1259–1261*
Re'em (Elijah Mizrahi), responsa literature of, *1487*
Reference works, for Jewish law
on abbreviations, *1566–1567*
bibliographies, *1560–1564*
biographies of halakhic authorities, *1556–1560*
concordances, *1568*
encyclopedias, *1551–1556*
guidebooks, *1541–1551*
journals and periodicals, *1570–1572*
lexicons, *1564–1566*
lists of, *1540–1572*
as literary source, *1102–1103*
mishpat ivri scholarly research, *1569–1570*
source references, sayings and aphorisms, *1568–1569*
textual variants, *1567*
Reform Movement, responsa literature and, *1492*
regi'ah (agreement), enforcement of communal enactments and, *680–681*
regional enactments, territorial scope of, *672–675*
See also countrywide enactments
Rehabilitation of Offenders Law, *1707–1709*
religious and ritual laws. *See issur* (religious and ritual law)
religious leadership, Jewish law and, *1605–1606*
religious persecution
agunot legislation and, *525–526*
See also pogroms.
Rema (Moses Isserles). *See* Isserles, Moses
rental property, laws regarding

territorial scope of communal enactments and, *675n.36*
See also property law; tenancy laws
repentance (*teshuvah*)
a fortiori inference and, *351*
expunction of criminal records and, *1708–1709*
literary sources on, *1198*
rescission of support, rabbinical courts' jurisdiction over, *1759n.21*
research in Jewish law
vs. adjudication, *1909–1914*
approaches to, *80–91*
objections to, *83n.35*
Resh Lakish, integrative interpretations of, *297–298*
Reshimat Ma'amarim be-Madda'ei ha-Yahadut, *1563*
reshut
disputes over terminology of, *1936*
Israeli statutory interpretation and, *1743–1751*
lacuna and, *1836n.32*
uncertainty of statutory interpretation and, *1868–1871*
unique terminology of Jewish law and, *1874–1875*
"resident alien" (*ger toshav*), Jewish heritage and, *1855–1856*
Responsa Asheri, *1522*
Responsa Binyamin Ze'ev, *1522*
responsa literature
of *aharonim*, *1482–1491*
authorship questions, *216, 1520nn.213*
Be'er Heitev, *1437*
Birkei Yosef, *1439*
codificatory literature and, *1138–1139*
commentary and novellae in, *1105*
communal enactment interpretation in, *445–448*
compared with other post-Talmudic literature, *1456–1457*
Darkhei Teshuvah, *1442*
defined, *1454*
development of Babylonian Talmud and, *1089–1090*
digest of, *90–91, 1525–1528*
documentary interpretation guidelines in, *442–443*
earnings of wife from her employment, rabbinical court decisions regarding, *1786*
in eighteenth century, *1489–1491*
during Emancipation, *1491–1495*
fictitious persons and places, *1512–1515*
in fifteenth centuries, *1479–1480*
on fraudulent conveyances law, *1891–1894*
in geonic era, *1114, 1158, 1468–1472*
Halakhah Pesukah, *1442*
halakhic-aggadic reciprocity in, *96*
as historical source, *43–44, 1464–1466*
hypothetical responsa, *1516–1517*
indexes to, *1934n.98*
Judah al-Bargeloni's works and, *1178n.107*
Keneset ha-Gedolah of Hayyim Benveniste, *1434–1437*
legislative material in, *783*
Leket ha-Kemah, *1437–1438*
as literary source, *1102–1103*
ma'aseh and, *975–978*
magnitude of, *1462*
of Maimonides, *1186*
Matteh Shim'on, *1439–1440*
methodology, structure and form, *1501–1517*
mishpat ivri as dominant subject, *1462–1463*
nature and content of, *1456–1468*
Orah Mishpat, *1442*
organization and structure of, *12–13*
Ozar ha-Posekim, *1442*
Panim Hadashot by Isaac Jesurun, *1433–1434*
parallels with other legal systems, *1466–1468*
Pithei Teshuvah, *1441*
in post-Talmudic era, *54, 418–421*
prohibition against litigation in non-Jewish courts, *1916n.46*
questioners and submission of questions in, *1501–1506*
redaction and organization of compilations, *1517–1523*
research and digest of literature, *1523–1528*
in *rishonim* era, *1473–1482*
role in development of Jewish law, *1461*
scientific legal research and, *89–90*
on *Sefer ha-Turim* codification, *1304*
in seventeenth century, *1488–1489*
Sha'arei Teshuvah, *1440–1441*
significance and weight of rulings in, *1457–1459*

responsa literature *continued*
in sixteenth century, *1486–1488*
as source for enactments, customs, legal documents and non-Jewish law, *1463*
structure, form, style, transmittal and copying of questions and responses, *1507–1512*
supreme judicial tribunal and, *1460–1461*
tables of contents in, *1435n.37, 1472*
in Talmudic literature, *1454–1456*
textual interpretation, philosophy and religious beliefs, *1464*
topical compilations according to *Shulhan Arukh*, *1432–1443*
in *Tosafot*, *1122–1123*
in twelfth to fourteenth centuries, *1477–1479*
during twentieth century, *1494–1499*
use of, during Polish diaspora, *9*
Yad Aharon, *1438–1439*
of Yehudai Gaon, *1154*
Responsa Maharibal, *1522*
responsa prudentium, responsa compared with, *1466–1468*
"responsibility of property" (*aharayut nekhasim*), law of obligations and, *590–591*
Restatements, in U.S. Law, *1144n.7*
Restoration of Lost Property Law, statutory interpretation of, according to Jewish law, *1746–1751, 1865–1866*
See also property law.
restrictive interpretation
acceptance of proselytes from forbidden groups, *361–364*
idolatrous town example, *367–369*
of communal enactments, opposition to, *461*
of thirteen canons, *360–370*
opposition to, *369–370*
rebellious son example, *365–366*
tort law, *413–414*
retroactive enactments
communal enactments, *772–777*
legal norms and, *176*
"rewards" concept, in Penal Law Revision (Bribery) law, *1642n.91*
Rezah (Zerahiah ha-Levi Gerondi), *1173–1174*
Ri, (Isaac b. Samuel, the Elder)
"all who marry do so subject to conditions laid down by the Rabbis and the Rabbis annul this marriage" legislation, *639n.63*
career as teacher, *1120n.68*
circumvention of *kum va-Aseh* in criminal law, *531–533*
codificatory literature, *1239–1240*
commentary on *Piskei ha-Rosh*, *1254*
as leading Tosafist, *1120*
Ri Berab (Jacob Berab)
legislative enactments, *1311*
as literary source, *1486*
Ri Migash (Joseph ibn Migash), *1168*
on books of *halakhot*, *1230*
"distinguished person's" approval, *758–759*
encouragement of codification by, *1382*
on geonic responsa, *1471n.56*
novellae and commentaries of, *1123*
on *Mishneh Torah*, *1227n.136*
responsa of, *1181–1184*
Riaz (Isaac b. Moses), *1241*
Riba (Isaac b. Asher ha-Levi), *1119n.63*
Ribash (Isaac b. Sheshet Perfet)
admonition of witnesses, *1700–1702, 1707*
abstention from exercise of legislative powers, *871–872*
"all who marry do so subject to conditions laid down by the Rabbis and the Rabbis annul this marriage" legislation, *639n.63*
"approval of all halakhic authorities of region," 856–857
binding force of communal enactments on minor, future generations, and subsequent community members, *732–734*
communal representatives, communal enactments by, *729–730*
criminal communal enactments and, *694–695*
"distinguished person's" approval, *754*
as exile leader, *1482*
explanatory remarks in communal enactments, *462–464*
on *issur* vs. communal enactments, *708–710*
"law of the land is law," *132–134*
legal reasoning (*sevarah*) and, *1006*
limitation of actions legislation, *1725*
migration to Algeria, *805*
proof of custom, *928*

on questioning methods in responsa, *1503*
responsa literature of, *1476, 1478, 1519n.211*
tax laws, prospective vs. retroactive enactments, *775–777*
ribbit kezuzah concept,
rabbinic law and, *221n. 149*
halakhic authorities and, *244–247*
law and equity in, *247–261*
Rif. *See* Alfasi, Isaac b. Jacob ha-Kohen
"right of the people," law of the land is law and, *134–135*
right of way law, just adjudication and, *169–170*
rishonim, *44*
agunot legislation and, *527–528*
"all who marry do so subject to conditions laid down by the Rabbis and the Rabbis annul this marriage" legislation, *632n.47, 638n.61, 614n.65*
annulment enactments of eighteenth and nineteenth centuries, *876–877*
authority of, *267–268*
circumvention of *kum va-Aseh* and, *521*
custom as source of law, *918*
"distinguished person's" approval, *752n.275*
exegetical interpretation by, *391*
get (bill of divorcement), *563n.81*
halakhic *midrashim* commentaries, *1110–1111*
hefker bet din hefker, *509n.72*
Hiddushei Halakhot and, *1128*
husband's inheritance rights, restrictions, *840n.223*
issur vs. communal enactments and, *712*
labor law, *617*
legal interpretations of, *277–278*
literary legal sources of, *1101–1102*
novellae of *aharonim* compared with, *1127–1128*
oral vs. documented debt, encumbered property and, *595*
responsa literature during, *1473–1482*
on responsibility of property, *590–591*
in *Shittah Mekubbezet*, *1126–1127*
stolen property legislation, *602n.243*
Talmudic research during, *44*
terminology of, *268n.102*
Tosefta commentaries of, *1111n.37*
Rindfleisch Massacres, *1249, 1345*
rishumiyyim, terminology of, *235n.25*
Ritba (Yom Tov b. Abraham Ishbili)
agunot legislation and, *528n.144*
communal enactments, equity in, *771*
custom as source of *sitomta*, *915n.70*
equal inheritance rights for sons and daughters, enactments for, *842–846*
interpretation of communal enactments by, *445–448*
on literary sources, *1125, 1305*
ritual bath. *See mikveh* (ritual bath)
ritual law. *See issur* (religious and ritual law)
Riva, Jacob, *1514n.187*
Rivkes, Moses
on *Even ha-Ezer*, *1430*
on *Hoshen Mishpat*, *1426*
on *Orah Hayyim* and *Yoreh De'ah*, *1431*
Rizag (Isaac ibn Ghayyat), *1177*
robbery. *See* theft, laws regarding
Rosh Hodesh, interpretation of, *438–439*
Roman law
Adoption of Children Law as departure from, *1664n.171*
classification of Jewish law and, *76n.4*
differences with Jewish law, *1628*
historical fate of, *101*
interpretatio extensa, *321*
interpretatio grammatica, *297, 319n.121*
interpretatio logica, *296*
interpretatio restricta, *321*
interpretive function in, *290–292*
Land Law legislation and, *1710, 1714–1716*
majority rule and communal enactments, *716n.154*
oral vs. written law in, *191*
pontifices in, *311–312*
power of custom in, *903*
precedent in Jewish law and, *980*
religious/legal dichotomy in, *93n.2*
responsa, compared with *responsa prudentium*, *1466–1468*
Succession Law influenced by, *1673n.219, 1674nn.226*
Twelve Tables of, *310–311, 589*
Rosanes, Judah
glosses on *Sefer ha-Hinnukh*, *1267n.134*
literary sources, *1234*
Rosen, Pinhas (Minister of Justice)
on Capacity and Guardianship Law, *1667*
Family Law Amendment (Maintenance) Law, *1661n.160*

Rosen, Pinhas *continued*
imprisonment for debt legislation, *1635n.54*
on Marriage Age Law, *1655*
on Penal Law Revision (Bribery) law, *1642n.90*
on statutory incorporation, *1625–1626, 1627n.15*
Rosenstein v. Solomon, Land Law legislation, *1710–1711, 1715–1716*
Rosenthal v. Tomashevski, statutory incorporation, *1881*
Rosh Ha-Shanah, caution regarding *ma'aseh* and, *950*
Roshei Besamin, *1432*
roshei ha-yeshivah (heads of academies), *799*
Roth v. Yeshufeh, laws regarding possession, *1745–1746*
Rozin, Joseph (Rogachover), *1496*
Rubinstein, Judah, *1232n.145*
Rules of Evidence Amendment (Warning of Witnesses and Abolition of Oath) Law, *1697–1707, 1707n.337*
witnesses' admonition and, *1706*
Ruppin, Dr. Arthur, *1593n.33*
Russia, responsa from, *1495*
Ruth, Book of
as literary source for law, *1022–1023*
symbolic barter (*kinyan sudar*) in, *582*

S
Saadiah b. David Adani (al-Adani), *1232n.145*
Saadiah Gaon
Arabic monographs of, *1207n.75*
monograph of, *1159–1161*
Sefer ha-Shetarot of, *1535–1536*
Saalschütz, Joseph Levy, *81*
Sabbateanism, *1426n.13*
sabbath, laws regarding
blocking out light during, *958*
caution regarding *ma'aseh* and, *950*
Prophets as literary source for law, *1021–1022*
midrashic compilations of, *1047–1049*
prohibition against waging war on, *1035–1036*
unreasonable or illogical custom, *940*
See also issur (religious or ritual law)
sabbatical (seventh) year, in Mishnah, *1053, 1058–1059*
sacrificial offerings
hora'at sha'ah (temporary measures) and, *520*
See also issur (religious or ritual law)
sacrilege (*me'ilah*), committed by courts, *486n.44*
Sadducees, interpretation of Torah, *314–315*
"Safed Period"
Jewish population decreases in Israel during, *1133*
responsa from, *1486*
Safekeeping of Property Law (*Hok Shemirat Nekhasim*), *1691–1693*
Sages
"all who marry do so subject to conditions laid down by the Rabbis and the Rabbis annul this marriage" legislation, *632n.47, 636–38*
annulment enactments, *852–853*
Biblical law and, *214–217*
communal representatives, communal enactments by, *728n.193*
criticism of symbolic interpretation by, *380–383*
custom (*minhag*), power of, *909n.47*
custom based on error, rulings regarding, *937–938*
interpretation of Torah by, *311, 313–314*
law of interest and, *967–968*
legal source of halakhic rules and, *889–891*
legislation of, *481–485, 668*
ma'aseh and, *948*
marriage laws of, *785*
minority rights, protection of, *763n.315*
moral-religious sanctions of, *149–154*
omission of names, in *Mishneh Torah*, *1218–1219*
Orders of the Mishnah and, *52*
redaction of Mishnah and, *1051n.50, 1059–1060*
rules for disagreement among, *1089–1090*
on sacrifice of life to save another, *969–972*
Sefer ha-Turim's omission of, *1285–1287*
tanna and, *1042*
witnesses, inquiry and examination procedures, *608*
Zugot generations of, *1043–1044*
See also specific sages.
"sages are displeased with him"
communal enactments equated with courts, *705n.99*

lost or stolen property legislation, *602n.243*
modern inheritance laws, *1673–1674*
as moral-religious sanction, *149–154*
Sahula, Ibn, commentaries on *Tosefta*, *1111n.37*
Sale Law, good faith (*tom lev*) and, *183*
Salmond, J. W., precedent in Jewish law and, *979*
Salonika, Jewish community in,
legislative enactments, *865–866*
responsa literature from, *1486–1487*, *1489–1490*
Salvdor, Joseph, *81*
Samson b. Zadok, *1255*, *1315n.21*
Samson of Chinon, *1544–1545*
Samson of Sens
legislative enactments and, *811n.120*
justice and equity discussed by, *259*
Samuel (*amora*), *65*, *95n.10*, *127*, *131n.167*, *132n.168*, *409–411*, *428n.24*, *523*, *564*, *570*, *573n.126*, *596n.220*, *617*, *642n.66*, *887–888*, *1088*, *1090*, *1821*
Samuel, Book of,
as literary source for law, *554*, *1024–1025*
Samuel b. Alexander, *1413n.143*
Samuel b. Azriel of Lenzberg, *1402n.114*
Samuel b. Hophni Gaon
Arabic monographs of, *1207n.75*
monographs of, *1161–1164*
Samuel b. Meshullam Yerudani, *1305*
Samuel b. Uri Shraga Phoebus, *1419*
Samuel ha-Levi, *Nahalat Shiv'ah* of, *1539*
Samuel ha-Nagid of Egypt, *1543*
Samuel ha-Nagid of Spain, *1543*
Samuel of Bamberg, *101n.36*
Samuel, Herbert, *1608*
sanctions, imposition of (*lehassi'a al kizatan*), *679–680*, *794n.54*
sanctuary, holiness of, murder and, *199–200*
sandal, *halizah* rules, *907–908*
Sanhedrin
arka'ot she-be-Suria and, *24n.80*
child support laws, *831*
court system organization and, *6–7*
criminal communal enactments and, *696*
equating communal legislation with court, *699–702*
exile in Usha, *1008n.73*, *1009*
hefker bet din hefker, *514n.90*
interpretation of Torah, *315*
king's law and, *58n.27*
lay tribunals and, *22*
"laying on of hands", laws regarding, *1062–1063*
legislative enactments, *486–490*, *558–569*
reestablishment of, in State of Israel, *1615n.101*
Sanhedrin Tractate
legislative enactments, *606–607*
as literary source, *1054*
Sapir, Jacob, *1582n.15*, *1585*
Saragossa Jewish community (Spain), *431–432*
Sardi, Samuel, *1244–1246*
Sarei ha-Elef, *1561*
Sasportas, Jacob
legal research and, *34n.104*
legislative enactments, *859–860*
as literary source, *1489*
Sassoon, David, *1153n.16*
Sassoon, Solomon (Mekizei Nirdamim), *1153n.16*
savir, lay tribunals and, *22n.72*
savoraim
Babylonian Talmud redaction and, *1093–1094*
moredet legislation, *659–660*
reduction of Talmudic literature, *227*
"scheming witness," 397–399
Schneerson, Menahem Mendel, *1495*
Schochetman, E., *Kelalei ha-Talmud* and, *1547*
scholars, tax exemptions of (*talmid hakham*), *1289n.206*
Schor, Alexander Sender, *1447*
Schwadron, Shalom Mordecai, *1495*
scientific legal research
academic aspects of, *84–85*
Ha-Mishpat Ha-Ivri (Jewish Law) Society and, *1589–1590*
need for, in Jewish law, *80–91*
responsa as source for, *1464n.34*
scriptural analogy canon (*hekkesh ha-Katuv*), *344–347*
explicit analogy, *344–345*
implicit analogy, *346–347*
priority of, *360*
Scriptures
Aramaic translation of, as legal source, *1045–1046*
Sefer ha-She'iltot and, *1151–1153*
"scrupulously careful" (*nekiyyei ha-da'at*)

"scrupulously careful" *continued*
custom as legal source of law and, *882n.8*
Second Jewish Commonwealth, *88n.47*
Second Temple period, *prosbul* enactment and, *513*
sedeh bet ha-shelahin, *1333–1334*
Sedeh Yehoshu'a, *1134*
Sedei Hemed, *1552–1553*
Seder ha-Dorot, *1558*
Seder ha-Hakhamim ve-Korot ha-Yamim, *1557*
Seder Nezikin (Order of Damages), *1199*
Seder Olam Zuta, *1156*
Seder Rav Amram Gaon, *1158n.31*
Seder Tannaim va-Amoraim, *1541–1542*
Sefer Abudarham, *1305*
Sefer Ahavah (The Book of Love (of God)), *1198*
Sefer al ha-Katnut ve ha-Bagrut (Book on Minority and Adulthood), *1162*
Sefer Ammudei Golah. See Sefer Mizvot Katan
Sefer Asheri. See Piskei ha-Rosh
Sefer Avi ha-Ezri, *1238–1239*
Sefer Avi'asaf, *1238–1239*
Sefer Avodah (The Book of Temple Service), *1198*
Sefer Avodat ha-Kodesh, *1275n.160*
Sefer be-Dinei ha-Kinyanim (Book of the Laws of Acquisition), *1161*
Sefer be-Dinei ha-Neharot, he-Te'alot ve-ha-Borot (Book of the Laws of Rivers, Canals, and Cisterns), *1162*
Sefer be-Dinei Ishut (Book of Family Law), *1162*
Sefer be-Dinei Mazranut (Book of the Law of Adjoining Property Owners), *1165*
Sefer be-Hilkhot Gezelah (Book on the Laws of Robbery), *1161*
Sefer be-Hilkhot Shekhenim (Book on the Law of Neighbors), *1161*
Sefer be-Hilkhot Zavva'ot (Book of the Laws of Wills), *1162*
Sefer be-Mikah u-Mimkar (Book of Purchase and Sale), *1161*
Sefer Bet Yisra'el u-Me'irat Einayim (Sema), *1207n.74*
commentaries on *Hoshen Mishpat* in, *1424–1425*
Shulhan Arukh codification and, *1408–1414, 1417–1418*
Sefer Eliyahu Zuta, *1403n.115*
Sefer Emunot ve-De'ot, *1474–1475*
Sefer Ez Hayyim, *1255–1256*
Sefer ha-Agudah, *1306*
Sefer ha-Agur, *1305*
Sefer ha-Agur ha-Shalem, *1305n.292*
Sefer ha-Arvut ve-ha-Kabbelanut (Book of Ordinary and Special Contractual Suretyship), *1162*
topical arrangement and classification of, *1196*
Sefer ha-Darshan. See Sefer Mizvot Gadol
Sefer ha-Dayyanim (Book of Judges), *1165*
Sefer ha-Din (Book of Law), *1178*
Sefer ha-Eshkol, *1178n.106, 1179n.113*
Sefer Hafla'ah (The Book of Asseveration), *1198*
Sefer Hakhmei Ahu, *1559*
Sefer ha-Halakhot
as codificatory literature, *1139–1140*
legal research, *82*
as model for Nahmanides, *1242*
commentaries on, *1173–1176*
dominance of, as codificatory source, *1179*
Falk's commentaries on, *1408–1414*
Hanukkah laws compiled in, *1192n.34*
nature and content of, *1167–1172*
Piskei ha-Rosh as complementary work, *1251–1255*
tax law compilations, *1444*
topical arrangement and classification in, *1196*
Sefer ha-Hashlamah, *1243–1244*
Sefer ha-Hinnukh
bailees' law and, *1695n.300*
enumeration of Biblical commandments in, *1259n.100*
as literary source, *1265–1267*
modern labor law and, *1632–1633*
severance pay, *924–925*
Sefer ha-Ittim (Book of the Seasons), *1177, 1178n.106*
Sefer ha-Ittur,
legal instruments compiled in, *1537*
as literary source, *1179n.113, 1267–1269, 1537*
Sefer ha-Hokhmah, *788*
Sefer ha-Kabbalah, *1557*
commentary on *She'eiltot*, *1152–1153*
Sefer ha-Madda (Book of Knowledge)
enumerations in, *1191, 1262n.111*
organization of, *1198*
Sefer ha-Maharil, *1305*
Sefer ha-Makhri'a, *1258n.98*
Sefer ha-Manhig, *1240–1241*

Sefer ha-Ma'or (Book of the Luminary), *1173, 1244*
Mishnah interpreted in, *1106–1107*
Sefer ha-Mashkon (Book of Pledges), *1161*
Sefer ha-Mattanah (Book of Gifts), *1161*
Sefer ha-Mattanot (Book of Gifts), *1159*
Sefer ha-Mikah ve-ha-Mimkar (Book of Purchase and Sale), *1165*
topical arrangement and classification of, *1196*
Sefer ha-Minhagim (Klauser), *1305*
Sefer ha-Minhagim (Tirna), *1305*
Sefer ha-Mishpat, 108n.70
Sefer ha-Mizvot (Book of the Commandments)
goals of, *1184*
halakhic material compiled in, *1184, 1186–1188, 1191*
lack of reference to sources in, *1204–1206*
topical arrangement and classification, *1195–1203, 1259*
Sefer ha-Mordekhai, 1249–1250
Sefer ha-Neyar, 1248
Sefer ha-Orah, 1178
Sefer ha-Pardes, 1178
Sefer ha-Parnas, 1255
Sefer ha-Pikkadon (Book of Bailments), *1159–1160*
Sefer ha-Remazim (The Book of Hints), *1285*
Sefer ha-Roke'ah, 1239
Sefer ha-She'iltot
as literary source, *1150–1153*
topical arrangement and classification, *1196*
Sefer ha-Shetarot
of Hai b. Sherira Gaon, *1166n.60, 1536*
of Judah al-Bargeloni, *1178, 1536–1537*
as literary source, *1160*
of Lucena, Spain, *1536*
of Saadiah Gaon, *1535–1536*
Sefer ha-Shevu'ot (Book of Oaths), *1162*
Sefer ha-Shutafut (Book of Partnership), *1161*
Sefer ha-Tanya, 1248
Sefer ha-Tashbaz, 973–974
Sefer ha-Tashbez, 1255, 1315n.21
Sefer ha-Tena'im (Book of Contracts), *1161*
Sefer ha-Terumah of Baruch b. Isaac, *1239–1240*
Sefer ha-Terumot of Samuel Sardi, *1244–1246*
Sefer ha-Torah, 108n.70
Sefer ha-Turim
Alfasi's influence on, *1172*
Bet Yosef as extension of, *1313–1316*
codification methodology of, *1277–1303*
commentaries on, *1302–1304*
comparison of language and style with *Mishneh Torah* and *Shulhan Arukh*, *1327–1340*
criminal communal enactments, *697–698*
Darkhei Moshe codification, *1351–1356*
Falk's commentaries on, *1408–1414*
Heller's commentary on, *1404–1407*
Hanukkah laws compilation in, *1192n.34*
hilkheta ke-vatra'ei, 1359n.182
idolatry laws codification, *1327–1329*
influence of *Sefer ha-Terumot* on, *1246*
legal research, *54, 76, 82*
mishpat terminology in, *108n.70*
overrefined classification of, *1293–1295*
possession (*hazakah*) codification, *1331–1335*
preeminence of, as codificatory literature, *1272*
property laws codification, *1330–1331*
responsa compilations, *1304, 1433, 1489*
scope of codification in, *1300–1302*
sedeh bet ha-shelahin, 1333–1334
Sefer ha-Ittur quoted in, *1269*
Shulhan Arukh modeled on, *1323–1327*
Sirkes' commentary on, *1416–1417*
structure and organization of, *1287–1303*
table of contents (*simanim*), *1287n.196*
tax law compilations, *1444*
To'en ve-Nit'an in, *1293n.217*
various editions of, *1288n.200*
word play in, *1291n.214*
Sefer ha-Yashar, 1486n.96
responsa literature and, *1518*
Sefer ha-Yerushot (Book of Inheritances)
Saadiah Gaon's monograph, *1159–1161, 1196*
Samuel b. Hophni's monograph, *1162*
Sefer ha-Zekut (Book of Merit), *1175*
Sefer Hukkot ha-Dayyanim (The Book of the Laws of the Judges), *1306–1308*
Sefer Issur ve-Hetter ha-Arokh, 1305
Sefer Kedushah (The Book of Holiness), *1198*
Sefer Keritut, 1544–1545, 1547
Sefer Kinyan (The Book of Acquisitions)
as literary source, *1199–1201, 1262n.111*
Tur Hoshen Mishpat compared with, *1294*
Sefer Kol Bo, 1258
Sefer Korbanot (The Book of Sacrifices), *1198*

Sefer Meisharim (The Book of Equity), *1269–1272*
Sefer Metivot, 1156n.24
Sefer Minhagim de-vei Maharam b. Baruch mi-Rothenburg, 1305
Sefer Mishpat ha-Tena'im (Book of the Law of Contracts), *1165*
Sefer Mishpatim (The Book of Civil Laws), *1199–1201, 1262n.111*
  Tur Hoshen Mishpat compared with, *1294–1295*
Sefer Mishpetei Halva'ot (Book of the Laws of Loans), *1165*
Sefer Mizvot Gadol (Semag), *1261–1263*
  codificatory methodology of, *1279*
  enumeration of Biblical commandments in, *1259n.100*
Sefer Mizvot Katan (Semak), 1263–1265
  enumeration of Biblical commandments in, *1259n.100*
Sefer Mizvot Kazar. See Sefer Mizvot Katan
Sefer Nashim (The Book of Women)
  organization and compilation of, *1198–1199, 1262n.111*
  Sefer ha-Turim codification compared with, *1291*
Sefer Nezikin (The Book of Damages), *1199, 1262n.111*
Sefer Nir, 1137
Sefer Notarikon, Simanim ve-Khinuyim, 1566
Sefer Ohel Mo'ed, 1305
Sefer Orhot Hayyim (The Ways of Life), *1257–1258*
Sefer Sha'arei Dura ha-Shalem ha-Nikra Issur ve-Hetter. See Sha'arei Dura
Sefer Shevu'ot (Book of Oaths)
  of Hai Gaon, *1165*
  of Saadiah Gaon, *1159*
Sefer Shibbolei ha-Leket, 1247–1248
Sefer Shofetim (The Book of Judges), *1199, 1201–1202, 1262n.111*
Sefer Tanya Rabbati, 1248n.51
Sefer Tohorah (The Book of Purity), *1198*
Sefer Yere'im (Book of the God-Fearing), *1259–1261*
Sefer Yuhasin ha-Shalem, 1557
Sefer Zemanim (The Book of Seasons), *1198, 1262n.111*
Sefer Zera'im (The Book of Seeds), *1198*
Sefer Zevadin de-Urha-Zeidah la-Derekh, 1307–1308
Selden, John, *81*
self-defense, laws regarding, subjective factors affecting recourse to Jewish law, *1924–1931*
self-executing actions, in Foundations of Law Act, *1886–1894*
Self-Government, 1532n.17
self-government, halakhic authorities and, *60–61*
self-sufficiency
  of Israeli state legislation, *1728–1729*
  Land Law and, *1709–1716*
Sema. See Sefer Bet Yisrael u-Me'irat Einayim
Semag. See Sefer Mizvot Gadol
Semak. See Sefer Mizvot Katan
semikhah, in *Arukh ha-Shulhan, 1449*
Sephardic communities
  attitude toward enactment barring levirate marriage and requiring *halizah, 1809n.185*
  commentaries on *Sefer ha-Turim, 1302–1304*
  halakhic interpretation of legislation and, *1809*
  novellae and commentaries of, *1123–1127*
  responsa literature from, *1490, 1496n.127*
  territorial legislation, *674–675*
Septuagint
  as literary source of law, *1019, 1029, 1037*
  Letter of Aristeas on origin of, *1036*
Seridei ha-Yerushalmi, 1137
"settled law" (*halakhah pesukah*), custom as source of, *891n.48*
sevarah. See legal reasoning
Seven Noahide laws. *See* noahide laws
severance pay
  custom as source of law regarding, *924–926.*
  Israeli legislation concerning, *1631–1634*
  lifenim mi-shurat ha-din, 158n.272
  See also labor law.
sexual intercourse
  marriage effected by, *535n.172*
  See also coerced marriage; rape
Sha'ar ha-Gemul (The Gate of Recompense), *1243*
Sha'ar ha-Mayim, 1276n.160
Sha'ar Yosef, 1129n.104
Sha'arei Dura
  as literary source, *1248–1249*
Sha'arei ha-Mishpat ha-Ivri (The Gates of Jewish Law), *1588–1591*
Sha'arei Simhah (Gates of Joy), *1177*
Sha'arei Torat Erez Yisra'el, 1137

Sha'arei Teshuvah
as literary source, *1178n.107, 1440–1441*
responsa compilation, *1458n.18*
Sha'arei Yosher, 1129n.104
Sha'arei Zedek, 1447n.86
Shabbetai b. Meir ha-Kohen
commentaries on *Hoshen Mishpat, 1425–1426*
hypothetical responsa of, *1516–1517*
on *Orah Hayyim* and *Yoreh De'ah, 1431*
prohibition against litigation in non-Jewish courts, *17–18, 1914n.44*
Shabbetai Zevi, *1426n.13*
Sha'beid nafsheih, law of obligations and, *589n.197*
Shagav v. District Rabbinical Court of Safed
"natural justice," violation of, *1759n.21*
statutory incorporation and, *1781–1782*
shaharit (morning prayer), custom as law regarding, *898–899*
Shakdiel v. Minister of Religions, 1794n.127, 1900
Shakh (Siftei Kohen). See Shabbetai b. Meir ha-Kohen
Shakhna, Israel, *1348*
Shakhna, Shalom
codification methodology of, *1345–1348, 1355–1356, 1362*
rejection of codification by, *1374–1376*
responsa literature of, *1487–1488*
Shaki, A. H., *1688n.288*
Shalit v. Minister of the Interior, 1688–1690
Shalom, Judah b., *225–226*
Shalshelet Rabbanei me-Ir Sofiyah, 1559
Shalshelet Rabbanei Salonik, 1559
Shamgar, Meir (Justice)
lifenim mi-shurat ha-din, 162–163
statutory incorporation and, *1689n.289, 1762n.33, 1802*
Shammai, School of
agunot legislation and, *402, 524–525*
civil law, communal enactments in, *687*
on collection of *ketubbah, 426–427*
on divorce law, *293–294*
halakhic decision making and, *1900–1901*
Hebrew spelling of, *1043n.11*
hefker bet din hefker, 514n.88
interpretation of Torah by, *315–316*
issur-mamon distinction, *123*
justice and equity in, *258–259*
"laying on of hands", laws regarding, *1062–1063*
olah, laws regarding, *349*
Oral Law terminology and, *191–192*
as part of *Zugot, 1043*
recitation of *Shema, 320–321*
sectarian disputes and, *1064–1070, 1900–1901*
sukkah, laws regarding, *959*
suprahuman influence interpretation, *264–265*
tannaitic legislation classification, *546–547*
Shapira, Avraham, *1810n.189, 1815n.195*
Shapira, Hayyim Eleazar, *1442*
Shapira, I. S., on Defamation Law, *1644n.103*
Shapira, Zevi Hirsch, *1442*
sharecropping lease laws
doreshin leshon hedyot applied to, *428–429*
legislative enactments, *930–932*
She'elot u-Teshuvot, on hypothetical responsa, *1517n.201*
she'er, spousal support legislation, *571*
she-ha-kol nihyeh bi-devaro ("by whose word all things exist), *898*
she'ilta, contents of, *1151–1152*
she-kakh kotev lo phrase, sharecropping lease laws, *429n.28*
shekhiv me-ra (deathbed)
authenticity of wills and, *1877–1884*
estate law and, *150–154*
modern Succession Law and, *1682–1683*
provisions of will of, *102*
succession law and, *1673n.218*
testamentary disposition and, *1671n.210*
See also estates and wills
Shelihim Niskharim le-Teiman, 1501n.131
shema
laws regarding recitation of, *1059–1060*
passage in Torah, *320–321*
recitation of, *ma'aseh* concerning, *969*
Shema Project, *1934n.98*
Shemaiah, as part of *Zugot, 1043*
Shem ha-Gedolim, Va'ad la-Hakhamim
commentary on *Shulhan Arukh, 1372n.18*
as literary source, *1558, 1561*
Shemonah Perakim, 1190n.28
Shemoneh Esreh prayer, *675n.34*
Shem Tov ibn Gaon, commentaries on *Mishneh Torah, 1232*
Shenaton ha-Mishpat ha-Ivri, 1570
Shenaton le-Mishpat Ivri u-le-Dinei Mishpahah be-Yisra'el, 1564
Shenei Luhot ha-Beirit, 1393n.78, 1418n.161

sheniyyot mi-divrei soferim, Ezra's legislative enactments, *557*
sheniyyot (secondary relationships), *483–485*
Sher'erit Yosef, *1545*
Sherira (Gaon). *See* Hai b. Sherira Gaon
shetar. *See* legal document (legal instrument)
shetar hazzalah See indemnification agreement
shetar hov. *See* promissory note
Shetilei Zeitim, *1432*
shevah karka'ot, property lien legislation and, *592n.210*
shev ve-al ta'aseh (sit and do nothing)
  court's authority, *505–506, 521*
  as literary source, *1494*
Sheyarei Keneset ha-Gedolah, *1436*
Sheyarei Korban, *1135*
she-yigzeru, terminology of, *255n.63*
Shibbolei ha-Leket ha-Shalem. *See Sefer Shibbolei ha-Leket*
shi-bud ha-guf, law of obligations and, *589n.197*
shi'bud nekhasim (lien)
  modern legislation, *1874*
  property lien legislation, *591–597*
shiddukhin (marriage agreement), *208n.92*
  See also ketubbah
shikkul hada'at (disputed point of law), *982*
Shiltei Gibborim, *1176*
shimmush (serving), *ma'aseh* and, *947–948*
Shittah Mekubbezet
  contents of, *1126–1127*
  on *divrei kabbalah*, *203n.65*
  legal reasoning (*sevarah*) and, *989n.5*
  as literary source, *1547*
  Rabad's commentaries in, *1123–1124*
  Ritba's commentaries in, *1125n.90*
shi'urim (measurement standards)
  Oral Law tradition and, *205*
  rabbinical vs. Biblical law and, *208n.92*
Shiyyurei Berakhah, *1439*
Shkop, Shimon
  on halakhic religious-legal interactions, *119n.115*
  issur-mamon distinction and, *136–137*
shofar
  affirmative commandments for, *505–506*
  laws regarding, *497–498*
Shor, Abraham Hayyim, justice as supplement to law, *171–172*
shufra de-shetara (adornments of the shetar), *1534*
Shulhan Arukh, *26*
  acceptance of, as definitive authority, *1417–1422*
  admonition of witnesses in, *1699–1702*
  alternative codes to, *1385–1407*
  Arukh ha-Shulhan of Epstein on, *1448–1450*
  Ashkenazic *halakhot* contained in, *1306*
  Bet Yosef as contradiction to, *1370–1372*
  Capacity and Guardianship Law and, *1668–1669*
  classification of Jewish law in, *76*
  codification methodology in, *1319–1322, 1417–1419*
  codificatory literature after, *1443–1452*
  commentaries on, *1407–1417*
  on competence of judges, *740*
  criminal communal enactments, *698*
  on custom as source of contract agreement, *916*
  decline of codificatory activity following, *1450–1451*
  eastern Jewish communities' reaction to, *1368–1373*
  Falk's commentaries on, *1408–1414*
  halakhic competence of witnesses, *739*
  halakhic decision making mandated by, *1911–1912*
  historical circumstances surrounding, *1419–1422*
  idolatry laws codification, *1327–1329*
  Jaffe's commentary on, *1397–1403*
  just adjudication and, *169*
  kim li plea, *1283n.180*
  language and style compared with *Mishneh Torah* and *Turim*, *1327–1340*
  laws omitted in, *1323n.39*
  legal research on, *82*
  limitation of actions legislation, *1725–1726*
  as literary source, *1072, 1172*
  Maharam of Lublin's commentaries on, *1384–1385*
  Maharsha's commentaries on, *1383–1385*
  Maimonides' influence on, *1231, 1337–1340*

mishpat ivri and, *105*
omissions in Babylonian Talmud and, *1095*
opposition to, without proposing any alternatives, *1375–1385*
organization of, *12*
possession (*hazakah*) codification, *1331–1335*
practical application of laws and, *54*
preeminence as codification literature, *1365–1366*
procedural enactments and, *826*
property laws codification, *1330–1331*
Rema's glosses to, *1363–1365*
responsa on, *1432–1443, 1488–1489*
Sefer Hukkot ha-Dayyanim cross-referenced with, *1307n.295*
Sephardic authorities' acceptance of, *1373*
Sirkes' commentary on, *1415–1416*
specific laws critiqued in, *1370–1372*
stolen property legislation, *602n.243*
structure and arrangement of, *1323–1327*
table metaphor in, *1322n.36*
tax law compilations, *1444–1446*
teaching Torah to women and, *1799*
Tiferet Yisra'el influenced by, *1110*
various editions of, *1323n.41*
will of *shekhiv me-ra* and, *1881*
Women's Equal Rights Law and, *1659–1660*
Shulhan Arukh Hoshen Mishpat. See Hoshen Mishpat (Shulhan Arukh)
Shulhan Arukh of Shneur Zalman of Lyady, *1447*
"Shum" enactments (Speyer, Worms, and Mainz), *1258*
mamzerim and, *789*
origins of, *788–789*
restriction of husband's inheritance rights, *836–838*
shuma hadra (return of appraised property) legislation, *627–628*
Shushan, Jacob, on halakhic authority, *270n.109*
shutafut (partnership), *1874*
See also partnership, laws regarding
Siddur Rashi, 1178–1179
Siddur (Saadiah Gaon), *1159–1160*
Siev, on nomenclature of Rema (Moses Isserles), *1349n.142*
Sifra
Akiva's compilation of (*Torat Kohanim*), *1048–1049*
as source of law, *1047*
commentaries on, *1110–1111*
customs (*minhag*) in, *886*
development and redaction of Mishnah and, *1051*
on halakhic authority, *243, 266–267*
literary sources for, *1047–1049*
Rabad's commentary on, *1110–1111*
Rabbenu Hillel's commentary on, *1111*
Sifrei
Akiva's compilation of, *1048–1409*
as source of law, *1047*
commentaries on, *1110–1111*
development and redaction of Mishnah and, *1051*
literary sources for, *1047–1049*
R. Ishmael's compilations of, *1048*
Rabbenu Hillel's commentary on, *1111*
rape laws in, *1031*
Siftei Kohen (Shakh), 1419
commentaries on *Hoshen Mishpat* in, *1425–1426*
on *Orah Hayyim* and *Yoreh De'ah, 1431*
Siftei Yeshenim, 1561n.112
Silberg, M. (Justice)
British Mandatory legal system and, *1612*
evidence and procedure legislation, *1767–1768*
legal research and, *181n.360*
marriage between *kohen* and divorcee, Jewish law incorporated in state legislation, *1771–1772, 1774–1782*
"natural justice," *1794n.126*
"public interest," *1779*
wife's income from employment and property and, *1804n.167*
silluk (renunciation of interest), *739n.228*
Simanei Asheri (Highlights of Asheri), *1285*
Simanei Or Zaru'a, 1241n.21
Simeon, R.
amoraic view of Mishnah and, *1061*
development and redaction of Mishnah and, *1051*
mishnayot compilations, *1051*
Simeon b. Azzai, *1044*
Simeon b. Eleazar
as literary source, *1033*
on power of custom, *909n.47*
Simeon b. Gamaliel II, *1044*

Simeon b. Hillel, as major *tannaim*, ***1043***
Simeon b. Shatah
  ketubbah enactment, ***559–561***
  legislative authority not prescribed in Torah, ***517n.104***
  as part of *Zugot*, ***1043***
  on sacrifice of life to save another, ***971***
Simeon b. Yohai, R.
  as leading *tanna*, ***7, 19, 1044***
Simeon b. Zoma, ***1044***
Simeon of Mizpeh, R.
  development and redaction of Mishna and, ***1050–1052***
  tractates of, ***1050***
Simeon the Just
  Great Assembly and, ***1043***
  Oral Law and, ***41, 192***
Simhah b. Samuel of Speyer, ***788***
Simhah b. Samuel of Vitry, ***1179, 1537***
Simon Mordecai b. Solomon Bekemoharar, ***1439–1440***
Simona, R., ***1094***
simultaneous death, modern Succession Law and, ***1680–1683***
Sinaitic revelation
  codification of Jewish law and, ***1145–1146***
  integrative interpretation and, ***385***
  legal norms and, ***233–234***
  legislative enactments, ***546***
  in *Mishneh Torah*, ***1186***
  as origin of Oral Law, ***192–203***
  prerogatives of halakhic authorities and, ***241–242***
  restrictive interpretations of Torah and, ***363n.264***
  "you shall not add or take away," ***500–502***
  See also halakhah le-Moshe mi-Sinai
Sirillo, Solomon, ***1132–1133***
Sirkes, Joel (Bah)
  commentaries of, ***1415–1416***
  on custom regarding modes of acquisition, ***916–917***
  "distinguished person" approval, ***757n.293***
  lifenim mi-shurat ha-din, ***157–159, 167***
  responsa literature of, ***1489***
  on *Sefer ha-Turim*, ***1303–1304***
sitomta (mark of ownership)
  custom as source of law, ***911n.56, 913–920, 943–944***
  origin of term, ***914n.68***
  power of custom in, ***911n.56, 914–920***
  property law research, ***211n.110***
  Wiloszni case and, ***1822–1824***
siyyata di-shemaya, ***977***
Skornik case, ***5n.7, 1946n.136***
slander laws, Septuagint as source for, ***1029***
slavery, laws regarding
  codification methods compared, ***1333–1340***
  contradictory passages in Torah regarding, ***338–339***
  custom as source of law regarding, ***924–925***
  enslaving of debtors, ***310–311***
  general principle canon and, ***356–357***
  influence of Oral Law and, ***200–201***
  integrative interpretation of, ***377n.337, 378–379***
  Onkelos' translations as source for, ***1046n.28***
  post-Talmudic halakhic interpretation, ***415n.41***
  severance pay legislation based on, ***1632–1634***
socioeconomic conditions
  Capacity and Guardianship Law, ***1665–1666***
  civil procedure and, ***1604–1605***
  communal tax enactments, ***750–751***
  grundnorm and, ***231–232***
  impact of, on Jewish legal system, ***46–49***
  king's law and, ***58n.27***
  lay tribunals and, ***24–29***
  in non-Jewish countries, ***36–37***
Sofer, Moses (Hatam Sofer)
  "distinguished person's" approval, ***758***
  as literary source, ***1495***
  majority rule and communal enactments, ***720–722***
  modern legislation and, ***1584n.18***
  on territorial scope of legislation, ***673n.30***
Soferim period of Talmudic research, ***40–41***
  interpretative methods, ***311, 313–314***
  legal interpretations of, ***40***
  Oral Law and, ***192***
sof hora'ah (end of instruction), Babylonian Talmud redaction and, ***1092***
Solomon b. Hasdai
  appoints Yehudai Gaon to Sura academy, ***1154***
  as literary source, ***1150***
Solomon Ephraim of Luntshitz, ***256–259***

Solomon (King), consanguinity laws, *557n.49*
Sorotzkin, Zalman (Rabbi), on teaching Torah to women, *1799*
source references, lack of, in Maimonides' work, *1204–1206*
sources of law
  defined, *228–230*
  difficulties with access to, *1931–1932*
  historical sources, *228–230*
  legal sources, *229–230*
  literary sources, *228*
sovereignty
  conflict of laws and, *78–79*
  decline of Jewish law and, *1609–1611*
  economic-social relationship and, *36–37*
  impact of on juridical autonomy, *15*
  "law of the land is law," 75
  legal norms and (*ribbon ha-le'um, ribbon ha-olam*), *234n.24*
Spain, Jewish communities in
  admonition of witnesses in, *1700*
  codificatory works from, *1177–1178*
  countrywide communal legislation in, *796–804*
  destruction of Jewish community in, *804–805*
  Expulsion in 1492, *1482*
  husband's inheritance rights, restriction of, *838–840*
  juridical autonomy of, *8–9*
  lay tribunals in, *23–24*
  legal instrument compilations of, *1538, 1540*
  proliferation of *halakhot* in, *1279*
  responsa literature from, *1478–1479, 1500n.131, 1525–1526*
  restriction on marriage and divorce legislation, *847*
  Sefer ha-Shetarot of Lucena, *1536*
  Torah centers in, *43*
De Specialibus Legibus, as literary source for Jewish law, *1030–1031*
specification, in thirteen canons, *330–333*
  explicative exegesis, *323–330*
  generalization required by, *328, 330*
  post-Talmudic halakhic interpretations and, *418–421*
  relationship to other canons, *327–328*
  requiring a generalization, *328–330*
  See also generalization
Spektor, Isaac Elchanan, *1495*
Speyer, Jewish community in, *848–850*
  See also "Shum" enactments.
spiritual hegemony, rise of *kehillah* and, *666–668*
spoiled goods, *Tosefta* legal rules regarding, *1080–1081*
spoils of war. *See* military law
spousal support
  debt obligations and, *1635n.58, 1636n.69*
  earnings of wife from her employment, rabbinical court decisions regarding, *1787–1789*
  Family Law Amendment (Maintenance) Law, *1660–1663*
  legislation concerning, *570–571*
  wife's income from employment and property and, *1802–1805*
spouse, priority of, in Succession Law, *1676n.233*
stability, in legal systems, *177–178*
stare decisis
  distinguishing process and, *961n.63*
  precedent in Jewish law and, *979*
State of Israel v. Avi Zur, freedom from detention issues in, *1843*
status quo ante, Land Law legislation and, *1710–1711, 1714*
statute of limitations, limitation of actions legislation and, *1724–1727*
statutes
  codification and, *1142–1144*
  vs. judicial decisions, *1459n.20*
  revision and codification, *1143–1144*
  See also communal enactments
statutory incorporation of Jewish heritage, in Israeli law
  communal enactments and, *449–450*
  fears concerning, *1938–1940*
  court decisions as examples of, *1739–1743n.435*
  Capacity and Guardianship Law, *1666–1671*
  direct vs. general incorporation and extent of incorporation, *1906n.18*
  Foundations of Law Act and, *1896–1897*
  general principle of, *1652–1653*
  halakhic decision making and, *1900–1906*
  illegal contract legislation, *1719–1720*
  interpretive approaches to Israeli legislation and, *1732–1735*
  Koenig case, additional hearing, *1875–1884*

statutory incorporation of Jewish heritage, in Israeli law *continued*
"legal issue requiring decision," *1838n.40*
provisions contrary to Jewish law, *1685–1688, 1838n.40*
rabbinical courts' jurisdiction over, *1761–1765*
secularization of *Halakhah*, *1906–1914*
subjective factors affecting recourse to Jewish law, *1928–1931*
uncertainty as to meaning, additional *Hendeles* hearing, *1863–1871*
unique terminology of, *1874–1875*
value-laden legal terms, *1871–1874*
"statutory share" (*Pflichtteil*), inheritance law and, *1678–1680*
Steinsaltz, Adin, *1130n.105*
stolen property. *See* lost or stolen property.
Streit v. Chief Rabbi of Israel, natural justice and, *1759n.20*
strict law, merger with king's law and, *57–58n.27*
Student's Guide Through the Talmud, *548n.10*
students, as halakhic authorities, *270n.111*
sub judice
Foundations of Law Act and, *1834–1835*
statutory interpretation, according to Jewish law, *1746–1751, 1780*
uncertainty of statutory interpretation and, *1864–1865*
subsequent expressions, as explanation, in thirteen canons, *334*
subordinate legislation
of Knesset, *478–479*
"you shall not add or take away," *502*
Succession Law (1965)
adoption of, *1625*
definition of a Jew in, *1688–1690*
equality of sexes in, *1683–1688*
"family provision" allowance, *1678–1679*
incorporation of Jewish heritage in, *1671–1688*
legislative enactments and, *829n.183*
murderer prohibited from inheriting from victim, *1677–1678*
provisions not in accord with Jewish law, *1683–1688*
"Quasi-Will" provision of, *1687–1688*
rabbinical courts' jurisdiction and, *1760–1765*
"reserved portion" of estate under, *1678–1681*
"Self-Sufficiency of this Law," *1672*
severing of ties to English law, *1728*
State as legal heir in, *1676–1677*
will of *shekhiv me-ra* and, *1882*
See also inheritance law.
sudar (kerchief), property transfer and, *221n.145*
suicide, statutory interpretation of Jewish law and, *1875–1884*
sukkah (*sukkot*)
customs (*minhag*) regarding, *886–887*
interpretation of Torah regarding, *387–389*
laws regarding, *497–498*
lulav prohibition, *889*
ma'aseh and, *959*
as religious-legal obligation, *118*
See also lulav.
supplements (*hashlamot*) to commentaries, *1110*
sumptuary legislation, Forli enactments regarding, *815–816*
suprahuman authorities
halakhic authorities' concessions to, *264–265*
power of, *260–261*
Supreme Court of Israel
amendment of Woman's Equal Rights Law, *1805–1807*
communal enactments equated with courts, *704n.97*
conflict of laws, *1483n.93*
criminal communal enactments and, *692, 696n.83*
Defamation Law in, *1645n.103*
documentary interpretation by, *443n.87*
education of children, parents' rights and responsibilities, *1795–1802*
freedom from detention issues, *1842–1845*
freedom of thought and speech, *1846–1850*
generalization and specification canons, *328n.149*
good faith (*tom lev*), *184, 187–188*
Israeli Declaration of Independence and, *1833–1834*
Land Law legislation and, *1710–1711*
"legal issue requiring decision," *1835–1838*
legal standards and, *178–180*
lifenim mi-shurat ha-din, *161–164*
limitation of actions legislation, *1727n.412*

marriage between *kohen* and divorcee, Jewish heritage and, *1776–1782*
personal status issues, *1758–1759*
reliance on Jewish law in, *1691–1692, 1729–1730, 1758–1759, 1872–1874, 1933–1934*
severance pay legislation, *1633*
severing of ties to English law, *1728–1729*
tort liability of spouses, *629n.37*
use of Jewish law as legal system by, *1920–1923*
wife's income from employment and property and, *1803–1805*
will of *shekhiv me-ra* and, *1884n.232*
Wiloszni case and, *1820–1824*
on witnesses' oaths or affirmations and, *1705–1706*
Women's Equal Rights Law and, *1656n.144*
Supreme legislation, Written law as, *479–480*
Sura academy (Babylonia)
influence of, *645*
legal research at, *43*
suretyship, laws regarding
Book of Ben Sira as source for, *1035*
Book of Proverbs as source for, *1026–1027*
chattels and, *1026n.28*
freedom of contract and, *127n.145*
Jerusalem Talmud and, *1096n.63*
legal-moral reciprocity and, *144n.214*
legislation contrary to Jewish law and, *1721–1724*
ma'aseh concerning, *953–954*
ordinary surety and *arev kabbelan*, *1163n.48*
Samuel b. Hophni's statements on, *1162–1164*
Sefer ha-She'iltot and, *1151–1152*
Suslin ha-Kohen, Alexander, *1306*
Sussman (President)
"justice" terminology and, *1837n.37*
subjective factors affecting recourse to Jewish law, *1925–1927*
Swiss Civil Code, suretyship law and, *1721–1722*
Symbolic interpretation, Sages' criticism of, *380–383*
Symmachus b. Joseph, *1044*
Syrian courts, prohibition against litigation in non-Jewish courts, *1915n.46*

T
ta'arovet, laws regarding, *1357–1359*
takkanah (*takkanot*)
as codification, *1140–1141*
conflict of laws and, *79*
defined, *29n.93*
establishment of Chief Rabbinate and, *1598*
historical background for, *504*
interchangeable use of, with *minhag* and *halakhah*, *888*
legal norms and, *233*
Leghorn, Italy lay tribunals, *28–29*
as literary source, *1102–1103*
Lithuanian lay tribunals and, *28, 30*
on marriage age, *1654–1656*
in *Mishneh Torah*, *1202*
role of, in State of Israel, *1616–1617*
scientific legal research and, *85*
terminology of, *490–492*
See also legislation
takkanot ha-kahal. *See* communal enactment
Takkanat ha-Shavim, expunction of criminal records and, *1708–1709*
takkanat ha-shuk enactment, *596–601*
takkanot kevu'ot, labor law, *617*
takkanat kiyyum shetarot, *611–614*
Takkanot of Shum, *1258*
Talmud
admonition of witnesses in, *1698*
Asheri's commentary on, *1251–1252*
"be killed rather than transgress," *990–991*
codificatory literature following order of, *1238–1258*
conversion to Judaism, *954–956*
cross-fertilization of Babylonian and Jerusalem teachings, *1090–1091*
custom as legal source of law and, *882n.8, 931–932*
defined, *1084*
dispute over printing rights, *673n.30*
"distinguished person's" approval, *752–754*
earnings of wife from her employment, rabbinical court decisions regarding, *1786n.103*
edict for burning of, *1247n.46, 1263*
enforcement of communal enactments, *682*
geonic legislative enactments compared with, *645n.6*

Talmud *continued*
halakhic authorities, legislative power of, *481–485, 517n.100*
husband's inheritance rights, restriction of, *837–838*
labor law and, *618–620*
as literary legal source, *1038–1039,1083*
ma'aseh regarding release from vows, *952–953*
Maimonides' omissions from, *1193n.93, 1204–1206*
market overt legislation, *599*
melog property, *486n.44*
Mishneh Torah as source, *1145–1146, 1211–1214*
modern severance pay legislation and, *1631–1634*
possession, laws regarding, *1009–1014*
precedent and judgment in Jewish law, *982–983*
role of, in Jewish legal system, *1098–1100*
suretyship law in, *1027n.35*
Wiloszni case and, *1823*
See also Babylonian Talmud; Jerusalem Talmud

Talmud Bavli im Targum Ivri u-Ferush Hadash, 1130n.105
Talmud Katan (Abridged Talmud), *1171*
Talmud, A Reference Guide, The, 1550
Talmud Yerushalmi, Order of Zera'im According to Readings of Elijah, the Gaon of Vilna, 1137

Talmudic literature
comparisons of codification methodology and, *1336–1340*
dating of reduction to writing, *227*
as dividing line for periods of Jewish law, *39–40*
Halakhah-Aggadah reciprocity in, *95–96*
justice as supplement to law, *169–170*
laws regarding Sukkot in, *388–389*
Maharshal's commentary and, *1386–1388*
on ordained judges, *20*
resolution against obligee, for legal ambiguity, *434–436*
responsa, *1454–1456*
Sages's law vs. Biblical law and, *215–216*
scientific legal research and, *87*
Sefer ha-Turim's omission of, *1285–1287*
terminology for lay tribunals, *20–22*
tort law interpretations, *412–413*
See also Babylonian Talmud; Jerusalem Talmud

Talmudic period
legal research into, *81*
scientific legal research and, *88n.47*

Tam, Rabbenu (Meir, Jacob b.)
arbitration procedures and, *17, 19*
authentication of witnesses' testimony, *613n.285*
"bad custom" (*minhag garu'a*), *941–942*
commentary of, *1117n.58*
custom as source of legislation, *891*
customs based on error and, *939*
divorce enactments, *787*
enactments of, *786–788, 1258*
explanation of writing legal instruments, *1267*
holkhei Usha, 1008n.73
husband's inheritance rights, restriction of, *836–838*
"I have nothing" oath to enforce civil judgments, *651n.29*
issur-mamon distinction in *Halakhah* and, *125–126*
justice as supplement to law, *170–171, 174*
literary source, *1258*
ma'aseh and, *947–948*
majority rule and communal enactments, *715–716, 722–723*
moredet legislation, *660n.68, 661*
origin of Tam appelation, *1120n.66*
responsa of, *1279, 1476, 1478, 1486n.96*
sharecropping lease laws, *428–429*
stolen property legislation, *602n.243*
Tosafists and, *1119n.63, 1120*
on untithed fruit, *938–939*
Yom Kippur, custom as law regarding, *899*

Tamar, levirate marriage of, *197–199*
Tanhuma, on ordained judges, *20n.64*
tanna, terminology of, *1042*
tannaitic era (*tannaim*)
acquisition (kinyan) legislation during, *580–587*
Aramaic translations of Scripture in, *1045–1046*
asmakhta (supportive interpretation) and, *303–305*
Bar Kokhba rebellion and, *13n.33*
Biblical vs. rabbinical law in, *211*
classification of Jewish law during, *76*
codification of Mishnah, *1057–1078*
criminal legislation during, *605*
on debt law, *295–296*
"do what is right and good," *623–624*

family legislation during, *570–580*
five generations of, *1044*
get (bill of divorcement), *566*
halakhic interpretation by, *268, 402–407, 1047–1049*
inheritance law during, *575–578*
integrative interpretations of, *297–300*
issur-mamon distinction in *Halakhah* and, *124–125*
judicial decision making *ma'aseh* regarding, *951–954*
labor legislation, *614–621*
"law of the land is law," *65*
law of obligations legislation during, *587–601*
lay tribunals during, *22*
legal instrument authentication and certification, *610–614*
legislation concerning procedure and evidence, *605–614*
literary sources in, *40, 1042–1082*
ma'aseh in the conduct of halakhic authorities, *958–959*
Mishna as legal source in, *1049–1056*
as Oral Law recipient, *192*
practice of *pilpul* and, *1381*
role of public in legislation, *539–540*
spousal support legislation, *570–571*
survival of Jewish law during, *2*
Talmudic research in, *41–42*
tort legislation, *601–605*
Tosefta as legal source in, *1078–1081*
zugot generations, *1043–1044*

Tarfon, R.
criminal communal enactments and, *692–694*
on custom as determination of law, *898*
debate with Akiva, *381–382*
legal research and, *6, 13*
as literary source, *1044*
ma'aseh and, *948*
on ordained judges, *20n.64*
witnesses, inquiry and examination procedures, *609*

Targum Yerushalmi, *1045–1046*

Targum Yonatan, *1045–1046*

Targumim (Scripture translations), *1040*

tax laws
codificatory literature on, *1444–1447*
collective levy of, on whole Jewish communities, *37*
communal enactments, *450–452, 703–704, 745–751, 772*
courts equated with communal enactments, *706n.110*
custom as source of, *920–923, 944*
Forli enactments regarding, *813–814*
halakhic decision making, *1912n.39*
individual rights, in communal enactments, *770–771*
king's law and, *56n.22*
"law of the land is law," *68*
lay tribunals and, *28*
legal-moral reciprocity and, *142n.206*
marriage dowries, interpretation of, *446–448*
Moroccan enactments concerning, *809*
non-Jewish courts and, *17*
prospective vs. retroactive enactments, *774–777*
protection of minority rights, *766–768*
Rashi, enactments of, *786*
in *Tur Yoreh De'ah*, *1289n.206*
Valladolid enactments concerning, *803*

Tazarti, Abraham b. Solomon ibn, civil law commentaries, *1306–1308*

Tchernowitz, Chaim (Rav Za'ir), correspondence of, *86n.44, 88n.47*

technology, right to privacy and, *1859–160*

Tedeschi, G. (Prof), *1835n.29, 1887n.237*

tefillin (phylacteries), laws regarding
Onkelos' translations as source for, *1046*

Tekufat ha-Geonim ve-Sifrutah, *1550*

Temple, judicial tribunals in, *287–288*

temporary measures (*hora'at sha'ah*)
Hisda's commentaries on, *520n.117*
legislation and, *519–520, 533–536*
"you shall not add or take away," *502*

Ten Commandments
context as basis of explanation in, *334–335*
copying of, into communal register, *1907–1908*
legal-moral reciprocity and, *142–144*
modern legislation on testimony and, *1697–1707*
religious and national characteristics in, *4–5*
use of non-Jewish courts as transgression of, *14–15*
See also Sinaitic revelation

tenai bet din
Joshua's property enactments as, *551n.28*
terminology of, *492–493*

tenants' law
  enactments of Candia regarding, *811–813*
  See also property law.
Tenants Protection law
  "justice" terminology in, *1837n.36*
  lifenim mi-shurat ha-din and, *166*
  Wiloszni case and, *1820*
Tenes, legislative enactments, *859n.280*
Teomim, Joseph, on *Orah Hayyim* and *Yoreh De'ah*, *1432*
terefah/terefot (unfit animals), laws regarding
  codification of, in *Tur Yoreh De'ah*, *1289–1290*
  Saadiah Gaon's monograph on, *1159*
  in *Torat ha-Bayit*, *1273–1275*
  in *Torat Hattat*, *1357–1359*
  Yemenite responsa on, *1500n.131*
Terikala, communal enactments in, *756n.292*
terumah (priestly tithes)
  "all who marry do so subject to conditions laid down by the Rabbis and the Rabbis annul this marriage" legislation, *634–636*
  in *Arukh ha-Shulhan*, *1449*
  custom as law regarding, *898, 902*
  on fruit, custom based on error regarding, *938–939*
  latent damage legislation, *603*
  laws regarding, *389*
  legal presumptions and, *996n.28*
  Mishnah compared with cognate sources, *1059–1060*
  of produce, *ma'aseh* and, *949n.19*
Terumat ha-Deshen
  codificatory literature, *750n.267*
  as literary source, *1253, 1486n.96*
  questioning methods in responsa and, *1505n.149*
  responsa in, *1516–1517, 1519n.206*
teshuvah. *See* repentance
Teshuvot Maimuniyyot, *1235n.158*
testimony
  agunot legislation and, *523–530*
  halakhic competence of witnesses and, *737–739*
  "mouth that has prohibited is the mouth that has permitted," *994–995*
  woman's competency and, *1656n.144*
  See also witnesses
Tevu'at Shor, *1447*
textual ambiguities, in communal enactments, *464–468*
theft, laws regarding
  asmakhta (supportive interpretation of), *302–304*
  compilation of, in *Mishneh Torah*, *1199*
  context as basis of explanation in, *335*
  halakhic religious-legal interactions, *119n.115*
  kelal u-ferat u-khelal canon and, *326–327*
  legal enforcement of rabbinic law and, *218–222*
  oath of robbery victims and, *616*
  See also lost or stolen property.
third party, protection of, *596–601*
thirteen canons of interpretation
  analogical exegesis, *343–360*
  context and subsequent expression in, *333–335*
  contradictory passages, *335–339*
  explicative exegesis of, *319–339*
  generalization and specification in, *323–333*
  logical interpretation, *339–343*
  post-Talmudic halakhic interpretation with, *415–421*
  R. Akiva's vs. R. Ishmael's interpretations, *373–374*
  restrictive interpretation, *360–370*
  See also entries under specific interpretations
"Three Communities" (Altona, Hamburg, and Wandsbeck), *1426*
"three pillars of instruction"
  Alfasi as first pillar, *1172*
  Asheri as third pillar, *1253*
  Bet Yosef codification and, *1314n.15*
  decision making disputes among, *1317–1319*
  hilkheta ke-vatra'ei, *1354–1356, 1359–1360*
  Maharshal's commentaries on, *1390–1394*
  Maimonides as second pillar, *1231*
  Nahmanides as third pillar, *1265n.129*
  Sefer ha-Mordekhai commentary and, *1250*
Tiferet Yisra'el
  legal research, *140*
  as literary source, *1109–1110*
tikkun ha-olam (social welfare), *504*
Tikkun Shetarot, *1538*
Tikkun Soferim
  of Moses Almosnino and Samuel Jaffe, *1538*
  of Rashbash, *1538*
Tiktin, enactments of, *823*

Tirna, Yizhak Isaac, *1305*
tithes
halakhah le-Moshe mi-Sinai concept and, *206–207*
laws regarding, in Mishnah, *1053*
See also charity, *terumah*
Tobit, Book of, as literary source for law, *1034*
Todros ha-Levi, Rabbenu, *842*
To'en ve-Nit'an (laws of plaintiff and defendant), comparisons in codification of, *1293n.217*
Tohorot Order, *1253n.69*
in Mishnah, *1054, 1056*
omission of, in Babylonian Talmud, *1095*
responsa literature and, *1491*
tohorot (Ritual Purity), abrogation of, *1583–1584*
"Tokhnit ha-Hukhah," *1613*
Toledo, Jewish community in
communal enactments in, *796–797*
equal inheritance rights for sons and daughters, *843–844*
husband's inheritance rights, restriction of, *838–840*
Toledo Trust Co. v. Simmons, laws regarding possession, *1745*
Toledot, *1558*
Toledot Adam ve-Havvah (The Chronicle of Adam and Eve), *1269–1272*
Toledot Gedolei Yisra'el u-Ge'onei Italyah, *1558*
Toledot ha-Halakhah, *1550*
Toledot ha-Posekim, *1347n.138, 1388n.62, 1550, 1561*
Toledot ha-Rabbanim le-Mishpahat Yisra'el mi-Rodos, *1559*
Toledot Hakhmei Yerushalayim, *1559*
Toledot Tannaim va-Amoraim, *1558*
"toleration money," taxes as source of, *920–921*
torah (custom), custom as source of law and, *883–885*
Torah
abandonment of law in, during Emancipation, *1580–1582*
Aramaic translation of, *1045*
arka'ot she-be-Suria and, *25n.80*
acceptance of as covenant, *234n.23*
binding authority of, *235n.24*
copyright law for Torah studies, *74n.87*
creative and integrative interpretation of, *285–286*
criminal communal enactments and, *692–696*
death penalty and, *61n.37*
divinity of, discussed, *240–242*
English translation as law, *191n.2*
entrusted to halakhic authorities, *243–247*
enumeration of commandments in, *1266–1267*
exegetical interpretation (*midrash ha-Torah*), *278–280, 283–300*
exemption of women from studying, *1798–1802*
Ezra's enactments regarding reading of, *556n.47*
freedom of contract law in, *123–127*
freedom from detention based on, *1845*
general courts' incorporation of, *1765n.46*
halakhic monographs seen as separation from, *1167*
interpretation (midrash) of, *276n.8*
king's law and, *54, 57*
lay tribunals as threat to, *31–33, 34–36*
legal-moral reciprocity and, *142–144*
as legal source for Jewish law, *237n.34*
legislation as preservation of, *503–505*
literary form of Mishnah and, *1050*
ma'aseh regarding judicial decision making and, *950–951*
marriage between *kohen* and divorcee, Jewish law incorporated in state legislation, *1772*
midrashic literature and, *1050*
modern severance pay legislation and, *1631–1634*
paschal sacrifice in, *112, 901*
prerogatives of halakhic authorities and, *240–242*
public reading of, laws regarding, *903n.27*
Rabbinical Court of Appeals and, *1811*
religious and legal solutions in, *4–5*
terminology of, *192n.7*
See also Biblical law
Torah ha-Ketuvah ve-ha-Mesurah, *1568–1569*
Torah Or le-ha-Rambam (Scriptural Index for Maimonides), *1198n.50*
Torat ha-Adam, *1243*
Torat ha-Bayit (Law of the House), *1273–1275, 1285, 1313*
Torat Hattat
codification methodology of, *1357–1359*
critical glosses to, *1347n.138*
Hayyim b. Bezalel's critique of, *1376*

Torat Hayyim, justice as supplement to law, ***171–172, 174***
Torat Hesed, ***1582n.14***
Torat Nevi'im, ***1549***
torot (instructions), terminology of, ***193***
tort law
abrogation of English sources, in Israeli legislation, ***1617n.110***
casuistic style of Mishnah and, ***1073–1074***
compilation of, in *Mishneh Torah*, ***1199***
encumbered property, legislation concerning, ***593n.213***
halakhah le-Moshe mi-Sinai concept and, ***207n.86***
halakhic interpretation, ***411–414***
law of obligations and, ***587–591***
legal commands vs. moral imperative in, ***145–147***
lifenim mi-shurat ha-din, ***161–164***
limits on, while acting on public authority, ***604–605***
mi-shum eivah (prevention of strife and enmity), ***629–630***
normative style of Mishnah and, ***1076–1078***
"religious" and "legal" aspects of *Halakhah* and, ***115***
Sefer Meisharim compared with *Mishneh Torah*, ***1272n.151***
tannaitic legislation concerning, ***601–605***
terminology for, in Jewish law, ***79***
in *Tosefta*, ***1078–1081***
Tortosa, Jewish community of, annulment enactments, ***856–858***
Torts Ordinance, ***1869n.183***
Tosafists
Ashkenazic novellae, ***1118–1123***
Caro's dispute with, ***1388n.62***
leading Tosafists listed, ***1120–1121***
Maharsha's commentaries on, ***1383***
responsa from, ***1279***
Tosafot
agunot legislation and, ***528–529***
commentaries on, ***1315n.19***
decisions and responsa in, ***1122–1123***
in *Sefer Ez Hayyim*, ***1256n.84***
Tosafot Rid, ***1258n.98***
Tosafot Yom Tov
commentary, ***1108–1109***
as literary source, ***1254, 1404–1407***
tosefet ketubbah (supplementary increment), widow's right to recover, ***841–842***
Tosefet Rishonim, ***1113n.44***
Tosefta
commentaries of, ***1111–1113***
communal enactments, ***679–681***
contents of Babylonian Talmud and, ***1088***
"distinguished person's" approval, ***752–753***
"do what is right and good," ***624–625***
"early Mishnah" (*mishnah rishonah*) and, ***1050–1051***
Ezra's legislative enactments, ***557***
on halakhic disputes, ***1065–1066***
issur-mamon distinction in *Halakhah* and, ***125***
interpretation of Torah and, ***284–285, 289n.19***
kilayim prohibition, ***507***
latent damage legislation, ***603***
law of Mishnah compared with cognate sources, ***1058–1059***
laws regarding fighting on the sabbath, ***1036***
legal commands vs. moral imperative in, ***146***
as literary source for law, ***1040, 1078–1081***
Pardo's *Hasdei David* commentary on, ***1112***
on property law, ***302n.56***
post-Talmudic halakhic interpretations, ***419–420***
sacrifice of life to save another, ***970–971***
in *Sefer Ez Hayyim*, ***1256n.84***
Wiloszni case and, ***1823***
"you shall not add or take away," ***497–498***
Tosefta Ki-Feshutah commentary, ***1112–1113***
Tov-Elem, Joseph
criminal communal enactments, ***688–690***
justice and equity in communal enactments, ***760***
town scribe, signature of, vs. witness' signature, ***741–744***
townspeople
consent (*hezkat ha-yishuv*), ***750–751***
legislation by. *See* communal enactments
tractates (*massekhtot*) of Talmud
juridical autonomy in, ***1586***
in Mishnaic Orders, ***1054***
omission of, in Babylonian Talmud, ***1094–1095***
responsa literature and, ***1472***

Yam Shel Shelomo and, *1389–1390*
See also specific Tractates
tradesmen associations
"distinguished person" approval, *752–753, 754n.280, 755–756*
force of communal enactment and, *702n.93*
majority rule and communal enactments, *717n.157*
tradition (*kabbalah*)
as legal source of Jewish law, *238–239*
prerogatives of halakhic authorities and, *241*
transgression, provisions of will as, *101–102*
trespass, post-Talmudic exegetical interpretation, *395–397*
Treu und Glauben, interpretive approaches to Israeli legislation, *1735n.422*
Treves, Wolf, *1584n.18*
Tribich, enactments of, *823*
Troyes, Jewish community of
enactments of, *786–788*
husband's inheritance rights, restriction of, *836–837*
trustees (*ne'emanim*), criminal communal enactments, *689–690*
truth, objective vs. legal, halakhic authorities and, *262–263*
Tshapui, defined, *28n.91*
Tudela enactment, *711n.134*
Tur Even ha-Ezer (The Stone of the Helper),
Jaffe's commentary on, *1401*
as literary source of, *1292–1293*
Turei Even, *1129n.104*
Turei Zahav (Taz), *1419*
commentaries on *Even ha-Ezer*, *1429*
commentaries on *Hoshen Mishpat*, *1425*
on *Orah Hayyim* and *Yoreh De'ah*, *1431*
Tur Hoshen Mishpat (The Breastplate of Decision)
codificatory structure of, *1291–1302*
Hoshen Mishpat in *Shulhan Arukh* and, *1323–1327*
influence of *Sefer ha-Terumot* on, *1246*
Jaffe's commentary on, *1401*
as literary source of law, *1281–1282*
role of law in Judaism discussed in, *1295–1300*
Sefer Hukkot ha-Dayyanim compared with, *1306–1308*
tax law compilations, *1445*
Turim. *See Sefer ha-Turim*
Turkey, Jewish communities in
juridical autonomy in, *1584–1586*
legal research and, *88n.49*
majority rule and communal enactments, *720*
Turkish language, British Mandatory legal system and, *1612*
Tur Orah Hayyim (The Path of Life), *1289*
Jaffe's commentaries on, *1400–1401*
organization and structure of, *1257*
Tur Yoreh De'ah (It Will Teach Knowledge), *1289–1290*
Jaffe's commentary on, *1401*
Tuv Mizrayim, *1559*
Tuvi, T., on Foundations of Law Act, *1832n.19*
Twelve Tables (in Roman law), *290–292*

U

u-lemadetem, education of children, parents' rights and responsibilities, *1798–1802*
Ulla, on oral vs. documented debt, *594–595*
unanimity, of community, majority rule and communal enactments, *717n.156*
"unguarded courtyard," in property law, *1748–1749*
uniformity of law
Jewish law and, *1377–1378*
legal research, *177–178*
Uniform Simultaneous Death Act (U.S.), *1681n.256*
Unjust Enrichment Law, 1696, lacuna in, *1837–1838*
United States law
codification in, *1144n.7*
law reporter systems compared with responsa, *1467*
responsa literature from, *1497–1499*
universally agreed intent, *459–460*
Unna, MK
Land Law legislation and, *1711–1716*
on Succession Law, *1676n.237*
"uprightness," interpretive approaches to Israeli legislation, *1735n.422*
unwritten laws, as source for Written Law, *1021–1022*
Urbach, E.E.
on midrash, *286*
on Tosafists, *1122–1123*
Urim ve-Thummim, commentaries on *Hoshen Mishpat* in, *1426–1427*

"usage" (*nohag*)
custom and, *896–897*
definition of, *885–888*
examples of, *930–932*
Usha, Jewish community in
legal reasoning, *1008–1009*
legislative enactments of, *566–569*
usufruct legislation, *melog* property, *572*
usury
laws regarding, codificatory literature on, *1290n.206*
rabbinic law and, *221–222*
"utilitarian" communal enactments, *688n.35*
ultra vires legislation, *536–538*
uvda. See ma'aseh
Uziel, Ben-Zion (Chief Rabbi)
on civil procedure, *1601, 1603n.70*
custom as source of law regarding severance pay, *925*
equality of inheritance rights among sexes and, *1684, 1755n.10*
on proof of custom, *929*
responsa literature of, *1499e*
on role of Jewish law in State of Israel, *1615n.101*
statutory incorporation, *1808–1809*
Woman's Equal Rights Law, jurisdiction over, *1760–1761*
Uzziel, Jonathan b.
Aramaic translations of, *1045–1046*
legal research, *304*

V

"vain plea," plea of limitations as, *1725*
Valladolid (Castilian Jewish community)
enactments, *798–804*
equal inheritance rights for sons and daughters, *842–846*
juridical autonomy of, *8*
lay tribunals in, *24–26*
value-laden legal terms
Foundations of Law Act and, *1895–1897*
statutory interpretation and, *1732–1737, 1871–1874*
Supreme Court's use of, *1730*
See also equity; justice; good faith
vav (Hebrew letter)
documentary interpretation and, *440–441*
explicative exegesis terminology and, *321–322*
halakhic interpretation by *amoraim* and, *407n.23*
ve-limmadetem, education of children, parents' rights and responsibilities, *1798–1802*
"verbal" bribery, *1640n.79*
ve-yesh she-horah, *1242–1243*
vice, Forli enactments regarding, *815–816*
Vidal of Tolosa
good faith (*tom lev*), *185*
lifenim mi-shurat ha-din, *159–160*
as literary source, *1232–1233*
viddui (confessional prayer before death), *1243*
Vikku'ah Mayim Hayyim
as literary source, *1347n.138*
rejection of codificatory literature in, *1376–1379*
Vilna, Gaon of
annulment, enactments concerning, *871n.316*
recitation of *shema*, *969*
violent crimes, use of non-Jewish courts and, *15–18*
voidness, concept of, illegal contract legislation, *1720n.379*
Volozhiner, Hayyim, *1494n.123*
voting rights, halakhic-aggadic reciprocity on, *96–99*
vows and oaths, obligations of
breaking of, local custom as law regarding, *934–935*
consecration of property and, *394*
halakhic religious-legal interactions, *119–120*
interpretation of communal enactments and, *451–452*
leshon benei adam (colloquial usage) interpretation, 437–438
ma'aseh regarding release from, *952–953*

W

Wage Protection Convention, *1629–1630*
Wage Protection Law (Wage Delay Prohibition Law) (*Hok Issur Halanat Sekhar*), *1629, 1694*
Waldenberg, Eliezer Judah, *1499*
war, laws regarding, *1035–1036*
Warhaftig, Z.
on civil procedure, *1603n.71*
on district courts, *1818n.206*
on Foundations of Law Act, *1832n.19*

on statutory incorporation of Jewish law, *1670n.207, 1908n.24*
on *takkanot* concerning succession, *1684n.270*
Weidenfeld, Dov Berish, responsa literature of, *1496*
Weil, Nethanel, *1255, 1432*
Weil v. State of Israel, rights of detainees and prisoners, *1841n.57*
Weinberg, Jehiel (Rabbi)
halakhic decision making by, *1901–1902*
responsa literature of, *1408*
Weiss, Judah (Judge), *1748*
Weizmann, Chaim, correspondence of, *86n.44*
Western countries, acceptance of *Shulhan Arukh* in, *1374–1417*
"Who is a Jew?" amendment, to Law of Return, *1688–1690*
"wickedness" concept, "sages are displeased" concept and, *154*
widow's rights
differing legal interpretations of, *296–297*
lay tribunals as judges for, *20n.65*
Succession Law regarding, *1679–1680*
See also inheritance laws; levirate marriage
"wife is not her husband's daily laborer," wife's earnings and, *1787*
wills and estates, laws regarding
daughters' inheritance rights in, *152–153*
disinheritance in place of charity, *99–102*
issur-mamon distinction in *Halakhah* and, *124–125*
freedom of contract and, *126n.140*
laws regarding, *1200–1201*
modern Succession Law and, *1681–1683*
"oral Will," modern Succession Law and, *1682–1683*
in suicide cases, *1875–1884*
support of daughters out of father's estate, *574–575*
Torah's provisions for, *152n.250*
validity of, *99–102, 1875–1884*
See also estate law; inheritance law
Wiloszni case
application of Jewish law, in personal status legislation, *1758–1759*
rabbinical courts and general legal system of state, *1820–1824*
statutory incorporation, *1944–1945*
wisdom literature, Book of Ben Sira as source for, *1034–1035*
Witkon, Justice, *1775–1776, 1767n.48*
witnesses, laws regarding
admonition of, in modern legislation, *1697–1707*
competency of, *1602–1603, 1776–1783*
general principle canon regarding, *356*
oath of (*shevu'at ha-edut*), *1697–1698*
scheming witnesses (*edim zomemim*), *397–399*
warning of, under Rules of Evidence Amendment, *1707n.337*
women
exclusion of, from prohibitions of marriage into Israelite community, *361–364*
study of Torah by, *1798–1802*
Woman's Equal Rights Law, *1653, 1656–1660*
amendment of, *1805–1807*
applicability to religious courts, *1757n.14*
Capacity and Guardianship Law linked with, *1665–1668, 1671n.211*
earnings of wife from her employment, decisions regarding, *1788n.109, 1789n.110, 1790n.113, 1791n.114*
rabbinical courts' jurisdiction and, *1758n.17, 1760–1765, 1824–1826*
Succession Law's equality of sexes and, *1684*
wife's income from employment and property and, *1802–1805*
work, prohibition of, on Sabbath, *202–203*
World Union of Agudat Israel, *1614*
Wörterbuch Über die Talmudim und Midraschim, *1565*
Written Law (*Torah she-bi-khetav*)
interpretation of, *277–278*
literary interpretation as bridge with Oral Law, *307*
as literary source, *1020*
Oral Law as supplement to, *200–203*
prerogatives of halakhic authorities and, *240–242*
"wrongdoer should not be rewarded," 1719–1720

Y

Yad Aharon, *1438–1439*
Yad Ephraim, *1432*
Yad Malakhi, *1546–1548*
Yad Ramah
legal instruments compiled in, *1537*
as literary source, *1124*

Yadayim Tractate, ***1056***
Yadlin v. State of Israel, freedom from detention issues in, ***1843n.63, 1844***
Yahadut Teiman-Pirkei Mehkar ve-Iyyun, ***1500n.131***
yahdav ("together"), explicative exegesis, ***322n.131***
Yalon, H., vowel points to Mishnah text, ***1110n.28***
Yam Shel Shelomo, ***1228n.136, 1386–1394, 1443***
Yavin Shemu'ah, ***1545, 1547***
Yavneh, halakhic center at, ***1066–1067, 1069***
Yedei Eliyahu, history of legislative activity, ***548n.10***
Yefeh Einayim, ***1128n.100***
Yefeh Mar'eh, ***1133n.119***
Yehaiah b. Joseph Zalah (Mahariz), ***1374n.20, 1491***
Yehudai Gaon, ***1300***
  authorship of *Halakhot Gedolot* attributed to, ***1155n.21***
  Halakhot Pesukot of, ***1153–1155***
  Karaism and, ***1156–1157***
Yekar Tiferet, ***1233***
Yemen, Jewish community in
  commentaries on *Shulhan Arukh* from, ***1432***
  resistance to *Shulhan Arukh*, ***1373n.20***
  responsa literature from, ***1464n.34, 1496n.127, 1499n.131***
Yerushalmi le-Seder Zera'im, ***1137***
Yerushalmi Massekhet Shekalim, ***1137***
Yerushalmi Shevi'it, ***1137***
yeshivot (academies)
  in Babylonia, ***1088, 1091–1093***
  enactments of Frankfurt and, ***794–796***
  establishment of, in Land of Israel, ***1096–1097***
  responsa literature of geonic period and, ***1468–1472***
  teaching Torah to women and, ***1799***
Yesodei ha-Mishpat ha-Ivri, ***82–83***
Yesodei ha-Torah (Fundamentals of the Torah), ***1198***
"Yesodot ha-Hukah be-Medinah ha-Yehudit," ***1614***
Yevamot Tractate
  court authority regarding legislation, ***506***
  equal inheritance rights for sons and daughters, ***844–845***
Yihus She'er (Consanguinous Relationships), ***1178***
Yihusei Tannaim va-Amoraim, ***1557***
yishuv institutions
  autonomy of, ***1609–1611***
  Mishpat Ha-Shalom Ha-Ivri (Jewish Court of Arbitration) and, ***1593–1596***
  national-religious leaders and, ***1605–1606***
  proposals requiring recourse to Jewish law, in State of Israel, ***1618***
  use of Hebrew in, ***1607–1608***
Yisraeli, Shaul (Rabbi), ***1907n.22, 1916n.46***
Yizhak Yeranen, ***1177n.101***
Yom Kippur (Day of Atonement)
  custom as law regarding, ***899–900***
Yom Tov b. Israel Jacob Algazi (Maharit Algazi) *See* Algazi, Yom Tov
Yom Tov Zahalon (Maharitaz), ***1372***
Yoma Tractate, Alfasi's *Sefer ha-Halakhot* and, ***1169–1170***
yored le-nikhsei havero, Unjust Enrichment Law, ***1696***
Yoreh De'ah
  commentaries on, ***1431–1432***
  contents and organization of, ***12***
  Darkhei Teshuvah on, ***1442***
  David b. Samuel ha-Levi's commentaries on, ***1425***
  legal research, ***105***
  literary sources, ***1280***
  responsa, ***1462, 1491–1492***
  Shabbetai b. Meir ha-Kohen's commentaries on, ***1426***
Yose, R.
  custom as source of legislation, ***891, 899***
  development and redaction of Mishnah, ***1051***
  on historical development of Jewish sectarianism, ***1063–1064***
  mishnayot compilations, ***1051***
Yose, R. (*amora*)
  as one of first *savoraim*, ***1086, 1093***
Yose b. Halafta, ***1044***
Yose b. Joezer
  halakhic studies of, ***1049–1050***
  "laying on of hands", laws regarding, ***1062***
  literary form of Mishnah, ***1049***
  as part of *Zugot*, ***1043***
Yose b. Johanan
  "laying on of hands," laws regarding, ***1062***
  as part of *Zugot*, ***1043***

Yose b. Tadai, on symbolic interpretation, *380–383*
Yose ha-Gelili, R., *1044*
Yosef, Ovadiah, responsa literature of, *1499*
"you shall not add or take away," *496–502*
Yunovitz, Y., Mishpat Ha-Shalom Ha-Ivri, *1595–1596*

Z
Zadok, R., *1044*
Zakkai, Johanan b. (R.), *950*
Zamora, Justice, *1078n.161*
zarot (fellow-wives), *agunot* legislation, *530n.153*
zav, restrictive interpretations of, *369–370*
Zavda, Abba b. (R.)
  legal research, *103*
  ma'aseh concerning lost or stolen property, *956–957*
Zechariah ha-Rofe, *1232n.145*
Zechariah Mendel b. Aryeh Leib, *1437*
Zedekiah (King), on legal reasoning, *1010–1011*
Zedekiah b. Abraham ha-Rofe, *1247–1248*
Ze'ev, Benjamin
  on custom as source of tax law, *923*
  responsa literature of, *1487*
zeh neheneh ve-zeh eino haser, Unjust Enrichment Law, *1696*
zekenim rishonim, *314*
Zeltner, Professor, *1896n.262*
  on Israeli Legislature and Jewish law, *1918–1920*
  on statutory incorporation, *1896n.262*
Zemah, Jacob, *1371n.13*
Zerahiah ha-Levi, *1244n.33*
Zera'im Order
  botanical questions, *1136*
  legal research, *54n.13*
  as literary source, *1133*, *1252n.69*
  in Mishnah, *1053*
  omission of, in Babylonian Talmud, *1094–1095*
Zeror ha-Hayyim, *1307*
Zeror ha-Kesef, *1307*
Zevi, Naftali, responsa literature of, *1495*
Zevin, Solomon Joseph, *1554*
Zilberberg, Moses Judah Leib, *1495*
Zionist movement
  Mishpat Ha-Shalom Ha-Ivri (The Jewish Court of Arbitration), *1592–1596*
  restoration of Hebrew language, *1607–1608*
  See also National Awakening
Zionist Organization, scientific legal research supported by, *86n.44*
Zirelson, Judah Leib, *1496*
Zivilgesetzbuch, interpretive approaches to legislation, *1733–1735*
Ziyyon be-Mishpat, *1580n.10*
Ziyyun le-Nefesh Hayyah, *1129n.104*
Ziyyun Yehoshu'a, *1128n.100*
zizit (fringes), overruling of legislation on, *543n.201*
Zofenat Pa'ne'ah (Revealer of Secrets), *1129n.104*, *1179*, *1486n.96*
Zohar, *1316n.23*
zorekh ha-sha'ah, terminology of, *255n.63*
Zugot ("pairs")
  interpretation of Torah during, *314–315*
  "laying on of hands," laws regarding, *1062*
  literary form of Mishnah, *1049–1050*
  as literary legal source, *1043–1044*
  as recipient of Oral Law, *192*
  Talmudic research, *41*
  See also specific "pairs," e.g. Hillel and Menahem
Zuri, J.S., *81*